THE HISTORY of PROFESSIONAL HOCKEY in VICTORIA B.C.

1911-2011

HELEN EDWARDS

◆ FriesenPress

Suite 300 - 990 Fort St
Victoria, BC, V8V 3K2
Canada

www.friesenpress.com

Copyright © 2019 by Helen Edwards
First Edition — 2019

All rights reserved.

No part of this publication may be reproduced in any form, or by any means, electronic or mechanical, including photocopying, recording, or any information browsing, storage, or retrieval system, without permission in writing from FriesenPress.

This book was produced after reading millions of words of microfilm. Any errors in fact or misinterpretations are my responsibility.

ISBN
978-1-5255-3806-3 (Hardcover)
978-1-5255-3807-0 (Paperback)
978-1-5255-3808-7 (eBook)

1. SPORTS & RECREATION, HOCKEY
2. SPORTS & RECREATION, HISTORY
3. HISTORY

Distributed to the trade by The Ingram Book Company

Exhaustive, almost encyclopedic, if that's a word—Helen Edwards has fully, thoroughly, completely compiled the details that give the most detailed and authoritative look possible at the incredible and entertaining history of professional hockey in Victoria. The names, the maneuvering through arena issues, and a Stanley Cup are all chronicled and this book is a must for anyone who grew up around Victoria's lone hockey rink. The one thing that shines through, and you'll say it at the end—man, did she do lot of arduous research to get this completed work. Impressive.

> Jim Swanson
> Managing Partner and General Manager
> VICTORIA HARBOURCATS BASEBALL CLUB

ACKNOWLEDGMENTS

They say it takes a village to raise a child, but I couldn't have written this book without my own "village." From its inception when the Victoria Salmon Kings folded in 2011 until I wrote the last word, it has been a long journey with a score of helpers.

I am particularly grateful to the former players (or relatives) and coaches who agreed to talk with me. Thanks to Gladys and Cory Shvetz (Bill Shvetz's widow and son), Dorothy Purvis and Rick Miller who told me the story of Clem Loughlin, Reg Abbott, Ryan Wade, Taylor Ellington, Rollie Wilcox, and Mark Morrison. Of particular note are Bob and Marilyn Barlow who helped me to get the stories about the Victoria Maple Leafs correct. They gave me access to Bob's hockey memorabilia, a real treasure trove of information.

My colleagues at the Society for International Hockey Research were particularly helpful, reading the opening chapter and offering advice, locating photographs, and encouraging me when I needed it.

It was a thrill to "talk hockey" with legendary broadcaster Jim Robson who gave freely of his time to answer my questions. In Victoria, Mel Cooper and Steve Duffy told me about the media end of hockey while former Mayor Alan Lowe gave me details of the construction of the current arena.

Thanks to RG Properties for allowing me to use images for the Victoria Salmon Kings and to Ernie Fitzsimmons who provided photographs for teams from the Victoria Cougars (all eras), the Victoria Cubs, and the Victoria Maple Leafs.

I could not have written this book without the assistance of John Ashbridge who shared information about players he had known, Ross MacKinnon who grew up just down the road from the Patrick family, and Rita Harvey who put me in touch with Reg Abbott. Sadly, they are no longer with us.

Sincere thanks to my ever-expanding group of friends on social media for their positive comments during the writing process.

This book would never have come to fruition without the amazing editing skills of Jim Swanson who read every word I wrote, made great suggestions, and offered incredible support throughout the entire process.

The team at Friesen's has been incredible, leading me throughout the publishing process.

Finally, thanks to my family who have put up with my lengthy absences during my research and writing. John, Susie, Edie, and Diana have been great, and my wonderful husband John has been a rock. To you all, I appreciate your love and support.

This book is dedicated to the 483 men who played professional hockey in Victoria (and to those who showed up to training camp but failed to make the team). Over the past eight years, I have come to know you all.

OFFICIAL PROGRAMME

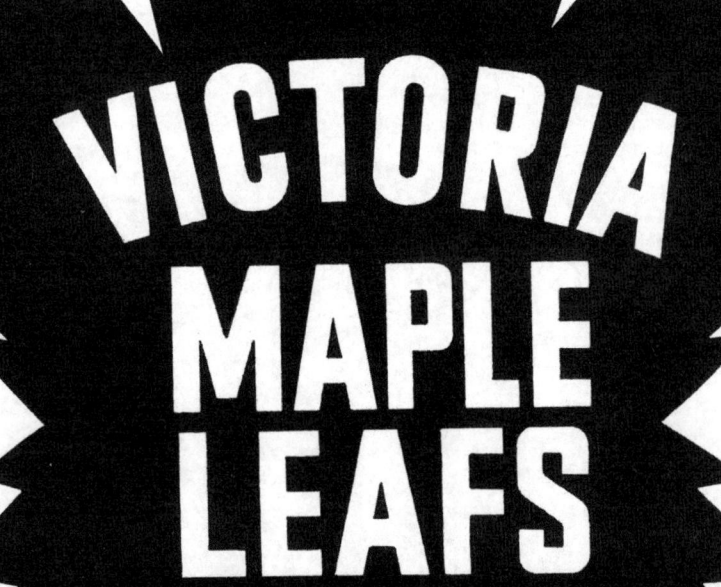

24 CENTS 25¢ PLUS 1¢ SALES TAX

VICTORIA MAPLE LEAFS

1964-65 SEASON

| SAN FRANCISCO SEALS | SEATTLE TOTEMS | PORTLAND BUCKAROOS | LOS ANGELES BLADES | VANCOUVER CANUCKS |

WESTERN HOCKEY LEAGUE

CONTENTS

1 - IN THE BEGINNING 1

2 - THE FIRST YEAR 10

3 - THE STANLEY CUP VICTORY THAT WASN'T 15

4 - CLOSE, BUT NO CIGAR 21

5 - THE LEAN YEARS 30

6 - NO HOCKEY IN VICTORIA 35

7 - HOCKEY RETURNS TO VICTORIA 37

8 - THE NEW GUARD TAKES OVER THE PCHA 43

9 - WINDS OF CHANGE BLOW THROUGH THE PCHA 49

10 - VICTORIA AND VANCOUVER JOIN THE WCHL 58

11 - THE QUEST FOR A SECOND CHAMPIONSHIP 68

12 - VICTORIA CUBS: SHORT-LIVED TEAM 77

13 - DARK DAYS FOR HOCKEY IN VICTORIA or
     HOW NOT TO BUILD AN ARENA 84

14 - PROFESSIONAL HOCKEY RETURNS TO VICTORIA 96

15 - COULD THE COUGARS REPEAT AS CHAMPS? 109

16 - A NEW LEAGUE—A NEW ERA 119

17 - THE NEW LOOK COUGARS. 126

18 - QUEST FOR ANOTHER CHAMPIONSHIP. 133

19 - ONE ERA ENDS—A NEW ONE STARTS 140

20 - WOULD THIS BE THE YEAR OF THE COUGAR? 151

21 - THE WINTER OF DISCONTENT 161

22 - NOWHERE TO GO BUT UP 171

23 - COUGARS UNDER NEW OWNERSHIP—AGAIN 180

24 - THE LAST HURRAH FOR THE COUGARS 194

25 - GO, LEAFS, GO! 206

26 - THE YEAR OF THE LEAFS! 220

27 - COULD THEY REPEAT? 240

28 - HOW NOT TO BUILD AN ARENA—VERSION TWO 253

29 - HOW TO BUILD AN ARENA SUCCESSFULLY **261**

30 - VICTORIA SALMON KINGS – NEW KIDS IN THE LEAGUE **275**

31 - THE SALMON KINGS PLAY IN THEIR NEW HOME **291**

32 - THE KINGS BECOME PART OF CANUCKS NATION **306**

33 - HIGH EXPECTATIONS FOR THE KINGS **320**

34 - RECORD-BREAKING SEASON **336**

35 - THE YEAR OF "THAT GOAL" **351**

36 - VICTORIA SALMON KINGS: THE LAST HURRAH **364**

Appendix A **381**
Selected Player Biographies

Appendix B **394**
Team Rosters

Appendix C **407**
Season Results

Sources **474**

Endnotes **477**

Index **572**

INTRODUCTION

If you had told me ten years ago that I would spend over seven years of my life researching and writing about professional hockey in Victoria, BC, I would not have believed you. However, I did, in fact, read millions of words on microfilm—and in print — and slowly, but surely, assembled a record of the professional game as played in Victoria between 1911 and 2011. As there were very few statistical records, particularly for the early teams, I produced schedules and results for every game played. I also compiled a list of the players and the franchises they skated with. The geek in me loves statistics so I had to include them. If they are not your bag, just skip those appendices.

I was struck by the connections between different eras of the game. Lester Patrick was the major influence on hockey here as the owner of both the original Cougars and the 1950s Cougars and his son managed the ill-fated Victoria Cubs. Eddy Mazur and Andy Hebenton played for both the Victoria Cougars and the Victoria Maple Leafs, while Dan Belisle Junior served as General Manager of the Victoria Salmon Kings; his father played here with the Maple Leafs.

I have been a fan of professional hockey in Victoria since the 1950s when the Victoria Cougars had a Kids' Club that sold tickets to games for one nickel. Attending those games was the start of my life-long love of the sport. When it was announced that the Victoria Salmon Kings were being disbanded, I was frustrated and annoyed. It seemed to me that I had been down this road before when the Victoria Maple Leafs were sold and moved to Phoenix. At about the same time, I learned of the death of Bill Shvetz who had played defence for the Victoria Maple Leafs in the 1960s. It seemed to me that time was of the essence if I wished to tell the story of the professional game in Victoria. I interviewed former players to get their unique views of the game and thoroughly enjoyed the process. As it would have been impossible to tell the story of every player, I have arbitrarily chosen players from different eras and written short biographies of them. I hope you enjoy reading them.

While there have been books written on hockey in BC and the old Western Hockey League, nobody, to my knowledge, has documented this issue from a strictly Victoria perspective. For this reason, I channelled my disappointment into a positive project. Although I was obviously not born when the Patricks' team won the Stanley Cup in 1925, I have been aware of this for many years. I watched the 1950s Victoria Cougars as a child and held season tickets for the Maple Leafs and Salmon Kings, so I possess the hockey knowledge to do this work.

I am an architectural historian and genealogist by trade, but this book combines my passion for hockey with my highly-developed research skills.

It took me almost eight years to write this book. I hope it takes you less time to read it!

1 - IN THE BEGINNING

The first game of professional hockey in Victoria was played between the New Westminster Royals and the hometown Victoria team at the new Victoria Arena on January 2, 1912.[1] However, the story starts many years earlier, in Québec.

Joseph Patrick was born August 4, 1857, to Thomas Patrick and his wife, Lucinda Watterson, who had immigrated to South Durham, Québec. He was one son of a large family. In the summer of 1881, Joseph moved to Drummondville to work in the general store. There, he met local schoolteacher Grace Nelson; they were married on May 7, 1883. Their first son, Curtis Lester, was born on December 31, 1883, and their second, Frank Alexis, on December 21, 1885. In 1887, Joseph moved his family to Carmel Hill, where he acquired a half-interest in a general store that he sold in 1892 for a profit. The family, by then numbering three sons and two daughters, moved to Daveluyville, and Joseph formed a lumber company and mill. The following year, the family moved to Montreal, and the boys were exposed to hockey, playing on frozen rivers and ponds and flooded land.

Lester played a season with Brandon in 1904, where he upset the precedent for defencemen by rushing the opposing goal. In those days, defencemen were ordered to stay on the defence and hoist the attacking forwards into the gallery. It was the duty of the forwards to get goals. Lester had played three years with the Montreal Wanderers when they won the Stanley Cup. On two of those years, he captained the Wanderers. During this time, Frank played with McGill University and the Montreal Victorias, and Lester and Frank were usually opponents.[2]

The Patrick family: Joseph and Grace with their children at their fiftieth-wedding anniversary celebration. Photo published in the *Victoria Daily Colonist*, May 9, 1933.

In 1906, Joseph sold his eastern interests and came west to open a new company. He acquired a tract of land in the Slocan district of British Columbia and established the Patrick Lumber Company. The family moved to Nelson in April 1907, leaving Lester behind in Montreal—although he joined the family by Labour Day. The brothers played together for the first time in Nelson and, together, led their team to a season of domination in the Kootenay league.[3] This was the first time the brothers played together; in the next season, they signed contracts with the fabulous Renfrew Millionaires.[4]

Joe Patrick was a businessman who could shrug off losses without a trace of emotion. During the spring of 1908, his lumberjacks put $100,000 worth of logs in the water. They floated down the Little Slocan River and into the Slocan River to the mill, where they were pooled by a series of piers. On a Saturday in June, a cloudburst hit the town and raised the level of the water. The north bank of the mill pond gave way and gradually the breach widened until logs were racing through into the Kootenay and then the Columbia River. There was no recovery; the season's output of logs was gone. As darkness settled over the scene, the sons felt sorry for their father. They awaited his reaction. He lit a cigar, said a few words, and went home to prepare his Sunday-school lesson. The next day, he taught the class and later his bible-study group, advocating faith, hard work, and fidelity to trust.[5]

However, Frank had a dream of operating a professional hockey team on the West Coast, and when his father retired in 1911—selling the Patrick Lumber Company to the British Canadian Lumber Corporation for $440,000—he presented the idea at a family meeting. Lester was unsure if they should follow Frank's plan, but Joseph voted in favour and the die was cast.[6] Together, they set up the Pacific Coast Hockey Association, with the original concept of four teams: Vancouver, Victoria, Calgary, and Edmonton. The *Victoria Daily Colonist* reported: "As far back as last November, Mr. [Frank] Patrick conceived the idea of putting in an artificial-ice rink in Vancouver, but he could not see how the proposition could be made to pay a legitimate interest on the capital invested until the idea of a four-club league cropped up."[7] Frank's brother, Lester, was expected to take up residence in Calgary or Edmonton.

The Patricks planned to build artificial-ice rinks in Vancouver and Victoria. "For the Victoria building and plant, which it is estimated will cost approximately $100,000, a site of three acres in the vicinity of the Willows Hotel has been purchased from M[ichael] B. Carlin."[8] Among the local men associated with the enterprise were real-estate agents Robert F. Green, Michael B. Carlin, and John A. Turner, along with architect Thomas Hooper (who designed the Victoria Arena), Dr. George A. B. Hall, and Harry Wright (the Member of the Legislative Assembly for Nelson).[9] In the end, there was not much interest in purchasing shares in the new team, so the Patricks incorporated the Victoria Arena Company on June 8, 1911. The first directors of the company were Joe Patrick, Fred Ritchie, Frank Buckley, Stuart G. Campbell, and Alex Pool. Lester Patrick was named manager of the arena.

On May 12, 1911, it was reported that Lester Patrick not only intended to make Victoria his home, but would manage the team and play for them, as well.[10]

On August 13, 1911, Victorians saw (for the first time) an architect's sketch of the proposed arena. The building was to be 322 feet long and 114 feet wide, with a seating capacity of 3,600. The ice surface was designed to be 210 feet by 85 feet. The foundation had been laid, and work on the timber frame was scheduled to start that week. Contractors had guaranteed that this rink and its counterpart in Vancouver would be ready by November 1, 1911.[11]

1 - IN THE BEGINNING

Sketch of Patrick Arena published in the *Victoria Daily Colonist,* August 13, 1911, page 17.

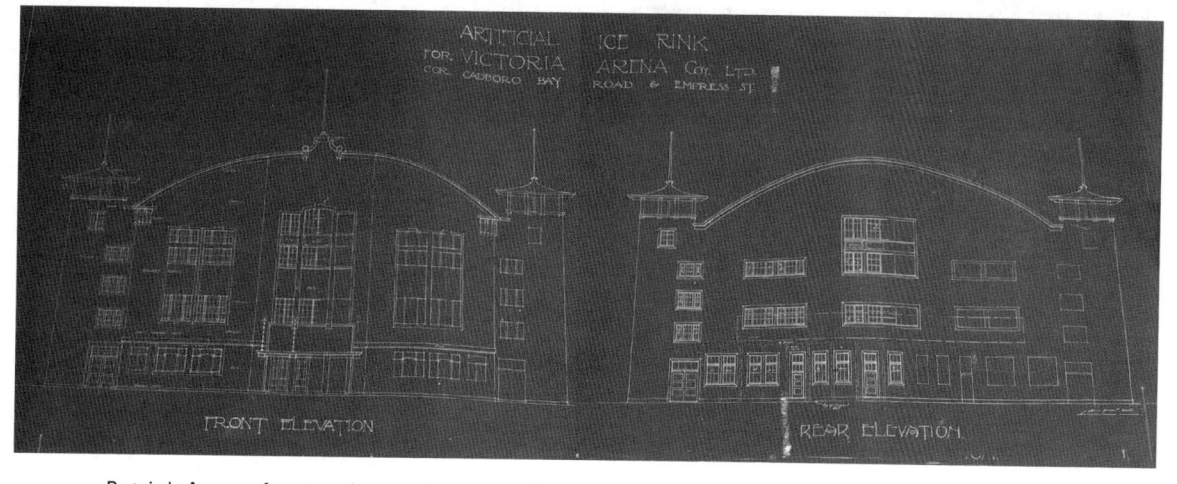

Patrick Arena, front and rear elevations. Image taken by the author at the Oak Bay Archives.

At this point, the composition of the new league had not been finalized.[12] Among the cities suggested for teams (in addition to Victoria, Vancouver, Calgary, and Edmonton) were Rossland, Nelson, and perhaps New Westminster.[13] In the end, the decision was made to start the new league with three teams: Victoria, Vancouver, and New Westminster, with the possibility of adding other teams later. As there was no rink yet in New Westminster, it was decided that New Westminster would play its "home" games in Vancouver.

The sports section of the November 19, 1911, *Victoria Daily Times* named (for the first time) possible players for the new Pacific Coast Hockey Association. Among these were the following: "Bobby" Rowe, who was one of the pillars of the Renfrew team the previous year and already residing in Victoria; Bert Lindsay, a crack goaltender for the Renfrew team; Jack Marshall, who was well known among eastern enthusiasts and a general favourite; Ernie "Moose" Johnson, a former member of the Montreal Wanderers and considered to be one of Canada's best players; Frank Glass, another former Montreal Wanderer with stick-handling talent; Walter Smaill, who was a star for the Wanderers and had come early to Victoria, assisting Lester Patrick in supervising the construction of the new ice rink; and "Newsy" Lalonde, one of the highest-rated players in Canada in both hockey and lacrosse.[14][15] Among those names were the early stars of professional hockey, many of whom would subsequently be elected to the Hockey Hall of Fame. Many players played both hockey and lacrosse, and it is thought that the Patricks expected to get revenue from lacrosse and other events to cover the cost of their arena investments. Lacrosse also provided year-round employment for some athletes.

With the new arena nearing completion—although it was not completed by November 1, as previously promised—players began to arrive in the West, ready to play with their new teams. Ernie Johnson, a star cover-point with the Montreal Wanderers for six years, arrived in Victoria to have a look at the new rink. He was signed to play for the New Westminster Royals and bet his old teammate Walter Smaill that the Royals would win the first game they played against Victoria. At the same time, it was noted that the Patricks had raided the stars from all the Eastern teams except Ottawa. The new Western players were confident they would be able to win the Stanley Cup (the symbol of hockey supremacy) in the spring and consequently transfer the hockey power centre to the West Coast.[16]

Although the idea of placing hockey teams in Edmonton and Calgary had not come to fruition, the Patricks were still looking for prairie players to bring to the coast. Tommy Dunderdale, a splendid Winnipeg player who had been rated one of the best forwards in the National Hockey Association the previous year, was encouraged to come to the coast with the promise of a better salary.[17]

Excitement continued to build as the arena grew near to completion, and by the second week of December, readers were presented with possible lists of players for the upcoming season. All three teams were well stocked with former Eastern stars, but the *Victoria Daily Colonist* waxed poetic about the Victoria players:

> *Victoria is also well stocked with stars. Bert Lindsay, of Renfrew, is carded for the goal position. The one and only Lester Patrick, whose brilliant defence playing in company with "Hod" Stuart in the Stanley Cup series in Winnipeg between the Montreal Wanderers and Kenora Thistles, has by no means been forgotten, will look after the point position. Two years ago Patrick's equal at point did not exist and if Lester is the same old Lester of old, Victoria will have a brainy and spectacular hockeyist guarding the position in front of Lindsay. Walter Smaill will play coverpoint for Victoria. Smaill also is an old Wanderer and when playing in Cobalt was one of the highest priced men. Donald Smith, formerly of Portage la Prairie, in the days of the Manitoba professional league and a star in the National Association in the past few years, will be on the forward line. Bobby Rowe, Odie Cleghorn, both National Association players, and Harris of Kenora are mentioned as the other forwards for the Victoria team.*[18]

Victoria hockey fans were thrilled to learn that the opening game of the new Pacific Coast Hockey Association would take place in Victoria against the New Westminster Royals on January 2, 1912.[19] Local sporting-goods stores took advantage of the growing interest in hockey to advertise hockey boots, skates, sticks, and other equipment.[20] Day by day, excitement grew as the start of the hockey season drew near. Readers of the *Victoria Daily Colonist* were advised: "The new ice rink is practically completed, and the power wires reached the plant today." The official name of the building was also announced: It was to be called the Victoria Arena, and large, four-foot high letters (spelling out ARENA) would be installed on the outside front of the building. The letters were designed to be lit with electric lights so they could be seen from some distance away.

It was expected that skaters would be able to use the ice surface by Wednesday, December 20.[21] With the arrival of Tommy Dunderdale in Victoria,[20] the team roster was complete. The Winnipeg star had been warned by the NHA officials that, because he was coming to play in the West, he would not be welcomed back to any Eastern team. He was not the only player to be warned, however; others were also banned from playing for any Eastern team. All these players would later appear on the rosters of the Pacific Coast Hockey Association teams. Dunderdale told the press that he was impressed with the new Western indoor rinks and expected that hockey on the West Coast would be successful, adding that "Victoria will have the best balanced team in the league."[22]

On December 20, 1911, Lester Patrick advised that the opening of the new rink had been delayed until Christmas Day, as workers were still getting things ready. There were to be two sessions for the public: an afternoon session from 3:00-5:30 and an evening session from 8:00-10:30. The hockey team was expected to have a few practices by the end of the week. Lester Patrick also announced that Lieutenant-Governor Thomas Wilson Paterson had donated the "Paterson Cup" to be presented to the winner of the Pacific Coast Hockey Association Championship.[23] The players selected for the team were shown in a full-page article with their photographs and positions. Showcased players were Lester Patrick, manager and point; Bert Lindsay, goal; Bobby Rowe, left wing; Walter Smaill, cover-point; George "Skinner" Poulin, right wing; and Tommy Dunderdale, rover.[24] Missing from the printed lineup was a centre. That error was corrected in the following day's edition, when Donald Smith's photograph was printed along with a notation that the omission of his name from the team listing had been an error.[25]

The first hockey practice was scheduled for the evening of December 22, 1911, providing (of course) that the ice was ready. The home dressing room was described in some detail: large bunks, one for each player, featuring the best of comfort, and with the player's name on a "nicely printed card." It was further noted that this area was for players only and was to be strictly private.[26]

At last, the ice was done, and Victoria was ready for professional hockey. The *Victoria Daily Colonist* proudly proclaimed:

> *All roads will lead to the Victoria Arena on Tuesday night, when the first ice hockey match of the Pacific Coast Hockey League for the Paterson Cup will take place between the fast Victoria team, captained by Mr. Lester Patrick, and the New Westminster septette under the direction of Jimmy Gardner. Lieutenant-Governor Paterson has consented to face-off the puck at 8:30 o'clock. It is expected that the Arena will be crowded with spectators keen to witness the introduction of the game that for years has held the enthusiasts on their toes in the east.... The city band will be in attendance and will provide an up-to-date musical programme. Mr. T. McPhillips of Vancouver will referee the match.... Special cars will be placed on the run by the B. C. Electric*

Railway Company early in the evening so that all attending can be in their seats by the appointed time of starting.[27]

With only a few days' practice under their belts, the Victoria hockey team opened the inaugural Pacific Coast Hockey Association season on January 2, 1912, with a home-ice loss to the New Westminster Royals by a score of 8-3. It was the first game played on artificial ice in Canada. According to media reports, it was a fast game, full of thrills, that was witnessed by a crowd of more than 2,500. As advertised, Lieutenant-Governor Paterson faced off the puck at the beginning of the game, the national anthem playing as he entered the arena. Some parts of the game were quite rough, with local player Walter Smaill sustaining a bad blow on the bridge of his nose after a collision. He left the ice but returned after medical attention and continued playing. It is important to note that hockey in 1911 was much different from the modern game, in that there was no substitution of players. All seven players played the entire sixty-minute game. That meant that injured players had to try to resume playing or their team would be one man short for the remainder of the game.

There was considerable trouble about each goal after it was scored, as there seemed to be doubt attached to them all. The difficulty arose because the proper goal netting had not arrived, and every time a goal was scored, the puck went through the netting. On several occasions, the puck went through so quickly it was hard for the goal umpires to tell whether it was a good goal. The Victoria team had some time to rest and practice before their next game, on January 9, 1912, in Vancouver.[28]

The line-ups for this historic game were:

	New Westminster	**Victoria**
Goal	Hugh Lehman	Bert Lindsay
Point	Archie McLean	Lester Patrick
Cover-point	Ernie Johnson	Walter Smaill
Rover	Ken Mallen	Tommy Dunderdale
Centre forward	Harry Hyland	Don Smith
Wings	Jimmy Gardner	Bobby Rowe
	Ran McDonald	Skinner Poulin[29]
Officials		
Referee	T. Phillips[30]	
Judge of Play	T. Hooper	
Timekeepers	F. W. Steele and J. A. Taylor	
Penalty Timekeeper	V. W. Odlum	
Goalkeepers	Bill Hooper and B. Reynolds	

It is interesting to compare Thomas Hooper's original drawing for the arena with its as-built appearance. The basic footprint was the same but much of the ornamentation was eliminated. It is likely that the cost to erect the Hooper design as originally conceived turned out to be higher than anticipated, and in addition, the building had to be ready for the start of the hockey season. The stairways at the corners had plain rooftops, rather than the open ones shown on Hooper's original drawing. The central entrance as built had a flat covering rather than the angled design. Perhaps the greatest difference was the name of the building. At some point, although the official name at that time was the Victoria Arena, only the word "ARENA" was erected (in the centre of the front façade). Nevertheless, the building became an instant landmark and was a popular destination for Victoria residents. The arena was called by several names, including the "Patrick Arena," the "Willows Arena," and simply "the arena." It was 1914 before the media settled on the name "Willows Arena."

Early photo of Patrick Arena. Courtesy Oak Bay Archives.

Newspapers accounts in 1912 did not use team names when reporting on hockey games. The official name for the Victoria team was "the Victoria Hockey Ice Hockey Club," but the media called it by many different names, including the Capitals, Lester Patrick's Puckchasers, and the Victorias. For the purposes of this history, I am using the most commonly accepted names for the Victoria team: Senators for 1911-12 and 1912-13, Aristocrats 1913-14 to 1915-1 and 1918-19 to 1921-22, and Cougars in subsequent years. The Vancouver team was called the Terminals and the Vancouvers but will called the Millionaires until the 1922-23 season when the name was changed to Maroons. Strangely, the New Westminster team was called the Royals from the beginning of the league. The *Victoria Daily Times* was the first Victoria newspaper to call the team the Capitals on a regular basis at the end of the first season. In the second season, when the *Victoria Daily Colonist* also began calling the team the Capitals, the *Victoria Daily Times* switched to calling them the Senators, and after that (for two years), it was the Capitals for reporters at the *Victoria Daily Colonist* and the Senators at the *Victoria Daily Times*.[31] The *Vancouver Province*, in its January 18, 1913, edition, began calling the Victoria team the Aristocrats, but the Victoria newspapers still used the old names. It was not until December 7, 1915, that the *Victoria Daily Colonist* adopted the Aristocrats[32] and the *Victoria Daily Times* followed suit on December 11, 1915.[33] It would appear that Lester Patrick had approved of the team being called Aristocrats, as that nickname was used until a final name change in 1922.[34]

In the early twentieth century, professional hockey teams appeared in unusual places in Canada, such as Cobalt and Haileybury, Ontario, where wealthy mine owners purchased the best players money could buy. John Ambrose O'Brien established a team in the town of Renfrew, Ontario, including Fred "Cyclone" Taylor and the Patrick brothers, Frank and Lester. Taylor was paid $5,250—more than twice the prime minister's salary![35] In 1909, O'Brien became a co-founder of the National Hockey Association, which was the forerunner of the National Hockey League. In 1909, three teams from the Eastern Canada Hockey Association (Ottawa, the Quebec Bulldogs, and the Montreal Shamrocks resigned and formed the new Canadian Hockey Association.[36] The new league opened membership to other teams, accepting All-Montreal and Montreal Le National. Attendance was poor, and owners talked about a merger with the National Hockey Association, but that did not happen.[37] Instead, the NHA admitted Ottawa, Quebec, and the Shamrocks; Quebec and Ottawa did not play until the 1910-11 season. The teams for the 1909-10 season were the Cobalt Silver Kings, Haileybury Comets, Montreal Canadiens, Montreal Wanderers, Renfrew Creamery Kings, and Montreal Shamrocks.

Bidding wars and the escalation of player salaries soon forced the Haileybury, Cobalt, and Montreal Shamrocks teams to fold. New teams were the Ottawa Senators and Quebec Bulldogs. For the 1910-11 season, NHA owners (who had all lost money in the 1909-10 season) established the first salary cap: $5,000 per team. That meant that players were now being paid about $500 each. However, competition for players within the NHA and with the new Pacific Coast Hockey Association led owners to ignore the regulations and negotiate higher salaries and bonuses with their top players.

As previously stated, hockey in 1912 was much different from the game played today. There were seven men to a team: a goaltender, a centre, and two wings on offence, two defencemen (who were called point and cover-point), and in between was the rover, playing both offensively and defensively. During regulation play, there would be fourteen men on the ice, unless there were penalties. Substitutions were rare, as the player leaving the ice was not allowed to return. Most players were on the ice for the entire sixty minutes of a game, unless they were sent off for a penalty or injured. In the case of an injury, the player was given ten minutes to be patched up, after which time his team would carry on shorthanded if he were unable to return. In the interest of sportsmanship, the opposing team would reduce their squad to make the number of players even.

Even coverage in the press was different. Today, articles concentrate on one sport and one league at a time. This was not the case in the early twentieth century, when an article might talk about the PCHA, an amateur hockey league, and a women's hockey league in the same story, with multiple linked headlines. This made reading accounts of games a little confusing, as the reader had to really concentrate on what was being said.[38]

Players had contracts for one year only and would often move from team to team. All players were signed by the league, not the individual teams, and their contracts were much different from today's multi-page documents, with astronomical salaries, bonuses, and incentives. The early versions were often merely letters signed by the player agreeing to whatever terms had been offered him. There were no player agents or other negotiators, although there are tales of a few wives doing the bargaining with the league management for their husbands. Often, contracts were little more than gentlemen's agreements. Players had jobs during the off-season. Many were farmers on the Prairies, and some ran businesses all year long.

Ticket prices were quite different from what we have now. Box seats for Victoria games cost two dollars, reserved seats were one dollar, and unreserved seats cost fifty cents. Local tickets were sold through merchants such as Richardson & Stephens and Fit-Rite Stores. They were also available at the arena on specific dates.[39]

In comparison, locally, three pounds of butter could be bought for a dollar, cured ham cost twenty cents per pound, and eggs were forty-five cents per dozen. Ladies' waterproof coats were eight dollars and fifty cents, while quality men's suits could be obtained for as little as twenty-five dollars. Building lots in Fairfield were priced at $1,500.[40]

The rules of play on the West Coast were designed to increase offence and make the game faster. For scoring records, only the scorer was given credit; there was no record of assists. If a game were tied at the end of three periods of play, the teams would play overtime until there was a winner. This would not change until the 1921-22 season,[41] and since most players were "sixty-minute men," they often played to the point of exhaustion. The rules, which were set at a league meeting just before the start of each season, were always being changed.[42]

2 - THE FIRST YEAR

Although the first game had not produced the desired result, the team was encouraged by the boisterous support they had received. It was the first time most Victorians had seen hockey live, and they were impressed by the speed and finesse of the game. The social benefits of game attendance were also reported in the *Victoria Daily Times*: "The new rink is quite a boon to Victorians and affords a popular and wholesome diversion to many who would otherwise be engaged in dancing, playing billiards, bridge, or idling away the time inactively in relatively small and confined rooms."[43]

The team travelled to Vancouver for an evening game on January 9, 1912, hoping to avenge the opening-game loss. There, they played "a splendid game"[44] and won the contest over the Vancouver team by a score of 8-4. Goal scorers for Victoria were Dunderdale and Poulin with singles, while Lester Patrick, Bobby Rowe, and Don Smith each scored twice. Scoring for Vancouver were "Newsy" Lalonde, Tommy Phillips, and Frank Patrick (2).[45]

The team now had its first victory under its belt and could move on to future games with more confidence. Their next game was against Vancouver, this time at home. In what the local media called "superior all-round playing," the locals won the game, 10-7. Frank Patrick attributed his team's loss to "the fog that rose from the ice in the third period."[46] Since both teams had to work around that issue, his comments fell on deaf ears. Tommy Dunderdale continued to shine for the home team, scoring four of the ten goals, while Walter Smaill and goaltender Bert Lindsay were also standouts. With the victory, Victoria moved into first place in the three-team league. Their next game was in Vancouver against the New Westminster team that had spoiled their home opener. Once again, the mainlanders were victorious, although it took 7:30 of overtime to settle the score. Ernie Johnson was the star of the game for New Westminster, with his aggressive play setting the tone. Bobby Rowe, Tommy Dunderdale, and Don Smith scored for Victoria.

Vancouver media carried the news that Frank Patrick was not happy with his team. He was thinking of playing a couple of amateurs, Jack Ulrich and Dissette (first name unknown), if they did not improve their play. With only three teams in the league, no team could afford to fall behind in the standings.[47] However, neither amateur player was willing to risk losing his amateur status without a guarantee of a permanent position on the team. Ulrich did eventually play in the PCHA for Vancouver and Victoria, but there's no record of any professional play for a Dissette from Vancouver.

From Vancouver came news that the league would expand to four teams. Seattle promoters were planning to build a $200,000 rink at the corner of Tenth and Madison in that city, and L. H. Griffiths

2 - THE FIRST YEAR

(a well-known real-estate man from Seattle) was in charge of that project. The rink in Seattle would (in all probability) be fashioned after the Victoria rink, which had a seating capacity of 3,500, and was the easiest and most up-to-date structure of its kind in the entire Dominion. The addition of Seattle would add a lot of prestige to the Patrick league. New Westminster was expected to have its own rink by the following winter so that the league would have four cities, all with powerful local backing.[48]

Once the Stanley Cup trustees decided that a challenge from the Pacific Coast Hockey Association would be accepted, Frank Patrick worried about the quality of ice for that series. The coast-league schedule ended on March 15, almost two weeks after the finish of the National Hockey Association in the East, causing uncertainty about the availability of natural ice in eastern locations.[49]

On January 23, the Victoria team finally beat their New Westminster rivals. Playing to an enthusiastic home crowd of 2,800, the team skated to a 3-2 victory. It was not an easy game, as the visitors led 2-0 at the end of the first period. However, Victoria came storming back with one goal by Walter Smaill in the second period and two by Don Smith in the third. The winning goal was scored with only four minutes to play in the game and sent the crowd home happy.[50] League officials were pleased with the crowds so far in Vancouver and Victoria, noting that (although Victoria was a smaller city) crowds there had been about the same as in Vancouver.[51]

The next game was on the mainland against Vancouver. This time, the home team prevailed by a 10-8 score, despite hat tricks by Lester Patrick and Don Smith. Of interest was the appearance of John Ulrich in his first professional game.[52] Given the nicknames "Dummy" (which he hated) and "Silent," he was the first deaf-mute player to suit up in the professional ranks. He played for Vancouver in the 1912 season and would play for Victoria in the two following seasons before returning to the East to play for the Montreal Wanderers and the Toronto Blueshirts.[53] Victoria lost its next game, this time 5-2 to the New Westminster Royals. Tommy Dunderdale scored both goals for Victoria.[54]

Jack Ulrich as a Victoria Aristocrat.
Photo courtesy Ernie Fitzsimmons.

On February 2, 1912, Victoria fans were able to see the Vancouver team play the New Westminster team. Local fans were urged to cheer for "Vancouver against Westminster for obvious reasons."[55] The game was an exciting contest, with Vancouver winning, 7-6, in overtime. The only bad news from the game was the injury to Westminster star Ernie "Moose" Johnson. His eye was hurt, but he refused to leave the game despite being advised by a doctor to do so. He scored the tying goal with under a minute left in regulation time.[56]

Victoria's next game was a real thriller and went 7:15 into overtime before they defeated Vancouver 8-7 after 7:15. More than 3,200 fans watched the close contest, cheering when Tommy Dunderdale scored four goals, and going home happy when

Skinner Poulin scored the overtime winner.[57] The next game also produced a winning result as Victoria defeated Vancouver, 6-4. Tommy Dunderdale scored another three goals, Lester Patrick notched two, and Bobby Rowe scored one. With the win, Victoria went back into first place in the league,[58] but the standings changed with each game played.

The Senators (the most commonly used name for the team at that time) would not fare so well in the next contest. New Westminster came from behind to win, 4-2. Victoria's poor shooting contributed to the defeat as they missed the net on countless opportunities. Don Smith and Skinner Poulin scored the first two goals of the game, but the team could not beat New Westminster goaltender Hugh Lehman again. On February 23, they again fell to New Westminster, clearly the best team in the league at that point. This time, the score was 4-3, with Smaill, Dunderdale, and Rowe scoring the goals. The team mounted a furious rally in the last seven minutes but could not put the puck in the net.[59] The next game was not much better. The team lost to Vancouver, 7-3, in a game that was described as "nothing to write home about."[60] The best players for Victoria were Lester Patrick and Don Smith, but their efforts were not enough to secure a victory. With the loss, Victoria was all but eliminated from league-championship contention.

In the next game, the Victoria team handed Vancouver a 7-3 defeat, reversing the tables on the previous encounter. This time, Vancouver was handicapped by the loss of Tommy Phillips from the lineup and an injury to the eye of Frank Patrick that limited his effectiveness. Dunderdale, Smaill, and Rowe scored two goals each while Poulin added one.[61] The loss slowed down Vancouver's hope of a league championship, but on March 5, 1912, Vancouver defeated New Westminster 10-6 to re-take first place.[62]

Victoria was officially eliminated from championship contention when they lost a game to New Westminster on March 8. The result was never in doubt, as the Royals outscored the home side 5-1. It was a fast, well-played game, but Victoria could not score more than once. Bobby Rowe was the only player to get a puck past Lehman, who played very well for the Royals. Four days later, the result was the same, but the score was 10-6. Victoria was clearly outclassed in this game, despite Tommy Dunderdale's hat trick and Smith's two-goal performance. The game set a record with twelve goals scored in the third period.[63]

The final game of Victoria's inaugural season was played at home on March 15, 1912. Much to the delight of their fans, they defeated the Vancouver team by a score of 8-6. They set a record for going an entire game without being penalized. The local team took the lead early in the first period and added three more goals by the end of the frame. Tommy Dunderdale and Poulin scored two each. In the second period, Vancouver found the net five times, but Walter Smaill scored twice and Lester Patrick once to make the score 7-5. The teams exchanged goals in the final period, with Don Smith notching the goal for Victoria. Tommy Dunderdale finished the season as the top scorer for Victoria with sixteen goals in twenty-four games.[64] He was named to the all-star team that would face a similar team from the East. The rest of the team left for their homes and some never played in Victoria again. Walter Smaill is quoted as saying he had played his last game of hockey and would take up a position as a physical director with the YMCA.[65]

New Westminster defeated Vancouver 7-5 on March 19 and was declared league champion. A scheduled game between those teams was cancelled, as it would not affect the standings.[66]

Art Ross announced the make-up of the "Art Ross All-Stars" that would come west for a series. Team members were: Paddy Moran (Quebec), Skene Ronan (Ottawa), Fred "Cyclone" Taylor (Ottawa), Odie Cleghorn (Montreal), Albert Kerr (Ottawa), Jack Laviolette (Canadiens), with Samuel Shore (Ottawa) in goal.[67] The Western team was made up of Hugh Lehman (New Westminster), Frank Patrick (Vancouver) with Lester Patrick (Victoria) as a substitute, Ernie Johnson (New Westminster), Tommy Dunderdale (Victoria), Newsy Lalonde (Vancouver), and Harry Hyland (New Westminster) with Jimmy Gardner (Westminster) as spare.[68] The games were played between April 2 and 6, under Western rules, with the PCHA team winning two of the three games. In the first games played in Vancouver, the Western team won 10-4.[69] The middle game of the series was played in Victoria before a huge crowd (estimated between 3,000 and 4,000). They were further encouraged to cheer with the addition of Bobby Rowe at left wing, replacing Ran McDonald, and Lester Patrick replacing his brother at point.[70]

There was no scoring in the first period, but local-favourite Tommy Dunderdale found the net early in the second period. This was followed by goals from Newsy Lalonde, another by Dunderdale, and two by Hyland, to make the score 5-0 at the end of the second period. In the third period, Hyland scored two goals for the West, while McDonald and Art Ross scored for the East. Victoria player Bobby Rowe scored the final goal. The final score was 8-2. In the final game played in Vancouver, the East finally won a game by a score of 6-5.

When Victoria goaltender Bert Lindsay was interviewed in Montreal after the season was over, he predicted a great next season. He noted that all hockey games were well attended and said that more Eastern players would likely move to play in the West. He attributed the losses by the Victoria team to a hard schedule and the fact that they carried no spares. "The ex-Renfrew goaltender regards hockey on the Coast as a big thing and will pretty soon be the Mecca of all puck-chasers."[71]

The season was over, but hockey news continued.

Since the Patricks had introduced the artificial-ice rink on the West Coast and had a successful hockey season, Eastern centres had shown much interest in building their own indoor rinks for skating and hockey. Hamilton, Toronto, and Quebec were all said to be considering new rinks.[72]

On August 15, it was reported that Don Smith (who played centre for the club the last season) was currently playing lacrosse in Toronto and would remain and play hockey there. He was "very popular here during his short stay, and the local hockey fans will miss his dazzling rushes up the ice."[73] There was good news on August 23, when it was announced that Tommy Dunderdale had arrived in Victoria with his sister and was expected to sign a contract with Lester Patrick before the start of the season.[74] Lester set off on a tour of the East, looking to convince more hockey players to come West. According to reports: "He is after Taylor, Benedict, Ronan, Gerrard, Kendall, Lowery, and Leseur."[75]

He later wired that he had talked with the best players in Ottawa, and they were not interested in coming West. He might, however, be able to sign Clint Benedict, a talented amateur.[76] On his return from the Eastern trip, Lester Patrick announced that New Westminster would have the same roster as last year, Vancouver would likely lose two players—Newsy Lalonde was reported to have signed a contract with Montreal and Phillips retired from hockey—and gain one in Carl Kendall. Lindsay, Patrick, Smaill, Dunderdale, Smith, Rowe, and Poulin were expected to return (Smaill's "retirement" having been short-lived).[77] At the end of October, it was announced that Newsy Lalonde and Donald Smith, who had played for Vancouver and Victoria the last year, would be playing in the Western league after all.[78]

It was not all smooth sailing in preparation for the new season. On November 1 PCHA officials issued an ultimatum to the National Hockey Association, saying, "unless the Eastern association takes a more favourable view of the term to govern a commission as submitted by the coast league at the annual meeting in Montreal on Saturday, November 3, a hockey war is assured." The PCHA was prepared to amalgamate if Eastern clubs waived all rights to Hyland and Johnson, who had jumped to the West. They further noted: "If this request is refused, the PCHA magnates will immediately take steps to sign

Eastern players. This will mean a war and a general scramble . . . for the best players in the game."[79] By November 12, the PCHA announced that there would be neither a war nor a commission for hockey, as NHA officials had not responded in time to the proposal put forth by the PCHA. Lester Patrick said that there were three or four Eastern players that he was negotiating with and that the teams were almost full. Named in a different article were Laviolette, Didier Pitre, Walsh, and "Cyclone" Taylor.[80]

By November 16, 1912, all the haggling was done, and the schedule for the upcoming year was drafted at the PCHA annual meeting in Vancouver. The schedule was to start on December 10, 1912, with New Westminster playing at Victoria, and end on March 7, 1913, with Victoria playing at New Westminster.[81]

3 - THE STANLEY CUP VICTORY THAT WASN'T

As usual, the local newspapers were full of rumours about the upcoming season. Who would play? Who would not? Fans were kept advised of player arrivals, injuries, and off-ice events. The *Victoria Daily Colonist* reported that the first practice of the season was held on November 5, 1912, with four professionals and a number of amateurs.[82] On the good-news side, the severe attack of pneumonia suffered by Albert (Dubbie) Kerr was not as serious as thought, and he would be coming West to play, after all. Donald Smith asked for his release, but this was not granted.[83] "Cyclone" Taylor turned down a large Eastern contract to instead play for Vancouver on the West Coast, and this led to others following his example.[84] Skinner Poulin arrived in Victoria near the end of November, followed by Goldie Prodger.[85] By December 3, there were eight players on the ice: Prodger, Poulin, Lindsay, Smaill, Patrick, Dunderdale, and Rowe for the professionals, along with talented amateur Joe Gorman.[86]

In other business activities, the Patricks reserved a large tract of land on the grounds of the Panama-Pacific Exhibition in San Francisco. They wanted to build an ice rink there to show visitors the joys of ice hockey. They felt that this would grow the popularity of the sport in the United States. Construction was to start in 1914 for the 1915 exhibition.[87]

Excitement was already building for the first home game of the season, when it was announced that the first in a series of skating races for the Wilkerson Trophy would be held between periods. Open to all amateurs, the races were one mile long—or eleven laps of the hockey rink.[88] This was one of many extra activities used to bring spectators out to hockey games.

The first game of the 1912-13 season was held in Vancouver and featured New Westminster as the visitors. The home team outplayed the league champions and skated to a 7-2 victory before a record crowd of more than 6,000 spectators. "Cyclone" Taylor was the star of the show.[89] Attention then shifted to Victoria, where Lieutenant-Governor Paterson dropped the first puck. The opponents were the New Westminster Royals, still smarting from their earlier defeat. Much to the delight of the 4,000 fans in attendance, the Victoria team won the game, 6-4. Tommy Dunderdale was the star for the local team, scoring three goals.[90]

The History of Professional Hockey in Victoria, BC: 1911-2011

Patrick Arena in 1912, photo taken from behind 1770 Rockland Avenue, looking northeast. Arrow marks the arena building. Image AM1376-: CVA 1376-545.16. Courtesy Vancouver Archives.

The next game was not successful, as Vancouver defeated Victoria, 6-3. Goaltender Lindsay was the star of the game, despite allowing six goals, while Dunderdale scored another three.[91] Victoria rebounded in their next encounter against the Vancouver team when "Silent" Ulrich scored a goal after 14:15 of overtime to take the contest 5-4, sending 4,000 fans home happy. The home side had fallen behind, 3-1, after one period, but outscored their opponents, 2-1, in the second to narrow the deficit to 4-3. Tommy Dunderdale tied the game halfway through the third period, paving the way for Ulrich's heroics.[92] Vancouver edged back into first place in league standings when they defeated the New Westminster Royals 10-5.[93] The previous-season champions were having trouble getting their game together, having failed to win in four attempts. They did not fare any better in the January 9 game in Victoria, as the home team prevailed, 3-2, in another overtime thriller. The hero again was the "Silent One," who scored 13:45 into the extra session—the second game in a row he scored an overtime winner.[94]

Victoria continued its winning ways with a close 4-3 decision over Vancouver. Skinner Poulin, a brand-new father, played the finest game of his career.[95] The result put the home team in first place in the standings and set up the rematch to come in Vancouver. In this game, Victoria again prevailed, this time with a 5-4 score. The goal scorers were Lester Patrick, Walter Smaill, Bobby Rowe, and Tommy Dunderdale (who scored twice). The other good news for the league came from New Westminster, where it was announced that "the new rink is ready and Victoria will play the first game there against the Royals. That optimism was short-lived, however, as the ice-making machinery failed to work, and the game had to be played in Vancouver.[96] Victoria's winning streak came to an end when the Royals notched their first victory of the season, 3-1, over a tired opponent. Three hard games in eight days appeared to have tired the team, and having two players down with "la grippe" did not help.

3 - THE STANLEY CUP VICTORY THAT WASN'T

Bert Lindsay

Tommy Dunderdale

Bobby Rowe

Walter Smaill

All images are of hockey trading cards from the author's collection.

Victoria retained their first-place standings atop the league, and Tommy Dunderdale led the scoring race with eleven goals in seven games.[97] According to local reports, the team was not upset by the loss, but were determined to win the next game.[98] Before that game was played, however, Vancouver beat the New Westminster team, 8-2, to move closer to Victoria in the standings.[99] The woes of the New Westminster team continued when they travelled to Victoria for a game on January 31. Victoria won easily, 7-3, solidifying their place at the top of the standings. Lester Patrick was the star of the game, scoring four times—the highest number of goals scored by one player in one game that season—while Dunderdale added two of his own to increase his lead atop the scoring race.[100]

Local fans were growing increasingly excited about their team's chance to become league champions. A victory in their upcoming game against Vancouver would give them a sizeable lead in the standings with only seven games to be played. As if on cue, the team travelled to Vancouver and loudly defeated them, 7-4, before more than 6,000 fans. The win gave Victoria a 7-2 record and a stranglehold on the Paterson Cup Championship. With three goals, Goldie Prodger was the star of the contest, while Bert Lindsay in goal played a stellar contest.[101]

The local press lauded the team, giving three reasons why Lester Patrick's team was leading the league. First, they were playing an unexcelled system of teamwork, with much unselfish play. Next, the defence was nearly impenetrable, backstopped by Bert Lindsay, who was having his best season ever. The final reason was the league's leading scorer, Tommy Dunderdale, who "combines his adeptness at propelling accurate and lightning-fast shots into the net with an ability to handle his stick second to none."[102]

However, all was not rosy for the Victoria team. Point-player Goldie Prodger was taken to the Jubilee Hospital suffering from acute and persistent pains in the head. He had complained of pains on his return from the game in Vancouver, and Lester Patrick had advised him to see a doctor. It was felt that the pain was the result of all the hard knocks he received during the course of games. He was ordered to rest completely for a number of days and would definitely miss the next game. Bobby Genge was named as his replacement at the point position.[103]

In New Westminster, the first professional hockey game was finally played, on February 7, 1913, before a capacity crowd. Vancouver defeated the Royals 3-2, in overtime to eliminate the defending champions from championship contention.[104]

Victoria consolidated its lead in the PCHA standings with a 7-2 victory over Vancouver in front of more than 4,000 fans. Goldie Prodger was released from the hospital in time to play in the game, and he scored the first goal. Bobby Rowe added one in the second period, during which Vancouver also scored. Vancouver tied the game early in the third period, but Victoria then scored five goals in quick succession (Lester Patrick with two, Skinner Poulin with two, Tommy Dunderdale with one) to secure the win. Pandemonium reigned as the Victoria team could no longer be caught in the standings and would win the Paterson Cup, and likely play the Eastern champion for the Stanley Cup.[105]

However, another injury struck the club. Walter Smaill had suffered a concussion in the previous game and was hurt more seriously than was thought at the time. "He was delirious all Tuesday night, and did not properly recover consciousness until noon yesterday [Wednesday]."[106] [107]

The discussion about which hockey system (the Western system of seven players or the Eastern system of six), heated up when "an old expert" said:

"Six-man hockey is like baseball without the shortstop—a big hole in the line without rhyme or reason. The prettiest thing about hockey is the combination team attack, the passing and the re-passing and the back checking, which are apparently impossible under the six-man rule. Baseball could be played with eight men a side or seven or six,

3 - THE STANLEY CUP VICTORY THAT WASN'T

but it wouldn't be baseball; the same applies to lacrosse and football as well as hockey."[108]

However, there was serious discussion about the possibility of the Western league adopting the six-man game. In fact, the next game between New Westminster and Vancouver would be played under this system. The penalty rules were also modified for this game. When a player was sent off, his place would be taken by another player. Teams would always play at full strength. For a first offence, the player would be warned, and for the second, he would be sent off for ten minutes, with another playing coming on. He would then be entitled to another warning, but the fourth offence would result in being benched for the game. Local reporters worried that a change to the six-man game would lessen the effectiveness of the Victoria team, as they depended on fine combination passing.[109]

In the game played with the six-man system, the New Westminster Royals defeated the Vancouver team, 5-3, to secure the top spot in the league for the Victoria septette. According to media reports, the six-man game was a hit with the spectators, as there was more room for brilliant individual efforts from the skilled players.[110]

Just as the Victoria team and its fans were celebrating a league championship and a trip to battle for the Stanley Cup, Lester Patrick announced that, unless the Quebec team agreed to play on neutral ice, there would be no Stanley Cup series between East and West. He noted: "The Quebec rink is about two-thirds the size of the one here, which would make it impossible for us to do our best, and while I believe Victoria to be a stronger team than Quebec, I don't think we would stand a chance in a series for the world's title in their stronghold." Toronto was suggested as an alternative rink, but Quebec would not agree to this. The players were disappointed and hoped that a better solution would be found.[111]

In a Tuesday game that meant nothing in the standings, New Westminster defeated Victoria in the Queen City, 6-1. The star of the game for the winning side was Ernie "Moose" Johnson, who returned to play after a series of injuries. Walter Smaill did not play, and his place was taken by "Silent" Ulrich.[112] The rematch was played the following Saturday in Victoria, and the result was a total reversal of the prior game. Victoria dominated in all facets of the game, outscoring their opponents, 7-1, for their most one-sided contest of that season. League scoring leader Tommy Dunderdale[113] scored a hat trick, while Lester Patrick netted two goals.[114]

In an attempt to hold a national-championship series, the Pacific Coast Hockey Association invited the National Hockey Association champions from Quebec to play in Victoria for a series; however, the winner would not receive the Stanley Cup.[115] Quebec agreed to the terms and arrived in Vancouver on March 22. They left on the night boat for Victoria and arrived the next day. While they were in Victoria, the team was housed at the Westholme Hotel. The first game was to be played under the seven-man system, and the second with six men a side.[116] In the first game on March 24, 1913, the Victoria team defeated the Quebec team in what was called a "cyclonic" game. The outstanding players for Victoria were Bobby Genge, Skinner Poulin, and Bobby Rowe. In between periods, Norval Baptie gave a fine exhibition of skating and jumped over eleven barrels to set a new record for that event.[117]

The second game (using the six-man system) was played on March 27, and this time, the Quebec team won the game, 6-3. Both teams used their substitutes, sometimes causing confusion during the changes as changing on the fly had not yet been perfected.[118] Victoria won the third game easily, 6-1, in what reporters labelled as "full of scintillating brilliant plays and thrilling moments." It was noted that this was the triumph of the West over the East, in a sport that had its birth in the East, and in which the Easterners were once considered invincible. Tommy Dunderdale recovered his scoring form, netting two for the winners, while Lester Patrick and Bob Genge added two of their own. The victory was seen as a feather in the cap of Lester Patrick, who had assembled a team of good players and taught them how to play as a team.[119]

It was indeed unfortunate that this series was played for the World Championship rather than the Stanley Cup, as it would have been a coup for the Patricks. However, it was enough for the team to know that they could beat the current cup-holders, and that they had won a hard-fought series against the best team the NHA had to offer.

A grateful City of Victoria held a banquet on April 1, 1913, at the Songhees Grill, to honour the team and present them with souvenirs of their accomplishment. The organizing committee undertook a subscription to raise the $500 to cover the costs of the souvenirs. Interested citizens could sign subscription lists at the *Victoria Daily Colonist*, the *Victoria Daily Times*, the Army and Navy Store, the Fit-Rite store, W. H. Wilkerson's jewellery store, and the "Two Jacks." Players were given were diamond-studded fobs. After the banquet, many of the players left for their homes: Goldie Prodger, Tommy Dunderdale, Bobby Genge, Jack Ulrich, and Bert Lindsay. Lester Patrick, Bobby Rowe, and Walter Smaill lived in Victoria year-round, while Skinner Poulin was expected to remain for the summer.[120]

Victoria Cougars 1912-13 team. Photo from the author's collection.

4 - CLOSE, BUT NO CIGAR

Although there were no games played during the summer, the Patricks spent the season travelling to the Prairies and back East to try to secure more players for their teams. On his return, Lester Patrick reported the formation of a hockey commission that would protect the club from being held up by its players, and at the same time, make ample provisions for the safeguarding of the players. One of the rules of the commission was that the Western teams could draw from players from west of Fort William, while the NHA could draw from east of the same city. At the same time, he announced that there would not be much of a change in the Victoria team this year, except for the departure of Goldie Prodger, who wished to play in Quebec and had been sold to that team.[121]

Skating season opened at the arena on October 17, with sessions starting at 8:15 p.m. Players who were in town would be taking the ice for practices.[122] In other news, Tommy Dunderdale was reported to be holding out for more money. Despite being the highest-paid player on the team, he felt he was worth more. His position was strange as he had verbally agreed to terms during the summer. However, had he decided not to play in Victoria that season, he would not have been able to play anywhere else either, as Lester Patrick would not give him a release.[123]

Several rule changes for the 1913-14 season were announced on November 6, after the league meeting. The most comprehensive changes were to the rules of foul play. Referees could impose penalties of ten minutes for a major foul with a substitute allowed for the following fouls:

> *"Deliberately disabling an opponent by hitting, hooking, or cross-checking with the stick; tripping an opponent to save a goal; kicking an opponent with skate; throwing stick which might prevent scoring of goal; abusive or profane language to officials, players, or spectators. If the foul is committed in the last ten minutes of play, the referee may impose a fine not exceeding $25. For minor fouls, there is a three-minute penalty imposed with no substitute. These may be given by the referee for deliberately tripping an opponent—no warning; deliberately charging an opponent—no warning; deliberately holding an opponent by the body, uniform or stick—no warning; goalkeeper deliberately kicking puck, which might prevent scoring of a goal—one warning; hooking an opponent with the stick—no warning; loafing offside and offside interference; goalkeeper must not during play lie, kneel, or sit upon the ice, but must maintain a standing position—one warning."*[124]

Other rules stated that every club must have at least eight men in uniform and available for play, and included a definition of a good body check. Positions of face-offs were also defined: "When a puck goes off the ice or a foul occurs behind the goals, it shall be taken by the referee to five yards from the goal on a line with the goal posts. When the puck goes over the side fences, it shall be faced at least ten feet from the fence."

A major announcement was the naming of an official scorer in each city who would keep a record of goals scored, assists, and penalties. Also included were amendments to rules for rinks and dressing rooms. Each rink now had to provide a separate dressing room for the referee and judge of play. A ten-minute intermission was allowed between periods, and the referee was allowed to start the play whether the teams were ready or not.[125]

Frank Patrick was the originator of the new offside rule, which was tested at Victoria on Friday, November 28. Local papers noted "If the rule proves a success, it will be adopted not only by the Pacific Coast Hockey League but also by the National Hockey Association. The rule provided for the division of the ice into three sections, each of seventy feet, a line being drawn across the ice that distance from each end of the rink. In the middle section, there will be no offsides and the players may pass the puck in any direction. Between the lines and goal nets, however, the old offside rule would be in effect. It was believed that the change in the rules would speed up the game."[126]

This season was also the first time that an assist was given to the player who had passed the puck to the goal scorer, although assists would not appear in the scoring statistics for some time. The league formed the Boundary Hockey League with teams in Grand Forks, Greenwood, and Phoenix. This was to serve as a "farm" system for the PCHA.[127]

There was a movement in the East to have the Stanley Cup rules modified to make this trophy emblematic of the world's hockey championship. Under the present rules, various clauses prohibited any inter-league struggles between the West and East Coast for this trophy. With the national commission in force, the Quebec club was taking a leading part in having the rules changed so that the Cup could be played for on a different basis from that which had existed in the past. The champions of the coast league were to travel eastward that spring and clash with the NHA champions, the latter coming westward in 1915. If the Stanley Cup were to remain the emblem of the coast hockey title, it would be seen that rules covering these transcontinental trips were required.[128]

Tommy Dunderdale. Courtesy Oak Bay Archives.

It turned out that Lester Patrick had been right about Tommy Dunderdale, as he signed his contract and was on his way to Victoria. Salaries had been sliced right and left in the East, with none of the stars drawing more than $1,000 for the season. This was a big difference from the coast league, where that sum was about the lowest paid.[129] Patrick also signed up a new player who would add considerably to the playing strength of the side. His name was Bernie Morris, and he lived in Moose Jaw and had for the greater part of his life. He came to the coast with an excellent reputation.[130] Another new player was Bob Genge, a Fort William sensation.[131]

But before the hockey season could begin, it was time for the skating carnival. Norval Baptie was in charge of festivities. Skaters in costume were advised to line up by the main entrance to form the grand march, led by Baptie and Mrs. David Spencer. It was estimated that there were 1,000 skaters in all colours and manners of costumes with an additional 800 spectators in the stands. Rowland's Music supplied special music. Prizes were given for the best costumes in various categories, with Mrs. Spencer winning a prize for her costume as a *"Vivandiere."*[132] Skaters without costumes were allowed on the ice after the grand march.[133]

Lester Patrick said that he would not announce his lineup until after the exhibition games had been played. The Senators had eleven players battling for places on the team, and the game on November 28 would help him make his decisions.[134] On the business side, season tickets were going well, and almost 500 had been sold from the office at 1019 Cook Street.[135] Tickets for single games were sold at Rowe and Poulin's tobacco shop[136] and at the arena. The regular players all played; "Silent" Ulrich and Mike Mitchell played a few minutes and "Dubbie" Kerr, who was still not in prime shape, played very little. The Senators defeated Vancouver 4-3 in overtime, with both teams displaying mid-season form.[137] The trial of the new offside rule went well by all reports, but the players seemed to be unfamiliar with the new rules. It was decided that more time would be needed to make a definitive decision. The rule would be tested at the first league game in Vancouver between Vancouver and New Westminster. After that, league officials would make a final decision.[138]

According to press reports, there was no doubt that the new rule would prove successful. "Both teams played faster hockey as a result of the adoption of the new system, and when they become more accustomed to this style, there will be more speed to the play." It was also popular with the fans, who hoped it would be adopted.[139]

Before the Senators started play that season, they received bad news. Lester Patrick had collided with Joe Gorman in a light workout and had fallen awkwardly on his arm. An X-ray showed that a small bone had been broken. He would be out of action for some time. As a result, changes had to be made for the opening game, with Walter Smaill and Bob Genge on defence, and Dubbie Kerr on left wing. Jack Ulrich had recovered from the injury to his foot and was expected to see some ice time.[140] The team did, however, suffer from the loss of Patrick, and despite Tommy Dunderdale's four goals, fell to the New Westminster Royals 6-5.[141] The Senators won the rematch three days later, with newcomer Dubbie Kerr scoring three goals in a 6-2 result. Victoria also had a goal disallowed, as it went right through the net.

Walter Smaill looked more like a war veteran than a hockey player. Playing with a stitched-up lip, he took a cut over the left eye and a gash on his head. Of note in the report of this game is the first appearance of Frederick James "Mickey" Ion as an official.[142] In prior games, referees and judges of play had been hockey players from the team not in action.[143]

The team did not fare as well in their next game, falling to the Vancouver Millionaires, 11-3. Vancouver had added players during the off-season who had strengthened the team. Frank "the Pembroke Peach" Nighbor had played for the Toronto Blueshirts the previous season, while "Cannonball" Didier Pitre came from the Montreal Canadiens.[144]

In off-ice news, George Rochon and Bernie Morris had been suspended for the season by the PCHA. These players were still under reservation by the coast league, and if they were again to play professional hockey, they would have to report to the coast clubs. In suspending these players, the coast league was setting a precedent that they would follow in the future with players who refused to accept terms offered and did not live up to the laws of professional hockey. There was little doubt that Portland would be represented in the coast hockey league the next season. Negotiations were underway to establish a team in that city. The arena was progressing fairly well, and it was thought that, by the next season, the coast league would also have an arena in Seattle.[145]

Regarding the rough play in the league, League President Frank Patrick noted: "We will have clean hockey in the coast league, if we have to get rid of the players who persist in roughing matters.... We cannot afford to lose the patronage of the coast sporting enthusiasts simply because one or two of the players have a grudge to settle, and I have ordered the referees to tack on stiff fines, in addition to long rests in the penalty box."[146] There was also the question of rowdy fans. Lester Patrick wanted to eliminate rowdy fans from the rink. The latter question was one that had to be handled with care, because if the rabid Victoria hockey fan refused to acknowledge the good playing of an opponent, who could make him change his view? He noted: "In all public pastimes there are those who go to the games purely and simply because they've a chance to heap the abuse on some poor unfortunate athlete. This has been demonstrated time and time again in baseball and is creeping into hockey." Manager Patrick said that there was a limit to real enthusiasm and he intended to have objectionable "rooters" placed under a ban for future games at the arena.[147]

On the ice, Victoria returned to its previous form and defeated Vancouver, 9-4, in the rematch at the home arena. The game was fast and well-played, with goaltender Bert Lindsay the star of the game. The forwards played much better as a unit and their shooting improved. The results left all three teams in the league tied with two victories and two defeats.[148] In the next game against the Royals, the Senators appeared listless and did not provide much opposition to the visitors. After scoring the first two goals and ending that period with the score tied, the team went to pieces in the second period, when they enabled the Royals to score a couple of goals that spelled defeat for the champions. The final score was 5-4, but it does not reflect the quality of play by the Royals, as the final Victoria goal was scored near the end of the contest.[149]

In order to be in better condition for their game in Vancouver, the team left on the morning boat, so they would have time to rest before playing. That strategy seemed to work, as the Senators won the game, 6-5. Despite giving up the first two goals, they stormed back to score two of their own, gave up a Vancouver goal, then scored four in a row before allowing another. In the third period, Vancouver scored two goals, but it was too little, too late for them.[150] In a game in Vancouver, the Millionaires defeated the Royals, 3-2, to sit atop the standings again.[151] Victoria won their fourth game, 5-3, over the New Westminster Royals to join Vancouver on top of the standings. Much of the game was played with six men, as there was no replacement for Charlie Tobin of the Royals when he had to leave the ice. To make the teams even, Bobby Rowe also left the ice. It was confusing to the players for a while, but by the third period, the teams were skating at top speed.[152] Vancouver regained the league lead with an 8-5 win over the Royals.[153]

It was beginning to look as if any team could win the championship that year. The Senators' hopes for a repeat of the PCHA Championship took a tumble when they were defeated, 7-6, by the Vancouver Millionaires. By all accounts, this was one of the best hockey games seen in Victoria, requiring almost fifteen minutes of overtime before "Cyclone" Taylor scored the goal that sent the locals home unhappy. Victoria thought they had scored early in overtime, but judge of play MacDonald disallowed the goal as being offside.[154] The Senators would now face two games in four days, and the results could make or break their championship hopes.

In their next game, which was a Saturday event at New Westminster, the Senators failed to show their top form and lost by a score of 6-4, despite another

4 - CLOSE, BUT NO CIGAR

two goals from Tommy Dunderdale. He continued to lead the league in scoring with sixteen goals in nine games.[155] Victoria had a better result in the second game, which was played in Vancouver the following Tuesday. Before 5,500 Millionaires' supporters, the Senators dominated play and emerged as victors by a 5-3 score. It was a close encounter, with the teams exchanging goals until midway through the second period, when Victoria scored twice to take the lead, 3-2. Two goals in the third period to Vancouver's one sealed the victory. The Senators were back in the championship race, now only one game behind Vancouver.[156]

Their chances improved even more when they beat the New Westminster Royals 7-5, before more than 3,000 spectators at the Victoria Arena. The result was even more impressive given that goaltender Bert Lindsay was severely cut under the eye just after play started and had to play the majority of the game with only one good eye. As a result of the victory, the Senators were now tied in points with the Millionaires for the league lead, and the Royals had been eliminated from championship contention. The Victoria team would now have ten days' rest, while Vancouver and New Westminster played each other twice during that time.[157] To everyone's surprise, the Royals won both of those games—8-2 and 3-1. Those results meant that the Victoria Senators were in first place in the PCHA standings, with a half-game lead on the Vancouver Millionaires.[158]

Excitement was building as the end of the season neared. Vancouver had lost its last three games and badly needed victories to get back in the race. The rest had done the Victoria team good. Bert Lindsay was back in top form, as were the rest of the team. The game was expected to be sold out, so arena management added standing-room places on a limited basis. A special streetcar service made sure all patrons arrived and departed safely.[159] Outplaying Vancouver in all phases of the game, the Senators thrilled their capacity home crowd with a 5-2 victory. They built up a three-goal lead before Vancouver scored, making the score 3-1 at the end of two periods. They continued their success, outscoring the Millionaires 2-1 in the third period.[160]

To create more interest in the championship race, readers of the *Victoria Daily Times* were offered a chance to win a pair of hockey tickets for the final New Westminster game in Victoria on February 20. All the fans had to do was guess the total number of goals that would be scored by the three clubs in the league in the next two games. Each of the first 100 correct answers mailed into the *Times*, along with coupons from the newspaper, would have two reserved hockey seats set aside at Rowe and Poulin. Fans had to have their guesses in before 6:00 p.m., on Tuesday, February 17; winners were drawn two days later.[161]

In the greatest exhibition of professional hockey seen in New Westminster, the Victoria Senators defeated the Royals 2-1. It was a thrilling contest, with the teams playing almost two full overtime periods before Tommy Dunderdale took a pass from Bobby Rowe and broke through to slam the puck into the net for the winning goal. The strain upon the players, mentally and physically, was such that the men had difficulty keeping their footing in overtime. Frank Patrick was asked to have the game called and replayed if it affected the championship, but he ordered the game to be completed as the constitution of the league called for the playing-off of all ties.[162]

Although Victoria now had a two-and-a-half-game lead over Vancouver in the championship race, the title was still not officially theirs. Lester Patrick noted, "While our prospects are now exceptionally bright, I do not intend making any preparations for a trip east until the Victoria team absolutely clinches the championship." He was referring to the trip east of the coast champions to play for the Stanley Cup and World Championship. President Quinn, of the national commission, was to forward the coast champions $2,500 to defray the expenses of the trip east, and complete financial arrangements would be made once the coast champions arrived in the East. There would be a private Pullman for

25

the entire party and special arrangements for food. It was expected that several coast hockey fans would book accommodations on the trip and many of the players would bring their wives. The coast champions would leave on March 2, and the first game would likely be played in the East on March 9.[163]

When Walter Smaill scored a goal nearly eight minutes into overtime in Vancouver, the Victoria Senators defeated the Vancouver Millionaires, 5-4, and secured the championship of the Pacific Coast Hockey Association for a second season. The game was played before more than 6,000 fans and was one of the most bitterly fought games that had ever been witnessed in this league. Individual stars for Victoria were goaltender Bert Lindsay and Lester Patrick, whose leadership and puck-carrying abilities were (to a large degree) responsible for the victory.[164]

Now that the league championship had been clinched, Lester Patrick planned to play his substitutes more, to give them game experience. That meant that Jack Ulrich would get his longed-for test in senior ranks. He had played in many games but had yet to start one. Kerr and Dunderdale would be rested during the last two league games, with Poulin and Smaill also taking turns on the bench.[165]

In one of the roughest games played in the PCHA, Victoria defeated New Westminster, 8-3. Referee Mickey Ion had his hands full with both teams. Ran MacDonald was fined ten dollars and ordered from the game for insulting the referee, while Eddie Oatman had several penalties including his final one: a cross check on Dunderdale, for which he was fined fifteen dollars and ejected for the remainder of the game. Tommy Dunderdale and Ken Mallen were fined five dollars each for fighting.[166] The rough play enraged one fan in attendance so much that he wrote a letter to the sports editor of the *Victoria Daily Times* condemning the rough play, particularly that of Eddie Oatman.[167]

The Senators lost the last game of their very successful season, 13-6, to the Vancouver Millionaires. "Cyclone" Taylor scored six goals for the winners. The Senators were weakened by the resting of Skinner Poulin.[168]

As New Westminster had been losing money ($4,000 in the first season and $9,000 in the second), the league was considering transferring the franchise to Portland and also adding the long-promised Seattle team.[169]

All three teams started on tours after the season closed. Victoria would, of course, go east to play Toronto for the World Championship and Stanley Cup. They played an exhibition game against Vancouver in Winnipeg to break their journey. New Westminster left on a five-game tour of the Prairie provinces and Vancouver left for a tour of Eastern Canada.[170]

The team lost the exhibition game in Winnipeg, which was played on very sticky ice. The game was played under the six-man system and the score was 8-6. Due to the poor play of the Toronto team near the end of their season, they did not clinch the championship and had to play an extra home-and-home series with the Montreal Canadiens to decide who would play Victoria for the Stanley Cup. As a result, the start of the final series was delayed until March 14. Lester Patrick used the time to practice his players to keep them in shape, and even arranged a practice in Montreal on the natural ice, in case that team won the title.[171] Toronto won the series against Montreal and got ready to play Victoria for the Stanley Cup.[172]

For Victoria fans who wanted to listen to the play-by-play of the championship series, arrangements were made with the Victoria Theatre to flash the results on the curtain as they were transmitted via direct wire from the Toronto rink. Reserved seats were offered for twenty-five cents each.[173]

4 - CLOSE, BUT NO CIGAR

VICTORIA, PACIFIC COAST CHAMPIONS, 1914-15

Top row, left to right—B. Rowe, J. Ulrich, W. Smaill, D. Kerr, J. Dunderdale. Bottom row—S. Poulin, B. Lindsay, L. Patrick, B. Genge, J. Ward.

Members of the 1914-15 Victoria Cougars. Note the typo of J. Dunderdale rather than T. Dunderdale.

Toronto won the first game of the series (played under the six-man rule), 5-2, with only Tommy Dunderdale and Skinner Poulin scoring for the PCHA champions. Toronto goaltender Harry Holmes was reported as the reason for the victory.[174] The second game was played under the seven-man system. This time, the Senators lost, 6-5, but the game went to overtime and only the stellar work of Harry Holmes kept them from victory. Walter Smaill and Lester Patrick were the stars of the game for Victoria.[175]

Toronto won the third game, again by one goal (this time by a 2-1 score). It was one of the most strenuous games of the season, with Lester Patrick and Bobby Genge playing despite the team physician's orders. After the game, Cup trustees announced that they would not have allowed the Stanley Cup to go west even had Victoria won, as somehow the team had failed to file a challenge form. Members of the winning team won $350 each; losing team members received $200.[176]

Victoria players left for their homes the day after the last game: Poulin came straight to the coast; Kerr, Dunderdale, and Ulrich stopped in Winnipeg; Genge and Lindsay would stay in the east all summer; and Bobby Rowe and Lester Patrick would return in a couple of weeks.[177]

The local press reported the off-season activities of players: Bert Lindsay was in business in Renfrew, Ontario; Bob Genge worked on the elevators at Fort William; Lester Patrick was also a director of the Victoria baseball club; Skinner Poulin and

27

Bobby Rowe owned a tobacco shop in Victoria; Dubbie Kerr worked for the CPR in Edmonton; Walter Smaill worked at the gymnastic department at Victoria playgrounds; Tommy Dunderdale joined his father's business in Winnipeg; and Silent Ulrich worked as a carpenter.[178]

The season had been successful, but the team had failed to retain the World Championship. Little did they know that it would be ten years before they would again play for the title and the Stanley Cup.

As in past years, hockey talk went on through the off-season. Peter Muldoon, the Vancouver Club's trainer, thought it likely that Portland would replace New Westminster in the PCHA for the 1914-15 season.[179] From Toronto came word that "Toronto critics think that the offside rule is a good style for [an] old men's home, but not for a young team with any speed." They felt that the rule impeded the player showing their skill and speed.[180] Concerning the planned hockey rink at the Panama Exposition, the newspaper noted: "Victoria will expect Mr. Patrick to bring back from the South a fine assortment of pennants or whatever else may be the reward of prowess with the sticks."[181]

News came that Skinner Poulin was going to replace Lester Patrick as manager of the local lacrosse team.[182] Frank Patrick announced, on June 9, that there would definitely be a Seattle club in the PCHA the next season. The Seattle Arena Company had been incorporated, and a twenty-year lease had been obtained on a site on East Jefferson Street, between Fourteenth and Fifteenth Avenues. Construction began immediately, with an estimated cost of $100,000. The new rink would hold 3,500 spectators.[183] With the declaration of war on August 8, there was concern over the loss of athletes to the war effort. It was noted that, in "France, Germany, Austria, and Belgium, practically every athlete of note has already taken up arms. . . . As Canada is sending a relatively small army, its athletic circles will not be affected to so great an extent as those countries at the seat of the disturbance." The article went on to note that numerous athletes had already signed up and that sports such as hockey, lacrosse, and football usually played by young men would suffer the most.[184]

The question of New Westminster having a PCHA franchise for the upcoming season was discussed yet again at the end of August. The Seattle franchise would not be ready for the upcoming season, while Portland's rink would be ready in October.[185] On October 1, Lester Patrick announced that the New Westminster franchise players would be transferred to Portland, with one exception—but he would not name it. He also said that contracts had been sent to all those who had played for Victoria the previous year. There were rumours that Bobby Rowe and Walter Smaill would retire, but Lester would not know until signed contracts were returned to him.[186] By the end of October, all of the prior year's players had been signed except for Tommy Dunderdale and Bobby Genge—Rowe and Smaill had decided to play once more.[187] However, Walter Smaill would only be able to play home games because of his duties at the high-school gymnasium.[188]

At the PCHA annual meeting, the New Westminster franchise was officially transferred to Portland. Negotiations were ongoing with that franchise to have the contact of Ran McDonald transferred to Victoria. The league would continue to play the seven-man game and rule changes for the upcoming season were as follows: the prohibition of body-checking a player within ten feet of the boards, and no offside would be called from a goalkeeper from the first section from his own goal. The schedule would start on December 8, when Vancouver would play the first game in Portland and would end on March 9, with Vancouver at Victoria.[189]

Lester Patrick announced that Bernie Morris, the best forward in the Boundary Hockey League, would receive a tryout with Victoria that year. It had been expected that he would play in Victoria the previous year, but he had not signed a contract then.[190] By mid-November, both Bobby Genge and Tommy Dunderdale had returned signed contracts, so the team was ready to defend its championship.[191] Early in December, Lester Patrick sold the contract of Jack "Silent" Ulrich to the Montreal Wanderers, as his deafness was a handicap in the seven-man system but wasn't expected to be as much of a difficulty in the six-man system played in the East.[192] According to Portland reports, Mickey Ion had been named official referee for PCHA games that season.[193] He had worked a few games in the last season; now he would officiate in almost every game.

5 - THE LEAN YEARS

Much to the disappointment of the Portland fans, the Vancouver Millionaires defeated the Rosebuds by a score of 6-3 in the opening game of the 1914-1915 season. Vancouver won their second game of the season, this time at the expense of the Victoria Senators (as they were being called at the time). Bernie Morris started the game at centre and played well, but was held off the scoresheet. The game was close, but Vancouver scored two goals in the third period to Victoria's one, for a 5-3 victory.[194] Victoria did not fare any better in the next game, falling 8-4 to Portland. There were outplayed at all stages of the game, while the Portland team played superior hockey all the way through and had a big edge in speed. Victoria, on the other hand, gave a weird display of goal-getting, their attack being the crudest of which the local septette had ever been guilty. Victoria failed utterly in helping out their defence, with the result that the goals came thick and fast against them.[195] This was obviously not the start that a championship team wanted.

On December 20, 1914, at the arena, team members were presented with handsome travelling bags—the city's gift to its champions. Following the presentation, which reminded them of happier days, the team was put through a strenuous workout against a local amateur squad. Lester Patrick was not happy with the lack of back checking and acknowledged that the team missed Walter Smaill at away games.[196] Things would have to get better, or changes would be made. For some reason, the past year's scoring leaders, Tommy Dunderdale and Dubbie Kerr, had yet to return to form. As they had scored three-quarters of the goals the previous year, this was a growing concern.[197]

The team travelled to Portland and promptly lost the game 8-1, despite Walter Smaill making the trip. Poor shooting was blamed for the defeat.[198] The next game, against Vancouver, was not much better, although the game was settled in overtime when Mickey McKay broke through the Victoria defence and scored with over twelve minutes played.[199] It was the fourth straight victory for the Millionaires and the fourth defeat for the Senators. Things were not looking good for a repeat of the Paterson Cup Championship. Lester Patrick issued a statement to the press that read, in part: "I am not prepared to state just how far my plans for strengthening the Victoria Hockey club have gone, but the fans may rest assured that if the present team is incapable of holding up Victoria's good name in the PCHA, they will be replaced by men who will."[200] Help would be needed very soon, as the Senators lost their next game, in Vancouver, by a whopping score of 9-2. Victoria goals were scored by Genge and Dunderdale.[201]

The Senators finally scored a victory, waiting until their sixth game to do so. By all accounts, it was an exciting game. Portland scored the first two goals, but Victoria stormed back with three to take the lead. That was short-lived, as Portland tied the game, sending it to overtime. Bobby Rowe was the hero for the locals, as he scored at 3:55 of overtime to send the crowd home happy.[202] In Vancouver, Portland handed the Millionaires their first defeat with a score of 3-2. The likely reason was that star "Cyclone" Taylor was unable to play.[203] Clubs still had to approve the naming of referees, and the Portland club did not want head-referee Mickey Ion working their games, as he was "too strict."[204] This was causing problems for the league, as Portland coach Muldoon had previously said he did not want his players acting as referees as "officiating is a severe mental strain on a player" and tired them out for games.[205] There was no comment from league officials at the time.

It appeared the champions had returned to form when they won their second game, outworking the Millionaires in a 4-1 victory. Dunderdale, with one goal and two assists, and Lindsay in net were the stars of the game.[206] It was looking better for Victoria when Vancouver lost another game, this time to Portland, 10-4.[207] The standings were looking more favourable to Portland and Victoria, as both teams had beaten the Millionaires. The local newspapers were talking about how their team could make a comeback. However, the bubble burst in the next game, when the Millionaires bested the Senators, 12-5, in a game in Vancouver.[208] Playing at home before several hundred public-school cadets,[209] the team played a determined game and outlasted the Portland team, 6-5, in an overtime thriller, with Dubbie Kerr scoring three goals, including the winner. Dunderdale also played well, netting two goals and an assist.[210]

League owners met in Vancouver in early February to discuss the question of rough play in the league. The officiating situation became worse when Tommy Phillips, who had been handling many of the games, resigned from the league. President Frank Patrick said that he had a tough time satisfying Portland in the matter of referees, and there had to be a solution or games could not be played.[211] Frank Patrick convinced Tommy Phillips to return to the league to officiate games for the rest of the season.[212]

Victoria's hopes of repeating as league champions took a tumble as Portland easily defeated the Millionaires, 8-3.[213] Portland pulled to within half a game of the Millionaires by winning a home game against Victoria, 3-2. It was a fast game with good plays from both teams. Portland's captain, Eddie Oatman, was the star of the game for his team, while Dubbie Kerr shone for Victoria.[214] The losing continued with a 6-4 loss to Vancouver. This was the team's ninth loss of the season and fairly well assured that they would not repeat as champions. Their effort was limited when Skinner Poulin was hurt in the third period, while the Vancouver team was aided by the return of Frank Patrick to the ice.[215] Local media were still calling the Senators "champions," but it was evident that they would no longer be champions after the season ended.

The Senators suffered another loss to Vancouver. This time the score was 10-3. They were in the game, and actually leading, 1-0, when Skinner Poulin had his hand broken. The floodgates then opened, and Vancouver scored ten goals, five in each of the last two periods, to win easily.[216] Just when local fans thought they would never see another victory, the Senators came to life and defeated the Portland Rosebuds, 4-3. Skinner Poulin coached the team from the bench, changing men as they tired. Dubbie Kerr played centre and Dunderdale was put back to rover. The changes seemed to work, as the team gave a much better effort.[217]

As he could not play hockey, Skinner Poulin was selected to referee the Vancouver-Portland series, with Portland still not pleased with the work of Mickey Ion.[218] Although his broken hand was still in a splint, he would be able to officiate.

On February 25, Lester Patrick announced that the arena would be shut down for the season after the game against Vancouver. The last game of the season (Victoria at Vancouver on March 9) was cancelled, as he said there would be no interest in a game that meant nothing in the standings.[219]

Meanwhile, over in Vancouver, the Millionaires clinched the championship of the PCHA. They would play the Eastern winner for the World Championship. The game was not close at all, with the Millionaires completely dominating in all phases to record a 13-3 score. Frank Patrick was greatly elated over the result and stated that it was his first time, in twelve years of hockey, that he had been on a championship team.[220] The next day, his team followed that victory with another over Portland, winning, 11-3.[221]

In the last game of the season in Victoria, the new champions from Vancouver outplayed the home side, 14-11. Both teams played loose defensive hockey, and players took full advantage of the circumstances. "Cyclone" Taylor had four goals and four assists for Vancouver, while Dunderdale had five goals and one assist for Victoria. Between them, the teams set a PCHA record for total goals scored in a game, eclipsing the prior mark of seventeen by a wide margin. Wearing a cast on his damaged hand, Skinner Poulin scored the first goal of the game, but that was the last time the local team had a lead.[222] The Senators made a final trip to Portland to play two games. They did not fare any better in those games than they had during the rest of the season, falling 9-1 and 6-2.[223] Thus, the Victoria Senators went from first to last place in one season, winning only four games.

At the end of the season for Portland and Victoria, the league formed an all-star team to play a six-man-style exhibition game against Vancouver to get them ready for the World Championship against the Ottawa team. Vancouver also played a two-game series in Portland as a warm-up.[224]

The Millionaires were in great shape by the time the Ottawa club arrived to play the series for the Stanley Cup. In games played on March 22, 24, and 25, they defeated the Ottawa Senators to win the series, three games to zero.[225] It was the first Stanley Cup for Vancouver and the PCHA. Seven of the Millionaires' players would end up in the Hockey Hall of Fame, and they were considered the best team to ever play in the PCHA's fifteen-year history.[226]

There were two big news items in the summer. The first was the decision to add Seattle to the league, and the second was the hockey "war" between the PCHA and the NHA.

Frank Patrick announced in April that Seattle would definitely be a member of the league for the next season. He said, "We planned to start up here last season and had the Seattle proposition all lined up, and were on the verge of letting the contract [for a new franchise] when the war broke out and I had to return to Vancouver. However, all the required capital is now available, and this city will certainly be in our league this year."[227] By June, contracts were signed to build an arena on Fifth Avenue, between Seneca and University Streets. In the summer time, the arena would be used as an auditorium for large gatherings. The seating capacity for hockey games was to be 4,000, and for conventions (with the ice area filled with chairs), 7,000. The ice surface was to be 85 by 200 feet.[228] Discussions were held during the summer with potential candidates for manager of the new team, the Metropolitans. In the end, Pete Muldoon was hired away from Portland and began to assemble a team.[229] The new arena opened for skating on November 12, with 1,800 in attendance.[230]

There was some talk that Victoria would not field a team in the new season,[231] but Lester Patrick convinced the league that the Victoria team should continue. It was felt that attendance in Victoria and Vancouver would be decreased because of the war, but that Seattle and Portland should draw fans.[232]

The big news of the summer was the hockey war between the PCHA and the NHA. It began when Frank Patrick announced that he had signed almost the entire Toronto team, most of whom would play in Seattle. In retaliation, George Kennedy of Montreal said he would make offers to Pacific-coast players, claiming that at least three were ready for the jump.[233] Threats went back and forth for some time, but in the end, peace prevailed, and hockey went on much as it had in prior years. Some Western players moved East, some Eastern players came West, but nothing major happened.[234] In local news, Tommy Dunderdale was traded to Portland for Ran McDonald before the season started.[235] This was also the first year that assists were shown in the scoring records, although they had been noted in newspaper accounts the year before.

In a move to generate interest in the hockey team, Lester Patrick opened team practices to the public.[236] It was a very different Victoria team that started the 1915-16 season. Fred McCullough was in goal, with Bobby Genge and Lester Patrick on defence (unchanged), Mickey O'Leary at centre, Dubbie Kerr at left wing, Ken Mallen at rover, Ran McDonald at right wing, and Jim Riley and George Box as substitutes.[237]

The Aristocrats were the visitors for the first game played in Seattle. It was estimated that ninety percent of the 2,500 spectators had never seen a hockey game before. It was a back and forth affair with very even play. The winning goal for Seattle was scored by former Senator Bernie Morris, lifting the new team to a 3-2 victory.[238] Next, it was time for Victoria's home opener. Col. Lorne Ross (commanding officer of the 67 Battalion, West Scots) faced off the puck. There was a large contingent of soldiers at the game, as they were given extended leave to be able to attend.[239] Although favoured, the Aristocrats lost the game to Seattle, 4-3, aided by a strange goal when goaltender McCullough put the puck into his own net in a botched clearing attempt.[240] It was not the start the local team wanted, falling twice to the new Seattle team. However, the team got a more favourable result their next game in Vancouver. Lester Patrick changed the lineup slightly, placing Riley on right wing and switching McDonald to centre. The strategy seemed to work, as the team was able to overcome a two-goal lead by the Millionaires and defeat them, 7-5. At one point, Lester Patrick was knocked unconscious, but he recovered and returned to play. Young McCulloch in the net played a good game, stopping many close-in shots.[241] In the return match three days later in Victoria, the Aristocrats again dominated the Millionaires, this time by a score of 8-2. George Box was the star of the game, scoring two goals and getting three assists.[242]

Lester Patrick, who had previously encouraged members of the public to visit the dressing room between periods, cancelled that privilege when the players and team doctors protested. It turned out that too many people jammed the room (some of them smoking) and the players could not breathe properly.[243]

The team then travelled to Portland for their first game against the Rosebuds. It was thought that Lester Patrick would be unable to play, having wrenched a ligament in his knee, but he jumped into the game near the end of the first period. The game was a close one, with Portland scoring two goals in the second period, and Victoria answering with two of their own in the third. The game went to overtime, with Portland prevailing, 3-2, on a goal by Harris. As the game had started late and gone to overtime, the Victoria team barely made the northbound train.[244] By the next game versus Portland, George Box was unable to play, as he had a broken collarbone (and would be out for three weeks), and Lester Patrick saw limited action. This weakened the team, and they fell, 10-5, to the Rosebuds.[245] The Aristocrats travelled to Vancouver to play the Millionaires. They took a 3-1 lead in the first period and looked good. Unfortunately, Kenny Mallen was injured in the second period when the puck opened up a gash behind his ear, and Mickey O'Leary took his place. This proved to be the turning point in the game, as Vancouver tied it before the end of the period and scored five more in the third, winning 8-3.[246]

There was good news in the acquisition of centre Sibby Nichols, who was transferred from Vancouver (as they already had two spares and did not need him). The change to the lineup turned out well as the team defeated the Seattle Metropolitans in the next game. With three goals and one assist, Dubbie

Kerr was the star of the night for Victoria, leading them to a 5-3 victory.[247] Victoria was once again in the cellar of the league standings after they dropped a 5-3 decision in Seattle. It was a clean game with no penalties called and plenty of good rushes.[248] Portland reinforced its position atop the PCHA standings with a hard-fought 3-1 victory over the Aristocrats at the arena. All the goals were scored in the second period, and only good goaltending by Murray in the Rosebud net kept Victoria from scoring.[249] In a subsequent game in Portland, the Aristocrats held a 5-4 lead, but Portland scored three goals late in the game to take the contest, 7-5.[250]

The Victoria hockey home season came to an abrupt halt when the Victoria Arena was taken over by the military authorities for the accommodation of troops and closed to hockey on Saturday, February 5. The arena was going to be converted to hold two battalions while the ice surface would be made into a drill hall. Its location, close to the largest military barracks in Victoria, made it the ideal site for training. The immediate access to open country for land training was another benefit. This announcement meant that there would only be one more home game played in Victoria, and that the majority of the remaining "home" games would be played in Seattle.[251] For a team already weakened by injuries, the need to play all games on the road was devastating, as they depended on the support of local fans to encourage good play.

The Aristocrats really wanted to win the final game in front of their home supporters, but it was not to be. They scored the first three goals, but could not hold Vancouver back for long. The Millionaires scored sixteen of the next seventeen goals to take the game easily, 16-4.[252] It was indeed a dark day for hockey in Victoria. They had no idea when the arena would again be available for hockey. The war that was supposed to be over by Christmas (1914)[253] was still being fought in mud-filled trenches and on the high seas, and would not be concluded until November 11, 1918.

The team played its remaining games, but their hearts were not in it and results were not good. They lost to Seattle, 6-3, on February 4[254] and again to Seattle, 8-4, on February 8.[255] A February 11 game against Vancouver did go to ten minutes of overtime before they lost again, 7-6, to the Millionaires.[256] In a bizarre game played in Seattle on February 15, Portland and Victoria were tied, 4-4, when a heavy mist spread over the ice surface, making it impossible for players and spectators to see.[257] The game was replayed on February 16, but neither Victoria newspaper reported the result—a rare victory for the Aristocrats over Portland, 5-2.[258] Portland would clinch the league championship by virtue of their 4-1 win over Victoria on February 19.[259] Victoria closed a losing season on a winning note, defeating the Vancouver Millionaires, 7-6, in a game played in Seattle on February 25.[260]

Portland played Montreal for the Stanley Cup, losing three games to two.[261]

6 - NO HOCKEY IN VICTORIA

With the Victoria Arena commandeered by the military for the duration of World War I, Lester Patrick had a PCHA franchise and nowhere to play. He decided to move the franchise to Spokane, Washington State's second-largest city. It seemed a logical move at the time, given the Patrick family's connections to that part of the world and the neutrality of the United States at that time. Spokane had been part of the family enterprise in the Kootenays, and although it was located south of the border, it was the transportation hub of the region. More rail traffic travelled north-south than east-west.[262] The family would have had business contacts in Spokane, having made several business trips there.[263]

There were rumours that Los Angeles wanted a PCHA franchise, although Frank Patrick thought that travel costs would be too high. The idea was backed by Alex Pantages, a Seattle vaudeville magnate. However, nothing came of this proposal.[264] By August, the Patricks had found support in Spokane but also had to invest some of their own funds. Together with Thaddeus S. Lane, W. H. Wraight, and W. H. Cowles, Frank and Joseph Patrick formed the Spokane Arena Company, with $100,000 in capital stock divided into 1,000 shares of $100 each. All these men were local businessmen who wanted their city to grow and were keen to bring a hockey franchise to their area. They represented the communication, media, and entertainment sectors of the city.[265] This arrangement was similar to the companies set up in Vancouver and Victoria when the league was formed.

Lester Patrick arrived in Spokane in October to personally supervise the erection of the Spokane Arena, intending to remain there permanently.[266] As the Patricks had done in Victoria and Vancouver, they welcomed local skating clubs and amateur hockey leagues to participate in arena activities.[267] It was announced that Spokane would have almost all the Victoria players from the previous year, except for Fred McCulloch and George Box.[268] There would likely be twenty-four games in a season that would open around December 1. Final schedules would be drawn up at the league's upcoming annual general meeting.[269]

The Spokane team won its first two games but eventually lost more than they won. Attendance was poor, with only 700 spectators at the first home game, so a local group of "boosters" was formed to try to entice people to come to the arena for games.

> *"The purpose of the . . . club is to get local sport lovers behind the Spokane hockey team and give support to the management of the team. Hockey in Spokane won't pay on the crowd that turned out for the first game of the season last Tuesday, and as the game is a new one in Spokane, the boosters' club will try to get the fans going to the games."* [270]

The strategy did not work, however, partly since the rink was located far from the downtown core, making just getting there difficult. The *Spokesman-Review* noted that "[o]nly once this season have the receipts of the games played in Spokane been great enough to pay the expenses of the team."[271] On February 15, 1917, the Spokane Arena announced that the remaining home games would be played in the other teams' arenas.[272] The Spokane experiment had proven to be a failure, and the team was disbanded at the end of the season, with the players being dispersed to the other clubs.[273]

In league play that season, the Seattle Metropolitans won the league title and played the Stanley Cup series against the visiting Montreal Canadiens. Seattle won the series three games to one to become the first United-States-based team to win the Cup.[274]

During the off-season, the league brought in new rules, including the delayed penalty so that teams would never be more than two men short. It also brought about a playoff series in which the first-place team would meet the second-place team in a series to decide the league championship. The winner of that series would go on to play for the Stanley Cup.

The first-place team for 1917-18 was the Seattle Metropolitans, coached by Lester Patrick. They were defeated in the two-game, total-goals-playoff series by the Vancouver Millionaires, coached by Frank Patrick. The Millionaires went to Toronto to play the Arenas (their official name although the press still called them the Blueshirts) of the new National Hockey League for the Stanley Cup but lost the final series three games to two.[275]

7 - HOCKEY RETURNS TO VICTORIA

In early October 1918, PCHA officials met in Seattle to discuss hockey for the upcoming season. Four teams were represented at the meeting: Victoria, Vancouver, Seattle, and Portland. The big concern was the number of hockey players still overseas fighting in the war. It was felt that the huge crews of shipbuilders working for the war effort would support hockey, but it was not yet known if Victoria's Arena would be available.[276] By October 27, Lester Patrick announced that, although the ice plant had been shut down for almost three years, he would have it refurbished and then open the arena for skating, likely in early December.[277] There still was no confirmation that Victoria would have a hockey team for the upcoming season, but as Portland had dropped out of the league, there was a good chance that hockey would indeed return to the capital city.[278] On November 12, the welcome news finally came that Victoria would have a team and that there would be a three-team league with Seattle and Vancouver. Play would start on January 1 and end in early March. Vancouver's Arena would be opened as soon as the "flu" epidemic subsided and the closing order was rescinded.[279][280]

The PCHA adopted the deferred-penalty system, which had been experimented with in the past and had recently been adopted by the NHA. "When a player is ruled off, he remains out of play until his time has expired. In the event of a second penalty being committed while one player is off, the second offender remains on the ice until the first penalty has expired, at which time he then goes to the bench." Portland players were made available to the Victoria team, and Lester Patrick was given permission to negotiate their services. Each team would play ten home games, as nearly as possible following this schedule: on Mondays in Vancouver, on Wednesdays in Seattle, and on Fridays in Victoria.[281]

The Victoria Arena opened for skating on December 10, and plans were made for six skating sessions a week,[282] with Monday evenings reserved for amateur hockey and Friday evenings for professional games.[283] Now it was time for Lester Patrick to negotiate with players to play for the reborn Aristocrats.

The first players to skate in an exhibition game were Lester Patrick, Dubbie Kerr, and Bobby Genge.[284] They were joined by Clem Loughlin, Moose Johnson, Charlie Tobin, and Tommy Murray, who arrived on Christmas Day, with Tommy Dunderdale and Alf Barbour expected the next day.[285] Skinner Poulin made an appearance on December 27, and Eddie Oatman, who had been ill, was expected to be released from hospital soon. Season tickets went on sale at the club office: 113 Pemberton Building.[286]

League play opened in Seattle on January 1, with the Vancouver Millionaires the visitors. The league champion Metropolitans defeated their opponents 4-1.[287] Seattle then travelled to Victoria to open the Aristocrats' home season. For the first time since February 1, 1915, there was professional hockey in Victoria. Fans came back in moderate numbers but cheered when Major Robert Gilmour Edwards Leckie dropped the puck for a ceremonial face-off at the start of the match. As to the game, there was not much to cheer about, as the Seattle team was virtually intact from the previous season, and knew how to play with each other, while the Victoria team was new, and the players did not know each other well enough yet to make great plays. The final score was 7-1, with Alf Barbour the only goal-scorer for Victoria.[288] It did not get any better in the second game, this time against Vancouver, as the Aristocrats lost 6-1.[289] They had scored only two goals in two games, and that was just not enough to win on most nights.

The team was bolstered by the arrival in Victoria of Eddie Oatman. He had recovered from his severe attack of the flu but was not expected to play for a couple of weeks. In the meantime, he was travelling with the team and helping to coach.[290] However, he did more than coach in the next game; he played, despite not being in game shape, and helped the team win their road encounter in Seattle. They again only scored one goal, by Ernie "Moose" Johnson, but this time it was enough to win the game, 1-0.[291] The Aristocrats' next game was against Vancouver on home ice, but the team could not improve on its effort in Seattle, again scoring one goal—not enough to beat the Millionaires, who put the puck in the net four times. Moose Johnson had a severe injury in which his eye was completely turned around, but he played the remainder of the game in spite of feeling a bit groggy.[292] The team welcomed the Seattle Metropolitans for a game at the Victoria Arena and, much to the delight of the huge crowd in attendance, scored three goals and defeated the Mets 3-1. Former Portland Rosebud Charlie Tobin was the star of the game with two goals and one assist. He had not missed one minute of a game so far in the season but seemed to get stronger as he got more work.[293] The team was rounding into form with better combination play and renewed energy. Local enthusiasts were cautiously optimistic that good results would be just around the corner.

Good results were indeed to come, but first, there was a game in Vancouver that the team lost 4-1. A slight lineup switch found Moose Johnson at rover, and he used his skill with the poke check to good advantage, but the team overall could not solve the problem of "Cyclone" Taylor, who once again, was a star for the Millionaires.[294]

Stanley Marples was discharged from the army and joined the team, strengthening the left-wing position that had been of concern for Manager Lester Patrick. In a show of courage and fighting spirit, the manager continued to fine-tune his team, despite suffering from a bad case of influenza himself.[295] Stan Marples had an immediate impact on the team's play, even though he had not played for some time, replacing Eddie Oatman in the second period and skating for twenty minutes. The team scored one goal, but that was all that they needed in this game, as the final score was 1-0. It was their third win over the Metropolitans that season.[296]

On January 24, the *Empress of Asia* brought Vancouver Island soldiers home from the war. All were invited to attend the game at the arena that night as guests of management, as were about a hundred convalescing men from the Esquimalt Military Hospital. One veteran said, "I have been only been back a few days, and one of the things I promised myself, as soon as I got a chance, was to watch a real good game of hockey, like we had in the Pacific-coast race before I went away." His sentiment was echoed by many others.[297] For Charlie Tobin, the homecoming was very personal, as his brother Gerald arrived on the ship, despite not being named on the manifest. The brothers had a great time together, with Gerald eating everything that was set in front of him at a fine dinner. In the game that evening, the Millionaires scored the only goal of the first period, but Dunderdale and Marples scored early in the second to give the Aristocrats the lead. Vancouver's Mickey McKay found the net halfway through the period to tie the score, but Moose Johnson beat Lehman in the Vancouver net in the third period, and the home team was victorious. Victoria and Seattle were now tied for the lead in the league—a position Victoria had not held for years.[298]

Before the Aristocrats played their next game, Vancouver and Seattle played each other twice, with each team winning a game.[299] Those results vaulted Seattle into first place in the league and set up another battle for first place when the Metropolitans visited Victoria at the end of January. Much to the delight of local fans, the Aristocrats won the game 2-1, with Moose Johnson playing a "sensational" game. It was reported as the "hardest, swiftest brand of hockey seen on local ice since the season opened." Both goaltenders played well, and Lester Patrick was pleased with the play of his younger skaters, Clem Loughlin and Stan Marples.[300]

Unfortunately, the winning record came to an end with the next game in Seattle when the Metropolitans soundly trounced the Aristocrats, 9-1. Lester Patrick, recovered from the flu, played his first game of the season.[301] The team focused on the upcoming home-and-home series with the Vancouver Millionaires. With both Bobby Genge and Clem Loughlin in hospital with influenza, the team lost the first game 1-0.[302] Before the second game in Vancouver, Moose Johnson and Alf Barbour were also admitted to hospital, leaving the team four men short.[303] Despite this adversity, the team played a marvellous game. Vancouver substitute Alex Irwin, who had been warming the bench for Vancouver, was loaned to the Aristocrats to make up a full complement of players. In a delightful irony, he scored the winning goal for Victoria after 3:35 of overtime. The result meant that all three teams were now tied for the league lead. From now on, every game would be important. Vancouver fans went home disappointed by the 2-1 defeat.

Irvin would continue to play the next three games for Victoria until their regulars were recovered from illness.[304] After that improbable victory, Captain Eddie Oatman of the Aristocrats said, "We are out after the world's championship." Off the ice, Lester Patrick had signed two new players, Leo Cook and Trooper Box, both of whom would be used as utility players.[305] They were looking forward to their next game against Seattle, as the hospitalized players were slowly returning to action. In that game, the team held a brief 2-1 lead, before the Metropolitans poured in seven straight goals to take the game 8-2.[306] The quest for the championship had taken a step backward. The results left Victoria just out of first place in the standings, but they would have to win the majority of their remaining games to have a chance. The league was so evenly balanced that year that any misstep could mean the loss of a chance at the championship.

The team's 4-1 loss to Seattle in their next game put them in a precarious position with regard to the standings. When Lester Patrick was asked to explain the troubles his team was having, he pointed out that most of the team, at one point or another, had suffered sufficiently from influenza to be hospitalized. He had just signed Wilf Loughlin, the Winnipeg Monarchs' star and younger brother of Clem Loughlin, and that meant that he had signed sixteen players to the team for that season. Of the sixteen players signed, nine had suffered from influenza during the season, causing havoc with combination play and consistency.[307] As they often did during that season, the team bounced back after the losses with an impressive 3-2 win over the Millionaires. It was Wilf Loughlin's first game, and he did not disappoint, playing with speed and effective checking. However, it was big brother Clem who would be the hero on that night, scoring the overtime winner on a pass from Oatman after 37:20 of overtime.[308]

Little did the team know that that would be the last time they would taste victory that season. They lost the remaining five games on the schedule, two to Seattle and three to Vancouver, to finish the season with a 7-13 record. It was small consolation to the Aristocrats that they had improved on their record before the war—having won only five games that year.

In a new feature for the league that year, referee Mickey Ion named an all-star team for the league. His choices were:

	First team	Second team
Goal:	Lehman, Vancouver	Holmes, Seattle
Defence:	Johnson, Victoria	Cook, Vancouver
	Rowe, Seattle	Duncan, Vancouver
Rover:	McKay, Vancouver	Walker, Seattle
Centre:	Morris, Seattle	Taylor, Vancouver
Right Wing:	Wilson, Seattle	Oatman, Victoria
Left Wing:	Harris, Vancouver	Foyston, Seattle[309]

In the league playoffs, second-place Seattle beat Vancouver 7-5 in a two-game total-point series. That gave the Metropolitans the right to host the Stanley Cup final that year against the Montreal Canadiens. With the series sitting with two victories for each team and one tie, it was suspended as so many players on both teams had contracted influenza. Five Montreal players were so sick from the 'flu that they could not play and Corbeau was so injured that he could not play either. Montreal Manager Kennedy suggested that gaps in the Montreal lineup could be filled by players from Victoria, but Seattle would not endorse this idea. For the first time, there was no Stanley Cup champion for a year, and the cup holder remained the Toronto Arenas, who had won the year before. On April 5, the real tragedy of the series was revealed when it was announced that Montreal defenceman Joe Hall had died in hospital. The remaining players who had been struck by the disease all eventually recovered, but it took some time. The deadly disease that had killed tens of millions of people around the world had a terrible impact on the 1919 Stanley Cup playoffs.[310]

In the off-season, Eddie Oatman, who was now a permanent resident of Victoria, had a try-out with the local professional baseball team, the Tyees.[311] History does not record him playing in any games, but he did umpire several amateur baseball games in the summer.[312] It was not unusual for hockey players to play a second sport, although the most-recorded choice was lacrosse.

In other news, it was suggested that ice hockey be included as entertainment for the Prince of Wales when he visited in September. Initial meetings made little progress on the issue, although Lester Patrick did agree to pick up the cost of any such event.[313] This plan never came to fruition, as it would have taken months of organization and officials noted that the prince was tired after a two-month trip across Canada. The only events he attended were at the legislative buildings on his arrival on the CPR Ship *Princess Alice* from Vancouver, a parade up Government Street and Fort Street, and a private dinner at Government House.[314] In hindsight, it is hard to imagine where a trip to the arena to view a hockey game would have fit into the schedule.

Local skating enthusiasts were excited to learn the arena would possibly be opening as early as Halloween. The rink was being repaired, with the boards painted white so that spectators would be able to see the black puck better.[315] In reality, the rink opened for skating on November 6, and some 1,000 people attended. Among the attractions were Seattle Metropolitans' Manager Pete Muldoon and George Brain, demonstrating fancy skating. The latter skated on twenty-six-inch stilts, a feat not seen anywhere else in North America.[316]

The PCHA announced that the league would again operate with three teams. The rumoured application from Con Jones[317] for a second Vancouver franchise would be turned down as "the conditions were not right for a second team in Vancouver."[318]

There were expected to be changes throughout the league as older players retired and younger ones took their place. Ran McDonald, Cully Wilson, and Tommy Dunderdale were expected to retire, and Dick Irwin would join the Aristocrats.[319] However, most of the rumours were not exactly true, as Dick Irwin was reinstated as an amateur,[320]

Wilson returned to play for the Metropolitans,[321] and Dunderdale was again an Aristocrat. Stan Marples, a former Victoria player, also returned to amateur ranks.[322]

On the local scene, Lester Patrick mailed contracts to all the players from the previous year and expected most of them to report. The first to sign a new contract was Eddie Oatman, who had spent some time helping to build ships for the French government.[323] Local players Dubbie Kerr, Bobby Genge, Eddie Oatman, and Lester Patrick began to work out with the amateur teams to get in shape before the rest of the team arrived.[324] One by one, players signed contracts and returned to Victoria. First to arrive was Moose Johnson, followed by new goaltender Norman "Hec" Fowler[325] and Wilf Loughlin.[326] Wilf's brother Clem signed, as well.[327]

At the PCHA annual meeting, the league announced that the season would start in Victoria on December 26, with Seattle as the visitors, with the rest of the schedule to be outlined later.[328] In the final schedule, released on December 13, there were thirty-three games for each team this year, with the season ending on March 10, with Victoria at Seattle.[329]

Former Toronto player Harry Meeking signed with the Aristocrats and joined the club on December 21, with goaltender Hec Fowler due a day later.[330] Finally, the season began, and the Aristocrats did not disappoint the 4,000 fans (including 400 who stood through the entire game), who turned out to watch them play the Metropolitans. After surrendering the first goal, the team came to life and scored two goals in the second period to secure the 2-1 victory. Wilf Loughlin was the star of the game, scoring one goal and assisting on the other. Harry Meeking was hit in the mouth by a stick and lost four teeth but was expected to play after a session in the dentist's chair.[331] It was a good start to the season.

The next game was in Vancouver, and the Aristocrats scored the first two goals of the game. However, they could not hold the lead and the teams battled to a 3-3 score at the end of regulation play. Unfortunately, just twenty-four seconds into overtime, Vancouver's Lloyd Cook found the net and the game was over. It was a disappointing end to a promising game.[332] In the return match in Victoria, the Aristocrats dominated the game and won handily 7-4. Ironically, the Millionaires scored the first goal of the game but did not score another until the home team had netted three of their own. Tommy Dunderdale scored four goals, returning to his form of prior years, and Harry Meeking scored his first goal as an Aristocrat.[333]

The team next played a home-and-home series against the Metropolitans. The Seattle team took the first game 5-2, with Dunderdale scoring both goals, while the Aristocrats took the second game, 2-0, with Dubbie Kerr scoring both goals.[334] When they won the game in Vancouver, the Aristocrats moved into first place in the standings. The pace was fast and furious, but the Victoria defence held firm while the Victoria shooters peppered Lehman in the Vancouver net with shot after shot. The final score of 4-3 flattered the losing team.[335] The Millionaires won the next game in Victoria 2-1 to move to the top of the standings, tied with Victoria. Star goal scorer Dunderdale played the game with a bandage around his head to project an injury, yet still managed to score the only goal and maintained his lead atop the scoring race.[336] A loss to Seattle in their next game left all three teams tied for the lead. It was a tight, clean, well-played game, with the Mets scoring the 3-1 victory.[337] It was obvious from the games played so far that the teams were very evenly matched, and there was no clear favourite to win the championship. That meant good hockey for the rest of the season with an exciting race.

The seesaw battle for the top spot in the standings continued when the Aristocrats defeated the Millionaires 4-1 in Victoria. It was the first game on the ice for Lester Patrick and his presence inspired the rest of the team. Dunderdale scored twice and had an assist. The game was notable as the teams played eleven minutes from the start of the game with no whistle and there were few blown in the rest of the game.[338] After the game, Lester said that, unless there was an emergency, he would not put on his skates but would stay behind the bench.[339] League president Frank Patrick placed a large ad in the newspaper stating: "The Pacific Coast Hockey Association will pay to anyone the sum of $1,000 for evidence that will lead to the conviction of anyone circulating slanderous statements that games in this association are 'fixed' or decided on other than their merits."[340] He also wrote a long letter to the editor outlying the situation.[341] It seemed that there were people who could not believe that three teams could have almost identical records. No one came forward, and the reward was never paid out.[342]

The next four games were not good to the Aristocrats. They lost in Vancouver 7-5, to Seattle 4-2, in Seattle 3-0, and to Vancouver 3-1.[343] Despite the team's poor efforts over the last few games, Dunderdale still led the scoring race with eighteen goals and three assists.[344] With Lester Patrick again playing and leading by example, the Aristocrats won a close game in Vancouver 3-2[345] to get back into the championship race and continued that success in Seattle, where they defeated the Metropolitans 6-1. Dunderdale scored three goals while Oatman had two goals and two assists.[346] Seattle turned the tables in the next encounter, outscoring the Aristocrats 6-0.[347] It was a costly loss, but it did not eliminate the team from championship contention. Their 3-1 victory over the Millionaires two days later put them back in the race. The game featured a fight between Tommy Dunderdale and Gord Roberts; referee Mickey Ion gave both warnings.[348] The Millionaires dealt a blow to the Aristocrats' chance for the lead with a 10-4 drubbing in Vancouver. The team was missing Moose Johnson, who could not play.[349]

While first place was out of reach, the team could still place second if everything fell into place. They responded to the challenge and rebounded to win a very close game against Seattle, 3-2. The game required more than seven minutes of overtime to settle the score, and the home fans jumped for joy when Dunderdale scored the winner.[350] With second place on the line, the Aristocrats lost a hard-fought match to Seattle, 2-0. At that point, they had only two games left and would have to win them both to secure a playoff spot.[351] In their last home game of the season, the Aristocrats sent the fans home happy with a 3-2 victory. Captain Eddie Oatman scored two brilliant goals and led his team to victory.[352] They were now tied with Seattle for second place and would be playing them in the last game of the season. A victory would mean second place and a playoff spot. Alas, it was not to be, as the Metropolitans defeated Victoria 5-1 to jump ahead of Vancouver and win the league championship.[353] It was without a doubt the closest finish in league history; Seattle finished first with twelve victories, Vancouver had eleven, and Victoria had ten. With just one more win, the Aristocrats would have reached the playoffs.

In the league playoff, Vancouver won the first game, 3-0, but couldn't duplicate the effort and fell, 6-0, to Seattle so the Metropolitans won the league championship, 6-3. They played the Ottawa Senators in the Stanley Cup finals but lost three games to two. The first three games were played in the Ottawa Arena, but the ice was very slushy as the rink did not have artificial ice. The remaining two games were played in the Arena Gardens in Toronto. This would be the last time a team from the West Coast of the United States played in a Stanley Cup final until 1993.[354]

8 - THE NEW GUARD TAKES OVER THE PCHA

There were two big hockey stories in the summer of 1920. The first was the Olympic Games in Antwerp, Belgium where the Winnipeg Falcons won the hockey championship in that event (and the gold medal), with Icelander Frank Fredrickson the star of the tournament. His success was noted in a cable from Iceland: "The Icelandic Sporting Association is banqueting Captain Frank Fredrickson, of the Falcons Hockey Club, tonight, and send congratulations to the rest of the boys, thanking them for their brilliant victory at Antwerp. (Signed) P. J. Torshon."[355]

Lester spent considerable effort persuading Fredrickson to turn pro and join the Aristocrats. The NHL was also interested in his services, but he said that if he decided to play professional hockey, it would be on the coast.[356] Aristocrat fans got a huge Christmas present when Fredrickson signed with the club. He brought with him youth, speed, and terrific hockey ability, in addition to a brilliant war record as a flier.[357]

The other off-season event was a controversy regarding the amateur status of the Alberta Big Four League. Frank Patrick wrote a letter to the Attorney-General of Alberta alleging that many of the league's players had been given money for their services the previous year, and thus were a semi-professional league, not amateur. He was supported in his beliefs by Manitoba amateur-hockey officials.[358] [359] More evidence was received from Montreal, where it was reported "a representative of the Big Four connected with Hustlers' Team of Edmonton . . . has been making offers to amateur players." The emissary was offering $1,500 or up to $2,000 for players to move west in "straight cash transactions."[360]

When the Province of Alberta would not investigate the charges, Mr. Patrick wrote a letter to *The Calgary Herald*, in which he offered a cheque of $1,000 (to be given to an Alberta charity) if he could not prove that at least ten players received money for their services.[361] Governors of the Alberta Amateur Athletic Union then opened an investigation into the charges with Frank Patrick and several players were called before the board to testify.[362] In the end, the Canadian Amateur Hockey Association sided with the Patrick allegations and declared the Big Four league professional. The league declined to appeal and operated as an independent league in 1920-21.[363]

Regarding the upcoming season for the Aristocrats, Lester Patrick announced that the arena would be open for skating on November 2. He noted: "Prices are to remain the same. Although the overhead expenses have gone up by leaps and bounds in common with other businesses, it is the intention of the management to keep the pre-war prices in effect."[364] He also sent out contracts to the players he wished to have play for the upcoming season.[365] One by one, players returned their signed contracts. First was Captain Eddie Oatman, who was determined to bring a title to Victoria.[366] He was followed closely by Harry Meeking, a great stick-handler who played aggressively.[367] Next to sign was Clem Loughlin, one of the most popular players with the locals.[368] Hec Fowler returned to defend the Victoria net. He was the youngest goaltender in professional hockey at the time and was expected to play a large part in the team's success.[369] The greatest defence player of his era, Moose Johnson, was the next to commit to the new season. He noted in his acceptance that: "I started with you and I know who I'll finish with."[370] [371] Dubbie Kerr announced his retirement, due to injuries received while playing hockey.[372] Wilf Loughlin signed as well, determined to play better than he had done the previous year.[373] The arrival of Tommy Dunderdale[374] and Bobby Genge[375] completed the roster of returning players.

The 1920-21 season opened on December 20, in Vancouver, with Seattle as the visitors. There were only six original players of the PCHA still in the league: Lester Patrick, Moose Johnson, Hughie Lehman, Bobby Rowe, Tommy Dunderdale, and Fred Harris.[376] The Millionaires won the game, 2-0, on a strong defensive game.[377] Victoria travelled to Seattle on December 22, to play the Metropolitans. The Aristocrats played well for two periods but collapsed in the third and lost the game 7-2.[378]

The next game was a matinee affair, on Christmas Day, when Victoria hosted Seattle. This first-ever afternoon game drew a huge crowd to the arena, and they were excited when the home team scored the first two goals. Unfortunately, they could not hold the lead and ended up losing 4-3 after 6:42 of overtime.[379] It did not get any better in Vancouver for the next game. Played under less-than-ideal conditions, with a dense fog over the ice, the Millionaires skated to a 6-3 victory.[380] This was not the start the club had anticipated. Victoria placed its faith in their newest member, Frank Fredrickson, to lead them to victory.

The talented Icelander played his first game on New Year's Day when Vancouver came to town. Vancouver scored the first two goals, but the Aristocrats got one back before the end of the second period. The third period belonged to the Victoria team as they outscored their opponents four goals to one to win the game 5-3.[381] Once Fredrickson took the ice, the game changed, and he dazzled the spectators with his skating ability and hockey skills. He scored one goal and added two assists in his debut. The Aristocrats played well in the next game too but fell to Seattle 2-1 after 3:35 of overtime.[382] What the fans had to realize was that Fredrickson was not the total answer, but he would help once he got used to playing with the rest of the team.

The Aristocrats rebounded from that loss and defeated the Metropolitans, 2-0. The defence played well, despite Moose Johnson playing with a broken rib.[383] The good effort, however, did not last over the next three games, as they lost twice to the Millionaires, 5-3 and 4-3, and to the Metropolitans, 9-2.[384] After a shakeup in the team, with players moved to new positions, the Aristocrats responded with a 4-1 victory over Vancouver.[385] Fredrickson and Dunderdale were the best players for that game, but the whole team concentrated on teamwork. Fans were hoping that this was the start of a winning streak, but there was a slight blip with a 5-2 loss to Vancouver.[386] However, the team managed to beat Seattle again, 5-3, with Johnson and Clem Loughlin leading the way. The Mets kept Fredrickson from scoring, but they put two checkers on him, leaving other players able to score.[387] Despite the overall losing record, individual players were doing well in the scoring race. Fredrickson was only two points out of first place, and Dunderdale was in the top ten.[388] The next game continued the winning streak, as the Aristocrats defeated the Metropolitans in a classic overtime victory. Seattle twice took the lead only to have the Aristocrats tie it up. Wilf Loughlin scored the winning goal after 31:14 of overtime, the second longest game in PCHA history. Team managers substituted in the first period of overtime as the players became very tired.[389]

After that effort, the team went into decline, losing five of their next seven games before recovering to defeat Seattle 3-0. In that game, Fredrickson scored all the Aristocrat goals, and the defence played very well. However, they were still two games back of Seattle in the league standings.[390] The team continued its mastery of the Metropolitans by winning their sixth straight over that team, 3-0 in Seattle.[391]

The entire city of Victoria was excited about the next home game. Based on a suggestion from a young fan, the Aristocrats held "Moose Johnson night." Five hundred young fans who had stood in line for free tickets made the crowd noisier than ever. It was a game for the ages.

The evening began with presentations to Ernie "Moose" Johnson, reported in the *Victoria Daily Times* as:

> *As Referee Ion poised the puck over the crossed sticks in centre ice, Murray Patrick, a wee youth, pushed off from the boards bearing in his hands a huge loving cup. He handed it to the Moose and immediately a great chorus of applause went up from the gods, where the 500 boys were quartered. The cup was inscribed: "Presented to Ernie 'Moose' Johnson by his pals, the Kids of Victoria, BC." Referee Ion tried to start the game again, but a stalwart man skipped out onto the ice and handed "Moose" a beautiful pair of diamond cuff-links, a present from the fans of Victoria. Referee Ion then took a hand in making presentations and waltzed out with a huge silver cup, which was engraved as follows: "Presented by PCHA to 'Moose' Johnson as a token of appreciation for his brilliant career as the greatest defence hockey player in the PCHA during the past ten years." The Kewpies ladies hockey team then presented the "Moose" with a big kewpie, and some dear mother trotted out a big birthday cake for Ernie. The proceedings wound up with the new police commissioner, Joe North, doing a skating act on the ice and announcing a bouquet of beautiful flowers for "Mrs. Moose."*[392]

The game did not start well for the Aristocrats, as Seattle scored the first two goals. However, Victoria outscored the opponents, 2-1, in the second period to trail by only two goals. In the third period, Victoria's offence came to life, and they scored twice, which put them in the lead, 4-3. Unfortunately, Seattle scored just before the end of the game, making overtime necessary. The first overtime period solved nothing. Nor did the second. The teams played a third overtime period, at which point they were totally exhausted. The managers of both teams agreed to call off the game, with the understanding that it would be played again if it would make a difference in the final league standing. It was the longest game ever played in the Pacific Coast Hockey Association, and perhaps, in the whole of professional hockey. Victoria had played in the four longest games in PCHA history.[393] They had won three and tied one of them.[394]

The team got terrible news the next morning. Their captain, Eddie Oatman, would not be able to play for the rest of the season. He had injured his spine in a collision with the goalpost the previous night, and the damage was more severe than was first reported.[395] Exhausted from their recent marathon game and missing their captain, the Aristocrats put up a good fight for two periods in Vancouver in their next game but could not hold the Millionaires back. The final score was 5-0.[396]

The 1919-20 PCHA season came to an end on March 11 when Vancouver visited Victoria. Despite having been eliminated from playoff contention, the Aristocrats played one of their better games of the season as the two clubs combined for nineteen goals—the largest total of the season and one of the largest in league history—and the home team emerged victorious by an 11-8 score. The contest featured a showdown between Vancouver scoring sensation Fred "Cyclone" Taylor, who scored three goals, and Frank Fredrickson. However, it was young Fredrickson who was the star of the show, with his three goals and two assists.[397] The Aristocrats ended the season with ten victories, two less than Seattle, and missed the playoffs for another year. On the bright side, Frank Fredrickson won the league scoring title with twenty goals and twelve assists in twenty-one games.[398]

In the league playoffs, first-place Vancouver defeated Seattle in the two-game total-points series 13-2, to win the right to play the Ottawa Senators for the Stanley Cup. Vancouver fans were disappointed when the Senators won the series 3-2. Average attendance for the series was 10,000, a record for the time. All games were close, being decided by one goal.[399]

The influence that the PCHA had on hockey in Canada was illustrated when the NHL decided, in 1921, to adopt some Western rules. The first was the playoff system used in the PCHA, where the first and second finishing team played a home-and-home two-game total-point series for the championship. The second was to adopt the penalty rule, where a team played one man short while a player was serving a penalty; previously, a different player had substituted so the team still played at full strength—really not much of a deterrent. Lastly, they would adopt the rule that allowed the goalkeeper to pass from his crease to the red line, forty feet away.[400]

There were changes to the Stanley Cup format, as well. The PCHA champion was no longer automatically named to play the NHL champion. A new professional league, the Western Canada Hockey League, had been formed on the Prairies, primarily out of the remains of the Big Four League. As the new league was considered comparable to the PCHA, there would be a playoff between the PCHA champion and the WCHL champion, with the winner playing the NHL champion for the Stanley Cup.[401] This meant that the PCHA had to start its schedule three weeks earlier to accommodate the additional playoff.

The major rule change for the 1921 season involved the awarding of a penalty shot if a player were fouled while he had a clear goal-scoring chance. Three dots were painted on each end of the rink, thirty-five feet from the net. The player could choose from which he would shoot on the goaltender. The first penalty-shot goal in history was scored by Tommy Dunderdale, on December 12, 1921.[402] In the entire season, there were ninety-eight attempts, of which only twenty-eight ended up in the net.[403] Another change was the limiting of games to one overtime period.[404] It was generally felt that the three-overtime game, played the previous season between Seattle and Victoria, had such an effect on the players that it took them days to recover, and that was not good for the health of the players, or indeed, the game itself.

On the home front, Lester Patrick mailed contracts to the players he wished to sign that year but would not reveal the individual names. All had to report between November 28 and December 1. He also announced that the arena would be open for skating on November 1, with a new band in attendance.[405]

The first new player to sign with the Aristocrats was Harold "Slim" Halderson. The former Winnipeg Falcon teammate of Frank Fredrickson was a marvellous stickhandler[406] and would bring his youthful enthusiasm to the club. The ageless Moose Johnson and Captain Eddie Oatman sent in their contracts.[407] Next to sign was Frank Fredrickson,[408] Clem Loughlin,[409] Wilf Loughlin,[410] Harry Meeking, and Tommy Dunderdale.[411] Goaltender Hec Fowler, who had expressed a wish to sign with his hometown Saskatoon Crescents, agreed to terms with the Aristocrats and would join the team for another season.[412] His decision was likely influenced by the fact that the Victoria club would not give him a release, and if he did not play for the PCHA, he would have been suspended from hockey for a year. He did not have a good time at his first practice, either, as his luggage had been delayed. He took to the ice wearing civvies, with a borrowed goal stick. Evidently, the players were supposed to take it easy on him, but Tommy Dunderdale conveniently "forgot" and fired a shot that definitely hurt Hec's leg. Hec said nothing.[413]

Lester Patrick started a new type of practice in which he "takes each player in turn to one end of the rink for fifteen minutes of unique practice. He makes the boys coming on the net try to get by him and then he alternates and tests his hired men in stopping him from getting in. Halts are called, and the manager explains to his pupils the points they should be observing. As a result, the checking and stick-handling ability of the team is being greatly improved."[414] Local fans were encouraged when Lester noted that his substitutes were just as good as his regulars. He also said that he had not picked a starting seven other than, of course, the goaltender.[415]

The new season opened in Vancouver on December 5, when the Millionaires defeated the Metropolitans, 2-1.[416] The opener for Victoria was on December 7, where the Aristocrats defeated the Millionaires, 4-1. This result was in direct contrast to their first game of the previous season when they returned from their first away game a dejected crew. Slim Halderson, playing as a substitute, was the first rookie to score a goal when he found the net behind Holmes in the first period.[417] Victoria fans eagerly awaited the home opener on December 8. The game did not disappoint in its excitement, but the teams played one full overtime period, and the result was declared a 1-1 tie.[418]

The Aristocrats rebounded in their next game in Vancouver and defeated the Millionaires, 2-0. Hec Fowler was the outstanding player of the game, stopping three penalty shots and not letting anyone else score.[419] As noted previously, Dunderdale scored on his penalty shot—called a "free shot" in the newspaper account. It was the first successful such goal in league history. When Vancouver travelled to the island for their next match, the Aristocrats again prevailed with Clem Loughlin's shot near the end of the third period breaking a 3-3 tie and sending the local fans home happy with a 4-3 win.[420]

After such a great start to the season, everyone was disappointed when the team lost their next four games,[421] falling out of first place in the league standings. With Frank Fredrickson and Eddie Oatman injured, the Aristocrats went into Seattle and staged a comeback from three goals down. Oatman, playing on one good leg, scored the tying goal with seconds left on the clock, setting the stage for Slim Halderson's winning goal at 14:34 of overtime.[422] The winning continued for another game when the Millionaires went down to defeat, 5-2. Manager Patrick made changes in his lineup, necessary because of the injury to Fredrickson: Meeking to rover, Oatman on defence, and Wilf Loughlin at forward. The juggling seemed to work. The team now had six men on the ice who could not only score but defend, as well. With the victory, the Aristocrats moved back into a first-place tie in the standings with Vancouver.[423]

The team received terrible news that week. The team doctor said that Eddie Oatman could not play for at least a week. This was not good news, as Moose Johnson was still ailing and unable to play an entire game.[424] They lost the next game to Vancouver, 4-0,[425] as the depleted team was unable to mount much of an offence. A feature of the game was manager Patrick playing goal in place of Fowler, who had been sent off the ice for fighting. With no goalie pads, Lester stopped the puck every way he could, dropping to his knees on several occasions. His unorthodox style of play earned him the nickname of the "Praying Colonel."[426]

The team got back to its winning ways with a 5-2 victory over the Metropolitans in Victoria. Although Seattle scored the first goal of the game, Harry Meeking scored shortly after to tie the score. The Aristocrats then peppered Holmes in the Seattle net with shot after shot, and four more ended up behind him, with Fredrickson the individual star of the night.[427] At the halfway point of the season, Victoria was in first place in the standings, but there were only two points between first and last, the teams being so evenly matched. The return engagement in Seattle was also a Victoria victory, although the score was much closer at 4-3. Down 2-1 with less than five minutes to play, the Aristocrats poured in three goals in four minutes to take the game and remain atop the standings.[428] Their winning streak was stopped by Vancouver, who took the next game, 4-3, in overtime. However, that was not the news of the day. Management and fans alike were stunned when Moose Johnson left the team, saying he was retiring and returning to work as a brakeman on the Portland railway. It was a slap in the face to the fans who had showered him with gifts the year before, but there was nothing anyone could do about the situation.[429] [430]

Things turned around again with a 5-4 victory over Vancouver in the mainland city. Dunderdale and Fredrickson found their old form in the cleanly played game.[431] Two consecutive losses to Seattle, 4-0 and 3-1,[432] moved the Aristocrats out of first place, but a subsequent 2-1 close victory over Vancouver returned them to top spot in the standings. Slim Halderson was the best player on the ice for the game, playing the best defensive hockey of the season.[433] However, championship hopes hit a roadblock when the Aristocrats lost their next three games: 3-2 to Vancouver,[434] 2-0 to Seattle,[435] and 7-0 to Seattle.[436] It was the third recent shutout by the Metropolitans, and the team could not figure out where their vaunted scoring had gone.

The results left the team in last place in the league, albeit only three points out of a playoff spot. Lester Patrick tried a new combination for the next game against Seattle. As reported in the press: "Wilf Loughlin, who has been warming the bench of late, was sent to right defence, a position he played earlier in the season, Eddie Oatman returned to right wing, Halderson went over to left, and Meeking and Fredrickson changed positions. Tommy Dunderdale went to the bench to view the proceedings. About halfway through the period, 'Freddie' went back to centre and Meeking to rover." The changes were effective as the team played with new energy to a 3-2 victory.[437] A victory in the next game would have gained the team a share of first place, but they fell to Vancouver 5-1 in a game in which they just never got going. They did not score until the final frame, by which time the result was already decided.[438]

The final game of the Aristocrats season was a successful one, as they defeated the Millionaires 7-4.[439] It was perhaps the closest finish in league history. Seattle finished in first place with twenty-five points, Vancouver in second with twenty-four, and Victoria with twenty-three. If they had earned one point in any of the games they lost, Victoria would have had a successful season. Alas, it was not to be, and the players departed to their off-season homes.[440]

In the playoffs, the Vancouver Millionaires won the two-game total-goals series against Seattle by identical 1-0 scores. They then played the Regina Capitals, the champions of the Western Canada Hockey League in a two-game total-goals series for the right to play the NHL champion for the Stanley Cup. Vancouver won that series five goals to two and advanced to play the Toronto St. Patricks. Eddie Oatman and Lester Patrick were added to the Vancouver squad; Oatman was to replace Harris, who was injured, and Patrick was to coach behind the bench.[441] In Toronto, with the series tied two games all, the St. Pats scored a 5-1 win to take the series and win their only Stanley Cup.[442]

9 - WINDS OF CHANGE BLOW THROUGH THE PCHA

In the 1922-23 season, the Pacific Coast Hockey Association eliminated the position of rover, putting an end to seven-man-a-side hockey, eleven years after the National Hockey Association had dropped it. Now there would be no further arguments about what system should be played during the Stanley Cup games; all leagues would play six-man hockey.[443] With the adoption of that system, new rules needed to be drafted:

Many of the feature rules, introduced by the Patricks, were retained, including the blue lines, the penalty shot, and the body check. The new rules were as follows:

> *(1) a team shall be composed of six players, who shall be bona fide of members of the club they represent. No team shall have more than nine men in uniform, the personnel of whom shall not be changed during the game. Each player shall wear a number on the back of his sweater, which number he shall retain while he is under contract with respective clubs.*

> *(2) The game shall be commenced and renewed by a faceoff in the centre of the rink. The home club shall have the privilege of choosing the goals to defend at the start of the game. The puck shall be faced off by being placed on the ice between the sticks of the opponents or by the referee dropping the puck on the ice between the sticks of the players facing, and the referee giving signal to play.*

> *(3) Three twenty-minute periods of actual play, with an intermission of ten minutes between each period, shall be decided by the team scoring the greatest number of goals during the sixty minutes. Goals shall be changed every twenty minutes. In case of a tie after playing the specified sixty minutes, after ten minutes' rest, play will continue for not more than twenty minutes, without change of goals or until one side scores a goal, it being understood that any extra time played shall be considered part of the match and all unexpired penalties shall remain in force. In case of a tie at the end of the overtime period, the match shall be considered a draw. In playoff games, the play will be limited to sixty minutes for the first game. If a tie exists at the end of sixty minutes play in the second game, the game will be continued until one team secures a goal, provided that not more than two twenty-minute periods shall be played, with ten minutes rest and change of goal between periods. In case of a tie at the*

end of the second game, one game will be ordered played on neutral ice and be played to a finish.

(4) The standing of clubs shall be figured by the point system, i.e., Two points for a win, one point each for a draw. If two teams in the same league tie for first place, they will, of course, take place in the league playoff. Should two teams tie for second place, the club scoring the highest average of goals in comparison with goals scored, shall be the team eligible to play off with the team standing highest in the league.

(5) Players may be changed at any whistle or bell interval. During the match by the captain or manager of a club and said substitute may be placed on the ice and the original player removed without interruption of the match. The substitute shall not get on the ice until the original players holding off the ice, or within three feet of the players' bench.

(6) There shall be a referee for each match. The duties of the referee are to impose the rules, adjudicate upon disputes or cases unprovided for by rules, supervise removed umpires or team timekeepers, assist the official scorer in recording names of players scoring goals and assisting in scoring goals as provided for under scoring rules . The puck shall be considered in play until the referee stops the game, which he may do it any time by sending the whistle or bell. And there shall be no appeal by any players. Capt. may appeal on a question of proper interpretation of the playing rules. The referee may have an assistant to aid him in enforcing rules and imposing penalties, reversal by the referee. The assistant shall be called Judge of Play.

(7) In the event of players being injured or compelled to leave the ice during the match, the referee may order play to be continued immediately without the team s leaving the ice, a substitute taking the injured man's position on the ice. Should a goalkeeper be injured, he shall be allowed ten minutes to recuperate, or a substitute shall be provided.

(8) Each rink shall divide the ice surface into three equal sections by drawing a blank coloured line, six inches or more in width, across the ice and the side fences at right angles to the length of the ice. This division will make one centre section and to end sections. All players shall be considered on side in the centre section. When a player passes the puck in either of the end sections, anyone of the same side who is at such moment of passing is nearer the opponent's goal line is out of play shall not touch the puck himself with the one exception as provided for in section 14. No player shall take the puck offside in the centre section if it has been played by one of his own side from the end section.[444]

Two clubs changed their names. The Vancouver Millionaires became the Maroons while the Victoria Aristocrats became the Cougars, the name chosen after a public contest to find a new name. Local press reported the entire procedure:

> "Cougars!" That is the new name for the Victoria pro hockey team. The old name "Aristocrats," which took a sober man half an hour to get his tongue around, now passes into history and takes its place with a lot of other useless things. Cougar is the local name by which the panther, a wild animal belonging to the cat family, is recognized. It is found on Vancouver Island. The quest for a new name for the Victoria Hockey Club resulted in many names being submitted.

The committee entrusted with the responsibility of setting a name reviewed them all. They found some difficulty in selecting the winning name from "Oaks," "Sunbeams," "Roses" and "Cougars." They believed that the club should have a name that no other club possessed and yet one which at the same time would denote something very virile and active. The committee considered the names "Vics" and "'Caps" but found that there were a great number of other towns in the country which boasted of those names and when for want of a change these names were often applied by sporting writers in regard to the activities of the Victoria club. Hereafter the name "Cougars" will always be associated with the capital of British Columbia and it would be the fond hope of every fan that the "Cougars" this year pounce upon the other teams in the league, give them a good trimming and wind up by snubbing the Eastern and Prairie champions and give Victoria the world's championship.[445]

For the first time, the PCHA would play an interlocking schedule with games against the Western Canada League. The Edmonton Eskimos, Calgary Tigers, Regina Capitals, and Saskatoon Crescents would play games against Vancouver, Victoria, and Seattle with the results showing in their league standings.[446,447] The Saskatoon team had poor attendance and moved to Moose Jaw on February 3, but was back in Saskatoon the next year as the Crescents.[448]

As usual, Manager Lester Patrick made a trip to the East to search out new talent for the team. On his return, he mailed contracts to the previous year's players. It was expected that most of the players would come back, but Lester would not announce his lineup until the signed contracts were returned. Harry Meeking, Wilf Loughlin, and Dunderdale were still in town and would likely make the team. Fredrickson was in Winnipeg and Halderson in Detroit. Oatman was in St. Paul. Hec Fowler was with his dad's printing business in Saskatoon, while Clem Loughlin was harvesting his crops in Viking, Alberta.[449]

Lester Patrick hired staff to overhaul the arena equipment to make the earliest opening ever—October 31. If the team played well and made the playoffs, skaters would have almost six months of exercise on their blades.[450] Hockey fans also looked forward to an early start to the season. Excitement grew as players returned their contracts. First to sign was Frank Fredrickson, the talented Winnipeg forward.[451] He was followed by Eddie Oatman, one of the few original PCHA players still active,[452] and Hec Fowler, who would again guard the net. He was looking forward to a season in which the goaltender had more responsibility, due to the elimination of the rover position. He felt he would be able to see the puck better with fewer players on the ice.[453] Harry Meeking was next to agree to terms; the six-man game was better suited to his offensive skills.[454] Slim Halderson quit his job in Detroit and made his way to Victoria. He intended to take up where he had left off the previous season.[455] Clem Loughlin finished harvesting his summer crops and made his way to the coast. He liked to live in Victoria in the winters, as the weather was nicer than in Alberta.[456] Tommy Dunderdale came back for another season, expecting to alternate at centre with Fredrickson. He wanted to score his two-hundredth goal during the season, needing only eight to achieve that mark.[457] Local hockey star Charles Albert Dieldal was hoping to find a place with the Victoria team. He had been the best amateur hockey player in Victoria over the last few years.[458] John "Jocko" Anderson star forward of the Calgary Tigers, was traded to Victoria and was expected to be one of the leading scorers. He came from a family of six hockey players, all of whom had made their mark in the game.[459] The signing of Wilf Loughlin completed the squad for the upcoming season. He would be the largest player on the team and a stalwart on defence.[460]

With the start of the hockey season, referee Mickey Ion (who had handled all the games in the PCHA for several years) would be joined by one or two additional referees, due to the increased schedule and the interlocking games with the WCHL.[461] League fans were curious about the six-man game, as many had never seen it played before. Teams were now able to carry three substitutes so that players could have some rest during the game.[462] The season started in Vancouver with the Maroons losing 8-2 to the Metropolitans.[463] The Victoria team opened their season in Seattle and lost to the high-flying Mets by a 4-0 score. Seattle goaltender Hap Holmes stymied multiple scoring efforts.[464]

Victoria played its first home game under the new name "Cougars" on November 17. The result was a 5-3 win over the Vancouver Maroons. The passing of Oatman, Fredrickson, and Meeking was a joy to watch, and defenceman Wilf Loughlin scored two pretty goals. Ever the innovator, Lester Patrick installed a scoreboard at the arena upon which spectators could follow the score and the elapsed time. It was declared "a good innovation."[465]

The Cougars then travelled to Vancouver, where they edged out the Maroons, 4-3. Frank Fredrickson scored four goals for Victoria, and Hec Fowler stymied the Vancouver efforts to tie the game.[466] The good play did not continue, however, as the team lost their next four league games by very close scores.[467] In a strange turn of fate, the Cougars defeated the touring Stanley Cup champions, the Toronto St. Pats, 7-3 in an exhibition game on December 1. After the game, St. Pats' Manager George O'Donoghue said he could not understand how the Cougars were having problems in the league. He was sure they would turn things around based on their play against his team. The St. Pats played in Vancouver and Seattle before making a round of the Prairie cities.[468]

On December 15, the Cougars put an end to their own losing streak and Seattle's winning streak with a hard-fought 2-1 victory in front of an appreciative home crowd.[469] With the win, they moved into a tie with Vancouver for second place in the league standings. The Cougars' next game was their first interlocking match—against the Regina Capitals. They lost 3-2, giving the Capitals two victories and one defeat on their coastal swing.[470] The Cougars then ended the Vancouver Maroons' winning streak when they defeated the mainland crew, 4-3. Harry Meeking scored the winning goal in the third period, on a pass from Fredrickson in front of the net.[471]

The Cougars started the new year optimistic that they had turned the corner and could challenge for a playoff position after so many years of finishing third in the standings. They took a step in the right direction with a thrilling 2-1 victory over Vancouver, their second consecutive win in two games over the Maroons. Vancouver's Cook scored the first goal of the game, but Halderson tied the score four minutes later. There was no further scoring, so the game went to overtime. Clem Loughlin took the puck deep in his own end and skated through the Vancouver defenders to fire a shot that eluded Lehman and gave the Cougars the victory after 8:20 of overtime.[472] The next game was just as exciting when Frank Fredrickson scored the only goal of the game against Seattle and vaulted the Cougars into a three-way tie atop the league standings.[473] The Cougars set records in their next home game.

The game, a 5-1 shellacking of the Metropolitans, was their fifth victory in a row (including the exhibition game) and their fourth in seven days. Every player was in top form, and they kept away from the rough stuff, preferring to stay on the ice and score. Lester Patrick substituted freely to keep his players fresh, and they produced a great effort as a result.[474]

The next game against Seattle was played in Vancouver, as the Maroons were off on their Prairie swing. The Cougars' bid for six wins in a row was halted when the Mets outscored them, 2-0. Perhaps the Metropolitans were afraid that their manager, Pete Muldoon had been serious when he told them: "You'll beat Victoria, or you'll walk home." In any event, the Mets played a rough game and came out on top.[475] The second interlocking game of the season featured the Calgary Tigers, handicapped by the loss of their regular goaltender, who had been clipped between the eyes with a stick in a league game against Edmonton. He played in Seattle on January 10, but afterward complained of severe pain. Doctors removed him from play, and as a result, a player who had never played goal before donned the pads and faced the deadly shooters of the Cougars. The result was predictable: a Cougar victory, 4-0. "Freddie" Fredrickson scored one goal and two assists to lead the team in scoring; the results moved him into first place in the league's scoring race.[476] In the next game, Victoria outlasted Vancouver, 3-2, after eight minutes of overtime. The hero was again Clem Loughlin, who scored this time on a long, bouncing shot.[477] The Maroons brought the Cougars back down to earth when they scored a 4-1 victory in Vancouver.[478] They followed this up with an 8-4 victory in a game played in Seattle while the Mets were on the Prairies.[479]

Victoria's next match was against the Saskatoon Crescents. The visitors just about did not make it to the game, as the train to the coast was delayed by four hours. As a result, they missed the scheduled boat to the island. In order to ensure a game in Victoria, league president Frank Patrick chartered the steamer *Charmer* to bring the team to the island in time for their game. Despite having Newsy Lalonde, one of the best hockey players in the world at that time, on their team, Saskatoon was unable to solve the goaltending of Hec Fowler. "Freddie" was again the most prominent player on the ice, with three goals and an assist.[480] With first place in the standings on the line, the Cougars fell to the Maroons, 4-3, after eleven minutes of overtime. The goal was hotly disputed by the home team, as the net was moving out of position at the time the shot was taken. Replacement referee George Irvine overruled the goal umpire who did not raise his arm to signify a goal. Lester Patrick protested the result to league officials[481] and the protest was allowed. The points from the game were deducted from Vancouver's total and all scoring points were taken away from both teams. It was decided that the game would be replayed on March 5, if it had any effect on the league standings.[482]

In response to the protest, the league declared that Mickey Ion would referee all future games in Victoria.[483] The next game was played in Seattle. The Mets came through with a 5-2 victory, as Victoria took too long to get their game going and their rally fell short.[484] Two days later, the Cougars handed the Mets their worst defeat of the season, outscoring them, 6-1. Seattle had scored the first goal of the game on a penalty shot in the first period, but after that, the Cougars took over, scoring two goals in the second period and four more in the third. Freddie had three goals and added two assists to increase his lead atop the league-scoring race.[485] Victoria got into penalty trouble in their next game and fell, 5-3, to the Maroons.[486] This loss put the team in last place in the league. They would have to win a lot more games if they were to make the playoffs. The Edmonton Eskimos were the next opponent for the Cougars. One of the best teams in the WCHL, they were unable to solve the Victoria defence and lost, 4-0. Clem Loughlin was the best player on the ice, scoring two goals unassisted.[487]

After that match, the Cougars left on their Eastern swing. They were the only PCHA team to score a victory on Regina ice, winning, 2-1; Harry Meeking scored the winning goal in the third period. Lester Patrick sent a "Lestergram" after the game that read:

> *"Fighting an uphill battle on sticky ice and handicapped by penalties, we outlasted and outgamed Regina tonight. Our boys repeatedly overskated the puck during the first period but readily adapted themselves to conditions for the balance of the game. The break did not come until halfway through the third period when Laird seemingly stopped a hard shot from Meeking only to discover that the puck had crossed the*

line. Fowler, Halderson, Clem Loughlin, Fredrickson, Meeking and Oatman played great hockey, with Fowler the most brilliant on the ice. Irvin and Moran scintillated for Regina. The rink was packed to the roof and the fans state that the game was the most thrilling of the season. All our players are in splendid shape and feel good to have a number one tucked away. We leave for Saskatoon tonight."[488]

Two days later, the Cougars won another game on the Prairies, besting the Saskatoon Crescents, 1-0, with Fredrickson scoring the only goal in the third period, under a minute from the end of regulation play. Just before the game, the mayor stepped out and made a speech to Saskatoon native Hec Fowler, and then handed him a cabinet containing $200 worth of silverware. Hec got married just before he came to the coast, and the fans had decided to show their respect for him in a substantial matter.

Then what does Hec do? He shuts out the home team.[489] While the Cougars were out of town, Victoria fans watched the Maroons defeat the Metropolitans. The Cougars' next game on the Prairies was in Edmonton. The Eskimos could not solve Fredrickson, and the Cougars ended up winning the game, 5-4. The Icelander scored three goals in the third period to salt the game away.[490] The last game of the gruelling Prairie swing was in Calgary. Playing on slushy ice, the speedy Cougars could not get their footing, and they lost the game, 4-2.[491] This was the only loss of their Prairie swing, so the team returned home quite satisfied with their results.

Tired after their long road trip and exhausted from the delayed train trip, the Cougars lost their next game in Seattle, 5-3. The result meant that Victoria and Seattle were again tied for second place in the league.[492] It would take the last scheduled game of the season to settle the playoff positions. Before the game, Mayor Hayward welcomed the team back to Victoria and congratulated them on playing seven games in fourteen days.[493] In the game that evening, the Cougars put up a magnificent offensive display and humbled the visiting Mets, 9-2. Fredrickson scored four goals and two assists to win the scoring race easily over MacKay of the Maroons. He finished the season with thirty-nine goals and fifteen assists in twenty-nine games.[494] As the Cougars finished ahead of the Metropolitans, there was no need for the replaying of the protested game from February 7. The finals standings showed the Maroons in first place and the Cougars in second place; both would go on to the two-game total-goals playoff for the league championship.

The Vancouver Maroons won the first game of the playoff, scoring a 3-0 win over the Cougars.[495] Victoria won the second game 5-3 but could not overcome the three-goal lead that Vancouver had carried into the game. Thus, they lost the series, 6-5. Vancouver would then go on to play the Ottawa Senators for the right to play the Edmonton Eskimos for the Stanley Cup. The Senators won the series against the Maroons 3-1, and then defeated the Eskimos, 2-0, to win the Stanley Cup.[496]

An analysis of the interlocking schedule played by PCHA teams against the Prairie teams showed that the Coast teams won fifteen out of twenty-four games, with the Cougars leading the way with six victories in the eight games they played. Regina had the best record of the Prairie clubs, while Saskatoon played six games and had only one tie to show for their efforts. The series had proven interesting to local fans, and they welcomed an interlocking schedule again the next year.[497] Almost as if they had read the fans' minds, the WCHL decided at its September meeting to increase the number of interlocking games in the upcoming season. Each Prairie team would make two trips to the Coast, doubling what had happened the year before.[498] The schedule for the upcoming PCHA season included no hockey on the Coast from December 10 until the afternoon of Christmas Day. All three Coast clubs would be on the Prairies for this fortnight, and there would be two and three games in Prairie cities on several nights during that period. Minor rule changes were made that affected goaltenders. "Goaltenders must wear standard equipment, may not be assisted by mechanical or extraordinary contrivance, their leg pads must not exceed twelve inches and he may not go behind his own goal at any time."[499]

Changes were coming to the Cougars lineup for 1923-24. Five-year-captain Eddie Oatman realized he could no longer play a full season, so was traded to Calgary as a playing manager in return for Jimmy Gibson and Bill Speck. Gibson was only twenty-four years old and had scored nineteen goals with Calgary the previous season. Bill Speck had injured his knee that same season and had to be examined by a doctor before being added to the roster. Lester also announced that he had signed Clem Trihey, a talented amateur from Montreal who had played in the Eastern American League the previous year.[500] Gibson, at first, refused to come to Victoria as he would lose his job, but arrangements were eventually made that would allow his job to be waiting in the off-season, and he agreed to join the team.[501] Wilf Loughlin was sold to the Toronto St. Pats. He had never reached his potential as a defender in Victoria, and Lester Patrick felt he would be better suited to play in the NHL.[502]

Lester Patrick looked to have better substitutes for the upcoming year as he felt the lack of production from his subs the last year had cost the team a playoff spot. He brought in several players to try for the backup positions and would not guarantee players would make the team, even if they held a signed contract.[503] He wanted to have a younger team that could withstand the rough play and the extensive travel that hockey in that era demanded. By the end of October, Lester had in hand signed contracts from Clem Loughlin, Slim Halderson, Harry Meeking, Frank Fredrickson, Jocko Anderson, Jimmy Gibson, Bill Speck, Clem Trihey, Harold "Gizzy" Hart, and Carson Thompson. Only Hec Fowler remained unsigned.[504] The first practice of the new season was held on November 5, and two days later, Hec signed his contract. The team was now complete, and young players were looking to make the team.[505] Clem Loughlin was named the new captain of the Cougars, with Frank Fredrickson as vice-captain. Harold Hart was named one of the permanent team, leaving four players scrambling to secure the remaining spaces.[506]

The new season started with the Metropolitans defeating the Maroons 3-2 before 6,000 fans in Vancouver.[507] The Cougars travelled to Seattle to open their season, as they had done for several years. The starters were Fowler, Halderson, Loughlin, Fredrickson, Meeking, and Anderson; the substitutes were Gibson, Trihey, and Hart. The team was unable to hold the lead and lost the game 6-5 when former Aristocrat Bobby Rowe scored after just over a minute of overtime.[508] The home opener featured a game against Vancouver, which the Cougars won 5-1. Jimmy Gibson started at left wing—his first professional game—and had a good game with several good shots on goal.[509] The next game in Vancouver did not go the Cougars' way. They lost 7-1 in a game where their only goal was scored on a penalty shot by Fredrickson.[510]

In the next game against Seattle, Fredrickson put on quite a display. He scored three goals and threw the Seattle defence off so that Gibson could score the fourth, but was rested after every goal. The team played well together and outscored their opponents 4-2. Both goaltenders were kept busy with Fowler stopping twenty-seven shots while Holmes in the Seattle net stopped forty-eight.[511] The Saskatoon Crescents came to town and put up a fight for one period, then wilted under the relentless Cougar attack and lost to the home team 7-1. Once the game was apparently in hand, Lester made frequent use of his subs, and at one point, pulled his two defencemen off the ice for a rest. It was the first time all season that Clem Loughlin had been off the ice during a game.[512] Next to come to town were the Calgary Tigers, who defeated the Cougars 3-1. Trihey missed two penalty shots for Victoria, and Fredrickson suffered an injury.

After the game, the Cougars left for their Prairie swing.[513] Their first game was in Edmonton against the Eskimos. The conditions were terrible because, in many parts of the outdoor rink, the sawdust was barely covered with ice, and before the contest was well underway, the players had cut through it and had to perform all kinds of maneuvers to keep on their feet. The players still managed to put on a passable exhibition of hockey, and the Cougars emerged with a 3-1 win. Loughlin, Fredrickson, and Hart scored the goals, all in the first period, while Sparrow scored for Edmonton.[514] There was no further scoring, likely due to the deteriorating conditions. The next game was in Saskatoon, where the tiny rink caused a problem for the speedy Cougars skaters, as they did not have as much room to make their moves. The Crescents won their first game of the season, outscoring the Victoria team 9-3. The Cougars' shooting was poor, as they missed the net on numerous occasions and just did not play well together.[515] The Prairie woes continued in Regina, where the Capitals emerged victorious, 4-2, in a high-speed game. Despite the loss, it was likely one of the best games the Cougars played in the season.[516] In a game played in Winnipeg, the Capitals again bested the Cougars, this time by a 4-1 score.[517]

This year's Prairie swing was nothing like the previous year's edition, in which the PCHA teams had been superior in every way. Either the WCHL teams had improved significantly, or the PCHA teams had lost their edge. With one game left for each Western team on the Prairie circuit, the WCHL teams had won thirteen of the sixteen games played so far, with one tied.[518] In the last game of their long road trip, the Cougars revisited Newsy Lalonde's Saskatoon team. This time, they played well and won the game in overtime, 3-2, twice coming back from a one-goal deficit and tying the game with only seventeen seconds left in regulation time. That set the stage for Clem Loughlin's overtime winner after just one minute of extra play. The result gave Victoria the best record on that Prairie swing. They won two out of five, Vancouver won one out of five, and Seattle lost all six.[519]

After returning from the Prairies, PCHA clubs returned to regular play. The Cougars and Maroons played a game on Christmas Day in Vancouver and, from all accounts, it was a great display of skill and finesse. The Maroons won the contest, 3-1, and regained first place in the league standings.[520] In the return match, played three days later in Victoria, the Cougars turned the tables on the Maroons and defeated them, 3-2. Victoria took the early lead on a goal by Jocko Anderson, but the Maroons tied it up before the end of the first period. In the third period, Vancouver took the lead only to have Meeking dash up the ice and score just twenty-eight seconds later. That set the stage for an extra period of hockey. Young Harold "Gizzy" Hart, playing his first year of professional hockey, was the overtime hero, scoring on a brilliant solo rush up the ice and beating Lehman cleanly. Lester Patrick had been impressed with the youngster's play as a sub in the first part of the game and so started him in place of Gibson in the overtime period. His hunch paid off, and the local fans were "delirious with joy" at the result.[521]

Then it was off to Seattle for the team. They played hard but still fell to the Mets, 2-1. Fredrickson had the tying goal on his stick but could not beat the acrobatics of Mets goaltender Holmes, who twisted to block the shot. "Freddie" was tightly checked throughout the game and never got a chance to show his talent. Clem Loughlin was outstanding for the Cougars, stopping rush after rush, and leading by example. Hart scored the sole goal for Victoria and was fast becoming a fan favourite in Victoria.[522]

When the Mets came to Victoria for the next contest, the result was different. The Cougars won a tightly contested game, 3-2. It took terrific saves by Fowler in the net to keep the game tied in regulation time, setting the stage for Fredrickson to score the winner after 15:32 of overtime. Victoria was back on top of the league standings.[523] Lester Patrick was so impressed by the work of "Gizzy" Hart that he named the young player to the starting group for the game against the Edmonton Eskimos. As the manager had predicted early in the season, the Cougar substitutes were as competent as his starters.[524] Despite the best efforts of the entire team, the Eskimos defeated them 4-2. Harry Meeking scored both Victoria goals but missed a wide-open net when a goal would have tied the score. It was the only victory for Edmonton on their PCHA swing.[525] The Cougars rebounded in the next game at Vancouver and won in overtime against the Maroons. Harry Meeking again scored the tying goal. The fans were barely in their seats for the extra play when "Gizzy" Hart scored after only twenty-six seconds of overtime.[526]

Between games, Lester Patrick bought in another young player, Archie Briden. He felt that the addition would give him two complete forward lines, either of which could score.[527] Having a player skate for the whole game was becoming less common, as the number of games increased and the need for extended Prairie travel took a toll on players' health and stamina.

The Cougars went into their next game against the Calgary Tigers needing a victory to regain first place in the standings. It was not to be, as Hec Fowler had an off night and allowed several long, soft shots to get past him. Victoria lost the game, 7-3. "Gizzy" Hart did all the scoring for the Cougars, but his effort was wasted.[528] The Cougars then travelled to Seattle to play the Maroons in a neutral-site game. The game was close, and when the dust was cleared, Vancouver had emerged victorious after 1:44 of overtime. Victoria was upset when Mickey Ion ruled a goal scored by Fredrickson offside, so it did not count. This was the sixth overtime game that Victoria had played that season, and this was only their second loss in extra time.[529]

The addition of Archie Briden paid dividends in the next encounter against the Maroons. The Maroons scored the only goal of the first period, and Briden the only goal of the third period. Again, the end came quickly as Briden notched the winner after only twenty-five seconds. Victoria fans went home happy as Victoria was once again in top spot in the standings, tied with the Mets.[530] Unfortunately, the Cougars could not build on that great victory and lost their next two games, 2-1 to Regina[531] and 8-1 in Seattle against the Mets.[532] Victoria was now in third place in the league and out of a playoff spot. Seattle came to Victoria and beat them again by a score of 4-1. The *Victoria Daily Colonist* described the game with their usual flair: "Visions of the Victoria Cougars entering the Pacific Coast Hockey Championship play-off competitions were rudely shattered and almost extinguished last night at the Willows Arena, when the Islanders on their home territory, hopelessly failed to check the Seattle puckchasers' terrific onslaught."[533]

The Cougars did manage to get some revenge on Seattle when they defeated the Mets, 4-1, in a game played in Vancouver. The game was very rough, with three penalty shots awarded to Victoria by Mickey Ion. Despite missing them all, the Cougars still came home with a victory.[534] They played their last home game of the season on February 15. The Cougars used their speed and shooting accuracy to beat the visiting Eskimos, 5-1. Hart scored twice while Briden, Fredrickson, and Anderson added singles.[535] Fans were hopeful that the team could repeat the previous year's success on their long Prairie road trip and get back to the playoffs. The WCHL teams had much better records that season than the previous one, and that was obvious when the Cougars could only manage a single point—a tie with Edmonton—on the whole, five-game road trip.[536] It was not the ending to the season that the team wanted, as they missed the playoffs by four points.

In the league playoffs, Vancouver beat Seattle and earned the right to play the WCHL champion Calgary for the chance to go directly to the Stanley Cup playoffs. Calgary won that series, while Vancouver had to play Montreal in a semi-final game, which they lost, 5-3. Montreal then defeated Calgary handily in the Stanley Cup finals.[537]

10 - VICTORIA AND VANCOUVER JOIN THE WCHL

Little did PCHA fans know that the 1923-24 season would be the last for the once-dominant league. Shortly after the season ended, ice was removed from the Seattle Arena, and it was used briefly as a roller rink before being remodelled into a parking garage. It was torn down in 1963 to make way for the IBM building.[538] The loss of the ice surface meant that the Seattle Metropolitans had no home, and the PCHA was left with only two teams. The Patricks had no choice but to join the Prairie league so that their franchises would survive. The merger was announced at the Calgary meeting of the WCHL, at which the owners called the "applications from Vancouver and Victoria . . . somewhat of a surprise." Other items of note from that meeting included a change to the offside rule so that there would be "no offsides in any section of the ice, excepting when crossing from one section to another." There would also be a new system for the playoffs at the end of the season. The four teams standing highest at the end of the schedule would form two groups to play home-and-home games, and the two winners would play another series to determine the championship. The winner of that series would advance to play the NHL winner in the Stanley Cup playoffs, which would be played in the West that year.[539]

With the suspension of the Seattle franchise, their players became available to the other teams in the expanded league. Media outlets speculated on just where the former Mets would play, and many different scenarios were proposed. In the end, forwards Frank Foyston, Gord Fraser, and Jack Walker joined the Cougars. The big signing for the team was former Seattle goaltender Harry "Hap" Holmes after Lester Patrick sold Hec Fowler to the new Boston team in the NHL.[540] Several former PCHL players were placed on waivers and could be picked up by any team in any league for the asking price. Victoria would lose Anderson, Trihey, and Gibson, none of whom had been very consistent in the league.[541]

It took some time for the schedule for the upcoming season of the expanded league to be confirmed. Play would start later than in the old PCHA, as the Prairie teams used natural ice and the weather had to be cold enough to produce a good skating surface. The schedule was finally released on November 3, and it featured twelve home games for each team, with the Victoria opener on Christmas Day. No longer would Friday be the "night" for hockey as in past seasons, as seven games would be played on Saturdays. It was felt this was beneficial to the club, as up-island fans would be able to drive down to attend such matches.[542]

Victoria fans were relieved when Fredrickson signed a new contract with the Cougars. He had always been a good goal scorer, and it was felt that he would fit in well with the acquisitions from Seattle.[543] With the return of Clem Loughlin and

10 - VICTORIA AND VANCOUVER JOIN THE WCHL

"Gizzy" Hart, the team was rounding into shape. Clem was noted as being a very durable player. The previous season, he had left the ice only three times for a rest, in addition to any penalties called on him.[544] By the time all the contracts were signed, the Cougars looked like a combination of the best of the Victoria and Seattle teams from the previous season.[545] Fans wondered if "this could be the year." They had been disappointed so many times in the past, but they felt the new playoff system might be to their benefit.

For the first time ever, the Victoria Cougars held a training camp in Winnipeg. Many of the players had connections to the Manitoba capital, and it was felt they could find more opposition for exhibition games there than at home.[546] It was becoming evident that players were trying to be in shape before training camp, rather than trying to lose excess weight and tone up their muscles in the short pre-season camp. Many players told of working out at their local "Y" or other facility, while Clem Loughlin kept in shape all summer long on his farm in Alberta.[547] Lester Patrick announced the signing of young Wally Elmer, who had played for Saskatoon the previous season.[548]

The Cougars played two exhibition games against the Calgary Tigers in Port William, both finishing in ties.[549] They closed out the exhibition season with a match in Regina against the Capitals. This game, too, ended in a draw.[550]

In other league news, Mickey Ion was named as one of the three referees who would work games in the expanded league. He was considered to be the most outstanding referee in any league, and his services were much in demand. He was expected to be joined by Bill Cook and Harry Gardner.[551]

Finally, it was time for the season to open. The schedule was one of the most gruelling ever designed, with games on consecutive nights and long train trips. It would take a team in great physical shape with good stamina to win the championship. On paper, the Cougars certainly looked very strong. For the past two seasons, however, the Cougars had seemed ready for a championship bid but fell short when something went wrong. Victoria opened its season in Winnipeg with a game against the Regina Capitals. Lester Patrick sent back a telegram to the Victoria media saying:

> "The lid is off and we are away with number one. Calgary used the same tactics as last year but found a fighting aggregation of Cougars opposed to them. Cougars came from behind with a winning punch. Walker starred. His needle was there when there were openings and the Foyston-Walker goal was a knockout. Fredrickson played brilliantly but was unfortunate in getting goals. All other players played to form and our defence looked good."

As Lester had noted, the team played very well against the prior year's champions. The final score of 4-1 did not reflect the level of play, as, without Holmes in goal and his spectacular saves, the score could have been very different.[552] The second game was also played in Winnipeg, but this time the opponents were the Maroons. The Cougars won again, 4-3, after a high-spirited, fast-paced game. Lester Patrick (as he had done in the previous season) assembled six forwards, divided into two lines, and not much was lost when the second line took to the ice. Players other than the starting crew were no longer reported as "subs," but were merely forwards and defence.[553] The era of the player who never came off the ice was ending.

After the opening games, the Cougars began their first Prairie circuit. They suffered their first loss of the season at Saskatoon by a score of 4-1. Without Hap Holmes, the score would have been more one-sided. The Cougars had trouble getting to the net and were stymied time after time by the Crescent defence and the small ice surface.[554] The next game, in Edmonton, did not go much better. The Cougars took too many penalties and had real problems playing in minus-forty-degree-Fahrenheit weather. They lost the contest 2-0. It was obvious that they could not adapt to the frigid conditions, and it hampered their play.[555]

In their third game against a Prairie team, the Cougars played much better, but could not hold the lead and fell, 4-2 to the Calgary Tigers.[556] The team was very happy to get home to a more moderate climate. On the trip, they had actually been snowbound while travelling to Edmonton, so had to play the next day under terrible conditions. They did not have the stamina to play two games on two nights with train travel in between. Clem Loughlin's ear had frozen, and other players had suffered similar fates. The team would practice in their home rink, then travel to Vancouver for their next game.[557] Playing the Maroons was just the trick for the Cougars, as they won a close game, 1-0. Holmes was the star of the game, stopping every shot that came his way, and Fredrickson scored the only goal the Cougars needed.[558]

After six games on the road, Victoria finally got their home opener on Christmas Day. Santa was good to the team as they outscored the Maroons 4-2 for their second victory in a row. In this game, Vancouver took the lead with two goals early in the first period but could not withstand the Cougar onslaught of four straight goals, including three by Fredrickson.[559] Regina came to town for the next encounter, and the Cougars were ready for them. Harry Meeking scored two goals in seven seconds in the first period, and the rout was on. Foyston notched a goal in the second period, and Fraser counted two in the third frame. The game was never close as the Cougars dominated in all phases of the game.[560] The Cougars then travelled to Vancouver for a matinee New Year's Day game. Once again, they won the game, but this time the score was 11-2. The only players who did not score at least one point were Clem Loughlin and Jack Walker. Fredrickson led the way with four goals and one assist; Foyston and Elmer had two goals and one assist; Meeking scored two goals in eight seconds and added an assist; Hart and Fraser each had one assist; and Halderson had one goal.[561]

Before the next game, Lester Patrick decided to put together another forward line, made up of Foyston, Fredrickson, and Meeking, to see what would happen. It probably would not have mattered who played the game, the Cougars were flat and lost on home ice to the Maroons, 3-0.[562] However, Victoria got back on the winning track with their next game, when the Calgary Tigers (managed by former Cougar captain, Eddie Oatman) came to town. Jocko Anderson, whose brother Ernie played for Calgary, led the way with two goals. Clem Loughlin had his best game of the season on defence, adding a goal and an assist to his statistics. The Cougars played well as a team and were very unselfish with the puck, often passing to a teammate who was in a better position to shoot.[563] The winning continued when the Saskatoon Crescents battled the Cougars. According to reports, this was the best game played at the arena all year, with speed, good defence, and stellar goaltending. Two regulars, Fraser and Meeking, were both playing hurt, and Halderson hurt his knee during the game and had to leave, but the other team members filled in admirably. Victoria was now on top of the standings, just ahead of Edmonton and Calgary.[564] The Cougars then left on another Prairie circuit. In their first game at Regina, they lost to the Capitals when George Hay scored the only three goals of the game in a 3-0 shutout. The Cougars were out of sorts after their long train ride and did not play well.[565]

They played much better in their next game in Saskatoon but could not catch the Crescents, who outscored them 5-2 in a face-paced, exciting match.[566] Things turned around at the next stop: Edmonton. The Cougars gave up three goals, then found their skating legs and scored five straight goals to take the lead. Edmonton scored once more, but two more Victoria goals sealed the deal. It was back to first place in the standings after the victory.[567]

Victoria came home and got ready to face the Edmonton Eskimos. In the evenly played game, the Eskimos got their revenge for an earlier defeat when they got past the Cougars, 3-2. Goaltender Stuart saved the day time and time again for the visitors, as he stopped shots from Cougar snipers.[568] The teams played again just two days later, and the result was totally different. The Cougars won the encounter 3-1. Jocko Anderson scored a beautiful goal in the third period on a pass from Jack Walker to put the team ahead for good, and then "Gizzy" Hart put in an insurance goal late in the game.[569] That season, the Cougars were finally winning more games than they were losing and were remaining close to the top of the WCHL standings. Fans were cautiously optimistic that they would finally play in the post-season for the first time in years.

The winning continued with a hard-fought victory over the Regina Capitals. In that match, Fredrickson, Loughlin, and Fraser scored to give the Cougars a lead they never relinquished in a 3-1 victory.[570] The same teams played two days later, and again, Victoria came out on top. This game was not particularly well played, but Fraser and Walker scored to give the home team a 2-1 victory.[571] It was particularly important for the team to have some wins under their belts, as they were heading out for their last Prairie trip of the season. They ran into bad ice in Calgary and were not able to score, losing to the Tigers 1-0.[572] It was on to Edmonton next, where the Eskimos scored a goal with a Cougar player serving a penalty and went on to defeat Victoria 4-1.[573] The Cougars then travelled to Saskatoon, where they lost again—the third time that the Crescents had won on their small ice surface. The score was 5-1, and the Cougars did not play well. Jocko Anderson was the only player to beat the Saskatoon goaltender.[574] The long road trip continued with a contest in Regina. Finally, the Cougars were able to get a victory. After being held in check by the other Prairie teams, Fredrickson managed to get back to his prior form and dazzled the spectators with his incredible talent. He scored four goals and added an assist, breaking out of his goal-scoring slump in great style, despite having to miss the entire second period to get repaired when his nose was broken.[575] The Cougars looked like real champions in this game, showcasing their talent to advantage.

In their first game home after the trip, they hit a roadblock in their encounter with the Calgary Tigers, losing 2-1. Calgary's aggressive forward Emory Sparrow was ejected from the game and fined $100 for arguing on several occasions with referee Mickey Ion. Despite his absence, the Tigers eked out a close win to return to first place in the league standings.[576] Little did Victoria fans know that the Cougars would win their final three games to clinch a playoff spot finally.

They started with a 4-0 shutout of their old nemesis, the Maroons. For the first time in four weeks, the Cougars scored first and never looked back. Single goals came from Walker, Halderson, Anderson, and Loughlin. However excited Victoria fans might be,[577] a reporter cautioned: "Well done, Cougars! But remember, the end of the road is a long way off yet and there are two hard hills to climb. Vancouver must be beaten in Vancouver on Monday night and Saskatoon must be humbled here a week from Saturday." The team took the advice to heart and defeated the Maroons 3-2 in the return game on the mainland. It was their sixth victory over their Vancouver opponents in the season[578] and was likely the reason they were playoff bound. "Gizzy" Hart scored twice for the Cougars, using his hard shot to advantage. In the final game of the season, with a playoff berth ensured, the Cougars entertained the Saskatoon Crescents and won that game 5-1, scoring four goals in ten minutes in the second period and adding one more in the third. Foyston notched two goals for the winners, proving once again the value of the former Seattle players who had been added to the Cougar roster.[579] The team had now finished play for the season—in first place in the standings—but could only watch as their competitors completed their seasons. Saskatoon won their game over the Maroons to jump ahead of Victoria in the standings then Calgary outscored the Regina Capitals 3-2 to jump ahead of Saskatoon to finish in first place in the standings.[580] Those results meant that the Cougars would have to play Saskatoon in a two-game, total-goals series for the right to meet Calgary in the WCHL final.

The first game was played in Victoria and hockey fever was in the air. It had been twelve years since there had been this type of excitement about hockey in the capital city. Victoria's defence was considered superior to Saskatoon's, but the forward lines were equal in talent. The Cougars would have to put together two good games to get past the Crescents. Much to the delight of local fans who packed the arena, the Cougars used their speed to skate away with a 3-1 victory. Fredrickson and Halderson set the stage early, and the team withstood a Saskatoon rush at the end of the game.[581]

The teams then travelled via train to Saskatoon for the second game of the series. This time, the Cougars scored a goal only to have the Crescents tie the game. This happened three times, so regulation time ended with the score tied 3-3. With this decision, Victoria won the series six goals to four and moved on to play the Calgary Tigers in the league final. It was estimated that 10,000 fans in Victoria and lower Vancouver Island sat in on the game, getting commentary as it came in off the wire by George Warren. The broadcast was sponsored by Fletcher Bros and the Hudson's Bay Company.[582]

Then it was off to Calgary for the opening game of the final series. The first game ended in a 1-1 tie, so the winner of the return match in Victoria would win the league championship.[583] Tickets went on sale on March 16, at 10 a.m., and some fans stood in line for two hours for tickets. Reserved seats were sold out by noon, and the remaining fans would have to stand in another line at the arena on game night for gallery seats and standing room only. Although the Cougars said they were in good shape, a look in the dressing rooms would reveal bumps and bruises on almost every body.[584] The game was played on March 18 with 4,000 spectators jammed to the rafters and thousands more listening to the play-by-play on their radios. It was the first home game broadcast in league history, as Lester Patrick realized just how many fans were disappointed to not have tickets for the big game.[585]

The game was one of the best very played on Victoria ice. Victoria took the lead in the second period when Fredrickson was left unchecked in front of the net and put the puck past goaltender Winkler. The Cougars sealed the victory when Walker scored on a pass from Fredrickson with less than three minutes remaining. The crowd went wild, cheering wildly for the best team to ever wear Victoria jerseys. Next would come the Stanley Cup series, and they were confident their team could win. Tickets for that series went on sale on March 20th, and a full capacity crowd was expected again. It was noted that Walker had scored in all four games of the playoffs, while Fredrickson had scored in three. It was also the first time in thirteen years that the normally stoic Lester Patrick actually got excited about a series. After the game, the WCHL announced that Mickey Ion would referee the Stanley Cup final, as Montreal had agreed to his selection. The Prairie teams did not like his style, so he had not been involved in the league playoffs.[586]

When tickets went on sale for the final series at Plimley and Ritchie's on View Street, the first fans arrived at 6:30 a.m., prepared to stay in line until they got the choice seats. At 9:50 a.m., the line stretched down View Street, along Government Street, and halfway up Fort Street. In response to the intense demand, Lester Patrick opened the doors early, and with police in attendance, admitted four patrons at a time. Most asked for the maximum of four tickets, so the reserved seats were sold out by noon, with the rush seats and ring seats sold out early in the afternoon. Businessmen who could not leave their jobs hired men from the employment bureau to acquire tickets on their behalf. The makeup of the line was mostly male, but there were a few women, as well. Leo Dandurand and the Montreal Canadiens had arrived in Vancouver, where they held a practice and were expected to arrive in Victoria the next morning.[587]

Excitement was building, and Victoria fans were not amused by the news from the Canadiens camp that they "expect[ed] to win the series in the first three games."[588] It seemed that they would not be paid for more than three games, so they had a financial incentive, as well. Victoria newspapers were filled with information on the players who would vie for the championship—still called the "world series" by many. It would be the sixth cup appearance for goaltender Harry "Hap" Holmes and the fifth for Jack Walker and Frank Foyston. Harry Meeking, the only other Cougar to have Cup final experience, had played in one. Two Cougars—Frank Fredrickson and "Slim" Halderson—were the only players to have played in the Allan Cup,[589] won an Olympic gold medal,[590] and now to play in the Stanley Cup final. It was quite an achievement for the Icelanders, now a vital part of the Cougars' roster. Short biographies of each of the Cougars players were also printed in the media, bringing a human face to the on-ice struggle.[591]

When Mickey Ion dropped the puck at nine p.m. on March 21, the final was finally on. Played under Western rules, the Cougars won the first game, 5-2. They put on an offensive display that baffled Georges Vezina in the Montreal net, and after Walker and Halderson scored first-period goals, they kept up the offensive pressure until Walker added another in the second period. The third period featured two Cougar goals by Fraser and singles for Montreal from William Coutu and Howie Morenz. The Canadiens seemed confused by the Cougars players changing lines on the fly, as was done in the WCHL, not waiting until a stoppage in play to do so as the NHL did. The result was announced to Victoria in a banner headline on the first page of The *Victoria Daily Colonist*, with great details of the entire game.[592]

The next game was played in Vancouver, using Eastern rules. Montreal would have been assumed to have had the advantage, but the Cougars prevailed before the largest crowd ever to watch a game at the Denman Street Arena. Walker and Fredrickson scored in the first period for the early lead, but Montreal found its legs in the second period, and Auriel Joliat scored, to make the score 2-1. Luckily, the Cougars rebounded, and Walker found the net in the third period to ensure the 3-1 victory.[593] The Cougars were coming home with a 2-0 lead in games, but there was still work to do. It is often said that the clinching game in any series is the hardest to win. This proved true when the teams came back to Victoria for game three. Although the match was played under Western rules, Montreal changed their strategy, using three defencemen in an effort to beat the Cougars at their own game.[594] The technique worked for that game, and Howie Morenz scored three goals and Joliat added one, to lead Montreal to a 4-2 victory. Victoria had actually been ahead 2-1 early in the third period on goals by Anderson and Hart, but could not hold the lead, surrendering three straight scores to Montreal. The series was now 2-1 in games for Victoria, and it was crucial that they win the next game to prevent Montreal from getting more confidence.[595]

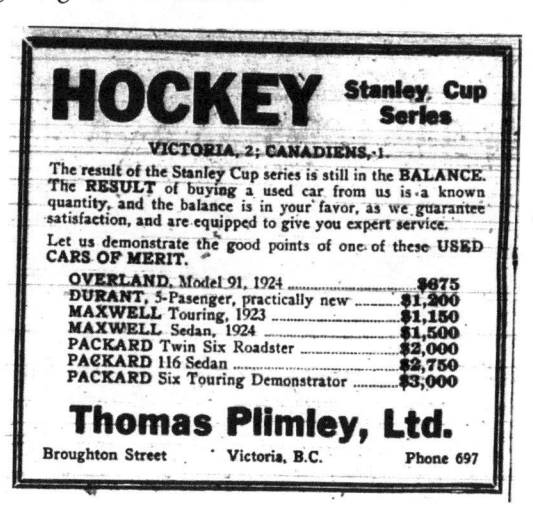

Plimley Ad, *Victoria Daily Colonist*, March 29, 1925, page 6.

Local advertisers used the hockey series to sell their merchandise. Thomas Plimley Ltd. placed an in the *Victoria Daily Colonist*, which read in part: "The results of the Stanley Cup series is still in the BALANCE. The RESULT of buying a used car from us is a known quality, and the balance is in your favour, as we guarantee satisfaction, and are equipped to give you expert advice."[596]

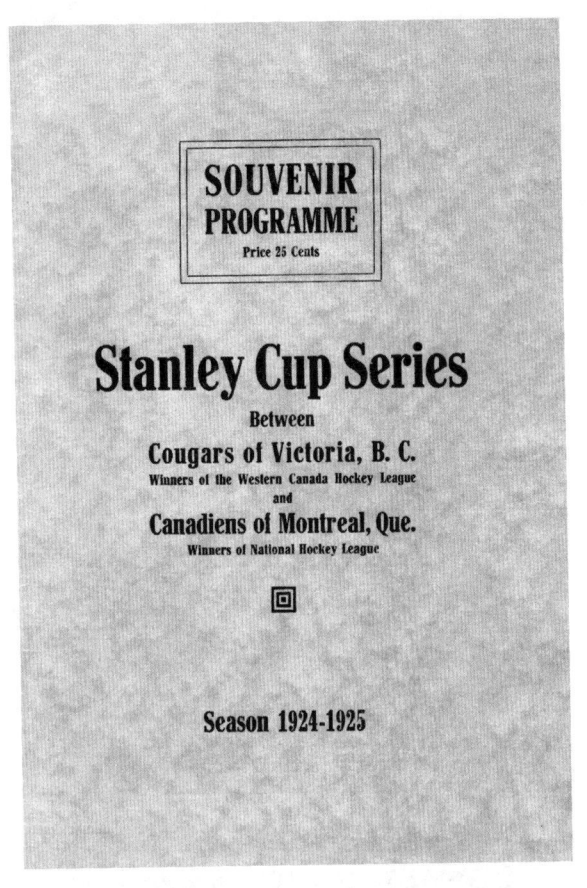

The History of Professional Hockey in Victoria, BC: 1911-2011

Stanley Cup Series, reproduction program.
From the author's collection.

Original Stanley Cup ticket, front.
From the author's collection.

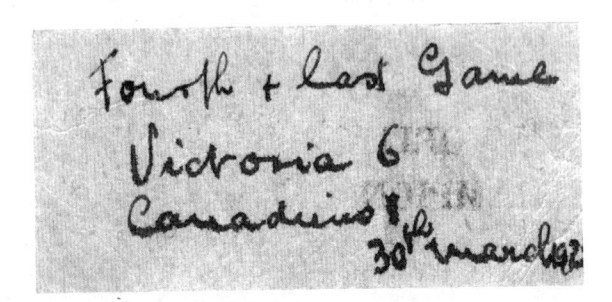

Original Stanley Cup ticket, back.
From the author's collection.

Souvenir hockey stick from the Stanley Cup series.

64

The fourth game would be played under Eastern rules, and for some Victorians, it would their first look at the different system. Under the Eastern code, the puck could only be passed forward or kicked inside the centre-ice section, players could not be substituted except after a whistle was blown, there was no deferred penalty, and there was no penalty shot. Canadiens' manager, Leo Dandurand, fully expected to win the game to send the series to a fifth and deciding game.[597] What he had not figured on was the speed and determination of the Cougars to finally win the Stanley Cup for Victoria. They had won the series against Quebec in 1913, but that was not considered a challenge. This time, the Cup was the prize, and Victoria was determined to win it. The Cougars skated rings around Montreal defenders, passed the puck with great skill, and dominated in all phases of the game. Fredrickson scored in the first period to give Victoria the lead. Hart notched a goal early in the second period for a 2-0 lead. Montreal's Boucher got that one back, but Halderson and Foyston closed out the scoring in the second period. With a 4-1 lead, the Cougars kept the pressure on the Canadiens, adding goals by Fredrickson and Loughlin to skate to a convincing 6-1 victory.[598]

Lester Patrick had brought the Stanley Cup to Victoria. He had finally assembled a team that could do the job. Hap Holmes was easily the better goalie in the series, and team captain Clem Loughlin led by example. Victoria City Council was deep in deliberation over the consolidation of sewer bylaws when City Clerk Bradley left the room, only to return a moment later to whisper in the mayor's ear. His Worship then announced, "Gentleman. The score's four to one in the second period." At the end of the game, council passed a resolution offering heartfelt congratulations to the team.[599]

Page 1 of the *Victoria Daily Colonist*, on March 31, had a huge banner headline:[600]

Cougars win Stanley Cup headline from the *Victoria Daily Colonist*, March 31, 1925.

Commentators were struck by the way Mickey Ion had handled the series with his usual iron fist. There had been little rough stuff, as both teams stuck to good hockey. It made the series more enjoyable to watch and one reporter mused: ". . . yet the Prairie scribes laugh at Mickey. Perhaps they've never been away from home."[601]

A civic banquet to honour the team was held at the Chamber of Commerce Auditorium on April 2, with about 300 in attendance. Mayor Pendray's remarks concluded with: "We appreciate all that they have done. We know of their strenuous efforts to bring the championship to Victoria and we wish to say thank you for it all. It may be too much to hope for, but I know we all wish that Victoria will win its second consecutive championship next year. But whether we have a championship team or not, I trust that the people of Victoria will patronize the team in a like manner to that which they have done in the latter part of the season. The Patricks have done a great deal for us here, and sometimes I do not think we fully appreciate it."

Then, one by one, the players were introduced to the assembled throng. The mayor then presented to Gordon Fraser and Frank Foyston with golden fobs on behalf of the city. He explained that there had only been time to produce two in the short time since the championship was won, but that all players would have one sent to their homes. Harold "Gizzy" Hart was given the puck with which he had scored the winning goal. It was decorated in the club colours of blue and gold and suitably engraved. Lester Patrick spoke next and told the guests, "It may interest you to know that the players have said that no other event in their playing careers has given them so much pleasure as winning the world's championship for Victoria. I do not know what the future holds for some members of the team, but they close their present season with the happiest recollections of a pleasant season in Victoria, one unmarred by any untoward act in the dressing room, on the ice, or as ordinary citizens."

Then it was time for former Alderman Joseph Patrick (Lester's father and the man who had financed the teams in the PCHA) to address the crowd. "I never played hockey," he said, "but I have been following it pretty closely for thirty-three years and I want to say that I have never seen a smoother machine than that which Victoria has had this year. And more than all that, they are the cleanest bunch I have ever seen. They have played the game and proved the rough tactics are not essential to success. We play clean out here and to the Cougars goes the palm for being the cleanest and the fairest." Other speakers including Dr. Davies, who had broadcast the games, and reporters Archie Wills of the *Victoria Daily Times* and Harold McDonald of the *Victoria Daily Colonist*. Team Captain Clem Loughlin was asked to speak on behalf of the team but passed the microphone to Fredrickson, who noted that the victory had shown the world that "Victoria is not only on an island but also populated." Musical entertainment was provided by the combined orchestras of the Kiwanis, Rotary, and Gyro Clubs along with vocalists.[602] It was a fitting celebration for the club that had reached the pinnacle of success. Years afterward, citizens would tell their stories of this once-in-a-lifetime experience and would proudly reveal the keepsakes of the Stanley Cup victory.

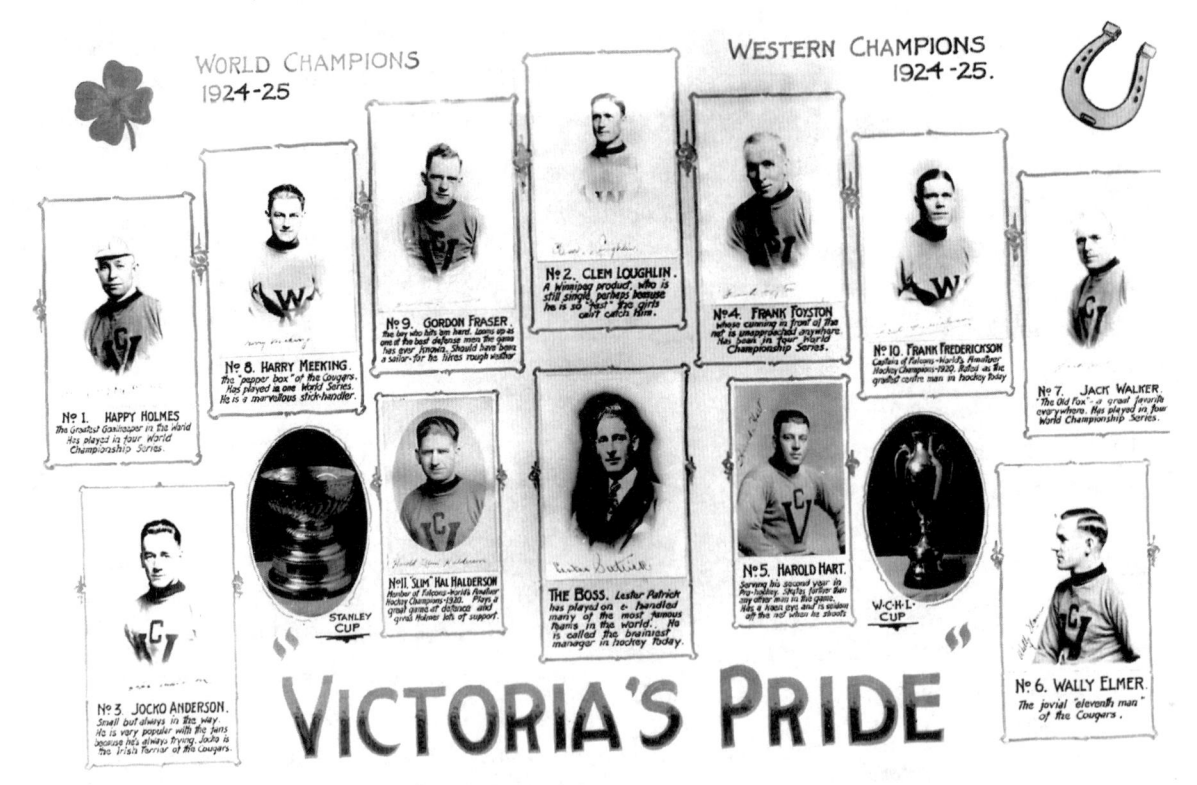

Victoria's pride: Victoria Cougars Stanley Cup champions. Photo courtesy BC Sports Hall of Fame, image 7311.1.

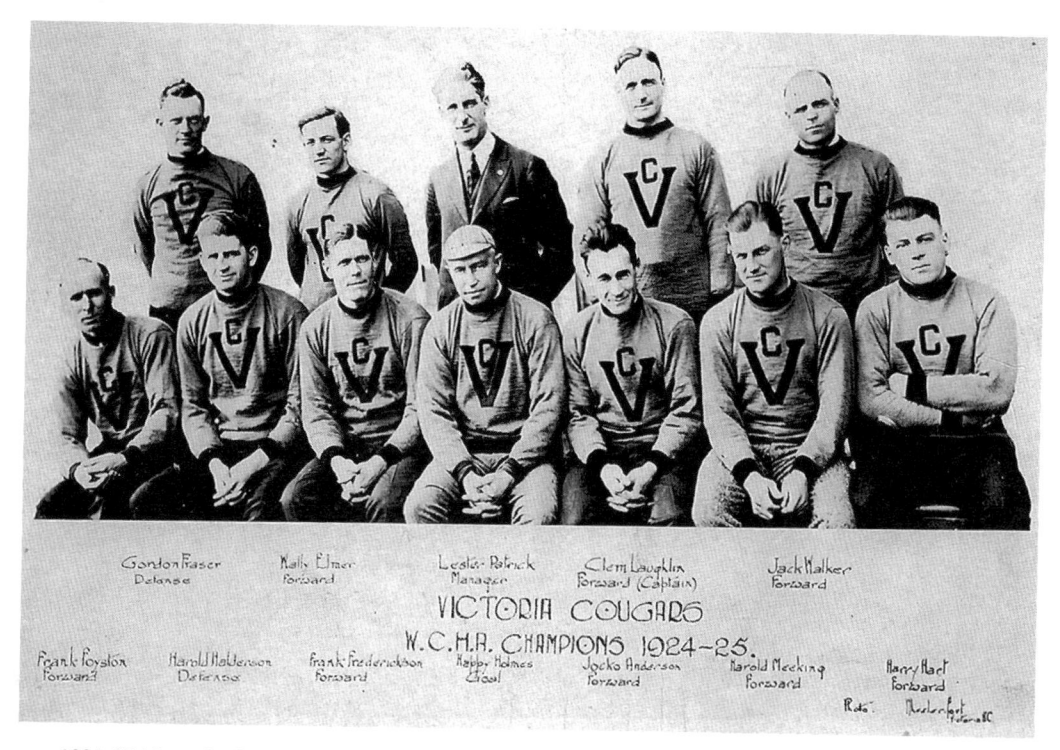

10 - VICTORIA AND VANCOUVER JOIN THE WCHL

1924-25 Victoria Cougars in uniform. Photo courtesy BC Sports Hall of Fame, image 7311.2.

Stanley Cup champions in formal portrait. Back row: left to right; Dr. Grant, Frank Fredrickson, Gordon Fraser, Harold Halderson, Frank Foyston, Harry Meeking, Wally Elmer. Front row, left to right: Jocko Anderson, Harold Hart, Harry Holmes, Lester Patrick, Clem Loughlin, Jack Walker. Photo courtesy BC Sports Hall of Fame, image 7311.3.

11 - THE QUEST FOR A SECOND CHAMPIONSHIP

Much of the off-season was spent discussing the makeup of the league for the upcoming season. First, there was talk about the possibility of Seattle coming back into the league.[603] By the end of July, it was clear that there would still be no building suitable for hockey in Seattle. A proposed project had been placed on hold pending funding issues, and would not (in any case) be ready for the start of the season.[604] Next came news from Regina that the Capitals might be moved to the Coast. The owner had received an offer of $25,000 for his franchise but had yet to make a decision.[605]

All the questions were resolved at the annual meeting of the Western Canada Hockey League in Calgary on September 15. The Regina franchise had been transferred to Portland after Regina investors failed to purchase the club. The Rosebuds were again in the league and were making improvements to their rink, the Hippodrome (later to be renamed the Coliseum).

To accommodate the fact that there was now an American franchise in the league, the league changed its name to the Western Hockey League.[606] Changes were also made to the rules. In overtime, rather than playing twenty minutes extra time with a ten-minute intermission and change of ends, play would stop for only two minutes, and play would continue for not more than ten minutes, or until one team scored. An anti-defence rule was adopted. It would now be illegal for any team to use more than two defencemen. When not back checking, two of the forwards had to be advancing toward the opponent's goal or have the puck actually in play. The third forward could not come back past own blue line until play was at least halfway between centre and the defending blue line. A change was also made to the playoff at the end of the regular season. If any team had a margin of five points more than the second-place team, they would receive an automatic bye into the final with the second and third place teams playing a home-and-home, two-game, total-goals series to determine who would play the first-place team in the final.[607]

Before the opening of the 1925-26 season, the Victoria Cougars played a series of exhibition games against Eastern teams. The club assembled in Winnipeg on November 4 for a short training session, then left for games in Ottawa, Montreal, and Toronto. Proceeds from the games in Ottawa were given to the Ottawa Humane Society at the request of Lady Byng, wife of the Governor-General of Canada.[608]

To have a team available to play the exhibition series, Lester Patrick had to sign his players earlier than usual. Many of his players now lived in Victoria, so contact with them was an easy phone call. He sent telegrams to the others, requesting them to reply right away so he would know who was available. At the same time, he gave Wally Elmer his unconditional release, so that he could find a place with another club. "Hap" Holmes was the first to sign.[609] Lester Patrick then signed talented amateur Russell Oatman, brother of former Cougar Eddie Oatman, to a professional contract. He was the first player developed in Victoria to sign with the club.[610] Returning players Gordon Fraser, Jocko Anderson,[611] "Gizzy" Hart, and Jack Walker soon committed to the club,[612] as did Harold Halderson[613] and Captain Clem Loughlin.[614] That left only three returning players to accept contracts, and Harry Meeking soon joined the team.[615] Frank Foyston announced his retirement from hockey,[616] and Frank Fredrickson finally signed when the club had already started workouts in Winnipeg.[617]

The team left Winnipeg on November 12 and made their way to Montreal for their first game on November 16.[618] The Cougars opened their series with a win over the Montreal Maroons. There was no score until the third period when Hart, Loughlin, and Halderson each scored before the Maroons notched their only goal.[619] Next on the schedule was a match against the Canadiens, the club that the Cougars had defeated in the Stanley Cup playoffs. Again, the Cougars prevailed, this time by a score of 5-3. Montreal sportswriters dubbed the Cougars "the greatest team to come out of the West."[620] Playing their third game in four days, the Cougars faltered in Ottawa in a game played under Eastern rules and lost by a score of 6-2.[621] Playing under Western rules in the next game did not help, as the Cougars again went down to Ottawa 2-0.[622] The next two games were played in Toronto, and although the Cougars played well, their fatigue showed, and they lost both games, 4-3[623] and 10-5, despite Fredrickson scoring three goals in each game.[624] The team then played the New York Americans in Windsor, where they lost 1-0.[625]

Although the team had not won as many games as they had expected to, Lester Patrick considered the trip a success. They had played seven games in twelve days, travelling between venues, and had not disappointed the Eastern fans who had been impressed with the speed of the play under Western rules.[626]

While the team was rattling across the country on the rails, season tickets went on sale at Plimley and Ritchie's. Patrons did not have to pay for the whole season in advance but were expected to pick up and pay for the tickets for each game. Failure to honour their contracts would result in the tickets being released to the general public. Fans who had held season tickets the previous season were able to reserve the same seats again.[627]

The Cougars opened the season in Vancouver, where the Maroons won handily 4-1. The Cougars missed several chances in front of the net that would have made a difference.[628] They disappointed their home fans when they lost their home opener 3-1 to Saskatoon.[629] The team seemed tired. Perhaps the Eastern trip had taken too much out of them. "Slim" Halderson was badly injured in that game and needed hospital treatment for a cut over the ankle.[630] The next game was interesting as the original result was a 2-1 victory for Vancouver over Victoria on a penalty shot goal in overtime. The shot was awarded after Jack Walker threw his stick. Unfortunately for the Cougars, Mickey Ion was not refereeing the game. It was Gord Meeking (incidentally the brother of Harry Meeking) who had made the call. According to league rules, "a penalty shot could only be awarded if a stick is thrown at a man who has beaten the defence and has only the goalie to face."[631] Lester Patrick protested the result saying that, in his opinion, Fraser should have been assessed a ten-minute penalty, as the shooter had not yet cleared the defence. League President H. L. Richardson ruled on the protest and reached the decision that a wrong call had been made and the penalty shot should not have been awarded. He removed the overtime goal from the records and declared the game a 1-1 tie. The Cougars finally got their first point of the season.[632]

Eddie Oatman brought his Calgary Tigers to town to play against his brother's Cougars. The teams played to a 0-0 overtime tie to each pick up a point, but the lack of scoring did not mean it was a poor game. Gord Fraser could not play much of the game due to an ankle injury, so the Cougars had only eight men for most of the contest. Just after overtime started, Jocko Anderson had to leave the ice to get stitches for a cut on the back of his head. That left only seven players on the ice against a full Calgary team, but they played like champions and held their opponents off the scoreboard.[633] With Halderson out of the lineup, a gallant band of Cougars travelled to Portland, where they battled the Rosebuds hard, only to lose 2-1 in overtime. It was their third overtime game in a week, and the shorthanded team had battled hard but come up short. Fraser tried to play but had to leave the game with a broken leg. He would be out for at least three weeks.[634]

When the Cougars got home, they were a tired and injured bunch. In addition to Halderson and Fraser, they had new injuries: Meeking had a bad thigh injury, and Fredrickson had a head wound and injured jaw.[635] Faced with a shortage of healthy players, manager Lester Patrick put on his skates and played for the first time in four years. He played as a substitute, relieving his tired defence when necessary. After the game, a reporter noted: "Lester is now far past the playing stage and the fact that he went out there last night proves he is still game." In a young man's game, Lester was forty-two and still able to perform. It might have been his play that inspired the team, but they scored the first two goals and held on for a well-deserved 2-1 victory—their first of the season.[636]

The crippled team left for a tour of the Prairies and played their first game in Saskatoon on the tiny rink. Meeking was unable to play, so Lester again donned the gear. This time, his magic did not work, and the team fell 3-0 to the Crescents.[637] The injury woes continued when Jocko Anderson suffered a broken nose. Lester tried to find players to fill the gaps, but it was becoming increasingly difficult for Western teams to compete against the NHL teams with their wide-open cheque books.[638]

The story did not get any better in the next game against Edmonton. Lester again had to play, and when Clem Loughlin (the team's only healthy defenceman) was sent off for a ten-minute penalty in the second period, the team had real troubles. Saskatoon scored the first three goals, but a counter by Lester Patrick gave the team hope. Alas, it was too little, too late, and the Cougars went down to defeat 3-1.[639] Things were not looking good for the Stanley Cup champions. They had played eight games, with just one win and two ties to show for their effort. They were severely handicapped by injury, having only one healthy defenceman, and had a forty-two-year-old trying to fill in. However, they dug deep and came out of Calgary with a decisive 4-1 victory.

The game was not without controversy. Jocko Anderson scored a beautiful goal that made the score 5-1. Referee Ion recorded the goal with the official scorer, then two minutes later, ordered the goal removed. Ion felt he had banished Anderson from the game for fighting, but the scorer said that he had recorded a major penalty and had allowed Jocko back on the ice after the penalty had expired. The goal was not needed for the victory, but it was the first time the Cougars had scored more than two goals.[640] The team limped home from the Prairies and had a week off before their New Year's Day afternoon contest against the Eskimos.

The Cougars started 1926 in fine form, as they shut out Edmonton 4-0 to win their second game of the season before an enthusiastic crowd of 3,000. Fredrickson scored two goals, with singles from Oatman and Loughlin. The team was buoyed by the return of Halderson and Meeking, although Fraser was still out of action.[641] In the next game in Vancouver, the Cougars held the edge in the first two periods, but could not handle the Millionaires in the third frame, and lost the game 1-0.[642] They lost the return match in Victoria by an identical score.[643] That the team was in a scoring drought was obvious. They had scored only fifteen goals in twelve games. They had been shut out four times, scored just one goal five times, and scored two goals once.

Only once did they score four goals. The truth of hockey is that, if you can't score goals, you can't win. The team needed to get its offence going quickly or the chance of a second championship would be out of reach.

A trip to Portland seemed to be what the Cougars needed. They scored the first goal, surrendered two, then roared back with two more within the last two minutes of the game to take it 3-2.[644] The Rosebuds got their revenge in the return match in Victoria, defeating the home team by the same score.[645] Local fans were getting restless. They did not like the way the team was playing and wanted better results. "It was a nice game but would have been nicer had the score been the other way," remarked one fan.[646] Unfortunately, that had been the theme for most of the season. The Cougars would win a game and lose a game, but never really put a winning streak together. They were a mere shadow of the team that had won the Stanley Cup. The team sat in fifth place in the league standings and were not likely to catch first-place Saskatoon, but a good hot streak could still move them up the standings.

The Edmonton Eskimos came to town, sitting four points ahead of the Cougars in the standings. Victoria could not be held back in this match. They got off to a good start when Clem Loughlin scored in the first two minutes and Oatman near the end of the first period. Edmonton scored early in the second period, but Halderson notched another goal, so the score was 3-1. Walker closed out the scoring in the third period, making the final tally 4-1.[647] Next to come to town was Saskatoon. The teams battled to a 1-1 overtime tie.

Fredrickson was the star in the next match in Portland. He set up one goal and scored the winner in a tight 3-2 victory. It was the Rosebuds' fifth straight loss at home, and they no longer looked like a second-place team.[648] The Cougars got some good news when Frank Foyston joined the club, coming out of retirement. After signing Foyston to a contract, Lester Patrick called him "good insurance against illness or accident in our drive for a championship, as Fraser's usefulness during the rest of the season is very uncertain."[649] Foyston did not play in the next game against Calgary, but the rest of the team put in a stellar effort. The Tigers scored first at only ten seconds of the third period and held that lead until a rainbow shot from Clem Loughlin deflected off the defender and found the net behind Winkler with only slightly more than a minute left in regulation time. The crowd roared its approval. It was the fourth tie between the two clubs this year; neither team could get the advantage over the other.[650] Now the team was building momentum. They had managed to get eight points in their last five games and had not lost a game since mid-January. They still sat in fifth place in the league, but now they were only one point behind Portland and Vancouver, and two points behind Saskatoon. Suddenly, a run for the championship seemed reasonable.

The Cougars embarked on another Prairie road trip. Frank Foyston played his first game of the season and scored one goal. However, the star of the game was Lester Patrick, the "Silver Fox," who not only scored the tying goal in the period but also notched the winner after 1:15 of overtime. It was a great victory for the team, and it moved them into third place in the league.[651] The Cougars rolled into Edmonton and had a setback when the Eskimos beat them 4-1. The defence did not play well, and without the great work of Holmes in goal, Edmonton's score would have been higher.[652] The next game was in Calgary, and the Cougars scored an impressive 4-3 overtime win when Jocko Anderson took a pass from Jack Walker and shot the puck while sprawling on his face. After the game, Calgary management protested that the referee had been about to blow his whistle for a penalty just before the winning goal was scored. The protest was disallowed by League president Richardson, and the result was allowed to stand. The two points jumped the Cougars into second place in the standings.[653] The tired team rolled into Vancouver, and a lone goal by Lester Patrick early in the first period gave them a win. Lester made full use of his subs, often changing an entire line on the fly.[654]

They then had to travel to play at Portland. With a slim lead late in the third period, the Cougars were unable to hold it and surrendered two late goals, giving the Rosebuds the victory. Victoria fans were eagerly awaiting the first home game of the season for Frank Foyston.[655] Lester Patrick had found the Prairie trip strenuous, and had not played in Portland, but would be suited up for the home encounter with Portland. Harry Meeking would be the only Cougar not playing in the game.[656] Victoria started the game quickly with Loughlin and Oatman striking in the first period. The second period was a total reversal, as Portland scored twice to tie the score. However, the Cougars would not be denied. They poured in four goals in the third period to Portland's one and won the contest, 6-3. Clem Loughlin was the outstanding player in the game, scoring twice and firing hot shots so that Oatman could score on the rebound.

It was a good victory and left the Cougars tied with Edmonton for second place in the standings.[657] The Cougars won their next five games to secure a playoff spot. They shut out the Maroons 4-0 in front of their appreciative home fans. Fredrickson returned to form, scoring three goals, while Foyston added a single.[658] Next to come to town were the Eskimos. The Cougars played at the top of their game and skated to a 4-1 victory. Fredrickson was the star of the contest, notching one goal and two assists. He was back to playing the way he had the previous season, and that was good news for the home team.[659] The Rosebuds were the next visitors, and they met the same fate. The Cougars, firing on all cylinders, defeated them 4-1, and effectively knocked them out of playoff contention, while virtually assuring themselves of a spot. Frank Foyston scored two goals and assisted on another to lead the team. Much mention was made of the Cougars' record since January 15. They had won nine games, tied two, and lost only two.[660] This was a far cry from the team at the beginning of the season that had struggled to score goals.

The Cougars travelled to Vancouver to play the Maroons. The game was not that interesting to the Vancouver fans, but Victoria certainly enjoyed the result. Vancouver scored the first goal in the second period. However, Oatman scored early in the third period to tie the score, and Lester Patrick scored the winner two minutes from the end of the game. After the game, Lester Patrick made an announcement of interest to hockey fans who did not hold season tickets. Any person who attended the upcoming game of the season against Vancouver and purchased their tickets at the club office would have seats saved for them for the playoffs. Thus, they would not have to stand in line when the playoff tickets were offered for sale.[661]

With Gord Fraser in the lineup for the first time in weeks, the Cougars forever put an end to the idea that Vancouver goaltender Hughie Lehman had the "evil eye" over them. Fredrickson scored in the first period, and Foyston got a goal in the second period, but it was in the third period that their offence really got going. Walker scored twice, while Fredrickson and Fraser added singles. The Maroons could only manage one goal, long after the result of the game was no longer in doubt. The six goals were the most that the Cougars had scored in the season.[662]

Before the playoffs began, the Cougars had one last road trip to Calgary. This turned out to be the first loss for Victoria since February 10. The ice was very heavy from an accumulation of water on the surface. The Tigers won 2-0, perhaps being better used to the bad ice than the Cougars. Despite the loss, Victoria finished third in the league, only three points behind Saskatoon, and four behind first-place Edmonton.[663]

The playoffs started on March 12, in Saskatoon. This series was notable because the two managers, Lester Patrick and Newsy Lalonde, had played together for the Renfrew Millionaires twenty years earlier. Fletcher Bros. arranged to broadcast the game on radio station CFCT. The details of the play by play would be transmitted via wire and *Victoria Daily Times* sports reporter Archie Wills would be the announcer.[664] The Cougars, who generally had trouble playing on the smaller rink in Saskatoon, played a good game and held the Crescents to a 3-3 tie. The bad news from the game was that Lester Patrick broke his thumb and could no longer hold his stick. He would not be able to play in future games but would remain behind the bench.[665] Four thousand fans packed the arena for the second game of the series. It was one of the best games played in Victoria, as neither team could score in regulation time. It remained for young Gordon Fraser to be the hero when he fired a hard shot behind Saskatoon goalie George Hainsworth after 8:10 of overtime. The Cougars had won the series four goals to three and were now slated to play Edmonton.[666]

Line-up for playoff hockey tickets for the Victoria Cougars vs. the Edmonton Eskimos, Government Street, March 1926. Courtesy City of Victoria Archives, image M06814.

Both games of the league final were played in the West, as there was no ice left in Edmonton. The series opened in Victoria on March 20, and neither team could score in the first period. Finally, Foyston scored on a pass from Loughlin and Halderson added a second. Hart notched a third goal for the Cougars in the final period, and Edmonton could only manage a single goal. Thus, Victoria had a two-goal lead going into the second game that would be played in Vancouver.[667] About 150 Victoria fans travelled to Vancouver to watch the second game of the series. The Canadian Pacific Railway arranged a special rate for the 2:15 boat and fans could take advantage of it by showing their hockey ticket at the office on Government Street.[668] Ten thousand fans crowded into the Denman Street Arena in Vancouver to watch the second game of the series. Most of the crowd seemed to favour the Eskimos, but that did not bother the Cougars. Edmonton took an early two-goal lead, but Foyston, who appeared have become rejuvenated, scored a goal in the second frame to narrow the score. His second goal, late in the third period, tied the score. There was no further scoring by either team, so the Cougars took the series five goals to three. Although the Victoria fans would not see their team play again on home ice, they wished them well on their trip to the East and were confident that the team could repeat as Stanley Cup champions.[669]

The Cougars left on the train for the East, not yet knowing who their opponent would be. The Montreal Maroons and Ottawa Senators were engaged in the NHL final series. The *Victoria Daily Times* sports editor Archie Wills travelled with the team and sent back reports on a regular basis. He noted that the team was spending a lot of time resting and trying to overcome their injuries. Jocko Anderson got the word that he might be able to play, but Lester Patrick had to leave his skates at home under doctor's orders.[670] The special train pulled into Winnipeg, where the players were able to get some good exercise during a seventeen-hour layover. They watched a junior hockey game, then strapped on the skates to work the kinks out of their legs. The team noted that they would prefer to play in Montreal, as the rink in Ottawa had oval ends, and that gave the Senators the advantage.[671] The Cougars got their wish when the Maroons defeated Ottawa in the NHL final.

They arrived in Montreal on March 29, and prepared to play the first game, but were advised that it would not happen until the next day. They took advantage of the delay by having a full work-out at the Forum, where the games would be played. Clem Loughlin's shoulder acted up, and he needed x-rays to diagnose the problem. He had the shoulder strapped up and would play in the first game. Anderson had the splints removed from his hand and was expected to play.[672]

The Stanley Cup final was a best-of-five series. The first game would be played under Eastern rules, the second under Western rules, with the rest of the games alternating. The total receipts for the first three games would be pooled, and after rink expenses, officials' salaries, and the travelling expenses of the visiting team were deducted, the remainder would be divided among the players, with sixty percent going to the winners, and forty percent to members of the losing team.[673]

The Cougars entered their first game against Montreal with some injuries but played gamely throughout. Their championship hopes took a tumble when Jocko Anderson, just returned to the lineup from an injured hand, dislocated his right hip and broke his leg. That put the Cougars down a man for the rest of the series and severely hampered their teamwork. They were likely tired from the long train trip and could not hold the charging Maroons back, falling to them by a 3-0 score.[674] The second game was played under Western rules, and the Cougars expected a better result. However, they fell again by the same score as the first game, 3-0. The team did play a lot better hockey but were unable to beat Clint Benedict in the Montreal net. Jocko Anderson had surgery on his hip and leg and was expected to make a full recovery.[675]

The Cougars were determined to show their talent in the next game, and they did so before 11,000 fans in the Forum. The Maroons scored the first goal, but Halderson scored the Cougars' first goal of the series to tie the game. Clem Loughlin scored in the second period to regain the lead, and Fredrickson's goal in the third period gave them a 3-1 lead. Montreal got one back but was unable to tie the game. Victoria had won the game 3-2 and was now back in the hunt for the Stanley Cup.[676] Unfortunately, the Cougars were unable to score in the fourth game, and the Stanley Cup went to the Montreal Maroons[677]

Where the team's scoring had gone was a mystery, as they had scored in only one contest: the game they won. However, when Lester Patrick got home, he gave some more details. He said the team was never more than sixty percent due to their injuries: Lester with his broken thumb, Anderson with a broken leg, Fraser unable to skate because of his leg not being entirely healed, and Loughlin with his sore shoulder. One good thing that came out of the series was that Eastern fans discovered that they liked the Western system of play better, as it was faster and showed

11 - THE QUEST FOR A SECOND CHAMPIONSHIP

more skill. Patrick also updated fans on Anderson's condition, and let them know that Montreal teams had raised money for his care and made sure he had visitors.[678][679]

An added benefit of the series was the increased interest in Victoria as a tourist destination. Montreal newspapers called Victoria the "City of Sunshine."[680]

It was becoming evident that hockey had become big business in the NHL. Many of the owners were millionaires and could afford additional expenses. Clubs had large arenas and paid huge salaries to attract new players. In contrast, the WCHL clubs were usually locally owned, with small budgets and an inability to pay inflated salaries. The larger population centres were in the East, with more modest-sized centres in the West.[681] For some time, there had been talk from Montreal that the NHL wanted the Western league broken up to provide more players for their teams, but nothing was announced at that time.[682] In the West, the Patrick family already owned three teams, and Frank Patrick convinced Calgary and Edmonton to let him act as their agent. Thus, when the Cougars were playing Montreal, Frank Patrick made overtures to the NHL, stating that he represented five clubs and subtly threatened that, if the NHL would not meet his terms, he would set up a rival league out West.[683] His idea might have been a bluff, but he got results.

On May 4, Victoria fans learned that their team had been sold to the new NHL franchise in Detroit for $100,000. In addition, the Portland Rosebuds had been sold to Chicago for $150,000 in a deal that also included some Vancouver Maroons. Saskatoon had also been sold, to E. L. Gary of New York.[684] Also, Eddie Shore and Duke Keats of Edmonton, and Harry Oliver and Archie Briden of Calgary, were sold to Boston for $50,000. Frank took a percentage of that sale.[685] The Western Hockey League ceased to exist, and Victoria fans lost the man who had been their face of hockey for so many years. Lester went to New York to run the Rangers franchise.

The loss of the team was a significant blow to Victoria, having just won the Stanley Cup a year before. They were, however, happy for some of their players who became members of the Detroit Cougars: Frank Foyston, Frank Fredrickson, Slim Halderson, Gizzy Hart, Clem Loughlin, Harry Meeking, Russell Oatman, and Jack Walker. Another Cougar, Gord Fraser, signed with Chicago.[686]

Lester Patrick in his office at Madison Square Garden. Photo courtesy BC Sports Hall of Fame, image 6753.20.

Although the Patricks no longer controlled hockey on the West Coast, their contributions to the game would never be forgotten. With the sale of the teams, they had barely broken even on their hockey "experiment," but looking back from over a century later, they had laid the foundation for the hockey of the future. While their revolutionary ideas seemed strange to some owners, most of their western rules were eventually adopted by the NHL. Lester Patrick would coach the New York Rangers until 1939, although he maintained his home in Victoria and died there on June 1, 1960.

Little did the Cougars know that they would go down in history as the last non-NHL team to win the Stanley Cup, and the last non-NHL team to play in a Stanley Cup series. They were also the last West Coast team to win the Stanley Cup until Anaheim did it in 2007. Victorians still talk about the "old" Cougars, who reached the pinnacle of success in the hockey world.

The History of Professional Hockey in Victoria, BC: 1911-2011

On May 25, 2001, local citizens erected a cairn to commemorate the Stanley Cup win. The monument was erected on the grounds of Oak Bay High School, across the street from the location of the original Patrick Arena, now the site of the Canmore Apartments. Former NHL players Russ and Geoff Courtnall, who were raised in Oak Bay, accompanied the Stanley Cup for the ceremony, although only Geoff could raise it above his head, having won the trophy in 1988 with the Edmonton Oilers. Several hundred fans attended the commemoration, which honoured those long-ago Cougars who put Victoria on the hockey map.[687][688]

Stanley Cup cairn and banner. Photo courtesy Oak Bay Archives.

12 - VICTORIA CUBS: SHORT-LIVED TEAM

In 1928, Frank Patrick purchased the entire Winnipeg team, as a member of the American Hockey Association. Before Lester left for his job with the New York Rangers, he assured Victoria fans that he had made sure that the team would make the capital city its home. The new league would be somewhat of a revival of the old Pacific Coast Hockey Association, but called the Pacific Coast Hockey League instead.[689] The teams were the Portland Buckaroos, the Seattle Eskimos, the Vancouver Lions, and the Victoria Cubs. Lester's brother Stanley Patrick was named president of the club, and Joe Smith was hired as manager. Early in October, Frank announced that Vancouver would play home games on Mondays, Victoria on Tuesdays, Portland on Thursdays, and Seattle on Fridays. The first game of the season would be played on November 19, in Vancouver.[690]

The Cubs would be a minor-pro club, with none of the cachet of its predecessor. When the schedule was released, it was noted that teams would play eighteen home games each and that several matches would be broadcast on the radio. The playoff format was as follows: The top two teams would play for the championship, except in the case where the third-place team finished within five points of second, in which case those two teams would play a series to determine who would play the first-place team.[691]

Victoria fans were delighted to discover that "Moose" Johnson would be seen in the league this year—not as a player, but as a referee. Gordon Meeking, another former Cougar, along with former Rosebud and Millionaire Charlie Uksila, would join Mickey Ion's officiating crew.[692]

Ernie Leacock, Victoria Cubs, 1928.
Photo courtesy Ernie Fitzsimmons.

77

When the season started, there were only six players from the Winnipeg team. They were: Bill Borland, Jack Kelly, Cliff O'Meara, Ollie Redpath, Herman Runge, and goaltender Earl Robertson.[693] Also in the lineup on opening day in Vancouver were Dave Downie, Ernie Leacock, and Jim Evans.[694] Redpath scored two goals to lead the team to a 4-3 victory with the winning goal off the stick of Jack Kelly. The two best players on the ice were the two young goaltenders, Earl Robertson and Percy Jackson.[695]

A packed house watched the first game against the Vancouver Lions. Premier Simon Fraser Tolmie dropped the puck to start the game. Both teams played hard and skated to a 3-3 overtime tie. Herman Runge scored two goals, and Oliver Redpath got the tying goal with just three minutes left in regulation time. The season was off to a good start.[696] The Cubs suffered their first loss of the season when Bobby Rowe's Portland Buckaroos came to town. Cliff O'Meara played his first game for the Cubs, coming off the injury list from a cracked cheekbone, but he did not appear in the scoring summary. The final score was 3-1, with Borland counting the only goal for the home team.[697] The Cubs then travelled to Portland, where they battled the Buckaroos to a 3-3 tie. Victoria twice had the lead, but could not hold it, surrendering the tying goal in the third period.[698] The next two games were against the Seattle Eskimos. The Cubs lost the first one in overtime, 4-3, to spoil a great game by Jack Kelly.[699] They also lost the return match in Victoria, failing to score in a 2-0 shutout.[700] In the next contest, in Vancouver, the Cubs again failed to score and fell 1-0 to the Lions in overtime. They were no longer in first place in the standings, sitting in third instead.[701] The Cubs got back on the winning track with a decisive 5-1 home victory over the Lions. This was the most goals they had scored all year; Kelly scored three with Downie and Leacock adding singles.[702]

Former Cougar "Moose" Johnson returned to active player status with Portland and was greeted warmly when his Buckaroos took the ice. The game was a close contest with both goaltenders performing well from the start. Runge and Evans scored for the Cubs in a 2-2 draw.[703] Victoria won the return engagement in Portland by a score of 1-0, with Runge counting the only goal.[704] The unbeaten streak continued with a 5-2 victory over the Eskimos in Seattle. Herman Runge's brother, Paul, was traded from the Buckaroos for Dave Downie and played in the game, scoring a goal. Kelly counted two goals, and Herman Runge and Asmundson scored singles. The Cubs were now in second place in the standings, and Jack Kelly was leading the scoring race.[705] The Cubs moved closer to the Lions and the league lead by holding the Eskimos to a draw in their next home game. It was one of the fastest games played for some time, and after a listless first period, the team came alive and pressed the net. Kelly, Paul Runge, and Evans all scored in a 3-3 tie.[706]

Little did Victoria fans know that their team was about to embark on a lengthy losing streak. They were defeated in their next five games, to fall out of championship contention. Vancouver beat the Cubs on New Year's Day 1929, 3-1. Herman Runge scored the only goal.[707] The team made a trade with Seattle, sending Bill Borland to the Emerald City in return for Norm Pridham and cash.[708] The Lions again proved too strong for the Cubs in a game in Victoria and beat them 2-1. Newcomer Pridham scored the only goal for the Cubs.[709] The Buckaroos came to town and shut out the Cubs 3-0. Former Cub Dave Downie scored the winning goal against his old mates.[710] The next game in Portland featured a fistfight between Herman Runge and Red Conn. Police had to intervene to separate the two combatants. The Cubs lost 2-0, as they seemed to have forgotten how to score goals.[711] The Cubs then travelled to Seattle, where they were able to score two goals, but the Eskimos found the net three times to win 3-2. Kelly and Evans were the goal scorers in a losing cause.[712] The team also lost a valuable player when Paul Runge suffered three fractures to his hand.[713]

12 - VICTORIA CUBS: SHORT-LIVED TEAM

Finally, the Cubs got their act together and played a game with good teamwork. They defeated the Seattle Eskimos, 3-1. Evans scored twice, and Redpath added a single. It was the first victory for the team since Christmas Day. The result moved the Cubs into third place in the standings.[714]

Cartoon of Vancouver Lions, who played the Victoria Cubs. Photo courtesy Vancouver Sun.

In Vancouver, the Cubs scored an overtime win over the Lions. Kelly scored two goals, including the overtime winner. It was a very clean game until the third period when Mickey Ion had to call six penalties to keep order.[715] In the next home game, the Cubs entertained the Lions and battled to an overtime draw. The game was thrilling and exciting, and reporters recalled old Victoria/Vancouver battles in the old PCHA. Leacock and Kelly were the Victoria marksmen.[716] The next game in the Willows Arena had the same score, but the opposition was the Portland Buckaroos. The Cubs had the lead in the game until there were only two minutes left in the third period but allowed a Portland goal and neither team could find the net in overtime.[717]

Just when everybody thought the Cubs were going to win more games and possibly gain a playoff berth, they went on to lose all but two games of their last fifteen. For some unexplained reason, the team could not score goals, nor could they keep the puck out of their own net. Over the next ten games, they were shut out twice, scored only one goal five times, and managed two goals three times.[718] At a game in Vancouver on February 11, the local crowd was in a constant uproar after referee Mickey Ion disallowed a goal. Fans littered the ice with debris, and the game had to be stopped so the ice could be cleared. At the end of the second period, when Ion was leaving the ice, he was stopped by a fan. Unfortunately for the spectator, Mickey Ion planted a fist in his nose, drawing blood.[719] [720]

The game in Victoria on February 26, was also a wild affair, with very little good hockey being played. Mickey Ion was not available to act as referee, so Charlie Uksila was placed in charge of the game. It was a very rough affair, with two fist fights in the second period—Herman Runge vs. Dan Daly and Ernie Kenny vs. Smokey Harris. All the combatants received five-minute penalties. Fans were upset with a number of calls and littered the ice with a variety of items, including onions and tacks. None of the projectiles hit the referee, but an innocent penalty timekeeper was hit in the head by a box of tacks. The rink rats had to come out many times to clear the ice. In the little hockey that was played, the Eskimos outscored the Cubs 3-1. The hope for a playoff berth was fading quickly.[721] [722] Manager Joe Smith resigned from the club and Cliff O'Meara, who had been named playing manager in January,[723] was named to replace him. Smith had "urgent business in the South" and was planning a trip there in the near future.[724]

It was not until March 5 that the Cubs would win another game. In that contest, the league's backup goaltender, "Red" Hardaker, replaced young Earl Robertson, who was suffering from the flu.

Smarting from a 5-2 defeat in Vancouver the night before, the Cubs put together a good effort and shut out the Lions at Willows Arena. Jack Kelly, who had been forced out of the game the night before when his skate broke, used a replacement pair, but could not perform at his usual high level. Hardaker was clearly the star of the game and quickly became a fan favourite. Victoria goals were scored by Redpath, Kelly, and Paul Runge. Mickey Ion was the referee, and there was no fan unrest in this match.[725] The Cubs lost their next match against Portland 2-1, but that game had controversy as well. After Timmins, the Portland goaltender, complained that Frank Saunders, the goal judge, was interfering in his game, Mickey Ion ordered Saunders off the ice and Charlie Jasper, the judge at the other end of the ice, quit in protest. The fans littered the ice in a show of support for the goal judges, and rink rats had to clear the surface to make it safe for play. Ion put two of the rink rats in as goal umpires to finish the game. Once again, there was little good hockey played.[726][727]

Replica jersey, Victoria Cubs, 1928-29. Photographed at the BC Sports Hall of Fame by the author.

There was sadness throughout hockey at the news that Pete Muldoon manager of the Seattle Eskimos, had died suddenly of a heart attack. Muldoon, who had started as a trainer of the Vancouver lacrosse team, came to the attention of the Patricks when they were forming the PCHA, due to his clean living and sportsmanship. Pete often advised his young athletes to live the good life; he never drank nor smoked. He had played hockey in the OHA in the 1900s, then moved to the Pacific coast to follow a boxing career. He also played lacrosse and was famous for being able to skate on stilts. He was likely best known as manager of the Seattle Metropolitans when they won the Stanley Cup. When the Seattle club folded, he went with players to Portland, and when that team was sold to Chicago, he went to work there before resigning and returning to Seattle, where he and a group of investors brought hockey back to Seattle.[728][729]

The Cubs achieved their last victory of the season when they travelled to Portland and outscored the Buckaroos 4-2. Redpath had a hat trick, and Kelly added a single.[730] The team then travelled to Seattle where they went down in defeat 3-1 to the Eskimos.

12 - VICTORIA CUBS: SHORT-LIVED TEAM

During the game, play was stopped, and a bugler played "Taps" in honour of Pete Muldoon.[731] The Cubs closed out their unproductive season at home on March 19, 1929, where they fell to the Eskimos 4-3 in an exciting overtime game.[732] Neither the players nor the fans knew that this would be the last professional hockey game played in the Willows Arena. In the league playoffs, second-place Seattle beat third-place Portland and went on to play the league-leading Vancouver team. The Lions won the league championship.

Plans for the 1929-1930 season of the PCHL were finalized at the annual meeting of the league on November 4, 1929. Frank Patrick was re-elected president of the league, Bobby Rowe of Portland was named vice-president. Lloyd Turner and Nate Druxman represented Seattle, and Stan Patrick, Victoria. In rule changes, each team would now be able to dress eleven men rather than the ten of the previous seasons. A two-minute penalty would be given for a goaltender who deliberately delayed the game by holding the puck for longer than three seconds. However, any offender would receive two warnings before a penalty was assessed.

The Victoria Cubs were "strengthened by the addition of Jocko Anderson as manager."[733] The teams would play eighteen games at home and the same away, with the first game in Victoria on November 19 against the Seattle Eskimos. The Cubs added Odie Lowe to the roster; he had played the previous year in Seattle.[734] Seven members of the Cubs attended the first workout of the season. Returnees from the previous year were: Kelly, Kenny, and the Runge brothers. New to the team were Odie Lowe, Tommy McInenly, and Ken Williamson. Ernie Leacock was hospitalized with chicken pox so was isolated for two weeks. Jimmy Evans and Earl Robertson were on their way from Vancouver and would join the team the next day.[735] Oliver Redpath, who had tried out with Pittsburgh, was ordered to report to the Cubs and did so. The last team member to arrive was Oscar Asmundson. The team was now essentially complete.[736]

Disaster struck Victoria hockey in the early hours of Sunday, November 10, 1929.[737]

"Arena destroyed in early morning blaze," *Victoria Daily Colonist*, November 12, 1929.

The Willows Arena was destroyed in a spectacular fire. The blaze was believed to have started in the engine room of the arena and spread quickly through the wooden structure. The first intimation of the blaze was seen by Robert Smith, driver of a Palm Dairy milk wagon, at about 4:35 on Sunday morning. His first thought was to notify Chief Syme, of the Oak Bay police, who in turn informed the fire departments of Oak Bay and Victoria. Four nearby residences and a small store were also gutted. The loss to the arena was partially covered by insurance.[738] The estimate of damage to all structures was as follows:

> VICTORIA Arena, 2110 Cadboro Bay Road, totally destroyed. Estimated loss: $100,000 (of which $40,000 insurance is carried in board companies). In addition, it was estimated that there was $5,000 worth of privately owned patrons' clothing, skates, and equipment lost in the blaze.
>
> Dwelling, 2184 Epworth Street, occupied by Mr. Robert Day, badly damaged, furniture completely destroyed, together with Ford coupe standing near the curb. Estimated loss: $3,000.
>
> Dwelling at 2162 Epworth Street, occupied by Mrs. Beatrice Godfrey, badly damaged but a few articles of furniture saved. Estimated loss: $3,000.
>
> Dwelling at 2140 Epworth Street, occupied by Mr. George Robertson, damage

to building and effects. Estimated loss: $2,500.

Dwelling at 2090 Cadboro Bay Road, occupied by Mrs. L. F. Louridge, damaged roof and walls. Estimated loss: $1,000.

Store on Cadboro Bay Road, opposite Victoria Arena, owned by Mr. V. Casnave, completely burned to ground. Estimated loss: $1,100.

Refreshment stand operated by Mr. Ray Keep. Estimated loss: $500.

Telephone equipment. Estimated loss: $2,500.[739]

Witnesses to the fire told how quickly it had spread, with sparks flying 300 feet in the air. Several bits of tar paper were picked up on Collinson Street, miles away from the fire site. The Robert Day family told firsthand the story of their remarkable escape when their residence was completely destroyed. The fire was coming through a window when Robert Day called his wife and daughter and hustled them out of the house. In five more minutes, it would have been too late. The family lost everything in the blaze, including all their clothes and money, service medals, discharge papers, war souvenirs, and other irreplaceable items.[740] Also lost in the conflagration was a collection of early hockey photographs and records from the early days of hockey in Victoria. The wall of fame, with its photos not only of Victoria teams but also the teams they had played over the years and Lester Patrick's personal records, including the activities of the PCHA teams since 1911, could never be replaced.[741]

Preliminary investigation of the fire indicated that it had been deliberately set. Stan Patrick advised that strict rules governed all patrons and staff at the arena, and no smoking was allowed at all. The arena engineer, Fred Sandiford, had carefully checked the arena on Saturday night after a Rotary carnival and ensured that the power was turned off. There had been a previous fire, also suspicious, at the arena during the summer, but it had been confined to the southeast corner of the building and had been quickly extinguished.[742]

The loss of the arena presented a tough problem for the PCHL executives. What would they do with the Victoria Cubs? Now homeless and with a new arena not likely to be built, where could they go? There were three options presented at the league meeting in Seattle: the Cubs could become a road team for the season, their players could be absorbed by the three other teams, or the team could be transferred to Tacoma, which had wanted a franchise for some time.[743] In the meantime, the Cubs travelled to Vancouver, where they obtained some new equipment and began to practice in preparation for a new season. Rookie Tommy McInenly was cut from the team and left for his home in Ottawa.[744]

Back in Victoria, a local group was interested in building a combination auditorium and skating rink. They felt that, as Victoria was advertised in tourist publications as the winter playground of the Pacific, an arena of some type was needed. From a business perspective, a downtown rink would be more profitable than one located out of the downtown area, as the Willows Arena had been. One possible site was the city-owned land across from the Crystal Garden. The group's leaders tried to arrange a meeting with CPR officials to get them interested in the project.[745] The Chamber of Commerce wanted an auditorium for the region, and it was thought that perhaps a dual-purpose structure could be designed.

Alderman Litchfield said, "When a calamity like the arena fire occurs, I think the City Fathers should spring to attention, and initiate a plan for a building that will give ample accommodation for the requirements of the community."[746] By February 11, Victoria Council had adopted the request of the Chamber of Commerce to ask the CPR to erect a combined auditorium and skating rink on the southeast corner of Belleville and Douglas Streets. A six-lot parcel was removed from sale for six months to allow time for negotiation. Preliminary plans drawn by Spurgin and Semeyn showed a fireproof building, with 138 feet of frontage on Douglas Street and 312 feet on Belleville. The ice rink would measure 80-x-200 feet and would hold 3,000 people, with a capacity of 5,000 when the ice was removed. The cost was estimated at between $200,000 and $250,000.[747] Although the Chamber of Commerce held meetings with the CPR officials, that company said they had already invested considerable funds in the city, and it was not likely that they would want to build yet another building.[748] The project never was built, so the dream of a new skating facility faded into obscurity.

Meanwhile, back in the Cubs' season, the league decided that the Cubs would be a road team with their "home" games split between Vancouver and Seattle. It was generally thought that the club would be transferred to Tacoma the following season, but no firm decision was made.[749]

The 1929-1930 season opened on November 18, with the Victoria Cubs visiting the Vancouver Lions. Although young net minder Earl Robertson played well, his team went down to defeat 2-1 when they were unable to score more than one goal.[750] In their second game, the Cubs again scored only once and lost to Seattle, 3-1.[751] In their first eight games, the Cubs only managed a total of six goals. During that time, they lost six games and tied two. It was not until December 17 that they won their first game of the season, a 3-0 shutout of the Portland Buckaroos.[752] The team followed up that victory with an impressive 2-1 win over Seattle when Asmundson scored the winning goal just twenty-seven seconds before the end of the game.[753] The rest of the season was an exercise in futility. The Cubs would win only three more games by the end of the season, ending with a dismal record of five wins, twenty-nine losses, and two ties. From February 10 to March 20, they played eleven games and were shut out in ten of them.[754] Following this team as a fan must have been very hard.

To create interest in the Cubs, the *Victoria Daily Colonist* ran a series of columns entitled "Some Sidelights on the Orphaned Victoria Icemen." The author was former Cubs' manager Joe Smith. In his December 1 article, he outlined how difficult it was for Jocko Anderson to manage a club with no home rink, no home fans, and playing in front of often hostile crowds.[755] He reinforced this notion in a later article, in which he said: "Every third week, the Cubs have a nasty trip. They leave . . . on Wednesday night, leave Seattle 9:30 a.m., arrive at Portland just after 3:00 p.m., play at 8:30, catch a train out for Seattle again at 11:30 that same night, arrive Seattle 7:00 a.m., breakfast and start for Vancouver, and at 8:30 Friday night, play in Vancouver."[756] Eventually, this column no longer appeared. It would appear that, despite the best efforts of some media outlets, there was little or no interest in the Cubs in Victoria.

The franchise was transferred to Tacoma for the 1930-31 season, but local backers never secured sufficient financing to build an arena. The team was homeless, as the Cubs had been before them, and league president Frank Patrick did not want a similar situation for a second year. However, the Tigers made history before they faded into history. On January 1, they played a rare hockey double-header with two forty-minute games against the Vancouver Lions. After the game, they were disbanded, and players were sold, with teams in the Pacific-Coast league having first choice.[757]

A detailed examination of coverage of the Cubs in the reborn league shows that even the local newspapers were not that supportive as play went on. When the first season started, there were banner headlines and complete stories, but as the season went on, reports were often placed on the secondary pages of the sports section, as the NHL was now the hockey league of choice. The Detroit Cougars and the New York Rangers ("Lester's Boys") received most of the coverage. In some cases, the scores of Cubs' games were difficult to find, making it almost impossible to compile a complete record of team statistics. The league was not that successful, folding after the 1930-1931 season. Public taste had moved on, and the media coverage reflected that.

13 - DARK DAYS FOR HOCKEY IN VICTORIA OR HOW NOT TO BUILD AN ARENA

After the loss of the Willows Arena, there was a desire for a new rink. First news appeared in the February 29, 1936, *Victoria Daily Colonist*, where it was announced that service clubs and other organizations who thought an arena was necessary were invited to a meeting hosted by the Kinsman Club. The Gyro Club and the Rotary Club had already begun investigations, but it was felt that a united action would be better for the community. The motto for the organizing committee was "The City Needs It. The People Want It. Let's Build It."[758] The site of an old wool mill near Ogden Point docks was suggested as a possible arena location, but it was rehabilitated and occupied by the Department of National Defence.[759] Another suggestion was a site on Douglas Street near the Hudson's Bay store, but that, too, failed. Then came the Second World War, and attention was diverted to overseas matters. In January 1940, the Junior Chamber of Commerce pledged to build an ice arena and forum on Pandora Avenue at Blanshard. They passed a resolution that read: "Resolved that the Victoria Junior Chamber of Commerce will sponsor the promotion and erection of an arena to completion, in the city of Victoria, in 1940." The former Civic Auditorium and Sports Arena Committee turned over to the Chamber all plans and information on a potential arena that had been gathered to that date.[760]

Mayor Andrew McGavin was appointed chairman of the Junior Chamber Commerce Campaign for Forum Funds and expressed his support for the project.[761] The Chamber issued a prospectus for the arena to be built on the north side of Pandora Avenue, between Blanshard and Quadra. Among the specifications were that the building be fireproof with a seating capacity of 3,500 and built to allow for expansion. They also announced that the best way to raise money for the project was by public subscription. Citizens donating more than twenty-five dollars would receive benefits such as reduced admissions.[762] They were also desirous that no mortgage be put on the arena, and noted "construction should only be commenced when all moneys had been collected."[763]

There was considerable public support for the project, and local organizations pledged their support.[764] By March 17, $20,000 had been raised, including $1,000 from BAPCO paint,[765] and by April 2, had reached $28,000.[766] With subscriptions at $32,000, the Chamber was determined to continue with the project and were expanding their canvassing area downtown, looking for business support.[767] However, on June 1, 1940, the

13 - DARK DAYS FOR HOCKEY IN VICTORIA or HOW NOT TO BUILD AN ARENA

Chamber announced that the arena plan would be suspended due to the war and that funds would be held in trust for two years.[768] Focus then shifted to the rehabilitation of the Horse Show Buildings at the Willows Fairgrounds for use as an arena. Those who had made pledges for the previous plan were asked for their consent or refusal of the new plan.[769] Large ads were placed in local newspapers outlining the costs and asking for citizen support.[770]

It was not until local businessman Barney Olson got involved that the project moved forward. He offered to lease the Horse Show Building for ten years to turn it into an ice arena.[771] The terms of the lease were agreed upon at $1,800 per year,[772] and the City of Victoria joined Mr. Olson "in an application to the priorities office at Ottawa for a licence to proceed with the necessary alternation to covert the Horse Show Building at Willows Park into an ice arena."[773] Permission was received by early July, and Mr. Olson announced that the arena would open on October 15.[774] He issued tenders for "soft drinks, confectionery, ladies' checking concessions" at the arena, as well as same for "skate rental, sharpening and repairs, and men's checking concessions."[775]

By August 20, the stalls had been removed, and the laying of the floor had commenced. It was noted that the city was spending $6,000 on the building for its conversion to an ice arena[776] while Mr. Olson was contributing the cost of the ice-making system. On November 11, 1941, the newspapers carried an announcement of the official opening of the ice arena.[777] The event, a colourful affair from all accounts, featured three bands, the Victoria Girls Drill Team, and provincial, civic, and municipal representatives. Once the official ceremony was over, the ice was cleared, and Mayor McGavin faced off the puck between the Victoria Bapcos and Vancouver Norvans. It was the first hockey game played in Victoria since 1929.[778] [779]

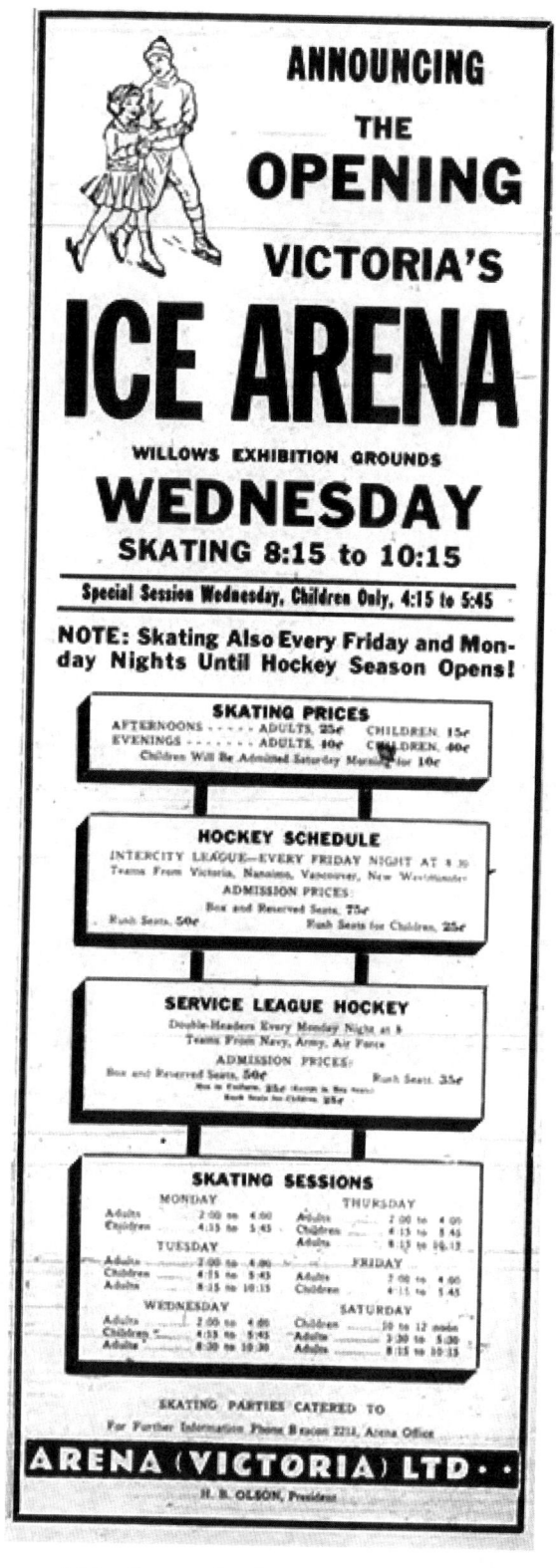

Ad for the opening for the new arena in the former Horse Show Building, *Victoria Daily Colonist,* November 11, 1941, page 9.

The History of Professional Hockey in Victoria, BC: 1911-2011

New Ice Arena Will Open Tomorrow

OUTSIDE VIEW OF NEW ARENA
This Picture Shows the Approach and Main Entrance to Victoria's New Winter Sports Centre, Formerly the Horse Show Building, at the Willows Exhibition Grounds

Conversion of horse show building to arena – *Victoria Daily Colonist*, November 11, 1941, page 9.

Second arena burning down April 24, 1944. Photo courtesy Oak Archives, image 1994-002-073.

13 - DARK DAYS FOR HOCKEY IN VICTORIA or HOW NOT TO BUILD AN ARENA

Once again Victoria became prominent in amateur hockey, as a Pacific Coast Amateur League was formed with teams from Victoria, Nanaimo, Vancouver, and New Westminster. Amateur hockey thrived at the new arena, with many military personnel joining teams while they were located on the coast. However, in December 1941, play was halted until the windows and doors of the arena could be painted out to meet the blackout regulations of the war.[780] Hockey continued to be played at the arena, and the Victoria Figure Skating Club (originally started by Lester Patrick) was revived.[781]

Then tragedy struck a Victoria hockey arena for the second time. The Willows Sports Centre and adjacent ice arena were destroyed by a spectacular fire on the evening of April 24, 1944. The buildings, owned by the City of Victoria, were fully insured; the loss was estimated at $100,000. The ice-arena equipment, valued at $50,000, was partially insured by owner Barney Olson. The fire brought back memories of the 1929 fire that had destroyed the Willows Arena. Mr. Olson announced that he would be interested in building a new arena in town.[782]

It was back to square one for an arena for Victoria, and it would take some time before a suitable building was erected.

The final report on the blaze, conducted by Assistant Fire Marshall W. Percy Nicholls with assistance from Oak Bay Fire Chief Edward Claywards and W. Ward of the Fire Underwriters Investigation Bureau from Vancouver, established that it was caused by a gas leak from an old stove at the southwest corner of the sports complex. Gas had accumulated to the point where it was ignited by the pilot light; any idea of sabotage was dismissed as there were frequent military patrols in the area.[783]

The first suggestion to come out of the aftermath of the fire came from the Victoria and District Labour Trades Council and was that the City of Victoria should build a new arena. Operating costs for a year were estimated at $34,000.[784] Next came the news that Barney Olson was willing to construct a combined arena/sports complex on the northeast corner of Pandora Avenue and Blanshard Street at an estimated cost of $125,000, provided he received concessions from the city. He wanted the land free from the city, tax concessions, and free water for twenty years. The concessions could not be granted without permission from the legislature, but the council was generally supportive of the idea.[785] However, that site was deemed too small, and council was considering other sites including city-owned property at Douglas Street and Garbally Road.[786]

The *Victoria Daily Colonist* printed an editorial that urged caution in the selection of a new arena site and also questioned the need to have it in concert with a sports complex. Their suggestion to council was to "sift the whole matter thoroughly, avoid 'in camera' sitting with anyone, and report on its findings as and when that is found practicable."[787]

By June 3, Barney Olson had withdrawn his former plans and was now pledging support of a municipally built arena. One member of the Victoria Citizens' Committee for a Civic Arena said that the building of a sports complex would be a "means of curbing juvenile delinquency."[788] The Citizens' Committee decided to act immediately to seek grants from the provincial and federal governments. As well, the Labour Council, one of the larger groups represented on the committee, would ask its member unions to donate funds, and businesses and citizens would be asked to raise $65,000, equal to the insurance proceeds from the old arena fire.[789]

On June 22, 1944, Victoria City Council, sitting as Committee of the Whole, endorsed in principle the idea of a civic arena and passed a motion to be submitted to the next council meeting. The motion also requested the property surrounded by Blanshard, Cormorant, and Pandora as the proposed site of the building, and that council "recognize the Citizens' Committee and that the proposals advanced by that committee be submitted in writing at the next meeting of the City Council."[790] Official endorsement was never gained, and the Citizens' Committee became increasingly frustrated with the delays. On July 4, they placed a large ad in the newspapers with the headline: "Victoria Must Have An Arena! Let's Stop Bickering and Start Building."[791] Still, there was no action from council. They claimed they were waiting for a report from the British Columbia Agricultural Association (to see if it wanted to rebuild on the Willows site) and permission from the province to use the insurance money for a new building in the downtown area. Some aldermen were in favour of a downtown arena, and others wanted a new arena on the Willows site.[792] Council was split and at an impasse. Citizens, becoming increasingly frustrated with the delays, wrote letters to the editor expressing their views in no uncertain terms.

On August 18, the Citizens' Committee placed another ad in the newspaper, this one asking residents to send in a form on which they indicated support for an arena to City Council.[793] Council continued to delay, prompting Alderman Archie Wills to say, "The public thinks the city is holding the matter up. There has been a lot of debate, and the question should not be allowed to die. If we cannot get it their way, we should see if we can get a rink by private ownership." Council eventually agreed to a meeting on September 27, 1944, but unfortunately, there was no progress made at that meeting. They tabled (for another two weeks) a "report of city representatives on the British Columba Agricultural Association recommending rebuilding of the horse show structure and the earmarking of the insurance money for that purpose."[794] Council decided to ask city taxpayers to support borrowing $150,000 toward the cost of construction of the arena, with the proviso that the Citizens' Arena Committee would raise $65,000 toward the final cost. The site of the new arena was determined to be property between Blanshard and Quadra Street at Galt Street.[795] For the first time, the community saw a possible design for the arena, in a large ad placed by many local companies. It said, "Vote for an Arena and You'll Get an Arena." The ad also solicited donations from the public.[796] However, this vision was far different from what was actually built.

The civic election was held on December 14, with 4,791 citizens voting in favour of the arena and 1,039 voting against it. Members of the Citizens' Committee noted, "Members of the committee are grateful to electors for supporting the by-law. An arena and auditorium will fill a long-felt want."[797] Mayor McGavin, who had not been that supportive of the arena, was defeated by Percy George.[798]

The city decided to use a barrel roof on the new arena but had to receive permission from the Chicago firm that held the patent rights.[799] At the same time, the Citizens' Committee began an active canvass for funds from the public. Residential areas were being canvassed by members of the parent-teacher association, and youth groups would try to raise funds, as well.[800] Over the next months, the newspaper reported on donations, large and small, from businesses, individual citizens, and young people. The Citizens' Committee placed another ad in the newspaper encouraging citizens to contribute.[801] Student canvassers at Victoria High School held a rally where they kicked off the campaign.[802] By February 2, the canvassers had raised $31,000.[803] Local businesses inserted requests for donations into their newspaper advertising[804] and organized a "silver trail" for March 2, with one last push to put the campaign over the top.[805] That enterprise netted $4,018, to bring the total donated to the area fund to $62,000; thus, only $3,000 remained to be found. Once that was done, the city would float a bond issue for $150,000 on April 1.[806]

Finally, progress on the building of a new arena was made. A meeting of the city's special committee and the Citizens' Arena Committee recommended that Hubert Savage, Percy Leonard James, David C. Frame, and Douglas James be appointed as associate architects to prepare plans for the arena.[807] F. E. Winslow, representative of the Citizens' Arena Committee, presented a cheque for $65,000 to Mayor Percy George. This was the amount raised by public subscription to assist in the payment of construction costs.[808] In perhaps one of their more intelligent moves, the City Council Arena

13 - DARK DAYS FOR HOCKEY IN VICTORIA or HOW NOT TO BUILD AN ARENA

Committee and the architects met with Lester Patrick, vice-president of Madison Square Garden (and the builder of the first arena in Victoria). Patrick was able to give advice based on his lifetime of experience, including information on the laying of pipes and planning of entrances and dressing rooms.[809] The purchase of a lot at Blanshard Street and Caledonia Avenue completed the assembling of the land needed to build the arena.[810] Clearing of the site started on June 18, so that the sinking of test holes for the foundation could be done later.[811] This was great news to the hundreds of supporters of the arena project, as they could see proof that the project was, indeed, going ahead. By August, the team of architects had submitted plans to the city for approval. The design called for an ultra-modern design "built of reinforced concrete throughout. Floor space of the planned ice rink will total 16,000 square feet, being 200 feet long and 85 feet wide." It was noted that the design and footage of the arena met with the approval of Lester Patrick.

By the end of September, final plans and estimates for the new building had been completed, and it was discovered that an additional $50,000 would be necessary to complete the project, bringing the total cost to $265,000.[812] Just when everything seemed to be running smoothly, word came from Ottawa that the city could not receive a permit for construction of an arena for several months. The reason given was that it was "contrary to regulations to build ice arenas at the present time." Housing for returning veterans was a priority of the government.[813] Local citizens were upset with the news and could not understand why the arena could not be built, especially as money had been collected from ratepayers, and it was an asset that the community needed badly.[814] On November 1, citizens saw an image of the proposed design for the arena. It would feature a barrel roof and unrestricted views from any seat.[815] The choice of the barrel roof over a steel-truss roof cost the project one of its architects. Percy Leonard James resigned from the design team, as he could not support the new design. According to reports received by council, the "maintenance of a concrete roof would be substantially less, and insurance costs would be cut one-third."[816]

However, the true cost of the arena could not be determined until the specifications were complete. This was complicated by the fact that the barrel roof had to be designed in Chicago, and those plans forwarded to the local team, who would add them to their work.[817] The whole process was time-consuming and expensive, and citizens who had already approved spending and had raised additional funds themselves were frustrated at the glacial-like speed of the whole project. By the end of the year, the City was negotiating a contract with Vancouver engineer C. T. Hamilton to supervise the concrete roof work.[818] The only progress made during the first part of the new year was the demolition of the Railway Avenue School on the site of the new arena.[819] Council was told that the plans for the concrete roof had been delayed until the end of May.[820] A call for tenders went out for the excavation and construction of footings and columns[821] and two bids were received. G. H. Wheaton's bid of $29,870 was accepted, with the work expected to take about two months.[822]

Council thought the Willows Fairground issue was one step closer to being settled when City Council unanimously endorsed the sale of the site to Colwood Park Association Ltd. for $86,000 cash, with the proceeds to be used for the completion of the Memorial Arena. All that remained for this to become official was the passage of a by-law by ratepayers.[823] However, the ratepayers turned down the by-law, and it was not until October 24 that a successful by-law was passed.[824]

Despite the failure of the first by-law to gain approval, progress was made. Ground was turned in a ceremony on June 12, 1946,[825] and C. T. Hamilton of Vancouver was named supervisor for the entire Memorial Arena project.[826] However, it was not all smooth sailing, as delays were reported due to the large amount of rock to be removed. Most of this work was completed by September.[827] Further work was hampered by shortages of building materials, particularly reinforcing steel. A partial shipment in mid-October meant that work could continue on the footings and columns.[828 829 830] By the end of January 1947, citizens were advised by the project manager that they would be skating that winter.[831]

It was great to start the new year with optimism but, given the history of the project to date, it was a false promise. Tenders for the construction of the roof and walls were called early in February[832] with four bids received by the deadline. The contract was let to Crowley Construction Ltd., whose bid of $118,315 was nearly $20,000 lower than the second-lowest bid. The work was to be completed in ninety days.[833] Early in March, the *Victoria Daily Colonist* published an image of an arena being built in Washington, supposedly to show what the Victoria one might look like. Of course, it would be a different size but of similar construction.[834] Perhaps this was intended to placate the citizens, who were growing impatient with the delays and excuses. Finally, work on the structure itself commenced, and a skeleton of steel and concrete rose above the building site on Blanshard Street.[835]

Good news for the future came when Al Leader, managing director of the Pacific Coast Hockey League and Kenny McKenzie, owner of the New Westminster Royals, visited Victoria to view the progress on the arena. The league was interested in adding a Victoria team and were hoping that the rink would be ready for their next season.[836] It was the first time in many years that "hockey" and "Victoria" had been mentioned in the same article, and it boded well for the future of professional hockey in the city.

Victoria City Council had, up to this point, been managing the construction of the arena as part of its regular business, and as such, lacked the expertise to do the job properly. To solve this problem, they decided to create an independent five-man commission to operate the arena.[837] Thirteen citizens were nominated for the commission and city council voted by secret ballot to select John Baxter, Barney Olson, J. C. Pendray, Archie Wills, and Douglas Fletcher as the initial members.[838] However, things did not go well. Pendray and Wills resigned a week after being selected,[839] and Olson followed a couple of weeks later.[840] The commission held its first meeting in mid-July and elected Douglas Fletcher as its chairman. The resigned members were replaced by Colonel Russell Ker, Dr. Arthur Poynter, and Bill Bridgewood.[841]

Council members were growing increasingly worried about the rising cost of the arena. To date, $75,000 had been spent on excavations, construction of footings, and architect's fees; $139,000 had been allocated for the roof and supporting columns; and $63,000 was estimated for the cost of the refrigeration system, engineers, and inspectors. In addition, the cost of interior walls, seating, and finishes could exceed $140,000.[842] This meant that there were insufficient funds to complete the job, so another funding by-law loomed on the horizon. On the positive side, the roof was now taking shape, as revealed to citizens with a page-one photo.[843] Forms were removed from the first completed roof section in early August.[844] This was real progress and citizens began to hope that the project would be completed with no further delays. The pouring of the third roof section was completed in mid-September, and work was expected to be finished by mid-October.[845] In early October, a model of the completed arena, showing interior features, was delivered to City Hall. The building was billed as the "most modern in Canada."[846] An editorial in the *Victoria Daily Colonist* summarized the public frustration with the delays in construction when it noted:

> "Three or four years is a long time to wait after a public subscription initiates a project and the Memorial Arena has been in the balance all that time.... Many building delays are legitimate enough these days, what with material shortages and labor difficulties, although it does not seem that the construction has been pushed as it might

have been. Periodic and piecemeal calls for tenders do not suggest a comprehensive plan of action or any great sense of urgency. It is difficult to escape the conclusion that in private hands the project would have gone ahead much later than it has done."[847]

It seemed that every time progress was being made, council found another issue. The question of how to honour the war dead appeared to cause no end of concern. It looked like they were "thinking out loud" rather than considering options and making a decision. Their major concern was who to add to the list of names of war dead: those who enlisted in Victoria, those who were born and educated here but entered the service elsewhere; those who may have been trained here; or a combination of all three.[848]

The arena project was once again an election issue, with different candidates announcing their position in their campaign literature.[849] The year ended with no discernible progress made in the construction, as contractors were becoming reluctant to bid on parts of the project before the previous contracts were completed. It was becoming obvious that city council lacked the expertise necessary to oversee a major construction site.

Completion of the arena ignited a major battle on the new council. At their first meeting of 1948, aldermen Diggon and Skillings led a fight to rescind a motion the council had passed at the last meeting of the previous year, wherein "the city would undertake completion of the structure without calling for any further major contracts." After several disagreements, the former decision was allowed to remain.[850] Local hockey fans expressed sadness when the city did not apply for a Victoria franchise in the Pacific Coast Hockey League for the 1948-49 season. Sports commentator Jim Tang asked "Is this a tacit admission by the city council that they have given up any hope of having the arena ready for the next hockey season? . . . Seldom has such a fiasco been seen as the attempt to construct a municipally owned arena in Victoria. Right from the time it was decided upon, the project has been handled with a lack of foresight and determination."[851] The financial report issued in January showed only $104,992 left in the arena account.[852]

Many citizens wondered if they would have approved the construction of the arena if they had known that it would be handled so poorly. Editorials put their arguments in writing.[853] There was much dissatisfaction throughout the city. News of a request for additional funds for the arena roof fuelled the fire of discontent.[854] The city issued calls for tenders for heating and ventilation,[855] electrical work,[856] and plumbing.[857] People thought work was set to begin again. However, there were still serious issues with the figures for the project. Final numbers were supposed to be available by the end of March,[858] but there was the continuing problem of where to find more money for the burgeoning budget. There was only enough money left to fund work to the end of April.[859] At a mid-April meeting, city council decided to raise the $325,000 needed to finish the arena by selling debentures. However, this had to be approved by voters and would result in a delay in further construction.[860] The *Victoria Daily Colonist* responded to the shortage of money by printing:

> *"The by-law will be unpalatable medicine in view of the sorry progress that has attended the building of the arena, and there seems to be no alternative. The primary consideration is that the arena must be finished, and no other method of financing its completion has appeared. When at last the doors of the ice arena are thrown open for long-awaited use, however, one must trust that its administration will prove to be a much more efficient affair than its construction."* [861]

Council decided that Victoria taxpayers would vote to approve the arena funding by-law on May 27.[862] Advertisements in the media showed a photo of the half-completed building with the message to vote "yes" to finish the job.[863] Faced with no other alternative, ratepayers approved the by-law, 2,120 to 923.[864] What was disappointing was the very low turnout. There were 15,000 citizens eligible to vote on the measure, but only 3,059 cast a ballot.[865] It was later revealed that there was only $1,000 left in the arena fund on the day the vote passed. The decision to hire city workers to do much of the work had reduced overall costs.[866]

Problems arose when unionized workers decided to work an extra half-day without pay to help make the project move forward.[867] The union stepped in and stopped the volunteer work, as such an effort was not in the agreed contract.[868] The whole matter turned into a fiasco when alderman Skillings said he had been talking with the workers on the day and they had offered to work some time for free. He was accused of "exploiting" the workers.[869] Further council chaos ensured when Skillings and Mayor George disagreed on the arena opening date. The mayor wanted the building to be dedicated in a ceremony held on November 11, to honour veterans, and Skillings said he did not like being pushed around.[870] The uncomfortable confrontation was noted in a *Victoria Daily Colonist* editorial, entitled "Arena Dignitaries Should Remain Unruffled." The article concluded with the words "Meanwhile, tiffs seem out of place."[871]

By mid-September, there were more concerns about money.[872] There were calls for a thorough probe into the building process as the fund had now run dry. Mayor George reported: "Anonymous letters and rumours alleging that serious civic irregularities have resulted in the high cost" had reached his office.[873] A series of photographs outlining the failed project appeared on page three of the *Victoria Daily Colonist*. It emphasized the slow progress of building and how poor management had contributed to the problems.[874] Then came the news that the consulting engineer, Charles Hamilton, was annoyed that he had not been consulted before the council announcement.[875] When the first of three reports commissioned by council was received, the amount of money needed to complete the arena was estimated at $150,000.[876] At the same time, the Victoria Builders' Exchange advised the city to get out as a contractor and described how money had been wasted by not using qualified personnel to do the work.[877]

On October 20, the city completed the last of its work on the arena and cleared the way for a private contractor to finish the building[878] and a call for tenders "for Completion of Victoria Memorial Arena" was made on October 23.[879] The comedy of errors that was the arena project continued when the bids received were higher than had been budgeted for. Council rejected them all, then decided to call for more tenders and ask taxpayers to pass another by-law to borrow $265,000.[880] The vote on this issue would be made at the same time as the elections for council in December.[881] In the meantime, the arena's clock arrived from the East, but there was nowhere to hang it.[882]

Citizens were urged to support the arena funding with ads such as "Just Suppose We DIDN'T Finish Our Arena!"[883] and "Let's Stop Arguing AND FINISH THE JOB."[884] In the December 9 election, all incumbent aldermen were re-elected, and the arena by-law passed by a count of 3,744 to 1,534. Just more than one-third of eligible voters made their way to the polls. Mayor George vowed to "try to have the arena finished as quickly as possible."[885] The funds allocated for the arena now totalled $1 million—far more than the original optimistic estimates—and citizens wondered if requests for more money would ever end.

Council called for tenders to finish the arena with sealed bids to be submitted by January 17.[886] The bid of $160,000, submitted by well-known Victoria firm Luney Brothers & Hamilton, was accepted so that work could commence once again. They estimated that the work would be completed by May 15.[887] Fred Bolton, an employee of the firm, was appointed superintendent for the completion of the arena.[888] The *Victoria Daily Colonist* editorial commented: "End of Arena Project in Sight." The

13 - DARK DAYS FOR HOCKEY IN VICTORIA or HOW NOT TO BUILD AN ARENA

column concluded with the statement: "Having cost a million dollars, it will be imperative that the Memorial Arena be efficiently managed."[889] It is likely that the majority of Victoria taxpayers echoed these sentiments.

Victoria City Council filled vacancies on the Arena Commission, appointing Fred Cabeldu, D. Grubb, Stanley Moore, and Richard Field to join Bill Bridgewood, whose term had not expired. Alderman Aubrey Kent warned council that, if they did not support the commission, all members might resign as they had done in the past.[890] The commission gained credibility when they were endorsed by Barney Olson. He noted that operating an ice arena was a big business and said, "I am glad to see that the members of the commission are proven businessmen of the community."[891] The next step was to advertise for a secretary for the commission. Applications were accepted from males only.[892]

Memorial Arena just after completion. Photo by W. Atkins, courtesy City of Victoria Archives, image M0547.

For the first team in years, there was positive news about the arena project. The contractor reported that the work was progressing on schedule.[893] This was indeed good news as previous reports had talked of delays and shortages of funds. The city advertised for a manager for the arena on March 20,[894] and by the end of the month, had received almost a hundred applications. Although no names had been divulged, rumours said that two and possibly three applications were from members of the Patrick family. Applications had been received from as far away as Halifax, and many were from the United States.[895] Eventually, Joe Dutkowski from Regina was hired.[896]

The first indication of trouble with the roof of the arena came when the contractor said that sheets of fibrerock were falling down.[897] A plan to use wire mesh to hold them in place was not successful, so another method had to be found.[898] The Chicago firm of engineers who designed the roof advised that loose ceiling sheets "could be fixed by the use of a gun that drives heavy nails deep into fibrerock sheets, fastening them in the cement roof above."[899] The roof dilemma meant that the contract would not be completed on schedule, as work had to come to a standstill while a solution was found.[900 901] An independent firm from Seattle was brought in to assess the ceiling situation and work on the arena floor was stopped until the ceiling issue was solved.[902] On receipt of the report from the ceiling experts, council decided to have the entire roof bolted up, to ensure safety.[903] A week later, they said that their decision had not been final[904] and decided to test different methods of securing the ceiling panels before making a final decision. So, the soap opera continued—one step forward, two steps back.

By the end of the month, the refrigeration pipes had been installed, and the pouring of the floor could commence. Once that had been finished, it was hoped that the work on the ceiling remediation could start.[905] By the end of June, the floor was finished, and work could begin on the ceiling. Bennett and White Construction Co. Ltd. of Vancouver submitted a bid of $7,400 to "fasten each ceiling sheet with a minimum of five bolts fired from a riveting gun."[906] Work commenced immediately, and a photo in the June 29 newspaper showed workers high above the floor on scaffolding.[907]

In the meantime, the arena had been rented for a stage show entitled "Theatre Under the Stars," from July 25-30. Would it be ready in time?[908] That was the question of the day. In a series of well-researched articles, The *Victoria Daily Colonist* presented arguments in favour of a council-manager form of administration. Using the arena fiasco as an example, the articles showed how the project would have been better served by having one person in charge, rather than an ever-changing slate of elected officials.[909 910]

At long last, the building was far enough along in construction to be safe for public use. The Victoria Theatre Foundation presented "The Merry Widow" at the arena on the evening of July 25, 1949. To promote the presentation, the Starlight Theatre cast and crew held a preview parade on July 23, complete with floats carrying actors in costume, with the star of the production carried in a horse-drawn carriage. The parade began at 2:30 p.m., at the CPR Docks, and made its way along Belleville Street to Humboldt, up Douglas to City Hall, and then along Cormorant Street to Blanshard, where it finished at the Memorial Arena.[911 912] By all accounts, the first performance in the arena went well. There was a huge crowd on hand to view the operetta.[913] Prices for seats ranged from fifty cents to a dollar fifty.[914] Not even a power failure between the first and second acts could dampen the enthusiasm for the performance.[915]

Opening ceremony at Memorial Arena. September 25, 1949. Courtesy City of Victoria Archives, image M06919.

For the next two months, very little was written about problems with the arena. The building was opened on September 25, 1949, with a ceremony that honoured the memory of Victoria's war dead. Their families were in attendance as honoured guests. The celebration began with the singing of

13 - DARK DAYS FOR HOCKEY IN VICTORIA or HOW NOT TO BUILD AN ARENA

"O Canada," followed by speeches and hymns. Command Chaplain G. L. Gillard delivered the address of dedication. He asked that future patrons remember the heroic deeds of those honoured by a plaque installed in the lobby of the building. It read: "IN CONSTANT REMEMBRANCE OF THOSE WHO GAVE THEIR LIVES IN DEFENCE OF JUSTICE, FREEDOM AND RIGHTEOUSNESS IN THE SECOND WORLD WAR." After the plaque dedication, playing of the "Last Post" was followed by two minutes of silence in memory of the fallen, and then reveille. Wreaths were laid at the base of the monument by dignitaries and veterans' groups.[916] The arena was finally a reality, and even the worst skeptic rejoiced when the first ice was laid after the dedication ceremony.[917]

14 - PROFESSIONAL HOCKEY RETURNS TO VICTORIA

While the problems with arena construction were going on, almost lost in the news was the fact that Victoria had been awarded a franchise in the Pacific Coast Hockey League. However, the league had not named the person who would operate the club. Applications were received from Lester Patrick and a group headed by former Premier John Hart.[918] In late May 1949, Al Leader, president of the PCHL, announced that Lester Patrick had been awarded the Victoria franchise.[919] Thus, Victoria hockey was back in the hands of the man who had first brought the professional game to the area. The first player he signed was Bernie Strongman, who had played here with the navy during the war.[920] As Lester was retaining his position as vice-president of Madison Square Garden, he hired Fred Hutchinson, former business manager of the Minneapolis Millers baseball team, to be the Cougars' general manager. Next on the agenda was the naming of a player-coach. As did many minor-league professional teams, the Cougars would have an affiliation with an NHL team, likely the Montreal Canadiens.[921] Next to sign were Fred Hildebrand, Roy McKay, and Donald James. The team learned that they would be able to train at the arena, as the ice would be ready by September 26.[922] Early in September, Fiori Goegan and Pat Dockery were added to the roster.[923] Eddie Wares was named the player-coach of the Cougars, bringing the roster total to seven.[924] Veteran PCHL player Joe Evans also joined the club.

Eddie Wares as a Cougar. Photo courtesy Ernie Fitzsimmons.

The Cougars opened a local office at 825 Fort Street and began the sale of season tickets. Hockey-starved fans bought 627 tickets on the first day of sales.[925] Meanwhile, Lester had reached an agreement with Montreal to send some of their players to the Cougars to gain experience. Georges Bougie and Larry Thibeault were the first to arrive, followed by Eddie Marineau and Jacques Deslaurier.[926] When training camp opened, Tom Rockey and goaltender Jerry Fodey were also on hand, along with about ten amateurs who were trying to make the team.[927] Although there was only one-quarter inch of ice in the arena, the Cougars tested it with a practice.[928]

First hockey game in Memorial Arena, October 6, 1949. Photo courtesy BC Archives, image I-02195.

On October 6, 1949, Victoria watched its first professional hockey game in five years when the Cougars hosted the Tacoma Rockets in a pre-season match. The team showed its lack of familiarity with each other and lost the game 6-0.[929] The Cougars dressed the youngest player in the league as newcomer Eddie Mazur was twenty.[930]

The team opened the 1949-50 season in New Westminster on October 8. They did not play well and lost 10-2. According to reports of the game, the Cougars were aggressive but lacked finish.[931] The home opener was played on October 10. Mayor Percy George dropped the puck to start the game, and the Cougars delighted the 4,133 fans with a 4-1 victory over the visiting Portland Penguins. Captain Bernie Strongman scored the first goal for the home team at 2:37 of the first period.[932] The next three games did not go as well as the Cougars visited Vancouver, where they lost 7-4, and then came home, where they lost consecutive games to the New Westminster Royals and the Tacoma Rockets, 7-2 and 7-3.[933][934][935]

In the next game in Victoria, the Cougars found their scoring touch and soundly defeated the visiting Vancouver Canucks, 8-4. Georges Bougie became the first Cougar to score a hat trick, and added an assist for four points, while Eddie Mazur scored two goals and had two assists.[936] The good play continued with the next game, this time with Tacoma the opponents. Defencemen Fiori Geogan and Eddie Marineau led the effort with their speedy play in a 3-1 win.[937] The Los Angeles Monarchs came to town for the first inter-division play, and this time, goalkeeper Jerry Fodey was the star in a convincing 3-1 victory.[938] After the game, the Cougars purchased centre-ice player Bob Wiest from the Oakland Oaks. He came to the club on a fifteen-day conditional basis.[939] Also signed was Russ Kopak, who had been released by Seattle. The team was preparing to play five games in seven nights.[940] Player-coach Eddie Wares scored his first goal of the season in yet another victory, a 5-3 defeat of the Portland Penguins. The win meant the team had won four games in a row and five out of the six they had played at home.[941]

Now they were heading out on the road where the fans would not be supportive. The first game was in Portland, and the Cougars fell 5-1.[942] The league-leading Seattle Ironmen scored early in the next game and handed the Cougars another road defeat 4-2. New team member Kopak scored in a losing cause.[943] The Cougars finally won a road game when they defeated the Vancouver Canucks 8-6 on November 1. Roy McKay scored four goals to lead his team, while Fodey was strong in the second period when the team was badly outshot.[944] The road trip ended on a sour note as New Westminster scored nine goals to Victoria's seven.[945]

Larry Thibeault returned to the roster, and Eddie Dorohoy joined as a recent acquisition sent from the Montreal Canadiens.[946] The home crowd was happy to welcome the team back to Memorial Arena and were thrilled when Eddie Mazur scored in the last minute to secure a 6-5 win.[947] The next game, played on November 5, was watched by a record crowd of 4,781, surpassing the hockey attendance record set during the Stanley Cup playoffs in 1925. Several hundred were turned away at the door, and they missed a victory over the visiting Vancouver Canucks. Kopak was the star of the game in a tight 5-4 win.[948] The new attendance record was broken in the next game when 5,039 saw the Cougars lose to the Seattle Ironmen 3-2.[949] The Cougars only won one game out of their next three—a 6-1 trouncing of the Vancouver Canucks in which Eddie Mazur scored two goals in seven seconds—to fall out of third place in the standings.[950 951 952]

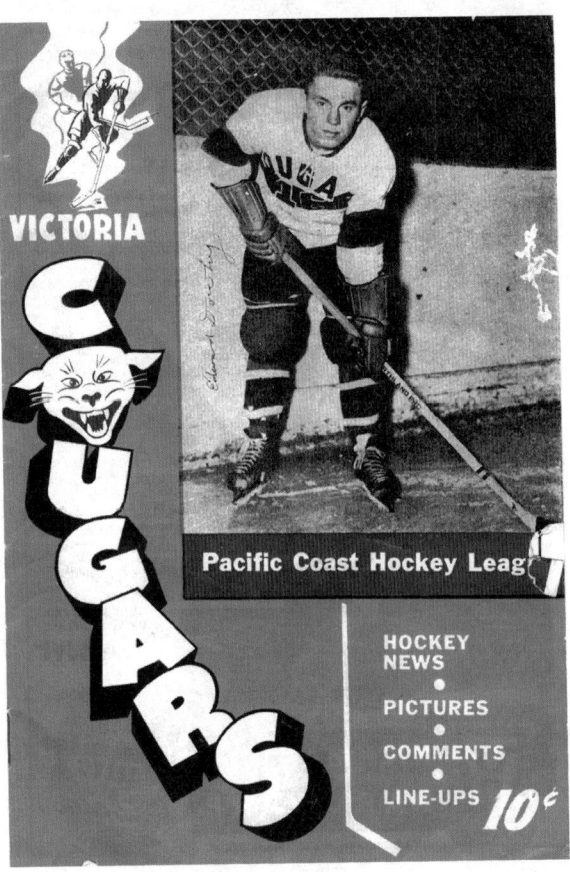

Cougars program 1949-50. From the author's collection.

Joe Evans broke out of a three-year scoring slump and scored two goals to lead his team to a 5-2 victory over the Tacoma Rockets.[953] That win started a successful set of games with only one loss in the rest of November. The prior season's league champions, the San Diego Skyhawks, came to town and left with a loss when Eddie Dorohoy scored the winning goal in a 5-3 Cougar victory.[954] Hockey in Victoria proved to be pretty tame compared to a game in New Westminster, where the police had to be called to calm down the fans after they reacted to a vicious check that left one of their players injured.[955] Meanwhile, back in Victoria, the Royals came to town and were narrowly beaten by the Cougars, 3-2. Had it not been for a spectacular save by Jerry Fodey in the waning seconds, the result could have been different.[956] The return match played in New Westminster ended with the same score, but the Royals were the victors.[957] The Cougars ended November with their thirteenth home victory, a 5-3 decision over the Fresno Falcons. Coach Wares tried moving defenceman Marineau up to the forward line to gain more scoring. However, this left only three players left on defence,[958] and the experiment did not work well.[959]

Montreal sent Charles Gagnon to Victoria, and Murray Richardson was purchased from the Fresno Falcons, while Alan Senior was released.[960] December started reasonably well, with a 3-3 tie against New Westminster[961] and a 4-1 victory over the Seattle Ironmen. Eddie Dorohoy scored a hat trick in that game to lead the team.[962] The Cougars lost the next battle against Vancouver 5-3, and also lost Murray Richardson to injury. George Robertson flew in from the East to replace him in the lineup,[963] but the team still lost the next game 9-0 to Tacoma. The team thought they were back on the right track with a 1-1 tie with Seattle,[964] but lost the next game to Vancouver by a score of 7-5.[965] The Cougars played much better hockey in their next home game, when they defeated the Tacoma Rockets 6-5 in a wild contest, with Eddie Dorohoy scoring two goals, including the winner.[966] The Cougars followed that victory with another one against Seattle. Defenceman Tom Rockey was the star of the game in the 4-1 score.[967] The next game on the Cougars' schedule was not played, as the Oakland Oaks franchise had withdrawn from the league. The remaining schedule for all teams was adjusted to allow for games that had been scheduled against Oakland.[968]

The rest of December was not very successful for the Cougars. Due to the schedule changes, they had to play three games in a row against Portland and lost all of them: 3-1, 5-0, and 5-2.[969] [970] [971] Finally, the Cougars played a good game, finishing the 1949 season with a tie in a game—a contest with the first-place New Westminster Royals. Coach Wares put together a new line—George Robertson, Eddie Mazur, and Roy McKay—and that seemed to spur the team as that line scored both goals.[972]

Georges Bougie as a Cougar. Photo courtesy of Ernie Fitzsimmons.

The 1950 season started well for the Cougars when they defeated the Vancouver Canucks, 4-2. Coach Wares noted that they had to skate quickly "to keep warm," and skate they did. He put together another new line combination—Russ Kopak between George Hayes and Georges Bougie—and they scored three goals.[973] However, the next game was a disaster as the Cougars lost 8-2 to the Canucks. After the loss, Coach Wares called out his team:

"We've got too many players on this club with no ambition. They seem to think that playing hockey is one big party with no reckoning. You just get out of hockey what

you put in and you're going to find out pretty quick. You can't tell me there is any reason for a club to fall apart like we did last night after the first period last night. For twenty minutes the Canucks were never in the game despite the fact they led 2-1 at the bell. Our players just quit playing after that opening period."

After the game, the team purchased left-winger Jack McIntyre from the Seattle Ironmen.[974] The coach's message had some effect on the team, as they won their next game against the New Westminster Royals. Defensive play was the hallmark of that game, along with steady goaltending.[975] The rest of January, however, was a great disappointment to club management, with only two ties in the next ten games.[976 977 978 979 980 981 982] The month ended with an embarrassing loss to the New Westminster Royals, 11-1.[983]

An unusual weather-related occurrence in January affected Cougars hockey. A cold snap on January 12 rendered Victoria and the lower mainland snowbound. A blizzard came down from Alaska and covered the region with snow and ice. Schools and many businesses were closed. The Cougars were due to play Vancouver on the mainland, but the *Princess Marguerite* (the steamship on which they regularly travelled) was unable to leave the dock at 2:35 p.m., due to poor visibility and raging winds. They tried to fly, even driving out to the airport, but that mode of transportation was unavailable, as well, so they came back into town. The ship finally sailed at 8:00 p.m., so they got to Vancouver the next morning, long after the scheduled game time. The game was rescheduled to a later date, and the team managed to reach New Westminster in time for their next game, but they were tired, and as a result, did not play well.[984]

February was not much better than January that year. Three Cougars were injured, and their absence was affecting the team's play. Coach Eddie Wares, Murray Richardson, and Eddie Dorohoy needed more tests to determine when they could return. To bolster the club, manager Hutchinson signed forward Len Mutcheson, who had played earlier in the season with Vancouver and Seattle.[985]

The Cougars won their first game in a convincing 6-2 contest over the San Francisco Shamrocks. The score was tied 2-2 at the end of the second period, but the home team scored four goals in the third period to win going away. There was an unexpected thrill for the crowd when the power in the arena went out with only 2:26 left to play. Patrons were generally well behaved during the outage and cheered when power was restored, and their team had won.[986] The rest of the month, however, was a dead loss as the team failed to win even one more game.[987 988 989 990] Included in the month was a long road trip to the southern division. The Cougars lost all of those games.[991 992 993 994] They just could not win away from home, it seemed. Futility continued in games in Portland and Seattle.[995 996] The team finally played a home game on February 28, when the Vancouver Canucks came to town. Despite a supportive home crowd, the Cougars played a miserable game and fell 8-0 to their mainland opponents.[997] It was their twelfth loss in a row, and, quite frankly, the home crowd had nothing to cheer about.

March did not start any better than February had ended. The Cougars lost a close 1-0 decision to the Tacoma Rockets—their best showing in almost a month.[998] Victoria then travelled to Vancouver to play the game that had been cancelled in January. They managed a 5-5 tie, gaining their first point since February 3.[999] The Seattle Ironmen came to town, and the Cougars played very well, winning the game handily, 6-1. Bougie scored a hat trick to help the team record its first victory in five weeks.[1000] The talent of young Cougar Eddie Mazur was recognized when he was named to the second all-star team.[1001] New Westminster clinched a playoff berth when they defeated the Cougars 5-2 in the Royals' city.[1002] The last two home games of the 1949-50 season were, surprisingly, victories for the reborn Cougars. They beat Vancouver 5-2 with the crowd razzing Canucks' owner Coley Hall. After police had been called, the crowd settled down.[1003] The final home game of the season was a sell-out, and the Cougars easily defeated the New Westminster Royals by a count of 7-2. When attendance numbers were totalled, they revealed that the Cougars had played to 117,000 fans, far more than had been expected. Winners of the most valuable awards, as voted by the fans, were: Larry Thibeault, Georges Bougie, Roy McKay, and Eddie Mazur.[1004] The final road game was played in Tacoma, where the Cougars lost another road contest, 8-2.[1005] Despite the losing season, hockey in Victoria had been a financial success and was here to stay.

The new season began with significant changes. Three southern teams—Fresno, San Francisco, and San Diego—had applied to withdraw from the league. As it would now be impossible to have a southern division, the league was reduced to the six northern teams. New rules were agreed upon at a league meeting and included a provision that only one man could be off the ice for each team at one time. A new icing rule meant that, whether or not the team was at full strength, the puck would be brought back and faced at the end face-off spot of the offending team.[1006] Another change was the player limit. Teams were now able to carry sixteen players, along with a spare goaltender, and could dress fourteen men, inclusive of goalies.[1007]

The first player transaction of the new season was the purchase of utility player Maurice Duffy from the New Westminster Royals.[1008][1009] Next, the Boston Bruins sold the contracts of Fred Hildebrand and Fiori Goegan to the Cougars.[1010][1011] In mid-September, the Canadiens announced that they had selected Roger Leger as the new player-coach of the Cougars, to replace Eddie Wares, who had accepted a new job as sport supervisor for the town of Nelson.[1012] However, Leger had not yet discussed a contract with Lester Patrick, so the local club felt the announcement was a bit premature.[1013] Next, the contract of goaltender Hec Highton was purchased from the Los Angeles Monarchs.[1014]

When the Cougars opened training camp in late September 1950, there were eight players on hand: professionals Bernie Strongman, Hec Highton, Fiori Goegan, Joe Evans, Roy McKay, Jack McIntyre, and Fred Hildebrand, along with lacrosse-star Denny Huddleston, who was trying for a spot on the team. More players were expected when the Montreal Canadiens reduced their rosters and sent seven or eight players to Victoria.[1015] Eddie Dorohoy and Eddie Mazur, returning players, arrived in camp shortly thereafter, and Montreal announced that the first three players to be sent from their camp would be Lorne Davis, Morley MacNeill, and Reg Abbott.[1016] Late arrivals to the roster were Andy Hebenton and Bob Frampton, with Joe Lepine arriving a bit later.[1017] The team played its first pre-season game in Nanaimo, where they defeated the Vancouver Canucks, 4-3,[1018] then followed that up with a 6-3 victory over the Canucks before the home fans. The club gave door prizes to lucky fans and announced that prizes would be presented at all games during the season.[1019]

The big news of the pre-season was not the play of the Cougars but the crash of the arena clock to the ice on the afternoon of September 28. Alderman Mulliner said a "structural defect" involving the metal ceiling inserts had caused the 1,200-pound clock to crash to the ice surface. It was fortunate that there was nobody on the ice at the time. The clock, owned by Imperial Tobacco Company, was to be repaired and rehung at some future date. There was considerable discussion about who would pay for the repairs and reinstallation.[1020] The clock finally reappeared in its familiar location on December 6, more than two months after it had fallen. Local hockey fans had been unhappy with the manual scoring system that had been used for games.[1021] Now all would be well again.

The season opened on October 6, with the New Westminster Royals visiting Victoria. The Cougars were one player short of the roster limit, as amateurs Fred Hildebrand and Denny Huddleston had decided not to turn professional.[1022] Much to the delight of the 4,146 fans in attendance, the Cougars won the game, 4-3. They never trailed, but the score was tied three times. The winning goal was notched by winger Joe Evans at the 18:17 mark of the third period.[1023] The second game did not go the Cougars' way, as they lost 5-2 to the Seattle Ironmen. After the game, the Cougars added a new defenceman, Don Webster, who had previously played for the Los Angeles Monarchs.[1024]

Trouble continued in the next game with the Portland Eagles in town. The Cougars failed to play as a team, and as a result, fell 7-2. The best players for the home team were their youngest players, Reg Abbott and Bobby Frampton.[1025] When the Cougars decided to ship Morley MacNeill and Lorne Davis back to Montreal so they could regain their amateur status, the Canadiens promised to send replacements. In the first road game of the season, the "two Eddies"—Mazur and Dorohoy—led the Cougars to a 2-2 tie.[1026]

In their next road game, the Cougars were shut out, 2-0, by the Vancouver Canucks. Joe Lepine was injured in the third period when he pulled a ligament, while goaltender Highton needed five stitches to repair a gash in his right elbow.[1027] Despite being only able to dress fourteen players, the Cougars manhandled the Tacoma Rockets, 9-1. Bobby Frampton scored two goals in twelve seconds, while his team was short-handed, but there was no one star of the game, as it was a real team effort.[1028] The next match, played in New Westminster, was a total reversal as the Cougars were soundly defeated, 8-4.[1029] When Vancouver came to town, the Cougars started slowly but gained momentum as the game went along and won a narrow decision, 5-3. They were led by the "youth" line of Hebenton, Frampton, and Abbott, as well as the "oldies" Strongman and McIntyre.[1030] The good play continued with a 1-1 tie against the Royals. That single point moved the Cougars into third place in the league standings.[1031] However, the results of the next three games were not what the team wanted, as they fell 5-2 in Portland when the team had to play shorthanded when Dorohoy was assessed a game misconduct and Stan Long received a misconduct penalty.[1032] Playing their next game at home did not help the Cougars, as the Portland Eagles beat them again, this time by a 6-3 score. In an effort to improve the team, general manager Hutchison purchased the contract of forward Joe Medynski, who played a few minutes in that game.[1033]

After that loss, the Cougars turned their season around. Led by their "kid line," they started a string of successful games with a 3-1 victory over the New Westminster Royals.[1034] Vancouver came to town and lost to the Cougars, 4-1. After the game, the Cougars bought the contract of Jerry Cotnoir from the Seattle Ironmen on a conditional basis. Manager Hutchinson was quick to note that this was not a slight against current net-minder Hec Highton, but merely insurance (since he was still the property of Los Angeles, and there was no guarantee that he would be able to remain with the club).[1035] For the next match, against Tacoma, the Cougars dressed two goalies, a first for Victoria hockey. They also acquired forward Geoff Berman, who had played for the San Francisco Shamrocks the year before.[1036] Before a near-capacity crowd, the Cougars skated well and downed the Tacoma Rockets 4-1 for their third consecutive victory.[1037] Roy McKay, who had not regained his prior form since recovering from a leg injury, was released by the club and returned to his home in Ontario.[1038] The Cougars got bad news when young star Andy Hebenton was rushed to hospital for an emergency appendectomy. He was expected to be out of action for a month, with his spot on the kid line being taken by Berman.[1039]

The Cougars travelled to Vancouver and managed a 6-6 tie with the Canucks to keep their unbeaten streak alive.[1040] Seattle came to town and fell 3-1 to the Cougars. The game featured a brawl in the third period, sparked when Fiori Goegan high-sticked Taillefer. When the dust settled, both teams ended up with several penalties. However, Goegan was also a valuable scorer with a goal and an assist.[1041] The Cougars lost their first game in two weeks when

14 - PROFESSIONAL HOCKEY RETURNS TO VICTORIA

they dropped a 7-3 decision in Tacoma.[1042] They were missing their young stars Andy Hebenton and Bob Frampton. The Cougars managed a 3-3 tie in Portland when Reg Abbott scored the tying goal with just more than five minutes left in the game. The result halted the Eagles' thirteen-game victory streak against the Cougars.[1043]

Gerry Cotnoir as a Cougar. Photo courtesy Ernie Fitzsimmons.

Local fans formed a Booster Club to support the club and made plans to travel to some of the road games.[1044] The Eagles got their revenge in the return game at the Memorial Arena, when they beat the Cougars 7-3. Jerry Cotnoir played in goal for the first time, and his play was rated as "fair."[1045] However, he rebounded in the next game and backstopped the Cougars to a 4-1 victory over the New Westminster Royals.[1046] The Cougars closed out November with a 2-2 tie at Portland when Eddie Mazur scored the tying goal at the 18:27 mark of the third period.[1047]

The Cougars began December with their first victory at Tacoma. The 4-1 victory evened their season record at .500, and they were pressing for third place in the standings.[1048] They followed that win with a 5-5 tie in Seattle. They kept taking the lead, only to have the Ironmen tie the game again. Seattle's last goal came on a fluke deflection past Cotnoir.[1049] Hec Highton was sold to the Vancouver Canucks and got his revenge in his first game for his new club when they defeated the Cougars 2-1 in a rough game on the mainland.[1050] Returning home, the Cougars entertained the Tacoma Rockets. The team played a very poor game and lost the match 4-1.[1051] A trip to New Westminster seemed to be just what the Cougars needed. They won their fourth game of the season against the league leaders, with Eddie Mazur scoring two goals and Abbott and Frampton adding one each in a 4-1 decision.[1052] Hec Highton played his first game in Victoria since being traded to Vancouver and was again the victor, shutting out the Cougars, 4-0.[1053]

The game was a very rough one, and more Cougars joined the casualty list. There were now seven Cougars either out of the lineup or playing with injuries. Joe Medynski had a fractured cheekbone, Eddie Dorohoy had possible blood poisoning in his arm, and Andy Hebenton was still recovering from appendicitis. Playing injured were Eddie Mazur with a bad knee, Stan Long with a charleyhorse in his leg, Joe Evans with an injured back, and Bob Frampton playing with an injured leg.[1054] It was not much wonder that the team was having trouble putting a winning streak together. Things got worse in Seattle, where Bernie Strongman suffered a badly bruised heel, and Joe Lepine swallowed his tongue and was taken to hospital. To make matters even worse, the Cougars lost the game 4-2 to slip in the standings.[1055] [1056] Despite their short bench, with three out of commission and six playing hurt, the Cougars dug deep and managed a 3-3 tie in a game with Seattle. Andy Hebenton returned to the lineup and appeared to be fully recovered.[1057]

The team travelled to Portland and managed a 3-3 tie with the Eagles. It was a rough-and-tumble game, with Coach Roger Leger being ejected for arguing with an official. In the third period, Portland's Danny Nixon slugged Don Webster, and the entire Victoria bench came to his aid. The Portland bench emptied, and the brawl was on. There was even fighting in the stands. Hebenton got his first goal since his return to the lineup and added an assist.[1058] The bright spot for the team was the scoring prowess of Eddie Dorohoy, who was in the top ten of the league. After thirty-one games, he had thirteen goals and sixteen assists.[1059] The Cougars led 4-0 in their next game in Vancouver but could not hold back the Canucks, who came back to tie the game, 4-4. Again, the kid line was the best group on the ice.[1060] After the game, Coach Leger fined Eddie Dorohoy and Eddie Mazur fifty dollars each as a "disciplinary measure."[1061]

On December 22, the Cougars honoured a special guest when they played the Tacoma Rockets. "Moose" Johnson returned to the city where he was a beloved member of the "old" Cougars. It was his first trip back to Victoria since 1923, and he recalled the special night the team had held for him.[1062] It was a shame that the game did not reflect well-played hockey. The game started well, with Reg Abbott scoring a spectacular goal, and play was fast and furious. However, it deteriorated in the third period when referee Eddie Powers whistled a penalty on Fiori Goegan. Fans littered the ice with anything they could find to throw, including steel chairs. Police got involved and, eventually, order was restored. The game ended with a 3-2 score in favour of the Rockets.[1063]

On Christmas Day 1950, Eddie Dorohoy scored a hat trick to lead the Cougars to a 6-3 victory over the Portland Eagles. They were the first team to defeat the Eagles, shattering a seventeen-game Portland unbeaten streak that had started October 28, 1949. It was the best game played on home ice since the season had begun but was marred by rough play in the first period. Coach Leger was upset after referee Powers called a series of penalties on the Cougars. Leger followed Powers all over the ice, eventually knocking him down. He was ejected from the game for the infraction, and Don Webster took over on the bench. That seemed to spark the team, and from that point on, they were flying down the ice and thoroughly outplayed the opposition.[1064] To no one's surprise, Leger was fined $200 and suspended indefinitely by League President Al Leader for his attack on the official. The good news, however, was that Bernie Strongman was almost ready to return to play.[1065]

Little did the team know it, but that game marked the turning point in the Cougars' season. Finally healthy, they went on a winning streak, in which they won ten games with one tie. In their last game of 1950, the team shut out the Ironmen, 3-0. It was the first shutout for the franchise, coming in the team's one hundred-and-fifth game. Two former Ironmen players were the stars of the game, with Cotnoir closing the door on Seattle shooters and Medynski scoring the winning goal.[1066] Coach Leger sat out the first of his two-game suspension, the decision having been made before the game. Defenceman Don Webster served as bench coach; he was not allowed to play because of a knee injury.[1067] By the end of the year, Eddie Dorohoy had climbed up the scoring statistics and sat in fourth place, just eight points away from the lead.[1068]

A sold-out crowd watched the Cougars roll over the New Westminster Royals, 3-1, on New Year's Day 1951. The game was won when Mazur and Medynski scored goals forty-two seconds apart in the second period.[1069] The winning continued when the Tacoma Rockets came to town. Cotnoir recorded his second shutout of the season, and the "Pistol Line" of Eddie Dorohoy, Eddie Mazur, and Jack McIntyre were the scoring stars of the game, with McIntyre notching a hat trick in a 6-0 decision. One of the advertising gimmicks for the season was the presentation of a new hat to a goaltender who shut out the opposing team or to a skater who notched a hat trick. Lately, it had become expensive for that business, as shutouts and hat tricks became the usual fare.[1070] Cotnoir gained another hat in the next game in Seattle, when he shut out the Ironmen, 3-0. He had not surrendered a goal in a hundred and sixty-three minutes and fifty seconds.

Eddie Mazur picked up assists on all three Cougar goals.[1071] Cotnoir's streak ended in the next game when Portland scored at 18:44 of the first period, but the Cougars won the game by a score of 3-2.[1072] The win moved the Cougars into second place in league standings. The team travelled to Portland and won another game, this time, 5-2. The star of this game was Fiori Goegan, who scored one goal and assisted on three others.[1073]

The winning streak continued with a convincing 5-1 victory over the Vancouver Canucks. There had always been bad blood between the two teams, but in this case, there was (at one point in the third period) more action in the stands than on the ice. It started when a Victoria fan yelled something that angered Vancouver coach Murph Chamberlain, and he shot off the bench and into the stands to the mezzanine concourse to solve the problem with a well-placed fist. Close on his heels was club owner Coley Hall, although he did not land a punch. Involved in another scuffle was Canucks trainer Reggie Wallis. Once order was restored, Chamberlain was ejected from the game and play resumed, although there was plenty of rough stuff for the remainder of the game.[1074] The winning streak came to an end on January 17, when the Cougars played the Ironmen in Seattle. The teams battled to a 3-3 tie, with Mazur scoring a pair of goals.[1075] In the return game in Victoria, the Cougars got back on the winning track with a 4-1 win before a sellout crowd.[1076]

All good things come to an end, and the Cougars' incredible streak did that when the team lost a 6-1 match in New Westminster. Weather played a part in that loss, as they had survived a very rough five-hour ferry crossing that got them into the arena at 9:46, long after the scheduled start.[1077] As good teams do, the Cougars rebounded from their loss and beat the Canucks soundly, 8-3. This was their first victory in Vancouver since November 1949, and it was a very satisfying one for the club. With Victoria leading 4-3 and playing shorthanded, Vancouver coach Chamberlain pulled his goaltender and had six skaters on the ice. That strategy backfired when Bob Frampton poked the puck into the empty net. Chamberlain tried it again, and Leger stepped out of the penalty box and scored on the unguarded goal. Shortly after these two gift goals, Mazur and Dorohoy then scored in rapid succession. All four goals were scored within 1:49, one second short of a league record.[1078]

The Cougars won another game in front of a large home crowd. It was a close match, with the Cougars beating Portland, 2-1.[1079] The result pulled the Cougars to within eight points of the league lead. In the next match, Andy Hebenton scored a spectacular goal, with fifty-four seconds left, to give the Cougars a narrow 2-1 victory over the Eagles.[1080] The much-awaited return match with the Vancouver Canucks, on January 30, proved to be an anti-climax. The visitors were never in the game after the eight-minute mark of the second period, when the score was tied 2-2. The second Vancouver goal seemed to ignite the Cougars, and they scored two goals in the next two minutes to regain the lead, then added two more before the period was over. They then added three goals in the third period to complete the rout.[1081] The Cougars had achieved a fantastic record in January: eleven wins, one tie, and only one loss. They had moved from fourth place in league standings to within six points of the lead—and the best was yet to come!

February began much the same way January had ended. Playing the league-leading New Westminster Royals with a chance to get closer to the lead, the Cougars tied the score, 2-2. The 4,461 ticket holders went home knowing they had seen one of the best games played in Victoria that season.[1082] The Cougars played their next game in Tacoma and came from behind twice to gain a 3-3 tie with the Rockets.[1083] In their next home game, the Cougars set a new record for total home attendance (101,573) and then went on to defeat the Tacoma Rockets, 4-3. Reg Abbott scored the winning goal that extended the home unbeaten streak.[1084]

The Cougars lost their next game, 7-2, to Portland, but the Royals also lost, so the club retained its position in the league standings.[1085] A smaller crowd of 3,200 witnessed the 4-3 victory over the Seattle Ironmen. The Cougars played well enough to win, but it was not a great effort. With the two points, they moved to within five points of the league-leading Royals.[1086] The Portland Eagles came to Victoria and played the Cougars to a 3-3 tie. The Cougars had not been beaten at home in thirteen games—quite a feat.[1087] In their next game in Tacoma, the Cougars gained another point with a 1-1 tie. They were now only six points behind the Royals in the standings and had played fewer games.[1088] The Cougars won a game in Vancouver, 4-3, to drive the Canucks further into the league cellar. Eddie Mazur scored twice and added an assist to spark the team.[1089]

The next game against New Westminster offered the Cougars a chance to draw closer to the Royals in the league standings. The Cougars responded to the challenge and won the game, 6-2, to pull within four points of the lead. Geoff Burman scored once and assisted twice in leading the charge.[1090] Unfortunately, the Cougars could not beat the Royals in the return match, and fell by the identical score of 6-2, losing the advantage they had gained the previous game.[1091] The Canucks came to Victoria and left with their tails between their legs, as they were defeated, 5-3, by the home team. It was fans' night at the Memorial Arena, and the crowd enjoyed the prizes, and of course, the game on the ice—the fifteenth without a defeat at home. Victoria moved to within four points of the Royals.[1092]

As the Cougars were now assured of a playoff berth, they announced a deal for playoff tickets. Any person purchasing tickets in advance at the club office for each of the last three games on the regular schedule would have the option to reserve two tickets in the same classification for any playoff games played in Victoria.[1093] The lineup for tickets started forming at 1:30 p.m. and, by 3:00 p.m., there were some 500 persons in line, four hours before they were due to go on sale. In the end, fans purchased all but 800 tickets for the last three home games and the playoffs. The lineup brought back memories of the 1925 lineups when the Cougars played in the Stanley Cup, but there was more diversity in the patrons this time—more women and youngsters than in 1925 when the lineup had been predominately male.[1094]

The Cougars continued to win, moving up the league standings. They defeated the Tacoma Tigers 5-3, to bring their home unbeaten streak to sixteen. Mazur and Long were the standouts in this game, which moved the Cougars to within two points of the league lead.[1095] They played their next game in Tacoma and managed a 4-4 tie, but had a disappointing loss in Portland, when the Eagles scored six goals, and the Cougars could only manage four.[1096] However, that would be their last defeat in the regular season. They went on a winning spree with six victories to end the season.

Roger Leger as a Cougar. Photo courtesy Ernie Fitzsimmons.

The new streak started with a game in Vancouver where Eddie Dorohoy scored four goals and added two assists in a 7-5 victory.[1097] New Westminster then played in Victoria, and the Cougars extended their unbeaten streak to seventeen, by outscoring their opponents, 3-1. The win moved the team to within a single point of the league lead.[1098] They moved into first place with a convincing 5-2 win in the Royals City. Stars of that match were Jerry Cotnoir and Dorohoy.[1099] Vancouver was the next team to lose to the Cougars, with the home team outscoring the Canucks four goals to one. At the same time, Tacoma beat the Royals, so the Cougars retained their position as league leaders.[1100] In the last home game of the season, the Cougars won again, shutting out the visiting Seattle Ironmen. Eddie Mazur scored his forty-second goal of the season, and Roger Leger set up two goals. The home unbeaten streak was now at nineteen.

Earlier in the day, Leger had been named the Pacific Coast Hockey League's "Most Valuable Player" for the 1950-51 season.[1101] In the final regular season game, the Cougars (led by Eddie Dorohoy's three goals and an assist) defeated the Seattle Ironmen 7-4 in the Emerald City and won the league championship.[1102] Dorohoy also won the scoring title by one point over New Westminster's Ken Uliyot.[1103] More than 200 fans were on hand to give the team a hero's welcome when they stepped off the *M.V. Chinook* early in the morning.[1104]

The Cougars did not have much time to celebrate their league championship, as the first round of the playoffs started the day after they arrived home. The first game of the best-of-seven series against the Portland Eagles was held on March 20. The game went into overtime and was not over until almost midnight, at 6:53 of overtime. The home crowd was stunned when the Eagles won the game to take a 1-0 lead in the series.[1105] The second game, three days later, also went to overtime. Neither team could score in regulation time, and it took until 6:45 of the second overtime period until a goal was scored. Unfortunately, the Portland team was the victor again, giving them a 2-0 series lead.[1106] Victoria fans were stunned that their team, who had gone so many games at home with no defeats, was in real danger of losing the series. They would need to regain their scoring touch and win on the road.

Travelling to Portland seemed to have energized the Cougars, as they played a great checking game and Fiori Goegan killed penalties with a vengeance. The team scored four goals while surrendering only one; Goegan scored twice, and Abbott and Evans added singles. The Portland lead in the series was reduced to 2-1.[1107] The fourth game, in Portland, also went to overtime, but this time the Cougars emerged triumphant. The prettiest goal of the game was scored by the kid line, who had come of age during the season. The hero of the night was Joe Medynski, who scored the winning goal at 6:19 of overtime. The series was now tied 2-2, and either team could win.[1108]

The next game was played in Victoria in front of a capacity crowd of 5,000. The Cougars played very well but had minor lapses that ended up costing them goals. However, their skill and good goaltending prevailed, and they won the game 4-3 for their first lead in the series.[1109] Just when local fans thought the series was won, Portland threw a monkey wrench into the celebration. Supported by their home fans, the Eagles won a hard fought 2-1 overtime victory to tie the series 3-3.[1110] Now the series came down to one game, with the winner taking the series and moving on to the final. Before the game, Coach Leger said his team would win by three goals. How right he was! The Cougars rose to the occasion and shut out the Eagles 3-0. Cougars goals were notched by Joe Medynski (quickly becoming the star of the post-season), Hebenton, and Dorohoy.[1111] Now the first series was over, and the Cougars moved on to face the New Westminster Royals, who had won their series over the Tacoma Rockets.

The league final series opened in Victoria on April 5. This time, the Cougars played good hockey and won the game, 4-0. Eddie Dorohoy scored two goals while Hebenton and Medynski added singles. Cotnoir made some spectacular saves to preserve the shutout.[1112] The second game was played in New Westminster, and the Cougars again prevailed. The

Royals scored the first goal, then Burman tied the score for the Cougars. Again, New Westminster pulled ahead, but Dorohoy scored early in the third period to knot the game again. The one hundred Victoria fans in the New Westminster rink jumped for joy when Eddie Mazur scored the winning goal at 15:52 of the third period and they rejoiced when two point-blank saves by Cotnoir late in the game sealed the victory. Team owner Lester Patrick did not travel with the team, as they had never won a game in New Westminster when he had been in attendance. Superstition or fact? Whatever the reason, the strategy worked.[1113] The Cougars were now up 2-0 in the series and were playing much better hockey than they had in the first round.

Cougars program 1950-51. From the author's collection.

The third game of the final series was a somewhat listless affair with the Cougars playing marginally better than their opponents. Long, Burman, and McIntyre scored for the home team, giving them a 3-2 victory and a 3-0 lead in the series.[1114] Needing only one more victory to win the league championship, the Cougars travelled again to the mainland. However, they came up flat and lost the match 7-3 to the Royals. They were down 2-0 early and just could not get the puck into the net.[1115] The series shifted back to Victoria, and the Cougars were hoping that Friday the thirteenth would be lucky for them. The game was a sellout with fans jammed to the rafters. The Cougars did not disappoint the crowd, as they shut out their rivals 3-0 to win the series and take the league championship, four games to one. Showing none of the playoff strain expected of a team with an average age of twenty-two, the Cougars, led by their kid line, skated furiously and would not let their opponents near the net. Andy Hebenton scored the first and third goals, while Stan Long notched the second.[1116] Coach Roger Leger had led by example, and his young charges had followed his lead.

It was the first hockey championship for Victoria since the heady days when the 1925 Cougars had won the Stanley Cup. The team had undoubtedly faced adversity, with injuries and a lack of team play, but they had turned it around on Christmas Day, losing only five games after that while winning twenty-five and tying six. They garnered fifty-six points out of a possible seventy-two during that run for a winning record of 78 percent, an incredible record in any sport. Season-end numbers showed that the Cougars had played to nearly a quarter million fans during the season. This figure included both home and away attendance and led the league. Home attendance totalled 137,019.[1117]

After the series ended, many players left for other locations: Roger Leger to Montreal, Don Webster to Los Angeles, and Jerry Cotnoir to play catcher for a Granby baseball team. Joe Evans, Bernie Strongman, Jack McIntyre, and Fiori Goegan made their homes in Victoria, and (it was rumoured) Andy Hebenton would be soon returning for a wedding. Eddie Mazur was called up to their parent-team Montreal Canadiens and dressed for a Stanley Cup game.[1118]

15 - COULD THE COUGARS REPEAT AS CHAMPS?

After the Portland Hippodrome was condemned, that franchise was returned to the league. The team that benefited most from the Portland demise was the Seattle Ironmen, as the AHL Cleveland Barons shifted their affiliation northward to the Emerald City and sent many Eagles players there.[1119] Faced with only five remaining teams, scheduling would be difficult, so the PCHL merged with the Western Canada Senior Hockey League, adding three franchises on the Canadian Prairies: the Calgary Stampeders, the Edmonton Flyers, and the Saskatoon Quakers. The PCHL was experiencing the same issues as those of a prior incarnation of the league and had solved them in the same manner. Western teams would play three games in each Prairie city, and Eastern teams would play three games in each Western city.[1120]

With the new season on the horizon, Lester Patrick asked the Montreal Canadiens for help for the Cougars. The retirement of defenceman Don Webster, who had decided that having a permanent career in television with a steady income was preferable to the uncertainty of a professional hockey contract, left a hole on the blueline.[1121] Many of the previous year's team would be returning, but details were not firm in early September. The team decided to hold a training camp in Saskatoon so that they could play a series of exhibition games on the Prairies. For old-timers, this was very familiar, as the Stanley-Cup winning Cougars had played games on the Prairies before the 1925-26 season.

From Quebec came the sad news that goaltender Cotnoir had broken his leg while playing baseball, and would be lost for the first half of the season.[1122] General Manager Hutchinson then purchased former Portland players, goaltender Tom Karakas, defenceman Hugh Sutherland, and left-winger Joe Cluman.[1123] None of those players ever suited up for the Cougars: Cluman and Sutherland retired, and Karakas took a job as a schoolteacher.[1124] Season tickets went on sale at the club office on September 10, and by the end of the day, a total of 1,500 packages had been sold, surpassing the prior year's total of 1,122.[1125]

Local players Reg Abbott, Joe Evans, Bernie Strongman, Andy Hebenton, and Joe Medynski, along with general Manager Hutchinson and trainer George Wilkinson, left for training camp in Saskatoon.[1126] Players coming from other points were Roger Leger, Joe Lepine, Ed Dorohoy, Bob Frampton, and Jack McIntyre from the previous year, as well as new goaltender, Jim Shirley. After a short training camp, the Cougars played three exhibition games, two against Saskatoon and one in Edmonton.[1127] While club preparation was going well, there was some concern about the lack of ice in the Memorial Arena due to issues with the ice-making machinery.[1128] Fred Hildebrand, a Maritime

Hockey League top scorer, joined the Cougars in Edmonton.[1129]

After playing their exhibition series, the Cougars opened the season with a game in Vancouver. As they had done in previous years, they beat the Canucks, this time by a whopping 8-2 score. The kid line provided most of the offence. Bob Frampton, twenty-two, set a league record when he scored three goals and assisted on three others; Reg Abbott, twenty, scored one goal and added four assists; and Andy Hebenton, twenty-two, scored two goals and added one assist. Newcomer Bob Bowness and veteran Jack McIntyre completed the scoring. Montreal assigned centre Dewar Thomson and Douglas McNeill to the Cougars; they would compete for a spot on the team.[1130] The Cougars remained in Nanaimo, so they could practice while their home arena in Victoria was being readied for the season ahead. The game originally scheduled for October 8 against the Vancouver Canucks had to be rescheduled, as there was no ice.[1131]

Finally, there was sufficient ice for teams to skate on, and the home opener was held on October 12. The quality of the ice was not good, becoming slushy in spots, but it did hold out until the end of the game in which the Cougars bested the Seattle Ironmen by a score of 4-3.[1132] The cause of the poor ice was given as poor coils in the brine tank, which were only operating at twenty-five-percent capacity by the end of the game. City crews worked all weekend to ensure that there was good ice for the next game.[1133] In the meantime, the Cougars took their show on the road and managed a 2-2 tie in New Westminster to keep their unbeaten streak alive. Goaltender Jim Shirley was the star of the game and prevented the Royals from snatching a victory.[1134]

After the second period of the game against the Saskatoon Quakers, league president Al Leader presented the Cougars with two trophies: the Shipstads and Johnson Ice Follies Trophy for the northern-division championship and the Phil Henderson Memorial Trophy for the PCHL Championship. In the game, the Cougars crushed the visiting Quakers by a score of 8-2. Victoria scorers were Anderson, Doherty, and Hebenton with two goals each, and Thomson and Leger with singles.[1135] The next visitors to Memorial Arena were the Tacoma Rockets, and the Cougars rolled along. They squashed the Rockets 9-4, and in the process, set a record for remaining unbeaten in twenty-two regular-season games at home over two seasons. Dorohoy was again the top scorer with two goals and one assist.[1136] The Cougars lost their first game of the season when the Seattle Ironmen defeated them 5-4.[1137] Defenceman Ernie Roche was sent to the team by Montreal and was expected to play in the next game.[1138]

The home unbeaten streak came to an end when the New Westminster Royals prevailed 5-3 over the home team. It was the first home defeat since December 22, 1950, and nobody from the Cougars wanted to discuss it in detail.[1139] The Cougars suffered their third straight loss when the Tacoma Rockets came from behind to win 4-1 and move one point ahead of Victoria in the standings.[1140] The Cougars then started on a series of ten games in fifteen days. This portion of the schedule could make or break their season.

The Calgary Stampeders were the visitors in the first game of November, and they went down to defeat 3-0. Unfortunately, Reg Abbott suffered a separated shoulder when he was hit in the first period and was lost to the team for six weeks.[1141] This meant line juggling that definitely affected team chemistry and scoring. The Cougars beat the winless Vancouver Canucks, extending that team's losing streak to nineteen games in league competition. Fiori Goegan was the star of the show with two goals.[1142] Vancouver's losing streak came to an end when they played the Cougars on the mainland and won the game, 4-3. Canucks goaltender Red McAtee was the best player on the ice and was undoubtedly responsible for his team's victory.[1143] The Cougars travelled to Seattle and were twenty-five seconds from victory when the Ironmen scored the tying goal for a 5-5 final score. Three times Victoria went ahead in the game, but they could not hold the lead.[1144] In

15 - COULD THE COUGARS REPEAT AS CHAMPS?

the return game in Victoria, the defence let the team down, and they fell 4-2 to the Ironmen. The game was marred by Jack McIntyre's attack on linesman Ken Gunter when he did not agree with a call in the second period. Some colourful language resulted in a game misconduct, and a slash across the official's leg followed.[1145] In the next game in New Westminster, the Cougars scored the first three goals, then their defence lapsed, and the Royals scored three goals in six minutes in the second period. However, that was the end of their offence, and the Cougars scored twice in the final frame to win the game.[1146]

The team then went on the road to the Prairies. The first game was a great success, as they won over the Calgary Stampeders, 7-4. They did not start well, surrendering the first two goals, but came back with a well-played third period.[1147] The rest of the trip did not produce the desired results. Edmonton outscored the Cougars 6-2, but that was not the worst news. Bob Frampton sprained the arch in his foot, and Fiori Goegan sprained a knee. Goaltender Shirley needed stitches for a cut over his eye, but after the game was delayed ten minutes, returned to action.[1148] The depleted team moved on to Saskatoon, where a breakaway goal with less than two minutes left in the game broke a 1-1 tie and cost them the game.[1149]

The first game home turned out to be a disaster for the Cougars. There were sixty-five minutes in penalties, and some very sloppy play, and the Tacoma Rockets won the game, 6-1.[1150] A trip to Seattle did not help, as the Ironmen soundly defeated the Cougars, 8-5. The loss dropped the Victoria team to sixth place in the standings—not where the defending champions wanted to be.[1151] Compounding the misery for the Cougars was the need for Goegan to have surgery on his knee; he would be out for six weeks.[1152] Just when everything looked bleak, the team dug down deep and came up with a disciplined game where they defeated the Edmonton Flyers by a score of 4-3. They also received the good news that Reg Abbott would return before their next match.[1153] The lack of a full defence roster showed to disadvantage when the Cougars were able to score five goals but surrendered six to the New Westminster Royals for another loss. Coach Leger could not understand why there was no help coming from Montreal.[1154]

Due to injuries, the team had been dressing under the maximum number of players, and those who were able to play were becoming exhausted. This was evident in the game they played against Vancouver on November 27. Although the Canucks had arrived late due to a severe storm that delayed their ferry crossing, they crushed the Cougars, 10-2, and in the process, injured Dorohoy's eye. He received immediate medical attention and would play within a week. Reg Abbott returned from his injury to spot duty, and after Dorohoy's injury, he played full shifts.

A bit of news was the acquisition of high-scoring Bob Ballance from the Canucks. He had fallen out of favour with Coach Chamberlain and had been warming the bench.[1155] In the next game, Ballance proved to be a great addition, as he scored the winning goal in the Cougars' 3-1 triumph over the Tacoma Rockets.[1156] Unfortunately, he was injured in the return engagement in Tacoma and would be lost to the team for ten days. The team lost the game as well, 4-1.[1157]

In other news, Jerry Cotnoir, spare Cougar goaltender, was loaned to the Edmonton Flyers for one week on an emergency basis after their netminder developed pneumonia.[1158] Calgary came to town and played the Cougars even for two periods, but the home team scored three goals in the third period to win, 5-2.[1159] The next night, the visitors were the Canucks, who won a close game, 4-3.[1160] There was still no help forthcoming from Montreal, although promises had been made.

Victoria travelled to Vancouver and engaged in a goaltenders' duel. McAtee held the high-scoring Cougars in check, and the teams played to a 2-2 tie. The highlight of the game was the improved play of Leon Bouchard. The young man continued to get better every day.[1161] Local fans were very disappointed with the result of the next encounter with New Westminster. The Royals dominated in all phases of the game, scoring a 7-2 victory. The star of the match was goaltender Lucien Duschenes, who blocked shot after shot until his team could get going and score their goals.[1162] Once again, the Cougars rebounded from a disappointing defeat and managed a 6-6 tie in Tacoma. With a little bit of luck (or better defensive play, to be honest), they would have won the game. Trailing 6-4 in the third period, the Rockets pulled their goaltender and scored twice in the final minute of regulation time.[1163] In their game in Seattle, the Cougars dominated in a 7-2 decision. Goal scorers were Medynski, McIntyre, Evans with two, Dorohoy, Leger, and Frampton. In the third period, Coach Leger shortened his bench, playing only two forward lines but using four centres.[1164]

Better play continued in the next home game, where a combination of age and youth led the team to victory. Doug Anderson set up Bowness for two goals, Strongman found the net for one goal, Leger tied the game with a shot off a rebound about halfway through the last period, and Shirley closed the door after that.[1165] Just before Christmas, the Cougars visited New Westminster and took a 4-2 decision from the league-leading Royals. Hebenton scored a hat trick, Dorohoy had four assists, and Medynski had the other goal. Jerry Cotnoir, playing his first full-time game of the season, was as strong as he had been the previous year.[1166] However, the streak of successful results came to a crashing halt over the next twenty games. The Cougars lost their next three home games: 4-3 for Vancouver;[1167] 6-0 for Saskatoon;[1168] and 3-1 for Tacoma.[1169]

Walt Atanas was sent to the club by Montreal and was inserted into the lineup. It was rumoured that Paul Masnick would also be joining the team, but that never happened.[1170] Would this give the Cougars the spark necessary to get their game on track? The only home victory in a month was a 5-2 decision over the Edmonton Flyers. The kid line was reunited at the start of the second period, and that seemed to spark the team. Bob Ballance returned to play after a lung injury, and newcomer Atanas also contributed to the effort. The two points moved the Cougars into fifth place in the league standings.[1171] Despite the lack of victories by the team, Eddie Dorohoy was once again back on top of the scoring race. He had been picking up points at a steady rate in a bid to repeat as league scoring champion.[1172] One victory does not turn a season around, and this became evident over the next five weeks.

Dealing with the business of hockey, the owners in the PCHL were confident that their league could achieve major status and compete with the NHL. They noted that the AHL, based in the eastern United States, was experiencing extremely small attendances and might fold. The owners felt that they could get larger rinks in some of their cities to bring all centres up to NHL condition. They recalled the heady days when the best of the West played the best of the East for the Stanley Cup and hoped to have that situation again.[1173] Their optimism was, in reality, not founded on facts. The AHL went on to become very successful, serving as a farm system for the NHL and is still operating today. The PCHL was the league that could not continue, although it would be some years before the end would come.

In the last home game before an extended road trip, the Cougars lost a tough contest, 8-4, to the Seattle Ironmen. They did get good news that left-winger Don Ashbee would be joining the team, having been assigned by the Canadiens. Fiori Goegan joined the team on the trip, although it was not known when he would be able to play.[1174] To make room on the roster for Ashbee, the Cougars released Bob Bowness, who returned to Halifax of the Maritime League.[1175] The road trip started with rumours of possible trades if performance did not improve. General Manager Hutchinson had the best quote when he said, "Our defence would not look so bad if some of the forwards were doing their job." The team failed to jell as the previous year's had, and they were in danger of missing the playoffs.[1176]

In the first game, Victoria was trounced by Vancouver, 6-4, in a game where they were totally disorganized and badly outplayed.[1177] Not even the return of Fiori Goegan could alleviate the extremely poor play and lack of teamwork that the Cougars exhibited in a 14-3 demolishing by the Calgary Stampeders. Goaltender Shirley was left with no defensive support on several occasions.[1178] Matters did not get any better in Edmonton, where the Flyers won, 3-1. The only Cougar to find the net was Doug Anderson.[1179] The Saskatoon Quakers completed the crushing of the Cougars when they won their game, 4-2.[1180] The young stars of the team could no longer score as they had done, and the rest of the team could not seem to work together.

The Cougars came home from their unsuccessful road trip and prepared to meet the Canucks. Different day, same result, as Vancouver prevailed, 8-5.[1181] The team was now tied with Calgary for last place in the league. A return to the playoffs seemed to be a remote possibility and a repeat of the championship only a dream. For the January 25 game against the New Westminster Royals, a familiar face appeared behind the bench. It was Lester Patrick, who had decided to try his hand at coaching again. Much to the surprise of everyone, including the opposing team, the Cougars managed a 3-3 tie, garnering their first point since January 4.[1182] However, they fell into their old ways and lost the next match in Tacoma to the Rockets, 5-2. As unbelievable as it might have seemed, they still had a chance to make the playoffs, as they had five games in hand on the Vancouver Canucks and one on Calgary, the teams they were trying to pass in the standings.[1183] Things took a turn for the better when the Cougars salvaged a 3-3 tie with Calgary. However, Anderson and McIntyre were injured and had to miss the game.[1184]

While the Canadiens did not send further assistance in the form of players, they did send Kenny Reardon to try to figure out why the club was playing so poorly. He observed the Calgary game and then coached the team for their next game.

15 - COULD THE COUGARS REPEAT AS CHAMPS?

Whatever he discovered and put into action, it worked, as the Cougars played very well and shut out the Canucks, 4-0. Perhaps his influence was felt most on the defence, as that is where he had starred in the NHL. Ernie Roche and Fiori Goegan played their best hockey of the season and this, coupled with aggressive forechecking by the forwards, led to a successful outing.[1185]

Unfortunately, the respite was temporary, as the Cougars fell back into some of their old ways. They lost a close 1-0 encounter to Edmonton, with Reardon again behind the bench. However, he noted that, if the team continued to play with such effort, they would win more games. He left for Montreal but promised to return for the playoffs.[1186] Now the team had to get into at least sixth place; not impossible, but unlikely. Over the next twenty-two days, they would play thirteen games: four against New Westminster, two against Tacoma, Seattle, and Vancouver, and one each against the Prairie clubs.[1187] The string did not start well, with the Cougars losing a 6-3 home decision to New Westminster,[1188] followed by a 7-3 loss in the Royal City the next evening.[1189] A critical game in Vancouver did not go the Cougars' way, either. The game was tied at the end of the first period, but the team was unable to handle the Canucks' sharpshooters and ended up losing the game, 7-2.[1190] As a result, the Cougars trailed the Canucks by seven points in the standings. The team needed a minor miracle.

Due to the burial of King George VI on February 15, all games in the league were rescheduled. The Cougars played in Tacoma on February 14, but they were unable to secure a victory, falling, 4-2, and losing ground in the bid for a playoff spot. The only highlight of the game was Eddie Dorohoy and Bob Frampton scoring within thirty-one seconds of each other, but it was a case of too little, too late, as the Rockets were already ahead 4-0 by that time.[1191] Returning home to play the Rockets did not help the situation, as the home team fell 9-2 in a poor effort at the Memorial Arena.[1192] The faint hope for a place in the playoffs flickered when the

Cougars came up with an inspired effort in Seattle and defeated the Ironmen, 7-3. The Cougars were led by Reg Abbott and Jack McIntyre, who scored two goals each with singles added by Frampton, Dorohoy, and Atanas. New Cougar right-winger Les Hickey, acquired from Buffalo, played in his first game.[1193] Any momentum gained in that game was side-railed when the Canucks came up with a 1-0 victory in Victoria.[1194]

The Ironmen came to town, and once again, the Cougars rallied for a well-earned 6-4 victory. In the game, the Cougars would take the lead, only to have the Ironmen tie the score. In the third period, Atanas and Goegan scored, and Seattle could not beat goaltender Cotnoir.[1195] At New Westminster, the Cougars fell, 5-2, unable to stop the high-scoring Royals,[1196] but they scored an impressive 6-4 victory over the Stampeders in Calgary. Atanas scored a hat trick, while Dorohoy scored two goals. In the league scoring race, Dorohoy was only four points behind Calgary's Agar; it was ironic that the two leading scorers in the league were playing for the bottom-dwelling teams.[1197]

Playoff dreams took a step backward when the Cougars dropped a 4-3 decision to the Flyers in Edmonton[1198] and 6-2 in Saskatoon. Even more disturbing was the loss of Andy Hebenton and Walt Atanas to injuries during the trip.[1199]

Just when everyone except the most rabid fans thought the Cougars would never make the playoff round, the team seemed to find its scoring touch and went on a winning streak—just at the right time. In their first home game on February 29, the Cougars upended the league-leading Royals 7-4. They built up a 6-1 lead, then held on for the win. Doug Anderson led the attack with three goals and an assist. Other marksmen were Goegan, Frampton, Evans, and Atanas.[1200][1201] The next Prairie opponent to visit Victoria was Saskatoon, and they, too, fell to the surging Cougars. Eddie Dorohoy, who had just been named the "most valuable player to his team" in a radio poll, set up the go-ahead goal by Bob Frampton in the third period of a 5-3 victory.[1202]

Seattle came to town, and the Cougars escaped with a narrow 3-2 victory. In the last few seconds of the game, Ironman forward Maxwell broke in on Cotnoir and seemed to be home free, but out of nowhere came the leg of Roche to deflect the puck and preserve the score.[1203] The Cougars won their fourth game in a row when they shut out the Rockets 2-0, while at the same time, the Stampeders were losing. The results left Victoria, Vancouver, and Calgary all with fifty-one points, and only one of them would secure a playoff spot.[1204]

Ed Dorohoy as a Victoria Cougar. Photo courtesy Ernie Fitzsimmons.

When the Cougars dropped their next game, in Vancouver, 4-2, they lost a bit of ground.[1205] The Cougars failed to improve their position in their next match, against Tacoma, losing 7-1. However, both Calgary and Vancouver lost, so the playoff hopes were still alive.[1206] With one week left in the regular season, the Cougars travelled to New

Westminster and beat the Royals, 2-1, while Calgary and Vancouver were losing.[1207] In a game where they should have played good hockey, the Cougars faltered and lost crucial points to the Canucks when they went down to defeat 3-2.[1208] Now, securing a playoff spot would be more difficult.

The Cougars closed out their home schedule before 4,114 fans, with a hard-fought 7-3 defeat of the New Westminster Royals. Anderson scored just forty seconds into the game, setting the tone for the rest of the match. All the team could do now was to wait for the results from other games. When the dust had settled, all the Cougars had to do was win their next game at Seattle on the last day of the season, and the sixth playoff spot would be theirs.[1209] It was also reported that the team had broken their old attendance record, as 152,580 fans had viewed their home games.[1210]

When their backs were against the wall, the Cougars rose to the challenge and did what they had to do. After a scoreless first period, Andy Hebenton opened the scoring just twelve seconds into the second frame; then the Cougars allowed the Ironmen to score three goals to take the lead. In the third period, the Ironmen scored their fourth goal and seemed to have the game in hand. However, the Cougars stormed back with goals by Atanas, Strongman, and Roche to tie the score. Coach Leger scored the winning goal at 14:45 of the third period and the Cougars held the Ironmen off the scoresheet for the rest of the game. The headline in the *Victoria Daily Times* newspaper screamed, "It Seemed Impossible, But Cougars Did It . . . They're In!" Eddie Dorohoy finished second in the scoring race, although somewhat consoled that he did lead the league in assists.[1211]

The PCHL playoffs started on March 25, with a rather complicated format. Saskatoon would play Edmonton, and Seattle would play Tacoma in best-of-five series, with the winners playing a best-of-seven series for the right to meet the winner of the best-of-seven series between Victoria and New Westminster. The Royals, as first-place finishers, were supposedly given an easier route to the finals.[1212]

The Cougars travelled to New Westminster to play their first game. The breaks of the game went against them, and they narrowly lost 3-2. Anderson had a chance to score the tying goal, but his shot went wide. The team was confident they could rebound and still win the series.[1213] The next game was played in Victoria, and, indeed, the Cougars did prevail, tying the series. The home team outplayed the visitors and emerged on the right side of a 3-2 score. League President Al Leader was heard to comment after the game, "I have never seen the Royals look so bad."[1214] The third game was played on the mainland, and the Royals outscored the Cougars 4-1 to win the game and take a lead in the series.

In the other series, the Rockets eliminated the Ironmen and would play the winner of the Edmonton/Saskatoon series.[1215] The next day, the Quakers won in overtime and began their series with Tacoma.[1216] With the series returning to Victoria, the Cougars hoped for a repeat of game two. The game was much different from the previous matches, as it went to overtime. Victoria took the lead in the first period when Les Hickey scored on a pass from Roche. Frampton increased the lead to 2-0, but then the Royals scored two goals to tie the score. Hebenton scored early in the second frame, but the Royals tied the game in the third period. That set the stage for Reg Abbott to be the hero when he scored a beautiful goal after 30:17 of overtime.[1217]

It was not an April Fool's joke—the series was now tied, and the Cougars had a real chance to win it. The series shifted back to New Westminster, and Victoria thought they had won the game when Les Hickey put the puck in the net in overtime. However, the officials did not see the play, so there was no stoppage. The Royals scored on the next rush to take the game, 5-4. Referee Eddie Powers, who was no stranger to controversy, said it was not a goal, as did the local goal judge. However, reporters from the *Province* and *Sun* newspapers said it was a goal.[1218]

As there was no system of replay or review in those days, decisions made on the ice were not changed. In today's game, there would be a video review and the correct decision would be made. Victoria was the site of game six in the series. Leon Bouchard, who had been injured in the previous game, scored the first marker and Hickey, the centre of controversy in the disputed game, notched the second goal in the middle frame. The Royals managed only one goal past Cotnoir, and Dorohoy sealed the victory with an empty-net goal.[1219]

Cougars program 1951-52. From the author's collection.

The whole season came down to one game, with the victor moving on to face the winner of the other semi-final series. The Cougars travelled to the mainland and played the most important game of their season. The Royals thought they had scored a goal early in the second period, but it was disallowed as the puck had been hit with a high stick. Halfway through the period, Frampton scored on a pass from Dorohoy. Cotnoir stopped a penalty shot to keep the Royals off the scoreboard, and Dorohoy put the puck in the net with four minutes left. The Royals managed to score and draw within one goal; then they pulled their goaltender. The Cougar defence stiffened and would not allow another goal.[1220] The lowly sixth-finishing Victoria Cougars had defeated the league leaders in a seven-game series and had a chance to win the championship again. Now they had to wait for the other semi-final series to be complete. Finally, the Saskatoon Quakers bested the Tacoma Rockets in their series, and the final could start.[1221]

The first game was played in Victoria as Saskatoon was already on the coast. The Cougars won the first game, 4-3. The game was not without controversy. Quakers' coach Doug Bentley claimed that Roger Leger was in the crease interfering with goalie Gump Worsley when the winning goal was scored. He also criticized the ice at the Memorial Arena, saying it was like "cheese."[1222] Game two was a classic goaltenders duel, and on this night, Worsley emerged as the victor in a 3-1 Quakers' decision. Once again there was a goal that the Cougars thought they had scored but was disallowed by referee Powers.[1223] What turned out to be the final home game of the season was played before a sold-out crowd. It looked as if the Cougars had run out of energy. They had been playing at a high level for the past month, barely making it into the playoffs and then knocking off the league leaders. Game three was no contest, as the Quakers downed Victoria 5-2. Despite the heroic efforts or Jerry Cotnoir. However, he could not stop everything, and his team went down to defeat.[1224] The Quakers now led the series 2-1 and headed home confident they could win the series in five games.

The Quakers easily won the next game, 7-2, and were poised to win the championship in the next match. Once again, missed chances cost the Cougars, as their sharpshooters could not find the net. Their defensive play was nowhere near the standard that they had played in the New Westminster series.[1225] With Saskatoon on the verge of clinching the series, the Cougars rebounded as they had done so often during the season, and won a game 6-4. They took a 3-0 lead in the first period, but let their defences down in the second frame, surrendering four goals in ten minutes, which gave the Quakers the lead. However, in this game, they would not be denied, and Dorohoy tied the score 4-4. In the third period, Andy Hebenton got the winning goal at 16:09 on great passing from Frampton and Abbott. The victory was sealed when Frampton scored into the empty net.[1226]

Victoria Cougars 1951-52 team portrait. Photo by Bill Halkett, courtesy City of Victoria Archives, image M04348.

On April 23, the Cinderella run of the Cougars came to an end when they lost 8-4 to the Quakers. Leading 3-2 at the end of the second period, the Cougars again suffered a disallowed goal. It would have given them a two-goal lead and who knows what might have happened after that. What occurred instead was that they were still upset about the referee's decision and let Saskatoon score the tying goal. They never seemed to recover their composure after that incident and did not play well in the third period. The best players for the Cougars were on the kid line, with Reg Abbott playing his best game of the series, but they could not handle the "explosive power" of the Quakers.[1227] Saskatoon may have won the series, but hockey fans would never forget the 1951-52 Cougars and how they turned their season around, and with a bit of puck luck, would have repeated as champions.

Most of the team made its way back to Victoria. Bernie Strongman, Joe Evans, Eddie Dorohoy, Reg Abbott, Andy Hebenton, Jerry Cotnoir, Joe Medynski, and Bob Ballance travelled home with team management, the club trainer, and members of the media. Jack McIntyre left for Regina; Roger Leger, Ernie Roche, and Leon Bouchard for Montreal; and Walt Atanas and Les Hickey for their homes in Ontario. Doug Anderson left the train at Edmonton. Fiori Goegan flew back to Victoria for his wedding, while Dorohoy and Hebenton had wedding plans as well.[1228]

16 - A NEW LEAGUE—A NEW ERA

Before the 1952-53 season, the name of the league changed to the Western Hockey League, a moniker that better described the geographical extent of the cities involved. For that season, the teams were the same as had played in the prior season, so there was little difference in how things were managed.

Unlike previous years, there was not much media speculation regarding prospective players for this edition of the Cougars. Owner Lester Patrick attended the NHL meetings in September and talked with several teams about supplying players.[1229] Local sports fans were not that concerned about the lack of hockey information, as their baseball team, the Tyees, were winning the Western International League pennant.[1230]

Reg Abbott autograph. From the author's collection.

Reg Abbott attended the Montreal Canadiens training camp and was considered to be a "hot prospect."[1231] He played exhibition games on a line with Bernie Geoffrion and Paul Meger, as Coach Dick Irvin wanted to see what the younger players could do. Stan Long was also in the Habs' camp.[1232] Cougar coach Roger Leger decided to remain in the East, so a new coach was named later. General Manager Hutchison advised that he had heard nothing about players or a new coach. The only player signed to play in the new season was Jerry Cotnoir, but once the Montreal training camp was concluded, there would be a roster of players for local fans to watch.[1233]

On September 24, Montreal announced that six players from the previous year's team would be sent to Victoria. Eddie Dorohoy, Reg Abbott, Andy Hebenton, Ernie Roche, Doug Anderson, and Leon Bouchard would report, along with newcomer, Ivan Irwin. Montreal also promised that either Eddie Mazur or Colin Kilburn would be on the Cougars' roster when the season began.[1234] On September 25, Eddie Dorohoy was named the player-coach of the Cougars, putting to rest the many rumours about who would be selected. Only twenty-three years of age, he was believed to be the youngest coach in professional hockey. Team owner Lester Patrick expressed confidence in Eddie's ability to lead the team,[1235] and local fans welcomed the selection of one of Victoria's favourite players to a leadership position.

Training camp started the following week and players arrived, most of them in good physical shape. Particularly fit was Fiori Goegan, who spent the summer on a construction crew.[1236] The first exhibition game, billed as a "Get Acquainted Jamboree," featured door prizes worth a total of $1,000.[1237] The team received great news when it was announced that former Edmonton Flyer star Colin Kilburn would be sent to Victoria. He was expected to add scoring punch to the Cougars, something they had needed in prior years.[1238]

By the time of the first exhibition game, the team roster stood at thirteen: Hebenton, Abbott, Dorohoy, Roche, Strongman, Evans, Goegan, Cotnoir, Bouchard, Medynski, McIntyre, and Anderson. The team would be wearing new uniforms featuring a snarling cougar on the crest.[1239] Stan Long was named to the team, and Eddie Mazur was en route from Montreal, but it appeared that Ivan Irwin would not come west, after all.[1240]

In the long-awaited exhibition game, the Cougars tied the Royals, 1-1. Unfortunately for the local fans, Cotnoir knocked the puck into his own net for the Royals' goal.[1241] In the return game, played on the mainland, the Royals outscored the Cougars 5-1.[1242]

As usual, there were changes to the rules before the start of the regular season. Some of them were as follows: the number of face-off zones in the neutral zone was reduced from six to four, thus dividing the ice surface into three equal parts; players other than the two involved in the face-off were required to be fifteen feet from the face-off location; any goal scored when the puck was batted into the net with a hand would be disallowed; and goals scored when a player was illegally on the ice would be disallowed.[1243] The 1952-53 Western Hockey League season opened on October 8, but the Cougars played their first game the following night.[1244] Much to the delight of the almost-capacity crowd at the Memorial Arena, the Cougars won a very close 3-2 decision over their mainland rivals from Vancouver. Newcomer Colin Kilburn had three points to lead the team.[1245] In the return game the next evening, the Canucks won 5-1 in a game that featured very rough play in the third period. Luckily, nobody was hurt in the melee, in which several players were given misconducts, and the penalty box was filled to overflowing.[1246]

The Tacoma Rockets came to town on Thanksgiving Day and lost to the Cougars by a score of 7-2. Tacoma scored the first goal, but that lead was short-lived as Evans scored ten seconds later to tie the game. Other goal-scorers for the winning team were Dorohoy and Mazur with singles, while Hebenton and Abbott notched two goals each.[1247] Jim Fairburn was acquired from Seattle before the next game with New Westminster and played an integral part in the Cougars' 6-3 victory.[1248] The team had now won three out of their first four games. The winning streak continued when the Cougars travelled to New Westminster and narrowly defeated the Royals 3-2. The victory put them into a tie for first place in the league standings, a position they had not been in for some time.[1249]

However, the bubble burst with the next fifteen games when the Cougars won only two games and tied once. They lost games to the Edmonton Flyers,[1250] the Tacoma Rockets, and the Seattle Bombers. Defencemen Long was injured in the Edmonton game, while Webster was hurt in the Tacoma game.[1251] Those injuries put further pressure on the remaining defenders. Lester Patrick issued a statement that the Cougars had asked Montreal for help.[1252] They received good news the next day that defender Ivan Irwin would report to the club by the end of the week. In the meantime, the Cougars played Vancouver and lost 5-1.[1253] Just when everything looked bleak for the team, they played a great game against the Seattle Bombers and emerged with an 8-4 victory. It was their largest offensive output since the start of the season, with Kilburn and Anderson working well together, the former with three goals and the latter with a goal and two assists. Newcomer Irwin played well on defence, despite having only an hour's skating with the club before the game.[1254]

The next game was a loss of 5-2 to New Westminster. After the contest, general manager Hutchinson announced that, by November 15, the Cougars had to cut their roster from seventeen to fifteen, so two players had to go. He would make the decisions after a detailed assessment of how each player contributed to the team effort over the next four home games.[1255] When the Cougars acquired Bob Goodacre, that meant that three players would need to be cut at the deadline.[1256] After a 4-2 loss to the league-leading Saskatoon Quakers, Eddie Dorohoy read the riot act to his team. "We'll find out if we have a club or not. If we haven't, there'll be some changes made. We outplay 'em in the first period, then go to sleep in the next two periods." He had benched Evans, Strongman, and Goegan before the game and advised they would be in the stands for the next one as well.[1257]

Victoria came up with a better effort in the next match and left the Memorial Arena with a 1-1 tie against Vancouver. Reg Abbott scored the only goal, tying the game in the second period. The Cougars then employed "the box," in which they played defensive hockey. It might have been boring to the fans, but it prevented the Canucks from scoring again.[1258] Although the Cougars put forth effort in their next game, they fell to the Calgary Stampeders, 5-4. Colin Kilburn did not play for the Cougars, as his sprained ankle was bothering him.[1259] In the next game, a 7-4 loss to Tacoma, nobody on the team played well, with the possible exception of Eddie Dorohoy, who lost two teeth and took ten stitches to the lip, then returned to play. As a result of the less-than-desired results, team management delayed the decision on who would be dropped from the roster.[1260] Eventually, the team released Bob Goodacre and Jack Kirk, but still had one extra player on the roster. Management was tight-lipped about any further changes.[1261] At this point, the *Victoria Daily Times* polled hockey fans to get their input on "What's Wrong With the Cougars?" Although there were differing opinions, most agreed that Dorohoy was too young to be a coach and that his players were not giving him their best effort. Fans also felt that the team needed more players with experience, as the current team seemed to lack cohesiveness.[1262]

Cougars program 1952-53. From the author's collection.

The Cougars got down to the league limit by placing forward Jack McIntyre on the inactive list; he had been bothered by foot issues in recent games.[1263] Kilburn and Evans were the only scorers in the next match: a 3-2 loss to the Seattle Bombers. Comments in the media were how about how the Cats had lost, but not by much.[1264] Reports gave excuse after excuse for the poor play. Just when everybody had written the Cougars off, they responded with their first shutout of the season, 2-0 over New Westminster. Andy Hebenton broke out of a slump, scoring both goals. The second period produced not much in the way of hockey, but lots in the way of fisticuffs.[1265] Kenny Reardon came west to check out the Cougars and accompanied Lester Patrick and the team on their eastern road swing.[1266] Local fans were likely hoping he could work his magic on this year's team the way he had done only a year ago.

However, the trip was anything but successful, as the Cougars lost all three games. They dropped a 7-4 decision to the Saskatoon Quakers,[1267] lost 5-2 to the Edmonton Flyers,[1268] and were totally dominated by the Calgary Stampeders, 9-2. It was the team's worst beating of the year and their twelfth loss in their last fifteen games.[1269] The season was not going well, and there seemed to be no way to get the team out of its poor play. Even the sports editor of the *Victoria Daily Times* got into the act and wrote an article saying how frustrated he was with the team's lack of success.[1270]

Ed. Dorohoy

Eddie Dorohoy autograph. From the author's collection.

In their next game, the Cougars scored two goals within fifteen seconds, and then held the Seattle Bombers to only one goal, registering a 2-1 win.[1271] Fans wondered if this was the game that would turn their season around but knew not to get their hopes up with this team. Several factors played into the next match: Coach Dorohoy had one-on-one interviews with the players while travelling on the ship to Vancouver, the coach and the owner had discussions, and Reg Abbott received news that he had been recalled to Montreal for a three-game trial, where he would take the place of injured Elmer Lach. The Cougars lost the game by a score of 4-2, as they never recovered from an early 2-0 Canucks' lead.[1272] However, the teams played the next night in Victoria, and the Cougars emerged with a 2-1 victory. Stan Long scored both goals and was easily the star of the game.[1273]

Playoff hopes suffered a setback when the Cougars travelled to Seattle and lost to the Bombers, 5-3. Victoria actually had a two-goal lead in the first period, but ran into penalty trouble and could not hold back the Seattle power play.[1274]

Jack McIntyre was sold to the New Westminster Royals and would play his old team for the first time.[1275] The Cougars emerged from that game with a well-deserved 5-3 win. By the end of the second period, they had a 4-0 lead and went on from there to win convincingly.[1276] Although they did not know it yet, that was to be the first of six victories in a row. The Cougars moved out of the league basement with a decisive 7-0 thrashing of the Tacoma Rockets. They were playing under stress as their bus had been involved in an accident outside Seattle. Channelling their anger, they scored early and often. Dorohoy ended the night with two goals and three assists, while Hebenton added a goal and two assists. In all, ten different players hit the scoresheet. Stan Maxwell, playing in his first game since being bought from New Westminster, scored one goal.[1277] Skating before a full house for the first time in a while, the Cougars took care of the league-leading Saskatoon Quakers 4-1 at the Memorial Arena. Maxwell scored two goals, bringing his total to three in two games.[1278] Winning continued with a 3-1 decision over the New Westminster Royals.[1279]

The Cougars received some bad news when they learned that Eddie Mazur might require surgery on his damaged knee, but that was balanced by the good news that Reg Abbott would be returning from Montreal to rejoin the team for the next game.[1280] It was first thought Mazur did not need surgery and would be able to play by the end of the week. However, it was later decided that surgery was necessary, and he would be lost to the team for at least three weeks.[1281] The Cougars gained their fifth straight victory when they overcame the visiting Calgary Stampeders, 6-3. Rising-star Maxwell notched yet another goal; he was joined by Kilburn, Hebenton, Fairburn, Roche, and Goegan.[1282] The Seattle Bombers came into Victoria riding an eight-game unbeaten streak but ran into a brick wall in the form of the Victoria Cougars. Jim Fairburn scored four goals to lead his team to an 8-2 victory. Colin Kilburn added one goal and three assists. With the two points, the team moved into sixth place in league standings.[1283]

However, the magic of previous years was not to happen as the Cougars proceeded to win only four and tie four of their next twenty games to fall from playoff contention. The losing streak started with a 6-1 loss to the Tacoma Rockets on Boxing Day.[1284] This was followed by a defeat in Tacoma[1285] and a 4-3 home loss to the Canucks, which put them back in the league basement. In that match, the Cougars had a two-goal lead but could not hold it.[1286] The team managed a 1-1 tie with the Canucks to break the losing streak,[1287] but gained no momentum from that moral victory, and fell to the Royals in a game where they looked bad at times, but for brief periods, played very well.[1288]

It was the inconsistency of the team that was frustrating the fans. In their last home game before a long road trip, the Cougars came up with their best effort and shut out the Seattle Bombers, 4-0.[1289] In the first game of the long trip, the Cougars fell behind 4-0 in the first period, and although they scored the next three goals, could not find a way to win.[1290] Two days later, Vancouver outscored Victoria 5-3, to move the Canucks into a second-place tie, and Victoria fell farther away from a playoff spot. Kilburn scored two goals and Fairburn had the other but it was not enough.[1291] On January 15, 1953, the Cougars became the first Coast team to beat Calgary in their home rink when they downed the Stampeders, 2-1. Kilburn and Abbott scored for Victoria, with the team playing its best game in some time.[1292] However, the team went back to its old habits and dropped a 6-2 decision to Edmonton. Hebenton and Abbott scored to give Victoria a 2-0 lead, but that was all the team could produce, and the Flyers scored six unanswered goals.[1293] The Cougars closed out their road trip with a 7-3 drubbing at the hands of the Saskatoon Quakers. Only Goegan, Roche, and Strongman scored for Victoria.[1294]

Victoria Cougars puck. From the author's collection.

In their first home game after the road trip, Victoria managed a 1-1 tie with the Vancouver Canucks. It turned out to be a goaltending duel between Emile "The Cat" Francis in the Vancouver nets and the hometown's Jerry Cotnoir. It was the best game the team had played in some time, and in some ways, they were unfortunate not to gain a victory as the lone Canucks goal deflected in off Goegan's glove in the third period. The game featured a brawl when Francis got involved with several Cougars and later accosted an official.[1295]

In the next match, the Bombers extended their win streak, securing their fifteenth straight home victory with a 7-5 defeat of the Victoria team. Hebenton scored three goals for the Cougars, but they could not outscore the Bombers in the third period.[1296] The "pony line" of Anderson, Kilburn, and Fairburn led the team to a decisive victory over the Tacoma Rockets before 4,338 fans.[1297] Fans wondered if the team could repeat the success they'd had the previous year but knew that the chance of that happening was growing slim. Playoff hopes took a dip when New Westminster beat Victoria 4-2 on the mainland. Defender Ivan Irwin was injured and needed stitches to repair a cut over his eye and across his nose, and Stan Long re-injured his back.[1298] Things were not looking good. Mazur returned to the lineup and was one of the stars as the Cougars tied the Tacoma Rockets 4-4. Colin Kilburn scored a pair of goals to sit fifth in the league scoring race.[1299]

In their next game, the Cougars came from being a goal down twice to gain a tie with the Calgary Stampeders.[1300] Their efforts were paying off, but they were not gaining ground on the clubs they had to pass to achieve a playoff spot. Any momentum the Cougars might have gained in their last games came to a crashing halt when the Edmonton Flyers came to town and handed them a horrendous 11-2 loss. One of the stars for Edmonton was former Cougar Leon Bouchard.[1301] The team rebounded from that terrible loss and humbled the Royals 6-2 in the next match. The game featured a series of penalties to New Westminster's Jackie Hamilton. He first received a penalty for slashing Hebenton. He then attacked the public-address announcer, Ernie Fox, who reported his actions to the referee. That cost him a ten-minute misconduct. He then made threats to Mr. Fox, not realizing that the announcer stood 6'5", and could withstand any attack from Hamilton's 5'7".[1302]

Team euphoria was short-lived, however, as the Cougars went on a five-game losing streak that all but eliminated them from playoff contention. They lost, 6-4, in the return match in New Westminster,[1303] and were shut out, 7-0, in Vancouver in a game where a reporter said they "fell apart like a Christmas toy."[1304] Even the local media was getting cynical. This team was a real paradox; they would play like world-beaters one night, then do the opposite the next. It was difficult to remain confident about their chances for success. Victoria next played a home-and-home series against Tacoma, losing both games, 6-3, at home[1305] and 5-4 on the road.[1306] Returning home to face the Saskatoon Quakers, the Cougars needed a good effort. Unfortunately, they were utterly outplayed and ended up losing 7-2.[1307] There was still a mathematical chance for the Cougars to make the playoffs, but they would have to win all fifteen remaining games and get a bit of help from other teams. It was a long shot, but they had done it before—just a year before.

As if on cue, the Cougars began to play competitive hockey. They shut out Seattle 1-0 in the next home game, with Montreal representative Kenny Reardon in attendance. After an assessment, he could not understand why the team was having so much trouble as they were strong "down the centre."[1308] His presence the year before had turned the season around. Could he work his magic again? Vancouver came to town and left a defeated team with the Cougars on the right end of a 6-2 score. The goal scorers were Anderson, Maxwell, Hebenton, Fairburn, and Mazur (with two).[1309] The Cougars then went on a Prairie road trip, and, much to everyone's surprise, did very well. The trip started with a 5-4 win over the Calgary Stampeders,[1310] followed by a 2-2 tie in Edmonton,[1311] and a 3-3 draw in Saskatoon.[1312] The streak continued in a home-and-home series with the Royals, where the Cougars won 7-3 in Victoria[1313] and 4-2 in New Westminster.[1314] The team was now unbeaten in seven games and were only six points back of a playoff spot.

March began with an 8-5 victory over Tacoma, where the goal judge and linesmen were attacked by Rockets' goaltender.[1315] Three days later, the winning streak continued with a 5-2 win over Seattle.[1316] The Cougars were still five points from a playoff position and time was running out. The great streak came to an end when the Tacoma Rockets handed the Cougars a 5-2 defeat.[1317] Faint playoff hopes revived with a 3-3 tie with Edmonton,[1318] but a subsequent 5-2 defeat at the hands of the Vancouver Canucks meant Victoria was out of the playoffs for sure.[1319] It was evident that the Cougars had lost the will to win, as they dropped the next game 9-5 to Vancouver. That game featured Colin Kilburn taking his frustrations out on referee Powers and receiving a misconduct for his actions.[1320]

The Cougars played out the rest of the season, beating New Westminster 8-6, in a game where Reg Abbott scored his first hat trick,[1321] and losing the final game of the season 8-7 to Seattle.[1322] The season was not over for goaltender Jerry Cotnoir, who was named an emergency replacement for the entire league. He played for the Royals, whose regular netminders had been injured.[1323] Eddie Mazur headed back to Montreal, where he played for the Canadiens in their playoff series against Chicago, scoring two goals in the game that moved the Habs into the final series against Boston.[1324] He also played in that series, notching two assists.[1325]

An analysis of the season revealed that, despite their mediocre record, the Cougars played before 152,745 fans, more than in any other year of operation. The streakiness of their play led to their lack of overall success; one day they were unbeatable, and the next could not win anything. A team needs consistency to win, and this version of the Cougars was severely lacking in this regard. The discussion then turned to which players would be back for another season, and who would move on.

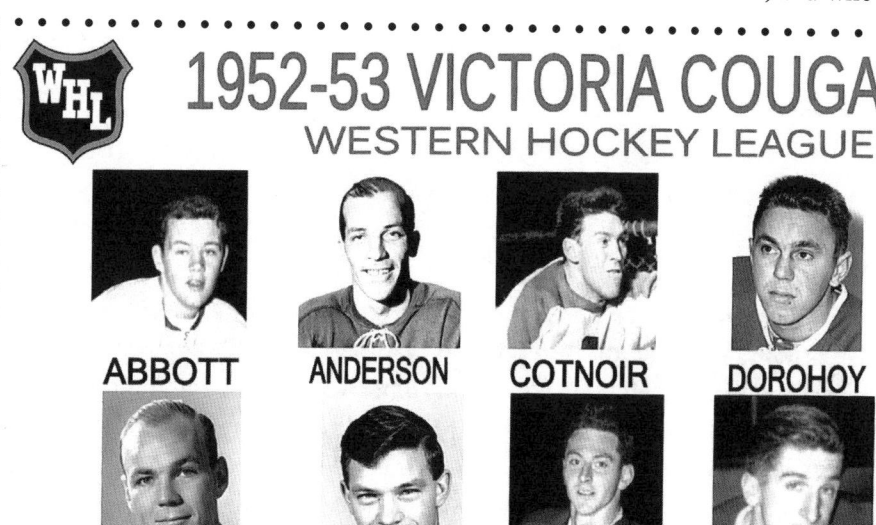

Victoria Cougars 1952-53 team photo. From the author's collection.

17 - THE NEW LOOK COUGARS

The Tacoma Rockets franchise folded, leaving seven franchises in the WHL. Coach Muzz Patrick and several of his players were signed by the Seattle Bombers.[1326] One of the most popular Cougars players, goaltender Jerry Cotnoir, was sold to Sherbrooke of the Quebec Hockey League, while goaltender Ralph Almas, recently acquired by the Montreal Canadiens was assigned to Victoria. Earlier, there had been rumours that Charlie Hodge would join the Cougars, but he was now expected to be sent elsewhere. Another change for the 1953-54 season was the naming of Billy Reay as player-coach, replacing Eddie Dorohoy, whose youth and inexperience had worked against him the previous season.[1327]

Cougars fan-club patch. From the author's collection.

Loyal Victoria fans showed their support for the home team by signing up for season tickets once again. It was expected that they would reach the prior year's total of 2,700.[1328] As the Memorial Arena was being used for the Canadian Lacrosse Championship, the Cougars training camp took place in Seattle. Fifteen players accompanied Billy Reay to the American city: goaltender Ralph Almas; defencemen Ross Lowe, Sam Levitt, Ernie Roche, Fiori Goegan, and Tony Schneider; and forwards Colin Kilburn, Sam Bettio, Gordie Cowan, Andy Hebenton, Eddie Dorohoy, Reg Abbott, Gene Achtymichuk, and Bill Sinnett. Local amateur Norm Jones was named as a backup goaltender.[1329]

The team moved to Nanaimo to play an exhibition game on September 26. They played the Seattle Bombers and edged them out, 5-4. They then prepared for a home game against the touring New York Rangers.[1330] Although the Cougars lost the game 3-1, they gave their NHL opponents a good fight. Stan Maxwell, a late addition to the team, scored the only goal for the home side before a sold-out crowd.[1331] The Cougars lost their next exhibition game against the Bombers 8-5 in Nanaimo.[1332] They won the return match in Victoria by a score of 3-2 but lost a player when key off-season acquisition Pentti Lund decided to retire due to problems with an eye that had been injured in a game in November 1951.[1333] That left the team one man short with management scrambling to find a replacement. In the last exhibition game, the Cougars defeated Seattle, 3-2.[1334]

The 1953-54 season opened on October 5, with the Cougars' first game on October 6. They travelled to Vancouver and lost a close game to the Canucks 2-1, with the home goalie, Lorne "Gump" Worsley, the star of the contest.[1335] The home season opened on the following Friday when they entertained the New Westminster Royals. Although the Cougars lost the game 4-3 before a crowd of 4,981, the team did establish one line with certainty: Kilburn, Dorohoy, and Hebenton.[1336] It would be up to Coach Reay to find two other scoring combinations. Fans wondered how long it would take for the team to become competitive.

The Calgary Stampeders came to town on Thanksgiving Day and left with a 7-3 victory over the Cougars. The team was competitive but faded in the third period.[1337] Defensive help arrived shortly after that when Montreal sent Joe Conn and Walter Clune to Victoria. Conn (who had played two seasons with Seattle) arrived the next day, but Clune was driving to the coast, so would arrive later.[1338] Ralph Almas played a solid game to help the Cougars win their first game of the season, and Bob Manson (who had just been traded from Seattle in return for Fiori Goegan) scored the winner in a 4-3 defeat of the Edmonton Flyers.[1339]

The celebration was short-lived, however, as the team managed to lose the next three games. In the next home game, Seattle outscored Victoria 7-2, with former Cougar Goegan scoring two goals for the Bombers. Forward Alex Kuzma joined the team, having been obtained on waivers from Vancouver.[1340] He played in the next game but did not help much, as the Canucks downed the Cougars, 4-1.[1341] Canadiens' chief scout, Kenny Reardon, made his annual scouting trip to Victoria and was in the stands when the Cougars dropped a 3-1 decision to the Seattle Bombers.[1342] In the two previous years, his visit had sparked an improvement in the team's play. It remained to be seen if he would work his magic this season.

He accompanied the team on their four-game road trip, which began with a 1-1 tie in New Westminster. Off the ice, Lester Patrick and Reardon met to discuss possible changes to the club in order to produce a winning product.[1343] The first surprise on the trip occurred in Calgary, where the last-place Cougars upended the second-place Stampeders 6-4. It was their second victory of the season and featured scoring from Hebenton, Maxwell, Manson, Kilburn, Clune, and Reay.[1344] The winning continued in Edmonton, where the Cougars defeated the Flyers, 3-2. Doug Anderson joined the team for that game and notched one assist. Defenceman Ernie Roche was sent to the Montreal Royals of the Quebec Hockey League.[1345] The Cougars closed out their road trip with a 3-3 tie in Saskatoon. Sam Bettio had two goals, and Achtymichuk added the other.[1346] After the game, both teams boarded the train to travel to Victoria for the return match on October 30. That game, a penalty-filled affair, ended in yet another tie. This time the score was 1-1, with Lavitt the only scorer for the home team. Defenceman Ross Lowe was hit in the eye in the first period, stitched up, and returned to play in the third period.[1347] It was later determined that he came very close to losing the eye.[1348]

The string of ties continued with a 1-1 deadlock with the Vancouver Canucks. Coach Reay noted that ties were nice, but they were not enough.[1349] He was pleased with the result of the next game when former Seattle player Manson led the Cougars to a 3-0 blanking of the Bombers, scoring two goals. Goaltender Almas was good when he needed to be and earned his first shutout of the season.[1350]

The starting time for the next game in New Westminster was delayed, as the boat from Victoria was caught in a winter storm in the Strait of Georgia. What today's fans might not know is that boat trips to Vancouver took five hours in the daytime and seven at night. Weather played a huge role in travel, and many sporting events were delayed due to storms. Unfortunately for the Cougars, their unbeaten streak came to an end when the Royals defeated them, 3-2.[1351] In Vancouver, the Cougars played one of their worst games of the season and lost the contest, 4-3. The usually reliable line of Kilburn, Anderson, and Hebenton was on the ice for three of the Canucks goals and were criticized by Coach Reay after the game. The Cougars' last victory on Vancouver ice had been October 5, 1951, and the team had wanted desperately to end that streak of futility.[1352]

The team played a more disciplined game at home and defeated New Westminster, 5-3. The line that had drawn Reay's fire two days before responded to the comments, and they were on the ice for all five goals, scoring or assisting on four of them.[1353] The offence continued in Seattle, where the Cougars easily beat the Bombers 6-3. Colin Kilburn scored three goals, becoming the first Cougar to collect a hat trick that season.[1354] In the next home game against Calgary, Hebenton scored four goals and added an assist, which combined with the two goals and an assist he'd had in the Seattle game, gave him nine points in only two games.[1355] The flurry of points brought him to within three points of the scoring lead in the WHL.[1356] However, Coach Billy Reay did not feel the team was playing well enough to gain ground in the playoff race, and he set goals for the upcoming games. In his opinion, the weekend series with New Westminster could set the tone for the rest of the season.[1357] Unfortunately, the good results came to an end with the next three games. The Cougars lost a chance to move into a higher playoff spot when they lost 5-3 to the Royals, despite outshooting them, 35-23.[1358] In the next two games, at New Westminster and Seattle, the Cougars were shut out, 2-0 and 3-0, respectively.[1359] That was definitely not the result that Coach Reay had wanted, and the team had to dig deep and try to turn things around.

In the final game of the road trip, the Cougars almost beat Vancouver but had to settle for a 2-2 tie when the Canucks scored with seventy seconds left in the match. On the positive side, the team finally scored a goal after having been blanked for 167:44.[1360] When the Bombers came to town, the Cougars were battling to make it into fourth place in the standings. The team responded with a superb effort, outscoring Seattle, 7-1. Dorohoy had one goal and added four assists, Bettio had two goals and one assist, and Kuzma had one goal and three assists. The Cougars were now in fourth place in the league, two points ahead of Seattle.[1361] They consolidated that position in the next contest, a home game against Edmonton. Their offence continued to play well, firing six goals past Glenn Hall, in a 6-4 victory. Bettio and Lowe scored two goals each with Clune and Kuzma adding singles.[1362] The brief winning streak ended before 4,923 local fans when the Quakers shut out the Cougars, 3-0. Coach Reay said that the team lost because they were outskated and outworked.[1363] In the next two home games, the Cougars regained their scoring touch and defeated the Vancouver Canucks 3-1 in a game that resembled a prize fight more than a hockey match.[1364] Victoria followed that win with a 3-2 edging of the Seattle Bombers. Bettio, Clune, and Hebenton were the marksmen, while Almas sparkled in the nets.[1365]

However, all good things must come to an end, and the good play did. Over the next eight games, the Cougars won only one game. During that stretch, they lost road games, 7-3 to the Royals[1366] and 3-1 to the Canucks.[1367] In Victoria, the coach shuffled his lines in an attempt to regain the scoring touch. That technique did not work, as they lost 4-2 to New Westminster to drop to the league basement. Reay called Montreal personally to get some help. With defenceman Tony Schneider still injured and Lowe not fully recovered from his injury, he pleaded with the Canadiens to send at least one defenceman to shore up the injury-riddled crew.[1368] Following a 2-0 shut out in Seattle, the coach again called Frank Selke in Montreal, stressing the need for immediate help.[1369] The response from Montreal? "Sorry, we can't help you just now." There would be no Christmas help from the East.

17 - THE NEW LOOK COUGARS

Cougars program 1953-54. From the author's collection.

Left to seek talent from within the league, the Cougars acquired Doug Macauley from Seattle.[1370] On Christmas Day, the Bombers provided the opposition and narrowly defeated the home team, 3-2. The Cougars again outshot Seattle, but just could not find the back of the net when a goal would have made all the difference in the game.[1371] Just when everything looked bleak for the Cougars, they found their scoring touch and defeated the Bombers in a game played in the small arena in Nanaimo on Boxing Day. Bettio and Dorohoy scored in the first period, and Victoria added four more goals in the second frame while surrendering only one. Lax play in the third period let Seattle score three goals to Victoria's one, to make the final score 7-4. Dorohoy led all scorers with one goal and three assists.[1372] However, the team could not build on that victory and fell 3-1 to the league-leading Canucks. Neither offence nor defence played well. After the game, the team released Bob Manson.[1373]

The Cougars turned over a new leaf as 1954 dawned and handily beat the Royals 6-2, in front of an appreciative New Year's Day crowd of 4,500 fans. Bettio, Lowe, and Dorohoy each recorded three points, and the entire team played well.[1374] Next on the agenda was a four-game road trip, with the team playing those games in just five nights. First was a contest in Vancouver where a minor miracle occurred. The Cougars finally beat the Canucks in their arena for the first time in twenty-seven months. Lavitt scored in the first period, Achtymichuk in the second, and Lowe in the third, to lead the team to a 3-2 victory. Ralph Almas played his best game of the season to strengthen his hold on the third-best goals-against-average in the league.[1375] The trip continued on a positive note with a 3-3 tie in Calgary. Dorohoy, Kuzma, and Lowe scored for the Cougars, as they started 1954 with an unbeaten record.[1376] That streak came to an end when Edmonton nipped the Cougars 3-2. It was the first time since January 17, 1953, that the Cougars had lost a game on the Prairies.[1377] In Saskatoon, the Quakers continued their mastery of Victoria by handing them a 4-2 defeat.[1378]

On their return home, the Cougars played a disciplined game and upended the Vancouver Canucks 3-2. Dorohoy was the scoring hero with two goals that moved him closer to the league scoring lead, while Almas starred in net.[1379] In the next game, the Cougars took an early lead on Seattle, but could not hold it, and settled for a 5-5 tie.[1380] The unbeaten streak continued in New Westminster, where the Cougars' scorers found the net seven times in a 7-3 victory. Dorohoy notched another hat trick to lead the team. The next night, it was Kilburn's turn to score a hat trick, as the Cougars went into Seattle and tied the Bombers, 4-4.[1381] After having not won a game in Vancouver for months before January 5, the Cougars finally won another one with a score of 4-1. Eddie Dorohoy was again the team leader and moved into a tie for the league scoring lead.[1382] That

129

unbeaten streak came to crashing end when New Westminster routed the Cougars, 6-3. Media reports of the game were more interested in an honoured guest behind the home bench. Swimmer Florence Chadwick was well known throughout the world for her swimming prowess but had been unsuccessful in her bid to swim the Strait of Juan de Fuca.[1383]

The league-leading Calgary Stampeders came to town and were summarily shut out by the Cougars, 2-0. Dorohoy scored once and assisted on the other goal to take the lead in the scoring race.[1384] In the final game of the homestand, the Cougars were narrowly defeated by the Flyers, 4-2. The team was particularly upset by the officials missing an offside pass on a play that led to the 3-2 goal for Edmonton. That call was the turning point for the game, and it left the Cougars "hopping mad."[1385]

It was then time for another Prairie road trip. In a game in Saskatoon, in which the Cougars had not played well, they managed to hold the Quakers to a 1-1 tie. This game, too, had a controversial play, but this time the decision was made to disallow a Quakers goal.[1386] The following night, there were more fights in the game than goals, as Edmonton downed the Cougars, 8-2. Ironically, the game was penalty-free until late in the second period, when Lowe engaged with Marcel Bonin, with both receiving major penalties. Next, it was Kilburn with Bonin, and while Kilburn was leaving the ice, he fought with some of the fans. There were other encounters with officials and fans, and the game seemed almost inconsequential.[1387] The trip concluded with a game in Calgary, where the Cougars took an early 1-0 lead but could not hold it and surrendered the tying goal late in the third period.[1388]

Back home again, the Cougars hosted the Quakers. This time, they were victorious in a very close match, outscoring Saskatoon, 4-3. The game was not without incident as numerous high sticks went undetected by the officiating crew.[1389] Vancouver came to town, and the league-leaders handed the home team a 4-2 loss. It was likely the worst game that the Cougars had played in a while, and reports say they were "in a fog like the weather outside."[1390]

February 12, 1954, was a special day in Victoria Cougar history. It was Eddie Dorohoy Night, as the team honoured their best scorer for his five years' service. He was presented with a new car by the Booster Club, among other gifts. In true Dorohoy fashion, he was the catalyst in the team's 2-1 victory over Seattle.[1391] That game seemed to provide the spark for the team, and they went on to win seven of their next eight games.

In an unexpected move, Montreal assigned goaltender Almas to Buffalo, their AHL farm team, and sent Claude Evans to Victoria in his place. Coach Reay also juggled his lines, moving Kilburn to play with Achtymichuk and Sinnett, while he had Anderson playing with Reay and Hebenton.[1392] According to media accounts, fans were prepared to dislike their new goaltender. He was very short, standing just 5' 6" tall, and noted as "smaller than [Vancouver's] Lorne Worsley." However, Claude played very well in his Victoria debut, leading the Cougars to a 3-1 decision over the Bombers, and became the toast of the town overnight.[1393] The Cougars played their next game in Seattle and defeated the Bombers 3-1, to move within one point of fifth place in the standings. The game was marred by fights in the stands behind the Cougars' bench, and police had to restore order.[1394] Calgary was the next team to play in Victoria, and the Cougars continued their winning ways with a 4-3 victory. Ross Lowe was unable to play due to a stomach ailment for which rest was the only cure, so Lavitt, Clune, and Schneider carried the defensive load; Lavitt played a total of forty-five minutes in the contest.[1395]

Playoff hopes took a step backward when the Vancouver team delighted its home fans with a decisive 7-3 win over the visiting Cougars. The game was another rough contest, with Sam Bettio as the primary combatant for Victoria, chalking up two majors and an automatic ten-minute misconduct for his efforts.[1396] Returning home, the Cougars played lacklustre hockey for the first two periods of their game with Seattle, but came alive in the final frame, scoring four goals (three of them in a span of forty-five seconds) to win the game, 4-2. Evans again played a stellar game in net.[1397]

On-ice success continued when Edmonton played in Victoria. With a playoff spot assured, the team was trying to finish fifth for a better chance in post-season play. The third period once again was the difference, as the Cougars overcame a 1-0 deficit, scoring three goals in 3:33, and added a fourth for the victory, with a score of 4-3.[1398] Victoria beat New Westminster 8-1 in one of the more lopsided games of the season. Kilburn opened the scoring at 1:29 of the first period, and the only mistake was allowing the Royals to score a single goal. The Cougars outshot the Royals 50-16 and were full value for the victory.[1399] Seattle gained a bit of revenge for their earlier defeat when they edged Victoria at the Memorial Arena 4-2. The Cougars scored first and last but could not produce in the second period.[1400] In the next game, in New Westminster, the Royals came out on top of a 5-4 score. Again, it was scoring goals in rapid succession in the third period that made the game interesting. Dorohoy picked up three points to move within two points of league-leader Guyle Fielder.[1401] Defenceman Sam Lavitt was injured, breaking his heel, and was lost to the team for some time. That put additional pressure on Lowe, Schneider, and Clune, as rosters were now set and could only be changed if the total number of players dropped below thirteen men.[1402]

Just when the team could use the loss of a key player as an excuse for sloppy play, they dug deep and played a gritty game against Saskatoon, defeating the Quakers, 4-3. Kilburn scored the opening goal thirteen seconds in, before many of the patrons were even in their seats. Bettio and Abbott added goals to give the Cougars a 3-0 lead, but they then had to withstand a furious Quaker attack.[1403]

In their last home game of the season, the Cougars fell 3-1 to the Vancouver Canucks. However, it was the loss of defenceman Schneider that was of grave concern. He suffered a sprained ankle and would be assessed on a game-to-game basis. That left the Cougars with only two defencemen, and Lowe was playing with a corset to protect his back. The only healthy player, Clune, was said to be "very tired."[1404]

The Cougars then embarked on the last Prairie trip of the season. When they lost December 4 to Calgary, they lost the chance to finish fourth in the league. Kilburn and Reay tried to play defence to help the two legitimate defenders.[1405] It apparently did not work. The Cougars played Edmonton to a 3-3 tie to gain at least one point on the trip. Kuzma scored two goals, with Macauley scoring the third. It was now established that the Cougars would play the Calgary Stampeders in the first round of the playoffs.[1406] The final game of the season was a 5-3 loss to the Quakers in Saskatoon.[1407]

The playoffs started in Calgary, and the Cougars won the first game, much to everyone's surprise. Playing before 5,800 fans, Sinnett, Achtymichuk, Bettio, and Hebenton scored for the home team in a 4-2 victory.[1408] Coach Reay was concerned about the condition of Colin Kilburn, who had injured his right ankle in the first game. It was still badly swollen, although x-rays had revealed no damage to the bones. His ability to play in the second game was unknown.[1409] Unfortunately, the Cougars could not carry forward the momentum from game one and fell 8-1 in game two. Kilburn did play but was not effective due to his injury. Lowe had to leave the game, as he was hit in the wrist (to add to his other injuries), and forward Kuzma was shaken up by a check from Bill Shvetz in the first period.[1410] Victoria was severely short-handed, and this definitely led to their defeat. However, the series was now tied, 1-1, and play would resume in Victoria.

The team's health was assessed when the Cougars returned to Victoria, and the news was better than expected. All the injured players would be able to play in some fashion, although not at one-hundred-percent ability. The only Cougar not able to dress was Sam Lavitt, whose broken heel was nowhere near healed.[1411] Game three was a hard-hitting affair with violence extending into the stands. The Cougars could not find the net in the first period, and their defence was suspect, as the Stampeders won easily 6-1 to take a 2-1 series lead. The injury parade continued, as Reg Abbott was tripped, falling into the goalpost and injuring his thigh. He was taken to hospital where he was diagnosed with a torn muscle.[1412] In game four, the Cougars worked hard, outshooting their opponents, but they had no finish around the net and lost the game 5-2.[1413]

The fifth game of the series was played in the Calgary Corral. The Cougars had only three defencemen, so were severely taxed. Ross Lowe played forty minutes, despite his many injuries, but the team had run out of energy as their multiple injuries had taken their toll. The final score was 7-4, and the Cougars were eliminated from further playoff action.[1414]

Fans wondered if the team could have done better if they had been healthy. Injuries certainly played a part in the disappointing playoff exit, but, quite frankly, their play had been inconsistent all year. They got off to a slow start, and never really regained full momentum. There would be no miracle finish to the 1953-54 season.

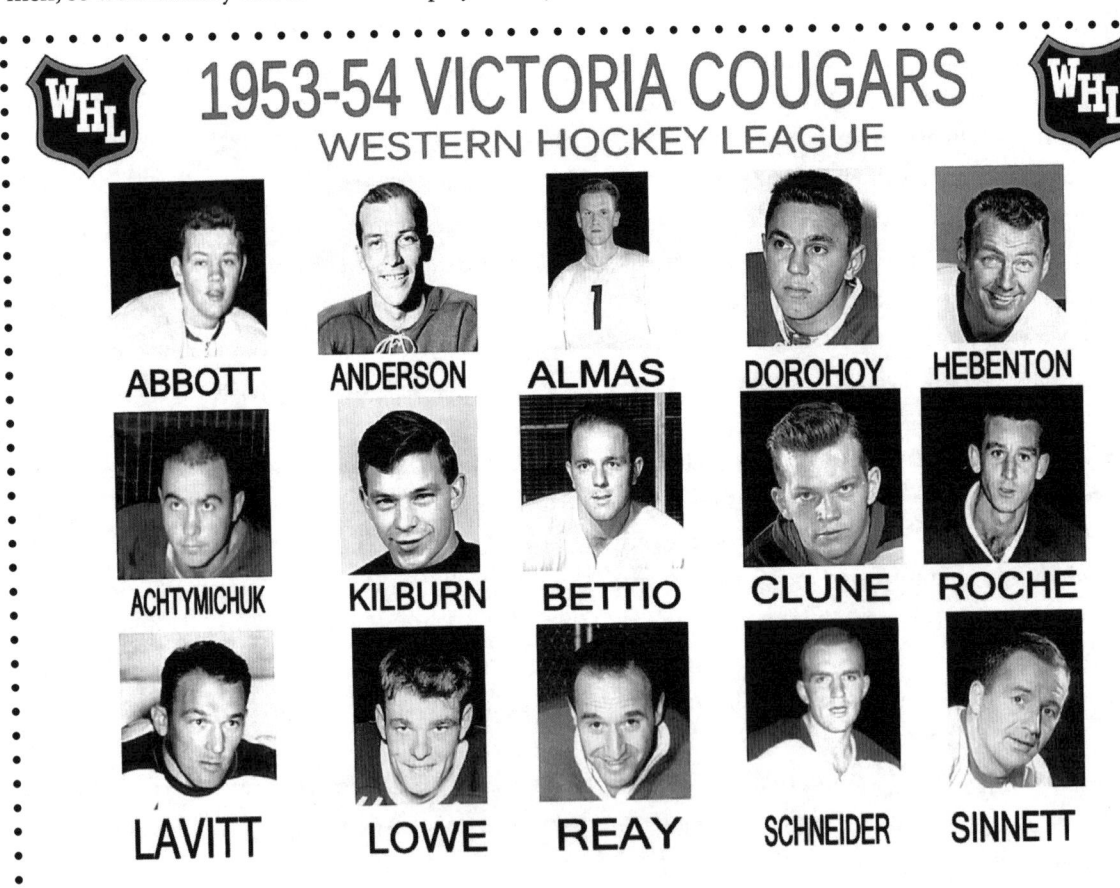

Victoria Cougars 1953-54 team photo. From the author's collection.

18 - QUEST FOR ANOTHER CHAMPIONSHIP

Sale of season tickets for the 1954-55 schedule opened on September 7, 1954, at the Central Ticket Bureau at 817 Fort Street. Prices ranged from $35 for the $1 seats, to $43.75 for the $1.25 seats, $52.50 for the $1.50 seats, and $70 for the $2.00 seats. Prior season-ticket holders could renew until September 18, with all unsold seats becoming available on September 20.[1415] Training camp opened in Kamloops, BC, on September 21, with fourteen players on hand: goaltender Marcel Pelletier; defencemen Bill Davidson, Wally Clune, and Mike Keating; and forwards Colin Kilburn, Wayne Brown, Dave Wall, Andy Hebenton, Alex Kuzma, Mark Marquess, Doug Anderson, Billy Reay, Gene Achtymichuk, and Doug Macauley. Defender Joe Conn was missing, as he was still farming near Calgary while Pete Durham declined to report to the Cougars. Moe Young refused to accept an invitation to the camp. Newcomer Mike Keating arrived in camp weighing twenty-five pounds more than his regular playing weight of 160.[1416] He had lots of work to do to get in shape.

The team played a pair of exhibition games in Kelowna, then came home for an exhibition game against the NHL's New York Rangers. Former Cougars Eddie Dorohoy and Ivan Irwin suited up for the Rangers. Bill Bucyk joined the Cougars, on loan from the Detroit Red Wings,[1417] and played in the exhibition game. To the disappointment of the Victoria crowd, the NHL club came out ahead of the local favourites by a score of 5-1.[1418] When the Rangers left town, Dorohoy was not with them, as his contract status was up in the air.[1419]

The Cougars opened the season in Vancouver against the Canucks. The short-handed team did not play well and lost 5-3. Kilburn and Hebenton were the best players for Victoria.[1420] Now it was time for the home opener against the league-champion Calgary Stampeders. Before 3,200 fans, the smallest opening-night crowd in their history, the Cougars defeated the Calgary team, 3-2. Goaltender Pelletier was the star of the game, keeping the onrushing Stampeders at bay. The team also filed an official protest over the first game of the season, contending that the Canucks had used an ineligible player, Billy Dea. Their position was backed by Central Registry,[1421] but the final decision would be made by league president Al Leader.[1422] In other off-ice news, Eddie Dorohoy had been offered a contract to return to the Cougars and was in negotiations with club management.[1423] Al Leader released his decision on the Billy Dea matter, saying,

> *"Although Dea was on the protected list of the National Hockey League club [New York Rangers], neither the Vancouver Hockey Club nor the WHL was aware of this. Therefore, the Canucks did not*

'knowingly' use an ineligible player. The fault lies with the Rangers in loaning Dea before he had been waived from the NHL, and the central registry for not notifying the WHL." [1424]

In the game played in Victoria, New Westminster beat the Cougars 4-3, in a match that featured the return of fan-favourite Eddie Dorohoy. Victoria got off to a 2-0 lead on two goals by Kilburn but surrendered three in the second period and never recovered. Injuries reared their ugly head again. X-rays revealed that Bill Bucyk had cracked his kneecap and would be out of action for at least five weeks. Wayne Brown broke his leg in the game and would be lost to the club for some time.[1425] This bad news could not have come at a worse time to the already depleted lineup.

Peter Durham, who had been traded for Sam Bettio in the off-season, decided to join the club after all and arrived in Victoria, ready to play. Management was still trying to find additional players to replace the injured ones.[1426] He suited up for the game against Edmonton but did not figure in the scoring. The depleted defence had a tough time with the Flyers, and Victoria lost the game, 6-4.[1427] Twenty-four-year-old Don Ashbee, a star lacrosse player as well as a hockey player, was acquired by the Cougars on loan from the Cleveland Barons and was driving across Canada with his family.[1428] As far as the Cougars were concerned, he could not arrive fast enough. The lack of a solid defence was evident as New Westminster shelled Victoria 7-2, in the mainland city. The Cougars scored the first goal, but never got the lead back. Club management had hoped to make a deal with the Royals' management to acquire a defenceman, but that was not to be, and they would have to look elsewhere.[1429]

Returning home, the Cougars beat their arch-rivals from Vancouver 3-1, in a game that featured hard, heavy hitting paired with a scintillating offence. Hebenton, Macauley, and Durham scored for the Cougars, with Kilburn adding two assists. The victory ended the losing streak at three games.[1430] Little did the club know that that would be longest losing streak they would have all season.[1431] However, there was no winning streak either, as the Cougars lost their game in Vancouver, 3-1. They also lost a player they had been negotiating with; Steve Black decided not to come out of retirement to join the club, so they would be looking to somebody else for help.[1432] The next game was in Victoria and was the third in a row between the rivals. This time, the Cougars found the secret to beating Canuck goaltender Johnny Bower and scored a 5-2 win. Macauley opened the scoring at 1:47 of the first period, Hebenton followed at 3:22, and Macauley found the net again at 6:12, to give Victoria a lead they would not surrender.[1433] So far in the young season, Victoria had played the Canucks four times, and each team had won two games.

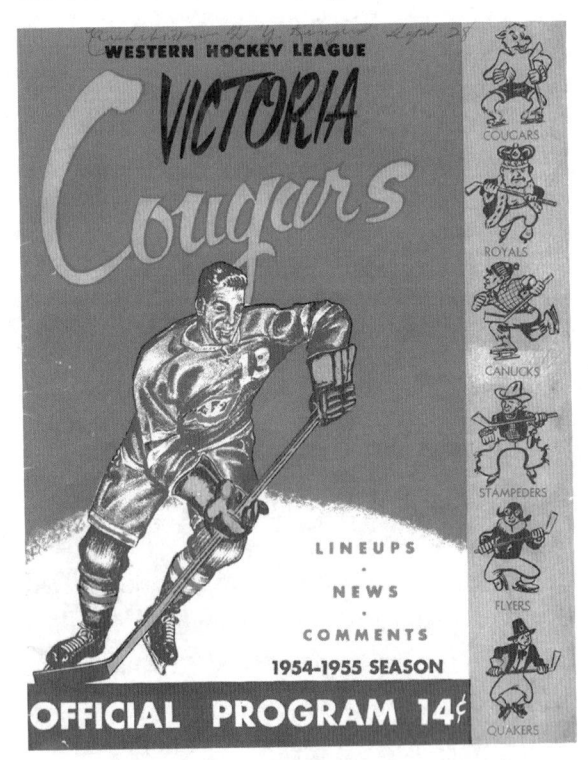

Cougars program 1954-55. From the author's collection.

Don Ashbee finally arrived in Victoria, having encountered Hurricane Hazel, which had devastated his hometown. He had delayed his departure while he worked on rescue operations and finally got on the road, using secondary roads because the main highways were still under water. No matter what he found on the ice, it could never compare to the gruesome sights he had seen during the rescue work.[1434]

The next game was a decisive 8-2 victory for the Cougars over the Quakers. Dorohoy, Hebenton, and Kuzma all scored five points to lead the team to a lopsided win. The game deteriorated in the third period when the result was not in question, with numerous penalties and even a Saskatoon player trying to fight local fans while he was in the penalty box.[1435] Unfortunately, the momentum from the huge victory did not carry forward to the next two games, a home-and-home series against New Westminster. They lost the first one, in Victoria 5-3. After the game, Coach Reay said,

> "You would have thought that two or three players wearing red sweaters [the Cougars wore red] were playing for the other team. Some of them don't know what it is to check. Anybody can skate when they're going one way. Why the Royals didn't get four more goals, I'll never know."[1436]

In the return match in New Westminster, the Cougars fell again, 5-3, before a crowd of only 1,000 fans. This was the fourth loss to the Royals this season and was having an effect on the standings.[1437] As luck would have it, the visitor for the next home game was again New Westminster. Finally, the Cougars got their act together and defeated the Royals, 6-1. The defence played very well, limiting their opponent to just nine shots on goal and gave up only one goal. Hebenton scored twice, while Marquess, Durham, Keating, and Kuzma added singles.[1438] The next game, again in New Westminster, would be the last game for one of the players, as teams had to reduce their rosters to fifteen by Sunday, November 7.[1439] Victoria won the game 4-0, with Pelletier earning his first shutout of the season. Hebenton again led the scoring with two goals. After the game, Don Ashbee (who was called a "disappointment" by general manager Hutchinson) was returned to the Cleveland Barons of the American Hockey League.[1440]

The next two games were more about violence than hockey. Victoria entertained Edmonton and gave up four goals before they got untracked. Hockey got sidetracked amid high sticking and fighting, and the Cougars lost the game, 5-2. Virtually the same scenario took place at Vancouver the next evening. In the first period, the teams played fundamental hockey, although there was no scoring. The second frame was only three minutes old when the trouble began. Numerous fights broke out, and the game deteriorated even further when the Canucks built up a 3-0 lead. Vancouver fans threw bags of peanuts at the Cougars' players, and when Kilburn went into the crowd, he was heavily penalized. Media reports blamed referee Paul Bozak, who had also officiated at the Edmonton game, for the lack of control in the game.[1441]

The next three games were played in Memorial Arena. First, the Cougars edged the Flyers 4-2. Dorohoy again led the scoring parade with two goals, while Hebenton added two assists.[1442] The next game resulted in an impressive 6-0 shutout of the Calgary Stampeders. Anderson had the best night of his career, counting four goals and two assists to lead the team. Kilburn added one goal and four assists and Macauley notched three assists, for a total of fourteen points from the one line.[1443] Before the next match, Dave Wall was released from the club to make room for the injured Bill Bucyk to return.[1444] Once again, the Cougars played well in a second consecutive shutout, this time 5-0 over the Canucks.[1445] Having completed a successful homestand, the team went on the Prairie swing, where they would play four games in five nights. The trip started on a positive note with a 4-2 decision over the Stampeders. Unfortunately, Pelletier did not record a shutout that would have given him a league mark, but the team played good hockey and secured their fourth consecutive win.[1446] The next night, the Cougars did not play as well and fell 5-1 to league-leading Edmonton. Goaltender Glenn

Hall was outstanding for the Flyers, while Bronco Horvath provided the offence with three goals and an assist.[1447]

In the morning of November 25, Ed Dorohoy's wife, Shirley, gave birth to their first child. In the evening, the new dad led his Cougars to a rare victory over the Quakers in Saskatoon—their first win there since the 1952-53 playoffs—scoring two goals and adding two assists on the way to a 5-2 final score.[1448] The Quakers got their revenge two days later, when they thumped the Cougars, 7-0, giving them only their second loss in the last seven games.[1449] The Prairie swing over, the Cougars played a game in Vancouver before coming home. Young defenceman Bucyk was moved to the forward line after an injury to right-winger Marquess and scored two goals in just more than four minutes, to lead the scoring parade.[1450]

Next on the schedule were three games against New Westminster. The first, in Victoria, was a 9-2 Cougar victory over the Royals. Dorohoy scored three goals and two assists, Macauley got his first hat trick, Hebenton added four points, and Marquess counted three. It was the most one-sided game the Cougars had won that season.[1451] Two days later, the Royals gained revenge with a close 3-2 victory over the home team.[1452] The scene then shifted to New Westminster, where the Cougars won, 3-2. Defenceman Clune scored two goals to lead the attack. The victory moved the Cougars to within three points of the league lead.[1453] The club returned home and hosted the Canucks. They made goaltender Johnny Bower look ordinary in a 4-1 contest. Bill Davidson, known best for his defensive talent, scored his first goal of the season. Dorohoy acquired two points, which put him in first place in the scoring race for the first time all season.[1454]

The road trip continued in Saskatoon, where the Cougars shut out the Quakers, 3-0. Alex Kuzma notched two goals for the Cougars, and Walter Clune added a single.[1455] Returning home, the Cougars drubbed the Canucks 6-1 before setting off on the road again. The team sported a record of ten wins and one tie in their last fourteen games and had moved to third place in the league standings, just two points away from the league lead.[1456]

The road trip started with a return encounter with the Canucks in Vancouver. The Cougars scored a 4-2 victory to move into second place in the league, only one point behind the leading Edmonton Flyers.[1457] The Prairie portion of the road trip was not a success for the team. Calgary ended the Cougars' winning streak by defeating the Cougars, 6-2.[1458] In the next game, Edmonton's Bronco Horvath scored four goals, while the Cougars only got one, and Edmonton won the game, 4-1.[1459] The team managed a 5-5 tie with the Saskatoon Quakers before falling again 5-2 to Calgary, in a Christmas Day matinee, to end the trip on a sour note. They had dropped to fourth place in the standings.[1460]

Home cooking did the trick, as the Cougars won their first game back from the road trip with a 4-0 shutout of the Calgary Stampeders. It was the fifth blanking of the year by Marcel Pelletier. Gene Achtymichuk scored two goals to lead his team to victory.[1461] However, the year did not end well for Victoria when they fell 3-2 to New Westminster. The team seemed sluggish in the first two periods, and when they got their plays working, did not have enough time to complete the comeback.[1462] The new year was not much better, as the Stampeders came to town and defeated the Cougars, 4-1. Ironically, the home team scored the first goal, but could not add to their total.[1463]

Next up was a home-and-home series against the Canucks. The home teams prevailed in each game; Vancouver winning 4-2 in the first game and Victoria 7-2 in the return engagement. Hebenton scored once in the first game and three times in the second, to lead the club in scoring with twenty-eight goals.[1464][1465] A short road trip produced a 2-0 loss to Vancouver and a 6-0 victory over New Westminster. Against the Canucks, the Cougars could not get a puck past Johnny Bower, but it was Vancouver who came away the biggest losers as their star, Bill Ezinicki, was injured in a fight.[1466] However, the team scored early and often for a well-deserved victory. Hebenton again scored—his twenty-ninth of the season.[1467] Doug Bentley's last-place Saskatoon Quakers came to town and outscored the Cougars, 5-2.[1468] The losing continued in New Westminster, where the Royals edged the Cougars, 6-4. The team had only won three games out of their last twelve, to fall further out of title contention.[1469] In a home game against the Royals, the Cougars managed a 5-5 tie, although they took the lead three times and could not hold it.[1470]

This result set a somewhat positive note as the Cougars left on a four-game Prairie trip. The first game in Edmonton also produced a tie, this time 2-2, with Hebenton and Macauley finding the net.[1471] In Saskatoon, the Cougars were shut out 5-0 by the Quakers, who built up a four-goal first-period lead, then held on for the victory.[1472] The Cougars managed a 6-2 win in Calgary for their first victory in almost two weeks. Kilburn, Hebenton, Anderson, Kuzma, Macauley, and Marquess found the net for Victoria, while Gerry Couture and Fred Hucul were the Calgary scorers.[1473] However, the team could not get a second win, and they fell 3-0 to Edmonton.[1474] As the playoff race continued, the Cougars would be playing six of their next eight games at home, where they had terrific fan support.

The homestand began on a positive note with the Cougars demolishing the New Westminster Royals, 8-1. They outshot their opponents 42-22, including a twenty-one-shot second period. Hebenton scored two goals to bring his season total to thirty-four, tying him with Bronco Horvath for the league lead.[1475] Once again, the Cougars could not continue the momentum, and they lost, 6-2, to New Westminster.[1476] The next three games were played at home, and the Cougars took advantage of crowd support to win two of them. In the first contest, they dominated the Stampeders, 6-2. The bad news after the game was that Doug Anderson had cracked a bone in his ankle and would be lost to the team for six to eight weeks.[1477] However, the rest of the team picked up the slack and won their second consecutive game, 5-3 over Vancouver. Hebenton led the way, as he usually did, with two goals. Victoria now had a seven-point lead over Vancouver in the race for a playoff position.[1478] The Cougars held the visiting Flyers to a rare scoreless tie,[1479] giving Marcel Pelletier his sixth shutout of the season, only one short of the league record.[1480] The Cougars travelled to New Westminster and handed the Royals a 4-1 defeat.[1481] Returning home, Victoria fell 4-1 to Vancouver, giving the Canucks a faint hope of making the playoff round. Rumours flew about a possible working agreement with the Boston Bruins when Lynn Patrick visited Victoria. General manager Hutchinson would not elaborate on the future plans but would not deny the idea, either.[1482]

In preparation for the playoffs, the Cougars acquired centre Barton Bradley from New Westminster and received permission from the league to include "injured players Doug Anderson and Wayne Brown on their list of eligible players." That meant that, if the players recovered, they would be allowed to play playoff games.[1483]

The Cougars entered the last fifteen games of their season sitting in fourth place in the standings, but able to move up one or two positions. It was evident that Edmonton would win the league title, as they had a substantial lead over the second-place team. The Cougars left the best for last, accumulating seventeen points out of a possible thirty.[1484] In their last home game before the final trip of the year, the Canucks upended New Westminster, 3-2. Hebenton, Dorohoy, and Bucyk scored for the Cougars.[1485]

Calgary stopped the Cougar march to the playoffs when they edged them, 2-1.[1486] In league news, president Al Leader announced that Winnipeg had been granted a franchise for the next season, joining Regina, which had previously been approved. There were also rumours of Seattle and Spokane being added, possibly expanding the league to ten teams. The 1955-56 season could see an exciting new league format.[1487]

The Cougars got back on the winning track with their first win in Edmonton that season, with a 3-1 victory. Bill Bucyk, Gene Achtymichuk, and Doug Macauley scored for Victoria, who moved to within one point of second-place Calgary.[1488] The unbeaten streak continued with a 2-2 tie in Saskatoon. The Cougars had built up a 2-0 lead, but tired in the third period, playing their fourth game in four nights, and surrendered two goals, the last just over a minute from the final whistle.[1489]

Having had a solid rest, the Cougars played at home and overpowered the Royals, 10-4. They scored three goals in the first ten minutes of the first period, and the rout was on. Hebenton had a huge night, with two goals and two assists. Dorohoy and Kilburn had two goals and three assists, while Barton Bradley, Alex Kuzma, and Doug Macauley added a goal and an assist each. It was the most goals scored by the Cougars in the season, and the victory moved them into second place in the standings.[1490] In the next game, on the mainland, they held the Royals to a 1-1 tie, with Eddie Dorohoy the only Cougar marksman.[1491] The unbeaten streak continued with a 4-2 over the first-place Flyers,[1492] a 1-1 tie with the Canucks in Vancouver,[1493] and a home victory of 4-3 over the Canucks.[1494]

As the season moved into its last ten days, several team records could be broken. Andy Hebenton was within one goal of Ed Mazur's single-season mark of forty-three goals. Dorohoy only needed nine points in the last six games to record his best season of scoring. Marcel Pelletier was one shutout away from a league record and close to a record-setting goals-against average. And Pete Durham needed only one goal to set a new Cougar record for goals by a defenceman, and was two goals short of a league record.[1495]

March 9, 1955, was a special night for Victoria hockey. The Cougars Booster Club held Andy Hebenton Night, to thank the talented player for his five years of service. He and his family were showered with gifts in honour of the occasion. Felicitations also came by telegram from ex-Cougars Roger Leger, Bob Frampton, Sam Lavitt, Reg Abbott, Tony Schneider, WHL President Al Leader, and others.[1496] In the game against Saskatoon, the Cougars prevailed, 6-2, with Hebenton scoring a goal on "his night."[1497] Three nights later, the Cougars again played Saskatoon, and the result was a one-sided 7-1 win. That victory clinched a playoff spot for the team, with their seeding and opponent yet to be determined. Pete Durham tied the record for goals by a defenceman at eighteen and Pelletier became the first goaltender to record an assist when he passed the puck to Gene Achtymichuk, who put it in the net.[1498]

The long unbeaten streak ended abruptly when the Canucks shut out the Cougars 3-0 on the mainland. Johnny Bower recorded his sixth shutout of the season, tying Pelletier for the league lead.[1499] In their last home game of the regular season, Victoria again lost to the Canucks, this time by a narrow 3-2 margin. The Cougars had taken a two-goal lead but were unable to beat Bower after the first period and could not hold Vancouver off the scoresheet.[1500] The Canucks won their third game in a week over the Cougars when they shut them out 1-0 on the mainland.[1501] That loss ensured that Pelletier would not have the lowest goals-against-average in the league, losing that honour to Bower. In the last game of the regular season, Victoria outlasted New Westminster in a 9-7 game. Hebenton scored one goal and added five assists to lead the club in scoring, while defenceman Durham notched his nineteenth goal of the season, setting a new league record for goals by a defender. Ten goals were scored in the third period: six by Victoria and four by New Westminster.[1502]

The Cougars met the Stampeders in the playoffs for the second consecutive year. In regular season play, Victoria had won six out of ten games with Calgary and was therefore deemed to have a slight advantage going into the series.[1503] However, the expected advantage in goal did not materialize, when Pelletier was injured in a freak home accident and could not play for much of the first game. Series goaltender replacement Bev Bentley of Saskatoon had to enter the game at 7:43 of the period when Pelletier had to retire. Victoria scored the first goal, but then surrendered two by the end of the first period. The teams exchanged goals in the second frame, but the final period was all Calgary, as they fired four pucks past Bentley to win the game easily, 7-2.[1504] Pelletier played in the second game, but the Stampeders still prevailed, 5-2. The Cougars could not get untracked until the third period, by which time it was too late. Local media tried to put a positive spin on the situation, with a reminder that the 1951 league champions also lost their first two games, but that was a different era.[1505]

The series then moved to Calgary. Here, the Cougars played well, coming back from a one-goal deficit twice to end regulation time tied, 2-2. At 5:43 of overtime, local hero Andy Hebenton scored the winning goal to give the team a 3-2 victory.[1506] Local fans thought perhaps the team had regained their legs and would be able to win the series. However, the optimism soon faded as Calgary whitewashed Victoria 5-0 in the next game to take a 3-1 lead in the series. Injuries were taking their toll on the team, with many players also suffering from illness.[1507] Jack Evans was brought in to replace Durham, who was too ill to play, but even that did not help as the Cougars lost the game 2-1 to give Calgary the series win.[1508] It was the second year that the playoffs had ended abruptly—and to the same opponent. It was a bitter pill to swallow, but players resolved to do better in the future. In league honours, Hebenton and Durham were named to the all-star team, recognizing their outstanding play during the season.[1509]

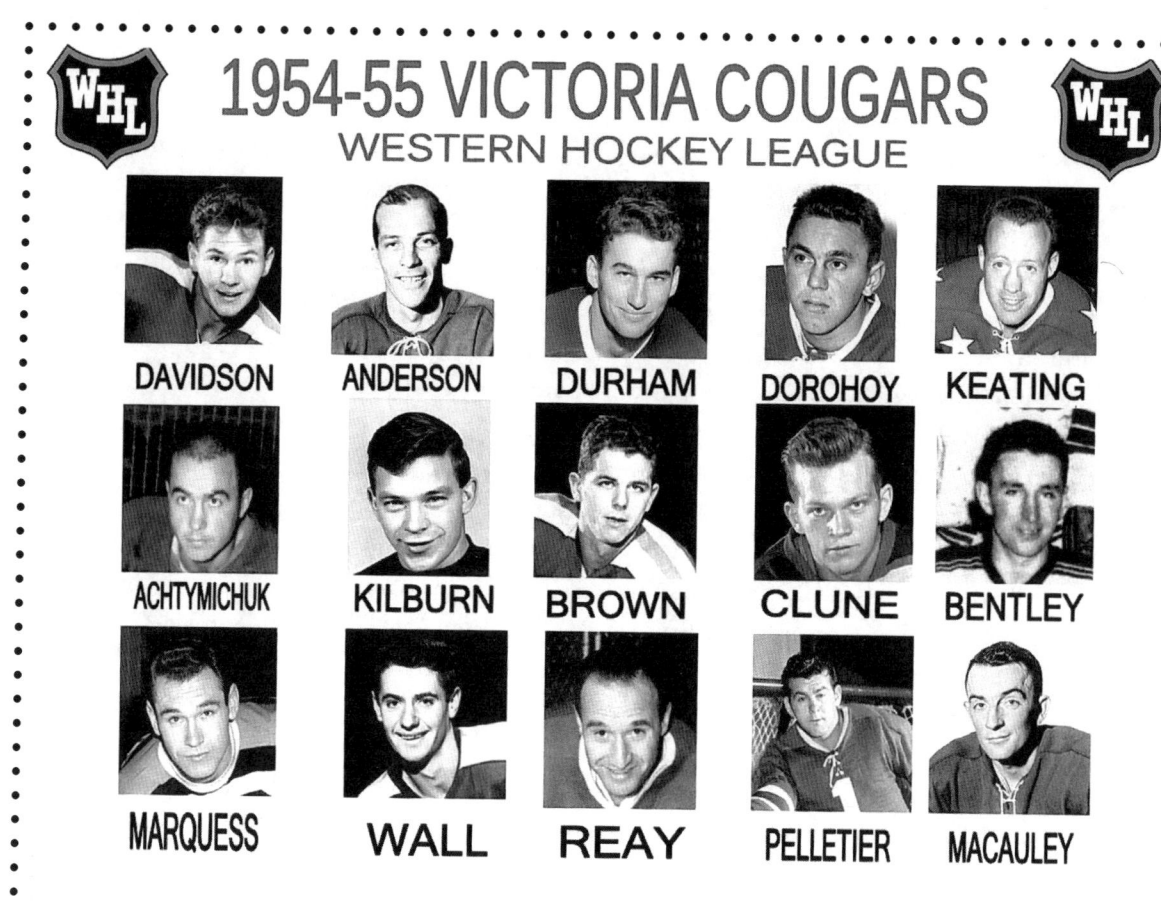

Victoria Cougars 1954-55 team photo. From the author's collection.

19 - ONE ERA ENDS—A NEW ONE STARTS

On September 2, 1955, Lester Patrick relinquished ownership of the Victoria Cougars to his sons, Murray and Lynn, and twelve local businessmen. This ended his association with Victoria hockey, which had started in 1910. At age seventy-two, his health was an issue, and the day-to-day rigours of running a hockey franchise were too much for him to handle. The identity of the businessmen was not revealed at the time, but Dr. Reginald Wride was named club president.[1510 1511] Meanwhile, the business of assembling a hockey team for the upcoming year continued with club staff. General manager Hutchinson reported that the Cougars now had a working relationship with the Boston Bruins of the NHL and that all Boston players who would be attending the local training camp had been signed. Also signed to contracts were returning players Bill Davidson, Colin Kilburn, Wayne Brown, and Mark Marquess, as well as Eddie Olson and Skip Teal. A newcomer to the club was eighteen-year-old Gordie Matheson of New Westminster.[1512]

Alex Kuzma and Dave Wall were sold to Trois-Rivières of the Quebec Hockey League, and the New York Rangers had to submit a list of three or four names from which the Cougars could pick the two players promised in the Andy Hebenton deal.[1513] Four players were sent: Bill Dobbyn, Don McGregor, Cornelius Madigan, and Wendy Keller.[1514] Training camp opened in Seattle on September 24, and Victoria would work out there until ice was available back home.[1515] The team returned to Victoria to play an exhibition game with the world-champion Penticton Vees. There were only seven returning players, and the team was heavy with rookies.[1516] The team played to a 1-1 tie with the Vees in Victoria,[1517] but emerged victorious in a game in Penticton. The Cougars were clearly the better team, as they skated to a 5-1 win.[1518] In their last exhibition game in Nanaimo, the Cougars lost 5-3 to the Vancouver Canucks.[1519]

The Cougars opened the 1955-56 season at home with a 4-1 victory over the New Westminster Royals. New coach Eddie Olson had six rookies in the lineup: Danny Wong, Floyd Hillman, Bill Dobbyn, Paul Strasser, Reg Belliveau, and Don Chiupka.[1520] Although the veteran line of Anderson, Kilburn, and Macauley accounted for three goals, Coach Olson noted that the three rookies on defence had played their positions very well. It was a "real nice" start to the season.[1521] The next match was on the road in Seattle, and the Cougars did not disappoint, outscoring the Americans, 4-2. Ironically, three of the Cougar goals came from former Seattle players—Macauley and Marquess—while both Seattle goals were counted by former Cougars—Lavitt and Bradley.

Cougars program 1955-56. From the author's collection.

Skip Teal as a Cougar. Photo courtesy Ernie Fitzsimmons.

Wayne Brown as a Cougar. Photo courtesy Ernie Fitzsimmons.

Mark Marquess as a Cougar. Photo courtesy Ernie Fitzsimmons.

In a Thanksgiving Day matinee back at home, the Cougars continued their winning ways with a 3-2 decision over the Vancouver Canucks. The line of Wayne Brown, Skip Teal, and Mark Marquess accounted for all the scoring.[1522] The next day, the Cougars played the Canucks in Vancouver and continued the streak with a close 4-3 victory. Danny Wong scored his first professional goal on a deflection halfway through the third frame to break the 3-3 tie and gave his team the win.[1523] There was no better way to start a season than with four consecutive wins.

All good things come to an end, and the win streak was no exception. The Cougars lost consecutive home games, 3-2 to Seattle and 5-4 to Edmonton. In the first game, former Cougars Dorohoy, Kuzma, and Bradley led their new team to the victory.[1524] In the second match, the Cougars played very sloppy defensive hockey in front of Pelletier, and he often had to leave the net to play the puck, at which point Edmonton would score.[1525] In the third game of the homestand, the Cougars got their game together and defeated New Westminster, 6-4. The Anderson, Kilburn, and Macauley line was the star of the game; Macauley scored a hat trick, while Anderson added two assists and Kilburn added one.[1526] The action then switched to the mainland, where the Royals outscored Victoria, 4-3. The Cougars fell behind, 3-0, and managed to tie the game, before Motto McLean hit the net for the winning goal.[1527]

The new Winnipeg team came to town, only to be shut out 3-0 by the Cougars. The game was fast, rough, and rugged. Victoria's free-wheeling forward Doug Anderson counted two goals to lead the team to victory.[1528] Next, Seattle entertained the Cougars and defeated them, 5-2, thanks to the efforts of the Americans' goaltender Charlie Hodge.[1529]

During November 1955, the Cougars played twelve games, winning only four and tying one to drop out of first-place consideration. The month started on a winning note, with a 3-1 defeat of Saskatoon. Marcel Pelletier played very well in the nets, and his defence stood their ground while Anderson, Olson, and Teal scored for the winners.[1530] Then the Cougars travelled to Seattle, where Pelletier shut them out 6-0. Three Victoria players scored two goals each: Skip Teal, Doug Macauley, and rookie Don Chiupka.[1531] The Americans came to Victoria where the Cougars again prevailed, this time 2-1. Coach Olson praised his young defence corps, led by Bill Davidson, for their stellar play.[1532] The Cougars were sitting in first place in the league standings and were off to their best start in years. However, things were about to change. The next game was a battle of division leaders, and Calgary came away with a 7-1 decision. Victoria scored the first goal, but that was the end of their offence for the night.[1533] Victoria lost the next two games. In New Westminster, the Cougars scored the first two goals but could not hold back the Royals and fell, 4-2.[1534] Two days later, Vancouver won, 5-2. Playing before the smallest crowd since the 1949-50 season, Victoria neglected the fundamentals of hockey and were never in the game.[1535]

After the three losses, team general manager Hutchinson warned his players that paycheques might be a bit reduced if they did not play a better, more disciplined game and earn their money.[1536] The threat affected play (for one game at least), as the Cougars rallied to defeat the visiting Seattle team, 4-1. The game was filled with fights, with more penalties than goals by a wide margin. The Cougars won the fights—and what hockey was played—then left for a trip to Seattle where the show would continue.[1537] That game was just as rough, and when Seattle won, 3-2, the Cougars filed a protest with the league.

> The Cougars protested the Saturday game on the basis that referee Blair Peters erred in his interpretation of rules 42F, 66A, and 66B.
>
> The points in question concern Peters's rulings following a penalty box fight between Victoria Cougar Bill Davidson and Seattle coach Billy Reay.

The ruckus began following a penalty to Davidson, when Reay blocked the entrance to the penalty box, which is adjacent to, and actually part of the Seattle players' box.

Davidson shoved Reay out of the way and Reay responded with a headlock. Seattle players joined the melee and Victoria players skated across the ice and also entered the altercation.

The Cougars were penalized for their part in the fracas (jumping on the ice to enter a fight) while the Americans got off scot free. Cougars claim both teams should have been penalized.

In addition, Reay was ruled off the bench. However, despite Cougar protests, he was allowed to sit in the section adjacent to the Seattle bench from where he continued to handle the club.

Cougars protested that Reay should have been removed from the immediate vicinity of the bench. "In our opinion, Peters is guilty of misinterpretation of the rules," team managing director Fred Hutchinson said when announcing the protest.[1538]

Unfortunately for the Cougars, the protest was unsuccessful, and the loss remained on their record. Bad luck seemed to follow the club, as they had a horrendous trip to Vancouver for their next game. Their plane had internal issues that kept it on the tarmac for an hour and fifteen minutes. When they finally arrived in Vancouver, they travelled on a bus with a police escort. Somehow, the bus was in collision with a car, further delaying their arrival at the game. Just when they thought they would escape with a 2-2 tie, the Canucks scored the winning goal at 19:44 of the third period, and added insult to injury with an empty-net goal to make the final score 4-2.[1539] Against New Westminster, the Cougars managed to get the game to overtime, but then lost 3-2 after 2:25 of the extra session. Manager Hutchinson once again read his team the riot act and warned that changes would be made if play did not improve.[1540] In New Westminster, the Cougars rallied somewhat and managed a 3-3 tie for their first point in a week. With a bit of luck, they would have had a victory, though, as the Royals did not tie the game until there was less than a minute to go.[1541]

The Regina Regals, the newest club in the WHL, played their first game against the Cougars in Victoria, and although they had the worst record in the entire league, easily dispatched Victoria 4-1. After the game, Coach Olson said that the club was still making too many mistakes, and this was costing them games.[1542] [1543] They had now failed to win in five consecutive games, and first place was now a distant memory, though they currently held a slim lead for second. November had not been a good month.

December started with a better result when the Cougars put together a much better effort and defeated the Western-division-leading Vancouver Canucks, 4-2. Once again, it was the top line that did the scoring, with Kilburn and Anderson scoring two goals each. Macauley assisted on two goals, and Anderson had two assists as well. The line had now scored thirty-seven of the sixty-nine Cougar goals that season, but they could not do it alone. The team left for a Prairie road trip wondering if they would return with the same team or if the threatened changes would be made.[1544]

In Winnipeg, the top line again did all the scoring, but could not match the Warriors' team, who scored six goals to defeat the Cougars, 6-3. Pelletier played well in goal, but the rest of team was abysmal.[1545] Things got marginally better in Regina, where the Cougars defeated the Regals, 4-1. Goals came from Ceresino, Marquess, Brown, and Anderson. Finally, somebody other than the top line was able to put the puck in the net as the team outshot their opponents, 44-26.[1546] With a return to second-place in the standings in their grasp, the Cougars failed to take advantage of the opportunity and fell 4-1 to Saskatoon. Chiupka scored early in the game, but that was the end of the offence, as the Quakers checked the top line well, not allowing them to get close to scoring.[1547] In Edmonton, the Cougars skated to a 2-2 tie with the Flyers, with Brown and Kilburn finding the net. The Boston Bruins sent a new player to the club; Jim Robertson (who had played with Skip Teal at St. Catherines) was expected to join the club shortly. To make room for him on the roster, the Cougars sold Mark Marquess to Vancouver.[1548] The road trip ended in Calgary, where the home team emerged victorious, 6-2. Only Anderson and Brown could score for the Cougars. On the positive side, Boston was sending yet another player to the team. Arnott Whitney was scheduled to arrive in time for a Friday game against Seattle.[1549] However, the first game back home was not a good one either. Vancouver scored at seventeen seconds into the first period and added another at 7:58. That would be all they would need, as the only Victoria goal came halfway through the period. That concluded the scoring for the game with neither team able to put a puck past the goaltenders. Victoria was eagerly awaiting the arrival of the new players, as it was felt that the team needed a shake-up to get them going.[1550]

In league news, it was announced that the Regina Regals would be playing their next home game at the Brandon Wheat City Arena. This was intended to determine if Brandon could support a hockey team, as the owners were losing a lot of money in Regina. Rather than withdraw from the league, the team owners were trying to find a new location.[1551]

The Cougars returned home and played their first game against Winnipeg, defeating the Warriors, 4-2. Several player changes were made: Reg Belliveau returned to the Boston Bruins to make way for Jim Robertson, while Floyd Hillman went to Hershey in exchange for Arnott Whitney. Victoria built up a four-goal lead before Winnipeg scored and then had to withstand an onslaught by the Warriors in the third period.[1552] The new players had an immediate impact on the next home game against Seattle. Whitney wasted no time impressing the local fans. He scored at 2:14 of the first period, approximately seven seconds after he stepped onto the ice for the first time. Jim Robertson scored the game's second goal, at 7:36. Other Cougar marksmen were Kilburn, Davidson, Chiupka, Anderson, and Brown, as the locals defeated Seattle, 7-3.[1553] The Cougars finally found consistency in their play, but the question was whether it would continue. In New Westminster, Pelletier and the Cougars shut out the Royals, 3-0, to solidify their hold on second place in the standings. Kilburn (headed for his best season as a Cougar) scored his twenty-second and twenty-third goals of the season and ran his point total to thirty-eight. Defenceman Nelson Bulloch scored his first goal as a professional and also assisted on one of Kilburn's goals.[1554]

With five days' rest, it would be assumed that the Cougar would be ready for crucial contests. Nothing could be further from the truth. Needing a victory over the Royals to inch closer to first place in the league, the Cougars went down in a 4-3 defeat in the last home game before Christmas. Not only was first place now almost out of reach, but the Royals were getting closer to the Cougars for second.[1555] Vancouver strengthened its hold on top spot with a 2-0 shutout of Victoria on the mainland. The close-checking game featured a fight early in the third period between Dobbyn and Earl Johnson of the Canucks.[1556] In the return engagement in Victoria the next day, the Cougars got a bit of revenge with a 1-0 shutout of the Canucks. The lone goal came from Chiupka late in the second period. The game was very rough and deteriorated into a free-for-all when Nels Bulloch of the Cougars and Mark Marquess, (an ex-Cougar) tangled and both benches cleared.[1557]

In the last home game of 1955, fans were treated to a display of exciting hockey when the Americans came to town. Every time Seattle scored in regulation time, the Cougars answered, including the tying goal at 19:42 of the third period with the goaltender pulled for an extra attacker. However, the local crowd went home disappointed when Seattle scored at 3:38 of overtime to win the contest, 4-3.[1558]

In a matinee affair on January 2, the Cougars started the new year off in style with a 3-1 victory over Edmonton. Victoria scored all its goals in the first period and held the Flyers at bay for the rest of the game. The win was even more impressive because Teal and Ceresino were sidelined with troublesome leg injuries.[1559]

In league news, the owner of the Regina Regals announced that he had moved the franchise to Brandon, effective immediately. The club had been playing all their home games there since December 17 and had garnered some local support. They were drawing close to 3,000 fans in Brandon, far better than the average of 900 in Regina. The Cougars would be playing there later in January.[1560][1561]

Marcel Pelletier as a Cougar. Photo courtesy Ernie Fitzsimmons.

The good play continued when Victoria defeated New Westminster, 4-0. It was Pelletier's fifth shutout of the season and was well deserved. Brown scored two goals for the Cougars, with Kilburn and Robertson adding singles. Royals' coach Max McNab commented, "They really played as a team tonight, and played very well." His comments were echoed by Cougar coach Eddie Olson who said, "That was one of our best—by everybody."[1562] The homestand ended with a scoreless tie with Vancouver. Over the last three games between these teams, Vancouver had scored two goals and Victoria one. This lack of scoring was mostly due to the outstanding goaltending of Mikulan of the Canucks and Pelletier of the Cougars. Both had been very stingy in allowing goals.[1563] Marcel Pelletier's bubble burst at forty seconds of the first period when Vancouver scored in the next game on the mainland. The Cougars scored two goals but allowed four, losing that important match, 4-2. After the game, managing director Hutchinson advised that Fred Wonoski, a nineteen-year-old centre from the Barrie Junior club, would join the team in Winnipeg. Defenceman Arnott Whitney further injured his ankle and would be lost to the club while he took additional treatment. Injured player Ceresino was given his release from the club.[1564]

The Cougars started their next game in New Westminster two men under the roster limit, and lost their captain, Colin Kilburn, when he suffered an eye injury in the first period. Doug Macauley scored three goals, Teal got two, and Robertson added a single for the 6-2 win. The Cougars added another junior player to their roster when they called up left-winger Larry Berg from the Humboldt-Melfort Indians, of the Saskatchewan Junior Hockey League, for a three-game pro tryout.[1565][1566] He was in the lineup when the Cougars defeated Edmonton, 5-2. The Cougars took charge early in the game with two goals in the first period and another early in the second. The team played great defensive of hockey, frustrating Edmonton's efforts. It was the Flyers' first loss in six games, and coincidentally, the first since the Cougar had scored a 3-1 victory over the Flyers in Victoria.[1567] The stellar play continued in Saskatoon, where Victoria outscored the Quakers, 4-3. Teal led the scoring with two goals, while Anderson notched one. The Cougars' final goal, and the game-winner, was Bill Dobbyn's first goal of the season.[1568]

In Winnipeg, the road-weary Cougars lost a close game to the Warriors, 3-2. Boston Bruins general manager Lynn Patrick was at the game to evaluate the Boston-owned talent. His choice for the best player of the game was Nelson Bulloch. Young Fred Wonoski made his first start for the Cougars and did well; he stayed with the club for three more games.[1569] After a two-day rest, the Cougars were ready to do battle again. They got back on the winning track with a 4-1 victory in Brandon. The game was completely sold out, showing the support that Brandon had for its adopted team. After surrendering the first goal, Victoria stormed back with three in the second period to take a lead they never relinquished. Macauley put the icing on the cake when he scored his second goal of the game in the third period.[1570]

A reasonably successful road trip ended on a sour note in Calgary, when the Stampeders blasted the Cougars, 9-3. Tired from the long trip, they looked sluggish and had too many passes intercepted. Skip Teal was injured in the game and had to miss the third period, while goaltender Pelletier suffered a groin injury but was still able to play, although his effectiveness was somewhat affected.[1571]

Being at home seemed to spark the Cougars, as they shut out the Americans, 4-0, at Memorial Arena. Kilburn, Bulloch, Chiupka, and Teal scored for Victoria, and Pelletier recorded his seventh shutout of the season, tying a league record. It was also a momentous day for Marcel in a different way, as he became a father for the second time, just an hour before the game. Little Cheryl Anne was likely the inspiration for his stellar play.[1572] The Cougars were missing Anderson (influenza) and Strasser (damaged eye) from their lineup for the next game against Saskatoon but recovered from a two-goal deficit to emerge victorious. Skip Teal was the offensive star of the match with two goals, bringing his recent record to eight goals in the last nine games. The Cougars were given permission to use centre Howie Hornby of the Kamloops Elks in their next three games and acquired winger Bruce Carmichael on loan from the New York Rangers.[1573]

The Cougars travelled to Seattle for two games against the Americans. In the first, they were shut out 4-0 but rebounded to take the second game 2-1 in an overtime thriller. Macauley was the hero, scoring at 6:59 of extra time.[1574] January finished on a winning note when Victoria edged out the Eastern-division-leading Calgary team 2-1. The Stampeders took a 1-0 lead in the first period when Fred Hucul's shot eluded Pelletier, but the Cougars tied the game on a goal from Robertson in the second period. That set the stage for Macauley's winner at forty-nine seconds into the third period. It was the team's first victory over Calgary in four attempts that season; they seemed to get stronger as the game progressed.[1575]

In off-ice news, Al Leader confirmed that the league had received an application from a Los Angeles entry. He noted that a new arena, with a seating capacity of 18,000, would be completed by April of 1957. He added that a new arena would be ready in Portland by the same time, opening the way for future expansion of the league.[1576]

February began on a losing note as the Americans shut out the Cougars, 2-0. Seattle goaltender Charlie Hodge was the star of the game, stopping every shot fired at him. To add insult to injury, both Seattle goals were scored by former Cougars: Kuzma and Bradley.[1577] If the Cougars' desire to finish first in the league standings were to become a reality, they would have to take both games from the Canucks. And that is precisely what they did. In Vancouver, Victoria emerged with a narrow 2-1 decision, handing the Canucks only their fifth loss at home. Goal scorers for Victoria were Kilburn and Chiupka.[1578] In Victoria, the home team again won by one goal, but the score this time was 5-4. The teams were tied 1-1 at the end of the first period, and Victoria held a 2-1 lead after the second. An onslaught of goals in the final frame (three by each team) made the difference, as Bulloch found the net at 13:03 for the winning goal.

The points gained put the Cougars only three points back of first-place—the closest they had been to the top in some time. Despite the team's success on the ice, attendance at the rink had been declining, and team officials had no idea how to get fans to attend games again. There were only 2,490 fans in the stands.[1579]

Next on the schedule were home-and-home games against the Royals. In the game in Victoria, only 2,448 fans watched the Cougars whip New Westminster handily (9-3) to move within one point of the division lead. Chiupka scored his first hat trick to lead his team to victory. Anderson and Brown contributed two goals each, and Davidson and Kilburn added singles.[1580] In New Westminster, the Royals turned the tables and defeated the Cougars, 6-4. The game was tied 4-4 early in the third period, but Max McNab scored the go-ahead goal, and the Royals added an empty-net goal to seal the victory.[1581] That result was soon remembered as only a minor impediment in the race for first when the Cougars trounced the Americans 7-1 in Seattle. Carmichael had two goals for Victoria, with singles scored by Bulloch, Brown, Kilburn, Macauley, and Davidson.[1582] Brandon played the Cougars tough in the next game and emerged with a 4-4 tie. The single point moved Victoria to within one point of Vancouver, with the Canucks their next opponent.[1583]

In the thirteenth meeting between Victoria and Vancouver that season, the Cougars outscored their opponents, 3-2, to jump into first place in the Western-division standings for the first time since November 19, 1955. Phil Maloney scored the first goal for Vancouver, but Teal tied it up before the end of the first period. Anderson put Victoria ahead, only to have Brown tie the score at 2-2 at the end of the second frame. Kilburn scored the winner at 18:43 of the final period to send the 3,427 fans in attendance home ecstatic.[1584] The great play (and winning) continued with a 5-3 decision over Seattle. Colin Kilburn got out of his sickbed to play and did not disappoint, scoring two goals including the game winner. Other Victoria marksmen were Teal, Anderson, and Bulloch. The team was now three points ahead of Vancouver in the standings.[1585] In their next game, the Cougars lost, 7-3, to New Westminster, but the Canucks lost as well, so there was no change in the standings.[1586]

In a battle between the division leaders, neither team could claim victory, as the game ended in a 2-2 tie. Olson and Macauley scored for the Cougars, while Ray Cyr and Fred Brown replied for the Canucks. Goaltender Pelletier was the best player on the ice, as Vancouver outshot Victoria 40-18.[1587] With a thrilling 3-2 overtime victory over the Royals, the Cougars secured a playoff position. They also retained their three-point lead atop the western division and realized that young Fred Wonoski, who had to replace injured Coach Olson, had the ability to play in the upcoming playoff round; he fired the winning goal at 5:00 of overtime. The only bad news was that Doug Anderson had hurt his shoulder and might be lost for some time.[1588] In the next game in Seattle, the Cougars lost, 3-1. With Seattle leading 2-1 in the third period, Kilburn appeared to tie the score when he put the puck behind Charlie Hodge. Referee Peters disallowed the goal, first saying that Kilburn had kicked the puck into the net, then changing his mind to say that the Cougar player was in the crease when the goal was scored. It was ironic that the goal judge ruled the goal to be legal. That was the turning point of the game, and the Cougars never really recovered after that.[1589]

In the next game against Vancouver, the Cougars came up short and were shut out 3-0. They were hampered in their efforts by injuries to key players. Coach Olson re-injured his leg in the third period, and Anderson could not play as he could not shoot the puck. Pelletier suffered a facial gash and play was stopped while he was stitched up. With all the injuries, there was a possibility that juniors would be called up for the balance of the season; the rules had been changed, and juniors were now able to play six games without sacrificing their amateur status.[1590] Lawrence Leach and Pete Panagabko from Humboldt of the Saskatchewan Junior Hockey League were brought to Victoria, ready to play if needed.[1591]

Doug Anderson as a Cougar. Photo courtesy Ernie Fitzsimmons.

The Cougars got back on the winning track with a close 3-2 win over the Americans. The junior players played very well, with Leach scoring the first goal, but it was veteran Colin Kilburn (who had been sold to the Boston Bruins of the NHL) who was the scoring leader with two goals. The game was rugged from start to finish with twenty-two penalties being called by referee Dalton MacArthur.[1592] In the final head-to-head match against the Canucks in Vancouver, the Cougars came up short and were shut out, 7-0.[1593]

First place was now out of reach, but the Cougars were solidly in second, and in the playoffs, anything could happen. In the last home game of the regular season, the Cougars shut out New Westminster 1-0. It was a special night for the "Gold Dust Trio" of Doug Anderson, Doug Macauley, and Colin Kilburn, who were presented with gifts in recognition of their scoring prowess. Macauley scored the only goal of the game, assisted by his linemates. Marcel Pelletier set a new league record with his eighth shutout of the season.[1594] The final game was played in Seattle, where the Americans eked out a 3-2 overtime win. Rookie goaltender Don Hamilton had to come into the game when Pelletier was injured in the first period. The Coast playoff format was a round-robin, home-and-home series. The top three teams—Vancouver, Victoria, and New Westminster—would play each other twice, with the top two teams advancing to the best-of-seven Western final.[1595]

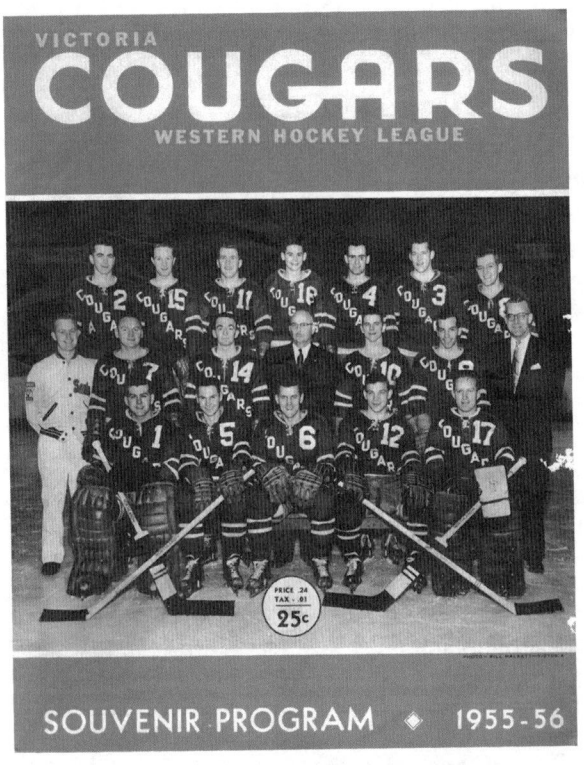

Victoria Cougar 1955-56 program. From the author's collection.

Victoria opened the playoffs at home against New Westminster. The Cougars' assignment for the game was to stop the high-scoring Royals trio of Gord Fashoway, Blinky Boyce, and Bob Love. Cougars Chiupka, Teal, and Robertson were very successful. Chiupka also provided the offence for the home team, along with Brown and Olson.[1596] The Royals shocked Vancouver by defeating them 4-3 in New Westminster.[1597] Next, the Cougars travelled to Vancouver and beat the Canucks, 5-2, to take the lead in total points in the series. Nelson Bulloch scored one goal and assisted on the others, all of which were scored when the team was shorthanded.[1598] Victoria next played the Royals in New Westminster and emerged with a 3-0 victory to clinch a berth in the division final. Pelletier closed the door on the Royals' scorers, while the Cougars took advantage of their chances to score.[1599] Victoria completed the series when they outscored the Canucks, 3-2, to finish the series with four victories. Brown, Davidson, and Carmichael scored goals for the home team.[1600] In the final game of the opening series, Vancouver trounced New Westminster to finish second in the round robin and advance to the final against Victoria.[1601]

The Cougars entered the division final, confident they could win the best-of-seven series. They were undefeated in post-season play and could see no reason why they could not go all the way. The problem was that nobody told the Canucks they were supposed to lose. The first game was played in Vancouver, and Victoria played its worst game in a long time, being swamped 7-1. The Cougars took an early lead but were unable to withstand an offensive onslaught by the Canucks. Coach Olson said, "I don't think we can be that bad again."[1602] The team played better in the second game but were affected by some questionable officiating and a lack of attention to details. Leading 2-1, they forgot to check Jerry Ehman, and he swooped in to score the tying goal. In the overtime period, the Cougars just could not score (despite many chances), while the Canucks scored on their first shot (at 7:19), to win the game.[1603] The hometown fans were in disbelief that their team was now down 2-0 in the series and badly needed a victory to retain any hope of winning.

Media coverage reflected on the similarity of this year's situation to that of the 1950-51 Cougars, who came back from a 2-0 deficit to win. However, the reality was that this was a different time and circumstances were not the same.[1604]

Despite the enthusiasm of their supporters, the Cougars travelled to Vancouver and lost again. The game was never close, as the Canucks took a 2-0 lead and never looked back. Former Cougar Marquess did most of the damage, with two goals. Reality now set in, as no WHL team had ever come back from a 3-0 deficit to win a series. The Toronto Maple Leafs had done it in the NHL to win the Stanley Cup, but it was perhaps one of the most challenging tasks in any sport.[1605] Just when even the most ardent fans were prepared for disappointment, the Cougars found their hockey legs and shut out the Canucks 2-0, to climb back into the series. The goaltenders, Mikulan and Pelletier, were the stars of the show with several sensational saves. Bruce Carmichael scored the opening goal, and Kilburn got the clincher.[1606] Now the series moved back to Vancouver, with the Cougars needing a victory to prolong the series. Unfortunately, Victoria played a flat game with no offence and ended up losing the game, 5-0, and the series four games to one.[1607] Cougar goaltender Marcel Pelletier was named the spare goalie for the Western Hockey League playoffs between Vancouver and Winnipeg.[1608]

It was a sad ending to a reasonably successful hockey season, but there had been bright points, as well. Marcel Pelletier and Colin Kilburn were named to the league all-star team, joining Canuck Maloney, Stampeders Fred Hucul and Art Michaluk, and Quaker Jackie McLeod on the team. Members of the all-star team received payment of $100 (the equivalent of $900 today).[1609] This is far from what today's all-star hockey players receive for their selection.

In the league finals, the Winnipeg Warriors upset the Vancouver Canucks to take the league title and advance to the Edinburgh Trophy series against the Montreal Royals.[1610] [1611]

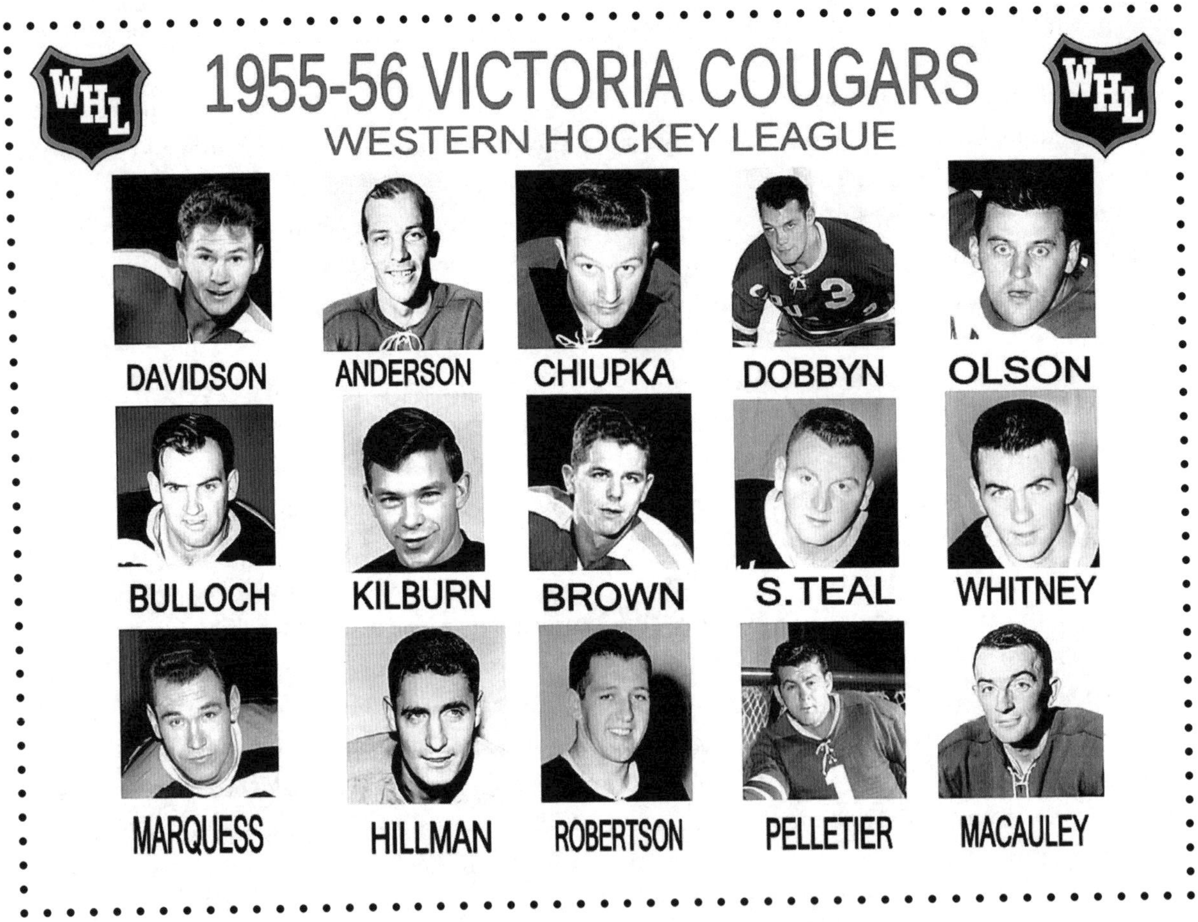

The History of Professional Hockey in Victoria, BC: 1911-2011

1955-56 VICTORIA COUGARS
WESTERN HOCKEY LEAGUE

DAVIDSON — ANDERSON — CHIUPKA — DOBBYN — OLSON
BULLOCH — KILBURN — BROWN — S. TEAL — WHITNEY
MARQUESS — HILLMAN — ROBERTSON — PELLETIER — MACAULEY

Victoria Cougars 1955-56 team photo. From the author's collection.

20 - WOULD THIS BE THE YEAR OF THE COUGAR?

The Cougars started the 1956-57 season with optimism, feeling they had the team to win the league championship. Acutely aware of the declining attendance over the past few years, they decided to "sweeten the pot" to encourage local citizens to purchase season tickets. Among the deals offered were a ten-percent discount on the price of individual games, a deposit contract plan, and free reserved and supervised parking at the Hudson's Bay parking lot for the first 250 subscribers who reserved at least two tickets. In addition, one purchaser would win a Plymouth Plaza Sedan.[1612]

In the plan was a special pre-season series against the Allan Cup champion Vernon Canadians, with a game in Nanaimo on October 4 and in Victoria on October 5.[1613][1614]

The Cougar organization was devastated when managing director and vice-president Fred Hutchinson died unexpectedly at forty-four. He passed away as he had lived, with gusto for sport, actually dying in the midst of a round of golf. He had come to Victoria in 1949 when the team was established and had been instrumental in the club ever since. Hutchinson had worked hard to get the upcoming season planned, and the remainder of the board decided to carry on as he had wished.[1615] He was remembered as having a detailed memory of every player who had worn a Cougar uniform and could relay information without reference to any notes. He was much admired by everyone involved in hockey in Victoria and throughout the league.[1616]

The Cougars opened training camp in Nanaimo on September 23.[1617] Colin Kilburn turned down a chance for a playing career with the Boston Bruins of the NHL to become playing coach of the Cougars.[1618] He made it clear to his players that they would be expected to be in shape and work hard. Two new players, Lionel Heinrich and Gordy Haworth, were singled out for praise by the coach. Other attendees were goaltenders Don Hamilton and Earl Anshelm; defenders Bill Dobbyn and Gordie Matheson; centres Doug Anderson and Larry Leach; left-wingers Don Chiupka, Wayne Brown, and Larry Berg; and right-wingers Doug Macauley, Bruce Carmichael, and Ed Varga.[1619] Holdover goaltender Marcel Pelletier arrived late to camp, as did Bill Davidson.[1620] Good news came from Boston when Kilburn was advised that the parent club would send players to the camp. Nelson Bulloch would return, along with two former Barrie Flyers, George Ranieri and Roy Partridge.[1621]

For the first game against Vernon, only Bill Dobbyn would be unable to play as he required some treatment for tendonitis. The game was a good workout for the Cougars, as they upended the Canadians, 5-1.[1622] In the second match in Victoria, the home team again won the game. At 3-2, it was a closer decision, with young Partridge impressing the coach with his good play.[1623]

The regular season opened on October 8, 1956, with a Thanksgiving Day matinee. Much to the delight of the 3,178 fans in attendance, the Cougars topped the Vancouver Canucks, 5-2. It was Kilburn's first victory as a coach, and he even scored a goal to help the team win. Haworth opened the scoring while the team was short-handed, and Ranieri, Anderson, and Macauley also put the puck past Mikulan in the Vancouver net.[1624] The coach asked for centre-ice help from Boston, and Bob Beckett was sent to the Cougars on a twenty-four-hour recall. In forty-eight games with the Barrie Flyers the previous season, he had scored sixteen goals and added twenty-six assists.[1625] With Beckett in the lineup, Victoria fell to the Americans, 6-4. The young Cougars fell victim to a series of errors, including untimely penalties that gave their opponents chances to score.[1626] The Cougars then left on the first of three Prairie road trips, stopping first at Seattle, where they had an opportunity to get their second victory of the season. They were leading the game, 3-2, but surrendered the tying goal to Fred Creighton at 19:38 of the final frame, and then allowed the winning overtime goal, at 1:34. It was a disappointing end to a reasonably well-played game.[1627]

Next, it was on to Winnipeg, where the Cougars came from behind to gain a 4-4 tie with the Warriors. The game was marked by the use of a $10,000 ice-clearing machine that seemed to make the ice slow. After the second period, the ice was cleaned by hand as the machinery failed, and the Cougars finally found their legs and rallied for the single point. There were a few injuries: Pelletier pulled a tendon in his knee, Haworth got a charley-horse, and Carmichael received a gash under his chin.[1628] The next stop of the trip was Brandon, where the Cougars were beaten, 5-0, by the Regals. Coach Kilburn was heard to say, "Some players won't be on this team when we make the next Prairie trip (December)."[1629] Things did not get better in Edmonton or Calgary as the Cougars lost both games by a single goal each. Edmonton fans loved the free-wheeling style of Victoria but were happy that their team prevailed 2-1. Coach Kilburn scored the only goal for his team.[1630] In Calgary, the coach again supplied the total Cougar offence, but his team could not hold the Stampeders off the scoresheet and fell 3-2.[1631]

After a road trip that produced only one point, the Cougars were glad to return to the friendly confines of the Memorial Arena. Their first opponent was the Stampeders, and, this time, the result was different. Victoria shut out Calgary, 1-0, behind the stellar goaltending of Pelletier. The only goal of the game was a strange one, as Kilburn was clearly offside on the play before Bulloch put the puck behind Hank Bassen. However, the call was not made, and the goal stood.[1632] Perhaps luck had turned in the Cougars' favour, as they now had their second victory of the season.

The Edmonton Flyers were the next to visit Victoria, and they left with a 4-3 win. It was the first game to use their new pucks. Each puck had the club monogram stamped on one side to make it more collectible.[1633] Flyers rookie Cummings Burton scored the first two goals of his professional career, including the overtime winner at 3:45 of extra time. Anderson scored two Cougar goals, and Kilburn scored one.[1634]

Colin Kilburn was not pleased with the lacklustre play of many on his team, and he gave Nelson Bulloch an ultimatum: lose ten pounds in two weeks, or you will be out.[1635] October ended with another set of mistakes that cost the team a win, as they fell, 3-2, to the Vancouver Canucks. Even a juggling of lines failed to get the desired result. However, Coach Kilburn saw some good play and was hopeful that the team would begin to win with a little more effort.[1636]

November started on a winning note when the Royals came to town. A much lighter Nelson Bulloch, Chiupka, and Carmichael scored for the Cougars, with Kilburn assisting on two of the goals in a hard-fought 3-1 decision. Players were obviously determined to keep their places on the team, as they all played hard.[1637] The scene shifted to New Westminster, where the teams battled to a 2-2 overtime tie. The new line combinations seemed to be working.[1638] The scoring came alive in the next game with the woeful Winnipeg Warriors. It was the kind of game in which everything went well—the kind of game that the coach had been claiming would happen soon. Wayne Brown, who had not scored a goal all season, broke out of his slump in a huge way with four goals. His linemates were equally prolific. Macauley had a goal and four assists, while Kilburn notched two goals and an assist. Carmichael and Leach completed the rout. According to most observers, the Warriors just refused to play good hockey in the last five minutes of the game, repeatedly icing the puck.[1639] The stalling tactic was reported to league president Leader, but he took no action, as referee Vern Buffey had not made an official report to the league. Also, Winnipeg president J. D. Perrin apologized for the behaviour, noting that he had reprimanded the coach and players, and saying that it would not happen again.[1640]

The Cougars then began a set of home-and-home series. The first was against Seattle. In Victoria, the Americans shut out the Cougars, 4-0, with a display of skill that overwhelmed the home team.[1641] In Seattle, the result was familiar: a 6-2 defeat. Guyle Fielder and former Cougar Kuzma scored two goals each before 4,729 supportive fans. It was a very clean game, with only two penalties called.[1642] In the next series, the Cougars' opponent was the Royals. In Victoria, the Royals won, 4-2, with Kilburn scoring the only Cougar goals.[1643] In New Westminster, the Royals again won, this time by a 3-0 score. With the four losses in a row, Coach Kilburn saw red. He asked Boston for help, noting that some players might be moved by the end of the week. In the meantime, he had to get the team ready for a game against Vancouver.[1644]

The game was billed as "Rotary Night," and there were more than the usual number of fans on hand. The Cougars ended their goal drought as they manhandled the Canucks, 6-3. Macauley and Brown got the Cougars off to a good start in the opening period. Haworth had returned from injury, and in the second frame, he scored a couple of goals within forty-five seconds. Carmichael and Brown found the net in the third period.[1645] In Vancouver, the Cougars again played a good game. They checked efficiently and made the most of their chances in a 5-2 victory. Coach Kilburn scored a hat trick to lead by example, while Anderson and Haworth added singles. It was the first road win for the Cougars and their first two-game winning streak of the season. These were small accomplishments, but they provided a base upon which to build further success.[1646]

The Cougars continued their good play against Seattle. New Cougar Ray Powell was in the lineup when the teams battled to a 3-3 overtime tie. The only downside of the game was an injury to Nels Bulloch. He suffered a fractured jaw in the overtime period and was scheduled to have tests to determine the extent of the break.[1647]

The scene then switched to Seattle, where the Cougars extended their unbeaten streak to four games, with a 4-2 win over the Americans. Anderson led the way with his second hat trick of the season, and Brown added a single goal. The victory moved the Cougars into third place in the division standings.[1648] The Cougar train suffered a minor setback with a narrow 2-1 loss to Edmonton. Surrendering the first two goals, the Cougars never recovered and fell short, despite Anderson's goal.[1649] Next, the team rebounded with a 3-0 shutout of Calgary. Pelletier recorded his second shutout of the season and got offensive help from Powell, Haworth, and Kilburn.[1650]

The Cougars then left on a four-game Prairie road trip that ended marginally better than their first one in October. In Brandon, they gave up two goals to the Regals in the first period and did not score until the third period, when it was too late. A late Brandon goal assured the Regals of a 3-2 win.[1651] In Winnipeg, Coach Kilburn led by example, as he had done in many past games. Not only did he notch a goal and an assist, but he wrenched his knee in the second period, was carried off the ice on a stretcher, got patched up with some tape and a bandage, and then returned to play the final frame. This 3-2 victory was the first win for the Cougars on the Prairies that season. Haworth and Chiupka were the other Victoria marksmen.[1652]

Next on the agenda for the Cougars was a game in Edmonton. As he had done earlier in Victoria on October 26, Flyers' rookie Cummings Burton scored the winning goal in overtime, to lead his time to a 2-1 victory. Coach Kilburn praised the young Flyer, noting that "rookies are liable to knock you dead any time."[1653] As usually happened in Calgary, the Cougars came up short in a 4-1 decision for the Stampeders. Only Macauley could score for Victoria.[1654]

In off-ice news in Vancouver, the Pacific National Exhibition announced that it had completed the purchase of the Vancouver Canucks team from Coley Hall. The exhibition had acquired fifty percent of the club in 1954, and it was agreed at that time that they could purchase the remainder at a later date.[1655]

The Cougars came home from their road trip to face a Prairie team, the Brandon Regals. The Cougars were tired, having endured two days on a train and a boat trip that got them home only six hours before game time, while the Regals had been on the coast. Victoria's fatigue showed in the gameplay, as Brandon won, 3-1. Coach Kilburn did everything but play goal but could not do it alone. He even got into a ruckus with an official after a goal was disallowed, resulting in a misconduct, a game misconduct, and a thirty-five-dollar fine. To make matters worse, Lionel Heinrich suffered a sprained back, leaving the team very short of defenders.[1656] The Boston Bruins responded to the request for a player and agreed to send Arnott Whitney, who had played thirty-nine games for the Cougars the previous season, as soon as possible. Tests on Heinrich's back revealed a wrenched muscle in the sacroiliac region that would keep him out of the lineup for seven to ten days, and Nels Bulloch would have to wait until Christmas to have his jaw unwired.[1657]

In their next home game, the Cougars made fewer mistakes than the Royals, and they escaped with a 6-4 victory. Off to an early 3-0 lead, Victoria got sloppy and let New Westminster back into the game. The winner was scored by Macauley, while Brown scored a hat trick—including the insurance goal on a penalty shot late in the contest. Referee Joey Johns made one of the strangest calls ever seen when he penalized Brown for delay of game when he skated to the bench to have a cut earlobe repaired. The fact that Brown required medical attention in the penalty box further confused the issue. After the game, Brown was reputed to have said that he would bleed to death next time, just to be on the safe side.[1658] The Cougars then played a home-and-home series with the Americans. In Seattle, the team battled to a 2-2 tie. It was the Cougars' seventh overtime that season, and they had yet to win in extra time.[1659]

In Victoria, the home team stretched their unbeaten streak to three games, with a 4-1 victory over the Americans before only 2,000 fans. Coach Kilburn scored two goals, Davidson notched his first goal of the season, and Anderson added a single. The game got rough at the final whistle when Kilburn and Pete Wright tangled near the Seattle goal. Both benches emptied, and it took some time for order to be restored.[1660] The unbeaten streak continued in New Westminster, where the Cougars upended the Royals, 4-3. Following a scoreless first period, the Royals took a one-goal lead in the second. However, Victoria outscored the home team, 4-2, in the final frame. Wayne Brown and Ray Powell each scored twice, supplying all the offence the team needed.[1661]

The next action was scheduled for Boxing Day. The schedule called for Victoria and Vancouver to play two games on the same day: a 2:00 p.m. matinee in Victoria and an 8:00 p.m. start on the mainland. The afternoon game was played at Memorial Arena, and sloppy play by the home team led to a 4-2 victory by the visitors. The teams were unable to play the night game, as their planes could not leave due to dense fog at the Victoria airport. The game was rescheduled for later in the season.[1662] The Cougars learned that they would be receiving a new player: Gordon Wilson, a centre, who was recuperating from knee surgery and so would not see game action until January.[1663]

Although the Cougars won their next game versus New Westminster, by a score of 3-0, it was a bittersweet victory, as the Royals' Pete Durham ran amuck with his stick. He hit Anderson across the arch of his foot, with further tests necessary to determine the extent of the injury, and put Ray Powell out of action for at least a month with a broken arm. Coach Kilburn said that the club might ask the league for action on the actions of Durham, who was well known across the league for his undisciplined play. In the game itself, Pelletier stopped fifty shots en route to his third shutout of the year, while Anderson, Kilburn, and Haworth provided the margin of victory.[1664] December ended the way it had started, with a Cougar loss. In Seattle, Victoria was outscored, 7-4, by the Americans, in a game where punches and goals were exchanged at will. Carmichael and Kilburn each scored a pair of goals in a losing cause.[1665]

The New Year's Day game in Vancouver began well for the Cougars, as Anderson scored two goals in six seconds in the first period. However, the Canucks tied the score before the end of the second frame. In the third, Carmichael gave Victoria a 3-2 lead, but Phil Maloney tied the game, and Earl Johnson scored at 6:50 of overtime to give the Canucks a 4-3 victory. This was the ninth overtime game the Cougar had played without tasting success. Victoria was now in last place in the standings.[1666]

The Cougars then opened a three-game homestand with a game against Winnipeg. Although the Warriors were the worst team in the Eastern division, having equalled the Cougars' record of futility with fifteen straight losses, Victoria knew they would have to play well to defeat them. In the game, Victoria survived the rough play and scored three goals to emerge with a 3-1 victory. Macauley, Haworth, and Brown provided all the offence they needed, while Pelletier stopped all but one of the twenty-three shots fired his way.[1667]

The Boston Bruins' Lynn Patrick arrived in Victoria to have a look at his charges playing for the Cougars, and other WHL players as well. He talked with his father, Lester, who was still involved in club operations. At the top of his mind was a desire to solve the lack of overtime success.[1668] Perhaps his visit would serve as inspiration, as the visits of Canadiens' scout Kenny Reardon had in the early 1950s.

In the game against Vancouver, Victoria started poorly, surrendering a goal to Maloney in the first period. Then they tied the game on Carmichael's goal early in the second and gave up a goal to Henry Syverson to trail 2-1 at the end of the second frame. However, the team came alive late in the final period, when George Ranieri scored at 17:44, Macauley at 17:27, and Ranieri at 19:41, to lead the team to victory.[1669] Just when the team thought they had momentum, they faced Seattle and ended up on the wrong end of a 5-4 decision. In the game, they held leads of 2-1, 3-1, and 4-3, but made too many mistakes and let the Americans back in the game, with the winning goal scored with just seven seconds remaining.[1670] These teams were on the opposite end of the standings: Seattle in the lead and Victoria bringing up the rear. Based on the play in this game, that situation was not likely to change.

On their trip to New Westminster, Victoria was shut out 3-0. Coach Kilburn was upset over the antics of Pete Durham, who again injured a Cougars' player, this time Macauley (on the ankle). Referee Vern Buffey was kept busy, handing out forty-six minutes in penalties to the clubs.[1671] The scene shifted to Victoria, and the result was a total reversal. The Cougars dominated the Royals, 7-1, in one of their strongest showings of the season. The onslaught began when Bulloch scored at 3:31 of the first period. Carmichael and Brown added goals to make the score 3-0 after one. Victoria outscored

New Westminster two to one in the second period and had the only scores in the third frame. Lynn Patrick left for Boston, having seen the team at its best and also its worst.[1672]

The Cougars lost a player when Boston re-assigned Arnott Whitney to Winnipeg. With the league's most dismal record, the Warriors hoped he would bring some life to their team.[1673] Roy Partridge was cut by the Cougars as they had to cut their roster down to fifteen by the middle of February. They still had another player to cut, but Coach Kilburn did share his thoughts with the media.[1674]

The Cougars continued their winning ways with a narrow 3-2 victory over Vancouver on the mainland. They started well with goals by Kilburn and Bulloch in the first period, surrendered a goal in the second period, then clinched the victory with a third-period goal by Brown on a breakaway from centre ice.[1675] A game in New Westminster was not as successful, as the Cougars could not score and so went down to a 4-0 defeat. In a strange turn of fate, Vancouver goaltender Ray Mikulan had to play for Victoria, as Pelletier was unable to start with a cut hand.[1676] Two days later, Mikulan was back with his regular team, playing against Victoria. Much to the delight of the home crowd, the Cougars came from behind and defeated the Canucks, 5-2. It did not look good for the first two periods of the game. Victoria trailed, 2-1, and was not playing well. All that changed in the last period, as Brown scored to tie the game, and then the offence caught fire, netting three goals in the last 2:18 to put the game away. The victory was significant, as it meant that Victoria was only one point behind the Canucks in the division playoff race.[1677]

In their last home game before their last Prairie road trip of the season, the Cougars fell, 3-2, to the Brandon Regals. The winning goal was certainly controversial. The Cougars felt that goaltender Pelletier had caught the puck, had possession, and so play should have been stopped. However, referee Vern Buffey allowed play to continue, and Royals' player Norman Johnson came into the crease and slashed the puck out of Pelletier's glove and into the net. Against Cougar protests, the goal was allowed to stand, and it made the difference in the game.[1678]

The big local story was the rumour that the Cougars would suspend operations, as they were losing money at the gate. While acknowledging the financial problems, club management assured the public that they would continue to operate the club. One of the issues was the scheduling change, moving some games to Monday, which had not been a success at all. Another was the addition of a third Prairie road trip, which proved very expensive. Coach Kilburn assured local fans that his team was working hard to win games and entice fans back to the Memorial Arena.[1679]

In Edmonton, the Cougars got the road swing off to a good start with an 8-7 overtime victory. It was their first decision over the Eastern-division-leading Flyers that season and much of the scoring for Victoria was done by players who had started their careers in the Alberta city. Kilburn scored two goals and two assists; Macauley, who grew up steps from the Edmonton Gardens, notched a hat trick and added an assist, while Anderson counted four assists. Edmonton had a 4-2 lead at the end of the first period, each team scored two in the second, and Victoria outscored Edmonton, 3-1, in the third to send the game to overtime. At the 2:35 mark, Kilburn got the winning goal, with assists to Haworth and Carmichael.[1680] The team moved on next to Calgary, where they played poorly for the first two periods, going down 3-0, before turning on the offence in the third. Carmichael scored two goals, while Kilburn got one to take the game to overtime. Neither team managed to score in extra time, so the game ended in a 3-3 tie.[1681] The Cougars' luck ran out in Winnipeg, where they scored the first goal of the game, and then could not find the net the rest of the way and fell 3-1 to the lowly Warriors, in a penalty-filled game.[1682]

The next game in Brandon was a bit unusual. Although the Regals had been near the top of the Eastern-division standings, attendance was dangerously low, and owner Piggott had threatened to move the franchise elsewhere if fans did not support the team. For "save hockey night," all tickets were sold for five dollars, with all patrons eligible to win a new car and other prizes. The Cougars were in a "giving" mood, and lost the game, 4-1.[1683]

Returning home from the road trip, the Cougars played a home-and-home series against the Royals. In the first game, they shut out the Royals, 2-0, on goals by Carmichael and Anderson. With the victory, they climbed into third place in the Western-division standings.[1684] On the mainland the next evening, the Cougars did not disappoint, as they held the Royals to a 2-2 tie to remain in possession of third place in the standings.[1685] Next on the schedule was a home-and-home series against Seattle. In the home game, the Americans' goaltender Emile Francis was the star of the show, as he shut out the Cougars, 2-0.[1686] In Seattle, the teams tied, 2-2, with Cougars' scoring coming from Macauley and Kilburn. The single point tied Victoria with Vancouver for third place.[1687]

In league business, the Brandon Regals played a test game in St. Paul, Minnesota. More than 7,000 fans showed up at the game, where the Regals won 5-2 over Winnipeg. The area had been without hockey since their team, the St. Paul Saints, had left the United States Hockey League in 1951.[1688][1689]

Meanwhile, back in Cougar hockey, the next three games would be against Prairie opponents. First, Edmonton came to town. In one of the most exciting games of the season, the Cougars edged the Flyers, 2-1, with utility player Don Chiupka scoring the winning goal midway through the final period. Edmonton pulled their goaltender in a concentrated effort to tie the score but were unsuccessful.[1690] In their next game, just over a minute of sloppy play in the first period allowed Brandon to score three goals, which cost the Cougars the game. They were able to respond with two goals but just could not tie the score. It was the sixth time that season that Brandon had defeated Victoria and was the likely reason why they were not higher placed in the standings.[1691]

The final Prairie team to visit Victoria was Calgary. Carmichael scored in the first period, Vancouver tied it in the second, and Leach fired the winner at 11:50 of the final frame. Now the playoff race could come down to the upcoming head-to-head games against Vancouver.[1692]

Victoria did precisely what they had to do in the home game, demolishing the Canucks, 6-2. There was no scoring in the first period, although the Cougars pressed hard. Chiupka, Brown, Powell, and Carmichael scored for Victoria in the second period, while Gord Hudson replied for Vancouver. Third-period goals by Leach and Haworth sealed the victory, and the home fans went home happy. Victoria was now one point ahead of Vancouver in the standings.[1693] All that changed when the teams played on the mainland. The Cougars were guilty of inconsistent play, and their effort bore little or no resemblance to that which they had produced the previous evening. On the other hand, the Canuck defence, which had been terrible in the first game, tightened up and protected their goal well. The final score of 4-2 for Vancouver tells the tale. The Canucks were back in third place.[1694] Just when things looked bad for the Cougars and their hope of a playoff berth, they came up with a masterful performance against Seattle, defeating the first-place Americans, 6-2. After surrendering the first goal early in the first period, the Cats stormed back to score six consecutive goals before giving up a late (and meaningless) one to Seattle. Carmichael led the scoring parade with two goals, while Leach, Dobbyn, Heinrich, and Davidson added singles.[1695] Two days later, in Seattle, the Americans got their revenge with a close 3-2 victory in overtime. Once again, the Cougars had built up a two-goal lead, but could not hold it and lost when former Cougar Kuzma beat Pelletier at 7:40 of extra time.[1696]

It was quite amusing to read the sports columns of the day, as the writers changed their minds on an almost daily basis about whether the Cougars would finish third in the Western-division standings. Their comments reflected the up-and-down characteristics of the team: world beaters one night and doormats the next.

The Cougars next travelled to Vancouver to play a game to replace the Boxing Day match that had been cancelled due to fog. The team seemed to be in a fog mentally, as they were thoroughly outplayed and could not even score a single goal, being shut out by the Canucks, 5-0. To make the defeat even more humiliating, the Canucks had several injuries to key players and were using some players called up from interior leagues. It was a feeble effort for Victoria when any sort of good play would have improved their playoff standing.[1697] In New Westminster, the Royals held off a furious charge in the third period to down the Cougars, 4-2. Chiupka had opened the scoring goal, but the team allowed three consecutive goals to the Royals, falling behind 3-1. Chiupka scored again in the third period but could not do it all himself. The Cougars' inability to keep the puck out of their own net was the key to the loss.[1698] After the game, Coach Kilburn expressed disappointment with two of his players (though he declined to name them), while praising the efforts of Chiupka, whom he called "the best forward I have at this time." He also announced that defenceman Heinrich would take injured forward Leach's spot in the lineup and would skate as a forward with Haworth and Carmichael.[1699]

New Westminster came to Victoria, and their agitator, Pete Durham, did not disappoint. Being heckled by fans in the south end of the rink after a particularly nasty hit on Kilburn, Durham did the unthinkable and climbed the wire to get closer to his tormentor, actually diving head first into the fans. Luckily, the heckler in question left in a hurry, and there was no serious damage to the others. Durham ended up with two minor penalties, along with two ten-minute misconducts for his actions. In the hockey game played on the ice, the Cougars won the game, 5-2. Carmichael led the scoring with a pair of goals, and Davidson, Macauley, and Anderson added another goal each.[1700][1701] In their next game, Victoria played a good game and showed their superiority over the lowly Winnipeg team. Emerging scoring star Don Chiupka scored his first hat trick of the season and added an assist, while his teammate Gord Haworth had two goals and two assists. The victory was ensured when the Cougars scored three goals in just over four-and-a-half minutes on their way to a 7-1 decision.[1702]

With a three-point lead over the Canucks, the Cougars travelled to Vancouver for a crucial game. They played reasonably well but were unable to match the Canucks in scoring, falling 7-5 in a high-scoring game. Vancouver took an early lead and never relinquished it, peppering Pelletier with thirty-four shots while Victoria could only manage seventeen at the other end. The once-comfortable cushion was now down to a single point, as it had been for most of the spring.[1703] However, as they had done numerous times before during the season, the Cougars rebounded from a bad game, this time demolishing the Americans, 7-1. As was typical with a game between these rivals, there was more action off the ice than on. In the second period, Kilburn and Amerks' goalie, Emile Francis, had a set-to in front of the net, and while this was going on, Davidson skated in from behind the goal, found the puck, and put it in the net. It took referee Andy Gurba about five minutes to defuse the situation in the ensuing fracas, and he ended up being slashed by Francis's stick. From the penalty box, Kilburn had altercations with Ray Kinasewich and Pete Wright, the latter punching Kilburn in the face. In the game itself, Kilburn scored twice with one assist, Chiupka had one goal and three assists, Anderson had three assists, and Davidson had a goal and two assists, while single goals came from Haworth, Powell, and Macauley. After the game, tempers flared again outside the Cougars' dressing-room door. Seattle player Art Hart, who just happened to be a Golden Gloves champion, wanted to attack Kilburn, but the other Cougars got their coach into the room. All the remaining players got into the melee, and it was not over until some Americans' players removed Hart from the scene. After that, cooler heads prevailed, and the incident was over.[1704][1705]

The next night, with a chance to clinch third place in the Western-division standings, the Cougars played a terrible game and lost, 8-3, to the Royals. Powell opened the scoring in the game, but that was the last time Victoria would have the lead.[1706] In what was perhaps the most important game of the year, the Cougars finally won a game on the road in Vancouver. With the 3-1 victory over the Canucks, Victoria clinched third place in the Western-division standings. Coach Kilburn led by example, scoring the opening goal. Vancouver tied the game before the end of the first period, but Anderson put the Cougars ahead in the second. Chiupka's score in the third period was the icing on the cake.[1707] In the last home game of the season, Victoria nipped the Royals in an overtime thriller. The game lead went back and forth and was tied 4-4 at the end of regular time. Goal scorers for the Cougars were Brown (with two), Macauley, and Carmichael, setting the stage for the coach to win the game after 6:01 of extra time.[1708] The 1956-57 regular season closed with a game in Seattle, where Victoria lost, 4-1, extending their streak of futility on the road. In the thirty-five road games this season, the Cougars managed to lose twenty-nine of them.[1709]

The playoff format this season had changed and now featured a first-round, best-of-three series. Victoria would play New Westminster starting on the mainland. Would the dreaded road streak continue?

As they had done most of the season, the Cougars scored the first two goals. It looked like the bad luck on the road would end, but they let the Royals back in the game and could not score even when they had a one-man advantage for a full five minutes. The game went to overtime, and it was over quickly, as Arnie Schmautz found the net behind Pelletier at thirty-three seconds, and, just like that, New Westminster had a 1-0 lead in the series.[1710] Much to the delight of the local fans, the Cougars won the second game in the series. Brown scored in the first period, and then Powell and Chiupka counted before the Royals got their lone goal. Carmichael sealed the victory with a score early in the third period, and the defence and goaltender Pelletier played very well to secure the victory that tied the series. During the game, the Royals' Pete Durham was seriously injured. He was trying to check Carmichael on a breakaway but missed the player and crashed head-first into the boards. He was transported to a local hospital and diagnosed with a broken neck. It was likely that he would never play hockey again.[1711]

In the deciding game of the series, the Royals edged the Cougars, 2-1, in overtime. The defeat magnified the troubles the club had during the season: the inability to win on the road and also the lack of success in overtime. Both factors came into play in the last game of the playoffs, and New Westminster would go on to play Seattle in the Western final, while the Cougars would go home.[1712] It was a sad end to a mediocre season. Coach Kilburn, when reflecting on the season, noted that the team had bright spots, including the emergence of Chiupka as a star, but the defence had been too inconsistent for a good winning percentage. In conclusion, Kilburn said that he wished the team had done better, both on the ice and at the gate, but he was still hoping to be involved the next season, although he knew that no decision had been made.[1713]

Lester Patrick, who had "retired" eighteen months before but returned to assist the Cougars after the death of Fred Hutchinson, decided to make his retirement permanent in mid-March. He said he would dispose of his remaining shares in the club and leave the job to younger men.[1714] As a tribute to Lester Patrick and his contribution to local hockey over more than half a century, *Victoria Daily Times* columnist Archie Wills wrote an eleven-part series. As Wills had travelled with the original Cougars in their early years, including the Stanley Cup-winning season, he was perhaps the only writer who could have given 1950s Victorians a glimpse into the man who had done so much for his adopted hometown.[1715]

The History of Professional Hockey in Victoria, BC: 1911-2011

After the defeat in the playoffs, the stockholders of the Cougars announced that they had decided to return the franchise to the league. Colin Kilburn then stepped in and led a reorganization of the team, raising $50,000 (at twenty-five dollars per share) from the local businesses and fans to keep the team afloat. The team now belonged to the community, and locals were more inclined to support what they owned. The list of shareholders is quite revealing, as it shows support from a diverse number of sources. Holding eighty shares was the Victoria Hockey Club (the former owners), while the British Columbia Electric Railway Co. Ltd. purchased forty shares, as did Lester Patrick, Harold Husband, Dr. Andy N. Reid, and Sidney Belither. Those with between twenty and thirty-nine shares included Dr. Gordon Grant, Island Broadcasting Co. Ltd., Island Decorators Co. Ltd., C. F. S. Mackenzie, George Straith Ltd., Derek C. Todd, and Victoria Press Ltd. The balance of shares belonged to everyone from wealthy businessmen to ordinary citizens who wanted to keep hockey in Victoria. The list reads like a who's who in Victoria. The Victoria Hockey Club (1957) was incorporated on August 19, 1957. Hockey would stay in the capital city.[1716]

Victoria Cougars 1956-57 team photo. From the author's collection.

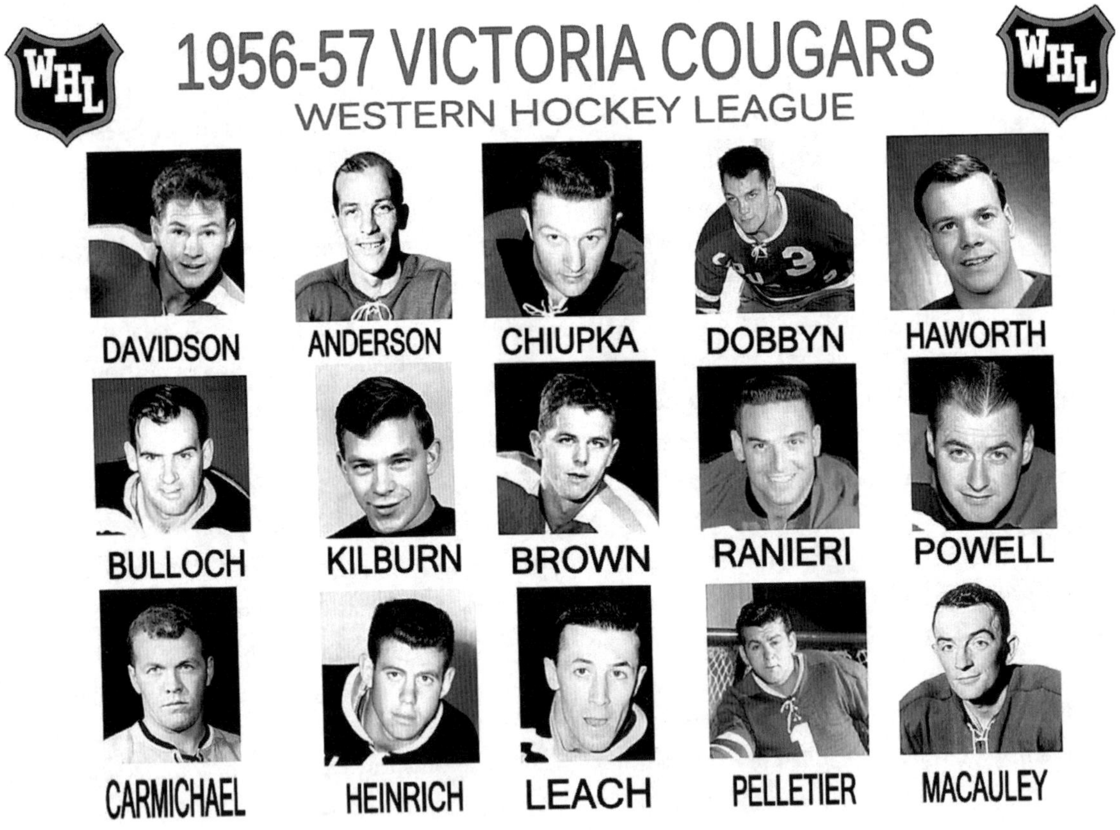

21 - THE WINTER OF DISCONTENT

The WHL had a significant change for the 1957-58 season. The Brandon Regals, who had suffered financial problems in the previous season, would now be called the Saskatoon-St. Paul Regals, and become the first ever team to have home bases in two cities in two countries. Home games would be divided equally between the two locations.[1717]

Plans for the Cougars' new season began in September when Boston assigned them veteran Nelson Bulloch and newcomer Warren Back. Both joined the training camp in Nanaimo. Also on hand were goaltenders Don Hamilton and Earl Anshelm; defencemen Carl Kaiser, Gordon Matheson, and Bob Cowan; and forwards Eddie Dorohoy, Doug Macauley, Doug Kilburn, Gordon Haworth, Gord Wilson, Fred Brown, and Larry Berg.[1718] Larry Leach was sent out by Boston and raised the roster count to sixteen. In August, fan-favourite goaltender Marcel Pelletier had been traded to Vancouver in return for Kaiser and Fred Brown, so there would be a new goaltender for the Cougars this season.[1719] After a few pre-season games, it was time for the regular season to start.

The Cougars opened their season in Seattle where the Americans shut out the young Victoria team, 2-0.[1720] The home opener was scheduled for Thanksgiving Day in the afternoon, but all was not well with Victoria Memorial Arena. Necessary repairs to the pipes under the floor were delayed, and the brine solution required twenty hours to be cooled before circulating through the pipes to create the ice surface.[1721] City staff worked over the weekend, and the ice was somewhat ready for the opener. Officials had to use bags of cracked ice to help out their ice-making equipment. The ice was placed over a bare strip at the south end of the arena and frozen with carbon-dioxide spray. Crushed ice was also used to repair the ice during the game.

"Play was delayed at the start of the second period to allow some New Westminster players to have skates re-sharpened. Poor ice made puck control and skating difficult, and the teams switched ends midway through the final period to even conditions as much as possible."[1722] In the game itself, the Royals defeated the home team, 5-2, as the wily veterans showed their skill (despite the ice conditions) and won easily.[1723] The new season was off to a miserable start, and a crushing 7-1 defeat at New Westminster led Coach Kilburn to purchase goaltender Emile Francis from the Saskatoon-St. Paul Regals to try to stop the losing. He said he had confidence in young Donnie Hamilton, but the defence was too weak to give him the support he needed. Eddie Dorohoy, who had returned to the Cougars after playing two seasons for the Seattle Americans, scored the only goal in the game.[1724]

EMILE "CAT" FRANCIS

ELECTED INTO HOCKEY HALL OF FAME 1982

Emile Francis' autograph. From the author's collection.

Emile Francis returned to Vancouver, the site of his greatest years in the WHL, and although he was now playing for Victoria, was well received. He made thirty-nine saves in a close 3-2 overtime loss to Vancouver. He barely made it to the game, as the Vancouver airport was fogged in, so he had to land in Victoria and take a ferry to the mainland. Phil Maloney scored the first goal for Vancouver on the power play, but Wilson tied it before the first period was over. Vancouver went ahead in the second, but new Cougar Blinky Boyce tied the game, sending it to overtime. A seemingly harmless shot at 8:23 bounced over Francis' shoulder and into the net. Victoria was still winless, although they were playing better hockey.[1725] Despite the good effort in the prior game, the Cougars fell back into their poor habits and lost their fifth straight game, 5-2, to Vancouver. They built up a 2-0 lead on Dorohoy goals but forgot that there were three periods in a game; they seemed to take the last one off and allowed Vancouver to score four goals to win easily.[1726] Although the Cougars had yet to win a game, the 1,500 citizens who had purchased shares in the club remained generally optimistic. There was concern about the failure of the defence to keep the puck out of their net.[1727] At a shareholders' meeting at Victoria High School, citizens asked questions about the business of running a team and planned a booster club to build more interest in the team locally.[1728] Coach Kilburn announced the acquisition of young centre Frank Milne from the American Hockey League's Cleveland Barons on a tryout basis.[1729]

Five bad minutes ruined a good effort in the next game. It was not without controversy, either. The Cougars filed a protest on a Royals' goal; they said a penalty should have been called when the New Westminster coach Hal Laycoe threw a towel on the ice. Victoria fired fifty-four shots at goaltender Bentley and came from behind three times but fell just short in a 7-6 loss.[1730] The winless streak continued with a 5-2 loss to Seattle. The Cougars were able to only dress eleven players due to an outbreak of influenza that hit the team. League president Al Leader went so far as to postpone the Cougars' next scheduled game in Vancouver, as they could not field a competitive team.[1731] The search continued for a veteran defender who could help the club, but there was no definite news from Coach Kilburn.[1732]

By the end of October, most of the team was healthy again and ready to take on the next challenge. The league decided that the game against New Westminster, where Coach Laycoe threw a towel on the ice, "would be replayed from the 7:13 mark of the third period with the score 5-4 in New Westminster's favour."[1733] After a disastrous 7-0 shut out at the hands of the Canucks, Colin Kilburn quit as coach of the team. He remained as general manager and player but yielded the coaching reins to Pat Egan, who had coached Vancouver two years before. The former NHL defender brought his defensive skills to the team at a time when they were sorely needed. Club management acknowledged that Kilburn had been expected to handle three jobs, and it had just been too much for him.[1734] On his arrival, new coach Egan met with his players as well as club management. He decided to add thirty minutes to the length of previous practices so that players would have a ninety-minute workout.[1735] Whether the extra work would produce results on the ice remained to be seen.

The Cougars finally won a hockey game when they defeated the Calgary Stampeders, 4-1, in front of an appreciative local audience. Doug Kilburn opened the scoring, and Blinky Boyce added a goal before the end of the first period. Calgary counted one goal at the start of the second frame, but Colin Kilburn replied for the Cougars. Eddie Dorohoy put the game away with a third-period score.[1736] It was Pat Egan's first victory as a coach, and the team hoped it was the first of many. However, in the next match against Seattle, the team fired thirty-five shots at the Americans' goaltender Hank Bassen but could only register three goals. As they had in many other games that season, they took an early lead but faltered in the third period and lost the game, 5-3. In Vancouver, the Cougars played hard and were unfortunate not to score the winning goal in the third period. The game went to overtime, and Orland Kurtenbach fired the winner for the Canucks at 3:49 of extra time.[1737] Having seen his new charges in action, Coach Egan set goals for the next three games, asking his players to produce at least four points. He announced that Gordie Wilson would return to the lineup from a knee injury and that Frank Milne, who had been injured in the overtime loss in Vancouver, would be out of action for at least two games.[1738]

In league news, fans would choose teams to play in the first-ever all-star game between the divisions. All proceeds of the January 9, 2017, game were directed to the WHL Player Benefit Fund, set up to assist needy hockey players. All fines collected by the league were also directed to the fund, totalling $9,000 to that date.[1739]

The league increased the player limit on clubs to fifteen, which immediately played a part in the Cougars' next game. The second win of the season came in New Westminster, where the Cougars outscored the Royals 5-3. Macauley got the team off to a 2-0 lead in the first period, and Boyce increased the lead to 3-0 before the Royals were able to score. A brief letdown let the Royals tie the game, but third-period goals by Leach and Eddie Dorohoy sealed the victory for the Cougars.[1740] The trip continued to be somewhat successful, when Victoria skated to an overtime 2-2 tie with Seattle. Again, the Cougars got off to a good start, with a 2-0 lead on goals by Boyce and Wilson, but penalties at inopportune times let the Americans tie the game.[1741] The Cougars had now earned three of the four points that their coach had asked for, but the next game against Vancouver would be a difficult one. During the game, local fans were enraged when referee Al Paradice failed to call a penalty shot in the second period, when Haworth was tripped while on a clear path to the goal. Instead of the most exciting play in hockey, the official called a minor penalty, and the Cougars could not score on the ensuing power play. The Cougars took an early 2-0 lead, but as they had done in so many other games, were unable to hold it and fell in a 4-3 defeat. Coach Egan was disappointed in his defence crew and resolved to work them harder in practice.[1742]

In a move that could only be described as strange, the Cougars (for a short period of time) owned the rights to Toronto Maple Leafs' Sid Smith, when they claimed him off the waiver wire. It was the first time in history that a minor-league team had claimed an NHL player on waivers. There was no chance that Smith would ever play in Victoria, but Manager Kilburn used the opportunity to deal with Toronto coach Billy Reay in his search for a defenceman. In return for releasing the player, Kilburn hoped to acquire a player to help.[1743]

Defensive lapses cost the Cougars dearly in their game against New Westminster. As they had so often in recent games, Victoria took a 2-0 lead on goals by Brown and Milne and led 3-1 early in the third period. However, a lack of good play in the third period let the Royals tie the score and eventually win it, 4-3, after 7:59 of overtime. Coach Egan was clearly disappointed in the poor effort defensively, and he noted that some of them "played like amateurs and if they aren't careful, they're going to be replaced by amateurs."[1744] The coach met with some of his players, and during that session, Carl Kaiser asked to be relieved of the captaincy. That job was transferred to Colin Kilburn, who was switched to play defence, with Nelson Bulloch moving to the wing position.[1745] In Vancouver, the Cougars surprised everyone and defeated the Canucks, 2-1. Even Vancouver coach Chapman praised the Victoria team's effort when he said, "The club that has given us the most trouble at home this season is

Victoria." Kilburn played well in his new position on defence, rejuvenated forward Haworth scored the two goals, and goaltender Emile Francis allowed only one goal.[1746] As Seattle's goaltender Hank Bassen had been given leave to deal with the death of his parents, young Don Hamilton was loaned to the Americans for Friday's game. In an all-too-familiar story, the Cougars got a good start with a 2-0 lead, but "played like amateurs" in the second period and let Seattle score five times to take the lead in the game. To the Cougars' credit, they did manage to score three goals of their own in the third period to tie the score but fell after 6:43 of overtime, when former Cougar Chiupka found the top of the net to give Seattle a 6-5 victory.[1747] The New Westminster Royals pounded the hapless Cougars 5-1 in the Royal City. The game was briefly tied at 1-1, but that was the end of the Victoria offence.[1748]

Victoria Cougars program 1957-58.
From the author's collection.

After the game, Steve Baliuk joined the team, and Nelson Bulloch was returned to his defence position. In a report to Cougars' shareholders, general manager Kilburn announced that the Cougars had made a profit of $1,180.20 for their first ten home games; attendance averaged 2,758, which was a little lower than the previous year, but expenses were lower, as well. Fred Brown was suspended by the club. He had been given permission to visit his ailing wife but sent a telegram that read, "In the interest of all concerned, I am retiring from professional hockey." He felt his sub-par performance was hurting the club; however, he was not the only player to play below his potential.[1749]

Next on the agenda were home-and-home games against the Canucks. In Vancouver, rookie Orland Kurtenbach sparked the home team to a 4-2 victory. Steve Baliuk played his first game with the Cougars, assisting on one goal and coming close to tying the score in the third period. Dorohoy, recently recovered from a bad case of the flu, collected five points.[1750] In Victoria, the Cougars won their game, 6-5, before 3,017 fans at Memorial Arena. After they built up a two-goal lead on scores by Macauley and Dorohoy, they surrendered two goals that tied the score, but this time, instead of wilting as they had in previous games, they poured on the offence, firing four goals in the second period to build their lead to 6-2. Vancouver scored three times in the last frame but could not tie the score.

Next, Victoria travelled to Seattle, where they upended the Americans, 4-2. Dorohoy was again the star of the show, with two goals and an assist.[1751] It was the first two-game winning streak for the Cougars that season, and they hoped to continue on this productive path.

Despite the lack of success by the Cougars as a team, Eddie Dorohoy was quietly closing in on a league record. He started the season in second place in all-time league scoring and was now only four points away from the lead. If he continued at his recent pace, he could set a new record in the next game or two.[1752] He came very close to that achievement in the next game, as the Cougars upended the Royals 6-3. Dorohoy had a goal and two assists to move within one point of the record. This was undoubtedly the best home game of the season and increased the winning streak to three games. General manager Kilburn advised that he had been in contact with Doug Anderson, who had retired at the end of the previous season and had convinced him to return to the team.[1753] The Cougars extended their winning streak to four games with a 9-6 defeat of the Americans. Victoria outplayed their opponents for the first two periods, building up an 8-1 lead before they collapsed in the final frame and surrendered five goals to make the 3,805 fans in the Memorial Arena very nervous. Dorohoy not only matched the old record, but he also blew through it, scoring three goals and adding an assist.[1754]

After a period of success on the ice, the Cougars started on a gruelling schedule of four games in five nights. First was an encounter in New Westminster, where the home team edged the Cougars, 4-3. Victoria missed several chances to win the game when they were unable to find the net on breakaways. Macauley scored twice for the Cougars, with Boyce adding a single.[1755] Two days later, the Cougars lost another one-goal game, 4-3, to Vancouver. Spotting the Canucks a four-goal lead, Victoria mounted a furious finish that just fell short.[1756] In the return engagement in Victoria, the game was as tight as it could be. The teams scored a goal each in the first period, and there was no more scoring until the 5:42 mark of overtime when Jackie McLeod scored to give Vancouver a 2-1 victory.[1757] The Cougars had lost their last three games but by one goal each time. With a bit of finish around the net, the results could have been victories rather than defeats.

Right in the middle of the season, the ice was removed from the arena for a bingo program. To keep his players in game shape, Coach Egan resorted to dry-land training at nearby Central Park. He led the team in calisthenics and simple soccer moves.[1758] The next game against New Westminster was "Shrine Hockey Night." The Shrine Band provided musical entertainment while the husband-and-wife team of Mr. and Mrs. Clem Patterson demonstrated figure skating. All proceeds benefitted Shrine charities.[1759] In the game, the Royals snatched a 3-1 win from the Cougars. Poor marksmanship hurt Victoria, and New Westminster goaltender Bentley was at the top of his game, as well.[1760] The Cougar manager announced that Warren Back was reassigned to Kingston of the Ontario senior amateur league to make way for Bud Syverson acquired from Calgary.[1761]

Saturday night, December 21, 1957, was the Cougars' Christmas party. Fans were able to win one of twenty hams or turkeys, there were 500 bags of candy for the kids, and Dean Pan Pete, a clown formerly with the Ringling Bros. Circus, entertained the crowd during the game.[1762] Unfortunately, the action on the ice was not of high quality. Linesman Laurie Ludlow was pressed into service as a referee at the last minute, and his inexperience was evident throughout the game. The Americans built up a 6-0 lead before the Cougars even hit the score sheet, so the result was clear early. However, the decision of the official not to call penalties just after the beginning of the game led to a riotous free-for-all in the third period. The Americans' goaltender Bassen slashed Cougars forward Leach and both benches cleared for an altercation that lasted twenty-five minutes. Although league rules called for players who left the bench to enter a fight to receive misconduct penalties, the referee chose not to enforce that rule.[1763][1764] It was certainly not the type of game that youngsters should have to view and definitely not a display of good hockey.

Christmas Day was not a good day for the Cougars. They played in New Westminster, where the Royals built up a 4-1 lead and held on for a decisive 6-3 victory. The game was very chippy, with several outbreaks between players. In the Boxing Day match, the Royals had a 2-0 lead before the game was seven minutes old. Try as they might, the Cougars could only score once and lost another game by a single goal. This contest was also cluttered with penalties that disrupted the flow of the play. Dorohoy got into a confrontation with referee Lloyd Gilmour and was penalized for his actions.[1765] The Cougars were pleased that Dorohoy would likely be able to play in the next game, as league president Al Leader had not yet received a report from the referee so could not decide on further discipline.[1766]

The Canucks came to Victoria for a December 28 game, and much to the delight of 3,042 local fans, the Cougars won the game in a 5-0 shutout, the first of the season for Emile Francis. The scoring punch came from Kilburn, Dorohoy, Macauley, Milne, and Baliuk. In the final game of 1957, Victoria travelled to Seattle, where the Americans won the game, 3-1.[1767]

Looking back on the first half of the 1957-58 season, there were some encouraging elements. First, there was the club itself, which had survived by becoming a community-owned operation.[1768] Although the Cougars' record had been dismal—nine wins, twenty-four losses, and one tie—there had been some highlights. Eddie Dorohoy set a new record for total points in the league, and several of the younger players were beginning to find their stride. The team looked forward to 1958 (British Columbia's centennial year) with hope and anticipation.

Unfortunately, the season continued with turmoil both on and off the ice. Of the remaining thirty-six games of the season, the Cougars won only nine and tied one. The once-successful team had fallen on hard times, indeed. In the first game of the new year, the Cougars scored first but gave up three second-period goals to the Americans and ended up losing 5-2. After the game, Coach Egan was furious with his team and said that it was no longer possible to blame "bad luck." He added that, if the club had more players available, he would replace four of his team immediately. However, he did not list the names of the players who were on the hot seat.[1769] On the player front, the Cats acquired John Yanchuk on loan from New Westminster, but Kilburn aggravated a groin injury in the previous game and might not be able to play.[1770] In Vancouver, the team lost its eighth game in a row, 5-3. Again, it was the inability to play well in the second period that led to the defeat.[1771] Even a line juggling by the coach could not inspire the team to play a full game, and they fell, 3-1, to New Westminster for their ninth consecutive loss. Defenceman Clare "Rags" Raglin was signed as a free agent after his release by the Saskatoon-St. Paul Regals. There were no WHL games scheduled until the end of the week, due to the all-star game in Calgary on January 8. Kilburn and Dorohoy were chosen to the Coast-division team, and the general manager took the opportunity to scout other players from Alberta who might be available to the Cougars.[1772] The game featured close, exciting play with great goaltending. The Coast All-Stars won the game, 5-3, over the Prairie All-Stars.[1773]

In league meetings, held in conjunction with the all-star game, league officials agreed to a strict enforcement of connected play stoppages, and more movement of officials between the two divisions, and adopted a new playoff formula. This season, the top teams in each division would compete in a best-of-seven series for the Governor's Cup; the second and third teams would play a best-of-five series, with the winners of those two series playing each other in another series, with the winner earning the right to play the Governor's Cup winner in a league final. Coastal teams had been playing with a fifteen-man limit for some time, while the Prairies favoured the twelve-man limit. This was causing problems in inter-divisional play, so the Prairie teams were allowed to increase their rosters, but until they were able to, any teams they were playing had to reduce their own rosters, so that each team had the same number of players.[1774]

In local hockey news, Cec Rawlings and Cec Rhodes donated the Wally Smith Memorial Trophy to be presented at the end of the season, to the Cougar "best combining playing ability and sportsmanship." Players worthy of consideration included Gord Wilson, with twenty-two points and zero penalty minutes; Doug Macauley, with twenty-four points and six penalty minutes; Gord Haworth, with twenty-three points and twenty-two penalty minutes; and Blinky Boyce, with twenty-five points and six penalty minutes.[1775]

Coach Egan announced the release of Yanchuk, although he would be available on a recall basis. Syverson was moved from defence to forward to shake up the team.[1776] The juggling seemed to have had little effect on the Cougars, as they dropped a game in Vancouver, 4-1. Former Cougar goaltender Pelletier was the star of the game for the Canucks, stopping all shooters but Syverson.[1777] More than a hundred New Westminster fans travelled to Victoria for the next game. Pete Durham, disabled during the playoffs in the spring, dropped the puck for a ceremonial face-off. The Cougars took a 3-2 lead into the third period, but, once again, their inability to play a full sixty-minute game came back to haunt them. They gave the Royals two third-period goals and the 4-3 victory.[1778]

However, the big news of the day was not the game result. The page-one headline screamed, "Hockey Board Ousts Kilburn as Manager." Club president Dr. Andy N. Reid said the board took the action to "ensure the future of good hockey in Victoria," citing the lack of the team's ability to play up to its "paper strength" in the WHL.[1779] The news took the shareholders by surprise, and heated debates were held all over town. What disturbed some fans was that it was Kilburn who had led the fight to keep the Cougars in Victoria, serving as chair of the fundraising committee, and the fact that he had not had much luck in obtaining new players that season. Some of the directors apparently felt that better leadership could have kept the community-owned Cougars in a contending position. Treasurer Fred Mackenzie was appointed as interim general manager.[1780] For his part, Colin Kilburn resolved not to play for the team under the current board of directors. Kilburn said that some of the directors were not notified of the meeting in time to attend, and he expressed disbelief that some members felt he had not given a hundred percent in all his dealings with the club.[1781] The directors called a general meeting to be held as soon as all shareholders could be notified by mail. The main reason cited for the dissatisfaction with Kilburn centred around the deal that had sent Marcel Pelletier to Vancouver.[1782] After a discussion with Coach Egan, Colin Kilburn agreed to play for the club until he could be traded elsewhere.[1783]

In the game against Seattle, former Cougar Chiupka was the star of the game in a 4-3 Seattle win. Fans throughout the Memorial Arena held signs supporting Kilburn—evidence of the affection they held for him.[1784] Several WHL clubs were interested in obtaining the Kilburn's services; Vancouver, Seattle, New Westminster, Calgary, and Edmonton all submitted potential deals.[1785] The next morning, Mackenzie announced that Colin had been sent to Edmonton in return for centre Dennis Olson and winger Tom McCarthy, both twenty-three years old. Kilburn was back where his hockey career had started.[1786] [1787]

The new players did not arrive in time for the game in New Westminster, where the Cougars dropped a 6-3 decision to the Royals. However, they were both in the lineup in Seattle as the Cougars finally got their first victory of 1958: a 4-1 decision over the Americans. Olson made his presence felt, scoring the first goal of the game at 6:49 of the first period, and assisting on the 2-0 counter by Haworth. The other newcomer, McCarthy, had an assist on the 3-1 goal by Wilson. Dorohoy completed the scoring. Emile Francis made twenty-five stops, allowing only one goal by Don Chiupka.[1788] Victoria fans flocked to the arena to see Colin Kilburn with his new team. A record crowd of 5,443 watched the Flyers defeat the Cougars, 5-4. Colin Kilburn scored the first goal of the game on the power play, and fans applauded, but for the most part, they were cheering for their hometown Cougars.[1789]

The club made another trade, sending Frank Milne and Blinky Boyce to Seattle in exchange for Art Hart. They felt his speed would help the Cougars win on a more consistent basis.[1790] The trade seemed to have injected new energy into the club, as the Cougars shut out the Royals, 2-0, in their next home game. The defence played a stellar game in front of goaltender Francis and made fewer mistakes than usual. Egan and Dorohoy provided all the scoring Victoria needed.[1791]

The Cougars received good news when Doug Anderson returned to the team after his "retirement." He played on a line between Hart and Baliuk.[1792] The Cougars won that game against Seattle, 7-6. Scorers in regulation time were Baliuk, Raglin, Macauley, McCarthy, Haworth, and Dorohoy. Gordon Wilson scored the winning goal at 1:01 of overtime to give the team its third win in four games.[1793] Unfortunately, the improved play came to an end in a game against Vancouver. According to Coach Egan, the team played like a group of strangers. There were several individual standouts, but team play was conspicuous by its absence in the 4-3 loss to the Canucks.[1794] The Winnipeg Warriors played a game at Victoria, and the teams battled to a 6-6 overtime tie. It was an exciting affair, with plenty of goals scored, and the 4,466 local fans cheered when Gordie Wilson scored the tying goal with only forty-four seconds left in regular time.[1795] The Cougars then went on a four-game losing streak: 6-1 in Vancouver,[1796] 7-2 in New Westminster (in what was described as a listless effort),[1797] a 5-4 Valentine's Day loss in Seattle,[1798] and a narrow 1-0 loss to the Canucks. The Cougars lost the services of Stan Baliuk when he broke his ankle—just the news the club did not need.[1799]

The Cougars won their first game in ten days when they defeated New Westminster at the Memorial Arena. There were only 1,524 fans in the stands when the Cougars overcame a 2-0 deficit to win the game, 4-3. There was no scoring in the first period; the Royals scored a couple early in the second period, but Haworth and Macauley tied the score by the end of that frame. The Royals took the lead at 4:45 of the third, but two goals by Hart gave the home team the victory.[1800] The next three games were not successful, but each had its own brand of excitement. In Vancouver, the teams battled in a rough game that escalated to a full-scale brawl in the third period. It started with Art Hart and Rob Robinson but quickly grew to the point that police were needed to restore order. Despite the heroic efforts of Emile Francis in goal, the Cougars lost the game, 4-3.[1801] The next game was a 3-1 loss to Seattle at the Memorial Arena. Haworth scored the first goal of the game, but that was all the offence the Cougars could manage. The next night, the Cougars were snowed under by Seattle, who fired ten goals while Victoria could only manage five. McCarthy had two goals, while Wilson, Dorohoy, and Yanchuk added singles.[1802]

Due to the Canadian curling championship in Victoria, the game originally scheduled for February 28 was moved to February 24. The change worked well for the Cougars, as they defeated the Royals 8-6. Now that they were mathematically eliminated from playoff contention, Victoria could only play the role of spoiler. New Cougar Barrie Ross, who was signed as a free agent after his release by the Canucks, scored his first goal as a Cougar. McCarthy had two goals, while Dorohoy, Kaiser, Yanchuk, Bulloch, and Macauley had a goal each.[1803] However, it would be three more games before there would be another victory. During that stretch, the Cougars were badly outplayed and outscored. They closed out February 1958 at Queen's Park Arena in New Westminster, where the Royals pounded them, 9-3.[1804]

It did not get any better in March, as the Cougars again lost to the Royals, this time by a score of 10-6. Left behind as the team embarked on their Prairie trip were Eddie Dorohoy and Nelson Bulloch, who were suspended by the team for "conduct detrimental to professional hockey."[1805] Although the newspaper account said that there would be a statement in a few days, no details of the suspensions were ever released.

The first stop on the Prairie swing was in Winnipeg. The Cougars got off to a 3-0 start, but after that, the wheels fell off. The Warriors scored eleven of the next twelve goals to win the game easily, 11-4. Roster-addition Clare Wakshinski, from Penticton, picked up his first professional point with an assist on the third Victoria goal.[1806] In Saskatoon, the team picked up a rare road victory, with a 6-5 decision over the Regals. Olson and Macauley hammered home two goals each for the Cougars, with Haworth and Wilson rounding out the scoring.[1807] The team then travelled to Edmonton, where they faced former Cougar Colin Kilburn, who managed to score the winning goal in a 5-4 Flyer victory. Former-Flyer Olson notched two goals for his new team, and Wakshinski had his first goal as a Cougar; Kaiser scored the other goal.[1808] The Prairie swing ended in Calgary, where the visitors dominated the first period but could not score. The Stampeders took a 2-0 lead into the second period and cruised to an easy 5-2 victory.[1809]

For the next home game against Saskatoon, the Cougars had to reduce their playing roster to twelve, as the Regals had retained the twelve-man limit that had been abolished at the league meeting. Coach Egan decided to use two forward lines: Olson between Anderson and Haworth, and Wilson between McCarthy and Macauley, Egan and Yanchuk were one defence pairing, while Kaiser and Raglin were the other. Either Ross or Hart would be the twelfth man.[1810] The Regals scored the first goal of the game, but McCarthy tied it before the end of the first period. Haworth put Victoria ahead, only to have Saskatoon-St. Paul tie it up again. Kaiser had the only goal of the third period, and it proved to be the winner in a 3-2 win.[1811] The Cougars won a second consecutive game four days later against Vancouver. Jim Powers scored four goals for the Canucks, becoming the second player to notch four goals in a game this year. Unfortunately for his team, Victoria scored seven goals to win the game: Gordie Wilson had a hat trick, while other goals were scored by Ross, Anderson, McCarthy, and Wakshinski. It was one of the better games played in Memorial Arena that season.[1812]

The March 19 game was a special day for several reasons. First, the Royals and Cougars would replay the last portion of the game that had been protested, starting at 7:13 of the third period with the score 5-4 for New Westminster. There was a regularly scheduled game, and it was "Pete Durham Night." The Cougar management donated $250 to the fund, and the Cougar Fan club added another $100. In addition, fans would be able to donate to help Durham, who had suffered a serious injury in the playoffs the previous season when he went head-first into the boards—a "hat" would be passed around the stands during the game.[1813] Winger McCarthy was ordered to report to the Providence Reds of the American Hockey League, and two players were brought in from the Nelson Maple Leafs. Jim Pilla and Dave Stewart were added to the roster for the rest of the season.[1814] In game action, the protested game was replayed, and the Royals won the game, 7-5. The Royals also won the regular game, outscoring Victoria, 3-2. Despite a furious effort in the third period, the Cougars were not able to tie the game. A total of $562.28 was raised to help Pete Durham.[1815]

In the next game, young Clare Wakshinski scored once and added two assists in the Cougars' 4-3 overtime win over the visiting Americans. Emile Francis was a star in the nets, stopping twenty-five shots. Little did the club know that this would be their last victory of a disastrous season.[1816] The next game was in New Westminster, on their version of "Pete Durham Night." Donations for the semi-paralyzed player came from most professional hockey leagues and fans. Durham received a cheque for $5,000 and several gifts in a ceremony between periods. The Cougars were generous in the game, too, blowing a 3-0 lead and losing the match, 6-4.[1817] The Vancouver Canucks won both games of a home-and-home series against Victoria. In Vancouver, they won 5-4, and in Victoria, the Canucks prevailed, 6-5.[1818] In the final game of the regular season, the hometown Seattle Americans defeated the Cougars, 6-3.[1819]

The worst season in Cougar history was finally over. In a full seventy-game schedule, the Cougars had set five new team records during the year: the most losses (50), the fewest victories (18), the fewest home victories (12), the most home losses (22), and the lowest point total (38). Although Eddie Dorohoy had been suspended for the last twelve games of the season, he still had the best scoring season of his career, with thirty-four goals, adding forty-one assists, to finish in eighth place in league scoring.[1820]

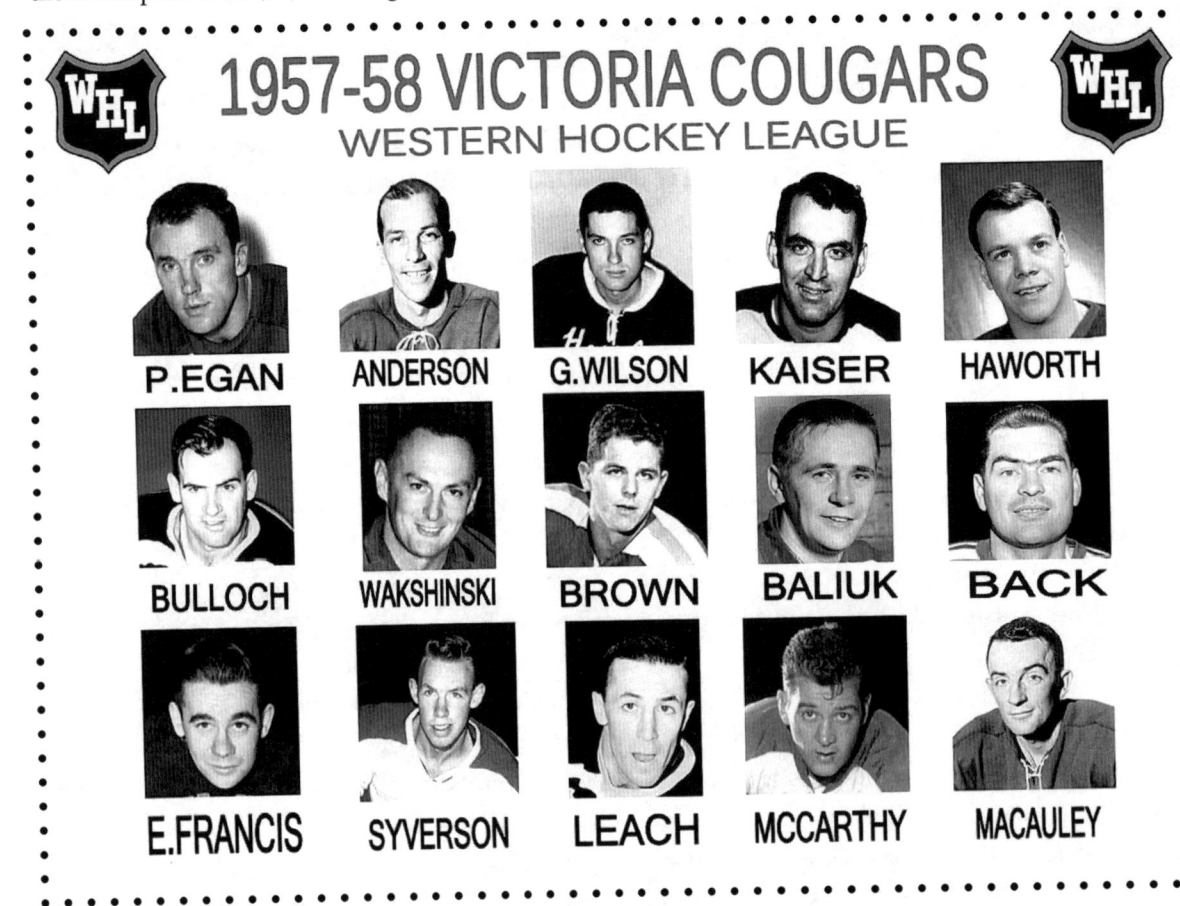

Victoria Cougars 1957-58 team photo. From the author's collection.

22 - NOWHERE TO GO BUT UP

After the worst season in the Cougars' history, the locals hoped there would be a much-improved group of players in the new season. Local media reported every possible player considered for the team, as everyone knew that changes were necessary. Clare Wakshinski, who had played briefly for the club at the end of the last season, was due to report to training camp, although other teams wanted his services, as well.[1821] The next rumour concerned Jack Bionda, well known in lacrosse circles, who had played for the Boston Bruins the previous season. His rugged play would certainly add punch to the listless defence, but he would have to be waived through the NHL before Victoria could purchase his rights.[1822] Nanaimo lacrosse player Skip McKay was invited to training camp on a tryout contract.[1823] When camp opened in Nelson on September 27, the roster included Doug Anderson, Doug Macauley, Al Nicholson, Don Blackburn, Jean-Marc Picard, Skip McKay, Barry Zajak, Gordie Matheson, Doug Stewart, Frank Milne, George Ford, Murray Wilkie, Enio Sclisizzi, Jim Pilla, Carl Forster, Art Stone, Gord Garrant, and Marcel Pelletier.[1824] Defender Lionel Repka was acquired from Seattle.[1825] Dave Rimstad was loaned from Edmonton, and Carl Kaiser arrived in camp.[1826] The team played one exhibition game against the Trail Smoke Eaters, losing 3-2. Then it was time to come back to the coast to start the season in Vancouver.[1827] Coach Egan announced that defenders Jim "Red Eye" Hay and Don McLeod had joined the team. Forward lines were expected to be Ford, Anderson, and Wilkie; Sclisizzi, Haworth, and Blackburn; and Baliuk, Nicholson, and Macauley, with Warshinski as an extra forward.[1828]

Enio Sclisizzi as a Cougar. Photo courtesy Ernie Fitzsimmons.

Gord Haworth as a Cougar. Photo courtesy Ernie Fitzsimmons.

The 1958-59 season opened with a narrow 3-2 loss in Vancouver. The game turned in the Canucks' favour when defenceman Picard was injured in the first minute, putting pressure on the remaining three defenders. George Ford scored the two goals for Victoria.[1829] The Calgary Stampeders were the visitors as the Cougars opened their home season with a Thanksgiving Day matinee. Former Cougar Eddie Dorohoy, who had been traded during the off-season to Calgary, led his new team to a 5-3 victory. Victoria had an early two-goal lead when Al Nicholson scored both counters within thirty-seven seconds, but the depleted defence corps could not hold the powerful Stamps off the scoresheet.[1830] In preparation for the next home game against Vancouver, Coach Egan shuffled his forward lines, putting George Ford, Clare Wakshinski, and Murray Wilkie together.[1831] The tactic seemed to work, as the Cougars won their first game of the season, upending the Canucks 5-3. Haworth and Sclisizzi scored two goals each, and Ford added a single (his fourth of the young season).

The next match was the first Sunday professional hockey game played in Vancouver. It is uncertain if the 2,000 local fans enjoyed the game, but the Cougars supporters did, as Victoria won 5-4 when Stan Baliuk scored after 5:24 of overtime.[1832] The winning streak reached three games when Victoria trounced New Westminster, 7-3, behind the two-goal efforts of Sclisizzi and Baliuk, with singles added by Ford, Haworth, and Macauley[1833] The Cougars gained a 5-5 tie in New Westminster, to run their unbeaten streak to four. In this game, the team came back from a 2-0 deficit to earn the single point.[1834] For the first time in years, the Cougars had a chance to move into first place in the league standings when they entertained the Seattle Totems, formerly known as the Americans. However, it was not to be, as the league-leading Totems knocked off Victoria, 4-2. The speed of the Seattle team proved to be too much for the Cougars, and it became apparent why the Totems were leading the league.[1835] The Edmonton Flyers then invaded Memorial Arena and shut out the Cougars, 4-0. Victoria played well in the second period, but in the third, managed only two shots on goal.[1836] That lack of performance was not the way to win games. Lines were shuffled once again before a game in Seattle, resulting in a 3-2 Cougar victory. Kaiser put Victoria on the scoreboard first, but the Totems tied the game before the end of the first period. After a scoreless second frame, Seattle took the lead early in the third period, but Blackburn tied it shortly thereafter with his first professional goal, and Macauley put the Cougars ahead to stay at 14:12.[1837]

Victoria got its first look at the new franchise in the league when they travelled to Spokane to play the Flyers,[1838] and emerged on the wrong end of a 6-1 score. Only a goal by McLeod spoiled a shutout for Emile Francis, now playing goal for the Flyers.[1839] The Cougars received good news on

November 4, 1958, when the Springfield Indians (AHL) loaned young defenceman Ted Harris to the team for cash.[1840] Marcel Pelletier recorded his first shutout of the season when the Cougars squeaked by the Saskatoon Quakers 1-0. It was a real goaltenders' duel with Lucien Deschenes giving up only one goal (to Macauley), but that was enough for him to lose the game. There was bad news on the injury front, as McLeod suffered a cartilage injury when he collided with Bill Bucyk behind the Saskatoon goal in the final period.[1841] The poor ice at the south end of the Memorial Arena was the site of another injury, this time to Vancouver's ace scorer Phil Maloney. Doug Macauley led the Cougars to a 3-3 tie with two goals, including the tying marker in the last period.[1842]

With a 5-5-2 record, the Cougars embarked on their first Prairie swing. The first game in Winnipeg was a heartbreaking overtime loss to the Warriors. Victoria was unable to hold a three-goal lead, letting the Warriors tie the score and surrendering the winning goal, by former NHL player Bill Mosienko, after 8:42 of extra time.[1843] The rest of the Prairie road trip was a disaster, as the Cougars lost consecutive games to Saskatoon, Edmonton, and Calgary. The Quakers scored the first three goals, then withstood a furious Victoria surge in the third period to escape with a 3-2 victory.[1844] In Edmonton, the Cougars came close but failed to score with the goaltender removed for the extra attacker, and the Flyers scored into an empty net to seal a 5-3 victory.[1845] Calgary dominated their game from the opening whistle, skating to an easy 5-1 win. Coach Egan was disappointed in the results of the trip but was encouraged by the strong play of Stan Baliuk.[1846]

The team came home, tired from their long train trip, and played Edmonton before a disappointing crowd of 1,790 fans in Memorial Arena. The young Flyers showed more finish around the net and emerged with a 4-2 win.[1847] The Cougars were buoyed by the news that Gordie Wilson would be returning to the club after two months of negotiations with Eddie Shore of the Springfield Indians.

The team would need all the help it could get, as the next ten days of the schedule would be hectic, with six games before the second Prairie swing of the season.[1848]

In league news, the talk was of the possibility of a franchise for Portland. A new exposition recreation centre was being built at the Rose City at the cost of $7 million, and it was likely that one of the smaller teams would be transferred there if all conditions were met.[1849]

Back in league play, Victoria and Vancouver played a weekend home-and-home series. In Victoria, the teams played to a 2-2 overtime tie. Sclisizzi scored both goals for the Cougars. On Sunday in Vancouver, Victoria played one of their best games of the season, as they shut out the Canucks 1-0, behind the skillful goaltending of Marcel Pelletier and the timely scoring of Baliuk. The three points put the Cougars in third place in the Western-division standings.[1850] At home against New Westminster, Pelletier and Baliuk again starred as the Cougars shut out the Royals 2-0. Baliuk had the first goal, and Ford added insurance. Pelletier notched his second consecutive shutout in an impressive display of skill.[1851] However, the shutout streak came to a crashing end when Victoria travelled to New Westminster. The Royals dominated in all phases of the game, crushing the Cougars 11-3.[1852] The team rebounded well against Seattle, as George Ford scored three goals (the last into an empty net) in a 4-3 victory. This was the third win in the previous five games, and it moved the Cougars into third place in the Western standings.[1853]

Next on the agenda was the second Prairie road trip. The Cougars hoped they would have better results than they had on the first one. In Saskatoon, the home team emerged victorious, 4-1, as their goaltender Duschenes played a skillful game, stopping all Victoria shooters except Anderson.[1854] Two days later in Winnipeg, Ford and Blackburn scored two goals each, and Marcel Pelletier again sparkled in the nets, as the Cougars defeated the Warriors, 4-3.[1855] The next night, the Cats lost a 5-4 heartbreaker to Edmonton in overtime, despite Ford scoring two more goals.[1856] Gordie Wilson flew to Calgary to play in the next game. He had reported to camp out of shape, and Coach Egan refused to play him until he was in game condition.[1857] The Cougars, playing their third game in three nights, ran out of steam and fell 6-2. In the second period, the Stampeders scored four goals in 3:25 of play to salt away the victory.[1858]

Now it was time to play at home. After some well-deserved rest, the Cougars played their first home game against the Western Hockey League's newest team, the Spokane Flyers. For that game, Coach Egan put Haworth, Baliuk, and Nicholson (his top point-getter) on a single line, and it paid dividends as they figured in three of the team's five goals. Although the defence had a few lapses, they played well enough for the Cougars to record a 5-3 victory.[1859] The next encounter, against Winnipeg, was also successful. The Cats played one of their best games of the year, building up a three-goal lead, then withstanding a Warrior push in the third period, to emerge victorious, 4-3. Wilson scored twice for Victoria, Ford added his fourteenth of the season, and Baliuk added the final score.[1860]

Two games on the road did not go well for Victoria. First, Spokane took advantage of sloppy defensive play and, led by Al Johnson and Ching Johnson, skated to a 7-4 decision over the Cats. The loss was the tenth road loss in twelve games that season.[1861] Two days later in Seattle, the Cougars fell again—this time, 5-2. The real problem in this game was that Victoria took too many penalties and was unable to keep the Totems' power play off the scoresheet.[1862] On Boxing Day 1958, the Cougars entertained New Westminster in an afternoon match and sent 3,212 fans home happy when they outlasted the Royals, 6-4. Doug Anderson played his best game of the season, notching the winning goal and adding an assist, but it was his defensive work with Doug Macauley that made him the star of the game. They often had to bail out defencemen who neglected to play their positions.[1863] Fans could not understand how the team could be so successful at home yet be a disaster on the road. If the Cougars could not find a solution to this problem, they would not go far in the playoffs—if they even made them. The next evening, the Cats played in New Westminster and won that game, 5-2. They fell behind, 2-0, then scored five straight goals to take the victory. Sharpshooters were Haworth, Wilson, Macauley, Ford, and Baliuk. Goaltender Pelletier received an assist on the goal by Ford.

On Sunday afternoon, the Cougars again came from behind, this time against Vancouver. Danny Belisle scored for the Canucks in the second period, but Nicholson tied the game early in the third frame, and Baliuk found the back of the net just fifty-one seconds later to end all scoring.[1864] At the end of 1958, Stan Baliuk had climbed into a tie for the league scoring lead with Guyle Fielder. He was enjoying his best professional season since breaking his leg at the end of the 1957-58 season.[1865]

In league business, Hal Laycoe, coach of the New Westminster Royals, announced that his club was heading for a $50,190 loss that year and noted, "unless fan support improves, I will be looking for a job." He cited major issues with Saturday home games conflicting with NHL telecasts on the same night, and a shorter schedule, with thirty-two home games that year compared to thirty-five the previous year. The travel was what was killing the financial bottom line, and this was not restricted to New Westminster but also affected all league teams. His closing comment was this: "Travelwise, we have an NHL operation on a WHL budget. It's impossible."[1866]

The league listened to the complaints from the Western clubs and promised to look into a return to a seventy-game schedule. League president Al Leader noted that "the WHL's twenty-percent fund, which saw each of the five Coast clubs contributing twenty percent of home games [revenue] to a common fund, is continuing this season to aid clubs having financial difficulties."[1867] Also up for discussion was a request from the Quebec League that the

Edinburgh Cup series be revived. The WHL teams did not feel that the Quebec league was of the same calibre, and thought that (if there were to be any such series) it should be between the WHL and the AHL. In addition, the timing of the series would not be beneficial, as it conflicted with Stanley Cup playoffs and the start of baseball season.[1868]

The year 1959 did not start well for the Victoria Cougars. They travelled to New Westminster, where they lost 4-2 to end their road unbeaten streak. According to Coach Egan, they had put forth a great effort but had been unable to put the puck in the net.[1869] Next on the agenda were two games in Spokane. They lost the first, 3-1, with Wilson counting the only goal.[1870] The next game was unusual, as it was a "double game" in which the winner would receive two victories and the loser would have two losses. This situation had occurred as the Spokane team had been unable to book the three additional dates they needed for home games. Here was a golden opportunity for the Cougars to pick up four points in one game. However, they could not rise to the occasion and lost the game, 5-4. As they had in many games that season, the Cats fell behind 2-0 before Harris scored. The team put up a fierce fight in the third period, with a rally that fell just short. The double win for Spokane brought the Flyers to within one point of the Cougars in the standings.[1871] The Cats would be glad to get home where they had had a good record in recent weeks.

Playing in the friendly confines of the Memorial Arena, the Cougars regained their scoring touch and won a thrilling overtime game over Spokane. Although goaltender Francis disputed the winning goal, saying he had the puck under control and it had not crossed the line, the goal judge did not agree. Trailing 2-1 going into the third period, the Cougars rallied, and Haworth tied the score at 3-3, with under five minutes left. That set the stage for the controversial tally, scored by Baliuk at the fifty-eight-second mark of extra time. The only downside to the game was an eye injury to Gordie Wilson.[1872][1873] In their only road match out of the next ten games on the schedule. Victoria took the New Westminster Royals to overtime and, again, managed to win. Trailing 5-1 in the second period, the Cougars got their act together, scoring four straight goals to end the period in a 5-5 tie. After a scoreless third period, the game went to extra time, in which Nicholson fired the winning goal after 1:58. Although falling behind was not the way the coach wanted the team to play, he was pleased with the comeback.[1874]

Victoria then played their next eight games at home, where they had a decent record. If they were going to make a serious play for a high playoff position, this would be the opportune time. Unfortunately, things did not go according to plan, and the team won only two games, lost five, and tied one.[1875] The first was a 5-3 loss to New Westminster. Despite facing a goaltender playing his first professional game, the team was unable to cash in on their chances, and the defensive lapses cost them dearly. After the game, Dave Rimstad was released to Seattle.[1876] Next, Al Nicholson assisted on three goals as the Cougars tied Spokane, 4-4. Anderson was unable to play due to the flu, and Baliuk (the team's leading goal-scorer) was injured during the game.[1877] Coach Egan announced that Murray Wilkie had been traded to the Calgary Stampeders for Bruce Lea; both were left-wingers.[1878] High-scoring Seattle came to town and shut out Victoria 3-0 behind the excellent goaltending of Bev Bentley. Pelletier played well in the Cougar net and had little chance on any of the pucks that beat him.[1879]

When Saskatoon came to town, the Cougars played before a sparse crowd of 1,596 and bested the Quakers 3-1. Nicholson scored two goals, and Haworth added one. Fred Hucul broke up Pelletier's bid for a shutout.[1880] However, Victoria lost the next two games: 6-2 to Edmonton with Doug Anderson counting the only goals for the Cougars,[1881] and 4-1 to Seattle where Ford was the only Cougar to find the net. Fans were beginning to wonder what had happened to the team that had done so well at home earlier in the season.[1882]

When Calgary invaded the Memorial Arena for the next game, bringing with them former Cougar star Eddie Dorohoy, Victoria remembered how to play good hockey and defeated the Stampeders, 5-2. Not only did the victory enhance the Cougars' playoff hopes, but it put to an end the visitors' sixteen-game winning streak. The largest crowd of the season turned out to watch Cougar players check their opponents into the ice. The coach's plan was to stop Dorohoy, and it worked, as Doug Anderson marked him on every play and Eddie had no points at all. Nicholson continued his scoring with two goals, and Macauley, Hay, and Forhan added the others. Ford strained an abdominal muscle halfway through the game and had to leave, reducing the scoring power of the home team.[1883] The referee was injured near the end of the next game against Winnipeg. Bing Jukes was clipped in the head when the Warriors' Bill Folk swung his stick at Al Nicholson and missed. The referee was knocked unconscious and needed four stitches in his head, finishing the game with blood running down his back. In the hockey portion of the game, Hynes had four goals for Winnipeg to lead his team to victory. Cougar marksmen were Blackburn and Forhan, both with two goals.[1884]

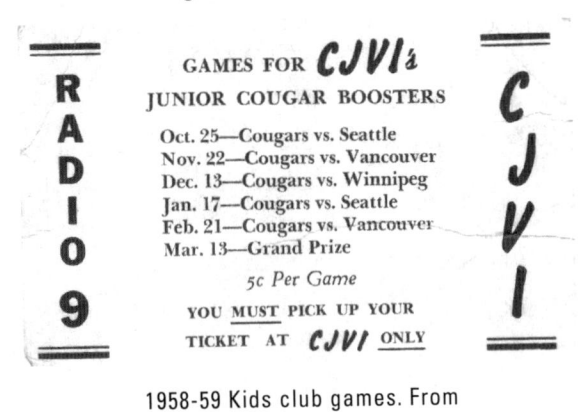

GAMES FOR CJVI's JUNIOR COUGAR BOOSTERS
RADIO 9 — CJVI

Oct. 25—Cougars vs. Seattle
Nov. 22—Cougars vs. Vancouver
Dec. 13—Cougars vs. Winnipeg
Jan. 17—Cougars vs. Seattle
Feb. 21—Cougars vs. Vancouver
Mar. 13—Grand Prize

5c Per Game

YOU MUST PICK UP YOUR TICKET AT CJVI ONLY

1958-59 Kids club games. From the author's collection.

The scene shifted to the Vancouver Forum, where the Cougars won their fourth straight game in that arena, 4-1, over the Canucks. The key to the victory was hard skating and tenacious checking. Al Nicholson scored a hat trick and added an assist on a goal by Haworth, while Pelletier made twenty-six saves to secure the win.[1885] The Canucks turned the tables in a game in Victoria. The hot-and-cold Cougars were definitely cold in an 8-4 loss. The defence did not play well, and goaltending was suspect. The next game was played in Seattle, and the Cougars were hot again, upsetting the Coast-division-leading Totems, 4-2. Macauley had two goals for Victoria, while Nicholson and Wilson had one each. Defenceman McLeod was injured when he was slammed into the boards.[1886] The good play continued in a home game against Spokane. Playing before a sparse crowd of 1,488 fans, the Cougars dozed through the first period, then caught fire and outscored the Flyers, 4-1. Macauley had two goals and an assist to lead the offence.[1887] Right-winger Bill Forhan was released by the club and was scheduled to join Indianapolis in the International League. As the team would now be one player short, Coach Egan said that he would dress if it became absolutely necessary.[1888]

Victoria and Seattle played a home-and-home series. In Seattle, the home team won the game, 7-5, when the defensive play let the Cats down again. Haworth, Nicholson, and Macauley continued their good play, but it was not enough to compensate for the errors.[1889] In the game in Victoria, both the defencemen and forwards forgot the basic rule of hockey: protect your own net. The Cougars started the game well, building up a 3-0 lead on goals by Anderson, Lea, and Macauley, then defensive lapses allowed the Totems to tie the score. In overtime, Bill McFarland scored the winner for Seattle after only 5:25 of extra time.[1890] Against Calgary, the Cougars gave up a goal to the Stampeders, then fired three goals in under three minutes. But they could not hold the lead and fell 6-4 to the leading Eastern-division team.[1891]

Just like a pendulum, the Cats swung back to playing well. Playing the hapless Royals in New Westminster, the Cougars scored four second-period goals, then added a fifth in the third period before giving up just one. Doug Anderson led the attack with two goals, while Blackburn, Haworth, and Nicholson scored singles.[1892] Later, the team received the good news that Stan Baliuk would be available to play again, after six weeks off due to his broken ankle. If Don Blackburn, who was hit in the face in the New Westminster game, could play, Baliuk would not dress.[1893] The Cougars entertained Vancouver and shut out the Canucks, 2-0. Goaltender Bruce Gamble went for a wander behind his net, and that mistake allowed Baliuk to put the puck into the empty net for the first goal. Lea scored the insurance goal into an empty net when the Canucks pulled their goaltender for an extra attacker, and Pelletier made thirty-two stops for his fourth shutout of the season. In Vancouver, it was Marcel Pelletier's turn to wander away from his net, and it cost his team the game. Nicholson scored the only goal for Victoria in a 3-1 loss.[1894]

The Cougars then embarked on their final Prairie swing of the season. In Saskatoon, Victoria was in the game right up to the end and was down 2-1 when Coach Egan pulled Pelletier for an extra attacker to try to tie the score. The only problem was that the Quakers put the puck into the empty net to secure a 3-1 win.[1895] Then the Cougars came up just a bit short in a 6-5 loss to Winnipeg. They fell three goals behind twice and could not get the tying goal, even with the goaltender out of the net for an extra attacker. The Cougars remained in a tie for third place in the standings.[1896] The following evening, Victoria rebounded to defeat Edmonton, 2-1. The Flyers opened the scoring in the first period, but Anderson scored the tying goal in the third period, sending the game to overtime. Nicholson was the scoring hero, with his marker at 6:56 of the extra period.[1897] Victoria got off to a poor start in the final game of the trip in Calgary, then found their scoring touch in the second period. Anderson scored at 9:28 of the third to pull the team within one goal, but the optimism was short-lived, as Lou Jankowski scored less than a minute later to restore the lead and seal the 6-5 victory for the Stamps.[1898]

League play was suspended for the all-star game on March 3, at the Vancouver Forum. Cougar winger Al Nicholson was selected to the Coast-division team. Proceeds from the game were added to the players' fund that had been established to help needy players.[1899] In the contest, the Coast Stars easily defeated the Prairie Stars, 6-3. Nicholson scored one of the Coast goals.[1900]

When regular season play resumed, the Cougars played one of their worst games of the season when they were shut out, 7-0, at home by the lowly Saskatoon Quakers. The team was never in the game and suffered from one of their "cold nights" that puzzled Coach Egan.[1901] After the game, Coach Egan fined ten members of the team fifty dollars each for "indifferent play." He said that he would return the fines if the players in question showed well over the balance of the season. Enio Sclisizzi (who did not play that game), Doug Anderson, and Doug Macauley were not fined, and it was believed that goaltender Pelletier was the fourth player who escaped punishment.[1902]

As they usually did, the Cougars rebounded from a poor effort and defeated the visiting Warriors, 4-2. Winnipeg opened the scoring, but goals by Nicholson and Ford gave the Cougars a 2-1 lead by the end of the first period. Haworth had the only counter in the middle frame, and Macauley closed out the scoring into an empty net after Winnipeg had notched their second goal at the start of the third period.[1903] The Cougars continued their good play in a 4-0 shutout of Spokane. Lea scored two goals for Victoria, and McLeod and Nicholson added singles. Goaltender Pelletier stopped thirty-six shots and earned his fifth shutout of the year.[1904]

Victoria took its show on the road to Seattle and handed the Totems a 7-3 defeat. Haworth and Ford opened the scoring for the Cougars, but Seattle tied it before the end of the first period. Sclisizzi and Baliuk had the only scores in the second frame, and Baliuk, Anderson, and Macauley added third-period goals, while the team surrendered only one in the final frame. With the victory, the Cougars clinched a playoff spot.[1905]

In the return game back in Victoria, the home team emerged victorious in a thrilling 2-1 overtime game. Seattle opened the scoring, to the delight of some ninety fans who had accompanied their team north of the border, but Macauley tied the score just over two minutes later. There was no further scoring in regulation time, setting the stage for Nicholson to be the hero when he found the back of the net at 4:04. This was the first time all season that the Cougars had won four consecutive games, and it was a good time for the team to get hot.[1906]

The question on everyone's mind was whether the Cougars could extend their winning streak to five games when they entertained New Westminster. It was a special night for the fans as all seats were priced at one dollar and there was entertainment between periods when the Victoria Shamrocks and Foul Bay boxla (box lacrosse) teams played a mini lacrosse game on ice. It was too bad that the play on the ice did not match the enthusiasm of the large crowd, as the Cougars were shut out 4-0.[1907] There would be no five-game winning streak this season. However, they got back on the winning track in New Westminster. Baliuk, Sclisizzi, and Wilson led the scoring parade. The game was held up at the beginning of the third period when Royals' goaltender Reno Zanier had to leave the game to have a chest wound stitched up. He returned to play, but perhaps his injury affected his play. With the game tied at the end of regulation time, the Cougars wasted no time securing the victory, as Baliuk found the back of the net at ten seconds of extra time. Pelletier played a great game in net for Victoria; it was a genuine team effort.[1908]

Having secured a playoff berth, team management focused their attention on the poor financial performance of the team. Although the community had supported the team by purchasing shares in its operation and the team was having one of its better seasons on the ice, the attendance at games was abysmal, and the team was losing money at the gate.

They needed a total attendance of 90,000 to break even and had no chance of getting that. With one game to go, only 82,152 fans had attended games. Inter-divisional games were the most popular, and the largest crowd had been for Eddie Dorohoy's return with Calgary. All the Cougars could hope for was a huge crowd at playoff games and a long run in the playoffs to help balance the books.[1909]

There were 2,296 fans in attendance at the last regular-season game, where the Cougars downed the Spokane Flyers, 5-2. Enio Sclisizzi paced the team with two goals and an assist, Baliuk added a goal and two assists, and Nicholson and Lea added a goal each. At the game, Doug Anderson was named the winner of the Wally Smith Memorial Trophy as the player to have "best combined sportsmanship, ability, and value to his team during the season." The final game was played in Seattle against the Cougars' first-round playoff opponent. It was a wild affair, with several brawls. Al Nicholson picked up two assists to equal the club scoring record set by Eddie Dorohoy eight years before. Victoria took a 2-1 lead into the second period, but Seattle scorers proved too strong, and the Cougars ended the game on the losing end of an 8-4 score. In the second period, the league's penalty leader, Seattle's Frank Arnett, elbowed Harris and that set off no less than four different fights. There were eight players in the penalty box after that altercation. Trouble broke out in the third period as well, when Nicholson felt he had been speared by Arnett and attacked him with a stick. A total of ninety-eight minutes in penalties were assessed by referee Joey Johns.[1910]

The first round of the playoffs, a best-of-five series, began on March 27, in Seattle. Coach Egan was not pleased that the first three games would be played on consecutive nights after four days' rest, but he said the team would be ready.[1911] The series opened with a 3-1 victory for the Totems. Although Doug Anderson held prolific scorer Guyle Fielder off the scoresheet, Rudy Filion led the way for Seattle with two goals. The Cougars' offence was ineffective, and they would need a better effort in future games if they wanted to advance to the second round.¹⁹¹² Back at home, Victoria played a sluggish game through most of the contest but came alive late in the third period. However, they were unable to overcome the deficit and fell 5-3 to drop their second game of the playoffs. The game featured a strange situation. In the last thirty seconds, Coach Egan pulled Pelletier for an extra attacker, then sent a seventh man onto the ice. Referee Vern Buffey did not see the additional skater in the furious play, but the Cougars did not score even with two more players than their opponents. Back in Seattle, the Totems outhustled the Cougars en route to a series-clinching 4-2 win. Seattle built up a 3-0 lead before Sclisizzi scored to bring the count to 3-1. Haworth narrowed the score to 3-2 midway through the third period, but Bill MacFarland found the back of the net to give Seattle the edge they needed. The series was over, and the better team had won.¹⁹¹³ As they had all season, the lack of consistent scoring and defensive lapses had cost the Cougars a chance to advance.

At the end of the season, WHL president, Al Leader revealed that the league wanted to improve its play to present "an alternative to the National Hockey League." He said, "People won't support minor-league sport to any great extent. I think it's got to come to the place where we'll have to consider becoming a major league." He saw an expansion of the league first, then an upgrade to major-league status in three to five years. Los Angeles was building a new arena, Portland would have a new arena ready by 1960, Seattle was expected to build a new arena, and San Francisco could already hold a major-league audience once an ice-making plant was installed. He noted that Portland, Los Angeles, and San Francisco had all played in the league in earlier days but had withdrawn by the 1951-52 season as their facilities were inadequate. The main benefit of upgrading the league would be that teams would own their players rather than having them under the control of NHL teams, so there would be less player movement and more consistency to each franchise.¹⁹¹⁴

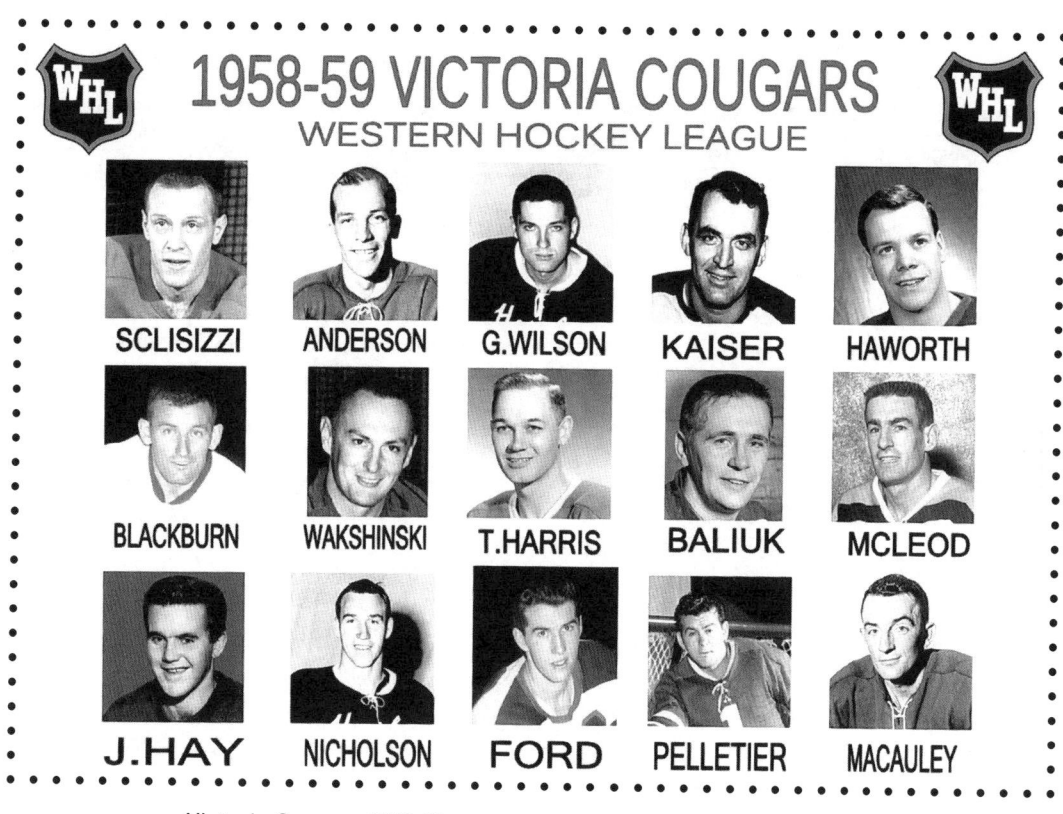

Victoria Cougars 1958-59 team photo. From the author's collection.

23 - COUGARS UNDER NEW OWNERSHIP—AGAIN

After a very weak financial year in 1958-59, the community-owned Cougars knew something had to change. However, until the books of the club were audited, shareholders had no idea just how bad their situation was. Only two months earlier, it had appeared that there was nothing wrong with the club that a good year at the gate wouldn't cure. The problem seems to have been poor management of the club through the last season, with too much control given to Manager-Coach Pat Egan. Even club directors were stunned when the real financial picture was revealed. Club assets were $10,543, made up of the $7,500 league deposit, $868 as the club's share of league funds, $458 in office furniture, $448 in accounts payable, $1,200 in supplies and equipment, and $69 in cash. Liabilities totalled $24,209, made up of a bank loan and overdraft of $10,693 and accounts payable of $13,336. The club had a loss of $50,711 in the two years it operated as a community-owned enterprise. League president Al Leader urged directors to find "fresh money" from local sources when he met with them on September 5. When directors were unable to secure the $50,000 they needed to keep the club afloat, they asked the president to search out other potential backers. Saskatoon contractor Jim Piggott was the only person interested in acquiring the team. Although it was suggested that shareholders had two choices—to sell the franchise to Piggott or refuse the offer and suspend pro hockey in Victoria for the upcoming season—the door was still open to local ownership at the cost of $25,000.[1915]

A meeting of the 587 shareholders was held on September 17, 1959. At that meeting, the shareholders voted to sell the franchise to Jim Piggott for $25,000 by a count of 759-27 (one vote being assigned to each twenty-five-dollar share held). New manager Hal Laycoe advised that he had not received any salary for the month since he had been hired and that there were insufficient funds to print tickets for the upcoming exhibition games.[1916] The sale of the club was approved by a meeting of the WHL board of governors the day after the Victoria meeting.[1917] Piggott now owned two franchises in the WHL and could only operate one. He decided to suspend the operations of the Saskatoon Quakers and committed to the Victoria Cougars. In a telegram to former Victoria president Dr. Reid, he said:

> *"In exercising my option for the purchase of the Victoria hockey franchise, please convey to your shareholders my sincere appreciation for the confidence they have placed in my ability to take over and successfully operate the Victoria franchise.*
>
> *Please convey also to the Victoria hockey fans, through the medium of the press and radio, a pledge by myself to concentrate with*

23 - COUGARS UNDER NEW OWNERSHIP—AGAIN

the utmost of my ability on icing for them a club worthy of representing Victoria.

My one aim will be the winning of the President's Cup this season."[1918]

Now that the question of ownership of the team had been settled, manager Laycoe was able to get down to the business of securing players for the upcoming season. He arranged exhibition games against two NHL teams, the New York Rangers on September 26, and the Detroit Red Wings on September 30.[1919] He announced that Pelletier had agreed to contract terms. Signed contracts were also received from Gordie Wilson and Jack Bionda. Players on the way to the West were George Ford and Pete Wright, the latter who had to arrange for winter help for his Grande Prairie, Alberta, sporting goods store.[1920] Players present for the first workout of the season were Pete Wright; Jack Bionda; Gordie Haworth; Arlo, John, and Charlie Goodwin; Gordie Wilson; Doug Macauley; and Jim Hay.[1921] Arnie Schmautz and Gordie Fashoway, formerly of New Westminster, hit the ice along with Reno Zanier (backup goaltender), Gordon Tansley, Carl Kaiser, Doug Anderson, and Art Jones.[1922] As camp proceeded, Hal Laycoe experimented with different line combinations. He put the three Goodwin brothers on one line and put Gordie Wilson between Arnie Schmautz and Gordie Fashoway. The Cougars received good news on September 24 when they learned that Boston was sending Al Nicholson, Victoria's leading scorer last season, back to the Cougars for another season.[1923] Former Cougar Andy Hebenton "came home" with the New York Rangers for an exhibition game.[1924]

A record crowd of 5,509 attended the game. The Cougars played very well, and the Rangers had to play a disciplined game to escape with a 5-4 victory. In a delicious irony, Andy Hebenton scored the winning goal.[1925] The club added defensive talent when Ron Matthews, formerly with the Royals, signed a contract.[1926] Next on the agenda was an exhibition game against the Detroit Red Wings.

Fans mobbed Gordie Howe before and after the game, which the Red Wings won, 2-1.[1927] In the end, only one Goodwin brother made the team: Arlo.

George Ford arrived in camp two weeks late but in game shape and ready to play, having worked all summer as a stonemason. However, Gordie Wilson was contemplating retirement as he was unsure if his previously injured leg would be able to withstand the rigours of a full season of hockey. In their final pre-season game played in Chilliwack, the Cougars lost, 6-3, to the Seattle Totems. Hay, Nicholson, and Haworth scored for Victoria.[1928]

In league business, the Spokane franchise changed its name to the Comets after the league decided that Edmonton had priority for the Flyer name, on September 21, 1959. The team held a contest and picked the new name from over 400 suggestions sent in by 2,000 fans.[1929] The Western Hockey League revamped its organizational structure, with seven teams playing in one division. Gone were the Saskatoon Quakers and the New Westminster Royals, with their players distributed to teams in this league and other professional leagues. The problem of travel expenses was solved by having Prairie teams play two games in Western cities on selected trips, with Coast teams doing the same on their Eastern swings. This plan reduced considerably the costs associated with these extensive —and expensive—trips.[1930]

The Cougars' 1959-60 season opened in Vancouver on October 9. The Canucks won the game, 3-1, taking advantage of slack Cougar checking. Art Jones scored the only Victoria goal, on passes from Fashoway and Wright. Arlo Goodwin suffered a five-stitch cut on his elbow, and Arnie Schmautz needed stitches for a head cut. The larger Vancouver defenders kept the diminutive Cougar forwards off their game with bruising hits.[1931] The home opener was a close affair. Down 1-0 in the second period, Ford tied the score, assisted by Bionda and Haworth. Unfortunately, the Canucks scored a fluky goal just over a minute later to close out the scoring. The defence played much better in this 2-1 loss, so Coach Laycoe was optimistic about future games.[1932]

For the Thanksgiving Day matinee, the Cougars decided to award a hamper of food to the largest family group in attendance.[1933] A disappointing audience of only 2,394 watched a thrilling come-from-behind victory. Both teams played at a fast and furious pace, with the defence delivering body checks to deter the Canucks' forwards from taking chances. Vancouver got on the scoreboard in the first period when McNab fired a shot past Pelletier. Macauley tied the game in the third period; there was no further scoring in regulation time. The crowd rose to its feet when Art Jones scored a power-play goal at 4:14 of overtime to win the first game of the season.[1934] The good play continued when Calgary made its first appearance in Victoria. Although the Cougars had not discovered their scoring punch, their defensive play was outstanding in this game, particularly the penalty killing. The line of Doug Anderson, Arlo Goodwin, and Doug Macauley was the most consistent throughout the game with their tenacious checking, and they scored the third goal; Haworth had scored in the first period and Wilson one in the second, for a final score of 3-1.[1935]

Manager Hal Laycoe announced that the Victoria Cougars would become the first team in Canada to issue credit cards. He said, "You can buy nearly everything else on credit, why not hockey tickets?" Under the plan, fans would be able to come down, purchase tickets, and get billed at the end of each month for the tickets they had used. He noted that fans' budgets were often strained when the team played three or four games in a week and he said he hoped that the credit-card system would help alleviate that strain.[1936] Three weeks after the cards were made available, 900 fans had acquired one. However, attendance was not much better than it had been before, so it was not the lack of money that was keeping fans away.[1937] There was mixed reaction from other WHL teams to the credit-card idea. Only Vancouver's Coley Hall dismissed it as not worthy. Edmonton and Winnipeg were the most interested and reportedly asked Laycoe for details on how it worked. In Seattle, they were already using restaurant credit cards for hockey purchases, and it was working well.[1938]

Seattle made its first trip to Victoria, and the game featured outstanding goaltending by both Pelletier and Bentley. Once again, the game was played at a rapid pace, with both teams using their speed to advantage. Ford scored in the second period to give Victoria the lead, but Seattle tied the game halfway through the third frame. There was no scoring in overtime; the final game score was 1-1. The Cougars still had not found their scoring touch but would be back at full strength by Wednesday, when Arnie Schmautz (who had missed two games while attending his father's funeral) would be back in the lineup.[1939] Next in town were the Edmonton Flyers. For the first time this season, the Cougars found their scoring touch, with six goals on their way to a 6-4 victory. Nicholson had two, with singles added by Schmautz, Hay, Bionda, and Jones. With the win, Victoria extended its unbeaten streak to four and moved into a second-place tie with Edmonton.[1940] Three days later, the same teams played, and the Cougars won by a 4-1 score. Fashoway notched a goal and two assists to lead the scoring, while Pelletier was magnificent in the nets.[1941]

Now it was time to take the show on the road to see if the winning could continue. Playing in Spokane, the Cougars scored seven goals en route to a 7-2 routing of the Comets. Arnie Schmautz had two goals, and singles came from Arlo Goodwin, Gord Haworth, Al Nicholson, Pete Wright, and Art Jones. Wright's goal was his second in as many games, after not scoring for more than three years.[1942][1943] The teams travelled to Victoria for a game the next day, and, again, the Cougars came out on the right side of the score. Gord Fashoway made the difference in the contest, scoring twice as the club skated to a 3-1 victory. The score could have been higher had it not been for the heroics of Comet goaltender Emile Francis, who had thirty-eight shots fired at him, many of the spectacular variety. He stopped all but three.[1944] The Cougars were now unbeaten in seven games, a feat that had not been seen since the 1953-54 season, and were off to their best start ever. However, they would have to keep winning to equal the ten-game unbeaten streak put up by the championship-winning 1950-51 Cougars.[1945]

All good things must come to an end, and the unbeaten streak did with two losses in one weekend. First, the Cougars lost 2-1 in Spokane, and then another close one, 3-2, in Seattle. Against the Comets, the Cougars tied the game in the first period on a goal by Nicholson, but Pelletier could not stop Tom Hodges, who fired the winning goal early in the third frame. The game featured two free-for-alls in the first period, including one where every player on the ice except the goaltenders got into the action. The next night, the Cougars seemed to have forgotten how to shoot, as they registered only twelve shots on goal in the game, including only one in the middle frame. The Totems outscored Victoria 2-1 in the first period with Schmautz as the marksman for the Cougars. Both teams had a goal each in the final period, with Bionda finding the back of the net for the Cougars.[1946]

The next two games were on home ice, and the Cougars had mixed results. First, they defeated the Winnipeg Warriors, 6-5, in a thrilling overtime game. With their highly regarded rookie reargards Teddy Green and Gary Bergman, and rookie forward Norm Waslowski, Winnipeg had a mix of young and old players.[1947][1948] Doug Anderson, who had been played sparingly due to a shoulder injury, notched the winning goal after only 1:50 of overtime.[1949] In the second game, Victoria played at Vancouver and was shut out 6-0 in their worst game of the season. They were sluggish in the final two periods and seemed to lack the will or energy to perform at an acceptable level.[1950]

However, the team rebounded and defeated the Canucks, 4-1, in Victoria. Checking ferociously and paying attention to detail, the team dominated in all phases of the game. Art Jones led the scoring with a couple of goals, and Pelletier stopped all but one of the twenty-five shots he faced. In Seattle the next night, the Cougars were again victorious. They completed their weekend with a 4-2 decision over the Totems. Falling behind twice, they came from behind, scoring three unanswered goals to overcome a 2-1 deficit. Seattle star Guyle Fielder scored his 700th point, but it was not enough to beat the surging Cougars.[1951]

In their final home game before an extended Prairie road trip, Victoria finally ran out of steam and lost, 5-2, to Spokane. Emile Francis made the difference, as he snagged almost every puck that was fired his way. The long unbeaten streak of home victories for the Cougars was over, as the Comets won their first road game of the season.[1952]

The Cougars then left on a six-game Prairie trip, during which they would play each club twice. In prior years, this trip had been a dismal experience for the club, as they had never had much success. In Edmonton, they took time warming up and allowed the Flyers to score two goals in thirty-four seconds in the opening period to fall behind quickly. After Edmonton scored again for a 3-0 lead, the Cougars finally found their legs and put up a fight. But it was a little too late, as they dropped a 3-2 decision. Only Goodwin and Matthews could score. The Flyers fired forty-one shots at Pelletier, and he made several good saves to keep his team in the game.[1953] In Calgary, the Cougars came up with a better effort, twice coming from behind to tie the game, but eventually losing 3-2 when the Stampeders scored after 2:30 of overtime. Coach Laycoe was given a misconduct penalty for his choice of words while protesting Calgary's second goal. This penalty carried an automatic fine of twenty-five dollars, so it was an expensive game for him.[1954]

The next stop was in Winnipeg, where the Cougars won, 4-2. Victoria outplayed the Warriors in all facets of the game, and only outstanding goaltending from Rollins kept the score from being even higher. Jones scored two goals, including the winner, with Fashoway and Ford adding the others.[1955] Unfortunately, the Cougars could not produce a winning result two days later. About 4,500 fans watched as Winnipeg dominated Victoria and recorded a 5-1 victory. Coach Laycoe was concerned about the lack of scoring from all but one line. Jones, Schmautz, and Fashoway had accounted for twenty-six of the Cougars' fifty-six total goals that season.[1956]

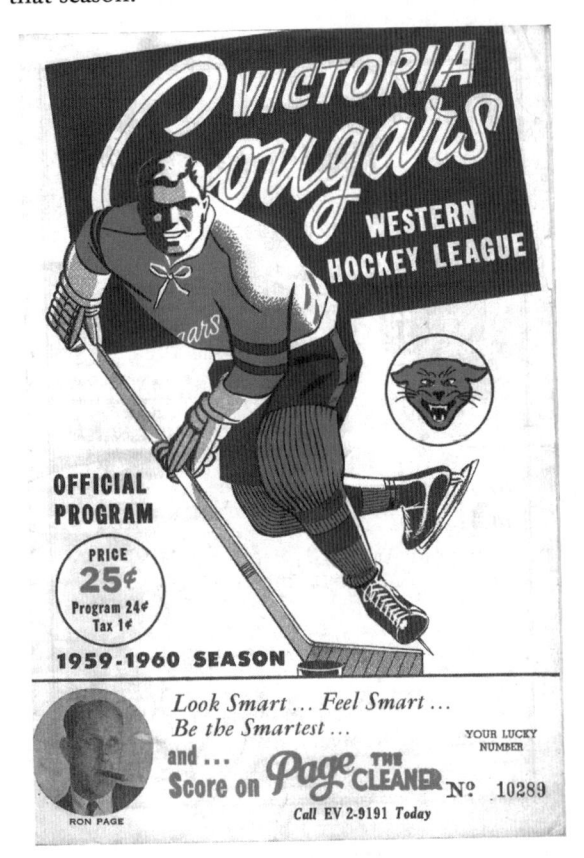

Cougars program 1959-60. From the author's collection.

In the next game at Edmonton, the Haworth-Ford-Nicholson line found their scoring touch and produced two goals in a game where Victoria had to come from behind three times to earn a 3-3 tie with the Flyers. They now had three points on the trip, which was not the record they wanted, though it was better than they had done in the past.[1957] In the final game of the trip in Calgary, the offence came alive again, and Victoria skated to a 7-4 win. Arnie Schmautz had a four-goal evening, equalling the Stampeders' output by himself. Jones, Ford, and Wilson rounded out the scoring.[1958] The Cougars were sitting nine points behind Vancouver in the standings and would have a chance to move closer, as they had two games against the Canucks coming up. In a game in Victoria, the Cougars outplayed the Canucks but could only manage a 1-1 tie. Danny Belisle scored for Vancouver, and Haworth replied for Victoria. Had the Cougars been able to cash in on the power play, they would have won easily.[1959] The scene shifted to Vancouver, and there the Canucks won a close one 2-1. Only Schmautz put a puck behind Vancouver goaltender Hank Bassen.[1960] Next up was a game against the Seattle Totems. Guyle Fielder, who was usually the hero of a game, actually gave up the puck to Doug Anderson who set up the winning goal.[1961] The Cougars then went on the road to Spokane for two games. In the first encounter, Victoria outlasted the Comets, 5-2. Gord Haworth had three goals for the Cougars while Jones and Schmautz added others. Coach Laycoe was particularly pleased that this line was finally getting going. He predicted that his team would battle Vancouver down to the wire for the league championship.[1962]

While they were in the Spokane area, the Cougars travelled to Trail, BC, to play an exhibition game against the Smoke Eaters of the Western International Hockey League. Victoria had to really work to defeat this team, 7-5. The lead changed many times in the game, but the skill of the WHL team was apparent. Fashoway led the team with two goals, with singles coming from Schmautz, Haworth, Matthews, Macauley, and Nicholson. The last goal was scored into an empty net and gained Pelletier an assist.[1963] Hal Laycoe called the result of the next game in Spokane "ridiculous." He noted, "We had the puck in front of their net at least eighty percent of the time and outshot them 39-28, but they outscored us. The boys played a whale of a game, but they couldn't put the puck in the net. And then they take a silly chance by pulling their goaltender with almost three minutes left and scramble in the tying goal, then beat us in overtime with a blind shot." The Comets scored first with Ford in the penalty box, but Fashoway tied the score in the second period. Anderson put the Cougars ahead in the third period, and it looked as if they would win the game. However, that is when Spokane coach Joe Crozier took the chance to pull the goaltender very early—and it paid off. The final score of 3-2 flattered the Comets.[1964] Then it was on to Seattle for the last game on the road trip. The lack of scoring reared its ugly head again, as the Cougars were shut out 4-0 by the Totems. Their inability to score in close games had cost them many games that season, and, given the talent on the team, it was perplexing. When they put three or more goals in the net, they had a good record, but there were so many losses where a single goal would have made the difference. Coach Laycoe did not have the answer, but if the team did not find its offence again, they could be out of a playoff berth.[1965]

Back at home in the friendly confines of Memorial Arena, the Cougars shut out Spokane, 4-0, to set up a battle for second place in their next game against Seattle. Although the team played most of the game with only three defencemen after Ron Matthews suffered a charley-horse, Jack Bionda double-shifted on defence, and the forwards helped with checking to secure the first shutout of the season for Pelletier. Once again, the top line did most of the scoring. Jones had two goals, Schmautz had three assists, and Fashoway had two assists. Other goal scorers were Bionda and Ford. The crowd of 1,792 cheered the home team as they skated to what the fans called an "easy victory."[1966] The previous season's scoring sensation Al Nicholson, who had failed to produce much offence this year, was shipped to Winnipeg in return for Don Blackburn, who had played fifty games for the Cougars the previous season.[1967] The consistent play continued with a 4-1 victory over Seattle. Goodwin was put in Nicholson's old spot, and the move paid immediate dividends. The new line of Haworth-Goodwin-Ford led the way to the win. After a scoreless first period, Haworth scored two goals, and Goodwin added a third for a 3-1 lead. A goal by Ford in the final frame sealed the deal. The Cougars were now back in second place in the standings, tied for points with the Totems, having increased their leads over both Calgary and Edmonton.[1968] In Seattle, Victoria came from behind to defeat the Totems, 3-2. Twelve players figured in the scoring, and no one player counted more than one point. Cougar goals came from Matthews, Fashoway, and Macauley. The teams remained tied in points with thirty-five each.[1969]

Colourful Cougar goalie Marcel Pelletier talked about the possibility of following the example of Montreal's Jacques Plante and wearing a mask during games. He said he would likely wear a mask if other professionals began to wear them, but noted that he had never been cut by a puck, though he had received his share of stick cuts. He also declared that "goalies wearing masks would take something out of professional hockey, but goalies wouldn't be scared to dive into a play." Gil Meyer of the Cleveland Barons of the AHL wore a mask to protect a broken jaw, and Dennis Riggin of the Edmonton Flyers wore one to protect an eye injury. Other NHL goalies were experimenting with masks, and most junior clubs required them.[1970]

In a strange turn of events, the Edmonton goaltender was cut in the ear and needed repairs. Before the injury, the Cougars were pressing, but while he was away for repairs, the Flyers seemed to have gotten organized and skated to a 3-1 win over Victoria. Jones fired the only goal for Victoria, his eighteenth of the season.[1971] On Boxing Day, the Cougars and Canucks played a doubleheader, with one game in each city. This idea had been scheduled in the 1956-57 season, but the second game that year was cancelled, as fog had prevented airplanes from taking players to the mainland. In 1959, there were no such issues, and both games were played. In the afternoon, Victoria edged Vancouver, 4-3. Coming off a six-day break, the Cougars showed no ill effects from the time away from gameplay and thrilled the good crowd of 3,346 with a 4-3 win. Goals by Macauley and Ford, in the first period, got the home team off to a good start. Vancouver's

Cyr scored twice in the second period, while Fashoway counted for Victoria. The Canucks tied the game in the first minute of the third period, but Schmautz scored on a rebound from an Anderson shot midway through the period, and there was no more scoring. The teams then made their way to the mainland, where the Canucks turned the tables on the Cougars, defeating them 4-2 in the nightcap. Former Cougar Colin Kilburn led the way for Vancouver with two goals; Haworth and Wilson answered for Victoria.[1972]

Seattle and Victoria played a home-and-home series, but the games were three days apart. In the American city, the home team outscored the visitors, 4-1. Only Schmautz fired a goal for the Cougars, long after the game result was decided.[1973] In Victoria, the Cougars won one of the roughest games played at home in some time. The action started late in the first period when Gerry Goyer (now playing for Seattle) made the mistake of cross-checking Jack Bionda under the chin. When he was in danger of being hurt, his teammates joined the fray, followed closely by the Cougars on the ice. Cougar forward Ford came off the bench to join in, and the north end of the arena resembled a wrestling ring, rather than a hockey rink. Referee Al Paradice let the fight draw to a conclusion and then penalized all the combatants. The twenty-minute delay in game action seemed to calm the remaining players down, and hockey resumed at the high quality often seen at the Memorial Arena during that season. Jones again led the Cougar attack with two goals, with Ford, Haworth, and Schmautz contributing the others. The largest mid-week crowd of the season—2,702—certainly got their money's worth.[1974] As seemed to happen with regularity this season, the Cougars then played a series of games against the Canucks. In Vancouver, the teams played on New Year's Day, and the home team won 4-2. Gord Fashoway opened the scoring in the game, but the Canucks counted two in the second period for a 2-1 lead. Fashoway's second goal, early in the third period, briefly tied the score, but two more by Vancouver ended any hope of a Cougar victory.[1975]

In Victoria, two days later, the Cougars were on the right end of a 6-2 score. Vancouver's Hank Cahan opened the scoring, but goals by Ford and Jones gave Victoria the lead at the end of the first period. There were no goals in the middle frame, but the Cougars rammed in four (by Goodwin, Wright, Macauley, and Blackburn) to Vancouver's one in the third period to win handily.[1976] Finally, the team was getting scoring from different players. Now it was back to the Vancouver Forum, where the Cougars had lost all five of the games played that season. In one of the best defensive efforts of the season, the teams battled to a 1-1 draw, with former Cougar Bruce Carmichael scoring for the Canucks and Art Jones answering for the Cougars.[1977]

Victoria played the next four games against Spokane, the first two in Memorial Arena and the second pair in Spokane. The first game, billed as "Student Night," attracted 4,000 fans. Some of the youngsters in attendance won prizes, including autographed hockey sticks, a lacrosse stick autographed by Bionda, skates, transistor radios, and bicycles. Anderson, Haworth, and Fashoway each scored twice for the Cougars in a 6-3 victory. Comets' manager Roy McBride was travelling with his team and complained that his players were not in shape. However, they were playing a club that had finally found its scoring stride, and the Comets did not have the speed to keep up, tiring in the final period, when Victoria notched two goals to put the game away.[1978] Three days later, the Comets upended the Cougars, 3-1, with Jones the only marksman for Victoria.[1979]

The league all-star game was played in Edmonton on January 12, 1960. A disappointing crowd of only 3,127 watched the Coast squad defeat the Prairie representatives, 5-3, for their third consecutive win in the annual affair. The Cougars were represented by Jones, Schmautz, and Fashoway.[1980][1981]

After the all-star break, the Cougars played the first of two in Spokane. The first period was

23 - COUGARS UNDER NEW OWNERSHIP—AGAIN

scoreless, but Victoria outscored the Comets, 4-1, in the second period and added the only score in the final frame to take the contest, 5-2. Macauley, Matthews, Blackburn, Fashoway, and Anderson scored for the Cougars. The Spokane loss spoiled the debut of manager Roy McBride, who had taken over the coaching job from Joe Crozier, who stayed with the club as a player.[1982] Three days later, Victoria won again by a 5-1 score. Victoria marksmen were Haworth (with two), Jones, Schmautz, and Matthews. Goaltender Marcel Pelletier's head was injured by a loose puck, and the game was held up for ten minutes to allow him to be repaired. Perhaps he would rethink his decision to forego wearing a mask.[1983]

Jack Bionda as a Cougar. Photo courtesy Ernie Fitzsimmons.

Returning home, the Cougars entertained Edmonton. Their good play continued, as Pelletier recorded another shutout, and the scorers fired five goals past the Flyer goalie. Fashoway scored twice, while Haworth, Schmautz, and Jones added singles.[1984] Since the beginning of January, the Cougars had played eight games, winning five and tying one, with only two losses. Marcel Pelletier had a low goals-against average, and their scoring was improving. Victoria travelled to Vancouver for their next match. All their good play came to a crashing end when they lost the game, 6-1. Ford scored for the Cougars, but the Canucks were already up by five goals by that time, so it was almost meaningless.[1985] All the club could do was to regroup and come up with a better effort in the next game.

Next on the agenda were five straight home games. This would be the time to get much-needed points to climb up the standings. The star of the first game against Seattle was 5' 7" Arnie Schmautz, whose skillful goal ignited the offence and led to the 6-4 victory. Jack Bionda had three assists, while Doug Anderson sealed the win with a goal into the empty net.[1986] Calgary came to Victoria for two games. In the first, the Stampeders scored first and held on for a close 3-2 victory. Starring for the visitors was their goaltender, Lucien Deschenes, who stymied the Cats' shooters time after time. The only players to put pucks past him were Blackburn and Goodwin.[1987] The Cougars then had three days to rest before meeting Calgary again. About 400 Duncan residents came down the island for the Saturday night game, and they brought the Cougars good luck. Mayor Jack Dobson dropped the ceremonial face-off, and Duncan area athletes were introduced to the crowd between periods. Blackburn opened the scoring, and Fashoway led the way to victory with his best effort of the season, notching a hat trick. The Cougars were playing a man under the roster limit, as Gordie Wilson had declined to play. His future with the team was up in the air.[1988]

Winnipeg invaded Memorial Arena for two games in early February. Featuring former Cougar Al Nicholson's return to Victoria with his new team, the first game was a thrilling affair. He opened the scoring for the Warriors in the second period, and that slim lead lasted until Schmautz tied the game with less than three minutes left in regulation time. Both Pelletier and Rollins made spectacular stops during the game. Overtime was almost over when

Macauley fired a shot past Rollins to give Victoria a 3-2 win.[1989] Three days later, the tables were turned, and the Warriors upended the Cougars, 6-4. Victoria came from behind three times to tie the score, but Rollins made exceptional saves on shots by Matthews, Bionda, and Fashoway near the end of the game, to keep Victoria off the scoresheet while his teammates were firing two goals past Pelletier at the other end.

With the loss, the Cougars lost ground in their bid to finish second in the standings.[1990] In Vancouver, the Cougars squeaked out a 2-1 win over the Canucks. It was their first victory in the Vancouver Forum that season and came at the right time. Orland Kurtenbach opened the scoring for Vancouver in the first period, and that lead held until Schmautz and Fashoway scored, nineteen seconds apart, to give Victoria the lead. There was no further scoring after that in an exciting, fast-paced match.[1991]

The February 10 game against Spokane proved to be one of the loudest on record. A huge crowd of more than 5,000 (many of them children) jammed Memorial Arena, eager to watch the game and to (perhaps) win the pony offered as a draw prize.[1992] The game's result was never in doubt, as Fashoway notched a natural hat trick in the first period. Haworth added a couple, and Blackburn and Schmautz contributed singles. Only Jim Moro ruined Marcel Pelletier's bid for a shutout.[1993] Young George Gerrard won the pony when his ticket was drawn from the 6,361 raffle tickets sold. However, as he lived in the city, his father said they did not know what they would do with the animal, as they had no place to keep him. Other children won hockey sticks, bicycles, sweater sets, binoculars, a half-dozen cases of soft drinks, skates, a portrait, and a Western riding suit.[1994]

The Cougars took their show on the road to Seattle, where the Totems won the game, 5-3. Victoria had a 3-1 lead at the end of the second period on two goals by red-hot Fashoway, and one by Haworth, but surrendered four goals to Seattle in the last ten minutes of the game, while being unable to increase their lead. The loss dropped the Cougars to fourth place in the standings.[1995] The league-leading Canucks were the next visitors to Victoria, and they left with a 3-2 win—their first victory on Victoria ice that season. The large Vancouver defenders made life miserable for the much smaller Victoria forwards, hitting them with bruising blows, seemingly at will. Macauley and Haworth had goals for the Cougars, who actually held a 2-1 lead at the end of the first period, but they seemed to tire after the punishment they were taking and failed to score on any of their subsequent chances.[1996]

The Cougars then left on their extended Prairie road trip, where they would play six league games in eight days. In Winnipeg, the team won the game, 3-1, but lost the services of the talented Schmautz when he suffered a hairline skull fracture. He was rushed to hospital and was expected to be kept there for a week. Coach Laycoe put Blackburn in Schmautz' spot, and he scored the third goal. Others came from Gerry Goyer (acquired from Seattle on February 4) and Ford. The only Warrior to beat Pelletier was Gordie Redahl.[1997] The team received the unwelcome news that Schmautz would be lost to the team for the rest of the season, as he would not be permitted to skate for at least eight weeks. The injury was more severe than initially thought, as he had also sustained a "slight tear in the brain cover."[1998]

In the next game in Winnipeg, the Warriors ended up the winners by a 4-2 score. Two long shots that eluded Pelletier made the difference in the match. Jones and Ford had goals for the Cougars, but Warrior goaltender Rollins was at his best stopping all the other shots. After the game, he was called up to play for the New York Rangers. The Cougars likely wished he had left before the game, rather than after.[1999] The next stop on the trip was in Edmonton, where the Flyers downed the Cougars, 5-2. Gerry Goyer, working between Anderson and Macauley, scored twice for Victoria, but the rest of the team was unable to beat goaltender Gilles Boisvert.[2000]

In Calgary the next night, the Cougars found their scoring touch again and came from behind to edge the Stampeders, 2-1, in a thrilling overtime game. Colwill put the home team ahead, but Ford tied it before the end of the first period. From then on, the goaltenders took over, and neither team could score. It took 5:39 of overtime before Matthews fired the shot that won the game.[2001]

The Cougars also received the news that Arnie Schmautz had successful surgery to repair the damage suffered in Winnipeg.[2002] Taking a break from league games, the Cougars stopped in Saskatchewan to play an exhibition game against the Quakers. Saskatoon-born Arlo Goodwin scored twice and Fashoway once, for a rather easy victory.[2003] Then it was on to Edmonton for another encounter with the Flyers. This time, the Cougars came out on top of a 3-1 score, ending the Flyers' home-ice winning streak at fourteen. Jones and Haworth scored in the first period, and Ford added one in the second frame. Marcel Pelletier was spectacular in net and was unlucky not to record a shutout; the only shot that eluded him came from Solinger when the score was already 3-0.[2004]

The final Prairie stop was the next evening in Calgary, where the Stampeders avenged an earlier defeat with a 5-3 decision over the Cougars. Norm Johnson and Lou Jankowski scored twice for the Stampeders, with a single from Grey. All the Cougars could manage were goals by Fashoway, Goodwin, and Matthews. They ended the gruelling Prairie swing with a 3-3 record, marginally better than they had done before.[2005] Before returning home, the team played a game in Vancouver. They seemed tired from the ardours of travel and dropped a 6-1 decision to the Canucks. In the game, playing hard, and trailing by one goal in the second period, they gave up a goal to Sandy Hucul at the end of the frame and ran out of steam, while Vancouver poured in three unanswered goals in the final period to win the game easily.

Manager-Coach Laycoe announced that former NHL player Paul Masnick would join the club for the rest of the season.[2006] In the final game of February, to acknowledge the leap year, *Victoria Daily Times* women's editor Elizabeth Forbes was given the assignment of covering the game, writing it in the style of the social pages of the day. The sports editor was sent to cover a meeting of the University Women's Club. Forbes's column was a work of parody and well worth reading just for a chuckle. In the game itself, it was no contest, as the Cougars rolled to an impressive 8-4 victory. Haworth had the only goal of the first period, but Fashoway, Jones, Matthews, Bionda, and Macauley got on the scoreboard in the second, before Hutchinson replied for Vancouver. Matthews (with his second goal) and Ford rounded out the scoring. Masnick, playing in his first game for Victoria, had two assists.[2007] It was a good win for the team, as it proved to them that they could play with the league leaders.

The Cougars held Shrine Hockey Night on March 2, and six lucky fans won door prizes, including a "four-day, expenses-paid trip for two to attend Cougars games at Seattle and Spokane on March 13 and 15."[2008] The game was a whitewash for the home team, as they swamped the hapless Warriors, 9-2. Even the defencemen got in on the scoring spree. Jack Bionda took only forty-four seconds to open the scoring in the first period, and Hay, Jones, and Haworth added others, while Winnipeg only scored two in response. The second period was all Cougars, as Ford scored twice while Hay and Masnick added singles. Matthews had the sole goal in the final frame. The 3,401 fans in attendance were pleased with the game result (especially the Duncan fan who ended up winning the trip).[2009]

Calgary was the next visitor to Victoria, and they left with a 3-1 win. The individual star of the game was Stampeder goaltender Deschenes who stopped everything fired at him except one shot by Jones. Although Calgary had almost been eliminated from playoff contention, they put up a good fight and were the better team on that night's play.[2010] Seattle played the next game in Victoria. The Cougars took a 2-0 lead on goals by Hay and Jones. In the second frame, the wire screen at the north end of the building came into play when a puck bounced off it and ended up behind Pelletier. That incensed Coach Laycoe, as he had complained about this issue for some time, but fortunately the fluky goal did not cost the Cougars the win. Goyer scored in the middle frame, and Jones notched the final score in the last period. With the 4-2 victory, the Cougars clinched a playoff spot.[2011]

The Western Hockey League announced the establishment of a $500 award for the player voted most valuable in the league by players and coaches. To qualify, the player had to participate in at least forty games. Each team would receive sixteen votes, with players and coaches only able to vote for opposing team members. The result of the voting would be announced at the end of the season.[2012]

The Cougars had an up-and-down weekend. On Saturday night in Victoria, they defeated the league-leading Canucks 3-1. Anderson and Goyer scored in the second period to take the lead, and after Vancouver went ahead early in the third period, Haworth fired the winner just under two minutes later. It was a solid team effort. On Sunday in Seattle, the Cougars came up short against the team they were battling with for second place in the standings, ending on the short end of a 7-5 score. Macauley, Fashoway, Goyer, Haworth, and Matthews had goals in a losing cause. Coach Laycoe said that some players had "their worst performance of the year."[2013] The Cougars took their frustration out on the Comets when they played their last road game of the season. They thumped their opponents, 9-2, setting a record for the most victories in a season with thirty-six, exceeding the record of the 1950-51 champion Cougars which had been tied by the 1955-56 team. They played their best road game of the season. Pelletier stopped thirty-three shots to backstop the team to victory. Jones notched his thirty-fourth and thirty-fifth goals of the season and added four assists; Fashoway got his thirty-second and thirty-third and added two assists, while Masnick had one goal and three assists.

Other Cougar scorers were Ford, Blackburn, Goyer, and Haworth.[2014]

The next game, on March 16, was Ladies Night at Memorial Arena. The first 100 women through the doors received nylon hosiery, and the next 300, miniature orchids. There was also a free draw for more prizes, with tickets given to all women in attendance. In the intermission, selected Cougars players competed against Comets player in speed and shooting contests.[2015] The opponents were the same Spokane Comets who had been humiliated the night before. The Comets took advantage of an over-confident bunch of Cougars and defeated them, 6-3, spoiling the night for the many ladies in the crowd. Masnick, Bionda, and Haworth were the only players to get pucks past Spokane goaltender Emile Francis.[2016] The Cougars closed out the regular season with a game against the Seattle Totems, the team they would also face in the first round of the playoffs. Fashoway opened the scoring, but the Cougars surrendered three goals to Seattle to enter the second period with a deficit of 3-1. However, Masnick and Wright counted goals in that period, and neither team was able to score in the final frame. It was then that Don Blackburn had his finest play as a Cougar when he shot the puck past Bentley to win the game for the Cougars, 3-2. It was the thirty-seventh victory of the season for the Cougars, setting a new club mark.[2017] Doug Anderson repeated as winner of the Wally Smith Memorial Trophy for best combining of sportsmanship and ability, while Arnie Schmautz was voted the most valuable player on the team.[2018]

The first round of the playoff was a best-of-seven series. Victoria, as the fourth-place finisher, opened the playoffs in Seattle. The Cougars won in spectacular fashion, coming from behind to snatch victory from the jaws of defeat. Seattle scored first, and then Haworth tied the score. Then Seattle scored again to finish the first period up 2-1. After a scoreless second frame, Haworth hit the back of the net early in the final frame to end the scoring in regulation time. It was then up to Haworth to be the hero

23 - COUGARS UNDER NEW OWNERSHIP—AGAIN

of this game, as he fired the winner after 9:21 of extra time.[2019] The second game was played back in Victoria, and, again, the Cougars won the day. After an outstanding team effort, they emerged with a 5-0 decision over the Totems, to take a 2-0 lead in the series. Checking tenaciously, they kept the Totems scorers at bay—a feat that had been accomplished only once during the regular season. After a scoreless first frame, Goyer, Ford, and Wright came through in the second period to give the home team a 3-0 lead. Blackburn and Goodwin completed the rout with goals in the third period. Back in Seattle, the Cougars surrendered an early goal to scoring leader Guyle Fielder, just as a Cougar penalty expired, but Jones tied the game before the end of the first period. The middle frame belonged to Victoria, as the only goals were scored by Masnick and Fashoway. The Totems scored in the third period, but Goyer got that one back. The final score of 4-2 could have been entirely different had Pelletier not played an outstanding game.[2020]

Victoria now had a commanding 3-0 lead in the series: one game away from advancing to the second round for the first time since the 1955-56 season. The series returned to Victoria, where 4,012 fans watched their beloved Cougars go ahead in the game when Macauley scored the first goal at 4:28 of the third period. It turned out that was all the Cats needed to win the game, but Arlo Goodwin put the icing on the cake when he found the back of the net near the end of play. The 2-0 shutout gave the series win to the Cougars, and they moved on to face Vancouver in the league championship. The Canucks had disposed of Edmonton in four straight games.[2021]

The league final was a best-of-nine series. For the first time, two games of the series would be played in Los Angeles, as the WHL wanted to gauge the popularity of hockey in the California city with a view to possible expansion in the future. There was some concern over the health of goaltender Pelletier, who had sustained a cut over his eye in a previous game, then had played the next night. The club doctor said that the swelling had gone down enough for him to play, but Coach Laycoe brought in Emile Francis to be used in an emergency.[2022]

The first game of the series was played in Vancouver. Belisle opened the scoring for the Canucks, but Goyer tied it for the Cougars before the end of the first period. After a scoreless second period, Fashoway put the Cougars ahead. However, Vancouver tied the score in the last minute when they pulled their goaltender and Carmichael flipped the puck over Pelletier from right in front of the net. That sent the game to overtime, where Anderson ended it after only 2:12 to give Victoria a 1-0 lead in the series.[2023] The next two games were played at the 16,000-seat Los Angeles Arena, giving the California city its first taste of professional hockey since 1950. Executives from all teams in the WHL were on hand to view the games, and they would be the topic of discussion at the upcoming league meetings. This was the first time in league history that games were played in a neutral location.[2024]

The first game drew a crowd of only 5,000, who watched the Cougars win again. Despite the humid conditions and sticky ice, it took only thirty-one seconds for Gerry Goyer to get the Cougars on the board. The Canucks tied the score before the period was over and took the lead after six minutes of play in the middle frame. Minutes later, Goyer scored his second goal, this time on the power play, and the game was tied. Anderson got the next goal that proved to be the winner, and Jones added insurance just after the halfway point of the third period. Pelletier played well in goal and was assisted by his forwards, who checked tenaciously, and the defence, who played a great game in the last two periods. Victoria won the game, 4-2, and took a 2-0 lead in the series.[2025] Team owner Jim Piggott, who was considering moving the Cougars to Los Angeles for the next season, said it was not yet time to make a decision. He noted that the Los Angeles Coliseum Commission must determine if it wished to have a team, and the WHL would have to approve any shift.[2026]

Game three was a close affair. Falling behind 2-0 after the second period, the Cougars finally got untracked and got on the scoreboard with goals by Matthews and Haworth. However, they could not hold the Canucks offence back, and at 18:43, Danny Belisle fired home the winning goal. It was a heartbreaking loss for Victoria, and they would have to regroup for the next game at home. Coach Laycoe blamed the heat for the loss, as he said his team ran out of energy.[2027] From that point on, the Cougars seemed to have lost their fire-power, and their play deteriorated. In the game back in Victoria, where the fans expected great things from their club, the Cougars played a listless game and forgot about teamwork, letting the Canucks walk over them in a 6-2 victory for the mainland team. It was a disappointing loss, but Coach Laycoe felt his team could recover.[2028]

The series switched back to Vancouver, now tied at two games apiece. It was a whole new scenario, with the team that won three more games winning the final round. Vancouver opened the scoring when former Cougar Kilburn found the back of the net early in the game. Jones scored the only marker of the middle frame, setting the stage for Canucks' Belisle to score the winning goal for the third game in a row. Vancouver now held a 3-2 series lead.[2029] Despite what he had said a few days earlier, Jim Piggott decided to apply for permission to shift the Cougars to Los Angeles, with the decision to be made at a league directors' meeting in Calgary, May 12-13.[2030] A crowd of only 3,590 fans attended the next game in Victoria. They were most upset with referee Scott Morrison, who disallowed two goals that the Cougars felt they had scored, making the difference in the close game. The first was a shot that Hay fired at the net at the same time as Fashoway was checked into the net by Kurtenbach. It was ruled that the net was off its pegs when the puck crossed the goal line. The second instance came in the last minute of play, when the Cougars had an extra attacker on the ice. Masnick put the puck in the net, but the referee blew his whistle for penalties at the same time. Verdict: no goal. It was a disappointing end to a well-played game, and it left the Cougars on the wrong end of a 2-1 score, facing elimination in Vancouver in the next game.[2031] Playing before a sell-out crowd of 5,500 at the Vancouver Forum, the Canucks got off to a 2-0 lead, but the plucky Cougars tied the game at 3-3 on goals by Goyer, Matthews, and Fashoway. However, three unanswered goals by the Canucks in the third period secured the 6-3 victory for them, and they won the President's Cup for the second time.

After the game, Coach Laycoe said,

> *"The whole series was a nightmare for us. There was no resemblance between our team against Vancouver and the one that beat Seattle in the semi-final. We just made too many errors in the final round. And, in that last game, we had most of the play and all Vancouver did was to score six goals. It was disappointing to get a team into the final and not be able to play our best hockey. Defensively, we were possibly the worst we've been all season. But you've got to give credit to the Canucks. Their defence, both legally and illegally, was tremendous."*[2032]

All that remained now for Victoria fans to do was to wait for the decisions of the WHL meetings in Calgary. On May 12, the league announced that a Portland franchise would be added to the league for the 1960-61 season. Franchises were issued to Los Angeles and San Francisco, but they would remain league property until "suitable dates are arranged and until an application can gain approval from the league." California teams would likely join the league in the 1961-62 season. In the meantime, there would be eight teams in the WHL for the 1960-61 season. Other decisions reached by the meeting were that "each team will dress fourteen players for each game, and each team must carry and play two rookies until November 15." The league would operate on a seventy-game schedule from about mid-October to mid-April.[2033] This meant there would be hockey in Victoria for at least one more season.

23 - COUGARS UNDER NEW OWNERSHIP—AGAIN

Victoria Cougars, 1959-60. Photo from the author's collection.

24 - THE LAST HURRAH FOR THE COUGARS

With the change to eight teams, the league looked entirely different in the 1960-61 season. For the Cougars, the addition of the Portland Buckaroos, who took over the former New Westminster Royals franchise, meant the loss of a significant number of players who had been loaned to Victoria, as well as their manager-coach. Moving with Hal Laycoe to Portland were: Jack Bionda, Gordie Fashoway, Arlo Goodwin, Gord Haworth, Art Jones, Ron Matthews, and Arnie Schmautz. These moves left considerable gaps in the team, particularly on offence, as these players had accounted for 61.25 percent of the total Cougar offence the last season. Only seven players played for both the 1959-60 Cougars and the 1960-61 version.[2034] New coach George Agar had his work cut out for him.

Season tickets went on sale, and patrons had until September 30 to secure the same seats as they had the last season. There were two choices for fans: They could pay a deposit at the beginning of the season, reserve the seats, and pick up and pay for them before every game; or they could pre-pay for the entire season and have the tickets mailed to them.[2035]

Among the expected additions to the veterans at training camp at Vernon were junior standouts Bert Fizzell and Don Wilson, Hugh Currie, Jack McLeod, Don McLeod, Art Hart, and Bill Swarbrick.[2036] Later additions to the roster were: Lionel Repka, Pete Wright, Wayne North, Jim Moro, Pat Ginnell, and Don Makaw. Junior goaltender Gary Waugh attended to gain experience.[2037] The coach got a pleasant surprise when Charlie Goodwin arrived at training camp without being invited. That offset the worry about not hearing from Jack McLeod, who had threatened to retire from hockey.[2038] Fizzell and Don Mcleod were the best players at early scrimmages, and Coach Agar said that Waugh and Macaw were good prospects but would not likely make the club that year.[2039] After a sweep of their exhibition series against interior senior teams and Nanaimo Clippers by huge margins, the Cougars returned to Victoria to face the reality of the new season.[2040]

The opening lineup for what would be the last season of professional hockey in Victoria (for a few years) was goaltender Marcel Pelletier; defencemen Hugh Currie, Don McLeod, Jim Hay, and Wayne North; and forwards Doug Anderson, Don Wilson, Bert Fizzell, Gerry Goyer, Pat Ginnell, Jim Moro, Doug Macauley, George Ford, and Bill Swarbrick.[2041]

The new-look Cougars fell behind, 2-0, and did not score their first goal (by Hay) until midway through the second period. However, the youngsters took over in the final frame, and Don Wilson tied the score just before the five-minute mark of the third period and Bert Fizzell won the game with a shot off a pass by Anderson at the eight-minute mark. Pelletier held the Totems off the score sheet after that, and the Cougars had their first home victory of the season.[2042] For their first road game, the Cougars tackled the Seattle Totems. Victoria scored the first and last goals, but Seattle scored three in between for a 3-2 victory. Goyer and Anderson led the way for Victoria, while Marc Boileau had two for the home team and Tom McVie added a third.[2043] Colin Kilburn came to town with his new team, the Comets, and did not let stitches in his head prevent him from playing. In attendance at the game were club-owner Jim Piggott, league president Al Leader, and Montreal Canadiens vice-president Kenny Reardon. The game was entertaining, and the 2,124 fans in attendance got their money's worth. Veteran Macauley scored the opening goal for the Cougars, but Spokane counted a pair to take the lead. Fizzell tied the game midway through the third period, sending the game to overtime. Spokane had early chances, but Pelletier turned them all aside. Macauley notched his second goal at 2:29 to win the game. Kilburn was held off the scoresheet.[2044]

After watching the team, Piggott agreed that the Cougars needed help if they were to have a successful season. Coach Agar released Bill Swarbrick (who had played only three games of his five-game trial) back to Kelowna of the Okanagan Senior League.[2045] Victoria then entertained Winnipeg for two games. In the first, goaltender Pelletier made the difference for the Cats. He stopped all but one of the thirty-three shots fired at him, while his opponent Lumley allowed four goals. The Warriors opened the scoring, but that was the end of their offence for the evening. Jim Moro tied the game and assisted on the next goal by Bill Johansen. Goals by Fizzell and North in the third period put the game on ice, and the Cougars had another victory by a 4-1 score.[2046]

In the second game, the Cougars gave up the first goal, then scored twice to take the lead. However, they seemed to switch defensive tactics in the third period, and it proved their undoing as the Warriors outscored Victoria, 4-1, in that final frame to win the game 5-3.[2047] The Cougars got back on the winning track against Spokane with a 5-3 win. George Ford led the way with two goals; others came from Johansen, Moro, and Wilson. Victoria had a 5-1 lead at one point and allowed a couple of late goals to make the score a little closer.[2048] The next night in Spokane, the tables were reversed. The Comets scored first, a goal by Chorley tied the game, but Spokane went ahead for good before the end of the second period. Chorley scored in the third period, but it was too little, too late, and the Cougars lost the game, 4-2.[2049]

Bill Saunders was added to the Cougars' roster, although he was not expected to be in the lineup for the next match.[2050] Bert Fizzell was again the hero when the Cougars played Calgary. The game started with Hay counting in the first period. Calgary tied the game early in the second frame, but a goal by Ginnell put Victoria ahead again. In the third period, Calgary scored two goals, and only Wilson could find the back of the net for the Cougars. That set up overtime, and that is where Fizzell came through again, scoring the winner, at 3:38, for a 4-3 victory for the home team. He had already notched some important goals for the Cats, and fans hoped he continued his excellent work.[2051]

It was like old home week when the Portland Buckaroos came to town. Former Cougars Schmautz, Haworth, and Jones scored for Portland with only Chorley and Wilson replying for Victoria. The Laycoe-coached Buckaroos checked the Cougars into the ice and emerged with a 5-2 victory, witnessed by 3,215 fans.[2052] The Cougars got their first road win of the season in Vancouver, as Pelletier was absolutely brilliant in stopping all but two of the thirty-seven shots fired his way. Macauley, Saunders, and McLeod provided the offence for Victoria.[2053] The drive for a second road win came close but was unsuccessful as the Cougars lost their game, 4-3, to Spokane. The Comets scored the first two goals, but Moro replied for the Cats before the end of the first period. After a scoreless second frame, Spokane added two more goals before Moro scored another two for the hat trick. Despite storming the net in the dying minutes, the Cougars were unable to tie the score.[2054]

Memorial Arena manager Joe Dutkowski announced that all remaining home games, except for the December 26 and January 2 afternoon games, would start at 8:30 p.m. Friday and Saturday games were starting at 9:00 p.m. while weekday games started at 8:00 p.m. This would make the start times of all games the same and reduce confusion.[2055] The first game under the new starting time was against Spokane. Saunders scored both of the Cougar goals, as they lost 3-2 to the Comets. The game featured a weird penalty-shot play. As reported in the *Victoria Daily Times*:

"Colin Kilburn, former Victoria manager-coach, got a break with Wayne North the only Victoria defender barring his way to the goal. Kilburn, getting by the defenceman as North's stick broke, had a clear path to the goal and North dropped the remaining portion of a shattered weapon as the rules dictate. However, the chunk of lumber dropping from North's hands slid ahead and momentarily hampered Kilburn's goalward flight. Referee Juckes whistled for a penalty shot, one of the few ever called at the arena. Johnson was elected to take the shot and the puck placed at the Victoria blueline. When Juckes sounded his whistle, Marcel dashed from his goal and slapped the puck down the ice. Juckes, apparently ruling that the puck was in play when the whistle sounded, called for a face-off. That brought a torrid protest from the Comets and Kilburn immediately informed the official scorer the game was being played under protest. Rule 31, Section B, of the WHL rulebook, states: 'the goaltender must remain in the goal crease until the attacking player has contacted the puck in his own attempt to score . . .' It is probable that if the game had ended in a tie or a Victoria victory, the protest would have been upheld and a replay ordered, which would've been downright embarrassing to the referee." [2056]

In player changes, Pat Ginnell was sent to Portland after a disappointing start,[2057] and defenceman Georges Roy was added on loan from the Chicago Blackhawks.[2058]

In a wide-open game with plenty of scoring, the Cougars defeated Edmonton, 5-3, at Memorial Arena. Fizzell scored his first hat trick in professional hockey to lead the hometown scoring; Goyer and Saunders added one each. A total of eighty-nine shots were fired on the two goaltenders, evidence of the open play that was very exciting to the 3,376 fans on hand to watch the game. They left the arena impressed by their new-look Cougars.[2059] The Cats travelled to Portland, where they were hammered, 7-3 (by their former teammates). Among the Portland scorers were Ginnell, Haworth, and Fashoway. McLeod, Johansen, and Ford replied for Victoria.[2060] Back home, the Cougars finally solved the Portland problem. Moro opened the scoring, then Ford scored two goals in twenty-one seconds to lead the Cats' attack. Macauley and Goyer added two third-period goals in fifty seconds to secure the 5-2 victory.[2061]

After a relatively successful start to the season, at 8-7, the Cougars lost their next four games to fall well below .500 on the season. First, they dropped an 8-6 decision in Vancouver, despite a hat trick by Saunders.[2062] Next, Vancouver won a game, 2-0, in Victoria, as the Cougars were unable to put a puck in the net.[2063] The next game would be remembered as the highest-scoring match to date in the WHL, but unfortunately for the Cougars, they were on the short end of a 9-7 score. They seemed to forget the defensive work that had carried them to victories earlier in the season and allowed the Stampeders to break in on net. On the positive side, Saunders continued his scoring with two goals and an assist, Goyer had two goals, and Ford had two assists. Other goals came from Fizzell, McLeod, and Moro.[2064] In Seattle, the Cats could kill penalties, but the need to cost them dearly in a 4-2 loss. Only Macauley and Johansen found the back of the net for Victoria.[2065] The coach and his players knew that

24 - THE LAST HURRAH FOR THE COUGARS

they would have to improve, or it would be a very long season of disappointment. In the last game before a Prairie swing, the Cougars found their game and defeated Winnipeg, 3-1. Falling behind 1-0 in the first period, they found their skating legs and scoring powers, and goals by Fizzell, Goyer, and Saunders carried the team to its first victory in five games.[2066] It was just the result they needed before heading out on a seven-game road trip.

The first game was at Calgary, where the Stampeders eked out a 2-1 victory over Victoria, who ran into a hot goaltender in Lucien Deschenes, who stopped their shooters time after time. Macauley had tied the game for Victoria, but Leopold scored under two minutes later to give the home team the win.[2067] The next night in Edmonton, the Cats played an even better game and got the result they wanted. Falling behind 2-0 by the end of the first period, the Cougars rallied, scoring the next four goals to win the game, 4-2. Cougar marksmen were Chorley, McLeod, Macauley, and Ford, the last into an empty net.[2068] However, the game two days later was an Edmonton victory. Victoria fell behind, 4-0, and could not catch up. Edmonton goaltender Riggin played well, stymying the Cougar attack and only allowing goals by McLeod, Goyer, and Fizzell.[2069] The next game in Calgary was a disaster, as the Stampeders stomped the hapless Cougars, 7-2. Calgary outshot Victoria by a 49-19 margin—and the score reflects that play.[2070] It was the kind of game that was best forgotten, except as a spur to improve play.

While the team was in the midst of their road trip, the league held a directors' meeting. President Al Leader denied rumours that Winnipeg and Victoria would be withdrawing from the league. He said that, although attendance was down in those cities, as well as Calgary, there was no proof of any team leaving the league at this time. In other league business, WHL owners had an issue with the NHL televising games on Saturday nights, as it meant fewer fans at their local games. Winnipeg owner Jack Perrin suggested that the NHL compensate WHL teams each time an NHL game was televised in their area on the same Saturday night that there was a local hockey game. The directors felt that "territorial rights should include television compensation." Officials were instructed to enforce the "freezing-the-puck rule and unnecessarily holding of the puck by goaltenders." The league would have a new trophy, donated by the former owner of the New Westminster Bruins, Fred Hume, for the most sportsmanlike player as judged by the print and radio reporters.[2071]

Cougars program 1960-61. From the author's collection.

A trip to Winnipeg proved to be just what the Cougars needed as they took both games there to improve their overall record slightly. The defence led them in the first game, playing their best game of the trip, and even got in on the scoring. After falling behind, 1-0, the Cougars stormed back with goals by North, Hay, and Fizzell to take the lead. Saunders sealed the 4-1 victory when he fired the puck into the empty net just before the end of the game.[2072] On the day between games in Winnipeg, Coach Agar made player changes. He cut Roy from the team as he felt the player had reported out of shape and had not contributed much in the four games he had played, then announced that Paul Masnick, who had played for the team the prior season, would be rejoining the Cougars.[2073]

The second game against the Warriors was a 3-0 shutout for Marcel Pelletier, his first of the season. Two goals by Goyer and one by Anderson gave the Cougars all the offence they needed. Victoria was now six points ahead of Winnipeg, who occupied the league basement.[2074] The last game on the extended trip was in Vancouver, where the Canucks shut out the weary Cats, 5-0. It had been one of their better road trips as they split, 3-3, on the Prairies, where wins were hard to come by.[2075]

In a Boxing Day matinee, the Cougars upended Portland, 6-4, before 3,557 fans. The liner of Goyer, Ford, and Saunders led the Cougar offensive with eleven points: Goyer and Ford each had two goals and an assist, while Saunders added four assists. Portland had a 2-1 lead by the end of the first period and each time had two goals in the second frame. It was in the third period that the Cougars won the game when they scored three unanswered goals to secure the win.[2076]

The final game of 1960, against Spokane, was a wild, penalty-filled affair. Gone was the spirit of Christmas! The game was late in starting as youngsters tossed shot pellets onto the ice and they had to be carefully removed. Skating well in the first period, the Cats ran into a brick wall named Cesare Maniago in the Comet net, and he held them off the scoresheet. However, in the middle frame, the Cougars scored twice on goals by Ford and Saunders, but the Comets managed to tie the game after each goal. In the third period, the roof caved in on Maniago as the Cats scored four goals in less than four minutes to secure the 6-2 victory: Macauley at :35, Goyer at 2:49, Johansen at 5:17, and North at 6:39.

The donnybrook began at 18:37 of the third period as a two-man event when Spokane's Dick Lamoureux tangled with Victoria's Wayne North. Then, two other fights broke out, followed quickly by the Spokane bench door opening and all their players coming onto the ice, followed seconds later by the Victoria bench clearing, as well. The fighting erupted in a thirty-man brawl, and when the linesmen tried to break it up, they were in danger of being hurt, so retreated to let the players tire themselves out. Tempers calmed down after about fifteen minutes. A fan came out of the stands to pick up a couple of discarded Comet sticks, but Spokane's trainer tackled the would-be thief and dropped him to the ice. Referee Lou Farelli handed out five-minute penalties to Hay, North, and Currie of Victoria and Folk, Lamoureux, and Steve Witiuk from Spokane. Also, each player who left the bench to enter the brawl was assessed a ten-minute misconduct penalty. The 220 penalty minutes for the game set a new record for the league. The total of eighteen misconducts, six majors, and the six minors called earlier in the game, far exceeded the 147 minutes assessed to Seattle and New Westminster in a match in March 1956. Also, each misconduct penalty carried with it a fine of ten dollars, so the league coffers ended up $180 richer. The clubs played the last ninety-three seconds with four men for each team—and no further incidents.[2077]

The first game of 1961 was a much tamer affair. The Cougars stuck to good hockey with short, crisp passes and tight checking as they upended the Edmonton Flyers, 6-1, in an afternoon matinee. Goyer, Ford, Saunders, Macauley, Wilson, and Hay all scored single goals for Victoria as they dominated their opponent in all phases of the game.[2078] Their recent success moved them from the league basement to sixth place, but they were only seven points behind the league-leading Vancouver and Calgary teams. A playoff spot that had seemed unattainable in November was now entirely possible.

Victoria's playoff plans took a step backward when they travelled to Spokane and were shut out,

5-0, by the Comets. The Cougars played with enthusiasm in the first period but were unable to solve goaltender Gilles Boisvert. In the last two periods of the game, they fired only thirteen shots in total, and none found the back of the net.[2079] Returning home, the Cougars found their scoring legs again and defeated Vancouver, 3-1. The Canucks scored in the first period, but the Cougars shut the door after that while scoring three goals of their own by Goyer, Johansen, and Ford.

However, the club took its show on the road to Portland and played one of their worst games of the season in being shut out by the Buckaroos, 9-0. There was some justification for their poor play as they encountered transportation problems and did not arrive at the arena until the time at which the game was supposed to start. Given thirty minutes to get ready, they had no energy and played very poorly.[2080] They would have to start winning more games on the road if they wished to do well in the latter part of the schedule.

Fans wondered what would happen the next time Spokane came to town. They would find out on Kids' Gifts Night, on January 10. This game had none of the fireworks of the previous encounter and was a listless, dull affair. The Cougars seemed to be half asleep through most of the evening and even the presence of 5,178 fans, most of them screaming youngsters, could not spur them to a better effort. Ford had the only goal for the home team in what had to be one of the worst home games of the season. More than thirty prizes donated by local merchants and the hockey club were given away to youngsters between periods. Young Betty Gray won the top prize, a go-cart.[2081]

The uninspired play continued when Seattle visited Victoria. The Totems outscored the Cougars, 8-2, on their way to their first victory in the capital city since February 15, 1969. The play was so bad that many of the 2,422 fans in attendance booed their efforts. Ford and Fizzell scored in a losing cause.[2082] The Cats then headed to Portland, where they had been shellshocked, 9-0, a week before.

The result was a bit closer this time but was still a 6-4 loss.

The Cougars got off to a good start with an early goal by Saunders, then watched Portland tie the score by the end of the first period. Goyer scored to put them ahead again, but the Buckaroos scored three goals before Saunders notched his second. The only other Victoria goal came late in the third period off the stick of Ford, but it was too late to be of any consequence.[2083] The Cougars had now lost four consecutive games and had slipped down in the standings. They would now play four games on home ice, hoping to snap out of the losing streak.

In the first game before a woeful crowd of 1,641, they outworked Edmonton on their way to a 5-3 victory. It was a close game with the lead changing hands many times. Edmonton opened the scoring, but Macauley got that one back at the end of the first period. The Flyers scored early in the second period, but goals by Goyer and Fizzell put the Cougars in the lead. However, Edmonton scored early in the third frame to tie the score at 3-3. A goal by Anderson just 2:08 later put the Cougars in the lead to stay. An empty-net goal by Ford sealed the victory.[2084]

New Cougar Leo Amadio was in the lineup for the game against Portland. He had been traded on January 17, from the Sudbury Wolves of the Eastern Professional Hockey League, for Paul Masnick who had not produced as expected.[2085] Even a new player could not help the Cougars as they lost a close game, 1-0, to the Buckaroos. The lone goal was scored by former Cougar Gord Fashoway, adding insult to injury.[2086] The Cats got back on the winning track again with a 5-3 decision over Calgary. They scored the first three goals on their way to the victory. Ford, Saunders, and Fizzell had goals in the first period, but Calgary had the only score of the middle frame. Macauley and Fizzell had the first goals in the final period; then the Stampeders mounted a furious attack that fell just short. Doug Anderson had his best game since the beginning of the season. He checked tenaciously and had assists on three of the goals.[2087] Unfortunately, Portland came to town, and they went home with a 3-1 victory. Close checking by the Buckaroos kept the Cougars off-balance, and they never really got going.[2088] Penalty trouble was costly against Seattle, and when the dust settled, the Totems had skated their way to a 5-1 victory. The Cougars had their chances but could not beat their old nemesis Bentley in the Seattle net. Victoria was now in sixth place in the standings, but the gap between them and the teams in front of them was growing wider.[2089]

George Agar finally landed Barrie Ross. In a complicated transaction, Ross was traded to the Cougars from Winnipeg by the Toronto Maple Leafs, for the rights to Gerry James, a two-sport (hockey and baseball) athlete. Agar was also considering playing defenceman Wayne North on the forward line as he had done so well in that position in recent games.[2090] A special visitor to the next game against Winnipeg was Montreal Canadiens' star Maurice Richard, who received a tray as a gift from the city and presented prizes during the intermissions. Coach Agar shuffled his lines before the game, and it certainly worked this time. As they had with disturbing regularity lately, the Cougars fell behind, 2-0, then came back to take the lead on goals by North and two by Goyer. Winnipeg then tied the game, forcing it to overtime. Much to the delight of the 2,770 fans at Memorial Arena, Macauley scored his thirteenth goal of the season to give the Cougars a 4-3 win.[2091] The improved play continued in the next game. Seattle came to town, and the Cougars blasted them, 7-1. Victoria had a 3-1 lead by the end of the second period and cruised to the victory. Nine Cougars had at least one point. Saunders had two goals and two assists, Macauley had two goals and an assist, and Ross had three assists to lead the charge.[2092]

The Cougars then left on an eight-game road trip that could make or break their season. In Winnipeg, they won their third consecutive game with a 4-1 decision over the Warriors. Former Warriors Red Johansen and Barrie Ross along with Winnipeg-born Bill Saunders handled the scoring for the Cougars. Pelletier lost his shutout bid when Winnipeg scored with less than five minutes left in the game.[2093] Two days later, the Warriors got their revenge when they beat the Cougars, 4-3. Johansen and Anderson gave Victoria a 2-1 lead by the end of the first period and extended the lead to 3-1 when North found the back of the net early in the third period. Then, Winnipeg scored three straight goals to win the game and put an end to the Cougars' winning streak.[2094]

The team moved to Alberta, where they faced the Flyers. Victoria recovered from their loss the night before and outscored Edmonton, six goals to three. George Ford scored two goals, while Fizzell, Saunders, Johansen, and Amadio had singles. Pelletier was a standout in net as the team moved closer to a playoff spot. They were now eight points ahead of both Edmonton and Winnipeg and had games in hand on both of them.[2095] In Calgary, Wayne North showed why he had been converted to a forward when he scored his fifth goal in six games to give his team a 4-3 lead going into the final frame. Unfortunately, the Stampeders scored three goals in the third period to win the game, 6-4.[2096] Little did the Cats know that they had embarked on a seven-game losing streak.

Three days later, Calgary demolished Victoria by a score of 8-1. The game was briefly tied in the first period when Ford scored, but that was the end of the Cougar offence. It was not a good game at all.[2097] Edmonton, with still a slight chance to make the playoffs, upended the Cougars, 5-3. Again, Victoria got on the board first, with a goal by North, Edmonton scored two goals, then Macauley tied the game again. The third period was the downfall for the Cougars as they could only score a goal by Goyer while the Flyers pumped three goals past Pelletier.[2098] Victoria's woes continued in Vancouver, where the Canucks shut them out, 4-0.[2099] The great scoring touch from mid-January had vanished, and Victoria was having difficulty scoring again. The losing streak reached five with a 5-4 loss to the Totems. The team played a much better game, but could not cash in on their chances. Goals by Macauley, Ross, and Currie kept them in the game and a score by North midway through the third period got the Cougars within one goal, but they could not score the equalizer. Failure to clear rebounds from in front of the net was the team's undoing as three of Seattle's goals were scored on rebounds. The only good thing to come out of the trip was that Edmonton failed to make up ground and was still six points back in the standings.[2100]

The road-weary Cats returned from their eighteen-day trip to face the Vancouver Canucks. It was Navy Night, with several hundred sailors in attendance and entertainment provided by the Naden Band. The Canucks opened the scoring in the second period, and the Cougars tied the game on a goal by Goyer late in the third period. Unfortunately for the home team, Vancouver won the game in overtime when former Cougar Bruce Carmichael beat Pelletier after 1:15 of extra time. The Cougars were guilty of defensive lapses and could not cash in on the scoring chances they had. That combination led to a 2-1 loss.[2101]

For some unknown reason, the Cats had yet another road game—in Spokane. Victoria took the lead on a goal by North, but Spokane tied the score before the end of the first period, then took the lead on a goal by Steve Witiuk early in the middle frame. The Cougars stormed back when Goyer and Macauley scored to begin the third period, but former Cougar Colin Kilburn notched two goals to give his new team the victory by a 4-3 score.[2102] The losing streak had now reached seven games and fans were beginning to wonder if the team would ever win another match. The team came home for a three-game homestand, hoping for a bit of "puck luck" to get them on the winning track again.

Their first opponents were Seattle Totems. For two-and-one-half periods, the team played very poorly, falling behind, 3-1, with only North able to beat Bentley. However, the Cats came alive, and Goyer and Saunders fired goals to tie the score. There was no scoring in the overtime period, so the game ended in a 3-3 tie. The Cougars had not lost, but they had not won, either. They were still five points ahead of Edmonton in the battle for sixth place in the standings and the final playoff spot.[2103]

Vancouver came to town, and the Cougars played a very passive game, letting the play come to them, rather than being the aggressors. In addition, they had great trouble clearing the puck from their own end and seemed to forget what team play was. They were a disorganized bunch with only Moro and Ross able to find the back of the net. Former Cougar Bruce Carmichael had two goals and an assist to lead his team to a 4-2 victory.[2104]

The Victoria club had now played nine games with only one point to show for their efforts. The only reason they were still in sixth place was that Edmonton was not playing much better than they were. In preparation for the next game, Coach Agar shuffled his lineup. Leaving the Goyer-North-Ford threesome intact, he moved Saunders between Moro and Macauley and put Ross with Anderson and Johansen. Fizzell who was nursing a charley-horse was named as a spare. Agar also changed his defensive pairings, putting Hay with Currie and McLeod with Amadio. He also told his team to play better positional hockey and to make it difficult for opponents to come into the defensive zone.[2105]

The changes seemed to have worked, for, on March 3, the Cougars won their first game since February 10, when they defeated Seattle by a score of 3-2. It did not look good for the home team early in the game, as they gave up the first goal. However, league penalty leader Frank Arnett cross-checked Currie, then skated down the ice to take on Ford. He received a penalty for his misdeeds, and that seemed to wake up the Cougars. North scored on the ensuing power play to tie the game. After a scoreless second frame, Macauley and Johansen scored in the third period to put the home team ahead by two goals. Seattle scored late in the final period but was unable to tie the score. Pelletier was again the star in the Victoria net, as he stopped almost everything the Totems fired his way.[2106]

The Cougars then travelled to Portland for two weekend games. On Saturday night, the Buckaroos scored a goal in each of the three periods, en route to a 3-1 victory. The only Cougar to beat Don Head in the Portland net was Ford. On Sunday, it looked as if the same thing would happen as former Cougar Art Jones scored two early goals. Moro's goal near the end of the first period narrowed the deficit, and Ford found the back of the net in the third period to tie the score. Neither team could score in overtime, so the result was a 2-2 tie.[2107]

Returning home, the Cougars next played Calgary. It was a high-scoring affair, but the 7-3 loss was not what the home team wanted. Calgary had opened the scoring, but two goals by Ross and one by Saunders had given Victoria the lead. Then the roof fell in on the Cougars. Calgary scored three more goals in ninety-three seconds before the end of the first period, added one in the second period, and two more in the third to win easily. The hot-and-cold Cougars were suddenly in danger of missing the playoffs, as they now only had a two-point lead on Edmonton with only one game in hand. Victoria was disorganized and allowed the Calgary forwards to enter the scoring zone almost at will.[2108] In their last thirteen games, the Cougars had won only once, tied twice, and lost ten. This was not the quality of play that would secure a berth in the playoffs.

Using bonuses as an incentive, Coach Agar put Saunders and Ross on the same line again. Saunders needed only four more goals to collect his bonus, while Ross needed three. The coach hoped that both players would be inspired to score more goals and that increased scoring would help pull the Cougars out of their terrible slump.[2109] The change paid immediate dividends in the next game against Spokane, as Ross scored two goals and added two assists, Saunders picked up a goal and three assists, and so did their line-mate Macauley. Other Cougar goals were notched by Hay and North. The Cougars were still in sixth place, as a result of their 6-3 victory, but Edmonton had also won their game, so every point from then on was crucial.[2110]

The Cougars travelled to Spokane for a return engagement, and the result was another win. Saunders opened the scoring with his twenty-sixth goal of the year, but Steve Witiuk tied the game with two seconds left in the first period. Ross (with his twentieth) and Fizzell (with his nineteenth) scored in the second period to give the Cougars a 3-1 lead. Goyer scored his twenty-ninth goal early in the third period to increase the lead, but Spokane counted two goals in sixty-nine seconds to bring the Comets closer. When their coach pulled the goaltender for an extra attacker, it backfired as Saunders fired a goal into the empty net. Marcel Pelletier sparkled in goal, stopping forty shots en route to the 5-3 victory. He even got in on the scoring, with an assist on the empty-net goal that clinched the game.[2111]

Things did not look good for Victoria in the first period of their game against Portland. Former Cougar Gord Fashoway had two goals in the first period to take his team to a 2-0 lead. However, it turned out he was the only Buckaroo able to get a puck past Pelletier, and the Cougars turned the game around in the second period with three goals (by Goyer, MacLeod, and Saunders) in just over four minutes. The game deteriorated when a penalty was assessed to Schmautz, which was followed by a call against goaltender Don Head, 1:06 later. Perhaps in an attempt to get a Cougar into the penalty box so the team would not be two men short, Tom Thurlby started swinging his stick at Goyer right after a face-off at 19:18. Within seconds, there were other fights all over the ice, a couple of players from each bench got into the action, and then Schmautz and Barney Krake (who was serving Head's penalty) left the penalty box to enter the fray. Referee Ross Valliere handed out fighting majors to the Buckaroos' Bionda, Thurlby, Rolfe, and Haworth as well as the Cougars' Ford, Hay, Saunders, and Goyer. In addition, Head was assessed an automatic misconduct for leaving his crease and fined ten dollars. It was quite an end to an exciting game, and the 3,000 fans at Memorial Arena went home happy, having got their money's worth for the evening.[2112]

Next on the agenda was a weekend road trip to Seattle and Portland. On Saturday, the Totems got the first goal, but Saunders tied it up at the beginning of the second period. Unfortunately for the Cougars, they gave away three goals in seven minutes to give Seattle the lead, which they never relinquished. Macauley scored for the Cougars in the third period to make it interesting, but a Seattle goal near the end of the game gave the Totems a 5-2 victory. On Sunday, first-period goals by Goyer, Hay, and Macauley got the Cougars off to a 3-1 lead. Despite playing short-handed, as Amadio and Ross were injured, the Cougars stuck to a checking game, and the three remaining defenders played additional time each. Fashoway scored early in the second period to bring Portland closer, but Saunders got a goal shortly thereafter to restore the two-point lead. Macauley added a second goal in the third period, so Portland's last goal had little effect on the final score of 5-3.[2113] When the dust settled, the Cougars had won their fourth game in five outings, and had a six-point edge on Edmonton, with both having played the same number of games. It should have been an easy run to a playoff spot, but the Cougars never seemed to do anything the easy way. They went on to lose their last six games and still managed to finish sixth; Edmonton played just as poorly as they had.

Coach Agar called up two junior players to fill in for injured players and to shake up the lineup a bit. Arriving on amateur tryouts were centre Ed Lawson and left-winger Don Makaw, both outstanding players in the Saskatchewan Junior Hockey League that season.[2114]

In league news, Jack Perrin offered his Winnipeg Warriors team for sale less than twenty-four hours after only 424 fans attended a game where the team beat Spokane, 4-2. Less than a hundred fans attended the game the next night. He wanted to move to San Francisco, but there was no proper ice surface there. The fate of the franchise was undecided as of yet, but it would likely not be located in Winnipeg.[2115]

Back in league play, Seattle visited Victoria and left with a 5-3 victory. The Cougars were led by Macauley, who scored two goals and added an assist, Ross with one goal and an assist, and Saunders who collected three assists. Victoria was in the game until the third period when the Ed Stankiewicz scored to give his team the lead, and an empty-net goal sealed the victory for the visitors.[2116] The Cougars moved closer to a playoff berth, despite losing in Portland, when Edmonton also lost. The Buckaroos scored first, Anderson tied it for Victoria, then Portland fired four straight goals to take a 5-1 lead before North fired a goal. In the third period, Saunders got his team a little closer, but Jones put the game away with the last goal in a 6-3 Buckaroo victory. The headline in the game account reminded fans that a tie in the upcoming game against Edmonton would clinch a playoff spot.[2117]

The start of that game was delayed to 9:00 p.m., so that hockey fans could watch the NHL Stanley Cup coverage of the game between Montreal and Chicago and then make their way to the Memorial Arena.[2118] The Cougars were playing the most important game of their season. All they needed was a tie to clinch a playoff spot. They started off well, as Ford scored two and Ross one for a 3-0 lead halfway through the second period. Three Edmonton goals in the span of three minutes erased the lead and a goal late in the third period gave the Flyers a 4-3 win and kept them mathematically alive in the playoff hunt. Victoria fans were disgusted that their team had a lead and were playing well, they could not hold that lead or find the winning goal themselves.[2119] All the Cougars could do now was hope they could win one more game, or else that the Flyers would lose one. That is exactly what happened, when Vancouver defeated Edmonton, 7-5, to eliminate them from the playoffs. The Cougars made it in through the "back door."[2120]

In their final home game of the season, Victoria fought hard but could not hold off the Buckaroos and wound up on the losing end of a 5-4 score. Matthews opened the scoring for Portland, but

Moro had two goals to give the Cougars a 2-1 lead going into the second period. Goyer increased the lead to 3-1 with a score early in the second period, but Portland had three goals to take the lead, 4-3, going into the third period. Saunders fired a goal in the final frame to tie the game, but former Cougar Arlo Goodwin fired the winner at 14:31, sending the Cougars to a 5-4 defeat before their home fans.[2121] It was yet another one-goal loss in a season where an odd goal here and there would have made all the difference between a fair season and a good one. In Spokane, the Cougars were trampled by the Comets and lost the game, 7-2. Only Ross and Fizzell scored for Victoria in one of their poorest games all season. The last game of the year was equally disastrous, as the Cougars dropped an 8-3 decision to the Totems. The game was tied 3-3 in the second period, with the Cougar goals coming from Fizzell, Ford, and Macauley, but Seattle scored the next three goals, and late Victoria scores by Saunders and Macauley did little more than make the score more respectable. The Cougars ended the season with a record of twenty-seven wins, forty-one losses, and two ties. Their total of fifty-six points was far from the first-place Stampeders' total of ninety-two.[2122]

The Cougars began the first round of the playoffs with a game in Vancouver. Playing with only three defencemen, Victoria opened the scoring on a goal by Ford, but they could not hold back the offence of the Canucks, who counted twice in the second period. There was no scoring in the final frame, but the Cats could not get the equalizer, even with Pelletier pulled for the extra attacker. Currie was an offensive spark while North was outstanding on defence in a losing cause.[2123] The second game was played in Victoria before a small crowd of 2,900. Doug Anderson got the opening goal; Macauley and Fizzell added counters in the middle frame. Hank Cahan got the Canucks on the board early in the third period, but Johansen fired a puck past Evans to give Victoria a 4-1 win and a 1-1 tie in the series. Barrie Ross and Jim Moro were unable to play, so injured defenceman Don McLeod had his sore chest treated with novocaine to kill the pain so that he could play. He delivered many hard hits throughout the game and was the individual star.[2124]

Game three was back in the Vancouver Forum before 2,481 fans. There was no scoring until Amadio hit the net in the second period, followed quickly by Saunders, and Macauley. Unfortunately, the Cougars let their defensive efforts lapse, and the Canucks got two goals to make the game close. Former Cougar Bruce Carmichael scored the tying goal at 19:34 (with the goaltender pulled for the extra attacker), sending the game to overtime. The teams played a full twenty minutes of extra time with no result, so the match went to a second overtime period. At 14:55 of that frame, George Ford took a pass from Gerry Goyer and fired a thirty-foot shot into the Vancouver net. Victoria now had a 2-1 lead in the series.[2125]

Back in Victoria, the Cats had a chance to win the series, if only they could use the home crowd as inspiration. However, it was not to be, as the Canucks upended Victoria, 3-1, with only Johansen scoring for Victoria.[2126] The series was now tied 2-2, with the final game being played in Vancouver. It would take good play with attention to detail to win the series and move on. Either team could win.

Great goaltending by Claude Evans carried the Canucks to a 3-1 victory, and the series win. Ford scored the first goal of the game, but it was the last one that Evans gave up. He stopped shot after shot, while his team was able to score three times on Pelletier.[2127] The season was over for the Cougars. It had been an up-and-down year, but considering that they were picked to finish last, they had a better record than had been forecast. No decision had been made on another season of hockey in Victoria, and none would be made until after the league meetings.

Ironically, the Portland Buckaroos were unable to play in their own arena, so made their temporary home in Victoria so local fans could still watch playoff hockey, regardless of the league's decision.[2128]

In league news, the rumours of a Los Angeles entry in the NFL were revived, but local fans hoped

24 - THE LAST HURRAH FOR THE COUGARS

that Victoria would remain as a part of the league. "The Coliseum Commission at Los Angeles reported today that it has instructed general manager Bill Nicholas to inform the National Hockey League that if it does not admit Los Angeles, the city will affiliate with the Western circuit." It was likely that teams would appear in Los Angeles and San Francisco with the Victoria and Winnipeg franchises moving. When Jim Piggott first purchased the Cougars, the WHL passed a resolution that he would get first chance to place a team in Los Angeles if the league expanded to California.[2129] Finally, on April 23, 1961, the WHL announced that Jim Piggott had been granted rights to Los Angeles and would move the Victoria franchise there for the next season. Winnipeg and Spokane would stay for at least one more season, as the WHL tried to gain the same status as the NHL. The prepared statement read:

> *"The WHL today took the first giant stride toward achieving major-league status when it voted to expand to Los Angeles and San Francisco. In unanimously approving this action, the governors of the league announced that they intend to reach major-league status in three to five years and to challenge the National Hockey League for the Stanley Cup."*[2130]

The *Victoria Daily Times* printed a short history of hockey in Victoria, stressing the early Cougars in 1912 and speaking with pride of the Stanley Cup win in 1925. It did not look good for professional hockey returning to Victoria, as the Memorial Arena was not large enough for the major-league status the WHL sought to achieve.[2131] For a while, there was a rumour that the Winnipeg franchise would be transferred to Victoria, but businessmen in Winnipeg banded together to keep the team in Manitoba.[2132]

There would be no professional hockey in Victoria for the 1961-62 season, and fans wondered if the city would ever have a pro team again. The wait would be a painful one.

The Victoria Cougars' name next appeared as the name of a team in the British Columbia Junior Hockey League, then of a junior franchise in the Western Hockey League for sixteen seasons. Many future NHL stars played in Victoria during that time. That team was sold in 1994 and moved to Prince George, taking the name "Cougars" with it. The local Vancouver Island Junior Hockey League - Junior B team now bears the name "Victoria Cougars," and uses a logo much like that of the 1960s-era professional team, so the name carries on, although it will likely never be used for a professional team again.

25 - GO, LEAFS, GO!

Professional hockey returned to Victoria in the fall of 1964 by a circuitous route. In June 1963, a group led by the NHL's Toronto Maple Leafs purchased the Spokane Comets—players, franchise, and all other assets—from principal owner, Mel Smith, after rising travel costs were making it difficult for the team to stay financially afloat. According to local press covering the team's move to Denver, the "move came suddenly and rather unexpectedly."[2133] The team was given the name "Invaders," and played regular-season games at the Denver Coliseum and playoff games at the arena at the University of Denver. However, after the team lost about $150,000 in their first season, Toronto's owner, Stafford Smythe, announced that the team would be moved to a new location (Victoria, BC, was the rumoured destination), because Denver hockey fans had not been able to guarantee 2,000 season tickets by a June 19, 1964, deadline.[2134] Once the move to Victoria was confirmed, the decision was met with favour by the other teams remaining in the league, as travel costs to Spokane had been very high. Thus, the Victoria Maple Leafs were born. Their uniforms were the same as their parent club, using blue and white and featuring a stylized maple leaf on the chest of the jersey.

The league had changed since the time of the Cougars. Edmonton and Calgary were gone, and now there were the two California franchises that had begun operating in 1961: the San Francisco Seals and the Los Angeles Blades (the former Victoria Cougars).

Victoria Maple Leafs sticker. From the author's collection.

In preparation for the start of the 1964-65 season, new theatre-style wooden seats were installed in parts of the Memorial Arena.[2135] Excitement built up as season tickets went on sale and fans looked forward to professional hockey again. Coach Rudy Pilous had fourteen of the players he had coached at Denver the previous year, when they had topped the league standings, before losing the championship to the Los Angeles Blades. Returning players were: Al Millar in goal; defencemen Sandy Hucul, Fred Hucul, Bill Shvetz, John Sleaver, Barry Trapp, and Ralph Winfeld; and forwards Bill Flett, Lou

Jankowski, Larry Keenan, Dick Lamoureux, Milan Marcetta, Gordie Redahl, and Steve Witiuk.

After a series of exhibition games, including one in Nanaimo before 666 fans,[2136] the Leafs got ready for their first league game in Los Angeles. Added to the team were rookie Rollie Wilcox and veteran Ed Mazur (formerly a Cougar).[2137]

The season opened on October 9, 1964, with a 7-3 loss in Los Angeles. Bill Shvetz scored the first goal for the new team, but the Leafs had already given up three goals at that point. Eddie Mazur found the net early in the second frame, but Los Angeles got that one back less than two minutes later. The Leaf to score in the third period was John Sleaver, while the Blades fired three past Millar to win easily.[2138] The next night, the Leafs were forced to play one defenceman short when Fred Hucul was unable to play. That put tremendous pressure on the three remaining defenders, and they were simply unable to hold back the Blades' scorers. In this game, the Leafs opened the scoring when Marcetta fired the puck past Norris in the Los Angeles net, but the Blades scored three straight goals to lead, 3-1, by the end of the middle frame. Marcetta and Keenan scored in the third period, but the Blades had two of their own and won the game, 6-3. It was not the start that Coach Pilous wanted, but he was keen to get home and show his team to the Victoria crowd.[2139]

The first professional hockey game in Victoria in three years—although it felt like a lot longer—was played before a disappointing crowd of only 1,732. City of Victoria Alderman Alfred Toone and league president Al Leader took place in the ceremonial face-off. Bob Barlow scored first for Seattle, then Lou Jankowski had two goals to give Victoria a lead. Two goals by the Totems gave them a 3-1 lead at the end of the middle frame. Seattle took a two-goal lead early in the final period, but Redahl hit the net to make it close. That set the stage for Jankowski to tie the game, with just over a minute left. However, Barlow notched his second score of the game at :58 of overtime, to give Seattle the victory and send the Victoria fans home sad.[2140]

Autographed hockey stick, Victoria Maple Leafs, 1964-65 team. From the author's collection. Photo by Heather McKeen-Edwards. Details of autographs in inset.

The History of Professional Hockey in Victoria, BC: 1911-2011

In news relating to the original Victoria Cougars, Fred Sandiford died in Victoria, on October 12, 1964. He had been the first man to install artificial ice in North America, laying the ice for the opening of the Patrick Arena and continuing to work there until the rink burned down in 1929. He also worked in Vancouver, Seattle, and New Westminster. Fred moved back to Victoria in retirement and was well-known in the local sports fraternity.[2141]

1964-65 Victoria Maple Leafs program. From the author's collection.

Back on the contemporary ice, the Maple Leafs won their first game of the season when they edged the San Francisco Seals, 3-2. Larry Keenan got the home team off to a good start with a goal early in the second period, but the Seals came back with two scores to take the lead. However, the final frame was all Victoria. Keenan scored his second to tie the game, and Redahl fired the winner, at 15:40. After three losses, it was good to get a win, and fans hoped for more of the same in the next match.[2142 2143]

For the next game, the Los Angeles Blades came to town. Al Millar played a great game, stopping thirty-two shots to backstop Victoria to a 3-1 victory. After Leo Labine had given the Blades a lead, Marcetta tied the game with less than a minute left in the opening period. After a scoreless second frame, the Leafs (Mazur and Sleaver) scored twice in the third period to secure the win. It was the second "W" in a row and moved the team into a third-place tie in the league standings.[2144] Vancouver came to town and left with a hard-fought 3-2 victory. The Canucks took a 2-0 lead in the first period, but goals by Redahl and Marcetta tied the game going into the final frame. There, the Leafs ran into penalty trouble and surrendered a goal with one man in the penalty box and one just released and not yet into the play.[2145] Despite their 2-4 record, the team had been in most of their games until the end, and with a bit of luck, could have won all those one-goal losses.

The team got back on the winning track with a thrilling 4-3 overtime win over Los Angeles. After allowing the first goal on a long shot by Willie O'Ree, the Maple Leafs buckled down and took the lead with scores by Marcetta and Fred Hucul. After a scoreless middle frame, the Blades regained the lead with two goals in the first half of the final frame, setting the stage for Bill Shvetz to score from a scramble in front of the net to tie the game. It took 8:41 of overtime before Jankowski took a pass from Sleaver and fired the puck into the net. The Leafs were back on a winning track and sent 1,935 fans home with smiles on their faces.[2146]

Added to the roster before the next game was defenceman Claude Labrosse, while Larry Keenan returned to the lineup after recovering from a toe injury.[2147] Going back on the road, Victoria dropped a game in Vancouver. The high-scoring Canucks fired six goals and only Keenan, Redahl, and Jankowski replied for the Maple Leafs.[2148] Portland came to town with several former Cougars in the lineup. Goals by Sandy Hucul, Keenan, and Sleaver gave the Leafs a 3-0 lead after two periods, but they could not sustain the effort in the third frame and allowed two

208

goals by former Cougar Arnie Schmautz, as well as Doug Messier and Mike Donaldson, and Portland escaped with a 4-3 win.[2149] The teams then travelled to Portland, and the Leafs lost another one-goal game, this one in overtime. After Leach had counted for the Buckaroos, Jankowski and Fred Hucul gave the Leafs a lead. However, they could not hold the lead even after Sleaver found the net, as they allowed Hebenton and Goyer to score twenty seconds apart. Jankowski fired the tying goal just before the end of regulation time, but Pat Stapleton put the puck past Millar at 6:30 of extra time to send the Leafs home with another loss, this time, 4-3.[2150]

Then it was on to Seattle for a date with the Totems. Penalties at inopportune times cost the Leafs this game, as they yielded three power-play goals on their way to a 4-3 defeat. Goals by Marcetta, Wilcox, and Jankowski were not enough to overcome the lack of discipline on the ice.[2151] So far in the season, Victoria had played eight one-goal games and won only two of them. This would have to change if they wanted to have a winning record.

Much to the relief of the team and its fans, the Maple Leafs won the next home game when they shut out Seattle, 2-0. They dominated the play but could not score until Sleaver fired a shot with under three minutes left to play. An empty-net goal by Redahl ensured the victory and ended the winless streak at four. After the game, the team sent Ed Lawson to Tulsa Oilers of the Central Professional Hockey League, leading to speculation about his replacement.[2152]

Against Los Angeles, the Leafs gave up an early first-period goal but came back on scores by Wilcox, Redahl, Lamoureux, and Keenan to take a 4-1 lead to the third frame. The Blades notched two goals to make the game close, but Millar stood his ground and the game finished with a 4-3 victory for Victoria.[2153] The homestand continued with a

Larry Keenan as a Maple Leaf.
Photo courtesy Ernie Fitzsimmons.

Claude Labrosse as a Maple Leaf.
Photo courtesy Ernie Fitzsimmons.

match against San Francisco. Despite two goals by Marcetta and Redahl and one by Keenan, they fell, 6-5, in overtime. It was yet another one-goal loss.[2154] The team received good news when Steve Witiuk, who had scored twenty-nine goals the last season for Denver, changed his mind about retiring and agreed to join the club.[2155] In their final home game before a four-game road trip, Victoria did not play very well and dropped a 5-2 decision to Portland. Diminutive Rollie Wilcox was the only Leaf to beat Don Head in the Portland net.[2156]

Victoria did not play much better in San Francisco. After taking a 2-0 lead on scores by Redahl and Keenan, they got sloppy and allowed the Seals to take a 3-2 lead. Jankowski tied the score, but San Francisco scored the last three goals in the game to win easily 6-3.[2157] The next evening, Victoria played much better and won its first road game of the season, 5-3, at San Francisco. Milan Marcetta led the scoring with two, Flett and Trapp scored their first goals of the season, and Sleaver added a single.[2158] Before the game in Seattle, manager Buck Houle announced that high-scoring Danny Belisle would be joining the team as soon as possible.[2159] The Maple Leafs travelled to Seattle and upset the first-place Totems, 4-1, before the largest crowd in Seattle's Western Hockey League history (9,008 fans). After a scoreless first frame, Bob Barlow scored the opening goal to put the home team ahead. However, Jankowski tied the score about four minutes later, and Marcetta, Keenan, and Wilcox put the game on ice in the final period. Belisle had an assist in his first action for Victoria; the team was finding its scoring touch.[2160] The modest two-game winning streak came to an end in Vancouver, where the Canucks upended Victoria, 5-3, in one of the most exciting games of the season. With the contest tied, 3-3, Billy McNeill got a lucky goal when he banked it into the net off Millar's equipment. An empty-net goal with a second left sealed the victory for the mainland team.[2161]

At Victoria, shaky defensive play cost the Leafs a game against Seattle. It was an up-and-down game with several lead changes. Gordie Redahl had a hat trick, and Lou Jankowski scored a pair, but two late-third-period scores by the Totems gave them a 7-5 win.[2162] The team gained another new player when goaltender Gary Smith was assigned from Toronto. He had played the previous season for the Memorial Cup-winning Toronto Marlboros and had been playing in Rochester. Also new in town was defenceman Bobby Taylor, better known as a flanker-back for the CFL Calgary Stampeders. The extra players meant that there could be a trade in the works, but management said nothing.[2163] The next day, the press reported that Fred Hucul had retired from the Maple Leafs and returned to his farm in Caroline, Alberta. Fred felt he was not playing up to the standard he expected of himself and thought he was hurting the club. His absence meant that Taylor would start the next game.[2164]

Victoria Maple Leafs puck

Vancouver came to town and spanked the Leafs, 6-2. It became apparent that goaltending was not the issue, as Smith replaced Millar and not much changed. The defence did not play well, and only Jankowski and Belisle could put a puck behind Gilles Villeneuve. It was a case of too many changes, and a total lack of cohesion by the Leafs and the fans let them know of their displeasure by booing loudly as the team left the ice.[2165] A trip to Portland did nothing to help the Leafs' cause when they dropped a heartbreaking 3-2 overtime loss to the Buckaroos. After spotting Portland a one-goal lead, the Leafs came back with scores by Belisle and Keenan but could not hold the lead and surrendered the tying goal before the end of the second frame. In overtime, McVie hit the net at 1:11, sending the Cougars down to their seventh one-goal loss that season.[2166] The team had now lost four games in a row and had to turn their game around if they wished to have a successful season.

Returning home to the friendly confines of Memorial Arena, the Leafs came up with a more disciplined effort and downed the Los Angeles Blades, 7-3. Rookie Wilcox had two goals while singles came from Belisle, Lamoureux, Marcetta, Keenan, and Mazur.[2167][2168] The next night, the Leafs played in Seattle and looked fatigued and could only manage a single goal from Redahl that came after the Totems had built up a three-goal lead.[2169] Next on the agenda was a four-game California road trip. In San Francisco, the Leafs rode a hat trick by Larry Keenan to a 6-5 victory over the Seals. His third goal gave Victoria the victory, while Shvetz and Labrosse led the defence in a concerted effort to protect goaltender Smith from the Los Angeles sharpshooters.[2170] The remainder of the trip did not go well for the Leafs. First, they lost, 6-4, in Los Angeles. Victoria had a brief 2-1 lead on goals by Jankowski and Mazur, but the Blades notched three straight counters to take the lead. The team then exchanged goals, with Redahl and Belisle finding the net for the Leafs while Maxwell and Young replied for Los Angeles. The Blades fired forty-two shots at Gary Smith, and the Leafs managed only thirty-one on Jack Norris.[2171]

Returning to San Francisco, the Leafs showed the effects of so much travel and dropped a 6-3 decision to the Seals. Briefly tied at 2-2 on goals by Redahl and Sleaver, the Leafs failed defensively after that, allowing their opponents to score four goals to their one (by Marcetta). Once again, Smith was the busiest player on the ice, facing fifty-three shots—twenty-four of them in the third period alone.[2172] The trip ended in Los Angeles with another loss. Al Millar started in goal but twisted his knee in the third period and had to leave the game. The Blades opened the scoring, and Sleaver responded three minutes later to end the first period tied, 1-1. However, Los Angeles had a goal in each of the remaining frames, while Victoria had no offence at all. They also received news that there would be no further help from the parent Toronto team, as they had suffered injuries and were playing short-handed themselves.[2173]

Starting a short homestand with a 10-19 record, the Leafs knew they had to start winning those close games to make their way up the standings. Things did not look good at the beginning of the game, as San Francisco took a 2-0 lead. Marcetta narrowed the lead to one, but the Seals added another score to restore the two-goal lead. The final period showcased an aggressive Leafs offence, and they stormed back with three goals to win the game. Witiuk, Redahl, and Keenan found the net behind Perreault, and for the first time in a while, the Leafs were able to hold the lead. Millar came up with several spectacular saves to preserve the victory.[2174] On Boxing Day, 1964, the Maple Leafs finally defeated the Buckaroos. Victoria took a 2-0 lead in the first period when Wilcox and Lamoureux found the back of the net, surrendered one Portland goal in the middle frame, and then traded single goals in the final period (Marcetta for Victoria) to win their first game in five against the Bucks.[2175] The Leafs won their third consecutive game when they upended the Totems, 4-1, in Seattle. Two goals by Wilcox, along with singles by Jankowski, and Marcetta powered Victoria to the victory. Millar lost his bid for a shutout when a puck deflected behind him off a teammate's body.[2176] For his efforts and stellar play, Victoria's Milan Marcetta earned "player of the week," accumulating three goals and two assists to move into sixth place in the league scoring race.[2177] The last game of 1964 was another win. A more respectable crowd of 3,160 watched their home team down Seattle by a score of 6-4. Led by the Keenan-Mazur-Witiuk line, the Leafs outscored the Totems two goals to one in each period, to secure their fourth straight win.[2178]

Junior player Paul Laurent was called up from the Toronto Marlboros for a two-game trial during a school break. In a game played on New Year's Day, 1965, Portland ended the Leafs' winning streak when they battled to a 1-1 tie. Former Cougar Bill Saunders counted for the Buckaroos, and Lamoureux answered just more than five minutes later. There was no further scoring for the remainder of the game, including overtime.[2179][2180]

The Leafs were now unbeaten in five games, which was just what they needed to move up the standings. A home victory over Vancouver resulted in a front-page announcement that read, "Leafs Go to Six as 4,000 Roar."[2181] Playing with speed and skating hard, Victoria outlasted Vancouver, 6-3, as the huge crowd chanted, "Go, Leafs, go" at every opportunity. Mazur had the first goal to give Victoria the early lead, only to have Bob McCusker tie it up. The middle frame belonged to the Leafs, as Jankowski and Keenan had the only scores. In the final period, Wilcox, Mazur, and Witiuk had Leaf goals, while the Canucks could only manage two goals.[2182] Al Millar played his best game of the season in a decisive 4-1 victory over Portland. The Leafs were clearly the best team in the opening period, and it was unfortunate that they were no more than one goal ahead on Witiuk's score. Portland tied the game on a defensive mistake early in the middle frame, but Shvetz restored the Victoria lead. Keenan and Marcetta had the only goals in the final period, giving the Leafs all the offence they needed, while Millar kept the Vancouver shots out of his net. The unbeaten streak was now at seven, and the Leafs were moving up the standings.[2183]

Victoria travelled to Vancouver, where the Canucks put an end to Victoria's unbeaten streak when they upended the Leafs, 5-3. The Leafs were never really in the game, giving up the first three goals. They mounted a middle-frame comeback with goals by Redahl and Keenan, but failed to score in the final period, when the Canucks scored twice on plays that were clearly offside. There was a lot more than hockey toward the end of the game, as Mazur received a major penalty: He was high-sticked by Bob Plager, and while falling, slashed his stick across his opponent's face, giving him a broken jaw.[2184] From this point in the season, the Leafs won many more games than they lost, never dropping more than two in a row, except in early March when they had a three-game losing streak.

The return encounter in Victoria was a tense affair, but some of the tension was released when Keenan scored after only sixty-two seconds of play on a pass from Mazur, the protagonist in the prior game. The same combination had a second goal 3:29 later, to give the Leafs a lead they would never relinquish. Marcetta and Mazur had second-period goals before Phil Maloney scored the only Canuck counter, and Jankowski put the icing on the cake at 11:35 of the final frame.[2185] The team also announced that Gary Smith had been sent to Tulsa as an emergency replacement. He would likely be away from Victoria for two weeks.[2186] The Maple Leafs took a short trip to Portland and upended the Buckaroos, 3-1. Three goals in less than three minutes, midway through the first period, were enough to send the 6,934 fans home very disappointed. Keenan had the first goal, then Belisle fired two. Millar in net did the rest, leading the Leafs to their fourth consecutive win over Portland, after having lost the first four contests of the season.[2187] The winning streak took a minor rest when the Blades came to town and handed the Leafs a 4-2 defeat. Playing their fourth game in five nights, Victoria ran out of steam, and only Belisle and Keenan could put a puck past Jack McCartan. Claude Labrosse was unable to play, and his steady work on defence was missed.[2188]

Former Cougar Don Chiupka joined the team on a tryout and was used for the upcoming four games in a five-night test.[2189] The team received more good news: Fred Hucul was back with the Maple Leafs, just in time for the brutal trip.[2190] A game in

Vancouver was not productive. Goaltender Gilles Villeneuve stoned the Leafs, allowing only Keenan and Redahl to put pucks past him.[2191] The Leafs had now lost two in a row and knew they would have to improve if they wanted to move up in the standings. Victoria got revenge on the Canucks the next night, as it was Millar's turn to shine. He stopped a breakaway just twenty-five seconds into the game, and that inspired the rest of the team to play very well. Fred Hucul wasted little time getting back into the action, scoring on a breakaway at 3:48 of the first period. Marcetta also added one before the period was over. Belisle scored twice in the second frame, twenty seconds apart, and completed the hat trick in the final period. Labrosse, recovered from his injury, scored his first goal of the season just before the end of the game.

The Leafs were now sitting in fourth place but were a single point behind Vancouver and only ten behind Seattle in first place.[2192] The Leafs then won two games against the league-leading Totems: 3-2 in Seattle and 5-1 back at home. Lamoureux, Belisle, and Witiuk had goals in the first game to move the team into fourth place in the standings.[2193] Back at home, there was no doubt who would win the game. Jankowski had two first-period goals, and singles by Witiuk, Keenan, and Belisle carried the Leafs to victory. Shvetz, Labrosse, and the Huculs played as well as any defence corps could, and Millar held the fort in goal.[2194] Now sitting in third place, this was a team on the move—gone were the early season inconsistencies.

A mid-season assessment of WHL attendance confirmed that Toronto had been correct in moving the Leafs from Denver, as they had been drawing well, particularly lately when they began to win on a consistent basis. Close to 50,000 fans had attended the club's twenty-two home games, which was a 36.5-percent increase over what had happened in Denver the year before. Total attendance for that year was estimated at 100,000.[2195]

Gordon Redahl as a Maple Leaf. Photo courtesy Ernie Fitzsimmons

In the next game, Coach Pilous said his team "didn't work quite hard enough," and they lost a close one, 3-2, to the Seals. However, the results had more to do with the goaltending of Bob Perreault than with the Leafs' inability to score. He stopped several point-blank shots from Redahl, Belisle, and Witiuk to lead his team, surrendering only goals by Fred Hucul and Wilcox.[2196] Three days later, the Leafs got their revenge on the Seals, upending them, 6-3. The game was not the best played of the season, but after surrendering an early San Francisco goal, the home team pumped in four consecutive goals—Eddie Mazur with two and singles by Lamoureux and Sleaver—to take a 4-1 lead into the second period. The Seals narrowed the lead early in the second frame, but Belisle and Marcetta increased the lead while the Seals could only manage one more score in the final period.[2197] The largest crowd of the season in Victoria (4,708) watched the Leafs upend the Buckaroos, 7-4. Three of the Buckaroo goals came on the power play (two with Victoria, two-men short), but a clever short-handed play by Hucul, Redahl, and Jankowski put an end to the Portland threat. Victoria sharpshooters were Marcetta with two, Jankowski, Keenan, Mazur, Redahl and Witiuk.[2198]

What a turnaround for the Leafs! They now had won four games and tied one against the Buckaroos since December. However, that streak came to a crashing end in the final game of January, in Portland when the Buckaroos demolished the Leafs, 7-2. Held to only two shots in the second period, the Leafs were never really in the game. An early goal by Fred Hucul and a late one by Jankowski were nowhere near enough. The game featured some rough stuff near the end, as Marcetta and Doug Messier tangled, and their teammates joined in. When the dust settled, they both were assessed major penalties, as were secondary combatants Witiuk and Connie Madigan.[2199]

Eddie Mazur as a Maple Leaf. Photo courtesy Ernie Fitzsimmons.

Having had nine days off to think about the loss, the Leafs took out their frustration on Los Angeles in their next game. It was no contest as Victoria demolished the Blades, 8-2. It was difficult to pick individual stars in a true team effort, but some did stand out. Bill Shvetz intercepted a pass deep in the Los Angeles zone and fired it home for the second goal that started the onslaught. Fred Hucul had four assists, Eddie Mazur had a hat trick, Keenan had a goal and three assists, and Millar played well in goal.[2200] A trip to Seattle did not have the desired result, as the Totems squeaked out a 4-3 decision. The Maple Leafs took a two-goal lead when Redahl and Marcetta scored in under a minute, but the team ran into penalty trouble that allowed the Totems to score four consecutive goals to take a lead they never relinquished. A late goal by Jankowski made it close, but the Leafs could not get the tying marker they needed, despite terrific pressure in the dying seconds.[2201]

A home-and-home series against Portland was next on the schedule. In Victoria, the Leafs upended the Buckaroos, 6-3. Building up a 3-0 lead on goals by Sleaver, Keenan, and Redahl, they surrendered a single goal to Portland, but Witiuk got that one back. In the final frame, Portland fired two scores to make it closer, but Sandy Hucul put the game away with a late goal.[2202] Then it was on to Portland, where the home team won the game, 4-1. The game turned on a call when the score was 2-1 for the Buckaroos. Referee Willie Papp ruled that a shot by Pat Stapleton had crossed the red line, and when Fred Hucul protested too much, he was assessed a misconduct. The goal was allowed to stand, and the Buckaroos scored once more to complete the victory.[2203]

Two home games against Seattle were up next. First, the Leafs defeated the Totems, 4-2, to regain third place in the standings. The first period was a penalty-filled affair with little flow to the action. Jankowski opened the scoring, but perennial scoring-leader Guyle Fielder responded with one of his own. After a scoreless middle frame, Seattle went ahead only to have Fred Hucul and Lamoureux give the Leafs back the lead, and Jankowski got the insurance with an empty-net goal.[2204] Three days later, the Totems shut out the Leafs, 1-0, when the offence could not beat goaltender Jim McLeod. Bob Barlow scored the only Seattle goal early in the final frame.[2205] The Maple Leafs welcomed a new winger, Edgar Ehrenverth, who had previously played for the Totems and was currently studying at the University of Alberta in Edmonton.[2206]

Victoria lost its second game in a row when the team travelled to Vancouver. Trailing 1-0 on a Belisle goal, the Canucks, led by former Cougar Bruce Carmichael, scored three times to take the lead. Eddie Mazur, who had just returned to the lineup from a knee injury, had to leave shortly after scoring a goal in the third period, having hurt the knee again. Vancouver had one more goal, and a late score by Redahl got the Leafs close but there was no further scoring, and the Canucks won 4-3.[2207] The return match in Victoria was just as close. Newcomer Ehrenverth had his first goal as a Leaf, but Danny Belisle (a former Canuck) was the star of the game, scoring a pair of goals and assisting on the overtime winner by Wilcox.[2208]

Just when they needed a lot of wins, the Maple Leafs had their longest losing streak of the second half of the season (three games), which put an end to any hope of finishing first in the standings. First, they lost a very close 4-3 home decision to Portland. The Leafs fell behind, 2-0, then Marcetta's three straight goals gave his team the lead. Unfortunately, the Buckaroos had the only scores in the final frame, and Victoria could not tie the game.[2209] Second, they dropped a 4-1 game in Vancouver. The Canucks built up a 3-0 lead before Marcetta scored early in the final period, and then Vancouver added another score to ensure their victory.[2210] The third loss came at the hands of San Francisco back in Victoria. Once again, the Leafs fell behind, and the Seals had a 4-0 lead before Belisle and Marcetta found the back of the net. Marcetta had scored five of the Leaf's last six goals, bringing his season total to thirty-two, tying him with Wayne Connelly and Tommy McVie for the league lead.[2211] Luckily, this would be the last time that the Maple Leafs would lose more than two games in a row. The team left on their final California road trip of the season.

Two games in Los Angeles seemed to be just what the Leafs needed. Ed Ehrenverth, who had been inserted into the lineup to play with Sleaver and Redahl, set up three goals—two by Sleaver and a single by Redahl—to pave the way to a 3-2 victory. Although the Blades pushed hard in the third period, they were unable to score more than two goals, as Millar stood firm in the Victoria net.[2212] Two days later, the Leafs were again victorious when they shut out the Blades, 6-0. Redahl scored in the first minute of play, and Jankowski, Sandy Hucul, and Keenan had goals before the end of the first period. Wilcox had a marker in the second frame, and Marcetta closed out the scoring in the final period. It was the second win in a row for the Leafs and got them back on track for a playoff spot.[2213]

Feeling a bit travel-weary, Victoria played in San Francisco and ended up on the short end of a 5-3 score. They fell behind, 3-0, and could only manage goals by Labrosse, Witiuk, and Keenan. Former Cougar Al Nicholson fired the winning goal for the Seals.[2214] Needing a win to take back fourth place and a playoff position, the Leafs rallied the next night and shut out the Seals, 4-0. Redahl led the way for Victoria with a hat trick and an assist on a goal by Sleaver.[2215] With only two games left on the extended road trip, the team headed north to Portland. The Buckaroos, who were playing just their fourth game in eleven nights, upended the Maple Leafs, 8-3, in a weak effort all around by the visiting team. Portland scored three times before the game was four minutes old, and the rout was on. Jankowski, Wilcox, and Belisle were the only Leafs to hit the scoresheet.[2216] It was the kind of game to learn from, then forget.

The final game on the trip was in Vancouver, where the Leafs had trouble winning. This game was no exception as they were outscored, 4-2. Penalties at inopportune times cost Victoria, and after the first period, they did not play very well. Keenan scored the first and last goals of the game, but he was the only Leaf to beat Villeneuve.[2217] Just when everybody thought the Leafs were out of the playoff picture, they dominated Vancouver in front of 3,553 rabid home fans. They fired fifty-four shots at Villeneuve and managed to get four pucks behind him. Millar surrendered the first goal of the game to Bob McCusker, then closed the door. Redahl had two goals while Belisle and Witiuk added singles. The Leafs were back in fourth place.[2218] Seattle then dealt Victoria a minor blow, defeating the Leafs, 2-1. Mazur was the only Leaf to find the back of the net.[2219]

Victoria responded to adversity with a 5-0 shut out of the Blades. After a scoreless first period, Keenan got the Leafs on the board in the middle frame, and Marcetta, Keenan, Redahl, and Jankowski finished the scoring with a third-period rush. Al Millar stopped all thirty-seven shots fired his way and deserved the shutout. With the victory, Victoria needed only one more win (or a San Francisco loss) to clinch the fourth and final playoff spot.[2220] Never a team to do it the easy way, they edged closer to clinching a spot when they tied Seattle, 3-3, in the Emerald City. The game was an entertaining affair with the lead changing hands several times. Tied 1-1 at the end of the first period, Seattle took a 3-1 lead into the final frame, but Wilcox scored twice to give his team the draw.[2221]

In the penultimate game of the regular season, the Leafs finally clinched a playoff position by dumping the Canucks, 5-3. Despite falling behind early in the contest, they recovered and were in control once they tied the score and went ahead. Fred Hucul was the star of the game with a smoking shot for a goal, adding an assist and playing a stellar game on defence. Victoria took advantage of Vancouver penalties to score on the power play to increase their lead.[2222] Needing a victory over the Canucks in Vancouver to finish third in the standings, the Leafs could not do it, falling 7-4 to their dreaded rivals and ending up in fourth place. Fred Hucul had two goals, with Lamoureux and Wilcox adding singles.[2223] It was Victoria's eighth straight defeat in Vancouver, so they were likely pleased to be playing Seattle in the first round of the playoffs.

Fred Hucul as a Maple Leaf.
Photo courtesy Ernie Fitzsimmons.

When asked who would win the upcoming playoff series, Coach Pilous picked his team, the Victoria Maple Leafs, "if we stay sound." He credited Ed Ehrenverth with the improvement in the power play and noted that Sleaver and Fred Hucul were also valuable players in the odd-man situations.[2224]

The playoffs started on March 31, 1965, with Victoria playing in Seattle. The Totems took a 2-0 lead on goals by Mantha and Barlow before Belisle found the net for Victoria. There was no scoring in the middle frame, but Sabourin's early third-period goal put the Totems up, 3-1. Redahl narrowed the lead on the power play, but when Millar was pulled for an extra attacker, the gamble backfired, and Leonard fired the final goal into an empty net.[2225] In the second game, Seattle shut out the Leafs, 3-0, to take a two-game lead in the series. Victoria managed only eighteen shots on goal in a poor effort.[2226]

Back at home, the Leafs came back with a vengeance and upended Seattle, 5-2, to get back into the series. The first three goals were described in the media as three of the "prettiest goals" seen in a while. *Victoria Daily Colonist* columnist Jim Tang called the play this way:

> *"Defenceman Claude Labrosse started the play each time, and the first one took some stubborn stickhandling in his own zone and a fine middle move by John Sleaver to end in success. Labrosse stickhandled past three Totems between his goal and the blue-line, fed a pass to Sleaver near the centre line. The puck was slightly behind Sleaver but a neat move got it up front. Sleaver crossed the Seattle blue-line and hit Lou Jankowski, cutting in from the left perfectly.*
>
> *Jankowski hit the puck the first time, literally rattling the piping behind McLeod.*
>
> *Sixty-three seconds later, it was 2-0. Labrosse rifled a pass from the left side, which Larry Keenan grabbed at the Seattle blue-line. Keenan moved over and in, then fired perfectly to McLeod's left.*
>
> *Still pressuring, the Leafs forced a Seattle penalty and Larry Hale had been in the box only thirty seconds when two passes put Rollie Wilcox out front and the rookie winger hit the opening on his right."*[2227]

Keenan scored his second goal to open the middle frame, the Leafs let down a bit defensively and allowed the Totems to notch two goals, then John Sleaver finished the game off with a score less than two minutes from the end of regulation time.[2228] The 5-2 victory cut Seattle's lead in the series to 2-1, and with a similar effort in the next game, the series could be tied. However, things did not go as planned, and the Leafs lost the game, 5-3. Victoria's game seemed out of sync, as their passes were not crisp, their shots missed the net, and their defensive lapses cost them goals. Millar was not his usual reliable self in goal, and the lack of consistency seemed to permeate the entire team. Wilcox, Mazur, and Jankowski finally scored in the third period to briefly tie the score, but two subsequent Seattle goals put an end to any comeback.[2229] Now down 3-1 in the best-of-seven series, the Leafs needed a minor miracle to advance to the next round.

Step one of the comeback happened in Seattle where the Maple Leafs upended the Totems, 3-1. Fred Hucul opened the scoring in the first period on the power play, Seattle tied it in the middle frame, and two goals by John Sleaver in the final period (the last into an empty net) sealed the victory. Al Millar injured his back in the third frame, but after medication, climbed back into play. His grit seemed to inspire the rest of the team.[2230] Game six was played in Victoria, with 3,641 fans in attendance. Larry Keenan led the way to a Leafs 2-1 victory, scoring once and assisting on Steve Witiuk's winning goal. Bob Barlow had the Seattle goal early in the final frame, but Millar and the defence corps held the fort, and the series was now tied at 3-3.[2231]

Al Millar as a Maple Leaf.
Photo courtesy Ernie Fitzsimmons.

The Leafs completed their remarkable comeback with a decisive 4-1 defeat of the Totems in a game played in Seattle, to win the semi-final series and move on to the final round against Portland. Al Millar, despite his aching back, was spectacular in goal, frustrating the Seattle sharpshooters time after time. Jankowski and Redahl gave the Leafs an early two-goal lead, but Barlow scored for Seattle on a power play to make the score close. Marcetta got that goal back before the end of the middle frame, and Belisle finished the scoring on a nice pass from Marcetta less than seven minutes from the end of regulation time.[2232] The Leafs had held Seattle superstar Guyle Fielder in check throughout most of the series, and their determination to win when the games were on the line made the difference in this series.

Perhaps the stress of the previous series had worn them out, but the Leafs did not play well in the first game in Portland. Playing without injured defencemen Shvetz and Sandy Hucul, they had trouble keeping the high-flying Buckaroos off the scoresheet. Bobby Taylor was inserted into the lineup but took some critical penalties, and in fact, hurt his team. Former Cougar Andy Hebenton scored two goals to lead the Buckaroos to a one-sided 5-1 victory. The only Cougar to beat Don McLeod in the Portland net was Belisle.[2233] The scene shifted to Victoria for the second game. The result was much the same, as Portland upended the Leafs, 3-1. Sandy Hucul played only the first period, and Mazur did not dress at all, leaving the team perilously short. They seemed to have forgotten how to move the puck, shoot, or check effectively. Only Keenan scored for Victoria—not nearly enough offence to win a game.[2234]

Down two games to none, the Leafs knew they had to come up with a better effort in game three, or the end would be nigh. Bud Poile was a big fan of Norman Vincent Peale's *Power of Positive Thinking*, and read excerpts to his team. There was an immediate effect, as the Leafs won their next game in spectacular fashion, 4-3 in overtime in Portland when Gordie Redahl fired the puck past Don McLeod after 4:53 of extra play.[2235] Now the series was closer, and a good effort in the next game could tie the series. However, that was not to be. Back home in Victoria, the team fell behind, 3-0, and could only score two goals, falling 3-2. Injuries were catching up with the team. Millar had been replaced by Jean-Guy Morissette, and Marcetta, Keenan, and Sandy Hucul were all playing hurt. It was just too much to ask of the remaining players. Witiuk and Sandy Hucul had scored in the third period, but it was too little too late, as the Leafs went down 3-1 in the series.[2236]

In the last game played in Victoria, Portland won the Lester Patrick Trophy with a 3-0 shutout of the Maple Leafs. The game was much closer than the score indicates, as there was one goal in the first period and that held up until an early power-play goal in the final frame game that gave the Buckaroos a 2-0 lead. The second score came while Jack Chipchase was serving a somewhat dubious penalty, and was the straw that broke the camel's back. An empty-net goal completed the scoring, and the Leafs went down to defeat.[2237] However, the team could look back on the season with some satisfaction, as they were not picked to do well and did well to recover after a poor start. There had been many bright spots during the season and fans hoped that things would be better next year.

In year-end awards, former Cougar Andy Hebenton, now playing for the Portland Buckaroos, was named the winner of the Fred Hume Trophy, given to the WHL player "adjudged to have exhibited the best type of sportsmanship and gentlemanly conduct combined with a high standard of playing ability." He became the first player in history to be chosen as the most gentlemanly players in two leagues, having won the Lady Byng Trophy in the NHL in the 1956-57 season.[2238]

The Western league approved a plan to have four teams make application for franchises in an expanded NHL. Los Angeles, San Francisco, Portland, and Seattle had large enough arenas to hold NHL-sized crowds and were ready to go. Vancouver was not included, as their arena was too small and there was not enough time to build a new one before the application deadline. Victoria was rejected outright, as "it does not have the population to support major hockey" and did not have a major-sized facility.[2239]

Next to surface were rumours of the Vancouver franchise being purchased and moved to Phoenix, Arizona. Canucks general manager Max McNab said that he had heard of an offer of $100,000, but that was a ridiculous price, and it would have to be a lot better offer even to be considered. NHL president Clarence Campbell said that professional hockey would return to the Prairies at the same time as NHL expansion. There would be a new league, including some WHL clubs, and it would be modelled on the Central Hockey League. Campbell also noted that Seattle and Portland would likely be left out of NHL expansion plans.[2240]

In a year-end review of the Victoria Maple Leafs, manager Buck Houle announced that the team would be playing the next year, as NHL plans for expansion had not yet come to fruition. He noted that the team hoped to hold the majority of games on Saturday nights, with most of the balance on Wednesdays. The media speculated on which players would be back for another season and who would be gone. They had many choices: Fred Hucul, who might become a playing coach elsewhere; Bill Shvetz, who would turn thirty-five before training camp; Claude Labrosse, who might be playing the AHL next season; Bob Taylor, who needed experience at a lower level; Steve Witiuk, who was thirty-six years old; Ed Mazur, who would turn thirty-six in July, Larry Keenan, who was expected to move up to a higher league; Danny Belisle, who would be returned to the New York Rangers; Rollie Wilcox, who would likely move up to a different league; and Dick Lamoureux and Ed Ehrenverth, who were utility players this season and would need to prove they had WHL ability. This was a lengthy list, and it would remain to be seen just how accurate the forecast was. Those players expected to return were Al Millar, Sandy Hucul, Lou Jankowski, John Sleaver, Milan Marcetta, and Gordie Redahl. It was also unlikely that Coach Rudy Pilous would return.[2241]

26 - THE YEAR OF THE LEAFS!

In the fall, the topic of conversation in hockey circles was the same as at the end of the season, revolving around whether the NHL would expand or the WHL would gain major-league status and compete with the NHL. Al Leader noted that four clubs (Los Angeles, San Francisco, Seattle, and Portland) already owned more than half their players, so were ready to compete. Also, the California franchises had set up farm systems but were growing tired of waiting for something to happen. Vancouver would need a larger building to be considered in expansion talks, and San Diego was in the process of building a new arena. As the WHL held the hockey territorial rights on the West Coast, the NHL could not expand into this area without paying a healthy fee. In preparation for a WHL expansion, the league had decided to play an interlocking schedule with the American Hockey League, with each team playing eight games against clubs from the other league.[2242]

In the meantime, with its small arena and a population deemed insufficient to support major-league hockey, Victoria quietly got on with the business of preparing for another season. Buck Houle announced that Mike Labadie had been assigned by Toronto, and he insisted on a French-language kindergarten so that his child could learn in his native tongue. Fred Hucul decided to play again and had arrived early so that his three children could be registered for school. Most of the players had to report to training camp the last week of September.[2243] From Toronto came the bad news that Larry Keenan needed surgery on his right knee, so he failed the physical for the Toronto Maple Leafs, ending his dream of playing in the NHL for the season. He would be coming back to Victoria once his surgery and rehab were over.[2244]

Mike Labadie as a Maple Leaf.
Photo courtesy Ernie Fitzsimmons.

26 - THE YEAR OF THE LEAFS!

The Leafs' new coach was Frank Mario, and he welcomed players to Victoria for training camp. Goaltenders present were Al Millar, Mike Berridge (from Calgary juniors), and Gary Holland (from Flin Flon juniors). Defencemen were Fred and Sandy Hucul, Claude Labrosse, and Bill Shvetz. Forwards in camp were holdovers Lou Jankowski, John Sleaver, Milan Marcetta, Steve Witiuk, and Dick Lamoureux. Newcomers were Mike Labadie and Bob Barlow, who had played for Seattle the last season. Two players were trying for a rookie position on the team: Mike Laughton and Fred Purvis. If Andy Hebenton did not stay with Toronto, he could come west, as well.[2245] Defenceman Autrey Erickson would be joining the team later.

In the first pre-season game in Nanaimo, in front of about 1,400 fans, Victoria was a bit sluggish and lost to Vancouver, 5-3, with all but one goal coming on the power play.[2246] Then it was back to work at the Memorial Arena, in preparation for another exhibition match. Mike Laughton decided to leave the team to go back to school, then try for the team next season.[2247]

New Leaf Bob Barlow was determined to score thirty goals that season if only to demonstrate that he could score without having Guyle Fielder feeding him the puck. For the pre-season game against his old team, Seattle, he played on a line with Milan Marcetta and Mike Labadie.[2248]

From Winnipeg came news that Eddie "Spider" Mazur had decided to retire from professional hockey after seventeen seasons. His battered right knee was just not strong enough to continue to play at the high level he had always done. Over the course of his career, Mazur had played for the Montreal Canadiens, scoring the winning goal in the seventh game of the Stanley Cup semi-final against the Chicago Blackhawks. He had played for the Cougars in the 1950s and the Leafs the previous season. One benefit of his bad knee was that he had met his wife in a Winnipeg hospital while recuperating from his third knee surgery.[2249]

The Leafs looked very sharp in their game against Seattle, defeating the Totems, 6-2. Victoria goals were scored by Ehrenverth, Marcetta, Labadie, Fred Hucul, Sleaver, and Lamoureux. Manager Houle said there would be more announcements from Toronto soon.[2250] The Leafs received the good news that Andy Hebenton would be coming to play for the Leafs, as would Eddie Litzenberger. Hebenton was the current hockey iron man, having not missed a game in thirteen seasons, and would be a valuable addition to the team. In their final pre-season games, the Leafs lost, 6-3, to the Spokane Jets, coached by former Cougar Colin Kilburn, and then defeated the Trail Smoke Eaters, 8-3.[2251]

The season opened on October 15, 1965, at Vancouver. It was a good start for the Maple Leafs, as they upended the Canucks, 4-2. The newly-formed forward line of Hebenton, Marcetta, and Barlow led the way with five points, and Fred Hucul had two goals as Victoria dominated the game, particularly in the third period. Millar stopped thirty-two shots in the net.[2252] The next night, the teams played in Victoria, where the Leafs dominated the Canucks and emerged with a decisive 7-2 victory. What made the game remarkable is that the team had to kill off seven penalties, including a major, in the middle frame and only gave up one power-play goal to Vancouver (with the team two men short), while scoring two themselves. Litzenberger had the only score of the first period, and Lamoureux and Barlow added goals in the middle frame. The third frame was a dominant performance, with Hebenton, Jankowski, Lamoureux, and Sleaver finding the net, while only Larry Popein beat Millar.[2253]

The third game of the season was played in Seattle, and the winning streak came to an end when the Totems upended the Leafs, 3-1. Coach Mario announced that two new players had joined the team. Defenceman Autrey Erickson, who had been working out with the team since training camp, agreed to a contract and would play immediately. Rookie Marty Desmarais (son of Tony Desmarais, a well-known player in Allan Cup senior hockey) joined the team on a five-game tryout.²²⁵⁴ Next, the Leafs took on the Buckaroos in a home-and-home series. In Victoria, Marcetta scored two goals, and Labadie added another to give the home team a 3-0 lead going into the final frame. They let up a bit defensively, allowing Portland to notch two goals, but managed to hang on and win their third game of the season. They were tied with the Buckaroos for first place in the league—a place they had rarely been the previous year—and were determined to stay there as long as possible. Redahl was injured in the game and would be unable to dress for the rematch. Lamoureux and Sleaver had minor injuries, but both were expected to play.²²⁵⁵ As it turned out, Lamoureux was unable to play past the first period, and Bill Shvetz moved from defence to play forward in his place. Portland opened the scoring when Art Jones beat Millar early in the second period, but Shvetz and Sleaver beat McLeod to give the Leafs the lead. Goals in the third frame by Witiuk and Shvetz put Victoria up 4-1, but again they faltered and surrendered a pair of goals. However, Millar stood tall in the nets, and the Leafs ended up with a 4-3 victory to sit alone atop the standings.²²⁵⁶ Next to visit Victoria were the San Francisco Seals, expected to be one of the league's top clubs. In this match, the Leafs gave up the first three goals, then needed a comeback to gain a 3-3 tie. Shvetz, Sleaver, and Marcetta were the home team's scorers. Neither team could find the net in overtime, although there were several good chances. Henderson stopped fifty Victoria shots, while Millar handled thirty-six.²²⁵⁷ Up next was the first of eight interlocking games against AHL clubs. The Cleveland Barons came to town, and the Leafs handed them a 7-3 thumping. Litzenberger opened the scoring, but Cleveland tied the game by the end of the first period. It was a completely different scenario in the middle frame when Barlow had a natural hat trick, and Fred Hucul and Lamoureux added singles, while Millar only gave up one marker to the Barons, to make the score 6-2 at that point. The team exchanged goals in the final period, with Litzenberger scoring his second of the night. It was an impressive performance by the entire team, who seemed to be hitting their stride at the right time.

Lou Jankowski as a Maple Leaf.
Photo courtesy Ernie Fitzsimmons.

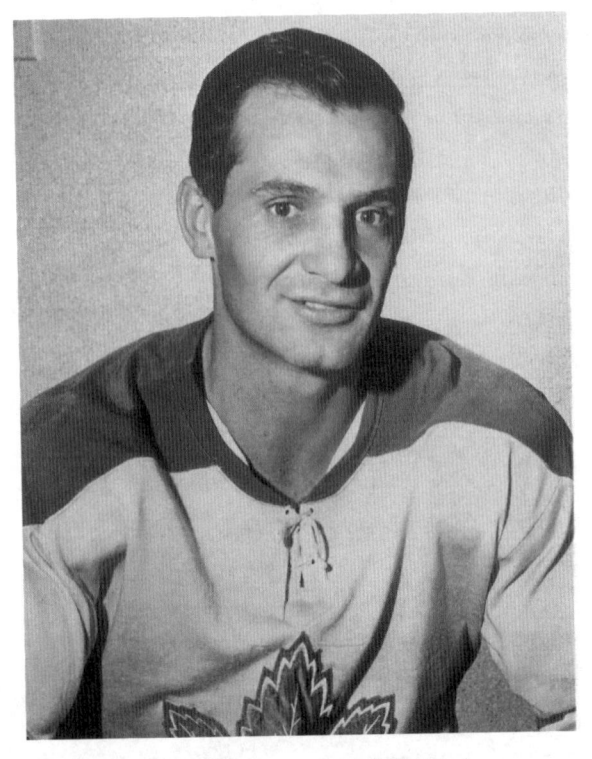

Milan Marcetta as a Maple Leaf.
Photo courtesy Ernie Fitzsimmons.

Then it was time for another encounter with the Seals. This game was a low-scoring affair with Marcetta counting for Victoria and Maxner for San Francisco. Although there was no further scoring, both teams had their chances, and McCartan and Millar played well in their nets.[2258] Next on the agenda was a home-and-home series against Seattle. In Victoria, the Leafs cashed in on Totem mistakes and easily won the game, 7-3. Seattle came out aggressively but could not get the puck past Millar. The game turned around when former Totem Barlow scored a goal for his new team and added a second seven minutes later. From then on, the Leafs offence took over. Jankowski and Sandy Hucul added singles before the first period was over. Hebenton and Jankowski had middle-frame scores, and Redahl finished the task with one early in the final period. Millar stopped thirty-one shots and allowed only three goals.[2259]

In team changes, rookie Dave Parenteau, a former Saskatchewan Junior Hockey League scoring ace with Flin Flon, was named to the team, replacing Desmarais, who returned to Calgary.[2260] In the return match in Seattle, the Leaf penalty killers were the stars of the show in a 5-3 Victoria victory. Coach Mario noted that the team had only given up three goals while shorthanded, thanks to the efforts of Witiuk, Sleaver, Labadie, and Lamoureux, along with the defence corps. Barlow and Hebenton each had a goal and two assists, and single goals came from Marcetta, Sleaver, and Redahl.[2261] Over the first ten games of the season, the team had won seven, tied two, and lost only two.

This remarkable record came to a crashing end when the Leafs travelled to Portland and played the Buckaroos. The game was not a good one for the Leafs, as they were shut out, 6-0.[2262] The Leafs got their revenge in the next game in Victoria. Portland scored first, but Redahl and Erickson gave Victoria the lead at the end of the first period. In the middle frame, Barlow had two goals, and Marcetta had one to put the Leafs in front. Al Millar played despite being ill and made the difference in the game. By the time he had to leave the match with ten minutes to go, the Leafs were up, 5-1, and on their way to victory. Gary Holland came into the game to finish it off and yielded one goal—not bad for somebody who had to get ready to play with little notice.[2263] The Los Angeles Blades came to town with former Cougar Marcel Pelletier in goal. Although that team was near the bottom of the league standings, they gave the Leafs all they could handle. Up, 2-0, at the end of the first period, the Blades let the Leafs back in the game, allowing Redahl, Marcetta, and Hebenton to score, while they could only put one puck past Millar. Barlow scored the winner on a play in front of Pelletier when both tried to play the puck at the same time. The disk slipped up and went into the net. Game over, with a 4-3 win for Victoria.[2264]

Dick Lamoureux as a Maple Leaf.
Photo courtesy Ernie Fitzsimmons.

Next on the schedule was a home-and-home series against the Canucks. In Vancouver, the Leafs came from behind to win the game, 5-4. Hebenton and Sleaver had goals in the first period, while

Vancouver had only one. In the middle frame, Vancouver scored twice, while only Marcetta replied for the Leafs. With the score tied at that point, the Canucks went ahead again only to have Litzenberger tie it up once more. Lamoureux scored the winning goal with just forty-two seconds left on the clock and the Leafs playing shorthanded. That play alone sent the 5,080 Forum fans home shaking their heads in disbelief.[2265] Back at home, the Leafs continued their mastery of the Canucks with a 4-2 win. After surrendering the opening goal, the Leafs came back with a score by Barlow, fell behind again in the first period, then scored three consecutive goals over the last two periods to win going away (two by Jankowski and one by Marcetta completed the comeback).[2266] In an impressive display of shooting, the Leafs fired nine goals past Pelletier—their best offensive performance that season—and upended the Blades, 9-5. There was a total of eighty-eight shots on goal: fifty-two by Victoria and thirty-six by Los Angeles. Marcetta had a hat trick and an assist, Litzenberger had one goal and three assists, while Sleaver, Labadie, Jankowski, Hebenton, and Redahl each had single goals. In all, twelve Leafs got at least one point.

Victoria was now alone in first place in the league, two points ahead of Portland.[2267] A quick trip to California produced a win and a rare loss. In San Francisco, the Leafs edged the Seals, 4-3. Barlow scored the Leafs' first three goals for a natural hat trick, and Lamoureux had the winner early in the third period after Wayne Connelly scored to tie the game. The Leafs played without Fred Hucul, who had stayed home due to a back injury.[2268]

In Los Angeles, the Blades found a way to upend the Leafs, 3-1, ending their unbeaten streak at six. Redahl got the Leafs off to the races with a goal early in the game, but that was the last of the offence as the usual high-scoring team fired blanks all night.[2269]

One-quarter of the way through the WHL season, league officials were pleased with the interlocking play against what most considered a "higher-ranked league." Nineteen games had been played, and the AHL had won ten. Home ice was a huge advantage, with most teams winning in their own arenas while struggling in the other team's arena.[2270] The long distances to be travelled were obviously a factor, as was player fatigue on long road trips. However, the experiment had been a success so far, and that had helped to showcase the talent level of the WHL. The Leafs would be the last team to make the eastern trek, so it was to their advantage to gain as many points as they could in the west, before that trip.

The Springfield Indians were the next AHL team to visit Victoria. Owned and coached by infamous NHL defenceman Eddie Shore,[2271] the team scored the first goal of the game. After that, it went downhill, as the Leafs poured in five straight scores en route to an 8-3 drubbing of the Indians. John Sleaver led the way for Victoria, with two goals and two assists, Claude Labrosse notched his first goal of the season, and rookie Dave Parenteau scored the first goal of his professional career. Other marksmen were Fred Hucul, Redahl, Barlow, and Lamoureux.[2272] A home-and-home series with Seattle offered an opportunity for the Leafs to put space between themselves and the rest of the teams in the standings. Playing with speed—the first period was likely the fastest period of hockey ever played in Victoria—the Leafs took a 3-0 lead on goals by Fred Hucul, Barlow, and Jankowski. In the middle frame, the teams each had two goals (Redahl and Marcetta for the Leafs), and Litzenberger finished it off with a late third-period goal that made the final count 6-2.[2273]

The match in Seattle was a lot closer, with the Leafs edging the Totems, 3-2. Sleaver and Jankowski scored before the Totems got on the board with a goal by Len Haley, with the Leafs two-men short, but Hebenton fired a shot in the third period to give the Leafs a lead they did not surrender. Seattle's only other score came just six seconds from the end of the game, making the final count 3-2.[2274] In a "sweet" promotion for the upcoming game against the Hershey Bears, a newspaper ad announced that "everyone attending Saturday night's game will receive a Hershey bar. Compliments of the Hershey

Chocolate Company."[2275] More than chocolate got licked in the game itself, as the Leafs dominated the Bears, thumping them 5-2. Redahl had two goals, while Shvetz, Hebenton, and Litzenberger added singles. It was to be the last home game for Eddie Litzenberger, as he rejoined the Rochester Americans to make way for Larry Keenan to return to the Victoria lineup.[2276]

On December 12, the Leafs suffered their fourth loss of the season in Seattle, where the Totems shut them out, 2-0. Missing Claude Labrosse (who had been sent to the Rochester Americans), the team had too few defencemen, and for some reason, the scorers could not find the net.[2277] Back at home, they had to play the Blades without defender Autrey Erickson, who had left to be with his family who had been injured in a severe car crash, and Mike Labadie had to be used sparingly as he'd pulled a muscle. Despite being understaffed, the Leafs responded with a spirited effort as they upended Los Angeles, 5-1. Marcetta scored the first of two goals just fifteen seconds into the second period, and the Blades did not threaten much after that. Jankowski recorded another hat trick to complete the scoring.[2278]

Victoria Maple Leafs pennant. From the author's collection.

All was going well for the Victoria Maple Leafs, but the next road trip was not a success. The team lost two games by identical scores of 4-3 to the San Francisco Seals. In the first game, the Leafs built up a 3-1 lead on two goals by Jankowski and one by Marcetta but allowed the Seals to score twice in the final period to tie the game. The winning goal was scored at 5:41 of overtime, just after a Leaf penalty had expired.[2279] The next night, the Leafs lost a second game in a row for the first time all season. This game was a back-and-forth affair with the lead changing hands. Wayne Connelly opened the scoring for the Seals, but Marcetta got that one back just before the end of period one. After a scoreless middle frame, Barlow put the Leafs ahead. However, the Seals scored three consecutive goals to take the lead, and a late goal by Barlow was not enough to tie the game.[2280]

Victoria Maple Leafs button. From the author's collection.

Game twenty-seven of the season was played in Victoria against Seattle, and the Leafs suffered their first home loss. Still playing shorthanded with Labrosse still in Rochester and Fred Hucul bothered by a sore foot, they came up with a poor effort. It was a third consecutive loss—not the way the team wanted to play. A trip to Portland helped a bit, as the Leafs were able to secure a 2-2 tie against the Buckaroos. Dick Lamoureux suffered a torn knee ligament in that game and would be lost to the team for at least a month.[2281] Back in Victoria, the Leafs lost again to the surging Seals. Feeling the effects of playing under the roster limit, they could not overcome their mistakes or untimely penalties. Keenan tied the game in the first period, Marcetta had a goal in the second, and Labadie found the net early in the third frame, but that was all the offence they could muster. The winless streak was now at five, and their lead atop the league standing had dwindled to only four points.[2282]

All that the Leafs needed to get back on the winning track was to play their old nemesis the Vancouver Canucks. What a turnaround this season had been! Last year, the Canucks had won all eight games played in Vancouver and two in Victoria, and this year had the Leafs winning all four games they played. This number increased to six after a home-and-home series. In Victoria on New Year's Day, the Leafs upended the Canucks, 4-1. Marcetta and Jankowski scored power-play goals to give the Leafs a lead they never relinquished. After a single goal by Vancouver, Barlow and Redahl put the game on ice.

The next night on the mainland, the Leafs came back from a 3-1 deficit to win the game, 5-3. Hebenton scored in the first period, and Vancouver netted three straight goals. However, the Leafs did not give up, and Redahl and Barlow tied the score. Mike Labadie had the winner at 15:51 of the third period and Hebenton sealed the 5-3 victory with an empty-net marker in the last minute of play.[2283] Victoria gained two much-needed points when it finally beat San Francisco, 6-1, before an appreciative home crowd of only 2,458. The Seals scored the first goal of the game, but Millar and the Leafs shut the door after that. Jankowski had two goals with singles added by Barlow, Redahl, Hebenton, and Parenteau. The difference in the game was penalty killing, as the Leafs kept the Seals from getting shots on goal, while on the other side of the ledger, they scored two power-play goals of their own.[2284]

Next on the schedule was a three-game road trip. In Los Angeles, the Leafs built up a 4-0 lead, then held on for a 4-3 victory. Blades "bad man" Howie Young was part of the reason for the victory, as he was in the penalty box for two of Victoria's goals. John Sleaver scored twice for the Leafs, while Marcetta and Keenan added singles. The win left the Leafs six points ahead of Portland in the league standings, although the Buckaroos had two games in hand.[2285] The downside to the win was that the league's leading scorer, Milan Marcetta, was injured and sent to hospital with a ruptured thigh.[2286]

San Francisco got its first shutout in 184 WHL games when the injury-depleted Maple Leafs were unable to score a single goal, and the Seals managed six. With scoring stars Marcetta and Jankowski on the sidelines, Victoria had little in the way of offence, as the lines were juggled and the new combinations were ineffective.[2287] The injury report got longer when the Leafs limped into Portland. Mike Labadie, Claude Labrosse, and Steve Witiuk would all play despite nagging injuries, but there was no fight left in the Leafs, and they suffered their second consecutive shutout, 4-0 to the Buckaroos. The league lead was down to two points, and Portland still had two games in hand.[2288] Before a disappointing crowd of 3,055 at the Memorial Arena, the Leafs never gave up and stormed back in the third period to win the game, 5-4, to retain first place. Despite having Dick Lamoureux and Aut Erickson added to the injury list, the team dug deep and found a way to win. After Goyer opened the scoring for Portland, Keenan got that one back four minutes later. Barlow put the Leafs ahead, only to have Art Jones tie it up. Before the end of the second period, the Buckaroos added two more goals, giving then a 4-2 lead. Fred

Hucul found the net on the power play, and his brother added a goal four minutes later to tie the score, setting the stage for Rollie Wilcox—just back from Tulsa—to streak down the ice to fire off a pass to Hebenton, who buried it behind McLeod for the winning goal. It was one of the most exciting games to date, and team management was disappointed at the poor attendance.[2289]

The Providence Reds were the next AHL team to visit Victoria. Coached by former Cougar Ivan Irwin, they were no match for the hometown Leafs. Firing fifty-two shots on Marcel Paille, Victoria had an easy game for the first time in weeks in a 5-1 victory. Jankowski, back in the lineup after his injury, led the team with two goals and an assist. Other scores came from Labadie, Barlow, and Sleaver. Millar lost his shutout bid on a Providence power play.[2290] The next game was an overtime thriller against Vancouver. Barlow opened the scoring with his twenty-fifth goal. Phil Maloney tied the game in the second frame, but Sleaver scored to give Victoria the lead under a minute later. Larry Popein had a third-period score for the Canucks to tie the contest again. That set the stage for the wily veteran Andy Hebenton to take a pass from Marcetta, deke out a defender, and then (after 3:22 of extra time), pull Villeneuve to one side of the net while depositing the puck in the other. The 2,656 fans in attendance were left limp with excitement from one of the closest games of the year, ending with a 3-2 victory.[2291] Before the next game, there were changes to the lineup. Rollie Wilcox was called up to Rochester as an emergency replacement, so lines had to be juggled. Keenan was put with Sleaver and Jankowski in an attacking unit. Thankfully, Marcetta was back on the ice, so that the top line would remain intact.[2292]

The next game was shrouded in controversy, as the Blades contended that the winning goal was offside and should not have counted. Labrosse opened the scoring on a nice passing play from Barlow and Marcetta, Los Angeles tied the score, and then went ahead on a goal by Willie O'Ree in the second frame. Erickson got Victoria even, early in the third period, setting the stage for the controversial goal. As reported in the local press, "The puck went from Fred Hucul in his own zone, to Bob Barlow at the Victoria blue line, and out to Marcetta over the red line." The Blades claimed that Barlow was inside the blue line when he touched the puck. Linesman Bunker Hill said "no," and referee Lloyd Gilmour agreed with him—and the goal stood.[2293]

Victoria then travelled to Vancouver where they'd had great success that season. For some reason, they forgot how to score or defend and left as 10-3 losers.[2294] Moving on to Seattle, the Leafs rebounded as they had for most of the season and edged the Totems, 3-2. The game was close and fast-skating. Hebenton had the first goal, and then Powers tied it for Seattle. In the second frame, the Totems took the lead only to have Keenan score for Victoria to tie the game again. The winning goal—the only score of the final period—came off the stick of Barlow after Marcetta stole the puck from a Totem player and passed to his line-mate for the score.[2295]

A sold-out crowd of 5,269 jammed the Memorial Arena to watch the Leafs play Portland. Inspired by their fans, the Leafs upended the Buckaroos to retain their first-place standing. The game started slowly, with Marcetta notching the only goal in the opening period. The middle frame was all Victoria, as Witiuk had one goal and Fred Hucul scored a pair. Jankowski and Hebenton closed out the Victoria scoring in the final frame. The Leafs got a bit sloppy late in the game and surrendered two late goals to make the final count 6-2.[2296] The Buckaroos got their revenge the next evening, beating the Leafs, 2-1, in the return match.

In an unprecedented move, Leafs management decided to hold an advanced ticket sale for the February 26 game against the Rochester Americans, Toronto's AHL franchise. Interested fans were invited to mail in a coupon with full payment for tickets, enclosing a stamped, self-addressed envelope, starting on February 6. The game was billed as "the clash of the top teams outside of the NHL."[2297]

Back on home ice, Victoria entertained San Francisco. Before the game, the Toronto Maple Leaf management ordered that Milan Marcetta and Fred Hucul—unquestionably two of Victoria's best players—be sent to Tulsa to try to secure a playoff berth for the CPHL club. In return, Victoria would receive Ed Ehrenverth and Jack Chipchase, which was certainly not a fair deal as far as local fans were concerned.[2298] Likely upset by the news that the team would be losing significant talent, along with the ability to retain first place in the standings, the players did not perform as well as they had in recent games and lost, 4-2, to the Seals. Only Hebenton and Jankowski were able to find the net for the Leafs, with the players about to leave adding one assist each. WHL president Al Leader was upset at the player move and called it "another example of the monopolistic outlook the NHL has on hockey." He added that "despite rumours, Toronto could not shift its WHL franchise to San Diego, which has a 13,900-seat arena under construction and due to be completed by October 1. San Diego already has a franchise [and] it's for next year."[2299]

With the imminent player shuffle leaving a bad taste in their mouths, the Leafs headed to Los Angeles for two games. For some strange reason, the team's equipment was not placed on the same aeroplane as they were on, so it arrived in Los Angeles ninety minutes after they did. The game did not start well, and the Leafs were down 2-0 at the end of the second period. Then Redahl suffered a stitch in his side, and his place was taken by Labadie. Like magic, that move ignited the team, and they stormed back to tie the game on goals by Erickson and Hebenton. In overtime, it was no contest, as Jankowski fired the winner, assisted by Sleaver and Labadie, at the 6:54 mark.[2300] Two days later, the teams played again, this time, minus the departed stars, and the result was a humiliating 7-2 defeat at the hands of the lowly Blades. The score was 4-0 before Keenan found the net, and 7-1 before Erickson scored, one minute from the end of the game. Once again, it was time to learn from the mistakes, and then move on to a contest in Portland. The Leafs found some of their old vitality and managed a 3-3 tie with the Buckaroos, leaving the two teams tied for the league lead. Hebenton, Keenan, and Sandy Hucul found the back of the net for Victoria, while Millar stopped thirty-three shots. Bill Shvetz was a stand-out on defence and was so tired after the game that he could hardly get onto the bus.[2301]

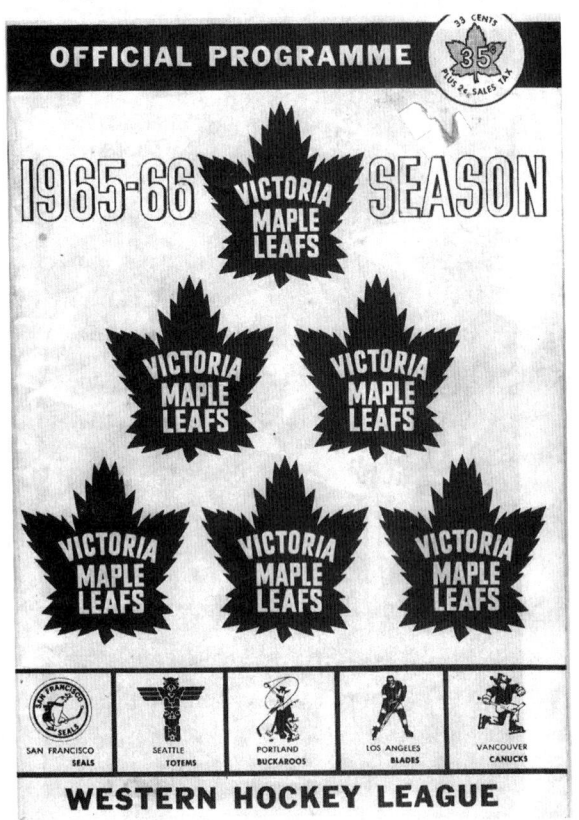

Victoria Maple Leafs 1965-66 program.

Victoria's next home game was against the Buckaroos, and, this time, Portland won in an overtime thriller. However, there was controversy over a goal that the Leafs claimed to have scored, only to have the officials disagree. The team was on a power play with a 2-1 lead when Sandy Hucul boomed a shot from the right side that went past Dave Kelly in the Portland net and travelled right through the mesh. The goal judge flashed the red light, but referee Lloyd Gilmour allowed the play to continue. Had the goal counted, it would have made the score 3-1 for the Leafs, and the game likely would have never gone to overtime. As it was, Bill Saunders scored 1:11 into extra time to give the Buckaroos the victory and sole possession of first place. After the game, players from both teams acknowledged that a goal had been scored, but there was nothing that could be done at that point.[2302] Little did the Leafs know that that game was the first of a six-game losing streak—their longest of the season by far—that moved them into second place in the league for good. It was not a coincidence that the losing took place while Marcetta and Fred Hucul were banished to Tulsa, and this enraged loyal Leafs fans, who felt their team should have been treated more fairly by the parent Toronto team.[2303]

In Vancouver, the Leafs fell behind, 2-0, but Jankowski scored to make the game close. However, the Canucks regained their two-goal lead by the end of the first period. Keenan, playing in Marcetta's place between Hebenton and Barlow, had two second-frame goals to tie the score. When Barlow found the back of the net, the Leafs went ahead, but they could not hold the Canucks back, and two quick goals gave Vancouver a close 5-4 victory.[2304] Back home, the Leafs played their worst game of the season and lost, 5-3, to the cellar-dwelling Blades. The game was filled with errors, with Victoria making more than their share. Only Hebenton, Sleaver, and Barlow could beat Marcel Pelletier in the Los Angeles net.[2305]

In Los Angeles, the losing continued. Hebenton opened the scoring, but the Blades had the next three goals to take the lead. He scored again, but Los Angeles got that one back quickly. Labrosse ended the middle frame with a goal, but the Blades scored two early in the third period to take a commanding lead. Two late counters by Jankowski were too little, too late as Victoria lost, 6-5.[2306] In San Francisco, Coach Mario switched goaltenders, playing Gary Holland in place of Millar. That tactic did not make much difference, as the Seals built up a two-goal lead, allowed a single score by Ehrenverth, then held on for a narrow 2-1 victory. The only good news to come out of that game was that Marcetta and Fred Hucul would be back with the team in time for their next game against Seattle.[2307]

Controversy then reared its ugly head about goaltending with the Leafs. According to reports, Al Millar had been on poor terms with several of his teammates, and at one point, had argued violently with John Sleaver. Millar made several disparaging comments about the team, calling them "prize sheep without a shepherd" and the coach "a puppet coach," which did not endear him to the rest of the club. Buck Houle, general manager, asked Toronto to send trade Millar for somebody who could be a team player, but no immediate help would be coming. Young Gary Holland was expected to assume full-time goaltending duties.[2308]

In the first home game since all the controversy, the Leafs were shut out, 3-0, by Seattle. Gary Holland played well in the net, but the rest of the players seemed to have forgotten how to play as a team. That was the sixth consecutive loss and the eighth in the last nine games. If the team wanted to go anywhere in the postseason, they would have to figure out how to regain their scoring touch.[2309] When the vaunted Rochester Americans came to town, the Leafs were in disarray but somehow managed to come up with a fabulous game and downed the AHL leaders, 6-4. Holland was given the start in goal, as team management was trying to make a deal for Millar. His inexperience showed at times, but he did come up with big saves when they were needed. The game was exciting, and the record crowd of 5,394 cheered every Leaf move. It was ten minutes before the Amerks got their first shot on goal, and by that time, Redahl and Lamoureux had found the net for a 2-0 lead. In the middle frame, Jim Pappin and Ed Litzenberger scored for Rochester, while Redahl and Marcetta replied for the home team. Al Arbour got an early third-period score to narrow the count to 4-3. Marcetta and Pappin scored their second goals. The result of the game was in doubt until Sandy Hucul fired the clinching goal on a power play with less than four minutes left.[2310] In the war between the Toronto farm teams, this battle went to the Victoria Maple Leafs.

In the goaltender fracas, Holland had already played four games and had only one left before his five-game trial was up. At that point, he would have to be signed as a professional, unless Houle could secure a three-game emergency extension.[2311] The situation grew more interesting as Millar was sent to Tulsa on orders from Toronto management.[2312]

Things got back to regular league play when the Seals came to town. Although San Francisco opened the scoring ten seconds after the game started, Barlow got that one back at forty-four seconds. Labadie and Labrosse had goals to give the Leafs a 3-1 lead going into the final frame. Jankowski's early score gave the Leafs the margin of victory they needed, and a late Seal goal had little effect on the final result of 4-2 for Victoria.[2313] In a game in Vancouver, the Leafs team forgot everything about how to play good hockey (and Holland had a poor effort) and were trampled, 8-1. Fred Hucul was the only skater to beat Villeneuve.[2314] Back at Memorial Arena, in their last game before a road trip that included an eastern swing through the AHL, the Leafs played good hockey and upended the Totems, 6-2. Seattle scored the first and third goals of the game, while Barlow and Parenteau had the second and fourth, tying the score at 2-2 at the end of one period. The Leafs won the game with four goals in the middle frame, with Erickson, Barlow, Jankowski, and Redahl beating McLeod, to end the scoring. For Barlow (a former Totem who had been told he would not be as effective a scorer without Guyle Fielder to pass the puck to him), this was a satisfying effort, as he now had thirty goals, matching his output of the previous season. Coach Mario had good news on the goaltending front when he learned that San Francisco backup goalie John Henderson would now be playing for the Leafs when the teams tangled in four days.[2315]

Holland was still in goal when the Leafs played the Seals. As they had on numerous other occasions, San Francisco dominated Victoria, upending them, 7-2. The Seals took an early 2-0 lead and were ahead 5-1 after two periods. Former Cougar Al Nicholson fired a hat trick to lead his team to victory, and only Redahl and Barlow were able to beat Jack McCartan in the San Francisco net.[2316] In their last game before the AHL trip, the Leafs defeated the Blades, 5-3, to move within three points of first-place Portland. New goaltender "Long John" Henderson played a crucial role in the game, stopping several Blades' chances. The Leafs team found its scoring touch, notching twice in four attempts, with Fred Hucul and Barlow doing the honours. Hebenton, Labrosse, and Witiuk added goals for Victoria. Lamoureux and Witiuk led the penalty killers, who negated the Blades' odd-men advantages.[2317]

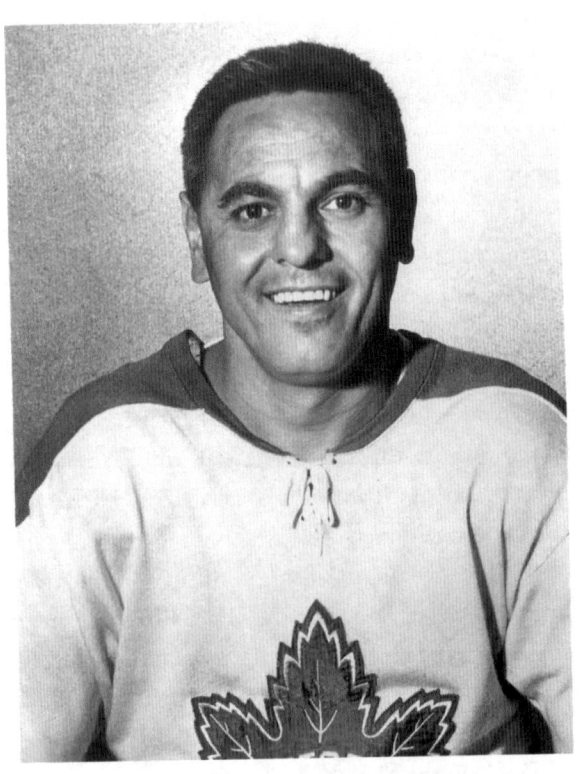

Steve Witiuk as a Maple Leaf. Photo courtesy Ernie Fitzsimmons.

The Leafs extended their winning record over AHL teams to six with a thrilling 2-1 overtime victory over the Pittsburgh Hornets. Hebenton scored the first Victoria goal only to have Pittsburgh tie the game under a minute later. There was no further scoring until overtime when Sleaver found the net at 4:52. As might be expected in a close game, the stars were the two goaltenders, John Henderson and George Gardner. Then it was on to Providence, where the Leafs ran into bad luck and lost, 4-3. First-period goals by Redahl and Barlow staked Victoria to a 2-0 lead, but a Providence score narrowed the lead to 2-1 by the end of the middle frame. Jankowski found the net to increase the lead, but two goals from the Reds tied the score. It took only eighteen seconds of overtime for Providence to win the game.[2318]

In Baltimore, the Leafs dominated the play for most of the game but fell just short in a 4-3 loss. Witiuk opened the scoring, but the Clippers notched three straight goals to take the lead. Labadie and Marcetta had Victoria goals, but could not find the tying marker.[2319] It was the second disappointing loss when a bit of luck might have turned the tables. Playing their sixth game in eight days, and without the services of Jankowski and Barlow, who had been injured in the Baltimore game, the Leafs played a dismal game in Hershey and lost 9-3, for their worst defeat of the season. Hebenton, Lamoureux, and Parenteau were the only Leafs to hit the back of the net.[2320] Victoria closed out its AHL trip with two losses. In Springfield, the Indians upended the Leafs 3-1 with only Hebenton able to score. The last game of the trip was played in Quebec, and a tired Leaf team lost 7-1. Nursing several injuries, Victoria ran out of steam after the long trip and did not put up much of a fight. Witiuk had briefly tied the score in the opening period, but that was the last score they could manage. The team limped home, having lost five games in a row, with the knowledge that Portland would likely finish in first place.[2321]

The Maple Leafs returned to Victoria confident that they could regain their scoring prowess and win the majority of their remaining seven games, six of which would be played on home ice. Coach Mario also hoped the team could gain some momentum heading into the post-season.[2322]

The Leafs, glad to be home, played like they had at the beginning of the season and upended the Canucks, 4-2. Rookie Parenteau, playing his best hockey, got the Leafs on the scoreboard first. Jankowski and Barlow added second-frame goals, and Labrosse had a third-period counter to give the Leafs a 4-0 lead. Then came a controversial play. Referee Lloyd Gilmour claimed that Sandy Hucul had closed his hand on the puck in the crease during a scramble. Sandy maintained that he had merely swept the puck out and protested the call, but a penalty shot was awarded. Sadly, Phil Maloney beat Henderson on that play, breaking the shutout bid. A late Canuck goal made the score closer but did not hurt the Leafs. It was a satisfying victory for the team and reversed the losing trend.[2323] After the game, Coach Mario singled out the efforts of Bill Shvetz and his many hits as the reason that the Leafs had won their last game. He was hoping that the stellar play would continue in the upcoming games, particularly against Portland.[2324]

Fred Hucul played against Portland although his ailing back was sore, proving once again his value to the team, as he notched two third-period goals that opened up a close game and secured a 4-1 victory for the Leafs. He also played well on defence, frustrating the Buckaroos at every turn. Barlow scored his thirty-fifth of the year, and Hebenton added his twenty-ninth.[2325] Tragedy struck the team when Gordon Redahl's daughter died in hospital. She had been ill for some time, and he had taken leave from the team to be with her.[2326]

The third game of the homestand was against the Buffalo Bisons. The Leafs built a 3-1 lead in the opening period and held on for the victory.[2327] Victoria opened April with a 6-4 win over Seattle. The Totems took a 2-0 lead before Fred Hucul scored with just seven seconds left in the opening period. Seattle had two goals in the middle frame, with Barlow answering for the Leafs. However, the third period was all Maple Leafs, as Jankowski had two goals and Hebenton and Lamoureux added singles. It was the team's fourth consecutive win after the disastrous road trip.[2328] Redahl returned to the lineup after the death of his daughter and scored four goals to lead the way to a 10-0 shutout of the Blades. Barlow had two goals, while Lamoureux, Hebenton, Sleaver, and Marcetta added singles. Henderson played a magnificent game, as he recorded the first Leaf shutout of the season.[2329] Victoria travelled to Seattle and dropped a 7-3 decision to the Totems. Parenteau scored two goals, and Barlow added one.

The game was 4-3 for Seattle at the end of the second period, but the Totems broke the game wide open with three unanswered scores in the final frame to win relatively easily.[2330] Victoria closed out the season with a home game against Vancouver. Andy Hebenton played his thirteenth consecutive complete season, having missed three games back in 1950-51, and none since. The Canucks opened the scoring with a first-period goal and one early in the second, but the Leafs roared back with three goals of their own—two by Barlow and one by Sleaver—before the Canucks scored again. Redahl added a goal late in the middle frame to tie the game 4-4. After Vancouver again took the lead in the final period, Barlow and Sleaver found the net to give the Leafs the victory.[2331] It was an excellent way to end the regular season, winning six out of the last seven games. However, the team that Victoria would face in the playoffs had not been determined. It would take the final game of the schedule to settle that issue. In the end, the San Francisco Seals finished fourth in the standings and would face the second-place Leafs in a best-of-season series. Third-place Vancouver would play Portland in the other semi-final.[2332]

The Leafs played well in the first game against the Seals. After San Francisco opened the scoring, Jankowski, Marcetta (with two), and Hebenton fired goals to give Victoria a 4-1 lead before the Seals added another before the end of the first period. In the middle frame, Fred Hucul had a pair of scores, and the Seals could only manage one more, to make the final count 6-3.[2333] Manager Poile of the Seals protested the loss as the team was forced to use an amateur when regular goaltender McCartan was injured and unable to play. He claimed that all other clubs would be able to use Marcel Pelletier if their regular goalie was out of action.[2334] The league ruled that Pelletier would play in game two, as the three other clubs had agreed, but that the result of game one would stand.[2335]

In game two, the Leafs' top line—Barlow, Marcetta, and Hebenton—scored goals in that order and the checking forwards and defence limited the Seals to only two scores. With the victory, Victoria took a two-game lead in the series.[2336]

Game action then shifted to California for a maximum of three games, the last one only played if necessary. In game three, the Seals took advantage of Victoria errors to emerge with a 4-2 victory before their home fans. San Francisco put together a checking line to handle the Leafs' top line, and it worked in this match as that trio had only one goal. Wayne Connelly opened the scoring for the Seals, then Labadie and Barlow gave Victoria a brief lead. However, San Francisco added two goals in the middle frame and a single near the end of the game, to win handily. The game got a bit chippy near the end, and it seemed likely that the level of intensity would be turned up in the next contest.[2337]

Although the attendance in San Francisco was not very high, the fans who were in the stands for game four saw a preview of what hockey would be like when they had an NHL franchise. Both clubs skated well, and there was end-to-end action with first one team having the advantage, then the other. Barlow got the first Leaf goal on a seemingly harmless shot that Pelletier misjudged. The Seals had two second-frame goals to take the lead, which they held until Fred Hucul took a pass from Hebenton late in that period to tie the game. After a scoreless third period, Larry McNabb found the net behind Henderson at 2:29 of overtime to give the Seals the victory. The series now sat at two games each.[2338] After the game, Coach Mario said that the Leafs had missed several chances to win that game and were really missing Steve Witiuk, who had an injured knee and was unable to play. "Without Steve, we have no flexibility at all," he said. "I'm going to have to try something new, but there aren't too many changes I can make."[2339]

Marcel Pelletier was no longer allowed to play for the Seals, as Doug Favell became available when Oklahoma City won the CPHL Championship. However, he did not arrive in time for game five, so amateur Bob Gray was forced into the net. He certainly looked to be of professional status as he backstopped the Seals to a 5-4 victory, giving San Francisco a 3-2 lead in the semi-final series. San Francisco took the early lead, then Hebenton tied it up. Again, the Seals took the lead only to have Jankowski knot the score. In the third period, San Francisco scored twice, but Barlow and Redahl replied to tie the game again. Unfortunately for the Leafs, rookie Stan Gilbertson took a pass from Wayne Connelly and Larry McNabb and fired it past Henderson. The Seals had won all three of their home games and could win the series in the next game in Victoria.[2340]

Back in Victoria, 4,903 fans in the Memorial Arena saw the most exciting game played there in two seasons. The Leafs did not disappoint, skating aggressively and playing with determination. Redahl found the net just twenty-eight seconds into the game, and Sandy Hucul followed that with a goal at 7:11. Jankowski beat Doug Favell in the Seals' net to put the Leafs up, 3-0, midway through the middle frame, but Victoria had a brief meltdown and surrendered three straight goals to tie the score. Barlow put the Leafs ahead at 14:42 of the third period, but the Seals tied it up when a John Sleaver pass was intercepted and fired past Henderson. That goal set up an agonizing overtime period. Knowing that if they lost the game, they would be out of the playoffs, the Leafs pressed hard, missing several chances. At the other end of the ice, San Francisco was doing the same to Henderson. Finally, at 12:37, Barlow scored on a rebound from a Marcetta shot, and the fans went wild. From the size of the line-up at the arena box office after the game, it was clear that most of the fans would be back two days later for the deciding game seven.[2341]

Before the final game, Seals' coach Charlie Burns said that either team could win but acknowledged that he was worried about Bob Barlow, who seemed to be everywhere on the ice, having notched six goals and adding six assists in the series, including the overtime winner in the last game. He said, "That Barlow keeps on popping up. He has had a great series. He's scoring goals, and he is back there doing his checking all the time."[2342] As it turned out, the game was the most one-sided contest of the entire series. With Toronto Maple Leafs' assistant manager King Clancy in attendance, the Leafs dominated the game, with Marcetta scoring on Favell just forty-seven seconds after the opening whistle. The Seals carried out their threat to hassle Barlow and did so with poor sportsmanship in the seventh minute of play. McNabb cross-checked Barlow, then Harris knocked him to the ice, cutting the back of his head. Referee Gilmour could have called a misconduct penalty but chose to assess a major penalty to Harris and a minor to McNabb. Fred Hucul scored with the two-man advantage, and Lamoureux added a single before the Seals managed to beat Henderson. After that, it was all over for the Seals. Redahl and Fred Hucul had second-period goals, and the team defended their net with ferocity, determined to win. Lamoureux's second of the night into an empty net was the icing on the cake. Victoria had won the game, 6-1, and the series four games to three. In the other league semi-final, Portland had come from behind to defeat Vancouver. Now the top two teams in the league would play each other for the championship.[2343]

Just in time for the final, a new player joined the Leafs. Mike Corrigan (who had played for Tulsa) was brought in as a replacement for Steve Witiuk, who was still unable to play.[2344] When asked which team would prevail in the final, Coach Mario noted that regular season records really did not count. Victoria had only managed three wins and two ties against the Seals but had defeated them in the semi-final. Their record against Portland was much better—six wins, four losses, and two ties—but all those games were in the past.[2345]

Tickets were at a premium for the first game in Victoria. Manager Poile advised that only 500 seats remained, and they were going fast.[2346] Fans were hoping for a different result this year, with memories of last year's 4-1 series defeat still in their minds.

The first game of the series exceeded everyone's expectations. Victoria fell behind, 2-0, and in fact, did not score until Labadie fired a shot at 4:18 of the second period. The Buckaroos added another goal ten minutes later to take a 3-1 lead. Marcetta scored on the power play to narrow the deficit. Fred Hucul opened the third period with a power-play goal to tie the score, but Portland scored again to take the lead. Fred Hucul made a perfect pass to Marcetta for the fourth Victoria goal midway through the third period to again knot the score. There was no further scoring in regulation time, so the game went to overtime. The teams skated up and down the ice, firing shots at the goaltenders, both of whom played well. The game went well past one overtime period, while the fans sat on the edge of their seats. The clock had passed midnight when the end came. Claude Labrosse took a pass from goaltender Henderson, skated down the ice, and fired a shot that went over Dave Kelly's shoulder, bounced off a goal post, and fell into the net. The time was 14:56 of the second overtime and the crowd let out a collective sigh of relief and erupted in joyful cheering. Game one was over—and the Leafs had won![2347]

The second game was played in Portland, and the Leafs did not play as well as they had in the first game. Hebenton opened the scoring while the Leafs were shorthanded, but the Buckaroos replied with two goals before the end of the first period. Hebenton's second score early in the middle frame tied the game, but that was the end of Victoria's offence, as Portland notched four straight goals to win, 6-2. The series was now tied 1-1, and either team could win.[2348]

The Leafs put up a much better effort in game three and won, 4-1, in Portland. There was no scoring in the opening period, as the teams played cautiously, feeling each other out. Fred Hucul put the Leafs ahead early in the middle frame only to have Goyer respond for the Buckaroos. It was in the third period that Victoria won the game. Barlow had the eventual winner on passes from Hebenton and Marcetta, Erickson added an insurance goal less than five minutes from the end of the game, and Jankowski put the game on ice with a score at 16:12.[2349] The victory meant that there would be at least two more games on Victoria ice. Tickets went on sale for what would be the last hockey games in Memorial Arena that season.[2350]

The Leafs came out well in game four but could not beat Rick Charron in the Portland net. After the first period, they played their worst game of the playoffs. The Buckaroos controlled the high-scoring Leaf trio, and as a result, ended Victoria's home winning streak at thirty-three games with a 3-0 shutout. The series was now square at two games each, and the whole season came down to the last three games.[2351] Victoria rebounded in the next game, as it had all season, with a hard-fought 4-2 win in front of 5,030 cheering fans.[2352] After a slow start, during which they surrendered two goals to the Buckaroos, the Leafs roared back in the final two periods. Barlow notched two power-play goals in the middle frame to tie the score. John Sleaver fired the winning goal in the ninth minute of the final period, and Marcetta hit an empty net for insurance.

With a 3-2 series lead, the Leafs travelled to Portland for game six.[2353] Never a team to do things the easy way, Victoria built up a 2-0 lead on goals by Lamoureux and Barlow and seemed to be on their way to a victory. However, Portland tied the game on two goals by Gerry Goyer, setting the stage for the winning score by Arnie Schmautz. How ironic that former Victoria Cougars scored all three goals in a 3-2 victory for Portland.[2354]

Now the whole season came down to one game, and the way the games were being played, either team could win. Working against Victoria was the fact that they would be skating at the Memorial Coliseum, where the fans were not on their side.

You could have cut the tension in the air at game seven with a knife. Larry Keenan scored the first goal of the game at 14:16 of the first period. Former Cougar Art Jones tied it up midway through the second frame, but Mike Labadie gave the Leafs the lead again six minutes later. The final period was all Victoria. Labadie, Keenan, and Marcetta all notched goals to give the Leafs the victory, 5-1. John Henderson stood tall in the nets and stymied the Buckaroos time after time. With that win came the Lester Patrick Trophy, reconnecting the Patrick name with Victoria hockey.[2355]

I attended the last two games in Portland, and it was an experience I will never forget. My feeling of euphoria at the decisive game-seven victory will last with me forever. I still get goosebumps when I think about it. I know I was one of very few Leafs fans in attendance. The downside was that I missed the welcome home for the team, as I was still on the road.

.es Maple Leafs de Victoria·ligue de hockey de l'Ouest·gagnants du trophée Lester Patrick
1965-1966
Victoria Maple Leafs Lester Patrick Trophy Winners Western Hockey League
1ère rangée—1st row: John Henderson, Bill Shvetz, Frank Mario, instructeur—Coach, Sandy Hucul, Capt., A.J. "Buck" Houle, gérant général—General Manager, Lou Jankowski, Gary Holland. 2ème rangée—2nd row: Gord Marchant, entraîneur—Trainer, Gord Redahl, Dick Lamoureux, John Sleaver, Aut Erickson, Claude Labrosse, Mike Corrigan. 3ème rangée—3rd row: Steve Witiuk, Andy Hebenton, Bob Barlow, Mike Labadie, Milan Marcetta, Fred Hucul, Larry Keenan, Dave Parenteau.

1965-66 Victoria Maple Leafs team photo. From the author's collection.

Gone was the frustration of the final series' loss of the previous season. The City of Victoria had another hockey championship, matching the 1924-25 Cougars and the 1950-51 Cougars. The Leafs flew back home and were welcomed home at Victoria International Airport by their families and about a hundred fans.

Five members of the Victoria Maple Leafs with the Lester Patrick Trophy. John Henderson, Bud Poile, Frank Mario, Bob Barlow, and one unidentified player. Photo courtesy Bob Barlow.

They travelled on to Memorial Arena, where they were cheered by an appreciative crowd of more than 600 fans. Entertainment was provided by the S. J. Willis Junior High School band. Alderman Geoffrey Edgelow welcomed the team on behalf of the city. Players received gifts from local merchants, and then all the players were introduced on a small stage in front of the arena doors.[2356] The sign on the Memorial Arena said it all: "Leafs, You are the Greatest."[2357]

In the evening, the players and their wives were feted at a civic dinner, at which each team member was given a suitcase with a small plaque that said, simply, "Thanks." The most cheers—and a standing ovation—were reserved for Andy Hebenton, who had played for the Cougars in the 1950-51 championship.[2358]

26 - THE YEAR OF THE LEAFS!

Victoria fans welcome the Victoria Maple Leafs as champions. Photo courtesy Bob Barlow.

After the series was over, fans learned of a local enthusiast who had erected signs of encouragement in the Barlow family's yard.[2359]

The City of Victoria loved the Leafs, and, it turned out, the Leafs loved the city back. In fact, Barlow and Shvetz joined Hebenton as full-time residents after the season and others were planning to do so, as well. It was plain that Victoria wanted the Leafs to come back for another season and that the team wanted to be there, too. The decision was in the hands of the Western Hockey League.[2360]

Sign supporting the Victoria Maple Leafs in a yard neighbouring the Barlows' home. Photo courtesy Bob Barlow.

Fred Hucul and Bob Barlow were named to the league all-star team, with Sandy Hucul on the second team. Manager Houle wondered why Andy Hebenton had not been selected. Toronto's King Clancy had said earlier that he thought Hebenton was the best player he had seen in the WHL, but of course, he did not get a vote. Each of the first-team choices received a cash award of $300 plus a trophy, while second-team stars won $150.[2361]

26 - THE YEAR OF THE LEAFS!

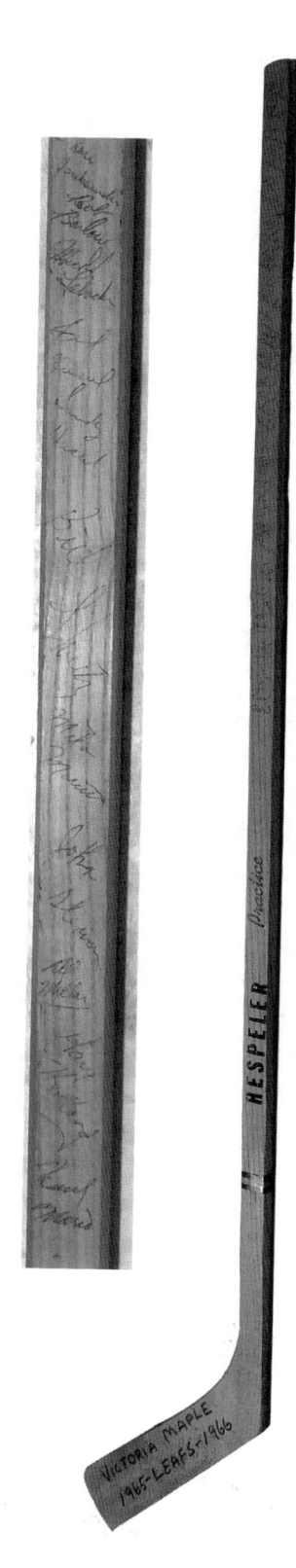

Autographed hockey stick, Victoria Maple Leafs, 1965-66 team. From the author's collection. Photo by Heather McKeen-Edwards. Detail of signatures in inset.

27 - COULD THEY REPEAT?

The training camp for the 1966-67 season opened on a positive note. Coach Frank Mario announced that several players would be returning—assuming the Toronto Maple Leafs did not throw a monkey wrench into the works. The big line of Andy Hebenton, Milan Marcetta, and Bob Barlow would be back for sure, along with forwards Lou Jankowski, Gord Redahl, Dick Lamoureux, Steve Witiuk, Mike Labadie, Rollie Wilcox, and Dave Parenteau. Defenders returning were Fred Hucul, Sandy Hucul, Claude Labrosse, Bill Shvetz, and Aut Erickson. Among the newcomers trying to make the team were Mike Laughton and Don Borgeson (who had played in Nelson the previous season), Neil Clark, and Jack Chipchase. Larry Keenan was at the Toronto training camp and could play for Victoria, and there was an outside chance that Ed Litzenberger would come west, as well. In goal, Gary Holland and Mike Beveridge would be in camp along with Gary Smith, son of former NHL defenceman Des Smith.[2362]

The first open practice drew a crowd of more than 1,000 fans, eager to see the latest edition of their team.[2363] The team played its first exhibition game against the San Diego Gulls, the league's newest team, in Chilliwack. The Leafs won the game, 3-2, in front of more than 1,500 fans. Rookie Mike Laughton scored his first professional goal, while Marcetta and Barlow scored the others.[2364] In the first home exhibition game, the Leafs upended the Gulls, 3-1, in a game designed to showcase the rookies trying to make the team.[2365] In the final home exhibition game, the Leafs defeated Seattle, 7-4. Manager Buck Houle announced that goalie Al Smith, who played with the Toronto Marlboros the previous year, would join the team.[2366] In Spokane, the Leafs defeated the Spokane Jets of the Western International Hockey League, 5-1.[2367] The final exhibition game was played in Trail against the Trail Smoke Eaters of the WIHL. The Leafs ended the pre-season with a perfect 5-0 record when they upended Trail, 6-2. Goaltender Al Smith arrived in Victoria, and Larry Keenan was on his way. All that remained was for Coach Mario to decide on his final lineup.[2368]

A pre-season analysis of the WHL named Portland and Victoria as the top teams but said there could be surprises with some of the other teams.[2369] Victoria fans were thrilled with the rosy predictions but knew that there would be a lot of hard work necessary to repeat as champions.

Victoria started the regular season with a 2-0 shutout of the California Seals. Mayor Alf Toone dropped the puck at centre ice to start proceedings and young Al Smith backstopped the team to victory while Redahl scored both goals. Manager Houle scrambled to sign players during the day, but the team had to play without the services of Fred and

Sandy Hucul, Milan Marcetta, and Bob Barlow.[2370] The forwards were signed the next day,[2371] and the Huculs before the second game of the season.[2372]

Mike Laughton as a Maple Leaf. Photo courtesy Ernie Fitzsimmons.

In a rematch of the prior season's championship, Portland came to town, and the Leafs and Al Smith recorded their second shutout of the season, with a score of 5-0. Marcetta had the prettiest goal of the night, skating the length of the ice, avoiding two defenders, and beating goaltender Don Head. Witiuk, Carmichael, and Hebenton scored before Neil Clark finished the scoring with his first professional goal.[2373] Victoria travelled to Seattle to play the Totems. An opponent finally scored on rookie Al Smith—Howie Hughes had three—but Carmichael, Marcetta, and Jankowski counted for the Leafs to end the game in a 3-3 tie.[2374] Victoria extended its unbeaten streak to four games with a close 3-1 victory over San Diego. Les Binkley, in the Gulls' net, kept the Leafs' scorers at bay and gave his team a chance to win. Hebenton scored two goals, and Marcetta had a single, as the top line continued the success they'd had the previous season.[2375]

Before the next game, the Leafs sent Dave Parenteau to the Totems, as they had an overabundance of forward talent. The success of rookies Clark and Laughton and the return of Larry Keenan to the lineup made the second-year player expendable.[2376]

San Diego earned its franchise's first point when it tied the Leafs, 4-4. Binkley stopped fifty shots in the net and held the Leafs shooters at bay, while the Victoria defence was anything but stellar. The Leafs built up a 4-2 lead on goals by Keenan, Lamoureux, Carmichael, and Fred Hucul but got sloppy around their own net and let Len Haley find the loose puck and score; then MacMillan intercepted a pass and fired home the tying goal. Although the Leafs had the edge in the overtime period, there was no further scoring.[2377]

Fans entering Memorial Arena for the next home game saw a new booth in the lobby. It was connected with "Andy Hebenton Night" at the Arena. Fans were asked to donate one dollar each with the goal of collecting $1,000—one dollar for every regular season game[2378] that Hebenton had played in his iron-man streak, dating back to 1952 with the Victoria Cougars. The name of each donor would be placed on a scroll that would be presented to this remarkable player during the night's festivities. It was unfortunate that the record of 1,000 consecutive games would be set on the road in Oakland, but local organizers decided to honour this remarkable achievement with festivities on October 30.[2379]

The Leafs lost their first game of the season when they fell, 5-3, to the visiting Los Angeles Blades. After a scoreless first period, the Blades fired four straight goals (after Hebenton found the net for Victoria) to take a lead they never relinquished. Redahl and Carmichael had third-period scores for the Leafs to pull them to within a single goal, but Los Angeles had an empty-net goal to put the game away.[2380] The Leafs then received the terrible news that Larry Keenan would be lost to the team for about eight weeks, as he had fractured his heel in a freak accident while trying on a new pair of skates. The loss of this talented centre left the Leafs a bit lean down the middle, with Marcetta the only veteran.[2381]

Victoria lost its second game of the season when Seattle came to town and defeated them, 3-2. The Leafs' positional play was not as good as it should have been, and their passing was atrocious, leading to scoring chances by their opponents. After surrendering the game's first two goals, the Leafs got on the scoreboard when Witiuk fired a shot past Jim Armstrong. The Totems got that one back in the middle frame. Shvetz got the team close with a counter early in the third period, but that was the end of the offence. With the loss, the Leafs dropped into a third-place tie with California.[2382] In their last game before a long road trip, Victoria battled to a 3-3 tie with the Seals. The Leafs were led by the veteran Hebenton and the rookie Clark. The team held a 3-1 lead by the end of the second period but let down their defences and gave up a pair of scores to the Seals in the final frame. Overtime solved nothing, but if not for the spectacular saves by Smith, it could have been a very different story. Having played all but one game at home this season, the Leafs left for a five-game road trip that could make or break their season.[2383]

The Toronto Maple Leafs sent Britt Selby to the WHL, but Selby, who had played fifty-one games with the NHL the previous season, was assigned to Vancouver, rather than Victoria. Local management was understandably upset at this move, as they were struggling to find a replacement for the injured Keenan. On the ice, the Leafs opened their road trip with a 1-1 tie in Portland. Goaltender Smith was outstanding in yielding only one goal, but the Victoria defence was depleted, as Sandy Hucul was unable to play due to a foot injury suffered in the last home game. The sole Leaf goal was notched by Fred Hucul, while the power-play goal by the Buckaroos was only the second surrendered by Victoria this season.[2384] In Los Angeles, the Leafs won, 7-5, over the Blades. Neil Clark and Milan Marcetta scored two goals each, with others by Jankowski, Hebenton,

and Fred Hucul. The game was close until the third period when Victoria notched the last three goals of the game to win relatively easily.[2385] Two days later, the Leafs defeated the Blades, this time by a 4-1 count. Rollie Wilcox led the way with his first hat trick as a professional, while Barlow added the other goal. Goaltender Smith played very well, allowing only a third-period goal by Willie O'Ree.[2386]

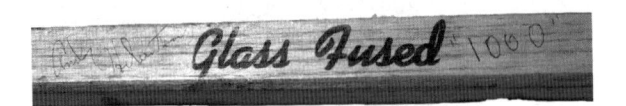

Close up of autograph by Andy Hebenton on a stick used in the game where he hit 1,000 consecutive regular-season games. From the author's collection. Photo by Heather McKeen-Edwards.

STATISTICAL STORY OF THE 1,000 GAMES

Following is the statistical story of Andy Hebenton's 1,000 consecutive professional games, combining regular schedule and playoff games. Symbols: PCHL, Pacific Coast Hockey League; WHL, Western Hockey League; NHL, National Hockey League; GP, games played; G, goals; A, assists, and TP, total points.

Season	Club	League	GP	G	A	TP
1951-52	Victoria (starting March 10)	PCHL	19	9	8	17
1952-53	Victoria	WHL	70	27	24	51
1953-54	Victoria	WHL	75	24	25	49
1954-55	Victoria	WHL	75	47	35	82
1955-56	N.Y. Rangers	NHL	75	25	14	39
1956-57	N.Y. Rangers	NHL	75	23	23	46
1957-58	N.Y. Rangers	NHL	76	23	27	50
1958-59	N.Y. Rangers	NHL	70	33	29	62
1959-60	N.Y. Rangers	NHL	70	19	27	46
1960-61	N.Y. Rangers	NHL	70	26	28	54
1961-62	N.Y. Rangers	NHL	76	19	26	45
1962-63	N.Y. Rangers	NHL	70	15	22	37
1963-64	Boston	NHL	70	12	11	23
1964-65	Portland	WHL	80	41	46	87
1965-66	Victoria (including Dec. 29)	WHL	29	9	21	30
Pro hockey totals:			1,000	352	366	718

NOTE: Prior to March 10, 1952, he played 129 games with Victoria and 44 with Cincinnati (1949-50) of the American Hockey League. His 630 regular schedule games in the NHL set a consecutive record that still stands. ◁

Details of Andy Hebenton's 1,000 consecutive regular-season games. From the author's collection.

The next game marked a milestone for Andy Hebenton when he achieved the mark of 1,000 professional hockey games without missing a single one. He had also played sixty-nine playoff games during the streak, which were not included in the official endurance record.[2387] However, the Leafs did not win the game, falling to the Seals, 2-1. All the scoring came in the second period, in one of the closest games of the season. Hebenton was honoured in a brief ceremony in the first intermission of the game. The Seals flew his wife, Gail, from Victoria for the ceremony, where California's co-owner read several congratulatory messages, including one from NHL president Clarence Campbell, and another from the New York Rangers where Andy played eight seasons. A more personal celebration was held in Victoria later in the month.[2388]

The Leafs got back on their winning ways the next evening when they blasted the Seals, 7-2. However, it did not start well, as they were down, 2-0, by the 7:12 mark of the first period. The game turned around when Clark and Hebenton found the net to tie the game before the end of the frame, and from then on, the Leafs coasted to an easy victory. Wilcox, Jankowski, Redahl, Carmichael, and Marcetta scored over the last two periods. The Leafs took four penalties but were able to kill them off with no damage, and Al Smith again played a stellar game in goal. Everything was working well.[2389]

At the league level, the WHL owners were discussing a possible merger with the AHL, as the NHL had plans to expand that would take Los Angeles and Oakland (California) from the WHL and Pittsburgh from the AHL. Preliminary plans included one league under the AHL banner but with a Western division made up of the WHL teams. Portland, Seattle, San Diego, and Vancouver were to be included, for sure, with Victoria a possibility.[2390]

For some reason, just when the team was within reach of first place in the WHL, the Leafs' play took a nosedive, and they lost eight consecutive games to fall out of contention. Were they tired from the California road trip? Had they suddenly forgotten how to play as a team? Had their good luck all been used up?

The slide began with a game against Vancouver. The Canucks silenced the 2,795 fans at the Memorial Arena, defeating the Leafs, 5-2. Victoria's play was sloppy at times, giving Vancouver chances to score. Marcetta and Erickson scored for Victoria, but the rest of the team took the night off.[2391] The next night in Vancouver was even worse—an embarrassing 9-1 loss to the Canucks. The only Leaf to find the back of the net was Wilcox. It was the kind of game that was best forgotten, except as an example of how not to play hockey.[2392] Meanwhile, Portland just kept winning, extending their lead over Victoria and Vancouver to ten points. They were on the verge of making the league-title race a runaway.[2393]

Victoria Maple Leafs program from November 26, 1966. From the author's collection.

The Leafs' road trip woes continued in Seattle, where the Totems narrowly edged the Leafs, 4-3.

The game was tied 1-1 after the first period, but Seattle notched three goals in the middle frame to take a 4-1 lead. The Leafs mounted a comeback with two scores in the last period, but it was a case of "too little, too late." Scoring goals for Victoria were Carmichael, Wilcox, and Erickson. This was the third loss in a row, and they had now slipped to fourth place in the standings.[2394]

In Vancouver, the Canucks emerged with a close 3-2 defeat of the Leafs. Things looked good after the Laughton and Redahl scored to give the Leafs an early lead. Unfortunately, that was the only scoring for Victoria, while the Canucks came from behind with three goals to take the victory. The most they could hope for now was a bounce-back game when the teams played the next night in Victoria.[2395] The team looked a lot better back at home, but still came up two goals short, losing, 6-4, to the Canucks. Vancouver scored three goals before Jankowski got the Leafs on the board. Carmichael got Victoria a bit closer, but the Canucks poured in three more goals in the middle frame to take a 6-2 lead. Third-period scores by Laughton and Hebenton made the score closer by the midway point of the third period, but that was all the home team could manage, and they fell for the fifth consecutive game.[2396]

Victoria was excited about the November 30 game against Seattle. All of hockey would be honouring Iron Man Andy Hebenton, as he reached the lofty total of 1,007 regular-season games without missing a single one. The last game Andy did not play in was on March 8, 1962, when the Victoria Cougars shut out Tacoma, 2-0. The closest he came to sitting out a game was when he was with New York Rangers and had an eye injury. He received treatment and was able to continue. Hebenton's streak in hockey was compared to the baseball streak of 2,130 games by Lou Gehrig but was considered a harder feat to accomplish given the physical nature of the game of hockey.[2397]

On November 30, 1966, the formal ceremony was held at the Memorial Arena before 3,564 fans. After accolades from the NHL, the New York Rangers, and the Montreal Canadiens, it was the local fans' turn to pay tribute. Over the previous six weeks, fans attending games had been asked to donate one dollar in the hopes that $1,000 would be raised to acknowledge the 1,000 consecutive games played. The fund was over-subscribed with over $2,000 raised, along with donations from the NHL ($620 to represents the 620 consecutive games Hebenton had played in the NHL), the Montreal Canadiens (who owned his rights early in his career), and the New York Rangers (who also sent a jersey he had worn while playing with them). Andy and his wife, Gail, received over $6,000 in gifts, including a trip to Hawaii, a colour television, golf clubs, and stereo equipment. His response was "Thank you very much, but I really don't deserve all this."

Line drawing honouring Andy Hebenton on the occasion of the celebration of his playing 1,008 consecutive games. Photo courtesy *Victoria Daily Times*.

One of the most gentlemanly players ever to lace on skates, he won the Lady Byng Trophy in the NHL and its WHL equivalent, the Fred Hume Trophy.[2398][2399] The only damper on the evening was that the Leafs just could not win their game against

Seattle. Goaltender Jim Armstrong was the star of the match, stopping Hebenton on a point-blank shot that would have written the fairy tale ending to the game. The Totems took advantage of their chances and won the game, 2-1. It was yet another one-goal defeat for the hard-luck Leafs with Jankowski the only Victoria player to beat Armstrong.[2400]

In Seattle, the Leafs took a 2-0 lead on first-period goals by Hebenton and Redahl. Seattle scored once in the middle frame, then Carmichael increased the Victoria lead to 3-1. However, the Leafs were not able to hold that lead, allowing Seattle to tie the score. In overtime, Earl Heiskala scored the winning goal at the 7:48 mark. It was the seventh consecutive defeat for Victoria, and they had slipped down to sixth place in the league standings.[2401] Now, even making the playoffs was going to be difficult.

Portland, the hottest team in the league, visited Victoria and handed the Leafs their eighth defeat in a row with a 3-1 decision. All the scoring came in the second period, and despite a valiant effort in the final frame, the Leafs could not add to Jankowski's goal. They shot wide, hit the post, and made poor decisions on passes. It was evident that they were missing stars Fred Hucul and Larry Keenan. After the game, manager Buck Houle said that changes would be made, as this team was not living up to its potential. The team had a full week before their next game, so there was time to make changes and work any new players into the system.[2402] By game time, no changes had been made, but the club had worked hard during the week, and the players were determined to be more aggressive in their play. During the losing streak, they had lost four games by a single goal and two others by two goals. A little extra effort in any of those games would have brought a different result.[2403]

The Leafs responded to the extra work and shut out the Totems, 3-0, before an appreciative—and relieved—home crowd. Witiuk and Marcetta scored in the second period to give Victoria a 2-0 lead, and a short-handed score by Erickson in the final frame sealed the deal. Al Smith returned to his early-season form and made several excellent saves to earn the shutout.[2404] It was the first victory on home ice since October 22, and their first points since November 13, when they had shut out the Seals.

Victoria followed that streak-breaker with another victory at the expense of the California Seals. Despite missing four regulars, when Sandy Hucul and Lou Jankowski were added to the injured list where Fred Hucul and Larry Keenan had been for some time, the Leafs dug deep and played a hard-hitting game. The first line of Hebenton, Marcetta, and Barlow got back some of their former prowess, combining for the first goal of the game. Laughton and Carmichael added singles in the final frame, while the defence stiffened to allow only one goal to the Seals. The 3-1 victory moved the Leafs out of the league basement.[2405] Plans for an extended winning streak hit a bump when hockey's "bad boy," Howie Young had one goal and two assists to lead the Blades to a 5-2 victory over the Leafs. Marcetta scored to tie the game in the first period, and Carmichael's goal in the second brought the team to a 2-2 tie. However, Victoria was unable to put any more pucks past Norris while Los Angeles scored three. It was not the way the team wanted to start an extended road trip.[2406]

The Leafs rebounded the next night in San Diego as they edged the Gulls, 4-3. Rookie Mike Laughton had two goals to lead his team to victory. Playing with only three defencemen when Bill Shvetz was hurt, the Leafs dug deep, with the forwards coming back to assist the depleted defence corps. San Diego opened the scoring with the only goal of the first period. Second-frame scores by Jankowski and Laughton gave Victoria the lead. The Gulls closed the gap with an early third-period goal, but the Leafs responded with goals by Laughton and Erickson to regain the lead. A late goal by San Diego made the score close, but they were unable to get the tying goal.[2407]

Playing the next night without injured forward Bob Barlow and defenceman Bill Shvetz, the Leafs shut out the Gulls, 2-0, behind the excellent goaltending of Al Smith. Tom Polanic was added to the roster from Tulsa and saw immediate action, partnered with Sandy Hucul. Marcetta scored both goals (the second into an empty net) to ensure the win. With two days off before their next game, the team hoped to get injured players back.[2408]

The last two games of the road trip were not successful. In a game in Los Angeles, they were more like a team of walking wounded than a hockey team. Marcetta, who was just gaining his scoring touch, suffered a two-inch cut and a concussion and had to leave the game. Goaltender Smith was cut by a skate and needed five stitches before he returned to play. Sandy Hucul was playing with a broken toe, Lou Jankowski with a badly bruised toe, and Labrosse with a bad elbow. Erickson came down with strep throat and was unable to play. The remaining players put forth a good effort but could not find the back of the net and ended up on the wrong side of a 4-0 score.[2409]

The final game was in Portland against the runaway league leaders. Down to one centre (Laughton), Coach Mario had to juggle his lines, but nothing seemed to work. There were just too few bodies to get the job done. The Leafs put up a good fight but were clearly outclassed in all phases of the game by the Buckaroos. Wilcox had the first and last scores for Victoria, while Carmichael and Hebenton added the others.[2410] The Leafs would be happy to get home and get their injured players recovered.

In their first game home, the Leafs entertained Vancouver. Before the game, they got the bad news that Fred Hucul was gone for the season and would need surgery on a spinal disc. The team put forth a good effort but were unable to score timely goals and fell, 5-2, to their BC rivals. Marcetta and Carmichael had the only Leaf scores, even though they outshot their opponents, 29-24. When would the scoring touch return?[2411]

The Leafs travelled to Vancouver for a game on Boxing Day and emerged with a narrow 3-2 victory. It was their first defeat of the Canucks that season, and, coupled with the welcome news that Larry Keenan would soon be back on the ice, it made loyal fans optimistic that the team had turned the corner and would now be successful. Vancouver opened the scoring, but three Victoria goals—two by Laughton and one by Marcetta—gave the Leafs a lead they would not relinquish. Vancouver scored halfway through the final frame to make the score close, but the Leafs held on for the win. Manager Buck Houle was behind the bench, as Frank Mario had left for Regina to attend his sister's funeral.[2412]

Back in Victoria, the Leafs were almost back to their previous form, and they upended the Gulls, 5-2, on "Parents' Night." In a marketing ploy, the team offered two half-price adult tickets to the parents (or accompanying adults) of any child who bought a ticket for the game. Marcetta opened the scoring, and he and Erickson added goals in the second period to give the Leafs a 3-0 lead at that point. San Diego managed two goals, but Carmichael got one back. A third-frame score by Labadie put the game on ice for Victoria to give them a modest two-game winning streak.[2413] On New Year's Eve, the same teams played again. This time, neither team prevailed, and the game ended in a 3-3 tie. Victoria fired fifty-six shots at Bob Champoux, and he stopped all but three. After the Gulls opened the scoring, Keenan got that one back for the Leafs. Carmichael gave Victoria the lead, but it was short-lived. The Gulls went ahead in the third period only to have Labrosse tie it once more. Overtime solved nothing, with both goaltenders standing tall. Next on the schedule was a trip to Portland, where the Buckaroos upended the Leafs, 4-1. Victoria shooters were constantly frustrated by the efforts of Don Head in goal, as he allowed only Mike Labadie to put a puck past him. The next evening, the Totems demolished the Leafs, 8-3. Seattle had a 5-0 lead before Wilcox scored, and third-period goals by Hebenton and Laughton were far too little to make much of a dent in the score.[2414]

Back at home, the Leafs played the Buckaroos.[2415] Portland scored the first two goals, then Carmichael got on the board. The middle frame was all

Buckaroos, as they scored two goals to take a 4-1 lead to the final period. Victoria mounted a stellar comeback, with Barlow, Laughton, and Keenan scoring in 3:14 to tie the score. Unfortunately, Len Lunde was left alone in front of the net, and he fired the puck past Gary Smith for the victory.[2416] Despite the three losses, Coach Mario liked the effort he had seen from his team, particularly in the Portland game, and decided not to changes the lines for the next game.[2417] Vancouver came to Victoria and left as 4-1 losers. The Leafs came up with a tremendous defensive effort, holding the Canucks to only seventeen shots on goal while firing thirty of their own. Hebenton and Erickson gave the team a 2-0 lead before the end of the first period. After a scoreless middle frame, Hebenton scored his second goal and Jankowski had the final goal of the evening, while only Gordie Vejprava beat Gary Smith in the Leafs' net.[2418]

The next evening, in Vancouver, Victoria came up with another inspired effort and shut out the Canucks, 7-0. Labadie had the only goal of the first period. In the middle frame, Marcetta, Barlow, and Carmichael added to the Victoria lead and the game finished with goals by Wilcox, Marcetta, and Laughton in the final period. Seven goals were the largest number that the Leafs had scored in a game that season.[2419]

Next to come to town were the Blades, and they were upended by the Leafs, 3-1. Leo Labine opened the scoring for Los Angeles, and it looked as if that goal would stand up for the entire game. It was not until the third period that Barlow found the back of the net to tie the game. The turning point came when Blades defenceman Al Lebrun made a crucial mistake that allowed Lou Jankowski to skate around him and fire the puck past Norris. Less than a minute later, Keenan scored the clinching goal, assisted by Wilcox and Jankowski.

The Blades headed off to Vancouver for another game there but would return three days later to play Victoria again.[2420] That game was even better for the home team, as they demolished the Blades, 6-1.

Norm Johnson opened the scoring for the Blades, but Hebenton got that one back before the end of the opening period. From that point on, it was all Victoria, as they poured in five more goals—Marcetta had two, Hebenton added a second, while Laughton and Wilcox added singles. Mike Laughton was the star of the game, as he absorbed punishment from the Blades and still managed to play a large part in the offence. The "goat" from the first game, Al Lebrun, was on the ice for all six Victoria goals.[2421] He was likely glad to leave Victoria behind.

The *Victoria Daily Colonist* wrote an excellent article on the Leaf rookie Mike Laughton, which told how his father had encouraged him to take figure-skating lessons to improve his balance on the ice. That seemed to have worked, as he more than held his own in the corners and caused Portland coach Hal Laycoe to wonder where they had been hiding Laughton. He was not hidden. He was out in plain view, but it took a while for opponents to notice him.[2422]

The next home game was against Seattle. For some reason, the Leafs (who had been playing so well in recent contests) forgot how to pressure a defence and ended up losing 5-2. Hebenton scored twice to tie the score briefly in the second period, but defensive lapses cost the Leafs, as they surrendered three straight goals in the final frame. As a result, they lost ground in their bid for a playoff spot, falling further behind the Totems.[2423] In the next game against California, Milan Marcetta set a league record, when he scored five goals as the Maple Leafs crushed the Seals, 7-2. Mike Labadie and Bruce Carmichael had the other Victoria counters. However, it was one of Marcetta's goals that folks would be talking about for a long time. The game report says it best:

> "In one of the most fantastic plays ever witnessed at Memorial Arena, [Gary] Smith charged his crease after making a save, promptly dropped the puck and stick handled across the blue line, then fired a

pass that put Marcetta into the clear for a breakaway run at Seals' goaltender Jack McCartan. ... The pass that put Marcetta in the clear was accurate and sharp, and an embarrassment to the average playmaker. It had to be good because Seals' Charlie Burns caught up to Victoria's rover and dropped him with a body check at centre ice. ... Most hockey experts don't favor a goaltender roaming to the extent that Smith does, but Mario isn't ready to put any chains on big Gary. Not yet, at least." [2424] [2425]

There was nowhere as much excitement in the game three days later. First, the Leafs learned that Keenan was injured again and would be out of action for the fourth time in two years with the Leafs. As well, Gary Smith had been ordered by the Toronto Maple Leafs to report to Rochester and would leave as soon as Al Smith arrived in Victoria.[2426] Marcetta continued his torrid scoring pace with a pair of goals in the next game against California. Jankowski added the other in a 3-3 tie with the Seals. Both goaltenders wandered from their nets, making for some interesting plays. The Leafs left for a four-game California road trip that would help to determine their place in the league standings.[2427]

Just when playing four good games was so important, Victoria did not have a successful California trip. First, they dropped a 5-1 decision to San Diego. They were understandably tired, as they had arrived just a few hours before game time. It was the second period that did them in, as the Gulls scored three times to take a 4-0 lead to the final frame. The score was 5-0 before Laughton fired the lone Leaf goal. Al Smith played his first game since arriving from the East.[2428]

Two days later, Victoria was again only able to score a single goal in a 6-1 loss to the Blades. Barlow was the lone Leaf marksman.[2429] Victoria scored its only victory on the trip, when they upended the Gulls 4-2. Jankowski had the first goal for the Leafs, with singles added by Witiuk, Marcetta, and Carmichael. Due to the absence of Mike Laughton (who was ill), Coach Mario had to juggle lines, but it worked (for this game at least). The trip finished in Los Angeles, where the Blades edged the Leafs, 5-3. The game started on a good note when Redahl put Victoria ahead early in the game. The Blades scored twice to take the lead, but Carmichael tied the score before the end of the first period. The Blades scored the only middle-frame goal and added two more in the third before Carmichael notched his second. Victoria's defence did not play well, leaving Los Angeles players alone in the front of the net.[2430]

Bob Barlow as a Maple Leaf.
Photo courtesy Ernie Fitzsimmons.

The first game of February featured the league-leading Buckaroos. Playing inspired hockey, Victoria checked Portland's every move, while the forwards regained their scoring touch. It was one of the best games played in Memorial Arena that season and kept the 2,444 fans on the edge of their seats. Larry Leach scored the first goal for Portland but Barlow—playing centre in place of Larry Keenan—tied it ten minutes later on a fifty-foot slap shot. Twice Victoria took the lead, on goals by Redahl and Lamoureux, only to have the Buckaroos even the score shortly after. The home team took the lead for the final time on a late second-period goal by Carmichael and clinched the game when Jankowski scored just 1:56 into the final frame. The close checking and stellar goaltending kept Portland off the scoresheet after that and ensured the well-earned victory.[2431]

Just when they could have moved up at least one position in the league standings with a few victories, the Leafs went into a tailspin and lost their next five games. Los Angeles came to town, and they upended the Leafs, 6-1. Marcetta got the game off to a good start when he scored at fifteen seconds of the first period. However, nobody else could beat Dave Kelly, while the Blades fired six shots past Al Smith in the Victoria net. The next night, Portland was the opposition, and they edged the home team, 7-5. The Buckaroos took the lead, only to have Labadie tied the score. Portland again scored, but Barlow got that one back. Victoria took a brief lead when Marcetta found the back of the net, but the Buckaroos fired three goals in the final period to win. Unlike the previous game against this opponent, the Leafs did not play well.[2432] Nor did they put up a good effort in the next match against Seattle. The Totems outscored the Leafs, 2-1, in the first period—Marcetta had the Victoria score—and got the only counter of the middle frame to take a 3-1 lead. Erickson found the net halfway through the final frame, but despite a tremendous effort in the closing minutes, could not tie the score.[2433]

Before the next game, Coach Mario moved Mike Labadie to a line with Bob Barlow and Lou Jankowski to try to get the team out of its losing streak.[2434] Despite outshooting the Blades, 52-20, the Leafs lost the game, 3-1. A goal by Wilcox briefly tied the score in the first period, but Victoria could not find the net again. A trip to Portland did not improve the Leafs record, as it was their fifth loss in a row and their eighth in their last ten games. The Buckaroos had a three-goal lead before Marcetta notched a goal. Jankowski and Labadie also scored to tie the score by 8:20 of the second period. However, Portland had the next three goals to win going away.[2435]

Dreams of a playoff berth were fading fast, as the Leafs were still in freefall.

A two-game trip to Oakland to play the Seals proved to be successful, as Victoria played much better hockey and won both games. Led by three players who had scoring success on the road this year (Wilcox, Labadie, and Carmichael), the Leafs broke their losing streak in a good way with a 4-1 victory. Carmichael scored twice, while the other road warriors had singles. Only a late goal by Charlie Burns spoiled Al Smith's bid for a shutout.[2436] Two days later, the Leafs again prevailed, but this time, they were able to shut out the Seals. Hebenton and Jankowski scored first-period goals, and that was all the team needed for the 2-0 victory. The playoffs were once again a possibility.[2437]

Returning home, Victoria played another strong game, led by the "Blah-Blah" line of Barlow, Jankowski, and Labadie. Barlow had always had a reputation for non-stop chatter during games, and now he was "talking" with his hockey stick in his new role as a centre, replacing Keenan. The line was working well as a unit, and it showed on the scoreboard. Barlow had three goals and an assist, Labadie had one goal and four assists, and Jankowski added a goal and three assists. Lamoureux added the final goal in the Leafs' third consecutive victory with a 6-3 decision.[2438] The mighty Buckaroos came to town, and when the game was over, Al Smith had recorded a 4-0 shutout—his sixth and the team's seventh—and the Leafs had won four games in a row. It was a solid team effort, with everyone contributing to the successful outcome. Marcetta, Lamoureux, Barlow, and Labadie beat Rick Charron in the Buckaroo net.[2439]

All good things come to an end and the Leafs' winning streak did so in Portland where the Buckaroos got revenge for their recent defeat and clobbered Victoria, 7-2. A three-minute stretch in the second, caused by ill-timed penalties, proved to be the Leafs' downfall. At that point, they were trailing in the game 2-1 and were pressing for the tying marker. Given a power play, they failed to cash in; then two Leafs took penalties seconds apart and opened the door for the powerful Buckaroos, who scored two power-play goals to take a commanding 4-1 lead, from which the Leafs never recovered. Hebenton and Labadie were the only scorers for Victoria, and despite the seven goals, Al Smith turned in a good performance in goal, stopping thirty-six shots, including sixteen in the first period alone.[2440]

In the second game of the short road trip, Victoria built up a three-goal lead and handed the Canucks a 5-2 loss. Barlow notched two goals, while Carmichael, Jankowski, and Sandy Hucul had singles. Sandy Hucul was, without a doubt, the player of the game for Victoria. He hit everything he could find and made it difficult for Canuck skaters to get close to the net. After the game, manager Houle announced that the Leafs would now have two Smiths, as Gary "Suitcase" Smith was being sent back to Victoria by Toronto to join Al as a second goaltender.[2441] This could be the spark that propelled the team into a playoff spot, as having two good goalies is good insurance for a team.

Back at home, the visitors were the Canucks, and again, the Leafs prevailed. The home team built up a four-goal lead by the end of the second period, on goals by Lamoureux, Marcetta, Jankowski, and Barlow, before seeming to relax and let the Canucks score two third-period goals to come close. Al Smith was in goal for Victoria and made thirty-one stops on the way to the 4-2 victory. The Leafs actually could have won more easily, if they had been able to score on their two breakaway chances: Hebenton hit the post and Wilcox had his shot deflected by the goaltender. Nevertheless, it was another victory at a time when the Leafs had to win at least half of their remaining games to have a chance at a playoff berth.[2442] In the next match, the Leafs vaulted into fourth place with a heart-stopping 5-4 overtime win over the Seals. California scored the first two goals of the game before Carmichael had the first Leaf goal. After the Seals increased their lead, he scored again to bring Victoria closer. California scored again, ten minutes later, only to have Jankowski score twice (the second with the goaltender out for an extra attacker), to tie the game. In overtime, Jankowski set up the winning goal by Barlow to give the Leafs the hard-fought two points.[2443]

In Seattle, the game resembled the Friday Night Fights more than professional hockey. Tempers were short all evening, with many encounters. Sandy Hucul tangled with Earl Heiskala, each drawing seven minutes in penalties. Then it was the turn of Tom Polanic and Larry Lund, who drew major penalties. Gary Smith played in goal for Victoria and made several saves to keep his team in contention. Carmichael and Hebenton found the back of the net for the Leafs, who pressed hard in the final period to get the equalizer. Alas, it was not to be, as the Totem defenders stood tall, notably when their team was shorthanded, and came away with a 3-2 victory. With the loss, Victoria slipped back into fifth place in the standings.[2444]

In their next home game, the Leafs lost a close 4-3 decision to the improving Gulls. Playing with only four defencemen, as Labrosse was injured, Victoria did not have enough healthy bodies to keep up the pace throughout the game. Winger Mike Labadie aggravated a troublesome back injury, so his place was taken by newly-arrived Gary Veneruzzo. Carmichael suffered a nasty cut on his chin to join the injury parade. Once again, the Leafs surrendered two goals before they got on the scoreboard. Barlow had two goals after Marcetta opened the Victoria scoring, but the team could not hold the 3-2 lead, allowing San Diego to count twice in the final period to win, 4-2. There were only 2,988 fans in attendance.[2445]

The next match against Seattle ended in a rare 0-0 tie with both goaltenders, Gary Smith and Jim McLeod, playing well in their respective nets. Before the game, Coach Mario shuffled his lines, moving in veterans Witiuk and Redahl, as they "had played well against Seattle." In addition to his stellar net play, Smith also got involved in a skirmish with Seattle's Howie Hughes. Both received fighting majors. Forwards from both teams had several chances to score, but none were successful.[2446] Victoria finally managed to get a victory and the valuable two points when they outlasted the Blades, 7-5, at Memorial Arena. Veneruzzo had two goals with singles coming from Marcetta, Barlow, Erickson, Witiuk, and Jankowski. The Blades took a 2-0 lead, but the Leafs kept coming back to secure the victory.

However, the Leafs were not so lucky in Seattle, where they were shut out, 7-0, by the Totems. The loss dealt a bitter blow to their playoff hopes, as they dropped further out of contention.[2447] When the Leafs played their next game on the road trip in Oakland, they had 200 sailors from the Royal Canadian Navy in the stands cheering for them. The five ships were the destroyer-escorts *Algonquin, Crescent,* and *Columbia,* being transferred from Halifax to join the Pacific Maritime Command at Esquimalt; and the destroyer-escorts *Mackenzie* and *Saskatchewan,* returning from a three-month training cruise in the Caribbean.[2448] The Leafs skated to a 2-2 tie with the Seals, the single point giving them a flickering hope of moving up in the standings. Barlow opened the scoring; then the Seals scored twice, setting the stage for Marcetta to get the tying goal in the third period.[2449]

Losses in the next three California games spelled the end to the playoffs for the defending champions. First, San Diego beat them, 3-1. Gulls' coach Max McNab rotated his goaltenders throughout the game, changing them every five minutes or so. The strategy seemed to have worked, as the Leafs could only manage a single goal.[2450] Two days later, the same teams played, and the Leafs lost again, this time by a 4-2 score. In the final game of the road trip, California put an end to any hope of a Victoria playoff berth when they upended the Leafs, 6-4. Victoria came from behind to take the lead, but in the end, were beaten by player-coach Charlie Burns'

two goals in the third period. Laughton, Carmichael, Hebenton, and Marcetta scored the Leaf goals, but they had little life left in their travel-weary legs and could not respond to the Seals' pressure. There were now only three games left on the schedule—two at home and one on the road.[2451]

Aut Erickson as a Maple Leaf.
Photo courtesy Ernie Fitzsimmons.

In the first game after the California trip, Al Smith decided not to wear the goalie mask, as he said he played better without it. Perhaps he was right, as he led the Leafs to a come-from-behind victory over the Vancouver Canucks. As they had so often this season, the Leafs fell behind, 2-0. Marcetta cut the lead in half, and then Laughton tied the game, all before the end of the first period. After a scoreless middle frame, Victoria took over the game. Carmichael, Witiuk, and Labadie all scored to make the final count 5-2.[2452] The final road game of the season was played in Vancouver, and Victoria found a way to win a close 7-6 overtime decision. The Leafs came out shooting: Jankowski and Barlow gave the Leafs a lead, but it was short-lived. Vancouver scored three straight goals to take the lead, only to have Wilcox tie the score again. The lead changed often during the game, with Laughton, Redahl, and Polanic adding more goals for Victoria. The game was tied 6-6 at the end of regulation time, and it went to overtime. Rollie Wilcox fired the winner at 3:17, crushing the spirit of the Vancouver fans.[2453]

In the final home game of the season, Victoria saved the best for last and defeated the league-champion Portland team, 2-1, before a disappointing crowd of 2,672. Hebenton opened the scoring, but Cliff Schmautz tied the score before the end of the first period. Marcetta notched the only other score in the third frame. It was only fitting that the last goal of the season be scored by the team's scoring ace—it was his fortieth goal and capped his best season as a professional. Now the question on everyone's lips was "Will the Leafs be back?"[2454] On the good news side of the ledger, Milan Marcetta and Autrey Erickson were called up to the parent Toronto Maple Leafs for the playoffs. Also, Al Smith was named the stand-by goaltender for the WHL playoffs.

Hockey became of secondary importance when manager Buck Houle was rushed to Royal Jubilee Hospital after suffering a heart attack. He had been planning a scouting trip on behalf of the parent club, but that became impossible.[2455]

News in May 1967, was that Toronto would transfer the Victoria franchise to Phoenix but would continue to operate the team.[2456] However, this changed in June 1967, a month after winning the Stanley Cup, when Maple Leaf Gardens, operator of the Toronto Maple Leafs, sold the team for $500,000 to a group from Phoenix.[2457] The team was renamed the Roadrunners after a "name-the-team" contest.[2458] They played there until the WHL ceased operations in 1974, winning league championships in 1973 and 1974. In a delicious irony, the first training camp of the Phoenix team was held at Victoria in September 1967.[2459]

Professional hockey had left Victoria once again, and local citizens wondered when, and if, it would ever return.

In the meantime, local fans could support a Junior A team, the Victoria Cougars of the British Columbia Junior Hockey League, from 1967-1971, and a major junior hockey team, also named the Cougars, from 1971 to 1994, when that franchise was transferred to Prince George.

28 - HOW NOT TO BUILD AN ARENA—VERSION TWO

By the 1990s, it was evident that the Memorial Arena was no longer an asset to the City of Victoria. Poorly constructed in 1949, its infrastructure was failing fast, and ongoing maintenance and operations were costing the city $500,000 annually. The only hockey team using the facility was the junior Victoria Salsa, who were drawing about 2,000 fans per game.[2460]

In 1996, the City selected Vancouver-based Pilot Pacific to be their partner in the construction of a new arena complex. Plans called for that group to contribute $5 million to the project, while the City would provide the land on the site of the Memorial Arena and an operating budget of no more than $500,000 per year (the current cost to keep the ageing building functional). Completion date was forecast at fall of 1999. As the new building would need an anchor tenant, Jake Bergen, president of Pilot Pacific, was interested in acquiring a hockey team that would bring revenue to the new venture. In December, it was rumoured that he was speaking with David Pasant, the owner of the International Hockey League's San Francisco Spiders, which had suspended operations after one year in the league.[2461]

The Spiders had lost about $6 million, despite winning forty-two games in their inaugural (and only) season. The IHL was interested in placing franchises in Canadian cities to join franchises moved to Winnipeg and Quebec, with Victoria and Saskatoon the frontrunners.[2462] "Solid local ownership, proof of a devoted fan base, and a proper building, are three main requirements for an IHL franchise," league spokesman Tim Bryant told the *Victoria Times Colonist* in July. Teams in that league operated on a budget of $3-5 million, with player salaries averaging $62,000. League rules stipulated that at least fifty percent of the seats must be sold at a price of ten dollars or less, making it family-friendly.[2463] The bid for an IHL team gained local support from Bob Barlow, a former Victoria Maple Leaf who compared this league to the old WHL in its heyday, with young players on the way up to the NHL and veterans hoping to get back to the top.[2464]

Negotiations continued between Jake Bergen and the City of Victoria, as he now wanted to construct a 10,000-seat arena at a cost of $57 million. However, that deal hinged on a legislative change from the provincial government to allow a long-term lease and a forty-five-year tax break. There was still hope that a deal would be finalized by the end of April, with construction complete by the start of the 1999/2000 season.[2465]

Back with the IHL, David Pasant noted that the IHL was essentially a league of free agents. Very few had long-term contracts, and you could build a competitive product almost immediately. He was encouraged by city-based research that revealed that the average Victoria citizen spends about $350 on sporting events. With IHL tickets starting at ten dollars, it would seem to be a good fit for Victoria. When asked about the team name "Spiders," he said "keeping it makes the franchise unique. There's Grizzlies, Cubs, Bears, Bruins. . . . I mean, how many different times can you say 'Bears'? There's no other pro sports team named the Spiders."

Pasant said he would like to keep the webbed uniforms and the mascot, which rappelled from the ceiling into the fans when the team was in California.[2466] By April 11, 1997, David Pasant of the San Francisco Spiders announced that he was now a half-owner in the building and would share his hockey team with David Bergen of Pilot Pacific, the developers of the new arena complex. Bergen added that the deal provides better security for Victorians. Their hockey team would be tied to their facility, so the team wouldn't threaten to move to another city offering better arena-lease arrangements, a problem endemic to all pro sports. Both owners claimed they would be moving to Victoria and buying homes here. Victoria Sports Entertainment Associates (VSEA) was formed to deal with the City. Harry Stokes, chief financial officer, was named to continue negotiation on behalf of the group.

Good progress was being made on provincial legislation with both Premier Glen Clark and municipal affairs minister, Mike Farnsworth, supporting it. Once the legislation was in place, the City was planning to negotiate a master agreement with the two owners. Demolition was slated to begin in April.[2467]

Next on the agenda was a visit to Victoria by an IHL delegation, led by Robert Ufer, commissioner of the IHL, and including four team owners from the eighteen-team league. In addition to meeting with local VSEA officials to discuss the proposed arena deal, they wanted to get an idea of Victoria and the surrounding region. To gauge public support for the Spiders as a local franchise, they planned a rally at Centennial Square at 11:30 on October 29.[2468] Financing would rely on securing an anchor tenant, and IHL approval was critical. Victoria Sports Entertainment Associates had until the November 14 deadline to get financing and league approvals in place.

At the rally, before 600 cheering fans, IHL commissioner Bob Ufer said that the relocation committee was ready to recommend, unanimously, that the Spiders be allowed to move to Victoria. Victoria Sports Entertainment Associates released a study that Monday, by the accounting firm Arthur Anderson, which showed the arena would generate $117 million in annual spending. Robert Leib, Arthur Anderson pro-sports specialist, said the Victoria groundwork so far equalled or bettered preparations made for franchise bids in the National Hockey League or National Basketball Association."[2469] However, there were dissenters in the crowd, with signs reading "Show Me the Money" and "Insolvent Hockey League." Some questioned the economic value placed by Arthur Anderson and wondered if the franchise would lose money as it had in San Francisco. Ufer said, "The success of an IHL franchise is generated by the intangibles like the emotional feel of the community and in that sense, Victoria ranks with the league's top cities."[2470]

Details of the economic-impact study were released and showed the new Victoria arena would create 569 jobs and generate spending of $117 million a year when it was built. Construction was expected to generate 515 person-years of employment, while direct spending by the arena and team would be $78 million, generating spin-off spending of $39 million. The Spiders would represent about half of the projected arena attendance, assuming an average of 10,500 persons at each game.[2471]

An editorial in the *Victoria Times Colonist* supported David Pasant and wondered what he had to do to convince locals that the arena project was a good idea. The final paragraph says it all: "Will he do it? We certainly hope so. We're looking forward to the fall of 1999 when we'll be watching Spiders hockey in the new arena from the *Victoria Times Colonist* box."[2472]

On November 3, 1997, the first in a series of articles examining the arena deal in detail appeared in the *Victoria Times Colonist*. It was the first column to openly question the ability of VSEA to deliver both a building and a hockey team. The opening lines sum up the position perfectly:

"It's the final minutes of the third period. Either the guys in the suits score financing for a new arena by Nov. 14, or the fans start leaving the building.

I don't want to hear any more extensions or letter of interest. If the arena developers want the community support they're salivating for, they have to deliver. If they can't do that in the next 12 days, they have to be more forthcoming than 'we're working on it.'"

The article continued in a similar vein, casting doubt on claims made by various players in the arena game, and for the first time, pointing out potential conflicts of interest and asking probing questions, including about the ability of VSEA to raise the funds necessary for construction to proceed. With the deadline of November 14, 1997, drawing near, it was time for facts, not projections of feel-good statistics. The columns pointed out that "people, not numbers on paper, are needed to fill those 12,500 seats" and that VSEA ultimately needed community support to make the project successful.[2473]

Almost as if in answer to those questions, VSEA released the findings of a survey conducted by Venture Market Research, with 605 people, that showed a very high level of community support. Among the results were:

"A total of fifty-two percent of respondents indicated they would be willing to attend a game for fourteen dollars. And thirty-six percent said they would very likely attend. The average number of games they would see was twelve.

Twenty percent said they would likely be willing to buy a season ticket of $500. And seven percent said they would very likely buy one."

The firm was so surprised at the level of support for a new arena that they went back and conducted a follow-up survey to double-check the results. However, the survey showed that three conditions had to be met before the community would fully support an IHL team. First was good-quality hockey, next was the team's performance, and third was ticket prices.[2474] Victoria had a record of only supporting winning teams, so if the Spiders expected good crowds, they would have to ice a competitive team and keep prices reasonable for families. The proponents guaranteed both, but it would remain to be seen if they could deliver on their promises.

The November 14 deadline for having sufficient financing for the project came and went. Mayor Bob Cross announced that the developers had been given another extension to come up with financing for the $30-million arena. The new deadline was set for December 15. However, Councillor Bob Friedland said that the real deadline was much later as "there is no obligation on the developer, the promoter to do anything, or to put any money at risk or put any surety or bond until February 15, 1998." He also noted that the city had been "demolishing Memorial Arena from the inside out" as 4,000 seats had been removed, bookings had been cancelled, and ice time had had to be purchased elsewhere. In response, VSEA officials said that a financing deal could be signed "as early as today." The article concluded with a chart showing the original dates, the amended dates, and the extended completion dates.[2475] An editorial on the same day noted that "deadline after deadline has been missed" and that David Pasant and Harry Stokes, president of VSEA, had not put forward even a rough financial statement and were still renting their local offices month to month. The editorial asked where the commitment was and why taxpayers were being told to "trust" when little of substance had been provided.[2476]

In the meantime, the delays in demolition of the old arena were causing problems for the Victoria Salsa. When VSEA missed the first deadline of August 29, the city delayed removing the seats from the old arena, some of which had been promised to the Salsa for use in their new home, Esquimalt's Archie Browning Sports Centre.[2477] At the same time, one member of the arena-project team resigned. Mark Timmis had worked as the franchise-development officer but said he didn't believe that the developers had much use for his area of expertise at this time.[2478]

Cartoon: "Sports complex developers get another one more extension." Printed in the *Victoria Times Colonist,* November 17, 1997, page 2. Used with the permission of Adrian Raeside.

Cartoon: Hockey Hall of Fame. Printed in the *Victoria Times Colonist,* December 14, 1997, page A10. Used with the permission of Adrian Raeside.

Adrian Raeside made readers laugh when he drew a cartoon with an imaginary headline from 2010 that read "Sports complex developers get another one-month extension."[2479] Sports columnist Cleve Dheenshaw reminded local citizens that, if they wanted a new arena but were not willing to pay for it, they had to realize that the public developers were not required to report their financial details in the same way that a publicly-funded project did.[2480]

December 15—the date by which VSEA was supposed to have financing in place for the arena project—came and went, with neither proof that loans of $85 million had been secured nor that official approval for the transfer of the Spiders franchise to Victoria had been received. However, the project officials assured council that everything was on track when they met behind closed doors. A new deadline of February 15, 1998, was set, but it could be extended "if both parties agreed."[2481] Raeside's cartoon again hit the nail on the head when he branded the "Arena deal between City of Victoria and Victoria Sports & Entertainment" as the Hockey Hall of Fame's "biggest screw-up."[2482] An editorial asked if the public trusted council's decision to grant further extensions. The last paragraph said it all: "Makes you wonder what will happen to the September 1998 'deadline' for opening a recreational arena at the site. If that turns out to be a 'target,' too, we can set our sights on a new city council."[2483]

The next "target day" was February 16, 1998, and there was optimism that financing would be in place. Mayor Bob Cross said, "I'm confident that we are right on the apex and we are coming down the home stretch."[2484] In a special meeting with council, VSEA reported that it needed more time to negotiate financing terms with a major Canadian bank. Based on this request, council voted seven-to-one to grant a sixty-day extension. Councillor Bob Friedland, an opponent of the project from the beginning, voted against the extension but councillors Helen Hughes and Jane Lunt said this was the last request they would support.[2485] The public was not really surprised when that deadline was not met. Victoria Sports Entertainment Associates advised that the bankers would not make a loan unless the province came up with a revenue guarantee. Council again caved in and permitted a fourteen-day extension.[2486]

28 - HOW NOT TO BUILD AN ARENA—VERSION TWO

An editorial in the *Victoria Times Colonist* suggested that there was no way that taxpayers should be liable for deficits. It went on to add the following: "If rumour proves true, and the taxpayers are asked to underwrite the deal, then it's time to pull the plug."[2487]

Premier Glen Clark declared that the province of BC would not guarantee a loan to the arena developers. He noted that they had made changes to the municipal act "to allow the municipality to enter a long-term lease with a private developer and that's as far as we will go." A UVic sports economist questioned the numbers provided by the developer and said, "If the banks are asking for guarantees, they must have some suspicions about the revenue-generating ability of the operation.[2488]

Arguments were made by both sides, and further extensions were granted, but public support gradually began to slip away. The lack of concrete funding in place and promises that were never kept meant that the developers and the city felt they were making progress, but this was not reflected in the court of public opinion. The Toronto Dominion Bank and the Bank of Nova Scotia set mid-December as a deadline for their conditions to be met for a $70-million loan. To try to regain public support, VSEA planned a huge public-relations campaign.[2489]

By mid-October, a group of businessmen spoke openly about their concerns with the VSEA proposal.[2490] At the same time, former provincial cabinet minister Hugh Curtis said he'd never seen "a project bungled as badly as Victoria's planned multiplex," and said, "It's just been a complete foul-up from the earliest times." Former mayor Peter Pollen also criticized the project, saying it was a "turkey that won't fly."[2491]

In anticipation of the demolishing of the Memorial Arena, veterans took part in a "Standing down Ceremony and Parade" in which the marble plaque and flags were removed from the building and stored by the City until a new building was erected.[2492]

David Pasant advised that VSEA's chance of meeting bank-financing conditions by December 15 was excellent. He noted they had already had $5,000 deposits for sixteen luxury suites and had advertisers and sponsors coming on board at a rapid rate. He claimed the group was still talking with provincial minister Moe Sihota about provincial support for the development.[2493] However, Sihota ruled out any provincial cash for the new arena until the developers "nailed down" revenue projections. On another note, Risser International of Atlanta and Johnston Sport Architecture of Victoria were named as the new team of architects for the complex.[2494]

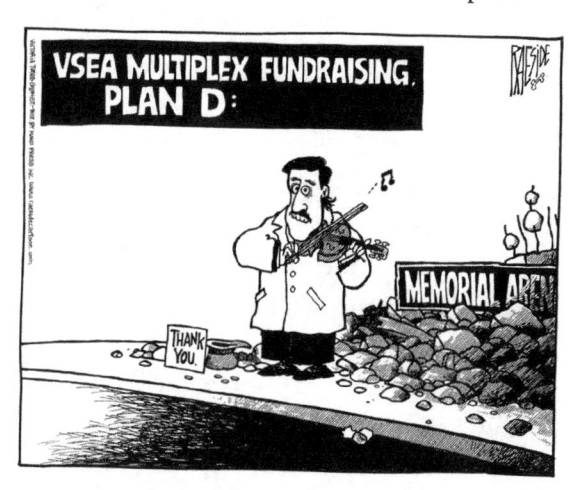

Cartoon: VSEA multiplex fundraising, Plan D. Used with the permission of Adrian Raeside.

At the end of November, VSEA mounted an advertising program designed to garner support for the project, stressing the benefits to the community, including top music shows, international sporting events, and family shows like *Disney on Ice*. In addition to banner ads in the *Victoria Times Colonist*,[2495] they produced a glossy full-colour brochure that further expanded on the public benefits. Victoria Sports Entertainment Associates spokespersons appeared on radio talk shows, continuing to paint a rosy picture of the project.

Cartoon: One way the provincial government can help out Victoria in the VSEA arena fiasco. Printed in the *Victoria Times Colonist,* April 17, 1998, page A16. Used with the permission of Adrian Raeside.

On December 2, 1998, a group of forty prominent Victoria citizens wrote a letter to Premier Glen Clark, asking for a meeting with him and Moe Sihota to express their opinion that the project would fail and that any provincial support would lead to higher taxes across the province. They also wrote to Mayor Bob Cross and council, requesting a public meeting where all points of view could be expressed. The signatories represented a cross-section of business interests and included real-estate professionals, accountants, developers, contractors, business owners, and former hockey players.[2496] However, Clark said he would not meet with the group, as he had no intention of getting the province involved in the project. Mayor Cross announced that there would be a public meeting on December 10, at which the developer and city staff would make presentations followed by questions from the public, with citizens limited to five minutes each.[2497]

An editorial in the *Victoria News* expressed the opinion that the multiplex saga was "like a hockey game that's been dragged out far beyond regulation time but refuses to conclude." The article ended with "It's time someone picked up the puck, told the team wearing VSEA jerseys to go home, and try to put a better team for the future. A team we can all afford."[2498] Despite growing opposition, including former finance minister Mel Couvelier and Victoria's Geoff Courtnall, a player for the NHL's St. Louis Blues (who said the project was too big for the city), Mayor Cross remained optimistic.[2499]

By December 10, forty citizens had already signed up to speak, and others would follow from the audience. Many written submissions had been sent to the city, and they would be placed into the record. Victoria Sports Entertainment Associates made a ten-year deal with Coca-Cola for beverage rights for an unspecified amount; they felt this would satisfy the banks' requirement for advertising.[2500] The meeting was packed with more than 200 people, who spoke both for and against the multiplex. Despite assurances that the "project's viability is not reliant upon attendance at events," many of the speakers worried about having to pay additional taxes if revenue did not meet expectations.[2501] *Monday Magazine* put a photo of Mayor Cross on its cover and asked the question, "If the arena deal collapses, will Mayor Cross find himself in the Political Penalty Box?" The article further noted that councillors who supported the multiplex deal might be caught in the political backwash, as well.[2502] Councillor Jane Lunt joined Councillor Friedland in asking for details of arena financing, citing what she believed was a serious financial liability for the city.[2503]

Mayor Cross refused a suggestion from his supporters that he put together a team of business leaders to critique the multiplex project. They felt he was often overshadowed by City Manager Don Roughley, and he should assert his authority. In the meantime, some former councillors were thinking about running in the 1999 civic election. However, no decisions would be made until the multiplex issue was finally settled.[2504]

On December 15, the so-called "D-Day" for the multiplex, VSEA met with council in camera at 9:00 a.m. before proceedings were open to the public at 3:00 p.m. At the morning meeting, VSEA was granted a final extension to secure financing but was given a "hard" date of February 25, 1999. The master agreement was amended for, hopefully, the last time.[2505][2506]

In a last-ditch effort to secure additional financing, VSEA tried to draw Vancouver-based developers Greystone Properties into the fold; the move was unsuccessful. The multiplex developer was negotiating for the rights to name the building; this was intended to secure much-needed cash.[2507] In early February, VSEA made changes to the design of the multiplex in a bid to generate more revenue; more high-end suites were planned.[2508] Ogden Entertainment of New York, the company that handled concessionaire services for the Kingdome in Seattle, was signed to provide the same for the new multiplex. This deal fulfilled one of the conditions for loan financing, but there was still the matter of a loan guarantee.[2509] Naming rights were finally granted to a small internet company based in Esquimalt, Pacific Coast Net Inc. Terms of the fifteen-year, multi-million-dollar deal were not released. The new complex was tentatively named Pacific Coast Net Place.[2510][2511][2512] The irony of Spiders playing in a facility named for a "web" company was not lost on members of the general public.

However, there was still no news of the required financing, and sports columnists doubted that the multiplex would ever be built. David Pasant still insisted that reporters would be writing a "nice story" at the deadline but would provide no details. The reality was that, if there were no loan by February 25, 1999, council would have "no choice but to serve notice on VSEA."[2513]

At a private meeting with VSEA, council decided not to extend the deadline another two weeks. Mayor Cross and councillors David McLean, Bob Friedland, Helen Hughes, Jane Lunt, and Pamela Madoff voted in favour of sending notice immediately; councillors Geoff Young and Chris Coleman were opposed, and councillor Bea Holland was absent. Victoria Sports Entertainment Associates left the meeting via a private staircase and did not talk to the media until the afternoon when they still hoped to have a financing deal before the two-week deadline.[2514][2515] The head of the city's parks and recreation selection committee said that, if the deal did not go through, it would take six or seven years to get us "back to where we are now." In the meantime, Vancouver developer Graham Lee, who had submitted a bid for the original project, indicated that he was still interested in building an arena in Victoria.[2516]

It seemed, however, that deadlines were not worth the paper they were written on, as Council granted an extension for multiplex financing just before the "drop-dead" date. In return for an extension to May 31, VSEA deposited a cheque for $200,000 with the city. If the project were to proceed, the money would be returned to the developer, but if the multiplex were never built, the city would retain the funds. Mayor Cross said in an interview that "we would be fools" not to give the extension.[2517] The developers were now dealing with the Bank of America, which replaced the Toronto Dominion Bank in loan negotiations. Scotiabank remained as the second bank involved, but the developers were confident that they would secure a $70-million loan.[2518] On May 31, a majority of council accepted a VSEA financing agreement and pushed the deadline to June 30. Victoria Sports Entertainment Associates representative Carl Hirsch said, "We are no longer pursuing an agreement, we are documenting an agreement."[2519]

Finally, Mayor Cross announced that, as no funding was in place on June 30, the agreement would be terminated at midnight. He said he was "very disappointed . . . we've bent over backwards to make this project work." In the wake of the death of the multiplex deal, there were calls for a review of the failed bid. Mayoral candidate Alan Lowe said that he supported a smaller, less-expensive arena that could house "a Western Hockey League junior team rather than an IHL professional franchise."[2520]

VSEA retained its Victoria office while it dealt with the fallout from the failed bid. Deposits on luxury suites had to be returned, and other financial matters to be settled.[2521] They finally closed the office at the end of August; gone were the giant toy spiders and other promotional material.[2522]

On the practical front, Memorial Arena was being booked through August 2000. The Victoria Salsa junior hockey team, who had temporarily moved to Archie Browning Arena in Esquimalt, came back to Memorial Arena and staff hoped that other regular events would be held in the old building while it was still standing.[2523]

In the aftermath of the multiplex failure, former Victoria Cougars' part-owner Fraser McColl and Vancouver arena developer Graham Lee expressed interest in building a new arena and having the junior Western Hockey League return to Victoria.[2524] At the same time, WHL executives expressed interest in having a team back in Victoria. However, no decision could be made until a suitable arena had been built.[2525]

Determined that the city would control the construction of a new arena, council authorized a study to assess what went wrong with the multiplex project. After much debate, they eventually settled on a "two-phase independent consultant review process that will wrap with a presentation of finding to the new city council on December 2." The review would focus on the original terms of reference, the proposal call, and the decision-making process over the last three years, and would include a general review of similar, successful projects in other regions.[2526,2527]

Mayor Cross decided not to run in the November election, and Alan Lowe was elected as mayor, defeating Bob Friedland and Geoff Young. His campaign slogan was "Aim High, Vote Lowe." He garnered 43.59 percent of the vote.[2528]

Jonathan Huggett, the consultant hired to examine the failure of the multiplex project, noted in his December 15 report that the deal was "botched from the beginning." He added that the city did not really know what it wanted, and as a result, could not explain what it wanted to potential developers. As well, the city did not seek specialist advice that would have protected the public interest and gave too much power to the city manager.[2529,2530]

The failed VSEA project finally came to an end when a decision was made in the Supreme Court of British Columbia on July 6, 2006. Victoria Sports/Entertainment Associates and Arachnid Hockey Canada, U.L.C. claimed that The Toronto-Dominion Bank and the Bank of Nova Scotia had caused them to lose the deal to build the multiplex. The judge ruled that the plaintiffs had not proven their case, saying "in short, the banks made no false representations to the plaintiffs," and he dismissed the action with costs.[2531]

29 - HOW TO BUILD AN ARENA SUCCESSFULLY

Victoria citizens needed only to look to Kelowna, where RG Properties' Graham Lee had built a new arena in a public-private partnership. It had cost $20 million and seated 6,500. "It's put us on the map as far as getting big-name acts, and it's become the centre of our cultural district," said a reporter with the *Kelowna Daily Courier*.[2532]

Determined to develop sound guidelines for the construction of a new arena, the City of Victoria hired Indaba Communications and Training Inc., in June 2000, to "develop a public consultation plan and communication strategy to assist the city in determining what the community wants in a new arena (which is now being referred to at City Hall as a "multipurpose facility"), what groups may wish to partner in the project and to assure the public that the process is open and transparent." Indaba was told to consult widely in the community with both local governments and user groups. Their first meeting would be with the ten community members selected for "the multipurpose arena community advisory committee." That committee included local neighbourhood representatives, business people, and members of the community at large. The consultation process was to be completed by November 2000, at which time Indaba would report to council.[2533]

The consultants' report was presented to council in mid-November. Public support for a multipurpose facility was strong throughout the region, based on a telephone poll and other responses. More than 1,000 questionnaires were completed, fifty-four email responses and letters were received, and three open houses attracted sixty people. The consultants made several presentations and contacted 450 community groups. According to the report, "the top three uses for a multiplex should be major spectator events, recreational ice, and consumer shows." City of Victoria Mayor Alan Lowe said that he felt an arena with 7,500 to 10,000 seats would probably be suitable, rather than the 12,500 seats in the prior proposal. The report was given to city hall staff, who were instructed to examine the details and to respond with suggestions by December 7.[2534]

At their next meeting, councillors "supported staff recommendations to choose an independent accounting agency to conduct, over a six-month period, a $25,000 market assessment and financial analysis of a public multiplex." This action would ensure that the city controlled the finances in any future project. At the same time, arena consultant Jonathan Huggett would "draft a request for qualifications."[2535]

By the end of February, the city issued a request for letters of interest. By that time, several developers had already contacted the city, expressing a desire to build a multiplex.[2536] On March 19, 2001, Grant Thornton presented the market feasibility study to the city manager. The extensive document made several recommendations for a new facility. A capacity of 6,500 fixed seats, with 2,000 floor seats, was deemed to be the most cost-effective for a new building, based on an average of 115 events per year. They decided that a larger-capacity building would not draw many more events. A facility of this size would generate a twenty-five-percent revenue stream under the "management and direction of City employees." The facility should be 90,000-95,000 square feet to allow for "optimum amount of lease space and fixed seating capacity." This would include 15,000 square feet of lease space, including food and beverage, and retail. Their recommended next steps were "to evaluate private sector proposals, negotiate terms suitable to the City, in terms of utilization, quality of facility and costs, and fast-track the development process to minimize the lag time between closure of Memorial Arena and the opening of the new complex."[2537]

On approval of the report by council, Mayor Lowe appointed the Mayor's Blue-Ribbon Panel (six members of the public from different areas of expertise) "to provide sound business advice as a means of facilitating a fair and equitable decision-making process that protects the interest of local taxpayers." Their role was to review the market study and financial analysis, review and provide feedback on expressions of interest and staff recommendations, make recommendations on a preferred funding model, review and provide feedback on any subsequent "Request for Proposals" document, review and provide feedback on all proposals received, and recommend a business model as a basis for negotiations with the preferred proponent.[2538]

This panel would prove to be key in the selection process. Unlike the failed VSEA proposal, the advisory power did not rest with city staff. From the beginning, there was community consultation, and that continued throughout the entire process.

Out of fifty-six information packages that had been mailed out by the city, only four groups submitted expressions of interest by the deadline of April 6, 2001: Mel Kowalchuk acting as spokesman for Miami businessman Dan Orlich; MKT Development Group; RG Properties; and The RPA Group. MKT had built projects in Ottawa and Surrey. RG Properties had constructed Skyreach Place in Kelowna, as well as projects in Coquitlam and Maple Ridge. The RPA Group was responsible for the Air Canada Centre in Toronto and GM Place in Vancouver, as well as smaller projects elsewhere. Orlich was unavailable for comment.[2539]

After a detailed review of all the proposals as outlined in the Grant Thornton report, only one (by RG Properties) met the city's criteria. The proposal included building, designing, financing, managing, and operating a sports and entertainment facility on the Memorial Arena site. It would provide around 7,000 seats for hockey, with an additional 2,000 for concerts. A WHL team would be the prime tenant. The building would also include a restaurant/sports bar, concession areas, dressing rooms, retail space, and removable seating for trade shows and exhibitions.[2540] The selection of RG Properties to build the arena meant that there was no need to call for additional proposals so that the project could be speeded up somewhat. On June 14, 2001, council passed "a motion to undertake negotiations with RG Properties for the design/build/financing and operation of a new entertainment and sport centre for Victoria."[2541] Mayor Lowe noted that there could be a deal by September, and if so, shovels could be in the ground by early fall 2002. The mayor would make one last attempt to secure financial support from other municipalities, whose citizens would use the facility.[2542]

From this point on, the significant difference between this project and the failed multiplex project became even more evident. There was little debate of issues in the media, as negotiations were held behind closed doors and only results were released to the public. This was in decided contrast to the previous multiplex plan where every move was detailed in the media. When I interviewed now-former-mayor Alan Lowe (he served from November 20, 1999, to December 2, 2008), he was very proud of the fact that the negotiations had been handled in a very professional manner.[2543]

At a meeting on October 25, 2001, council endorsed "recommendations for the multiplex facility:

- That the City's Negotiation Team be directed to continue to negotiate an Agreement in Principle to Design, Build and Operate a Multipurpose Facility with RG Properties to be concluded on or before November 30, 2001;
- That in the event that an agreement is approved with RG Properties that the City will retain ownership of the Facility and contract the Management and Operation of the Facility to RG Properties;
- That in the event that the Agreement in Principle with RG Properties is not deemed satisfactory by City Council on or before November 30, 2001, that the City will proceed on the basis of a publicly owned and operated facility, and
- That final agreement with RG Properties or a decision to proceed with a publicly owned and operated facility will be subject to the assent of the electors."[2544]

Councillors were impressed with the strong business plan and the proven ability of the developer to produce a quality arena. The most significant hurdle was the need to secure a WHL franchise, but Graham Lee remained confident that he could secure a team as the anchor tenant of the arena. Financial details would be put to the public for approval in a referendum.[2545]

On November 22, 2001, council endorsed a public-private partnership for the new facility with the following conditions:

- "The City will finance and own the asset
- The employment of existing regular Arena staff is protected
- The operating risks are borne by the Private Sector"[2546]

Cartoon: Arena Referendum. Used with the permission of Adrian Raeside.

Victoria taxpayers would be asked in an April referendum to approve a property-tax hike of between one and three percent to finance construction of the facility. A proposed thirty-year agreement, broken into ten-year terms, would ensure that all current employees would retain their jobs.[2547] Financial terms of the agreement were outlined in a lengthy partnership agreement.

In early April 2002, Mayor Lowe urged all citizens to support the funding referendum. On Saturday, April 20, the polls would be open from 8:00 a.m. to 8:00 p.m. An information sheet outlining the need for an arena and the details of the project was sent to all households in the city,[2548] and advertisements were placed in local newspapers.[2549] Four municipalities voted to contribute toward the cost of the facility: the District of Saanich, the Municipality of Oak Bay, the Township of Esquimalt, and the Township of View Royal.[2550]

City of Victoria taxpayers went to the polls on April 20, 2002. The question was simple:

> Do you approve of the proposed Partnering Agreement (the synopsis of the key terms are noted on the back of this ballot including the matters requiring the assent of the electors) between the City of Victoria and the RG Group of Companies, a copy of which is attached to

the City of Victoria *Multipurpose Facility Partnering Agreement Authorization Bylaw No. 02-40*? Under the copy of this Agreement the members of the RG Group of Companies would design and build a multipurpose arena with no less than 7,000 seat (the "Multipurpose Facility") for the City of Victoria, and then operate the Multipurpose Facility on behalf of the City of Victoria for a period up to thirty years.

The proposed Partnering Agreement requires among other terms that the City pay the costs of design and construction of the Multipurpose Facility, and your approval of the Partnering Agreement will authorize the City to borrow for that purpose up to $30 million under proposed City of Victoria *Loan Authorization (Multipurpose Facility) Bylaw No. 02-12.*

YES [ ] NO [ ] [2551]

Cartoon: Memorial Arena closing soon. Printed in the *Victoria Times Colonist*, April 20, 2002, page A12. Used with the permission of Adrian Raeside.

Citizens overwhelmingly approved the borrowing of funds. Total votes cast were 13,819 with 71.45 percent voting "yes." The mayor was ecstatic, noting that this vote had moved the city forward.[2552] In July 2002, council voted to remove the requirement for a WHL franchise by September 1, from the master agreement. Also, RG Properties guaranteed ticket-surcharge revenue that had been projected for WHL attendance and an increase in the non-refundable security deposit on the first $2 million payment from $300,000 to $1.1 million.[2553] Developer Graham Lee said that he was "comfortable to go ahead with [construction] and take the risk." Mayor Lowe said that council would decide on the final design of the arena within a month.[2554] A group of disgruntled taxpayers filed a legal challenge of the referendum result, but the case was dismissed in July 2002. This decision cleared the way for construction of the much-needed arena.[2555]

"Thanks for the Memories" program, exterior, September 28, 2002. From the author's collection.

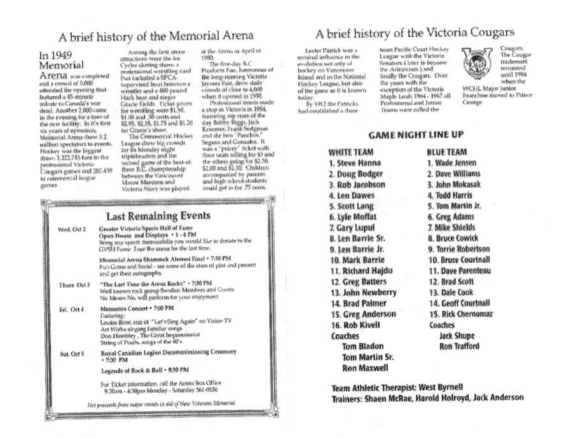

"Thanks for the Memories" program, interior, September 28, 2002. From the author's collection.

The last weekend of September 2002 and the first week of October were set aside to celebrate all the events that had been at the Memorial Arena. From the Victoria Salsa Junior A opening game on September 26 to the Royal Canadian Legion Decommissioning Ceremony on October 5, there was an event for everybody.[2556] For hockey fans, the highlight was the return of former hockey players to Memorial Arena for one last event. Three members of the 1949-50 Cougars: Bernie Strongman, Ken Gunter, and Al Senior were joined on the ice by Cougars from the 1950s: Eddie Dorohoy, Reg Abbott, and Don McLeod, while Bill Shvetz, Bob Barlow, and Dave Parenteau represented the Victoria Maple Leafs. Andy Hebenton who had played for both the Cougars and the Maple Leafs was a crowd favourite.

For me, that celebration was the best event of the commemoration. Members of the Victoria Cougars from the 1970s to 1990s played an exhibition game, which was the last ice event in the storied arena. All proceeds from the many events were earmarked for an updated veterans' memorial in the new building.[2557]

On October 10, council passed a motion approving the design-build agreement, operating agreement, and guarantee agreement.[2558] The arena was slowly dismantled, with much of the equipment sold to neighbouring recreational partners and private companies. Esquimalt purchased the arena boards and glass, some hockey and lacrosse nets, as well as goal lights and a thirty-second score clock system. Oak Bay, Saanich, and Panorama took seats, ice paint, and cleaning materials. The red carpet went to a new home in Saanich, the Victoria Salsa purchased the Nevco score clock, and RG Properties bought the Zamboni and the skate sharpener for use in their other properties around BC. An Olympia resurfacing machine went to Alberta. The sale of arena assets, in high demand throughout the region, raised about $140,000.

As demolition of the old arena neared, RG Properties advised that contamination studies were underway and that any asbestos or other hazardous materials would be disposed of safely. Once all contaminants were gone, the building would be demolished piece by piece by a wrecking ball, rather than by implosion.[2559] The loss of Memorial Arena was potentially disastrous to the Victoria Salsa and Shamrocks when a plan for a new facility on the Westshore was defeated in a referendum in November. Both teams would move to the smaller Archie Browning Arena in Esquimalt for the next season but hoped that there would be a new arena in place, somewhere in the region, by the 2004 season.[2560]

In early February, the *Victoria Times Colonist* published a set of "Memorial Memories" that focussed on sports and music as held in the old building. The sports memories included stories from pro and junior hockey players, lacrosse players, and fans who had seen celebrated pros like Wayne Gretzky and Marcel Dionne there, as well as their local heroes. The article made special mention of Andy Hebenton, who had played for both the Cougars and the Maple Leafs. Of course, nobody who ever attended an event at the Memorial Arena would ever forget the smell of those arena hotdogs. It seemed to permeate the building itself.[2561] The second article covered the numerous musical events that had been held over the years in the arena. In the 1960s, 1970s, and 1980s, the big names in various genres of music came to town. That changed when the cost to bring big-name acts to town could not be covered by the ticket prices. There was also the less-than-perfect acoustics in the old barn. Sounds reverberated off the barrel ceiling and the walls.[2562]

On February 17, 2003, thousands of citizens gathered outside the protective fence to watch the start of the demolition of the Memorial Arena. The event began when Mayor Alan Lowe and RG Properties' Graham Lee were hoisted to the top of the north end in a fire-department bucket. As they struck the building with gold-toned sledgehammers, absolutely nothing happened—the old girl was not going down without a fight. It took a 2,000-kilogram wrecking ball to make any headway on the work.[2563] By February 20, the arena looked like an open-dome structure, as the entire roof structure had been removed.[2564] Finally, it was all over, when the last wall came down on March 1.[2565] The structure may have been demolished, but it would live on in the new structure as 12,000 tonnes of concrete were being recycled as backfill or as a component of the new concrete for the multiplex. Site cleanup was expected to take two weeks, after which the new structure would begin to rise from the rubble.[2566] The deconstruction of Memorial Arena was broadcast on the city's website and had over 10,000 hits in March 2003, alone.[2567]

Meanwhile, on the West Shore, their much smaller arena was beginning to take shape on the site. It was anticipated to be the new home of the Victoria Salsa hockey team and the Victoria Shamrocks lacrosse team.[2568] The building of the two arenas soon became a political football, as Westshore politicians gloated over the fact that their arena had "walls" while the downtown Victoria site remained "flat."[2569] That would change on June 6, the anniversary of the D-Day invasion of Normandy, when Mayor Lowe and Graham Lee joined Jack Cockrell, chair of the local veterans' memorial committee, and young student Amory Hall, who was battling leukemia, in a "hand-joining" ceremony. The event was held at the spot of the future public plaza. The four placed their handprints in concrete that commemorated the foundation of "new entertainment and recreational choices in Victoria."

Cockrell had arrived in France two days after D-Day, so was well-placed to represent those troops while Amory represented the youth of today. Veterans were raising funds to erect a new memorial with marble plaques honouring the South African campaign, both world wars, Korea, and peacekeeping missions. A sculpture by local artist Maarten Schaddelee would form an integral part of the memorial.[2570] [2571]

Now that the arena was to become a reality, the question was who would be the anchor hockey tenant. From the US came the news that the Baton Rouge Kingfish of the ECHL were for sale, and that Graham Lee had indicated an interest in the team. That league was the third-ranked pro league in North America and should provide competitive hockey for the citizens of Victoria. However, league officials cautioned that "nothing is firm at this time." With thirty-two teams in eighteen US states, the ECHL was (at that time) the largest league in pro hockey.[2572]

The next news was the awarding of the contract for the work of public art to be placed on the plaza outside the arena. This quickly became the most controversial component of the arena project. After a four-month jurying process, artist Mowry Baden was chosen to create the public art to be placed on the civic plaza near the main entrance to the arena. The work, titled "Pavilion Rock and Shell," cost $120,000, and according to the artist, represented somebody leaning against a boulder while drinking coffee and reading the sports pages of a newspaper.[2573] Public response, for the most part, was outrage. Mayor Alan Lowe said that he had received over fifty emails opposed to the art, and as a result, was going to see if council could reverse the decision.[2574] On July 3, a Seattle art director said that Victorians should give the sculpture a chance,[2575] while in another area of the same newspaper, letters both for and against the project filled an entire page.[2576] The matter was decided when the city received a legal opinion that the contract must be honoured. It was suggested, however, that the process for public art acquisitions be examined.[2577]

Once again, the pouring of the arena foundation was delayed due to the need for more site preparation. There were problems with the amount of rock on the site, and the hardness of the ground on which the arena would be situated was also a concern.[2578] Despite the issues, developer Graham Lee assured Victorians that the building would open on August 28, 2004. The work completed up to now had been mainly underground, to give the structure stability. The only question left about the anchor tenant was

29 - HOW TO BUILD AN ARENA SUCCESSFULLY

whether Lee would own the ECHL team or merely be the landlord and have someone else own it.[2579] In a special report in the Weekend Monitor section of the *Victoria Times Colonist*, readers were shown the details of the arena, both inside and out. The new building was designed to be accessible on one level, creating ease of entry for both commercial users and the public. The only stairs that spectators would encounter would be when they went to their seats. This was particularly welcome in a city where the population was ageing.[2580]

On the inside, the major difference between the old Memorial Arena and the new structure was the absence of a concourse and walkway between two layers of seating. This social interaction place would be replaced by a large concourse entirely surrounding the main bowl of the arena, with concessions situated all around and ample space for meetings and conversation. In addition, the sloping columns and sweeping concrete stairwells were designed to protect the building from damage during an earthquake.[2581]

At long last came the official news of the anchor tenant: The ECHL franchise, formerly of Baton Rouge, Louisiana, would be transferred to Victoria and operated under a different name. Management announced a contest to name the team, the same as had been done in 1922 when the Victoria team in the PCHL was given the name "Cougars."[2582][2583]

More than 2,700 entries were received for the "name the team" contest. Among the choices were Islanders, Victoria Secrets, Orcas, Killer Whales, Seals, Sockeyes, Mighty Oaks, Marmots, Venom, Vipers, Valiant, Valour, Vanguard, Vampires, Royals, Monarchs, Rain, Rainforest, and Rainmen. There was even a suggestion of "Spiders." The name "Cougars" was also selected, but RG Properties wanted to establish their own identity with a totally new name.[2584] Team executives chose the name "Salmon Kings," suggesting that it combined royalty and marine life. As this name was suggested by ten different persons, a draw was made from their names with the winner securing a pair of season tickets for their efforts.[2585] Public reaction to the name was varied. A *Victoria Times Colonist* editorial made fun of the name,[2586] but it remained to be seen how the name would fit the team that was eventually assembled.

Ken Noakes was hired as the general manager for the new arena, chosen from over 450 applicants for the position. This was the fourth opening he would supervise, having done the same at the Corel Centre, SkyDome, and the Hershey Centre. He noted that he planned on securing as many local players as he could for the team. However, hockey wouldn't be his only responsibility, as he would oversee every event in the new arena from trade shows to concerts. He joked that he would be spending as much time with major concert promoters as with ECHL governors.[2587] Former NHL defenceman Bryan Maxwell was named as coach of the new ECHL franchise. After his professional-hockey career ended, he had taken up coaching, first with the Medicine Hat Tigers of the WHL and then with the Los Angeles Kings of the NHL. He then returned to the WHL to coach the Spokane Chiefs.[2588]

The yet-unbuilt arena scored a coup when the 2005 men's world curling championship was awarded to Victoria. Scheduled to run between April 2 and April 10, 2005, it would be the first international event in the new facility. Local organizers were "honoured" that this event would be held in Victoria and looked forward to hosting similar events in future years.[2589] The championship would give local fans a look at the top men's teams from twelve countries, less than a year before the 2006 Winter Olympics in Turin, Italy.[2590]

There was also good news for the Greater Victoria Sports Hall of Fame. The ten-year-old organization would be moving into the new facility. Arena developer RG Properties donated $25,000 for display cases, but the group would have to raise funds to mount their artifacts in proper displays. No longer would the story of sport be hidden in cases and lockers but would instead be on display to anyone who attended an event at the arena. The area's rich sports history would now be celebrated in a very public way.[2591]

On the construction front, Graham Lee said that he wasn't worried about the "hole on Blanshard," assuring the public that the new arena would open on August 28, 2004, as scheduled. He based his assessment on the firm's history of completion of arena projects, and the fact that much of the material would be prefabricated offsite and assembled at a later date.[2592]

From the veterans came news that they were closer to the $80,000 needed for the new memorial at the arena. A grant of $5,000 from the provincial Ministry of Community, Aboriginal and Women's services put the total over $50,000. A major donation came from Thrifty Foods ($10,000), eighteen veterans' groups contributed $20,000, and individual donations came from local citizens, including widows of veterans.[2593]

Luxury boxes went on sale in late November 2003—and they were not cheap. The sole double suite cost $75,000, while smaller suites were priced from $42,500 to $56,000 per year. Each suite came with bar service, food service from the caterers, padded seats, and televisions, as well as tickets for every Salmon Kings game, concert, or other events, along with two on-site parking spots. There was room for thirty-one luxury boxes in the arena plans.[2594] The first fourteen luxury boxes were leased out in less than a week, and names were put on a waiting list for the remain seventeen suites, if and when they were built.[2595]

Finally, there was evidence that a building would, indeed, rise on Blanshard Street. The last of the concrete foundation was poured on December 19, and crews were working six days a week to meet deadlines. Arena manager Ken Noakes commented that "everything is vertical after this," referring to work starting on the walls.[2596] As had long been suspected, the new arena was not likely to be completed by August 28. Citing delays in demolition, removal of contaminated soil, and removal of hazardous material, the City set a new target date of November 15, 2003, although Graham Lee insisted it would be ready earlier.[2597]

Now that the building was well underway, it was time to select a sponsor to name the arena. One of the firms in the running was Save-On-Foods, the grocery giant owned by Jim Pattison. However, the bidding process was still actively underway, with an expected price tag of $100,000 to $150,000 per year. Results would be released "within a few weeks."[2598] The actual release came on March 31, 2004, when it was announced that Save-On-Foods would be granted naming rights, having been chosen from four or five candidates. Public reaction of the new name, "Save-On-Foods Centre," was mixed, with most of those questioned saying it was not very creative. The firm paid $1.25 million for a ten-year deal, joining corporations all over North America in sponsoring major sporting venues.[2599]

Under the deal, the City of Victoria would retain "ten percent of the first $100,000 earned from naming rights each year, with twenty-five percent of any additional amounts above that. The sponsor gained the right to have two large signs on the exterior of the building, with other signage inside, as well.[2600] However, the veterans' group who was planning the permanent display in the new building did not give up, and worked with Save-On-Foods and city officials to reach an agreement to rename the structure the "Save-On-Foods Memorial Centre." As Jack Cockrell, chair of the Veterans Memorial Committee said, "When we knew the building had to go down, we were determined that the building might go down, but the memorial aspects had to live on. The one thing that was missing was that link, before people ever entered the building, that there was a memorial aspect. That link is now complete. We're happy as can be."[2601] The new name was overwhelmingly supported by the community, with citizens anxious to recognize the memorial aspect of the site.[2602] An editorial in the *Victoria Times Colonist* applauded Save-On-Foods for doing the "right thing."[2603]

There had been rumours of a time capsule somewhere in the old Memorial Arena, but it was never found during demolition. However, the Veterans

Committee of the Royal Canadian Legion was determined to have one in the new building. The city issued a call for memorabilia, including short, written stories outlining memories of the arena, photos, ticket stubs, handbills, or any other historic documents. The best items, as selected by the committee and city, would be placed in a capsule that would be placed in one of the new arena's beams. Citizens were given just over a week to make their submissions.[2604]

On the business side of arena operations, the city tentatively set rental rates for the new arena—and in all cases, their proposed rates were higher than those charged by the neighbouring municipalities. For example, school students would be charged $3 per hour in Victoria, while they currently paid $1 in Esquimalt and $1.50 in Saanich. Under the agreement with RG Properties, the city negotiated 950 "prime time" hours per year and 750 hours outside of prime time.[2605]

The construction continued with prefabricated concrete columns being installed; these would support the main arena seating and the roof trusses. Roof trusses were being manufactured and were expected to be delivered by the end of June. The opening was still set for November 15, 2004.[2606]

Traveller's Inn Hotels launched a multi-million-dollar lawsuit over the naming of the arena, naming Graham Lee, two of his RG groups of companies, and one of his employees. Traveller's representative Harvey Stevenson claimed he "met with [Dave] Dakers at the downtown offices of the Salmon Kings hockey team, the anchor tenant of the arena, on December 22, 2003. At that time, he said he signed a ten-year agreement in writing for the Traveller's Inn to hold the naming right to the arena." The agreement was subject to "appropriate approval" by the RG Properties board within three business days of the alleged meeting. In the meantime, the deal went sideways, and the scheduled January 2 press conference was cancelled. None of the claims had been proven in court to that date.[2607] That case was later dismissed by the judge in the British Columbia Supreme Court.

By mid-August, it was evident that the arena would not be ready for the Salmon Kings' first home game. According to Dave Dakers, they had fallen behind schedule as they had difficulty in securing skilled labour and construction materials. However, roof construction was underway, and things were moving along at a moderate pace.[2608] The developer faced extra costs and lost revenues from the delay, so it was in their best interest to complete the project as soon as possible. The new completion date was set for February 2005, when Graham Lee made a trip to Victoria to view the progress on the site. Although hockey would likely not be played there this season, there was no way it would not be ready for the 2005 Men's World Curling Championship in May, seven months after the original opening date.[2609]

The changes in completion date brought out the best in columnist Jack Knox, who wrote a column in which he recalled the name "David Pasant." However, he did note that Graham Lee did not appear to be worried about the delays, as he has thirty years to make money on the arena and these delays are minor when compared to that time frame. Lee admitted that he should not have been so firm on the August 28 deadline and vowed to improve communication with the public as the project neared completion.[2610]

In mid-October, the target date was changed again, this time to March 31. Some members of city council were critical of the unending delays and wondered if the building would ever be finished. Among the projects yet to be completed were the roof, exterior wall cladding and finishes, elevators, the rink slab, seating, the suites, installation of ice-making equipment, and completion of the main lobby. Mayor Lowe said that the developer made it clear that some finishing touches would not be ready until after the primary facility opened. When the arena was finally finished, a "performance verification list" would compare the final project to the contracted performance specifications.[2611]

Two huge video screens were planned for the corner of Caledonia Avenue and Blanshard Street. They were intended to identify sponsors and also to advertise events happening in the arena. Council had to bend a municipal by-law to permit approval of the signs. The signs had to go to a public hearing before construction but was expected to be approved and then built before the arena opened. There was also some concern about the builders' liens, filed because of payment disputes between subcontractors. Sierd Hortsang, the city's arena project manager, noted that two liens had been discharged and other problems were being addressed.[2612] By the end of October, there was progress on major items. All structural steel had been installed except one section on the north end where it was in progress, the roofing contractor started the installation of the main domed-roof membrane, all underground plumbing was substantially complete, underground electrical rough-in had commenced, casting of concrete slabs and casting of concrete topping over the floor metal deck had started, installation of seating sections on the west side of the arena was in progress, and installation of the curtain wall was expected to commence shortly. RG Properties supplied written confirmation to the city that they would open the arena before all tenant improvements were complete, but the arena bowl, concessions, washrooms, concourse, lobbies, and public spaces would be complete by the opening date.[2613]

In mid-November came the news that Sarah McLachlan had been booked to perform April 13, 2005, at the Save-On-Foods Memorial Centre. The concert would be one of the final dates of her *Afterglow* tour, which began July 5, in Seattle. Tickets went on sale on November 22.[2614] However, this concert was delayed to June 7 and 8, so that Rod Stewart's concert on March 25 was the first event at the new arena. A photograph in the *Victoria Times Colonist* showed the building with its new roof in place. Now it looked like a real arena and citizens could imagine attending events and games there in the not-too-distant future.[2615] By the end of December, the interior of the arena was taking shape.[2616] Over 120 workers were on site, with jobs being done in two shifts per day, seven days a week. Heating and air-conditioning ducts had been hung from the roof, the sprinkler system was in, ice-making equipment was on site, some seats had been delivered, and interior framing had started on private suites and media areas. While some contractors thought the work would be delayed yet again, city officials had confidence that everything would be ready on time.[2617]

For every month that the completion of the arena was delayed, the city lost about $35,000 from ticket sales, community ice-rental time, and operating fees, but that was more than offset by more than $500,000 in interest earned on the money not advanced to the project developers. As a result, the delays were not costing the city any money. RG Properties blamed several factors, including a difficulty in finding skilled workers and obtaining material when the province was in the midst of a building boom. Many of the finishing touches, including many landscape features, would not be completed by the time of Rod Stewart's concert but would be added later. Inside the building, three concessions would be ready, but the restaurant, kitchen, and retail spaces would be incomplete. By the end of January 2005, twenty percent of the spectator seats had been installed, and work was continuing.[2618]

The developer gave the city a list of 501 tasks that had to be completed for the new arena. Of these, there were more than 400 yet to be done. One of the main tasks that remained was the pouring of the concrete rink slab that would form the base for the ice surface. It was scheduled for March 2, with preliminary work starting early in February. Ice-making was planned to begin on March 23.[2619] The organizers of the 2010 Winter Olympics in Vancouver arrived in Victoria for a tour of the new building. John Furlong was very impressed with the work to date and expressed faith in the ability of Graham Lee to get the job done. Construction Superintendent Leo Mariotto said that 230 people were currently working at the site, almost ten times the number that was working there a year ago. The crews were now working seven days a week in two shifts from 7:00 a.m. to 11:00 p.m. to get as much done as possible.[2620]

In mid-February, RG Properties was looking for 300 persons to work at the arena, including concessions, customer service, ushers, and ice-floor conversion crews. All positions would be part-time with flexible hours and pay about eight dollars per hour. A Duncan-based coffee vendor, Serious Coffee, won the contract to supply coffee to the concessions, while Villages Pizza secured a four-year contract to provide the arena with 10,000-15,000 pizzas per year. Coco-Cola and Molson would supply beverages to the arena. Twenty-three of the twenty-six luxury boxes had been sold, with all the purchasers local. Much of the advertising spots in the arena had also been sold.[2621]

With one month to go before the Rod Stewart concert, the concrete rink slab had been poured a week ahead of schedule, and other work was proceeding at a rapid pace.[2622] The often-criticized sculpture by Mowry Baden had been installed in front of the Save-On-Foods Memorial Centre by the end of February. Entitled "Pavilion, Rock and Shell," it took eighteen months to complete and stood 4.3 metres tall.[2623] Patrons of the new arena would have a problem with parking, as the on-site parking would not be ready and they could have to walk up to ten blocks. Evening parking rates at city-owned parkades were increased to $2 per evening. City staff identified 2,000 parking spaces in the five nearest city-owned parkades; there were also some private lots close by as well, but parking there would be more expensive. On-street parking in the North Park neighbourhood would be prohibited, and streets would be rigidly patrolled.[2624]

To address potential parking problems at the new arena, BC Transit offered free bus rides to anyone holding a ticket for the Rod Stewart concert. Costs were covered by RG Properties, the City of Victoria, and Robbins Parking.[2625] The new identification sign was installed on the front of the new building, and RG Properties began the process of hiring workers. From over 4,000 applications that had been received, selected candidates had been interviewed, hired, and were being trained in their new duties.[2626] On March 26, the date of the Rod Stewart concert, fans had to wait to see if they would be allowed to enter the arena when city inspectors found "minor deficiencies" in the construction. Between 350 and 400 workers were on the site to get the work done. Much to the delight of all concerned, the building was given an occupancy permit just six hours before the concert, and everything went well.[2627] Graham Lee noted that all the missed deadlines would soon be a "distant memory," once the arena was open and operating at peak capacity. He reflected on the last few months and outlined how many of the delays were beyond his control. His one disappointment was the way that his workers were disparaged in some news stories. He noted that they had been first-rate, and their work had been done to high standards.[2628]

A *Victoria Times Colonist* editorial advised its readers that the arena was a "place to create fresh memories." It told the story of the building of the Memorial Arena and how it had construction delays, but that was not what citizens remembered about the buildings; it was the concerts, hockey games, lacrosse matches, and other events that came to mind. It would be the same with the new arena; missed deadlines would be forgotten, and new memories would be forged.[2629]

Just after 8:00 p.m., on March 26, 2005, concert patrons heard the skirl of bagpipes that led Rod Stewart to the stage, where he opened the concert with a rendition of *Forever Young*. He sported a green hard hat and joked with the audience that "the roof is still on." Some of the concert goers wore construction helmets, as well, getting into the spirit of the evening. The crowd was mostly middle-aged, but they stood and cheered throughout the evening, transported back to when they were younger.[2630] [2631]

Victoria had a great response to the opening of the arena: "It rocks!" Those living near the site were thankful that patrons did not block their driveways or park on their streets. They were also grateful that the construction noise was over for the most part, and they could now open their windows in good weather. Even those who had been unable to attend the concert were impressed and were looking forward to the official opening to be held later. Local restaurants reported a dramatic increase in customers before and after the concert and expected to see the same results with future events. Business was also good for taxi companies, as many of the audience chose that method of transportation. Perhaps the new arena would become a much-needed economic generator for the area around it.[2632] Local citizens flooded the *Victoria Times Colonist* with their impressions of the arena. Among the comments were:

- This venue will bring people of all ages together for years to come.
- Small, intimate setting . . . not a bad seat in the house.
- A little late, but worth the wait.
- The stairways are very steep and perhaps need a handrail.
- It was exciting to attend the very first event in Victoria's Save-On-Foods Memorial Centre. It's a wonderful building.
- Every parent should breathe a sigh of relief. Older teens may now attend concerts on their own without the usual dilemma of time/money/chaperone it took to go to something out of town.
- It reminded me of a mini-GM Place.
- Having seen the new Save-On-Foods Memorial Centre rise from the rubble over the last two years, with the anticipation of finally having a state-of-the-art concert venue in Victoria, you could feel the buzz amongst the crowd on Saturday night.[2633]

Not many of the concert goers took advantage of the free bus service, preferring to arrive on foot or in a vehicle. It appeared that many were being dropped off at the venue and being picked up after the concert. BC Transit estimated that 500-600 people rode the bus for free, over half of whom took the shuttles operating from CanWest Mall in Langford and from Sidney, using double-decker buses. Mayor Alan Lowe said that the concert was a great test for the transportation system, and it seemed to have worked smoothly. There were even empty spaces in lots across from the arena.[2634]

In the aftermath of the opening of the new arena, Duncan Stevenson, the city building inspector, assured the public that "no rules were bent to allow the opening-day permit." He and his team worked on Good Friday and Easter Monday to ensure that everything was ready. They gave RG Properties a list of deficiencies that had to be addressed before an occupancy certificate could be issued, and all were dealt with. Permits had not yet been issued for the luxury boxes, a restaurant-lounge, retail spaces in the building, and offices. All were expected to be complete by May 30.[2635]

The new arena was shown off to the world when the 2005 Men's World Curling Championship was held there from April 2-10. In addition to those watching live, the event was streamed to fifty-two different countries, showcasing Victoria in the same way that the 1994 Commonwealth Games had done.[2636] Although there were minor glitches during the event—lack of electricity at some outlets, media internet stations not working, toilet paper dispensers that didn't dispense, and the occasional seat that had not been installed—the facility had good ice, and the curlers were satisfied. From a spectator point of view, the poor sightlines from the premium seats were an issue. One patron said he had not paid $400 to sit on plastic. All those who complained were relocated, leaving the premium seating area almost empty.[2637] Local fans went home thrilled when Canada's Randy Ferbey rink won the final match against Scotland's David Murdoch.[2638] The event was a success off the ice, as well, generating $20 million in economic spinoffs and showing a profit of $500,000. Those funds were split three ways, with $145,000 going to both the World Curling Federation and the Canadian Curling Federation, and the remainder to a special program in Victoria to assist young curlers to improve their game by travelling to out-of-town events. Managed by PacificSport, it would be similar to what they offered for rowing, rugby, and triathlon. The championship might be over, but its legacy would live on.[2639]

In the arena lobby, a crew from Mortimer's Monumental Works installed five plaques made of Carrera marble from Italy, as part of the new memorial. One plaque had been carved for the original Memorial Arena and honoured those who gave their lives in the Second World War. It was restored and was joined by new plaques that recognized casualties of the Boer War, the First World War, and the Korean War. A final plaque was dedicated to Canadian peacekeepers. A sculpture entitled "When Peace Comes" by local artist Maarten Schaddelee, was installed next to the wall along with six flagpoles. The entire project was financed through funds raised by veterans' groups and grants from various sources, including $10,000 from the city.[2640]

The memorial was dedicated by Lieutenant Governor Iona Campagnola on April 17, 2005. For retired captain Jack Cockrell, it was the end of an emotional five-year effort to preserve the "memorial" aspect of the site. Besides the local and provincial politicians, there were members of the general public of all ages. Visitors ranged from war veterans to young children, who were all asked to remember the sacrifice of our veterans and "carry the torch" forward. The mood was upbeat, with music supplied by the Naden Band and many tapped their toes along to the music.[2641]

By October 2005, the arena was still not finished, as work had been halted while subcontractors tried to get paid by RG Properties. Work on the restaurant and press had not even started, elevators were not working, baseboards had not been installed, concrete was cracked in places, and some interior walls had not been painted. Outside, construction debris was piled up, and landscaping was incomplete. Apparently, the city had held back monies from the developer to the point where he was unable to pay the contractors. The matter was in the hands of lawyers, and a resolution was expected soon.[2642] On the political front, mayoralty candidate Ben Isitt said that there might be grounds to tear up the operating agreement between the city and the developer of the Save-On-Foods Memorial Centre. He maintained that the citizens had been shortchanged and most were unhappy with the arena. However, Mayor Alan Lowe pointed out that the facility had generated millions of dollars in spin-off economic benefit, and more than 500,000 people had enjoyed events there in its first six months of operation.[2643] The electorate must have agreed with Lowe, as it returned him as mayor with 51.9 percent of the total vote.[2644]

A deal to end the dispute was announced on November 10, in which the arena developer was allowed to defer for five years half of a $2 million lease prepayment. The money would be paid back with interest. RG Properties agreed to release $1.5 million of its funds to enable the work on the building to be completed. Mayor Alan Lowe noted that the city was holding back $4.7 million until the building was finished, but would give $1.5 million to RG to be placed in trust and used for the needed payments.[2645]

The end to major construction came two days before the deadline of March 11, 2005. The arena restaurant, a preparation kitchen, and a ground-floor lounge were given occupancy permits. Mayor Lowe pointed out that RG Properties had managed to get the facility operational at a fixed price at a time when construction costs were rising, and skilled workers were in short supply.[2646]

The arena hosted eighty events in its first year and has continued to host a variety of events in addition to hockey. Concerts, children's shows, car sales, skating championships and exhibitions, and even monster trucks have drawn visitors to the building.[2647] It is now a familiar sight on the city landscape, and most of the early issues have long been forgotten. Victoria needed an arena and now has one that it can be proud of.

Shaw TV moved its entire television production operations to the Save-On-Foods Memorial Centre in March 2008, but they did not expect to start broadcasting Salmon Kings games in the near future. Shaw developed more than 4,000 square feet over two floors on the south side of the arena. Included was a full studio, five editing suites, master-control and engineering areas, and other offices for management and accounting inside the arena.[2648]

30 - VICTORIA SALMON KINGS – NEW KIDS IN THE LEAGUE

Season tickets for the Salmon Kings inaugural season went on sale on October 14, 2003, priced at $478.26 for adults and $318.45 for children, seniors, and students.[2649] Sales were brisk, with a down payment of twenty-five dollars put down on 1,005 seats. Most of the people in the lineup were excited to be able to view professional hockey in Victoria again.[2650] Now that there was a team with a name, albeit with nowhere to play, thoughts turned to who would the players be. Would the team focus on home-grown talent? There were plenty of Vancouver Island and BC players currently toiling in the ECHL who would possibly like to play closer to home. The article listed nine players who might suit up for the Salmon Kings.[2651] However, only three,—Jason Stone, David Brumby, and David Neale—ever played for the local team.[2652]

With only four veterans (players with five or more seasons of pro-hockey experience) allowed per team, Coach Bryan Maxwell would need to draw on his experience with developing young players.[2653] In a press conference, he noted that his father, Stan Maxwell, had played for Lester Patrick's Cougars when the Memorial Arena was new, and now he would lead the Salmon Kings in another new arena.[2654]

Although the start of the season was months away, Coach Maxwell began to assemble his team in April. He spent time scouting ECHL teams for potential players, using his contacts within the hockey milieu. He was disappointed by the decision of the Vancouver Canucks to retain their affiliation with an ECHL team in Columbus, SC.[2655] Maxwell said that he would enter discussions with the Vancouver team once their season was over. He also announced that the Salmon Kings would hold open tryouts in August and that only twenty-six or twenty-seven players would be invited to a training camp in the fall.[2656]

At ECHL league meetings in June, the renamed conferences and divisions were announced. The Salmon Kings would play in the western division of the National Conference. The season would start on October 22, 2004, against the Bakersfield Condors. After an extended road trip, during which they expected the arena to be completed, they would play their first home game on December 5.[2657] Among fans who made the original twenty-five-dollar deposits to hold season tickets, less than fifty of them failed to pay the first deposit of one-third of the cost of the full season. Many wondered if the arena would be completed in time, but they were advised that there would be a full refund for ticket holders "unable to attend any home games that couldn't be played) at Save-On-Foods Memorial Centre." Just in case the building was not ready, the Victoria Salsa had drawn up their schedule for Bear Mountain Arena working around the Kings' dates.[2658]

By July, the team was signing players. The first rumoured signing was Victoria-native David Brumby, who had first suited up in Oak Bay as a five-year-old. He had played for Coach Maxwell at Lethbridge, and thus had a relationship that could prove valuable for the Salmon Kings. He was expected to be the first of the four "veteran" players that each team could carry.[2659] In fact, he did not sign until the end of July, giving the honour of the first signings to Ryan Finnerty, Rob Voltera, and Ryan Wade. They were the first players to sign contracts in Victoria since the Victoria Maple Leafs had left in 1967. At the same time, the team revealed the design of their jersey, which featured a crowned salmon with the word "Kings" beneath. Victoria was acknowledged in arm patches. Ken Noakes, directors of sales and marketing for the Salmon Kings, said, "We consider ourselves traditionalists and went with a classic hockey sweater." Home jerseys were white while the road versions were a very dark blue.[2660]

Coach Maxwell continued to negotiate with players for the team. For him, it was the first time he had to worry about salaries, as junior hockey players are not paid. Also, he had to keep the total salaries under the league-mandated $10,000 US per week. Most players in the ECHL earned between $350 US to $500 US per week. However, they received apartments, utilities, groceries, and insurance, as well as selected entertainment packages. Maxwell said that he didn't care what route the players took to get to pro hockey, as long as they were good. He also noted that he preferred to sign Canadians.[2661] By the end of July, a total of eight players had been signed. Adding to Finnerty, Voltera, and Wade were David Brumby from Victoria, Kyle Stanton from Chemainus, Jason Hegberg from Stettler, Alberta, Oak Bay fireman Mike Josephson, and Calgary's Blue Bennefield.[2662] Next to join the team were Jeff Williams from Point-Claire, Quebec, and defenceman Corey Smith, a former Victoria Salsa player.[2663]

When it was announced that the arena would not be complete for the home opener, the owners negotiated dates with Bear Mountain Arena. Among the issues were that fact that 3,000 season tickets had been sold, and there were not that many seats at Bear Mountain, and of course, no luxury boxes.[2664] On September 9, 2004, the rumour was confirmed as truth. The Salmon Kings would play the start of the season at Bear Mountain Arena and might play there all season, depending on when the downtown arena was completed. Although there were not enough seats there to accommodate all those who had purchased season tickets, the team announced that twenty percent of the ticket holders would not be attending games at the outlying arena, freeing up space for walk-up traffic. Season-ticket holders had three options: attend games at Bear Mountain Arena and be given a hundred-dollar Salmon Kings gift certificate, not attend at Bear Mountain but hold seats at the new arena with the funds paid rolling over to the next season, or to give up the season ticket all together with a full refund of amounts paid. As part of the deal, the Salmon Kings had to compensate old-timers and minor hockey leagues who had to give up ice time. The only revenue stream for RG Properties would be from ticket sales, as West Shore Parks and Recreation retained all revenue from concessions.[2665]

There was an upside to local hockey in the fall of 2004, however. Talks between the National Hockey League Players Association and the NHL had stalled, with a lockout of the players a likely outcome. That would mean that hockey-starved fans could flock to local games, as they would have nothing to view on TV.[2666]

Another locally developed player signed with the Salmon Kings in September. Mike Barrie was excited to be back playing in his hometown, having laced up his skates for the WHL Cougars in the early 1990s.[2667] Late September signings included former Cowichan Valley Capitals player Jim Gattolliat,

Brad Dexter of Brockville, Ontario, and Robert Busch, who had played eight seasons of pro hockey in Germany.[2668]

The Salmon Kings held their inaugural training camp at CFB Naden, from October 8-20, at the Wurtele Arena ice rink and its adjacent pool, weight room, gymnasium, cardiovascular machines, therapeutic tubs, and a dining mess hall. The facilities rivalled those of many NHL teams. Coach Maxwell promised that the players would have to be in shape to play hard or somebody else would take their spots. He had twenty-three players signed and expected a total of twenty-four or twenty-five players at the camp. He anticipated competition for every spot on the roster, and lively scrimmages that would be open to the public on a limited basis.[2669]

Among the new players was Seth Leonard, who had been labelled "too small" all his life. He was determined to show that he belonged at the pro level.[2670] For Ryan Wade, it was a homecoming, as he would be able to play in front of family and friends in his hometown. He initially thought he might be playing at a higher level, but the NHL lockout meant that they were not signing anyone new and that trickled down to the minor leagues as well. He was now part of a small but very speedy hockey team.[2671] Robert Busch had to make the difficult adjustment from the larger ice surface in Europe but thought he could overcome the lack of space by playing a physical style of hockey.[2672] Goaltender Jason Stone represented the drive to succeed at any cost. Cut by many teams, he never gave up and was now in a battle with Kyle Stanton for the number two spot at goal, believing that Brumby would be named the starter.[2673] Kristjan Jefkins who had been a featured storyline in some episodes of CBC's series *Making the Cut,* was now trying to "make the cut" with the Salmon Kings.[2674]

The Salmon Kings played their first exhibition game on October 15, 2004, at Prospera Centre in Chilliwack, against the defending league-champion, Idaho Steelheads. Despite losing the game, 7-2, the Kings played a fast, crisp game. Their effort was marred by "bonehead" penalties, which gave the powerful Steelheads too many chances with the man advantage. Jeff Williams scored the first exhibition goal for the team, with Ryan Wade adding the second. David Brumby seems to have played his way to the number one position in goal as he stood tall and made several good saves.[2675] [2676] The second exhibition game was played in Duncan at "The Stick." Again, the Kings fell short, losing, 7-4. Forward Ryan Finnerty was injured and would be lost to the team for up to three weeks. Then Mike Josephson went down with an injury when he went head first into the end boards, not the news that the team needed to hear as they began a dreadful road trip to start the season.[2677]

Teams had until October 20 to finalize their rosters. They were able to keep as many players as they could while fitting under the $10,000 US per week cap. The rest of the players would be placed on waivers, and the Salmon Kings would pick first in the waiver draft.[2678] Just before the first game of the road trip, the Kings signed Jeremy Cheyne, a twenty-three-year-old scorer from Calgary.

As this would be the first ECHL game by a Canadian team, the Hockey Hall of Fame asked for items to be sent to them, including a jersey worn in the inaugural game and the stick of the player who scored the first-ever Salmon King regular-season goal.[2679] Getting to the game proved to be an adventure, as the team's flight from Vancouver to Los Angeles had to turn back due to a mechanical failure. After the plane left again, it did make it to Los Angeles, but then the bus driver got lost on the trip to Bakersfield Centennial Arena. That meant that the team travelled for fifteen hours and arrived very late and were tired.[2680]

After a rendition of *O Canada,* where the singer needed a "cheat sheet" containing the words, the Salmon Kings' inaugural season began. The Bakersfield Condors scored two goals before the game was one minute old on their way to a 7-2 victory. On the positive side, the first Salmon Kings goal was scored at 6:40 of the first period by Victoria-raised

Ryan Wade, and former Condor Mike Barrie added the second in the middle frame. The team did not play well overall, with their coach noting that they would have to play a lot better in future games if they wanted to be successful.[2681][2682][2683] The next night, the Kings played a lot better and were within forty-five seconds of their first point when Vlad Serov scored the winner for Bakersfield in a 2-1 victory. Bryan Maxwell said that his team "deserved a better fate." Oak Bay fireman Mike Josephson had the lone counter for the Kings. Goaltender Brumby was outstanding in net and likely deserved to win.[2684] The Salmon Kings finally won their first game on October 24, 2004, with a 5-0 shutout of the Fresno Falcons. Jason Hegberg put the Kings on the board at 4:07 of the first period and Jeff Williams found the back of the net at 8:20 to give the visitors a 2-0 lead at the first intermission. Robert Busch hit the scoresheet at 2:22 of the middle frame and Williams added his second at 4:49. Blue Bennefield added a power-play goal with five seconds left in the game to ensure the historic victory. The team would now fly home for an eleven-day break before their next match.[2685][2686]

Although the Salmon Kings were unable to secure the services of locked-out Victoria homegrown NHL star Matt Pettinger, the Alaska Aces landed their favourite son, Scott Gomez of the New Jersey Devils. In Kings' player moves, the team released Kristjan Jefkins and signed Ryan Watson, a twenty-three-year-old who had been placed on waivers by the Trenton Titans.[2687]

In preparation for the first home game for the Salmon Kings, management announced that there would be about 1,000 tickets available for each game, 500 of which would be standing room. Only 1,800 season ticket holders had purchased seats at Bear Mountain Arena, while most of the remainder chose to transfer their tickets to the following season when the new downtown arena would be complete.[2688]

The merry-go-round roster moves continued. Forward Robert Busch retired to go to work for his father-in-law, leaving the team with seventeen skaters and two goalies. The team practiced at Naden and prepared for their upcoming trip to Boise to play the Idaho Steelheads.[2689] Ryan Watson and Duncan's Duncan Campbell joined the club, along with former Cowichan Valley Capital Ryan Finnerty who returned from injury. The roster now had a real Vancouver Island flavour as twelve of the current nineteen players were from the Island or had played for Island teams in junior.[2690]

The addition of Finnerty paid immediate dividends, as he scored twice as the Kings upended the Steelheads 4-1. Rob Voltera scored the third goal and added one into the empty net to secure the win.[2691] Unfortunately, the Kings were unable to maintain their intensity the next night and fell, 6-2, to Idaho. The Steelheads put pressure on the Salmon Kings while controlling the puck and showing more desire to win. Goaltender Brumby had an off-night for the Kings, but he was not alone in less-than-stellar play.[2692] After being fogged in at the Idaho airport, the team was unable to return home for a quick practice, travelling instead to Los Angeles for their next game against the Long Beach Ice Dogs.[2693]

Playing on ice with a peculiar blue hue, the Kings fell behind, 2-0, in the first period and were unable to mount a comeback, although they outplayed their opponents in the final two frames. The Ice Dogs, the ECHL affiliate of the Montreal Canadiens, got a stellar effort in goal from Olivier Michaud, as they narrowly edged the visitors, 2-1. Jason Stone of Duncan got the start in net for Victoria as the coach felt he had earned the right to a start. He could only be faulted for one goal, but in a close game, that made all the difference. Ryan Finnerty had the lone counter for the Kings.[2694] The team then travelled to Las Vegas for an encounter with the Wranglers. Once again, the Kings fell behind early and never really recovered. Their slow start was partially due to untimely penalties, including having to play two men short. They were also badly outshot, 16-5, and ended up trailing, 4-0, at the end of the first period. They began to apply pressure on the Wranglers in the middle frame, but it was a case of too little, too late.

The only marksmen for the Kings were Rob Voltera and Ryan Watson. The bright lights of Las Vegas did not shine on the road-weary Salmon Kings.[2695]

The interminable road trip continued in Fresno. In this game, the Kings put a good effort and managed to tie the game, 4-4, in the third period. However, the Falcons scored twice in the final 1:29 of the third period, including one into the empty net, to win the game, 6-4, and send the Kings to their fourth consecutive loss.[2696] From sunny California, the Salmon Kings travelled to Alaska to play the Aces. The Kings took an early lead on a goal by Brad Dexter but could only manage two more counters in the third period—after the score was 5-1 for the Aces—by Ryan Watson and Ryan Finnerty. Locked-out NHL player Scott Gomez was the star for his hometown team.[2697] Three days later, the Kings again fell behind and struggled to come back. Unfortunately, they could only score twice—Bennefield and Voltera—en route to a 5-2 loss. The defence was just not good enough for hockey at this level and hope was expected in the person of Nate Forster, who was going to join the team for their California games.[2698]

The third game in Alaska was a different one for the Salmon Kings. Spurred by a two-goal effort from Seth Leonard, the team finally defeated the Aces. Brad Dexter had the 3-0 goal, and Jason Hegberg found the empty net in a 4-1 victory. Jason Stone played in goal and was outstanding, holding the Aces off the scoresheet until 9:41 of the third period.[2699]

The team had a short time at home before departing on the road again, for California this time, to end the unending fourteen-game road trip. Jeremy Cheyne left the team on November 22, having decided to switch to pro lacrosse.[2700]

With only three games left on the road trip, the Kings headed down to Fresno. Unlike their last trip there, the team played poorly and ended up on the wrong side of a 4-2 score. Falling behind, 3-0, they could not find the back of the net until Blue Bennefield scored at 17:12 of the second period. Mike Barrie made the score 3-2, but Victoria squandered several chances to tie the score. An empty-net goal by the Falcons sealed the deal.[2701] It did not get any better in the next game, as the Falcons won, 5-2.[2702] The road trip finally ended back where it had begun thirty-seven days before, in Bakersfield. The team put up a good effort and had a 2-0 lead thanks to goals by Dexter and Barrie but could not hold it, and the Condors tied the game before the end of regulation time. When overtime solved nothing, the match went to a shootout. Unfortunately, the Kings could not prevail, losing the game, 3-2. However, they did pick up a single point, their first one since November 21.[2703] The team then rode the bus six hours to San Francisco from which they flew home.

The Salmon Kings had amassed a record of 3-10-1 on their season-opening road trip and would now play fourteen games at home. Even the most optimistic fan realized that the team was in a deep hole and needed to win most of their games at home to get back into the playoff race.

Former number-one goaltender David Brumby was waived after struggling in recent games and replaced by Jason Stone. Coach Maxwell's position was that the four veteran players should be the four best on the team, and Brumby was nowhere near being one of the best players. Maxwell hoped to fill the veteran space with a defenceman.[2704] That is precisely what he did a few days later, when Dale Purinton, a locked-out New York Ranger, decided to join the team to play for Maxwell, his old junior coach. In other player moves, the Salmon Kings waived defenceman Trent Frandvold, brought goaltender Kyle Stanton of Chemainus back to practice, and signed former Salsa player David Neale. Out with injuries were Hegberg, Josephson, and Williams.[2705] Victoria's Grant Sjerven was signed as an emergency backup goaltender before the opening game.[2706] An article in the *Victoria Times Colonist* explained the difference between ECHL hockey in Canada and the US. Here and in the northern American states, fans generally knew the rules of hockey and would attend to see the game. Down

South, where the weather is warm and there is not much hockey played, the teams have to have special promotions to draw fans. NASCAR drivers are a big draw, as are rides on a Zamboni. As Bear Mountain Arena was likely to be sold out for each game, there was no need locally to have exotic promotions.[2707]

Fans holding tickets for the inaugural game were invited to a family tailgate party starting at 11:00 a.m. Doors opened at noon for the game and fans received a collector puck when they entered. Seats were still available at game time.[2708] The *Victoria Times Colonist* featured the team in its Monitor section and printed photos of the current team members, along with short biographies. There was also a story about Coach Maxwell and an explanation of the ECHL and what kind of hockey could be expected.[2709]

Victoria Salmon Kings first home game puck.

The first ECHL game in Victoria—and the first professional hockey game since the 1967 Victoria Maple Leafs—was played before a packed house at Bear Mountain Arena on December 5, 2004. A hardy group of Condors fans travelled from Bakersfield to watch their team play, driving 1,200 miles for a road trip of their own. Hometown-favourite Ryan Wade scored the first home goal in Salmon Kings' history at 4:57 of the first period. He noted that the team fed off the energy in the arena. David Neale put the home team up, 2-0, but they could not hold the lead and regulation time finished with the score tied, 2-2. In overtime, the Condors' Brad Mehalko fired a puck past Jason Stone, and the game was over. Although the Salmon Kings had lost the game in overtime, they did nab a single point and were given a standing ovation as they left the ice. Professional hockey was back in Victoria, and the fans were delighted.[2710] [2711]

Two days later, the Salmon Kings played their second home game, with Bakersfield the opponent again. This time, the home team won, with veteran Jeff Williams notching two goals to lead his team to the victory. Other Salmon King marksmen were Ryan Finnerty and Ryan Watson, with two apiece. At 5:16 of the third period, Dale Purinton hit Condor Krzysztof Wieckowski hard, slamming his head on the boards. Wieckowski was motionless on the ice for twenty minutes before being taken off the ice on a stretcher. Purinton received a major penalty and a game misconduct. This was only the second loss of the season for the Condors and moved the Salmon Kings to 4-10-2. They had earned four of a possible six points in their last three games, all against Bakersfield.[2712]

In their third straight game against the Condors, the Salmon Kings won a second consecutive match. Defenceman Purinton led the offence, with a goal and two assists in the first period of a lively game before 2,123 local fans. Other Victoria goals came from Ryan Wade (with two), Nate Forster, Brad Dexter, Seth Leonard, Derek Campbell, and Jeff Williams in the 8-6 victory.[2713] The Condor player injured in the prior game, after a hit by Purinton, was diagnosed with a concussion and a strained neck. He would not be able to play for at least thirty days.[2714] ECHL headquarters staff studied the tape of the incident and suspended the Kings' defenceman for six games, as they determined that he had elbowed the Condor player in the head. He would be able to play again on December 31, at home against Long Beach.[2715]

Next to come to town were the Mississippi Sea Wolves. The Kings played a strong game. Seth Leonard scored the first goal at 3:30 of the opening period. The middle frame was a more physical affair, with several boarding calls and rough play. After the Sea Wolves tied the game, the Kings roared back when Brad Dexter found the back of the net and sealed the deal in the third period when they scored three times in just over three minutes. Voltera and Finnerty scored on breakaways, while Wade fought off a check before roofing the puck. The final score was 5-1, and it gave the Kings three consecutive wins for the first time in their history.[2716]

The next night, the teams played another entertaining game, but this time the visitors nipped the locals, 4-3, in overtime. Trailing 2-0 at the end of the second period, the Salmon Kings tied the game on goals by Ryan Finnerty and Blue Bennefield. However, the Sea Wolves beat goaltender Stone with twenty-four seconds left in regulation time and looked to have won the game. The Kings pulled the goaltender, and Wade tied the game, 3-3, with just eleven seconds left in the period. Unfortunately for the home team, there was no Cinderella ending, as the visitors ended the game at 1:36 of overtime. The winning streak was over.[2717] In the third game against Mississippi, the Kings ran into penalty trouble and lost the contest, 4-2. Frustrated by a non-call on a slash to his ankle in the first period, Mike Barrie racked up two retaliation minors and a ten-minute misconduct in the middle frame. He later added a double minor and a second ten-minute misconduct when goaded by the Sea Wolves. The loss of their leading scorer did nothing to help the Kings' chances of winning. With the loss of Nate Forster to a possible concussion, the team was reduced to twelve skaters and two goaltenders. It was too much to ask the severely depleted lineup to keep up with the physically strong and positionally sound visitors, and they fell, 4-2. Only Bennefield and Campbell found the back of the net for the Kings.[2718]

On the business side of hockey, there was some concern about the low attendance for games at Bear Mountain Arena. Other than the inaugural game that had sold out, there had been low numbers. The average number of attendees for the first six home games had only been 2,141. Some commentators wondered how the team could fill a new 7,300-seat arena downtown when they were not attracting crowds right now. Team management remained optimistic, saying that it took time to build momentum.[2719] It was evident that many fans were not willing to drive the distance to the temporary home and would be more likely to attend if the action were closer to home. There was certainly a buzz in town with fans talking about the team, but it was not translating into "bums in seats."

In league news, the Salmon Kings' defenceman Brad Dexter was named the ECHL "player of the week" for December 6-12, for his two goals and three assists to lead his team to a record of seven out of eight points in their homestand. A case of pucks was donated to Greater Victoria minor hockey by Glas Co, the puck supplier for the ECHL and the sponsor of the "player of the week" award.[2720]

For the next series against the San Diego Gulls, the Kings had only fourteen skaters due to injuries and suspensions. They did a fairly good job of holding their opponents in check, except for Brian Gomick, who scored twice for the visitors and led them to a 2-1 victory over Victoria. The Kings fired thirty-five shots at the Gulls' goaltender Eddy Fehri, but only Ryan Wade got one past him for his seventh goal of the season.[2721] Two days later, the home team played better hockey but made a few mistakes that proved costly. Three times the Kings took the lead only to have the Gulls tie it up. Jeff Williams opened the scoring on the power play, but the Gulls tied it with the Kings short-handed. Just before the end of the first period, Seth Leonard put Victoria ahead. After the Gulls again tied the score, Brad Dexter put them ahead, finishing off a passing play from Leonard. Then the roof caved in, as the Gulls notched two goals, producing the final score of 5-4. Ironically, the winning goal was actually deflected behind goaltender Jason Stone by Finnerty.[2722]

The final game in the series was sold out, and the Salmon Kings did not disappoint the huge crowd. They used their speed and outworked their opponents en route to a 3-2 victory. Seth Leonard was brilliant on the ice, notching the first goal after skating through the Gulls' defence. Victoria native Sean O'Connor tied the game for San Diego, to the delight of over a hundred fans there to support him, but Rob Voltera scored twice to give the home team a 3-1 lead, and the team held on to win, despite having to play short-handed for the last minute and a half of the game. The defence and goaltender Stone managed to keep the puck out of their net to preserve the "W."[2723] The team then enjoyed a holiday break with their next game not being played until January 1.

It might have been a new year, but the month of January 2005 was one that the Salmon Kings would like to forget. They were unable to win a game and could not even garner a single point, going winless throughout the month to create an eighteen-game losing streak. The year 2005 opened with a home game against the Long Beach Ice Dogs. After surrendering the first goal on a bounce off a Kings' player, the team managed to tie the contest early in the second frame, when Derek Campbell streaked down the ice and put the puck behind Chris Madden. Again, the Ice Dogs went ahead, but Rob Voltera pulled the Kings even again. Both goaltenders played very well in the final frame, with Stone surrendering the winning goal with only 2:43 left in regulation time. It was another one-goal loss and was very hard to take.[2724] The final game of the series was played at 8:00 p.m., so that fans could watch the gold-medal game at the World Junior Hockey Championship. In a game they desperately wanted to win, the Salmon Kings took too many penalties and ended up losing 5-1. Ryan Finnerty had the only counter for the home team.[2725]

The next three-game series was against the Alaska Aces. Defenceman Corey Smith was placed on the injury list, with a lower-body injury, and would be out indefinitely.[2726] In the first game of the series, the Aces won the game, 6-3. The game was tied at 3-3 when Rob Voltera fired a shot past Peter Aubrey. However, that tie was broken when Alaska scored just thirty-two seconds later and then added a shorthanded marker seconds before the end of the game. The Kings sent Jeff Williams to the Wheeling Nailers, and in return secured the rights to former Victoria Salsa forward Mark Kosick. They also signed former Vernon Viper Cole Byers.[2727] The merry-go-round that was an ECHL roster continued.

The second game was a total disaster for the Kings. They were never in the match and ended up dropping a 10-3 decision. After the game, Coach Maxwell apologized to the fans while acknowledging the support of the near-capacity crowd. Another former Salsa player, Craig Zubersky, signed with the club just before the game and took a few shifts in the game.[2728] However, it would not have mattered who was playing that day; the team had no cohesion and showed little spirit.

Just before the team left for a road trip to Alaska, they received the news that Brad Dexter had been named to the ECHL all-star team. The all-star game would be played in Reading, Pennsylvania, on January 26.[2729] In the first match in Alaska, the Kings came up with a much better effort and came very close to a victory. The Aces opened the scoring early in the first period, but Mike Barrie notched a power-play goal to tie the score. Four minutes into the third frame, the Aces found the back of the net, and from then on, the Kings' offence disappeared, and they could not score despite having the last four minutes of the game on the power play.[2730] Chris Minard of the Aces scored five goals in the next game, setting an Alaska record. The crowd of 4,112 cheered each shot as their team overcame the Kings, 8-2. Only Blue Bennefield and Rob Voltera notched goals for Victoria. Brad Dexter did not play, as he had separated his shoulder in the previous game. Also out of action were Jason Hegberg, Ryan Watson, Aaron Plumb, Corey Smith, and David Neale. From Alaska, the Kings made their way to California where they would play Long Beach.[2731]

30 - VICTORIA SALMON KINGS – NEW KIDS IN THE LEAGUE

With injuries mounting, the team signed former junior WHL Portland Winter Hawk defenceman Robert McGregor. They also waived backup goaltender Grant Sjerven and replaced him with Victoria-raised Kelly Shields.[2732]

It was raining in California, and in the Salmon Kings' game, it was raining goals. The Kings ran into penalty trouble again, and it cost them, as they gave up three power-play goals. Only Rob Voltera and Seth Leonard found the back of the net for Victoria in a 6-2 loss. In personnel matters, Brad Dexter was moved from the seven-day disabled list to the thirty-day list, as his shoulder was not responding to treatment. Adam Campbell was added to the defensive corps. He had played the last three seasons for the University of Prince Edward Island, where he amassed 246 career penalty minutes. He would fit right in with the rest of the penalty-prone team. In a not-so-funny moment, the Ice Dogs' radio broadcast online went down during the game and fans were told to follow the Kings' broadcast. Whoops, they did not have one due to cost-cutting by management.[2733]

A trip to Las Vegas did nothing to stop the losing streak, as the Kings fell, 3-2, in overtime to the Wranglers. At least they garnered a single point—their first since December 11. Leading 2-0 going into the third period on goals by Forster and Finnerty, they surrendered a goal with just thirty-one seconds remaining in regulation time to allow the Wranglers to tie the score, 2-2. Newcomer Russian Alexei Glukhov played his first game and skated well. In overtime, the Kings found another way to lose, giving up a shorthanded goal after a giveaway while on the power play.[2734] Then it was back to Long Beach, where nothing changed except the margin of loss. This time, the Ice Dogs outscored the lowly Kings, 4-1, with Mike Josephson counting the lone Victoria goal. The losing streak was now at ten, and some fans wondered if the team would ever win a game again.[2735] Two days later, the Kings lost again, this time by a 4-2 score. Having tied the score 2-2 on goals by Rob McGregor and Mike Josephson, the team gave up a goal with only twenty-two seconds left in the middle frame and then at thirty-eight seconds of the third period. The Kings could not mount a comeback and recorded their eleventh consecutive loss.[2736]

Being back in the home confines of Bear Mountain Arena did not help the Salmon Kings, as the Long Beach Ice Dogs won another game by a score of 5-2. Although the Kings came out hard at the start of the game, they were stymied time and time again by goaltender Chris Madden, who had been the Memorial Cup MVP in 1998. Only Blue Bennefield and Rob Voltera found the back of the net. The Kings also ran into penalty trouble (again), which killed any momentum they might have had from their good play in the first period. Kelly Shields played well in the net for Victoria but could not hold back the onslaught from the Ice Dogs.[2737] The next night, the Ice Dogs ran their record against Victoria to 9-0, with a 3-1 victory. Using the Kings' aggressive play to their advantage, Long Beach drew several penalties and made the most of them, except for one penalty when newly-signed Princeton-grad Chris Corrinet intercepted a pass and streaked down the ice to notch a short-handed goal. Unfortunately, that was the only offence they could record, and the season of futility continued with their thirteenth consecutive loss.[2738]

Despite the string of losses, Victoria fans were not yet ready to give up on their team. Many did not expect the team to do well in its first year and were willing to give them a season's grace. Management had not been doing much marketing, as the smaller arena did not warrant it, but pledged to ramp it up the next season when they would be moving to the larger Save-On-Foods Memorial Arena, which would seat 7,000 for hockey.[2739]

A three-game set against the Alaska Aces was likely the last thing the Kings wanted to play, mired as they were in a long losing streak, but they showed up and played hard. A good crowd of 2,597 watched their home team take too many penalties and drop a 5-1 decision to the Aces. Alaska was a fast, slick-skating team and the locals could not keep up. Chris Corrinet was again the only Salmon King to register a goal. Before the game, the team announced that veteran Mike Barrie had retired due to a hand injury. Mark Smith, a locked-out San Jose Shark, was added to the roster and became the latest member of the revolving door of players.[2740] The misery continued for the Salmon Kings in the second game against the Aces, when they were shut out, 3-0, in front of a sold-out crowd. Coach Maxwell attributed the lack of success to the inept power play and the numerous off-sides on rushes. He said the players were working but were not being rewarded.[2741]

In the final game of the set, the Salmon Kings tied the ECHL winless streak at sixteen when they fell 5-2, in an afternoon contest at Bear Mountain Arena. They had a strong first period, in which Voltera and Forster scored to tie the game, 2-2, but they could not put any more pucks past Ace's goaltender Lance Mayes of Brentwood Bay. Locked-out Alaska-star Scott Gomez said that he had to admire the Kings' players for sticking to the plan and playing hard, even when they were not rewarded. He praised the fan support and said that the breaks would come at sometime.[2742]

The ECHL all-star game was played in Redding, Pennsylvania, and the sole Salmon King present was Nate Forster, who was selected as a replacement for the injured Brad Dexter. Although a Victoria native, he had been surfing in Australia and contemplating his future when a call came to play for his hometown team. He readily agreed, and now his hockey career was back on track. The coverage of the all-star game noted that "a Victoria Salmon King actually won an ECHL hockey game on Wednesday." Nate Forster was part of the National Conference team that defeated the American Conference, 6-2. In news from the league meetings held at the same time, ECHL commissioner Brian McKenna said that Stockton, California would be added as a new Western-division franchise for next year, and he envisioned the pro hockey ladder moving to a "30-30-30 system," whereby thirty teams in the ECHL would feed into thirty AHL teams, which would feed into thirty NHL teams.[2743]

After the break, the Victoria played two games at Las Vegas. Defencemen Ryan Esselmont and Dennis Mullen were added to shore up the injury-riddled defensive corps, while Rob McGregor was waived, although he continued to skate with the team in practice. He was a victim of "the numbers game."[2744] In the first match, the Kings came agonizingly close to a victory, losing, 2-1, in a shootout. In doing so, they set a record for the longest losing streak in ECHL history, not exactly the record they expected to have this season. After the Wranglers took a 1-0 lead, newcomer Mullen tied the game, but neither team could score in regulation time or overtime. In the shootout, Las Vegas goaltender Marc Magliarditi stopped all five Victoria shooters, while his teammate Dustin Johner beat Jason Stone to win the game.[2745] The Salmon Kings closed out January 2005 with a second game in Las Vegas. Once again, the Kings took too many penalties and ended up on the wrong side of a 4-1 score. Other teams in the league had not responded to the aggressive play of the Kings. Instead, they backed off and drew penalties. This tactic frustrated the Victoria players even more, and they took even more penalties. Ryan Watson had the only score for the Kings, who returned home, hopeful of a victory sometime in 2005.[2746]

In what was rapidly becoming a comedy of errors, the Salmon Kings reached a new low in a game versus the Fresno Falcons at Bear Mountain Arena. Dale Purinton, who had scored the opening goal for Victoria, was ejected in the second period for "instigating, refusing to stop fighting, and pulling hair in a battle with Clint Cabana." He also received a fighting major and a game misconduct, racking up forty-two minutes in penalties in one fell swoop. On the resulting seven-minute power play, the Falcons scored only once, but that made the score 5-2 and put the game out of reach for the powerless Kings. On the bright side, Alexei Glukhov scored his first goal in NorthAmerica since joining Victoria, and

Ryan Wade added the third goal. With the score 3-2, Jason Stone was pulled as the goaltender and replaced by Kelly Shields, but that did not make much difference, as he gave up four goals. The team was just not getting the level of goaltending that was necessary to win, but there were rumours that the situation would soon change.[2747]

Dan Blackburn with two blockers.

Locked-out New York Rangers goaltender Dan Blackburn made his debut as a Salmon King against the Fresno Falcons. He suffered from a chronic muscular and nerve injury that left him unable to use a catching glove on his left hand. He had to come down with the arm in a "strange swooping motion." The NHL gave permission for Blackburn to use an unusual contraption that "helps support movement in his left arm. His catching glove was essentially a converted blocker with a pocket built in underneath to snag the puck."[2748] He played his first game for the Kings against Fresno, but the team found yet another way to lose a game. Mark Smith could not play, as he had sustained a hand injury, and Purinton did not play, as he was suspended indefinitely pending league review of the prior game. Also, Blue Bennefield had been waived. With the suspension and seven players on the disabled list, the Kings could only ice thirteen skaters, and when Craig Zubersky was knocked out after being hit into the boards in the second period, they were down to twelve. The referee's calls were not popular with the team or the fans, as Dennis Mullen was assessed a game misconduct for disputing a call and the locals littered the ice with plastic bottles in protest. The Kings fell behind 2-0 before Ryan Wade converted a two-on-one shorthanded pass for their first goal. When Adam Campbell fired a shot from a strange angle, and it went in, the game was tied. The Falcons got the winning goal as time expired. That was the sort of the luck that Victoria had been having—all bad. The losing streak was now at twenty, and that was a new league record.[2749]

Finally, the stars aligned, and the Salmon Kings recorded a victory on February 5, 2005. However, it was not easy. Trailing, 1-0, at the end of the first period, the Kings scored two quick goals, by Glukhov and Smith, to take the lead. When Ryan Wade scored on a power-play, and the score went to 3-1, the local fans began to wonder if this would be the night. After the Falcons closed the gap to 3-2, Watson found the net on the power play to restore the two-goal lead. That, however, was short-lived, as the Falcons scored twice in eighteen seconds to tie the score at 4-4. After overtime solved nothing, it remained for the shootout produce a winner. Ryan Watson gave his team a 3-2 advantage in the shootout, and that was enough for a victory.[2750]

Having ended the ignominious streak of twenty consecutive losses, the Salmon Kings looked to get a win streak going against the Idaho Steelheads. Things started well when Ryan Wade fired home a shot to give the Kings a 1-0 lead, but that was the end of their scoring. The Steelheads tied it in the second. Minutes later, Blackburn stopped Dan Vandermeer on a penalty shot but could not stop Riley Riddell, who broke down the left side and fired a hot shot. Vandermeer got his revenge later in the frame when he scored the 3-1 goal, ending the scoring.[2751] The walking wounded of the Salmon Kings gave it a good effort but fell just a bit short.

The second game of the set started poorly, with the Steelheads up 2-0 in the second period. Derek Campbell narrowed the lead to 2-1 with a shot through the pads of the Idaho goaltender, and the team pressed for the equalizer, outshooting Idaho, 15-7, in the final frame, but could not get the goal they desperately needed. Coach Maxwell was furious with his charges during and after the game, saying "Maybe we're just not damn good enough to play at this level." The Kings then had six days off to prepare for the next set of games.[2752] It was a good bet that the practices were pretty tough.

During the break between games, team management was busy. They signed forward Scott Turner from the Peoria Rivermen for financial considerations. He had just recovered from hernia surgery, so hopefully would be able to contribute offensively. The team also announced that the days and time for the final homestand of the season against the Idaho Steelheads had been changed. The March 9 game was unchanged with a 7:00 p.m. start. The March 11 game had been moved to March 10 with a 7:00 p.m. start. The final home game was on March 12, with a starting time of 1:00 p.m. instead of 7:00 p.m.[2753] From the ECHL headquarters came news that the commissioner wanted a natural geographic rivalry for the Salmon Kings. Among the suggestions were Chilliwack and Nanaimo in BC, and sites in Washington and Oregon.[2754] In reality, none of these suggested locations acquired ECHL teams, and, for most of the Salmon Kings' existence, their main rival was the Alaska Aces.[2755]

Play resumed on February 15, when the Fresno Falcons came to town and history repeated itself. The game was similar to the one on February 3, also against Fresno. The Falcons were the only team the Salmon Kings had beaten in 2005, and they did it twice, both times in the shootout. The first goal was an all-Ryan affair: scored by Ryan Watson on assists from Wade and Finnerty. The Falcons tied the score less than a minute later, and the teams went into the first intermission tied 1-1. There was no further scoring in regulation time or overtime, so it was time for the shootout. Despite his obvious handicap, Dan Blackburn allowed only one shooter to score on him, while his team scored twice to secure the victory.[2756]

In the game the next day, the game featured a bench-clearing brawl at 1:20 of the third period. It started with Dale Purinton, as might be expected, when he tangled with the Falcon's tough guy Glenn Olson. By the time the affair was over, even the goaltenders had gotten into the action. Referee Max Battimo sent both teams to their dressing rooms, so he could get the penalties straightened out. When play resumed, the Kings were shorthanded, as Purinton was determined to have been the aggressor. It had been a pretty rough game in the second period, but that was tame compared to the third. Penalties were handed out for the brawl. Olson (Fresno) got a major for fighting, with a double-game misconduct. Majors for fighting, with game misconducts went to Fresno players Brisson, O'Dette, Lorentz, and Sheptak, and to Victoria players Forster, Gattolliat, and Josephson. Mullen from Victoria received roughing and fighting majors, with a game misconduct. Victoria's Purinton got majors for instigating and fighting with a game misconduct match penalty. Jaeger (Fresno) and Stone (Victoria) were penalized for leaving the crease and received majors for fighting, and game misconducts, and finally, Victoria's Finnerty received a misconduct.[2757] It was reported that the Salmon Kings had just four players left on the bench, while Fresno had six. In the hockey part of the game, the Falcons easily defeated the Kings 4-0.[2758]

The league came down hard on the brawlers. The ECHL prided itself on being family entertainment and deemed this type of play as unacceptable. Rod Pasma, the league's vice-president of hockey operations, including league discipline, said it was an isolated incident, but behaviour of this type would not be tolerated.[2759] Purinton received a seven-game suspension, Jim Gattollia and Dennis Mullen would miss six games, and Adam Campbell would be out for two. The Kings' coach Bryan Maxwell was suspended for three games for failing to control his bench and allowing the players over the boards first. As all four players were defencemen, the league let Campbell serve his sentence later. For Fresno, Joe Pereira would miss five games, Glenn Olson would miss four, Dustin VanBallegooie would miss two, and Matt O'Dette would miss one. Stick-swinging Coach Greg Spenreth also received an undisclosed penalty. Both teams were fined an undisclosed amount of cash.[2760]

The Kings then went on the road for a short two-game series. To add insult to injury, they were held up at the Peach Arch border crossing and missed their flight to Boise out of Sea-Tac in Seattle. They were forced to continue the trip via bus and arrived at the arena exhausted and anything but ready to play. There was so much news about the suspensions that, other than the score of the next game (12-3 for the Idaho Steelheads), there was no box score reported in local media.[2761] Perhaps it was best not to record the details of the worst defeat of the season. The next night, the Kings played better hockey but were short of players; the only defenders they had were Forster and Campbell. The Steelheads outshot the Salmon Kings, 29-13, and allowed only two goals, by Ryan Watson and Seth Leonard.[2762]

Before the next home game, defenceman Dennis Mullen was released by the Kings.[2763] In the game against San Diego, the Kings came up with a stellar effort. With only twelve skaters and three forwards (David Neale, Alexei Glukhov, and Chris Corrinet) playing defence, they dug deep and defeated the Gulls, 5-2. The offence was led by defensive forward Jason Hegberg, who recorded the team's first hat trick. Seth Leonard and Nate Forster had the other goals for the home team.[2764] Alas, the Kings could not carry the momentum into the next game and fell 4-1. By the end of the game, they were down to ten skaters, even though they had added Greg Keith from Chilliwack. Corey Smith and Nate Forster had been lost to injury in the second period. Corrinet had the only counter for the home side.[2765]

Brad Dexter returned from a separated shoulder, Ryan Esselmont from the flu, and Adam Campbell from suspension in time for the start of a three-game series against Las Vegas.[2766] The first game was a well-played affair that ended in dramatic fashion. The Wranglers opened the scoring at 1:28 of the first period, but Derek Campbell tied the score, and recently-signed Mike Ikeda briefly gave the Kings the lead. After Las Vegas tied the score, Jason Hegberg put the Salmon Kings ahead midway through the middle frame. However, the home team could not hold the lead, surrendering a goal at 6:24 of the final period and allowing the winning goal with only twenty-eight seconds on the clock. It was a heartbreaking defeat for a gallant team.[2767] The next game was another heartbreaker. Watson put the Kings on the board after just thirty-seven seconds of play, but the Wranglers scored twice to take a 2-1 lead into the second period. Early in that period, Las Vegas went ahead, 3-1, but Glukhov narrowed the lead to 3-2, only to have the Wranglers restore the two-goal lead with less than one second in the frame. Sean Turner got the score to 4-3, but the Kings were unable to get the equalizer. After the game, forward Mike Josephson said, "We got caught glancing at the clock (at the end of the second period) and that's the one that cost us."[2768] In the final game of the set, the Salmon Kings came up with a mediocre effort. This time, it was the poor penalty killing that gave the game away, as Las Vegas scored three power-play goals en route to a 5-2 victory. Scott Turner and Jim Gattolliat were the only Victoria marksmen.[2769]

The schedule was anything but friendly to the Salmon Kings. They had only five home games left before they left on a twelve-game road trip to finish the season. When the season began, it was thought that the Kings would be in the new arena by this point and would have to leave to allow the Men's World's Curling Championship to use the ice. Of course, the completion of the arena was delayed so long that the entire Kings' season was played at

Bear Mountain Arena. This was the team that just couldn't get a break.

When Dale Purinton finished his ECHL suspension, he would not be playing for the Salmon Kings, as they had suspended him for the balance of the season. Coach Maxwell said that he had not seen Purinton during his suspension and had no idea where he was. New York Rangers GM Glen Sather, who was in Victoria to watch Blackburn play, said that Purinton's heart was in the right place, but he sometimes got carried away in protecting his teammates.[2770] Among other player news was the decision of Dan Blackburn to leave the team in the hopes that he could get eighteen games in the AHL or NHL. He needed to restrict his play to collect on a reported $6-million insurance payout if he were unable to return to play in the NHL. To add to the team's problems, backup-goaltender Jason Stone came down with mononucleosis and Kelly Shields, the third goalie, had given up waiting to be used in the net and had signed with a team in Florida. Five new players suited up for the Kings: goaltender Robert Muntain, who played the first two periods; goaltender Jaime McCaig, who finished the game in net; Casey Bartzen; Geoff Rollins; and Kurtis Dulle. Greg Keith was waived by the team in what could only be considered a surprise move. On the injury list were Stone, Nate Forster, Aaron Plumb, Rob Voltera, Corey Smith, Craig Zubersky, and Mark Smith. The game was a disaster. The Kings were never really in it and lost, 7-3, in front of 2,422 fans at Bear Mountain Arena. Ryan Wade scored his thirteenth of the season, while Turner and Neale added singles.[2771] The second game of the set started well, as the Kings took a 1-0 lead into the third period. But as had happened too much that season, they could not hold the lead and gave up four unanswered goals to lose the match, 4-1.[2772]

The final home series of the season was played against the Idaho Steelheads. In the opening game, Victoria led, 2-1, after the first period, on goals from Hegberg and Corrinet. However, the Kings fell into their usual bad habits and let the visitors tie the score. Within moments, Idaho went ahead with a lead they never relinquished. Scott Turner's two goals in the final period made the score close, but once again, the home team failed to get the equalizer. It was the seventh loss in a row since February 16 and the forty-third defeat of the season.[2773] In the middle game of the set, the Salmon Kings pulled out a rare overtime win, 3-2, over Idaho. Goaltender Robert Muntain was the difference in the game, stopping several Steelhead shooters in spectacular fashion. Corrinet scored the opening goal for the Kings, but Idaho tied the game in the third period. Glukhov gave the home side the lead with a highlight-reel goal only to have the visitors knot the score with just twelve seconds left in regulation time. Much to the delight of the Bear Mountain crowd, Ryan Wade whipped home the winning goal after 1:36 of overtime to send the crowd home happy.[2774] In the final home game of the 2004-2005 season, the Salmon Kings were blown out by the Steelheads, 8-2. At the end of the game, the capacity crowd of 2,605 gave the team a standing ovation in thanks for their efforts over the season. In return, the Kings gave fans the jerseys off their back after having names drawn. Team members commented on how the fans had been supportive throughout the season, despite the lack of success.[2775]

Then the team left on the season-ending twelve-game road trip. Gattolliat was released by the team, and Jason Stone was waived, while Scott Borders and Brandon Elliott were added to the roster. Although the playoffs were out of reach and had been for some time, the players were playing for contracts for the next season—and nobody was guaranteed a spot.[2776]

The first game was played against the Florida Everblades. The Kings came out very flat and dropped a 7-1 decision. Ironically, the arena was sold out, likely as teams felt fairly confident of a victory when Victoria came to town.[2777] In the next encounter against the second-worst team in the ECHL, the Texas Wildcatters, the Kings emerged with a rare road victory. Leading the way was the line of Smith, Wade, and Turner, who accounted for two goals, with others coming from Leonard, Finnerty, and Borders in the 5-3 hard-fought victory.[2778] In Lafayette, Louisiana, the Kings won a second consecutive road game: this time 7-5 over the IceGators. Ryan Smith scored just thirty-six seconds into the game, and the rout was on. Ryan Wade had a hat trick, and Scott Turner had a six-point night, including a single goal, to lead the offence. Other goals were scored by Ryan Finnerty and Adam Campbell in one of the better games of the season.[2779] On the next day, the Gators got revenge with a close 2-1 victory. The Kings played hard and dominated the play, outshooting their opponents, 19-1, in one period, but could only manage a single goal by Turner.[2780]

In Pensacola, the Kings took an early lead at 2:30 of the second period on a goal by Mark Smith, but collapsed in the final frame and surrendered three goals in the last seventeen minutes of the game to lose the match 3-1.[2781] The Mississippi Sea Wolves won the next game in Biloxi. After the Kings fell behind 2-0, in the first period, Mark Smith got them within one on a power play. In the final frame, the Kings outshot their opponents but could not find the equalizer and fell, 2-1.[2782] The Kings then travelled back to Florida to play two more games against the Everblades. In the first encounter, the Kings fell behind, 3-1, in the second period but stormed back with three goals to win the game, 4-3. Finnerty, Josephson, Corrinet, and Dulle scored for Victoria, while Rob Muntain made thirty saves in net to even his record at 2-2.[2783] Florida got their revenge in the next game, when they upended the Kings, 5-2. Corrinet and Smith found the net for Victoria. Missing from the game were Scott Turner (shoulder), Alexei Glukhov (shoulder), Derek Campbell (wrist), Brandon Elliott (flu), and Craig Strain (ankle), as the injury bug continued to deplete the team.[2784]

With the road trip half over, Bryan Maxwell took time to reflect on the season. He had envisioned a team made up of Western Hockey League graduates, but that had not been possible as injuries laid waste to his lineup. He had no idea that he would end up with four foreign players. Corrinet and Turner were Americans, Glukhov was a Russian, and newcomer Tomas Micka was a Czech.[2785]

The road trip then made its way to Las Vegas. The travel-weary Salmon Kings fell, 4-1, to the Wranglers in an uninspired contest on April Fool's Day. Smith was the only Victoria player to find the back of the Vegas net.[2786] In Long Beach, the Kings' listless play continued, and they lost the game, 5-1, to the Ice Dogs. Captain Brad Dexter had the lone counter for Victoria in a losing cause.[2787] The Salmon Kings final loss of the season was recorded in San Diego, as the Gulls narrowly edged them, 3-2. Corrinet and Campbell scored for the Kings.[2788] In the last game of the season, the Kings dug deep and won an overtime contest against the Gulls. Newcomer Jan Sochor recorded a hat trick, while Ryan Wade, whom Maxwell called the best Salmon King that season, had a pair. Kurtis Dulle scored the overtime winner to give the team a good ending to a disastrous season. Their record of 15-52-5 was the worst record of the eighty-seven teams playing pro hockey that year. Coach Maxwell said the priority for next season was to secure an affiliation with an NHL team—the Vancouver Canucks being the logical choice as their ECHL affiliation with Columbus was soon coming to an end. Talks would take place after the season was over.[2789]

In a year-end assessment of the team, the consensus was that Brad Dexter and Ryan Wade should definitely stay as two of the eight players that each ECHL team was able to protect at the end of the season. Among others who should be protected were Nate Forster, Chris Corrinet, and Kurtis Dulle. Some players could be named as the last three on the list.[2790] Given how many players had suited up for the Salmon Kings over the season, it would be necessary to assess the skills of those who were still eligible to play. As it was likely that the NHL would return to action in the next season, any locked-out players would return to their rights-holders and would not play in the ECHL. It would be an interesting off-season.

Coach Bryan Maxwell was given a vote of support from RG Properties and was told that he would be back the next season. Dave Dakers, executive director of RG, said they were "happy with the effort. Neither Bryan nor the players ever quit despite the trying conditions." The team would likely add a full-time assistant coach and office staff to deal with the day-to-day details of running a hockey team.[2791]

When you look back at the season as a whole, the Salmon Kings did not really have much of a chance of success. They had no home arena, so had to find an alternative site for a training camp. They had to start the season on the road because the new arena was supposed to open in December. When their new home was not ready on time, they had to play at a much smaller venue out of town. Finally, they had another "road trip from hell" at the end of the season. When you add in the unusual amount of injuries, the suspensions for undisciplined play, and the travel issues, you have a blueprint for failure. To their credit, the players who were able to skate never gave up, and neither did the home fans. The honeymoon year of the new franchise was over; it would remain to be seen what would happen in the next season when they were able to play in their new home at the Save-On-Foods Memorial Arena.

31 - THE SALMON KINGS PLAY IN THEIR NEW HOME

The Salmon Kings began to prepare for what they thought would be a better season. They signed a pair of players who had travelled a lot in their careers. Steve Roberts, born in Connecticut, played in prep school and then with ECHL with the Atlantic City Boardwalk Bullies. He had attended NHL training camps (the Colorado Avalanche in 2002 and the Detroit Red Wings in 2003) and was trying to take that last huge step. Victoria-born Steve Roberts had not played at home since he was fifteen, and was thrilled to be back in Victoria. He had played for eight pro teams in North America and four in England. Coach Maxwell had wanted to sign him the previous season, but that had not worked out.[2792]

On the coaching side, the Kings brought in former junior Victoria Cougar Mark Morrison (nicknamed "Mighty Mouse") who had just hung up his skates the previous spring at age forty-two. He owned every Victoria Cougar junior scoring record and had also won three regular-season and two playoff titles in the British National League as a player/coach. He would be perhaps the best mentor the young Salmon Kings could have. The only reason he did not play much in the NHL was his height: five feet, eight inches. Also added to the staff was Dan Belisle Jr., who became the new director of hockey operations.[2793] His father had played for the old Victoria Maple Leafs, linking the Salmon Kings to an earlier era.

In a strange irony, the first hockey game played at the Save-On-Foods Memorial Centre was not a professional game, but a junior contest between the Victoria Salsa and the Alberni Valley Bulldogs. The Mann Cup lacrosse playoffs had precedence at Bear Mountain Arena, so the hockey game had to be moved downtown. Let the record show that the first hockey goal scored in the new arena came from the stick of Bulldog forward Andrew Estey of Fredericton, NB, at 13:19 of the first period of the game on September 10, 2005,[2794] and that the first victory went to a Victoria team. The arena was not yet finished, with the removable seats still not installed in the north end and the restaurant incomplete, but at least there was ice and hockey could be played.[2795]

Back in Salmon Kings news, popular forward Ryan Finnerty was traded to the Texas Wildcatters in return for two defencemen: Aaron MacInnis, nephew of the NHL's super shooter Al MacInnis, and former Fresno Falcon Simon Mangos.[2796]

The Mississippi Sea Wolves asked for a one-year suspension of their franchise after Hurricane Katrina hit Biloxi hard, demolishing most of the city, including their arena. They vowed to rebuild and return to play in the 2006-2007 season. Kings' director of hockey operations Dan Belisle was a resident of New Orleans, also hit by Katrina, but he was fortunate to have moved to Victoria to assume his new duties just three weeks before the devastation.[2797]

The next signing was Pete Gardiner, a 6'2", 225-pound forward who had been in Germany the prior season. He had size and could score, and so was an asset to any club. Maxwell also said he was interested in talking with some of the now-available Sea Wolves players but could not sign anyone until after the ECHL's governors' meeting on September 22.[2798] One of the four veteran spots became available when former Salsa Corey Smith was forced to retire. An ankle broken twice last season was not mending properly, so he would be unable to play hockey at all. He was expected to return to New Zealand to work in the family's business.[2799]

On the business side of hockey, the Salmon Kings were unable to find a radio station to broadcast their games. The only AM station in Victoria, C-FAX, was already carrying the Vancouver Canucks and could not cover two different leagues at the same time. Fans were able to follow most games by logging into the opponent's website, but they did not get local news on those broadcasts. The Salmon Kings were one of the few ECHL teams without an NHL affiliation or a play-by-play broadcast.[2800]

The next player the Kings signed was Dustan Heintz, whom they acquired from the Johnstown Chiefs for an undisclosed amount of cash. They also inked Derek Allan, who had played the last season in Germany. Scott Turner had signed with the Kalamazoo Wings of the United Hockey League and would not be returning to the Salmon Kings.[2801]

In ECHL business, the leagues adopted rule changes that had recently been made at the NHL level. These included allowing for two-line passes, the shrinking of goaltending equipment, and restriction of the area in which goalies could handle the puck behind the net. They also approved the one-season suspension of the Mississippi Sea Wolves franchise that had been hit so hard by Hurricane Katrina.[2802]

For hockey fans who could not commit to a full season of games, the Salmon Kings offered a selection of alternatives: a half season, super Saturdays, and Crazy 8s (eight games). These packages would only be available on October 1 and 2, 2005, from 10:00 a.m. to 4:00 p.m.[2803]

Coach Brian Maxwell at training camp, October 2005. Photo courtesy Victoria Salmon Kings.

Training camp 2005 at the Save-On-Foods Memorial Arena. Photo courtesy Victoria Salmon Kings.

Training camp opened on October 7, 2005, with thirty-one players in attendance, twenty-one of whom had signed contracts. No position was considered secure, and many jobs would have more than one player vying for it. The camp was divided into two groups who would work out separately in the morning and then scrimmage against each other in the evening. All sessions were open to the public with a full schedule published in the *Victoria Times Colonist*.[2804]

31 - THE SALMON KINGS PLAY IN THEIR NEW HOME

Steve Lingren, who was born in Lake Cowichan and played for the last Victoria Cougars junior team in 1993-94, came back home to play for the Salmon Kings as a veteran. The space opened up when Corey Smith suffered a career-ending injury. The Salmon Kings now had three veterans on defence, a position where players usually take longer to develop and fine-tune professional skills.[2805]

Mother Nature reared her ugly head again when Hurricane Rita tore through Beaumont, Texas, severely damaging Ford Arena, where the Wildcatters played. There would now be two teams suspending operations for the upcoming season because of hurricane damage. The Kings had played both teams the last season, so would not do so this season. Other teams would not be so lucky, as the schedules they had already printed would now have to be changed.[2806]

As training camp went on, returning players commented that this year's atmosphere was entirely different from the previous year's one. Most evident was the strength on defence, with six to eight good candidates, so that no player would have to log an excessive number of minutes.[2807] The team would hopefully be able to put behind them the horror of the 2004-2005 season.

By mid-October, the Kings had made the first cuts. Forwards Jason Beauchamp and Ryan Reeves and defencemen Ryan Bremner left the camp.[2808] Although the Florida Everblades had offered to pay two-thirds of the cost to bring the Kings to play in Naples, Florida, team management felt that a cross-country trip just before the season-opening road trip would tire the players unnecessarily. Instead, the team would play two exhibition games against the Senior A Powell River Regals.[2809] The only thing that went wrong in the weekend series was that Adam Taylor of Courtenay lost a skate and had to play on borrowed equipment. The Kings swept the games by scores of 7-2 and 6-2. The best players for Victoria were Lingren and Mangos on defence and forward Taylor. On the downside, veteran pro Steve Roberts suffered a shoulder injury and was expected to be out of action for a week.[2810]

With preseason over, the Kings set their roster. They had seventeen skaters with B. J. Boxma and Rob Muntain in goal. Roberts and Seth Leonard were placed on the seven-day injury-reserve list. Seven Vancouver Island products made the cut: Ryan Wade, K. C. Timmons, Nate Forster, Derek Campbell, Mike Josephson, and the injured Roberts[2811] The team featured six returnees and fifteen newcomers, including four rookies.[2812]

The second season started in Fresno, the home of the Falcons, the ECHL farm team of the San Jose Sharks. In sharp contrast to last year's first game, the result this year was much closer, with the final score, 2-1 for the Falcons. Goaltender Boxma faced forty shots and allowed only two goals to Derek Krestanovich and Fraser Claire. Derek Allan notched the only score for Victoria. The Kings certainly had their chances, but they went 0-7 on the power play, including three chances with a two-man advantage.[2813] Game two was played in Bakersfield, and the Kings again failed to win, falling 5-3 to the Condors. Rob Muntain started in goal but was pulled after he surrendered three goals in three minutes; Boxma came in and played the rest of the game. Mangos, Lingren, and K. C. Timmons scored a goal each to tie the score in the second period, but the Condors notched a pair of goals in the final frame to win the game. The team then returned home to prepare for another six-game road trip.[2814]

During the break between games, the *Victoria Times Colonist* printed a series of pages that educated citizens about the business side of hockey. The Salmon Kings had an operating budget of $2.2 million per season. They had lost between $1 million and $2 million the previous year when they had to play in the much smaller Bear Mountain Arena. Team management hoped that fans would flock to the new downtown arena to support their hockey team. They already had around 3,000 season-ticket holders, and there was growing interest in the team. The most pressing expenses for hockey operations were salaries, travel, and insurance. Victoria was second only to Alaska in distance travelled during a season.[2815] The ECHL had positioned itself as the feeder into the AHL, which feeds into the NHL. At this point, 264 former ECHL players had made it to the NHL, with more moving up the hockey ladder each year. This season, there were twenty-five teams in the league, with Victoria the only Canadian entry, with the American entries located in fourteen different states.[2816]

The Salmon Kings played their next road game at the E Center in Salt Lake City, Utah. This site had particular significance for Canadians, as it was where the men's and women's hockey teams won Olympic gold in 2002. The Kings were hoping some of the good luck would rub off on them, as they played their third road game of the season.[2817]

Regardless of whether it was good luck or good hockey skills, the Kings won their first game of the young season when they upended the Utah Grizzlies, 8-5. Victoria took an early 4-0 lead but could not prevent their opponents from tying the score. Wade put the Kings ahead, 5-4, but again, the Grizzlies knotted the score. Adam Taylor found the net at 7:15 of the final frame (one of three goals by the Kings in that final period) for his third point of the game, and Victoria won the game, 8-5. Lingren had a goal and two assists, while Mike Wirll, Peter Gardiner, Dustan Heintz, and Lanny Gare added single goals. Lance Mayes dressed as back-up to goaltender Rob Muntain, as Boxma was resting a minor leg strain.[2818] The next night, the Kings ran into penalty trouble and ended up losing the game to Utah by a score of 6-3. Falling behind, 2-0, in the first period, the Kings scored three times (Lingren, Wirll, and Timmons) in the middle frame, but could not hold the lead when they could not stay out of the penalty box and allowed Utah to score four times in the final frame to secure the victory. Victoria then flew across the country to play games in the Eastern United States.[2819]

The first Eastern game was played in Trenton, the home of the Titans, who had won the 2004-2005 ECHL Championship. Despite the intimidation and the long odds, the Kings rode the outstanding goaltending of Muntain to a 2-1 victory. He made twenty-eight saves and stopped many excellent chances by the Titans. New Salmon King Mike Henderson, who barely made it to the start of the game, scored at 4:24 of the second period and MacInnis added a second eight minutes later. The Titans managed a single goal in the final frame, but that was the only shot that got past Muntain.[2820] After an eight-hour bus ride to Dayton, Ohio, the Kings got ready for another road game. It was a close match on "Faith and Family Night," with Victoria unlucky not to tie the game and at least send it to extra time. Seth Leonard scored on a power play in the second period, but that was all the team could manage despite pressuring the Bombers. Coach Maxwell criticized his forwards after the 2-1 loss, saying that some did not get the job done.[2821]

The next game was in Toledo, Ohio. The Salmon Kings again ran into penalty trouble in a 5-3 loss in the seventh game of their season-opening road trip. The Storm scored three times in the final period to overcome the 3-2 lead the Salmon Kings had held after the second frame. The highlights of the evening for Victoria were the two power-play goals by Lingren.[2822] In the final game of the road trip, the Kings did not play well, likely suffering the effects of gruelling travel. Driving through the night and encountering a thunderstorm with rain that knocked out power in the area, they did not arrive at their hotel until 4:00 a.m. Once again, the Kings took a 2-0 lead but could not hold off the Wheeling Nailers and lost the game, 7-3. Wade and Drummond each had a goal and an assist, while Henderson added a goal.[2823] There was a familiar surname behind the bench for the Nailers. Glenn Patrick, son of Lynn Patrick and grandson of Lester, was the coach. He hadn't been to Victoria for twenty-five years but knew about his family's connection with sports in our city.[2824] The team would be glad to be back in Victoria for their much-anticipated home opener in the Save-On-Foods Memorial Centre.

31 - THE SALMON KINGS PLAY IN THEIR NEW HOME

Hampered by injuries to three key forwards (Lanny Gare, Steve Roberts, and Jan Sochor), the team hoped that the home crowd would give them a lift.[2825] Much as Victoria had done the previous year, the visiting Stockton Thunder had to start their season with an extended fifteen-game road trip, while their new 10,000-seat arena was being completed.[2826]

Ryan Wade, first game in SOFMC. Photo by Anne Marie Sorvin, courtesy Victoria Salmon Kings.

The long-anticipated Salmon Kings' home opener at the Save-On-Foods Memorial Centre took place on November 10, 2005, before 6,406 enthusiastic fans.[2827] Much to the delight of those in attendance, the home team won the game, 5-2.

The team wore throwback uniforms, similar to those worn by the 1925 Victoria Cougars, and raised a banner commemorating the Stanley Cup win to the rafters. In the game, newcomer Jade Galbraith had two goals, while singles came from Wirll, Wade, and Henderson. Muntain was again stellar in the net, stopping thirty-one Stockton shots. Hockey was back on Blanshard Street in Victoria, and the locals were happy.[2828]

Cougars banner raised at game versus Stockton. Photo by Anne-Marie Sorvin, courtesy of Victoria Salmon Kings.

On Remembrance Day, there was a short ceremony before the game to link the present memorial to the past. In game play, Adam Taylor scored early in the second period to give the home team the advantage. That lead held up until an unfortunate penalty—for shooting the puck over the netting—close to the end of regulation time, put Stockton on the power play, and they scored with only forty-three seconds left to tie the game. The Thunder then fired the winner after 1:05 of overtime to send the local fans home disappointed. Ryan Wade sustained a knee injury and was placed on the thirty-day injury list, joining Steve Roberts and his damaged shoulder.[2829]

In the third game of the series, the Kings came back from the recent defeat and upended the Thunder by a score of 6-4 before 4,770 fans. The event began with a fight between Josephson and Jason Konstadine after only two seconds of play, sending the crowd into a frenzy. However, Stockton scored first to take a 1-0 lead. The Kings fired in four goals in the middle frame, by Lingren, Taylor, Gare, and Timmons, while the Thunder added two to make the score 4-3 at the end of the second. After Stockton drew to within a goal in the final period, the Kings scored into an empty net to seal the deal.[2830]

Adam Taylor scores against Idaho, November 2005. Photo by Anne-Marie Sorvin, courtesy of Victoria Salmon Kings.

The next home series was a three-game set against Idaho. In the first game, the Steelheads' Mike Stutzel, who grew up in Victoria, led the way for his team, scoring the winning goal in a 5-2 victory for the visiting team. Seth Leonard and Pete Gardiner found the net for the Kings. Coach Maxwell lamented that his team did not come out well, and by the time they began to play, it was too late. He stressed the need for the team to play sixty minutes and said that, if they had worked as hard in the first period as they did in the second, they would have done much better.[2831] Game two did not start well at all for the Kings. By 10:34 of the opening period, the score was 3-0 for Idaho, and the Kings had been outshot, 14-0. By the end of the period, the score was 4-0 with the shots 22-9. By the time Galbraith found the back of the net, it was far too late for a reasonable comeback. A power-play goal by Forster and a penalty shot by Leonard completed the Victoria scoring, but they ended up losing 6-3. Before the game, the team exchanged future considerations for goaltender David Currie from the Johnstown Chiefs. Muntain had gone on the seven-day injury list, and the Kings needed goaltending help.[2832]

In the third game, Lingren was the hero, as he scored the winner at thirteen seconds of overtime in a thrilling 3-2 victory. It did not start well, as the Steelheads opened the scoring, but this time the Kings rebounded when Gare found the back of the net only twenty-five seconds later. Lingren put the Kings ahead, but Idaho tied the score to extend the match. In personnel moves, Victoria sent Gardiner to Pensacola in exchange for Dallas Anderson and Pat Sutton. All the new players were expected to join the Kings on their next road trip.[2833]

Even playing in front of Victoria's NBA MVP Steve Nash did not help the Salmon Kings in Phoenix. After building up a two-goal lead thanks to Dustan Heintz and Chad Damesworth, the Kings got sloppy and committed two glaring giveaways that led directly to Phoenix goals. With the game tied, the Roadrunners scored what could only be described as a fluky goal at 1:13 of the third period, which held up and gave the home team the win by a score of 3-2.[2834] This was not the way Victoria wanted to start the road trip, but they hoped to bounce back in subsequent games.

It was a completely different story two days later in San Diego, as the Salmon Kings upended the Gulls, 4-2. Victoria got off to a good start with a 3-0 lead on a goal by Heintz and two power-play markers by Kurt Drummond. However, the Gulls outshot the Kings, 18-5, in the final frame and made it close with two power-play goals of their own, to narrow the lead to one goal. Then Taylor found the net for the insurance goal at 17:10 to snuff out a San Diego comeback. David Currie made his first start in the net, blocking thirty shots.[2835] After a three-day break, the Kings were back in action, this time in

Las Vegas. The Wranglers scored first at 17:31 of the first period, but Heintz tied it up at 7:56 of the second. Then the roof fell in as Las Vegas scored two more goals to take the contest, 3-1.[2836]

The trip continued in Long Beach, where injuries that had piled up during the trip took their toll. Wirll, Henderson, Josephson, and Campbell were all hurt, and there was no relief in sight. Down to thirteen players, the Kings managed to notch two shorthanded goals by K. C. Timmons and Mangos and an even-strength marker by Galbraith but could not hold off the Ice Dogs, who fired six goals to take the contest, 6-3. Mangos was hurt in the game, making the manpower situation even worse.[2837] The road trip mercifully came to an end in Phoenix where the injury-riddled Kings fell, 3-1. Boxma let in three weak goals, and his team could only score once in support. The lone marksman for Victoria was Forster. The trip finished with a record of 1-3—not what the Kings had anticipated.[2838]

The December 2, 2005, game against the Utah Grizzlies had a special attraction. The Stanley Cup was on a tour of ECHL cities to raise funds for hurricane victims, and fans could have their pictures taken with the Cup in exchange for a donation.[2839] They could also find the name "Victoria Cougars" as the winners in 1925. Perhaps the association with that storied team would inspire the new generation of hockey players.

The Kings started the game well, with Gare scoring at 1:13 and Timmons at 2:28, but again, could not hold the lead. The Grizzlies had four straight goals to take a 4-2 lead. However, the Kings stormed back with a second marker by Gare on a pass from Wirll and a buzzer-beater by Galbraith that tied the score at 19:44 of the middle frame. After a scoreless third period, Taylor was the hero with an overtime goal to send the fans home happy with a 5-4 victory.[2840] Game two of the series followed an all-too-familiar pattern. After an early Utah goal, the Kings had counters by Mangos and Wirll, to lead, 2-1, at the end of the first period. Taylor added to the lead at 10:54 of the middle frame and missed a glorious opportunity to give the Kings a two-goal lead when he was awarded a penalty shot. Unfortunately, he fanned on the shot, and the puck slid harmlessly away. After an early third-period goal by Utah's Anthony Battaglia, Jeff Miles added a natural hat trick that left the fans stunned in their seats. Utah took the game, 5-3.[2841]

The final game of the series was played on Sunday, December 4 and was "Teddy Bear Toss" night. Timmons had an early goal that let the fans throw their bears onto the ice, but that was the end of their offence. Utah tied the score and then got two unanswered goals in the final frame to win, 3-1.[2842] This team seemed incapable of playing a full sixty-minute game, and it was frustrating to the players and fans alike. There had been so many third-period letdowns that had cost them games.

To aid the goaltending situation, the Vancouver Canucks shipped Rob McVicar to Victoria.[2843] That move paid immediate benefit for the Salmon Kings, as he backstopped the team to a 4-2 win in Idaho. After surrendering an early goal to the Steelheads, he settled down and gave his team a chance to win. Forster tied the game only to have Utah pull ahead again. Heintz replied for the Kings, knotting the score at 2-2. Gare fired the winner at 5:53 of the final period and Dallas Anderson added insurance at 19:29 to give Victoria a 4-2 win.[2844] Unfortunately, the Canucks recalled McVicar, and he was no longer available to play for Victoria. On the positive side, the team added forward Adam Huxley from Las Vegas in return for future considerations.[2845] In the next game, Victoria again won, this time by a 5-1 score. After surrendering an early goal, the Kings stormed back with five unanswered scores. Galbraith tied the score on the power-play, and Taylor notched another before the end of the opening period. Wirll, on the power-play, and Josephson had the middle-frame markers. Timmons closed out the scoring on the power-play in the final period.[2846] The Steelheads salvaged the series with a 5-2 victory over Victoria. Rob McVicar was back with the team and stopped thirty-four shots. Even his heroics were not enough, as the Kings' offence dried up; only Anderson and Taylor were able to beat Idaho's goaltender.[2847]

Victoria Salmon Kings versus Alaska, December 2005. Photo by Anne-Marie Sorvin, courtesy of Victoria Salmon Kings.

Back home, the Kings entertained the Aces, who were riding an eleven-game win streak. Victoria put an end to that record in dramatic fashion. Victoria was led by two goals from Lingren, with others by Timmons and Gare. With the game tied, 4-4, Mike Wirll was the overtime hero, firing a shot past Chris Beckford-Tseu in the Alaska net after only thirty-three seconds of play to send the crowd home happy. Wade returned to the lineup after having missed sixteen games with a knee injury, and he responded by setting up the winning goal.[2848] A day later, the Kings played one of their worst games of the season, as they were shut out, 8-0, by the Aces, who scored five power-play goals on eight chances. Coach Maxwell noted that his team had some chances but could not put them home. He added that Alaska had shown why they were the top team in the league.[2849] The series concluded with a third game in Victoria. The Aces played a smart offensive and defensive game while the Kings came out flat. Wirll opened the scoring for Victoria, but that was the end of their offence. The Aces scored four straight goals to win comfortably, 4-1.[2850]

The Salmon Kings closed out the year 2005 with five road games, starting in Utah. In the first game, Leonard opened the scoring for Victoria, but they could not beat goaltender Alfie Michaud. The Grizzlies poured in four straight goals to win the game, 4-1. Joel Anderson was added to the roster when Forster was put on the seven-day injured list.[2851] Game two was not much better. Galbraith opened the scoring, but Utah soon tied the score. The Grizzlies added two markers in the middle frame before Drummond narrowed the lead to 3-2. However, two unanswered goals for Utah in the final period sealed the 5-2 victory for them. The Kings now had a short Christmas break before resuming action in Alaska.[2852]

In their next game, 6,251 fans watched the Salmon Kings' killer Chris Minard score twice in a 4-0 shutout of the Kings by the Aces. Victoria had only nineteen shots on goal in the entire game, giving Matt Underhill a very easy game. Forward Dustan Heintz was suspended by the Salmon Kings when he failed to return to the club after the Christmas break.[2853] In the second game of the series, the Kings fell behind, 2-0, but fought back to tie the score at 5-5. Wade scored twice, with Gare, Drummond, and Galbraith adding singles. However, the Aces notched the final goal of the game to take the match, 6-5.[2854] Just when things looked bleak for Victoria, the Salmon Kings found their scoring touch again, and upended Alaska, 5-3, to end 2005 on a high note. Galbraith opened the scoring. After Alaska tied the game, Wirll and Wade put the Kings ahead, 3-1. The teams exchanged goals (Mangos for Victoria), and Wade added an empty-net goal to make the final count 5-3.[2855] It was a satisfying result for a team that had struggled so much all season.

As the new year began, the Salmon Kings' Dan Belisle assured local fans that the team was actually better than its record would indicate. He noted that the Kings had struggled when they had a lead and had often failed to put teams away in the third period, squandering valuable points in the standings. He added that there would be an assessment of team personnel and changes could be made. Belisle asked fans to be patient.[2856]

Victoria won its second consecutive game with a 5-3 clipping of the Fresno Falcons in front of 3,856 fans. They were led by a two-goal performance by Lingren and a goal and two assists by Gare. After a Victoria goal was disallowed when the referee ruled that the puck was kicked into the net, on the next shift, Wade notched his eighth of the year to restore a two-goal lead. The final goal came from the stick of Timmons. For the Falcons, it was their first loss in eleven games, and their first road loss since November 8, 2005.[2857] A day later, the Falcons got their revenge, when they scored two late goals to upend the Kings, 4-3. The inability to hold the lead was a factor in the Victoria loss. Wade opened the scoring, and after Fresno had tied it up, Gare put the puck in the net, only to have the Falcons score three straight to take the lead. Galbraith brought the score to 4-3 with a tricky shot at 13:09 of the third, but despite pressure on the goaltender, the Kings could not get the equalizer. Somehow, Victoria failed to carry the momentum of the prior game forward.[2858] The Kings' offence sputtered yet again in the final game of the series. They surrendered four goals in the first period, counted two goals of their own by Taylor and Wade, then gave up a pair of goals in the final period to fall 6-4. Victoria did not do well in any phase of the game; goaltending was weak, they lost far too many faceoffs, and their defence was virtually non-existent.[2859] For a team that was trying to make the playoffs for the first time, this was not the way they should be playing.

At the mid-point of the season, while the Salmon Kings were losing on the ice, they were winning on the business side of hockey. Their average attendance of 4,495 represented the best crowds in Victoria since the heady days of the Victoria Cougars of the 1950s. Advertising and sponsorship numbers were high, and the city was very supportive of the franchise. On the downside, the Kings were still without NHL affiliation and still had no radio broadcast.[2860]

There were calls from local fans to fire head coach, Bryan Maxwell, but RG representative Dave Dakers insisted that the coach was not solely to blame for the poor record. Maxwell was known as an old-school coach who stressed hard work and attention to detail, but his coaching style did not seem to be very effective this season. The team was giving up leads and neglecting to fore-check in many situations, and this was costing them games.[2861]

On the road in Idaho, the Salmon Kings came up with one of their better efforts and downed the Steelheads by a score of 7-5. As they often did, Victoria took the lead in the game. Wade notched his eighth goal in the last six games late in the first period. Mangos and Wirll both scored to extend the lead, but some sloppy play led to four straight Steelhead counters. However, the Kings stormed back with four goals to take a lead they would not relinquish. Gare (the star of the game) had two, while Lingren and Timmons added singles. Idaho had one last score but could not overcome the deficit. It was a good start to the road trip.[2862]

Victoria played another good game the next night. Idaho led, 1-0, going into the third period, but Wirll and Galbraith counted for the Kings to put them ahead. After Idaho tied the score, the game went to overtime. Lingren was the hero for the Kings, as he notched the winner after just thirty-seven seconds of play. B. J. Boxma started in goal, as David Currie was on the injured list, but he was injured halfway through the middle frame and was replaced by Rob McVicar.[2863]

Less than a week after publicly supporting coach and general manager Maxwell, the management team fired him. Assistant coach Troy Ward was named to succeed him as coach, while Dan Belisle took over as general manager. The reason given for the dismissal was the lack of consistent play by the team. Dave Dakers said that it was easier to fire one person than twenty, and the players could now start afresh with a new coach. Belisle added that the team was playing much better than its record indicated and a change in coaching philosophy would be good for the team.[2864] New coach Ward promised that the players would produce fast-paced, two-way hockey or they would be replaced. He said that they would all be "accountable" to themselves and their teammates.[2865] Players noticed a higher tempo at the first practice, with a complete change of system.[2866] For his part, Maxwell said that he had worked as hard as he could to try to make the team a success and thought that the team's recent success meant they had turned the corner. Though he was not granted the extra time he felt he needed, he was proud to have built the team from scratch.[2867]

Coach Troy Ward with Morrison in background, January 27-28, 2006. Photo by Anne-Marie Sorvin, courtesy of Victoria Salmon Kings.

As quite often happens when a new coach takes over a team, the Salmon Kings played an inspired game and defeated Bakersfield, 6-2. They scored five goals in the second period, their best output in a single frame this year. Gare and Josephson each notched a pair, while Wade added a single. After the Condors counted twice in the early third period, Mangos added a power-play goal late in the game to secure the victory. With their third win in a row, the Kings hoped to keep the streak going in their next match.[2868] Unfortunately, that did not happen, as the Condors tightened up their defensive game and shut out the Salmon Kings, 3-0 the next night. In the middle frame, Josephson suffered a concussion, and Galbraith a sore knee; defender Mangos was moved to the forward line, leaving only five defencemen to hold off the Condor attack.[2869] In the next game in Long Beach, the Kings were shut out again, this time by a 2-0 score. To add to the problems, forward Dallas Anderson had been suspended while the league investigated an incident just before the end of the prior game in Bakersfield when he had been assessed a match penalty and a game misconduct.[2870]

After the all-star game in which Taylor and Lingren represented Victoria, the Kings entertained Phoenix. After giving the Roadrunners a 3-0 lead in the first period, Victoria notched three of their own by Wade, Taylor and Forster, while giving up only one, to trail 4-3 at the end of two. Steve Roberts scored twice on the power-play to put the Kings ahead, but Phoenix tied it up just past the halfway mark of the third. Five minutes of overtime solved nothing, so the game went to a five-round shootout. In that extra time, Phoenix outscored Victoria, 2-1, to gain the extra point.[2871] The Kings gained a single point in the next game, losing, 1-0, to the Roadrunners with just sixteen seconds left in overtime. Goaltender Boxma called the winning goal "a pool shot" and said that it was bad luck that it went in. He noted that play as being the type of luck the team had been having lately.[2872]

In personnel matters, top-scorer Mike Wirll left the team to play hockey in Finland. Team management suspended Dallas Anderson "for violation of team rules and conduct unbecoming of the Salmon Kings organization," according to Coach Ward. He added, "You'd better adhere to team rules if you want to wear the Salmon Kings logo and he chose not to." Those changes left the team with nine healthy forwards, seven defencemen, and three goaltenders.[2873] Coach Ward said that the team was exploring options to trade one of the goalies because having three of them rotate in the net did not establish an identity in goal, and that was bad for team morale.[2874]

The homestand continued with three games against the Augusta Lynx. In the first one, Adam Huxley, better known for his physical play, notched his first goal of the season at 16:01 of the final period to secure a 4-3 victory for the Kings. The Lynx scored first, but Lingren, Taylor, and Roberts fired goals in the middle frame to take a 3-1 lead. Unfortunately, they let the Augusta back into the game. That set the stage for the unlikely hero.[2875] Game two saw the Kings outplay their opponents for most of the game but run into a hot goaltender in Mike Wall, a draft pick of the Anaheim Mighty Ducks. Wade scored twice, and Lingren added a single as Victoria came back from a 3-1 deficit to tie the game before the end of regulation time. Much to the disappointment of the 3,744 fans in attendance, Sam Ftorek (son of former NHL player Robbie Ftorek) beat Rob McVicar at 1:02.[2876] In the final game of the series, Victoria outshot their opponents, 31-19, but had trouble finding the net and ended up losing the match, 3-1. The sole King to beat Wall in the Lynx net was Josephson. For a team that was chasing a playoff spot, this type of play was not good enough. Their inability to score was costing them valuable points that were sorely needed at this point in the season.[2877]

On the deadline to sign players from Europe, the Salmon Kings added two to their lineup. British Columbia native Ryan Thrussell came from Stuttgart, Germany, while Alberta-native Tyler Shybunka came from Trondheim Ice Hockey Club in Norway. Both had played university hockey: Thrussell at UBC and Shybunka at the University of Alberta.[2878] In other personnel moves, the team dealt David Currie to the Dayton Bombers.[2879]

The next home series against Long Beach did not start well for the Kings, as they were shut out, 4-0. Soft goaltending and a lack of finish around the net were the major reasons for the defeat.[2880] Two days later, the Salmon Kings built up a two-goal lead on scores by Mangos and Roberts, but as they had done so many times that season, could not hold the lead and ended up losing the game, 5-2. The turning point came when the Ice Dogs scored a goal late in the second period. The Kings argued that the player had been in the crease, inhibiting the ability of the goaltender to make a save, but the referee overruled their objection and allowed the goal. That opened the floodgates for Long Beach, and they scored two more goals to put the game on ice. The Kelly Cup, emblematic of the ECHL Championship, was on display at the game. Unfortunately, for Victoria fans, that would likely be the only time they would view it that season.[2881]

In the final game of the series, the Kings came close to a victory, but could only garner a single point. They started off well with Josephson firing a goal just three minutes into the game, and Shybunka adding another five minutes later. However, the Ice Dogs scored twice on just four shots to knot the score. Gare put the Kings ahead only to have a puck bounce off the post behind goaltender Boxma. Lingren's power-play blast near the end of the middle frame put Victoria ahead, 4-3, but the Ice Dogs tied the game when Christian Larrivee found the back of the net with only twenty seconds left in regulation time. Boxma was brilliant in overtime, frustrating the Long Beach shooters, but he could not hold them off in the shootout, where the visitors scored three times and the home team only once. It was a bitter defeat and extended the Ice Dogs' winning streak over the Kings to fifteen games over the last two seasons.[2882]

Next on the agenda was a three-game road trip. Game one was played in Phoenix, and the Salmon Kings followed their usual script. Timmons, Huxley, and Gare had put the Kings ahead, 3-2, by 17:18 of the second period, but the Roadrunners tied it up with just eight seconds left. It stayed that way until 17:20 of the third with Soucy of Phoenix blasting a puck past Boxma's pads to put his team ahead. A goal at 18:17 provided the necessary insurance, and the Roadrunners stole a 5-3 decision. The failure of goaltending to make those crucial saves and defensive lapses cost Victoria yet another victory. The mathematical chance of the Kings' making the playoffs became very slim, as they were now twenty-three points out of a spot with only twenty-two games left.[2883]

Game two was played in San Diego. San Diego took a two-goal lead into the second period before Huxley found the net to narrow the count. The Gulls added two more power-play markers in the third period, leaving the Kings to try to come back. Leonard and Wade scored, but the team could not get the equalizer. Again, Coach Ward criticized his goaltender, saying, "The bottom line is if you can't stop the puck, you can't win hockey games." The Gulls, who were supported by a crowd of 12,240, scored all their goals on the power-play, going 4-9.[2884] Much to the surprise of hockey "experts," the Salmon Kings went into Las Vegas and defeated the Wranglers, 3-2. Timmons opened the scoring for Victoria, but the Kings surrendered two goals to trail, 2-1, at the end of the second period. Lingren fired home the tying goal at 7:40 of the final period to send the game to overtime. Lingren was the hero of the evening, when he fired home the winning goal at 4:20 of extra time, giving the Salmon Kings the unexpected victory.[2885]

Victoria then played an eleven-game homestand. They began with Timmons, Andresen, and Drummond out with injuries, but Galbraith would return. Huxley was serving the second game of a two-game suspension but would return for the next game. Chip Dunleavy, a former NCAA forward, was signed and would play in the opening game of the series.[2886] Over the next three weeks, the team played perhaps its best hockey of the season. The first game was against Alaska. Forster and Shybunka gave the home team a 2-0 lead that the home team held until the Aces scored at 8:23 of the third period. The tying goal came with only forty-seven seconds left and the winner at 3:56 of overtime. It was a game that Victoria should have won, but despite Boxma playing an outstanding game, the Kings just could not hold the lead nor add to it, even though they outshot the Aces, 38-17.[2887]

In game two, the scenario was somewhat similar, but the result was different. The Aces scored first, but Galbraith responded on the power-play. After Alaska scored again, Leonard notched his seventh of the season to tie the game again. Adam Taylor put the Kings ahead again with 3:20 left in regulation time, but as had happened the night before, the Aces tied the game with a late goal. After a scoreless overtime, Wade and Galbraith scored in the shootout, and Boxma blocked four of the five shots fired his way. The Kings had a 4-3 victory over the Aces.[2888] The team made another trade, this time acquiring Greg Black from the Florida Everblades in return for future considerations. The former Seattle Thunderbird was expected to join the team in time for the next game.[2889] Goaltender Boxma was recognized for his outstanding work in the previous week when he was named the Rbk Hockey ECHL "goaltender of the week." He had a save percentage of .924 against the top two teams in the league.[2890]

In the first of three games against Bakersfield, the visitors took an early lead on a shot that dribbled past Boxma. Shybunka got that one back only to have the Condors score another soft goal. After Victoria killed off a major penalty to newcomer Black, Lingren tied the score late in the middle frame. Taylor gave the Kings their first lead when he found the back of the net. Unfortunately, Victoria could not hold that lead, surrendering the tying goal in the last minute of regulation time. Overtime was scoreless, and Bakersfield outscored the Kings, 3-1, in the shootout to take the game, 4-3.[2891]

McVicar returned to the team after a two-week Olympic break, during which he had been on the roster of the Vancouver Canucks. He said that he noticed a considerable difference in the team's play. In the next game, Galbraith opened the scoring for Victoria only to have the Condors tie it up. Shybunka put the Kings ahead, 2-1, and newcomer Chip Dunleavy deflected a Josephson shot to put Victoria up, 3-1. With just over five minutes left in regulation time, Bakersfield scored to narrow the lead, but this time the Kings did not collapse and instead found the empty net for insurance, to ensure the 4-2 victory. This was the fifth game in which Victoria had garnered at least one point—their best record for some time.[2892] All good things come to an end, and the point streak did in an afternoon encounter that completed the Bakersfield series. The Kings were shut out by Bakersfield, 4-0, in one of their worst games of the year.[2893]

In the next series, the opponents were the Alaska Aces. In game one, the Kings played another substandard match and lost badly by a score of 6-2. Only Lingren and Roberts produced offence for the home team. It was the kind of game that was best forgotten.[2894] The second game was closer, but still not a victory, as the team reverted to its failure to prevent opponents from scoring near the end of regulation time. The Kings fell behind, 2-0, as they often did, but a goal from Lingren made it closer. Gare fired a shot with under four minutes remaining in regulation time to knot the score, but the Wranglers scored with 1:53 left, to take the game, 3-2.[2895]

Las Vegas completed the series sweep with a 4-1 trouncing of the Salmon Kings. Josephson was sick, Forster was hurt in the pre-game warmup, Pat Sutton received a concussion, and Black was injured in a fight. Drummond, Andresen, and Timmons were already out, so the team was playing very shorthanded. They just did not have the firepower to withstand the Wrangler attack, and their goaltending was also suspect. Only Shybunka found the net for Victoria.[2896] The loss formally removed the Salmon Kings from playoff contention, although nobody had expected them to come close this season. Management had already focused its attention on the next season, scouting WHL junior playoff games and the CIS National Championship to look for players that would be a good fit for the Victoria team. Another priority was an NHL affiliation. GM Belisle had started talks with the Nashville Predators, one of only five NHL teams without an affiliate.

He was also in contact with Dave Nonis of the Vancouver Canucks. He noted that being affiliated with an NHL team did help to attract players.[2897]

Before the next three-game series, Lingren was called up to the AHL to join the Milwaukee Admirals for the rest of the season and the playoffs. That meant he would soon not be a Salmon King.[2898] The final three games of the homestand were against San Diego. In the opening match, newcomer Taggart Desmet made a huge impact in his first professional game, scoring the overtime winner and adding three assists. Down 3-1 after the first period with only Gare able to find the back of the net, the Kings stormed back to tie the match on goals by Galbraith and Gare (with his second). Overtime did not last long as Desmet found the back of the net at the twenty-second mark. Mike Josephson, an original Salmon King, announced his retirement to pursue his career as an Oak Bay firefighter.[2899] Game two was also successful. After falling behind, 1-0, Steve Roberts and Seth Leonard scored seventeen seconds apart in the second to put the Kings in front. McVicar then closed the door on the Gulls, and when Roberts scored into the empty net, the victory was complete. Coach Ward called the game a "very solid team effort."[2900]

In the final game of the series, the Kings came close but lost to the Gulls. San Diego scored the first goal of the match and added another before Forster found the back of the net. After the Gulls fired another goal, Wade and Leonard notched markers forty-seven seconds apart to tie the score, 4-4. Overtime solved nothing, and in the shootout, the Gulls fired three while the Kings could only manage two.[2901] The loss was a disappointment, but the homestand had been fairly successful with four victories, four losses, one overtime loss, and two shootout losses.

Lingren finally left for the AHL, and the Salmon Kings signed another new player, Josh Garbutt, who had been playing with the University of Regina Cougars. At the same time, Tyler Shybunka retired at age twenty-seven to pursue a civilian career in Edmonton.[2902]

The Salmon Kings then left on their last road trip of the season, seven games in thirteen days. First on the schedule was Phoenix. McVicar stopped all twenty-four shots fired by the Roadrunners in a 5-0 shutout in the desert. Galbraith scored at forty-nine seconds of the middle frame, and Leonard added two goals, while Gare scored shorthanded and Roberts had the other score. Elias Godoy, a forward out of NCAA UMass-Lowell, joined the club and made his pro debut.[2903] Two days later in Long Beach, the Kings won another game, when they upended the Ice Dogs, 4-3. Galbraith scored twice, Taylor had a single, and Roberts had the winner with 1:29 remaining in regulation time.[2904] The Kings then played twice against Stockton. Game one was played before 10,117 fans. Godoy opened the scoring and assisted on Taylor's 2-0 goal. However, the Thunder scored four unanswered goals to take the victory. McVicar faced fifty-three shots while his opponent saw thirty-six.[2905] The next night, the Kings turned the tables on the Thunder and upended them, 3-2. Mangos and Roberts scored the first two goals for Victoria, and Godoy tallied the eventual winner at 6:21 of the third period. Boxma made thirty saves for the victory.[2906]

In the final game of the series, Desmet notched two goals and an assist to give him thirteen points in his first eight games of professional hockey. Galbraith had the other Victoria goal. Regulation time ended tied, 3-3, but there was no miracle comeback for the Kings this game, as the Falcons scored the winner on the power-play at 4:15 of extra time.[2907] Next, the Kings travelled to Alaska for their last two road games. In the first match, Victoria won the game, 4-3, in overtime, much to the dismay of the capacity crowd of 6,451 at the Sullivan Arena. The Kings took an early lead when Garbutt and Roberts scored in the first period. The Aces fired twenty-four shots at McVicar in the middle frame, but he only gave up one goal, narrowing the lead to 2-1. Early in the third period, the Aces scored again, but Taylor responded for the Kings. A late Alaska goal tied the game, 3-3, and sent the game to overtime. Gare proved to be the hero of the evening, as he found the back of the net with only thirteen seconds remaining in extra time to give the Kings a hard-fought victory.[2908] In the last game in Anchorage, the hometown Aces shut out the visiting Salmon Kings 3-0.[2909]

Although they lost the last road game, Victoria had played much better hockey over the last eighteen games, securing at least one point in all but six of them.

The Kings had two more games remaining, at home versus Utah. Two former Lethbridge Hurricanes, Mark Olafson and Mark Ashton, were signed by the team before game one.[2910] Victoria's offence completely dried up in game one, as they were shut out, 3-0, by the Grizzlies, who had secured the fourth playoff spot and were heading off to Alaska for the first round of the playoffs.[2911] Game two was a different game. It was Fan Appreciation Night, and 4,775 of them were in attendance to witness a 7-4 victory by the home team. Power-play goals by Seth Leonard and Adam Taylor, along with an even-strength marker by Ryan Wade, staked the Kings to a 3-0 first-period lead. The middle frame belonged to the Grizzlies, who poured in four goals while only Godoy counted for Victoria. In the final period of the season, Mangos found the net on a two-man advantage, Leonard added a power-play score at 14:17, and Roberts clinched the victory with an empty-net goal. Although the team had missed the playoffs for the second time, they had improved dramatically over their record from the prior year, and if their recent play were any indicator, they would be a much younger and stronger team the next season. In the 2004-2005 campaign, their record was 15-52-5, and this year it was 26-37-9, an improvement of thirty-five points. After the game, Steve Roberts announced his retirement after a ten-year professional career.[2912]

While the Salmon Kings might have had a poor record of play, they were a success at the gate. The average paid attendance for thirty-six home games was 4,230, placing them in the top half of attendance among the eighty-eight minor-pro hockey teams in North America. Now, the priority of the team was to re-sign Coach Troy Ward, who had led the team to a much-improved 12-14-8 record after taking over from Bryan Maxwell. Dan Belisle, club GM, said he was conducting "exit interviews" with all the players to determine what they planned to do next season. Although he noted that no spot on next season's roster was guaranteed, he was very pleased with the play of the late-season additions, with the emphasis on graduating WHL players.[2913] [2914]

In mid-April, the *National Post* reported that the AHL might be coming to Victoria. That was news to Dave Dakers of RG Properties, which had a thirty-year deal to manage the Save-On-Foods Memorial Arena. It was one of many rumours being floated about teams moved up to the AHL from the ECHL, most of which had no basis in truth.[2915] The next day, AHL president Dave Andrews said that there had been no discussion about an AHL team in Victoria, and there had not been an enquiry from an NHL team. Canucks GM Nonis said he was still talking with Manitoba about the Moose remaining there as Vancouver's AHL affiliate.[2916]

Dan Belisle announced that Troy Ward had turned down a two-year contract to coach the Salmon Kings, as he wished to be nearer to his sons who lived in Pittsburgh with his ex-wife. He said that he had enjoyed his time with Kings and enjoyed the city and its fans, but his family had to come first. He said that his replacement would have to be a "good teacher" as the ECHL is a development league, which should be open to young, aggressive players seeking to move up to the AHL. Belisle called Ward's decision "a tough day in the Salmon Kings organization and a new hurdle for us to overcome." He added that they had a few names on a list, but most were still coaching and could not be contacted. He was looking for a "strong recruiter and strong motivator."[2917] Tony MacAulay was named head coach and signed a two-year contract on June 8, 2006. He had been the coach of the Texas Wildcatters when Hurricane Rita wiped out their 2005-2006 season. He then moved to Trenton to coach the Titans. He was delighted to return to Canada to coach. Dan Belisle said that MacAulay had the qualities he was looking for in a coach being "knowledgeable and a good teacher and communicator."[2918] [2919]

32 - THE KINGS BECOME PART OF CANUCKS NATION

Finally, the Salmon Kings were named as the Vancouver Canucks' farm team in the ECHL. They were now the third rung on a ladder that led players to the AHL Manitoba Moose and the NHL Vancouver Canucks. Goaltender Bryan Bridges, who had played Junior B hockey with the Peninsula Panthers and the Victoria Salsa, was signed to play for the Kings. He said that he wanted to play for a competitive team in a competitive league and that playing in his hometown was a bonus. He had already been invited to the Moose training camp, where he would have a chance to impress Canucks' management.[2920]

The Kings signed a new player in Geoff Irwin of Kamloops, who had played the prior season for the Stockton Thunder. He joined Steve Lingren and newcomer Wes Goldie in the veteran category, leaving one space yet to fill.[2921]

The Vancouver Canucks were holding a prospects camp at 8 Rinks in Burnaby with three Victoria observers present: GM Belisle, Coach MacAulay, and Assistant Coach Morrison. They felt this was a good time to view the young players and determine if one or more would be a good fit for the Kings. Next on the agenda was a trip to the Manitoba Moose training camp, with MacAulay and Morrison having on-ice responsibilities for drills. Among the players who might come to Victoria were Elias Godoy and Milan Gajic, both former Burnaby Bulldogs.[2922] Young players who wondered if it were possible to move from the ECHL all the way to the NHL only needed to look at forward Alex Burrows and goaltender Alex Auld, who were now with the parent club, having made it all the way from the ECHL.[2923] While the prospects were being assessed, it was also a time for the management teams of the Moose and Kings to get to know each other, so that players could move from one team to another at any time during the year.[2924]

Adam Taylor became the first Salmon King to land an NHL deal when he signed a two-way contract with the Florida Panthers. He was expected to be assigned to their AHL affiliate, the Rochester Americans. His ECHL rights were retained by the Salmon Kings.[2925]

The Salmon Kings continued to sign new players. Mike Lefley, who had captained the University of Nebraska-Omaha team, was expected to bring leadership qualities to Victoria. He had a few other pro offers but was convinced by Coach MacAulay that he should come here. The Kings signed another former captain with Jason Williamson, who had played for the CHA conference-champion Niagara University.[2926] Next to sign was twenty-five-year-old

David Morisset. He had suffered many injuries, which had hampered his progress up the hockey ladder. His decision was influenced by the Kings' having an NHL affiliation and working with Mark Morrison at a summer hockey school in Langley.[2927] Just before the Manitoba Moose training camp, the Kings signed two more players: Corey Sabourin, a CIS star with the Brock University Badgers, and Chris Martini, who played for the University of Alabama-Huntsville. Former King Adam Huxley signed with the Stockton Thunder, so would not be returning to play in Victoria.[2928] Warren McCutcheon, a twenty-four-year-old from Carmen, Manitoba, was signed to a contract and was immediately invited to the Moose camp.[2929] Signings continued with the inking of Ryan Jorde, a 6'3" defenceman who had been playing for the Rochester Americans in the AHL but had been beset by injuries.[2930] A veteran goaltender, David Belitski was the next to be given a contract. He was expected to serve as a mentor to Bryan Bridges.[2931] The Moose sent goaltender Bryan Bridges, along with David Wrigley and Mike Lefley, to Victoria. Sticking with the Moose for pre-season games were McCutcheon, Julien Ellis, and Milan Gajic.[2932]

Early in October, the Canucks assigned forward Francois-Pierre Guenette, defenceman Matt Kell, and Warren McCutcheon. Kiel McLeod was signed as a free agent, bringing size and grit to the Kings. Milan Gajic of Burnaby was offered a two-way contract by the Moose and would be assigned to Victoria.[2933] Louis-Philippe Martin joined Guenette, his former friend from Laval, as a member of the Kings.[2934]

Rule changes for the upcoming season, to bring enforcement into line with that of the NHL, were introduced before the start of the year. Less obstruction would make the game faster, as had been seen in the NHL the previous year. The changes would make it easier for players to move up the chain, as the rules and their enforcement would be the same.[2935]

At the end of September 2006, the ECHL announced its new alignment. There were two conferences: National and American. Victoria would be in the western division with Idaho, Phoenix, Utah, and Alaska. The Pacific division of that conference was all the California and Nevada teams: Bakersfield, Fresno, Las Vegas, Long Beach, and Stockton.[2936]

Victoria Salmon Kings 2006-07 schedule. From the author's collection.

The Salmon Kings opened their training camp on October 6, 2006, with an on-ice session at 9:00 a.m. Coach MacAulay said that the management team "did a lot of homework on each individual before bringing them here and there are no character issues on this team." Two new defencemen were added to the team: Gustav Engman from Sweden, who had played two seasons with the WHL Spokane Chiefs and last year with the Columbia Inferno, and Jeff MacAulay of Charlottetown, who was a rookie pro.

Goaltenders reporting to camp were Bryan Bridges, Jacey Moore, and Dave Belitski.[2937] In the first intra-squad game, Pat Sutton scored on a penalty shot to give Team Blue the victory, 3-2. The Kings would not be able to practice on the ice the next day because of a Black Eyed Peas concert but would work out on dry land.[2938] The final intra-squad game was played on October 11, 2006, and five players were released after including Seth Leonard, who became an extra forward when Adam Taylor and Milan Gajic were sent to the Kings by Manitoba.[2939]

The first preseason game was played in Idaho, where the Steelheads upended the Salmon Kings, 4-2. Adam Taylor and Wes Goldie scored for Victoria, while Dave Belitski played in goal.[2940] The team did not show much better in the second game, losing badly, 8-1. The Kings outshot the Steelheads, 48-38, but were only able to record one goal by McCutcheon. Victoria had twenty-six players still in camp and had to pare the roster down to twenty before the season-opening game in Anchorage.[2941] Often-injured forward David Morisset and defenders Sutton and Thrussell were released from the roster.[2942] Louis-Phillippe Martin and Joel Irwin did not make the cut, but forward Darryl Lloyd was an unexpected survivor of training camp, making the team when others (who had been rated ahead of him when camp started) did not. The team roster for the first game was as follows: forwards: Ryan Wade, Adam Taylor, Mike Stutzel, Milan Gajic, Wes Goldie, David Wrigley, F. P. Guenette, Greg Hornby, Kiel McLeod, and Warren McCutcheon; defencemen Gustav Engman, Andrew Zulyniak, Seamus Young, Ryan Jorde, Steve Lingren, and Josh Garbutt; and goaltenders Bryan Bridges and Dave Belitski. As only eighteen players could suit up for each match, Garbutt and Hornby were not expected to play in Alaska.[2943]

The opening night of the 2006-2007 season did not go the way that the Salmon Kings hoped it would. Facing the league-champion Alaska team, they played hard but came up a bit short. McLeod opened the scoring, but the Aces fired in three straight goals to take a lead they would never relinquish. After the teams traded goals in the middle frame[2944] (Lloyd for Victoria), Guenette cut the lead to one with just under four minutes left in regulation time. With the Kings on the power play, Coach MacAulay pulled the goaltender for a two-man advantage, but that backfired when the Aces scored into the empty net.[2945] The second game of the series also went Alaska's way. The Kings had a 2-1 lead after period one, on goals by McLeod and Goldie, but they could not hold it, surrendering three goals to the Aces and losing the game, 4-2.[2946][2947]

Back in Victoria, fans were given hope for a good season in a series of articles in the *Victoria Times Colonist*. The fact that Victorians "know hockey" was seen as a positive sign that should fill seats to boost the business side of the game. On the players' side, affiliation with the Vancouver Canucks was anticipated to bring rising young stars to play for Victoria.[2948][2949] Before the home opener, defenceman James DeMone was assigned from the Manitoba Moose and Josh Garbutt was released. Gajic and Zulyniak were ill with the flu so would not play.[2950] The Salmon Kings new mascot was introduced at the home opener: a marmot that did not (as yet) have a name.[2951] In the game, Idaho shut out the Kings, 4-0. Coach MacAulay said that the team had played hard but had not paid attention to details and ended up with too many players in one area of the ice, freeing their opponents for a clear shot on net.[2952]

Game two was not well executed, either. After surrendering the first goal, the Kings tied the game on a shot by McLeod. Victoria took a 4-1 lead on scores by Lloyd, Stutzel, and Young and managed to lead, 4-2, after two frames. Penalty trouble led to Idaho's comeback in the third period, as a power-play goal reduced the lead to one, and a soft shot tied the game. Stutzel put the home team ahead at 16:21, but another weak shot by Idaho tied the score. Overtime was scoreless, but in the shootout, Idaho had two successful shots while the Kings had none.[2953] They did secure a single point for the 6-5 shootout loss but should have won. This was not the start the Salmon Kings wanted, but there was plenty of hockey left, and there was nowhere to go but up.

Finally, in game three of the series, the Kings got their first victory. They played their most complete game in a 7-3 effort. McCutcheon, McLeod, Gajic, and Goldie fired shots past Steelhead goaltender Daigneau, who was replaced in the second period by Silverthorn. The lead was increased to five when McCutcheon notched his second of the game before Idaho scored three straight goals to narrow the lead to 5-3. Guenette scored an insurance marker at 15:10 of the third period and Goldie sealed the deal on a two-man advantage at 19:03. The team left for a road trip as Skate Canada International took over the arena.[2954] Lloyd and Kelly were injured and would be out of action for the first game in Las Vegas.[2955]

Just when things were looking up on the ice for the team, it was revealed that the Victoria Police had raided the Salmon Kings' locker room. Team management was in the dark about the police action, noting that no one on the twenty-man roster had been charged with any offence.[2956] Police remained tight-lipped about the investigation, but it was alleged that a young woman had been sexually assaulted at training camp. Three players were detained but were not charged and were released.[2957] The crown prosecutor examined the evidence package from the Victoria Police Department, including witness statements. The local department did not express an opinion on the necessity for charges, leaving that to the senior officials. In the meantime, no player was prevented from games or travel.[2958] In February 2007, the crown prosecutor announced that they would not be pressing formal charges as the "evidence gathered by Victoria police more than three months ago didn't provide a substantial likelihood of conviction." The file was then closed.[2959] However, "experts" wondered if the image of the team had been damaged. After three months of delays and speculation, the decision not to proceed left the organization in limbo, but it was felt that loyal fans would still support the team.[2960]

On the hockey side of things, the team traded future considerations to the Augusta Lynx for Phil Cole. He had played the previous season for Augusta in the ECHL and the Philadelphia Phantoms in the AHL.[2961] Julien Ellis joined the team, having been sent from Manitoba;[2962] defenceman Shaun Heshka was also assigned.[2963]

The Kings advertised a contest to name the Salmon Kings' marmot mascot. The winner would receive a $250 shopping spree from "Kings Things." The first 200 entries would receive a pair of tickets to the November 17 game. The deadline was November 13.[2964] After entries were tabulated, the mascot was named Marty. He made his first appearance with his new name at the November 17 game.

The Kings travelled to Las Vegas to play the Wranglers, the ECHL farm team of the Calgary Flames. In the first game, Julien Ellis made his first start of the season, and his team staked him to a two-goal lead on the strength of scores by Guenette and Gajic. However, the Wranglers fired two goals to tie the score. With Victoria on the power play, Vegas scored a short-handed goal to put them ahead, and when the Kings pulled the goaltender to try to tie the game, the Wranglers found the empty net for a 4-2 victory.[2965]

In game two, Julien Ellis won his first professional game as he backstopped Victoria to a 5-4 overtime victory. King goals in regulation time came from Lloyd, Gajic, Goldie, and Guenette, while David Wrigley won the game with a goal with only 1:22 left in overtime.[2966] In the final game of the series, Bridges played very well in goal and led his team to an exciting 3-2 shootout win. Vegas had the only score of the first period, but McLeod and Lingren put the Kings ahead in the second only to have the Wranglers tie it up again. After overtime solved nothing, Bridges gave up two goals, while three Kings found the back of the net—Gajic, Wrigley, and Wade—to give Victoria the well-deserved win, which was its second in a row for the first time this season.[2967]

Before the homestand against Fresno, the Manitoba Moose recalled defenceman Shaun Heshka.[2968] Playing with Manitoba Moose GM Craig Heisinger in the crowd, the Salmon Kings won their third game in succession, with a 6-3 decision over the Fresno Falcons, led by two goals by Captain Kiel McLeod, and singles by Engman, Hornby, Gajic, and Young. Ellis faced forty-seven shots in net, allowing only three to get past him.[2969] The second game of the series was a complete reversal of the first. The Kings were outplayed in all aspects of the game, and were down, 4-0, after two frames before they managed to score two meaningless goals. Only Wrigley and Taylor beat the Falcons' goaltender, as the Kings fell, 4-2, to slip back below .500 on the season.[2970] In a Sunday matinee, the Salmon Kings rebounded from the poor effort the night before and upended the Falcons, 4-3. Goldie scored twice, including the winner that broke a 3-3 tie in the third period. Other Kings' marksmen were McLeod and Engman. After the match, the team skated with fans and their families. Such an event is always more fun when the team wins.[2971] [2972]

Victoria Salmon Kings puck with double image. From the author's collection.

In a game before 3,418 fans at Save-On-Foods Memorial Centre, Julien Ellis outdueled Devan Dubnyk, as the Kings managed an exciting overtime win over the Stockton Thunder, Edmonton Oilers' farm team. Goldie staked the Kings to a 1-0 first-period lead. Wade increased the lead, but then the Thunder scored a shorthanded goal to narrow the lead to 2-1. After Stockton tied the game again, Lloyd put the Kings ahead only to see the Thunder force overtime with a score with just forty-five seconds left in regulation time. Young notched the winner with 1:42 seconds left in extra time. Ellis faced fifty-three shots in the game, while Dubnyk had only twenty-two.[2973] The Kings were depleted on defence for the second game, as they had only four healthy players. Lingren, Cole, Zulyniak and Kelly were all on the injured list. Down 2-0, they got a goal by DeMone to narrow the deficit. Young added another Victoria marker and Gajic scored the third goal, but the team could not hold off the powerful Thunder.[2974]

The Kings faced a familiar face in the next two-game road series. Former Victoria goaltender Rob McVicar was now toiling for the Grizzlies at the E Center in Salt Lake City. Zulyniak returned from the injury list, but Brad Cook took his place. That left the defensive corps still undermanned, so Wade would have to play some time with the rearguard.[2975] Utah beat Bryan Bridges in the Victoria net at forty-six seconds to take an early lead, and the game was tied, 2-2, after one period, when Lloyd and Wrigley found the net for the Kings. Goldie scored his third shorthanded goal of the season to give Victoria a lead, but from that point on, the play was all Grizzlies, as they scored five unanswered goals to take the game, 7-3. After the game, Adam Keefe was sent down from the Moose and would soon join the team.[2976] As they had early in this season, the Salmon Kings rebounded from a poor game. Mike Stutzel scored three goals and had two assists to lead Victoria to a 5-3 victory over Utah. He tied an ECHL record for the most points in a game. Other Victoria scorers were Gajic and Guenette as the Kings scored four power-play goals while only surrendering one. Ellis was strong in the net, shutting the door on the Utah comeback bid.[2977] [2978]

Back home, the Kings looked to try to defeat the Aces. Adam Taylor who had wanted to be traded to Florida, got his wish when the Kings sent him and David Wrigley to the Pensacola Pilots in return for Derek and Jordan Krestanovich, brothers from Surrey.[2979] Those two were lucky to arrive in Victoria. En route, they were involved in a roll-over accident when a wheel flew off the rim of Jordan's vehicle. Ironically, there were four new tires on the car, and one became detached. One rental car and many more miles later, the brothers were ready to play for the Salmon Kings.[2980]

In the first game of the series against Alaska, the Kings came up flat and surrendered a four-goal second period en route to a 6-1 defeat. Some of the 3,834 fans in attendance expressed their displeasure, "booing" the team during that defensive lapse. McLeod had the only Victoria marker, but it came when the score was 6-0, and the game was out of hand.[2981] Game two was a bit different, but still not a success. Ellis made fifty-one saves, but he could not hold back the power of the Aces. The Kings got into penalty trouble with the game scoreless, and that opened the floodgates. Victoria was shut out, 3-0, to give Alaska a 4-0 season record over the Salmon Kings.[2982] The Aces completed the series sweep with a 9-6 defeat of Victoria. The Kings clawed their back from deficits of 4-1 and 5-2 to take a 6-5 lead when McLeod scored his second of the game at 8:20 of the third period, but that was quickly erased, as Alaska scored the final four goals to win easily. Other Kings scorers were Stutzel, Goldie with two, and McCutcheon.[2983] The Kings had started the series just one point behind the Aces for the division lead but were now seven points in arrears.

A set of brothers would be reunited and playing against each other when Long Beach came to town, Wes for the Salmon Kings and Ash for the Ice Dogs. Both grew up in London, Ontario, and had never played against each other at the professional level, until now.[2984] Unfortunately, Ash was unable to play and had to watch from the sidelines with his relatives, who had come west to see the brothers play. Round one went to the Ice Dogs, as they nipped the Kings, 5-4. Coach MacAulay said that it was inattention to detail in their own zone that led to the defeat. Victoria had taken a 2-0 lead on goals by Young and Jordan Krestanovich, but Long Beach fired in four straight goals to take a 4-2 lead. After DeMone scored a disputed goal to narrow the lead, the Ice Dogs got that one back. Krestanovich had the last Victoria counter, but it was too little, too late.[2985]

Game two was a different matter, as the Salmon Kings turned the tables and won the game, 3-2. Guenette opened the scoring early in the first period, but a questionable penalty call put the team shorthanded, and the Ice Dogs tied the score on the resulting power play. Jordan Krestanovich put the Kings ahead, only to have the Ice Dogs tie it up again. While killing a penalty, Stutzel broke down the ice, catching a glimpse of a jersey. He passed the puck to Kelly, who fired it past Dogs' goaltender Mike Brown for a dramatic winning goal. It was Kelly's first professional goal, and it could not have come at a better time.[2986] The rubber game of the series was also "Teddy Bear Toss" night. Derek Krestanovich opened the scoring marker, bringing forth a flood of bears from the fans in attendance. Wes Goldie, who had been cut for a substantial number of stitches in the previous game, scored twice to lead his team to victory. Victoria was down to fourteen skaters as McLeod, McCutcheon, Cole, and Cook were out with injuries, and Lloyd was serving a one-game suspension, but they buckled down and played a great defensive game.[2987]

Ellis practically stood on his head in Phoenix stopping fifty shots. However, his effort was not enough as the Roadrunners upended the Kings, 4-2, with two late goals. Lingren and Lloyd found the back of the net for Victoria, but defensive lapses cost the team the two points.[2988] In their next game in Long Beach, the Kings could not convert on the power play, going just one-for-seven, leaving potential scores behind. Goldie and Derek Krestanovich were the only Victoria players to beat Ice Dogs' goalie Mike Brown.[2989] The road trip continued in Bakersfield, where the Condors scored four second-period goals en route to a 6-4 victory. Ellis started in goal but was replaced by Bridges after allowing five goals. Lingren scored twice for Victoria, while Goldie and Stutzel added singles.[2990] The Kings had now lost three in a row and were dropping behind the playoff position leaders. Things would have to turn around soon, or the season would be considered a failure.

It was the same story in Fresno, where a questionable goal by the Falcons spurred them to a 3-1 victory over the Salmon Kings. After the Kings fell behind, 1-0, Guenette tied the score in the middle period. Coach MacAulay said that the team was not getting the "bounces." However, failing to get shots on goal has nothing to do with "bounces," and everything to do with execution.[2991] The Kings maintained their slim hold on the eighth and final playoff spot, but any more losses and that ranking could be in jeopardy. Just when help was needed, it arrived in the form of McLeod and Gajic returning to the lineup, the latter being returned from Manitoba.[2992] It was unfortunate that this "help" did not produce a victory, as the Salmon Kings dropped their fifth straight game, this time, 4-2, to the Roadrunners. While Gajic scored a goal and Derek Krestanovich added another, it was the two goals that bounced into the Victoria net off defenders that sealed the deal. Players were at a loss to understand why they worked so hard and got no rewards.[2993] Something was clearly wrong with the team, and it was up to management to right the ship and turn the season around.

In the midst of all the negativity, the league named Ellis as Victoria's representative on the all-star team. It was a singular honour for the first-year professional and rewarded him for facing so many shots.[2994]

The road trip ended with a second game in Phoenix with the same score as the one two days before: 4-2. Playing a team that had travelled to Long Beach and played a tough game there, the Kings who had been in Phoenix for a week did not play well. Gajic notched another goal and assisted on Wade's goal, but that was all the offence that Victoria could manage. After their sixth consecutive loss, the Kings needed the upcoming Christmas break.[2995] It was a time for players, coaches, and management to take some time to reflect on recent games and try to remedy the situation.

Club management certainly acted, firing Coach Tony MacAulay after he had led the Salmon Kings to a 9-17-0-1 record. General manager Dan Belisle said, "With the talent we have, we should be in the top half of the standings and not the bottom half. The team just wasn't gelling on the ice, and we had to make a change." The new coach was former assistant Mark Morrison, well known to Victoria fans for his prowess with the WHL Victoria Cougars. He was a hard worker as a player, and fans hoped he could get his team to work as hard as he did. He did not plan many changes before the next game.[2996] He would have one new player in the person of defenceman Justin Spencer, a former NCAA star with Colgate University. Spencer was described as a stay-at-home defender who should be able to relieve some of the pressure on goaltender Ellis, who often had to face fifty shots.[2997]

Going into a series with the Alaska Aces, who had dominated all the games that year and were riding a seven-game winning streak, the Kings dug deep and came up with an unexpected victory. The losing streak ended at six, with an exciting 3-2 win before 5,000 delighted fans. Stutzel opened the scoring at twenty-six seconds, and Goldie added a shorthanded goal four minutes later. That seemed to wake up the Aces, and they found the back of the net a minute later; they tied the score in the third period. Finally, Victoria retook the lead on a shot by Goldie, with 1:15 left in the game. Ellis made some remarkable saves to keep his team in the game and was the obvious first star. The team was thrilled to get their new coach a victory in his first game behind the bench.[2998]

Unfortunately, the Kings could not continue the winning, as the Aces rebounded in the second game of the series and downed Victoria, 5-4. Bryan Bridges played a good game in the net, but some team mistakes cost him a victory. Salmon Kings' goals came from Kelly, McLeod, Gajic, and Wade. The team dedicated the rest of the season to *Victoria Times Colonist* sports editor Gavin Fletcher, who had died in a car crash on the Malahat on December 11th.[2999] The final game of the series, an afternoon affair, did not start well, as the Aces scored early in the game on the power play and then took a 2-0 lead. They appeared to have put the game on ice, but Kelly found the net at 15:39 of the third period and Gajic, with the goaltender pulled for an extra attacker, tied the score at 19:36. Many fans, who were working their way to the exits, had to return to their seats. In overtime, the Kings outshot their opponents, but could not beat the goaltender. Ellis missed only one shot in the shootout, while Gajic and Goldie were successful for Victoria; it was a satisfying 3-2 win for the home team.[3000]

The Salmon Kings then took their show on the road. Opening in Long Beach, Wes Goldie finally got the chance to play against his brother Ash, who scored the first goal of the game. However, it was Wes who had the last laugh as the Kings downed the Ice Dogs, 6-4. He had three goals and an assist, while Lloyd, Kelly, and McLeod added singles. The three stars were Wes Goldie, Ash Goldie, and Julien Ellis. The latest addition to the Salmon Kings from Winnipeg, Marc Andrew Bernier, was on the ice for the game.[3001] As the road trip continued, the players noted that their new coach had brought an air of personal responsibility, with short shifts and discipline. They were still taking too many penalties that cost them games and were determined to change their ways.[3002] Just before the game in Fresno, Manitoba called up Julien Ellis, so Victoria had to use Bridges with an emergency backup in case of injury. The Falcons opened the scoring after just 1:45 of play, but Stutzel tied the game thirty-six seconds into the final frame on a two-man advantage. However, Fresno took the lead two minutes later and added insurance at 10:23 and 11:38 for a 4-1 victory.[3003]

In Bakersfield, the Salmon Kings ran into penalty troubles early in the game, on which the Condors scored two power-play goals to erase the lead that the Kings had taken when Goldie found the back of the net after 3:12 of play. Bakersfield added a third goal near the end of the opening period to take a 3-1 lead. After the Condors pulled ahead by two goals, McLeod scored at 17:10 of the middle frame to narrow the lead. Gajic assisted on that play for his fiftieth ECHL helper. New King Bernier scored on the power-play only to have the Condors notch one of their own. Gajic fired the final goal of the game, but it was not enough as Victoria fell, 6-4, for their second loss on the road trip.[3004]

Back in Fresno, the Kings again scored first, when McLeod converted passes from Gajic and Goldie early in the game. However, an untimely penalty gave the Falcons a power-play, and they cashed in at 4:43. The winning goal was scored midway through the final frame, and the Falcons sealed the victory with an empty-net goal.

This was the third consecutive loss, but Coach Morrison said that the team was playing well but not able to score that timely goal that would make a difference. They went 0-7 on the power play, playing against the best penalty-killing team, and it cost them dearly. Now it was on to Las Vegas, where the Kings had played well this season.[3005] The Kings rolled the dice and came up winners against the Wranglers. Vegas scored first, but McLeod knotted the score before the end of the first period. The winning goal (by Young at 8:14 of the middle frame) and insurance marker (by Kelly at 14:50 of the third) both came from pinching defencemen. The entire team played well with attention to detail.[3006] In league news, Gajic was named to replace Ellis on the all-star team, as the latter was playing in Manitoba.[3007]

Then it was off to Alaska to face the Kings' nemesis. In game one, the Kings opened the scoring on Wade's short-handed marker, but the Aces stormed back with three goals in the second period to take a lead they never relinquished. Gajic found the back of the net at the midway point of the final period, but that was the end of Victoria's offence. It was yet another loss in Anchorage.[3008] Game two was even worse. Again, the Kings took an early lead, this time on a shot by Bernier, but allowed the Aces to notch five straight to take the lead and win the game.[3009] Fans were beginning to wonder if Victoria would ever win a game in the Sullivan Arena. The road trip finished with a disastrous loss to the Aces by a 7-2 score. The only Kings to beat Alaska were McLeod and Gajic. With the victory, Alaska won the season series against Victoria 9-1-1, taking nineteen out of a possible twenty-two points. Those games could likely make the difference between the Salmon Kings making the playoffs or failing, yet again, to get to the postseason.[3010]

Just when everybody thought the ECHL was stable, there were rumours from Abbotsford that that community might be seeking an ECHL franchise to be the anchor tenant in their new 7,000-seat, $55-million arena, due to be completed in time for the 2008-2009 season. A franchise so close to home would be just what Victoria needed for several reasons. With the distances that other clubs had to travel to get there, the teams often played three-game series, and fan interest tended to lag by the end of a series, particularly if the home team was not doing well. On the flip side, the Kings had horrendous travel costs and were away from home so often that they never really connected with the local community.[3011][3012]

Before the next series, the Kings signed goaltender Alexandre Vincent, a Canucks' draft pick, to back up Bryan Bridges. The biggest news was that fans could finally listen to Salmon Kings home games on free audio or watch on pay-per-view. Lambrick Park grad Mike Walker was signed to handle the play-by-play.[3013]

Back on the ice, the Salmon Kings played a three-game series against Bakersfield. The first game was a real rout, as the visitors scored five goals on their first twelve shots on Bridges en route to an 8-1 thumping of Victoria. Only Bernier could beat the Condor netminder. Coach Morrison said the entire team had a bad game and hoped they could put this behind them and rebound in the next match.[3014] The next game was better in some regards, but it was not an easy triumph. Outshot 15-2 in the first period, and with no shot until the fifteen-minute mark, the Kings ended up tied at that point as Bernier's shot on a rebound eluded the Bakersfield goaltender. An undisciplined major penalty to McLeod opened the doors for the Condors, who notched two goals on that penalty to take a 3-1 lead. Cole had his first of the season, and Goldie added one early in the third period to tie the score. Bakersfield went ahead on a goal by Kevin Asselin and added another on a two-man advantage to take a 5-3 lead. However, Goldie fired a shorthanded marker at 15:23 of the final period, and Gajic added a power-play marker at 17:34. Overtime solved nothing, so the game went to a shootout. Bridges stopped the Condors shooters, while Gajic and Goldie scored for Victoria to give the 4,813 fans something to cheer for.[3015] The 6-5 victory was not a showpiece, but the team got the job done when it needed to.

With thirty-five games left in the season, games were becoming "must-win" for the Salmon Kings, if they wanted to gain a playoff spot. James DeMone left the team to play in England, but Rich Meloche from NCAA Bowling Green, and Robin Gomez, who had been playing in England, joined the Kings.[3016] In game three, the Condors, led by thirty-five-year-old Kevin St. Jacques, upended the Salmon Kings, 4-3, to knot the series at one game each. His two goals opened the game, and when the Kings could only manage goals by Bernier and Jordan Krestanovich, they paved the way to victory. Gajic missed on a penalty shot that could have turned the game Victoria's way, and Bridges let in a soft goal to make the difference.[3017] Taking only two points out of six was not going to get the Salmon Kings to the playoffs, as they were now falling behind Utah for the eighth and final playoff spot, with the Grizzlies holding two games in hand. Coach Morrison said of his team's play, "I can't stand to watch it anymore. We have some players who have a good game, followed by a game of [figuratively] not showing up, followed by a good game, followed by another game of not showing up. We have to be more consistent in our effort. I can't tell if some of our guys are going to show up or not every night." He indicated that changes would be made to try to improve the team.[3018]

In the first match of a four-game road trip, the Kings played a much better game. Goldie and McLeod staked the team to a 2-0 lead by the end of the first period, and they managed to hold Long Beach at bay with Bridges allowing only one power-play goal on a rebound. An empty-net goal by Goldie was the icing on the cake. Bridges made forty-three saves and was named the game's first star. It was a good start to a California trip, and the team hoped to carry the momentum forward as they travelled to Bakersfield.[3019] Game two was another successful effort, as the Kings defeated the Condors 4-3. After Victoria fell behind, 1-0, Goldie pulled the team even with his twenty-fifth goal of the season, and McLeod put them ahead. The Condors tied the game, but the Krestanovich brothers combined for a short-handed beauty that put the Kings ahead. Bernier notched the fourth goal, and the team held off Bakersfield, allowing them only one more score. It was Bernier's seventh goal in thirteen games since he had joined the team.[3020]

The next day at noon, the good play continued. Bernier had a hat trick, Guenette added a goal and two assists, and Kelly notched a single, while Alexandre Vincent made fifty stops in his professional hockey debut to lead the Salmon Kings over the Condors, 6-5. However, it was not easy, as Bakersfield scored an improbable, late shorthanded goal to tie the game and force it to overtime. There, Goldie took a pass from Guenette to fire home the winner at 4:16. The Kings were suddenly on a roll with three consecutive victories.[3021] Could it continue?

Back in Long Beach, the Kings kept their winning streak alive with a 6-3 thumping of the Ice Dogs. Goals came from Bernier, Gajic, Cole, Wade, McLeod, and Jordan Krestanovich. Coach Morrison noted that his veterans (Wade, Goldie, and Lingren) had led the way for the younger players to follow. Goldie added to his team-leading scoring total with three assists, bringing his total to forty-five points. Bridges had an easier day in the net, as his team outshot the Ice Dogs, 42-28.[3022] Having now won four in a row, the Salmon Kings came home for two games before heading out on the road for three more, all against Idaho.

The Kings made a trade with Phoenix acquiring Paul Ballantyne in exchange for Greg Hornby and future considerations. He was expected to add strength to the much-maligned blue line. In league news, Milan Gajic was named ECHL "player of the week" for his four goals and seven assists in the four-game road trip.[3023]

Back home in Victoria, the Kings won their fifth in a row when they beat Idaho, 3-1. Wes Goldie opened the scoring with a shorthanded goal in the opening period, and Lingren added a second in the middle frame. Salmon Kings special teams then went to work, holding the Steelheads off the scoreboard despite playing shorthanded for four minutes. Wade had a goal on the power play late in that period, and the Kings held the Steelheads to one goal in the third. Adam Keefe was assigned to the Kings from Manitoba and played in the game. To make room for him on the roster, forward Rich Meloche was traded to the Pensacola Ice Pilots for financial considerations.[3024] However, the win streak ended at five, when the Steelheads routed Victoria, 6-2. Goaltending was suspect, and Morrison pulled Bridges after he gave up five goals; he was replaced by Vincent, who allowed the final Idaho goal. Only Guenette and Young managed to score for the Kings.[3025]

In the first game in Idaho, the Steelheads downed the Kings, 2-1. Victoria took an early lead when Young fired a goal before the game was two minutes old, but that was the last time anyone beat Idaho goaltender Steve Silverthorn. The Steelheads tied the score, then fired the winner early in the third period.[3026] Much to the delight of Kings' fans, Ellis returned from Winnipeg and started the next game. He was helped by his teammates, who scored the first four goals of the game. Goldie had a pair, and Derek Krestanovich and Gajic added singles. After Idaho scored two in a row, Lloyd put the game on ice with a marker three minutes into the final frame, and Jordan Krestanovich added insurance with the net empty, as the Salmon Kings upended the Steelheads, 6-3, to crawl back into playoff contention.[3027] The next game was not as successful, as the Kings were blanked, 2-0, by Idaho. Both Steelhead goals came on the power play, and Victoria was unable to beat Silverthorn.[3028]

The Salmon Kings came home for six games. They opened a three-game set with Stockton with an impressive 4-0 victory. It was the first shutout of Ellis's career, and he scooped the puck up as a souvenir. McLeod scored the only goal Victoria really needed late in the first period. In the middle frame, the Kings gradually took control of the match, with Stutzel firing home a puck at 9:05 and Jordan Krestanovich adding one on a two-man advantage. The team withstood furious pressure from the Thunder, but Ellis stood tall in the net, stopping thirty-six shots. Bernier added another shorthanded goal with only twenty-four seconds left in the game to ensure the victory.[3029]

In the second game, the Kings found their offence and outscored the Thunder, 6-3, for their eighth win in their last eleven games. Stockton opened the scoring, but two goals in thirteen seconds (by Ballantyne and Engman) put the Kings ahead. Gajic fired a goal on a two-on-one opportunity midway through the middle frame, Goldie added his thirtieth of the season, and Guenette added one to give the home team a 5-1 lead at 2:34 of the third period. However, the Thunder fought back, scoring twice to narrow the lead. The win was secured when McLeod added an empty-netter at 18:44.[3030] Game three was a close affair with none of the high-scoring of the other games. McLeod and Goldie got Victoria off to a good start, scoring against Devan Dubnyk, an Oilers draft pick expected to play in the NHL before long. That lead was short-lived, as the Thunder tied the game and then went ahead, 3-2, late in the middle frame. That set the stage for the Krestanovich brothers to combine on the tying marker at 7:16 of the third, sending the game to extra time. Overtime was short and sweet, as Goldie fired his second goal of the night past Dubnyk at forty-seven seconds, to send the 4,417 fans home very happy.[3031]

Fresh off his ECHL "goaltender-of-the-week" honours, Ellis prepared to face Las Vegas.[3032] The first game did not go well at all, as the Salmon Kings seemed to forget how well they had been playing and reverted to their former bad form. Outshot, 16-4, in the first period, they were also down, 3-0, on the scoreboard. The Wranglers added singles in the two final periods to shut out the Kings, 5-0.[3033] It was not the way the home team wanted to start the series.

Game two was an entirely different affair. After Guenette put the Kings ahead, Vegas fired two past Ellis. McLeod tied the score on a nice pass from Goldie early in the third. Then it was up to Ellis to hold the fort and get the game to overtime. Despite a power play in the extra time, the Wranglers could not beat Ellis, so the game went to a shootout. Again, Ellis was the star, as he stopped all the Vegas shooters, while Gajic, Goldie, and Wade found the back of the net to give the Kings a 3-2 victory.[3034] The final game of the set belonged to the Wranglers, as Mike McKenna blanked the Kings, despite his team being outshot, 42-25. For some reason, Victoria was unable to solve his goaltending, despite seven chances with the man advantage. Coach Morrison stated the obvious when he said: "our power play has got to get better."[3035] The Kings finished the homestand with a 4-2 record and remained in the playoff hunt.

The Salmon Kings then went on the road again. With only fifteen games left on the schedule, the team had to win as many games as possible to secure a playoff spot.[3036] The first stop was in Fresno, where Victoria got off to the start they wanted, upending the Falcons, 3-1. Ballantyne got the Kings on the scoreboard at 17:06, then Guenette struck on the power play at 19:39 to give them a 2-0 lead after one. The only score of the second frame was a power-play marker by Young. Fresno did not score until Ellis lost his stick and was unable to stop a shot early in the final frame. However, he stood firm the rest of the way, and the Falcons could not beat him again.[3037]

The next night, the Kings won for the fifth time in six ECHL shootouts, this time, 4-3. Wade, Ballantyne, and Engman scored for Victoria in regulation time. Gajic and Bernier scored in the shootout while only one Falcon beat Ellis. The suddenly very strong Salmon Kings notched their twelfth victory in seventeen games and took a six-point lead over the Utah Grizzlies for the eighth and final playoff spot, sitting only two points out of seventh place.[3038]

The Kings' blue line was strengthened when the Canucks sent prospect Patrick Coulombe to Victoria. He was playing for the Moose but had been with the Vancouver Canucks for seven games. In junior, he had played for the Rimouski Océanic, quarterbacking a power play that included future superstar Sidney Crosby.[3039] He was in the lineup when Victoria played Stockton. McLeod put the Kings on the board first, with Goldie assisting to bring his point total to fifty-eight, eclipsing the mark set the previous year by Adam Taylor. Mathieu Melanson, son of former NHL goaltender Rollie Melanson, fired two goals for the Thunder, including the winner in overtime. With the overtime loss, the Kings gained a valuable point in the standings.[3040] Game two was a close one as well. Victoria scored three power-play goals (by McLeod, Gajic, and Goldie) and Stutzel added a fourth that tied the game at 4-4. Ellis stopped twenty-six shots in the second period alone. This time, the Salmon Kings were unable to win in the shootout and gained only a single point.[3041]

In the third game of the series, Stockton took an early lead, but goals by Bernier and Gajic put the Kings ahead in the first period. The Thunder roared back with two goals to take the lead back, setting the stage for Engman to knot the score with only 5:45 left in regulation time. Stockton scored twice in the shootout on Bridges, playing to give Ellis a rest, while Dubnyk blanked all Victoria shooters. This was the fourth game to go to extra time on this trip, and the usually hot Victoria shooters had gone cold at the wrong time.[3042]

Now, the Kings were home for five games that could determine their position in the standings. The first three games were against the Utah Grizzlies, who were sitting in ninth place in the standings, seven points behind the seventh-place Kings.[3043]

Former Salmon King Rob McVicar, who was now playing for Utah, would return to where he had played the last year, but his job was to make sure that his new team emerged victorious.[3044] In game one, the Kings did exactly what they needed to do. They upended Utah, 6-3, to take a stranglehold on a playoff position. Bernier scored the first goal of the game only to have the Grizzlies come back with two to take the lead. Phil Cole tied the score midway through the middle frame and went ahead on Goldie's thirty-fourth goal of the season. In the early third period, the Kings poured it on, as Bernier and Young scored in the first three minutes to give the home team a 5-2 lead. A shorthanded Utah goal narrowed the score, but a late goal by Kelly put the game on ice at 6-3.[3045]

The second game saw Utah rebound and beat the Kings, 3-2, before a season-high crowd of 5,070. Goldie opened the scoring at twenty-eight seconds, and it looked like Victoria had scored again at 1:56, but that was waved off due to a penalty call. Before the Kings could regroup, Utah fired two goals to take the lead. Stutzel tied the game midway through the game, but Jelitto had the winning goal at 10:10 of the final period. McVicar was given the day off, as

Ben Gray replaced him.[3046] Little did the team know that this would be their last loss in the regular season.

In the final game of the series, a matinee affair, Victoria got back to basics and thumped the Grizzlies, 4-1. Bridges played in net for the Kings and allowed a first-period goal but shut the door after that. Four unanswered goals in the last two periods, by Lingren and Gajic on the power play, a short-handed score by Wade, and a full-strength marker by Kelly, propelled the Kings to a well-deserved victory.[3047]

Just when things were going well, Manitoba goalie Wade Flaherty suffered an injury and would be out six to eight weeks. As a result, Ellis was called up to play in Winnipeg, leaving Bridges to handle goaltending duties for Victoria.[3048] Anticipating a run for the playoffs, the club offered special prices for upcoming games. Fans could buy three tickets for only forty-three dollars or six tickets for only ninety-six dollars, which included two playoff tickets for the first round. Zellers offered a family pack that included four tickets, a ten-dollar discount for the Old Spaghetti Factory, and twenty-four cans of a Coke product for only forty-eight dollars.[3049]

The Salmon Kings took another step toward a playoff spot when Bridges backstopped them to a win over the Ice Dogs. The Kings did not start well, and it was up to Bridges to keep them in the game, but McLeod fired a goal at 8:36 on a partial breakaway. The Ice Dogs tied the score with just twenty-six seconds left in the first period, but that was the last time Bridges yielded a goal. Wes Goldie scored on a breakaway at thirteen seconds of the second frame and added another at the end of the period. Jordan Krestanovich and Milan Gajic also scored for Victoria for a convincing 5-1 victory.[3050]

The Kings swept the two-game series with a 4-1 win over Long Beach. Lloyd brought the crowd to its feet with a hot shot after only thirty-three seconds of play. McLeod made it 2-0, and Lingren added a third. The Ice Dogs scored their only goal in the final frame, but it was matched by a marker from Jordan Krestanovich. Bridges withstood a barrage of shots, with the Kings shorthanded near the end of the game, and was named the first star of the game for the second game in a row.[3051]

The long wait was over, as the Salmon Kings clinched their first playoff berth with a timely 7-1 victory in Salt Lake City. Victoria scored on its first two shots to take a 2-0 lead after just thirty-four seconds of play: Goldie at twenty-one seconds and Gajic at thirty-four seconds set the tone for the rest of the game. Five other players also found the back of the net: Stutzel, Bernier, McCutcheon, and both Krestanovich brothers. Bridges was again stellar in the net, facing forty-six shots but allowing only one goal.[3052] The team received good news when Ellis was sent back to play for Victoria, although the team had not suffered during Bridges' run of consecutive victories.

On the ice, the Kings won their fifth game in a row with a thrilling 4-3 overtime decision. The first period featured a parade of penalties but only one power-play goal, by Utah. The Grizzlies went ahead, 2-0, on an early second-period power play, but Goldie got that one back on the power play with only four seconds left. Kelly narrowed the margin, and Gajic tied the game at 3-3 at the 14:42 mark of the third period, setting the stage for McLeod's overtime winner.[3053] [3054] Victoria swept the series with a 5-1 win in the third game. Goals by Ballantyne, Stutzel, and Gomez, in just two-and-a-half minutes, late in the second period, blew open what had been a close game. Guenette had a goal and two assists, and Goldie fired home his fortieth of the season, setting a new record. With the victory, Victoria was assured of finishing at least seventh in the standings, but their first-round opponent was yet to be determined.[3055]

The Salmon Kings marketing department put large ads in the newspaper announcing, "We're in the playoffs!" They were trying for a sell out on Saturday, April 7, and were offering tickets starting at only five dollars. According to the ad, "Salmon Kings hockey must be seen, heard, and felt live in person to truly appreciate all its excitement and passion that it has. Be a part of the team and join us for the Salmon Kings' march to the playoffs and witness live and first-hand the priceless experience that this time of the season offers."[3056] It was an exciting time to be a hockey fan in Victoria.

In the first game of the final homestand, the Salmon Kings defeated Phoenix, 6-4, for their seventh consecutive victory. Gomez opened the scoring, but the Roadrunners tied it up by the end of the first period. Gajic made it 2-1, and Stutzel, 3-1 before Phoenix scored twice in thirty-five seconds to knot the score. McLeod had the only score of the middle frame. Gajic scored the eventual winner at 9:39 of the final frame. Phoenix got one more goal to make it interesting, but McLeod found the empty net with six seconds left in the game.[3057] Bridges played in the middle game of the series and came within a whisker of his first professional shutout. The record crowd of 5,349 roared their approval of the team. Derek Krestanovich scored the only goal of the first period, despite the Kings' outshooting their opponent, 16-2. McLeod put Victoria ahead, 2-0, early in the second, and Lloyd put the team up 3-0 at 14:17 of that period. After Phoenix scored on a bad bounce, with 1:23 left in the game, Gajic finished the scoring with an empty-net goal with thirty-three seconds remaining.[3058]

A new record crowd of 7,006 saluted the Salmon Kings as they upended Phoenix, 6-1, for their ninth straight victory. Goals came from Wade, Derek Krestanovich, Bernier, Goldie, Lloyd, and Ballantyne. Ellis played in net, despite having been hit in the throat during the warmup, and yielded only one goal. The Salmon Kings played their best hockey over the last thirty-one games, going 22-6-3 during that period and finishing the season with a 36-32-4 record, the first time this franchise finished over .500. Now it was on to the playoffs against Alaska, their nemesis.[3059]

In the first playoff game, the Salmon Kings shocked the Aces, defeating them, 3-2. Gajic scored the first goal at 14:44 of the first period, but the Aces tied it just after the start of the middle frame. Goldie had the next two goals to lead his team to victory. A late Aces goal brought them closer, but Ellis held the fort, making fourteen third-period saves.[3060] In game two, Alaska roared back, upending the Kings 7-1 to tie the series at one game each. The Aces took advantage of Victoria mistakes and made the Kings pay dearly. Stutzel had the only score for the Kings.[3061]

Back in Victoria, the Aces were outshot, 37-30, but emerged victorious by a score of 5-2. Lingren and Derek Krestanovich were the only Salmon Kings to beat Alaska goaltender Derek Gustafson. The team made too many mistakes, and goaltending was not up to snuff.[3062] They would have to bounce back, or it would be a short series. Game four went to the Aces, mainly due to a controversial call by referee Tyler Johnson. McLeod fired a shot that beat the goaltender, but the official ruled that the puck went in off a high stick. Alaska television clearly showed it was a legal goal, but there was no video review, so the erroneous call stood. McLeod's second goal would have tied the game at 3-3 late in the game and could have changed the outcome of the match. The only two goals that counted for Victoria came from the sticks of Jordan Krestanovich and McLeod. Now, the Aces were up 3-1 in the series and only needed one more victory to take the series.[3063]

Just when the Aces were looking to win the series, the Salmon Kings came to life and upended Alaska, 9-4. Victoria built up a 4-0 lead on first-period markers by Goldie, Bernier, and Gajic and an early-middle-frame counter by McLeod. The Aces scored at 1:16 of the second, but Goldie, Wade, and Lingren made it 7-1 by 16:58. After Alaska counted twice, Goldie completed the hat trick at 1:14 of the third to make the score 8-3. It was the first hat trick ever for a Salmon Kings' player on home ice.[3064]

Back in Anchorage, the playoff magic came to an end when the Aces outscored the Salmon Kings, 5-2. Unfortunately, the Kings' rookie goaltending tandem could not rise to the occasion, often letting in soft goals during the series. Wade and Goldie found the back of the net for Victoria, but that was all the team could manage. Yes, the Kings lost the series, but they learned so much from it. Fans could look forward to the next season with some hope.[3065]

33 - HIGH EXPECTATIONS FOR THE KINGS

Now that the Salmon Kings had a taste of the play-offs, fans were looking forward to the new season. Who would be back? Could the team continue the type of hockey that they had played at the end of the regular season?

Among the first players signed for the 2007-2008 season were Phil Cole, Jordan and Derek Krestanovich, Ryan Wade,[3066] and Robin Gomez.[3067] Ash Goldie joined his brother Wes as a member of the team as well. The team also added a new assistant coach. Quentin Van Horlick, who had an eleven-year career as a professional player, was expected to bring enthusiasm to his first coaching job and be able to help with player development.[3068]

However, the real buzz in Victoria was the Vancouver Canucks' training camp at Bear Mountain Arena. Many of the Salmon Kings attended the prospects camp and were hoping to impress the Canucks brass and move up the ladder to the Manitoba Moose and even higher. Victoria hockey fans crammed the small arena and followed every move. There were plenty of chances to meet players and get autographs and photos.

Tickets to the intra-squad game sold out in four minutes.[3069] In the game itself, held at 11:00 a.m., on September 16, 2007, Team Blue defeated Team White, 4-3, but nobody really cared about the score. They were there to see the established stars and to have a look at the players who might have a chance to stick with the big club this season. To a man, the Canucks wanted to thank Victoria fans for their welcome and support and said they would like to come back again.[3070] Unfortunately, training camp was held elsewhere in subsequent years.

The Salmon Kings announced that their training camp would run October 5-14, at Save-On-Foods Memorial Centre with the Blue-Gold intra-squad game on October 9 and that they would play two pre-season games in Utah against the Grizzlies on October 12 and 13. Stan Smyl, the Canucks' director of player personnel, said there would be players coming to the Salmon Kings, as it was better for prospects to have more playing minutes at the ECHL level than having minimal playing time in the AHL. Those who played more would develop faster, and that would benefit the organization as a whole. Salmon Kings from last season invited to the Moose camp included Ellis, Gajic, Cole, Kelly, Coulombe, and Bernier. Newcomer Ash Goldie was there, as well. Belisle said he expected thirty to thirty-two players at the Kings' camp.[3071]

Added to the roster was Penticton's Matt Hanson, who had played NCAA hockey at the University of Alaska-Anchorage.[3072] Defenceman Seamus Young was traded to the Wheeling Nailers for financial considerations; he had requested to be moved for personal reasons.[3073] Next to be signed was Kevin Cooper, a forward who had played in the ECHL, UHL, and Europe. He brought speed and was an aggressive forechecker.[3074] The Moose assigned Gajic, Bernier, Cole, and Ash Goldie to Victoria after a preseason game. More would be coming as further cutdowns were made.[3075] The Kings signed goaltender Billy Thompson, as it was possible that Ellis would stay with Manitoba. He would compete with Bridges for the starting goalie position.[3076] Dylan Yeo, Julien Ellis, and Matt Kelly were the next players to be sent from Manitoba. Former Chilliwack Chief Kevin Estrada was inked for the Kings just before the start of training camp.

The roster for training camp:

Goalies	Forwards[3077]	
Bryan Bridges	Mike Bartlett	Derek Krestanovich
Julien Ellis	Marc-Andre Bernier	Jordan Krestanovich
Billy Thompson	Kevin Cooper	Alex Lalonde
Jordan Watt	Drew Davis	Danny LaPointe
	Kevin Estrada	Kiel McLeod
Defenceman	Milan Gajic	Ty Morris
Phil Cole	AshGoldie	Atsushi Ohata
Paul Ballantyne	WesGoldie	Tim Plett
Gary Gladue	Robin Gomez	Ryan Wade
Matt Hanson	Marco Guercio	
Jordan Little		
Matt Kelly		
Dylan Yeo		

Training camp was particularly significant for Danny LaPointe, whose father, Rick LaPointe, had toiled for the Victoria Cougars of the WCHL for four seasons and then played twelve seasons in the NHL for Detroit, Philadelphia, St. Louis, Quebec, and Los Angeles. Rick died of a heart attack in 1999, when he was only forty-four. Danny often walked past a plaque honouring his father and other notables in displays in the arena concourse. For him, it was an honour to skate on the site of his father's junior glory days, albeit in a new arena.[3078]

After the annual intra-squad game, team management had to cut six players from the roster. Gone were Jordan Watt, Atsushi Ohata, Drew Davis, Marco Guerico, and Tim Plett.[3079] The team would have to cut six more players before the opening game of the season. What happened in the two pre-season matches against the Utah Grizzlies would go a long way in determining who would remain on the active roster.[3080]

Two former members of the defunct Long Beach Ice Dogs, Gary Gladue and Ash Goldie, led the way in the first exhibition game, as the Kings defeated Utah, 3-2. Ellis did not make the trip, as the team wanted to give him some rest, so Thompson played in this game. He faced thirty-two shots, allowing only two goals. Five skaters who were assured of making the team (Bernier, Estrada, Kelly, Yeo, and McLeod) were given the night off so that management could have a serious look at the other hopefuls.[3081] Bryan Bridges played in goal for the second exhibition game and made thirty-five saves. However, his teammates could only manage to score one goal, by Ash Goldie, in a 4-1 defeat.[3082] Now it was up to management to make those tough decisions.

In a surprise move, the Kings released Bryan Bridges, having decided that Billy Thompson had more experience and would be a better back-up to Ellis. Canucks prospects Daniel Rahimi and Patrick Coulombe were assigned to Victoria and were expected to shore up the Kings' defence. Cut from the roster were Mike Bartlett, Danny LaPointe, Matt Hanson, Kevin Cooper, and Jordan Little.[3083] The ECHL rule that allowed only four veteran players cost Phil Cole his spot with the team. The four veterans retained were McLeod, Jordan Krestanovich, Gomez, and Wade.[3084]

The Salmon Kings opened the season in Boise, Idaho, having to watch a championship banner raising and the presentation of rings to the Kelly Cup-winning Steelheads.[3085] However, they got the last laugh, as they upended the champions, 2-1, in overtime. Ellis played a stellar game in the net, stopping thirty-five of thirty-six shots fired his way, while Wes Goldie fired his first of the season at just thirty-seven seconds, and Coulombe fired the winner on a power play at 1:02 of overtime. It was the first season-opening victory for the Kings, who had struggled early in the season in years past. Victoria's penalty killing made the difference in the match, as the Kings were shorthanded five consecutive times in the third period but gave up nothing.[3086] The next night, Idaho got a few lucky bounces, while the Kings could not convert on theirs, and the Steelheads upended Victoria, 4-2. Gajic had both goals for the Kings and noted that, with a bit of luck, he could have had more. Thompson played in the net, as Ellis was called up to Manitoba. Rahimi was also recalled to the Moose, leaving the roster a bit short.[3087]

Fans who wished to follow the team but could not attend games on the road were able to get an audio feed for free on the Salmon Kings website. Also available was a pay-per-view version.[3088]

The home opener, dubbed "Rock the Rink," featured music by The Usual Suspects and an interactive Kids' Zone.[3089] On the ice, the Kings lost an exciting match, 4-3, to the Las Vegas Wranglers, who ran their unbeaten streak in regulation play to seventeen. Wade gave the Kings a 1-0 lead on a power play with a two-man advantage at the 9:49 mark, but the Wranglers tied it with seconds left in the opening frame. After Vegas went ahead early in the second, Estrada drew the Kings even. The Wranglers pulled ahead again, but Ash Goldie got the 3-3 goal. A Wrangler score on the power play proved to be the winner, as a blast from Bernier with time running out rang off the post, denying him the tying marker. Both teams played well, but one took advantage of the breaks, and the other did not.[3090] The next game produced a much better result, as the Kings put an end to the Wranglers' streak in defeating them, 4-3. Wes Goldie led the way with a hat trick, and Dylan Yeo added his first goal as a professional. After building up a 4-1 lead, the Kings held on as the Wranglers stormed the net, beating Billy Thompson twice to narrow the lead. However, the Kings weathered the storm and sent the 3,675 fans home happy.[3091]

When Ballantyne injured his wrist and was placed on the seven-day injury list, the Kings acquired Bryan Nathe from the Johnstown Chiefs for future considerations. The team also added Chris St. Jacques off waivers when he was released by Stockton. Although only 5'8", he had put up big numbers in the WHL, and it was hoped he would do the same in the ECHL.[3092]

Julien Ellis returned from Manitoba and was in the net for the first game against Bakersfield. Ash Goldie accounted for the entire Victoria offence, scoring a hat trick as his brother had in the previous series. The third—and winning—goal in a 3-2 victory came with just twelve seconds remaining in the game, bouncing off his body into the net.[3093] It was the kind of break that the Kings did not get in prior years. Could the tide be turning in Victoria's favour?

The Goldie brothers got into the action in the second game of the Bakersfield series; both scored twice, and Ash added a pair of assists. Gajic had two goals, and Estrada added the seventh in a decisive 7-4 win. The Kings capitalized on their chances on the power play, scoring five with the extra attacker.[3094] In the final game of the series, the Salmon Kings nipped the Condors in a shootout. Ash Goldie had two goals, as did McLeod, while Gajic contributed three assists to lead Victoria. In the shootout, both Goldies and Gajic were successful, while Condors were blanked to give Victoria the series sweep with a 5-4 win.[3095] In recognition of his stellar work during the week, Ash Goldie was named ECHL "player of the week."[3096]

A significant change in the Salmon Kings' travel this year was that they did not spend all their travel time in busses; they flew to many destinations, saving time and keeping them relatively fresh. It also meant that there were no nine-game trips, as the longest trip this season was six games.[3097]

The Salmon Kings were hoping to continue their hot play with a fifth consecutive victory against Utah, but the streak came to a crashing halt when the Grizzlies upended the Kings, 7-1. Utah outshot Victoria 50-23, leaving Ellis on his own for most of the contest. The only bright point for the Kings was McLeod's power-play marker with 1:01 left in the game. Both the coaches and players felt the team would do better in the rest of the series.[3098] Julien Ellis was the best player in the next game, stopping forty-seven of the forty-eight shots fired his way, to lead the Kings to a tight 2-1 victory. His best save was on a two-man breakaway with six minutes left in the game. Wade and Estrada scored power-play goals for the only Victoria scoring, but on this night, two was enough.[3099]

In the final game of the series, the depleted defence came up big, and Ellis only had to make twenty-four saves. Ash Goldie fired the lone goal of the game in a tense 1-0 victory for Victoria. With the win, the Kings' record was 7-3, the best-ever start to a season, and they were sitting atop the National Conference for the first time in team history.[3100]

Back home, the improved play continued as the Kings defeated Stockton 7-4 before an appreciative crowd of 4,166 noisy fans. Gajic opened the scoring, then Bernier took over with two goals in 2:35 late in the first period. Stockton got on the board with eight seconds remaining to make the score 3-1 at the first intermission. Derek Krestanovich and Chris St. Jacques each scored their first goals of the season to increase the lead to 5-1 at the second break. A few defensive lapses let Stockton back in the game, but McLeod and Ash Goldie found the back of the net to seal the deal.[3101] At the second game of the series, the Salmon Kings held "Marty's Birthday Party" to recognize the efforts of their team mascot. For the last year, one dollar from the sale of every mini-Marty sold at the team store was earmarked for the Vancouver Island Marmot Recovery Fund, and a cheque for the year's sales was presented to the organization during the first intermission.[3102] In the game, Ellis was unable to play due to the flu, so Billy Thompson was in the net while Jordan Watt was called up as a backup. Defenders Gladue and Coulombe played an outstanding game, gaining praise from management. Gajic got his team on the scoreboard at 5:40 of the opening period, but then the Thunder pulled ahead with two goals of their own. However, Estrada deflected a Coulombe shot to tie the score at 2-2, and then Gajic put the home team ahead. Stockton managed to tie the score midway through the final frame, but Wes Goldie had a sneaky goal on the wrap-around to put the Kings in the lead for good. It was a good, hard-working 4-3 victory and pushed the season record to 9-3.[3103] The next night, Victoria completed the series sweep with a 2-1 overtime thriller. Stockton scored first, but Jordan Krestanovich tied it up just over five minutes later. Thompson was named the game's first star, as his team was outshot 42-28, but the hero of the evening was Dylan Yeo, who fired the winner at 2:00 of overtime, extending the team's winning streak to five.[3104] The team had now won ten games that season, whereas in the previous season they had not reached that mark until December 29. The Kings were very powerful, with eleven returning from last year's squad, and they worked very hard as a team to be successful. In preparation for the road series in Idaho, the Kings signed defenceman Eric Nelson to help shore up the depleted blueline.[3105]

The win streak reached six with a 4-1 victory over the defending-champion Steelheads. Ellis was back in net and was named the game's first star. Kings' goals came from Jordan Krestanovich, Bernier, Gajic, and Ash Goldie. After the game, Ash left to attend a funeral and would miss the remaining games in the series.[3106] In another personnel change, forward Milan Gajic was called up to the AHL's Houston Aeros.[3107] The win streak was snapped in game two of the series, as the team was missing its two top scorers. Bernier gave Victoria an early lead, but that was all the offence the team could manage, as they were outshot, 36-14, and looked sluggish in a 5-1 loss.[3108] The final game of the series served as a wake-up call for the Salmon Kings, as they were shut out, 3-0, and they outshot 40-23. McLeod said the team had not played well in the last two games, with the puck in their end most of the time. He added, "Our team defence was brutal."[3109]

The next home series had to be played on three consecutive nights, as a TOOL rock concert was already booked for December 1.[3110] The ECHL announced that rugged forward Robin Gomez had been suspended pending a review of an elbowing penalty on Steelhead Colin Sinclair.[3111] On the good news front, the Manitoba Moose sent Rahimi and Kelly back to Victoria to strengthen the blue line. With seven healthy defenders, the Kings waived Eric Nelson who had been filling in.[3112][3113]

The Salmon Kings got back on the winning track with a 4-3 overtime decision over the visiting Phoenix Roadrunners. Despite outshooting their opponents 10-3 in the first period, the Kings were down 1-0, at the first intermission. Ash Goldie then fired a shot at 7:29 of the second that beat Phoenix goalie Cody Rudkowsky cleanly, and Jordan Krestanovich had a short-handed marker on a pass from Rahimi to put the Kings up. However, Victoria-native Sean O'Connor scored on the power play to knot the score at 2-2. Both goals came on a five-minute major assessed to McLeod, who drew blood on a hit to Corey LeClair. The call was loudly booed by the crowd, as McLeod was also bleeding. Phoenix went ahead on another power play early in the final period, but Bernier snapped a shot at 5:09, to tie the score at 3-3. That set the stage for Wes Goldie to fire home the winner at 3:08 of overtime before a mid-week crowd of 4,205.[3114]

The next night, the Kings prevailed again, although they had to go to a shootout to earn the extra point. Phoenix took the lead in the second period, but Wes Goldie fired home the tying goal ten minutes later. Derek Krestanovich put the Kings ahead at 1:33 of the third frame to put Victoria up, 3-1, but the Roadrunners managed to score twice, the second with just forty-one seconds in regulation time. Overtime solved nothing, so the game went to a shootout. Each team had one goal after the mandatory five rounds, so it went to sudden death. McLeod fired a shot that went off the post and into the net, while Thompson held his ground and denied the Phoenix shooter. The Kings won, 4-3.[3115][3116]

The final game of the series was also "Teddy Bear Toss" night. After Phoenix scored at 1:18, St. Jacques got the Kings on the board at the 1:47 mark. That was the cue for the season-high number of 5,810 fans to litter the ice with stuffed animals that would be donated to Queen Alexandra Children's Hospital, the pediatric ward of Victoria General Hospital, and C-FAX's Santa's Anonymous. Unfortunately, the Roadrunners scored the next two goals to have a 3-1 lead before the game was five minutes old. Ellis had to leave the game when he took a shot off his hand; Thompson came in to replace him. Estrada reduced the Phoenix lead to 3-2, but a Kings' miscue cost them a goal. The Roadrunners made the mistake of trying to defend their lead in the third period, and it cost them dearly. Jordan Krestanovich reduced the lead to 4-3 with four minutes to go, and Ash Goldie fired the tying goal 1:22 later. That set the stage for his power-play goal at one minute of overtime, which won the game 5-4 for Victoria.[3117]

Before the Salmon Kings left for a road trip, they got good news. Milan Gajic had returned from his stint in Houston and would be available to play. Darryl Lloyd rejoined the club from the Bossier-Shreveport Mudbugs of the Central Hockey League. He was expected to add grit and aggressive forechecking.[3118]

At the US Airways Centre in Phoenix, the Salmon Kings fell behind 4-0, not scoring until McLeod fired his fifth goal of the season at 5:40 of the third period. Estrada brought the Kings closer at 7:33. Bernier made it a one-goal game at 14:24, and Jordan Krestanovich completed the comeback at 17:37. Overtime solved nothing, but in the shootout, McLeod and Gajic scored while Ellis allowed only one goal. The improbable victory was complete.[3119] The modest four-game winning streak came to an end when Phoenix won their first game of the season against the Salmon Kings. St. Jacques and Jordan Krestanovich had scored for Victoria in a 2-2 game when former Victoria Salsa Sean O'Connor fired the winning goal at 13:27 of the second period. There would be no miracle comeback today. All the games against Phoenix had been very close, with the previous four going to either overtime or a shootout. With a week between games, the Kings decided to come home before leaving for weekend games in California.[3120]

Before the Kings left, they received news from Manitoba. Due to an injury to Canucks' goalie Luongo, Drew McIntyre had been called up to Vancouver. That left a space open in Manitoba, which was filled by calling up Ellis from the Kings. Also, the Moose were short a forward, so they signed Gajic to a try-out contract. Billy Thompson was now the starting goalie for Victoria, with Jordan Watt being activated as a backup.[3121]

Game one in Fresno did not go well. When the Kings fell behind, 4-0, by the end of the second period, it was too much of a challenge to come all the way back. Wes Goldie scored his fifteenth goal of the season at 5:26 of the third, and Jordan Krestanovich added one 2:10 later. However, a Falcon goal at 18:11 put the game on ice for the home team.[3122] The next night, Victoria rebounded and edged the Bakersfield Condors 3-2. Rather than fall behind, the team was aggressive on offence. Jordan Krestanovich fired his seventh goal of the season at 3:18, and Gladue added his first before the game was five minutes old. After the Condors narrowed the lead, Bernier restored the two-goal margin, and Thompson allowed only one further score, stopping twenty-six shots along the way.[3123]

In a return engagement in Fresno, Victoria won in convincing fashion, 7-3, over the Falcons. Special teams were what determined the result, as the Salmon Kings killed off eleven of twelve Fresno power plays while scoring on three of their six opportunities with the extra man. Wade got the Kings on the board first, and Yeo added a second with under four minutes left in the opening period. The Falcons opened the middle frame with a spurt and managed to tie the score. However, Ballantyne, back from the injury list, blasted a shot past goaltender Moreland, only to have the Falcons score on a two-man advantage to again knot the game. In the final frame, it was all Salmon Kings as Bernier, Lloyd, Gladue, and Lloyd added markers before the end of the game. Victoria outshot Fresno, 38-36.[3124][3125]

Next, it was time for the teams on top of the standings to meet for the first time. Alaska came to town for a three-game set. Defencemen Coulombe and Kelly would miss the game due to injury, but Ellis was back from Manitoba, ready to take on the Aces.[3126] In game one, Bernier put the Kings ahead at 6:27, but they then made too many mistakes in the first period and ended it down, 3-1. Wes Goldie narrowed the lead to 3-2 on the power play midway through the middle frame and then looked to have tied it with a shorthanded goal. However, it was ruled to have gone off the crossbar. This play, and others like it, reinforced the issue of no video replay scoreboard in the arena. The Kings did manage to tie the score on a Yeo shot early in the third period, sending the game to extra time. Overtime was scoreless, and, in the shootout, Alaska scored three times to win the game, 4-3. Former King Guenette was the star for the Aces.[3127]

Game two was one for the ages. Victoria dominated in all aspects of the game to demolish Alaska, 8-1. Ash Goldie, just named as a starter in the ECHL all-star game, scored the first three goals to get the team off to a great start. Ryan Wade scored his fiftieth goal as a Salmon King, McLeod added his sixth of the season, Lloyd fired a pair, and Wes Goldie topped it off with his eleventh of the season. Ellis, also named as an all-star starter, made twenty-six saves for the win, running his record to 10-2-2. Victoria beat Alaska for only the fourth team in thirty-three regular-season games.[3128]

In the rubber match, it was another nail-biter as the Aces topped the Kings in a shootout. The first period was likely the worst hockey played by Victoria in a long time and ended with Alaska up, 1-0. After a very soft goal, Thompson was pulled and replaced by Ellis. In the middle frame, the Kings came alive and scored three times to take the lead. Wade at 12:10 (with a two-man advantage), Bernier at 17:20, and Wes Goldie at 19:52, all beat Kris Tebbs. However, an Alaska power-play goal tied the score and sent the game to extra time. After a scoreless overtime period, the game went to a shootout, where Pete Metcalf scored the only goal for the Aces (in the eighth round), propelling his team to victory.[3129]

After the Christmas break, Victoria finished out calendar year 2007 with a three-game trip to California. Playing before 6,866 fans in Stockton, Estrada got the first goal, but defensive lapses led to two-on-ones for the Thunder, and they buried two of them to lead after one. Estrada tied the game early in period two, and Jordan Krestanovich converted on the power play to put the Kings ahead, 3-2, after two. Ash Goldie gave Victoria a 4-2 lead before the Thunder scored on a power play. Derek Krestanovich had the final goal to ensure the 5-3 victory. Ellis stopped twenty-eight shots in recording his eleventh victory of the season against two losses and two shootout losses.[3130] In Fresno, the Kings won their twentieth game of the season, but they had to take it to a shootout to do so. Again, the Kings fell behind, 1-0, in the first period, but Estrada (with his third goal in as many nights) tied the game in the middle frame only to see the Falcons take the lead after forty minutes. Ash Goldie scored his twentieth of the season early in the final frame to tie the score again, but Fresno notched another on the power play. That set the stage for Ballantyne to get the equalizer with just under four minutes left in regulation time. Overtime solved nothing, and the game went to a shootout—and what an exciting shootout it was, going ten rounds before Yeo tallied the winner.[3131]

In the final game of the calendar year, the Kings fell to the Falcons. They were outshot, 11-4, in the first period, when Fresno notched two goals and did the same in the second. At twenty-six seconds of the final frame, Wes Goldie got the first Victoria score, followed by Estrada on the power play. Fresno notched their fifth goal, and Wes Goldie completed the scoring with a power-play marker at 16:57, but it was too little, too late, and Victoria lost 5-3.[3132] It was their first regulation-time loss in over two weeks.

The first news of 2008 was that Mark Morrison had been named as co-coach of the ECHL National Conference all-star team, sharing duties with the Wranglers' coach, Glen Gulutzan.[3133]

In the first home series of 2008, the Kings played Utah. In game one, they continued to perform well in racking up a 5-1 victory. Ash Goldie put the Kings on the board with his twenty-first goal of the season. Utah scored on the power play early in the middle frame, but the Grizzlies had no answer to St. Jacques and McLeod, who fired markers later in the frame to put the home team up 3-1. Captain McLeod scored his second of the game on a breakaway early in the third, and Ash Goldie completed the scoring with under six minutes left.[3134] The second game did not go Victoria's way, and they fell 2-1, to Utah in overtime. St. Jacques scored the first goal, but the Grizzlies tied it less than a minute later. The winning goal came in overtime on a shorthanded breakaway goal by Scott Burt, who stripped the puck and went in alone on Ellis. Coach Morrison said the team did not perform up to its standard.[3135]

The final game of the series, an afternoon affair, was much like the one the night before. Derek Krestanovich opened the scoring only to have the Grizzlies tie it up. Patrick Coulombe returned from injury and converted an Ash Goldie rebound on the power play to put the Kings up, 2-1, at the second intermission. The Grizzlies tied the score on the power play early in the third period and scored the winning goal on the power play at thirty-two seconds of overtime, sending the 4,539 fans home unhappy. Kevin Estrada and Bernier were unable to play due to injuries and Gajic was still with the Moose, so the team was playing with less than a full roster.[3136]

Before their next road trip, the Kings signed former junior star Nathan Barrett, who had won the WHL scoring title in 2001-02 with 45 goals and 107 points. Things had not worked out with the team he was playing for in Europe, so he signed with the Kings. As he was considered a "veteran" and Victoria already had the maximum four veterans, Gomez, Barrett, Wes Goldie, Jordan Krestanovich, or McLeod would have to sit out each game. In the meantime, Gomez was placed on the seven-day injury list.[3137]

Next on the schedule was a two-day trip to Las Vegas. The first game was a disaster, as the Kings could not score on Vegas goalie Daniel Manzato, and the Ferraro brothers, Peter and Chris, led the offence to a 5-0 shutout of Victoria. In the first period alone, the Kings were outshot, 17-4, but Ellis held the Wranglers off the board until the second frame when the dam burst and the rout was on.[3138] In the rematch, the Salmon Kings worked much harder and won the battles they had lost the night before. Down to four defencemen who could dress, the forwards helped where they could, and Ellis had a strong game in the net. New Salmon King Barrett opened the scoring on the power play. After the Wranglers tied it up on a shot off the post and Ellis's leg, McLeod got that one back just twenty-seven seconds later on a pass from Barrett. Wes Goldie completed the scoring with a shot just under the crossbar, and the defence held on from there to ensure the 3-1 victory.[3139]

Having an affiliation with an NHL club was not the solution to everything for the Salmon Kings. The downside was that, when a Canuck got injured, a replacement was called up from the Manitoba Moose, and that player had to be replaced with one from the Salmon Kings. In the second game at Las Vegas, Victoria had seven healthy defencemen, but that was reduced by two when the Canucks sent Yeo and Rahimi to Winnipeg. In addition, Gladue was out day-to-day with a low-body injury and Deschamps with a broken ankle. The search was on for anyone who could play defence in the upcoming home series.[3140]

In the first match of a two-game series against Bakersfield, Victoria lost a home game in regulation time for the first time in seventeen games. Gladue, who was playing despite being injured, notched the first goal of the game on a two-man advantage, but it was all downhill from there. Coach Morrison noted that the forwards did not forecheck, and the team did not play smart hockey, as there were far too many turnovers that led to chances for the Condors. The 5-1 score was one that was best forgotten—it was one of the worst games played that season. The Kings had to regroup quickly if they were going to get any points in the short series.[3141] Playing with just fourteen skaters and two goaltenders, the Salmon Kings dug deep and made the most of their chances. Jordan Krestanovich and Barrett had first-period goals to give the home team a 2-1 lead at the first intermission. Hemmed in their own zone and under intense pressure, the Kings finally broke out when Ash Goldie fed Estrada for a 3-1 goal. Bakersfield outshot Victoria 53-33, and notched two goals in the third period, but Thompson stood tall in the nets, giving his team a chance to come back. With the game tied, 4-4, at the end of regulation time, it took only twenty-nine seconds of overtime for Estrada to fire home the winner to the delight of the 5,802 fans in attendance.[3142]

Next on the agenda was a three-game series against the Fresno Falcons, who had been playing well of late and were now sitting just six points back of the Salmon Kings in the standings, with three games in hand. Things did not start well, as Fresno scored twice in the last three minutes of the opening period. However, power-play markers by Jordan Krestanovich and Ballantyne evened the score by the 6:44 mark of period two. In the final period, the teams exchanged goals; Lloyd and Ballantyne (with two to complete the hat trick) were the Victoria marksmen. Tied, 4-4, at the end of regulation time, the teams played extra time. Overtime was scoreless, but the Kings prevailed in the shootout as Dylan Yeo, just back from Manitoba, notched the winner.[3143] [3144] The Falcons got their revenge in the second match when they edged the Salmon Kings in overtime. Wade scored short-handed after 1:59 of play and Wes Goldie notched his seventh of the season while playing with a five-on-three advantage. Unfortunately, that was the end of the offence, as the Falcons eventually tied the score and then scored the 3-2 winner in overtime, playing short-handed. It was a bitter pill to swallow, but there was another game within a few hours for the team to get its act together.[3145] The Kings finished their homestand on a winning note when they clipped the Falcons, 3-1, in an afternoon matinee. Playing its seventh game in ten days, Victoria was led by Wes Goldie's two goals and one by the suddenly-offensive-minded Ballantyne, while Ellis made forty-two saves, giving up only one goal. After the game, the team had enough energy to skate around the ice with several fans.[3146]

Most of the players in the ECHL had a five-day break, but Ash Goldie, Julien Ellis, and Mark Morrison went to the all-star game in Stockton, California. In the skills competition the night before the game, Goldie set a record, becoming the first player in eleven years of ECHL history to hit all four of the targets in the accuracy challenge with only four shots.[3147] In the game itself, he continued to shine, scoring three goals on four shots and adding three assists to lead the National Conference to a 10-7 victory. He and Peter Ferraro of the Las Vegas Wranglers combined to record the fastest two goals in ECHL all-star history when they notched markers within sixteen seconds. Ellis was declared a co-winner in the breakaway relay. Goldie was then named the MVP of the game, attended by AHL and NHL scouts.[3148]

The team travelled north to Alaska, determined to break the mental block that seemed to prevent them from winning consistently against the Aces. One possible reason is that the Sullivan Arena in Anchorage was Olympic-sized and was well-suited to the game that Alaska played. In the first game, the Salmon Kings were shut out, 2-0, despite playing hard.[3149] Game two was a Victoria win by a score of 4-1. Bernier scored twice while Estrada, and Ash Goldie added singles. Thompson made thirty-six saves to record the victory.[3150] [3151] The Salmon Kings topped their effort from the night before, upending the Aces 7-4. Ash Goldie had a hat trick, Kelly had a pair, and Wes Goldie and Wade added singles. Estrada had three assists, and Bernier had two. The game started with a fight between Robin Gomez and the Aces' Eric Neilson, who had knocked out McLeod in the prior game, rendering him unable to play. The game had its ups and downs, but it was a satisfying win for Victoria, who now had an eight-day break before their next game.[3152] [3153]

Ash Goldie was named the ECHL "player of the week" for his prowess in the all-star game and the series in Alaska, where he notched four goals and two assists. It was the second time this season he had been honoured; he had also been recognized for the week of October 29-November 4.[3154]

On the road in California, the Salmon Kings were well-rested and ready to put forth a good effort to win their division. Milan Gajic was back from the Moose, but Kelly and Rahimi were still in Manitoba.[3155] In Bakersfield, the Kings took a lead, blew it, but came back to edge the Condors

7-6, in a shootout. Mark Derlago scored twice for Bakersfield, and Jason Kostadine added another, while only Yeo could find the back of the net for the Kings, who trailed, 3-1, at the first intermission. The first seven minutes of the middle frame were all Salmon Kings as Wes Goldie, Lloyd, and Derek Krestanovich scored to give the visitors a 4-3 lead. Coulombe gave the Kings a two-goal cushion at 15:00. In the third period, goals came with great frequency. Derlago scored at twenty-nine seconds to bring his team to within one, but Wade got that one back at 5:29. However, the Condors had two goals to tie the game and send it to extra time. Overtime was scoreless, but Wes Goldie and Milan Gajic fired goals in the shootout to give Victoria the victory.[3156]

Action then moved to Stockton, where the Kings continued their good play, winning, 4-3, in regulation time. Bernier got the team on the board first, but the Thunder tied it by the second intermission. Stockton went ahead early in the third period, but Gajic scored on the power play to knot the score at 2-2. Barrett's goal and Bernier's second gave Victoria a two-goal cushion that they needed, as the Thunder got another goal to bring them to within one. Ellis then held the fort, stopping forty-four shots in all, to preserve the victory.[3157] The final game of the road trip was not very successful, as Derlago had a hat trick to lead the Condors past the Kings. Gajic had a hat trick for Victoria, and Jordan Krestanovich and Coulombe added singles in a losing cause.[3158]

The Kings returned home for a two-game set against Fresno. In the first game, there was no miracle finish, as Victoria dropped a 3-2 decision to the Falcons. Wes Goldie's goal in the first period tied the game at 1-1, but the only scorers in the middle frame were from Stockton, giving them a 3-1 lead at the second intermission. Estrada brought the Kings within one and rang one off the post with seconds remaining, but it stayed out.[3159] Victoria was back in form for the next game, although they did not make it easy, needing overtime to get a 6-5 victory. After giving up the first goal, the Kings stormed back when Wade and Gajic scored fifty-seven seconds apart to put the team into the lead. Wes Goldie made it 3-1, and Lloyd scored the fourth goal. However, the Falcons came back and took the lead, 5-4, opening the way for Coulombe's tying goal with under a minute left in regulation time, with Thompson pulled for an extra attacker. It took just nineteen seconds of overtime play for Ash Goldie to fire the winner and send the 4,291 fans home happy.[3160]

The Salmon Kings then travelled to Las Vegas for a two-game set against the Wranglers that could go a long way toward the team finishing atop the conference. Vegas took a 2-0 lead, but Ash Goldie's power-play marker and McLeod's regular strength goal tied the game before the second intermission. Yeo fired the winner at 12:33 of the final frame, to give the Kings two precious points.[3161] Game two went Las Vegas's way as they upended Victoria, 5-3. Victoria took a 2-0 lead on goals by Gomez and McLeod, but the Wranglers got one back before the first intermission. Yeo restored Victoria's two-goal lead, but two power-play goals before 9:15 of the second tied the score again, setting the stage for two more Vegas goals for the win.

After the series, Victoria was in the same position as they had been before it: eight points behind the Wranglers with a game in hand. The last twenty-two games would be crucial.[3162] The next game was in Phoenix. It had to be rescheduled, as there was a conflict with the original date in March, so the Roadrunners let the Kings use their deluxe sleeper bus so they would be rested for the match.[3163] The well-rested Kings found their offensive skill and beat the Roadrunners, 6-4. Matt Kelly, just returned from Manitoba, got the show on the road with a goal just a minute into the game. Next came scores from Yeo and Lloyd, to give Victoria a 3-0 lead before the game was seven minutes old. Phoenix notched two quick goals, but McLeod restored a two-goal advantage with a power-play marker late in the first period. The second frame opened with another McLeod power-play score, but Phoenix got that back at the midway point. Wes Goldie added the final goal, his twenty-fourth of the season, shorthanded, to ensure the victory.[3164]

The next two series at home would very likely decide playoff positions. First up was a three-game set against the defending-champion Steelheads. Victoria was only three points ahead of Idaho, so it was essential to take as many points from them as possible.[3165] The Steelheads closed the gap on the Kings with a close 3-2 victory in game one. Victoria came up powerless, not getting a shot on goal until the fourteen-minute mark and almost unable to beat Kellen Briggs in the Idaho net. He stopped Gajic on a breakaway and was near-perfect the rest of the way, allowing only goals by Jordan Krestanovich and Ash Goldie.[3166] Two days later, the Salmon Kings found their scoring touch and rode a terrific performance by Ellis to a 6-0 shutout of the Steelheads. Victoria scored three times on the power play, twice shorthanded, and once at full strength. McLeod opened the scoring at 3:13 from in front of the net on a five-on-three advantage; that was all the offence until the third period when the floodgates opened. Jordan Krestanovich had a power-play marker at 1:21, Estrada a shorthanded goal at 7:32, Wes Goldie found the back of the net three minutes later, Bernier made it 5-0 at 11:59, and St. Jacques finished the scoring on the power play at 15:36. It was the widest margin of victory in some time, and it left the Kings three points up on the Steelheads.[3167]

Idaho took the rubber match, 4-2, and moved to within one point of Victoria. Special teams let the home team down, as they went zero-for-seven with the man advantage. The Steelheads played great defensive hockey, thwarting the Kings' offence at every turn. Only Lloyd and Yeo were able to break through for goals. The margin of the lead was down to a single point. Wade was suspended for two games for a hit in the prior game, reducing the number of forwards able to suit up. The team released Nathan Barrett, re-signed Chris Shaw, and activated forward Robin Gomez. Next up was a three-game set against the powerhouse Las Vegas team, currently in first place in the conference.[3168]

Victoria won the first game against Las Vegas, 5-3, but also lost, learning that their captain Kiel McLeod had been signed by the Albany River Rats of AHL and would be leaving immediately. The Wranglers started the game off well, with three goals in the first period offset by McLeod's last counter as a King. In the middle frame, Estrada scored at 7:57 and St. Jacques tied the game at 9:40. The final period was all Victoria, as St. Jacques's second goal of the game was the winner, and Estrada's second into an empty net sealed the deal.[3169] The team had to deal with the loss of McLeod, whose 6'6" frame and aggressive play would be missed. However, they had to come together and play like they had when he was injured earlier in the season.[3170]

Jordan Krestanovich was named team captain before the second game, which featured a heart-stopping finish. The Salmon Kings took a 3-0 first-period lead on goals by Wes Goldie, Ash Goldie, and Bernier. Las Vegas crawled back with a goal in the middle of the second frame and two in the third. Gajic put the Kings ahead, 4-3, but a shorthanded goal that went in off the skate of Gladue behind Ellis brought the teams level again. However, Yeo scored on the power play with .07 seconds left in overtime to send the 4,802 fans home happy. He said that he had never scored a last-second goal before, but this was an excellent time to do it.[3171]

The Wranglers won the third game in the series, but it featured an incident that should have never happened. With the home team down, 4-1 (only Ash Goldie had scored), Robin Gomez, apparently frustrated with how the game was progressing, came off the bench and sucker-punched Vegas star and former NHLer Chris Ferraro. The arena grew quiet as the fallen player lay in a pool of blood after hitting his head on the ice. Referee Jason Nissen threw the book at Gomez, assessing a game misconduct, match-fighting major, fighting major, and a minor penalty as the instigator. On the ensuing power play, Vegas scored what would be the eventual winner.

The Kings fought back when Wes Goldie fired two goals, and Yeo added one, but what would have been the tying goal off the stick of Wes Goldie just missed the net with six seconds left in the game. The Wranglers won the game, 5-4, but everyone was more concerned about the condition of the injured player. That the game had been played in front of hundreds of young hockey players, celebrating "Salute to Minor Hockey" night, made the incident even more disturbing.[3172] The ECHL took immediate action, suspending Gomez indefinitely. They also suspended Wrangler Marco Peluso for two games and fined him an unknown amount of money. He had punched Gomez while he was being held by the officials and unable to respond. The Victoria Police Department confirmed that they were investigating the incident to determine whether there was enough evidence to charge Gomez with assault. They had to examine the intent and also interview many witnesses, some of whom did not live there, so it would take some time to complete the process. Coach Morrison said he did not condone the behaviour and could not understand why Gomez did it.[3173]

Before a three-game series in Alaska, Manitoba called up defenceman Dylan Yeo. However, the team signed Brad Zanon, a former UBC Thunderbird, who was described as a solid all-round player.[3174] With a playoff spot clinched, the Salmon Kings set their sights higher and wanted to win their division. This plan was set back when the Alaska Aces topped the Kings, 3-2, in the first game of the set.[3175] Wes Goldie scored twice to run his season total to thirty, but he was the total offence for Victoria, as they lost their second game in a row. The next night, he added another goal, while his brother Ash and Gladue had singles, but they fell, 4-3. This was the first time all season that the Salmon Kings had lost three consecutive games in regulation time.[3176] The team would have to find some offence, or their plans for a division title would go up in smoke.

The losing streak came to an end when the Salmon Kings finally won a game in Alaska. Led by two shorthanded goals by Bernier and Estrada, a power-play marker by Gajic, and the thirty-second of the season by Wes Goldie, Victoria emerged as a 4-3 winner. Ellis played a strong game in the net to backstop his team to victory. Coach Morrison noted that all three games had been decided by one goal and either team could have won.[3177]

With Yeo, Rahimi, and Estrada still in Manitoba, the Canucks placed Nathan McIver on the Salmon Kings roster, although it was unlikely that he would ever play here.[3178] In the first of two games in Phoenix, the Salmon Kings came up flat, and their inability to score on the power play, despite seven opportunities, cost them the game. Only Bernier got on the scoreboard for Victoria. After Ellis surrendered four goals, he was replaced by Thompson who gave up one. The final score was 5-1; it was not a very good effort, and the Kings would need a much-improved game to gain the points they desperately needed.[3179] Phoenix won the second game, as well, sweeping the Kings in a series for the first time that season. Rookie Trevor Blanchard fired the only Victoria goal on a breakaway, but the Roadrunners scored six times to win handily 6-1. The Kings were again ineffective on the power play, going zero-for-five with the man advantage.[3180]

The Salmon Kings turned things around when Utah came to town for a three-game set. Two WHL grads, Kalvin Sagert from the Prince George Cougars and Jacob Dietrich from the Portland Winter Hawks, were added to the roster for the stretch run. Gajic was recalled to Houston of the AHL, so he was lost to the team for the immediate future. Derek Krestanovich was activated off the injury-reserve list, while Trevor Blanchard was placed on the three-day injury-reserve list.[3181] The first game was a decisive victory, 7-3, for the Salmon Kings. After losing five of their last six games, the Kings' special teams rose to the occasion, scoring four goals on the power play. They held the Grizzlies scoreless on the power play while notching one shorthanded. Wes Goldie had two power-play goals, and Derek Krestanovich added a single before the first intermission. Utah got on the scoreboard at

7:11 of the middle frame, but St. Jacques got that back 1:11 later. The Grizzlies narrowed the score to 4-2 by the second intermission, but Coulombe restored the three-goal margin—on the power play. Early in the final frame, Wade added a shorthanded marker, and Ash Goldie had the final goal, again on the power play, at 16:20.[3182]

The second game went Victoria's way, as Thompson backstopped his team to victory, making thirty saves for a well-earned shutout (his first of the season). Wes Goldie opened the scoring with his three-hundred-and-first professional goal early in the opening period. New King Jacob Dietrich had two goals in his second game with the team, and Kelly had the single score. The final score of 4-0 was an accurate indication of the run of the play.

Next on the agenda was "Pink in the Rink," to close out the series.[3183] The first 5,000 fans who made donations to breast-cancer research at the Saturday night game received a pink T-shirt. The game was a thrilling affair, as the Kings came back from a 2-0 deficit to send the game to overtime. Utah had the only score of the first period and added a second early in the third, but Ash Goldie and Wes Goldie scored on power plays to tie the score at 2-2. Overtime solved nothing, so the game went to the shootout. Out of ten shooters, only Ryan Wade was successful, but it was enough to give Victoria the victory 3-2, and the series sweep.[3184] Wes Goldie was named the ECHL "player of the week" for the week of March 17-23. He had four goals and six points against Utah, leading Victoria back to first place in the Western division.[3185]

The final road trip of the season took the Salmon Kings to California. Victoria opened in Stockton, where the team won despite being outshot, 40-25. St. Jacques opened the scoring at 4:48 only to have the Thunder tie it up twelve seconds later. A power-play marker by Bernier and an even-strength goal by Ash Goldie put the Kings ahead by two, but Stockton narrowed the lead by the first intermission. Early in the middle frame, the Thunder fired the 3-3 goal and went ahead, 4-3, on a power play.

Ash Goldie replied on a Victoria power play, and Coulombe added a man-advantage score as well to give the Kings a 5-4 lead after two. After Stockton evened the score again, Ash Goldie recorded the hat trick to put the Kings up in the seesaw match. The Thunder had one more goal, but West Goldie notched his thirty-seventh of the season at 19:09 of the third period to give his team the 7-6 victory. Newly-signed Salmon King Simon Lambert, a graduate of the Rochester Institute of Technology, and a finalist for the Hobey Baker Award as NCAA "player of the year," played his first game. The Salmon Kings reached the forty-win plateau for the first time in franchise history.[3186]

After four consecutive wins, the Kings could not handle Bakersfield and fell 6-3. The game started well with Kelly and Ash Goldie scoring in the first period. However, the Condors poured in four straight markers to take a lead they never relinquished. Wade had the third Victoria goal on the power play late in the second period, but Bakersfield added two more scores in the final frame to win easily.[3187]

Back in Stockton, the Kings managed a single point, as they lost in a shootout before 9,737 screaming fans. After the Thunder opened the scoring, Bernier and Coulombe put the Kings ahead, 2-1, at the second intermission. However, a power play midway through the final period knotted the score, sending the game to extra time. After a scoreless overtime, the game went to a shootout, where all five Victoria shooters were stopped, and the last shooter for Stockton scored, to give his team a 3-2 victory.[3188] In the final road game of the season, Fresno edged Victoria, 5-4, in overtime, but the Kings did pick up a valuable single point. The game was tied, 1-1, at the first intermission with Lloyd finding the back of the net for Victoria, but Fresno outscored the Kings, 2-1, in the middle frame to lead, 3-2, after two; Derek Krestanovich had pulled the Kings to within one. Fresno went ahead, 4-2, but a shorthanded marker by Wes Goldie and an even-strength goal by his brother tied the game with just under three minutes to play. However, Fresno found the back of the net after 2:28 of overtime to win, 5-4. This was not the time for the Salmon Kings to lose—they had picked up four points out of a possible eight on the road—but first place in the division was still up for grabs.[3189]

It all came down to the final homestand against Alaska to determine who would finish in first place and get home-ice advantage in the first round of the playoffs. Game one was a disappointment for the 5,056 fans who were expecting a better effort. The Goldie brothers staked Victoria to a 2-0 lead, but the Aces had tied it up by the thirty-seven-second mark of the middle frame. St. Jacques and Wes Goldie put the home team ahead again, but Alaska reeled off four straight goals to win the game, 6-4. The latest junior addition to the team was Brady Leavold, a star with the Kelowna Rockets, who was in the lineup for the opening game. Ironically, the winning goal was scored by former Salmon Kings forward Guenette, who had found a new home with the Aces.[3190] [3191]

Before the second game, Dylan Yeo was returned to the team from Manitoba.[3192] However, Jordan Krestanovich was out for a month with a leg injury. The race for first place in the Western division was going to come down to one game after the Salmon Kings found their offence and shut out the Aces, 2-0. The young players got the team on the scoreboard first, with Dietrich assisting on a goal by Leavold in the second period. Veteran Wes Goldie fired the second goal into an empty net to ensure the victory. Thompson made thirty-five saves, some of the spectacular variety, to backstop his crew to the win.[3193]

The success of the entire season came down to a single game between the two arch-rivals. Wes Goldie fired his forty-second goal of the season halfway through the second period to put Victoria on the board, only to see Alaska tie the score on the power play just seventeen seconds later. Derek Krestanovich got that one back about five minutes later to make the score 2-1 at the second intermission. Period three was all Salmon Kings, as Lloyd fired a puck past Brown, and Leavold cinched the game with an empty-net counter. The 4-1 victory gave Victoria first place in the western division and sent the loud crowd of 7,006 home very happy.[3194]

The Salmon Kings' opponent for the first round of the playoffs would be the Bakersfield Condors. Based on the teams' records, it should have been a short series. However, it turned out to be much closer than the experts predicted. Game one at home was a real shocker, as the visiting Condors edged the Salmon Kings, 2-1, in overtime.[3195] Thompson let in a very soft shot at forty-three seconds of the first period to give the visitors a 1-0 lead. Despite firing shots at Bakersfield goaltender Yutaka Fukufuji, the first Japanese-born player to make it to the NHL, they were unable to solve him until Eric Estrada fired a shot at 9:51 of the final frame to tie the score. In overtime, Keith Truelson fired a shot on the power play to win the game for Bakersfield.[3196] In the second, the Kings fell behind but played well enough to win the game, 4-3.

In the next game, Bakersfield scored the only goal of the first period, but Wade tied it up early in the second. However, the Condors scored the next two goals to take a 3-1 lead at the second intermission. Then it was time for the Ryan Wade show, as he scored shorthanded twice on the same Bakersfield power play (at 7:32 and 7:53 of the third), to tie the score. When Chris St. Jacques popped home the winner at 16:30, the 6,448 fans roared their approval. The series was now tied, 1-1, with the next three games in California.[3197]

Game three was another nail-biter. Yeo gave the Kings a 1-0 lead on a power play, but the Condors tied it up just thirty seconds later on a power play of their own. The second Victoria goal came off the stick of Yeo just as a two-man advantage was coming to an end, but a puck that bounced off players and into the net tied the score for Bakersfield. That set the stage for the overtime heroics of Bernier, who backhanded a shot past Fukufuji for the winning goal that sent the crowd of 5,197 home disappointed. Before the game, the team had received the good news that Gajic would be returned to Victoria in time to play, but he was a non-factor.[3198] [3199]

In the next game in Bakersfield, the Salmon Kings played like they had done most of the season and smothered the Condors, 4-1. Outshooting their opponent, 20-9, in the first period, they were only able to score once, when Ash Goldie hit the back of the net at 2:47. The Condors tied the match at 13:13 of the middle frame, but Yeo and Lloyd scored at 18:20 and 19:33, to open up a two-goal lead. In the final period, the Kings missed on breakaways by Wes Goldie and St. Jacques and on a penalty shot by Lloyd. However, Wes Goldie sealed the victory with his first of the series at 14:37. Victoria now led the series, 3-1, and was only one game away from a series victory.

Before the next game, the teams had two days off due to concerts by 3 Doors Down and Elton John.[3200] The rest seemed to have benefited the Condors, as they won, 5-4, to extend the series. Bakersfield opened the scoring, but Yeo notched his fourth of the series to tie the count. The Condors went ahead just before the first intermission, but Ash Goldie and Wade gave the Kings a 3-2 lead. Bakersfield came back, then Wes Goldie put the Kings up, 4-3. Then came a very soft goal that Thompson should have stopped and the eventual winner by Salmon King-killer Derlago, at 14:43. The Kings were unable to tie the game, despite exerting pressure on the Condors.[3201]

The series then shifted to Victoria for game six, with the Kings leading, 3-2. It was yet another heart-pounding one-goal decision. The game did not start well for Victoria, as Bakersfield opened the scoring and added a second on a strange bounce. Bernier got the Kings on the board on an assist from Lloyd, but the Condors got that one back about three minutes later. St. Jacques scored on the power play with just over a minute left in the first period. Ballantyne tied the score early in the second, but the Condors again took the lead. The final frame made the difference in the game, as the Kings outscored their opponents, 2-1, to end regulation time, 5-5. Bernier and Wade had given Victoria a lead, but the pesky Condors tied it at 13:16. Victoria outshot Bakersfield, 57-23, but could not get the extra goal they needed. There was no further scoring in regulation time, so the game went to extra time. The winner came shorthanded off the stick of Ash Goldie, who had taken a perfect pass from Estrada. That sixth goal brought the crowd of 6,701 to its feet to cheer the team who had just won their first playoff series.[3202] [3203] Now, it was on to the next round against the Utah Grizzlies, with the first game on April 25, 2008, in Victoria.[3204]

The Salmon Kings did not play well in the first game, failing to match the intensity of the Utah Grizzlies. As a result, they were shut out, 6-0. The usually-prolific power play went zero-for-ten, while their opponents had two goals in four chances. Thompson started the game but was replaced by Ellis in the third period. The change did not make any difference as, on this night, the Grizzlies scored almost at will.[3205] [3206] Victoria would have to play a complete game two days later, or it would be a short series. That game did not start well as Tyler Haskins scored on a penalty shot at 18:03 of the first period, but the Salmon Kings had an unbelievable third frame, notching six unanswered goals, to win the game, 6-1. Coach Morrison changed his lines, inserting Dietrich between Ash Goldie and Milan Gajic, and the strategy worked as they combined for four goals. Dietrich started the onslaught on the power play at 2:18. Goals then followed in quick succession: Wes Goldie at 8:30, Ash Goldie at 12:02, Gajic on the power play at 13:55, Wes Goldie again at 18:52, and Dietrich completing the rout at 19:24. Ellis made his first start of the playoffs and made twenty saves, some of them of the spectacular variety. The series was now tied, 1-1, with play shifting to Utah.[3207]

Kiel McLeod returned to the lineup as his AHL team, the Albany River Rats, had been eliminated from further playoff games.[3208] The next game started well but ended in disaster. Gajic and Wes Goldie scored before the game was nine minutes old, Utah responded, then McLeod had a pair and

Bernier a single to put the Kings up, 5-1. That's when the roof caved in, as the Grizzlies scored six unanswered goals in just over two minutes to play to win the game, 7-5. Utah was now leading the series, 2-1, with two more games left in the E Center.[3209]

Game four was a more subdued affair with only two goals scored. Unfortunately for Victoria fans, their team did not score either of them. The Grizzlies rode an early first-period goal by Kinasewich, and a hot goalie in Mike Mole, adding an empty-net counter to seal their victory. Coach Morrison said his team played really well but could not find the back of the net. Now down 3-1 in games, it was "do or die" the next night.[3210]

The fifth game of the series was one that the Salmon Kings wish had never happened. They were blasted, 8-3, by a team on a mission. Ballantyne's goal in the opening period had narrowed a Utah lead to 2-1, but six straight unanswered Grizzlies' goals put an end to any hope Victoria had of coming back. Bernier had two goals near the end of the contest, one on the power play, but it was all over long before that. For a team that had played so well most of the season, the collapse in this series was puzzling. Perhaps they just ran out of steam after playing short-staffed for most of the season.[3211]

In his post-season comments, Dave Dakers said that he thought the team would do better in Utah, but that it had been a successful season overall. In the first two seasons, playoff hopes were dead by Christmas, and this year, the team had won a division title and made it to the second round of the playoffs. Over the playoffs, the Salmon Kings led all minor hockey leagues (including the AHL) in attendance, with an average of 5,851 over five games. Gone were the days when you could literally count the fans. GM Dan Belisle would spend time trying to sign as many players as possible because the team was only able to put eight non-signed players on their protected list.[3212] With a new GM in Vancouver who favoured a three-tier system, it looked as if the affiliation with the Canucks would continue under Mike Gillis. There would be changes as players moved up to the AHL or took their skills to Europe, but there was a good core here that would form the basis for another exciting team.[3213]

In May, the Salmon Kings signed head coach Mark Morrison to a new three-year contract. In addition to his coaching duties, he would also assume the position of general manager. That move would allow him to speak to players with authority on all hockey matters. Dan Belisle would remain with the club as vice-president of hockey operations. Together, they hoped to build a winning team for the hockey fans of Victoria.[3214] In off-ice matters, the Salmon Kings organization was rewarded with National Conference Awards of Excellence for the ticketing department and media relations.[3215] Everything was in place for another successful season. It remained to be seen what would happen in the fall.

Victoria Salmon Kings 2007-2008 celebratory card. From the author's collection.

34 - RECORD-BREAKING SEASON

In July of 2008, the Salmon Kings announced that they had renewed their affiliation agreement with the Vancouver Canucks and the Manitoba Moose for the 2008-09 season. Steve Tambellini, Vancouver Canucks vice-president and assistant general manager, said, "The strong local connection between the Canucks and the Salmon Kings reinforces our commitment to further develop and support hockey in British Columbia." Craig Heisinger, senior vice-president and general manager of the Moose, said, "After the tremendous success of the Salmon Kings last season, we are looking forward to once again working with Mark Morrison and the rest of the organization in 2008-09. The Salmon Kings did a great job providing young players like Daniel Rahimi or Dylan Yeo with the type of atmosphere that we strive to provide here in Winnipeg with the Moose, so it is a good fit."[3216]

Throughout the summer, news of player signings was released. Veterans signed were Darryl Lloyd, Chris St. Jacques, Wes Goldie, Jacob Dietrich, and Matt Kelly, while newcomers Jeremy Swanson, Shaun Landolt, Jordan Foote, Marc Fulton, Jeremy Schenderling, and Mike Nesdill were also given contracts.[3217][3218] Three Kings players were invited to the Canucks prospect training camp in Vancouver: Julien Ellis, Patrick Coulombe, and Daniel Rahimi would suit up with other young players but could be returned to the Kings during the season.[3219] Ellis was injured during an exhibition game and would be out for about two months. The Canucks invited Victorians and draft picks Taylor Ellington and Dan Gendur to the main Vancouver camp, along with Daniel Rahimi, while Patrick Coulombe and Victorian Jordie Benn would attend the AHL camp of the Winnipeg Moose.[3220]

Early in September, assistant coach Quentin Van Horlick resigned, leaving a vacancy in the team's coaching ranks.[3221] The announcement of his replacement was a bittersweet moment for Victoria fans. Original Salmon King Ryan Wade announced his retirement from professional hockey but would remain with the organization as the new assistant coach. His knowledge and experience would prove valuable as the team began to take shape.[3222]

September saw some more signings as Tim Wedderburn, returning defenceman Darren Deschamps, and rookie Rob Jarvis all signed contracts.[3223] By the end of September, Coach Morrison said he expected eleven players contracted to the Vancouver Canucks or Manitoba Moose to be assigned to Victoria, up from just five in the last season. The goaltenders who would be present at the local camp were Todd Ford and Jonathan Boutin, with a further decision to be made when Ellis was able to return to the roster. Taylor Ellington was deemed "not ready for the pro game" and was returned to his WHL junior team in Everett.[3224]

Jordie Benn, the former captain of the Victoria Grizzlies, was assigned to Victoria by Manitoba just before the Kings' camp. Also sent to Victoria were Matt Kelly and Jacob Dietrich.[3225] Young goaltenders Blake Grenier from the University of Alberta and UVic goalie Gord Neave were expected to play in the nets until Ford and Boutin arrived. The Kings' training camp ran from October 3 to October 8, with two exhibition games against the Idaho Steelheads on October 10 and 11.[3226]

Former foe Olivier Labelle, who had played for the Utah Grizzlies the last season and was largely responsible for the Kings' exit from the playoffs, was assigned to Victoria from Manitoba, along with Yeo and Coulombe, both of whom had toiled here last season. Goaltenders Ford and Boutin were also sent to the Salmon Kings.[3227]

In the first exhibition game in Idaho, the Kings came out on top with a 4-2 decision over the Steelheads. Scoring for Victoria were Foote, Lloyd, Kelly, and Landolt.[3228] Game two went the same way, with Victoria winning, 4-3, in the shootout. Olivier Labelle scored twice in regulation time, and Kelly added a single. In the shootout, it was Labelle and St. Jacques finding the back of the net. Todd Ford played well in goal, stopping thirty-five shots in regulation and overtime and four out of five in the shootout.[3229] The team had one spot left in the veteran category and was looking to fill it before the start of the season.[3230] With former captains McLeod and Jordan Krestanovich playing now in Italy, the Kings needed a new leader. Wes Goldie was named the new captain just before the season opener, with Wedderburn and Kelly named as alternates. The opening day roster was confirmed as well. Forwards: Jacob Dietrich, Jordan Foote, Marc Fulton, Olivier Labelle, Shaun Landolt, Darryl Lloyd, Sean O'Connor, Chris St Jacques, Jeremy Schenderling, and Wes Goldie. Defencemen: Tim Wedderburn, Matt Kelly, Dylan Yeo, Patrick Coulombe, Gary Gladue, Jordie Benn, Mike Nesdill, and Jeremy Swanson. Goaltenders: Todd Ford and Jonathan Boutin.[3231] Jeff Harris's play-by-play call of each game was available on the Salmon King's website; a video version was on a pay-per-view basis.[3232]

The 2008-2009 season opened on the road in Phoenix. It did not go well for Victoria, as they tried to play a finesse game and that was not their style. Several defensive lapses proved to be costly in a 7-1 loss to the Roadrunners. Boutin got the start for the Kings but was replaced by Ford in the third period. Only O'Connor managed to beat Craig Kowalski in the Phoenix net.[3233] Game two did not go any better, as the Roadrunners edged the Kings, 2-1. Victoria started the game strongly with seven shots but was unable to score. Ironically, Phoenix got its first shot at 8:22, and ironically, it ended up in the net for a 1-0 lead. It was a strange game, as the usually calm Wes Goldie even got into a fight to try to inspire his team. Phoenix went up 2-0 early in the third period, and Kelly scored the only Kings' goal under a minute later, but that was all the offence for Victoria.[3234] In two games, they had scored two goals, a far cry from the way they had been able to score at the end of last season. The offence finally woke up in the third game of the season, when the Kings upended the Roadrunners 4-2. Labelle scored his first as a King at 3:22 of the opening period. Yeo had the second goal early in the middle frame, and Labelle added his second under five minutes later. However, the Roadrunners scored twice on the power play in just over three minutes to narrow the score and had a great chance near the end of the game, when they had a two-man advantage and pulled the goaltender, but Wes Goldie fired a short-handed goal into the empty net to seal the victory.[3235]

Before the home opener, local-product Dan Gendur was sent to the Kings from the Moose.[3236] Brady Leavold re-joined the team after some time in the AHL with Norfolk. He had played here in the playoffs last year, and the Kings had retained his ECHL rights. Two forwards, Fulton and Schenderling, were not under an NHL or AHL contract and were released by the Kings. The fourth veteran position was filled by Olivier Filion, who had played with the Alaska Aces. He had tried playing in France, but it had not worked out, so he had contacted Mark Morrison to see about a spot.[3237]

Salmon Kings commemorative pennant for Western Division Championship, 2008.

The first 4,000 fans through the gates for the home opener received a mini replica of the 2008 ECHL Championship banner, the original of which was raised to the rafters in a special ceremony. However, the evening went downhill from there. Stockton got on the board early in the first period, and it took until nearly the end for Wes Goldie to score on a power play to tie the game at the first intermission. Former WHL Vancouver Giant Gareth Hunt was a thorn in the side of the Kings all night, scoring twice and agitating throughout the game. Dan Gendur notched his first professional goal, but that was the end of the Victoria offence. The Thunder added two power-play markers in the final frame to win (quite easily), 5-2.[3238] Game two was a complete reversal of form, as the rookies led the way in a 5-2 Victoria win. Wes Goldie had the only marker of the first period, but Leavold and Gendur scored the next two to stake the home team to a 3-1 lead. Goldie's second increased the lead, and Labelle potted the insurance goal late in the third. Victoria outshot Stockton, 42-20, but took too many penalties, leading to the two Thunder scores. The team revealed their third jersey with a large V on the front and a crown hanging off one edge.[3239] The rubber match of the series was played with Oilers' assistant GM Kevin Prendergast in the stands, watching his farmhands with the Thunder, and he liked what he saw; Moose GM Craig Heisinger was not as impressed by what he saw. Wes Goldie scored his fifth of the season on a first-period power play, but the offence dried up after that, and Stockton notched three unanswered to take the match, 3-1. The Salmon Kings were now 2-4 to start the season—not where they were expected to be. Something was going to have to change, or it would be a long season.[3240]

Utah came to town for a three-game set and former Grizzlies' player Labelle fired the winning goal on a two-man advantage, with under three minutes left in regulation time, to give his new team a hard-fought 4-3 win. Wes Goldie scored the first goal, as he had been doing a lot that season and Yeo fired a shot on the power play to give the Kings a 2-0 lead at the first intermission. A few minutes of inattention at the start of the second period let Utah back in the game, as they scored twice before the period was three-minutes old to tie the game. Curtis Billsten, who had been picked up on waivers from the Idaho Steelheads just before the game, put the Kings ahead, only to have Utah tie it up again. That set the stage for the winner with 2:44 left in the game. The team was still not playing up to its potential, but there were flashes of brilliance.[3241] In player moves, Leavold hurt his leg and was placed on the thirty-day injury list; that allowed the Kings to reactivate Jordan Foote. Mike Nesdill was lost on waivers to the Cincinnati Cyclones when Travis Ramsey was sent down from Manitoba.[3242] In the second game, on Halloween, Utah edged Victoria,

3-2. After taking the lead midway through the first period on a goal by Labelle, the Kings gave up three straight to the Grizzlies, who led, 3-1, at the second intermission. A second goal by Labelle early in the final frame gave the home fans some hope that their team could come back, but they could not penetrate the Utah defence.[3243]

In the rubber game of the match, the Kings fell again, this time by a 4-3 score. Utah took the early lead, but Labelle tied it up. The Grizzlies went ahead, but Kelly scored on the power play to even the score again. Utah then fired two goals to take a 4-2 lead and a late goal by St. Jacques was too little, too late. The Kings were now an embarrassing 3-6 on the season, winning just one game in each of the first three series. There was an upsetting incident in the game when Utah's Evan Kotsopoulos kicked Sean O'Connor and cut him across the cheek. Coaches, players, and fans could not figure out how the Grizzlies player was not given a penalty for the infraction. It was expected that the league would have a look and decide on supplementary discipline.[3244 3245 3246] The league eventually handed Kotsopoulos a nine-game suspension and assessed an undisclosed fine for his kicking incident. The league noted that it found no intent to injure.[3247]

The next road trip started very early in Bakersfield. It was the annual "School Day," so the game began at 10:30 a.m., an ungodly hour for hockey. In personnel moves, the Kings released Foote and placed Gendur on the three-day injury list. Jordie Benn was activated for the upcoming games.[3248] Labelle continued his great play with a second-period goal to put his team on the board. O'Connor had the other two scores, the second one into an empty net to ensure the victory. Boutin played well in the early game, shutting out the Condors, 3-0, sending 8,000 screaming schoolchildren home unhappy.[3249] The newest Salmon King was Scott Howes, who was signed by Manitoba and was assigned to Victoria. In his first game, he was on a line with Goldie and Filion, which fired seventeen shots on goals but did not score.[3250] Once again, the Kings could not win two games in a row, as they dropped a 3-2 decision in the shootout to Stockton. Goldie fired the first goal to make the score 1-0 Kings at the first intermission. The teams traded goals in the middle frame (O'Connor for Victoria), and the Thunder had the only counter of the third. Overtime solved nothing, but in the shootout, Stockton outscored Victoria 3-1 to take the extra point.[3251] The next day, Victoria turned the tables and defeated the Thunder 3-1. Filion and Billsten gave the Kings a 2-0 lead before Stockton got on the board. It was a close 2-1 game until Landolt scored short-handed into the empty net with three seconds left to seal the deal. Todd Ford was named the game's first star for his stellar work in the net, stopping all but one of the twenty-five shots fired his way. This was the most successful road trip of the season, as the Kings picked up five of a possible six points.[3252]

Back home in Victoria, the Kings played a three-game set against Phoenix. In the first game, they finally figured out how to score on the power play and did it twice against the top-ranked penalty killers. Billsten opened the scoring at 8:04, and Goldie added a power-play marker just fifty-nine seconds later to give the home team a 2-0 lead. Phoenix had an early goal in the third period, but that was the only time they were able to beat Boutin. Filion scored twice, one on the power play, to put the game on ice.[3253] The second game showed total domination by the Salmon Kings, as they dumped Phoenix, 9-0. Gendur scored twice on the power play to open the scoring, and Howes added a single to give the Kings a 3-0 lead at the first intermission. Labelle and St. Jacques added second-period goals. St. Jacques completed his hat trick in the third period, while Lloyd and Goldie completed the rout. The Kings outshot the Roadrunners, 57-25, scoring the most goals in a game in franchise history.[3254] Goaltender Jonathan Boutin was named the ECHL "goaltender of the week" for November 10-16. Over his four starts in November, he was 3-0-0-1 with two shutouts, a goals-against-average of 0.73, and a save percentage of .975.[3255]

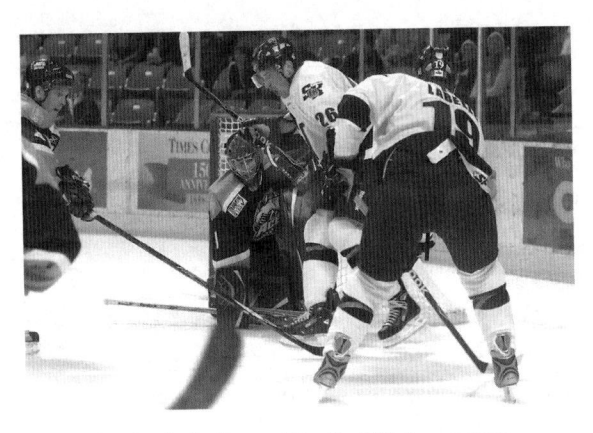

Olivier Labelle and Curtis Billsten versus the Alaska Aces, November 19, 2008. Photo courtesy the Victoria Salmon Kings.

The Alaska Aces came to town and cooled off the Salmon Kings. Victoria opened with a goal by Filion, but the Aces got that back before the end of the first period. In the middle frame, goals came in rapid succession. The Aces went ahead on the power play at twenty-five seconds, but Filion got that back just nine seconds later. Alaska retook the lead, and Goldie tied it up on the power play at 6:56. Two more Aces' goals gave the visitors a 5-3 lead at the second intermission. A single Alaska marker in the third period completed the scoring. The Kings' three-game winning streak had come to a crushing end.[3256] Victoria rebounded in the next game to upend the league-leading Aces, 3-1. Dietrich gave the Kings a 1-0 lead at 17:39 of the first period, scoring his first of the season. Lloyd added a single with just twenty-four seconds left in the middle frame to give his team a 2-0 lead. Boutin lost his shutout when Alaska beat him about nine minutes into the final period, and Goldie fired his eleventh of the season into the empty net to ensure the victory.[3257]

In the rubber match of the series, the Kings fell behind, rallied to tie the game, and then fell in overtime after a questionable penalty call in overtime. The Aces scored the first three goals of the game, but Landolt, Gendur, and Labelle scored in the late-second and early-third periods to tie the score. A high-sticking call of the very light variety (that usually would not be called) 1:45 into overtime gave the Aces the extra man, and they took full advantage of it. However, the team played hard and did not give up. They also took three out of six points from the Aces, matching them in intensity.[3258]

In player moves, Boutin was loaned to the Manitoba Moose, as their goaltender had been called up to replace injured Canucks goalie Roberto Luongo. Luckily, Julien Ellis had just come off the thirty-day injury list and would be available to play, but would be a bit rusty. Ford was expected to carry most of the goaltending load on the upcoming seven-games-in-fourteen-nights road trip.[3259] [3260] Olivier Labelle also left the team, as he was called up to Manitoba. So far this season, he had sixteen points in seventeen games for the Kings and was a threat to score at any time. His departure left Victoria with eleven forwards, seven defencemen, and two goalies.[3261] [3262]

The road trip started well. Playing at the E Centre for the first time since their collapse in the playoffs the previous year, the Kings spent most of the first period shorthanded and fell behind late on a power-play marker in the opening period. St. Jacques and Dietrich scored 1:09 apart in the middle frame to put the Kings in the lead. Utah then tied the score, only to have Landolt put Victoria back in front at the second intermission. A goal by Yeo midway through the final period gave the Kings a 4-2 victory. Ford stopped thirty of thirty-two shots fired his way.[3263]

Game two was a close affair, with Victoria emerging with a 3-2 overtime decision. Utah opened the scoring to lead 1-0 at the first intermission. Lloyd scored early in the second, but Utah went ahead five minutes later to take a 2-1 lead. With just over four minutes left in the game, Filion received a four-minute penalty. Despite playing one-man short, the Kings went on the offensive and were rewarded when Yeo tied the game with a short-handed marker at 16:15. In overtime, playing on the power play, Landolt fired the winner at 2:35 on passes from Filion and Goldie.[3264] The Salmon Kings swept the series with a 2-1 win over Utah. The only goal surrendered by Ellis, making his first start of the season after returning from an ankle injury, was a first-period penalty shot. He then closed the door, giving his team a chance to win. Goldie fired two goals to bring his season total to thirteen, which was all the offence that the team needed. Both were named stars of the game.[3265] Wes Goldie and his scoring prowess were featured in an article, in which he was compared to Guyle Fielder of the Seattle Totems, who was an amazing scorer but never made it to the NHL. As Goldie put it, "I can't control what happens off the ice and decisions that are made about your career by others." The benefit for Victoria fans was that they were able to watch Wes play in their hometown.[3266]

The Salmon Kings then played the Ontario Reign, the former Texas Wildcatters. Kelly opened the scoring for Victoria, but Ontario tied the score by the first intermission. In the second period, the Reign took the lead, but Yeo tied it up for the Kings. The only goal of the final frame was by the Reign, as they narrowly edged the Kings 3-2.[3267] The Augusta Lynx ECHL franchise became the first to fail to complete a season in the league when they folded. However, none of their players ended up in Victoria.[3268]

The troubles that the Kings had in Fresno continued in game two of the trip. After taking a 2-0 lead on goals by St. Jacques and Dietrich in the first period, Victoria sat back and surrendered three unanswered goals to the Falcons, who emerged as 3-2 victors.[3269] Rebounding from the loss the night before, the Salmon Kings played a nearly perfect game, limiting Fresno to just seventeen shots on goal on their way to a 5-1 victory. Landolt and Goldie fired goals in the first period to get the game underway. After a scoreless middle frame, O'Connor and Yeo beat Fresno-goaltender Michael Ouzas. After a shorthanded goal by Fresno, Goldie, with his fifteenth of the season, closed out the scoring. Ellis went the distance for a relatively easy win.[3270]

In the final game on the road, the Salmon Kings edged the Reign, 3-2. Captain Goldie notched the first goal on the power play to give the visitors a 1-0 lead at the first intermission. After Ontario scored twice to take the lead, Filion evened the count on the power play. The winner came off the stick of O'Connor with under five minutes left in regulation time. Yeo assisted on all three Victoria goals and Gendur on two.[3271] After fourteen days on the road, the Kings finished with a 5-2 record. Were they on track for even greater achievements?

Goaltender Julien Ellis in game versus Bakersfield Condors on December 9, 2008. Photo by Anne-Marie Sorvin, courtesy of Victoria Salmon Kings.

Back home, the Salmon Kings shut out the Condors, 2-0. With only nine forwards, Morrison moved defenceman Matt Kelly to a winger spot, and it paid off. The game was scoreless until Kelly found the net at 10:59 of the third period. Landolt ensured the victory with an empty-net goal at 19:00. Ellis made twenty-four saves en route to his first shutout of the season.[3272] The winning streak continued as the Kings bulldozed the Roadrunners, 7-0. Sean O'Connor scored at sixteen seconds, the quickest score after an opening faceoff in team history, and the rout was on. Lloyd added a pair, while St. Jacques, Dietrich, Yeo, and Billsten added singles. Ford went the distance for the shutout, stopping all twenty-six shots fired his way. Gendur and Ramsey had been called up to the Moose, but the team did not seem to miss them, at least for now. However, the big news was off the ice, as Abbotsford had been granted an AHL franchise that would play in an arena the same size as in Victoria. Many in Victoria wondered if their city would be next in line, but Dave Dakers noted that, in order to secure a team, the city would have to pay travel subsidies and underwrite a portion of the losses, and there was no appetite in Victoria to do that right now.[3273]

December 14, 2008, was a brutal winter night, but that did not stop 4,339 stalwart fans—including two who made their way to the game on cross-country skis—from braving the conditions to support their suddenly soaring team. It was also "Teddy Bear Toss" night, and the home fans did not have to wait long to cover the ice with stuffed animals that would be distributed to children in hospitals, as Goldie scored his first of three at 4:46 of the opening period. That goal was his one hundredth as a Salmon King, and he became the first to reach that milestone. Goldie's linemates, Filion and Gendur (just back from Manitoba), featured prominently in the play, the former with a goal and two assists and the latter with a pair of assists. Other markers came from Kelly and Dietrich, while Ellis stopped twenty-five of the twenty-seven shots fired his way.[3274] Just when everything was falling nicely into place, the Moose recalled Julien Ellis and reassigned Jonathan Boutin to Victoria.[3275] The Salmon Kings stayed on top of the Western division by defeating the Alaska Aces, 4-2. This rivalry always produced the most competitive games, likely because of their geographic proximity, and this series did not disappoint. Another good crowd of 4,162 made it to the arena to watch Goldie fire another hat trick, bringing his goal total for the season to twenty-two. His final score went into an empty net, with the Aces playing six-on-three after pulling their goaltender and with two Kings in the penalty box. Billsten added the other goal, and Ford stopped all but two of the shots he faced. It was the sixth consecutive win for the team and put them three points ahead of the Aces, in first place in the division.[3276]

Victoria moved five points up on Alaska, as they shut out the Aces, 5-0, with 4,772 fans in attendance. This time, a different line made the difference. Billsten recorded a pair of assists, Landolt had a goal, and O'Connor had a goal and an assist as their line played a dominant role in the victory. Other marksmen were St. Jacques and Scott Howes. Ford made twenty-six saves en route to his second shutout of the season. Kelly separated his shoulder in the second period and was expected to be out for at least two weeks.[3277] In the final game of the series—and the last before the Christmas break—the Salmon Kings completed the sweep, outlasting the Aces, 5-3. Alaska got on the board first, but Landolt and Goldie put the home team ahead at the first intermission. Two goals early in the middle frame put the visitors ahead, but a controversial penalty shot awarded to St. Jacques turned the game around. He was hooked from behind on a breakaway and still managed to get a shot away. Usually, in those cases, a penalty is assessed, but in this case, it was a penalty shot on which he made no mistake, knotting the score at 3-3. Coulombe found the net for his first of the season, and Goldie sealed the victory with an empty-net marker with fifty seconds left in the game. The winning streak was now up to eight, and fans wondered how long this magical ride would last.[3278]

For players trying to get home for Christmas, Mother Nature had different plans. Flights out of Victoria and Vancouver were cancelled, with repercussions all across Canada, and some players wondered if they would ever get home. The lucky ones were those who called Victoria home—Sean O'Connor, Jordie Benn, and Dan Gendur—and Gary Gladue and Shaun Landolt from the lower mainland.[3279]

ECHL officials were scrambling to redesign the schedule now that the Fresno Falcons, who had been in the league since 1946, had folded. The team cited the economic downturn in North America, reflected in the drop from average attendance to 3,284 this season from 5,035 in 2007-2008 and the decrease in season-ticket revenue and corporate sponsorship. As a result of the uneven number of teams in the National Conference, the proposed playoff system (with the top four from each division) had to be scrapped. The top eight finishers in the conference would now make the playoffs and would be seeded accordingly.[3280]

Todd Ford was named the ECHL "goaltender of the week" for December 15-21. He stopped eighty-one shots in a three-game series against the Alaska Aces. In his last five starts, he was 5-0 with two shutouts and goals-against-average of 1.40 and a save percentage of .952.[3281]

Back from the Christmas break, the Salmon Kings continued their red-hot play. In Stockton, they gave up the first goal, then came back with four unanswered to win the game, 4-1. Goldie added to his league-leading goal total with his fourteenth of the season and then assisted on one by Filion. Lloyd and O'Connor had the other markers; Goldie, Filion, and St. Jacques all had two points for Victoria. Boutin was in net for the Kings and stopped thirty-three of the thirty-four shots he faced.[3282] The next game produced yet another win, extending the streak to ten. Stockton was no match for the Salmon Kings, who came back from a 2-1 deficit to win, 5-2. Twice Goldie scored to put the Kings ahead, and twice the Thunder tied it up. However, Leavold and Dietrich put Victoria up, 4-2, and Billsten fired the puck into an empty net to secure the victory.[3283] The year ended on a high note when three Salmon Kings (Wes Goldie, Dylan Yeo, and Dan Gendur) were named to the ECHL all-star team.[3284]

The Salmon Kings opened 2009 the same way they closed 2008: with a victory. The streak was now at eleven, setting yet another team record.[3285] Bakersfield was the visitors this time, and they went down to defeat by a score of 5-2. Billsten opened the scoring, and Goldie made it 2-0 by the first intermission. After the Condors got on the board, Yeo restored the healthy lead. In the final frame, Dietrich made the score, 4-1. Bakersfield got that one back, but Billsten found the empty net for the clinching goal. Olivier Labelle rejoined the team from Manitoba, and former Victoria Grizzlies defenceman Devon Lang made his debut, collecting one assist on the night. Scott Howes was recalled by Manitoba.[3286] In the next match, Boutin turned aside thirty-one shots in Bakersfield to earn a narrow 2-1 victory. Victoria never trailed in the game, as Billsten notched his ninth with the Kings holding a two-man advantage in the first frame, and Lloyd added a second-period marker to lead the team to a 2-0 lead at the second intermission. The only Condor score came with under five minutes left in regulation time on the power play, but they were unable to beat Boutin again.[3287] The Salmon Kings' win streak reached thirteen with a decisive 6-1 win over Bakersfield, sweeping the series. It was the fourth-longest winning streak in ECHL history.[3288][3289] They scored four times on the power play and added one shorthanded to dominate on special teams. Billsten continued his strong play, notching his tenth goal of the season to open the scoring. In the middle frame, Coulombe on the power play, O'Connor shorthanded, and Goldie on the power play put the Kings up, 4-0. Lloyd and Leavold added scores with the man advantage to add to the lead. Boutin lost his shutout bid with under five minutes left to play. However, it was a satisfying win, and the coach was very pleased with the way that the veterans had helped the younger players gel as a cohesive team.[3290]

With the demise of the Fresno Falcons, the Salmon Kings schedule had to be changed. As travelling to Victoria is expensive for visiting teams, three-game series were changed to four games in three cases. The three-game set versus the Falcons, originally scheduled for April, was cancelled and the games added to series against other teams. The Wednesday, April 1 game was changed to February 8, versus Las Vegas at 5:05 p.m. The Friday, April 3 game was changed to March 15, versus Ontario at 1:05 pm, and the April 4 game was changed to March 22, against Idaho, at 1:05 p.m. This meant that the season would finish on March 28, in Stockton, and there would be a week's wait until the playoffs began.

In personnel changes, Gendur, Howes, and Ellis were returned from Manitoba. That created a three-way competition in the goal crease. Coach Morrison decided to keep all three for now, just in case there was an injury.[3291] The team received several honours for their great play over the last month. Wes Goldie was named the ECHL "player of the month," Todd Ford was named ECHL "saver of the month," and Mark Morrison was named as co-coach of the National Conference for the 2009 ECHL all-star game.[3292]

The beat went on as the winning streak continued, now reaching fourteen. Goldie hit the thirty-goal plateau with the opening goal of the game on the power play. Lloyd and Yeo also found the net. The three goals were scored in just 1:11, to set a new club record. Ontario narrowed the lead with a pair of goals in the middle frame, but Victoria notched a pair of their own in the final period, as Goldie and Lloyd scored their second of the match. The key to the game came when the score was 3-2, and the Kings were down two men. Led by Wedderburn, they killed those penalties off, blocking shots and frustrating the Reign shooters. Boutin played a stellar game in the net, stopping thirty-eight of the thirty-nine shots he faced.[3293] The next night, the Salmon Kings upended Ontario, 5-2, to extend their win streak to fifteen, the second longest in ECHL history. Falling behind on an Ontario power play at 5:20 of the opening period, the Kings rebounded with four straight scores in the middle frame, as O'Connor, Goldie, Labelle, and Coulombe all found the net. In the final period, Ontario scored early, but Gendur hit the empty net to seal the deal. Julien Ellis played his first game for Victoria since returning from Manitoba and got better as the game went on. He ended up with thirty-four saves and was named the first star of the game.[3294]

The Salmon Kings took their winning streak on the road to Alaska. Scott Howes was placed on the three-day injury list and Ford on the seven-day list.[3295] The streak ended in Alaska, as the Aces edged Victoria, 3-2, in a shootout. Twice, the Kings took the lead, only to have the Aces tie it up. Filion scored on the power play in the first period, and Coulombe in the second, but the team was unable to prevent the Aces from tying the score with under three minutes left in regulation time. Overtime was scoreless, and in the ensuing shootout, the Aces outscored Victoria, 2-0, to take the victory.[3296] In game two of the series, the Kings suffered their first regulation-time loss since December 5, 2008, when Alaska beat them, 5-3. It was another close encounter, with the outcome in doubt until the Aces hit the empty net with 1:04 left in regulation time. Three consecutive Alaska goals in the second period made the difference in the game, as the Kings were unable to match their intensity. Gendur had the first goal, but the Aces replied. Howes put the Kings ahead, 2-1, but then Alaska potted three to take a 4-2 lead. Lloyd brought the score closer, but the Aces fired on an empty net to put an end to the Victoria comeback.[3297] In the final game of the series, the game was scoreless through regulation time and overtime. In the shootout, only Billsten found the net for the Kings, but two Aces did, so Victoria lost 1-0. It was not the way the team wanted to enter the all-star break, but they had a 26-10-4 record, and that was none too shabby.[3298]

Wes Goldie decided not to play in the all-star game, as he wished to rest an upper-body injury, but Gendur and Yeo, along with Coach Morrison headed for Reading, California.[3299] In the ECHL skills competition, Gendur won the fastest skater with a speed of 13.686 seconds to win by .13 seconds, while Yeo had the hardest shot at 97.7 miles-per-hour (the runner-up fired at 97.1 mph).[3300] In the game itself, both players had five shots on goal but did not score. The American Conference outscored the National Conference 11-5.[3301]

The Salmon Kings started a new streak after the all-star game was done. They travelled to Las Vegas and won the first game of a three-game set, 2-1, in a shootout. Todd Ford was the star of the game, stopping thirty-one shots in regulation time and overtime and then allowing only two Wranglers to beat him in the shootout. Las Vegas took an early lead in the second period on a power play, but O'Connor tied it up, also on the power play, midway through the third frame. Overtime was scoreless, and the teams ended the mandatory five-player shootout tied, 2-2. It then went to sudden death, where Ford blanked the Wranglers while Landolt scored in the tenth round to win the game.[3302]

The next night was a bit easier, as the Kings outscored the Wrangler 4-2. O'Connor had two goals, while Landolt and St. Jacques added singles, the last into an empty net.[3303] Game three did not go well right from the start. Down 3-0 after the first period, St. Jacques scored in the middle frame to narrow the lead to 3-1, but the Wranglers scored three times in the third, while only Goldie could find the net for the Kings in the matinee game. It was one of those games where the bounces went the wrong way and often ended up behind Ellis. The final score of 6-2 pretty well reflected the play. It said a lot about the team that they were disappointed not to take all six points on the road.[3304]

Before the next homestand, Adam Taylor returned to the team after playing in China.[3305] The club sent Jonathan Boutin to the South Carolina Stingrays for future considerations. He was a victim of the three-goaltender scenario, as he was not under contract to either the Canucks or the Moose. In the first home game against Stockton, all three lines played well in the total team effort. The Kings were up 3-0, by the first intermission on goals by Gendur, Goldie, and Labelle. The Thunder scored twice early and once late in the middle frame, but Howes and Goldie responded for Victoria. Two goals in the final period, by Billsten and Howes, made the final score 7-3. Admittedly, Stockton was shorthanded on defence, because of injuries and suspensions from their previous game, but even if they had been at full strength, it is likely that the Kings would have won.[3306] The next game was a complete reversal, as Victoria had no offence and Stockton managed two goals to shut out the Kings, 2-0. Despite the loss, Ellis was strong in goal, stopping thirty-two shots and being named the third star of the match.[3307]

In personnel moves, Manitoba called up Dylan Yeo, and Jacob Dietrich was traded to the South Carolina Stingrays.[3308] Milan Gajic returned to the Salmon Kings when his team in Denmark was facing financial issues. He was one of seven players from the last year's team—Ash Goldie, Kevin Estrada, Paul Ballantyne, Kiel McLeod, Jordan Krestanovich, and Billy Thompson—who had gone to play in Europe.[3309] Coulombe was added to the injury list, so there were only four defencemen—Gladue, Wedderburn, Kelly, and Benn—able to play in the next series. Landolt, who had played some defence in junior hockey, would be dropping back to help when needed.[3310]

After a week off, the Kings appeared flat and did not play well in game one against Las Vegas. They fell behind, 3-0, and did not get their offence untracked until midway through the second period, when Goldie scored on the power play and St. Jacques added a single. Try as they might, they could not beat Wranglers' goalie Glenn Fisher, who made several scintillating stops. An empty-net goal ensured the 4-2 victory for the visitors.[3311]

The second game was just as close, although the Kings did play better hockey. After the Wranglers opened the scoring, Goldie tied it up with a shorthanded goal from an impossible angle. Las Vegas had the only goal of the middle frame and led off the third with another, to give them a 3-1 lead. Taylor notched his first since rejoining the Kings, but an empty-net marker by the Wranglers gave them a second consecutive 4-2 victory.[3312] The next game was "Pink in the Rink," and more than $19,000 was raised in the fight against breast cancer and other women's diseases. The Kings did not play well and lost their fourth in a row, with a score of 2-1. Taylor opened the scoring, but that was the end of Victoria's offence as they failed to convert on five power plays after going zero-for-six the night before. Of note was their inability to cash in on a two-minute, two-man advantage late in the second period with the score tied, 1-1. The winning marker came early in the third period off the stick of veteran Chris Ferraro and sent the crowd of over 6,000 home deflated. Victoria was still in first place in their division, but the lead was shrinking.[3313]

The Wranglers completed the series sweep with a 1-0 overtime victory in a late-afternoon match. It was a tense affair with the goaltenders near-perfect. The winning goal came, with just sixteen seconds left in the overtime period, off the stick of Victoria-product Sean Owens, who really enjoyed playing in his hometown. With the losing streak now at five, the Kings were headed out on the road for a twelve-game trip as the Save-On-Foods Memorial Centre was being used for the Scotties National Women's Curling Championship.[3314]

In a trade that shocked some of the Victoria fans, the Salmon Kings sent popular forward Milan Gajic to the Florida Everblades in return for defenceman Aaron Brocklehurst, a former Victoria Salsa player. The coaching staff noted that it was a difficult deal to make, given what Gajic had done for the Kings, but they needed to shore up the defence, and this trade would bring in a power-play specialist who could give the anemic Kings' power play a boost.[3315]

The first game in Alaska was a tense, hard-fought victory for the Aces. Alaska took a two-goal lead, but Taylor and St. Jacques tied the score at 2-2. The Aces again went ahead, but Lloyd knotted the score. A goal at 19:02 gave Alaska the victory and sent the Kings to their sixth straight loss.[3316] Defensive help was on the way for the beleaguered Salmon Kings, as Manitoba had assigned Travis Ramsey to Victoria. Coach Morrison was none too happy with his team's lack of wins. He noted that some players were just not trying hard enough, and for him, that was unacceptable.[3317] The players took his comments to heart and won the next game, 2-1. It was their first "W"

since January 27, 2009. After falling behind, 1-0, in the second period, the Kings made the final frame count, notching two goals (by Goldie and Lloyd) to emerge with the victory.[3318] In the third game of the series, it was "close, but no cigar," as the Aces edged the Kings, 3-2, in a shootout. Kelly got Victoria on the scoreboard early in the game, but Alaska notched two straight to take the lead. St. Jacques tied the game, 2-2, at 8:02 of the final frame, but nobody could beat a goaltender in the remainder of regulation time or overtime. In the shootout, the Aces outscored the Kings, 1-0, to take the game.[3319] The final game of the set was all Alaska, as they dumped Victoria, 5-2. The Kings, showing the effect of four games in five nights for a short bench, did not show much offensive power. Although they had the first eight shots of the game, they were unable to score, and Alaska got on the scoreboard first. By 2:08 of the third period, the score was 5-0, so the late goals by St. Jacques and Wedderburn merely made the score more respectable. Now, it was on to California and warmer weather.[3320]

In Ontario, the Kings failed to convert their many chances in the first period and fell, 5-3, to the Reign. Goldie notched his fortieth goal of the season to open the scoring, but Ontario then put three shots past Ellis with only St. Jacques replying for the Kings. In the final frame, Ontario had two more goals to only one (by Kelly) for Victoria. Their lead atop the western division was shrinking with every loss.[3321] Having finally fielded a full defence, the Salmon Kings were now going to be a man short on the blue line, as Ramsey was recalled by Manitoba. With the forwards, Brady Leavold was activated off the injured-reserve list, but Dan Gendur was placed on it.[3322]

In the next game, the Kings bumped the slump, edging Bakersfield in a shootout. Landolt and Labelle scored in the first period with one by the Condors sandwiched in between. Bakersfield took the lead with a pair of goals, but Goldie tied it, on the power play, with his forty-first of the season. After a scoreless overtime, the Kings edged their opponents, 2-1, in the shootout. Ford was outstanding in goal, making thirty-seven saves, including twenty-two in the middle frame.[3323]

The remainder of the road trip was unsuccessful, as Victoria lost all five games. On the next game in Bakersfield, the Kings ran into a potent offence and could not respond in kind. Goldie and St. Jacques were the only marksmen for Victoria in a 5-2 loss.[3324] In Ontario, the Reign took a five-goal lead before the Kings got going. Goals by Gendur and Howes were all that Victoria could manage in a 5-2 loss. Ellis faced fifty-two shots, many of the spectacular variety, but he did not have much support.[3325] Fans wondered what had happened to the team that had reeled off fifteen straight wins. It was like a tale of two different teams, with the current version in freefall. At the end of February, Gendur was recalled by Manitoba.[3326]

After a week off, the Kings resumed play with three matches in Idaho. Now out of first place, Victoria had to make sure that they made the playoffs, where anything could happen. For some reason, this was the first time that the Kings had played Idaho, and they would play seven of their last fifteen against the Steelheads.[3327] In game one, the Kings were tied after two periods with goals by Lloyd and Goldie, but a fluke score did them in. According to *Victoria Times Colonist* reporter Cleve Dheenshaw, "the puck chipped off Victoria forward Chris St. Jacques and flew so high into the air that most of the players lost sight of it. There was probably six inches of daylight between Victoria goaltender Todd Ford's back and the crossbar, yet somehow the puck found that tiny gap to bounce off Ford's back and into the net." That play was typical of the kind of luck the team was having lately: mostly bad.[3328]

Two days later, the Kings started well but faded in the late going to lose, 6-5. O'Connor started the game on a good note with a goal at seven seconds. That lead held until late in the period when Idaho tied it up. In the second frame, O'Connor, Labelle, Taylor and St. Jacques found the net for Victoria, while the Steelheads responded with two to make the score 5-3 at the second intermission. Then the roof caved in, as Idaho shot three pucks past Ford and the Kings had no response. It was a disappointing result and dropped Victoria into third place in the standings.[3329] Idaho completed the series sweep with a decisive 4-1 thumping of Victoria. The team had lost its confidence and was not playing well, firing shots that went wide and not capitalizing on their chances. Kelly had the only score for the Kings, and it opened the game. When Idaho notched three goals in less than three minutes in the second period, the game changed for the worse, and Victoria never recovered.[3330]

Returning home after a 2-8-1 road trip, the Salmon Kings looked to take advantage of being at home in front of their rabid fans.[3331] The team responded to the home response with a decisive 9-4 thumping of the Reign. Taylor led the way with a hat trick, and Jordie Benn scored his first professional goal, while singles came from O'Connor, Goldie, Brocklehurst, Labelle, and Filion. Billsten had four assists and was named the game's second star.[3332] The second game did not go well. Ford had a shaky first period, allowing three goals on only nine shots. Despite holding the edge in play, only O'Connor found the net for the Kings. His second narrowed the lead to 3-2, but an early third-period goal by the Reign gave them a two-goal lead. Goldie notched his forty-fifth of the season, but the team was unable to tie the score.[3333] With the Vancouver Canucks' director of player development Dave Gagner in the stands, the Kings played a spirited game and edged the Reign in a shootout. After surrendering the first goal, Kelly and Filion gave the home team a 2-1 lead. Ontario scored twice in the final frame to take the lead, but Brocklehurst fired a shot with just eleven seconds left to tie the score, 3-3. After a scoreless overtime, the game went to a shootout, where Ellis stoned the Reign, and three Victoria shooters were successful. The teams had a very short turnaround with the next game being played at 1:00 p.m. the next day.[3334] In the matinee, the Kings upended the Reign, 3-1. Howes, Leavold, and Taylor scored for the home team, and Ellis stopped all but one shot. It was a good victory and made the after-game skate with local fans much more enjoyable.[3335]

The last home series was a four-game affair against Idaho. Game one saw Goldie score his forty-sixth of the season to give the Kings an early lead. After Idaho tied the score, Leavold put the home team ahead again. However, a late first-period goal by the Steelheads made the score 2-2 at the first intermission. Adam Taylor put the Kings ahead in the middle frame, but Idaho tied the game with under a minute left in regulation time. In the shootout, Idaho outscored Victoria, 3-2, to win the game by a score of 4-3.[3336]

Game two was a low-scoring affair, as Ford and the Salmon Kings shut out the Reign, 2-0. Leavold had both goals for the winners, and Ford had to stop just twenty-two shots. Dylan Yeo was back in the lineup, as he had been returned from Manitoba and his presence was felt on the blue line.[3337] A crowd of 6,314 was ready to cheer their Kings to victory in the third game of the series, but something went terribly wrong. Victoria came out very flat, and the score was 5-0 before Landolt got the Kings on the board. The Steelheads added two more and embarrassed the home team, 7-1. It was the most lopsided loss of the season and virtually ensured that the Kings would finish third in the standings behind Alaska and Idaho.[3338]

The homestand ended on a sour note, as the Steelheads upended the Salmon Kings 4-2. Victoria was down, 2-0, midway through the second period, when Filion found the net to narrow the score. However, the Steelheads outscored the Kings 2-1 in the final frame to take the contest. Wes Goldie fired his forty-seventh goal in a losing cause.[3339][3340] With the home portion of the season over, an examination of attendance showed that the average number of fans per game rose slightly over the previous year, to 4,923. This ranked the team ninth best in the ECHL and better than seventeen teams in the American Hockey League.[3341]

On the final road trip of the regular season, the Salmon Kings travelled to California. In Stockton, Victoria scored three times in the third period to win the first game, 5-2. Lloyd had the first goal, and at the first intermission, the score was 1-0. In period two, the Thunder had two goals to the one for the Kings by Howes. Tied, 2-2, at the second intermission, the game was broken wide open when Lloyd, Landolt, and Coulombe found the net, the last into an empty cage, and Ford held firm in goal, despite facing sixteen shots in that period alone, and forty-seven overall.[3342]

Next on the schedule was Bakersfield, whose 16-4-1 record over their last twenty-one games made them the hottest team in the league. Leavold scored first only to see the Condors tie it up before the first intermission. Lloyd, O'Connor, and Labelle then scored in a span of 5:21 to lead, 4-1. The Condors got only one in that frame, leaving the score 4-2 at the second intermission. Lloyd notched his second of the game at 16:07 of the third period and the home team beat Ellis with fifteen seconds left in the game. Julien Ellis was the star of the match, facing fifty-five shots while his team could only manage twenty-three on Yutaka Fukufuji, the usually deadly Bakersfield netminder.[3343]

In the return match, Bakersfield showed why they had such a good record lately when they blitzed the Kings, 7-3. The Kings scored first, as Leavold and Kelly found the net, but three straight Condor goals gave them the lead. Goldie tied the game early in the middle frame, but Bakersfield notched four straight goals to win going away.[3344]

The Salmon Kings' regular season finished with a game in Stockton. Scott Howes led the way with his first professional hat trick, while Coulombe added a single. The game was tied, 4-4, after regulation time, but Leavold found the net just forty-four seconds into overtime to send the Salmon Kings off to the playoffs on a winning note.[3345]

Now all the Kings could do was sit and wait, as they had two weeks off (due to the changes in the schedule when the Falcons folded). Time was spent in practice and strategy sessions, as they prepared for round one. Their opponent would not be decided until the other Western teams had completed their schedules.[3346] In ECHL business, three teams folded. The Phoenix Roadrunners, Dayton Bombers, and Mississippi Sea Wolves would not be in the league the next year, making it five teams that had ceased operation in one season. On the positive side, the Toledo Walleye would be joining the league in the next season. There would, therefore, be nineteen teams in the ECHL for the 2009-2010 season.[3347]

Dylan Yeo made history when he was selected to the all-star first team—the first Salmon King to be so honoured. Wes Goldie was chosen for the second team—the third time a King had been on that list (Ash Goldie was chosen in 2007-2008 and Lingren in 2005-2006).[3348]

Finally, the Kings knew that they would play the Idaho Steelheads in the first round of the playoffs, with that team having finished second to the Alaska Aces. The series would start in Boise on April 11. The first two games would be in Idaho, with the series moving to Victoria for games three, four, and five (if necessary). Any further matches would be played in Boise.[3349] In preparation for their twenty-two-man rosters for playoff action, the Kings included Manitoba players Taylor Ellington and Travis Ramsey, neither of whom would be on the roster when play began.[3350] A pre-series analysis of the teams gave the edge to Idaho in goal and forwards, and to Victoria on defence and even for the coaching staff. Would the Kings be stale, having not played competitively for two weeks? Only time would tell.[3351]

In game one, Idaho opened the scoring, but then Ford shut the door, allowing no further pucks past him. Labelle and Leavold put the Kings ahead, 2-1, and Landolt iced the victory with an empty-net marker. Goldie missed a penalty shot, but fortunately, that did not affect the result of the game, which ended with a 3-1 victory. It was the first time Victoria had won at Idaho all season and could not have come at a better time.[3352]

Game two was also successful, as Ford shut out the Steelheads, 2-0. He stopped all fifty-one shots fired his way in a masterful performance. Labelle scored the first goal at 8:08 of the opening period, and there was no further scoring until Taylor hit the empty net. The Kings now led the series, 2-0, and were heading home, where the crowd would be on their side.[3353] With 4,086 fans roaring their approval, the Salmon Kings demolished Idaho, 9-2, in the first home game of the series. The nine goals tied a 2007 playoff mark set in a round against Alaska.

Coulombe got the game off to a good start with a marker at forty seconds. Idaho tied the game at the five-minute mark, then Brocklehurst, O'Connor, Filion, and Labelle fired goals to end the first period up, 5-1, despite having only nine shots on goal. Goldie, Howes, and Landolt beat Rejean Beauchemin, who had replaced Matt Climie in the Steelhead net after the third Kings goal. Idaho hit the net early in the final period, but Howes replied, ensuring the decisive victory. The Kings were now up 3-0, in the series and had to be careful not to be over-confident.[3354] In sports, the game to clinch a series is often the hardest to win. However, the Kings did, indeed, sweep the series with a nail-biting overtime decision. Idaho got on the board first, and that 1-0 lead held until the third period when Taylor scored his second of the series to tie the match. That set the stage for the winning goal in overtime. Matt Kelly notched it after 12:56 of extra time and sent the crowd of 4,973 into a frenzy. The Salmon Kings had won the first round of the playoffs when the "experts" had given them little chance. Ford stopped thirty-one shots, while Climie made thirty-eight saves for Idaho.[3355]

In the other series in the Western division, the Alaska Aces dispatched the Utah Grizzlies four games to one, setting up a series between two teams that were very familiar with each other. The question on everyone's minds was whether the Kings could overcome the mastery that the Aces had demonstrated over several seasons. To do so, they would have to play with the same grit they did against Idaho.[3356]

In the first game of the series at Sullivan Arena in Anchorage, the hometown Aces blanked the visiting Salmon Kings, 3-0. Victoria got into penalty trouble with two of the goals scored with the man advantage. Against a team as strong as the Aces, players just cannot take penalties. Now it was time to regroup and get ready for the next contest.[3357] Alaska capitalized on their power play chances in game two, notching five goals on their ten chances. The game was 3-0 for the Aces at the first intermission. In the middle frame, Alaska scored twice with the only Victoria response a power-play marker by Goldie. Down 5-1 at that point, Ford was replaced by Ellis, who surrendered the next three goals. A late goal by Howes with just over two minutes remaining was the only other Victoria score. Now down 2-0 in games, and having been outscored, 11-2, the Kings were going to have to bear down and play the gritty hockey that had carried them through the first series.[3358]

The series now shifted to the friendly confines of the Save-On-Foods Memorial Centre, where the crowd would be loud and in favour of the Salmon Kings. Coach Morrison said that his players had to step up and do what they had done to get them that far. He also noted that the goaltending had to improve.[3359] In game three, the Kings built up a 2-0 lead on first-period goals by Labelle and St. Jacques, but collapsed in the third period, surrendering five straight unanswered goals by the Aces, who took the match, 5-2. Ford allowed the five goals on just eleven shots, not the type of goaltending the team needed, and the defence did not play up to par either. Now down 3-0 in the series, the Kings would have to win the next game, or it would be all over.[3360]

History was against the Salmon Kings, as no team in ECHL history had come back to win a series after being down 3-0. However, the team was taking it one game at a time and was determined to fight to the last minute.[3361] In the next game, the Kings played like the home fans expected them to. With nothing left to lose, they were loose and relaxed as they skated and checked their way to shut out the Aces, 4-0. Goldie scored twice, while singles from Filion and St. Jacques gave the Kings the offence they needed. Gendur added two assists. Ellis, making his first start in over a month, stopped all twenty-eight shots from the potent Alaska shooters. The game deteriorated in the third period with roughing minors, fighting majors, and high-sticking among the infractions. Now with a victory in the series, it was up to the Kings to repeat that feat and send the series back up north.[3362] Game six started poorly for Victoria, as Alaska had two goals by the 7:35 mark. However, the Kings stormed back with scores by O'Connor and Filion on the power play to knot the score after one period. Filion and Brocklehurst had early second-period markers to put the home team ahead 4-2, but the Aces got one back before the second intermission and took the lead with a pair of final-frame markers. They added an empty-net goal to seal their victory. Alaska won the game, 6-4, and the series, 4-1, to move on to the next round.[3363]

For the Salmon Kings, it was time to clean out the lockers and disperse across the continent to their homes. The series had illustrated the lack of depth on the team, as when they lost Kelly on defence, there was nobody able to step up to take his place. On the other hand, Alaska had many players who could step up their game.[3364]

There were many questions to be answered, but in retrospect, the season certainly had its high points, including the fifteen-game winning streak. The second-half collapse that cost the Salmon Kings first place and home-ice advantage in the playoffs had to rank as the low mark of the season. Who would be back the next season? Some of this team undoubtedly would be, but many would play elsewhere.

35 - THE YEAR OF "THAT GOAL"

As the 2009-2010 season drew near, several players were signed to contracts. Wes Goldie and Curtis Billsten would be back and would be joined by Dirk Southern, an explosive forward from the Gwinnett Gladiators.[3365] Next to be inked were Olivier Filion and newcomer Rob Smith, who had played the last season in Germany. Tim Wedderburn would return, and the team would add Kaleb Betts who had spent the previous season with the Elmira Jackals.[3366] The Salmon Kings renewed their affiliation with both the Vancouver Canucks and the Manitoba Moose. The relationship had been good for the Kings, as they received quality players who had formed the nucleus of the team.[3367] The Salmon Kings' athletic therapist and strength and conditioning coach was hired by the Vancouver Canucks as an assistant athletic trainer, illustrating that there was upward movement of training staff, as well.[3368] Defenceman Matt Waddell, who had played the last season in Sweden, and defender Mike Burgoyne from the Belfast Giants were signed at the end of August.[3369]

Training camp would open in early October; there would be no pre-season games due to the distance that teams must travel to reach Victoria and the extra costs involved. In addition, Canadian players on US teams needed to have US work permits in place, and teams were reluctant to file applications for permits for players who were not likely to make the team. The latest signing was Bear Trapp who had been a Hobey Baker nominee for the past two years while playing at Sacred Heart in the NCAA.[3370] Yannick Tifu, who had survived a bus crash while playing with the Albany River Rats, was now fully rehabilitated from a back injury and ready to play for the Salmon Kings.[3371] Also returning was Patrick Coulombe, now signed by the Salmon Kings, as his three-years with the Canucks organization had expired. It was interesting to note that Coulombe had been voted the last season's Salmon Kings' team MVP by the coaching staff.[3372] Winger Jason Deleurme was also signed. He had a thirteen-year career, playing last in Germany. He was expected to bring leadership to the club.[3373] Former Condor Chad Painchaud also joined the Kings. Coach Morrison had been impressed with his play during the last season against Victoria.[3374] New signings in late September included all-star goalie John Murray, who had played for Ontario the last year and defenceman Brandon Roach.[3375] Manitoba sent four players to the Kings: Taylor Ellington, a former WHL player with Everett; Dan Gendur, Scott Howes, and newcomer Dirk Southern, an Anaheim draft pick.[3376]

Training camp opened with twenty forwards, eight defencemen, and four goaltenders. Included in the prospects was Lance Morrison, son of the coach. Management was awaiting word on goaltender David Shantz, now in the Calgary Flames system.[3377]

The annual Blue vs. White inter-squad game, on October 9, showcased the current season's talent and was used by the coaching staff to make decisions on which players to retain. Admission was free and hot dogs, pop, and popcorn were sold for one dollar.[3378] In the game itself, Blue won, 4-3, over White. Lance Morrison, Rob Smith, Kaleb Betts, and Brandon Lassiter scored for the winning team, and Scott Howes, Brandon Roach, and Taylor Ellington for the losers. Following a second inter-squad game, the roster would be reduced by eight.[3379] Local-product Tim Crowder, Kaleb Betts, Kyle Bruce, Jason Deleurme, Brandon Lassiter, Colin Patterson, Bear Trapp, Kevin Falloon, Stefan Drew, and Justin Grevious were released from the team, as the roster reached twenty-two players. A new addition was Olivier Latendresse, who had signed with Manitoba but did not make that team.[3380]

Victoria Salmon Kings puck with white background. From the author's collection.

The Salmon Kings opened the 2009-2010 ECHL season in Anchorage against the Aces. On the roster were goaltenders David Shantz and John Murray; defencemen Patrick Coulombe, Taylor Ellington, Gary Gladue, Brandon Roach, Rob Smith, Tim Wedderburn, Mike Burgoyne, and Noel Coultice; and forwards Andy Brandt, Olivier Filion, Dan Gendur, Wes Goldie, Mike Hamilton, Scott Howes, Olivier Latendresse, Lance Morrison, Chad Painchaud, Dirk Southern, Adam Taylor, and Yannick Tifu.[3381] The first game was a close encounter, but the Kings fell, 2-1, to the Aces. Goldie had the only goal, which tied the score, 1-1, at the time. The winning goal came with just fifty-seven seconds left in regulation time.[3382] Game two was another loss, this time, 5-3. Howes opened the scoring, but then the Aces notched three straight goals to take the lead. Filion and Painchaud tied the score at 14:33 of the middle frame, but a late second-period goal and one shorthanded in the third put the game on ice for Alaska.[3383]

The Aces swept the opening series with a narrow 2-1 victory. Latendresse scored early in the opening period to put the Kings on the board, but the Aces scored twice in the middle frame (the winner on the power play) to secure the victory. Victoria outshot Alaska, 35-25, but was unable to solve the goaltending of Scott Reid.[3384]

After losing three straight games to open the new season, the Salmon Kings came home to face Bakersfield. Unfortunately for Victoria, the Condors were the top farm team of the Anaheim Ducks, who did not have an AHL affiliate at that time and thus had ten top prospects in their lineup.[3385] The Kings' record slipped to 0-4, with a 3-1 loss in their home opener. Bakersfield scored first, but Taylor tied it just over seven minutes later. However, that was the end of Victoria's offence, and the Condors notched the winning goal on a soft shot late in the third period. An empty-net goal ensured their victory.[3386] [3387] The Salmon Kings won their first game of the new season when Fisher backstopped the team to a 3-0 whitewashing of the Condors. Wes Goldie led the way with two goals, while Brandt added a single. Filion and Gendur added a pair of assists. Goaltender Glenn Fisher, who was signed when David Shantz was called up to the AHL, made thirty-six saves for his first shutout of the season.[3388]

In the rubber game of the series, the Kings made "big mistakes," and it cost them dearly. After a scoreless first period, the Condors notched three goals to Victoria's two, with Hamilton and Ellington finding the back of the net for the Kings. The backbreaker came when the Condors scored a shorthanded marker to increase their lead to 4-2. A Kings' goal on the same power play made it close, but Justin Pogge closed the door, stopping all twelve shots in the final frame; his team managed only three on Murray in the Victoria net. With their record now at a dismal 1-5, the Kings knew that things would have to change.[3389] Coach Morrison put a claim on Riley Weselowski, who had been released by the Idaho Steelheads,[3390] but for some reason, the defenceman never came to Victoria.[3391] Yannick Tifu was traded to the Elmira Jackals for future considerations when the Kings realized they had too many small stick-handling forwards. His veteran spot on the team was filled by forward Jay Henderson, who had the distinction of being the last player taken in the 1997 NHL draft. He was expected in the lineup when the Stockton Thunder came to town.[3392]

In the first game against Stockton, the Kings scored first when Painchaud found the back of the net. However, the roof caved in when the Thunder notched five straight goals, including four in just six minutes and thirty-one seconds of the final frame. Scoring remained a problem for Victoria with only thirteen markers in seven games. The power play had been a disaster with just two goals in thirty-three chances that season.[3393] Latendresse was called up to the Manitoba Moose after the Kings' 5-2 loss to Stockton. Again, it was the inability to score and the taking of untimely penalties that cost the team a victory. The Thunder scored four goals with the man advantage, while Victoria had only one on eight attempts. Taylor's first-period goal had briefly tied the score, but three straight Thunder goals, all on the power play, put them up, 4-1. Burgoyne notched his first for the Kings to narrow the score in the final frame, but another power-play marker for the Thunder put the game away. The visitors outshot the home team, 46-30. The Salmon Kings' record was now 1-7, with no signs of them breaking out of the season-opening slump.[3394]

Up next on the schedule was a two-game road trip to Ontario. New signing forward Randall Gelech was expected to give the team a front of the net presence, while Neil Petruic joined the team as the "future considerations" portion of the Yannick Tifu deal with the Elmira Jackals.[3395] Once again, the Kings were tied, 1-1, at one point of the game before collapsing and allowing three consecutive goals by the Reign, to lose the game, 4-1. Latendresse, just returned from Manitoba, had the only Victoria marker of the match. The lack of offence was a real issue, with the Kings scoring less than two goals a game. That is not good enough in any league, and particularly not in the ECHL, where play is dominated by young skaters.[3396] The second game in the California city was not any more successful than the first, as the Kings fell, 4-3, to bring their season record to a league-worst 1-9. At least they scored three goals this time, as Painchaud had a pair and Brandt added a single, but it was not enough. The power play went an anemic one-for-ten, and although they outshot their opponents, 36-24, they could not put enough pucks in the net. Fans wondered if the team would ever win another game.[3397]

Coach Morrison shook up the team to try to turn their season around. Gone were promising forward Dan Gendur (who just had not produced that year) and defenceman Mike Burgoyne. New signings were defenceman Jimmy Sharrow, a power-play specialist; defender Mike Salekin, who had ECHL experience with Reading, Cincinnati, and Stockton; and goaltender Matt Keetley, a Calgary Flames draft pick sent to Victoria by the Abbotsford Heat for a conditioning stint.[3398]

Perhaps a new goaltender was what the Salmon Kings needed, as Keetley shut out the Reign, 2-0, for the Kings' second win of the season. A first-period power-play goal by Dirk Southern and one at even strength by Brandt in the second were all the offence needed on this night. Keetley made several sensational saves to preserve the victory.[3399] Just when things were looking up for the beleaguered Salmon Kings, they ran into a "hot" goaltender in

Curtis Darling, who stopped almost everything the Kings fired at him. Only Goldie and Gelech beat him; the closest that Victoria got in the score was 3-2. An empty-net marker by the Reign sealed the deal.[3400] The power play finally got it going in the third game of the set. The Kings scored three goals with the man advantage en route to a 4-0 shutout of the Reign. Brandt, Roach, and Howes clicked to give the Kings a 3-0 lead at the second intermission. Howes added his second in the third period to cement the win. Painchaud had three assists, and Sharrow had two as they quarterbacked the man advantage. Victoria outshot Ontario, 51-18, and was full value for the victory.[3401]

Just before a short trip to Idaho, Keetley was named ECHL "goaltender of the week" for his play against Ontario and was called back to Abbotsford; Shantz was sent to Victoria.[3402] In the first game against the Steelheads, the Kings prevailed by a score of 5-3. Despite being outshot, 22-8, in the first period, the Kings ended up tied, 2-2. Goldie had both goals, and Shantz held the fort in goal. Taylor put Victoria in the middle frame, and Latendresse and Gelech added third-period markers. A late goal by Idaho completed the scoring. The Salmon Kings had now won two consecutive games for the first time that season and had improved their record to 4-10.[3403]

The modest winning streak came to an end when Idaho shut out the Kings, 4-0. They were outshot, 42-22, and failed on four power-play chances.[3404] In the rubber match, it was "close, but no cigar," as the Kings fell in overtime, 6-5. After Idaho got on the board, Victoria notched three straight goals by Taylor, Sharrow, and Coulombe to take a 3-1 lead. That lead disappeared with the Steelheads responding with three of their own. Howes tied the game at 16:15 of the third period, sending the game to overtime. The Steelheads beat Shantz at 2:30 for the winner. However, the trip had been moderately successful, with three points out of a possible six against the league's top team.[3405] It would remain to be seen if the momentum could continue.

In a special game as part of the Subway Super Series, the WHL all-stars played the Russian team and defeated them, 2-1.[3406] The WHL controversy reared its head again when a headline proclaimed, "It's unanimous, Victoria wants WHL back." The article was slanted toward those who wanted a WHL team, and strangely, did not interview the many who preferred the ECHL.[3407]

Tim Wedderburn and Dirk Southern against the Ontario Reign, November 11, 2009. Photo courtesy the Victoria Salmon Kings.

Taylor Ellington was called up to the Moose just before the home series against the Reign.[3408] Down a goal when Ontario notched a shorthanded goal in the opening period, the Kings rallied back with Hamilton in the second and Howes in the third, firing goals to give the home team a gutsy 2-1 victory. Neither team scored on the power play, but on this night, it did not matter. Shantz made several key saves to ensure the win.[3409] Game two was a total team effort, as the Kings blanked Ontario, 5-0. Goals by Latendresse and Wedderburn in the opening period gave the team a great start. Southern, Coulombe, and Brandt completed the rout.[3410] Had the team turned the corner?

December opened with a trip to Las Vegas and Ontario. Noel Coultice was released without having played a game. He was kept as a backup for the defence, and never really got a chance to show what he could do.[3411] In the first game, things started well when Goldie and Gelech got the team off to a 2-0 lead. After the Wranglers got one back, Southern put the Kings up, 3-1. However, they could not hold the lead and surrendered two goals, the last with only fourteen seconds remaining in regulation time. In overtime, Vegas beat Shantz to win the game, 4-3. The single point moved Victoria out of the basement in league standings, but two points would have been better.[3412] Taylor Ellington was sent down by the Manitoba Moose and would play later in the series. Video evidence revealed that a Victoria goal that had been disallowed in the first game appeared to have gone in. That's the kind of bad luck that a team in the Kings' position often had.[3413] Small mistakes made the difference in the second game, which the Wranglers won, 7-3. Las Vegas got off to a 2-0 start with a shorthanded goal and one on the power play. Painchaud narrowed the score only to see the Wranglers move back in front by two. Third-period scores by Hamilton, Gelech, and Coulombe gave the Salmon Kings a 5-4 lead, but the Wranglers reeled off three straight goals, the last into an empty net, to secure the victory.[3414]

The Kings dropped their third straight close game to Las Vegas after losing a 2-1 decision. The teams exchanged goals in the middle period (Wedderburn for Victoria), but the Wranglers had the only score of the third frame to win the game. Now it was time for a single contest in Ontario to finish the trip.[3415] Painchaud opened the scoring, but the Reign notched three straight goals to take the lead. However, the Kings fought back, with Latendresse scoring on the power play to narrow the lead and Filion tying the game with under six minutes left in regulation time. In overtime, the Reign outshot the Kings, 4-0 and scored the winner at 1:44. It was yet another one-goal loss for Victoria, who needed to start winning or the playoffs would be far away.[3416]

Leavold was re-signed to bring some grit to the Kings. He had recovered from the H1N1 infection that had caused him to fail the physical examination in training camp. He had tried playing in Europe but quickly discovered their game was not for him. He was hoping to contribute to a rejuvenated Salmon Kings' team.[3417]

Back home for eight games, the Kings prepared for a series against Las Vegas. In the first match, they finally defeated the Wranglers. After falling behind, 1-0, Painchaud got the Kings on the board. An early second-period score put the Wranglers up again, but Brandt, Goldie, and Sharrow fired pucks into the net to give Victoria a 4-2 victory. Goldie's point was his four hundredth in ECHL play, a notable accomplishment.[3418]

In the second game, Las Vegas opened the scoring, but Howes tied it up five minutes later. Goldie scored his first of two to put the Kings ahead, and Painchaud broke away while killing a penalty and fired a shorthanded marker. The Wranglers got one back, but Goldie's second ensured that Victoria would win the game.[3419] The second game was played before a disappointing crowd of 3,831. Las Vegas scored the only goal of the opening period on the power play. Filion replied for Victoria with a shorthanded effort early in the middle frame. That was the signal for fans to litter the ice with teddy bears that would be delivered to children in local hospitals. However, the joy was short-lived as the Wranglers notched two quick goals to take a 3-2 lead. The third period was Victoria's time to shine, as Goldie and Painchaud found the net while Shantz allowed only one Las Vegas shot to beat him. With the game tied at the end of regulation time, it was up to Latendresse to fire the winner at 1:12. The Salmon Kings now had a modest three-game winning streak with a series against Stockton on the horizon.

With Stan Smyl, the Canucks' senior advisor to the GM, in the crowd, the Salmon Kings played a physical game and outscored the Thunder, 7-2. Goals came with rapidity in the first period. Howes got the Kings on the board after just twenty seconds of play. Stockton tied the score, but Gelech put Victoria back in front. The Thunder scored again at the 9:34 mark. Southern restored the Kings' lead with just over a minute left in that period. Victoria broke the game open with four goals in the second period; Latendresse had a pair, while Painchaud and Goldie added singles. Shantz stopped twenty-seven of the twenty-nine shots fired his way.[3420] The Salmon Kings had now their last seven home games and hoped to continue their success.[3421]

The rumours of a "race for Victoria between the AHL and WHL" surfaced again in an article in the *Province*. Kings management said there was nothing new in the story and that team ownership would talk about the situation when the time was right.[3422]

The great play continued in the second game against Stockton, as the Salmon Kings (with Shantz in the net) shut out the Thunder, 2-0, to run their win streak to five. Sharrow put the Kings on the board midway through the first period. The best chance for Stockton came when Shantz took a penalty at the 18:20 mark of the third period, and the Thunder pulled their goalie for a two-man advantage. However, he made some great saves and eventually Brandt fired the puck into the empty net for a shorthanded goal with only nine seconds left in the game.[3423] The Kings swept the series against Stockton with a narrow 4-3 victory. With Sharrow, Goldie, and Coulombe all scoring in the first period, Victoria built up an impressive 3-0 lead. Stockton narrowed the lead in the middle frame with two goals, but Gelech put the Kings up, 4-2, at the second intermission. A power-play marker by Stockton made the score 4-3, but Fisher, who had replaced Shantz at the 28:57 mark when a skate blade collided with his facemask, shut the door to preserve the victory.[3424] David Shantz was sore but happy when he was named the ECHL "goaltender of the week." He was riding an 8-2-3 record with a league-leading .927 save percentage, co-leading with two shootouts, and a league second-best goals-against average of 2.35.[3425]

Although the team was now doing well on the ice, attendance was down an average of 1,030 from the previous season. Part of the reason was the poor start the team had, but the downturn in the local economy was also a factor. In addition, it was well known that Victoria hockey fans are fickle, preferring to support a winning team. Management hoped that fans would again come to support the now-surging team.[3426] To encourage parents to come with their children, the Kings offered a special deal for the upcoming games against Alaska. Fans could buy a family combo, which cost thirty dollars and gave one ticket for an adult and one for a child, plus free popcorn.[3427]

In the opening game against Alaska, the Kings found their scoring touch and upended their arch-rivals, 7-3. They were led by Goldie's pair of goals, while Brandt, Latendresse, Ellington, Painchaud, and Roach all found the net. Fisher was stalwart in the net, stopping twenty-eight of the thirty-one shots fired his way. A good crowd of 4,660 attended the early evening contest.[3428] The Salmon Kings swept the two-game series with a narrow 5-4 victory over the Aces. They did not do it the easy way, falling behind, 4-0, in the first period. Brandt got the scoring started, followed in rapid succession by Sharrow, and Hamilton with two. Goldie got the only goal of the third period (the winner) at forty seconds. Fisher held the Aces off the scoresheet after that, including staving off a man advantage with the goaltender pulled as well for a 6-4 session. For the Kings to beat the Aces twice in a row was unusual, particularly in that season.[3429]

With an eight-game winning streak under their belts, the Salmon Kings hit the road for five games. In Utah, the Kings finally beat the Grizzlies at the E Centre. It was a close affair, with neither team holding more than a one-goal lead at any time. The clubs exchanged goals, resulting in a 4-4 score at 12:40 of the third period; Goldie had two goals, including the winner at 14:47 of the final frame. Other Victoria marksmen were Latendresse, Gelech, and Southern. The Kings went two-for-two on the power play while holding Utah to one-for-three.[3430] In the next game, the Salmon Kings won a narrow victory in a six-shooter shootout, to extend the winning streak to ten. Latendresse scored first, then the Grizzlies notched two to take the lead. Painchaud fired the tying marker midway through the final period. Overtime was scoreless. Goldie and

Southern scored in the shootout while the Grizzlies matched them in the first five shooters. Hamilton scored in extra time, and Shantz stopped the Utah shooter in the sixth round. Now, it was north to Alaska, savouring a tough 3-2 victory.[3431]

In the first game in Anchorage, the Salmon Kings upended the Aces by a score of 6-2. Gelech and Painchaud got the game off to a good start, while Filion, Goldie, and Sharrow notched scores in the middle frame. Gelech hit the net early in the final period; then the Aces beat Shantz twice to somewhat narrow the score.[3432] The streak reached twelve with a 3-2 shootout victory over Alaska. Victoria took a 2-0 lead on goals by Gelech and Painchaud, only to have the Aces tie the score by the third period. Overtime was scoreless, but in the shootout, Hamilton fired the winning shot for the second shootout in a row.[3433] All good things come to an end, and so did the Salmon Kings' winning streak when the Aces cooled them off, 5-3. Alaska would not be beaten, as they scored the first three goals. The second period saw Sharrow and Goldie narrow the lead. In the final frame, the Aces scored, then Latendresse found the net to make the score 4-3. Alaska put the game on ice with an empty-net goal on the power play with just over a minute left in regulation time.[3434] For the second time in three weeks, David Shantz was named the ECHL "goaltender of the week." His save percentage of .924 led the league, and his goals-against-average of 2.33 was second in the league.[3435]

Defenceman Neil Petruic was signed for the remainder of the season. He had played in thirteen games that season with the Manitoba Moose. Manitoba recalled Taylor Ellington, and the Kings loaned Jimmy Sharrow to the Moose for the balance of the season.[3436]

Back home, the Salmon Kings came back in game one against the Steelheads. Howes opened the scoring, then Idaho notched two to take a 2-1 lead. From then on, Victoria took over the game as Gladue scored his first goal in 120 games to tie the game; then Goldie took over, scoring a natural hat trick, the last into an empty net. In a league that was geared to young players on the way up, it was often the grizzled veterans who shone brightly. The Salmon Kings outshot the Steelheads, 35-30, and went three-for-nine on the power play.[3437] Victoria's twelve-game home winning streak came to an end when the Steelheads dumped the Salmon Kings, 8-2. Filion and Goldie had second-period goals, but by that time, they were down 4-0. Idaho scored another four in the third frame with no response from the Kings.[3438] Defenceman Andy Rogers joined the Salmon Kings from the Toronto Marlies. He was expected to strengthen the back-end.[3439]

In the first game against Las Vegas, Brandon Roach opened the scoring, and Las Vegas tied it up. Filion put the Kings ahead, 2-1, but the Wranglers notched a pair to take the lead, 3-2. The final period belonged to Victoria as Brandt, Latendresse, and Gelech put the Kings ahead to stay. Shantz stopped thirty-one of the thirty-four shots fired his way.[3440] Jimmy Sharrow was returned to Victoria from Manitoba to bring the roster to twelve forwards, eight defencemen, and two goaltenders.[3441]

The next night, Victoria again outscored Las Vegas, this time, 6-4. Filion opened the scoring with a nifty backhand shot after 1:26 of play. The Wranglers then had a puck deflect off a Victoria defender and into the net. Coulombe and Howes put the home team ahead 3-1 in the middle frame, but Las Vegas narrowed the lead before the second intermission. The third period featured a flurry of goals that began when the Wranglers scored at 3:25, Howes at 3:31, Las Vegas again at 3:52. While playing with a two-man advantage, Latendresse fired home a shot at 8:03, and just under three minutes later, Painchaud found the net with another 5-3 play. Shantz stopped twenty-six shots and was named the game's second star. Joel Gistedt in the Wrangler net faced forty-six shots in a losing cause.[3442]

Forward Andy Brandt and defenceman Tim Wedderburn were loaned to the Lake Erie Monsters of the AHL, who were playing a weekend series in Abbotsford. Andy Rogers, a 6'5", 230-pound defenceman who had played in the AHL for the Toronto Marlies and Norfolk Admirals, was added to the Salmon Kings' roster.[3443]

Next to come to town were the Bakersfield Condors. The first game will forever be remembered for "that goal." The Salmon Kings scored five times in the opening frame. Southern started things off with a marker at 5:01, Howes added one at 7:03, Latendresse at 8:15, and Painchaud at 11:15, before the Condors fired their first. Then it was time for the line of Howes, Southern, and Taylor to weave their magic as the puck went from player to player, sliding through legs as though it had eyes of its own, with Taylor finally putting it home. The goal was named the TSN "goal of the night," and tapes were requested by (and sent to) networks all over North America, including ESPN, SportsNet, and Yahoo Sports. It was also posted to YouTube, where it recorded over one million hits. It is still there and being watched, years later. The rest of the game was anti-climactic, as the Condors fired two goals and Gelech finished up for the Kings. It was a game for the ages, which anyone who was there will never forget, nor will the millions who watched it on TV or their computers.[3444] The goal eventually was named one of the best of the year at the end of 2010, securing the number five position on TSN's list of top ten plays of 2010.[3445] Rogers Sportsnet rated it the top play of 2010 and The Score named it number ten on its list of top-fifty plays.[3446]

January 15, 2010, was "Pink in the Rink" night with the Salmon Kings wearing special pink jerseys, which were auctioned off to raise money for the BC Cancer Foundation. The jerseys of Latendresse and Sharrow were available through an online auction, and those of Goldie and Coulombe through a silent auction with the jerseys presented after the game. There was also a live auction for the jersey of Shantz.[3447] The game was a tense affair, with the Kings taking the lead then falling behind. Coulombe and Painchaud had first period markers, but the Condors tied the score by the first intermission. Painchaud and Goldie put the Kings up by two, but the Condors got one back by the second intermission. Bakersfield scored first in the final period, but Lance Morrison notched one for Victoria to put them ahead, only to have the Condors tie the game, 5-5, with just twenty-nine seconds left in regulation time. Overtime solved nothing, and in the shootout, Goldie and Latendresse fired goals, while Shantz allowed only one Condor to beat him. The large crowd of 5,443 went home happy.[3448]

After all the jerseys were auctioned off and all other monies added in, the team had raised over $28,000, surpassing the previous year's total of $20,000. Gladue offered a quilt made by his grandmother; it was sold for $350.[3449]

The ECHL then broke for the all-star game in Ontario, California. The Salmon Kings' representatives were David Shantz and Taylor Ellington, who were on the National Conference team that won the skills competition.[3450] In the game itself, the American Conference edged the National Conference, 10-9, in a shootout. "The goal" was shown at the ECHL all-star game and was seen in the 66 million homes the broadcast reached.[3451]

Despite their terrible start, the Kings found themselves in second place in the Western-division standings. Since November 11, they had amassed a 22-6-3-0 record picking up forty-seven points over that stretch, and their eighteen home wins was the best record in the ECHL.[3452] After the short break, the Kings got back to work. Wedderburn and Brandt were returned from the Lake Erie Monsters, so were available for the upcoming California road trip.[3453] In Bakersfield, the Condors scored first, but Taylor tied it just under two minutes later. The Condors went ahead again three minutes later and led the game, 2-1, at the first intermission. Brandt and Roach put the Kings up, 3-2, after two periods, but Bakersfield tied the game with the goaltender out for an extra attacker at 19:17. In overtime, the Condors beat Shantz with a shot at 3:51.[3454] After the game, Chad Painchaud was loaned to the Manitoba Moose. In his forty games with the Kings, he had accumulated forty-six points on eighteen goals and twenty-eight assists.[3455]

Victoria rebounded from the loss and edged the Condors, 2-1, in the second game of the set. In the first period, Bakersfield opened the scoring at 2:08, but Coulombe tied it just 1:07 later. Filion hit the net on the power play midway through the middle frame to complete the scoring. Shantz made thirty-four stops, some of the remarkable variety, to preserve the victory and was named the game's first star.[3456] In the first of three games in Stockton, the Kings did not play well and lost, 7-3, to the Thunder. All the Victoria offence came off the stick of Wes Goldie, who recorded a hat trick. Despite outshooting the Thunder, 37-36, the Kings were unable to mount much of an attack.[3457]

In more player moves, the Moose assigned Eric Walsky to the Kings, while the Calgary Flames recalled David Shantz and assigned Leland Irving to Victoria. Neil Petruic was loaned to Binghamton of the AHL, while Scott Howes and Dirk Southern sustained lower-body injuries and were expected to be out of the lineup for most of the regular season. Brandon Roach was granted bereavement leave and went home to Bay Roberts, Newfoundland.[3458][3459]

With the team playing severely depleted, they not could muster much offence and fell, 7-1, to the Stockton Thunder. Gladue opened the scoring for Victoria, but that was all the team could manage, as they were down to fourteen skaters. Irving played his first game for the Kings but did not have a good outing.[3460] The second game in Stockton was one for the ages. Scoreless after regulation time and overtime due to the efforts of Fisher and Stockton's Pitton, the game went to a shootout. The third shooter for each team scored (Latendresse for Victoria), but there were no more goals until the sixteenth round, when Andy Brandt fired home the winning shot, sending the crowd of 9,158 home disappointed.[3461]

In a complicated deal involving future considerations, forward Matt Siddall was sent to the Kings from the Gwinnett Gladiators. He was familiar with the area, being from North Vancouver and having played for the Powell River Kings in junior. Painchaud was returned from Manitoba, and Roach had come back from his grandmother's funeral.[3462] Back home against Utah, the teams played extra time. The Grizzlies scored first, but the Kings notched three straight goals—Painchaud, Coulombe, and Filion—to take a 3-1 lead by the first intermission. Taylor found the net early in the middle frame to increase the lead to 4-1. Utah narrowed the lead, but Gelech scored his fourteenth of the season to restore the three-goal lead. Utah came back again; the score after two was 5-3. The Grizzlies scored first in the third period, but Gelech got that one back. However, Utah had the last two goals of regulation time to tie the score, 6-6. Overtime was scoreless, but in the shootout, Goldie, Latendresse, and Hamilton scored for Victoria, while only two Grizzlies beat Fisher in the Kings' net.[3463]

Game two was another close affair. Goldie fired a hat trick, but that was only enough to have the game tied after regulation time. After a scoreless overtime, the Kings were blanked in the shootout, while the Grizzlies scored twice on Irving.[3464] The next night, the tables were reversed as the teams played their fourth consecutive shootout contest. Sharrow scored the only goal of the first period. The middle frame was all Utah, as they had two markers to lead, 2-1, at the second intermission. Goldie tied the game early in the third period on the power play. The goaltenders held firm in overtime to send the game to a shootout. All four Salmon King shooters scored in the shootout, while Irving blanked the Grizzlies, and Victoria won 3-2.[3465]

Before the series against Alaska, Ellington was returned from Manitoba.[3466] However, Coulombe had a concussion so was unable to play.[3467] Wes Goldie, playing in his two-hundred-and-sixty-sixth contest for Victoria, without having missed one, had a pair of goals, while Olivier Filion had three points on a goal and two assists to lead the Kings to a 6-2 victory. Other Kings' marksmen were Morrison, Painchaud, and Siddall. Victoria outshot the Aces, 50-27, in the domination of their arch-rivals.[3468] In the next game, the Aces rebounded and edged the Kings, 5-3. Painchaud got Victoria on the board first, and Taylor scored after the Aces had tied it up; at the first intermission, Victoria was up, 2-1. The Aces had the only counter of the middle frame to knot the score, then added three in the third to go up, 5-2. A late goal by Hamilton narrowed the lead to 5-3, but the severely depleted team could not muster any more offence.[3469]

In the afternoon rubber game of the series, the Salmon Kings found their legs and thumped Alaska, 5-1. The Aces had actually opened the scoring on the power play, but Irving shut the door after that, stopping thirty-five shots. Siddall tied the game in the first period, Goldie with his thirty-fifth of the season in the second, and Gelech, Painchaud, and Sharrow in the third. Siddall had two assists as well and was named the game's first star. Now the Kings were on the road, playing eight games in twenty-three days, as it made no sense to have them play at home while the 2010 Winter Olympics were being held in Vancouver. Ironically, the first game would be played in the E Centre in Salt Lake City, the site of the 2002 Winter Olympics.[3470]

In game one in Utah, the Salmon Kings suffered yet another shootout loss. The Grizzlies took an early lead at 1:59, but Taylor tied it up thirty-two seconds later. Midway through the middle frame, Utah took a 2-1 lead, but Sharrow fired the equalizer, 2:30 into the third period. After a scoreless overtime, Goldie scored on the first shot in the shootout, but he was the only King to do so, while two Grizzlies managed to beat Irving. Games between these team seemed to always be tight, with eleven of the last twelve games decided by a single goal.[3471]

Jimmy Sharrow was loaned to the San Antonio Rampage of the AHL. He had previously played one game for the Moose.[3472] The Kings acquired defenceman Bobby Davey from the Bakersfield Condors in exchange for future considerations. He had also previously played for Fresno and Reading in the ECHL.[3473] Forward Bryan Leitch, a native of Coquitlam, BC, was assigned from the Milwaukee Admirals of the AHL. He had made ECHL stops in Cincinnati, Alaska, Florida, Kalamazoo, and Toledo.[3474]

The second game of the series had a more decisive score, as the Salmon Kings upended the Grizzlies, 5-2. Utah scored the first goal, but Gelech tied it up just before the end of the first period. Taylor notched a hat trick to lead the offence—his second goal was shorthanded—with the other goal coming from Painchaud into an empty net. Due to injuries and call-ups, Victoria was playing with just four defencemen and nine forwards. Leitch, the newest team member, had an assist in his first game.[3475] In the final game of the set, Utah came back to win, 3-1. Down, 1-0, in the second period after Siddall had scored for Victoria, the Grizzlies reeled off three straight scores to seal the victory. Again, the Kings' power play was ineffective, going one-for-eight.[3476]

The first game in Bakersfield turned out to be "too little, too late" for the Salmon Kings. Down 3-0 by the 5:21 mark of the third period, the team rallied, outshooting their opponents 23-8 in that frame. Two power-play goals by Goldie in twenty-four seconds brought them close, but time ran out before they could complete the comeback, as they fell 3-2.[3477] The next evening, the team pushed but could not make the most of their chances as they lost 4-2. Bakersfield opened the scoring, but Gelech tied it under eight minutes later. However, the Condors scored the next two to take a 3-1 lead. Goldie's thirty-eighth of the season made it close, but a late counter by Bakersfield gave them the "W."[3478]

The hockey world's attention was focussed on Vancouver and the men's hockey final between Canada and the US on February 28, 2010. The two American-born Salmon Kings, Brandt and Sharrow, were in the minority, as most of the Kings would be cheering for Canada. In the end, Sidney Crosby scored the "golden goal," and Canadians cheered with gusto. Then life got back to normal.

The Salmon Kings travelled to Stockton, where they would play a three-game set. Goalie switching continued, as Leland Irving was recalled to

Abbotsford, leaving only Glenn Fisher to play in goal for the Kings, with Matt Pamidi of San Jose as an emergency backup. Taylor notched the only goal for Victoria, as they were outscored by the Thunder, 4-1.[3479] Playing severely short-staffed, with eight players out due to injuries and call-ups, the Kings looked to rebound. Coach Morrison admitted that his team was tired, with players having to log more minutes that they were used to, and it had now caught up to them. However, they would have to continue putting out a good effort, as they needed points to secure a playoff spot.[3480]

To add insult to injury, Andy Brandt was called-up to the Moose, further depleting the roster.[3481] The Kings' four-game losing streak ended in Stockton when they squandered 2-0 and 4-1 leads to edge the Thunder, 5-3. The game started well for Victoria when Leitch and Gladue opened the scoring. The Thunder narrowed the lead, and Goldie replied for the Kings. In period two, Painchaud extended the lead but Stockton scored twice to get to within one. Then Gelech fired the puck into the empty net to give the Kings a 5-3 victory.[3482] The last game of the road trip was not a success. Stockton opened the scoring, but Goldie fired his fortieth of the season sixteen seconds later to tie the game. After two Thunder goals, Southern found the net. At the first intermission, Stockton was up 3-2. However, the Thunder fired four straight power-play goals to take a 7-2 lead, and Painchaud's twenty-fifth of the season, on the power play, was all the Kings could manage as they fell, 7-3.[3483]

The goalie merry-go-round continued, as Irving went to Abbotsford while Keetley came back to Victoria.[3484] In their first home game in some time, the Kings faced the first-place Idaho Steelheads. In the first match, the Kings started well when Painchaud and Gelech found the net. However, they then allowed the Steelheads to score five consecutive times to win easily by a score of 5-2.[3485] Before the middle game of the set, the Kings signed Jeff Lynch, formerly of the University of British Columbia Thunderbirds.[3486] The Steelheads showed why they were in the number-one position in the division when they demolished the Salmon Kings, 7-1. The Steelheads started slowly, with only one counter in the first period, then added a pair sandwiched around the sole Victoria goal by Wedderburn. To add insult to injury, Idaho fired four goals in the final frame.[3487] The Steelheads completed the sweep with a 5-3 victory, sending the Kings to their seventh loss in eight games. The game was 4-0 before Lynch fired his first goal as a Salmon King, and Gelech narrowed the score. However, Idaho got one back to restore the three-goal lead. Painchaud's twenty-seventh of the season closed out the game.[3488]

Wes Goldie plays against Idaho. Photo by Anne-Marie Sorvin, courtesy of Victoria Salmon Kings.

The Salmon Kings signed forward Mark Magnowski out of Princeton University. Andy Brandt was returned from Manitoba, Matt Siddall was set to return from short-term injury, and Eric Walsky from long-term injury. These moves should help the team, which had been severely depleted for some time.[3489] The Kings continued to struggle, taking a beating in Stockton by a score of 7-2. The game was close at the second intermission, as the Thunder had notched three goals while Sharrow and Painchaud had replied for Victoria. However, the final period was all Stockton, as they beat Keetley four times.[3490] The Salmon Kings rebounded against Bakersfield and beat the Condors, 5-1. Goldie fired his forty-first goal, while Southern added three assists; other Victoria marksmen were Gelech, Painchaud, Ellington, and Howes. Fisher was stellar in the nets, stopping thirty-one shots.[3491] The next evening, the tables were reversed, as the Condors edged the Kings, 3-2. Matt Siddall led the Victoria effort with a goal and an assist, while Lance Morrison had the other marker. Points were certainly becoming hard to come by in the highly competitive Western division.[3492]

Games now shifted to Idaho. Magnowski was released, as the race for a playoff space was not the time for a rookie to try to make an impact. Andy Brandt was recalled by Manitoba, and Bobby Davey was released as he was not playing the way he was expected to on the blue line.[3493] In the first game, Victoria was shut out, 5-0, by the Steelheads. Keetley started in the net for the Kings but was replaced by Fisher after the second Idaho goal. It did not seem to make much difference, as the Steelheads fired three past him. This was definitely not the way to get a playoff spot.[3494]

The player merry-go-round continued, as the Kings signed defenceman Paul Bezzo to an amateur tryout. He had played sixty-four games in the Ontario Hockey League that season with Owen Sound, Windsor, and Belleville.[3495] Brandt returned from Manitoba, bringing the roster to twenty-four players: fifteen forwards, seven defencemen, and two goaltenders.[3496] Just when the Salmon Kings needed a big game, they got it from Glenn Fisher, who stopped all thirty of the shots fired his way, and Walsky had the lone Victoria goal in a 1-0 shutout of the Steelheads. Bezzo played his first game as a professional and was held off the scoresheet.[3497] The Steelheads got their revenge when they upended the Kings, 5-2, in a game the next evening. It was close in the first period when Southern fired a goal to tie the contest, but Idaho pulled away with four straight to win convincingly. In the standings, Idaho was far on top with ninety-nine points, but the rest of the division was close. Bakersfield had seventy-five points followed by Alaska with seventy-four, Utah with seventy-three, Victoria and Las Vegas with seventy-two, Stockton with seventy-one, and Ontario with seventy. One team would miss the playoffs, and at that point, it could have been just about anybody in the chase pack.[3498]

Ellington was reassigned to the Moose, but his spot on the roster was taken by David Cianfrini, a graduate of Canisius College in Buffalo, New York.[3499] [3500] With the season ending against Utah at home, the Kings had to gain some points to ensure a playoff position. Their special teams would have to get more productive, as the power play had pretty well dried up, and the team had been surrendering too many shorthanded goals. The season came down to three games at the Save-On-Foods Memorial Centre.[3501] Ellington was returned from the Moose just in time for the final series.[3502] Much to the dismay of the 5,355 Victoria fans in the stands, the Utah Grizzlies clinched a playoff spot with a 2-1 victory over the hometown Kings. Siddall hit the scoresheet first with his nineteenth of the season, but two Grizzlies' markers in the final two periods gave them the narrow victory. Now Victoria had to win their last two games or rely on other teams to get them into a playoff position. Veteran Patrick Coulombe returned from a concussion and had two shots on goal and one minor penalty.[3503] Before the second game, Ellington rejoined the Moose.[3504] Former Moose Jaw Warrior Jason Bast joined the Salmon Kings before the second game of the series.[3505]

In the good news department, defenceman Jimmy Sharrow was named to the ECHL all-star second team. He completed a defensive club record on January 15, when he recorded a point in his twelfth straight game, during which he amassed sixteen points. It was also the longest point-scoring streak by a defenceman in the ECHL that year. He had the second-highest point total for defencemen in the league and was tied for the league-lead in power-play goals with eight.[3506]

The Salmon Kings clinched a playoff spot with a decisive victory over Utah. After the Grizzlies took an early lead, Goldie fired two to give the Kings the lead. He completed the hat trick, reaching forty-four for the season, and Southern fired a pair to lead Victoria to a 9-2 win. Other marksmen were Painchaud, Brandt, Siddall, and Filion. Victoria outshot their opponents, 32-18, and fired two power-play goals in seven chances.[3507]

The final game of the regular season was billed as "Sellout Saturday," with tickets offered for sale for just five dollars until March 30, after which the cost would increase by one dollar per day until they were ten dollars.[3508] That promotion worked, as the paid attendance was 7,006. Unfortunately, the crowd did not have much to cheer about as the Kings dropped the season finale to Utah, 5-2. The game was tied at the second intermission, with Morrison and Filion scoring for the home team, but three straight goals gave the Grizzlies the victory. Now it was on to the playoffs, where the Kings would play Bakersfield in the first round.[3509]

The Salmon Kings added defencemen Kris Fredheim of Campbell River to the twenty-man playoff roster.[3510] Goldie and Painchaud fired two goals each, while Southern and Filion added singles to lead the Kings to a 6-3 victory in game one in Victoria. A small crowd of 3,191 was in the stands.[3511] In the second game, Bakersfield upended the Kings, 4-2, to tie the series at a game apiece. Filion had opened the scoring, but two Condor markers put them ahead. Goldie narrowed the lead, but an empty-net goal put an end to the comeback.[3512]

The series then shifted to California. In game three, the Kings edged the Condors, 3-1. All the scoring took place in the third period. Bakersfield scored first, but three straight Victoria goals gave the visitors the victory. Painchaud's third of the series tied the game, and Sharrow notched the winner. Walsky fired a shot into the empty net to ensure the win. The Kings were now ahead 2-1 in the series, but they needed to win three games to move on to the next round.[3513]

Bakersfield won game four, 5-2, over the Kings. Painchaud had put Victoria on the board, but four straight Condor goals put them in control. His second narrowed the lead, but two late goals, the last into an empty net, tied the series, 2-2, with the final game to be played in Bakersfield.[3514]

The deciding game was a tight affair, as the Condors scored at fifty-nine seconds of the opening period and Brandt tied it up about ten minutes later. The score remained 1-1 until the last minute of play, when the Condors fired the winner at 19:11, to give them a series victory. The Kings' playoff run was over. They had fought hard but had just come up short.[3515] [3516]

As the players emptied their lockers, they had time to reflect on the season that had just been completed. The team had paid dearly for the AHL's carousel of call-ups, which had left them short-handed. Coach Morrison said that he was interested in returning for another season, but the decision would be made by team management. He noted that his team had outplayed the opposition for most of the games, but the bounces had gone against them. It was time for reflection, as there had been high points in the season after a disastrous start. Who would return next year and what would happen?[3517]

36 - VICTORIA SALMON KINGS: THE LAST HURRAH

After the disappointing 2009-2010 season, Kings' fans looked forward to the upcoming season with hope. As most of the decisions on player personnel were made further up the hockey chain by Manitoba or Vancouver, Victoria management often had limited say in which players they could put on the ice.

At the Canuck prospect camp in Penticton, Vancouver Island players Taylor Ellington, Kris Fredheim, and Dan Gendur were all there. Ellington remained in Penticton for the Canucks' camp, Gendur went to the Moose camp, and Fredheim would be at the Salmon Kings' camp. In other news, Coach Morrison announced that Daren Machesney, who would attend the Columbus Blue Jackets' main camp, would be the starting goaltender for the Salmon Kings.[3518]

The Kings' training camp ran from October 3-10, at the Save-On-Foods Memorial Centre. This was a more-focussed training camp, with each participant chosen to fit a pattern. This year, the team would play two exhibition games against the UBC Thunderbirds at home. Admission would be by donation with hot dogs, popcorn, and pop available for one dollar during the games.[3519] Another signing was North Vancouver's Michael Wilson, a defenceman who had spent time in the AHL with the Worcester Sharks.[3520] One player expected to play a leadership role that season was Pete Vandermeer, who had played briefly with the Phoenix Coyotes in the NHL and spent the last season with the Utah Grizzlies.[3521] Former Salmon Kings, like Kiel McLeod and Milan Gajic, came back because this was their last chance to win a Kelly Cup Championship. New faces in camp were defenceman Ryan Turek, centre Ryan Dingle, and defenceman P. J. Atherton.[3522] Port McNeill's Rick Cleaver was thrilled to come "home" to play hockey. He had left at age eighteen and was ready to retire if he could not play close to Vancouver Island. Ellington was sent to the Kings from Manitoba, while the Kings signed goaltender Jase Weslosky and added Victoria Grizzlies forward Jonathan Milhouse on a tryout contract.[3523] Rob Hennigar, former CIS star with the New Brunswick Varsity Reds, had formerly played in the ECHL with Utah and Florida, so he was familiar with the Salmon Kings' style of play.[3524]

For the first pre-season game, the lineup was as follows: forwards Matt Siddall, Rob Hennigar, Milan Gajic, Jonathan Milhouse, Derek Couture, Kiel McLeod, Matt Stefanishion, Ryan MacMurchy, Ryan Dingle, and Rick Cleaver; defencemen Derek Martin, Ryan Turek, P. J. Atherton, Mike Wilson, Peter Vandermeer, and Taylor Ellington; and goaltenders Jase Weslosky and Riley Gill.[3525] In the game, the Kings defeated UBC Thunderbirds, 8-6, before a small crowd of 1,421. Kings' goals came from Dingle with a hat trick, Gajic, Cleaver, Vandermeer,

Stefanishion, and Martin.[3526] In the second game, Cleaver had a hat trick, while McLeod, Stefanishion, and Wilson added singles as the Kings dominated the game, 6-2. As the AHL teams cut down their rosters, Coach Morrison expected new additions. Manitoba sent goaltender David Shantz and forward Josh Aspenlind to Victoria.[3527] Jonathan Milhouse was still in the mix after the exhibition games—the only rookie pro still on the roster.[3528] Pete Vandermeer was named captain of the Salmon Kings for the 2010-2011 season, replacing the popular Wes Goldie, who was now with the Alaska Aces.[3529]

The opening game of the season did not go the Salmon Kings' way, as they were shut out, 5-0, in Idaho. Special teams were a problem, as the Kings went zero-for-three while the Steelheads had three scores with the man advantage.[3530] In a reversal of form, the Kings rebounded with a shutout of their own, 4-0, over Idaho. Gajic had a pair, while Atherton and Couture added singles. Riley Gill, in his first game in the net, had an impressive game, stopping all thirty-nine shots fired at him, and was named the first star. Penalty killing was stellar, including nearly two minutes of five-on-three play in the second period.[3531]

Before the next games in Las Vegas, the Kings added two more players. Geoff Waugh, a native of Winnipeg, was a 6'4" defenceman who would enhance their blueline. Also signed was forward Gabe Gauthier, a former Chilliwack Chiefs junior star who had also won two NCAA Frozen Four titles with the University of Denver.[3532]

In Las Vegas, the Kings rode the sterling goaltending of rookie Riley Gill to a 3-1 victory over the Wranglers. Gajic opened the scoring midway through the first period, but the Wranglers tied it up six minutes later. Vandermeer notched his first of the season to put the Kings ahead. The game result was in doubt until Siddall hit the empty net with just over a minute left in regulation time.[3533] The next night, the Wranglers turned the tables and defeated the Kings, 3-1. Shantz made thirty-five saves, but his effort was not enough as only Siddall could find the back of the net. Victoria took far too many penalties—eleven in all—and although they surrendered only one goal, that amount of time playing shorthanded is very tiring for the special teams.[3534]

Prab Rai, a Canucks' draft pick, was assigned to the Salmon Kings, but he had injured his back during training camp and was placed on the twenty-one-day injury list.[3535] In the end, his injury prevented him from playing for the entire season.[3536]

The home season started on October 27, 2010. The Kings upended the Ontario Reign to win only their second home opener in franchise history. Turek opened the scoring on the power play, and MacMurchy made it 2-0 by the first intermission. After Ontario beat Shantz in the net, Painchaud scored the first of his pair to restore the lead. Gajic added his fourth of the season to secure the 5-2 victory. Victoria outshot their opponent, 39-29.[3537] The second game of the set also went to the Salmon Kings. Stefanishion scored on the power play, but Ontario tied it up before the first intermission. In the middle frame, Victoria scored four goals—McLeod, Painchaud, Couture, and Hennigar—in the first 9:35 of play, to take an insurmountable lead. Two Reign goals narrowed the score, but Cleaver gave the Kings the insurance they needed for a 6-3 win. P. J. Atherton had two assists and six shots on goal and was named the game's first star.[3538] Victoria completed the series sweep with a 4-1 victory. Quintin Laing, who had played thirty-six NHL games the previous season for the Washington Capitals, was added to the Kings just before the game. Siddall fired two goals, while Couture and McLeod added singles and Shantz stopped thirty-five of the thirty-six shots fired his way.[3539]

The win streak reached four with a 3-2 victory over the visiting Idaho Steelheads. Victoria got on the board when Couture found the back of the net at 15:11 of the opening period. Idaho tied the score early in the middle frame. Cleaver put the Kings up again, only to have the Steelheads tie it up again. A soft floater by Gajic found its way into the net with under five minutes left in the game to give Victoria the win.[3540] Young goaltender Riley Gill—ECHL "goaltender of the month" for October—was traded to Kalamazoo to satisfy the future considerations portion of the deal that had sent Cleaver to the Kings. On the injury front, Chad Painchaud and Ryan Dingle were placed on the seven-day and twenty-one-day injured-reserve list.[3541] The second game of the set did not produce the result that the 3,231 fans wanted. Atherton scored a first-period power-play goal, but Idaho tied the game just 1:04 later. Cleaver restored the one-goal lead, but the Steelheads notched four straight goals to take the game, 5-2.[3542] In the final game of the set, the Salmon Kings ran into penalty trouble, and Idaho scored three times with the man advantage to defeat the home team, 5-2. The only Kings to find the back of the net were Turek and McLeod.[3543]

Despite the early success on the ice, fans were staying away from hockey games in record numbers. The economic downtown in the province was one reason given for the decline, as fans did not have the same amount of disposable income they'd had in previous years. However, there was a misconception that the previous year's team had not been exciting. Nothing could have been further from the truth, but sometimes it was hard to explain why patrons did the things they did. In any event, attendance at Kings' games was down six percent from the previous year.[3544]

The Salmon Kings then took their show on the road—to Las Vegas. The first game did not go well, as the Wranglers outlasted Victoria, 4-2. Again, it was untimely penalties and the inability to kill them off that led to the defeat. The Wranglers scored three times in the first period, twice on the power play, before McLeod replied in the middle frame to narrow the lead. Couture got the Kings to within one goal, but a Vegas marker midway through the third period restored the two-goal lead. Of note was the inability of the Kings to score on their rare power-play opportunities, going zero-for-two with the man advantage.[3545] The losing streak hit four games as the Wranglers upended the Kings, 3-1. As had happened in prior games, Victoria took too many penalties—nine in all on this night—and it meant they were playing at less than full strength for a significant amount of time. This time, the game was a bit closer, as the Kings were only down 2-0, when MacMurchy gave them some hope. However, an empty-net goal put an end to the comeback, and Victoria could only hope they would become more disciplined in future games.[3546]

It was beginning to sound like a broken record, but too many penalties cost the Salmon Kings another game. Although the Wranglers did not score on the power play, it is hard to have any flow to the game if the team is spending so much time defending rather than attacking. Captain Pete Vandermeer had the book thrown at him for an incident in the second period. Having just served a spearing minor, he took a spearing major, a match penalty for deliberate attempt to injure, a game misconduct for abuse of an official, and a second game misconduct for the spearing penalty. Bryon Lewis, the supervisor of officials for the ECHL, was in attendance and would likely have more to say after reviewing what had happened. Wranglers' goaltender Joe Fallon was outstanding in making forty saves and lost his shutout bid with under thirty seconds remaining in the contest.[3547] Justice came swiftly for Vandermeer, as he was suspended for eight games and assessed an undisclosed fine for his actions in the last game in Las Vegas. Victoria led the league in penalties with 381 minutes. In second place was the team they would play next: the Bakersfield Condors.[3548]

Playing before a morning crowd of 5,051 screaming students, the Condors upended the Kings, 3-1. Both teams took the same amount of penalties, so that was not an issue in this match. However, the lack of scoring was beginning to be a real problem, as the Kings could not put the puck in the net with any regularity. Scoring one or two goals a game does not lead to winning hockey. MacMurchy's power-play goal in the second period tied the game at 1-1, but a marker by former Salmon Kings Mark Magnowski early in the third frame proved to be the winner.

An empty-net goal gave the Condors the insurance they needed. Coach Morrison said that he would have to shake up the team, as the way they were playing lately was just not good enough. He noted the lack of hunger and work ethic that was missing in their game.[3549]

Two days later, the Salmon Kings, minus Milhouse who had been released, finally won a game, as they continued their early-season mastery of the Ontario Reign. Although they fell behind in the first period, the team did not fold, as Stefanishion and MacMurchy fired goals to give them a 2-1 lead. After Ontario tied it up late in that period, Victoria got its act together, and Cleaver scored twice in 2:37 to put his team up for good. A late Reign goal narrowed the count, but that was the end of the offence for the night. Special teams played a much better game, with McMurchy's goal coming shorthanded, and Cleaver's second on the power play.[3550] The next stop on the road trip was Bakersfield, where the Kings got revenge for their earlier defeat by beating the Condors, 4-1. Atherton got the scoring going in the first period, Gajic added one in the second, and MacMurchy notched one on the power play in the third. An empty-net marker by Painchaud, just off the injury list, ensured the victory for the visitors. Shantz played well in the nets and was named the game's first star. Ryan Dingle returned from the injury list and had two shots on goal.[3551]

In Stockton, the Kings completed the road trip with a third consecutive win, as they dumped the Thunder, 4-1. By the 7:17 mark of the second period, the score was 3-0 for Victoria, as Siddall, McLeod, and MacMurchy had all found the back of the net. The Condors had the lone goal of the middle frame, and Painchaud wrapped it up with a third-period power-play marker. Shantz stopped thirty-one of the thirty-two shots fired his way, and was (again) the game's first star.[3552]

Just before a six-game homestand, the Kings signed twenty-eight-year-old forward Garth Murray. He had played for the Abbotsford Heat the previous season but had fallen victim to a youth movement and the veteran rule in the AHL.[3553] Idaho came to town for three games and swept them all. In game one, Victoria took the lead, when Murray notched his first goal of the season. Idaho tied the game late in the middle frame, and a fluky effort gave the Steelheads the victory. The puck went directly from a face-off to deflect off a Victoria's defenceman's skate. It was the first game for newly acquired Gord Burnett. Formerly of the Trenton Devils, he made his presence known with a first-period fight.[3554] With Taylor Ellington out with a concussion, his place was taken by Yann Sauve, assigned from Manitoba.[3555] In the second game of the set, Idaho scored early and often, as they dumped the Salmon Kings, 6-4. The Thunder scored twice in the first period, and Waugh narrowed the lead before the first intermission. The Steelheads had two more goals to open the middle frame, but Atherton and Siddall answered for Victoria. In the third period, Idaho regained their two-goal lead, Atherton replied for the Kings, and Idaho sealed the deal with a score with under three minutes left in the game.[3556]

In the final game, Stefanishion served the first game of a two-game suspension, reducing the roster to fourteen skaters. Victoria opened the scoring when Siddall notched a pair within 1:26. Idaho got one back late in the period, then added four straight goals in the middle frame to take a 5-2 lead. The clubs exchanged goals in the final period (Hennigar for Victoria) to make the final score, 6-3. The Kings had been a streaky and confusing team this year; winning four, then losing six, winning three, and losing three. That was not the way to have a winning season.[3557]

Next to come to town was the Stockton Thunder. The team was still depleted, with injured players Couture, McLeod, Rai, and Ellington out, so the pressure was on the remaining team members to carry the weight. MacMurchy scored first for Victoria; then the Thunder notched two straight to take the lead. Siddall notched his ninth of the season to tie the game. After a scoreless overtime, the teams went to the fourth round of the shootout before Stockton won the extra point. The team suffered another injury and Dingle had to leave the game.[3558] In game two, Stockton prevailed, 5-3. They scored the first two goals before Stefanishion, back from his suspension, replied for the Kings. Siddall tied the game for the Kings, but Stockton fired a pair to restore the lead. Cleaver narrowed that lead, but an empty-net goal sealed the deal for the Thunder. Vandermeer also returned from his suspension and had an assist and amassed seven minutes in penalties.[3559]

The third game was closer but still not a victory. The Thunder scored the first two goals to lead, 2-0, at the first intermission. In the middle frame, Stefanishion and Painchaud evened the score. Atherton put the Kings ahead in the third period, Stockton had a pair, then Turek tied the game, 4-4. In overtime, the Thunder put the game on ice with a score at 4:38.[3560] To say the homestand had been a disaster was an understatement. Victoria managed to gain only two points out of a possible twelve.

Just when the Kings were having issues, the question about a Western Hockey League move to Victoria surfaced. The WHL commissioner said that the league had an interest in the Victoria market, but nothing had moved along yet. RG Properties had until January 2012 to renew a three-extension in the ECHL, so there was a year in which the WHL could return. The other complication was the deal with the City of Victoria in which the city owned the facility, but RG Properties had a thirty-year contract to run it. Any changes would have to be approved by the city.[3561]

The team acquired Jeff Caister from the South Carolina Stingrays, in return for future considerations, to bolster the defence.[3562] Now it was "north to Alaska" for the Kings, where they would encounter their former teammate, Wes Goldie. In another deal, the Kings swapped goaltenders with Elmira. Machesney went to the Jackals for Zane Kalemba, a former player for the Princeton Tigers.[3563] Siddall fired a pair of first-period goals to open the scoring. After the Aces narrowed the lead, Murray notched the third Kings' goal to give them a hard-fought 3-1 victory. Rob Hennigar got an assist on the first goal to extend his points streak to ten games on a goal and fifteen assists. Shantz was outstanding in the net with thirty-two saves.[3564] The second game was a real nail-biter. Cleaver had the opening goal, but Alaska scored in the second and the third to take the lead. A power-play marker by Gajic tied the score with just seventeen seconds left in regulation time. Overtime solved nothing, and in the shootout, it took five rounds before an Ace shooter scored the only marker in the shootout. Picking up three out of four points in Alaska was a moral victory for the Kings, as they continued on the road.[3565]

Garth Murray and Josh Aspenlind were called up to the Manitoba Moose, reducing the healthy roster to sixteen. They had seven forwards, seven defencemen, and two goaltenders.[3566] Help was on the way in the person of Tim Kraus, a former Vancouver Giant and Ontario Reign. McLeod was returning from injury, so that would strengthen the forward lines.[3567]

After a rare weekend off, the team travelled to Idaho. In the first game against the Steelheads, the Kings came up short in a 4-1 loss. The score was 2-0 before Hennigar got the Kings on the board. The Steelheads added two more goals to win the game. The team made too many mistakes, and with a team as talented as Idaho, the result is often a puck in your net. Penalties were still an issue, as they had been all season, as two of the Steelhead goals came with the man advantage. Kraus played his first game as a Salmon King and picked up an assist.[3568] The Salmon Kings lost another player when the Moose recalled Yann Sauve. Thankfully, the team would have a long Christmas break after their next two games, and would likely have Couture, MacMurchy, and Dingle due back in the new year.[3569]

The second game was more successful for the Kings. Vandermeer scored first to put Victoria on the board. Idaho replied, then Burnett scored for the Kings. In the third period, Idaho notched two goals to take a 3-2 lead, but Siddall had his thirteenth of the season at 19:24 of the third period to send the game to extra time. After a scoreless overtime period, the game went to a shootout. Goaltenders Shantz and Mike Zacharias blanked the first five shooters, then Turek scored on his first-ever shootout attempt, and the Steelhead shooter missed. It was a great win for the short-staffed Victoria team; defencemen Burnett and Vandermeer had to play forward, and each scored.[3570]

In the final game before the break, the Salmon Kings edged the Utah Grizzlies, 4-3. Painchaud and Wilson gave the Kings a 2-0 lead, and Siddall added another in the second before Utah beat Shantz. Painchaud's second of the game restored the three-goal lead. Two Grizzlies' power-play goals in the final period made the score close, but they could not tie the score. The Kings headed for their break on a positive note.[3571]

After ten days off, the Salmon Kings were tied with Bakersfield for second place in the standings, only seven points behind Utah. Despite all their issues, they were having a reasonably good season. Shantz was apparently the best player on the team, as he often held his team in games until they could get their offence on track.[3572] Ontario came to town for a two-game set. In the first game, Victoria outplayed the Reign but still fell, 6-3. They had fifty shots on goal but failed to take advantage of their chances. Hennigar scored first, but Idaho notched three straight goals to take a 3-1 lead. Siddall got one back before the first intermission and Painchaud tied the score early in the second period. However, Ontario pulled away by scoring three times, including two in the final period within seventeen seconds. The defensive errors cost the Kings, and Coach Morrison said his team would have to improve.[3573]

The next night, the Salmon Kings erupted for eight goals and upended the Reign 8-4. They scored five goals in the third period to break open a 3-2 game and ensure the victory. Painchaud had a hat trick, while singles came from Turek, Caister, Kraus, Stefanishion, and Waugh. The eight goals were the most that the team had scored all season. Was the drought over? In league news, P. J. Atherton was named as a starter in the ECHL all-star game. Matt Butcher, son of NHLer Garth Butcher, played his first game for the Kings.[3574]

Back on the road in Utah, the Salmon Kings were shut out, 1-0, on New Year' Eve. The Grizzlies scored the only counter midway through the middle period and held off the Kings to preserve the low-scoring victory. The New Year's Day game was also a Utah shutout, this time, 2-0. For a team that had just scored a record number of goals, being shut out two games in a row was unacceptable. They then headed home for five straight games against Stockton and Las Vegas.[3575]

The goaltender roulette continued as Kalemba was released to make way for Chris Beckford-Tseu, who was familiar to Victoria fans for his work for Alaska and Phoenix.[3576] Stockton came to town and edged the Kings, 3-2. The Thunder scored short-handed in the second period, but Dingle notched his first of the season to tie the game at the second intermission. After the Thunder went ahead, Stefanishion knotted the score. A terrible defensive lapse allowed Stockton forward Bretton Cameron to break away and score the winning goal at 15:25 of the third. Despite storming the net, the Kings were unable to get the equalizer.[3577]

The middle game was more successful, as MacMurchy returned to the lineup after missing twelve games with a hand injury, and made his presence felt on the power play and as a penalty killer. His goal at 4:03, with the man advantage, opened the floodgates and Painchaud and Vandermeer added singles by 12:05. A Stockton goal just thirty-five seconds later narrowed the lead to 3-1. The teams played a scoreless middle frame; then Gajic found the back of the net from an almost impossible angle midway through the final period to increase the margin. The Thunder added a meaningless goal with two minutes left to play. The Salmon Kings victory ended Stockton's four-game winning streak on Blanshard Street.[3578] The Thunder got back on the winning side when they upended the Kings, 3-1, the next night. Stockton led all the way with goals in the first and second periods and an empty-net marker in the third. The Kings' only goal came off the stick of Caister with two seconds left in the game, spoiling Bryan Pitton's bid for a shutout. It was a relatively clean game, with only five minor penalties; no goals came on the power play.[3579] Victoria welcomed back a familiar face when Adam Taylor joined the team after leaving the financially-troubled Edinburgh Capitals. He had been pondering a career in Germany but opted for his hometown team, instead.[3580]

Next to visit were the Las Vegas Wranglers. In the first game, Jamie Bates led his team with two goals, the first on the power play. Cleaver and Taylor gave the Kings a short-lived 2-1 lead, but the Wranglers scored three straight to go ahead, 4-2. Markers by Siddall and Stefanishion tied the score in the third period, but the winner came just over two minutes later, and it seemed to deflate the Kings. A late goal gave the Wranglers a 6-4 victory. Victoria had outshot Las Vegas, 41-22, but played a very poor defensive game. Assistant coach Ryan Wade noted, "We have extra bodies in camp right now, and if the guys aren't playing, they will not get in the lineup." Even the players were frustrated with the lack of production and said they had to play better. The Salmon Kings now had a record of 0-15 that season when trailing after two periods.[3581]

The Wranglers swept the set with a 5-3 come-from-behind win over the Salmon Kings. Victoria opened the scoring when Siddall notched his seventeenth of the season, but Las Vegas tied it under six minutes later on the power play. The Kings scored twice in the second frame, when Cleaver and MacMurchy found the net, to take a 3-2 lead. However, the third period was all Wranglers, as they fired three goals, the last into an empty net, to win with relative ease. Coach Morrison said that he had never been so disappointed in a team in his coaching career. He questioned "some of the desire in that room" and noted that some decisions had to be made."[3582] Things went from bad to worse when the Kings lost their top defenceman. P. J. Atherton decided to move to play in Sweden, leaving the team in mid-season. He said that he had realized that the NHL dream was over for him at twenty-eight, and he needed to move on.[3583]

After a disastrous homestand where they won only one game out of five, the Salmon Kings went on the road. In Idaho, a wild-and-woolly contest ended in an overtime victory for the Kings. Painchaud got Victoria on the board early, but Idaho tied it before the end of the first period. Second-frame goals by Taylor, Turek, and Butcher put the visitors up, 4-1. In the third period, the Steelheads got their offence in gear and scored four straight goals to take a 5-4 lead. Vandermeer scored the tying goal just twenty-seven seconds later, sending the game to extra time. Cleaver found the net at 1:53 to give the Kings an exciting win.[3584] Why was this team so much better on the road than at home?

In the next contest, the Steelheads scored three times on the power play to demolish the Kings, 6-1. Only Taylor could find the net for Victoria. It was the Kings' eighth loss in twelve games, and their once-secure playoff position was in danger as the Ontario Reign were only seven points back, but with three games in hand.[3585] Before the rubber match, the players held a team meeting and decided to turn their season around. In the game, they put their money where their mouths were and blanked the Steelheads, 4-0. Marksmen were Caister, Cleaver, Dingle, and Stefanishion, while Shantz recorded his first shutout of the season.[3586]

After a four-day break, the Kings flew to Alaska for two games. In the first, they got two goals from MacMurchy, while Cleaver and Hennigar added singles. The lone goal for the Aces came off the stick of former King Wes Goldie.[3587] The next game was a complete reversal of form, as the Aces dumped the Kings, 6-1. Too many penalties gave Alaska eight power plays, and they scored on four of them. The game was 6-0 before Siddall scored his eighteenth of the season at 13:18 of the third period. The teams now had a break for the ECHL all-star game. Ryan

Turek was named as the Kings' representative, replacing Atherton, who had left for Europe.[3588]

Next on the schedule was a visit to Victoria by the first-place Las Vegas Wranglers. The old problems came back to haunt the Kings, as they took far too many penalties, so they were playing shorthanded for too much of the game. It is difficult to get any flow to a contest when the top players are sitting on the bench waiting for even-strength play. The Wranglers scored four goals on thirty-two shots while the Kings could only manage one (by Cleaver) on twenty-five shots.[3589] In the next game, the Wranglers had a 2-0 lead by the first intermission. Butcher had the first goal of the second period, but Las Vegas got that one back to lead, 3-1, after two. The Wranglers scored again on the power play, and Cleaver replied with the man advantage to make the final score 4-2. At one point in the game, four Salmon Kings were sitting in the penalty box.[3590] The Salmon Kings won the third game of the set to salvage some points. In the matinee affair, Victoria got off to a good start, scoring the first three goals of the game. Turek, Butcher, and Cleaver had the markers. The Wranglers scored twice, sandwiched around a Kings' goal from Gajic. Following the 4-2 victory, the team skated with several of their young fans.[3591]

Next to town were the Alaska Aces. In the first game, Caister scored two power-play goals to lead Victoria to a 6-3 victory. Gajic had two as well, the second into an empty net, while Dingle and Cleaver added singles. Former King captain Wes Goldie had one assist in his first trip back to Victoria. Shantz, playing in his two hundredth professional game, made twenty-nine saves.[3592] In the annual "Pink in the Rink" game, the Kings won their third in a row, as they upset the Aces, 6-2. Tim Kraus scored a hat trick, while MacMurchy added five assists to tie the franchise high set by Scott Turner in 2005. Gajic had a pair of assists and McLeod, Turek, and Cleaver completed the scoring.[3593] The Aces won the third game by a score of 3-1. MacMurchy was the only King to beat Aces goaltender Courchaine, while Alaska fired thirty-seven shots at the game's first star, Shantz. Wes Goldie fired his first goal of the series.[3594]

In personnel moves, Vandermeer was placed on the twenty-one-day injury list. The Salmon Kings signed another defenceman, Ed Snetsinger who had played for Florida and Utah in the ECHL, and spent August in the Southern Professional League.[3595] On the road in Las Vegas, the Salmon Kings blanked the Wranglers, 2-0, on the strength of goals by Cleaver and Dingle, the latter into an empty net to secure the victory. Despite taking seven penalties, the Kings killed them all off as the penalty killers did a remarkable job.[3596] The second game was also a win for the visitors, to bring their recent record to five wins in six games. MacMurchy and Butcher each had a pair of goals to lead the team to a 4-2 victory. Shantz stopped thirty of the thirty-two shots fired his way and was named the game's second star. This was the first-ever sweep of the Wranglers in Las Vegas, and it could not have come at a better time.[3597]

The Salmon Kings moved on to Bakersfield, where they kept their modest win streak intact with a decisive 7-2 victory. Hennigar scored the first goal of the game at forty-three seconds, followed by Painchaud on the power play. In the middle frame, McLeod, MacMurchy, and Couture found the back of the net to make the score 5-0 at the second intermission. The Condors scored twice in the third period, but Cleaver and Dingle answered back. The Kings scored four goals with the man advantage and only allowed one. Shantz, who had earlier been named ECHL "goaltender of the week," made twenty-three saves to secure the win.[3598] Defensive standout Geoff Waugh was called up to the Moose, but that would give the coaches a chance to see what recently signed Snetsinger could do. Yann Sauve, who had started the year with the Kings, made the huge jump to the Vancouver Canucks.[3599] Next on the schedule was a two-game set in Stockton. In the first game, the Salmon Kings edged the Thunder, 3-1. The Thunder had taken a 1-0 lead halfway through the opening period to lead at the first intermission. Cleaver scored on the power play and Hennigar at even strength to give Victoria the lead. MacMurchy got the needed insurance with an empty-net goal. Shantz who led the ECHL in minutes played, got his record to 19-18-3.[3600]

In game two, the roof caved in, as the Thunder demolished the Kings, 8-1. It was a fight-filled affair with the first encounter at ten seconds and eight more after that. Victoria ended up sixty-one minutes in penalties while Stockton had fifty-nine. The score was 6-0 before the Kings got on the board. Couture had the only Victoria goal, on the power play, but that was the only offence they were able to muster. Nevertheless, the Kings had still won seven of their last nine games for a respectable streak.[3601] The next evening, the score was not as outrageous, but the result was the same: a Stockton victory. Victoria was unable to score even once, as they were shut out, 4-0, by the Thunder. The Kings went zero-for-six on the power play, so they had chances but were unable to convert. On the injury front, Painchaud and McLeod went down again.[3602]

Kiel McLeod and Milan Gajic versus Utah Grizzlies. Photo by Jonathan Howe, courtesy of Victoria Salmon Kings.

The Salmon Kings then came home and prepared for a five-game stand against Utah and Bakersfield. Butcher and Cleaver both scored twice, while Turek and Bryan Cameron—who had just been sent to the club from Abbotsford—added singles to lead Victoria to a 6-2 win over the Grizzlies.[3603] Shantz was called up to Manitoba and MacMurchy to Abbotsford before the second game. This was a close, nail-biting affair, with the lead changing hands during the game. Utah opened the scoring at 5:19, then Painchaud and Couture replied for the Kings. Victoria product Tim Crowder scored for the Grizzlies to tie the game at 2-2 at the first intermission. Dingle put the Kings ahead again, but Utah scored to tie it up once more. Cameron's goal restored the lead, and the teams entered the second intermission with the Kings up, 4-3. In the third period, Gajic gave the Kings a two-goal lead, but they could not hold it, yielding two Utah markers that left the score 5-5 at the end of regulation time. After a scoreless overtime, the game went to a shootout. Cleaver and Gajic, the first two Victoria shooters, both scored, and Beckford-Tseu shut the door on the Grizzlies, giving the Salmon Kings a well-deserved 6-5 victory.[3604]

In the midst of the homestand, the rumours about Victoria's return to the WHL surfaced again. Nobody would confirm or deny the rumours, but several scenarios were presented. Which team could move to Victoria? Among the suggestions were the Prince George Cougars, Kootenay Ice, Chilliwack Bruins, Portland Winterhawks, and Saskatoon Blades. Evidently, RG Properties, when given a chance to decide between the AHL and the WHL, had favoured the latter. The story would unfold over the next few weeks.[3605]

In player roulette, the Salmon Kings lost Derek Couture to the Connecticut Wolf Pack of the AHL but got back Shantz and Aspenlind from Manitoba. The team also brought in Craig Lineker out of the UBC Thunderbirds via the WHL Chilliwack Bruins for a viewing.[3606] [3607] Shantz made the most of his first game back in Victoria, as he backstopped the team to a 3-0 whitewashing of the Bakersfield Condors. It was his fifth career shutout, a new record for the Kings' franchise. Turek opened the scoring on the power play, Stefanishion added one in the second period, and Gajic fired a puck into the empty net to complete the scoring.[3608] Two days later, the

Condors got their revenge when they edged the Kings, 2-1. Turek scored at forty-seven seconds to give the home team a 1-0 lead, but that was all the offence they could produce. Bakersfield had a goal in each of the second and third periods to take a lead they never surrendered. The Kings had their chances but could not convert on their power-play opportunities even with a two-man advantage, and that cost them the game.[3609]

Mark Donnelly sings the anthems at a Salmon Kings game on March 5, 2011. Photo by the author.

Saturday, March 5, 2011, was a night to remember. Not for the hockey, but for the anthem singer, as Vancouver Canucks' talented vocalist, Mark Donnelly, belted out the national anthems before the game. The game was an uninspired effort, as the Condors dumped the Kings, 5-2. Only Painchaud, on a spectacular shorthanded breakaway, and Cameron could score for the home team. The crowd of 4,229 went home disappointed.[3610] Veteran Tim Kraus was released by the team.[3611]

The Salmon Kings went back on the road for a three-game set in Alaska. It did not turn out well. In the first game, a pair of ex-Kings, Wes Goldie and Scott Howes, provided much of the offence needed to upend Victoria, 5-3 with two goals from the former and one from the latter. Siddall, Gajic, and Caister replied for the Kings, who lost their third straight game.[3612] Before the next game, the Kings signed Scott Freeman, formerly of the Clarkson University Golden Knights. He got one shot on goal in his first game. The rest of the team did not do much better, as they were pummelled by the Aces, 6-1. Painchaud scored midway through the third period, on the power play, to prevent a shutout, but that was all the offence the visitors could produce as they extended their losing streak to four. Alaska scored four goals with the man advantage as the "too many penalties" problem was evident once more.[3613] The Salmon Kings went "zero-for-Alaska," as they dropped the final game of the series, 3-1. They took ten penalties, and the Aces scored twice on the power play. Painchaud had narrowed the score to 2-1 in the second period, but Goldie iced the game with an empty-net goal.[3614]

Before the next home series against Utah, the Salmon Kings made personnel changes. Goaltender Beckford-Tseu was released to make room for Jimmy Spratt, from the AHL's Grand Rapids Griffins. Snetsinger and Lineker were also dropped from the roster. Cameron was recalled by the Abbotsford Heat, and Waugh was returned from Manitoba. New to the Salmon Kings was Tommy Maxwell, a former Medicine Hat Tiger, who was assigned by the Moose. A new signing was Cam Ritchie, a graduate of the Princeton Tigers. On the injury front, forward Cleaver went on the three-day list, where he joined Turek and Taylor while Ellington and Vandermeer were on the longer-term list. MacMurchy and Couture were still up in the AHL, and McLeod was suspended for two games for an incident in a game in Alaska. As was the case in the ECHL, it was up to the coaches to make the most of the players they had available for any match.[3615] Would the Salmon Kings cling to their playoff spot? The series against Utah might decide the issue.

Desperately needing a victory to get their season back on track, the Kings surrendered a power play early in the first period, then fired five straight of their own to take an insurmountable lead. Gajic scored his sixteenth, Caister his seventh, Dingle his seventh, Aspenlind his first, and Freeman his first professional goal. After the Grizzlies scored their second goal, Gajic completed the hat trick, while

Painchaud (with his one-hundredth goal in the ECHL) and Siddall added singles. The nine goals set a team record for offence. Victoria outshot Utah, 44-38, as Shantz recorded his one-hundredth win as professional. With the two points, the Kings moved nine points ahead of the Ontario Reign with nine games remaining. They controlled their own destiny but needed to keep winning.[3616] And win they did, as they upended the Grizzlies for a second straight time. Special teams played a vital role in the 5-2 victory. Dingle opened the game with a shorthanded effort at 4:44 of the first period. In the second frame, Freeman and McLeod fired power-play markers to give the Kings a 3-0 lead. Utah broke up the shutout bid with two goals in just over four minutes midway through the final frame, but Hennigar added a power-play goal and Taylor finished the game with a power-play goal into an empty net. Victoria outshot the Grizzlies, 33-19, giving Shantz a relatively easy victory.[3617] Game three was a close affair, with Utah edging the Salmon Kings in overtime. Victoria got off to a great start when Painchaud scored twice in the first 6:08 of the second period. However, Utah got one back and then added a second, shorthanded, early in the third. In overtime, Utah scored at 1:33 to send the 4,374 fans home disappointed.[3618] Yet, it had been a good homestand, with the home team picking up five out of a possible six points.

Now, it was back on the road for four games in California. With their playoff spot pretty well ensured, as they had a ten-point lead over Ontario, with a magic number of two, the team looked to fine-tune their offence and get ready for the post-season.[3619] In the final game in Bakersfield, the Condors edged the Kings, 2-1. The third-place Condors scored first, but Painchaud notched his twenty-third of the season to tie the contest. There was no further scoring until 19:41 of the middle frame when the Grizzlies got the winner. As much as the Kings pressed in the final period, they were unable to get the equalizer, but most players were pleased with the effort. Another addition to the roster was Jeff Terminesi, fresh from four years with the Mercyhurst College Lakers. Jimmy Spratt, who was acquired earlier in the month and had been warming the bench in the AHL, also joined the team.[3620] Now only one victory away from securing a playoff position, the Salmon Kings came from behind in the third period, the first time they had done so that season, and edged the Thunder, 7-6, in a shootout. Painchaud and Waugh got the Kings off to a good start with power-play goals, but Stockton counted one shorthanded, one on the power play, and two at even strength to take a 4-2 lead at the first intermission. Cleaver added a power-play marker to narrow the score, but Stockton got that one back to lead, 5-3, at the second intermission. Just twenty-nine seconds into the third period, the Thunder increased their lead, and it looked like the game was over for the Kings. However, they rallied with Caister and Hennigar scoring with the man advantage and Ritchie at even strength, sending the game to extra time. Both goaltenders held firm in overtime, sending the contest to a shootout. Cleaver, the first shooter for Victoria, put them up, 1-0, but Jason Pitton scored as the third shooter for Stockton. Painchaud, the final shooter for Victoria, fired home a goal, while Spratt put up a brick wall in his net. It was an exciting game that clinched a playoff spot.[3621]

As sports fans know, in the playoffs anything can happen—and often does. The next night, it was a reversal of form as far as scoring went, as the Salmon Kings took the lead and then let the Thunder back into the game. Siddall and Gajic had first-period markers, and Stefanishion added one early in the second period. Stockton added one in the middle frame to narrow the lead to 3-1. At 18:36 of the second period, there was an eight-player brawl that brought the crowd of 5,830 to its feet. Unfortunately, Victoria came out on the short end of the penalty calls and was reduced to only three defencemen, when Ritchie and Martin were ejected from the game. With a weakened corps of defenders in front of him, Shantz became vulnerable and surrendered two goals that tied the game. Overtime was scoreless, and in the shootout, the second shooter for each team (Gajic and Vanoosten) scored, but after the regulation five shooters, it was still tied. In the sixth round, Stefanishion beat former King Kalemba to give his team the 4-3 victory.[3622] In the final road game of the regular season, the Thunder got their revenge on the Salmon Kings, thumping them, 8-4. It did not start out that way, as a pair of goals by Caister and one by Painchaud staked the Kings to an early 3-0 lead. However, Stockton got two back before the end of the period and added three to start the second to give them a 5-3 lead. Gajic notched a goal on the power play to narrow the lead to a single goal, but four unanswered Thunder goals after that gave Stockton the victory.[3623]

In the final home series, the Salmon Kings would play their nemesis, the Alaska Aces. They were hoping for some success against the top team in their division. Game one went to the Aces, 4-2. Taylor and Painchaud put the Kings up by two, then the roof caved in, and the Aces scored four straight to take the win in impressive fashion.[3624] In the midst of the ECHL playoffs, a minority owner of the Chilliwack Bruins said that the team was being sold to RG Properties. Dave Dakers, president of RG Properties' sports and entertainment division, refused to confirm or deny the sale. If the rumour were true, then it would mean the demise of the Salmon Kings.[3625]

It was no April Fool's joke, as the Salmon Kings edged the Aces, 3-1, before 5,411 enthusiastic fans. Most of the scoring occurred in the first period, as Ritchie notched his second of the season at just thirty-three seconds and Turek at 6:13, while Wes Goldie responded for the Aces. That lead held up until the end of the game when Taylor scored shorthanded into an empty net at 19:59 of the third period. Spratt made twenty-four saves to record the victory.[3626] Needing a win over the Salmon Kings to clinch first place in the ECHL overall, the Aces took an early lead, allowed a goal by Painchaud, then added two more to win the game and secure the overall championship. With the regular season over, the Kings now knew they would play the Bakersfield Condors in the first round of the playoffs, a five-game set.[3627]

Salmon Kings ticket for game on April 2, 2011, versus Alaska Aces.

The Kings won game one, 3-1, to give the home team a lead in the series. Gajic scored in the first period, while Klassen and Painchaud added goals in the third. The Condors broke up Shantz's bid for a shutout with a power-play marker, five-on-three, with fifty-seven seconds left in the game.[3628] With the imminent announcement about the WHL returning to Victoria, many wondered if the game the next night would be the last home game ever for the Salmon Kings. That would only be true if the Kings failed to advance to the second round with the remaining games in Bakersfield.[3629] [3630]

The Western Hockey League approved the sale of the Chilliwack Bruins, issuing the statement that it had "granted conditional approval to a request from the ownership of the Chilliwack Bruins for the sale of their WHL franchise. Until such time as all of the conditions related to the sale have been satisfied the WHL is not in a position to make any further statement on this transaction." Not everyone was thrilled with the news, and many fans attending the Salmon Kings game expressed dismay. One woman said, "We feel bad for the Salmon Kings. They're supposed to be doing their best in the playoffs, and they don't know if they're just keeping the rink warm for the WHL."[3631] RG Properties refused to comment, leaving fans in limbo and feeling confused and disillusioned. The timing was terrible, to say the least, with the Kings still playing hockey.[3632]

In the game, which seemed almost secondary to the WHL rumours flying around, the Condors upended the Kings, 6-1, to tie the series, 1-1. Only Klassen and Gajic were able to find the back of the net. The series now shifted to Bakersfield for at least two games.[3633] The Salmon Kings took the series lead with a 2-0 shutout in Bakersfield. Siddall put the Kings on the board at 11:26 of the first period and Caister added another less than five minutes later. That score held up to the end of the game. Shantz made thirty saves, despite being crashed in his crease, and was named the game's first star. Victoria now had a 2-1 lead in the best-of-five series and needed only one more victory to win the series.[3634]

Meanwhile, back in Chilliwack, the Bruins were handing out pink slips to many of their employees. According to the *Kamloops Daily News*, the team would change hands on April 17. There was still no comment from RG Properties.[3635]

Back on the ice, the Salmon Kings edged the Condors, 3-2, in overtime to win the series. Bakersfield got on the board first and led, 1-0, at the first intermission. Gajic and Taylor scored in the second frame to give the Kings a 2-1 lead. The Condors tied the score early in the third period on a deflection, sending the game to overtime. Painchaud was the overtime hero, firing the puck into the net at 4:26. The number-seven team had upset the number-two seed, sending the Kings to the second round of the playoffs.[3636]

Round two was against the sixth-seeded Utah Grizzlies, with the series starting in Boise, on April 15. The Kings were ready to play and were gaining confidence with every victory.[3637] The first game was a good one for the Salmon Kings, as they upended the Grizzlies, 4-2, with 3,063 disappointed fans in the stands. Victoria had learned from past games in Boise, and skated away from confrontations rather than take stupid penalties. Utah ended up with twenty minutes in penalties, while the Kings had only six. Cleaver scored on the power play at 8:55 in the first period. Utah got that one back, but Caister fired a successful shot at 18:32, to give the Kings a 2-1 lead at the first intermission. Martin had the only score of the middle frame. In the third period, Utah narrowed the lead, but Taylor sealed the victory with a shot into the empty net.[3638] [3639] Victoria was coming home with a 2-0 series lead, after sweeping the Grizzlies in Utah, defeating them, 4-2, in the second game of the series. Utah took the lead midway through the first period, but Painchaud notched two goals in the middle frame. Utah tied the score, but McLeod scored his first of the playoffs to restore the Victoria lead. Tommy Maxwell, a late-season send-down from Manitoba, fired the insurance goal midway through the third period, and Shantz and the Kings defended well to ensure the win.[3640]

In the WHL soap opera, the Western Hockey League held a press conference for April 20, 2011, to confirm that the Chilliwack Bruins had been sold to RG Properties and would be playing in Victoria next season. WHL hockey would be back in the capital city for the first time since the Victoria Cougars moved to Prince George in 1994. The team would have a new nickname, as "Bruins" had no connection to Victoria. Dave Dakers said that the Salmon Kings would either fold or be sold, and that no decision would be made until the playoff run ended.[3641] An editorial lauded the return of the WHL, pointing out that the team would be more financially stable, as travel costs would be more modest than had been the case for the Salmon Kings. The City's deal with RG Properties was extended for another ten years. It closed with the statement, "The big thrill, however, comes in the fall. We've been waiting seventeen years for the WHL to return—and in just five months, our team will be on the ice."[3642]

Goal by Matt Siddall versus Utah, April 20, 2011. Photo by Jonathan Howe, courtesy of Victoria Salmon Kings.

On the ice, the now-disposable Salmon Kings' players called a press conference, in which they urged fans to come out to support them as they continued in the playoffs. They wanted 7,000 fans in the stands to give them a great send-off. They knew their futures were out of their control, but right now, they were in the playoffs and still representing the city of Victoria. Under normal circumstances, such a plea would not have been made, but this was not a normal time with the team about to be closed or sold.[3643] The players had support from fans, as several letters to the editor stressed that the timing of the demise of the team was unfair to the players and the loyal fans.[3644]

In game three of the second round of the playoffs, the Salmon Kings came back from a 2-0 deficit to defeat the Utah Grizzlies, 3-2, in overtime. Utah scored goals thirty seconds apart in the second period to take the lead. McLeod scored for the Kings at 18:57 to narrow the lead. Siddall found the net on the power play early in the third period to tie the score and send the contest to overtime. It did not take long for Aspenlind to become a hero, as he scored at eleven seconds of extra time to send the small crowd of 3,691 home very happy . With that goal, he tied a record for the fastest goal in overtime, originally set by Mark Derlago on April 18, 2009.[3645] The Kings now had a 3-0 lead in the series and could complete the sweep with a victory in game four.[3646 3647 3648]

Victoria Salmon Kings celebrate the series win over the Utah Grizzlies, April 22, 2011. Photo courtesy the Victoria Salmon Kings.

Game four, played in front of a season-high crowd of 6,095 fans, was a magical event as the Salmon Kings swept the Grizzlies with a dramatic double-overtime thriller. Utah opened the scoring at 2:44 of the opening period and that lead held until 18:55 of the middle frame. Both goaltenders played well and kept their teams in the game. Lamoureux stopped fifty Victoria shots, while Shantz made forty saves. Finally, at forty-eight seconds into the second overtime period, local-product Adam Taylor fired a shot into the net, releasing the tension and sending the fans into a frenzy. Up next was a series with their arch-rivals from Alaska.[3649 3650]

The Salmon Kings players told the media how special this playoff run had been to them, especially considering the circumstances. As seventh seed, they had gone on a 7-1 run to win two series against all the odds and were now going to play the team that they saw most often during the regular season. Games against the Alaska Aces had always been interesting, and the Kings had won more of them this season than ever before. The teams were connected through player moves. Wes Goldie and Scott Howes now played in Anchorage, while former Aces Derek Martin and Ryan Turek now skated for Victoria. Heading into this series, the Salmon Kings were the decided underdogs, as the Aces had won the league title, but in the playoffs, anything could happen.[3651] Before the series, the Kings added two AHL players, as Derek Couture and Ryan MacMurchy's teams had been eliminated from AHL playoffs and were able to return to Victoria.[3652 3653]

Game one of the Western final went to Alaska. It was a very close affair with goals late in the first and third periods, staking the Aces to a 2-1 victory. The opening score came with five seconds remaining in the opening frame. Caister notched a goal at 12:47 of the final period, and it looked like the game would go to overtime. However, the Aces' second goal, with just nine seconds left in regulation time, gave them the victory. It was demoralizing for the Kings to lose in that manner, but they had to regroup and get ready for the next encounter.[3654]

The second game was just as close. Alaska took an early lead at 4:11 and led, 1-0, at the first intermission. The middle frame belonged to the Salmon Kings, as Martin and Turek both found the net to give the team a 2-1 lead. The third period saw the Aces score twice to go ahead again, but MacMurchy tied the match again. In overtime, it was over quickly, as the Aces beat Shantz at 2:15. Hennigar led all shooters with three assists and was Victoria's star of the game.[3655] Two games had been played, and either team could have won. Unfortunately for Victoria, they did not get the bounces and were now down, 2-0, in the series.

Game three was played in Victoria, with a very disappointing crowd of 3,614 in attendance. The Kings took a one-goal lead to the first intermission on a shot from Siddall. However, they were unable to withstand an Aces' onslaught in the middle frame that saw them pull ahead, 4-1. When the score was 2-1, Victoria scored what seemed to be a good goal, but it was disallowed. Coach Morrison said he "watched it later on video and (saw) that it was a good goal. That was a big goal to have called off." The Aces added two more in the third, while Caister replied for Victoria.[3656] The Salmon Kings were now down, 3-0, in the series, and it would be a mammoth task to come back for a victory.

Face-off for final game against Alaska Aces, May 2, 2011. Photo by Jonathan Howe, courtesy of Victoria Salmon Kings.

The miracle was not to be, as the Aces did it again to the Kings. It was another close game, but the hockey gods did not give the hometown team a break. The Aces could smell blood and took a two-goal lead into the second intermission. However, the Kings were not done yet and mounted a comeback, as Couture and Klassen tied the score by the midway point of the third period. It was Scott Howes, a former King, who scored the winner with just thirty-five seconds left in regulation time, to send the Aces to the final and the Salmon Kings into history.[3657]

Salmon Kings salute the crowd at the end of the final game in their history, May 2, 2011. Photo by Jonathan Howe, courtesy of Victoria Salmon Kings.

The small crowd of 3,153 stood and applauded their hometown team, many with tears in their eyes. It was the end of a seven-year run that had had its ups and downs. Ironically, in a "looking back" article, *Victoria Times Colonist* sports reporter Cleve Dheenshaw listed the other professional hockey teams that had called Victoria home, including the PCHL Senators/Aristocrats/Cougars, the Cougars of the old WHL, and the Maple Leafs. For some reason, the Victoria Cubs were not mentioned.[3658]

When the Kings heard that the team was folding, it was hard for everybody involved. The coaches tried to inspire the players to go all the way to the championship, just to show the city and the owners what they were losing. However, not all the players got on board, so the team fell short in the series against the Aces. The lack of fan support was curious, as well, as the Salmon Kings were playing good hockey, and the building should have been full.[3659]

As the team cleaned out their lockers for the last time, Coach Morrison reflected on his time with the team, first as an assistant and then GM and head coach. He said that he would take some time to reflect on what had happened and then decide what he would do in the future. He noted that the Kings were the best team he had ever coached, and added that "Victoria fans never fully realized what they had the last seven seasons."[3660] Mark now enjoys coaching in the NHL, but he feels that his time with the Salmon Kings was the highlight of his career. He was able to reconnect with folks he had met when he was here as a junior player with the Cougars. He recalled the huge crowds when the Cougars were doing well and thought that the Kings would draw, as well. For some reason, that did not happen, even when they were a really good team. Mark said that to be able to coach in his home area was a real treat, as not many coaches get to do that.[3661]

Victoria pro hockey will be missed

Re: City scores another chance at WHL (*News*, April 22)

To say I am upset by the announcement of the return of the WHL to Victoria is an understatement. I find the timing of the announcement to be atrocious. At least the NHL had the courtesy to delay an announcement on the possible move of the Phoenix Coyotes back to Winnipeg until the 'Yotes were eliminated from the playoffs. Some of us are devoted Salmon Kings fans and would have preferred to keep the team here.

Last Wednesday, we learned RG Properties rejected the idea of moving the Manitoba Moose to Victoria. I much prefer the professional game – and am a great fan of the minor leagues. Some of the players earn their way to the NHL and have entertained audiences across North America at the same time.

I am still mad that we lost the Victoria Maple Leafs when Toronto moved the team to Phoenix – just a year after a championship season (1965-66). I did support the Victoria Cougars junior team for years but when they were sold and moved to Prince George, I decided that was it for junior hockey. What makes people think it will be any different now? Victoria fans are generally very fickle and only support a winning franchise.

I remember the fuss about the Victoria Spiders (who never actually made it here) – everyone holding jerseys for the photo-op. It was the same for the Salmon Kings when they arrived. Now they are being cast aside. I hope the Salmon Kings keep winning and embarrass their owners. Too bad a hockey decision comes down to the almighty dollar.

Go Kings Go – all the way to the cup.

Helen Edwards
Victoria

My letter to the editor about the demise of the Salmon Kings. Published in The *Victoria News*, April 27, 2011.

The era of the Salmon Kings came to an end on May 7, 2011, when RG Properties decided to fold the franchise with the approval of the ECHL's board of governors. All Victoria players then became free agents. Two hundred and thirty-five players had worn the Salmon Kings uniform, some for a short time, others for much longer. The team had raised money for local charities and community groups to the tune of over $1.5 million, and this gave Dave Dakers great pride. He noted, "The team reached thousands of people. I'm proud of that."

An analysis of the attendance at Salmon Kings' games over the seven seasons showed that Victoria fans' interest peaked in the 2008-2009 season when an announced average of 4,923 attended the games, and that had dropped to only 3,717 in the 2010-2011 season.

The Kings were gone, and given the overall preference for junior hockey in this market, it was highly unlikely that professional hockey would ever return. I was personally disappointed when the Salmon Kings were folded, and this, coupled with the death of former Victoria Maple Leaf Bill Shvetz, on April 21, 2011, awakened in me the need to document the story of professional hockey in Victoria. I have been researching ever since.

Professional hockey was first established in Victoria in 1911, and the final game was played in 2011. Over a century, 483 men plied their trade for a Victoria team; some were very successful, others not, but all deserve our thanks for the entertainment they brought us. This book is my thank you to those men, the organizations they played for, the coaches, and other staff.

APPENDIX A

Selected Player Biographies

Tommy Dunderdale

Tommy Dunderdale. Photo courtesy Ernie Fitzsimmons.

Tommy Dunderdale was born to English parents in Benalla, Australia, on May 6, 1887. The family moved to Ottawa, Ontario, in 1894, and it was there that the young Tommy discovered hockey. He first played with his high school team there but moved to Winnipeg in 1905, where he played one season of amateur hockey with the Winnipeg Ramblers before turning professional with the Winnipeg Strathconas. In 1910, Dunderdale joined the Montreal Shamrocks, recording twenty-one goals in fifteen games. He moved to the Quebec Bulldogs for the next season, where he counted thirteen goals in nine games.

His next move was to the newly-formed Pacific Coast Hockey Association, where he became a valued member of the Victoria Senators, later the Aristocrats. In the inaugural season, he scored twenty-four goals in sixteen games and was named to the all-star first team; this would be the first of six such selections and the first of four in a row in the PCHA. In the next two seasons, Dunderdale scored twenty-four goals in each season. In the 1914-15 season, he notched seventeen goals and assisted on ten others, for twenty-seven points in seventeen games. In 1915-16, Dunderdale was traded to the Portland Rosebuds in return for Ran McDonald; he played there for three seasons. With the Victoria Arena open after being closed for the war effort, the Aristocrats were reborn. Dunderdale rejoined the team, as the Portland Rosebuds had folded, and remained there until the end of the 1922-23 season. When the PCHA folded, he played one season in the West Coast Hockey league with the Saskatoon Crescents and the Edmonton Eskimos.

Dunderdale retired after the 1923-24 season, but he remained in hockey coaching and managing teams in Winnipeg, Los Angeles, and Edmonton.

His prowess as a hockey player was unquestioned. He was a fast skater and an exceptional stickhandler, whose name was all over the PCHA record book. He scored the first penalty shot in hockey history, beating Hugh Lehman on December 12, 1912. He notched 194 goals over his Western Canadian career, leading the league in goals in three seasons and points in two. Over his eighteen professional seasons, he played 309 games, scored 267 goals, and 366 total points.

Tommy Dunderdale died in Winnipeg on December 15, 1960, and was buried in Brookside Cemetery. In 1974, he was inducted into the Hockey Hall of Fame—the only Australian to be so honoured.

Frank Fredrickson

FrankFredrickson. Photo courtesy Ernie Fitzsimmons.

Frank Fredrickson was one of the most exciting and talented players to don a Cougars' uniform.

Born in Winnipeg on June 11, 1895, to Icelandic parents, he started skating on the family's backyard rink when he was five years old. After he finished grade eight, he got a job as an office boy in a law firm. That proved to be a good move, as the firm sponsored a hockey team with which he excelled. The lawyers encouraged Frank to attend law school, so in 1914, he began studies at the University of Manitoba, where he captained their hockey team. Frank played his violin in a dance orchestra to finance his education. He had joined the Winnipeg Falcons for the 1913-14 season and was named their captain.

In February 1916, he enlisted with the 19 Western Universities Battalion and was transferred to the 223 Battalion, where he played with several Falcon teammates on their hockey team. He was then sent to England, where he was transferred to the Royal Flying Corps. He survived several close calls, including having the ship on which he was returning to the Western Front hit by a torpedo. He spent many days in a lifeboat in the Mediterranean, clutching his beloved violin until he was rescued. He continued flying as a test pilot and instructor.

Back in Winnipeg, Fredrickson reformed the Winnipeg Falcons hockey club for the 1919-20 season and they won the Allen Cup, earning the right to represent Canada at the 1920 Olympics in Antwerp, where hockey was a demonstration sport. The Falcons easily won the gold medal in the first international hockey contest to include North America. In a game against the Swedes, Fredrickson scored seven goals en route to a 12-1 victory.

Recognizing his enormous talent, Lester Patrick made Fredrickson an offer he could not refuse. The talented Icelander played his first game for the Victoria Aristocrats on New Year's Day, 1921. The visiting Vancouver team scored the first two goals, but the Aristocrats got one back before the end of the second period. The third period belonged to the Victoria team, as they outscored their opponents four goals to one to win the game, 5-3. Once

Fredrickson took the ice, the game changed, and he dazzled the spectators with his skating ability and hockey skills. He scored one goal and added two assists in his debut. The team name changed to Cougars in the 1922-23 season, and Fredrickson stayed with them until the 1925-26 season, when they were sold to Detroit of the NHL. During that time, he contributed to the Stanley Cup victory in 1925 and the unsuccessful attempt a year later. Fredrickson was named to the league all-star team on five occasions and led the league in goals and total points in 1923. Two Cougars, Frank Fredrickson and "Slim" Halderson, were the only players up to that point to have won the Allan Cup, an Olympic gold medal, and also a Stanley Cup.

Fredrickson played for the Detroit Cougars, Boston Bruins, Pittsburgh Pirates, and Detroit Falcons in the NHL. He retired after the 1930-31 season and turned his skills to coaching, reorganizing the Falcons' junior team and coaching Princeton University's varsity and freshman teams from 1933 to 1935. Fredrickson then resigned his post at Princeton and moved to Victoria. He officiated and coached in the Western Canadian League, and later coached the University of British Columbia (UBC) Thunderbirds for the 1939-40 season. In 1941, he enlisted as a Flying Officer. He was sent to St. Catharines, Ontario, Calgary, Alberta, and Boundary Bay, BC. In the first two locations, he also coached hockey teams.

After his discharge in 1945, Fredrickson returned to UBC, as a volunteer hockey coach for six seasons. The 1949-50 team won the Humber Cup Championship. They then toured in the US and defeated the US college champions from Colorado College, as well as other highly ranked teams, effectively becoming the top college hockey team in North America.

In Vancouver, he worked as an insurance company executive, served on the school board in 1943, and was elected an alderman between 1959 and 1963, including a short period as acting mayor in 1961.

Fredrickson was instrumental in securing funding to send the UBC rowing crew to Henley, for the 1955 World Championships, and in the early 1960s, he raised funds for the construction of UBC's first Winter Sports Centre; Canada's 1964 Olympic hockey team later trained there. In his later years, he moved to Toronto, where he died on May 28, 1979, at Riverdale Hospital.

Fredrickson was inducted into the Hockey Hall of Fame in 1958. He was posthumously inducted into the Manitoba Sports Hall of Fame in 1981, the British Columbia Sports Hall of Fame in 1983, and the UBC Sports Hall of Fame in 2009.

Clem Loughlin

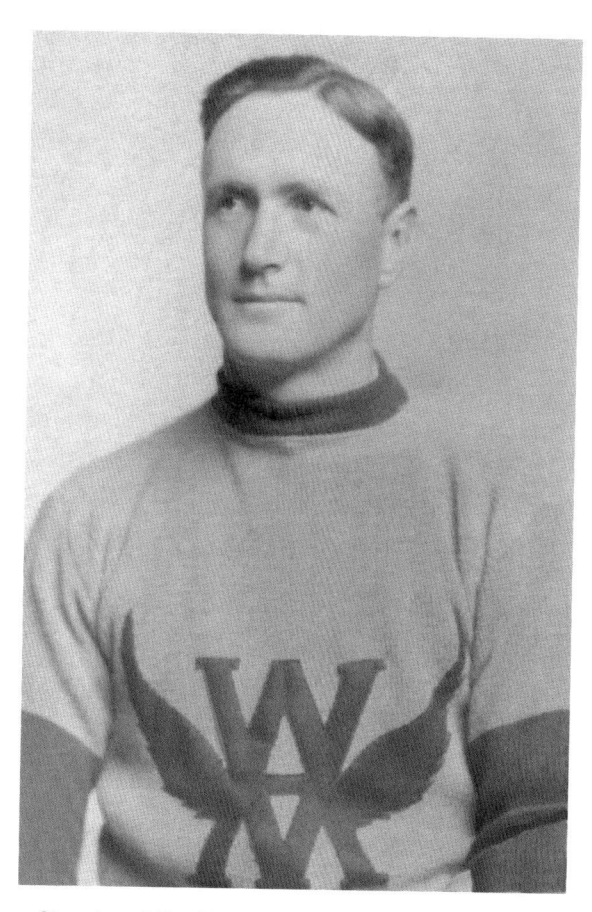

Clem Loughlin. Photo courtesy Ernie Fitzsimmons.

Clem Loughlin was born on November 15, 1892, in Carrol, Manitoba. He began his amateur hockey career in 1910-1911, playing forward at St. Boniface College in Winnipeg. The next season, he was with the Winnipeg Intermediates, and the following two with the Strathconas, where he played both forward and defence and was named team captain. In the 1914-15 season, he played with Dick and Alex Irwin and Stan Marples on the Winnipeg Monarchs' World Amateur Ice Hockey Championship team. He also played baseball with a batting average of over .305.

In 1916, the twenty-three-year-old Clem turned professional with the Portland Rosebuds; this was the first time he had skated on artificial ice. He played one more season, and when the team folded in 1918, he joined the Victoria Aristocrats. Clem had made a significant purchase in 1917, acquiring a farm in Viking, Alberta. He kept in good shape working the farm in the off-season and was occasionally late for training camp if his crops were late in maturing. He played eight seasons with Victoria, being named captain in his second season. Clem was named an all-star on the second team three times and a first-team all-star once, in 1924. He led the Victoria Cougars to a Stanley Cup victory in the 1924-25 season.

When the Victoria Cougars were sold to the Detroit Athletic Club, for $100,000, and became the Detroit Cougars, Clem moved to the Motor City. He played in the first hockey game at the historic Olympia Stadium, the "Old Red Barn," and was also the first captain in Detroit hockey history. In his first year there, he scored seven goals and played a solid game on defence. In 1928, he was sold to the Chicago Blackhawks but ended up in the minor leagues. He was traded to the Toronto Maple Leafs in 1929 but was sent to London of the International Hockey League the same day. He became the player-coach of the Tecumsehs, taking them from last place to the league championship in 1933-34.

Clem returned to the NHL as coach of the Chicago Blackhawks from 1934-37. After resigning from the Hawks, Clem returned to Viking, Alberta, where he had a farm and ran a hotel. He was very involved in youth hockey and was a mentor to the six Sutter brothers.

Clem passed away on February 8, 1977, while reading the hockey news in *Sports Illustrated*. He was inducted into the Manitoba Hockey Hall of Fame for his contribution to sport in that province.

Ernie "Moose" Johnson

Ernie "Moose" Johnson in a New Westminster Royals' jersey. Photo courtesy Vancouver Archives.

Ernie Johnson was born on February 26, 1886, in Montreal. After playing amateur hockey in Montreal, he played in 1905 with the Montreal Wanderers of the new Eastern Canada Amateur Hockey Association. With Lester Patrick scoring two late goals in the championship series, the team won the Stanley Cup—then the trophy for Canada's amateur champions. When the league became professional in 1906-07, the Wanderers signed Johnson to a contract. He and his teammates Jack Marshall, Hod Stuart, Frank Glass, and Riley Hern, became the first professional players to compete for the Stanley Cup. He would win a total of four Stanley Cups with the Wanderers.

When the Patricks formed the Pacific Coast Hockey Association, Johnson, who was considered a premier hockey player, came west to play for the New Westminster Royals. There, he switched positions from left wing to cover point (defence) and led the team to the inaugural league championship. Despite being declared an "outlaw" by the National Hockey Association, Johnson declined to return and remained with the Royals. When the franchise moved to Portland, he moved with them. The Rosebuds won the PCHA Championship that season and became the first American team to compete for the Stanley Cup. They did not win, losing to the Montreal Canadiens three games to two. Johnson stayed with the Rosebuds until the end of the 1917-18 season, when the team moved to Victoria to become the Aristocrats.

Victoria welcomed "Moose," and he quickly became a fan favourite. On March 4, 1921, based on a suggestion from a young fan, the Aristocrats held "Moose Johnson Night." In the stands were 500 young fans who had stood in line for free tickets. The evening began with presentations to the player and his wife. The game itself was epic, as it was the longest game played in the PCHA. With the game tied, 4-4, after regulation time, Victoria and Seattle played three overtime periods. As most players were on the ice for the entire game, they were exhausted after playing the equivalent of two consecutive games. The game was called off, with the understanding that it would be replayed at the end of the season if the points would make a difference in the standings. He retired from Victoria (then named the Cougars) after the 1921-22 season. He would return to the game in 1925, playing in California and one final time with the Buckaroos retiring for good at age forty-five.

Johnson had been shocked by a 2,300-volt electrical current in an accident when he was fourteen years old and lost two fingers on his right hand. It did not seem to have affected his hockey prowess. He was known for his skating speed and his ultra-long reach; he used a long stick that gave him a reach of around ninety inches. He also could skate equally well backward and forward, in an era where this was not common. He was not afraid to back down from gritty play, accumulating more than his share of penalties. He was named a second-team all-star in the ECAHA in 1908, and to the PCHA first-team all-stars in 1912, 1913, 1915, 1916, 1917, 1918, 1919, and 1921.

From the time he moved to Portland, Moose worked for the Union Pacific Railroad during the off-season, and once he retired from hockey, he worked full-time as a brakeman. Moose Johnson was inducted into the Hockey Hall of Fame in 1952. He retired to White Rock, BC, in 1954, and died there on March 24, 1963, after suffering a stroke in 1961.

Andy Hebenton

Andy Hebenton. Photo courtesy Ernie Fitzsimmons.

Andy Hebenton was born in Winnipeg, Manitoba, on October 3, 1929. After playing junior hockey in his hometown, he made his professional debut

The History of Professional Hockey in Victoria, BC: 1911-2011

with the Cincinnati Mohawks of the American Hockey League in 1949. The next season, he came to Victoria to play for the Cougars, where he became part of the "kid line" with Reg Abbott and Bob Frampton. Just when things were going well, he was rushed to the hospital with appendicitis. He missed a few games but returned to score spectacular goals, helping the Cougars bring home a league championship. He continued to live in Victoria, marrying a young Victoria lady. To keep in shape during the off-season, he worked for a cement contractor.

Hebenton would play four more seasons for the Cougars, then was signed by the New York Rangers for the 1955-56 season. He played eight seasons there, then was claimed by the Boston Bruins on the waiver wire. He then returned to the West coast, playing for the Portland Buckaroos of the Western Hockey League for the 1964-65 season. Victoria was the next stop on his hockey journey, and he played on the team's top line with Milan Marcetta and Bob Barlow. Together they formed one of the most potent scoring machines in the league. They accumulated a total of 101 goals, and a 138 assists, for a total of 239 points. Their efforts led the team to its only championship when they defeated the first-place Portland Buckaroos in a classic seven-game series that could have gone either way. After the 1966-67 season, the Leafs were sold, and Andy returned to Portland where he played for eight more seasons. He ended his professional career with four games for the Seattle Totems of the Central Hockey league and two years for a semi-pro team in

Other than his scoring ability, Hebenton was known for two things: his gentlemanly play and his durability. He won the NHL's Lady Byng trophy once and was the runner-up on another occasion. In the WHL, he won the Fred J. Hume Cup for the most gentlemanly player a total of six times. His streak of consecutive games was remarkable. He missed three games in 1951, while with the Cougars, then played every game for his subsequent teams until early in 1967, with the Victoria Maple Leafs, when he missed a game to attend his father's funeral. He returned after the service and never missed another game until 1974-75. Although the NHL does not include records from other leagues or playoff games in its statistics, this amazing athlete played an estimated 1,563 consecutive games. He was honoured during a game in Victoria on November 30, 1966, where he and his family were honoured and presented with over $6,000 in gifts.

Andy Hebenton won two championships with Victoria: one with the Cougars in 1951-52, and the second with the Maple Leafs in 1965-66. His type of player will never be seen again due to the gruelling schedules and the more physical game that is played today. Andy died in Portland on January 29, 2019.

Reg Abbott

Reg Abbott. Photo courtesy Ernie Fitzsimmons.

Reg Abbott was born in Winnipeg on February 4, 1930. He was an all-around athlete who played baseball with the Rosedales. The team operated between 1945 and 1950, until declining attendance and lack of an adequate playing diamond led them to fold. The organization was inducted into the Manitoba Baseball Hall of Fame in 2015. Abbott was also an almost-scratch golfer and played lacrosse. However, he committed to hockey as a teenager, playing two seasons with the Brandon Wheat Kings, on the top line with Gus Juckes and Brian Roche.

He was sent to the Victoria Cougars in 1950, after attending training camp with the Montreal Canadiens. He played on the "youth line" with Andy Hebenton and Bob Frampton. He played every game that first season, notching fourteen goals and twenty-four assists. The team won the President's Cup, emblematic of the Pacific Coast Hockey League Championship. Before the 1952-53 season, he attended the Montreal Canadiens' training camp and was considered a "hot prospect," playing on a line with Bernie Geoffrion and Paul Meger. The Habs sent him back to the Cougars but recalled him on December 1, 1952, when Elmer Lach was injured. He appeared in three games for Montreal—December 4, 6, and 7—on a line with Geoffrion and Meger but recorded no points. He was returned to Victoria when Lach was healthy, and finished the season there. He played four seasons with the Cougars in all, ending with the 1953-54 season.

Reg Abbott. Current photo taken by the author.

Abbott told me a story about how Lester Patrick helped his young players with the game. He would set up a sample rink with nickels for one team and dimes for the other and move the coins around the rink, illustrating plays. Patrick was very generous with his time, helping the young members of his team reach their potential. He also said that his time in Victoria proved to be important in his life, as he met his wife there. She was working at Eaton's at the time, and the romance bloomed. He was one of many Cougars who met their wives while playing hockey in Victoria.

Reg Abbott told me that he eventually realized his the dream of playing professional hockey was gone, and he needed to make a living to support his family. He switched to the insurance industry and was able to continue his love of hockey through playing with senior teams in Windsor and Winnipeg. The Winnipeg Maroons were a very powerful team, going to the Allan Cup finals three straight times, and winning the championship in 1964. The team then played for Canada in the World Championship, finishing fourth. Abbott scored two goals and gained four points in seven games. This would effectively be the end of his hockey career.

Bill Shvetz

Bill Shvetz was born August 27, 1930, in Hardieville, Alberta, the son of a coal miner. He credits hockey with saving him from a life underground. He grew up in the Crowsnest Pass area, and while playing hockey there for the Bellevue Lions, he met Gladys, his future wife.

Bill was drafted by the Chicago Blackhawksand turned pro in 1950. He played professional hockey for seventeen years. His first season was for the Milwaukee Sea Gulls of the United States Hockey League; he then returned to Western Canada to play three years for the Calgary Stampeders. He left for one season in the Quebec Hockey League with the Montreal Royals, then came back to Calgary for one more season. Bill then played four seasons in the American Hockey League with the Cleveland Barons. He then moved to the Spokane Comets for the 1961-62 season, staying with the franchise as it moved to Denver (as the Invaders) and on to Victoria (as the Maple Leafs). He finished his pro career with the Phoenix Roadrunners when the franchise moved to Arizona.

Bill Shvetz autographed photo.
Courtesy Gladys Shvetz

During his career, he won several trophies, including the President's Cup and the Edinburgh Trophy with the Calgary Stampeders in 1953-54, the Calder Cup with the Cleveland Barons in 1955-56, and the Lester Patrick Cup with the Victoria Maple Leafs in 1965-66.

While he was playing for the Montreal Royals, they were in a playoff series with Quebec. Their star player was Al Arbour, and during a game in Montreal, Bill and Al collided. Bill lost a couple of teeth, but Al separated his shoulder. The Royals then travelled to Quebec City via train and were met by the local police, who were there to protect Bill as there had been death threats against him. At the game, a punching bag was lowered from the rafters.

Bill was a tough defenceman who made his foes earn every move. He was called "the Destroyer," because his punishing body checks discouraged his opponents from taking chances. Don Cherry called him one of the best defencemen he had ever played with or against. Bill was known more for his penalty minutes than his scoring prowess but could find the back of the net on occasion, often when his team needed a boost. When the Maple Leafs were short of forwards, Bill moved to a new position for a few games, showing his versatility.

When the Maple Leafs moved to Phoenix, Gladys and their son stayed in Victoria, so the youngster could start school. Bill retired at Christmas, as he was not happy being apart from his family. He took a job with the City of Victoria but found that he worked faster than the rest of the crew, making them look bad. One winter during a cold spell, he turned a pond on Dallas Road into a skating rink for the kids. Bill worked at Colwood, mowing the greens, and then studied golf-course management via correspondence through the University of Guelph. He moved on to be the superintendent at Gorge Vale, then worked at Uplands for the rest of his working life. He would often get up in the middle of the night to check on the "water boys" (who watered the greens at night), as there were no automatic sprinkling systems in those days.

Bill Shvetz died in Victoria, BC, on April 21, 2011.

Bob Barlow

Bob Barlow was born in Hamilton, Ontario, on June 17, 1935, into a hockey-playing family. His father, Hugh Sr., played for the Hamilton Pats, Montreal Royals, and the Cornwallis Navy team during World War II. As a member of the Montreal Royals, Hugh Sr. won the Allan Cup in 1947. Bob's older brother Hugh Jr. played on the 1954 Memorial Cup Championship team (St. Catharines Teepees).

Bob played Senior A hockey in Northern Ontario (North Bay Trappers) and said that the best thing that came out of those days was meeting his wife, Marilyn, a very talented figure skater. Bob turned pro with the Cleveland Barons of the American Hockey League (AHL). He then continued in the AHL for three seasons with the Quebec Aces. In 1962, he moved west to play in the Western Hockey League (WHL). He became established as a prolific scorer (with forty-seven goals) with the Seattle Totems, playing on a line with Guyle Fielder and Jim Powers. Bob remained with the Totems for three years.

Bob Barlow. Photo courtesy Bob Barlow.

Bob moved to British Columbia to play for the Victoria Maple Leafs for the 1965-66 season. He was determined to score more than thirty goals that season to demonstrate that he could score without his Seattle centreman Guyle Fielder to feed him the puck. Coach Frank Mario put Bob on a line with Andy Hebenton and Milan Marcetta, and together they became one of the most potent scoring machines in the league. Their line accumulated a total of 101 goals and 138 assists, for a grand total of 239 points. Their scoring efforts led the team to its only WHL Championship when the Maple Leafs defeated the first-place Portland Buckaroos in a classic seven-game series that could have gone either way. Bob had ten goals and nine assists during that playoff run, which cumulated in winning the WHL Lester Patrick Cup that season. The next year was not as successful for the Leafs, as they missed the playoffs.

Rochester was his next stop, where he played one season back in the AHL, winning the Calder Cup trophy before moving west again to play for the Vancouver Canucks. Bob served as the captain of the 1968-69 Vancouver Canucks, where he won another WHL Lester Patrick Cup.

Bob's big break came in 1969 when he was signed by the Minnesota North Stars of the NHL. He played his first NHL game on October 12, 1969, becoming the oldest rookie (to that date) in the NHL at age thirty-four. Former Portland Buckaroo Connie Madigan would eclipse that record three years later when he broke into the NHL at thirty-eight. Bob has the distinction of scoring his first NHL goal on his first shot of his first shift, within six seconds! He played that full season with the North Stars and another seven games the following year. His career then took him back to the WHL, to Phoenix, where he was reunited with some of his Victoria teammates on the Phoenix Roadrunners, where he won two back-to-back WHL Lester Patrick Cup Championships, in 1972-73 and 1973-74. When Phoenix was granted a World Hockey Association (WHA) franchise in 1974-75, he made the move to the new league.

Bob Barlow shows his collection of hockey memorabilia. Photo courtesy Deddeda.

He played twenty-five games for the Tulsa Oilers of the Central Hockey League and finished his playing career with the Tucson Mavericks, also of the CHL, serving as a player-coach. His career spanned twenty-four years in five professional hockey leagues—the AHL, WHL, CHL, WHA, and NHL—accumulating a total of 1,052 points (including 522 goals), one AHL Championship, and four WHL Championships.

Bob purchased a house in Victoria with his Vancouver Canucks' playoff bonus. He and Marilyn still live there today. In the basement is a treasure trove of hockey memorabilia, with everything from the puck from his first NHL goal to hockey sticks, pennants, newspaper clippings, and his collection of championship rings. Bob can be seen at local junior hockey games watching the game he loves, socializing with his friends, and handing out Minnesota North Stars trading cards to the young fans.

Ryan Wade

Ryan as Salmon Kings' coach. Photo courtesy the Victoria Salmon Kings.

Ryan Wade has the distinction of being the only player or coach to be with the Salmon Kings throughout their entire seven-season run.

He first skated when he was two years old. He played other sports including baseball, basketball, and soccer, as well as track and field. Hockey always came first for him. He had a chance to play for the local Victoria Salsa but opted for the WHL, where he suited up for Tacoma and then Kelowna when the franchise moved there. He then attended the University of Alberta to get an education, using the WHL's Scholarship Package. During his time there, he played for the Golden Bears, where he won the CIS West points title in 2004 and was named MVP in the same year. The team won three straight CIS West Championships and one National Championship during his time there.

He played one game for the AHL's Houston Aeros when his college career was over, but they were not signing players due to the NHL lockout. Therefore, when an opportunity to play for the new Victoria ECHL pro team, the Salmon Kings, came up, it was a chance to play in front of friends and family in his hometown, and he eagerly signed up. Wade was a real leader in every sense of the word, leading by example rather than words.

The first year of the franchise was not easy as the new downtown arena was not ready, so the team had to play in the much-smaller Bear Mountain Arena in Colwood. The first ECHL game in Victoria—and the first professional hockey game since the 1967 Victoria Maple Leafs—was played before a packed house at Bear Mountain Arena. Hometown favourite Ryan Wade scored the first home goal in Salmon Kings' history, at 4:57 of the first period.

The next season saw the opening of the Save-On-Foods Memorial Arena, where the Salmon Kings began to build a loyal following. In November 2006, Ryan was pressed into service as a defender due to injuries on the blue line and filled in admirably. In a playoff game on April 12, 2008, against Bakersfield, he scored two short-handed goals on the same Condor power play to lead the team to a 4-3 victory that tied the series, 1-1.

After playing four years for the Salmon Kings, as their all-time leader in games played, assists, points, penalty minutes, and shots, Ryan hung up his skates. When assistant coach Quentin Van Horlick resigned suddenly, coach Mark Morrison asked Ryan to become his assistant. He said yes, and stayed with the team until its final season. Morrison noted that "even when he was a player, it always felt like Ryan was an assistant coach."

Ryan's coaching philosophy was to recognize the skill sets of each player and deal with each one on a personal basis. He expected players to work hard in the same way he had, and that paid off. The team had its best years between 2008-09 and 2010-11. When it was announced that team ownership had purchased the Chilliwack Bruins of the WHL and would be moving them to Victoria, the Salmon Kings were in the midst of an historic playoff run. Ryan said the motivation for the team was that they wanted to end it with a bang. They made it further in the playoffs that year than any other team but fell just short to the Alaska Aces. Even at the end of the franchise, there was pride in what the team had accomplished on the ice and in the community, including building a loyal fan base.

Ryan then went to the Pursuit of Excellence Hockey Academy in Kelowna, as a coach, and was there for three years. He is now working in the oil and gas industry.

Mark Morrison

Mark Morrison was announced as the assistant coach of the Victoria Salmon Kings on September 5, 2005. He was well known in Victoria for his junior-hockey exploits.

Mark joined the Victoria Cougars of the WHL as a sixteen-year-old, for the 1979-80 season. Over the next four years, he played 249 regular-season games, in which he accumulated 159 goals and 235 assists as well as forty-seven playoff games that resulted in nineteen goals and thirty-five assists. His total of 178 goals, 270 assists and total of 422 points were franchise records. The 1980-81 team won the WHL Championship and played in the Memorial Cup. Mark was named the Most Sportsmanlike Player at that tournament, won by the Cornwall Royals. He also represented Canada at the 1982 and 1983 World Junior Championships. Nicknamed "Mighty Mouse," he owned every Victoria Cougar junior-scoring record. His lack of size, at 5'8", worked against him, as he was thought to be too small and light to withstand the rigours of an NHL season. He was drafted by the New York Rangers in the third rounds, fifty-first overall in the 1981 entry draft, and played a total of ten games in the NHL.

Mark Morrison at 2005 training camp.
Photo courtesy Victoria Salmon Kings.

In 1985, he headed to Europe, where the bigger ice surface meant the emphasis was on speed rather than size, and he played there for eight years. He played in Italy before moving on to Britain in 1992, where he starred for the Fife Flyers through the 1999-2000 season. He took over as coach midway through the 1995-96 season. Mark won three regular-season and two playoff titles during his time in the British National LeagueHe still holds the record for most goals all-time (393) and ranks second in assists in one season with 189 in the 1993-94 season. His number—seventeen—was retired by the club.

Mark's coaching style merged well with that of head coach, Bryan Maxwell. Both stressed a strong work ethic, which would work well with young players eager to move up the hockey ladder.

When Tony MacAulay was fired as Salmon Kings coach in late December 2006, Mark was named to replace him. He signed a three-extension of his contract in May 2008 and added the position of general manager to his duties. He served in both capacities until the club folded in 2011.

Reflecting on his time with the Salmon Kings, he says that he felt that the quality of play in the was better than that of a WHL club, as most of the ECHL clubs had former junior stars and were put together for success. He felt that the Salmon Kings were a placeholder team and that club ownership really wanted a WHL team. When the Kings heard that the team was folding, it was hard for everybody.

On July 20, 2011, Mark was named assistant coach for the AHL affiliate of the Winnipeg Jets. The team was based in St. John's, Newfoundland, as the St. John's IceCaps until the end of the 2014-15 season, when they moved to Winnipeg as the Manitoba Moose.

Mark became an assistant coach with the NHL's Anaheim Ducks on June 28, 2017. He enjoys coaching in the NHL but feels that his time with the Salmon Kings was the highlight of his career. He was able to reconnect with people he had met there as a junior player. He recalled the huge crowds from when the Cougars were doing well and thought that the Salmon Kings would draw well. For some reason, this did not happen, even when they were a good, competitive team. Mark said it was a real treat to coach in his home area as not many coaches get to do that.

Taylor Ellington

Taylor Ellington plays against the Idaho Steelheads, March 13, 2010. Photo by Anne-Marie Sorvin, courtesy of Victoria Salmon Kings.

Taylor Ellington was born in Victoria, BC, on October 31, 1988. He played five years of WHL junior hockey with the Everett Silvertips, from 2004-05 to 2008-09. He was drafted by the Vancouver Canucks in the second round, thirty-third overall, in the 2007 NHL Entry Draft.

Taylor was invited to the Vancouver Canucks' 2008 training camp but was declared "not ready for the pro game," and was returned to the Silvertips. On March 16, 2009, the Canucks signed Taylor to a contract; he played one game in the AHL for the Manitoba Moose that season. He attended the training camp of the Vancouver Canucks in 2009 and felt that he had made a good impression. When he was assigned to the Salmon Kings, he was disappointed not to be playing for the Manitoba Moose in the

AHL, but enjoyed playing in Victoria as his friends and family could come to see him play regularly. What he really enjoyed was meeting members of the community, while many businesses were welcoming and made the players feel at home.

He played most of the 2009-10 season for the Salmon Kings, notching three goals and eleven assists, but was recalled to Manitoba on several occasions, where he played fourteen games. He suffered a concussion in the next season that kept him out of action for most of the season. The record shows he played only fourteen games for the Salmon Kings that year.

After the Salmon Kings folded, he played for four ECHL teams: the Kalamazoo Wings, the Chicago Express, the Florida Everblades, and the Cincinnati Cyclones.

When he realized that the NHL dream was over, he signed to play in Denmark. He had worked very hard, but it had not paid off the way he thought it would, and he retired after thirty-eight games.

Taylor is currently working in property management and is going back to school to complete his business degree . So far, he has not found a career path that gives him the same buzz that hockey did.

He said the bond between hockey players is unlike any other, as they are a tight-knit group. For many of them, Victoria will always be home.

APPENDIX B

Team Rosters

Victoria Senators/Aristocrats/Cougars

Name	Position	Birthdate	Death date	Years played
Jocko Anderson	LW	April 10, 1892	July 22, 1960	1922-23 to 1925-26
Alf Barbour	Rover	June 1, 1891	May 13, 1953	1918-19
Archie Briden	LW	July 16, 1898	June 8, 1974	1923-24
Charles Deildal	RW	May 8, 1894	October 19, 1971	1922-23
Tom Dunderdale	C	May 6, 1887	December 15, 1960	1911-12 to 1914-15 and 1918-19 to 1922-23
Wally Elmer	F	January 1, 1898	August 28, 1978	1924-25
Norman Fowler	G	October 14, 1892	July 30, 1987	1919-20 to 1923-24
FrankFoyston	C	February 2, 1891	January 19, 1966	1924-25 and 1925-26
Gord Fraser	C	March 3, 1894	October 1, 1964	1924-25 and 1925-26
FrankFrederickson	C	June 11, 1895	May 28, 1979	1920-21 to 1925-26
Robert Genge	D	December 20, 1889	September 20, 1937	1912-13 to 1914-15 and 1918-19 to 1920-21
Jimmy Gibson	C	March 2, 1896	May 28, 1964	1923-24
Harold Halderson	D	January 17, 1898	August 1, 1965	1921-22 to 1925-26
Harold Hart	LW	June 1, 1901	June 22, 1964	1923-24 to 1925-26
Harry Holmes	G	February 21, 1888	June 27, 1941	1924-25 and 1925-26
Alex Irvin	D	April 5, 1890	April 25, 1971	1918-19
Ernie Johnson	LW/D	February 26, 1886	March 24, 1963	1918-19 to 1921-22
Albert Kerr	LW	June 19, 1888	September 17, 1941	1913-14 to 1914-15 and 1918-19 to 1919-20
Bert Lindsay	G	July 23, 1881	November 11, 1960	1911-12 to 1914-15
Clem Loughlin	D	November 15, 1892	January 28, 1977	1918-19 to 1925-26
Wilf Loughlin	D	February 28, 1896	June 25, 1966	1918-19 to 1922-23
Stan Marples	LW	November 16, 1891	January 27, 1928	1918-19
Gord Meeking	C	August 26, 1890	December 21, 1965	1919-20 to 1923-24
Harold Meeking	LW	November 4, 1894	December 31, 1971	1920-21, 1924-25, and 1925-26

Name	Position	Birthdate	Death date	Years played
Bernie Morris	C	August 21, 1890	May 1, 1963	1914-15
Tommy Murray	G	February 17, 1893	October 25, 1963	1918-19
Eddie Oatman	D	June 10, 1889	November 5, 1973	1918-19 to 1922-23
Russell Oatman	LW	February 19, 1905	October 25, 1964	1925-26
Lester Patrick	D	December 30, 1883	June 1, 1960	1911-12 to 1914-15, 1918-19 to 1921-22, and 1925-26
George Poulin	F	September 17, 1887	May 3, 1971	1911-12 to 1914-15 and 1918-19
Samuel Prodger	D	February 18, 1891	October 25, 1935	1912-13
Bobby Rowe	D	August 19, 1885	September 21, 1948	1911-12 to 1914-15
Walter Smaill	CP	December 18, 1884	March 2, 1971	1911-12 to 1914-15
Donald Smith	Rover	June 4, 1887	May 13, 1959	1911-12
Charlie Tobin	RW	November 4, 1885	May 30, 1924	1918-19
Clem Trihey	RW	June 24, 1897	February 4, 1973	1923-24
Joseph Ulrich	RW	July 15, 1887	June 12, 1953	1912-13 to 1913-14
Jack Walker	F	November 19, 1888	February 16, 1950	1924-25 and 1925-26

Victoria Cubs

Name	Position	Birthdate	Death date	Years played
Oscar Asmundson	C	November 17, 1908	November 2, 1964	1928-29 and 1929-30
James Borland	D	March 17, 1892	November 23, 1977	1928-29
Daniel Carrigan	C	February 20, 1904	June 16, 1979	1928-29
Eugene Carrigan	C	July 5, 1907	March 15, 1945	1928-29
? Coleman	G			1929-30
David Downie	RW	March 11, 1909	March 18, 1963	1928-29
James Evans	C	June 26, 1904	June 10, 1957	1928-29 and 1929-30
Albert Hardaker	G	February 22, 1908	September 20, 1981	1928-29 and 1929-30
John Kelly	LW	August 7, 1904	September 22, 1936	1928-29 and 1929-30
Ernie Kenny	D	August 20, 1907	June 2, 1970	1928-29
Ernest Leacock	D	March 22, 1906	April 17, 1976	1928-29 and 1929-30
Odie Lowe	LW	September 25, 1904	March 17, 1995	1929-30
Clifford O'Meara	F	February 13, 1896	June 2, 1957	1928-29
Norm Pridham	D	October 18, 1906	December 5, 1972	1928-29
Oliver Redpath	D	February 16, 1904	August 2, 1986	1928-29 and 1929-30
Earl Robertson	G	November 24, 1910	January 19, 1979	1928-29 and 1929-30
Herman Runge	D	October 19, 1905	October 5, 1984	1928-29 and 1929-30
Paul Runge	C	September 10, 1908	April 27, 1972	1928-29 and 1929-30
Ken Williamson	RW	March 10, 1909	July 5, 1967	1929-30

The History of Professional Hockey in Victoria, BC: 1911-2011

Victoria Cougars 1949-50 to 1960-61

Name	Position	Birthdate	Death date	Seasons played
Reg Abbott	C	February 4, 1930		1950-51 to 1953-54
Leo Amadio	D	February 2, 1935	April 6, 1991	1960-61
Gene Achtymichuk	C	July 7, 1932		1953-54 and 1954-55
Ralph Almas	G	April 26, 1924	May 3, 2001	1953-54
Doug Anderson	C	October 20, 1927	January 8, 1998	1951-52 to 1960-61
Don Ashbee	LW	September 9, 1930		1954-55
Walter Atanas	RW	December 23, 1922	August 8, 1991	1951-53
Warren Back	D	November 15, 1936		1957-58
Bob Ballance	C	April 29, 1923	July 30, 1962	1951-52
Stan Baluik	C	October 5, 1935		1957-58 to 1958-59
Bob Beckett	C	April 8, 1936		1956-57
Reg Beliveau	LW	June 21, 1935		1955-56
Beverly Bentley	G	June 8, 1927		1954-55
Larry Berg	LW	April 2, 1936		1955-56 and 1957-58
Silvio Bettio	LW	December 1, 1928	June 14, 2006	1953-54
Jack Bionda	D	September 18, 1938	November 3, 1999	1959-60
Gordon Black	D	March 21, 1940		1958-59
Don Blackburn	LW	May 14, 1938		1958-59 and 1959-60
Leon Bouchard	D	May 3, 1929	July 4, 2011	1951-52
Georges Bougie	RW	April 10, 1927	February 1, 1971	1949-50
Bob Bowness	LW	May 7, 1928	February 16, 1994	1951-52
Nelson Boyce	RW	January 24, 1924	July 1, 2002	1957-58
Barton Bradley	C	July 29, 1930	September 16, 2006	1954-55
Fred Brown	RW	September 4, 1928		1957-58
Wayne Brown	RW	November 16, 1930		1954-55 to 1956-57
Bill Bucyk	D	January 26, 1933		1954-55
Nelson Bulloch	D	March 7, 1931		1955-56 to 1957-58
Geoff Burman	C		December 7, 2009	1950-51
Bruce Carmichael	RW	March 28, 1934		1955-56 and 1956-57
Ray Ceresino	LW	April 24, 1929	May 1, 2015	1955-56
Don Chiupka	C	August 14, 1934	December 21, 2013	1955-56 to 1956-57
Elliot Chorley	F	September 12, 1931	December 5, 2008	1960-61
Walter Clune	D	February 20, 1931	February 3, 1998	1953-54 and 1954-55
Joe Conn	D	March 21, 1927	April 15, 1978	1953-54
Jerome Cotnoir	G	October 8, 1924	February 16, 2018	1950-51 to 1952-53
Hugh Currie	D	October 22, 1925	November 1, 2017	1960-61
Bill Davidson	D	November 19, 1929	February 24, 2001	1954-55 to 1956-57
Lorne Davis	RW	July 20, 1930	December 20, 2007	1950-51

Appendix B

Bill Dobbyn	D	July 7, 1935		1955-56 to 1956-57
Ed Dorohoy	C	March 13, 1929	May 28, 2009	1949-50 to 1954-55 & 1957-58
Lloyd Durham	D	November 6, 1927		1954-55
Pete Egan	D	April 26, 1918	June 3, 2008	1957-58 to 1958-59
Claude Evans	G	April 28, 1983	July 7, 1982	1953-54
Jack Evans	D	April 21, 1928	November 10, 1996	1952-53 and 1954-55
Joe Evans	LW	May 23, 1922	March 23, 2005	1949-50 to 1951-52
Jim Fairburn	RW	September 12, 1927	March 28, 2015	1952-53
Gord Fashoway	LW	June 16, 1926	May 1, 2012	1959-60
Bert Fizzell	LW	January 18, 1941		1960-61
Jerry Fodey	G	July 27, 1924	December 4, 1992	1949-50
George Ford	F	June 8, 1930		1958-59 to 1960-61
Bill Forhan	RW	December 10, 1937		1958-59
Robert Frampton	LW	January 20, 1929	September 8, 2001	1950-51 to 1951-52
Emile Francis	G	September 13, 1926		1957-58
Pat Ginnell	RW	March 3, 1937	November 1, 2003	1960-61
Fiori Goegan	D	November 30, 1927	February 24, 1975	1949-50 to 1953-54
Robert Goodacre	RW	September 2, 1928	May 3, 1992	1952-53
Arlo Goodwin	C	January 22, 1935		1959-60
Gerry Goyer	C	October 20, 1936		1959-60 to 1960-61
Ken Gunter	C	June 25, 1920	October 16, 2011	1949-50
Donald Hamilton	G	February 18, 1937		1955-56 and 1957-58
Ted Harris	D	July 18, 1936		1957-58
Art Hart	W	September 30, 1934		1957-58
Gordie Haworth	C	February 20, 1932		1956-57 to 1959-60
Jim Hay	D	May 15, 1931		1959-60 to 1960-61
George Hayes	C	April 28, 1926	May 4, 1979	1949-50
Andy Hebenton	RW	October 3, 1929	January 29, 2019	1950-51 to 1954-55
Lionel Heinrich	LW	April 20, 1934	April 21, 2014	1956-57
Les Hickey	RW	February 2, 1921	August 8, 1990	1951-52
Hector Highton	G	December 10, 1923	September 28, 1985	1950-51
Ike Hildebrand	RW	May 27, 1927	August 27, 2006	1951-52
Floyd Hillman	D	November 19, 1933		1955-56
Howard Hornby	C	October 7, 1934	October 1, 2014	1955-56
Ivan Irwin	D	March 13, 1927	February 11, 2019	1952-53
Doug Jackson	G	December 12, 1924	April 26, 1980	1949-50
Bill Johansen	C	July 27, 1928	March 21, 2001	1960-61
Art Jones	C	January 31, 1935		1959-60
Carl Kaiser	D	April 8, 1927	April 29, 2010	1957-58 to 1959-60
Mickey Keating	D	April 12, 1931	January 19, 2004	1954-55

The History of Professional Hockey in Victoria, BC: 1911-2011

Colin Kilburn	LW	December 26, 1927	December 6, 1995	1952-53 to 1957-58
Doug Kilburn	RW	August 10, 1930		1957-58
Jack Kirk	D	August 13, 1925	December 29, 2001	1952-53
Russ Kopak	C	April 26, 1924	November 25, 1998	1949-50
Alex Kuzma	RW	February 9, 1929		1953-54 to 1954-55
Sam Lavitt	D	August 1, 1922	October 20, 2012	1953-54
Ed Lawson	C	November 7, 1940		1960-61
Bruce Lea	LW	February 12, 1933		1958-59
Larry Leach	C	June 18, 1936		1955-56 to 1957-58
Roger Leger	D	March 16, 1919	April 7, 1965	1950-51 to 1951-52
Stan Long	D	November 6, 1929	January 10, 1982	1950-51 and 1952-53
Ross Lowe	D/LW	September 21, 1928	August 8, 1955	1953-54
Con McBeth	RW	October 11 1926		1949-50
Tom McCarthy	LW	September 15, 1934	January 20, 1992	1957-58
Jack McIntyre	C	October 15, 1926	November 11, 1977	1949-50 to 1952-53
Roy McKay	RW	January 6, 1926	January 19, 2016	1949-50 to 1950-51
Don McLeod	D	August 19, 1932		1958-59 and 1960-61
Douglas McNeil	D	November 7, 1927	January 18, 2015	1951-52
Morley MacNeill	D	June 30, 1930		1950-51
Doug Macauley	RW	July 22, 1929	September 2, 2009	1953-54 to 1960-61
Don Makow	C	April 10, 1941		1960-61
Bobby Manson	C	December 22, 1927		1953-54
Ed Marineau	D	September 15, 1927	December 2, 2004	1949-50
Mark Marquess	RW	March 26, 1925	January 19, 2015	1954-55 to 1955-56
Paul Masnick	C	April 14, 1931		1959-60 to 1960-61
Gordie Matheson	D	August 31, 1938		1956-57
Ron Matthews	D	January 9, 1927	April 30, 2014	1959-60
Stan Maxwell	LW	September 5, 1925	April 28, 2008	1952-53 to 1953-54
Eddie Mazur	LW	July 25, 1929	July 3, 1995	1949-50 to 1950-51 and 1952-53
Joe Medynski	RW	July 6, 1922	March 30, 1981	1950-51 to 1951-52
Ray Mikulan	G	May 27, 1934		1956-57
Frank Milne	LW	June 28, 1933	June 13, 2008	1957-58 to 1958-59
Jim Moro	RW	March 31, 1934	July 1, 2003	1960-61
Len Mutcheson	LW	February 5, 1921	November 13, 2005	1949-50
Al Nicholson	LW	April 26, 1936	December 9, 1978	1858-59 to 1959-60
Wayne North	LW	March 3, 1938		1960-61
Dennis Olson	C	November 9, 1923		1957-58
Eddie Olson	LW	January 1, 1922	February 10, 1995	1955-56
Rudy Panagabko	RW	March 9, 1938		1955-56
Roy Partridge	RW	July 25, 1936	April 23, 2001	1956-57

Appendix B

Name	Pos	Born	Died	Seasons
Marcel Pelletier	G	December 6, 1927	May 13, 2017	1954-55 to 1956-57 and 1958-59 to 1960-61
Jean Marc Picard	D	November 9, 1936		1958-59
Jim Pilla	RW	November 1, 1935	October 24, 2014	1957-58
Ray Powell	C	November 16, 1925	September 30, 1998	1956-57
Gerry Prince	LW	November 11, 1933		1959-60
Clare Raglan	D	September 4, 1927	April 15, 2002	1957-58
George Ranieri	LW	January 14, 1936		1956-57
Billy Reay	C	August 21, 1918	September 23, 2004	1953-54 to 1954-55
Murray Richardson	LW	August 24, 1926	March 15, 1954	1949-50
George Robertson	C	May 11, 1927		1949-50
James Robertson	LW	November 22, 1933	April 23, 2014	1955-56
Ernie Roche	D	February 4, 1930	January 2, 1988	1951-52 to 1953-54
Tom Rockey	D	January 27, 1926		1949-50
Barrie Ross	C	January 22, 1936	January 2008	1957-58 and 1960-61
Georges Roy	D	September 28, 1927	December 15, 2010	1960-61
Bill Saunders	F	November 22, 1937		1960-61
Arnie Schmautz	RW	July 3, 1933	September 13, 2016	1959-60
Tony Schneider	D	May 17, 1933		1953-54
Enio Sclisizzi	LW	August 1, 1925	June 27, 2012	1958-59
Allan Senior	C	July 5, 1925	March 28, 2015	1949-50
Jim Shirley	G	January 19, 1929	January 11, 1996	1951-52
William Sinnet	RW	February 4, 1934		1953-54
Dave Stewart	D	June 20, 1936		1957-58
Paul Strasser	RW	January 26, 1935	2004	1955-56
Bernie Strongman	LW	March 15, 1919		1949-50 to 1952-53
George Swarbrick	RW	February 16, 1942		1960-61
Henry Syverson	D	August 1, 1934		1957-58
Allan Teal	C	July 17, 1933	July 8, 2006	1955-56
Larry Thibeault	LW	October 2, 1915	April 2, 1977	1949-50
Dewar Thomson	C	January 4, 1929	February 25, 2010	1951-52
Clare Wakshinski	C	April 24, 1936	August 1, 2016	1957-58 to 1958-59
Dave Wall	C	February 18, 1932		1954-55
Eddie Wares	RW	March 19, 1915	February 29, 1992	1949-50
Don Webster	LW	July 3, 1924	April 12, 1978	1950-51 and 1952-53
Arnott Whitney	D	November 16, 1931		1955-56
Bob Wiest	C	August 16, 1922	June 15, 1993	1949-50
Don Wilson	RW	December 6, 1939		1960-61
Gord Wilson	LW	August 13, 1932		1956-57 to 1959-60
Fred Wonoski	F	January 16, 1936		1955-56
Pete Wright	D	January 25, 1927	August 19, 1989	1959-60
John Yanchuk	D	July 20, 1936	January 1, 2017	1957-58

The History of Professional Hockey in Victoria, BC: 1911-2011

Victoria Maple Leafs 1964-65 to 1966-67

Name	Position	Birthdate	Death date	Years played
Bob Barlow	LW	June 17, 1935		1964-65 to 1965-66
Dan Belisle	RW	May 9, 1937		1966-67
Bruce Carmichael	RW	March 28, 1934		1964-65
Jack Chipchase	D	April 5, 1945		1965-66 to 1966-67
Don Chiupka	C	August 14, 1934	December 21, 2013	1964-65 and 1966-67
Neil Clarke	C	January 2, 1946		1964-65
Dwight Clunie	LW	May 29, 1946		1964-65
Mike Corbett	RW	October 4, 1942		1965-66
Marty Desmarais	RW	October 20, 1944		1965-66
Edgar Ehrenverth	RW	March 12, 1940	July 8, 2015	1965-66 to 1966-67
Autry Erickson	D	January 25, 1938	August 21, 2010	1964-66 to 1965-66
Bill Flett	RW	July 21, 1943	July 12, 1999	1966-67
Andy Hebenton	RW	October 3, 1929	January 29, 2019	1964-65 to 1965-66
John Henderson	G	March 25, 1933		1965-66
Gary Holland	G			1965-66
Alex "Sandy" Hucul	D	December 5, 1933		1964-65 to 1966-67
Fred Hucul	D	December 3, 1931		1964-65 to 1966-67
Lou Jankowski	RW	June 27, 1931	March 21, 2010	1964-65 to 1966-67
Larry Keenan	LW	October 1, 1940		1964-65 to 1966-67
Mike Labadie	RW	August 17, 1921	April 17, 1990	1964-65 to 1965-66
Claude Labrosse	D	August 31, 1934		1964-65 to 1966-67
Dick Lamoureux	LW	February 27, 1934	November 1, 2010	1965-66 to 1966-67
Mike Laughton	C	February 21, 1944		1964-65
Paul Laurent	C	March 20, 1946		1966-67
Ed Lawson	C	November 7, 1940		1966-67
Ed Litzenberger	RW	July 15, 1932	November 1, 2010	1965-66
Milan Marcetta	C	September 19, 1936	September 18, 2014	1964-65 to 1966-67
Eddie Mazur	LW	July 25, 1929	July 3, 1995	1966-67
Al Millar	G	September 18, 1929	December 20, 1987	1965-66 to 1966-67
Jean-Guy Morissette	G	December 16, 1937	March 22, 2011	1966-67
Dave Parenteau	LW	October 1, 1944		1965-66
Tom Polanic	D	April 2, 1943		1964-65
Gord Redahl	F	August 28, 1935	June 22, 2011	1964-65 to 1966-67
Bill Shvetz	D	August 27, 1930	April 21, 2011	1964-65 to 1966-67
John Sleaver	C	August 18, 1934	November 19, 2001	1965-66 to 1966-67
Al Smith	G	November 10, 1945	August 7, 2002	1964-65
Gary Smith	G	February 4, 1944		1964-65 and 1966-67
Bob Taylor	D	March 5, 1940		1966-67

Name	Position	Birthdate	Seasons played
Barry Trapp	D	August 14, 1941	1966-67
Gary Veneruzzo	LW	June 28, 1943	1964-65
Rollie Wilcox	LW	January 8, 1943	1964-65 to 1966-67
Ralph Winfield	D	December 8, 1942	1966-67
Steve Witiuk	LW	January 8, 1929	1964-65 to 1966-67

Victoria Salmon Kings 2004-05 to 2010-11

Name	Position	Birthdate	Seasons played
Derek Allan	RW	November 3, 1981	2005-06
Dallas Anderson	RW	September 17, 1979	2005-06
Joel Andresen	D	April 11, 1983	2005-06
Mark Ashton	D	April 11, 1983	2005-06
Josh Aspenlind	RW	April 19, 1986	2010-11
P J Atherton	D	August 16, 1982	2010-11
Paul Ballantyne	D	July 16, 1982	2006-07 and 2007-08
Nathan Barrett	C	August 3, 1981	2007-08
Mike Barrie	C	March 17, 1974	2004-05
Casey Bartzen	C	January 25, 1979	2004-05
Jason Bast	C	June 2, 1989	2009-10
Chris Beckford-Tseu	G	June 22, 1984	2010-11
David Belitski	G	February 20, 1977	2006-07
Jordie Benn	D	July 26, 1987	2008-09
Blue Bennefield	RW	July 5, 1979	2004-05
Marc-Andre Bernier	RW	February 5, 1985	2006-07 and 2007-08
Paul Bezzo	D	October 26, 1990	2009-10
Curtis Billsten	RW	September 10, 1986	2008-09
Greg Black	C	May 13, 1982	2005-06
Dan Blackburn	G	May 20, 1983	2004-05
Trevor Blanchard	LW	June 6, 1983	2007-08
Scott Borders	LW	August 31, 1981	2004-05
Jonathan Boutin	G	March 28, 1985	2008-09
B J Boxma	G	June 1, 1981	2005-06
Andy Brandt	RW	June 1, 1984	2009-10
Trent Brandvold	D	July 9, 1976	2004-05
Bryan Bridges	G	December 27, 1985	2006-07
Aaron Brocklehurst	D	June 10, 1985	2008-09
David Brumby	G	May 21, 1975	2004-05
Mike Burgoyne	D	December 28, 1980	2009-10
Gord Burnett	D	April 2, 1981	2010-11

The History of Professional Hockey in Victoria, BC: 1911-2011

Robert Busch	F	March 17, 1974	2004-05
Matt Butcher	C	January 1, 1987	2010-11
Cole Byers	D	April 16, 1983	2004-05
Jeff Caister	D	January 17, 1985	2010-11
Bryan Cameron	RW	February 25, 1989	2010-11
Adam Campbell	D	January 5, 1980	2004-05
Derek Campbell	LW	March 3, 1982	2004-05 and 2005-06
Jeremy Cheyne	F	July 10, 1980	2004-05
David Cianfrini	D	June 12, 1985	2009-10
Rick Cleaver	LW	August 10, 1983	2010-11
Phil Cole	D	September 6, 1982	2005-06 and 2006-07
Chris Corrinet	W	October 29, 1978	2004-05
Patrick Coulombe	D	April 23, 1985	2006-07 to 2009-10
Derek Couture	RW	April 24, 1984	2010-11
Matt Cowie	D	October 10, 1986	2010-11
David Currie	G	March 24, 1982	2005-06
Chad Dameworth	D	July 6, 1972	2005-06
Bobby Davey	D	April 20, 1987	2009-10
James DeMone	D	July 1, 1982	2006-07
Darren Deschamps	D	July 17, 1984	2007-08
Taggart Desmet	C	May 29, 1982	2005-06
Brad Dexter	D	March 29, 1972	2004-05
Jacob Dietrich	C	June 20, 1987	2007-08 and 2008-09
Ryan Dingle	F	April 4, 1984	2010-11
Kurt Drummond	D	April 12, 1978	2005-06
Kurtis Dulle	D	November 6, 1979	2004-05
Chip Dunleavy	F	July 31, 1982	2005-06
Taylor Ellington	D	October 31, 1988	2009-10 and 2010-11
Brandon Elliott	D	March 8, 1984	2004-05
Julien Ellis	G	January 27, 1986	2006-07 to 2008-09
Gustav Engman	D	January 17, 1985	2006-07
Ryan Esselmont	D	April 20, 1974	2004-05
Kevin Estrada	LW	May 28, 1982	2007-08
Olivier Filion	C	October 3, 1982	2008-09 and 2009-10
Ryan Finnerty	C	November 23, 1980	2004-05
Glenn Fisher	G	April 25, 1983	2009-10
Jordan Foote	W	March 7, 1985	2008-09
Todd Ford	G	May 1, 1984	2008-09
Nathan Forster	D	July 2, 1980	2004-05
Kris Fredheim	D	February 23, 1987	2009-10
Scott Freeman	F	January 12, 1988	2010-11

Appendix B

Marc Fulton	RW	February 23, 1983	2008-09 and 2010-11
Milan Gajic	RW	June 1, 1981	2006-07 to 2009-10
Jade Galbraith	RW	March 2, 1982	2005-06
Josh Garbutt	LW	July 18, 1984	2005-06
Pete Gardiner	F	September 29, 1977	2005-06
Lanny Gare	F	September 5, 1978	2005-06
Jim Gattolliat	D	December 18, 1976	2004-05
Gabe Gauthier	LW	January 20, 1984	2010-11
Randall Gelech	RW	February 2, 1984	2009-10
Dan Gendur	RW	May 21, 1987	2008-09 and 2009-10
Riley Gill	G	January 1, 1985	2010-11
Gary Gladue	D	April 9, 1984	2007-08 to 2009-10
Alexei Glukhov	F	April 5, 1984	2004-05
Elias Godoy	F	March 11, 1981	2005-06
Ash Goldie	F	March 11, 1981	2007-08
Wes Goldie	C	May 5, 1979	2006-07 to 2009-10
Robin Gomez	LW	October 15, 1981	2006-07 and 2007-08
Francois-Pierre Guenette	C	January 18, 1984	2006-07
Mike Hamilton	F	May 2, 1983	2009-10
Jason Hegberg	LW	January 9, 1979	2004-05
Dustan Heintz	C	March 23, 1981	2005-06
Jay Henderson	LW	September 17, 1978	2009-010
Mike Henderson	RW	November 22, 1980	2005-06
Rob Hennigar	C	April 4, 1983	2010-11
Shaun Heshka	D	June 30, 1985	2006-07
Kevin Hoffman	D	May 2, 1968	2004-05
Greg Hornby	LW	January 18, 1982	2006-07
Scott Howes	LW	September 3, 1987	2009-09 and 2009-10
Adam Huxley	LW	November 4, 1983	2005-06
Mike Ikeda	F		2004-05
Leland Irving	G	April 11, 1988	2009-10
Kristjan Jefkins	D	August 7, 1982	2004-05
Ryan Jorde	D	March 23, 1981	2006-07
Mike Josephson	LW	June 9, 1976	2004-05
Adam Keefe	RW	April 26, 1984	2006-07
Matt Keetley	G	April 27, 1986	2009-10
Greg Keith	F	July 26, 1980	2004-05
Matt Kelly	D	March 23, 1985	2006-07 to 2008-09
Chad Klassen	C	April 16, 1985	2010-11
Tim Kraus	C	February 21, 1987	2010-11
Derek Krestanovich	C	May 31, 1983	2006-07 and 2007-08

The History of Professional Hockey in Victoria, BC: 1911-2011

Jordan Krestanovich	C	June 14, 1981	2006-07 and 2007-08
Jonathan Labelle	LW	May 8, 1983	2007-08 and 2008-09
Quinton Laing	LW	June 8, 1979	2010-11
Alex Lalonde	C	June 21, 1983	2007-08
Simon Lambert	F	July 29, 1983	2007-08
Shaun Landolt	C	October 2, 1984	2008-09
Devon Lang	D	June 23, 1987	2008-09
Olivier Latendresse	C	January 12, 1986	2009-10
Brady Leavold	RW	August 21, 1987	2007-08 to 2009-10
Bryan Leitch	LW	June 17, 1984	2009-10
Seth Leonard	LW	October 29, 1983	2004-05
Brett Leone	G	March 28, 1977	2005-06
Craig Lineker	D	February 14, 1986	2010-11
Steve Lingren	D	April 15, 1973	2006-06 and 2006-07
Darryl Lloyd	C	February 10, 1984	2006-07 to 2008-09
Jeff Lynch	LW	November 20, 1985	2009-10
Aaron MacInnis	D	September 29, 1978	2005-06
Ryan MacMurchy	RW	April 27, 1983	2010-11
Jamie McCaig	G		2004-05
Warren McCutcheon	C	August 6, 1982	2006-07
Rob MacGregor	RW	April 7, 1983	2004-05
Kiel McLeod	C	December 30, 1982	2006-07 and 2007-08
Ryan McLeod	C	August 16, 1984	2005-06
Rob McVicar	G	January 15, 1982	2005-06
Daren Machesney	G	December 13, 1986	2010-11
Mark Magnowski	F	May 8, 1986	2009-10
Simon Mangos	D	February 15, 1980	2005-06
Derick Martin	D	December 17, 1981	2010-11
Tommy Maxwell	RW	November 19, 1985	2010-11
Lance Mayes	G	September 6, 1978	2005-06
Rich Meloche	F	January 17, 1985	2006-07
Tomas Micka	F	June 7, 1983	2004-05
Jonathan Milhouse	C	January 30, 1989	2010-11
Ty Morris	LW	February 2, 1984	2007-08
Lance Morrison	LW	October 29, 1983	2009-10
Dennis Mullen	D	August 14, 1977	2004-05
Robert Muntain	G	March 20, 1979	2004-05
Garth Murray	C	September 17, 1982	2010-11
John Murray	G	July 4, 1987	2009-10
Bryan Nathe	D	February 8, 1983	2007-08
David Neale	C	November 12, 1980	2004-05

Appendix B

Eric Nelson	D	June 11, 1979	2007-08
Mike Nesdill	D	February 7, 1984	2008-09
Sean O'Connor	RW	October 19, 1981	2008-09
Mark Olafson	RW	March 22, 1985	2005-06
Chad Painchaud	RW	May 27, 1986	2009-10 and 2010-11
Neil Petruic	D	July 30, 1982	2009-10
Aaron Plumb	LW	August 24, 1978	2004-05
Dale Purinton	D	October 11, 1976	2004-05
Daniel Rahimi	D	April 28, 1987	2007-08
Travis Ramsey	D	May 16, 1983	2008-09
Cam Ritchie	D	January 6, 1987	2010-11
Brandon Roach	D	June 9, 1985	2009-10
Steve Roberts	W	February 17, 1974	2005-06
Andy Rogers	D	August 25, 1986	2009-10
Geoff Rollins	W	March 31, 1982	2004-05
Adam Ross	D	October 15, 1986	2010-11
Kalvin Sagert	D	January 20, 1987	2007-08
Mike Salekin	D	August 17, 1985	2009-10
Yann Sauve	D	February 18, 1990	2010-11
Jeremy Schenderling	C	April 3, 1986	2008-09
David Shantz	G	May 5, 1986	2009-10 and 2010-11
Jim Sharrow	D	January 31, 1985	2009-10
Chris Shaw	D	April 19, 1981	2007-08
Kelly Shields	G	January 28, 1980	2004-05
Tyler Shybunka	C	January 21, 1979	2005-06
Matt Siddall	RW	September 26, 1984	2009-10 and 2010-11
Rob Simnor	F	May 18, 1979	2004-05
Grant Sjerven	G	March 13, 1970	2004-05
Corey Smith	LW	May 10, 1975	2004-05
Mark Smith	C	October 24, 1977	2004-05
Rob Smith	D	March 11, 1983	2009-10
Ed Snetsinger	D	February 17, 1986	2010-11
Jan Sochor	F	January 17, 1980	2004-05
Dirk Southern	F	August 9, 1983	2009-10
Justin Spencer	RW	May 25, 1981	2006-07
Jimmy Spratt	G	November 10, 1985	2010-11
Chris St. Jacques	C	January 22, 1983	2007-08 and 2008-09
Matt Stefanishion	RW	October 5, 1983	2010-11
Jason Stone	G	April 10, 1982	2004-05
Craig Strain	D	September 1, 1979	2004-05
Mike Stutzel	LW	February 28, 1979	2006-07

Pat Sutton	D	April 26, 1984	2005-06
Jeremy Swanson	D	June 21, 1984	2008-09
Adam Taylor	RW	June 24, 1984	2005-06 to 2006-07 and 2008-09 to 2010-11
Jeff Terminesi	D	January 7, 1987	2010-11
Billy Thompson	G	September 24, 1982	2007-08
Ryan Thrussel	D	March 15, 1981	2005-06
Yannick Tifu	C	October 12, 1984	2009-10
K C Timmons	D	April 6, 1980	2005-06
Peter Trumbley	D	December 25, 1979	2004-05
Ryan Turek	D	September 22, 1987	2010-11
Scott Turner	F	July 9, 1979	2004-05
Pete Vandermeer	LW	October 14, 1975	2010-11
Alexandre Vincent	G	December 11, 1986	2006-07
Rob Voltera	W	May 24, 1978	2004-05
Ryan Wade	F	May 11, 1978	2004-05 to 2007-08
Eric Walsky	F	September 30, 1984	2009-10
Ryan Watson	F	June 12, 1981	2004-05
Geoff Waugh	D	August 25, 1983	2010-11
Tim Wedderburn	D	June 29, 1981	2009-09 and 2009-10
Dean Whitney	G	December 8, 1974	2004-05
Jeff Williams	LW	February 11, 1976	2004-05
Michael Wilson	D	May 8, 1987	2010-11
Mike Wirll	RW	February 28, 1982	2005-06
David Wrigley	LW	June 1, 1980	2006-07
Dylan Yeo	D	July 16, 1986	2007-08 and 2008-09
Seamus Young	D	August 16, 1983	2006-07
Brad Zanon	D	April 29, 1983	2007-08
Craig Zubersky	D	May 31, 1983	2004-05
Andy Zulyniak	D	February 25, 1985	2006-07

APPENDIX C

Season Results

Victoria Senators 1911-1912

Date	Home	Score	Away	Score	Result	Pts	Notes	W	L
January 2, 1912	Victoria Senators	3	New Westminster Royals	8	L				1
January 9, 2012	Vancouver Millionaires	4	Victoria Senators	8	W	2		1	
January 12, 1912	Victoria Senators	10	Vancouver Millionaires	7	W	4		2	
January 16, 1912	New Westminster Royals	4	Victoria Senators	3	L				2
January 23, 1912	Victoria Senators	3	New Westminster Royals	2	W	6		3	
January 26, 1912	Vancouver Millionaires	10	Victoria Senators	8	L				3
January 30, 1912	New Westminster Royals	5	Victoria Senators	2	L				4
February 9, 1912	Victoria Senators	8	Vancouver Millionaires	7	W	8	Overtime: 7:20	4	
February 13, 1912	Vancouver Millionaires	4	Victoria Senators	6	W	10		5	
February 16, 1912	Victoria Senators	2	New Westminster Royals	4	L				5
February 23, 1912	New Westminster Royals	4	Victoria Senators	3	L				6
February 27, 1912	Victoria Senators	3	Vancouver Millionaires	7	L				7
March 1, 1912	Vancouver Millionaires	3	Victoria Senators	7	W	12		6	
March 8, 1912	Victoria Senators	1	New Westminster Royals	5	L				8
March 12, 1912	New Westminster Royals	9	Victoria Senators	7	L				9
March 15, 1912	Victoria Senators	8	Vancouver Millionaires	6	W	14		7	
Regular season total								7	9

The History of Professional Hockey in Victoria, BC: 1911-2011

Victoria Senators 1912-1913

Date	Home	Score	Away	Score	Result	Pts	Notes	W	L
December 13, 1912	Victoria Senators	6	New Westminster Royals	4	W	2		1	
December 17, 1912	Vancouver Millionaires	6	Victoria Senators	3	L				1
December 27, 1912	Victoria Senators	5	Vancouver Millionaires	4	W	4	Overtime: 14:15	2	
December 31, 1912	New Westminster Royals		Victoria Senators				Postponed due to new rink not being ready.		
January 9, 1913	Victoria Senators	3	New Westminster Royals	2	W	6	Overtime: 12:45	3	
January 17, 1913	Victoria Senators	4	Vancouver Millionaires	3	W	8		4	
January 21, 1913	Vancouver Millionaires	4	Victoria Senators	5	W	10		5	
January 31, 1913	Victoria Senators	7	New Westminster Royals	3	W	12		6	
February 4, 1913	Vancouver Millionaires	4	Victoria Senators	7	W	14		7	
February 11, 1913	Victoria Senators	7	Vancouver Millionaires	2	W	16		8	
February 13, 1913	New Westminster Royals	8	Victoria Senators	1	L				2
February 18, 1913	New Westminster Royals	6	Victoria Senators	1	L				3
February 21, 1913	Victoria Senators	8	New Westminster Royals	1	W	18		9	
February 25, 1913	Vancouver Millionaires	9	Victoria Senators	6	L				4
March 4, 1913	Victoria Senators	4	Vancouver Millionaires	5	L				5
March 7, 1913	New Westminster Royals	0	Victoria Senators	1	W	20		10	

Remaining games in the schedule cancelled as Victoria had clinched championship

Regular season total — 10 | 5

WORLD'S TITLE SERIES

March 26, 1913	Victoria Senators	7	Quebec	5	W				
March 27, 1913	Victoria Senators	3	Quebec	6	L				
March 29, 1913	Victoria Senators	6	Quebec	1	W				

WON WORLD'S CHAMPIONSHIP, BUT THIS WAS NOT A SERIES FOR THE STANLEY CUP

408

Victoria Senators 1913-14

Date	Home	Score	Away	Score	Result	Pts	Notes
December 9, 1913	New Westminster Royals	6	Victoria Senators	5	L		
December 12, 1913	Victoria Senators	6	New Westminster Royals	2	W	2	
December 16, 1913	Vancouver Millionaires	11	Victoria Senators	3	L		
December 26, 1913	Victoria Senators	9	Vancouver Millionaires	4	W	4	
January 2, 1914	Victoria Senators	4	New Westminster Royals	5	L		
January 6, 1914	Vancouver Millionaires	5	Victoria Senators	6	W	6	
January 13, 1914	Victoria Senators	5	New Westminster Royals	3	W	8	
January 20, 1914	Victoria Senators	6	Vancouver Millionaires	7	L		Lost at 14:45 of overtime
January 23, 1914	New Westminster Royals	6	Victoria Senators	4	L		
January 27, 1914	Vancouver Millionaires	3	Victoria Senators	5	W	10	
January 30, 1914	Victoria Senators	7	New Westminster Royals	5	W	12	
February 10, 1914	Victoria Senators	5	Vancouver Millionaires	2	W	14	
February 13, 1914	New Westminster Royals	1	Victoria Senators	2	W	16	Overtime: 36:49
February 17, 1914	Vancouver Millionaires	4	Victoria Senators	5	W	18	Overtime: 7:40
February 20, 1914	Victoria Senators	8	New Westminster Royals	3	W	20	
February 27, 1914	Victoria Senators	6	Vancouver Millionaires	13	L		
Regular season total							
WORLD'S TITLE SERIES							
March 14, 1913	Toronto	5	Victoria Senators	2	L		
March 17, 1913	Toronto	6	Victoria Senators	5	L		Lost at 18:00 of overtime
March 19, 1913	Toronto	1	Victoria Senators	2	L		
LOST SERIES, 3-0							

The History of Professional Hockey in Victoria, BC: 1911-2011

Victoria Aristocrats 1914-1915

Date	Home	Score	Away	Score	Result	Pts	Notes	W	L
December 11, 1914	Vancouver Millionaires	5	Victoria Aristocrats	3	L				1
December 15, 1914	Victoria Aristocrats	4	Portland Rosebuds	8	L				2
December 27, 1914	Portland Rosebuds	8	Victoria Aristocrats	1	L				3
December 29, 1914	Victoria Aristocrats	3	Vancouver Millionaires	4	L		Lost at 12:00 of overtime		4
January 8, 1915	Vancouver Millionaires	9	Victoria Aristocrats	2	L				5
January 12, 1915	Victoria Aristocrats	4	Portland Rosebuds	3	W	2	Overtime: 3:55	1	
January 19, 1915	Portland Rosebuds	10	Victoria Aristocrats	5	L				6
January 22, 1915	Victoria Aristocrats	4	Vancouver Millionaires	1	W	4		2	
January 29, 1915	Vancouver Millionaires	12	Victoria Aristocrats	5	L				7
February 2, 1915	Victoria Aristocrats	6	Portland Rosebuds	5	W	6	Overtime: 18:20	3	
February 9, 1915	Portland Rosebuds	3	Victoria Aristocrats	2	L				8
February 12, 1915	Victoria Aristocrats	4	Vancouver Millionaires	6	L				9
February 19, 1915	Vancouver Millionaires	10	Victoria Aristocrats	3	L				10
February 23, 1915	Victoria Aristocrats	4	Portland Rosebuds	3	W	8		4	
March 2, 1915	Victoria Aristocrats	11	Vancouver Millionaires	14	L				11
March 4, 1915	Portland Rosebuds	9	Victoria Aristocrats	1	L				12
March 7, 1915	Portland Rosebuds	6	Victoria Aristocrats	2	L				13
Regular season total								4	13

Victoria Aristocrats 1915-1916

Date	Home	Score	Away	Score	Result	Pts	Notes	W	L
December 7, 1915	Seattle Metropolitans	3	Victoria Aristocrats	2	L				1
December 11, 1915	Victoria Aristocrats	3	Seattle Metropolitans	4	L				2
December 14, 1915	Vancouver Millionaires	5	Victoria Aristocrats	7	W	2		1	
December 17, 1915	Victoria Aristocrats	8	Vancouver Millionaires	2	W	4		2	
December 28, 1915	Portland Rosebuds	3	Victoria Aristocrats	2	L		Lost in overtime: 11:30		3
January 4, 1916	Victoria Aristocrats	5	Portland Rosebuds	10	L				4
January 11, 1916	Vancouver Millionaires	8	Victoria Aristocrats	3	L				5
January 14, 1916	Victoria Aristocrats	5	Seattle Metropolitans	3	W	6		3	
January 18, 1916	Seattle Metropolitans	5	Victoria Aristocrats	3	L				6
January 21, 1916	Victoria Aristocrats	1	Portland Rosebuds	3	L				7
January 25, 1916	Portland Rosebuds	7	Victoria Aristocrats	5	L				8

Appendix C

Date	Home	Score	Away	Score	Result	Pts	Notes	W	L
February 1, 2016	Victoria Aristocrats	4	Vancouver Millionaires	16	L		Last game before arena is closed for military		9
February 4, 1916	Seattle Metropolitans	6	Victoria Aristocrats	3	L				10
February 8, 1916	Seattle Metropolitans	8	Victoria Aristocrats	4	L				11
February 11, 1916	Vancouver Millionaires	7	Victoria Aristocrats	6	L		Lost at 10:56 of overtime		12
February 15, 1916	Portland Rosebuds	4	Victoria Aristocrats	4			Game called after 3 periods due to dense fog on the ice		
February 17, 1916	Portland Rosebuds	4	Victoria Aristocrats	1	L				13
February 26, 1916	Vancouver Millionaires	6	Victoria Aristocrats	7	W	8	Played in Seattle	4	
Regular season total								4	13

Victoria Aristocrats 1918-1919

Date	Home	Score	Away	Score	Result	Pts	Notes	W	L
January 3, 1919	Victoria Aristocrats	1	Seattle Metropolitans	7	L				1
January 6, 1919	Vancouver Millionaires	6	Victoria Aristocrats	1	L				2
January 8, 1919	Seattle Metropolitans	0	Victoria Aristocrats	1	W	2		1	
January 10, 1919	Victoria Aristocrats	1	Vancouver Millionaires	4	L				3
January 17, 1919	Victoria Aristocrats	3	Seattle Metropolitans	1	W	4		2	
January 20, 1919	Vancouver Millionaires	4	Victoria Aristocrats	1	L				4
January 22, 1919	Seattle Metropolitans	0	Victoria Aristocrats	1	W	6		3	
January 24, 1919	Victoria Aristocrats	3	Vancouver Millionaires	2	W	8		4	
January 31, 1919	Victoria Aristocrats	2	Seattle Metropolitans	1	W	10		5	
February 5, 1919	Seattle Metropolitans	9	Victoria Aristocrats	1	L				5
February 7, 1919	Victoria Aristocrats	0	Vancouver Millionaires	1	L				6
February 10, 1919	Vancouver Millionaires	1	Victoria Aristocrats	2	W	12	Overtime: 3:35	6	
February 14, 1919	Victoria Aristocrats	2	Seattle Metropolitans	8	L				7
February 19, 1919	Seattle Metropolitans	4	Victoria Aristocrats	1	L				8
February 21, 1919	Victoria Aristocrats	3	Vancouver Millionaires	2	W	14	Overtime: 37:20	7	
February 24, 1919	Vancouver Millionaires	6	Victoria Aristocrats	3	L				9
February 28, 1919	Victoria Aristocrats	4	Seattle Metropolitans	5	L				10
March 5, 1919	Seattle Metropolitans	3	Victoria Aristocrats	1	L				11
March 7, 1919	Victoria Aristocrats	5	Vancouver Millionaires	6	L		Lost after 11:04 of overtime		12
March 10, 1919	Vancouver Millionaires	11	Victoria Aristocrats	8	L				13
Regular season total								7	13

411

The History of Professional Hockey in Victoria, BC: 1911-2011

Victoria Aristocrats 1919-1920

Date	Home	Score	Away	Score	Result	Pts	Notes	W	L
December 26, 1919	Victoria Aristocrats	2	Seattle Metropolitans	1	W	2		1	
December 29, 1919	Vancouver Millionaires	4	Victoria Aristocrats	3	L		Lost after 00:24 of overtime		1
January 2, 1920	Victoria Aristocrats	7	Vancouver Millionaires	4	W	4		2	
January 7, 1920	Seattle Metropolitans	5	Victoria Aristocrats	2	L				2
January 9, 1920	Victoria Aristocrats	2	Seattle Metropolitans	0	W	6		3	
January 12, 1920	Vancouver Millionaires	3	Victoria Aristocrats	4	W	8		4	
January 16, 1920	Victoria Aristocrats	1	Vancouver Millionaires	2	L				3
January 21, 1920	Seattle Metropolitans	3	Victoria Aristocrats	1	L				4
January 23, 1920	Victoria Aristocrats	4	Vancouver Millionaires	1	W	10		5	
January 26, 1920	Vancouver Millionaires	7	Victoria Aristocrats	5	L				5
January 30, 1920	Victoria Aristocrats	2	Seattle Metropolitans	4	L				6
February 4, 1920	Seattle Metropolitans	4	Victoria Aristocrats	0	L				7
February 6, 1920	Victoria Aristocrats	1	Vancouver Millionaires	3	L				8
February 9, 1920	Vancouver Millionaires	2	Victoria Aristocrats	3	W	12		6	
February 13, 1920	Victoria Aristocrats	6	Seattle Metropolitans	1	W	14		7	
February 18, 1920	Seattle Metropolitans	6	Victoria Aristocrats	0	L				9
February 20, 1920	Victoria Aristocrats	3	Vancouver Millionaires	1	W	16		8	
February 23, 1920	Vancouver Millionaires	10	Victoria Aristocrats	4	L				10
February 27, 1920	Victoria Aristocrats	3	Seattle Metropolitans	2	W	18	Overtime: 7:04	9	
March 3, 1920	Seattle Metropolitans	2	Victoria Aristocrats	0	L				11
March 5, 1920	Victoria Aristocrats	3	Vancouver Millionaires	2	W	20		10	
March 10, 1920	Seattle Metropolitans	5	Victoria Aristocrats	1	L				12
Regular season total								**10**	**12**

Victoria Aristocrats 1920-1921

Date	Home	Score	Away	Score	Result	Pts	Notes	W	L	T
December 22, 1920	Seattle Metropolitans	7	Victoria Aristocrats	2	L				1	
December 25, 1920	Victoria Aristocrats	3	Seattle Metropolitans	3	L		Lost after 6:42 of overtime		2	
December 27, 1920	Vancouver Millionaires	6	Victoria Aristocrats	3	L				3	
January 1, 1921	Victoria Aristocrats	5	Vancouver Millionaires	3	W	2		1		
January 5, 1921	Seattle Metropolitans	2	Victoria Aristocrats	1	L		Lost after 3:35 of overtime		4	
January 7, 1921	Victoria Aristocrats	2	Seattle Metropolitans	0	W	4		2		

Appendix C

Date	Home	Score	Away	Score	Result	Pts	Notes	W	L	T
January 10, 1921	Vancouver Millionaires	5	Victoria Aristocrats	3	L				5	
January 14, 1921	Victoria Aristocrats	3	Vancouver Millionaires	4	L				6	
January 19, 1921	Seattle Metropolitans	9	Victoria Aristocrats	2	L				7	
January 21, 1921	Victoria Aristocrats	4	Vancouver Millionaires	1	W	6		3		
January 24, 1921	Vancouver Millionaires	5	Victoria Aristocrats	2	L				8	
January 28, 1921	Victoria Aristocrats	5	Seattle Metropolitans	3	W	8		4		
February 2, 1921	Seattle Metropolitans	2	Victoria Aristocrats	3	W	10	Overtime: 31:14	5		
February 4, 1921	Victoria Aristocrats	3	Vancouver Millionaires	4	L				9	
February 7, 1921	Vancouver Millionaires	7	Victoria Aristocrats	2	L				10	
February 11, 1921	Victoria Aristocrats	3	Seattle Metropolitans	1	W	12		6		
February 16, 1921	Seattle Metropolitans	3	Victoria Aristocrats	4	W	14		7		
February 18, 1921	Victoria Aristocrats	0	Vancouver Millionaires	2	L				11	
February 21, 1921	Vancouver Millionaires	5	Victoria Aristocrats	1	L				12	
February 25, 1921	Victoria Aristocrats	3	Seattle Metropolitans	0	W	16		8		
March 2, 1921	Seattle Metropolitans	0	Victoria Aristocrats	3	W	18		9		
March 4, 1921	Victoria Aristocrats	4	Seattle Metropolitans	4	T	19	Tied after 60 minutes of overtime			1
March 7, 1921	Vancouver Millionaires	5	Victoria Aristocrats	0	L				13	
March 11, 1921	Victoria Aristocrats	11	Vancouver Millionaires	8	W	21		10		
Regular season total								10	13	1

Victoria Aristocrats 1921-1922

Date	Home	Score	Away	Score	Result	Pts	Notes	W	L	T
December 7, 1921	Seattle Metropolitans	1	Victoria Aristocrats	4	W	2		1		
December 9, 1921	Victoria Aristocrats	1	Seattle Metropolitans	1	T	3	Tied after 20 minutes of overtime			1
December 12, 1921	Vancouver Millionaires	0	Victoria Aristocrats	2	W	5	First ever penalty shot goal	2		
December 16, 1921	Victoria Aristocrats	4	Vancouver Millionaires	3	W	7		3		
December 21, 1921	Seattle Metropolitans	2	Victoria Aristocrats	1	L				1	
December 23, 1921	Victoria Aristocrats	2	Seattle Metropolitans	3	L		Lost at 1:15 of overtime		2	
December 26, 1921	Vancouver Millionaires	3	Victoria Aristocrats	2	L				3	
December 30, 1921	Victoria Aristocrats	3	Vancouver Millionaires	5	L				4	
January 4, 1922	Seattle Metropolitans	3	Victoria Aristocrats	4	W	9	Overtime: 14:34	4		
January 6, 1922	Victoria Aristocrats	5	Vancouver Millionaires	2	W	11		5		
January 9, 1922	Vancouver Millionaires	4	Victoria Aristocrats	0	L				5	
January 13, 1922	Victoria Aristocrats	5	Seattle Metropolitans	2	W	13		6		

The History of Professional Hockey in Victoria, BC: 1911-2011

Date	Home	Score	Away	Score	Result	Pts	Notes	W	L	T
January 18, 1922	Seattle Metropolitans	3	Victoria Aristocrats	4	W	15		7		
January 20, 1922	Victoria Aristocrats	3	Vancouver Millionaires	4	L		Lost at 5:22 of overtime		6	
January 23, 1922	Vancouver Millionaires	4	Victoria Aristocrats	5	W	17		8		
January 27, 1922	Victoria Aristocrats	0	Seattle Metropolitans	4	L				7	
February 1, 1922	Seattle Metropolitans	3	Victoria Aristocrats	1	L				8	
February 3, 1922	Victoria Aristocrats	2	Vancouver Millionaires	1	W	19		9		
February 6, 1922	Vancouver Millionaires	3	Victoria Aristocrats	2	L				9	
February 10, 1922	Victoria Aristocrats	0	Seattle Metropolitans	2	L				10	
February 15, 1922	Seattle Metropolitans	7	Victoria Aristocrats	0	L				11	
February 17, 1922	Victoria Aristocrats	3	Seattle Metropolitans	2	W	21		10		1
February 20, 1922	Vancouver Millionaires	5	Victoria Aristocrats	1	L				12	
February 24, 1922	Victoria Aristocrats	7	Vancouver Millionaires	4	W	23		11		
Regular season total								11	12	1

Victoria Cougars 1922-1923

Date	Home	Score	Away	Score	Result	Pts	Notes	W	L	T
November 15, 1922	Seattle Metropolitans	4	Victoria Cougars	0	L				1	
November 17, 1922	Victoria Cougars	5	Vancouver Maroons	3	W	2		1		
November 20, 1922	Vancouver Maroons	3	Victoria Cougars	4	W	4		2		
November 24, 1922	Victoria Cougars	4	Seattle Metropolitans	6	L				2	
November 29, 1922	Seattle Metropolitans	5	Victoria Cougars	4	L		Lost at 16:47 of overtime		3	
December 8, 1922	Victoria Cougars	3	Vancouver Maroons	4	L				4	
December 11, 1922	Vancouver Maroons	2	Victoria Cougars	1	L				5	
December 15, 1922	Victoria Cougars	2	Seattle Metropolitans	1	W	6		3		
December 22, 1922	Victoria Cougars	2	Regina Capitals	3	L				6	
December 29, 1922	Victoria Cougars	4	Vancouver Maroons	3	W	8		4		
January 1, 1923	Vancouver Maroons	1	Victoria Cougars	2	W	10	Overtime: 8:20	5		
January 3, 1923	Seattle Metropolitans	0	Victoria Cougars	1	W	12		6		
January 5, 1923	Victoria Cougars	5	Seattle Metropolitans	1	W	14		7		
January 8, 1923	Victoria Cougars	0	Seattle Metropolitans	2	L		Played at Vancouver		7	
January 12, 1923	Victoria Cougars	4	Calgary Tigers	0	W	16		8		
January 19, 1923	Victoria Cougars	3	Vancouver Maroons	2	W	18	Overtime: 8:00	9		
January 22, 1923	Vancouver Maroons	4	Victoria Cougars	1	L				8	
January 24, 1923	Vancouver Maroons	8	Victoria Cougars	4	L		Played at Seattle		9	

Appendix C

Date	Home	Score	Away	Score	Result	Pts	Notes	W	L	T
January 27, 1923	Victoria Cougars	5	Saskatoon Crescents	2	W	20		10		
February 2, 1923	Victoria Cougars	3	Vancouver Maroons	4			See "Note 1" below			
February 7, 1923	Seattle Metropolitans	5	Victoria Cougars	2	L				10	
February 9, 1923	Victoria Cougars	6	Seattle Metropolitans	1	W	22		11		
February 12, 1923	Vancouver Maroons	5	Victoria Cougars	3	L				11	
February 16, 1923	Victoria Cougars	4	Edmonton Eskimos	0	W	24		12		
February 19, 1923	Regina Capitals	1	Victoria Cougars	2	W	26		13		
February 21, 1923	Saskatoon Crescents	0	Victoria Cougars	1	W	28		14		
February 23, 1923	Edmonton Eskimos	4	Victoria Cougars	5	W	30		15		
February 26, 1923	Calgary Tigers	4	Victoria Cougars	0	L				12	
February 28, 1923	Seattle Metropolitans	5	Victoria Cougars	3	L				13	
March 2, 1923	Victoria Cougars	9	Seattle Metropolitans	2	W	32		16		
Regular season total								**16**	**13**	**0**

Note 1: The results of this game, which gave Vancouver a victory at 11:00 of overtime, were removed from the record after a successful Victoria protest. The game would have been played on March 5, if it would have changed the end results.

TWO GAME, TOTAL POINTS SERIES

March 7, 1923	Victoria Cougars	0	Vancouver Maroons	3						
March 12, 1923	Vancouver Maroons	2	Victoria Cougars	3						

LOST TOTAL GOALS SERIES, 5-3

Victoria Cougars 1923-1924

Date	Home	Score	Away	Score	Result	Pts	Notes	W	L	T
November 14, 1923	Seattle Metropolitans	7	Victoria Cougars	6	L		Lost at 1:42 of overtime		1	
November 16, 1923	Victoria Cougars	5	Vancouver Maroons	1	W	2		1		
November 19, 1923	Vancouver Maroons	7	Victoria Cougars	1	L				2	
November 23, 1923	Victoria Cougars	4	Seattle Metropolitans	2	W	4		2		
November 30, 1923	Victoria Cougars	7	Saskatoon Crescents	1	W	6		3		
December 7, 1923	Victoria Cougars	1	Calgary Tigers	3	L				3	
December 10, 1923	Edmonton Eskimos	1	Victoria Cougars	3	W	8		4		
December 12, 1923	Saskatoon Crescents	9	Victoria Cougars	3	L				4	
December 14, 1923	Regina Capitals	4	Victoria Cougars	2	L				5	
December 17, 1923	Regina Capitals	4	Victoria Cougars	1	L		Game played at Winnipeg		6	
December 21, 1923	Saskatoon Crescents	2	Victoria Cougars	3	W	10	Overtime: 1:00	5		
December 25, 1923	Vancouver Maroons	3	Victoria Cougars	1	L		Matinee		7	
December 28, 1923	Victoria Cougars	3	Vancouver Maroons	2	W	12	Overtime: 3:16	6		

415

The History of Professional Hockey in Victoria, BC: 1911-2011

Date	Visitor	Score	Home	Score	Result	Points	Notes	W	L	T
January 2, 1924	Seattle Metropolitans	2	Victoria Cougars	1	L				8	
January 4, 1924	Victoria Cougars	3	Seattle Metropolitans	2	W	14	Overtime: 15:32	7		
January 11, 1924	Victoria Cougars	2	Edmonton Eskimos	4	L				9	
January 14, 1924	Vancouver Maroons	3	Victoria Cougars	4	W	16	Overtime: 00:26	8		
January 18, 1924	Victoria Cougars	3	Calgary Tigers	7	L				10	
January 23, 1924	Victoria Cougars	3	Vancouver Maroons	4	L		Lost at 1:44 of overtime. Game played at Seattle		11	
January 25, 1924	Victoria Cougars	2	Vancouver Maroons	1	W	18	Overtime: 00:25	9		
February 1, 1924	Victoria Cougars	1	Regina Capitals	2	L				12	
February 6, 1924	Seattle Metropolitans	8	Victoria Cougars	1	L				13	
February 8, 1924	Victoria Cougars	1	Seattle Metropolitans	4	L				14	
February 11, 1924	Seattle Metropolitans	1	Victoria Cougars	4	W	20	Game played at Vancouver	10		
February 15, 1924	Victoria Cougars	5	Edmonton Eskimos	1	W	22		11		
February 18, 1924	Calgary Tigers	4	Victoria Cougars	3	L				15	
February 20, 1924	Regina Capitals	2	Victoria Cougars	1	L				16	
February 22, 1924	Saskatoon Crescents	4	Victoria Cougars	3	L				17	
February 25, 1924	Edmonton Eskimos	1	Victoria Cougars	1	T	23	Tied after 20 minutes of overtime			1
February 27, 1924	Calgary Tigers	7	Victoria Cougars	1	L				18	
Regular season total								11	18	1

Victoria Cougars 1924-25

Date	Visitor	Score	Home	Score	Result	Points	Notes	W	L	T
December 8, 1924	Victoria Cougars	4	Calgary Tigers	1	W	2	Played at Winnipeg	1		
December 11, 1924	Victoria Cougars	4	Calgary Tigers	3	W	4	Played at Winnipeg	2		
December 14, 1924	Victoria Cougars	1	Saskatoon Crescents	4	L				1	
December 16, 1924	Victoria Cougars	0	Edmonton Eskimos	2	L				2	
December 17, 1924	Victoria Cougars	2	Calgary Tigers	4	L				3	
December 22, 1924	Victoria Cougars	1	Vancouver Maroons	0	W	6		3		
December 25, 1924	Vancouver Maroons	2	Victoria Cougars	4	W	8		4		
December 28, 1924	Regina Capitals	0	Victoria Cougars	5	W	10		5		
January 1, 1925	Victoria Cougars	11	Vancouver Maroons	2	W	12		6		
January 4, 1925	Vancouver Maroons	3	Victoria Cougars	0	L				4	
January 7, 1925	Calgary Tigers	1	Victoria Cougars	5	W	14		7		
January 11, 1925	Saskatoon Crescents	2	Victoria Cougars	3	W	16		8		

Appendix C

Date	Team	Score	Team	Score	Result			
January 16, 1925	Victoria Cougars	1	Regina Capitals	3	L			5
January 18, 1925	Victoria Cougars	2	Saskatoon Crescents	4	L			6
January 19, 1925	Victoria Cougars	7	Edmonton Eskimos	4	W	18	9	
January 22, 1925	Edmonton Eskimos	3	Victoria Cougars	2	L			7
January 24, 1925	Edmonton Eskimos	1	Victoria Cougars	3	W	20	10	
January 30, 1925	Regina Capitals	1	Victoria Cougars	3	W	22	11	
January 31, 1925	Regina Capitals	1	Victoria Cougars	2	W	24	12	
February 4, 1925	Victoria Cougars	0	Calgary Tigers	1	L			8
February 6, 1925	Victoria Cougars	1	Edmonton Eskimos	4	L			9
February 9, 1925	Victoria Cougars	1	Saskatoon Crescents	5	L			10
February 11, 1925	Victoria Cougars	6	Regina Capitals	3	W	26	13	
February 14, 1925	Calgary Tigers	2	Victoria Cougars	1	L			11
February 18, 1925	Vancouver Maroons	0	Victoria Cougars	4	W	28	14	
February 24, 1925	Victoria Cougars	3	Vancouver Maroons	2	W	30	15	
February 28, 1925	Saskatoon Crescents	1	Victoria Cougars	5	W	32	16	
Regular season total						16	11	0
SEMI-FINAL	**WON TOTAL GOALS 6-4**							
March 6, 1925	Saskatoon Crescents	1	Victoria Cougars	3	W			
March 10, 1925	Victoria Cougars	3	Saskatoon Crescents	3	T			
FINAL	**WON TOTAL GOALS 3-1**							
March 14, 1925	Victoria Cougars	1	Calgary Tigers	1	T			
March 18, 1925	Calgary Tigers	0	Victoria Cougars	2	W			
STANLEY CUP FINAL								
March 21, 1925	Montreal Canadiens	2	Victoria Cougars	5	W			
March 23, 1925	Montreal Canadiens	1	Victoria Cougars	3	W	Played at Vancouver		
March 27, 1925	Montreal Canadiens	4	Victoria Cougars	2	L			
March 30, 1925	Montreal Canadiens	1	Victoria Cougars	6	W	Won Stanley Cup series, 3-1		
WON STANLEY CUP SERIES 3-1								

The History of Professional Hockey in Victoria, BC: 1911-2011

Victoria Cougars 1925-26

Date	Visitor		Home	Score	Result	Points	Notes	W	L	T
December 3, 1925	Victoria Cougars	1	Vancouver Maroons	4	L				1	
December 5, 1925	Saskatoon Crescents	3	Victoria Cougars	1	L				2	
December 9, 1925	Vancouver Maroons	1	Victoria Cougars	1	T		Overtime goal by Vancouver was disallowed after protest			1
December 12, 1925	Calgary Tigers	0	Victoria Cougars	0	T					2
December 16, 1925	Victoria Cougars	1	Portland Rosebuds	2	L		Lost at 1:20 of overtime		3	
December 18, 1925	Portland Rosebuds	1	Victoria Cougars	2	W			1		
December 21, 1925	Victoria Cougars	0	Saskatoon Crescents	3	L				4	
December 23, 1925	Victoria Cougars	1	Edmonton Eskimos	3	L				5	
December 25, 1925	Victoria Cougars	4	Calgary Tigers	1	W			2		
January 1, 1926	Edmonton Eskimos	0	Victoria Cougars	4	W			3		
January 4, 1926	Victoria Cougars	0	Vancouver Maroons	1	L				6	
January 8, 1926	Vancouver Maroons	0	Victoria Cougars	1	L				7	
January 13, 1926	Victoria Cougars	3	Portland Rosebuds	2	W			4		
January 15, 1926	Portland Rosebuds	3	Victoria Cougars	2	L				8	
January 18, 1926	Edmonton Eskimos	1	Victoria Cougars	4	W			5		
January 22, 1925	Saskatoon Crescents	1	Victoria Cougars	1	T		Overtime			3
January 25, 1926	Victoria Cougars	3	Portland Rosebuds	2	W			6		
January 29, 1926	Calgary Tigers	2	Victoria Cougars	2	T		Overtime			4
February 3, 1926	Victoria Cougars	3	Saskatoon Crescents	2	W		Overtime 1:15	7		
February 5, 1926	Victoria Cougars	1	Edmonton Eskimos	4	L				9	
February 6, 1926	Victoria Cougars	4	Calgary Tigers	3	W		Overtime 8:58	8		
February 8, 1926	Victoria Cougars	1	Vancouver Maroons	0	W			9		
February 10, 1926	Victoria Cougars	3	Portland Rosebuds	4	L				10	
February 12, 1926	Portland Rosebuds	3	Victoria Cougars	6	W			10		
February 16, 1925	Vancouver Maroons	0	Victoria Cougars	4	W			11		
February 19, 1926	Edmonton Eskimos	1	Victoria Cougars	4	W			12		
February 26, 1926	Portland Rosebuds	1	Victoria Cougars	4	W			13		
March 1, 1926	Victoria Cougars	2	Vancouver Maroons	1	W			14		
March 5, 1926	Vancouver Maroons	1	Victoria Cougars	6	W			15		
March 9, 1926	Victoria Cougars	0	Calgary Tigers	2	L				11	
Regular season total								15	11	4
SEMI-FINAL	**WON TOTAL GOALS 4-3**									
March 12, 1926	Victoria Cougars	3	Saskatoon Crescents	3	T					

418

Appendix C

Date	Visitor	Score	Home	Score	Result		
March 16, 1926	Saskatoon Crescents	0	Victoria Cougars	1	W 8:10 OT		
FINAL	**WON TOTAL GOALS 5-3**						
March 20, 1926	Edmonton Eskimos	1	Victoria Cougars	3	W		
March 22, 1926	Victoria Cougars	2	Edmonton Eskimos	2	T	Game played in Vancouver as Edmonton had no ice	
STANLEY CUP FINALS							
March 30, 1926	Victoria Cougars	0	Montreal Maroons	3	L		
April 1, 1926	Victoria Cougars	0	Montreal Maroons	3	L		
April 3, 1926	Victoria Cougars	3	Montreal Maroons	2	W		
April 6, 1926	Victoria Cougars	0	Montreal Maroons	2	L		
LOST STANLEY CUP SERIES 3-1							

Victoria Cubs 1928-29

Date	Visitor	Score	Home	Score	Result	Points	W	L	T
November 19, 1928	Victoria Cubs	4	Vancouver Lions	3	W	2	1		
November 20, 1928	Vancouver Lions	3	Victoria Cubs	3	T	3			1
November 27, 1928	Portland Buckaroos	3	Victoria Cubs	1	L			1	
November 29, 1928	Victoria Cubs	3	Portland Buckaroos	3	T	4			2
November 30, 1928	Victoria Cubs	3	Seattle Eskimos	4	L			2	
December 4, 1928	Seattle Eskimos	2	Victoria Cubs	0	L			3	
December 10, 1928	Victoria Cubs	0	Vancouver Lions	1	L			4	
December 11, 1928	Vancouver Lions	1	Victoria Cubs	5	W	6	2		
December 18, 1928	Portland Buckaroos	2	Victoria Cubs	2	T	7			3
December 20, 1928	Victoria Cubs	1	Portland Buckaroos	0	W	9	3		
December 21, 1928	Victoria Cubs	5	Seattle Eskimos	2	W	11	4		
December 25, 1928	Seattle Eskimos	3	Victoria Cubs	3	T	12			4
January 1, 1929	Vancouver Lions	3	Victoria Cubs	1	L			5	
January 2, 1929	Victoria Cubs	1	Vancouver Lions	2	L			6	
January 8, 1929	Portland Buckaroos	3	Victoria Cubs	0	L			7	
January 10, 1929	Victoria Cubs	0	Portland Buckaroos	2	L			8	
January 11, 1929	Victoria Cubs	2	Seattle Eskimos	3	L			9	
January 15, 1929	Seattle Eskimos	1	Victoria Cubs	3	W	14	5		
January 21, 1929	Victoria Cubs	3	Vancouver Lions	2	W	16	6		
January 22, 1929	Vancouver Lions	2	Victoria Cubs	2	T	17			5
January 29, 1929	Portland Buckaroos	2	Victoria Cubs	2	T	18			6

419

The History of Professional Hockey in Victoria, BC: 1911-2011

Date	Visitor	Score	Home	Score	Result	points		
January 31, 1929	Victoria Cubs	0	Portland Buckaroos	3	L			10
February 1, 1929	Victoria Cubs	1	Seattle Eskimos	7	L			11
February 5, 1929	Seattle Eskimos	2	Victoria Cubs	1	L			12
February 11, 1929	Victoria Cubs	1	Vancouver Lions	2	L			13
February 12, 1929	Vancouver Lions	2	Victoria Cubs	1	L			14
February 19, 1929	Portland Buckaroos	4	Victoria Cubs	0	L			15
February 21, 1929	Victoria Cubs	2	Portland Buckaroos	3	L			16
February 22, 1929	Victoria Cubs	2	Seattle Eskimos	3	L			17
February 26, 1929	Seattle Eskimos	3	Victoria Cubs	1	L			18
March 4, 1929	Victoria Cubs	2	Vancouver Lions	5	L			19
March 5, 1929	Vancouver Lions	0	Victoria Cubs	3	W	20	7	
March 12, 1929	Portland Buckaroos	2	Victoria Cubs	1	L			20
March 14, 1929	Victoria Cubs	4	Portland Buckaroos	2	W	22	8	
March 15, 1929	Victoria Cubs	1	Seattle Eskimos	3	L			21
March 19, 1929	Seattle Eskimos	4	Victoria Cubs	3	L			22
Regular season total						8	22	6

Victoria Cubs 1929-30

Date	Visitor	Score	Home	Score	Result	points	Played at	Notes	W	L	T
November 18, 1929	Victoria Cubs	1	Vancouver Lions	2	L					1	
November 19, 1929	Seattle Eskimos	3	Victoria Cubs	1	L		Seattle			2	
November 23, 1929	Portland Buckaroos	1	Victoria Cubs	0	L		Vancouver			3	
November 29, 1929	Victoria Cubs	1	Seattle Eskimos	2	L					4	
December 5, 1929	Victoria Cubs	0	Portland Buckaroos	0	T	1					1
December 6, 1929	Vancouver Lions	5	Victoria Cubs	1	L		Vancouver			5	
December 9, 1929	Victoria Cubs	1	Vancouver Lions	2	L					6	
December 10, 1929	Victoria Cubs	1	Seattle Eskimos	1	T	2		Overtime			2
December 17, 1929	Portland Buckaroos	0	Victoria Cubs	3	W	4	Seattle		1		
December 20, 1929	Victoria Cubs	2	Seattle Eskimos	1	W	6			2		
December 25, 1929	Victoria Cubs	2	Portland Buckaroos	3	L			Overtime		7	
December 27, 1929	Vancouver Lions	8	Victoria Cubs	0	L		Vancouver			8	
December 30, 1929	Victoria Cubs	2	Vancouver Lions	3	L					9	
January 1, 1930	Seattle Eskimos	1	Victoria Cubs	5	W	8	Seattle		3		
January 10, 1930	Victoria Cubs	2	Seattle Eskimos	6	L					10	
January 13, 1930	Victoria Cubs	1	Portland Buckaroos	4	L					11	
January 16, 1930	Victoria Cubs	1	Portland Buckaroos	3	L					12	

Appendix C

Date	Home	Score	Away	Score	W/L/T	Pts	Notes		
January 17, 1930	Victoria Cubs	3	Vancouver Lions	4	L		Overtime		13
January 20, 1930	Victoria Cubs	4	Vancouver Lions	3	W	10		4	
January 21, 1930	Seattle Eskimos	5	Victoria Cubs	0	L		Seattle		14
January 28, 1930	Portland Buckaroos	3	Victoria Cubs	2	L		Seattle	Overtime	15
January 31, 1930	Victoria Cubs	1	Seattle Eskimos	4	L				16
February 6, 1930	Victoria Cubs	2	Portland Buckaroos	3	L				17
February 7, 1930	Victoria Cubs	4	Vancouver Lions	3	W	12		5	
February 10, 1930	Victoria Cubs	0	Vancouver Lions	5	L				18
February 11, 1930	Seattle Eskimos	10	Victoria Cubs	0	L		Seattle		19
February 14, 1930	Victoria Cubs	0	Portland Buckaroos	4	L		Vancouver		20
February 18, 1930	Portland Buckaroos	4	Victoria Cubs	0	L		Vancouver		21
February 21, 1930	Victoria Cubs	0	Seattle Eskimos	5	L				22
February 27, 1930	Victoria Cubs	0	Portland Buckaroos	4	L				23
February 28, 1930	Victoria Cubs	1	Vancouver Lions	3	L				24
March 4, 1930	Seattle Eskimos	2	Victoria Cubs	0	L		Seattle		25
March 11, 1930	Portland Buckaroos	3	Victoria Cubs	0	L		Seattle		26
March 14, 1930	Victoria Cubs	0	Seattle Eskimos	8	L				27
March 20, 1930	Victoria Cubs	0	Portland Buckaroos	8	L				28
March 21, 1930	Victoria Cubs	2	Vancouver Lions	3	L				29
Regular season total				12			5	29	2

Victoria Cougars 1949-50

Date	Home	Score	Away	Score	W/L/T	Pts	Notes
October 8, 1949	New Westminster Royals	10	Victoria Cougars	2	L		
October 10, 1949	Victoria Cougars	4	Portland Penguins	1	W	2	
October 11, 1949	Vancouver Canucks	7	Victoria Cougars	4	L		
October 14, 1949	Victoria Cougars	2	New Westminster Royals	7	L		
October 15, 1949	Victoria Cougars	3	Tacoma Rockets	4	L		
October 18, 1949	Victoria Cougars	8	Vancouver Canucks	4	W	4	
October 21, 1949	Victoria Cougars	3	Tacoma Rockets	1	W	6	
October 25, 1949	Victoria Cougars	3	Los Angeles Monarchs	1	W	8	
October 28, 1949	Victoria Cougars	5	Portland Penguins	3	W	10	
October 29, 1949	Portland Penguins	5	Victoria Cougars	1	L		
October 30, 1949	Seattle Ironman	4	Victoria Cougars	2	L		
November 1, 1949	Vancouver Canucks	6	Victoria Cougars	8	W	12	

421

The History of Professional Hockey in Victoria, BC: 1911-2011

November 2, 1949	New Westminster Royals	9	Victoria Cougars	7	L	
November 4, 1949	Victoria Cougars	6	Tacoma Rockets	5	W	14
November 5, 1949	Victoria Cougars	5	Vancouver Canucks	4	W	16
November 11, 1949	Victoria Cougars	2	Seattle Ironmen	3	L	
November 12, 1949	Tacoma Rockets	6	Victoria Cougars	4	L	
November 15, 1949	Vancouver Canucks	1	Victoria Cougars	6	W	18
November 16, 1949	Seattle Ironman	6	Victoria Cougars	2	L	
November 18, 1949	Victoria Cougars	5	Tacoma Rockets	2	W	20
November 22, 1949	Victoria Cougars	5	San Diego Skyhawks	3	W	22
November 25, 1949	Victoria Cougars	8	New Westminster Royals	2	W	24
November 26, 1949	New Westminster Royals	3	Victoria Cougars	2	L	
November 29, 1949	Victoria Cougars	5	Fresno Falcons	3	W	26
December 2, 1949	Victoria Cougars	3	New Westminster Royals	3	T	27
December 6, 1949	Victoria Cougars	4	Seattle Ironmen	1	W	29
December 9, 1949	Victoria Cougars	3	Vancouver Canucks	5	L	
December 10, 1949	Tacoma Rockets	9	Victoria Cougars	0	L	
December 11, 1949	Seattle Ironman	1	Victoria Cougars	1	T	30
December 13, 1949	Vancouver Canucks	7	Victoria Cougars	5	L	
December 16, 1949	Victoria Cougars	6	Tacoma Rockets	5	W	32
December 20, 1949	Victoria Cougars	4	Seattle Ironmen	1	W	34
December 23, 1949	Victoria Cougars		Oakland Oaks			Game not played: franchise folded
December 24, 1949	Victoria Cougars	1	Portland Penguins	3	L	
December 26, 1949	Victoria Cougars	0	Portland Penguins	5	L	
December 28, 1949	Portland Penguins	5	Victoria Cougars	2	L	
December 30, 1949	Victoria Cougars	2	New Westminster Royals	2	T	35
January 2, 1950	Victoria Cougars	4	Vancouver Canucks	2	W	37
January 3, 1949	Vancouver Canucks	8	Victoria Cougars	2	L	
January 6, 1950	Victoria Cougars	4	New Westminster Royals	1	W	39
January 7, 1950	Portland Penguins	4	Victoria Cougars	1	L	
January 8, 1950	Seattle Ironman	8	Victoria Cougars	6	L	
January 13, 1950	Vancouver Canucks		Victoria Cougars			Team could not make it to Vancouver so game postponed
January 14, 1950	New WestminsterRoyals	7	Victoria Cougars	5	L	
January 17, 1950	Victoria Cougars	3	Seattle Ironmen	3	T	40
January 20, 1950	Victoria Cougars	3	Portland Penguins	2	L	
January 21, 1950	Tacoma Rockets	4	Victoria Cougars	3	L	
January 22, 1949	Portland Penguins	3	Victoria Cougars	2	L	

Appendix C

January 24, 1950	Victoria Cougars	3	New Westminster Royals	6	L		
January 27, 1950	Victoria Cougars	4	Tacoma Rockets	4	T	41	
January 28, 1950	New Westminster Royals	11	Victoria Cougars	1	L		
February 3, 1950	Victoria Cougars	6	San Francisco Shamrocks	2	W	43	
February 4, 1950	Victoria Cougars	3	Vancouver Canucks	7	L		
February 7, 1950	Vancouver Canucks	7	Victoria Cougars	1	L		
February 8, 1950	New Westminster Royals	4	Victoria Cougars	3	L		
February 10, 1950	Victoria Cougars	1	Portland Penguins	4	L		
February 11, 1950	Portland Penguins	2	Victoria Cougars	1	L		
February 14, 1950	San Diego Skyhawks	4	Victoria Cougars	1	L		
February 15, 1950	Los Angeles Monarchs	7	Victoria Cougars	1	L		
February 18, 1950	Fresco Falcons	3	Victoria Cougars	1	L		
February 22, 1950	San Francisco Shamrocks	7	Victoria Cougars	4	L		
February 25, 1950	Portland Penguins	6	Victoria Cougars	1	L		
February 26, 1950	Seattle Ironman	6	Victoria Cougars	2	L		
February 28, 1950	Victoria Cougars	0	Vancouver Canucks	3	L		
March 3, 1950	Victoria Cougars	0	Tacoma Rockets	1	L		
March 4, 1950	Tacoma Rockets	11	Victoria Cougars	1	L		
March 7, 1950	Vancouver Canucks	5	Victoria Cougars	5	T	44	Playing of postponed game
March 10, 1950	Victoria Cougars	6	Seattle Ironmen	1	W	46	
March 11, 1950	New Westminster Royals	5	Victoria Cougars	2	L		
March 14, 1950	Victoria Cougars	5	Vancouver Canucks	2	W	48	
March 17, 1950	Victoria Cougars	7	New Westminster Royals	4	W	50	
March 18, 1950	Tacoma Rockets	8	Victoria Cougars	2	L		

The History of Professional Hockey in Victoria, BC: 1911-2011

Victoria Cougars 1950-51

Date	Home	Score	Away	Score	Result	Pts	Notes
October 6, 1950	Victoria Cougars	4	New WestminsterRoyals	3	W	2	
October 9, 1950	Victoria Cougars	2	Seattle Ironmen	5	L		
October 13, 1950	Victoria Cougars	2	Portland Eagles	7	L		
October 14, 2016	Tacoma Rockets	2	Victoria Cougars	2	T	3	
October 17, 1950	Vancouver Canucks	2	Victoria Cougars	0	L		
October 20, 1950	Victoria Cougars	9	Tacoma Rockets	1	W	5	
October 22, 1950	New Westminster Royals	8	Victoria Cougars	4	L		
October 24, 1950	Victoria Cougars	5	Vancouver Canucks	3	W	7	
October 27, 1950	Victoria Cougars	1	New Westminster Royals	1	T	8	
October 29, 1950	Portland Eagles	5	Victoria Cougars	3	L		
October 31, 1950	Tacoma Rockets	5	Victoria Cougars	2	L		
November 3, 1950	Victoria Cougars	3	Portland Eagles	6	L		
November 4, 1950	New Westminster Royals	1	Victoria Cougars	3	W	10	
November 7, 1950	Victoria Cougars	4	Vancouver Canucks	1	W	12	
November 10, 1950	Victoria Cougars	4	Tacoma Rockets	1	W	14	
November 14, 1950	Vancouver Canucks	6	Victoria Cougars	6	T	15	
November 17, 1950	Victoria Cougars	3	Seattle Ironmen	1	W	17	
November 18, 1950	Tacoma Rockets	7	Victoria Cougars	3	L		
November 19, 1950	Portland Eagles	3	Victoria Cougars	3	T	18	
November 24, 1950	Victoria Cougars	3	Portland Eagles	7	L		
November 28, 1950	Victoria Cougars	1	New Westminster Royals	5	W	20	
November 30, 1950	Portland Eagles	2	Victoria Cougars	2	T	21	
December 2, 1950	Tacoma Rockets	1	Victoria Cougars	4	W	23	
December 3, 1950	Seattle Ironmen	5	Victoria Cougars	5	T	24	
December 5, 1950	Vancouver Canucks	2	Victoria Cougars	1	L		
December 8, 1950	Victoria Cougars	1	Tacoma Rockets	4	L		
December 9, 1950	New Westminster Royals	1	Victoria Cougars	4	W	26	
December 12, 1950	Victoria Cougars	0	Vancouver Canucks	4	L		
December 13, 1950	Seattle Ironmen	4	Victoria Cougars	2	L		
December 15, 1950	Victoria Cougars	3	Seattle Ironmen	3	T	27	
December 17, 1950	Portland Eagles	3	Victoria Cougars	3	T	28	
December 19, 1950	Vancouver Canucks	4	Victoria Cougars	4	T	29	
December 22, 1950	Victoria Cougars	2	Tacoma Rockets	3	L		
December 25, 1950	Victoria Cougars	6	Portland Eagles	3	W	31	

Appendix C

Date	Team	Score	Team	Score	Result	Points
December 29, 1950	Victoria Cougars	3	Seattle Ironmen	0	W	33
January 1, 1951	Victoria Cougars	3	New Westminster Royals	1	W	35
January 5, 1951	Victoria Cougars	6	Portland Eagles	0	W	37
January 7, 1951	Seattle Ironmen	0	Victoria Cougars	3	W	39
January 12, 1951	Victoria Cougars	3	Portland Eagles	2	W	41
January 14, 1951	Portland Eagles	2	Victoria Cougars	5	W	43
January 16, 1951	Victoria Cougars	5	Vancouver Canucks	1	W	45
January 17, 1951	Seattle Ironmen	3	Victoria Cougars	3	T	46
January 19, 1951	Victoria Cougars	4	Seattle Ironmen	1	W	48
January 21, 1951	New Westminster Royals	6	Victoria Cougars	1	L	
January 23, 1951	Vancouver Canucks	3	Victoria Cougars	8	W	50
January 26, 1951	Victoria Cougars	2	Portland Eagles	1	W	52
January 28, 1951	Seattle Ironmen	1	Victoria Cougars	2	W	54
January 30, 1951	Vancouver Canucks	3	Victoria Cougars	9	W	56
February 2, 1951	Victoria Cougars	2	New Westminster Royals	2	T	57
February 3, 1951	Tacoma Rockets	3	Victoria Cougars	3	T	58
February 9, 1951	Victoria Cougars	4	Tacoma Rockets	3	W	60
February 11, 1951	Portland Eagles	7	Victoria Cougars	2	L	
February 13, 1951	Victoria Cougars	4	Seattle Ironmen	3	W	62
February 14, 1951	Seattle Ironmen	8	Victoria Cougars	5	L	
February 16, 1951	Victoria Cougars	3	Portland Eagles	3	T	63
February 18, 1951	Tacoma Rockets	1	Victoria Cougars	1	T	64
February 20, 1951	Vancouver Canucks	3	Victoria Cougars	4	W	66
February 24, 1951	Victoria Cougars	6	New Westminster Royals	2	W	68
February 24, 1951	New Westminster Royals	6	Victoria Cougars	2	L	
February 27, 1951	Victoria Cougars	5	Vancouver Canucks	3	W	70
March 2, 1951	Victoria Cougars	5	Tacoma Rockets	3	W	72
March 3, 1951	Tacoma Rockets	4	Victoria Cougars	4	T	73
March 4, 1951	Portland Eagles	6	Victoria Cougars	4	L	
March 6, 1951	Vancouver Canucks	5	Victoria Cougars	7	W	75
March 9, 1951	Victoria Cougars	3	New Westminster Royals	1	W	77
March 10, 1951	New Westminster= Royals	2	Victoria Cougars	5	W	79
March 13, 1951	Victoria Cougars	4	Vancouver Canucks	1	W	81
March 16, 1951	Victoria Cougars	5	Seattle Ironmen	0	W	83
March 18, 1951	Seattle Ironmen	4	Victoria Cougars	7	W	85

PLAYOFFS—FIRST ROUND   **WON SERIES, 4-3**

The History of Professional Hockey in Victoria, BC: 1911-2011

March 20, 1951	Victoria Cougars	3	Portland Eagles	4	L	Overtime: 6:53
March 23, 1951	Victoria Cougars	0	Portland Eagles	1	L	Overtime: 26:45
March 25, 1951	Portland Eagles	1	Victoria Cougars	4	W	
March 27, 1951	Portland Eagles	2	Victoria Cougars	3	W	Overtime: 6:19
March 29, 1951	Victoria Cougars	4	Portland Eagles	3	W	
April 1, 1951	Portland Eagles	2	Victoria Cougars	1	L	Overtime: 18:18
April 3, 1951	Victoria Cougars	3	Portland Eagles	0	W	
PLAYOFFS—SECOND ROUND	WON SERIES 4-1					
April 5, 1951	Victoria Cougars	4	New Westminster Royals	0	W	
April 8, 1951	New Westminster Royals	2	Victoria Cougars	3	W	
April 10, 1951	Victoria Cougars	5	New Westminster Royals	2	W	
April 11, 1951	New Westminster Royals	7	Victoria Cougars	3	L	
April 13, 1951	Victoria Cougars	3	New WestminsterRoyals	0	W	

Victoria Cougars 1951-52

Date	Home	Score	Away	Score	Result	Pts	Notes
October 5, 1951	Vancouver Canucks	2	Victoria Cougars	8	W	2	
October 8, 1951	Victoria Cougars		Vancouver Canucks				Not played as there was no ice in the Memorial Arena
October 12, 1951	Victoria Cougars	4	Seattle Ironmen	3	W	4	
October 13, 1951	New WestminsterRoyals	2	Victoria Cougars	2	T	5	
October 16, 1951	Victoria Cougars	8	Saskatoon Quakers	3	W	7	Trophy presented
October 19, 1951	Victoria Cougars	9	Tacoma Rockets	4	W	9	
October 24, 1951	Seattle Ironmen	5	Victoria Cougars	4	L		
October 26, 1951	Victoria Cougars	3	New Westminster Royals	5	L		22-game-unbeaten-at-home streak ended
October 27, 1951	Tacoma Rockets	4	Victoria Cougars	1	L		
November 2, 1951	Victoria Cougars	3	Calgary Stampeders	0	W	11	
November 3, 1951	Victoria Cougars	4	Vancouver Canucks	3	W	13	
November 6, 1951	Vancouver Canucks	4	Victoria Cougars	3	L		
November 7, 1951	Seattle Ironmen	5	Victoria Cougars	5	T	14	
November 9, 1951	Victoria Cougars	2	Seattle Ironmen	4	L		
November 10, 1951	New Westminster Royals	3	Victoria Cougars	5	W	16	
November 12, 1951	Calgary Stampeders	4	Victoria Cougars	7	W	18	
November 13, 1951	Edmonton Flyers	6	Victoria Cougars	2	L		
November 14, 1951	Saskatoon Quakers	2	Victoria Cougars	1	L		

Appendix C

Date	Team	Score	Team	Score	Result	
November 16, 1951	Victoria Cougars	1	Tacoma Rockets	6	L	
November 18, 1951	Seattle Ironmen	8	Victoria Cougars	5	L	
November 20, 1951	Victoria Cougars	4	Edmonton Flyers	3	W	20
November 23, 1951	Victoria Cougars	5	New WestminsterRoyals	6	L	
November 27, 1951	Vancouver Canucks	10	Victoria Cougars	2	L	
November 30, 1951	Victoria Cougars	3	Tacoma Rockets	1	W	22
December 1, 1951	Tacoma Rockets	4	Victoria Cougars	1	L	
December 7, 1951	Victoria Cougars	5	Calgary Stampeders	2	W	24
December 8, 1951	Victoria Cougars	3	Vancouver Canucks	4	L	
December 11, 1951	Vancouver Canucks	2	Victoria Cougars	1	T	25
December 14, 1951	Victoria Cougars	2	New WestminsterRoyals	7	L	
December 15, 1951	Tacoma Rockets	6	Victoria Cougars	6	T	26
December 16, 1951	Seattle Ironmen	2	Victoria Cougars	7	W	28
December 21, 1951	Victoria Cougars	4	Seattle Ironmen	4	T	29
December 22, 1951	New Westminster Royals	2	Victoria Cougars	4	W	31
December 26, 1951	Victoria Cougars	2	Vancouver Canucks	3	L	
December 28, 1951	Victoria Cougars	0	Saskatoon Quakers	6	L	
January 1, 1952	Victoria Cougars	1	Tacoma Rockets	3	L	
January 4, 1952	Victoria Cougars	5	Edmonton Flyers	2	W	33
January 11, 1952	Victoria Cougars	4	Seattle Ironmen	8	L	
January 12, 1952	New Westminster Royals	9	Victoria Cougars	4	L	
January 15, 1952	Vancouver Canucks	6	Victoria Cougars	4	L	
January 17, 1952	Calgary Stampeders	14	Victoria Cougars	3	L	
January 18, 1952	Edmonton Flyers	3	Victoria Cougars	1	L	
January 19, 1952	Saskatoon Quakers	4	Victoria Cougars	2	L	
January 22, 1952	Victoria Cougars	5	Vancouver Canucks	8	L	
January 25, 1952	Victoria Cougars	3	New Westminster Royals	3	T	34
January 26, 1952	Tacoma Rockets	5	Victoria Cougars	2	L	
February 1, 1952	Victoria Cougars	4	Calgary Stampeders	3	W	36
February 5, 1952	Victoria Cougars	0	Edmonton Flyers	1	L	
February 8, 1952	Victoria Cougars	3	New Westminster Royals	6	L	
February 9, 1952	New WestminsterRoyals	7	Victoria Cougars	3	L	
February 12, 1952	Vancouver Canucks	7	Victoria Cougars	2	L	
February 14, 1952	Tacoma Rockets	4	Victoria Cougars	2	L	Originally scheduled for February 15, was moved due to burial of King George VI
February 16, 1951	Victoria Cougars	2	Tacoma Rockets	9	L	
February 17, 1952	Seattle Ironmen	3	Victoria Cougars	7	W	38

The History of Professional Hockey in Victoria, BC: 1911-2011

Date	Team	Score	Team	Score	Result	
February 19, 1952	Victoria Cougars		Vancouver Canucks		T	39
February 22, 1952	Victoria Cougars	6	Seattle Ironmen	4	W	41
February 23, 1952	New WestminsterRoyals	5	Victoria Cougars	2	L	
February 25, 1952	Calgary Stampeders	4	Victoria Cougars	6	W	43
February 26, 1952	Edmonton Flyers	4	Victoria Cougars	3	L	
February 27, 1952	Saskatoon Quakers	6	Victoria Cougars	2	L	
February 29, 1952	Victoria Cougars	7	New WestminsterRoyals	4	W	45
March 4, 1952	Victoria Cougars	5	Saskatoon Quakers	3	W	47
March 7, 1952	Victoria Cougars	3	Seattle Ironmen	2	W	49
March 8, 1952	Tacoma Rockets	0	Victoria Cougars	2	W	51
March 11, 1952	Vancouver Canucks	4	Victoria Cougars	2	L	
March 14, 1952	Victoria Cougars	1	Tacoma Rockets	7	L	
March 15, 1952	New WestminsterRoyals	1	Victoria Cougars	2	W	53
March 16, 1952	Victoria Cougars	2	Vancouver Canucks	3	L	
March 21, 1952	Victoria Cougars	7	New Westminster Royals	3	W	55
March 23, 1952	Seattle Ironmen	4	Victoria Cougars	5	W	57
PLAYOFFS—FIRST ROUND	**WON SERIES, 4-3**					
March 26, 1952	New Westminster Royals	3	Victoria Cougars	2	L	
March 28, 1952	Victoria Cougars	3	New Westminster Royals	2	W	
March 30, 1952	New Westminster Royals	4	Victoria Cougars	1	L	
April 1, 1952	Victoria Cougars	4	New Westminster Royals	3	W	Overtime: 30:17
April 2, 1952	New Westminster Royals	5	Victoria Cougars	4	L	Overtime: 21:28
April 4, 1952	Victoria Cougars	3	New Westminster Royals	1	W	
April 5, 1952	New Westminster Royals	1	Victoria Cougars	3	W	
PLAYOFFS—SECOND ROUND	**LOST SERIES, 4-2**					
April 12, 1952	Victoria Cougars	4	Saskatoon Quakers	3	W	
April 14, 1952	Victoria Cougars	1	Saskatoon Quakers	3	L	
April 16, 1952	Victoria Cougars	2	Saskatoon Quakers	5	L	
April 19, 1952	Saskatoon Quakers	7	Victoria Cougars	2	L	
April 21, 1952	Saskatoon Quakers	4	Victoria Cougars	6	W	
April 23, 1952	Saskatoon Quakers	8	Victoria Cougars	4	L	

Appendix C

Victoria Cougars 1952-53

Date	Home	Score	Away	Score	Result	Pts	Notes
October 9, 1952	Victoria Cougars	3	Vancouver Canucks	2	W	2	
October 11, 1952	Vancouver Canucks	5	Victoria Cougars	1	L		
October 13, 1952	Victoria Cougars	7	Tacoma Rockets	2	W	4	
October 17, 1952	Victoria Cougars	6	New Westminster Royals	3	W	6	
October 19, 1952	New Westminster Royals	3	Victoria Cougars	4	W	8	
October 24, 1952	Victoria Cougars	1	Edmonton Flyers	2	L		
October 25, 1952	Tacoma Rockets	7	Victoria Cougars	5	L		
October 26, 1952	Seattle Bombers	5	Victoria Cougars	2	L		
October 28, 1952	Vancouver Canucks	5	Victoria Cougars	1	L		
October 31, 1952	Victoria Cougars	8	Seattle Bombers	4	W	10	
November 1, 1952	New Westminster Royals	5	Victoria Cougars	2	L		
November 8, 1952	Victoria Cougars	2	Saskatoon Quakers	4	L		
November 9, 1952	Victoria Cougars	1	Vancouver Canucks	1	T	11	
November 11, 1952	Victoria Cougars	4	Calgary Stampeders	5	L		
November 14, 1952	Victoria Cougars	4	Tacoma Rockets	7	L		
November 19, 1952	Seattle Bombers	3	Victoria Cougars	2	L		
November 21, 1952	Victoria Cougars	2	New WestminsterRoyals	0	W	13	First shutout of the season
November 24, 1952	Saskatoon Quakers	7	Victoria Cougars	4	L		
November 25, 1952	Edmonton Flyers	5	Victoria Cougars	2	L		
November 26, 1952	Calgary Stampeders	9	Victoria Cougars	2	L		
November 29, 1952	Victoria Cougars	2	Seattle Bombers	1	W	15	
December 1, 1952	Vancouver Canucks	4	Victoria Cougars	2	L		
December 2, 1952	Victoria Cougars	2	Vancouver Canucks	1	W	17	
December 3, 1952	Seattle Bombers	5	Victoria Cougars	3	L		
December 5, 1952	Victoria Cougars	5	New Westminster Royals	3	W	19	
December 6, 1952	Tacoma Rockets	0	Victoria Cougars	7	W	21	
December 12, 1952	Victoria Cougars	4	Saskatoon Quakers	1	W	23	
December 13, 1952	New Westminster Royals	1	Victoria Cougars	3	W	25	
December 16, 1952	Victoria Cougars	6	Calgary Stampeders	3	W	27	
December 19, 1952	Victoria Cougars	8	Seattle Bombers	2	W	29	
December 26, 1952	Victoria Cougars	1	Tacoma Rockets	6	L		
December 27, 1952	Tacoma Rockets	3	Victoria Cougars	1	L		
January 1, 1953	Victoria Cougars	3	Vancouver Canucks	4	L		
January 2, 1953	Vancouver Canucks	1	Victoria Cougars	1	T	30	

The History of Professional Hockey in Victoria, BC: 1911-2011

January 6, 1953	Victoria Cougars	2	New Westminster	3	L	
January 9, 1953	Victoria Cougars	4	Seattle Bombers	0	W	32
January 11, 1953	New WestminsterRoyals	6	Victoria Cougars	4	L	
January 13, 1953	Vancouver Canucks	5	Victoria Cougars	3	L	
January 15, 1953	Calgary Stampeders	1	Victoria Cougars	2	W	34
January 16, 1953	Edmonton Flyers	6	Victoria Cougars	2	L	
January 17, 1953	Saskatoon Quakers	7	Victoria Cougars	3	L	
January 20, 1953	Victoria Cougars	1	Vancouver Canucks	1	T	35
January 21, 1953	Seattle Bombers	7	Victoria Cougars	5	L	
January 23, 1953	Victoria Cougars	5	Tacoma Rockets	1	W	37
January 25, 1953	New Westminster Royals	4	Victoria Cougars	2	L	
January 27, 1953	Tacoma Rockets	4	Victoria Cougars	4	T	38
January 30, 1953	Victoria Cougars	4	Calgary Stampeders	4	T	39
February 3, 1952	Victoria Cougars	2	Edmonton Flyers	11	L	
February 6, 1953	Victoria Cougars	6	New Westminster Royals	2	W	41
February 8, 1953	New Westminster Royals	6	Victoria Cougars	4	L	
February 10, 1953	Vancouver Canucks	7	Victoria Cougars	0	L	
February 13, 1953	Victoria Cougars	3	Tacoma Rockets	6	L	
February 14, 1953	Tacoma Rockets	5	Victoria Cougars	4	L	
February 17, 1953	Victoria Cougars	2	Saskatoon Quakers	7	L	
February 20, 1953	Victoria Cougars	1	Seattle Bombers	0	W	43
February 21, 1953	Victoria Cougars	6	Vancouver Canucks	2	W	45
February 23, 1953	Calgary Stampeders	4	Victoria Cougars	5	W	47
February 24, 1953	Edmonton Flyers	2	Victoria Cougars	2	T	48
February 25, 1953	Saskatoon Quakers	3	Victoria Cougars	3	T	49
February 27, 1953	Victoria Cougars	7	New Westminster Royals	3	W	51
February 28, 1953	New Westminster Royals	2	Victoria Cougars	4	W	53
March 3, 1953	Victoria Cougars	8	Tacoma Rockets	5	W	55
March 6, 1952	Victoria Cougars	5	Seattle Bombers	2	W	57
March 7, 1952	Tacoma Rockets	5	Victoria Cougars	2	L	
March 13, 1952	Victoria Cougars	3	Edmonton Flyers	3	T	58
March 14, 1952	Victoria Cougars	2	Vancouver Canucks	5	L	Out of playoffs
March 18, 1952	Vancouver Canucks	9	Victoria CougarsL			
March 20, 1952	Victoria Cougars	8	New Westminster Royals	6	W	60
March 22, 1952	Seattle Bombers	8	Victoria Cougars	7	L	

Appendix C

Victoria Cougars 1953-54

Date	Home	Score	Away	Score	Result	Pts	Notes
October 6, 1953	Victoria Cougars	1	Vancouver Canucks	2	L		
October 9, 1953	New Westminster Royals	4	Victoria Cougars	3	L		
October 12, 1953	Calgary Stampeders	7	Victoria Cougars	3	L		
October 16, 1953	Edmonton Flyers	3	Victoria Cougars	4	W	2	
October 18, 1953	Victoria Cougars	2	Seattle Bombers	7	L		
October 19, 1953	Victoria Cougars	1	Vancouver Canucks	4	L		
October 23, 1953	Victoria Cougars	1	Seattle Bombers	3	L		
October 24, 1953	Victoria Cougars	1	New WestminsterRoyals	1	T	3	
October 26, 1953	Victoria Cougars	6	Calgary Stampeders	4	W	5	
October 27, 1953	Victoria Cougars	3	Edmonton Flyers	2	W	7	
October 28, 1953	Victoria Cougars	3	Saskatoon Quakers	3	T	8	
October 30, 1953	Saskatoon Quakers	1	Victoria Cougars	1	T	9	
November 2, 1953	Vancouver Canucks	1	Victoria Cougars	1	T	10	
November 6, 1953	Seattle Bombers	0	Victoria Cougars	3	W	12	
November 8, 1953	New WestminsterRoyals	3	Victoria Cougars	2	L		
November 11, 1953	Vancouver Canucks	4	Victoria Cougars	3	L		
November 13, 1953	Victoria Cougars	5	New WestminsterRoyals	3	W	14	
November 14, 1953	Seattle Bombers	4	Victoria Cougars	6	W	16	
November 16, 1953	Victoria Cougars	5	Calgary Stampeders	3	W	18	
November 20, 1953	Victoria Cougars	3	New Westminster Royals	5	L		
November 21, 1953	New WestminsterRoyals	2	Victoria Cougars	0	L		
November 22, 1953	Seattle Bombers	3	Victoria Cougars	0	L		
November 24, 1953	Vancouver Canucks	2	Victoria Cougars	2	T	19	
November 27, 1953	Victoria Cougars	7	Seattle Bombers	1	W	21	
November 30, 1953	Victoria Cougars	6	Edmonton Flyers	4	W	23	
December 4, 1953	Victoria Cougars	0	Saskatoon Quakers	3	L		
December 7, 1953	Victoria Cougars	3	Vancouver Canucks	1	W	25	
December 11, 1953	Victoria Cougars	3	Seattle Bombers	2	W	27	
December 12, 1953	New Westminster Royals	7	Victoria Cougars	3	L		
December 15, 1953	Vancouver Canucks	3	Victoria Cougars	1	L		
December 18, 1953	Victoria Cougars	2	New Westminster Royals	4	L		
December 20, 1953	Seattle Bombers	2	Victoria Cougars	0	L		
December 25, 1953	Victoria Cougars	2	Seattle Bombers	3	L		
December 26, 1953	Victoria Cougars	7	Seattle Bombers	4	W	29	Played at Nanaimo

The History of Professional Hockey in Victoria, BC: 1911-2011

December 28, 1953	Victoria Cougars	1	Vancouver Canucks	3	L	
December 29, 1953	New WestminsterRoyals	6	Victoria Cougars	3	L	
January 1, 1954	Victoria Cougars	6	New Westminster Royals	2	W	31
January 5, 1954	Vancouver Canucks	1	Victoria Cougars	3	W	33
January 7, 1954	Calgary Stampeders	3	Victoria Cougars	3	T	34
January 8, 1954	Edmonton Flyers	3	Victoria Cougars	2	L	
January 9, 1954	Saskatoon Quakers	4	Victoria Cougars	2	L	
January 11, 1954	Victoria Cougars	3	Vancouver Canucks	2	W	36
January 14, 1954	Victoria Cougars	5	Seattle Bombers	5	T	37
January 16, 1954	New Westminster Royals	3	Victoria Cougars	7	W	39
January 17, 1954	Seattle Bombers	4	Victoria Cougars	4	T	40
January 19, 1954	Vancouver Canucks	1	Victoria Cougars	4	W	42
January 22, 1954	Victoria Cougars	3	New Westminster Royals	6	L	
January 25, 1954	Victoria Cougars	2	Calgary Stampeders	0	W	44
January 29, 1954	Victoria Cougars	2	Edmonton Flyers	4	L	
February 1, 1954	Saskatoon Quakers	1	Victoria Cougars	1	T	45
February 2, 1954	Edmonton Flyers	8	Victoria Cougars	2	L	
February 3, 1954	Calgary Stampeders	1	Victoria Cougars	1	T	46
February 5, 1954	Victoria Cougars	4	Saskatoon Quakers	3	W	48
February 8, 1954	Victoria Cougars	2	Vancouver Canucks	4	L	
February 12, 1954	Victoria Cougars	2	Seattle Bombers	1	W	50	Dorohoy Night
February 19, 1954	Victoria Cougars	3	New Westminster Royals	1	W	52
February 20, 1954	Seattle Bombers	1	Victoria Cougars	3	W	54
February 22, 1954	Victoria Cougars	4	Calgary Stampeders	3	W	56
February 23, 1954	Vancouver Canucks	7	Victoria Cougars	3	L	
February 26, 1954	Victoria Cougars	4	Seattle Bombers	2	W	58
March 1, 1954	Victoria Cougars	4	Edmonton Flyers	3	W	60
March 5, 1954	Victoria Cougars	8	New Westminster Royals	1	W	62
March 6, 1954	Victoria Cougars	2	Seattle Bombers	4	L	
March 10, 1954	New Westminster Royals	5	Victoria Cougars	4	L	
March 12, 1954	Victoria Cougars	4	Saskatoon Quakers	3	W	64
March 15, 1954	Victoria Cougars	1	Vancouver Canucks	3	L	
March 17, 1954	Calgary Stampeders	5	Victoria Cougars	1	L	
March 19, 1954	Edmonton Flyers	3	Victoria Cougars	3	T	65
March 20, 1954	Saskatoon Quakers	5	Victoria Cougars	3	L	
PLAYOFFS—FIRST ROUND	**LOST SERIES, 4-1**					

Appendix C

Date	Home	Score	Away	Score	Result
March 23, 1954	Calgary Stampeders	2	Victoria Cougars	4	W
March 25, 1954	Calgary Stampeders	8	Victoria Cougars	1	L
March 27, 1954	Victoria Cougars	1	Calgary Stampeders	6	L
March 29, 1954	Victoria Cougars	2	Calgary Stampeders	5	L
April 1, 1954	Calgary Stampeders	7	Victoria Cougars	4	L

Victoria Cougars 1954-55

Date	Home	Score	Away	Score	Result	Pts	Notes
October 5, 1954	Vancouver Canucks	5	Victoria Cougars	3	L		
October 6, 1954	Victoria Cougars	3	Calgary Stampeders	2	W	2	
October 11, 1954	Victoria Cougars	3	New Westminster Royals	4	L		
October 13, 1954	Victoria Cougars	4	Edmonton Flyers	6	L		
October 16, 1954	New Westminster Royals	7	Victoria Cougars	2	L		
October 20, 1954	Victoria Cougars	3	Vancouver Canucks	1	W	4	
October 22, 1954	Vancouver Canucks	3	Victoria Cougars	1	L		
October 23, 1954	Victoria Cougars	5	Vancouver Canucks	2	W	6	
October 27, 1954	Victoria Cougars	8	Saskatoon Quakers	2	W	8	
October 29, 1954	Victoria Cougars	3	New Westminster Royals	5	L		
November 2, 1954	New Westminster Royals	5	Victoria Cougars	3	L		
November 3, 1954	Victoria Cougars	6	New Westminster Royals	1	W	10	
November 6, 1954	New Westminster, Royals	0	Victoria Cougars	4	W	12	
November 10, 1954	Victoria Cougars	2	Edmonton Flyers	5	L		
November 12, 1954	Vancouver Canucks	3	Victoria Cougars	1	L		
November 13, 1954	Victoria Cougars	4	Edmonton Flyers	2	W	14	
November 17, 1954	Victoria Cougars	6	Calgary Stampeders	0	W	16	
November 20, 1954	Victoria Cougars	5	Vancouver Canucks	0	W	18	
November 23, 1954	Calgary Stampeders	2	Victoria Cougars	4	W	20	
November 24, 1954	Edmonton Flyers	5	Victoria Cougars	1	L		
November 25, 1954	Saskatoon Quakers	2	Victoria Cougars	5	W	22	
November 27, 1954	Saskatoon Quakers	7	Victoria Cougars	0	L		*Saskatoon Star-Phoenix, November 29, 1954, page 21.*
November 30, 1954	Vancouver Canucks	3	Victoria Cougars	3	T	23	
December 1, 1954	Victoria Cougars	9	New Westminster Royals	2	W	25	
December 3, 1954	Victoria Cougars	2	New Westminster Royals	3	L		
December 4, 1954	New Westminster Royals	2	Victoria Cougars	3	W	27	
December 8, 1954	Victoria Cougars	4	Vancouver Canucks	1	W	29	

433

The History of Professional Hockey in Victoria, BC: 1911-2011

Date	Team	Score	Team	Score	Result	#	Source
December 11, 1954	Victoria Cougars	3	Saskatoon Quakers	0	W	31	*Saskatoon Star-Phoenix, December 13, 1954, page 15.*
December 15, 1954	Victoria Cougars	5	Vancouver Canucks	1	W	33	
December 17, 1954	Vancouver Canucks	2	Victoria Cougars	4	W	35	
December 21, 1954	Calgary Stampeders	6	Victoria Cougars	2	L		
December 22, 1954	Edmonton Flyers	4	Victoria Cougars	1	L		*Saskatoon Star-Phoenix, December 23, 1954, page 12.*
December 23, 1954	Saskatoon Quakers	5	Victoria Cougars	5	T	36	
December 25, 1954	Calgary Stampeders	5	Victoria Cougars	2	L		
December 27, 1954	Victoria Cougars	4	Calgary Stampeders	0	W	38	
December 29, 1954	Victoria Cougars	2	New Westminster Royals	3	L		
January 1, 1955	Victoria Cougars	1	Calgary Stampeders	4	L		
January 4, 1955	Vancouver Canucks	4	Victoria Cougars	2	L		
January 5, 1955	Victoria Cougars	7	Vancouver Canucks	4	W	40	
January 7, 1955	Vancouver Canucks	2	Victoria Cougars	0	L		
January 8, 1955	New Westminster Royals	1	Victoria Cougars	6	W	42	
January 12, 1955	Victoria Cougars	2	Saskatoon Quakers	5	L		
January 13, 1955	New Westminster Royals	6	Victoria Cougars	4	L		
January 14, 1955	Victoria Cougars	5	New Westminster Royals	5	T	43	
January 18, 1955	Edmonton Flyers	2	Victoria Cougars	2	T	44	
January 19, 1955	Saskatoon Quakers	5	Victoria Cougars	0	L		*Saskatoon Star-Phoenix, January 20, 1955, page 13*
January 21, 1955	Calgary Stampeders	2	Victoria Cougars	6	W	46	
January 22, 1955	Edmonton Flyers	3	Victoria Cougars	0	L		
January 26, 1955	Victoria Cougars	8	New Westminster Royals	1	W	48	
January 29, 1955	New Westminster Royals	6	Victoria Cougars	2	L		
February 2, 1955	Victoria Cougars	4	Calgary Stampeders	1	W	50	
February 5, 1955	Victoria Cougars	5	Vancouver Canucks	3	W	52	
February 9, 1955	Victoria Cougars	0	Edmonton Flyers	0	T	53	
February 10, 1955	New Westminster Royals	1	Victoria Cougars	4	W	55	
February 13, 1955	Victoria Cougars	1	Vancouver Canucks	4	L		
February 16, 1955	Victoria Cougars	3	New Westminster Royals	2	W	57	
February 17, 1955	Calgary Stampeders	2	Victoria Cougars	1	L		
February 18, 1955	Edmonton Flyers	1	Victoria Cougars	3	W	59	
February 19, 1955	Saskatoon Quakers	2	Victoria Cougars	2	T	60	
February 23, 1955	Victoria Cougars	10	New Westminster Royals	4	W	62	
February 26, 1955	New Westminster Royals	1	Victoria Cougars	1	T	63	
March 2, 1955	Victoria Cougars	4	Edmonton Flyers	2	W	65	
March 4, 1955	Vancouver Canucks	1	Victoria Cougars	1	T	66	

Appendix C

March 5, 1955	Victoria Cougars	4	Vancouver Canucks	3	W	68	
March 9, 1955	Victoria Cougars	6	Saskatoon Quakers	2	W	70	Andy Hebenton Night
March 12, 1955	Victoria Cougars	7	Saskatoon Quakers	1	W	72	
March 15, 1955	Vancouver Canucks	3	Victoria Cougars	0	L		
March 16, 1955	Victoria Cougars	2	Vancouver Canucks	3	L		
March 18, 1955	Vancouver Canucks	1	Victoria Cougars	0	L		
March 19, 1955	New Westminster Royals	7	Victoria Cougars	9	W	74	*Saskatoon Star-Phoenix*, March 21, 1955, page 17.
PLAYOFFS—FIRST ROUND	**LOST SERES, 4-1**						
March 22, 1955	Victoria Cougars	2	Calgary Stampeders	7	L		
March 22, 1955	Victoria Cougars	2	Calgary Stampeders	5	L		
March 24, 1955	Calgary Stampeders	2	Victoria Cougars	3	W		Overtime, 5:43
March 29, 1955	Calgary Stampeders	5	Victoria Cougars	0	L		
March 31, 1955	Calgary Stampeders	2	Victoria Cougars	1	L		

Victoria Cougars 1955-56

Date	Home	Score	Away	Score	Result	Pts	Notes
October 7, 1955	Victoria Cougars	4	New WestminsterRoyals	1	W	2	
October 8, 1955	Seattle Americans	2	Victoria Cougars	4	W	4	
October 10, 1955	Victoria Cougars	3	Vancouver Canucks	2	W	6	Thanksgiving Day matinee
October 11, 1955	Vancouver Canucks	3	Victoria Cougars	4	W	8	
October 14, 1955	Victoria Cougars	2	Seattle Americans	3	L		
October 18, 1955	Victoria Cougars	4	Edmonton Flyers	5	L		
October 21, 1955	Victoria Cougars	6	New Westminster Royals	4	W	10	
October 22, 1955	New Westminster Royals	4	Victoria Cougars	3	L		
October 29, 1955	Victoria Cougars	3	Winnipeg Warriors	0	W	12	
October 30, 1955	Seattle Americans	5	Victoria Cougars	2	L		
November 4, 1955	Victoria Cougars	3	Saskatoon Quakers	1	W	14	
November 5, 1955	Seattle Americans	0	Victoria Cougars	6	W	16	
November 8, 1955	Victoria Cougars	2	Seattle Americans	1	W	18	
November 11, 1955	Victoria Cougars	1	Calgary Stampeders	7	L		
November 12, 1955	New Westminster Royals	4	Victoria Cougars	2	L		
November 14, 1955	Victoria Cougars	2	Vancouver Canucks	5	L		
November 18, 1955	Victoria Cougars	4	Seattle Americans	1	W	20	
November 19, 1955	Seattle Americans	3	Victoria Cougars	2	L		Result was protested, but not changed

The History of Professional Hockey in Victoria, BC: 1911-2011

Date	Team 1	Score	Team 2	Score	Result	Pts	Notes
November 22, 1955	Vancouver Canucks	4	Victoria Cougars	2	L		Plane issues and bus accident
November 25, 1955	Victoria Cougars	2	New Westminster Royals	3	L		Overtime 2:44
November 26, 1955	New WestminsterRoyals	3	Victoria Cougars	3	T	21	
November 29, 1955	Victoria Cougars	1	Regina Regals	4	L		
December 2, 1955	Victoria Cougars	4	Vancouver Canucks	2	W	23	
December 5, 1955	Winnipeg Warriors	6	Victoria Cougars	3	L		
December 6, 1955	Regina Regals	1	Victoria Cougars	4	W	25	
December 7, 1955	Saskatoon Quakers	4	Victoria Cougars	1	L		
December 9, 1955	Edmonton Flyers	2	Victoria Cougars	2	T	26	
December 10, 1955	Calgary Stampeders	6	Victoria Cougars	2	L		
December 12, 1955	Vancouver Canucks	2	Victoria Cougars	1	L		
December 13, 1955	Victoria Cougars	4	Winnipeg Warriors	2	W	28	
December 16, 1955	Victoria Cougars	7	Seattle Americans	3	W	30	
December 17, 1955	New Westminster Royals	0	Victoria Cougars	3	W	32	
December 23, 1955	Victoria Cougars	3	New Westminster Royals	4	L		
December 26, 1955	Vancouver Canucks	2	Victoria Cougars	0	L		
December 27, 1955	Victoria Cougars	1	Vancouver Canucks	0	W	34	
December 30, 1955	Victoria Cougars	3	Seattle Americans	4	L		Overtime 3:38
January 2, 1956	Victoria Cougars	3	Edmonton Flyers	1	W	36	Matinee
January 6, 1956	Victoria Cougars	4	New Westminster Royals	0	W	38	
January 10, 1956	Victoria Cougars	0	Vancouver Canucks	0	T	39	
January 13, 1956	Vancouver Canucks	4	Victoria Cougars	2	L		
January 14, 1956	New Westminster Royals	2	Victoria Cougars	6	W	41	
January 16, 1956	Edmonton Flyers	2	Victoria Cougars	5	W	43	
January 17, 1956	Saskatoon Quakers`	3	Victoria Cougars	4	W	45	
January 18, 1956	Winnipeg Warriors	3	Victoria Cougars	2	L		
January 20, 1956	Brandon Regals	1	Victoria Cougars	4	W	47	
January 21, 1956	Calgary Stampeders	9	Victoria Cougars	3	L		
January 24, 1956	Victoria Cougars	4	Seattle Americans	0	W	49	
January 27, 1956	Victoria Cougars	5	Saskatoon Quakers	3	W	51	
January 28, 1956	Seattle Americans	4	Victoria Cougars	0	L		
January 29, 1956	Seattle Americans	1	Victoria Cougars	2	W	53	Overtime 6:59
January 31, 1956	Victoria Cougars	2	Calgary Stampeders	1	W	55	
February 3, 1956	Victoria Cougars	0	Seattle Americans	2	L		
February 6, 1956	Vancouver Canucks	1	Victoria Cougars	2	W	57	
February 7, 1956	Victoria Cougars	5	Vancouver Canucks	4	W	59	

February 10, 1956	Victoria Cougars	9	New Westminster Royals	3	W	61	
February 11, 1956	New Westminster Royals	6	Victoria Cougars	4	L		
February 14, 1956	Seattle Americans	1	Victoria Cougars	7	W	63	
February 17, 1956	Victoria Cougars	4	Brandon Regals	4	T	64	
February 21, 1956	Victoria Cougars	3	Vancouver Canucks	2	W	66	
February 24, 1956	Victoria Cougars	5	Seattle Americans	3	W	68	
February 25, 1956	New Westminster Royals	7	Victoria Cougars	3	L		
February 28, 1956	Vancouver Canucks	2	Victoria Cougars	2	T	69	
March 2, 1956	Victoria Cougars	3	New Westminster Royals	2	W	71	Overtime 5:00
March 3, 1956	Seattle Americans	3	Victoria Cougars	1	L		
March 6, 1956	Victoria Cougars	0	Vancouver Canucks	3	L		
March 9, 1956	Victoria Cougars	3	Seattle Americans	2	W	73	Overtime 8:43
March 10, 1956	New Westminster Royals	4	Victoria Cougars	3	L		
March 13, 1956	Vancouver Canucks	7	Victoria Cougars	0	L		
March 16, 1956	Victoria Cougars	1	New Westminster Royals	0	W	75	
March 18, 1956	Seattle Americans	3	Victoria Cougars	2	L		Overtime 1:05
PLAYOFFS - FIRST ROUND	**VICTORIA AND VANCOUVER ADVANCE TO WESTERN FINAL**						
March 20, 1956	Victoria Cougars	3	New Westminster Royals	1			
March 21, 1956	New Westminster Royals	4	Vancouver Canucks	3			
March 23, 1956	Vancouver Canucks	2	Victoria Cougars	3			
March 24, 1956	New Westminster Royals	0	Victoria Cougars	3			
March 27, 1956	Victoria Cougars	3	Vancouver Canucks	2			
March 28, 1956	Vancouver Canucks	5	New Westminster Royals	1			
WESTERN FINAL	**LOST SERIES 4-1**						
March 30, 1956	Vancouver Canucks	7	Victoria Cougars	1	L		
April 1, 1956	Victoria Cougars	2	Vancouver Canucks	3	L		Overtime 7:19
April 3, 1956	Vancouver Canucks	7	Victoria Cougars	2	L		
April 6, 1956	Victoria Cougars	2	Vancouver Canucks	0	W		
April 8, 1956	Vancouver Canucks	5	Victoria Cougars	0	L		

The History of Professional Hockey in Victoria, BC: 1911-2011

Victoria Cougars 1956-57

Date	Home	Score	Away	Score	Result	Pts	Notes	W	L	T
October 8, 1956	Victoria Cougars	5	Vancouver Canucks	2	W	2		1		
October 12, 1956	Victoria Cougars	4	Seattle Americans	6	L				1	
October 13, 1956	Seattle Americans	3	Victoria Cougars	4	L		Overtime: 1:30		2	
October 16, 1956	Winnipeg Warriors	4	Victoria Cougars	4	T	3	Overtime: tie			1
October 17, 1956	Brandon Regals	5	Victoria Cougars	0	L				3	
October 19, 1956	Edmonton Flyers	2	Victoria Cougars	1	L				4	
October 20, 1956	Calgary Stampeders	3	Victoria Cougars	2	L				5	
October 22, 1956	Victoria Cougars	1	Calgary Stampeders	0	W	5		2		
October 26, 1956	Victoria Cougars	3	Edmonton Flyers	4	L		Overtime: 3:43		6	
October 30, 1956	Vancouver Canucks	3	Victoria Cougars	2	L				7	
November 2, 1956	Victoria Cougars	3	New Westminster Royals	1	W	7		3		
November 3, 1956	New Westminster Royals	2	Victoria Cougars	2	T	8	Overtime: tie			2
November 5, 1956	Victoria Cougars	9	Winnipeg Warriors	2	W	10		4		
November 9, 1956	Victoria Cougars	0	Seattle Americans	4	L				8	
November 10, 1956	Seattle Americans	6	Victoria Cougars	2	L				9	
November 16, 1956	Victoria Cougars	2	New Westminster Royals	4	L				10	
November 17, 1956	New Westminster Royals	3	Victoria Cougars	0	L				11	
November 19, 1956	Victoria Cougars	6	Vancouver Canucks	3	W	12	Rotary Night	5		
November 20, 1956	Vancouver Canucks	2	Victoria Cougars	5	W	14		6		
November 23, 1956	Victoria Cougars	3	Seattle Americans	3	T	15	Overtime: tie			3
November 24, 1956	Seattle Americans	2	Victoria Cougars	4	W	17		7		
November 26, 1956	Victoria Cougars	1	Edmonton Flyers	2	L				12	
November 30, 1956	Victoria Cougars	3	Calgary Stampeders	0	W	19		8		
December 4, 1956	Brandon Regals	3	Victoria Cougars	2	L				13	
December 5, 1956	Winnipeg Warriors	2	Victoria Cougars	3	W	21		9		
December 7, 1956	Edmonton Flyers	2	Victoria Cougars	1	L		Overtime: 3:30		14	
December 8, 1956	Calgary Stampeders	4	Victoria Cougars	1	L				15	
December 10, 1956	Victoria Cougars	1	Brandon Regals	3	L				16	
December 14, 1956	Victoria Cougars	6	New Westminster Royals	4	W	23		10		
December 15, 1956	Seattle Americans	2	Victoria Cougars	2	T	24	Overtime: tie			4
December 21, 1956	Victoria Cougars	4	Seattle Americans	1	W	26		11		
December 22, 1956	New Westminster Royals	3	Victoria Cougars	4	W	28		12		
December 26, 1956	Victoria Cougars	2	Vancouver Canucks	4	L		Matinee – 2:00 p.m.		17	

Appendix C

Date	Team 1	Score	Team 2	Score	W/L/T		Notes	
December 26, 1956	Vancouver Canucks		Victoria Cougars				An 8:00 p.m. game was planned but was cancelled because planes could not fly because of fog.	
December 28, 1956	Victoria Cougars	3	New Westminster Royals	0	W	30		13
December 29, 1956	Seattle Americans	7	Victoria Cougars	4	L			18
January 1, 1957	Vancouver Canucks	4	Victoria Cougars	3	L		Overtime: 6:55	19
January 4, 1957	Victoria Cougars	3	Winnipeg Warriors	1	W	32		14
January 7, 1957	Victoria Cougars	4	Vancouver Canucks	2	W	34		15
January 11, 1957	Victoria Cougars	4	Seattle Americans	5	L			20
January 12, 1957	New Westminster Royals	3	Victoria Cougars	0	L			21
January 14, 1957	Victoria Cougars	7	New Westminster Royals	1	W	36		16
January 18, 1957	Vancouver Canucks	2	Victoria Cougars	3	W	38		17
January 19, 1957	New Westminster	4	Victoria Cougars	0	L			22
January 21, 1957	Victoria Cougars	5	Vancouver Canucks	2	W	40		18
January 25, 1957	Victoria Cougars	2	Brandon Regals	3	L			23
January 29, 1957	Edmonton Flyers	7	Victoria Cougars	8	W	42	Overtime: 2:35	19
January 30, 1956	Calgary Stampeders	3	Victoria Cougars	3	T	43	Overtime: tie	5
February 1, 1957	Winnipeg Warriors	3	Victoria Cougars	1	L			24
February 2, 1957	Brandon Regals	4	Victoria Cougars	1	L			25
February 4, 1957	Victoria Cougars	2	New Westminster Royals	0	W	45		20
February 5, 1957	New Westminster Royals	2	Victoria Cougars	2	T	46	Overtime: tie	6
February 8, 1957	Victoria Cougars	0	Seattle Americans	2	L			26
February 9, 1957	Seattle Americans	2	Victoria Cougars	2	T	47	Overtime: tie	7
February 15, 1957	Victoria Cougars	2	Edmonton Flyers	1	W	49		21
February 18, 1957	Victoria Cougars	2	Brandon Regals	3	L			27
February 22, 1957	Victoria Cougars	2	Calgary Stampeders	1	W	51		22
February 25, 1957	Victoria Cougars	6	Vancouver Canucks	1	W	53		23
February 26, 1957	Vancouver Canucks	4	Victoria Cougars	2	L			28
March 1, 1957	Victoria Cougars	6	Seattle Americans	2	W	55		24
March 3, 1957	Seattle Americans	3	Victoria Cougars	2	L		Overtime: 7:40	29
March 5, 1957	Vancouver Canucks	5	Victoria Cougars	0	L		Boxing Day game rescheduled	30
March 6, 1957	New Westminster Royals	4	Victoria Cougars	2	L			31
March 8, 1957	Victoria Cougars	5	New Westminster Royals	2	W	57		25

The History of Professional Hockey in Victoria, BC: 1911-2011

March 11, 1957	Victoria Cougars	7	Winnipeg Warriors	1	W	59		26
March 12, 1957	Vancouver Canucks	7	Victoria Cougars	5	L			32
March 15, 1957	Victoria Cougars	7	Seattle Americans	1	W	61		27
March 16, 1957	Victoria Cougars	3	New Westminster Royals	8	L			33
March 18, 1957	Vancouver Canucks	1	Victoria Cougars	3	W	63	Clinched playoff spot	28
March 22, 1957	Victoria Cougars	5	New Westminster Royals	4	W	65	Overtime: 6:01	29
March 23, 1957	Seattle Americans	4	Victoria Cougars	1	L			34
BEST-OF-THREE—ROUND ONE	**LOST SERIES, 2-1**							
March 26, 1957	New Westminster Royals	3	Victoria Cougars	2	L		Overtime: 0:33	
March 28, 1957	Victoria Cougars	4	New Westminster Royals	1	W			
March 31, 1957	New Westminster Royals	2	Victoria Cougars	1	L		Overtime: 11:55	

Victoria Cougars 1957-58

Date	Home	Score	Away	Score	Result	Pts	Notes	W	L	T
October 13, 1957	Seattle Americans	2	Victoria Cougars	0	L				1	
October 14, 1957	Victoria Cougars	2	New Westminster Royals	5	L		Thanksgiving Day matinee — 2:00 p.m.		2	
October 16, 1957	New Westminster Royals	7	Victoria Cougars	1	L				3	
October 18, 1957	Vancouver Canucks	3	Victoria Cougars	2	L		Overtime: 8:23		4	
October 19, 1957	Victoria Cougars	2	Vancouver Canucks	5	L				5	
October 23, 1957	Victoria Cougars	6	New Westminster Royals	7	L		Protest filed		6	
October 26, 1957	Victoria Cougars	2	Seattle Americans	5	L				7	
October 27, 1957	Seattle Americans	5	Victoria Cougars	2	L		Flu outbreak		8	
October 29, 1957	Vancouver Canucks		Victoria Cougars				Postponed due to flu outbreak			
November 2, 1957	Victoria Cougars	0	Vancouver Canucks	7	L		Kilburn quits as coach; Pat Egan takes over		9	
November 6, 1957	Victoria Cougars	4	Calgary Stampeders	1	W	2		1		
November 9, 1957	Victoria Cougars	3	Seattle Americans	5	L				10	
November 11, 1957	Vancouver Canucks	3	Victoria Cougars	2	L		Overtime: 3:49		11	
November 13, 1957	New Westminster Royals	3	Victoria Cougars	5	W	4		2		
November 15, 1957	Seattle Americans	2	Victoria Cougars	2	T	5	Overtime			1
November 16, 1957	Victoria Cougars	3	Vancouver Canucks	4	L				12	
November 20, 1957	Victoria Cougars	3	New Westminster Royals	4	L		Overtime: 7:59		13	

Appendix C

Date	Team	Score	Team	Score	Result		Notes	
November 22, 1957	Vancouver Canucks	1	Victoria Cougars	2	W	7		3
November 24, 1957	Victoria Cougars	5	Seattle Americans	6	L		Overtime: 6:43	14
November 27, 1958	New Westminster Royals	5	Victoria Cougars	1	L			15
November 29, 1957	Vancouver Canucks	4	Victoria Cougars	2	L			16
November 30, 1957	Victoria Cougars	6	Vancouver Canucks	5	W	9		4
December 1, 1957	Seattle Americans	2	Victoria Cougars	4	W	11		5
December 4, 1957	Victoria Cougars	6	New Westminster Royals	3	W	13		6
December 7, 1957	Victoria Cougars	9	Seattle Americans	6	W	15		7
December 11, 1957	New Westminster	4	Victoria Cougars	3	L			17
December 13, 1957	Vancouver Canucks	4	Victoria Cougars	3	L			18
December 14, 1957	Victoria Cougars	1	Vancouver Canucks	2	L		Overtime: 5:42	19
December 15, 1957	Seattle Americans	3	Victoria Cougars	6	W	17		8
December 18, 1957	Victoria Cougars	1	New Westminster Royals	3	L		Christmas Party Night	20
December 21, 1957	Victoria Cougars	3	Seattle Americans	6	L			21
December 25, 1957	New Westminster Royals	6	Victoria Cougars	3	L			22
December 26, 1957	Victoria Cougars	1	New Westminster Royals	2	L			23
December 28, 1957	Victoria Cougars	5	Vancouver Canucks	0	W	19		9
December 29, 1957	Seattle Americans	3	Victoria Cougars	1	L			24
January 1, 1958	Victoria Cougars	2	Seattle Americans	5	L			25
January 3, 1958	Vancouver Canucks	5	Victoria Cougars	3	L			26
January 4, 1958	New Westminster Royals	3	Victoria Cougars	1	L			27
January 8, 1958	ALL-STAR GAME							
January 10, 1958	Vancouver Canucks	4	Victoria Cougars	1	L			28
January 11, 1958	Victoria Cougars	3	New WestminsterRoyals	4	L		Kilburn fired as manager	29
January 15, 1958	Victoria Cougars	3	Seattle Americans	4	L			30
January 18, 1958	New Westminster Royals	6	Victoria Cougars	3	L			31
January 19, 1958	Seattle Americans	1	Victoria Cougars	4	W	21		10
January 25, 1958	Victoria Cougars	4	Edmonton Flyers	5	L			32
January 29, 1958	Victoria Cougars	2	New Westminster Royals	0	W	23		11
February 1, 1958	Victoria Cougars	7	Seattle Americans	6	W	25	Overtime: 1:01	12
February 5, 1958	Victoria Cougars	3	Vancouver Canucks	4	L			33
February 8, 1958	Victoria Cougars	6	Winnipeg Warriors	6	T	26		2
February 11, 1958	Vancouver Canucks	6	Victoria Cougars	1	L			34
February 12, 1958	New Westminster Royals	7	Victoria Cougars	2	L			35
February 14, 1958	Seattle Americans	5	Victoria Cougars	4	L			36
February 15, 1958	Victoria Cougars	0	Vancouver Canucks	1	L			37

441

The History of Professional Hockey in Victoria, BC: 1911-2011

February 19, 1958	Victoria Cougars	4	New Westminster Royals	3	W	28	13
February 21, 1958	Vancouver Canucks	4	Victoria Cougars	2	L		38
February 22, 1958	Victoria Cougars	1	Seattle Americans	3	L		39
February 23, 1958	Seattle Americans	10	Victoria Cougars	5	L		40
February 25, 1968	Victoria Cougars	8	New Westminster Royals	6	W	30	14
February 26, 1958	New WestminsterRoyals	9	Victoria Cougars	3	L		41
March 2, 1958	New Westminster Royals	10	Victoria Cougars	6	L		42
March 4, 1958	Winnipeg Warriors	11	Victoria Cougars	4	L		43
March 6, 1958	Saskatoon-St. Paul	5	Victoria Cougars	6	W	32	15
March 7, 1958	Edmonton Flyers	5	Victoria Cougars	4	L		44
March 8, 1958	Calgary Stampeders	5	Victoria Cougars	2	L		45
March 12, 1958	Victoria Cougars	3	Saskatoon-St. Paul	2	W	34	16
March 16, 1958	Victoria Cougars	7	Vancouver Canucks	4	W	36	17
March 19, 1958	Victoria Cougars	6	New Westminster Royals	7		Replay of portion of October 23 game	
March 19, 1958	Victoria Cougars	2	New Westminster Royals	3	L	Pete Durham Night	46
March 22, 1958	Victoria Cougars	4	Seattle Americans	3	W	38 Overtime: 4:06	18
March 26, 1958	New Westminster Royals	6	Victoria Cougars	4	L		47
March 28, 1958	Vancouver Canucks	5	Victoria Cougars	4	L		48
March 29, 1958	Victoria Cougars	5	Vancouver Canucks	6	L		49
March 30, 1958	Seattle Americans	8	Victoria Cougars	3	L		50

Victoria Cougars 1958-59

Date	Home	Score	Away	Score	Result	Pts	Notes	W	L	T
October 10, 1958	Vancouver Canucks	3	Victoria Cougars	2	L				1	
October 13, 1958	Victoria Cougars	3	Calgary Stampeders	5	L		Thanksgiving Day matinee		2	
October 18, 1958	Victoria Cougars	5	Vancouver Canucks	3	W	2		1		
October 19, 1958	Vancouver Canucks	4	Victoria Cougars	5	W	4	Overtime: 5:24 First Sunday professional hockey game in Vancouver	2		
October 21, 1958	Victoria Cougars	7	New Westminster Royals	3	W	6		3		
October 22, 1958	New WestminsterRoyals	5	Victoria Cougars	5	T	7				1
October 25, 1958	Victoria Cougars	2	Seattle Totems	4	L				3	
October 28, 1958	Victoria Cougars	0	Edmonton Flyers	4	L				4	

442

Appendix C

Date	Team	Score	Team	Score	Result	Notes	Record
October 31, 1958	Seattle Totems	2	Victoria Cougars	3	W	9	4
November 1, 1958	Spokane Flyers	6	Victoria Cougars	1	L		5
November 5, 1958	Victoria Cougars	1	Saskatoon Quakers	0	W	11	5
November 8, 1958	Victoria Cougars	3	Vancouver Canucks	3	T	12	2
November 11, 1958	Winnipeg Warriors	5	Victoria Cougars	4	L	Overtime: 8:43	6
November 12, 1958	Saskatoon Quakers	3	Victoria Cougars	2	L		7
November 14, 1958	Edmonton Flyers	5	Victoria Cougars	3	L		8
November 15, 1958	Calgary Stampeders	5	Victoria Cougars	1	L		9
November 19, 1958	Victoria Cougars	2	Edmonton Flyers	4	L		10
November 22, 1958	Victoria Cougars	2	Vancouver Canucks	2	T	13	Overtime	3
November 23, 1958	Vancouver Canucks	0	Victoria Cougars	1	W	15	6
November 25, 1958	Victoria Cougars	2	New Westminster Royals	0	W	17	7
November 26, 1958	New Westminster Royals	11	Victoria Cougars	3	L		11
November 29, 1958	Victoria Cougars	3	Seattle Totems	1	W	19	8
December 2, 1958	Saskatoon Quakers	4	Victoria Cougars	1	L		12
December 4, 1958	Winnipeg Warriors	3	Victoria Cougars	4	W	21	9
December 5, 1958	Edmonton Flyers	5	Victoria Cougars	4	L	Overtime: 1:51	13
December 6, 1958	Calgary Stampeders	6	Victoria Cougars	2	L		14
December 10, 1958	Victoria Cougars	5	Spokane Flyers	3	W	23	10
December 13, 1958	Victoria Cougars	4	Winnipeg Warriors	3	W	25	11
December 17, 1958	Spokane Flyers	7	Victoria Cougars	4	L		15
December 19, 1958	Seattle Totems	5	Victoria Cougars	2	L		16
December 26, 1958	Victoria Cougars	6	New Westminster Royals	4	W	27	Boxing Day matinee	12
December 27, 1958	New WestminsterRoyals	2	Victoria Cougars	5	W	29	13
December 28, 1958	Vancouver Canucks	1	Victoria Cougars	2	W	31	14
January 1, 1959	Victoria Cougars	2	New Westminster Royals	4	L		17
January 3, 1959	Spokane Flyers	3	Victoria Cougars	1	L		18
January 4, 1959	Spokane Flyers	5	Victoria Cougars	4	L	This was a four-point game, so Cougars were given two losses	20 and 21
January 6, 1959	Victoria Cougars	4	Spokane Flyers	3	W	33	Overtime: 0:58	15
January 10, 1959	New Westminster Royals	5	Victoria Cougars	6	W	35	Overtime: 1:58	16
January 12, 1959	Victoria Cougars	3	New Westminster Royals	5	L		21
January 14, 1959	Victoria Cougars	4	Spokane Flyers	4	T	36	Overtime	4
January 17, 1959	Victoria Cougars	0	Seattle Totems	3	L		22
January 21, 1959	Victoria Cougars	3	Saskatoon Quakers	1	W	38	17

The History of Professional Hockey in Victoria, BC: 1911-2011

Date	Team 1	Score	Team 2	Score	W/L			#
January 24, 1959	Victoria Cougars	4	Edmonton Flyers	6	L			23
January 27, 1959	Victoria Cougars	1	Seattle Totems	4	L			24
January 31, 1959	Victoria Cougars	5	Calgary Stampeders	2	W	40		18
February 4, 1959	Victoria Cougars	4	Winnipeg Warriors	8	L			25
February 6, 1959	Vancouver Canucks	1	Victoria Cougars	4	W	42		19
February 7, 1959	Victoria Cougars	4	Vancouver Canucks	8	L			26
February 8, 1959	Seattle Totems	2	Victoria Cougars	4	W	44		20
February 11, 1959	Victoria Cougars	4	Spokane Flyers	1	W	46		21
February 12, 1959	Seattle Totems	7	Victoria Cougars	5	L			27
February 14, 1959	Victoria Cougars	4	Seattle Totems	5	L		Overtime: 5:25	28
February 17, 1959	Victoria Cougars	4	Calgary Stampeders	6	L			29
February 18, 1959	New WestminsterRoyals	1	Victoria Cougars	5	W	48		22
February 21, 1959	Victoria Cougars	2	Vancouver Canucks	0	W	50		23
February 22, 1959	Vancouver Canucks	3	Victoria Cougars	1	L			30
February 24, 1959	Saskatoon Quakers	3	Victoria Cougars	1	L			31
February 25, 1959	Winnipeg Warriors	6	Victoria Cougars	5	L			32
February 26, 1959	Edmonton Flyers	1	Victoria Cougars	2	W	52	Overtime: 6:56	24
February 28, 1959	Calgary Stampeders	6	Victoria Cougars	4	L			33
March 4, 1959	Victoria Cougars	0	Saskatoon Quakers	7	L			34
March 7, 1959	Victoria Cougars	4	Winnipeg Warriors	2	W	54		25
March 11, 1959	Victoria Cougars	4	Spokane Flyers	0	W	56		26
March 13, 1959	Seattle Totems	3	Victoria Cougars	7	W	58		27
March 14, 1959	Victoria Cougars	2	Seattle Totems	1	W	60	Overtime: 4:04	28
March 17, 1959	Victoria Cougars	0	New Westminster Royals	4	L		Bargain Night	35
March 18, 1959	New Westminster Royals	3	Victoria Cougars	4	W	62	Overtime: 0:10	29
March 21, 1959	Victoria Cougars	5	Spokane Flyers	2	W	64		30
March 22, 1959	Seattle Totems	8	Victoria Cougars	4	L			36
PLAYOFFS	**LOST SERIES 3-0**							
March 27, 1959	Seattle Totems	3	Victoria Cougars	1	L			
March 28, 1959	Victoria Cougars	3	Seattle Totems	5	L			
March 29, 1959	Seattle Totems	4	Victoria Cougars	2	L			
March 3, 1959	WHL All-star game							

Appendix C

Victoria Cougars 1959-1960

Date	Home	Score	Away	Score	Result	Pts	Notes	W	L	T
October 9, 1959	Vancouver Canucks	3	Victoria Cougars	1	L				1	
October 10, 1959	Victoria Cougars	1	Vancouver Canucks	2	L				2	
October 12, 1959	Victoria Cougars	2	Vancouver Canucks	1	W	2	Thanksgiving Day matinee Overtime: 4:14	1		
October 14, 1959	Victoria Cougars	3	Calgary Stampeders	1	W	4		2		
October 17, 1959	Victoria Cougars	1	Seattle Totems	1	T	5	Overtime			1
October 21, 1959	Victoria Cougars	5	Edmonton Flyers	4	W	7		3		
October 24, 1959	Victoria Cougars	4	Edmonton Flyers	1	W	9		4		
October 27, 1959	Spokane Comets	2	Victoria Cougars	7	W	11		5		
October 28, 1959	Victoria Cougars	3	Spokane Comets	1	W	13		6		
October 31, 1959	Spokane Comets	2	Victoria Cougars	1	L				3	
November 1, 1959	Seattle Totems	3	Victoria Cougars	2	L				4	
November 4, 1959	Victoria Cougars	6	Winnipeg Warriors	5	W	15	Overtime: 1:50	7		
November 6, 1959	Vancouver Canucks	6	Victoria Cougars	0	L				5	
November 7, 1959	Victoria Cougars	4	Vancouver Canucks	1	W	17		8		
November 8, 1959	Seattle Totems	2	Victoria Cougars	4	W	19		9		
November 11, 1959	Victoria Cougars	2	Spokane Comets	5	L				6	
November 13, 1959	Edmonton Flyers	3	Victoria Cougars	2	L				7	
November 14, 1959	Calgary Stampeders	3	Victoria Cougars	2	L		Overtime: 2:30		8	
November 17, 1959	Winnipeg Warriors	2	Victoria Cougars	4	W	21		10		
November 19, 1959	Winnipeg Warriors	5	Victoria Cougars	1	L				9	
November 20, 1959	Edmonton Flyers	3	Victoria Cougars	3	T	22	Overtime			2
November 21, 1959	Calgary Stampeders	7	Victoria Cougars	4	W	24		11		
November 28, 1959	Victoria Cougars	1	Vancouver Canucks	1	T	25				3
November 27, 1959	Vancouver Canucks	2	Victoria Cougars	1	L				10	
November 29, 1959	Victoria Cougars	2	Seattle Totems	1	W	27		12		
December 2, 1959	Spokane Comets	2	Victoria Cougars	5	W	29		13		
December 5, 1959	Spokane Comets	3	Victoria Cougars	2	L				11	
December 6, 1959	Seattle Totems	4	Victoria Cougars	0	L				12	
December 9, 1959	Victoria Cougars	4	Spokane Comets	0	W	31		14		
December 12, 1959	Victoria Cougars	4	Seattle Totems	1	W	33		15		
December 18, 1959	Seattle Totems	2	Victoria Cougars	3	W	35		16		
December 19, 1959	Victoria Cougars	1	Edmonton Flyers	3	L				13	
December 26, 1959	Victoria Cougars	3	Vancouver Canucks	4	W	37	Matinee game	17		

The History of Professional Hockey in Victoria, BC: 1911-2011

Date	Team	Score	Team	Score	Result			
December 26, 1959	Vancouver Canucks	4	Victoria Cougars	2	L		Evening game	14
December 27, 1959	Seattle Totems	4	Victoria Cougars	1	L			15
December 30, 1959	Victoria Cougars	5	Seattle Totems	3	W	39		18
January 1, 1960	Vancouver Canucks	4	Victoria Cougars	2	L			16
January 3, 1969	Victoria Cougars	6	Vancouver Canucks	2	W	41		19
January 5, 1960	Vancouver Canucks	1	Victoria Cougars	1	T	42		4
January 6, 1960	Victoria Cougars	6	Spokane Comets	3	W	44		20
January 9, 1960	Victoria Cougars	1	Spokane Comets	3	L			17
January 13, 1960	Spokane Comets	2	Victoria Cougars	5	W	46		21
January 16, 1960	Spokane Comets	1	Victoria Cougars	5	W	48		22
January 20, 1960	Victoria Cougars	5	Edmonton Flyers	0	W	50		23
January 22, 1960	Vancouver Canucks	6	Victoria Cougars	1	L			18
January 23, 1960	Victoria Cougars	6	Seattle Totems	4	W	52		24
January 27, 1960	Victoria Cougars	2	Calgary Stampeders	3	L			19
January 30, 1960	Victoria Cougars	4	Calgary Stampeders	1	W	54		25
February 3, 1960	Victoria Cougars	2	Winnipeg Warriors	1	W	56	Overtime: 9:00	26
February 6, 1959	Victoria Cougars	4	Winnipeg Warriors	6	L			20
February 9, 1960	Vancouver Canucks	1	Victoria Cougars	2	W	58		27
February 10, 1960	Victoria Cougars	7	Spokane Comets	1	W	60		28
February 12, 1960	Seattle Totems	5	Victoria Cougars	3	L			21
February 13, 1960	Victoria Cougars	2	Vancouver Canucks	3	L			22
February 16, 1960	Winnipeg Warriors	1	Victoria Cougars	3	W	62		29
February 18, 1960	Winnipeg Warriors	4	Victoria Cougars	2	L			23
February 19, 1960	Edmonton Flyers	5	Victoria Cougars	2	L			24
February 20, 1960	Calgary Stampeders	1	Victoria Cougars	2	W	64	Overtime: 5:39	30
February 23, 1960	Edmonton Flyers	1	Victoria Cougars	3	W	66		31
February 24, 1960	Calgary Stampeders	5	Victoria Cougars	3	L			25
February 26, 1960	Vancouver Canucks	6	Victoria Cougars	1	L			26
February 27, 1960	Victoria Cougars	8	Vancouver Canucks	4	W	66		32
March 2, 1960	Victoria Cougars	9	Winnipeg Warriors	2	W	68		33
March 5, 1960	Victoria Cougars	1	Calgary Stampeders	3	L			27
March 9, 1960	Victoria Cougars	4	Seattle Totems	2	W	70		34
March 12, 1960	Victoria Cougars	3	Vancouver Canucks	2	W	72		35
March 13, 1960	Seattle Totems	7	Victoria Cougars	5	L			28
March 15, 1960	Spokane Comets	2	Victoria Cougars	9	W	74		36
March 16, 1960	Victoria Cougars	3	Spokane Comets	6	L			29
March 19, 1960	Victoria Cougars	4	Seattle Totems	3	W	76		37

Appendix C

PLAYOFFS ROUND 1—BEST OF 7	WON SERIES 4-0						
March 25, 1960	Seattle Totems	2	Victoria Cougars	3	W	Overtime: 9:21	
March 27, 1960	Victoria Cougars	5	Seattle Totems	0	W		
March 28, 1960	Seattle Totems	2	Victoria Cougars	4	W		
March 30, 1960	Victoria Cougars	2	Seattle Totems	0	W		
PLAYOFFS ROUND 2—BEST OF 9	LOST SERIES 5-2						
April 2, 1960	Vancouver Canucks	2	Victoria Cougars	3	W	Overtime: 2:12	
April 6, 1960	Vancouver Canucks	2	Victoria Cougars	4	W	Game played in Los Angeles	
April 7, 1960	Vancouver Canucks	3	Victoria Cougars	2	L	Game played in Los Angeles	
April 9, 1960	Victoria Cougars	2	Vancouver Canucks	6	L		
April 12, 1960	Vancouver Canucks	2	Victoria Cougars	1	L		
April 13, 1960	Victoria Cougars	1	Vancouver Canucks	2	L		
April 15, 1960	Vancouver Canucks	6	Victoria Cougars	3	L		

Victoria Cougars 1960-1961

Date	Home	Score	Away	Score	Result	Pts	Notes	W	L	T
October 14, 1960	Victoria Cougars	3	Seattle Totems	2	W	2		1		
October 15, 1960	Seattle Totems	3	Victoria Cougars	2	L				1	
October 18, 1960	Victoria Cougars	3	Spokane Comets	2	W	4	Overtime: 2:29	2		
October 22, 1960	Victoria Cougars	4	Winnipeg Warriors	1	W	6		3		
October 26, 1960	Victoria Cougars	3	Winnipeg Warriors	5	L				2	
October 28, 1960	Victoria Cougars	5	Spokane Comets	3	W	8		4		
October 29, 1960	Spokane Comets	4	Victoria Cougars	3	L				3	
November 1, 1960	Victoria Cougars	4	Calgary Stampeders	3	W	10	Overtime: 3:38	5		
November 4, 1960	Victoria Cougars	2	Portland Buckaroos	5	L				4	
November 8, 1960	Vancouver Canucks	1	Victoria Cougars	3	W	12		6		
November 9, 1960	Spokane Comets	4	Victoria Cougars	3	L				5	
November 11, 1960	Victoria Cougars	2	Spokane Comets	3	L		Penalty-shot controversy		6	
November 18, 1960	Victoria Cougars	5	Edmonton Flyers	3	W	14		7		
November 20, 1950	Portland Buckaroos	7	Victoria Cougars	3	L				7	
November 22, 1960	Victoria Cougars	5	Portland Buckaroos	2	W	16		8		
November 25, 1960	Vancouver Canucks	8	Victoria Cougars	6	L				8	
November 26, 1960	Victoria Cougars	0	Vancouver Canucks	2	L				9	

447

The History of Professional Hockey in Victoria, BC: 1911-2011

Date	Team	Score	Team	Score	Result		Notes	
December 2, 1960	Victoria Cougars	7	Calgary Stampeders	9	L			10
December 4, 1960	Seattle Totems	4	Victoria Cougars	2	L			11
December 9, 1960	Victoria Cougars	3	Winnipeg Warriors	1	W	18		9
December 13, 1960	Calgary Stampeders	2	Victoria Cougars	1	L			12
December 14, 1960	Edmonton Flyers	2	Victoria Cougars	4	W	20		10
December 16, 1960	Edmonton Flyers	6	Victoria Cougars	3	L			13
December 17, 1960	Calgary Stampeders	7	Victoria Cougars	2	L			14
December 19, 1960	Winnipeg Warriors	1	Victoria Cougars	4	W	22		11
December 21, 1960	Winnipeg Warriors	0	Victoria Cougars	3	W	24		12
December 23, 1960	Vancouver Canucks	5	Victoria Cougars	0	L			15
December 26, 1960	Victoria Cougars	6	Portland Buckaroos	4	W	26		13
December 30, 1960	Victoria Cougars	6	Spokane Comets	2	W	28	Donnybrook with penalty record	14
January 2, 1961	Victoria Cougars	6	Edmonton Flyers	1	W	30	Matinee	15
January 4, 1961	Spokane Comets	5	Victoria Cougars	0	L			16
January 7, 1961	Victoria Cougars	3	Vancouver Canucks	1	W	32		16
January 8, 1961	Portland Buckaroos	9	Victoria Cougars	0	L			17
January 10, 1961	Victoria Cougars	1	Spokane Comets	4	L		Kids' Gifts Night	18
January 13, 1961	Victoria Cougars	2	Seattle Totems	8	L			19
January 15, 1961	Portland Buckaroos	6	Victoria Cougars	4	L			20
January 17, 1961	Victoria Cougars	5	Edmonton Flyers	3	W	34		17
January 20, 1961	Victoria Cougars	0	Portland Buckaroos	1	L			21
January 24, 1961	Victoria Cougars	5	Calgary Stampeders	3	W	36		18
January 27, 1961	Victoria Cougars	1	Portland Buckaroos	3	L			22
January 30, 1961	Seattle Totems	5	Victoria Cougars	1	L			23
January 31, 1961	Victoria Cougars	4	Winnipeg Warriors	3	W	38	Overtime: 1:30	19
February 3, 1961	Victoria Cougars	7	Seattle Totems	1	W	40		20
February 6, 1961	Winnipeg Warriors	1	Victoria Cougars	4	W	42		21
February 8, 1961	Winnipeg Warriors	4	Victoria Cougars	3	L			24
February 10, 1961	Edmonton Flyers	3	Victoria Cougars	6	W	44		22
February 11, 1961	Calgary Stampeders	6	Victoria Cougars	4	L			25
February 14, 1961	Calgary Stampeders	8	Victoria Cougars	1	L			26
February 15, 1961	Edmonton Flyers	5	Victoria Cougars	3	L			27
February 17, 1961	Vancouver Canucks	4	Victoria Cougars	0	L			28
February 19, 1961	Seattle Totems	5	Victoria Cougars	4	L			29
February 21, 1961	Victoria Cougars	1	Vancouver Canucks	2	L		Navy Night. Overtime: 1:15	30
February 22, 1961	Spokane Comets	4	Victoria Cougars	3	L			31

Appendix C

Date	Home	Score	Away	Score	Result	Pts	Notes	W	L	T
February 24, 1961	Victoria Cougars	3	Seattle Totems	3	T	45	Overtime			1
February 28, 1961	Victoria Cougars	2	Vancouver Canucks	4	L				32	
March 3, 1961	Victoria Cougars	3	Seattle Totems	2	W	47		23		
March 4, 1961	Portland Buckaroos	3	Victoria Cougars	1	L				33	
March 5, 1961	Portland Buckaroos	2	Victoria Cougars	2	T	48	Overtime			2
March 7, 1961	Victoria Cougars	3	Calgary Stampeders	7	L				34	
March 10, 1961	Victoria Cougars	6	Spokane Comets	3	W	50		24		
March 12, 1961	Spokane Comets	3	Victoria Cougars	5	W	52		25		
March 17, 1961	Victoria Cougars	3	Portland Buckaroos	2	W	54		26		
March 18, 1961	Seattle Totems	5	Victoria Cougars	2	L				35	
March 19, 1961	Portland Buckaroos	3	Victoria Cougars	5	W	56		27		
March 24, 1961	Victoria Cougars	3	Seattle Totems	5	L				36	
March 26, 1961	Portland Buckaroos	6	Victoria Cougars	3	L				37	
March 28, 1961	Victoria Cougars	3	Edmonton Flyers	4	L				38	
March 31, 1961	Victoria Cougars	4	Portland Buckaroos	5	L				39	
April 1, 1961	Spokane Comets	7	Victoria Cougars	2	L				40	
April 2, 1961	Seattle Totems	8	Victoria Cougars	3	L				41	
PLAYOFFS ROUND 1 - BEST OF 5	**LOST SERIES 3-2**									
April 4, 1961	Vancouver Canucks	2	Victoria Cougars	1	L					
April 5, 1961	Victoria Cougars	4	Vancouver Canucks	1	W					
April 7, 1961	Vancouver Canucks	3	Victoria Cougars	4	W		Overtime: 34:55 (second overtime)			
April 8, 1961	Victoria Cougars	1	Vancouver Canucks	3	L					
April 10, 1961	Vancouver Canucks	3	Victoria Cougars	1	L					

END OF HOCKEY IN VICTORIA UNTIL THE MAPLE LEAFS CAME TO TOWN

Victoria Maple Leafs 1964-65

Date	Home	Score	Away	Score	Result	Pts	Notes	W	L	T
October 9, 1964	Los Angeles Blades	7	Victoria Maple Leafs	3	L				1	
October 10, 1964	Los Angeles Blades	6	Victoria Maple Leafs	3	L				2	
October 13, 1964	Victoria Maple Leafs	4	Seattle Totems	5	L		Overtime: 0:57		3	
October 17, 1964	Victoria Maple Leafs	3	San Francisco Seals	2	W	2		1		
October 20, 1964	Victoria Maple Leafs	3	Los Angeles Blades	1	W	4		2		
October 24, 1964	Victoria Maple Leafs	2	Vancouver Canucks	3	L				4	
October 27, 1964	Victoria Maple Leafs	4	Los Angeles Blades	3	W	6	Overtime: 8:41	3		

449

The History of Professional Hockey in Victoria, BC: 1911-2011

October 30, 1964	Vancouver Canucks	6	Victoria Maple Leafs	3	L			5
October 31, 1964	Victoria Maple Leafs	3	Portland Buckaroos	4	L			6
November 1, 1964	Portland Buckaroos	5	Victoria Maple Leafs	4	L		Overtime: 6:30	7
November 6, 1964	Seattle Totems	4	Victoria Maple Leafs	3	L			8
November 7, 1964	Victoria Maple Leafs	2	Seattle Totems	0	W	8		4
November 10, 1964	Victoria Maple Leafs	4	Los Angeles Blades	3	W	10		5
November 14, 1964	Victoria Maple Leafs	5	San Francisco Seals	6	L		Overtime: 2:21	9
November 17, 1964	Victoria Maple Leafs	2	Portland Buckaroos	5	L			10
November 20, 1964	San Francisco Seals	6	Victoria Maple Leafs	3	L			11
November 21, 1964	San Francisco Seals	3	Victoria Maple Leafs	5	W	12		6
November 25, 1964	Seattle Totems	1	Victoria Maple Leafs	4	W	14		7
November 27, 1964	Vancouver Canucks	5	Victoria Maple Leafs	3	L			12
November 28, 1964	Victoria Maple Leafs	5	Seattle Totems	7	L			13
December 5, 1964	Victoria Maple Leafs	2	Vancouver Canucks	6	L			14
December 6, 1964	Portland Buckaroos	3	Victoria Maple Leafs	2	L		Overtime: 1:11	15
December 12, 1964	Victoria Maple Leafs	7	Los Angeles Blades	3	W	16		8
December 13, 1964	Seattle Totems	3	Victoria Maple Leafs	1	L			16
December 16, 1964	San Francisco Seals	5	Victoria Maple Leafs	6	W	18		9
December 18, 1964	Los Angeles Blades	6	Victoria Maple Leafs	4	L			17
December 19, 1964	San Francisco Seals	6	Victoria Maple Leafs	3	L			18
December 20, 1964	Los Angeles Blades	3	Victoria Maple Leafs	1	L			19
December 22, 1964	Victoria Maple Leafs	4	San Francisco Seals	3	W	20		10
December 26, 1964	Victoria Maple Leafs	3	Portland Buckaroos	2	W	22		11
December 27, 1964	Seattle Totems	1	Victoria Maple Leafs	4	W	24		12
December 29, 1964	Victoria Maple Leafs	6	Seattle Totems	4	W	26		13
January 1, 1965	Portland Buckaroos	1	Victoria Maple Leafs	1	T	27	Overtime: no scoring	1
January 2, 1965	Victoria Maple Leafs	6	Vancouver Canucks	3	W	29		14
January 5, 1964	Victoria Maple Leafs	4	Portland Buckaroos	1	W	31		15
January 8, 1965	Vancouver Canucks	5	Victoria Maple Leafs	3	L			20
January 9, 1965	Victoria Maple Leafs	5	Vancouver Canucks	2	W	33		16
January 10, 1965	Portland Buckaroos	1	Victoria Maple Leafs	3	W	35		17
January 12, 1965	Victoria Maple Leafs	2	Los Angeles Blades	4	L			21
January 15, 1965	Vancouver Canucks	5	Victoria Maple Leafs	2	L			22
January 16, 1965	Victoria Maple Leafs	6	Vancouver Canucks	2	W	37		18
January 17, 1965	Seattle Totems	2	Victoria Maple Leafs	3	W	39		19
January 19, 1965	Victoria Maple Leafs	5	Seattle Totems	1	W	41		20
January 23, 1965	Victoria Maple Leafs	2	San Francisco Seals	3	L			23

Appendix C

Date	Team	Score	Team	Score	Result			
January 26, 1965	Victoria Maple Leafs	6	San Francisco Seals	3	W	43	21	
January 30, 1965	Victoria Maple Leafs	7	Portland Buckaroos	4	W	45	22	
January 31, 1965	Portland Buckaroos	7	Victoria Maple Leafs	2	L			24
February 9, 1965	Victoria Maple Leafs	8	Los Angeles Blades	2	W	47	23	
February 12, 1965	Seattle Totems	4	Victoria Maple Leafs	3	L			25
February 13, 1965	Victoria Maple Leafs	6	Portland Buckaroos	3	W	49	24	
February 14, 1965	Portland Buckaroos	4	Victoria Maple Leafs	1	L			26
February 16, 1965	Victoria Maple Leafs	4	Seattle Totems	2	W	49	25	
February 20, 1965	Victoria Maple Leafs	0	Seattle Totems	1	L			27
February 26, 1965	Vancouver Canucks	4	Victoria Maple Leafs	3	L			28
February 27, 1965	Victoria Maple Leafs	4	Vancouver Canucks	3	W	51	Overtime: 5:46	26
March 6, 1965	Victoria Maple Leafs	3	Portland Buckaroos	4	L			29
March 7, 1965	Vancouver Canucks	4	Victoria Maple Leafs	1	L			30
March 9, 1965	Victoria Maple Leafs	2	San Francisco Seals	4	L			31
March 10, 1965	Los Angeles Blades	2	Victoria Maple Leafs	3	W	53	27	
March 12, 1965	Los Angeles Blades	0	Victoria Maple Leafs	6	W	55	28	
March 13, 1965	San Francisco Seals	5	Victoria Maple Leafs	3	L			32
March 14, 1965	San Francisco Seals	0	Victoria Maple Leafs	4	W	57	29	
March 17, 1965	Portland Buckaroos	8	Victoria Maple Leafs	3	L			33
March 19, 1965	Vancouver Canucks	4	Victoria Maple Leafs	2	L			34
March 20, 1965	Victoria Maple Leafs	4	Vancouver Canucks	1	W	59	30	
March 21, 1965	Seattle Totems	1	Victoria Maple Leafs	2	L			35
March 23, 1965	Victoria Maple Leafs	5	Los Angeles Blades	0	W	61	31	
March 26, 1965	Seattle Totems	3	Victoria Maple Leafs	3	T	62		2
March 27, 1965	Victoria Maple Leafs	5	Vancouver Canucks	3	W	64	32	
March 28, 1965	Vancouver Canucks	7	Victoria Maple Leafs	4	L			_36_
Regular season total							32 36	2

FIRST ROUND PLAYOFFS—WON SERIES 4-3

Date	Team	Score	Team	Score	Result			
March 31, 1965	Seattle Totems	4	Victoria Maple Leafs	2	L			1
April 2, 1965	Seattle Totems	3	Victoria Maple Leafs	0	L			2
April 3, 1965	Victoria Maple Leafs	5	Seattle Totems	2	W		1	
April 6, 1965	Victoria Maple Leafs	3	Seattle Totems	5	L			3
April 9, 1965	Seattle Totems	1	Victoria Maple Leafs	3	W		2	
April 10, 1965	Victoria Maple Leafs	2	Seattle Totems	1	W		3	
April 11, 1965	Seattle Totems	1	Victoria Maple Leafs	4	W		4	

SECOND ROUND PLAYOFFS—LOST SERIES 4-1

Date	Team	Score	Team	Score	Result			
April 14, 1965	Portland Buckaroos	5	Victoria Maple Leafs	1	L			1

The History of Professional Hockey in Victoria, BC: 1911-2011

Date	Home	Score	Away	Score	Result	Notes		
April 17, 1965	Victoria Maple Leafs	1	Portland Buckaroos	3	L			2
April 18, 1965	Portland Buckaroos	3	Victoria Maple Leafs	4	W	Overtime: 4:53	1	
April 21, 1965	Victoria Maple Leafs	2	Portland Buckaroos	3	L			3
April 24, 1965	Victoria Maple Leafs	0	Portland Buckaroos	3	L			4

Victoria Maple Leafs 1965-66

Date	Home	Score	Away	Score	Result	Pts	Notes	W	L	T
October 15, 1965	Vancouver Canucks	2	Victoria Maple Leafs	4	W	2		1		
October 16, 1965	Victoria Maple Leafs	7	Vancouver Canucks	2	W	4		2		
October 17, 1965	Seattle Totems	3	Victoria Maple Leafs	1	L				1	
October 23, 1965	Victoria Maple Leafs	3	Portland Buckaroos	2	W	6		3		
October 24, 1965	Portland Buckaroos	3	Victoria Maple Leafs	4	W	8		4		
October 27, 1965	Victoria Maple Leafs	3	San Francisco Seals	3	T	9				1
October 30, 1965	Victoria Maple Leafs	7	Cleveland Barons	3	W	11		5		
November 3, 1965	Victoria Maple Leafs	1	San Francisco Seals	1	T	12				2
November 6, 1965	Victoria Maple Leafs	7	Seattle Totems	3	W	14		6		
November 7, 1965	Seattle Totems	3	Victoria Maple Leafs	5	W	16		7		
November 10, 1965	Portland Buckaroos	6	Victoria Maple Leafs	0	L				2	
November 13, 1965	Victoria Maple Leafs	5	Portland Buckaroos	2	W	18		8		
November 17, 1965	Victoria Maple Leafs	4	Los Angeles Blades	3	W	20		9		
November 19, 1965	Vancouver Canucks	4	Victoria Maple Leafs	5	W	22		10		
November 20, 1965	Victoria Maple Leafs	4	Vancouver Canucks	2	W	24		11		
November 23, 1965	Victoria Maple Leafs	9	Los Angeles Blades	5	W	26		12		
November 26, 1965	San Francisco Seals	3	Victoria Maple Leafs	4	W	28		13		
November 27, 1965	Los Angeles Blades	3	Victoria Maple Leafs	1	L				3	
December 1, 1965	Victoria Maple Leafs	8	Springfield Indians	3	W	30		14		
December 4, 1965	Victoria Maple Leafs	6	Seattle Totems	2	W	32		15		
December 5, 1965	Seattle Totems	2	Victoria Maple Leafs	3	W	34		16		
December 11, 1965	Victoria Maple Leafs	5	Hershey Bears	2	W	36		17		
December 12, 1965	Seattle Totems	2	Victoria Maple Leafs	0	L				4	
December 14, 1965	Victoria Maple Leafs	5	Los Angeles Blades	1	W	38		18		
December 17, 1965	San Francisco Seals	4	Victoria Maple Leafs	3	L		Overtime: 5:41		5	
December 18, 1965	San Francisco Seals	4	Victoria Maple Leafs	3	L				6	
December 25, 1965	Victoria Maple Leafs	1	Seattle Totems	5	L				7	
December 26, 1965	Portland Buckaroos	2	Victoria Maple Leafs	2	T	39				3

452

Appendix C

December 29, 1965	Victoria Maple Leafs	3	San Francisco Seals	5	L			8
January 1, 1965	Victoria Maple Leafs	4	Vancouver Canucks	1	W	41		19
January 2, 1965	Vancouver Canucks	3	Victoria Maple Leafs	5	W	43		20
January 5, 1965	Victoria Maple Leafs	6	San Francisco Seals	1	W	45		21
January 6, 1966	Los Angeles Blades	3	Victoria Maple Leafs	4	W	47		22
January 7, 1966	San Francisco Seals	6	Victoria Maple Leafs	0	L			9
January 9, 1966	Portland Buckaroos	4	Victoria Maple Leafs	0	L			10
January 11, 1966	Victoria Maple Leafs	5	Portland Buckaroos	4	W	49		23
January 15, 1966	Victoria Maple Leafs	5	Providence Reds	1	W	51		24
January 19, 1966	Victoria Maple Leafs	3	Vancouver Canucks	2	W	53	Overtime: 3:22	25
January 22, 1966	Victoria Maple Leafs	3	Los Angeles Blades	2	W	55		26
January 23, 1966	Vancouver Canucks	10	Victoria Maple Leafs	3	L			11
January 28, 1966	Seattle Totems	2	Victoria Maple Leafs	3	W	57		27
January 29, 1966	Victoria Maple Leafs	6	Portland Buckaroos	2	W	59		28
January 30, 1966	Portland Buckaroos	2	Victoria Maple Leafs	1	L			12
February 2, 1966	Victoria Maple Leafs	2	San Francisco Seals	4	L			13
February 3, 1966	Los Angeles Blades	2	Victoria Maple Leafs	3	W	61	Overtime: 6:54	29
February 5, 1966	Los Angeles Blades	7	Victoria Maple Leafs	2	L			14
February 6, 1966	Portland Buckaroos	3	Victoria Maple Leafs	3	T	62		4
February 9, 1966	Victoria Maple Leafs	2	Portland Buckaroos	3	L		Overtime: 1:11	15
February 11, 1966	Vancouver Canucks	5	Victoria Maple Leafs	4	L			16
February 12, 1966	Victoria Maple Leafs	3	Los Angeles Blades	5	L			17
February 16, 1966	Los Angeles Blades	6	Victoria Maple Leafs	5	L			18
February 18, 1966	San Francisco Seals	2	Victoria Maple Leafs	1	L			19
February 23, 1966	Victoria Maple Leafs	0	Seattle Totems	3	L			20
February 26, 1966	Victoria Maple Leafs	6	Rochester Americans	4	W	64		30
March 2, 1966	Victoria Maple Leafs	4	San Francisco Seals	2	W	66		31
March 4, 1966	Vancouver Canucks	8	Victoria Maple Leafs	1	L			21
March 5, 1966	Victoria Maple Leafs	6	Seattle Totems	2	W	68		32
March 9, 1966	San Francisco Seals	7	Victoria Maple Leafs	2	L			22
March 10, 1966	Los Angeles Blades	3	Victoria Maple Leafs	5	W	70		33
March 12, 1966	Pittsburgh Hornets	1	Victoria Maple Leafs	2	W	72	Overtime: 4:52	34
March 13, 1966	Providence Reds	4	Victoria Maple Leafs	3	L			23
March 15, 1966	Baltimore Clippers	4	Victoria Maple Leafs	3	L			24
March 16, 1966	Hershey Bears	9	Victoria Maple Leafs	3	L			25
March 19, 1966	Springfield Indians	3	Victoria Maple Leafs	1	L			26
March 20, 1966	Quebec Aces	7	Victoria Maple Leafs	1	L			27

The History of Professional Hockey in Victoria, BC: 1911-2011

March 23, 1966	Victoria Maple Leafs	4	Vancouver Canucks	2	W	74	35		
March 26, 1966	Victoria Maple Leafs	4	Portland Buckaroos	1	W	76	36		
March 30, 1966	Victoria Maple Leafs	4	Buffalo Bisons	2	W	78	37		
April 2, 1966	Victoria Maple Leafs	6	Seattle Totems	4	W	80	38		
April 6, 1966	Victoria Maple Leafs	10	Los Angeles Blades	0	W	82	39		
April 8, 1966	Seattle Totems	7	Victoria Maple Leafs	3	L			28	
April 9, 1966	Victoria Maple Leafs	6	Vancouver Canucks	5	W	84	40		
Regular season total							39	28	4

FIRST ROUND PLAYOFFS—WON SERIES 4-3

April 13, 1966	Victoria Maple Leafs	6	San Francisco Seals	3	W	1-0
April 16, 1966	Victoria Maple Leafs	3	San Francisco Seals	1	W	2-0
April 18, 1966	San Francisco Seals	4	Victoria Maple Leafs	2	L	2-1
April 20, 1966	San Francisco Seals	3	Victoria Maple Leafs	2	L	Overtime: 2:29
April 22, 1966	San Francisco Seals	5	Victoria Maple Leafs	4	L	2-3
April 23, 1966	Victoria Maple Leafs	5	San Francisco Seals	4	W	Overtime: 12:37
April 26, 1966	Victoria Maple Leafs	6	San Francisco Seals	1	W	4-3

SECOND ROUND - PLAYOFFS – WON SERIES 4-3

April 30, 1966	Victoria Maple Leafs	6	Portland Buckaroos	5	W	Overtime: 34:56
May 2, 1966	Portland Buckaroos	6	Victoria Maple Leafs	2	L	
May 3, 1966	Portland Buckaroos	1	Victoria Maple Leafs	4	W	
May 6, 1966	Victoria Maple Leafs	0	Portland Buckaroos	3	L	
May 7, 1966	Victoria Maple Leafs	4	Portland Buckaroos	2	W	
May 9, 1966	Portland Buckaroos	3	Victoria Maple Leafs	2	L	
May 10, 1966	Portland Buckaroos	1	Victoria Maple Leafs	5	W	

WON LESTER PATRICK CUP FOR LEAGUE CHAMPIONSHIP

Victoria Maple Leafs 1966-67

Date	Home	Score	Away	Score	Result	Pts	Notes	W	L	T
October 15, 1966	Victoria Maple Leafs	2	California Seals	0	W	2		1		
October 19, 1966	Victoria Maple Leafs	5	Portland Buckaroos	0	W	4		2		
October 21, 1966	Seattle Totems	3	Victoria Maple Leafs	3	T	5				1
October 22, 1966	Victoria Maple Leafs	3	San Diego Gulls	1	W	7		3		
October 26, 1966	Victoria Maple Leafs	4	San Diego Gulls	4	T					2
October 29, 1966	Victoria Maple Leafs	3	Los Angeles Blades	5	L				1	
November 2, 1966	Victoria Maple Leafs	3	Seattle Totems	2	L				2	

Appendix C

Date	Team	Score	Team	Score	Result	Notes		
November 5, 1966	Victoria Maple Leafs	3	California Seals	3	T	9		3
November 6, 1966	Portland Buckaroos	1	Victoria Maple Leafs	1	T	10		4
November 9, 1966	Los Angeles Blades	5	Victoria Maple Leafs	7	W	12	4	
November 11, 1966	Los Angeles Blades	1	Victoria Maple Leafs	4	W	14	5	
November 12, 1966	California Seals	2	Victoria Maple Leafs	1	L			3
November 13, 1966	California Seals	2	Victoria Maple Leafs	7	W	16	6	
November 16, 1966	Victoria Maple Leafs	2	Vancouver Canucks	5	L			4
November 18, 1966	Vancouver Canucks	9	Victoria Maple Leafs	1	L			5
November 23, 1966	Seattle Totems	4	Victoria Maple Leafs	3	L			6
November 25, 1966	Vancouver Canucks	3	Victoria Maple Leafs	2	L			7
November 26, 1966	Victoria Maple Leafs	4	Vancouver Canucks	6	L			8
November 30, 1966	Victoria Maple Leafs	1	Seattle Totems	2	L	Andy Hebenton Night		9
December 2, 1966	Seattle Totems	4	Victoria Maple Leafs	3	L	Overtime: 7:48		10
December 3, 1966	Victoria Maple Leafs	1	PortlandBuckaroos	3	L			11
December 10, 1966	Victoria Maple Leafs	3	Seattle Totems	0	W	18	7	
December 13, 1966	Victoria Maple Leafs	3	California Seals	1	W	20	8	
December 15, 1966	Los Angeles Blades	5	Victoria Maple Leafs	2	L			12
December 16, 1966	San Diego Gulls	3	Victoria Maple Leafs	4	W	22	9	
December 17, 1966	San Diego Gulls	0	Victoria Maple Leafs	2	W	24	10	
December 20, 1966	Los Angeles Blades	4	Victoria Maple Leafs	0	L			13
December 21, 1966	Portland Buckaroos	6	Victoria Maple Leafs	4	L			14
December 23, 1966	Victoria Maple Leafs	2	Vancouver Canucks	5	L			15
December 26, 1966	Vancouver Canucks	2	Victoria Maple Leafs	3	W	26	11	
December 28, 1966	Victoria Maple Leafs	5	San Diego Gulls	2	W	28	12	
December 31, 1966	Victoria Maple Leafs	3	San Diego Gulls	3	T	29		5
January 1, 1967	Portland Buckaroos	4	Victoria Maple Leafs	1	L			16
January 2, 1967	Seattle Totems	8	Victoria Maple Leafs	3	L			17
January 4, 1967	Victoria Maple Leafs	4	Portland Buckaroos	5	L			18
January 6, 1967	Vancouver Canucks	1	Victoria Maple Leafs	4	W	31	13	
January 7, 1967	Victoria Maple Leafs	7	Vancouver Canucks	0	W	33	14	
January 11, 1967	Victoria Maple Leafs	3	Los Angeles Blades	1	W	35	15	
January 14, 1966	Victoria Maple Leafs	6	Los Angeles Blades	1	W	37	16	
January 18, 1966	Victoria Maple Leafs	2	Seattle Totems	5	L			19
January 21, 1967	Victoria Maple Leafs	7	California Seals	2	W	39	17	
January 24, 1967	Victoria Maple Leafs	3	California Seals	3	T	40		6
January 25, 1967	San Diego Gulls	5	Victoria Maple Leafs	1	L			20
January 27, 1967	Los Angeles Blades	6	Victoria Maple Leafs	1	L			21

The History of Professional Hockey in Victoria, BC: 1911-2011

Date	Team	Score	Team	Score	Result			
January 28, 1967	San Diego Gulls	2	Victoria Maple Leafs	4	W	42		18
January 29, 1967	Los Angeles Blades	5	Victoria Maple Leafs	3	L			22
February 2, 1967	Victoria Maple Leafs	5	Portland Buckaroos	3	W	44		19
February 4, 1967	Victoria Maple Leafs	1	Los Angeles Blades	6	L			23
February 5, 1967	Portland Buckaroos	5	Victoria Maple Leafs	3	L			24
February 8, 1967	Victoria Maple Leafs	3	Seattle Totems	2	L			25
February 11, 1967	Victoria Maple Leafs	3	Los Angeles Blades	1	L			26
February 12, 1967	Portland Buckaroos	6	Victoria Maple Leafs	3	L			27
February 15, 1967	California Seals	1	Victoria Maple Leafs	4	W	46		20
February 17, 1967	Californi Seals	0	Victoria Maple Leafs	2	W	48		21
February 22, 1967	Victoria Maple Leafs	6	San Diego Gulls	3	W	50		22
February 25, 1967	Victoria Maple Leafs	4	Portland Buckaroos	0	W	52		23
March 1, 1967	Portland Buckaroos	7	Victoria Maple Leafs	2	L			28
March 3, 1967	Vancouver Canucks	2	Victoria Maple Leafs	5	W	54		24
March 4, 1967	Victoria Maple Leafs	4	Vancouver Canucks	3	W	56		25
March 8, 1967	Victoria Maple Leafs	5	California Seals	4	W	58	Overtime: 1:49	26
March 10, 1967	Seattle Totems	3	Victoria Maple Leafs	2	L			29
March 11, 1967	Victoria Maple Leafs	3	San Diego Gulls	4	L			30
March 15, 1967	Victoria Maple Leafs	0	Seattle Totems	0	T	59		7
March 18, 1967	Victoria Maple Leafs	7	Los Angeles Blades	5	W	61		27
March 19, 1967	Seattle Totems	5	Victoria Maple Leafs	5	L			31
March 22, 1967	California Seals	2	Victoria Maple Leafs	2	T	62		8
March 23, 1967	San Diego Gulls	3	Victoria Maple Leafs	1	L			32
March 25, 1967	San Diego Gulls	4	Victoria Maple Leafs	2	L			33
March 26, 1967	California Seals	6	Victoria Maple Leafs	4	L			34
March 29, 1967	Victoria Maple Leafs	5	Vancouver Canucks	2	W	62		28
March 31, 1967	Vancouver Canucks	6	Victoria Maple Leafs	7	W	64	Overtime: 3:17	29
April 1, 1967	Victoria Maple Leafs	2	Portland Buckaroos	1	W	66		30

LAST PROFESSIONAL HOCKEY GAME IN VICTORIA UNTIL THE VICTORIA SALMON KINGS IN 2004.

Appendix C

Victoria Salmon Kings 2004-2005

Date	Home	Score	Away	Score	Result	Pts	Notes	W	L	OTL	SOL
October 22, 2004	Bakersfield Condors	7	Victoria Salmon Kings	2	L						
October 23, 2004	Bakersfield Condors	2	Victoria Salmon Kings	1	L				2		
October 24, 2004	Fresno Falcons	0	Victoria Salmon Kings	5	W	2		1			
November 5, 2004	Idaho Steelheads	1	Victoria Salmon Kings	4	W	4		2			
November 6, 2004	Idaho Steelheads	6	Victoria Salmon Kings	2	L				3		
November 10, 2004	Long Beach Ice Dogs	2	Victoria Salmon Kings	1	L				4		
November 12, 2004	Las Vegas Wranglers	5	Victoria Salmon Kings	2	L				5		
November 13, 2004	Fresno Falcons	6	Victoria Salmon Kings	4	L				6		
November 17, 2004	Alaska Aces	7	Victoria Salmon Kings	3	L				7		
November 20, 2004	Alaska Aces	5	Victoria Salmon Kings	2	L				8		
November 21, 2004	Alaska Aces	1	Victoria Salmon Kings	4	W	6		3			
November 25, 2004	Fresno Falcons	4	Victoria Salmon Kings	2	L				9		
November 26, 2004	Fresno Falcons	5	Victoria Salmon Kings	2	L				10		
November 27, 2004	Bakersfield Condors	3	Victoria Salmon Kings	2	SOL	7					1
December 5, 2004	Bakersfield Condors	4	Victoria Salmon Kings	3	OTL	8				1	
December 7, 2004	Bakersfield Condors	2	Victoria Salmon Kings	5	W	10		4			
December 8, 2004	Bakersfield Condors	6	Victoria Salmon Kings	8	W	12		5			
December 10, 2004	Mississippi Sea Wolves	1	Victoria Salmon Kings	5	W	14		6			
December 11, 2004	Mississippi Sea Wolves	4	Victoria Salmon Kings	3	OTL	15				2	
December 13, 2004	Mississippi Sea Wolves	4	Victoria Salmon Kings	2	L				11		
December 17, 2004	Victoria Salmon Kings	1	San DiegoGulls	2	L				12		
December 18, 2004	Victoria Salmon Kings	4	San Diego Gulls	5	L				13		
December 20, 2004	Victoria Salmon Kings	3	San Diego Gulls	2	W	17		7			
December 31, 2004	Victoria Salmon Kings	3	San Diego Gulls	4	L				14		
January 1, 2005	Victoria Salmon Kings	2	Long Beach Ice Dogs	3	L				15		
January 2, 2005	Victoria Salmon Kings	1	Long Beach Ice Dogs	5	L				16		
January 4, 2005	Victoria Salmon Kings	3	Alaska Aces	6	L				17		
January 5, 2005	Victoria Salmon Kings	3	Alaska Aces	10	L				18		
January 7, 2005	Alaska Aces	2	Victoria Salmon Kings	1	L				19		
January 8, 2005	Alaska Aces	8	Victoria Salmon Kings	2	L				20		
January 12, 2005	Long Beach Ice Dogs	6	Victoria Salmon Kings	2	L				21		
January 14, 2005	Las Vegas Wranglers	3	Victoria Salmon Kings	2	OTL	18				3	
January 15, 2005	Long Beach Ice Dogs	4	Victoria Salmon Kings	1	L				22		
January 16, 2005	Long Beach Ice Dogs	4	Victoria Salmon Kings	2	L				23		

The History of Professional Hockey in Victoria, BC: 1911-2011

January 18, 2005	Victoria Salmon Kings	2	Long Beach Ice Dogs	5	L			24
January 19, 2005	Victoria Salmon Kings	1	Long Beach Ice Dogs	3	L			25
January 21, 2005	Victoria Salmon Kings	1	Alaska Aces	5	L			26
January 22, 2005	Victoria Salmon Kings	0	Alaska Aces	3	L			27
January 23, 2005	Victoria Salmon Kings	2	Alaska Aces	5	L			28
January 29, 2005	Las Vegas Wranglers	2	Victoria Salmon Kings	1	SOL	19		2
January 31, 2005	Las Vegas Wranglers	4	Victoria Salmon Kings	1	L			29
February 2, 2005	Victoria Salmon Kings	3	Fresno Falcons	7	L			30
February 4, 2005	Victoria Salmon Kings	2	Fresno Falcons	3	L			31
February 5, 2005	Victoria Salmon Kings	5	Fresno Falcons	4	W	21	SO win	8
February 7, 2005	Victoria Salmon Kings	1	Idaho Steelheads	3	L			32
February 9, 2005	Victoria Salmon Kings	1	Idaho Steelheads	3	L			33
February 15, 2005	Victoria Salmon Kings	2	Fresno Falcons	1	W	23	SO win	9
February 16, 2005	Victoria Salmon Kings	0	Fresno Falcons	4	L			34
February 18, 2005	Idaho Steelheads	12	Victoria Salmon Kings	3	L			35
February 19, 2005	Idaho Steelheads	4	Victoria Salmon Kings	2	L			36
February 22, 2005	Victoria Salmon Kings	5	San DiegoGulls	2	W	25		10
February 23, 2005	Victoria Salmon Kings	1	San Diego Gulls	4	L			37
February 25, 2005	Victoria Salmon Kings	3	Las Vegas Wranglers	4	L			38
February 26, 2005	Victoria Salmon Kings	3	Las Vegas Wranglers	4	L			39
February 28, 2005	Victoria Salmon Kings	2	Las Vegas Wranglers	5	L			40
March 4, 2005	Victoria Salmon Kings	3	Bakersfield Condors	7	L			41
March 5, 2005	Victoria Salmon Kings	1	Bakersfield Condors	4	L			42
March 9, 2005	Victoria Salmon Kings	4	Idaho Steelheads	5	L			43
March 10, 2005	Victoria Salmon Kings	3	Idaho Steelheads	2	W	27	OT 1:36	11
March 12, 2005	Victoria Salmon Kings	2	Idaho Steelheads	8	L			44
March 15, 2005	Florida Everblades	7	Victoria Salmon Kings	1	L			45
March 17, 2005	Texas Wildcatters	3	Victoria Salmon Kings	5	W	29		12
March 19, 2005	Louisiana Ice Gators	5	Victoria Salmon Kings	7	W	31		13
March 20, 2005	Louisiana Ice Gators	2	Victoria Salmon Kings	1	L			46
March 22, 2005	Pensacola Ice Pilots	3	Victoria Salmon Kings	1	L			47
March 23, 2005	Mississippi Sea Wolves	2	Victoria Salmon Kings	1	L			48
March 25, 2005	Florida Everblades	3	Victoria Salmon Kings	4	W	33		14
March 26, 2005	Florida Everblades	5	Victoria Salmon Kings	2	L			49
April 1, 2005	Las Vegas Wranglers	4	Victoria Salmon Kings	1	L			50
April 2, 2005	Long Beach Ice Dogs	5	Victoria Salmon Kings	1	L			51
April 8, 2005	San Diego Gulls	3	Victoria Salmon Kings	2	L			52

Date	Home	Score	Away	Score	Result	Pts	Notes	W	L	OT L	SO L
April 9, 2005	San Diego Gulls	5	Victoria Salmon Kings	6	W	35	OT	15			
Regular season total								15	52	3	2

Victoria Salmon Kings 2005-2006

Date	Home	Score	Away	Score	Result	Pts	Notes	W	L	OT L	SO L
October 21, 2005	Fresno Falcons	2	Victoria Salmon Kings	1	L				1		
October 22, 2005	Bakersfield Condors	5	Victoria Salmon Kings	3	L				2		
October 28, 2005	Utah Grizzlies	5	Victoria Salmon Kings	8	W	2		1			
October 29, 2005	Utah Grizzlies	6	Victoria Salmon Kings	3	L				3		
November 2, 2005	Trenton Titans	1	Victoria Salmon Kings	2	W	4		2			
November 4, 2005	Dayton Bombers	2	Victoria Salmon Kings	1	L				4		
November 5, 2005	Toledo Storm	5	Victoria Salmon Kings	3	L				5		
November 6, 2005	Wheeling Nailers	7	Victoria Salmon Kings	3	L				6		
November 10, 2005	Victoria Salmon Kings	5	Stockton Thunder	2	W	6		3			
November 11, 2005	Victoria Salmon Kings	1	Stockton Thunder	2	OTL	7				1	
November 12, 2005	Victoria Salmon Kings	6	Stockton Thunder	4	W	9		4			
November 16, 2005	Victoria Salmon Kings	2	Idaho Steelheads	5	L				7		
November 18, 2005	Victoria Salmon Kings	3	Idaho Steelheads	6	L				8		
November 19, 2005	Victoria Salmon Kings	3	Idaho Steelheads	2	W	11	Overtime: 00:13	5			
November 21, 2005	Phoenix Roadrunners	3	Victoria Salmon Kings	2	L				9		
November 23, 2005	San Diego Gulls	2	Victoria Salmon Kings	4	W	13		6			
November 26, 2005	Las Vegas Wranglers	3	Victoria Salmon Kings	1	L				10		
November 27, 2005	Long Beach Ice Dogs	6	Victoria Salmon Kings	3	L				11		
November 29, 2005	Phoenix Roadrunners	3	Victoria Salmon Kings	1	L				12		
December 2, 2005	Victoria Salmon Kings	5	Utah Grizzlies	5	W	15	Overtime	7			
December 3, 2005	Victoria Salmon Kings	3	Utah Grizzlies	5	L				13		
December 4, 2005	Victoria Salmon Kings	1	Utah Grizzlies	3	L				14		
December 7, 2005	Idaho Steelheads	2	Victoria Salmon Kings	4	W	17		8			
December 9, 2005	Idaho Steelheads	1	Victoria Salmon Kings	5	W	19		9			
December 10, 2005	Idaho Steelheads	5	Victoria Salmon Kings	2	L				15		
December 16, 2005	Victoria Salmon Kings	5	Alaska Aces	4	W	21	Overtime: 00:33	10			
December 17, 2005	Victoria Salmon Kings	0	Alaska Aces	8	L				16		
December 19, 2005	Victoria Salmon Kings	1	Alaska Aces	4	L				17		
December 21, 2005	Utah Grizzlies	4	Victoria Salmon Kings	1	L				18		
December 22, 2005	Utah Grizzlies	5	Victoria Salmon Kings	2	L				19		

The History of Professional Hockey in Victoria, BC: 1911-2011

Date	Team	Score	Team	Score	Result			
December 28, 2005	Alaska Aces	4	Victoria Salmon Kings	0	L		20	
December 30, 2005	Alaska Aces	6	Victoria Salmon Kings	5	L		21	
December 31, 2005	Alaska Aces	3	Victoria Salmon Kings	5	W	23	11	
January 5, 2006	Victoria Salmon Kings	5	Fresno Falcons	3	W	25	12	
January 6, 2006	Victoria Salmon Kings	3	Fresno Falcons	4	L		22	
January 7, 2006	Victoria Salmon Kings	2	Fresno Falcons	6	L		23	
January 12, 2006	Idaho Steelheads	5	Victoria Salmon Kings	7	W	27	13	
January 13, 2006	Idaho Steelheads	2	Victoria Salmon Kings	3	W	29	14	
January 20, 2006	Bakersfield Condors	2	Victoria Salmon Kings	6	W	31	15	
January 21, 2006	Bakersfield Condors	3	Victoria Salmon Kings	0	L		24	
January 22, 2006	Long Beach Ice Dogs	2	Victoria Salmon Kings	0	L		25	
January 27, 2006	Victoria Salmon Kings	5	Phoenix Roadrunners	5	SOL	32		1
January 28, 2006	Victoria Salmon Kings	0	Phoenix Roadrunners	1	OTL	33		2
February 1, 2006	Victoria Salmon Kings	4	Augusta Lynx	3	W	35	16	
February 3, 2006	Victoria Salmon Kings	3	Augusta Lynx	4	OTL	36		3
February 4, 2006	Victoria Salmon Kings	1	Augusta Lynx	3	L		26	
February 8, 2006	Victoria Salmon Kings	0	Long Beach Ice Dogs	4	L		27	
February 10, 2006	Victoria Salmon Kings	2	Long Beach Ice Dogs	5	L		28	
February 11, 2006	Victoria Salmon Kings	4	Long Beach Ice Dogs	5	OTL	37		4
February 17, 2006	Phoenix Roadrunners	5	Victoria Salmon Kings	3	L		29	
February 18, 2006	San DiegoGulls	4	Victoria Salmon Kings	3	L		30	
February 21, 2006	Las Vegas Wranglers	2	Victoria Salmon Kings	3	W	39	Overtime: 4:20 17	
February 24, 2006	Victoria Salmon Kings	2	Alaska Aces	3	OTL	40		5
February 25, 2006	Victoria Salmon Kings	4	Alaska Aces	3	W	42	18	
March 3, 2006	Victoria Salmon Kings	3	Bakersfield Condors	4	SOL	43		2
March 4, 2006	Victoria Salmon Kings	4	Bakersfield Condors	2	W	45	19	
March 5, 2006	Victoria Salmon Kings	0	Bakersfield Condors	4	L		31	
March 8, 2006	Victoria Salmon Kings	2	Las VegasError! Bookmark not defined. Wranglers	6	L		32	
March 10, 2006	Victoria Salmon Kings	2	Las Vegas Wranglers	3	L		33	
March 11, 2006	Victoria Salmon Kings	1	Las Vegas Wranglers	4	L		34	
March 15, 2006	Victoria Salmon Kings	4	San Diego GullsError! Bookmark not defined.	3	W	47	Overtime: 00:20 20	
March 17, 2006	Victoria Salmon Kings	3	San Diego Gulls	1	W	49	21	
March 18, 2006	Victoria Salmon Kings	3	San Diego Gulls	6	SOL	50		3
March 20, 2006	Phoenix Roadrunners	0	Victoria Salmon Kings	5	W	52	22	
March 22, 2006	Long Beach Ice Dogs	3	Victoria Salmon Kings	4	W	54	23	

Appendix C

Date	Home	Score	Away	Score	Result	Pts	Notes			
March 24, 2006	Stockton Thunder	4	Victoria Salmon Kings	2	L				35	
March 25, 2006	Stockton Thunder	2	Victoria Salmon Kings	3	W	56		24		
March 27, 2006	Fresno Falcons	4	Victoria Salmon Kings	3	OTL	57				6
March 31, 2006	Alaska Aces	3	Victoria Salmon Kings	4	W	59	Overtime	25		
April 1, 2006	Alaska Aces	3	Victoria Salmon Kings	0	L				36	
April 7, 2006	Victoria Salmon Kings	0	Utah Grizzlies	3	L				37	
April 8, 2006	Victoria Salmon Kings	7	Utah Grizzlies	4	W	61		26		
Regular season total								**26**	**37**	**6**	**3**

Victoria Salmon Kings 2006-2007

Date	Home	Score	Away	Score	Result	Pts	Notes	W	L	OTL	SOL
October 20, 2006	Alaska Aces	5	Victoria Salmon Kings	3	L				1		
October 21, 2006	Alaska Aces	4	Victoria Salmon Kings	2	L				2		
October 25, 2006	Victoria Salmon Kings	0	Idaho Steelheads	4	L				3		
October 27, 2006	Victoria Salmon Kings	5	Idaho Steelheads	6	SOL	1					1
October 28, 2006	Victoria Salmon Kings	7	Idaho Steelheads	3	W	3		1			
November 3, 2006	Las Vegas Wranglers	4	Victoria Salmon Kings	2	L				4		
November 4, 2006	Las Vegas Wranglers	4	Victoria Salmon Kings	5	W	5	Overtime: 3:38	2			
November 7, 2006	Las Vegas Wranglers	2	Victoria Salmon Kings	3	W	7	Shootout win	3			
November 9, 2006	Victoria Salmon Kings	6	Fresno Falcons	3	W	9		4			
November 11, 2006	Victoria Salmon Kings	2	Fresno Falcons	5	L				5		
November 12, 2006	Victoria Salmon Kings	4	Fresno Falcons	3	W	11		5			
November 16, 2006	Victoria Salmon Kings	4	Stockton Thunder	3	W	13	Overtime: 4:58	6			
November 17, 2006	Victoria Salmon Kings	3	Stockton Thunder	6	L				6		
November 24, 2006	Utah Grizzlies	7	Victoria Salmon Kings	3	L				7		
November 25, 2006	Utah Grizzlies	3	Victoria Salmon Kings	5	W	15		7			
November 29, 2006	Victoria Salmon Kings	1	Alaska Aces	6	L				8		
December 1, 2006	Victoria Salmon Kings	0	Alaska Aces	3	L				9		
December 2, 2006	Victoria Salmon Kings	6	Alaska Aces	9	L				10		
December 6, 2006	Victoria Salmon Kings	4	Long Beach Ice Dogs	5	L				11		
December 8, 2006	Victoria Salmon Kings	3	Long Beach Ice Dogs	2	W	17		8			
December 9, 2006	Victoria Salmon Kings	3	Long Beach Ice Dogs	1	W	19		9			
December 12, 2006	Phoenix Roadrunners	4	Victoria Salmon Kings	2	L				12		
December 15, 2006	Long Beach Ice Dogs	4	Victoria Salmon Kings	2	L				13		
December 16, 2006	Bakersfield Condors	6	Victoria Salmon Kings	4	L				14		

The History of Professional Hockey in Victoria, BC: 1911-2011

Date	Team	Score	Team	Score	Result			
December 17, 2006	Fresno Falcons	3	Victoria Salmon Kings	1	L		15	
December 21, 2006	Phoenix Roadrunners	4	Victoria Salmon Kings	2	L		16	
December 23, 2006	Phoenix Roadrunners	2	Victoria Salmon Kings	4	L		17	
December 29, 2006	Victoria Salmon Kings	3	Alaska Aces	2	W	21	10	
December 30, 2006	Victoria Salmon Kings	4	Alaska Aces	6	L		18	
January 1, 2007	Victoria Salmon Kings	3	Alaska Aces	2	W	23	11	
January 3, 2007	Long Beach Ice Dogs	4	Victoria Salmon Kings	6	W	25	12	
January 5, 2007	Fresno Falcons	4	Victoria Salmon Kings	1	L		19	
January 6, 2007	Bakersfield Condors	6	Victoria Salmon Kings	4	L		20	
January 7, 2007	Fresno Falcons	3	Victoria Salmon Kings	1	L		21	
January 9, 2007	Las Vegas Wranglers	1	Victoria Salmon Kings	3	W	27	13	
January 12, 2007	Alaska Aces	3	Victoria Salmon Kings	2	L		22	
January 13, 3007	Alaska Aces	5	Victoria Salmon Kings	1	L		23	
January 14, 2007	Alaska Aces	7	Victoria Salmon Kings	2	L		24	
January 19, 2006	Victoria Salmon Kings	1	Bakersfield Condors	8	L		25	
January 20, 2007	Victoria Salmon Kings	6	Bakersfield Condors	5	W	29	14	
January 22, 2006	Victoria Salmon Kings	2	Bakersfield Condors	4	L		26	
January 24, 2007	Long Beach Ice Dogs	1	Victoria Salmon Kings	3	W	31	15	
January 26, 2007	Bakersfield Condors	3	Victoria Salmon Kings	4	W	33	16	
January 27, 2006	Bakersfield Condors	5	Victoria Salmon Kings	7	W	35	Overtime: 4:16	17
January 28, 2007	Long Beach Ice Dogs	5	Victoria Salmon Kings	6	W	37	18	
February 2, 2007	Victoria Salmon Kings	3	Idaho Steelheads	1	W	39	19	
February 3, 2007	Victoria Salmon Kings	2	Idaho Steelheads	6	L		27	
February 7, 2007	Idaho Steelheads	2	Victoria Salmon Kings	1	L		28	
February 9, 2007	Idaho Steelheads	3	Victoria Salmon Kings	6	W	41	20	
February 10, 2007	Idaho Steelheads	2	Victoria Salmon Kings	0	L		29	
February 14, 2007	Victoria Salmon Kings	4	Stockton Thunder	0	W	43	21	
February 16, 2007	Victoria Salmon Kings	6	Stockton Thunder	3	W	45	22	
February 17, 2007	Victoria Salmon Kings	4	Stockton Thunder	3	W	47	Overtime: 00:47	23
February 21, 2007	Victoria Salmon Kings	0	Las Vegas Wranglers	5	L		30	
February 23, 2007	Victoria Salmon Kings	3	Las Vegas Wranglers	2	W	49	Shootout win	24
February 24, 2007	Victoria Salmon Kings	0	Las Vegas Wranglers	3	L		31	
March 2, 2007	Fresno Falcons	1	Victoria Salmon Kings	3	W	51	25	
March 3, 2007	Fresno Falcons	3	Victoria Salmon Kings	4	W	53	Shootout win	26
March 7, 2007	Stockton Thunder	2	Victoria Salmon Kings	1	OTL	54		1
March 9, 2007	Stockton Thunder	5	Victoria Salmon Kings	4	SOL	55		2
March 10, 2007	StocktonThunder	4	Victoria Salmon Kings	3	SOL	56		3

Appendix C

Date	Home	Score	Away	Score	Result	Pts	Notes	W	L	OTL	SOL
March 15, 2007	Victoria Salmon Kings	6	Utah Grizzlies	3	W	58		27			
March 17, 2007	Victoria Salmon Kings	2	Utah Grizzlies	3	L				32		
March 18, 2007	Victoria Salmon Kings	4	Utah Grizzlies	1	W	60		28			
March 23, 2007	Victoria Salmon Kings	5	Long Beach Ice Dogs	1	W	62		29			
March 24, 2007	Victoria Salmon Kings	4	Long Beach Ice Dogs	1	W	64		30			
March 28, 2007	UtahGrizzlies	1	Victoria Salmon Kings	7	W	66		31			
March 30, 2007	Utah Grizzlies	3	Victoria Salmon Kings	4	W	68	Overtime: 4:19	33			
March 31, 2007	Utah Grizzlies	1	Victoria Salmon Kings	5	W	70		34			
April 4, 2007	Victoria Salmon Kings	6	Phoenix Roadrunners	4	W	72		34			
April 6, 2007	Victoria Salmon Kings	4	Phoenix Roadrunners	1	W	74		35			
April 7, 2007	Victoria Salmon Kings	6	Phoenix Roadrunners	1	W	76		36			
Regular season total								**36**	**32**	**1**	**3**

PLAYOFFS—ROUND ONE

Date	Home	Score	Away	Score							
April 9, 2007	Alaska Aces	2	Victoria Salmon Kings	3							
April 10, 2007	Alaska Aces	7	Victoria Salmon Kings	1							
April 12, 2007	Victoria Salmon Kings	2	Alaska Aces	5							
April 13, 2007	Victoria Salmon Kings	2	Alaska Aces	5							
April 14, 2007	Victoria Salmon Kings	9	AlaskaAces	4							
April 16, 2007	Alaska Aces	5	Victoria Salmon Kings	2							

LOST SERIES, 4-2

Victoria Salmon Kings 2007-2008

Date	Home	Score	Away	Score	Result	Pts	Notes	W	L	OTL	SOL
October 19, 2007	Idaho Steelheads	1	Victoria Salmon Kings	2	W	2	Overtime: 1:02	1			
October 20, 2007	Idaho Steelheads	4	Victoria Salmon Kings	2	L				1		
October 26, 2007	Victoria Salmon Kings	3	Las VegasWranglers	4	L				2		
October 27, 2007	Victoria Salmon Kings	4	Las Vegas Wranglers	3	W	4		2			
October 31, 2007	Victoria Salmon Kings	3	Bakersfield Condors	2	W	6		3			
November 2, 2007	Victoria Salmon Kings	7	Bakersfield Condors	4	W	8		4			
November 3, 2007	Victoria Salmon Kings	5	Bakersfield Condors	4	W	10	Shootout win	5			
November 9, 2007	Utah Grizzlies	7	Victoria Salmon Kings	1	L				3		
November 10, 2007	Utah Grizzlies	1	Victoria Salmon Kings	2	W	12		6			
November 12, 2007	Utah Grizzlies	0	Victoria Salmon Kings	1	W	14		7			
November 4, 2007	Victoria Salmon Kings	7	Stockton Thunder	4	W	16		8			
November 16, 2007	Victoria Salmon Kings	4	Stockton Thunder	3	W	18		9			

The History of Professional Hockey in Victoria, BC: 1911-2011

Date	Team 1	Score	Team 2	Score	Result			
November 17, 2007	Victoria Salmon Kings	2	Stockton Thunder	1	W	20	Overtime: 2:00	10
November 21, 2007	IdahoSteelheads	1	Victoria Salmon Kings	4	W	22		11
November 23, 2007	IdahoSteelheads	5	Victoria Salmon Kings	1	L			4
November 24, 2007	Idaho Steelheads	3	Victoria Salmon Kings	0	L			5
November 28, 2007	Victoria Salmon Kings	4	Phoenix Roadrunners	2	W	24	Overtime: 3:08	12
November 29, 2007	Victoria Salmon Kings	4	PhoenixRoadrunners	3	W	26	Shootout win	13
November 30, 2007	Victoria Salmon Kings	5	Phoenix Roadrunners	4	W	28	Overtime: 1:00	14
December 6, 2007	Phoenix Roadrunners	4	Victoria Salmon Kings	5	W	30	Shootout win	15
December 7, 2007	Phoenix Roadrunners	3	Victoria Salmon Kings	2	L			6
December 14, 2007	Fresno Falcons	5	Victoria Salmon Kings	2	L			7
December 15, 2007	Bakersfield Condors	2	Victoria Salmon Kings	3	W	32		16
December 16, 2007	Fresno Falcons	3	Victoria Salmon Kings	7	W	34		17
December 19, 2007	Victoria Salmon Kings	3	Alaska Aces	4	SOL	35		1
December 21, 2007	Victoria Salmon Kings	8	Alaska Aces	1	W	37		18
December 22, 2007	Victoria Salmon Kings	3	Alaska Aces	4	SOL	38		2
December 28, 2007	Stockton Thunder	3	Victoria Salmon Kings	5	W	40		19
December 29, 2007	Fresno Falcons	3	Victoria Salmon Kings	4	W	42	Shootout win	20
December 30, 2007	Fresno Falcons	5	Victoria Salmon Kings	3	L			8
January 3, 2008	Victoria Salmon Kings	5	Utah Grizzlies	2	W	44		21
January 5, 2008	Victoria Salmon Kings	2	Utah Grizzlies	1	OTL	45		1
January 6, 2008	Victoria Salmon Kings	3	Utah Grizzlies	2	OTL	46		2
January 11, 2008	Las Vegas Wranglers	5	Victoria Salmon Kings	0	L			9
January 12, 2008	Las Vegas Wranglers	1	Victoria Salmon Kings	3	W	48		22
January 15, 2008	Victoria Salmon Kings	1	BakersfieldCondors	5	L			10
January 16, 2008	Victoria Salmon Kings	5	Bakersfield Condors	4	W	50	Overtime: 00:29	23
January 18, 2008	Victoria Salmon Kings	6	Fresno Falcons	5	W	52	Shootout win	24
January 19, 2008	Victoria Salmon Kings	2	Fresno Falcons	3	OTL	53		3
January 20, 2008	Victoria Salmon Kings	3	Fresno Falcons	2	W	55		25
January 25, 2008	Alaska Aces	2	Victoria Salmon Kings	0	L			11
January 26, 2008	Alaska Aces	1	Victoria Salmon Kings	4	W	57		26
January 27, 2008	Alaska Aces	5	Victoria Salmon Kings	7	W	59		27
February 5, 2008	Bakersfield Condors	6	Victoria Salmon Kings	7	W	61	Shootout win	28
February 7, 2008	Stockton Thunder	3	Victoria Salmon Kings	4	W	63		29
February 8, 2008	Bakersfield Condors	7	Victoria Salmon Kings	5	L			12
February 11, 2008	Victoria Salmon Kings	2	Fresno Falcons	3	L			13
February 12, 2008	Victoria Salmon Kings	6	Fresno Falcons	5	W	65	Overtime: 00:19	30
February 15, 2008	Las Vegas Wranglers	2	Victoria Salmon Kings	3	W	67		31

Appendix C

Date	Team	Score	Opponent	Score	Result				
February 16, 2008	Las Vegas Wranglers	5	Victoria Salmon Kings	3	L			14	
February 18, 2008	Phoenix Roadrunners	4	Victoria Salmon Kings	6	W	69		32	
February 20, 2008	Victoria Salmon Kings	2	Idaho Steelheads	3	L			15	
February 22, 2008	Victoria Salmon Kings	6	Idaho Steelheads	0	W	71		33	
February 23, 2008	Victoria Salmon Kings	2	Idaho Steelheads	4	L			16	
February 27, 2008	Victoria Salmon Kings	5	Las Vegas Wranglers	4	W	73		34	
February 29, 2008	Victoria Salmon Kings	5	Las Vegas Wranglers	4	W	75	Overtime: 4:59	35	
March 1, 2008	Victoria Salmon Kings	4	Las Vegas Wranglers	6	L			17	
March 7, 2008	Alaska Aces	3	Victoria Salmon Kings	2	L			18	
March 8, 2008	Alaska Aces	4	Victoria Salmon Kings	3	L			19	
March 9, 2008	Alaska Aces	3	Victoria Salmon Kings	4	W	77		36	
March 14, 2008	Phoenix Roadrunners	4	Victoria Salmon Kings	1	L			20	
March 16, 2008	Phoenix Roadrunners	6	Victoria Salmon Kings	1	L			21	
March 19, 2008	Victoria Salmon Kings	7	Utah Grizzlies	3	W	79		37	
March 21, 2008	Victoria Salmon Kings	4	Utah Grizzlies	0	W	81		38	
March 22, 2008	Victoria Salmon Kings	3	Utah Grizzlies	2	W	83	Shootout win	39	
March 26, 2008	Stockton Thunder	6	Victoria Salmon Kings	7	W	85		40	
March 28, 3008	Bakersfield Condors	6	Victoria Salmon Kings	3	L			22	
March 29, 2008	Stockton Thunder	3	Victoria Salmon Kings	2	SOL	86			3
March 30, 2008	Fresno Falcons	5	Victoria Salmon Kings	4	OTL	87			4
April 2, 2008	Victoria Salmon Kings	4	Alaska Aces	6	L			23	
April 4, 2008	Victoria Salmon Kings	2	Alaska Aces	0	W	89		41	
April 5, 2008	Victoria Salmon Kings	4	Alaska Aces	1	W	91		42	
Regular season totals								42 23	4 3

PLAYOFFS - ROUND ONE

Date	Team	Score	Opponent	Score	Result		
April 10, 2007	Victoria Salmon Kings	1	Bakersfield Condors	2	OTL		
April 12, 2007	Victoria Salmon Kings	4	Bakersfield Condors	3	W		
April 15, 2007	Bakersfield Condors	2	Victoria Salmon Kings	3	W	Overtime: 2:51	
April 16, 2007	Bakersfield Condors	1	Victoria Salmon Kings	4	W		
April 19, 2007	Bakersfield Condors	5	Victoria Salmon Kings	4	L		
April 22, 2007	Victoria Salmon Kings	6	Bakersfield Condors	5	W	Overtime: 7:59	

WON FIRST FOUND OF THE PLAYOFFS, 4-1

PLAYOFFS—ROUND TWO

Date	Team	Score	Opponent	Score	Result
April 24, 2007	Victoria Salmon Kings	0	Idaho Steelheads	6	L
April 27, 2007	Victoria Salmon Kings	6	Idaho Steelheads	1	W
May 1, 2008	Utah Grizzlies	7	Victoria Salmon Kings	5	L
May 2, 2008	Utah Grizzlies	2	Victoria Salmon Kings	0	L

The History of Professional Hockey in Victoria, BC: 1911-2011

May 4, 2008	Utah Grizzlies	8	Victoria Salmon Kings	3	L
May 6, 2008	Victoria Salmon Kings		Idaho Steelheads		

LOST SECOND ROUND OF THE PLAYOFFS. ELIMINATED FROM FURTHER COMPETITION

Victoria Salmon Kings 2008-2009

Date	Home	Score	Away	Score	Result	Pts	Notes	W	L	OTL	SOL
October 17, 2008	Phoenix Roadrunners	7	Victoria Salmon Kings	1	L				1		
October 18, 2008	Phoenix Roadrunners	2	Victoria Salmon Kings	1	L				2		
October 19, 2008	Phoenix Roadrunners	2	Victoria Salmon Kings	4	W	2		1			
October 24, 2008	Victoria Salmon Kings	2	Stockton Thunder	5	L				3		
October 25, 2008	Victoria Salmon Kings	5	Stockton Thunder	2	W	4		2			
October 26, 2008	Victoria Salmon Kings	1	Stockton Thunder	3	L				4		
October 29, 2008	Victoria Salmon Kings	4	Utah Grizzlies	3	W	6		3			
October 31, 2008	Victoria Salmon Kings	2	Utah Grizzlies	3	L				5		
November 1, 2008	Victoria Salmon Kings	3	Utah Grizzlies	4	L				6		
November 5, 2008	Bakersfield Condors	0	Victoria Salmon Kings	3	W	8		4			
November 7, 2008	Stockton Thunder	3	Victoria Salmon Kings	2	SOL	9					1
November 8, 2008	Stockton Thunder	1	Victoria Salmon Kings	3	W	11		5			
November 14, 2008	Victoria Salmon Kings	4	Phoenix Roadrunners	1	W	13		6			
November 15, 2008	Victoria Salmon Kings	9	Phoenix Roadrunners	0	W	15		7			
November 19, 2008	Victoria Salmon Kings	3	Alaska Aces	6	L				7		
November 21, 2008	Victoria Salmon Kings	3	Alaska Aces	1	W	17		8			
November 22, 2008	Victoria Salmon Kings	3	Alaska Aces	4	OTL	18				1	
November 26, 2008	Utah Grizzlies	2	Victoria Salmon Kings	4	W	20		9			
November 28, 2008	Utah Grizzlies	2	Victoria Salmon Kings	3	W	22		10			
November 29, 2008	Utah Grizzlies	1	Victoria Salmon Kings	2	W	24		11			
December 3, 2008	Ontario Reign	3	Victoria Salmon Kings	2	L				8		
December 5, 2008	Fresno Falcons	3	Victoria Salmon Kings	2	L				9		
December 6, 2008	Fresno Falcons	1	Victoria Salmon Kings	5	W	26		12			
December 7, 2008	Ontario Reign	2	Victoria Salmon Kings	3	W	28		13			
December 9, 2008	Victoria Salmon Kings	2	Bakersfield Condors	0	W	30		14			
December 12, 2008	Victoria Salmon Kings	7	Phoenix Roadrunners	0	W	32		15			
December 14, 2008	Victoria Salmon Kings	6	Phoenix Roadrunners	2	W	34		16			
December 17, 2008	Victoria Salmon Kings	4	Alaska Aces	2	W	36		17			
December 19, 2008	Victoria Salmon Kings	4	Alaska Aces	0	W	38		18			

Date	Team 1	Score	Team 2	Score	Result				
December 20, 2008	Victoria Salmon Kings	5	Alaska Aces	3	W	40		19	
December 27, 2008	Stockton Thunder	1	Victoria Salmon Kings	7	W	42		20	
December 28, 2008	Stockton Thunder	2	Victoria Salmon Kings	5	W	44		21	
January 2, 2009	Victoria Salmon Kings	5	Bakersfield Condors	2	W	46		22	
January 3, 2009	Victoria Salmon Kings	2	Bakersfield Condors	1	W	48		23	
January 4, 2009	Victoria Salmon Kings	6	Bakersfield Condors	1	W	50		24	
January 9, 2009	Victoria Salmon Kings	5	Ontario Reign	2	W	52		25	
January 10, 2009	Victoria Salmon Kings	5	Ontario Reign	2	W	54		26	
January 14, 2009	Alaska Aces	3	Victoria Salmon Kings	2	SOL	55			2
January 16, 2009	Alaska Aces	5	Victoria Salmon Kings	3	L			10	
January 17, 2009	Alaska Aces	1	Victoria Salmon Kings	0	SOL	56			3
January 23, 2009	Las VegasWranglers	1	Victoria Salmon Kings	2	W	58		27	
January 24, 2009	Las Vegas Wranglers	2	Victoria Salmon Kings	4	W	60		28	
January 24, 2009	Las Vegas Wranglers	6	Victoria Salmon Kings	2	L			11	
January 27, 2009	Victoria Salmon Kings	7	Stockton Thunder	3	W	62		29	
January 28, 2009	Victoria Salmon Kings	0	Stockton Thunder	2	L			12	
February 4, 2009	Victoria Salmon Kings	2	Las Vegas Wranglers	4	L			13	
February 6, 2009	Victoria Salmon Kings	2	Las Vegas Wranglers	4	L			14	
February 7, 2009	Victoria Salmon Kings	1	Las Vegas Wranglers	2	L			15	
February 8, 2009	Victoria Salmon Kings	0	Las Vegas Wranglers	1	OTL	63			2
February 11, 2009	Alaska Aces	4	Victoria Salmon Kings	3	L			16	
February 13, 2009	Alaska Aces	1	Victoria Salmon Kings	2	W	65		30	
February 14, 2009	Alaska Aces	3	Victoria Salmon Kings	2	SOL	66			4
February 15, 2009	AlaskaAces	2	Victoria Salmon Kings	5	L			17	
February 18, 2009	Ontario Reign	5	Victoria Salmon Kings	3	L			18	
February 21, 2009	Bakersfield Condors	3	Victoria Salmon Kings	4	W	68	Shootout win	31	
February 22, 2009	Bakersfield Condors	5	Victoria Salmon Kings	2	L			19	
February 23, 2009	Ontario Reign	5	Victoria Salmon Kings	2	L			20	
March 4, 2009	Idaho Steelheads	3	Victoria Salmon Kings	2	L			21	
March 6, 2009	Idaho Steelheads	6	Victoria Salmon Kings	5	L			22	
March 7, 2009	Idaho Steelheads	4	Victoria Salmon Kings	1	L			23	
March 11, 2009	Victoria Salmon Kings	9	Ontario Reign	4	W	70		32	
March 13, 2009	Victoria Salmon Kings	3	Ontario Reign=	4	L			24	
March 14, 2009	Victoria Salmon Kings	4	Ontario Reign	3	W	72		33	
March 15, 2009	Victoria Salmon Kings	3	Ontario Reign	1	W	74		34	
March 18, 2009	Victoria Salmon Kings	3	Idaho Steelheads	4	SOL	75			5
March 20, 2009	Victoria Salmon Kings	2	Idaho Steelheads	0	W	77		35	

The History of Professional Hockey in Victoria, BC: 1911-2011

March 21, 2009	Victoria Salmon Kings	1	Idaho Steelheads	7	L			25	
March 22, 2009	Victoria Salmon Kings	2	Idaho Steelheads	4	L			26	
March 24, 2009	Stockton Thunder	2	Victoria Salmon Kings	5	W	79		36	
March 25, 2009	Bakersfield Condors	3	Victoria Salmon Kings	5	W	81		37	
March 27, 2009	Bakersfield Condors	7	Victoria Salmon Kings	3	L			27	
March 28, 2009	Stockton Thunder	4	Victoria Salmon Kings	5	W	83	Overtime: 00:44	38	
Regular season total								38	27	2	5

PLAYOFFS—ROUND ONE

April 11, 2009	Idaho Steelheads	1	Victoria Salmon Kings	3	W
April 12, 2007	Idaho Steelheads	0	Bakersfield Condors	2	W
April 15, 2007	Victoria Salmon Kings	9	Idaho Steelheads	2	W
April 17, 2009	Victoria Salmon Kings	2	Idaho Steelheads	1	W

WON FIRST FOUND OF THE PLAYOFFS, 4-0

PLAYOFFS—ROUND TWO

April 24, 2007	Alaska Aces	3	Victoria Salmon Kings	0	L
April 25, 2007	Alaska Aces	8	Victoria Salmon Kings	2	L
April 29, 2009	Victoria Salmon Kings	2	Alaska Aces	5	L
May 1, 2009	Victoria Salmon Kings	4	Alaska Aces	0	W
May 4, 2008	Victoria Salmon Kings	4	Alaska Aces	6	L

LOST SECOND ROUND, 4-1; ELIMINATED FROM PLAYOFFS

Victoria Salmon Kings 2009-2010

Date	Home	Score	Away	Score	Result	Pts	Notes	W	L	OTL	SOL
October 16, 2009	Alaska Aces	2	Victoria Salmon Kings	1	L				1		
October 17, 2009	Alaska Aces	5	Victoria Salmon Kings	3	L				2		
October 19, 2009	Alaska Aces	2	Victoria Salmon Kings	1	L				3		
October 21, 2009	Victoria Salmon Kings	1	Bakersfield Condors	3	L				4		
October 23, 2009	Victoria Salmon Kings	3	Bakersfield Condors	0	W	2		1			
October 24, 2009	Victoria Salmon Kings	1	Bakersfield Condors	4	L				5		
October 30, 2009	Victoria Salmon Kings	1	Stockton Thunder	5	L				6		
November 1, 2009	Victoria Salmon Kings	2	Stockton Thunder	5	L				7		
November 6, 2009	Ontario Reign	4	Victoria Salmon Kings	1	L				8		
November 7, 2009	Ontario Reign	4	Victoria Salmon Kings	3	L				9		
November 11, 2009	Victoria Salmon Kings	2	Ontario Reign	0	W	4		2			
November 13, 2009	Victoria Salmon Kings	2	Ontario Reign	4	L				10		

Appendix C

Date	Team 1	Score	Team 2	Score	Result				
November 14, 2009	Victoria Salmon Kings	4	Ontario Reign	0	W	6		3	
November 18, 2009	Idaho Steelheads	3	Victoria Salmon Kings	5	W	8		4	
November 20, 2009	Idaho Steelheads	4	Victoria Salmon Kings	0	L			11	
November 21, 2009	Idaho Steelheads	5	Victoria Salmon Kings	4	OTL	9			1
November 27, 2009	Victoria Salmon Kings	2	Ontario Reign	1	W	11		5	
November 28, 2009	Victoria Salmon Kings	5	Ontario Reign	0	W	13		6	
December 1, 2009	Las Vegas Wranglers	4	Victoria Salmon Kings	3	OTL	14			2
December 3, 2009	Las Vegas Wranglers	7	Victoria Salmon Kings	5	L			12	
December 4, 2009	Las Vegas Wranglers	2	Victoria Salmon Kings	1	L			13	
December 6, 2009	Ontario Reign	2	Victoria Salmon Kings	1	OTL	15			3
December 10, 2009	Victoria Salmon Kings	4	Las Vegas Wranglers	2	W	17		7	
December 11, 2009	Victoria Salmon Kings	4	Las Vegas Wranglers	2	W	19		8	
December 12, 2009	Victoria Salmon Kings	5	Las Vegas Wranglers	4	W	21		9	
December 16, 2009	Victoria Salmon Kings	7	Stockton Thunder	2	W	23		10	
December 18, 2009	Victoria Salmon Kings	2	Stockton Thunder	0	W	25		11	
December 19, 2009	Victoria Salmon Kings	4	Stockton Thunder	3	W	27		12	
December 27, 2009	Victoria Salmon Kings	7	Alaska Aces	3	W	29		13	
December 28, 2009	Victoria Salmon Kings	5	Alaska Aces	4	W	31		14	
December 30, 2009	Utah Grizzlies	4	Victoria Salmon Kings	5	W	33		15	
December 31, 2009	Utah Grizzlies	2	Victoria Salmon Kings	3	W	35		16	
January 2, 2010	Alaska Aces	2	Victoria Salmon Kings	6	W	37		17	
January 3, 2010	Alaska Aces	2	Victoria Salmon Kings	3	W	39		18	
January 4, 2010	Alaska Aces	5	Victoria Salmon Kings	3	L			14	
January 8, 2010	Victoria Salmon Kings	5	Idaho Steelheads	2	W	41		19	
January 9, 2010	Victoria Salmon Kings	2	Idaho Steelheads	8	L			15	
January 12, 2009	Victoria Salmon Kings	5	Las Vegas Wranglers	3	W	43		20	
January 13, 2009	Victoria Salmon Kings	6	Las VegasWranglers	4	W	45		21	
January 15, 2010	Victoria Salmon Kings	6	Bakersfield Condors	3	W	47		22	
January 16, 2010	Victoria Salmon Kings	6	Bakersfield Condors	5	W	49	Shootout win	23	
January 22, 2010	Bakersfield Condors	4	Victoria Salmon Kings	3	OTL	50			4
January 23, 2010	Bakersfield Condors	1	Victoria Salmon Kings	2	W	52		24	
January 27, 2010	Stockton Thunder	7	Victoria Salmon Kings	3	L			16	
January 29, 2010	Stockton Thunder	7	Victoria Salmon Kings	1	L			17	
January 30, 2010	Stockton Thunder	0	Victoria Salmon Kings	1	W	54		25	
February 2, 3010	Victoria Salmon Kings	7	Utah Grizzlies	6	W	56		26	
February 5, 2010	Victoria Salmon Kings	3	Utah Grizzlies	4	SOL	57			1
February 6, 2010	Victoria Salmon Kings	3	Utah Grizzlies	2	W	59		27	

469

The History of Professional Hockey in Victoria, BC: 1911-2011

February 11, 2010	Victoria Salmon Kings	6	Alaska Aces	2	W	61	28	
February 13, 2010	Victoria Salmon Kings	5	Alaska Aces	3	L		18	
February 14, 2010	Victoria Salmon Kings	5	Alaska Aces	1	W	63	29	
February 17, 2010	Utah Grizzlies	3	Victoria Salmon Kings	2	SOL	64		2
February 19, 2010	Utah Grizzlies	2	Victoria Salmon Kings	5	W	66	30	
February 20, 2010	Utah Grizzlies	3	Victoria Salmon Kings	1	L		19	
February 26, 2010	Bakersfield Condors	3	Victoria Salmon Kings	2	L		20	
February 27, 2010	Bakersfield Condors	4	Victoria Salmon Kings	2	L		21	
Much 3, 2010	Stockton Thunder	4	Victoria Salmon King	1	L		22	
March 5, 2010	Stockton Thunder	3	Victoria Salmon Kings	5	W	68	31	
March 6, 2010	Stockton Thunder	7	Victoria Salmon Kings	3	L		23	
March 10, 2010	Victoria Salmon Kings	5	Idaho Steelheads	2	L		24	
March 12, 2010	Victoria Salmon Kings	1	Idaho Steelheads	7	L		25	
March 13, 2010	Victoria Salmon Kings	3	Idaho Steelheads	5	L		26	
March 17, 2010	Stockton Thunder	7	Victoria Salmon Kings	2	L		27	
March 19, 2010	Bakersfield Condors	1	Victoria Salmon Kings	5	W	70	32	
March 20, 2010	Bakersfield Condors	3	Victoria Salmon Kings	2	L		28	
March 24, 2010	Idaho Steelheads	5	Victoria Salmon Kings	0	L		29	
March 26, 2010	Idaho Steelheads	0	Victoria Salmon Kings	1	W	72	33	
March 27, 2010	Idaho Steelheads	5	Victoria Salmon Kings	1	L		30	
March 31, 2010	Victoria Salmon Kings	1	Utah Grizzlies	2	L		31	
April 2, 2010	Victoria Salmon Kings	9	Utah Grizzlies	2	W	74	34	
April 3, 2010	Victoria Salmon Kings	2	Utah Grizzlies	5	L		32	
Regular season total							34 32 4 2	

PLAYOFFS—ROUND ONE

April 7, 2010	Victoria Salmon Kings	6	Bakersfield Condors	3	W	
April 8, 2010	Victoria Salmon Kings	2	Bakersfield Condors	4	L	
April 10, 2010	Bakersfield Condors	3	Victoria Salmon Kings	1	L	
April 15, 2007	Bakersfield Condors	5	Victoria Salmon Kings	2	L	
April 17, 2009	Bakersfield Condors	2	Victoria Salmon Kings	1	L	

LOST FIRST ROUND OF THE PLAYOFFS, 4-1

Appendix C

Victoria Salmon Kings 2010-2011

Date	Home	Score	Away	Score	Results	Pts	Notes	W	L	OTL	SOL
October 15, 2010	Idaho Steelheads	5	Victoria Salmon Kings	0	L				1		
October 16, 2010	Idaho Steelheads	0	Victoria Salmon Kings	4	W	2		1			
October 22, 2010	Las Vegas Wranglers	1	Victoria Salmon Kings	3	W	4		2			
October 23, 2010	Las Vegas Wranglers	3	Victoria Salmon Kings	1	L				2		
October 27, 2010	Victoria Salmon Kings	5	Ontario Reign	2	W	6		3			
October 29, 2010	Victoria Salmon Kings	6	Ontario Reign	3	W	8		4			
October 30, 2010	Victoria Salmon Kings	4	Ontario Reign	1	W	10		5			
November 3, 2010	Victoria Salmon Kings	3	Idaho Steelheads	2	W	12		6			
November 5, 2010	Victoria Salmon Kings	2	Idaho Steelheads	5	L				3		
November 6, 2010	Victoria Salmon Kings	2	Idaho Steelheads	4	L				4		
November 11, 2010	Las Vegas Wranglers	4	Victoria Salmon Kings	2	L				5		
November 12, 2010	Las Vegas Wranglers	3	Victoria Salmon Kings	1	L				6		
November 13, 2010	Las Vegas Wranglers	3	Victoria Salmon Kings	1	L				7		
November 17, 2010	Bakersfield Condors	3	Victoria Salmon Kings	1	L				8		
November 19, 2010	Ontario Reign	3	Victoria Salmon Kings	4	W	14		7			
November 20, 2010	Bakersfield Condors	1	Victoria Salmon Kings	4	W	16		8			
November 21, 2010	Stockton Thunder	1	Victoria Salmon Kings	4	W	18		9			
November 24, 2010	Victoria Salmon Kings	1	Idaho Steelheads	2	L				9		
November 26, 2010	Victoria Salmon Kings	4	Idaho Steelheads	6	L				10		
November 27, 2010	Victoria Salmon Kings	3	Idaho Steelheads	6	L				11		
December 1, 2010	Victoria Salmon Kings	2	Stockton Thunder	3	SOL	19					1
December 3, 2010	Victoria Salmon Kings	3	Stockton Thunder	5	L				12		
December 4, 2010	Victoria Salmon Kings	4	Stockton Thunder	5	OTL	20				1	
December 8, 2010	Alaska Aces	1	Victoria Salmon Kings	3	W	22		10			
December 9, 2010	Alaska Aces	2	Victoria Salmon Kings	3	SOL	23					2
December 15, 2010	Idaho Steelheads	4	Victoria Salmon Kings	1	L				13		
December 17, 2010	Idaho Steelheads	3	Victoria Salmon Kings	4	W	25		11			
December 18, 2010	Utah Grizzlies	3	Victoria Salmon Kings	4	W	27		12			
December 28, 2010	Victoria Salmon Kings	3	Ontario Reign	6	L				14		
December 29, 2010	Victoria Salmon Kings	8	Ontario Reign	4	W	29		13			
December 31, 2010	UtahGrizzlies	1	Victoria Salmon Kings	0	L				15		
January 1, 2011	UtahGrizzlies	2	Victoria Salmon Kings	0	L				16		
January 5, 2011	Victoria Salmon Kings	2	Stockton Thunder	3	L				17		
January 7, 2011	Victoria Salmon Kings	4	Stockton Thunder	2	W	31		14			

The History of Professional Hockey in Victoria, BC: 1911-2011

Date	Team 1		Team 2		Result			
January 8, 2011	Victoria Salmon Kings	1	Stockton Thunder	3	L			18
January 11, 2011	Victoria Salmon Kings	4	Las Vegas Wranglers	6	L			19
January 12, 2011	Victoria Salmon Kings	3	Las Vegas Wranglers	5	L			20
January 14, 2011	Idaho Steelheads	5	Victoria Salmon Kings	6	W	33	Overtime: 1:53	15
January 15, 2011	Idaho Steelheads	6	Victoria Salmon Kings	1	L			21
January 16, 2011	Idaho Steelheads	0	Victoria Salmon Kings	4	W	35		16
January 21, 2011	Alaska Aces	1	Victoria Salmon Kings	4	W	37		17
January 21, 2011	Alaska Aces	6	Victoria Salmon Kings	1	L			22
January 28, 2011	Victoria Salmon Kings	1	Las Vegas Wranglers	4	L			23
January 29, 2011	Victoria Salmon Kings	2	Las Vegas Wranglers	4	L			24
January 30, 2011	Victoria Salmon Kings	4	Las Vegas Wranglers	2	W	39		18
February 2, 2011	Victoria Salmon Kings	6	Alaska Aces	3	W	41		19
February 4, 2011	Victoria Salmon Kings	6	Alaska Aces	2	W	43		20
February 5, 2011	Victoria Salmon Kings	1	Alaska Aces	3	L			25
February 11, 2011	Las Vegas Wranglers	0	Victoria Salmon Kings	2	W	45		21
February 13, 2011	Las Vegas Wranglers	2	Victoria Salmon Kings	4	W	47		22
February 15, 2011	Bakersfield Condors	2	Victoria Salmon Kings	7	W	49		23
February 18, 2011	Stockton Thunder	1	Victoria Salmon Kings	3	W	51		24
February 19, 2011	Stockton Thunder	8	Victoria Salmon Kings	1	L			26
February 20, 2011	Stockton Thunder	4	Victoria Salmon Kings	0	L			27
February 25, 2011	Victoria Salmon Kings	6	Utah Grizzlies	2	W	53		25
February 26, 2011	Victoria Salmon Kings	6	Utah Grizzlies	5	W	55	Shootout win	26
March 2, 2011	Victoria Salmon Kings	3	Bakersfield Condors	0	W	57		27
March 4, 2011	Victoria Salmon Kings	1	Bakersfield Condors	2	L			28
March 5, 2011	Victoria Salmon Kings	2	Bakersfield Condors	5	L			29
March 9, 2011	Alaska Aces	5	Victoria Salmon Kings	3	L			30
March 11, 2011	Alaska Aces	6	Victoria Salmon Kings	1	L			31
March 12, 2011	Alaska Aces	3	Victoria Salmon Kings	1	L			32
March 16, 2011	Victoria Salmon Kings	9	Utah Grizzlies	2	W	59		28
March 18, 2011	Victoria Salmon Kings	5	Utah Grizzlies	2	W	61		29
March 19, 2011	Victoria Salmon Kings	2	Utah Grizzlies	3	OTL	62		2
March 23, 2011	Bakersfield Condors	2	Victoria Salmon Kings	1	L			33
March 25, 2011	Stockton Thunder	6	Victoria Salmon Kings	7	W	64		30
March 26, 2011	Stockton Thunder	3	Victoria Salmon Kings	4	W	66		31
March 27, 2011	Stockton Thunder	8	Victoria Salmon Kings	4	L			34

Appendix C

March 30, 2011	Victoria Salmon Kings	2	Alaska Aces	4	L			35	
April 1, 2011	Victoria Salmon Kings	3	Alaska Aces	1	W	68	32		
April 2, 2011	Victoria Salmon Kings	1	Alaska Aces	4	L			36	
Regular season total							32	36	2	2

PLAYOFFS—ROUND ONE

April 4, 2011	Victoria Salmon Kings	3	Bakersfield Condors	1	W
April 5, 2011	Victoria Salmon Kings	6	Bakersfield Condors	3	L
April 8, 2011	Bakersfield Condors	0	Victoria Salmon Kings	2	W
April 9, 2011	Bakersfield Condors	2	Victoria Salmon Kings	3	W

WON FIRST ROUND OF THE PLAYOFFS, 3-1

PLAYOFFS—ROUND TWO

April 15, 2011	Utah Grizzlies	2	Victoria Salmon Kings	4	W
April 16, 2011	Utah Grizzlies	2	Victoria Salmon Kings	4	W
April 20, 2011	Victoria Salmon Kings	3	Utah Grizzlies	2	W
April 22, 2011	Victoria Salmon Kings	2	Utah Grizzlies	1	W

WON SECOND ROUND OF THE PLAYOFFS, 4-0

PLAYOFFS—ROUND THREE

April 27, 2011	AlaskaAces	1	Victoria Salmon Kings	0	L
April 28, 2011	AlaskaAces	4	Victoria Salmon Kings	3	L
April 30, 2011	Victoria Salmon Kings	2	Alaska Aces	6	L
May 2, 2011	Victoria Salmon Kings	2	Alaska Aces	3	L

LOST THIRD ROUND OF THE PLAYOFFS, 4-0

LIKELY THE END OF PROFESSIONAL HOCKEY IN VICTORIA

SOURCES

Personal interviews and consultations

Reg Abbott
John Ashbridge
Bob and Marilyn Barlow
Mel Cooper
Marc Durand
Steve Duffy
Taylor Ellington
Ernie Fitzsimmons
Jeff Harris
Rita Harvey
Alan Lowe
Ross MacKinnon
Alan Livingstone MacLeod
John McKeachie
Rick Miller
Monika Moravan
Dorothy Purvis
Jim Robson
Cory Shvetz
Gladys Shvetz
Jim Swanson
Ryan Wade
Rollie Wilcox

Newspapers

Calgary Herald
Oak Bay News
Saskatoon Star-Phoenix
Spokane Daily Chronicle
Spokane Spokesman-Review
The Globe and Mail
Vancouver Sun
Victoria Daily Colonist
Victoria Daily Times
Victoria News
Victoria Times Colonist

Archives, Libraries, and Halls of Fame

British Columbia Archives
British Columbia Sports Hall of Fame
City of Victoria Archives
Greater Victoria Public Library
Greater Victoria Sports Hall of Fame
Hallmark Heritage Society Archives
Hockey Hall of Fame Archives, Toronto
Oak Bay Archives
University of Victoria Library
Vancouver Archives
Washington State Archives

Books and publications

Book of Champions, 1926. Undated and no publisher indicated.

Bowlsby, Craig H., *Empire of Ice: The Rise and Fall of the Pacific Coast Hockey Association 1911-1926.* Knights of Winter Publishing, 2012.

Bowlsby, Craig H. *The Knights of Winter: Hockey in British Columbia 1896-1911.* Published privately by Craig Bowlsby, 2006.

Coleman, Charles. *The Trail of the Stanley Cup, Volume I, 1893-1936*. National Hockey League, 1966.

Cox, Damien and Gord Stellick. *'67: The Maple Leafs, Their Sensational Victory, and the End of an Empire*. HarperCollins e-books, 2004.

Devaney, John and Burt Goldblatt. *The Stanley Cup: A Complete Pictorial History*. Rand McNally and Company, 1975.

Diamond, Dan. *Total Hockey*. Total Sports Publishing, 2000.

Dopp, Jamie and Richard Harrison. *Now is the Winter: Thinking About Hockey*. Wolsak and Wynn, 2009.

Elections BC. *Electoral History of British Columbia 1871-1986*. Victoria, 1986.

Frayne, Trent. *The Mad Men of Hockey*. McClelland and Stewart, 1978.

Henderson's Greater Victoria City Directory, 1910-1911.

Hollander, Zander and Hal Bock, editors. *The Complete Encyclopedia of Ice Hockey*. Prentice-Hall, Inc., 1970.

Andrew C. Holman, Editor. *Canada's Game*. McGill-Queens University Press, 2009.

Jenish, D'arcy. *The Stanley Cup, A Hundred Years of Hockey at its Best*. McClelland and Stewart, 1992.

McKinley, Michael. *Putting a Roof on Winter*. Greystone Books, 2002.

Mancuso, Jim and Scott Peterson. *Hockey in Portland*. Arcadia Publishing, 2007.

Purvis, Dorothy. *Clem Loughlin's Hockey Career*. Unpublished manuscript by his niece.

Robidoux, Michael A. *Men at Play*. McGill-Queens University Press, 2001.

Shubert, Howard. *Architecture on Ice: A History of the Hockey Arena*. McGill-Queens University Press, 2016.

Stott, Jon C. *Ice Warriors*. Heritage House Publishing Company Ltd., 2008.

Whitehead, Eric. *The Patricks*. Goodread Biographies, 1980.

Wong, John Chi-Kit. "Limitations of Entrepreneurship: The Birth and Death of the Spokane Canaries, 1916-1917." Paper presented at the 2010 "Hockey on the Border: An International Scholarly Conference" at Buffalo, New York, June 3-5, 2010.

Wong, John Chi-Kit. *Lords of the Rinks*. University of Toronto Press, 2005.

Zweig, Eric. *Hockey Night in the Dominion of Canada*. Lester Publishing Limited, 1992.

Electronic media and websites

"The story of the Renfrew Millionaires" at

http://www.nhlbirthplace.ca/renfrewMillionaires.html

Society for International Hockey Research at https://www.sihrhockey.org

Wikipedia on various topics

Imperial War Museum at https://www.iwm.org.uk/history/podcasts/voices-of-the-first-world-war/podcast-8-over-by-christmas

http://pasttensevancouver.tumblr.com/post/41881760680/dontargue1920s.

City of Victoria at http://www.victoria.ca/

Victoria Baseball 1946-2008 at http://www.vdba.ca/pages-added/victoria-baseball-1946---2006.php

The Canadian Encyclopedia at https://en.wikipedia.org/wiki/Canadian_Hockey_Association_(1909%E2%80%9310)

ECHL at https://www.echl.com/

Emails sent from the Salmon Kings to season ticket holders.

Salmon Kings media advisories.

Ancestry genealogical records at https://www.ancestry.ca/

Hockey database at http://www.hockeydb.com/

Hockey Hall of Fame at http://www.legendsofhockey.net

Hockey reference at http://www.legendsofhockey.net

*"Victoria Salmon Kings TSN highlight of the night"
at https://www.youtube.com/watch?v=U2mPuh41kgI*

The Daily Colonist newspaper at http://britishcolonist.ca/

Google newspapers at https://news.google.com/newspapers

Newspapers at https://www.newspapers.com/

ENDNOTES

1 *"Hockey makes its debut here," Victoria Daily Colonist, January 3, 1912, page 9.*

2 *Archie Wills, "B.C. Capital Pioneered Artificial Ice Skating in Canada," Daily Times, 1949, page 3.*

3 *Craig H. Bowlsby, "Empire of Ice: The Rise and Fall of the Pacific Coast Hockey Association, 1911-1926." Knights of Winter Publishing, 2012, page 3.*

4 *The Renfrew Millionaires were a professional hockey team that for two seasons, 1909-1910 and 1910-1911, would attract national attention to the small timber town of Renfrew, Ontario. It was the creation of railroad contractor and town founder, M. J. O'Brien and his son, Ambrose. They were originally called the Renfrew Creamery Kings, and were a small hockey team playing in the Upper Ottawa Valley League. Dreaming of having their hockey team win the Stanley Cup, the O'Briens fought to have the team recognized by the Eastern Canadian Hockey Association. After numerous rejections, the O'Briens just created their own league, and called it the National Hockey Association (NHA). M. J. financed four teams in the league: the Renfrew Creamery Kings, which became the Renfrew Millionaires, Cobalt, Haileybury, and Les Canadiens of Montreal. The Montreal Wanderers were the fifth team. By the time the Millionaires hit the ice on January 12, 1910, the 4,000-capacity crowd at the Renfrew hockey arena were on their feet. The crowds continued to fill the arena, despite the Millionaires' first-game loss of 11-9, to Cobalt. Adding to the excitement was the team roster. The O'Briens were paying huge cash salaries for a team of hockey stars, attracting attention and the best talent. Bert Lindsay was brought in to play goal for the Millionaires. Lester and Frank Patrick were signed at the outrageous cost of $3,000 and $2,000 a season. Frank "Cyclone" Taylor became the highest-paid athlete in the world when he joined the Renfrew Millionaires, for $5,250 a year. (Information taken from www.nhlbirthplace.ca/renfrewMillionaires.html accessed February 3, 2015, at 8:00 p.m.)*

5 *Archie Wills, "B.C. Capital Pioneered Artificial Ice Skating in Canada," Daily Times, 1949, page 3.*

6 *Archie Wills, "B.C. Capital Pioneered Artificial Ice Skating in Canada," Daily Times, 1949, page 3.*

7 *"Will Build Here Ice Hockey Rink," Victoria Daily Colonist, March 14, 1911, page 9.*

8 *Henderson's Greater Victoria City Directory, 1910-1911, page 210 accessed at http:// www.vpl.ca/bccd/index.php/browse/title/1910-1911/Henderson per cent27s_Greater_Victoria_City_Directory*

9 *Elections BC, "Electoral History of British Columbia 1871-1986." Victoria, 1986, page 112.*

10 *"Lester Patrick Will Make Home Here," Victoria Daily Colonist, May 12, 1911, page 7.*

11 *"Victoria to Have Ice Hockey Rink," Victoria Daily Colonist, August 13, 1911, page 17.*

12 *Howard Shubert, "Architecture on Ice: A History of the Hockey Arena," McGill-Queens University Press, 2016, page 76.*

13 *"Interest in Ice Hockey is Keen," Victoria Daily Colonist, October 19, 1911, page 9.*

14 *The Sporting World section, Victoria Daily Colonist, November 19, 1911, page 9.*

15 *Many players played both hockey and lacrosse, and it is thought that the Patricks expected to get revenue from lacrosse and other events to cover the cost of their arena investments. Lacrosse also provided year-round employment for a number of athletes.*

16 *"Wanderer Hockey Star Makes Visit to City," Victoria Daily Colonist, November 25, 1911, page 9.*

17 *"Winnipeg Hockeyists Wanted by Patricks," Victoria Daily Colonist, November 25, 1911, page 10.*

18 *"New Coast League a Powerful One," Victoria Daily Colonist, December 8, 1911, page 9.*

19 "Coast Hockey Given Birth in Victoria," *Victoria Daily Colonist*, December 9, 1911, page 9.

20 Advertising, *Victoria Daily Colonist*, December 9, 1911, page 9, and December 16, 1911, page 9.

21 20 "Tommy Dunderdale is in Vancouver," *Victoria Daily Colonist*, December 17, 1911, page 10.

22 "Professionals All Here Now," *Victoria Daily Colonist*, December 19, 1911, page 9.

23 "Rink Will Open Christmas Day," *Victoria Daily Colonist*, December 21, 1911, page 9.

24 The Sporting World Section, *Victoria Daily Colonist*, December 21, 1911, page 9.

25 The Sporting World Section, *Victoria Daily Colonist*, December 22, 1911, page 9.

26 "First Hockey Practice at Arena Rink Tonight," *Victoria Daily Colonist*, December 22, 1911, page 9.

27 "Wanderer Hockey Star Makes Visit to City," *Victoria Daily Colonist*, November 25, 1911, page 9.

28 "Hockey Makes its Debut Here," *Victoria Daily Colonist*, January 3, 1912, page 9.

29 *Players' full names were obtained from the Society for International Hockey Research website at* sihr.org.

30 *It is likely that the referee was noted hockey player Tommy Phillips. In the early days of the league, there were no professional referees and a player from the team not playing that night was used as a referee. Tommy Philipps, who had a career in Kenora and Montreal, moved to Nelson in 1909-10, where he would have met the Patricks, then joined the Vancouver team in its inaugural season.*

31 *Bowlsby, page 322.*

32 "Hockey Season Opens Tonight," *Victoria Daily Colonist*, December 7, 1915, page 17.

33 "Weird Goal Decides Hard-Fought Game in Favor of Visiting Team," *Victoria Daily Times*, December 11, 1915, page 8.

34 "What's in a Name? "Gr-r-r-r Says the 'Cougar,'" *Victoria Daily Times*, November 17, 1922, page 8s.

35 "The Birth of the National Hockey League (NHL) -https://www.thecanadianencyclopedia.ca/en/article/the-birth-of-the-national-hockey-league-feature/

36 https://en.wikipedia.org/wiki/Canadian_Hockey_Association_(1909%E2%80%9310)

37 Charles L. Coleman, "The Trail of the Stanley Cup Volume 1, National Hockey League 1966, pages 178-221.

38 *I can attest to this from personal experience. Throughout of my research, I read thousands of pages of reports on games, players, and the leagues. In later eras, reporting is more like what we have today.*

39 *Victoria Daily Times, January 12, 1912, page 6.*

40 *Victoria Daily Colonist, January 25, 1912, page 7 and 8.*

41 *Bowlsby, page194.*

42 "Relying Too Much on Hook-check Walker," *Victoria Daily Colonist*, March 21, 1912, page 11.

43 "Hockey Makes Debut Here," *Victoria Daily Times*, January 6, 1912, page 6.

44 "Victoria Won a Splendid Game," *Victoria Daily Times*, January 10, 1926, page 6.

45 "Victoria Wins Lively Game," *Victoria Daily Colonist*, January 10, 1912, page 9.

46 "Victoria Jumps into Lead in Hockey Race," *Victoria Daily Times*, January 13, 1912, page 6.

47 "May Be Changes in Vancouver," *Victoria Daily Times*, January 18, 1912, page 6.

48 "Four-Club Hockey League Next Year," *Victoria Daily Times*, January 22, 1912, page 6.

49 *Victoria Daily Times, January 28, 1912, page 6.*

50 "Spirit of Hockey Has Gripped Fans," *The Victoria Daily Colonist*, January 24, 1912, page 9.

51 "Vancouver Won from Victoria Last Night," *Victoria Daily Times*, January 25, 1912, page 6.

52 *Victoria Daily Times, January 27, 1912, page 6.*

53 http://sihr.ca/member_player_sheet.cfm?player_id=27176

54 "Royals Go into Tidy Lead in Hockey Race," *Victoria Daily Times*, January 31, 1912, page 6.

55 "Lots of Interest in Friday's Game," *Victoria Daily Times*, February 1, 1912, page 6.

56 "Vancouver is the Victor," *Victoria Daily Colonist*, February 3, 1912, page 9.

57 "Teams Neck and Neck with Race Half Won," *Victoria Daily Times*, February 10, 1912, page 6.

58 "Victoria Team Leads Again," *Victoria Daily Colonist*, February 14, 1912, page 9.

59 "In A Sizzling Finish, Royals Nose Out Ahead," *Victoria Daily Times*, February 24, 1912, page 6.

60 "Caps Just About Down and Out for Keeps," *Victoria Daily Times*, February 28, 1912, page 6.

61 "Capitals Win at Vancouver," *Victoria Daily Colonist*, March 2, 1912, page 9.

62 "Vancouver Again on Top of Coast League," *Victoria Daily Times*, March 6, 1912, page 6.

63 "Victoria Does Down Farther," *The Victoria Daily Colonist*, March 13, 1912, page 10.

64 "Victoria Makes Things Easier for The Royals," *Victoria Daily Times*, March 16, 1912, page 6.

65 "Hockey Players Leave for Home," *Victoria Daily Times*, March 19, 1912, page 6.

66 "All-Star Hockey Matches Assured," *Victoria Daily Times*, March 20, 1912, page 6.

67 "Eastern Hockey Stars Are Coming," *Victoria Daily Colonist*, March 20, 2012, page 10.

68 "Star N. H. A. Team Plays on Coast," *Victoria Daily Times*, March 13, 1912, page 6.

69 https://en.wikipedia.org/wiki/1911%E2%80%9312_NHA_season

70 "Hockey Game Here Tomorrow," *Victoria Daily Colonist*, April 3, 1912, page 9.

71 "Coast Starts Win Easily," *Victoria Daily Colonist*, April 5, 1912, page 9.

72 "Artificial Rinks," *Victoria Daily Colonist*, April 28, 1912, page 17.

73 "Don Smith to Remain in East," *Victoria Daily Colonist*, August 15, 1912, page 9.

74 "Hockey Player Visiting," *Victoria Daily Colonist*, August 23, 1912, page 11.

75 "Some Stars Lester Patrick is After," *Victoria Daily Colonist*, October 11, 1912, page 16.

76 "Hockey Clubs After Players," *Victoria Daily Colonist*, October 15, 1912, page 9.

77 "No Changes in Hockey Team," *Victoria Daily Colonist*, October 25, 1912, page 9.

78 "Will Play on Coast," *Victoria Daily Colonist*, October 30, 1912, page 1.

79 "League Issues an Ultimatum," *Victoria Daily Colonist*, November 2, 1912, page 9.

80 "Neither A War nor Commission," *Victoria Daily Colonist*, November 12, 1912, page 9.

81 "All Ready for Opening of Pacific Coast Hockey Season," *Victoria Daily Colonist*, November 16, 1912, page 9.

82 "Ice Hockey Practice," *Victoria Daily Colonist*, November 6, 1912, page 9.

83 "Kerr is Coming Strong as Ever," *Victoria Daily Colonist*, November 17, 1912, page 14.

84 As reported in *Victoria Daily Colonist*, November 23, 1912, page 9, players who might come west included Carl Kendall, Goldie Pronger, Eddie Oatman, and Jack McDonald. It was believed that Ernie Johnson would return, as well. Pronger was the only one to play for Victoria that year.

85 "Hockey Players Coming Fast," *Victoria Daily Colonist*, November 28, 1912, page 9.

86 "Hockeyists Go Through Paces," *Victoria Daily Colonist*, December 4, 1912, page 9.

87 "Patricks to Have Rink at San Francisco Exposition," *Victoria Daily Colonist*, December 4, 1912, page 9.

88 "Skating Races for Wilkerson Trophy," *Victoria Daily Colonist*, December 10, 1912, page 9.

89 "Record breaking Crowd Saw Vancouver Defeat Champions," *Victoria Daily Colonist*, December 11, 1912, page 9.

90 "Sensational Hockey Struggle Results in Win for Victoria," *Victoria Daily Colonist*, December 14, 1912, page 9.

91 "Sensational Overtime Victory for Senators," *Victoria Daily Colonist*, December 18, 1912, page 8.

92 "Victoria Wins Hockey Match with Whirlwind Finish," *Victoria Daily Colonist*, December 28, 1912, page 9.

93 "Vancouver Back into Lead in Coast Hockey Series," *Victoria Daily Colonist*, January 5, 1913, page 11.

94 "Capitals Gather in One More Overtime Contest," *Victoria Daily Colonist*, January 10, 1913, page 9.

95 "Capitals Lead in Coast Hockey League Race," *Victoria Daily Colonist*, January 18, 1913, page 9.

96 "Locals Play Hockey at Vancouver Tonight," *Victoria Daily Colonist*, January 25, 1913, page 9.

97 "Royals Go into the Win Column," *Victoria Daily Colonist*, January 26, 1913, page 20.

98 "Capitals Not Whit Dismayed," *Victoria Daily Colonist*, January 28, 1913, page 9.

99 "Vancouver Now Crowding Victoria in Hockey Race," *Victoria Daily Colonist*, January 29, 1913, page 9.

100 "Capitals Have Easy Time Against Worn-Out Royals," *Victoria Daily Colonist*, February 2, 1913, page 9.

101 "Capitals Rise Another Notch," *Victoria Daily Colonist*, February 5, 1913, page 9.

102 "Why Capitals Lead League," *Victoria Daily Colonist*, February 6, 1913, page 9.

103 "Prodgers In Hospital as Result of Hard Knocks," *Victoria Daily Colonist*, February 7, 1013, page 9.

104 "Vancouver Eliminates Champions from Race," *Victoria Daily Colonist*, February 8, 1913, page 9.

105 "Whirlwind Spurt Puts Capitals Far in Lead," *Victoria Daily Colonist*, February 12, 1913, page 9.

106 "Walter Smaill in Bad Shape," *Victoria Daily Colonist*, February 13, 1913, page 9.

107 *Victoria Daily Colonist*, February 14, 1913, page 9 reported that Walter Smaill was improving, but it was not known when he would be able to return to play.

108 *Victoria Daily Colonist*, February 6, 1913, page 9.

109 "Change in Penalty Rules for Hockey," *Victoria Daily Colonist*, February 13, 1913, page 9.

110 "Westminster vs. Victoria," *Victoria Daily Colonist*, February 16, 1913, page 9.

111 "Easy Victory for Victoria," *Victoria Daily Colonist*, February 18, 1913, page 9.

112 "Royals' Wonderful Defence Beat Capitals Last Night," *Victoria Daily Colonist*, February 19, 1913, page 9.

113 Much was made of the need for Tommy Dunderdale to learn how to drive a motor car, as he had been offered summer employment at Woods Motors in Victoria. In the end, he did not take the job and left town at the end of the season. It is not known if he did learn to drive.

114 "Capitals Take Full Revenge," *Victoria Daily Colonist*, February 22, 1913, pages 9 and 10.

115 "Invites Quebec to Come West," *Victoria Daily Colonist*, February 22, 1913, page 9.

116 *Victoria Daily Colonist*, March 21, 1913, page 9.

117 "Stanley Cupholders Are Downed in Cyclonic Game," *Victoria Daily Colonist*, March 25, 1913, page 9.

118 "Quebec Ties Series in Eastern Style of Game," *Victoria Daily Colonist*, March 28, 1913, page 9 and 10.

119 "Victoria Wins World's Ice Hockey Championship," *Victoria Daily Colonist*, March 30, 1913, page 9.

120 "Coast Stars Beat Quebec," *Victoria Daily Colonist*, April 1, 1913, page 9 and "Citizens Honor Hockey Players," *Victoria Daily Colonist*, April 2, 1913, page 9.

121 "Patricks in Search of Hockey Material," *Victoria Daily Colonist*, September 12, 1913, page 9 and "Hockey Leagues Work Together," *Victoria Daily Colonist*, September 16, 1913, page 9.

122 "Skating Season Will Open This Evening," *Victoria Daily Colonist*, October 17, 1913, page 9.

123 "Dunderdale is Real Hold-Out," *Victoria Daily Colonist*, October 25, 1913, page 9.

124 "Lester Patrick Announced Changes," *Victoria Daily Times*, November 6, 1913, page 8.

125 "Lester Patrick Announced Changes," *Victoria Daily Times*, November 6, 1913, page 8.

126 "Test Game Here," *Victoria Daily Times*, November 15, 1913, page 8.

127 Ron Boileau and Philip Wolf, "The Pacific Coast Hockey Association," in Dan Diamond, *Total Hockey*, Total Sports Publishing, 2000, pages 51–54.

128 "Ernie Johnson is The Latest Holdout," *Victoria Daily Times*, November 15, 1913, page 8.

129 "Genge and Ulrich on Deck," *Victoria Daily Times*, November 11, 1913, page 8.

130 "Bernie Morris Signs for Victoria," *Victoria Daily Times*, November 8, 1813, page 8.

131 "Genge and Ulrich on Deck," *Victoria Daily Times*, November 11, 1913, page 8.

132 Vivandière or Cantinière is a French name for women attached to military regiments as sutlers or canteen keepers. Definition found on Wikipedia, accessed July 12, 2016.

133 "Coast Ice Hockey League to Expand," *Victoria Daily Colonist*, November 15, 1913, page 8.

134 "Fight for Places on Champions," *Victoria Daily Times*, November 19, 1913, page 8.

135 *Victoria Daily Times*, November 19, 1913, page 8.

136 Both players had decided to stay in Victoria during the off-season and opened the tobacco shop in order to support themselves.

137 "Champions Won in Overtime," *Victoria Daily Times*, November 29, 1913, page 8.

138 "Champions Have Chance to Get Jump on Coast Clubs," *Victoria Daily Times,* December 2, 1913, page 8.

139 "Royals Win Game by Seven to Five," *Victoria Daily Colonist,* December 6, 1913, page 9.

140 "Victoria Star Break Forearm," *Victoria Daily Times,* December 9, 1913, page 8.

141 "Victoria Finished Strong, But Lost to Royals by Single Goal," *Victoria Daily Times,* December 10, 1913, page 8.

142 "Champions Easily Win from Royals In Strenuous Contest," *Victoria Daily Times,* December 13, 1913, page 9.

143 He would go on to become the head official, and would move to the NHL when the Western league folded. He was elected to the Hockey Hall of Fame as an official in 1961. For more information, see http://www.nhlofficials.com/halloffame.asp?member_id=8 and https://en.wikipedia.org/wiki/Mickey_Ion

144 Information on these players is from sihr.org. Nighbor would play with Vancouver for two seasons, then return to the East to play for the Ottawa Senators. Pitre played just this season for Vancouver before returning to Montreal.

145 "Coast League Suspensions: Portland Sure of Franchise," *Victoria Daily Times,* December 20, 1913, page 8.

146 "Clean Hockey at Any Cost," *Victoria Daily Times,* December 26, 1913, page 9.

147 "How Far Can Fans Go?" *Victoria Daily Times,* December 29, 1913, page 9.

148 "Champions Return to Form and Easily Beat Terminals," *Victoria Daily Times,* December 27, 1913, page 7.

149 "Champions Beaten by Royals," *Victoria Daily Times,* January 3, 1914, page 8 and "Westminster Wins Tame Hockey Match," *Victoria Daily Colonist,* January 3, 1914, page 8.

150 "Champions Win at Vancouver In Brilliant Hockey Struggle," *Victoria Daily Times,* January 7, 1914, page 8.

151 "Vancouver Again Won Over Royals," *Victoria Daily Times,* January 10, 1914, page 8.

152 "Champions Tied Terminals for Lead in Coast Hockey League," *Victoria Daily Times,* January 14, 1914, page 8.

153 "Royals Go Down Before Vancouver," *Victoria Daily Colonist,* January 17, 1914, page 9.

154 "Vancouver Wins Thrilling Overtime Hockey Struggle," *Victoria Daily Times,* January 21, 1914, page 8.

155 "Victoria Beaten at Royal City," *Victoria Daily Times,* January 24, 1914, page 8.

156 "Champions Beat Vancouver In Hard Fought Game Last Night," *Victoria Daily Times,* January 28, 1914, page 8.

157 "Senators Now Within Half a Game of the Terminal Seven," *Victoria Daily Times,* January 31, 1914, page 8.

158 "Westminster Won Over Terminals," *Victoria Daily Times,* February 4, 1914, page 9 and "Victoria Leading in Hockey League," *Victoria Daily Times,* February 7, 1914, page 8.

159 "Vancouver Plays Here Tonight," *Victoria Daily Times,* February 10, 1914, page 7.

160 "Senators Increase Lead in Race for Pacific Coast Hockey Title," *Victoria Daily Times,* February 11, 1914, page 8.

161 "Hockey Guessing Competition for Victoria Times Readers," *Victoria Daily Times,* February 12, 1914, page 7.

162 "Coast Championship Almost in Grasp of Triumphing Senators," *Victoria Daily Times,* February 14, 1914, page 8.

163 "Championship First in Now Motto of the Coast Leaders," *Victoria Daily Times,* February 16, 1914, page 9.

164 "Victoria Captures Coast Hockey Honors," *Victoria Daily Times,* February 18, 1914, page 8.

165 "Toronto Now Looms UP as Team Victoria Will Play," *Victoria Daily Times,* February 19, 1914, page 8.

166 "Champions Score Six Straight in Roughest Game of the Season," *Victoria Daily Times,* February 21, 1914, page 8.

167 The full text of the letter can be found on page 8 of the "Victoria Daily Times" of February 23, 1914.

168 "Champions Suffer Bad Slump," *Victoria Daily Times,* February 28, 1914, page 8.

169 "Changes in Coast League," *Victoria Daily Times,* February 28, 1914, page 8.

170 "Pacific Coast Will Be Well Advertised," *Victoria Daily Times,* February 24, 1914, page 7.

171 "Victoria Team Arrives in East," *Victoria Daily Times,* March 7, 1914, page 8.

172 "N.H.A. Final Booked Tonight," *Victoria Daily Times,* March 11, 1914, page 9.

173 *Victoria Daily Times,* March 12, 1914, page 8.

174 "Helped Toronto Win First Game," *Victoria Daily Times*, March 16, 1914, page 8.

175 "Grand Overtime Struggle Ends with Victoria Players Again Losers," *Victoria Daily Times*, March 18, 1914, page 8.

176 "Torontos Win Final Game in Sensational Contest with Locals," *Victoria Daily Times*, March 20, 1914, page 9.

177 "Torontos Win Final Game in Sensational Contest with Locals," *Victoria Daily Times*, March 20, 1914, page 9.

178 "Hockey Players Hold Various Jobs," *Victoria Daily Times*, March 25, 1914, page 8.

179 "Royal Will Lose Hockey Franchise," *Victoria Daily Colonist*, March 25, 1914, page 9.

180 "Coast Hockey Rules Disliked in East," *Victoria Daily Colonist*, March 26, 1914, page 8.

181 *Victoria Daily Colonist*, April 25, 1914, page 4.

182 "'Skinner' Poulin Is Manager of Team," *Victoria Daily Colonist*, May 7, 1914, page 8.

183 "Seattle Will Have an Ice Hockey Club," *Victoria Daily Colonist*, June 10, 1914, page 7.

184 "Legion of Noted Athletes Go to War," *Victoria Daily Colonist*, August 23, 1914, page 8.

185 "Westminster Doubtful About Hockey Prospect," *Victoria Daily Colonist*, August 29, 1914, page 10.

186 "Offering Contracts to All of Old Guard," *Victoria Daily Colonist*, October 2, 1914, page 8.

187 "Not Worrying Over Reported Holdouts," *Victoria Daily Colonist*, October 28, 1914, page 9.

188 "Coast Veteran," *Victoria Daily Times*, November 18, 1914, page 9.

189 "Coast Hockey Will Open on December 8," *Victoria Daily Colonist*, October 23, 1914, page 8.

190 "Boundary Forward to Be Tried Out Here," *Victoria Daily Colonist*, November 1, 1914, page 15.

191 "Dunderdale Accept Terms; Will Report," *Victoria Daily Colonist*, November 22, 1914, page 8.

192 "Jack Ulrich Sold to Wanderers," *Victoria Daily Times*, December 7, 1914, page 9.

193 "Poulin to Assist at Opening Game," *Victoria Daily Times*, December 7, 1914, page 9.

194 "Terminals Make It Two Straight," *Victoria Daily Times*, December 12, 1914, page 9.

195 "Rosebuds Play Champions at Arena To-night," *Victoria Daily Times*, December 16, 1914, page 10.

196 "Travelling Bags for Champions," *Victoria Daily Times*, December 21, 1914, page 10.

197 "Gold Dust Duo Off Their Stride," *Victoria Daily Times*, December 24, 1914, page 9.

198 "Champions Badly Beaten Saturday," *Victoria Daily Times*, December 28, 1914, page 9.

199 "Fourth Defeat for P.C.H.A. Champions," *Victoria Daily Times*, December 30, 1914, page 11.

200 "N.H.A. Club After Local Star," *Victoria Daily Times*, December 31, 1914, page 11.

201 "Six Straight for Vancouver Seven," *Victoria Daily Times*, January 9, 1915, page 9.

202 "Champions Win in Overtime," *Victoria Daily Times*, January 13, 1915, page 9.

203 "Champions Have Two Games for Next Week and Must Win Both," *Victoria Daily Times*, January 16, 1915, page 9.

204 "Roughest Game of Season Last Night," *Victoria Daily Times*, January 15, 1915, page 10.

205 "Muldoon Recalls Terrific Hockey Contest," *Victoria Daily Times*, January 11, 1915, page 9.

206 "League Leaders Easily Beaten," *Victoria Daily Times*, January 23, 1915, page 9.

207 "Portland Septette Won from Leaders," *Victoria Daily Times*, January 27, 1916, page 7.

208 "Champions Beaten in Exciting Clash," *Victoria Daily Times*, January 30, 1915, page 10.

209 As reported in the *Victoria Daily Times*, January 29, 1915, the cadets would meet at their air headquarters downtown and march to the rink, headed by their full band. The band would provide music during the intermissions. The cadets were the guests of Walter Smaill, local high-school employee and management of the team.

210 "Champions Out-Game Portland," *Victoria Daily Times*, February 3, 1915, page 7.

211 "Coast League Referee Has Resigned," *Victoria Daily Times*, February 5, 1915, page 9.

212 An examination of subsequent score sheets showed his name in many of them.

213 "Ions [sic] and Phillips To Handle Game," *Victoria Daily Times*, February 8, 1915, page 7.

214 "Rosebuds Victorious in Thrilling Game," *Victoria Daily Times*, February 10, 1915, page 10.

215 "Champion Beaten by Loose Hockey," *Victoria Daily Times*, February 13, 1915, page 9.

216 "Locals Beaten by Terrific Finish," *Victoria Daily Times*, February 20, 1915, page 11.

217 "Portland Expected to Win Tomorrow," *Victoria Daily Times*, February 24, 1915, page 7.

218 "Poulin to Handle Terminal Game," *Victoria Daily Times*, February 25, 1915, page 7.

219 "Monday Night Will Close Skating," *Victoria Daily Times*, February 25, 1915, page 9.

220 "Vancouver Wins Coast Honors," *Victoria Daily Times*, February 27, 1915, page 10.

221 "New Champions in by 11 Goals to 3," *Victoria Daily Colonist*, February 28, 1915, page 8.

222 "Last Local Game Won by Vancouver," *Victoria Daily Colonist*, March 3, 1915, page 9.

223 "Senators Were Beaten at Portland," *Victoria Daily Times*, March 5, 1915, page 10 and "Victoria Beaten by Portland Rosebud Seven," *Victoria Daily Times*, March 8, 1915, page 9.

224 "Six Man Exhibition Tomorrow," *Victoria Daily Times*, March 8, 1915, page 9.

225 *https://en.wikipedia.org/wiki/1914per centE2per cent80per cent9315_PCHA_season.*

226 Boileau, Ron; Wolf, Philip, "The Pacific Coast Hockey Association," in Diamond, Dan, *Total Hockey*, Total Sports Publishing, 2000, page 52.

227 "Seattle Will Play Hockey Next Year," *Victoria Daily Colonist*, April 15, 1915, page 11.

228 "Contract Signed for Ice Arena," *Victoria Daily Colonist*, June 13, 1915, page 11.

229 "Muldoon Is Proposed as Seattle Manager," *Victoria Daily Colonist*, October 3, 1915, page 12.

230 "Victoria Hockey Team Ordered to Report for Practice on November 17," *Victoria Daily Times*, November 13, 1915, page 8.

231 From the *Victoria Daily Colonist*, September 30, 1915, came this article: "We have not yet decided whether Victoria will be represented in Coast hockey this winter or not," said Manager Lester Patrick.

"There appears to be a sentiment in some quarters that we should abandon the sport this winter, and perhaps for the period of the war. On the other hand, there are large numbers or hockey enthusiasts of the Capital who are looking forward with keen anticipation to the enjoyment of their usual number of games. The sentiment, however, is not sufficiently pronounced at present for me to arrive at any definite conclusion as to the real wishes of the people of Victoria, and until a real expression of sentiment in the matter is obtained I am unable to say what the position of Victoria will be."

232 *Victoria Daily Colonist*, September 9, 1915, page 10.

233 "Spoils of War Go to Frank Patrick," *Victoria Daily Colonist*, November 6, 1915, page 12.

234 Eddie Carpenter, Jack Walker, Harry Holmes, Cully Wilson, and Frank Foyston came west to play for Seattle. Frank Nighbor, Bert Lindsay, Skinner Poulin, and Walter Smaill were signed by eastern clubs.

235 "Eastern Magnates Fail to Induce Coast Hockey Players to Jump," *Victoria Daily Times*, November 18, 1915, page 8.

236 "Public Are Invited to Witness Workout of Victoria Team Tonight," *Victoria Daily Times*, November 22, 1915, page 9.

237 "P. C. H. A. Season Opens To-morrow," *Victoria Daily Times*, December 6, 1915, page 9.

238 "Seattle Winners in Hair-Raising Opener with Victoria," *Victoria Daily Times*, December 8, 1915, page 8.

239 "Victoria 1915-16 Hockey Season Openings Tonight," *Victoria Daily Times*, December 10, 1915, page 9.

240 "Seattle Hockey Team is Winner," *Spokane Daily Chronicle*, December 11, 1915, page 12.

241 "Victoria Wins Sensational Game," *Victoria Daily Times*, December 15, 1915, page 9.

242 "Aristocrats Decisively Defeated Champions Last Night," *Victoria Daily Times*, December 18, 1915, page 8.

243 "Public Will Not Be Permitted into Dressing Rooms During Intervals," *Victoria Daily Times*, December 23, 1915, page 8.

244 "Portland Gain League Leadership by Defeating Victoria in Overtime Game," *Victoria Daily Times*, December 29, 1915, page 9.

245 "Crippled Local Team Was Badly Beaten by Portland Last Night," *Victoria Daily Times*, January 5, 1916, page 9.

246 "Victoria Hockey Team Beaten After Establishing Good Lead," *Victoria Daily Times*, January 12, 1916, page 9.

247 "Victoria Gain Footing in Hockey League Race," *Victoria Daily Times*, January 15, 1916, page 8.

248 "Seattle Turned the Tables on Victoria Last Night," *Victoria Daily Times*, January 19, 1916, page 9.

249 "Portland Strengthens Its Grip on First Placer in P. C. H. A.," *Victoria Daily Times*, January 22, 1916, page 8.

250 "Portland Maintains P. C. H. A. League Leadership by Defeating Victoria," *Victoria Daily Times*, January 26, 1916, page 9.

251 "Victoria Arena May Be Taken Over by Military Authorities," *Victoria Daily Times*, January 28, 1916, page 8.

252 "Victoria Completely Out played in Final Game of Local Season," *Victoria Daily Times*, February 2, 1916, page 9.

253 http://www.iwm.org.uk/history/podcasts/voices-of-the-first-world-war/podcast-8-over-by-christmas

254 "Seattle Won from Aristocrats In Last 10 Minutes of Play," *Victoria Daily Times*, February 5, 1916, page 9.

255 "Seattle Doubled the Score on Aristocrats," *Victoria Daily Times*, February 9, 1916, page 11.

256 "Aristocrats Lose to Champions in Thrilling Overtime Game," *Victoria Daily Times*, February 9, 1916, page 9.

257 "Hockey Game Called Owing to dense Fog," *Victoria Daily Times*, February 16, 1916, page 11.

258 https://en.wikipedia.org/wiki/1915%E2%80%9316_PCHA_season

259 "Portland Team New Coast Hockey Champs," *Victoria Daily Times*, February 19, 1916, page 9.

260 "Victoria Won from Vancouver Septette," *Victoria Daily Times*, February 26, 1916, page 9.

261 "Flying Frenchmen Won Deciding Game," *Victoria Daily Times*, March 31, 1916, page 8.

262 https://en.wikipedia.org/wiki/History_of_Spokane,_Washington

263 John Chi-Kit Wong, "Limitations of Entrepreneurship: The Birth and Death of the Spokane Canaries, 1916-1917" Paper presented at the 2010 "Hockey on the Border: An International Scholarly Conference" at Buffalo, New York, June 3-5, 2010.

264 John Chi-Kit Wong, "Limitations of Entrepreneurship: The Birth and Death of the Spokane Canaries, 1916-1917" Paper presented at the 2010 "Hockey on the Border: An International Scholarly Conference" at Buffalo, New York, June 3-5, 2010.

265 Spokane County Auditor Articles of Incorporation, Accession No. 979-0029. Spokane Arena Company, No. 480304, Box 77, August 8, 1916. Washington State Archives Eastern Region Archives.

266 "Lester Patrick in Spokane," *Spokane Spokesman-Review*, October 11, 1916, page 14.

267 "Amateur hockey league," *Spokane Spokesman-Review*, October 17, 1916, page 16; "Skating rink," *Spokane Spokesman-Review*, October 29, 1916, part 3, page 2.

268 In reality, Box, Mickey O'Leary, Jim Riley and McCulloch did not move with the team to Spokane. Information from sihrhockey.org team sheets.

269 "Spokane To Have Victoria Stars," *Spokane Spokesman-Review*, October 18, 1916, page 14.

270 "Form Club to Boost Hockey," *Spokane Daily Chronicle*, December 8, 1916, page 19.

271 *Spokane Spokesman-Review*, 21 January 1917, part 3, p. 2.

272 "Pro Hockey Fails to Make Good in Spokane," *Toronto Globe and Mail*, February 15, 1917, page 9.

273 "Scott Would Dispose of Spokane Franchise," *Spokane Daily Chronicle*, February 19, 1917, page 16.

274 Ron Boileau and Philip Wolf, "The Pacific Coast Hockey Association," in Diamond, Dan, "Total Hockey," Total Sports Publishing, 2000, page 53.

275 Boileau, Ron; Wolf, Philip (2000), "The Pacific Coast Hockey Association," in Diamond, Dan, "Total Hockey," Total Sports Publishing, 2000, page 53.

276 "Hockey Moguls Will Meet in Seattle," *Victoria Daily Colonist*, October 4, 1918, page 8.

277 "Skating Fans Will Ge Their Chance," *Victoria Daily Colonist*, October 27, 1918, page 8.

278 "Pro Hockey Probable," *Victoria Daily Colonist*, October 29, 1918, page 8.

279 "League Arranging for Hockey Season," *Victoria Daily Colonist*, November 12, 1918, page 10.

280 For more information on the influenza pandemic, see: https://virus.stanford.edu/uda/

281 "Three Clubs Only Will Play Hockey," *Victoria Daily Colonist*, November 20, 1918, page 8.

282 *Times for skating were: Tuesday, Thursday, and Saturday evenings, from 8:15 to 10:30 with Rowland's band in attendance; Wednesday evening, without the band, 8:15 to 10:30; Wednesday afternoon from 3 to 5:15, and Saturday afternoons from 3:00 to 5:15 with Rowland's band in attendance.*

283 *"Ice Skating Rink Will Open This Evening," Victoria Daily Colonist, December 10, 1918, page 8.*

284 *"First Hockey Game To-Night at Arena," Victoria Daily Times, December 20, 1918, page 13.*

285 *"Christmas Skating Record for Arena," Victoria Daily Times, December 26, 1918, page 7.*

286 *"Boys Looked Good in First Practice," Victoria Daily Times, December 27, 1918, page 11.*

287 *"Friday's Visitors to Local Arena Won Opening Game in Pacific Coast Hockey," Victoria Daily Times, January 2, 1919, page 11.*

288 *"Team Work Too Good Last Night for Aristocrats," Victoria Daily Times, January 4, 1919, page 10.*

289 *"Brilliant Hockey Game at Vancouver," Victoria Daily Times, January 7, 1919, page 8.*

290 *"Eddie Oatman Has Joined Aristocrats," Victoria Daily Times, January 8, 1919, page 10.*

291 *"Aristocrats First to Lower Colors Of Leaders In Pacific Coast Race," Victoria Daily Times, January 9, 1919, page 11.*

292 *"Old-Time Hockey Crowd Cheers Victoria Players Raining Shots on Lehman," Victoria Daily Times, January 11, 1919, page 12.*

293 *"Victoria Again Too Clever for League Leaders," Victoria Daily Times, January 18, 1919, page 10.*

294 *"Honors Go Again to Millionaires," Victoria Daily Times, January 21, 1919, page 8.*

295 *"Another Wing Man to Join Aristocrats," Victoria Daily Times, January 21, 1919, page 9.*

296 *"Aristocrats Third Win Over Seattle," Victoria Daily Times, January 23, 1919, page 11.*

297 *"Men on Empress of Asia Guests at Hockey Battle on Home Ice To-Night," Victoria Daily Times, January 24, 1919, page 10.*

298 *"Aristocrats Climb to Top of League," Victoria Daily Colonist, January 25, 1919, page 7, and "Tobin Entertained His Soldier Brother," Victoria Daily Times, January 27, 1919, page 8.*

299 *"1919 PCHA season" from https://en.wikipedia.org/wiki/1919_PCHA_season.*

300 *"Victoria League Leaders After A Strenuous Battle," Victoria Daily Times, February 1, 1919, page 13.*

301 *"Another Championship Fight After Seattle's Big Victory," Victoria Daily Times, February 6, 1919, page 10.*

302 *"Millionaires Won by Only Score in Exciting Battle," Victoria Daily Times, February 8, 1919, page 12.*

303 *"Aristocrat Have Two More Players with the Flu," Victoria Daily Times, February 10, 1919, page 8.*

304 *"Victoria Out of Cellar and Tied for Lead Again," Victoria Daily Times, February 11, 1919, page 8 and "Aristocrats Win with Crippled Team," Victoria Daily Colonist, February 11, 1919, page 7.*

305 *"Going to Get World's Pennant Says Eddie Oatman," Victoria Daily Times, February 14, 1919, page 10.*

306 *"Seattle Winner Over Victoria by Eight Goals to Two," Victoria Daily Times, February 15, 1918, page 11.*

307 *"Aristocrats' Manager Has Record for Signing Up Players," Victoria Daily Times, February 21, 1919, page 15.*

308 *"Victoria Wins in Record Overtime," Victoria Daily Colonist, February 22, 1919, page 7.*

309 *Mickey Ion's Selection for an All-Star Pacific Coast Team," Victoria Daily Times, March 5, 1919, page 10.*

310 *Material in this paragraph was sourced from: Victoria Daily Times, April 2, 1919, page 12; Victoria Daily Colonist, April 2, 1919, page 7; Victoria Daily Times, April 7, 1919, page 8; and Ron Boileau and Philip Wolf, "The Pacific Coast Hockey Association," in Diamond, Dan, "Total Hockey," Total Sports Publishing, 2000, page 53.*

311 *"Tiger Are guests of Tyees Here Today," Victoria Daily Colonist, May 23, 1919, page 9.*

312 *"Coal Miners Take Another Contest," Victoria Daily Colonist, June 17, 1919, page 9.*

313 *"Urge Ice Hockey for Royal Visit," Victoria Daily Colonist, August 30, 1919, page 7.*

314 *"Loyal Thousands Extend Welcome to Prince of Wales," Victoria Daily Colonist, September 24, 1919, page 3.*

315 *"Arena Season May Open at Hallowe'en," Victoria Daily Colonist, September 26, 1919, page 1110.*

316 *"Large Attendance at Opening of Rink," Victoria Daily Times, November 7, 1919, page 10.*

317 Con Jones was well known in Vancouver for his promotion of sports in Vancouver. For more information, see http://pasttensevancouver.tumblr.com/post/41881760680/dontargue1920s.

318 "Three Clubs Only for Coast Hockey," *Victoria Daily Colonist*, October 14, 1919, page 12 and October 17, 1919, page 9.

319 "New Blood Expected in Hockey Line-Up," *Victoria Daily Times*, October 16, 1919, page 10.

320 "Special Inducements for Hockey Players," *Victoria Daily Colonist*, October 22, 1919, page 22.

321 In fact, Cully Wilson would not only play for the Metropolitans for 1919-1920 season, but he would also move to the NHL the following season and play there with Toronto, Montreal, and Hamilton until he returned to the West and played in the WCHL with the Calgary Tigers. He had one last season with the Chicago Blackhawks, playing five games in 1926-17, and played minor-pro until he retired for good in 1932. Information sourced from http://sihr.ca/member_player_sheet.cfm?player_id=4104&CFID=49665097&CFTOKEN=16677430

322 "Marples Is Another Camouflaged Sport," *Victoria Daily Colonist*, October 25, 1919, page 10.

323 "Eddie Oatman Will Again Be Skipper," *Victoria Daily Colonist*, October 30, 1919, page 11.

324 "Hockey Players Will Work Out Tomorrow," *Victoria Daily Colonist*, November 9, 1919, page 11.

325 Fowler was supposed to play with the Aristocrats the previous season but went overseas with the Siberian Expeditionary Force. He had played for Spokane and then Seattle for one year each before joining the military.

326 "Fowler Will Guard Victoria's Nets," *Victoria Daily Colonist*, November 14, 1919, page 11.

327 "Hockey Players Will Be Out in Strength," *Victoria Daily Colonist*, November 16, 1919, page 11.

328 "Hockey Directors Fix Hockey Dates," *Victoria Daily Colonist*, November 22, 1919, page 10.

329 "Schedule of Coast Hockey Announced," *Victoria Daily Colonist*, December 14, 1919, page 10.

330 "Harry Meeking Has Joined the Roster," *Victoria Daily Colonist*, December 21, 1919, page 10.

331 "Four Thousand Fans See Aristocrats Win," *Victoria Daily Colonist*, December 27, 1919, page 10.

332 "Overtime Game Is Won By Vancouver," *Victoria Daily Colonist*, December 30, 1919, page 10.

333 "Aristocrats Show Championship Form," *Victoria Daily Colonist*, January 3, 1920, page 10 and "Seven To Four Win Over Vancouver Places Aristocrats on Top," *Victoria Daily Times*, January 3, 1920, page 11.

334 "Victoria Won Two to Nil," *Victoria Daily Times*, January 10, 1920, page 12.

335 "Victoria Defeats Vancouver at Home," *Victoria Daily Colonist*, January 13, 1920, page 11.

336 "Millionaires Won Two to One and Draw Even with Victoria in Race," *Victoria Daily Times*, January 17, 1920, page 16.

337 Metropolitans Won Three to One and Created Three-Cornered Tie," *Victoria Daily Times*, January 22, 1920, page 10.

338 "Aristocrats Are on Top Again," *Victoria Daily Times*, January 24, 1920, page 11.

339 "Patrick Prefers Managerial Role," *Victoria Daily Times*, January 26, 1920, page 10.

340 *Victoria Daily Times*, January 26, 1920, page 10.

341 "Frank Patrick Challenges 'Fixters,'" *Victoria Daily Times*, January 27, 1920, page 11.

342 Ron Boileau and Philip Wolf, "The Pacific Coast Hockey Association," in Diamond, Dan, "Total Hockey" Total Sports Publishing, 2000, page 53.

343 Information taken from *Victoria Daily Times*, January 27, 1920, page 10; January 31, 1920, page 10; February 5, 1920, page 10; and February 7, 1920, page 10.

344 "Records in Hockey to Half Way Mark," *Victoria Daily Times*, February 10, 1920, page 11.

345 "Aristocrats Put on The Brakes and Beat Vancouver Three to Two," *Victoria Daily Times*, February 10, 1920, page 11.

346 "Aristocrats Playing Like Championship Team," *Victoria Daily Times*, February 14, 1920, page 12.

347 "Bad Defeat but No Knockout," *Victoria Daily Times*, February 19, 1920, page 11.

348 "Aristocrats Come Back as Contenders for Big Honors," *Victoria Daily Times*, February 23, 1920, page 10.

349 "Vancouver Gets Highest Score of the Season," *Victoria Daily Times*, February 24, 1920, page 10.

350 "Aristocrats Beat Mets Three to two After Seven Minute Overtime," *Victoria Daily Times*, February 28, 1920, page 10.

351 *"Seattle Won Hard Game Two-Nil," Victoria Daily Times, March 4, 1920, page 10.*

352 *"Hat Still in the Ring For Coast Title," Victoria Daily Times, March 6, 1920, page 10.*

353 *"Met's Victory Put Vitoria Out of Coast Titular Series," Victoria Daily Times, March 11, 1920, page 10.*

354 *https://en.wikipedia.org/wiki/1920_Stanley_Cup_Finals*

355 *"Icelanders Convey Congrats to Falcons," Victoria Daily Colonist, June 11, 1920, page 11.*

356 *"F. Fredrickson, Falcon Star, May Come to Coast," Victoria Daily Times, December 9, 1920, page 12.*

357 *"Falcons Skipper Joins Aristocrats," Victoria Daily Colonist, December 23, 1920, page 10.*

358 The text of Mt. Patrick's letter read as follows:

The Honourable Attorney-General of Alberta, Edmonton, Alberta

Sir: I respectfully desire to draw your attention to a situation that exists in Alberta with regard to the game of hockey. Any kind of investigation will reveal the fact that the Big Four Amateur Hockey League of Alberta is nothing more than a semi-professional organization pertain under the guise of amateurism and, as such, is perpetrating a fraud on the public and evading the Alberta provincial amusement tax applicable to professional sport.

Your attention is directed to an editorial in The Morning Albertan of October 10 on "Honest Athletics," in which the resignation of Captain Robert Pearson as president of the "Big Four" Hockey Association is discussed, also the question or amateurism and professionalism in sport.

I make the positive assertion that last season the "Big Four" was a semi-professional organization and that many, if not the majority of players, were paid in money for their services as hockey players. The situation that existed last season will be even worse the coming season.

I feel quite confident that once your attention has been called to the state of affairs that exists at present in Alberta, you will open an investigation under oath and clean out those responsible for the conduct of Canada's National Winter game of hockey in Alberta.

The Pacific Coast Hockey Association has been operating a professional hockey league for the past nine years and the source of supply for players has been primarily from the prairie provinces. This source has been cut off due to the illegitimate opposition now operating a semi-professional league as an amateur organization, although paying players in excess, in some instances, of which highest paid professional player commands. No one resents legitimate competition in business, but illegitimate and unlawful competition should not be allowed to exist without some effort being made to remedy it.

It is not the wish of our association to project ourselves into the domestic affairs of another province, hence our desire to point out to the properly constituted officers of the crown the existence of a fraud and allow them to take the proper steps to prevent the recurrence of same, and protect the sports-loving public.

We feel that having an investment of substantially over half a million dollars and operating a legitimate enterprise that our position in the matter should be clear to you.

Trusting you will use your office to investigate the charges herein contained, we beg to remain,

Yours very truly,

PACIFIC COAST HOCKEY ASSOCIATION

FRANK A. PATRICK, President"

359 *"Charges Alberta 'Big Four' as Being Professional and Requests Investigation," Victoria Daily Times, November 10, 1920, page 10.*

360 *"Charges Repudiated by Hockey Official," Victoria Daily Times, November 13, 1920, page 10.*

361 *"Patrick Ready to Prove Ten Players in Alberta 'Big Four' Took Money," Victoria Daily Times, November 19, 1920, page 10.*

362 *"Patrick In Calgary to Prove His Charges," Victoria Daily Times, November 29, 1920, page 10.*

363 *"Big Four through with Amateur Union; to run as independent league," Calgary Herald, December 13, 1920, page 16.*

364 *"Announce Opening of Arena on November 2," Victoria Daily Times, October 25, 1920, page 10.*

365 *"Contracts Are sent to Victoria Puck-Chasers," Victoria Daily Times, October 28, 1920, page 10.*

366 *"Eddie Oatman to Captain Aristocrats This Season," Victoria Daily Times, October 30, 1920, page 10.*

367 "Meeking Will Be with Aristocrats This Year," *Victoria Daily Times*, November 5, 1920, page 10.

368 "Clem Loughlin Coming to Play With Victoria," *Victoria Daily Times*, November 9, 1920, page 10.

369 "Heck [sic] Fowler Will Be Back Defending Victoria's Net," *Victoria Daily Times*, November 13, 1920, page 10.

370 "Game Moose Johnson is to Play With Victoria," *Victoria Daily Times*, November 18, 1920, page 10.

371 Both Johnson and Lester Patrick had started their professional careers in 1904 with the Montreal Amateur Athletic Association.

372 "Through With Ice Hockey For Good," *Victoria Daily Times*, November 26, 1920, page 10.

373 "Wilf Loughlin Returning to Redeem His Lost Laurels," *Victoria Daily Times*, December 4, 1920, page 10.

374 "Dunderdale Going After Scoring Honours This Year," *Victoria Daily Times*, December 8, 1920, page 12.

375 "Patrick Signs Genge," *Victoria Daily Times*, December 11, 1920, page 12.

376 "Only Six Originals of P. C. H. A. Here This Year," *Victoria Daily Times*, December 2, 1920, page 13.

377 "Fine Defence Gave First Hockey Game to Vancouver," *Victoria Daily Times*, December 21, 1920, page 12.

378 "Victoria Held Mets For Two Periods, Then Broke," *Victoria Daily Times*, December 23, 1920, page 10.

379 "Mets Outgamed Aristocrats in Fierce Overtime Battle Which Marked Opening of Pro Hockey," *Victoria Daily Times*, December 27, 1920, page 10.

380 "Fowler Unable to See In Fog and Caps Lost," *Victoria Daily Times*, December 28, 1920, page 10.

381 "Fredrickson to Play in Big Game To-morrow," *Victoria Daily Times*, January 3, 1921, page 12.

382 "Foyston's Goal Gives Mets Overtime Battle," *Victoria Daily Times*, January 6, 1921, page 12.

383 "Aristocrats Give Mr. Jinx His Marching Orders and Win Their First Game From Seattle Mets," *Victoria Daily Times*, January 8, 1921, page 10.

384 *Victoria Daily Times*, January 11, 1921, page 12; January 15, 1921, page 10; and January 20, 1921, page 10.

385 "Team Work Carries Aristocrats to Victory in Another Wild and Woolly Game with Millionaires," *Victoria Daily Times*, January 22, 1921, page 10.

386 "Victoria Forwards Bring Home Victory," *Victoria Daily Times*, January 24, 1921, page 10.

387 "Splendid Defence and Good Shooting Bring Aristocrats Victory," *Victoria Daily Times*, January 29, 1921, page 10.

388 "Scoring Records," *Victoria Daily Times*, January 29, 1921, page 10.

389 "Victoria Humbles Seattle After Terrific Overtime Battle," *Victoria Daily Times*, February 3, 1921, page 10.

390 "Caps Hand Mets Fifth Straight Licking," *Victoria Daily Times*, February 26, 1921, page 10.

391 "Victoria Has Best of Mets in Rough Battle," *Victoria Daily Times*, March 3, 1921, page 10.

392 "Caps and Mets Scrap for Two Long Hours," *Victoria Daily Times*, March 5, 1921, page 10.

393 The first long game was played in 1914, when Victoria defeated Westminster on February 13 after 36:49 of overtime. Dunderdale scored the winning goal. Oatman and Johnson were on the losing team on that occasion. The next lengthy game was on February 21, 1919, between Victoria and Vancouver. That game lasted 37:20 of overtime before Clem Loughlin scored the deciding goal. On February 2 this year, Seattle and Victoria played 31:00 minutes of overtime before Wilf Loughlin scored.

394 "Victoria Has Played in Fur Marathon Games," *Victoria Daily Times*, March 5, 1921, page 10.

395 "Eddie Oatman Not to Play Again This Year," *Victoria Daily Times*, March 7, 1921, page 10.

396 "Crippled Aristocrats Put Up Strong Fight," *Victoria Daily Times*, March 8, 1921, page 10.

397 "Capitals Are Victors in Great Scoring Bee," *Victoria Daily Times*, March 12, 1921, page 10.

398 "Official Records for Year in Coat Hockey Show 'Freddie' on Top," *Victoria Daily Times*, March 15, 1921, page 10.

399 Ron Boileau and Philip Wolf, "The Pacific Coast Hockey Association in Diamond, Dan, "Total Hockey," Total Sports Publishing, 2000, page 53.

400 "Coast Procedures Favored by Ottawa," *Victoria Daily Colonist*, November 9, 1921, page 12.

401 Ron Boileau and Philip Wolf, "The Pacific Coast Hockey Association in Diamond, Dan, "Total Hockey," Total Sports Publishing, 2000, page 53.

402 "New Hockey Rules Coming Into Force," *Victoria Daily Colonist*, December 13, 1921, page 10.

403 Ron Boileau and Philip Wolf, "The Pacific Coast Hockey Association in Diamond, Dan, "Total Hockey," Total Sports Publishing, 2000, page 53.

404 "One Overtime Period to Be Limit In All Future Hockey Tilts," *Victoria Daily Times*, November 4, 1921, page 10.

405 "Contracts Mailed to All Hockey Players," *Victoria Daily Times*, October 17, 1921, page 12.

406 "'Slim' Halderson signs to Play With Victoria Pro Team This Year," *Victoria Daily Times*, October 21, 1921, page 8.

407 "'Moose' Johnson Will Be Back For Another Season With Victoria," *Victoria Daily Times*, October 29, 1921, page 18.

408 "Slim Halderson and Fredrickson Will Play With Victoria," *Victoria Daily Times*, November 5, 1921, page 12.

409 "Clem Loughlin Will Be Here This Winter," *Victoria Daily Times*, November 7, 1921, page 16.

410 "Wilf Loughlin Signs and Figures on This Being His Best Year," *Victoria Daily Times*, November 9, 1921, page 12.

411 "Harry Meeking Last Man on Local Squad," *Victoria Daily Times*, November 10, 1921, page 12.

412 "Hec Fowler Will Be Good Boy and Come to Play in Victoria," *Victoria Daily Times*, November 18, 1921, page 12.

413 "Aristocrats Begin To Show Fine Form," *Victoria Daily Times*, November 30, 1921, page 12.

414 "Aristocrats Will Be Fit for Fray After Four More Workouts," *Victoria Daily Times*, December 1, 1921, page 12.

415 "Victoria Substitutes Will Be As Good as Regulars Says Lester," *Victoria Daily Times*, December 2, 1921, page 12.

416 "MacKay Scored Goal Which Gave Game to Vancouver Squad," *Victoria Daily Times*, December 6, 1921, page 12.

417 "Slim Sets Record for Recruit Scoring," *Victoria Daily Times*, December 8, 1921, page 12.

418 "Close Checking Robbed Opening Game of Thrills," *Victoria Daily Times*, December 10, 1921, page 12.

419 "Clem's Shot in Last Minute Gives Great Win to Aristocrats," *Victoria Daily Times*, December 13, 1921, page 12.

420 *Victoria Daily Times*, December 17, 1921, page 12.

421 December 21, 1921 - Seattle 2, Victoria 1; December 23, 1921 - Seattle 3, Victoria 2 in overtime; December 26, 1921 - Vancouver 4, Victoria 2; and December 30, 1921 - Vancouver 5, Victoria 3. All information from the newspapers the day after the game.

422 "Oatman Playing on One Leg, Turns Tide and Victoria Wins," *Victoria Daily Times*, January 5, 1922, page 5.

423 "Juggling of Players Enables Vitoria to Score Sparking Win," *Victoria Daily Times*, January 7, 1922, page 14.

424 "Oatman Must Rest For Week, Game Tonight," *Victoria Daily Times*, January 9, 1922, page 5.

425 "Millionaires Take Comedy Game From Aristocrats at Home," *Victoria Daily Times*, January 10, 1922, page 12.

426 Coleman, Charles, "The Trail of the Stanley Cup, Volume I, 1893-1936" inc., page 399.

427 "Foyston Rings Bell Five Times and Mets Walk Off with Game," *Victoria Daily Times*, January 12, 1922, page 10.

428 "Three Goals In Last Four Minutes Handed Aries Game and Lead," *Victoria Daily Times*, January 19, 1922, page 10.

429 "Moose Johnson Quits Victoria For Keeps," *Victoria Daily Times*, January 21, 1922, page 12.

430 While Moose did not play any more for Victoria that season, he would play in different minor leagues off and on, returning for twenty-eight games with the Portland Buckaroos of the Pacific Coast Hockey League in 1928-29, before ending his career for good in the California Pro league in 1931. Information was taken from Society of International Hockey Research website at http://www.sihrhockey.org/member_player_sheet.cfm?player_id=17336.

431 "Aries' Speedy Rally Gives Them Exciting Win Over Vancouver," *Victoria Daily Times*, January 24, 1922, page 12.

432 "Mets Sensed Snow Storm and Gave Aries a Taste of It," *Victoria Daily Times*, January 28, 1922, page 12 and February 2, 1922, page 12.

433 "Aries Show Their Teeth and Fight Way Through to Greatest Win of the Season at Expense of Vancouver," *Victoria Daily Times*, February 4, 1922, page 12.

434 "Vancouver Victor in Second Rough Battle and Returns to Lead," *Victoria Daily Times*, February 7, 1922, page 12.

435 "Holmes and Morris Beat Millionaires," *Victoria Daily Times*, February 9, 1922, page 12.

436 "Mets Slip Rollers Under Aristocrats," *Victoria Daily Times*, February 16, 1922, page 12.

437 "New Combination Finds Its Way Through Mets' Defence For Win," *Victoria Daily Times*, February 18, 1922, page 12.

438 "Millionaires Got Off To An Early Lead," *Victoria Daily Times*, February 21, 1922, page 12.

439 "Curtain Is Dropping on Local Pro. Hockey After Game To-night," *Victoria Daily Times*, February 25, 1922, page 12.

440 "Aries Wind Up Their Season's Work With Win Over Vancouver," *Victoria Daily Times*, February 25, 1922, page 12.

441 "Les Patrick and Eddie Oatman Going East With Millionaires," *Victoria Daily Times*, March 8, 1922, page 12.

442 Ron Boileau and Philip Wolf, "The Pacific Coast Hockey Association," in Diamond, Dan, "Total Hockey," Total Sports Publishing, 2000, page 53.

443 Coleman, Charles, "The Trail of the Stanley Cup, Volume I, 1893-1936 inc.," page 421.

444 "Uniform Rules For Two Hockey Loops," *Victoria Daily Times*, October 18, 1922, page 10.

445 "What's In a Name? Gr-r-r-r- Says the 'Cougar'," *Victoria Daily Times*, November 17, 1922, page 10.

446 "Aristocrats Last Team to Take Road," *Victoria Daily Times*, October 4, 1922, page 10.

447 "Contracts Mailed to Hockey Players," *Victoria Daily Times*, October 3, 1922, page 10.

448 https://en.wikipedia.org/wiki/Saskatoon_Sheiks

449 "Contracts Mailed to Hockey Players," *Victoria Daily Times*, October 3, 1922, page 10.

450 "Arena Opening Up for Season Oct. 31," *Victoria Daily Times*, October 11, 1922, page 10.

451 "Looking For Early Opening of Hockey," *Victoria Daily Times*, October 14, 1922, page 10.

452 "Eddie Oatman Will Stage Wing Rushes, "*Victoria Daily Times*, October 17, 1922, page 10.

453 "Hec Fowler Will Handle The Hot Ones This Year," *Victoria Daily Times*, October 19, 1922, page 12.

454 "Harry Meeking Ready to Answer Call to Training," *Victoria Daily Times*, October 20, 1922, page 10.

455 "Halderson Coming To Claim Uniform," *Victoria Daily Times*, October 21, 1922, page 10.

456 "Clem Loughlin To Kick Up the Ice Flakes Again," *Victoria Daily Times*, October 25, 1922, page 12.

457 "Dunderdale Seeks New Scoring Mark," *Victoria Daily Times*, October 27, 1922, page 12.

458 "Skaters All Ready for Arena Opening," *Victoria Daily Times*, October 31, 1922, page 10.

459 "'Jocko' Arrives To Play With Victoria," *Victoria Daily Times*, November 4, 1922, page 10.

460 "Wilf Loughlin Comes Into Fold; Completes the Squad," *Victoria Daily Times*, November 8, 1922, page 12.

461 "Opening Hockey Game in Coat League Is Set for November 13," *Victoria Daily Times*, October 23, 1922, page 10.

462 "Hockey Show Will Open Monday Night," *Victoria Daily Times*, November 11, 1922, page 10.

463 "Maroons Severely Beaten in Seattle," *Victoria Daily Times*, November 14, 1922, page 10.

464 "Grim Ice Battle Is Won By Pesky Mets," *Victoria Daily Times*, November 16, 1922, page 12.

465 "Cougars Open Home Season With Win Over Vancouver," *Victoria Daily Times*, November 18, 1922, page 10.

466 "'Freddie' and Hec Made Maroons Weep," *Victoria Daily Times*, November 21, 1922, page 12.

467 The Cougars lost as follows: November 24 - Seattle 6, Victoria 4; November 29 - Seattle 5, Victoria 4 in overtime; December 8 - Vancouver 4, Victoria 3; December 11 - Vancouver 2, Victoria 1. All scores taken from the Victoria Daily Times in the next issue after the game.

468 "Speed Loosed in Right Path," *Victoria Daily Times*, December 2, 1922, page 12.

469 "Winning Streak of Seattle At Last Halted by Cougars," *Victoria Daily Times*, December 16, 1922, page 12.

470 "Regina Furnishes Another Sensation Beating Cougars," *Victoria Daily Times*, December 23, 1922, page 10.

471 "Maroons Winning Streak Is Shattered by Meeking's Goal," *Victoria Daily Times*, December 30, 1922, page 8.

472 "Cougars Start New Year Right By Winning a Bitter Battle," *Victoria Daily Times*, January 2, 1923, page 9.

473 "'Freddie's' Sensational Goal Moves Cougars to Top of Race," *Victoria Daily Times*, January 4, 1923, page 10.

474 "No Halting Cougars Who Walk Over Mets to New Coat Records," *Victoria Daily Times*, January 6, 1923, page 10.

Endnotes

475 "Cougars' Winning Streak Is Halted in Very Rough Battle," *Victoria Daily Times*, January 9, 1923, page 10.

476 "Cougars Prove Better Hockey Players Than Tigers, and Win," *Victoria Daily Times*, January 13, 1923, page 10.

477 "Cougars Recover in Time," *Victoria Daily Times*, January 20, 1923, page 10.

478 "Cougars' Mad Rush Halted by Maroons," *Victoria Daily Times*, January 23, 1923, page 10.

479 "Cougars' Claws Are Clipped by Maroons," *Victoria Daily Colonist*, January 25, 1923, page 10.

480 "Cougars Win Out in Goalies Battle," *Victoria Daily Times*, January 29, 1923, page 10.

481 "Cougars Nosed Out of Game By a Funny-Looking Goal by Boucher," *Victoria Daily Times*, February 3, 1923, page 10.

482 "Victoria's Protest on Friday's Game Upheld," *Victoria Daily Times*, February 5, 1922, page 8.

483 "Mickey Ion Will Be at Helm Again on Friday," *Victoria Daily Times*, February 6, 1923, page 10.

484 "Cougars Come To Life Too Late and Lose Out," *Victoria Daily Times*, February 8, 1923, page 10.

485 "Cougars in Fine Form, Hand Mets Their Worst Defeat of The Season," *Victoria Daily Times*, February 10, 1923, page 10.

486 "Cougars play Great Hockey But Lose Out," *Victoria Daily Times*, February 13, 1923, page 10.

487 "Cougars' Defence Too Strong for Edmonton," *Victoria Daily Times*, February 17, 1923, page 10.

488 "Cougars Tear Into Regina and Pick Off Very Spectacular Win," *Victoria Daily Times*, February 20, 1923, page 10.

489 "Saskatoon Mastered In a Terrific Battle," *Victoria Daily Times*, February 22, 1923, page 10.

490 "Eskimos Could Not Stop Fredrickson," *Victoria Daily Times*, February 24, 1923, page 10.

491 "Cougars Stumbled in Last Battle, And Lost," *Victoria Daily Times*, February 27, 1923, page 10.

492 "Terrific Battle Won By Mets, Ties Up Race," *Victoria Daily Times*, March 1, 1923, page 10.

493 "Teams With Backs To Wall Battle Hard," *Victoria Daily Times*, March 2, 1923, page 10.

494 "Cougars Swamp Seattle in Game Which Landed Them in Playoff," *Victoria Daily Times*, March 3, 1923, page 10.

495 "Maroons, Travelling in High Gear, Score Beautiful Win Over Cougars," *Victoria Daily Times*, March 8, 1923, page 10.

496 Boileau, Ron, and Wolf, Philip, "The Pacific Coast Hockey Association," in Diamond, Dan, "Total Hockey," Total Sports Publishing, 2000, page 53.

497 "Coast Teams Had Edge on Prairie Brethren," *Victoria Daily Times*, March 3, 1923, page 10.

498 "Looks Like Big Hockey Bill For Fans This Year," *Victoria Daily Times*, September 8, 1923, page 10.

499 "Maroons Will Open Season Here Nov. 16," *Victoria Daily Times*, October 22, 1923, page 10.

500 "Calgary Gets Oatman For Two Youngsters," *Victoria Daily Times*, October 1, 1923, page 10.

501 "Gibson Agrees to Play Hockey With Victoria," *Victoria Daily Times*, October 25, 1923, page 10.

502 "Sold To Toronto," *Victoria Daily Times*, October 25, 1923, page 10.

503 "Cougars Will Have Capable Reserves," *Victoria Daily Times*, October 27, 1923, page 10.

504 "Clem Loughlin Will Be Late Reporting," *Victoria Daily Times*, October 29, 1923, page 10.

505 "Activities in Hockey Camps Are Very Keen," *Victoria Daily Times*, November 8, 1923, page 10.

506 "Clem Loughlin Will Skipper The Cougars," *Victoria Daily Times*, November 10, 1923, page 10.

507 "Foyston's Shot Wins First Game for Mets," *Victoria Daily Times*, November 13, 1923, page 10.

508 "Wee Robert Slips In Goal That Did Trick," *Victoria Daily Times*, November 15, 1923, page 10.

509 "Cougars Dazzle Fans and Maroons By Their Play and Win Easily," *Victoria Daily Times*, November 17, 1923, page 10.

510 "Duncan Shows Squad Way To Beat Cougars," *Victoria Daily Times*, November 20, 1923, page 10.

511 "Cougars Apply Brakes To Seattle's Winning Streak," *Victoria Daily Times*, November 24, 1923, page 10.

512 "Crescents Battle Well For Period, Then Wilt in Fast Game," *Victoria Daily Times*, December 1, 1923, page 10.

513 "Tigers Go Both Ways at Terrific Clip, Muzzle the Victoria Attack and Win," *Victoria Daily Times*, December 8, 1923, page 10.

514 "Cougars Open Tour With Win Over Esks," *Victoria Daily Times*, December 11, 1923, page 10.

515 "Crescents Avenge Defeat on Coast," *Victoria Daily Times*, December 13, 1923, page 10.

516 "Cougars Are Defeated At Hands of Capitals," *Victoria Daily Times*, December 15, 1923, page 10.

517 "Wicked Pace At End Too Hot For Cougars," *Victoria Daily Times*, December 18, 1923, page 10.

518 "Prairie Clubs Have Gained a Big Edge," *Victoria Daily Times*, December 20, 1923, page 12.

519 "Cougars Wind UP Tour With A Thrilling Win Over Lalonde's Boys," *Victoria Daily Times*, December 22, 1923, page 10.

520 "Cougars Tamed in Great Ice Battle," *Victoria Daily Times*, December 26, 1923, page 10.

521 "Hart's Thrilling Rush Bring Great Victory to Tireless Cougars," *Victoria Daily Times*, December 29, 1923, page 10.

522 "Holmes' Great Save Gave Seattle A Win," *Victoria Daily Times*, January 3, 1924, page 8.

523 "Fowler's great Save Gave Fredrickson Chance To Win Furious Game," *Victoria Daily Times*, January 5, 1924, page 10.

524 "Hart Will Get Chance to Show as a Regular," *Victoria Daily Times*, January 9, 1924, page 10.

525 "Aided By Lucky Goal, Eskimos Score First Victory Over Cougars," *Victoria Daily Times*, January 12, 1924, age 10.

526 "Hart's Cane breaks UP Overtime Battle," *Victoria Daily Times*, January 15, 1924, page 10.

527 "Lester Now Has His Forward Line Nicely Balanced," *Victoria Daily Times*, January 16, 1924, page 10.

528 "Cougars Are Beaten On Long-Soft Shots," *Victoria Daily Times*, January 19, 1924, page 10.

529 "Cougars Force Game Into Overtime, Lose," *Victoria Daily Times*, January 24, 1924, page 8.

530 "Cougars Thrill Fans With Another Great Victory in Overtime," *The Daily Colonist*, January 26, 1924, page 10.

531 "Fiendish Luck Causes Downfall of Cougars In Terrific Battle," *Victoria Daily Times*, February 2, 1924, page 10.

532 "Cougars Are Badly Mauled By Seattle," *Victoria Daily Times*, February 9, 1924, page 10.

533 "Americans Outclass Lester's Hirelings," *Victoria Daily Colonist*, February 9, 1924, page 10.

534 "Cougars Beat Mets Despite Dirty Work," *Victoria Daily Times*, February 12, 1924, page 10.

535 "Cougars Right Back in Form, Defeat Esks," *Victoria Daily Times*, February 16, 1924, page 10.

536 "Cougars Badly Used In Their Last Game," *Victoria Daily Times*, February 28, 1923, page 8.

537 Boileau, Ron and Wolf, Philip, "The Pacific Coast Hockey Association in Diamond, Dan, "Total Hockey," Total Sports Publishing, 2000, page 54.

538 http://www.revolvy.com/main/index.php?s=Seattleper cent20Iceper cent20Arena&sr=50

539 "World Series To be In West," *Victoria Daily Colonist*, August 28, 1924, page 11.

540 "'Hec' Fowler Sold To Boston, And Holmes Is Signed To Replace Him," *Victoria Daily Times*, October 30, 1924, page 12.

541 "Four Cougars Are Placed On Waive List by L. Patrick," *Victoria Daily Times*, October 13, 1924, page 11.

542 "Cougars Play First Hockey Game Here Christmas Day," *Victoria Daily Times*, November 4, 1924, page 10.

543 "Goal-getting Ace Will Play Centre Fr the Cougars," *Victoria Daily Times*, November 6, 1924, page 9.

544 "Loughlin and Hart Sign For Another Term With Cougars," *Victoria Daily Times*, November 7, 1924, page 14.

545 "Foyston and Walker To Become Cougars," *Victoria Daily Times*, November 10, 1924, page 10.

546 "Cougars Hold Two Stiff Practices: Team Looks Smart," *Victoria Daily Times*, November 24, 1924, page 10.

547 "Meeking Showing Sensational Form in Hard Practices," *Victoria Daily Times*, November 26, 1924, page 10.

548 "Cougars To play Calgary Tigers at Fort To-night," *Victoria Daily Times*, December 1, 1924, page 9.

549 "Cougars Play To Draw Again With Calgary Tigers," *Victoria Daily Times*, December 3, 1924, page 10.

550 "Holmes's Fine Work Saved Regina From Defeating Cougars," *Victoria Daily Times*, December 5, 1924, page 10.

551 "'Mickey' Likely To Be On Deck," *Victoria Daily Colonist*, September 17, 1924, page 10.

552 "Cougars Give Dazzling Display Against Tigers, and Win Opener," *Victoria Daily Times*, December 9, 1924, page 10.

553 "Second Straight Win Is Scored By Cougars," *Victoria Daily Times*, December 12, 1924, page 10.

554 "Sheiks' Defence Proves Too Tough For Victoria Pets," *Victoria Daily Times*, December 15, 1924, page 10.

555 "Cougars Suffer Many Penalties and Go Under, 2-0," *Victoria Daily Times*, December 17, 1924, page 10.

556 "Furious Rally Near Close Beats Cougars," *Victoria Daily Times*, December 18, 1924, page 10.

557 "Cougars Glad To Say Bye-Bye To Prairies," *Victoria Daily Times*, December 19, 1924, page 10.

558 "Cougars' Style of Play Beat Maroons," *Victoria Daily Times*, December 23, 1924, page 9.

559 "Cougars' Superior Team-play and Speed Bring Victory in Opener," *Victoria Daily Times*, December 26, 1924, page 9.

560 "Cougars Are Far Too Good For Regina Caps," *Victoria Daily Times*, December 29, 1924, page 9.

561 "Scoring Record For Season For Cougars," *Victoria Daily Times*, January 2, 1925, page 9.

562 "Maroons Bounce Cougars Out of Stride," *Victoria Daily Times*, January 5, 1925, page 8.

563 "Cougars Play Their Real Game and Win," *Victoria Daily Times*, January 8, 1925, page 10.

564 "Cougars' Great Win Places Them On Top," *Victoria Daily Times*, January 12, 1925, page 8.

565 "Cougars Perform Well But Regina Out-scored Them," *Victoria Daily Times*, January 16, 1925, page 10.

566 "Cougars Nosed Out In Thrilling Encounter," *Victoria Daily Times*, January 19, 1925, page 13.

567 "Cougars Polish Off Tour With Fine Win," *Victoria Daily Times*, January 20, 1925, page 10.

568 "Cougars' Rally End With Victory In Sight," *Victoria Daily Times*, January 23, 1925, page 10.

569 "Jocko's Gal Gives Cougars Brilliant Win Over Eskimos," *The Daily Colonist*, January 25, 1925, page 10.

570 "Cougars Beat Regina And Now Lead League," *Victoria Daily Times*, January 31, 1925, page 9.

571 "Walker's Great Shot Brings Another Win," *Victoria Daily Times*, February 2, 1925, page 9.

572 "Poor Ice And Lucky Goal Beat Cougars," *Victoria Daily Times*, February 5, 1925, page 10.

573 "Simpson's Tally, With Fraser Off, A Winner," *Victoria Daily Times*, February 7, 1925, page 10.

574 "Cougars Meet Third Reverse on Prairies," *Victoria Daily Times*, February 10, 1925, page 10.

575 "Cougars Rip Through Regina For Fine Win," *Victoria Daily Times*, February 12, 1925, page 10.

576 "Cougars Nosed Out of A Crucial Battle," *Victoria Daily Times*, February 16, 1925, page 13.

577 "Victoria Stays On Top and Maroons Pass Out," *Victoria Daily Times*, February 19, 1925, page 10.

578 "Early Jump Helped Cougars Take Game," *Victoria Daily Times*, February 24, 1925, page 10.

579 "Four Goals In Ten Minutes Bring Win," *Victoria Daily Times*, March 2, 1925, page 10.

580 "Hockey Fever Holds Town In Tight Grip," *Victoria Daily Times*, March 5, 1925, page 9.

581 "Cougars Gain Two-Goal Lead in First Playoff Game," *Victoria Daily Times*, March 7, 1925, page 10.

582 "Cougar Defence Smothers Sheiks," *Victoria Daily Times*, March 11, 1925, page 10.

583 "Cougars Are Back Home After Spectacular Prairie Tour," *Victoria Daily Times*, March 16, 1925, page 10.

584 "Fans Gobble Up Seats Like Dish of Sweets," *Victoria Daily Times*, March 17, 1925, page 10.

585 "Hockey Game Is To Be Broadcast by 'Jim' and 'Les'," *Victoria Daily Times*, March 18, 1925, page 10.

586 "Cougars Bring First Hockey Title to Victoria In Twelve Years," *Victoria Daily Times*, March 19, 1925, page 10.

587 "Packed House Will Witness First Game of World's Series," *Victoria Daily Colonist*, March 20, 1925, page 10.

588 "Canadiens Expect To Win Series In Three First Games," *Victoria Daily Times*, March 19, 1925, page 10 and "World's Series Will Start Here Tomorrow," *Victoria Daily Colonist*, March 20, 1925, page 10.

589 The Allan Cup, symbolic of the national championship for men's ice hockey, was established in 1908. The Winnipeg Falcons had won this trophy in 1920.

590 The Winnipeg Falcons represented Canada in the inaugural ice-hockey tournament at the 1920 Olympics in Antwerp.

591 "Danderand Does Not Expect To Win Three Straight Games," Victoria Daily Times, March 21, 1925, page 10.

592 "Cougars Jump Into Lead in World's Ice Series," Victoria Daily Colonist, March 22, 1925, pages 1 and 11, and "Cougars Carry Winning Streak Into World's Series," Victoria Daily Times, March 23, 1925, page 8.

593 "Cougars Make It Two Straight In World's Series," Victoria Daily Times, March 24, 1925, page 10 and "Cougars Win Second of series," Victoria Daily Colonist, March 24, 1925, pages 1 and 6.

594 "Canadiens Will Adopt Victoria's System to-Night," Victoria Daily Times, March 27, 1925, page 11.

595 "Cougars' Winning Streak Is Finally Halted," Victoria Daily Times, March 28, 1925, page 10.

596 Victoria Daily Colonist, March 29, 1925, page 6.

597 "Fans Will See Hockey As Played Under Eastern Rules," Victoria Daily Times, March 30, 1925, page 10.

598 "Victoria Wins Stanley Cup in Decisive Manner," Victoria Daily Times, March 31, 1925, page 10.

599 "Cougars Swap Canadiens in Deciding Game," The Daily Colonist, March 31, 1925, page 10.

600 "Cougars Win Stanley Cup Victoria Daily Colonist, March 31, 1925, page 1.

601 "Canadiens Unable to Cope With Terrific Speed of Cougars," Victoria Daily Times, March 31, 1925, page 10.

602 "Victoria's Citizens Laud Lester Patrick and Band of Cougars," Victoria Daily Colonist, April 3, 1925, page 10 and "Hockey Furore Ends at Great Victory Banquet," Victoria Daily Times, April 3, 1925, page 10.

603 "Frank Patrick Wants Seattle Back Again," Victoria Daily Colonist, April 30, 1925, page 12.

604 "No Ice Hockey in Seattle Next Winter," Victoria Daily Colonist, July 28, 1925, page 10.

605 "Champ Says Capitals May Be Transferred," Victoria Daily Colonist, August 30, 1925, page 12.

606 "Portland Rosebuds Replace Regina in Hockey World," Victoria Daily Colonist, September 16, 1925, page 10.

607 "Alterations In Western Hockey Rules Are Made," Victoria Daily Colonist, September 17, 1925, page 10.

608 "Cougars to Tour Eastern Centres Shortly," Victoria Daily Colonist, October 16, 1925, page 11 and "Cougars Will Make Tour of East," Victoria Daily Times, October 15, 1925, page 10.

609 "Contracts Sent to All Cougars," Victoria Daily Times, October 17, 1925, page 8.

610 "Russel [sic] Oatman, Star Amateur, Is a Cougar," Victoria Daily Times, October 20, 1925, page 10.

611 "Jack 'Hookcheck' Walker Will Shine With Cougars Again," Victoria Daily Colonist, October 21, 1925, page 10.

612 "Cougars' Dynamo Is returning To Team," Victoria Daily Times, October 23, 1925, page 12.

613 "Halderson Coming Back To Cougars For Defence Work," Victoria Daily Times, October 24, 1925, page 10.

614 "Capt. Clem Loughlin Will Join World Champions at 'Peg Soon," Victoria Daily Colonist, October 25, 1925, page 10.

615 "Harry Meeking Is Ninth Man to Sign Up For Coming Season," Victoria Daily Colonist, October 28, 1925, page 10.

616 "May Quit Hockey," Victoria Daily Times, October 31, 1925, page 8.

617 "Cougars All Set With Fredrickson Signed," Victoria Daily Times, November 6, 1925, page 12.

618 "Victoria Cougars Left Winnipeg for Montreal To-day," Victoria Daily Times, November 12, 1925, page 10.

619 "Cougars Open Eyes of East," Victoria Daily Times, November 17, 1925, page 10.

620 "Greatest Team to Come Out of West, Say Fans," Victoria Daily Times, November 19, 1925, page 12.

621 "Ottawa Elated Over Defeat of The Cougars," Victoria Daily Times, November 20, 1925, page 12.

622 "Boucher Tried To Cut Halderson With Stick," Victoria Daily Times, November 23, 1925, page 12.

623 "Five-Man Defence All That Humbled Cougars," Victoria Daily Times, November 24, 1925, page 10.

624 "Cougars Play Another Great Game, But Lose," Victoria Daily Times, November 26, 1925, page 12.

625 "Simpson's Orphan Goal Put Cougars Down Again," Victoria Daily Times, November 27, 1925, page 12.

626 "Cougars Succeed As Hockey Missionaries," Victoria Daily Times, December 3, 1925, page 10.

627 "Hockey Fans May Reserve Seats for Season, Monday Morning," Victoria Daily Times, November 28, 1925, page 14.

628 "Lehman's Luck Held and Champions Lost," Victoria Daily Times, December 4, 1925, page 12.

629 "Cougars Disappoint Fans In First Game," *Victoria Daily Times*, December 7, 1925, page 14.

630 "Cougars Will Take Ice Without 'Slim'," *Victoria Daily Times*, December 9, 1925, page 12.

631 "Unusual Climax For Thrilling Game," *Victoria Daily Times*, December 10, 1925, page 12.

632 "Protest Is Upheld and Air Is Cleared On Stick Incident," *Victoria Daily Times*, December 11, 1925, page 12.

633 "Cougars Play Like Trojans of Old and Hold Calgary Even," *Victoria Daily Times*, December 14, 1925, page 12.

634 "Cougars Finally Lose In Overtime Struggle," *Victoria Daily Times*, December 17, 1925, page 12.

635 "Crippled Champs To Fight To Last Ditch," *Victoria Daily Times*, December 18, 1925, page 16.

636 "Cougars Win Their First League Game," *Victoria Daily Times*, December 19, 1925, page 10.

637 "Weakened Cougars Go Under in Hard Battle," *Victoria Daily Times*, December 22, 1925, page 12.

638 "Trying To Fill Gaps In Champions' Ranks," *Victoria Daily Times*, December 23, 1925, page 12.

639 "Cougars Play Gamely, But Lose Again," *Victoria Daily Times*, December 24, 1925, page 10.

640 "Cougars Defeat Calgary Tigers By Four to One," *The Daily Colonist*, December 27, 1925, page 12 and "Cougars Back From Strenuous Tour of Prairies With Win," *Victoria Daily Times*, December 28, 1925, page 1.

641 "Victoria Whitewashes Edmonton Eskimos in Great Holiday Battle," *Victoria Daily Colonist*, January 2, 1926, page 12.

642 "Cougars Have Edge In Two Periods, But Lose," *Victoria Daily Times*, January 5, 1925, page 10.

643 "Little Defence Man's Goal Beats Cougars," *Victoria Daily Times*, January 9, 1925, page 12.

644 "Cougars Dashing Rally Brings Great Victory," *Victoria Daily Times*, January 14, 1926, page 10.

645 "Too Much Trapp Puts Cougars Down and Out," *Victoria Daily Times*, January 16, 1926, page 8.

646 "Sidelights," *Victoria Daily Times*, January 16, 1926, page 8.

647 "No Holding Cougars In Thrilling Display Against Edmonton Esks," *Victoria Daily Times*, January 19, 1926, page 10.

648 "Fredrickson Again Brings Home a Win," *Victoria Daily Times*, January 26, 1926, page 10.

649 "Frank Foyston Puts On His Old Uniform As Fighting Cougar," *Victoria Daily Times*, January 27, 1926, page 10.

650 "Lucky Goal One Minute Before Time Gives Cougars One Point," *Victoria Daily Times*, January 16, 1926, page 10.

651 "Lester Patrick Hero In Win Over Sheiks," *Victoria Daily Times*, February 4, 1926, page 10.

652 "Esks Prove Far From Soft Spot For Champs," *Victoria Daily Times*, February 6, 1926, page 12.

653 "Wee Jocko Nets Great Goal and Cougars Win," *Victoria Daily Times*, February 8, 1926, page 12.

654 "Orphan Goal by Lester Gives Champs A Win," *Victoria Daily Times*, February 9, 1926, page 10.

655 "Two Goals In Last Two Minutes Beat Cougars," *Victoria Daily Times*, February 11, 1926, page 10.

656 "Frank Foyston Makes His First Bow To-night," *Victoria Daily Times*, February 12, 1926, page 14.

657 "Cougars' Furious Rally Clips Rosebuds," *Victoria Daily Times*, February 13, 1926, page 8.

658 "Cougars Have Too Much In Reserve For Maroons, And Win In A Gallop," *Victoria Daily Times*, February 17, 1926, page 10.

659 "Cougars Brush Edmonton Aside, 4-1," *Victoria Daily Times*, February 20, 1926, page 8.

660 "Cougars Almost Certain of Playoff," *Victoria Daily Times*, February 27, 1926, page 10.

661 "Lester's Goal Lifts Champs Into Playoff," *Victoria Daily Times*, March 2, 1926, page 10.

662 "Cougars Close Strong and Win Very Easily," *Victoria Daily Times*, March 6, 1926, page 10.

663 "Calgary Win From Cougars For First Time This Season," *Victoria Daily Times*, March 10, 1926, page 10.

664 "Former Team-mates To Lead Opposing Forces," *Victoria Daily, Times*, March 12, 1926, page 12.

665 "Saskatoon Fails To Gain The Advantage," *Victoria Daily Times*, March 13, 1926, page 10.

666 "Victoria Dusts Off Saskatoon," *Victoria Daily Times*, March 17, 1926, page 10.

667 "Cougars Enter Second Game of Playoff With a Two-Goal Lead," *Victoria Daily Times*, March 22, 1926, page 12.

668 "Victoria Fans Will Travel to Mainland To See Final Game," *Victoria Daily Times*, March 20, 1926, page 12.

669 "Victoria Vanquishes Western Rivals," *Victoria Daily Times*, March 23, 1926, page 10.

670 "Cougars To Clash With Montreal or Ottawa For World Hockey Title," *Victoria Daily Times*, March 24, 1926, page 10.

671 Archie Wills, "With The Cougars," *Victoria Daily Times*, March 26, 1926, page 12.

672 Archie Wills, "With The Cougars," *Victoria Daily Times*, March 29, 1926, page 12.

673 Archie Wills, "With The Cougars," *Victoria Daily Times*, March 30, 1926, page 10.

674 "Montreal 3, Victoria 1, In First Game," *Victoria Daily Times*, March 31, 1926, page 12.

675 "Montreal 3, Victoria 1, In Second," *Victoria Daily Times*, April 2, 1926, page 12.

676 "Westerners Almost Even Favorites In Stanley Cup Race," *Victoria Daily Times*, April 5, 1926, page 12.

677 "Montreal Played Better Hockey, Defeated Cougars As The Curtain Drops," *Victoria Daily Times*, April 7, 1926, page 12.

678 "Lester Back Smiling; No Alibis But Points To Cougar Injury List," *Victoria Daily Times*, April 13, 1926, page 10.

679 *In reality, Anderson had played his last game of hockey. He would return to Victoria to coach the Victoria Cubs for one season but returned to civilian life in 1930.*

680 "Ice Hockey Series Made 'Victoria' Household Word," *Victoria Daily Times*, April 14, 1926, page 10.

681 "Hockey In East Is Now In Big Business Class," *Victoria Daily Times*, April 15, 1926, page 12.

682 "Montreal Story Denied By Pres. Richardson," *Victoria Daily Times*, January 11, 1926, page 12.

683 Frayne, Trent, "The Mad Men of Hockey," McClelland and Stewart, 1978, page 170.

684 "Victoria Cougars Pass Into Control of Detroit," *Victoria Daily Colonist*, May 4, 1926, page 10.

685 *The deal never went through as initially announced, as the final price was not paid. Briden and Keats ended up with Detroit, while Shore and Oliver did sign with Boston.*

686 http://www.sihrhockey.org/member_team_sheet.cfm?team_id=23&season_id=52.

687 *Oak Bay News*, May 30, 2001, pages 1 and 3.

688 *Victoria Times Colonist*, May 26, 2001, page A1.

689 "Victoria Will Have Strong Team in New Coast Hockey League," *Victoria Daily Times*, September 26, 1928, page 8.

690 "Opening Dates For Pro Hockey League Announced To-day," *Victoria Daily Times*, October 2, 1928, page 9.

691 "Eighteen Games In Each Town; Radio To be Widely Used," *Victoria Daily Times*, October 22, 1928, page 8.

692 "'The Moose,' Hero of Victoria Fans, Will Return This Season," *Victoria Daily Times*, November 16, 1928, page 8.

693 http://www.sihrhockey.org/member_team_sheet.cfm?team_id=280&season_id=53 sand http://www.sihrhockey.org/member_team_sheet.cfm?team_id=323&season_id=54

694 "Victoria Cubs Take Opening Game," *Victoria Daily Colonist*, November 20, 1928, page 10.

695 "Red Kelly's Goal Give Cubs a Win In Opening Battle," *Victoria Daily Times*, November 20, 1928, page 8.

696 "Victoria Cubs Take Lead in the P.C.H.L.," *Victoria Daily Times*, November 22, 1928, page 10.

697 "Bucks Skate Their Heads Off to Hand Cubs a 3-1 Defeat," *Victoria Daily Times*, November 28, 1928, page 8.

698 "Buckaroos Rally In Last Period to Gain Draw With Victoria," *Victoria Daily Times*, November 30, 1928, page 8.

699 "Cubs Slip Badly In Third Period To Let Esks Win In Overtime," *Victoria Daily Times*, December 1, 1928, page 8.

700 "Seattle Eskimos Show Their Class To Blank Cubs By Score of 2-0," *Victoria Daily Times*, December 5, 1928, page 8.

701 "Sanderson's Goal In Overtime Gives Lions Sweet Win Over Cubs," *Victoria Daily Times*, December 11, 1928, page 9.

702 "Cubs Break Jackson's String of Shut-outs by Lacing Lions 5-1," *Victoria Daily Times*, December 12, 1928, page 8.

703 704 "Cubs and Buckaroos Battle to draw in a Thrilling Game," *Victoria Daily Times*, December 19, 1928, page 8.

704 "Victoria Cubs Jump Into Second Place by Win Over Bucks," *Victoria Daily Times*, December 21, 1928, page 8.

705 "Red-headed Kelly Leads Cubs to Win Over Seattle Esks," *Victoria Daily Times*, December 22, 1928, page 8.

706 "Cubs Creep Nearer Lions By Holding Eskimos to Draw," *Victoria Daily Times*, December 26, 1928, page 10.

707 "Cubs Fail to get By Stiff Defence And Vancouver Wins," *Victoria Daily Times*, January 2, 1929, page 8.

708 "Bill Borland Is Sold To Seattle Eskimos," *Victoria Daily Times*, January 2, 1929, page 8.

709 "Cubs Again Find Vancouver Lions A Goal Too Good," *Victoria Daily Times*, January 3, 1929, page 8.

710 "Portland Shutout Victoria to Stay In Second Place," *The Vancouver Sun*, January 9, 1929, page 12.

711 "Policeman's Aid is Called When Bucks Win From Victoria," *Victoria Daily Times*, January 11, 1929, page 9.

712 "Lady Luck Deserts Cubs and They Lose Tough One to Esks," *Victoria Daily Times*, January 12, 1929, page 8.

713 "A Casualty," *Victoria Daily Times*, January 12, 1929, page 8.

714 "Cubs Display Fine Improvement to Win From Seattle Club," *Victoria Daily Times*, January 16, 1929, page 10.

715 "Overtime Win Over Lions Lifts Cubs Out of the Cellar," *Victoria Daily Times*, January 22, 1929, page 8.

716 "Lions and Cubs Put Up Furious Battle In Overtime Draw," *The Vancouver Sun*, January 23, 1929, page 12.

717 "Bond's Goal With Two Minutes to Go Gives Bucks Draw," *Victoria Daily Times*, January 30, 1929, page 8.

718 Numbers were taken from my statistical analysis of all games played in the 1929-1930 season.

719 "Referee Ion Hits Fan As Climax to Wild Hockey Game," *Victoria Daily Times*, February 12, 1929, page 8.

720 "Vancouver Increases Lead by 2 to 1 Win; Ion Hits Spectator," *Victoria Daily Colonist*, February 12, 1929, page 13.

721 "Irate Fans Litter the Ice With Everything From Onions to Tacks," *Victoria Daily Times*, February 27, 1929, page 8.

722 "Eskimos Send Locals Down to Defeat for Ninth Straight Loss," *The Daily Colonist*, February 27, 1929, page 13.

723 "Fast Game Expected When Victoria Takes On Sound City Crew," *Victoria Daily Colonist*, January 15, 1929, page 12.

724 "Resigns as Manager of Victoria Cubs," *Victoria Daily Colonist*, February 27, 1929, page

725 "Red Hardaker Plays Spectacularly And Cubs Trounce Lions," *Victoria Daily Times*, March 6, 1929, page 10.

726 "Bucks Regain Second Position In League By Defeating Cubs," *Victoria Daily Times*, March 13, 1929, page 10.

727 "Portland Chalks Up 2-1 Victory in Last Fixture With Locals," *Victoria Daily Colonist*, March 13, 1929, page 10.

728 "Smiling and Happy, Pete Muldoon Had Not Single Enemy," *Victoria Daily Times*, March 14, 1929, page 8.

729 More details of Pete Muldoon's life are available at http://www.seattlehockey.net/Seattle_Hockey_Homepage/Articles_files/PeteMuldoon.pdf

730 "Redpath Sinks Puck Three Times as Cubs Hand Bucks Setback," *Victoria Daily Times*, March 15, 1929, page 8.

731 "Eskimos Win And Regain Second Place," *Victoria Daily Times*, March 6, 1929, page 8.

732 "Cubs Stage Finest Exhibition of Season But Lose to Seattle," *Victoria Daily Times*, March 20, 1929, page 10.

733 "Frank Patrick Re-elected," *Victoria Daily Times*, November 4, 1929, page 8.

734 "Victoria Cubs Oppose Seattle In First Game," *Victoria Daily Times*, November 4, 1929, page 8.

735 "Seven Members of Cubs Limber Up At Opening Practice," *Victoria Daily Times*, November 5, 1929, page 8.

736 "Roster Of Ice Team Completed," *Victoria Daily Times*, November 9, 1929, page 8.

737 There is considerable confusion regarding the date of the fire. Most online sources say the fire occurred on November 11, 1929. However, newspaper accounts published on November 12, 1929, talk about the fire on Sunday morning. A quick check of a 1929 calendar clearly shows Sunday's date as November 10. A report entitled "Fire Hits Hockey Arena" in the Spokane Spokesman-Review edition of November 12, 1929, is dated November 10.

738 "Arena Destroyed in Early Morning Blaze," *Victoria Daily Colonist*, November 12, 1929, page 1.

739 "Insurance Partially Covers Loss From Serious Outbreak," *Victoria Daily Colonist*, November 12, 1929, page 1.

The History of Professional Hockey in Victoria, BC: 1911-2011

740 "Fire Victims Miraculously Escape Death," *Victoria Daily Colonist*, November 12, 1929, page 2.

741 "Famous Set of Pictures Destroyed," *Victoria Daily Times*, November 12, 1929, page 6.

742 "Incendiarism in Arena Fire is Suggested," *Victoria Daily Times*, November 12, 1929, page 1.

743 "Cubs Will Become Road Team or Be Absorbed By Other Three Clubs," *Victoria Daily Times*, November 12, 1929, page 6.

744 "Cageless Cubs Workout in New Hockey Raiment," *Vancouver Sun*, November 13, 1929, page 20.

745 "Campaign Being Launched to Secure New Arena in Victoria," *Victoria Daily Times*, November 13, 1929, page 10.

746 "Great Need in City for Auditorium," *Victoria Daily Colonist*, November 28, 1929, page 2.

747 "Reserve Set on Site for Auditorium," *Victoria Daily Colonist*, February 11, 1939, pages 1 and 2.

748 "Mr. Coleman is Told Need of Auditorium," *Victoria Daily Colonist*, March 18, 1930, page 3.

749 "Cubs Will Play Games on the Road This Season," *Victoria Daily Times*, November 14, 1929, page 9.

750 "Lions Give Finished Display to Win Opening P.C.H.L. Game," *Victoria Daily Times*, November 19, 1929, page 8.

751 "Victoria Cubs Are Tossed for Their Second Straight Loss," *Victoria Daily Times*, November 20, 1929, page 8.

752 "Victoria Cubs Whitewash Portland Buckaroos," *Victoria Daily Colonist*, December 18, 1929, page 12.

753 "Cubs Display Real Form To Win Over Esks In Thriller," *Victoria Daily Times*, December 21, 1929, page 8.

754 In an effort to have some meaningful statistics, I read game summaries in the Victoria Daily Times, the Victoria Daily Colonist, and the Vancouver Sun, all local newspapers, and compiled a record of games played, the final score, as well as goals for and goals against the Cubs.

755 Joe Smith, "Some Sidelights on Victoria's Orphaned Ice Team," *Victoria Daily Colonist*, December 1, 1929, page 25.

756 Joe Smith, "Some Sidelights on Victoria's Orphaned Ice Team," *Victoria Daily Colonist*, January 5, 1930, page 25.

757 "Tacoma Dropped From Coast Ice Hockey," *Victoria Daily Colonist*, January 2, 1931, page 13.

758 "United Actions for Ice Arena," *Victoria Daily Colonist*. February 29, 1936, page 2.

759 "Mill Building," *Victoria Daily Colonist*, April 29, 1937, page 6.

760 "Resurrect Forum Idea," *Victoria Daily Colonist*, January 9, 1940, page 6.

761 "Mayor Is Head of Arena Drive," *Victoria Daily Colonist*, January 31, 1940, page 2.

762 "Arena Prospectus Is Issued by Junior Chamber Executive," *Victoria Daily Colonist*, February 7, 1940, page 6.

763 "Want No Lien On New Arena," *Victoria Daily Colonist*, February 13, 1940, page 9.

764 "More Groups In Favor of Arena," *Victoria Daily Colonist*, February 25, 1940, page 19.

765 "Drive Attains First $20,000," *Victoria Daily Colonist*, March 17, 1940, page 3.

766 "Will Continue Arena Efforts," *Victoria Daily Colonist*, April 2, 1940, page 3

767 "Staying With Arena Project," *Victoria Daily Colonist*, April 12, 1940, page 2.

768 "Arena Plan Dropped Due to War," *Victoria Daily Colonist*, June 1, 1940, page 1.

769 "New Hope For Arena," *Victoria Daily Colonist*, December 20, 1940, page 17.

770 "Now You Can Have An Arena Now," *Victoria Daily Colonist*, January 26, 1941, page 15.

771 "Building Terms," *Victoria Daily Colonist*, May 29, 1941, page 5.

772 "Arena Plans Going Ahead," *Victoria Daily Colonist*, May 30, 1941, page 14.

773 "Rink Permit," *Victoria Daily Colonist*, June 4, 1941, page 13.

774 "Arena Will Open Oct. 15 Says Olson," *The British Colonist*, June 7, 1941, page 11.

775 "Ice Arena Tenders," *Victoria Daily Colonist*, August 3, 1941, page 19.

776 "Pressure Stepped Up Through Pump," *Victoria Daily Colonist*, August 20, 1941, page 3.

777 "Announcing the Opening," *Victoria Daily Colonist*, November 11, 1941, page 9.

778 "Colorful Display To Feature Rink Opening in City," *Victoria Daily Colonist*, November 20, 1941, page 13.

Endnotes

779 "Official Opening of Victoria's New Arena," *Victoria Daily Colonist*, November 23, 1941, page 15.

780 "Sports Circles Feel Blackout," *Victoria Daily Colonist*, December 10, 1941, page 11.

781 "Figure Skating Club Organized," *Victoria Daily Colonist*, November 11, 1941, page 9.

782 "Spectacular Fire Destroys Sports Centre and Arena," *Victoria Daily Colonist*, April 25, 1944, page 1.

783 "Gas Leakage Caused Fire," *Victoria Daily Colonist*, April 27, 1944, page 11.

784 "Suggest Council Build Ice Arena," *Victoria Daily Colonist*, April 27, 1944, page 3.

785 "Seeks Concessions for Arena," *Victoria Daily Colonist*, April 27, 1944, page 11.

786 "Arena Proposals Under Discussion," *Victoria Daily Colonist*, May 21, 1944, page 17.

787 "Work It Out," *Victoria Daily Colonist*, May 24, 1944, page 4.

788 "Olson Offers to Co-operate In Building Public Arena," *Victoria Daily Colonist*, June 3, 1944, page 1.

789 "Arena Committee to Seek Grants," *Victoria Daily Colonist*, June 9, 1944, page 11.

790 "City in Favor of New Arena," *Victoria Daily Colonist*, June 23, 1944, page 5.

791 "Victoria Must Have an Arena," *Victoria Daily Colonist*, July 4, 1944, page 5.

792 "No Action on Arena Plans," *Victoria Daily Colonist*, August 3, 1944, page 8.

793 "Arena Now or Never," *Victoria Daily Colonist*, August 18, 1944, page 10.

794 "No Action Yet On Arena Plan," *Victoria Daily Colonist*, September 28, 1944, page 2.

795 "City Ratepayers to Vote On $150,000 Arena Loan," *Victoria Daily Colonist*, October 5, 1944, page 1 and 2.

796 "Vote for an Arena and You'll Get an Arena." *Victoria Daily Colonist*, December 13, 1944, page 9.

797 "Arena By-Law Is Endorsed," *Victoria Daily Colonist*, December 15, 1944, page 1.

798 "Decisive Vote," *Victoria Daily Colonist*, December 15, 1944, page 4.

799 "Arena May Be Ready For Winter Season," *Victoria Daily Colonist*, January 9, 1945, page 9.

800 "Canvass Planned For Arena Funds." *Victoria Daily Colonist*, January 11, 1945, page 12.

801 "It's Now or Never," *Victoria Daily Colonist*, January 21, 1945, page 5.

802 "Student Canvassers Hold Arena Campaign Rally," *Victoria Daily Colonist*, January 27, 1945, page 7.

803 "Over $31,000 Collected in Arena Drive," *Victoria Daily Colonist*, February 2, 1945, page 9.

804 "Charmingly Gay," *Victoria Daily Colonist*, February 8, 1945, page 3.

805 "Final Public Appeal Will Be Made March 3 - Gigantic Parade Slated - Committee Named," *Victoria Daily Colonist*, February 23, 1945, page 9.

806 "Memorial Arena Deemed Certain," *Victoria Daily Colonist*, March 4, 1945, page 1.

807 "Architects Named for Arena plans," *Victoria Daily Colonist*, April 21, 1945, page 9.

808 "Accepts $65,000 Cheque for Arena," *Victoria Daily Colonist*, April 25, 1945, page 9.

809 "City Arena Committee Confers With Patrick," *Victoria Daily Colonist*, May 23, 1945, page 9.

810 "Approve Purchase Of Lot for Arena," *Victoria Daily Colonist*, June 5, 1945, page 12.

811 "Work Gets Underway On Arena Site Here," *Victoria Daily Colonist*, June 19, 1945, page 9.

812 "Complete Plans and Estimates For Victoria's Memorial Arena," *Victoria Daily Colonist*, September 27, 1945, page 11.

813 "Local Arena May Be Ready Next Season," *Victoria Daily Colonist*, October 16, 1945, page 13.

814 Editorial, *Victoria Daily Colonist*, October 16, 1945, page 4.

815 *Victoria Daily Colonist*, November 1, 1945, page 1.

816 "Concrete Roof Approved by City Council," *Victoria Daily Colonist*, November 6, 1945, page 19.

817 "Cost of Arena To be Learned At Later Date," *Victoria Daily Colonist*, December 18, 1945, page 9.

818 "Arena Contract," *Victoria Daily Colonist*, December 29, 1945, page 9.

819 "Accept Tender," *Victoria Daily Colonist*, March 15, 1946, page 5.

820 "Arena Plans Held Up for Five Weeks," *Victoria Daily Colonist*, March 28, 1946, page 9.

821 "Council Will Not Delay Arena Project," *Victoria Daily Colonist*, May 14, 1946, page 3.

822 "To Commence Construction Of New Arena," *Victoria Daily Colonist*, May 21, 1946, page 1.

823 "Randall to Get Willows on Terms Reserving Ground as Sport Centre," *Victoria Daily Colonist*, May 28, 1945, page 5.

824 "Ratepayers Agree to Sale of Willows By Safe Majority," *Victoria Daily Colonist*, October 25, 1946, page 1.

825 "Soil at Arena Site to be Turned Today," *Victoria Daily Colonist*, June 12, 1946, page 14.

826 "Vancouver Man Supervises Arena," *Victoria Daily Colonist*, July 9, 1946, page 1.

827 "City Hall," *Victoria Daily Colonist*, September 7, 1946, page 19.

828 "Arena Progress Hampered By Shortages," *Victoria Daily Colonist*, October 11, 1946, page 20.

829 "Municipal Briefs Of the District," *Victoria Daily Colonist*, October 18, 1946, page 21.

830 "Steel Work Starts on Memorial Arena," *Victoria Daily Colonist*, October 26, 1946, page 3.

831 "Arena Ready Next Winter Engineer Says," *Victoria Daily Colonist*, January 30, 1947, page 3.

832 "Victoria Civic Memorial Ice Arena," *Victoria Daily Colonist*, February 4, 1947, page 5.

833 "Contract on Roof, Pillars Of Arena Let at $118,315," *Victoria Daily Colonist*, February 25, 1947, page 1.

834 "Arena to Be Similar to Washington Structure," *Victoria Daily Colonist*, March 9, 1947, page 1.

835 "Memorial Arena Construction Advances," *Victoria Daily Colonist*, April 19, 1947, page 3.

836 "Coast Hockey Head Interested in Victoria as League Member," *Victoria Daily Colonist*, May 3, 1947, page 11.

837 "Five-Man Commission To Operate City's Arena," *Victoria Daily Colonist*, May 7, 1947, page 1.

838 "Council Elects Arena Members," *Victoria Daily Colonist*, June 3, 1947, page 9.

839 "Two Resign From Membership In Five-Man Arena Commission," *Victoria Daily Colonist*, June 12, 1947, page 19.

840 "Olson Resigns as Member of Arena Body," *Victoria Daily Colonist*, June 26, 1947, page 3.

841 "Fletcher Chosen as Chairman Of Victoria Arena Commission," *Victoria Daily Colonist*, July 18, 1947, page 19.

842 "Council Members Worry Over Rising Arena Costs," *Victoria Daily Colonist*, May 17, 1947, page 1.

843 "Roof of Memorial Arena Takes Shape," *Victoria Daily Colonist*, July 26, 1947, page 1.

844 "Forms Removed From Completed Arena Roof Section," *Victoria Daily Colonist*, August 8, 1947, page 19.

845 "The Local Scene," *Victoria Daily Colonist*, September 19, 1947, page 3.

846 "Arena Will Be Most Modern in Canada," *Victoria Daily Colonist*, October 2, 1947, page 13.

847 Editorial, *Victoria Daily Colonist*, October 17, 1947, page 4.

848 "Council Group Faces New Arena Problem Of Honoring War Dead in Civic Building," *Victoria Daily Colonist*, October 19, 1947, page 21.

849 "Kiwanis Club Hears Hamilton Voice Staunch Defence of Arena Project," *Victoria Daily Colonist*, December 10, 1947, page 9.

850 "Completion of Arena Starts Council Battle," *Victoria Daily Colonist*, January 6, 1949, page 1.

851 Jim Tang, "The Hockey Franchise," *Victoria Daily Colonist*, January 7, 1948, page 9.

852 "Report Shows $104,992 All Left in Arena Fund," *Victoria Daily Colonist*, January 11, 1948, page 1.

853 "Arena Report," *Victoria Daily Colonist*, January 13, 1948, page 4.

854 "Additional Cost Of Arena Roof Parley Subject," *Victoria Daily Colonist*, February 15, 1948, page 3.

855 "Notice to Contractors," *Victoria Daily Colonist*, February 4, 1948, page 9.

856 "Notice to Contractors," *Victoria Daily Colonist*, February 21, 1948, page 12.

857 "Notice to Contractors," *Victoria Daily Colonist*, February 25, 1948, page 19.

858 "Final Figures On Arena Are Promised," *Victoria Daily Colonist*, March 13, 1948, page 5.

859 "Search for Arena Funds Still Worries Committee," *Victoria Daily Colonist*, March 16, 1948, page 1.

860 "City to Vote on Money By-Law To Complete Arena Financing," *Victoria Daily Colonist*, April 14, 1948, page 7.

861 *"Memorial Arena," Victoria Daily Colonist, April 15, 1948, page 4.*

862 *"Three City By-Laws To Face June Test," Victoria Daily Colonist, May 19, 1948, page 1.*

863 *Victoria Daily Colonist, May 26, 1948, page 3.*

864 *"Arena By-Law Wins Majority But Vote Light," Victoria Daily Colonist, May 28, 1944, page 1.*

865 *"Arena By-Law" Victoria Daily Colonist, May 28, 1948, page 4.*

866 *"$1,000 Left in Coffers," Victoria Daily Colonist, June 5, 1948, page 1.*

867 *"Arena Workmen Make Appreciated Gesture," Victoria Daily Colonist, June 22, 1948, page 4.*

868 *"Volunteer Arena Work Stopped by Union," Victoria Daily Colonist, June 26, 1948, page 10.*

869 *"Skillings Denies 'Exploitation' of Memorial Arena Workmen," Victoria Daily Colonist, July 6, 1948, page 3.*

870 *"Mayor, Skillings Clash On Arena Opening Date," Victoria Daily Colonist, July 20, 1948, page 23.*

871 *"Arena Dignitaries Should Remain Unruffled," Victoria Daily Colonist, July 21, 1948, page 4.*

872 *"City Council Meeting To Study Arena Cost," Victoria Daily Colonist, September 15, 1948, page 1.*

873 *"Complete Arena Inquiry Scheduled for Council May Be Held Next Week," Victoria Daily Colonist, September 16, 1948, page 1.*

874 *"Pictures Sketch Sad Arena History," Victoria Daily Colonist, September 16, 1948, page 3.*

875 *"Engineer Won't Talk On Arena Dispute," Victoria Daily Colonist, September 16, 1948, page 1.*

876 *"Cost to Complete Arena Estimated at $150,000 By Inspector, Foreman," Victoria Daily Colonist, October 7, 1948, page 1.*

877 *"'Get Out as Contractor' Builders Advise Council," Victoria Daily Colonist, October 7, 1948, page 1.*

878 *"City Work On Arena Ends Today," Victoria Daily Colonist, October 20, 1948, page 3.*

879 *"Notice to Contractors," Victoria Daily Colonist, October 23, 1948, page 5.*

880 *"Council Decides to Call More Arena Tenders; $265,000 Loan Needed," Victoria Daily Colonist, November 16, 1948, page 1.*

881 *"Civic Non-Partisan League Announces Slate of Candidates in Forthcoming Elections," Victoria Daily Colonist, November 21, 1948, page 3.*

882 *"Arena Clock Here," Victoria Daily Colonist, November 13, 1948, page 13.*

883 *Victoria Daily Colonist, December 7, 1948, page 11.*

884 *Victoria Daily Colonist, December 4, 1948, page 18.*

885 *"All Aldermen Re-elected; By-Law on Arena Passes," Victoria Daily Colonist, December 10, 1948, page 1.*

886 *"Tenders for Arena Completion Due Soon," Victoria Daily Colonist, January 9, 1949, page 31.*

887 *"Bid of $160,000 Nets City Firm Arena Contract," Victoria Daily Colonist, January 18, 1949, page 1.*

888 *"Name F. Bolton To Supervise Work on Arena," Victoria Daily Colonist, January 21, 1949, page 7.*

889 *"End of Arena Project in Sight," Victoria Daily Colonist, January 19, 1949, page 4.*

890 *"Arena Commission Gets Four Members," Victoria Daily Colonist, February 16, 1949, page 11.*

891 *"Support Arena Olson Urges," Victoria Daily Colonist, February 22, 1949, page 3.*

892 *Victoria Daily Colonist, March 6, 1949, page 23.*

893 *"Arena Work Progressing On Schedule, Is Report," Victoria Daily Colonist, February 27, 1949, page 3.*

894 *Victoria Daily Colonist, March 20, 1949, page 25.*

895 *"Applications Near 100 for Arena Managership," Victoria Daily Colonist, March 31, 1949, page 18.*

896 *"Arena Manager Speaks Tonight," Victoria Daily Colonist, May 6, 1949, page 11.*

897 *"Wire Mesh May Prevent Cave-In of Arena Ceiling," Victoria Daily Colonist, March 11, 1949, page 9.*

898 *"Wire Can't Hold Ceiling of Arena," Victoria Daily Colonist, March 25, 1949, page 1.*

899 *"Arena Repairs Discussed; Ask Date of Completion," Victoria Daily Colonist, April 29, 1949, page 3.*

900 *"Construction Phases 'Up in Air' Delaying Completion of Arena," Victoria Daily Colonist, April 22, 1949, page 3.*

901 *"Arena Workers Laid Off, Won't Finish Next Month," Victoria Daily Colonist, May 10, 1949, page 21.*

902 *"Order Halt to Work on Arena Floor Until Ceiling Repairs Carried Out," Victoria Daily Colonist, May 17, 1949, page 3.*

903 "To Bolt Up Ceiling For Arena Safety," *Victoria Daily Colonist*, May 20, 1949, page 1.

904 "Questions on Arena's Ceiling, Floor May Be Settled in Meeting Today." *Victoria Daily Colonist*, May 27, 1949, page 3.

905 "Complete Installation of Arena Pipes," *Victoria Daily Colonist*, May 31, 1949, page 3.

906 "City Takes Offer For Arena Work," *Victoria Daily Colonist*, June 22, 1949, page 1.

907 "Workmen Start 'Shooting Up' Arena Ceiling," *Victoria Daily Colonist*, June 29, 1949, page 1.

908 "Theatre Under the Stars To Be in Arena July 25," *Victoria Daily Colonist*, June 16, 1949, page 15.

909 "Arena Body's Personnel Shifts Seen Blocking Unified Control," *Victoria Daily Colonist*, July 8, 1949, pages 1 and 2.

910 "Council-Manager System is Best Hope," *Victoria Daily Colonist*, July 17, 1949, page 4.

911 "Starlight Theatre Cast Plans Parade Saturday," *Victoria Daily Colonist*, July 7, 1949, page 3.

912 "Second Starlight Season Opens in Arena Monday," *Victoria Daily Colonist*, July 24, 1949, page 3.

913 "Joint Arena-Starlight Theatre Opening Proves Big Success," *Victoria Daily Colonist*, July 26, 1949, page 5.

914 "Gala Opening," *Victoria Daily Colonist*, July 23, 1949, page 18.

915 "Power Break Darkens City," *Victoria Daily Colonist*, July 26, 1949, page 1.

916 "Throngs See Memorial Arena Given More than As Keystone of New, Greater Community," *Victoria Daily Colonist*, June 27, 1949, page 3.

917 "First Ice Put in Memorial Arena," *Victoria Daily Colonist*, September 27, 1949, page 1.

918 "P. C. H. L. Approves Victoria; Franchise Not Yet Granted," *Victoria Daily Colonist*, April 30, 1949, page 9.

919 "P. C. H. L. Gives City Franchise to Lester Patrick," *Victoria Daily Colonist*, May 24, 1949, page 9.

920 Jim Tang, "It Beats Me," *Victoria Daily Colonist*, June 14, 1949, page 15.

921 "Arrival of Victoria Manager Touches Off Hockey Activity—Cougars Hope to Train Here, May Get Help from N.H.L.," *Victoria Daily Colonist*, August 6, 1949, page 11.

922 "Patrick Obtains Winger, Guard for Cougars; Seeks Name Coach," *Victoria Daily Colonist*, August 16, 1949, page 13.

923 "Add Left-Wing To Cougar Roster," *Victoria Daily Colonist*, September 4, 1949, page 19.

924 "Name Eddie Wares Coach of Cougars," *Victoria Daily Colonist*, September 16, 1949, page 13.

925 "Big Rush for Season Hockey Ducats; Seating Capacity of Arena is 4,462," *Victoria Daily Colonist*, September 9, 1949, page 11.

926 "Victoria Cougars Will Sound Like Les Canadiens; Marineau, Deslaurier Join Thibeault and Bougie," *Victoria Daily Colonist*, September 18, 1949, page 21.

927 "Speedy Frenchman Enroute to Cougars," *Victoria Daily Colonist*, September 30, 1949, page 15.

928 "Cougars Loosen Up on Arena Ice," *Victoria Daily Colonist*, September 28, 1949, page 13.

929 "Hockey Returns After Five-Year Absence," *Victoria Daily Colonist*, October 7, 1949, page 13.

930 "Cougars Will Dress Youngest Line-Up in Coast League's Northern Division," *Victoria Daily Colonist*, October 4, 1949, page 15.

931 "Cougars Trounced In Season Opener," *Victoria Daily Colonist*, October 9, 1949, page 19.

932 "Cougars In Successful Home Debut Before Crowd of 4,133," *Victoria Daily Times*, October 11, 1949, page 13.

933 "Cougars Blow Lead to Canucks; Ironmen Win," *Victoria Daily Times*, October 12, 1949, page 12.

934 "Royals Score Easy Triumph," *Victoria Daily Times*, October 15, 1949, page 13.

935 "Seattle Back in League Lead; Canucks Face Cougars Tuesday," *Victoria Daily Times*, October 17, 1949, page 13.

936 "Bougie, Mazur Spearhead Cougars to Pleasing Win," *Victoria Daily Times*, October 19, 1949, page 13.

937 "Defencemen Marineau, Goegan Score Big Goals for Cougars," *Victoria Daily Times*, October 22, 1949, page 12.

938 "Fodey Sensational in Victoria Win," *Victoria Daily Times*, October 26, 1949, page 15.

939 "Cougars Purchase Centre From Oaks," *Victoria Daily Times*, October 26, 1949, page 15.

940 "Cougars Face Heavy Schedule," *Victoria Daily Times*, October 28, 1949, page 15.

941 "Eddie Wares' First Goal Proves Winner," *Victoria Daily Times*, October 29, 1949, page 13.

942 "Cougars Still Seek First Road Victory," *Victoria Daily Colonist*, October 30, 1949, page 21.

943 "Cougars Drop Close One To Loop Leaders," *Victoria Daily Times*, October 31, 1949, page 13.

944 "McKay Sparks Cougars Win; Wind Up Road Trip Tonight," *Victoria Daily Times*, November 2, 1949, page 15.

945 "Royals Maintain Hex Over Cougars," *Victoria Daily Times*, November 3, 1949, page 15.

946 "Tacoma Ice Six Here Tonight," *Victoria Daily Times*, November 4, 1949, page 15.

947 "Mazur's Last-Minute Goal Wins Thriller," *Victoria Daily Times*, November 5, 1949, page 12.

948 "Cougars Draw All-Time Record Crowd," *Victoria Daily Times*, November 7, 1949, page 13.

949 "Long Rest Catches Up With Cougars," *Victoria Daily Times*, November 12, 1949, page 13.

950 "Seattle Back In Lead; Cougars Meet Canucks," *Victoria Daily Times*, November 14, 1949, page 13.

951 "Cougars Rout Canucks; Tackle Seattle Tonight," *Victoria Daily Times*, November 16, 1949, page 17.

952 "Cougars Wilt In Closing Minutes Against Seattle," *Victoria Daily Times*, November 17, 1949, page 13.

953 "Evans Beats Jinx To Spark Cougars," *Victoria Daily Times*, November 19, 1949, page 13.

954 "Hustling Eddie Dorohoy Gets Big One in Cougars' Victory," *Victoria Daily Times*, November 23, 1949, page 15.

955 "Police Called As Hockey Game At New Westminster Blows Up," *Victoria Daily Times*, November 24, 1949, page 15.

956 "Battered Royals Drop Close One To Cougars," *Victoria Daily Times*, November 26, 1949, page 12.

957 "Seattle Boosts Lead; Fresno Here Tuesday," *Victoria Daily Times*, November 26, 1949, page 17.

958 "Cougars Eye Third Place In Tonight's Game With Fresno," *Victoria Daily Times*, November 29, 1949, page 13.

959 "'13' No Jinx To Cougars As They Knock Off Fresno," *Victoria Daily Times*, November 30, 1949, page 19.

960 "Gagnon En Route From East to Join Cougars," *Victoria Daily Times*, December 1, 1949, page 17.

961 "Dorohoy-Mazur Power Fails As Cougars Settle For Tie," *Victoria Daily Times*, December 3, 1949, page 13.

962 "Cougars Show Club Spirit To Give Dorohoy Hat-Trick," *Victoria Daily Times* December 7, 1949, page 17.

963 "George Robertson Flies From East To Join Cougars Sunday," *Victoria Daily Times*, December 10, 1949, page 13.

964 "Cougars Tie Ironmen To Regain Fourth Spot," *Victoria Daily Times*, December 13, 1949, page 13.

965 "Cougars Blow Chances, Hand Game To Canucks," *Victoria Daily Times*, December 14, 1949, page 19.

966 "Hustling Eddie Dorohoy Paces Cougars To Wild Hockey Win," *Victoria Daily Times*, December 17, 1949, page 15.

967 "Improving Rockey Stars As Cougars Regain Fourth," *Victoria Daily Times*, December 21, 1949, page 15.

968 "Oaks' Withdrawal Brings Player Changes; Ironmen Here Tonight," *Victoria Daily Times*, December 20, 1949, page 13.

969 "Clawless Cougars Bow To Rugged Penguins," *Victoria Daily Times*, December 24, 1949, page 12.

970 "Cougars Give Miserable Show In Shutout Defeat," *Victoria Daily Times*, December 27, 1949, page 9.

971 "Tailenders Prove Too Tough For Cougars; Road Ahead No Easier," *Victoria Daily Times*, *Victoria Daily Times*, December 29, 1949, page 12.

972 "Cougars Play Smart Hockey To Draw; Regain 4 Place," *Victoria Daily Times*, December 31, 1929, page 14.

973 "New Line Fires Three Goals As Cougars Wallop Vancouver," *Victoria Daily Times*, January 3, 1950, page 11.

974 "Cougars Buy Jack McIntyre; Wares Hot After Bad Defeat," *Victoria Daily Times*, January 4, 1950, page 13.

975 "Cougars Enjoy Upsetting Pratt In Beating Royals," *Victoria Daily Times*, January 7, 1950, page 13.

976 "Ironmen Push Cougars Nearer League Cellar," *Victoria Daily Times*, January 9, 1950, page 13.

977 Jim Tang, "It Beats Me," *Victoria Daily Colonist*, January 17, 1950, page 11.

978 "McKay, Mazur In Star Roles AS Cougars Tie," *Victoria Daily Times*, January 18, 1950, page 13.

979 "Three Mistakes Cost Cougars Close Battle," *Victoria Daily Times*, January 21, 1950, page 13.

980 "Cougars In Poor Shape Following Third Straight One-Goal Defeat," *Victoria Daily Times*, January 23, 1950, page 13.

981 "Cougars' Playoff Chances Reach Mathematical Stage," *Victoria Daily Times*, January 25, 1950, page 13.

982 "Clawing Cougars Hold Rockets To Draw," *Victoria Daily Times*, January 28, 1950, page 13.

983 "Stearns' Late Marker Gives Seattle Victory," *Victoria Daily Times* January 30, 1950, page 13.

984 "Storm-Bound Cougars Reach Mainland But Too Late," *Victoria Daily Times*, January 14, 1950, page 13.

985 "Injured Cougars May Know Fate By Monday," *Victoria Daily Times*, February 1, 1950, page 15.

986 "Third Period Rampage Earns Cougars Victory," *Victoria Daily Times*, February 4, 1950, page 13.

987 "Fan Comes Off Second Best In Fight With Ref; Cougars Lose," *Victoria Daily Times*, February 6, 1950, page 13.

988 "Impotent Cougars Again Badly Mauled," *Victoria Daily Times*, February 8, 1950, page 15.

989 "Cougars Drop Another; Penguins Here Friday," *Victoria Daily Times*, February 9, 1950, page 13.

990 "Cougars Show Nothing In Loss To Portland," *Victoria Daily Times*, February 11, 1950, page 14.

991 "Skyhawks Close Gap On Southern Leaders," *Victoria Daily Times*, February 15, 1950, page 17.

992 "Ironmen Nip Penguins; Cougars Beaten Again," *Victoria Daily Times*, February 16, 1950, page 14.

993 "Rockets Blast Canucks, Cougars Bow to Fresno," *Victoria Daily Colonist*, February 19, 1950, page 20.

994 "Coast Hockey League Standards Take Bad beating From Cougars," *Victoria Daily Times*, February 23, 1950, page 8.

995 "Canucks Beat, Says Hall But Royals Don't Agree," *Victoria Daily Times, The Daily Colonist*, February 26, 1950, page 21.

996 "Ironmen Extend Cougars' Streak," *Victoria Daily Times*, February 27, 1950, page 8.

997 "Home Crowd Fails To Rally Cougars," *Victoria Daily Times*, March 1, 1950, page 8.

998 "Rowe's Goal Big One For Rockets," *Victoria Daily Times*, March 4, 1950, page 8.

999 "Cougars Get Piece Of Canucks; Tacoma Wins," *Victoria Daily Times*, March 8, 1950, page 9.

1000 "Hustling Cougars On Seattle," *Victoria Daily Times*, March 11, 1950, page 8.

1001 "Mazur Named To Second Team In All-Star Poll," *Victoria Daily Times*, March 11, 1950, page 8.

1002 "Three Teams Tied In Playoff Battle," *Victoria Daily Colonist*, March 12, 1950, page 21.

1003 "Fans Force Hall To Yell For Cops," *Victoria Daily Times*, March 15, 1950, page 8.

1004 "Cougars Play To 117,000 Patrons," *Victoria Daily Times*, March 18, 1950, page 8.

1005 "Tacoma Rockets Clinch Second Place; Penguins Keep Chance To Top Seattle," *Victoria Daily Colonist*, March 19, 1950, page 22.

1006 "Eliminate Icing Puck In Coast Hockey Loop," *Victoria Daily Times*, September 1, 1956, page 8.

1007 "Cougars Buy Duffy In Opening Deal," *Victoria Daily Times*, September 9, 1950, page 8.

1008 "Cougars Buy Duffy In Opening Deal," *Victoria Daily Times*, September 9, 1950, page 8.

1009 Although Duffy was purchased by the Cougars, he never actually played a game for them.

1010 "Hildebrand, Goegan Cougars' Property," *Victoria Daily Times*, September 13, 1950, page 9.

1011 Goegan, who had played for the Cougars in the previous year, did play for the Cougars, eventually playing a total of five seasons. Hildebrand, on the other hand, did not play until the 1951-52 season, when he only appeared in eight games.

1012 Pete Sallaway, "From the Fanstand," *Victoria Daily Times*, September 23, 1950, page 9.

1013 "Roger Leger Canadiens' Choice As Coach of Victoria Cougars," *Victoria Daily Times*, September 14, 1950.

1014 "Cougars Procure Goal Insurance," *Victoria Daily Times*, September 15, 1950, page 9.

1015 "Eight Players In Fold As Cougars Open Camp," *Victoria Daily Times*, September 25, 1950, page 9.

1016 "Junior Ice Stars Coming To Cougars," *Victoria Daily Times*, September 28, 1950, page 8.

1017 "17 Players Now Listed On Roster of Cougars," *Victoria Daily Times*, September 26, 1950, page 9.

1018 "New Players To Strip Tuesday," *Victoria Daily Times*, October 2, 1950, page 9.

1019 *"Hustling Cougars Please Home Fans,"* Victoria Daily Times, October 4, 1950, page 8.

1020 *"Arena Timing Clock To Be Repaired And Suspended Again From Ceiling,"* Victoria Daily Times, September 30, 1950, page 1.

1021 *"Big Clock Finally Replaced At Arena,"* Victoria Daily Times, December 7, 1950, page 9.

1022 *"Cougars Face Test Against Champions,"* Victoria Daily Times, October 6, 1950, page 8.

1023 *"Opportunist Evans Spark For Cougars,"* Victoria Daily Times, October 7, 1950, page 8.

1024 *"Clawless Cougars Prey of Ironmen,"* Victoria Daily Times, October 10, 1950, page 8.

1025 *"Cougars Collapse In One-Sided Loss,"* Victoria Daily Times, October 14, 1950, page 8.

1026 *"Canadiens Will Ship Out Replacements To Cougars,"* Victoria Daily Times, October 16, 1950, page 9.

1027 *"Two Soft Goals Wreck Cougars,"* Victoria Daily Times, October 18, 1950, page 8.

1028 *"Cougars Break Out To Blast Tacoma,"* Victoria Daily Times, October 21, 1950, page 8.

1029 *"Cougars Tail Off As Royals Romp,"* Victoria Daily Times, October 23, 1950, page 9.

1030 *"Cougars Roll By Hallmen,"* Victoria Daily Times, October 25, 1950, page 8.

1031 *"Improving Cougars Settle For 1-1 Draw,"* Victoria Daily Colonist, October 28, 1950, page 13.

1032 *"What's In A Name? Cougars Still Hexed,"* Victoria Daily Times, October 30, 1950, page 8.

1033 *"Cougars Wilt To Drop 3 Straight,"* Victoria Daily Times, November 4, 1950, page 8.

1034 *"Cougars In Best Stand of Season,"* Victoria Daily Times, November 6, 1950, page 8.

1035 *"Cotnoir To Cougars As Canucks Routed,"* Victoria Daily Times, November 8, 1950, page 8.

1036 *"Cougars To Strip 2 Goalies Tonight,"* Victoria Daily Times, November 10, 1950, page 8.

1037 *"Tenacious Cougars Down Rockets, 4-1,"* Victoria Daily Colonist, November 11, 1950, page 11.

1038 *"Released,"* Victoria Daily Colonist, November 11, 1950, page 11.

1039 *"Healthy Looking Appendectomy Victim,"* Victoria Daily Times, November 14, 1950, page 9.

1040 *"How Lucky Can You Get? Cougars Cry,"* Victoria Daily Times, November 15, 1950, page 8.

1041 *"Goegan Adds Spice To Cougar Triumph,"* Victoria Daily Times, November 18, 1950, page 8.

1042 *"Cougar Lossless Streak Ends With Tacoma Win,"* Victoria Daily Colonist, November 19, 1950, page 21.

1043 *"Abbott Gives Cougars Tie,"* Victoria Daily Times, November 20, 1950, page 8.

1044 *"Booster Plan Trip To Seattle,"* Victoria Daily Times, November 22, 1950, page 9.

1045 *"Cotnoir Fair, Cougars Foul,"* Victoria Daily Times, November 25, 1950, page 8.

1046 *"'Tres Bien,' Said Cotnoir And The Cougars Agreed,"* Victoria Daily Times, November 29, 1950, page 8.

1047 *"Leger Gambles As Cougars Earn Tie,"* Victoria Daily Times, December 1, 1950, page 8.

1048 *"Cougars Win First Game at Tacoma Club at .500, Presses for Third Spot,"* Victoria Daily Colonist, December 3, 1950, page 23.

1049 *"Horse Shoes Help Seattle In Breaks,"* Victoria Daily Times, December 4, 1950, page 8.

1050 *"Hec Does It, But Gets Stiff Battle From Jerry,"* Victoria Daily Times, December 6, 1950, page 8.

1051 *"Kittenish Cougars Tamed By Rockets,"* Victoria Daily Times, December 9, 1950, page 8.

1052 *"Canucks Fail To Overtake Cougars,"* Victoria Daily Times, December 11, 1950, page 8.

1053 *"'Happy Hec' Returns To Haunt Crippled Cougars,"* Victoria Daily Times, December 13, 1950, page 8.

1054 *"Seven Cougars Now On Club's Casualty List,"* Victoria Daily Times, December 13, 1950, page 8.

1055 *"Cougar Casualty List Reaches Nine,"* Victoria Daily Times, December 14, 1950, page 10.

1056 *"Cougars Lose, 4-2; Two Players Hurt,"* Victoria Daily Colonist, December 14, 1950, page 19.

1057 *"McIntyre Mystery Remains Unsolved,"* Victoria Daily Times, December 16, 1950, page 8.

1058 *"Cougars Tie Eagles, Regain Fourth Spot,"* Victoria Daily Times, December 18, 1950, page 8.

1059 *"Dorohoy Remains In P. C. H. L.'s Top Ten,"* Victoria Daily Times, December 19, 1950, page 9.

1060 *"Tremendous Finish Give Canucks Tie,"* Victoria Daily Times, December 20, 1950, page 8.

1061 "Leger Fines Two Cougars," *Victoria Daily Times*, December 20, 1950, page 8.

1062 "Passing Years Fail to Dim Johnson's Memory," *Victoria Daily Times*, December 22, 1950, page 8.

1063 "Hockey Fans Show Christmas 'Spirit'," *Victoria Daily Times*, December 23, 1950, page 8.

1064 "Eagles Routed As Cougars Break Hex," *Victoria Daily Times*, December 264, 1950, page 8.

1065 "Leger Fined, Suspended For Attack On Powers," *Victoria Daily Times*, December 17, 1950, page 8.

1066 "Coachless Cougars Blank Ironmen, 3-0," *Victoria Daily Colonist*, December 30, 1950, page 11.

1067 "Two-Game Ban On Leger; Webster Relief Coach," *Victoria Daily Colonist*, December 29, 1950, page 9.

1068 "Eddie Dorohoy Moving Up In Scoring Race," *Victoria Daily Times*, December 28, 1950, page 8.

1069 "See Omen In Cougar Win," *Victoria Daily Times*, January 2, 1951, page 8.

1070 "'Hat Trick' Bounty Boon To Cougars," *Victoria Daily Times*, January 6, 1951, page 8.

1071 "Cotnoir Sets P. C. L. Goalkeeping Mark," *Victoria Daily Times*, January 8, 1951, page 8.

1072 "Karakas Stays Cool In Spite Of It All," *Victoria Daily Times*, January 13, 1951, page 8.

1073 "Cougars Clip Eagles For Fifth Straight," *Victoria Daily Times*, January 15, 1951, page 8.

1074 "Vancouver Canucks Play Cougars Again On Jan. 30," *Victoria Daily Times*, January 17, 1951, page 8.

1075 "Mazur Scored Pair As Cougar In Tie," *Victoria Daily Times*, January 18, 1951, page 8.

1076 "Ho Hum! Just Another Win," *Victoria Daily Times*, January 20, 1951, page 8.

1077 "Eagles Wing Way Back Up Ice Ladder," *Victoria Daily Times*, January 22, 1951, page 8.

1078 "Murph Mortified As Cougars Rub It In," *Victoria Daily Times*, January 24, 1950, page 8.

1079 "Joe Gets His The Hard Way," *Victoria Daily Times*, January 27, 1951, page 8.

1080 "Hebenton's 'Picture Goal' Gives Cougars Narrow Win," *Victoria Daily Times*, January 29, 1951, page 8.

1081 "Coley Missing As Cats Outdo Katie," *Victoria Daily Times*, January 31, 1951, page 8.

1082 "It Just Had To Be A Tie," *Victoria Daily Times*, *Victoria Daily Times*, February 3, 1951, page 8.

1083 "Ironmen, Canucks In 'Lost Week-End,'" *Victoria Daily Times*, February 5, 1951, page 8.

1084 "Cougars Set Crowd Mark," *Victoria Daily Times*, February 12, 1951, page 8.

1085 "Cougars Defeated, But So Are Royals," *Victoria Daily Times*, February 12, 1951, page 8.

1086 "Roger Agrees, Cougars They Not Play Too Well," *Victoria Daily Times*, February 14, 1951, page 8.

1087 "It Might Have Been Better Than It Was," *Victoria Daily Times*, February 17, 1951, page 8.

1088 "Ironmen In Serious Bid; Royals Draw With Eagles," *Victoria Daily Times*, February 19, 1951, page 8.

1089 "Canucks Get Dug In, But Properly," *Victoria Daily Times*, February 21, 1951, page 8.

1090 "Joe Boots Cougars Home By 3 Lengths," *Victoria Daily Times*, February 24, 1951, page 8.

1091 "Rockets Halt Seattle Streak," *Victoria Daily Times*, February 26, 1951, page 8.

1092 "Canucks Try Hard, But Get Outwaltzed," *Victoria Daily Times*, February 28, 1951, page 8.

1093 Advertisement in *Victoria Daily Times*, March 1, 1951, page 8.

1094 "Playoff Fever Grips City Hockey Fans," *Victoria Daily Times*, March 2, 1951, page 8.

1095 "Rockets Make '16' Tight Fit For Cats," *Victoria Daily Times*, March 3, 1951, page 9.

1096 "Cougars Clawed By Eagles; Royals Win," *Victoria Daily Times*, March 5, 1951, page 8.

1097 "Eddie's Show May Have Been Too Late," *Victoria Daily Times*, March 7, 1951, page 8.

1098 "Cougars Take '17' By Tripping Royals," *Victoria Daily Times*, March 10, 1951, page 8.

1099 "Royals Gain Lead By Clipping Eagles," *Victoria Daily Times*, March 12, 1951, page 8.

1100 "Hec Shines, Vows Even Greater Effort," *Victoria Daily Times*, March 14, 1951, page 8.

1101 "Big 'Rog' Named 'Most Valuable'," *Victoria Daily Times*, March 17, 1951, page 8.

1102 "Fighting Cougars Claw Way To P. C. H. L. Pennant," *Victoria Daily Times*, March 19, 1961, page 8.

1103 "Coast League Scoring Champion," *Victoria Daily Times*, March 19, 1961, page 8.

1104 "Fans Rise Early To Greet Return Of Triumphant Victoria Cougars," *Victoria Daily Times*, March 19, 1951, page 1.

1105 "Hopper Makes Highton Hero As Portland Grabs Series Opener," *Victoria Daily Times*, March 21, 1951, page 8.

1106 "Hopper Makes Tony Eat Crow—Like It," *Victoria Daily Times*, March 24, 1951, page 8.

1107 "Cougars Slug Their Way Back Into Contention," *Victoria Daily Times*, March 26, 1951, page 8.

1108 "'Fiji' Goegan Cats' Hero; P. C. H. L. Series Squared," *Victoria Daily Times*, March 28, 1951, page 8.

1109 "It Was Close, Too Close For Comfort," *Victoria Daily Times*, March 30, 1951, page 8.

1110 "'We'll Win The Hard Way' Is Grim Leger Vow Today," *Victoria Daily Times*, April 2, 1951, page 8.

1111 "Roger Said They Would And Do It The Cats Did," *Victoria Daily Times*, *Victoria Daily Times*, April 4, 1951, page 8.

1112 "Cougars Get Busy With Job At Hand," *Victoria Daily Times*, April 6, 1951, page 8.

1113 "Lester Superstitious? Knew When To Stay Home," *Victoria Daily Times*, April 9, 1951, page 8.

1114 "Cats' Whiskers Twitch And Westminster Wilts," *Victoria Daily Times*, April 11, 1951, page 8.

1115 "Royals Do It The Easy Way," *Victoria Daily Times*, April 12, 1951, page 8.

1116 "Cougars Come Through In Championship Style," *Victoria Daily Times*, April 14, 1951, page 8.

1117 "Cougars Play To Nearly Quarter-Million Fans," *Victoria Daily Times*, April 18, 1951, page 9.

1118 "Eddie Mazur to strip for Canadiens tonight," *Victoria Daily Times*, April 19, 1951, page 9.

1119 Stott, John C., "Ice Warriors," Heritage House Publishing Company Ltd., Surrey, BC, 2008, page 38.

1120 "Royal-Canucks Dominate Cougars' Home Schedule," *Victoria Daily Times*, September 4, 1951, page 9.

1121 "Cougars Seek Defence Aid," *Victoria Daily Times*, September 1, 1951, page 8.

1122 "Cotnoir Lost To Cougars; Has Broken Leg," *Victoria Daily Times*, September 5, 1951, page 8.

1123 "Portland Players Bought by Cougars," *Victoria Daily Times*, September 10, 1951, page 8.

1124 Bill Walker, "It's My View," *Victoria Daily Times*, September 14, 1951, page 8.

1125 "They'll See The Cougars This Winter," *Victoria Daily Times*, September 11, 1951, page 8.

1126 "The Cougars Proceed To Their Lair," *Victoria Daily Times*, September 18, 1951, page 8.

1127 "Cougars To Plan Three Pre-Season Exhibitions" *Victoria Daily Times*, September 20, 1951, page 8.

1128 "Cougars Officially In Dark About Arena" *Victoria Daily Times*, September 25, 1951, page 8.

1129 "Speedy Fred Hildebrand Bolsters Cougar Ranks," *Victoria Daily Times*, October 3, 1951, page 9.

1130 "There's Only One Real 'Kid Line' Cougars Say," *Victoria Daily Times*, October 6, 1951, page 8.

1131 Bill Walker, "It's My View," *Victoria Daily Times*, October 10, 1951, page 8.

1132 "Cats Slosh Way To Win," *Victoria Daily Times*, October 13, 1951, page 8.

1133 "There'll Be Hockey Here Tuesday Despite Further Trouble At Arena," *Victoria Daily Times*, October 13, 1951, page 8.

1134 "Ice To Be Ready For Quaker Visit," *Victoria Daily Times*, October 15, 1915, page 8.

1135 "Roger Says 'He'll Try To Repeat' Cougars Run Riot Over Quakers," *Victoria Daily Times*, October 17, 1951, page 8.

1136 "Rockets Not So Tough After All," *Victoria Daily Times*, October 20, 1951, page 8.

1137 "Ironmen Put Clamp On Cougars' Streak," *Victoria Daily Times*, October 25, 1951, page 8.

1138 "Cougars Acquire New Defenceman Ernie Roche," *Victoria Daily Times*, October 25, 1951, page 8.

1139 "'No Comment' Describes Cougar Defeat Perfectly," *Victoria Daily Times*, October 27, 1951, page 8.

1140 "Rockets Hurdle Over Cougars," *Victoria Daily Times*, October 29, 1951, page 8.

1141 "Abbott Out For Six Weeks As Cougars Topple Cowboys," *Victoria Daily Times*, November 3, 1951, page 8.

1142 "Cougars Run Canucks Skein To 19 games," *Victoria Daily Times*, November 5, 1951, page 8.

1143 "Cougars Mesmerized By McAtee's Mystic Magic," *Victoria Daily Times*, November 7, 1951, page 8.

1144 "Late Tally Evens Contest; Flyers Hold to Win Streak," *The Calgary Herald*, November 8, 1951, page 23.

1145 "Shirley Human After All; Proves He Needs A Defence," *Victoria Daily Times*, November 10, 1951, page 8.

1146 "Worsley Denies Calgary; Royals Big Lead Crumbles," *The Calgary Herald*, November 12, 1951, page 20.

1147 "Cougars Tour Cowboys; Move Into Second Place," *Victoria Daily Times*, November 13, 1951, page 8.

1148 "Flyers Trim Cats; Royals Blank Cats," *Victoria Daily Times*, November 14, 1915, page 8.

1149 "Quakers' in Gives Cats Split On Road," *Victoria Daily Times*, November 15, 1951, page 8.

1150 "There's Some Doubt If This Was Really Hockey," *Victoria Daily Times*, November 17, 1951, page 8.

1151 "Ironmen Paste Cougars To Close Gap On Royals," *Victoria Daily Times*, November 19, 1951, page 8.

1152 "Top-Rated Flyers Test Cats Tonight," *Victoria Daily Times*, November 20, 1951, page 8.

1153 "Fly Boys Get Wings Clipped," *Victoria Daily Times*, November 21, 1951, page 8.

1154 "Defeat Hangs Tough On Rog Who Just Doesn't Know Why," *Victoria Daily Times*, November 24, 1951, page 8.

1155 "Cats Savage Ballance From Vancouver Visit," *Victoria Daily Times*, November 28, 1951, page 8.

1156 "Ballance Handy Item To Have Ex-Canuck Proves To Cougars," *Victoria Daily Times*, December 1, 1951, page 8.

1157 "Fast Reason For Fat Lead," *Victoria Daily Times*, December 3, 1951, page 8.

1158 "Cotnoir To Flyers," *Victoria Daily Times*, December 3, 1951, page 8.

1159 "It Took Two Periods For The Cats To Roll," *Victoria Daily Times*, December 8, 1951, page 8.

1160 "Ironmen Lose Ground As Stamps Finally Win," *Victoria Daily Times*, December 10, 1951, page 8.

1161 "McAtee Was At His Best," *Victoria Daily Times*, December 12, 1951, page 8.

1162 "Dechene Plays Lead In Cougars' Puck Tragedy," *Victoria Daily Times*, December 15, 1951, page 8.

1163 "Hey, Our Cats Are Picking Up," *Victoria Daily Times*, December 17, 1951, page 8.

1164 "Hey, Our Cats Are Picking Up," *Victoria Daily Times*, December 17, 1951, page 8.

1165 "Bowness Got The Goals But Dougie Did The Heavy Work," *Victoria Daily Times*, December 22, 1951, page 8.

1166 "Home Sked Favors Cats," *Victoria Daily Times*, December 24, 1951, page 8.

1167 "Pity Murph Wasn't Here To See 'His Team' Win," *Victoria Daily Times*, December 27, 1951, page 8.

1168 "Quakers Preach; Cougars Listen," *Victoria Daily Times*, December 29, 1951, page 8.

1169 "Cougars Dip To Sixth In Defeat By Rockets," *Victoria Daily Times*, January 2, 1952, page 8.

1170 "This May Be a Future Cougar," *Victoria Daily Times*, January 4, 1952, page 7.

1171 "Long Vigil Finally Ends," *Victoria Daily Times*, January 5, 1952, page 8.

1172 "Dorohoy Back In Point Lead," *Victoria Daily Times*, January 8, 1952, page 7.

1173 "MacKenzie Sees P. C. H. L. Rising," *Victoria Daily Times*, January 10, 1952, page 7.

1174 "Even Ashbee Couldn't Have Helped Much Here," *Victoria Daily Times*, January 12, 1952, page 9.

1175 *Victoria Daily Times*, January 14, 1952, page 9.

1176 "Trade Winds In Air As Cougars Start Road Trip," *Victoria Daily Times*, January 15, 1952, page 7.

1177 "Cougars Reach Low Ebb In Losing To Vancouver," *Victoria Daily Times*, January 16, 1952, page 8.

1178 "Cats Slaughtered By Stormy Stamps," *Victoria Daily Times*, January 18, 1952, page 8.

1179 "Nick Pidsodny Fills The Bill As Vancouver's New Goalie," *Victoria Daily Times*, January 19, 1952, page 23.

1180 "Quakers Complete Prairie Debacle," *Victoria Daily Times*, January 20, 1952, page 8.

1181 "Plunging Cougars Get Another Healthy Push," *Victoria Daily Times*, January 23, 1952, page 8.

1182 "New Man On Cat's Bench," *Victoria Daily Times*, January 26, 1952, page 8.

1183 "Cougars Hit Rock Bottom," *Victoria Daily Times*, January 28, 1952, page 9.

1184 "Cougars Get Reprieve But Only Temporarily," *Victoria Daily Times*, February 2, 1952, page 8

1185 "Reardon Puts Finger On Cougars' Problem," *Victoria Daily Times*, February 4, 1952, page 9.

1186 "Reardon Sees Hope For Cougars As Visit Ends," *Victoria Daily Times*, February 6, 1952, page 12.

1187 "Royals First On Cougars' 'Make-Break' Schedule," *Victoria Daily Times*, February 8, 1952, page 8.

1188 "The Lesson Should Be Obvious To All," *Victoria Daily Times*, February 10, 1952, page 8.

1189 "Cougars Bow To Royals; Flyers Roughly Treated," *Victoria Daily Times*, February 11, 1952, page 8

1190 "Currie Returns, Haunts Cougars," *Victoria Daily Times*, February 13, 1952, page 8.

1191 "Cougars Frustrated As Rockets Add To Streak," *Victoria Daily Times*, February 15, 1952, page 8.

1192 "Royals Lose Game, Player and Ground While Quakers Enjoy Scoring Spree," *The Calgary Herald*, February 18, 1952, page 20.

1193 "Playoff Hopes Flicker Again," *Victoria Daily Times*, February 18, 1952, page 8.

1194 "Flyers Again Spoil Long Win Skein," *The Calgary Herald*, February 20, 1952, page 23.

1195 "Cats Keep Hopes Alive," *Victoria Daily Times*, February 23, 1952, page 8.

1196 "Tony Quits As Ironmen Coach," *Victoria Daily Times*, February 25, 1952, page 8.

1197 "Cougars Trample Stamps, Dorohoy In Point Game," *Victoria Daily Times*, February 26, 1952, page 8.

1198 "Cougars Lose More Ground," *Victoria Daily Times*, February 27, 1952, page 8.

1199 "Time Running Out For Cats," *Victoria Daily Times*, February 28, 1952, page 8.

1200 "Victoria Cougars Retain Hopes Of Making Playoffs," *The Calgary Herald*, March 1, 1952, page 24.

1201 "Cougars Give Faithful Good Reason To Cheer," *Victoria Daily Times*, March 1, 1952, page 8.

1202 "Eddie'll Give Luke Battle For Honors," *Victoria Daily Times*, March 5, 1952, page 8.

1203 "Cougars Win But One Moment Will Linger On," *Victoria Daily Times*, March 8, 1952, page 8.

1204 "Puck Race Tightens As Cats Win, Stamps Lose," *Victoria Daily Times*, March 10, 1952, page 8.

1205 "Deepest Gratitude Owed To Cougars From Canucks," *Victoria Daily Times*, March 12, 1952, page 8.

1206 "Yep, Hans Was Right; Things Were Off-Key," *Victoria Daily Times*, March 15, 1952, page 9.

1207 "Cougars Remain In Battle For Sixth Playoff Spot," *Victoria Daily Times*, March 17, 1952, page 8.

1208 "Cats' Playoff Dreams Just a Memory - Almost," *Victoria Daily Times*, March 19, 1952, page 8.

1209 "Cougars One Game From P.C.H.L. Playoff Berth," *Victoria Daily Times*, March 22, 1952, page 8.

1210 "Cougars' Attendance Reaches Record High," *Victoria Daily Times*, March 11, 1952, page 8.

1211 "It Seemed Impossible, But Cougars Did It … They're In!" *Victoria Daily Times*, March 24, 1952, page 8.

1212 "P.C.H.L. Playoff Get Away Tonight," *Victoria Daily Times*, March 25, 1952, page 8.

1213 "Lady Luck Favors Royals in Opener," *Victoria Daily Times*, March 22, 1952, page 8.

1214 "Kenny Worried as Cats Strike Back," *Victoria Daily Times*, March 29, 1952, page 8.

1215 "Cougars One Game Down to Royals; Rockets Oust Ironmen," *Victoria Daily Times*, March 31, 1952, page 8.

1216 "Doug Bentley Puts Quakers Into Semis," *Victoria Daily Times*, April 1, 1952, page 6.

1217 "Is Reggie Abbott Happy? 'You Darn Right I am'," *Victoria Daily Times*, April 2, 1952, page 10.

1218 "Cougars Furious as Royals Win After Dubious Decision," *Victoria Daily Times*, April 3, 1952, page 8.

1219 "'We'll Take 'Em for Sure' Says Roger of Royal Six," *Victoria Daily Times*, April 5, 1952, page 6.

1220 "'Bring On the Quakers' Cry Victorious Cougars," *Victoria Daily Times*, April 7, 1952, page 8.

1221 "Quakers Dump Rockets; Finals Here Saturday," *Victoria Daily Times*, April 10, 1952, page 8.

1222 "Bentley Bitter Over Cougars' Winning Goal," *Victoria Daily Times*, April 14, 1952, page 8.

1223 "Worsley Vs. Cotnoir And the 'Gump' Won It," *Victoria Daily Times*, April 15, 1952, page 8.

1224 "Rog: We're Not Beat Yet. Doug: Be All Over Monday," *Victoria Daily Times*, April 17, 1952, page 8.

1225 "60 Minutes Left To Make History," *Victoria Daily Times*, April 21, 1952, page 8.

1226 "Cats Still have Teeth; Quakers Have the Scars," *Victoria Daily Times*, April 22, 1952, page 8.

1227 "It's All Over But They Won't Forget The Cats," *Victoria Daily Times*, April 24, 1952, page 8.

1228 "Cougars Make Long Trek Home," *Victoria Daily Times*, April 25, 1952, page 8.

1229 Bill Walker, "It's My View," *Victoria Daily Times*, September 3, 1952, page 8.

1230 "Victoria Baseball 1946-2008," http://www.vdba.ca/pages-added/victoria-baseball-1946---2006.php

1231 *Victoria Daily Times*, September 19, 1952, page 8.

1232 "Abbott to Start as Habs Tackle Royals," *Victoria Daily Times*, September 20, 1952, page 6.

1233 "Leger Plans to Remain in East," *Victoria Daily Times*, September 22, 1952, page 8.

1234 "Cougars Assigned 7 Players; Mazur or Kilburn to Report," *Victoria Daily Times*, September 24, 1952, page 8.

1235 "Eddie Dorohoy Named Coach of Cougars," *Victoria Daily Times*, September 25, 1952, page 8.

1236 "Dorohoy Optimistic As Cats Open Training," *Victoria Daily Times*, September 29, 1952, page 8.

1237 *Victoria Daily Times*, September 29, 1952,

1238 "Kilburn Sent to Victoria," *Victoria Daily Times*, September 30, 1952, page 8.

1239 "Cougars Prep for Exhibition Game," *Victoria Daily Times*, October 1, 1952, page 8.

1240 "Long to Join Cougars; Exhibition Game Tonight," *Victoria Daily Times*, October 3, 1952, page 8.

1241 "Cats Give All for Eddie; Fans Lend Support, Too," *Victoria Daily Times*, October 4, 1952, page 8.

1242 "Mazur Here, Kilburn Due," *Victoria Daily Times*, October 6, 1952, page 8.

1243 "Dark Glasses Our For Goal Judges," *Victoria Daily Times* October 7, 1952, page 8.

1244 "Western Hockey League Season Opens Tonight," *Victoria Daily Times*, October 8, 1952, page 8.

1245 "Orders Are Orders, Ed Tells Victorious Cats," *Victoria Daily Times*, October 10, 1952, page 8.

1246 "Cougars Bop Best But Canucks Win," *Victoria Daily Times*, October 11, 1952, page 8.

1247 "Muzz Gambles, Loses; Cougars Sparkle, Win," *Victoria Daily Times*, October 14, 1952, page 8.

1248 "Cougars Give Fred Cause For Joy, But Also Alarm," *Victoria Daily Times*, October 18, 1952, page 8.

1249 "Cougars, Canucks In Tie For Western Hockey League," *Victoria Daily Times*, October 20, 1952, page 8.

1250 "Flyers Hang On As Cats Claw in Vain," *Victoria Daily Times*, October 25, 1952, page 8.

1251 "Bombers Hand Cougars Third Straight Defeat," *Victoria Daily Times*, October 27, 1952, page 6.

1252 "Something's Gotta Give, And Soon, For Cougars," *Victoria Daily Times*, October 28, 1952, page 8.

1253 "Hold That Towel, Irwin on His Way," *Victoria Daily Times*, October 29, 1952, page 8.

1254 "Kilburn-Anderson Find New Partner for Combine," *Victoria Daily Times*, November 1, 1952, page 8.

1255 "'Two Must Go,' Cats Warned," *Victoria Daily Times*, November 3, 1952, page 8.

1256 "Cougars Acquire Winger," *Victoria Daily Times*, November 5, 1952, page 8.

1257 "Yes, Boys Will Be Boys, But Eddie Prefers Men," *Victoria Daily Times*, November 8, 1952, page 8.

1258 "Quakers in League Lead as Cougars Tie Canucks," *Victoria Daily Times*, November 10, 1952, page 8.

1259 "Cougars Receive 'E' for Effort, But That's All," *Victoria Daily Times*, November 12, 1952, page 8.

1260 "Even Cougar Brass in Doubtful Mood," *Victoria Daily Times*, November 15, 1952, page 8.

1261 "Goodacre, Kirk Draw Release From Cougars," *Victoria Daily Times*, November 17, 1952, page 8.

1262 "Fan Consensus - Cougars Not Giving Dorohoy Their Best," *Victoria Daily Times*, November 18, 1952, page 8.

1263 *Victoria Daily Times*, November 19, 1952, page 8.

1264 "Cats Lose Again, But Not By Much," *Victoria Daily Times*, November 20, 1952, page 8.

1265 "Cougars Bounce Royals; Make Critics Eat Words," *Victoria Daily Times*, November 22, 1952, page 8.

1266 "Patrick, Reardon to Screen Cougar Problems," *Victoria Daily Times*, November 22, 1952, page 8.

1267 "Cats Get Four, Quakers More," *Victoria Daily Times*, November 25, 1952, page 8.

1268 "Basement Battle Goes to Cougars," *Victoria Daily Times*, November 26, 1952, page 8.

1269 "Stamps Corral Cougars, Then Put Boots to 'Em," *Victoria Daily Times*, November 27, 1952, page 8.

Endnotes

1270 Bill Walker, "So Help Me, Cougars, It's Up to You," *Victoria Daily Times, November 28, 1952, page 8.*

1271 *"Victory, Yes, But Not Neat or Gaudy," Victoria Daily Times, November 28, 1952, page 8.*

1272 *"Cougars Lose On All Counts," Victoria Daily Times, December 2, 1952, page 8.*

1273 *"Cougar Glitter Proves 24-Carat Over Canucks," Victoria Daily Times, December 3, 1952, page 8.*

1274 *"Thud! Cats Land In Basement Again," Victoria Daily Times, December 4, 1952, page 8.*

1275 *"Quakers Whip Rockets To Regain W.H.L. Lead," Victoria Daily Times, December 5, 1952, page 8.*

1276 *"Cougars Win, But Royals No Dynasty," Victoria Daily Times, December 6, 1952, page 8.*

1277 *"Cougars Soundly Whip Rockets; Injuries Hit Canucks, Quakers," Victoria Daily Times, December 5, 1952, page 8.*

1278 *"Stan Truly No Ingrate," Victoria Daily Times, December 13, 1952, page 8.*

1279 *"Cougars Bop Favorite 'Cousins' Once Again," Victoria Daily Times, December 15, 1952, page 10.*

1280 *"In the News," Victoria Daily Times, December 15, 1952, page 10.*

1281 *"Eddie Mazur To Feel Knife," Victoria Daily Times, December 18, 1952, page 10.*

1282 *"Cougars Mangle Stamps In Torrid Third Period," Victoria Daily Times, December 17, 1952, page 10.*

1283 *"Cougars Dissolve Bombers; Flyers, Canucks Tepid Too," Victoria Daily Times, December 20, 1952, page 8.*

1284 *"Rockets Rout Cougars Before Crowd of 5,500," Victoria Daily Times, December 27, 1952, page 8.*

1285 *"Cougars Falter Again; Bombers, Rockets Win," Victoria Daily Times, December 29, 1952, page 8.*

1286 *"Cougars Edged by Canucks' Replace Flyers in Basement," Victoria Daily Times, January 2, 1953, page 8.*

1287 *"Cougars Gain, But Remain in Cellar," Victoria Daily Times, January 3, 1953, page 8.*

1288 *"Cougar Confusion Confounds Critics," Victoria Daily Times, January 7, 1952, page 8.*

1289 *"Cougars Win, But Walkers Fights On," Victoria Daily Times, January 10, 1953, page 8.*

1290 *"Royals Unkind To Cats," Victoria Daily Times, January 12, 1953, page 8.*

1291 *"Cougars Lose, Canucks Gain," Victoria Daily Times, January 14, 1953, page 10.*

1292 *"Cougars Surprise Stamps in Corral," Victoria Daily Times, January 16, 1953, page 8.*

1293 *"Cats Fall Back," Victoria Daily Times, January 17, 1953, page 8.*

1294 *"Quakers Drub Cougars," Victoria Daily Times, January 19, 1953, page 8.*

1295 *"Francis Good, and Mad; Cotnoir Good, and Sore," Victoria Daily Times, January 21, 1953, page 8.*

1296 *"Cats Fail at Seattle," Victoria Daily Times, January 22, 1953, page 8.*

1297 *"Cougars Ride On Pony Line," Victoria Daily Times, January 24, 1953, page 8.*

1298 *"Cougars Bow to Royals; Canucks in League Lead," Victoria Daily Times, January 26, 1953, page 8.*

1299 *"Mazur Clicks as Cats Tie Rockets," Victoria Daily Times, January 28, 1953, page 8.*

1300 *"Cougars Not Dead In Abbott's Book," Victoria Daily Times, January 31, 1953, page 8.*

1301 *"Leon Was So Mean Doing What He Did," Victoria Daily Times, February 4, 1953, page 8.*

1302 *"Cougars Rebound To Whip Royals," Victoria Daily Times, February 7, 1953, page 8.*

1303 *"Flyers Thump Bombers; Cougars Bow to Royals," Victoria Daily Times, February 9, 1953, page 8.*

1304 *"It Won't Be Long Now Cougars Can Well Sing," Victoria Daily Times, February 11, 1953, page 8*

1305 *"Cougars Get Clubbed Again," Victoria Daily Times February 14, 2016, page 8.*

1306 *"Puck Race Close But For Cougars," Victoria Daily Times, February 16, 1953, page 8.*

1307 *"Quakers Flatten Cougars, But Good," Victoria Daily Times, February 8, 1953, page 8.*

1308 *"Cougars Click as Reardon Ponders," Victoria Daily Times, February 21, 1953, page 9.*

1309 *"Ken May Have Come Too Late," Victoria Daily Times, February 23, 1953, page 8.*

1310 *"Dorohoy Now Eighth In WHL Scoring Race," Victoria Daily Times, February 24, 1953, page 8.*

1311 *"Cougars Still Hopeful, Battle Flyers to Tie," Victoria Daily Times, February 26, 1953, page 8.*

1312 "Cougars Still Pitchin', Quakers Rally for Tie," *Victoria Daily Times*, February 26, 1953, page 8.

1313 "Cats Clip Royals," *Victoria Daily Times*, February 28, 1953, page 10.

1314 "Cats Still Alive," *Victoria Daily Times*, March 2, 1953, page 8.

1315 "Cats Thump Rockets Who Thump Officials," *Victoria Daily Times*, March 4, 1953, page 8.

1316 "Cougars Win, But Time May Hold Final Answer," *Victoria Daily Times*, March 7, 1953, page 8.

1317 "Bombers Help Cougar Cause," *Victoria Daily Times*, March 9, 1953, page 8.

1318 "Shirt-Tail Hold Only Cougar Hope," *Victoria Daily Times*, March 14, 1953, page 8.

1319 "Cats Fall by Wayside, Seattle May Join 'Em," *Victoria Daily Times*, March 16, 1953, page 8.

1320 "Kilburn Does Clipping, Too," *Victoria Daily Times*, March 18, 1953, page 8.

1321 "Cougars Could Scuttle Things," *Victoria Daily Times*, March 21, 1953, page 8.

1322 "Bombers In, Rockets Out," *Victoria Daily Times*, March 23, 1953, page 8.

1323 'Cotnoir May Appear For Royals, Bombers,' *Victoria Daily Times*, March 26, 1953, page 8.

1324 "Our Boy Ed Show 'Em As Habs Oust Chicago," *Victoria Daily Times*, April 8, 1953, page 8.

1325 http://www.sihrhockey.org/member_team_sheet.cfm?team_id=4&season_id=78

1326 Scott, John C., "Ice Warriors," Heritage House Publishing Limited, 2008, page 52.

1327 "Cougars Get Veteran Goalie," *Victoria Daily Times*, September 5, 1953, page 8.

1328 "Ticket Sales Boom as Hockey Season Nears," *Victoria Daily Times*, September 10, 1953, page 8.

1329 "Cougars Open Training Camp," *Victoria Daily Times*, September 21, 1953, page 8.

1330 "Cats Edge Seattle," *Victoria Daily Times*, September 28, 1953, page 8.

1331 "Cougar Home Debut Undimmed by Loss," *Victoria Daily Times*, September 30, 1953, page 10.

1332 "Bombers Turn on Cougars," *Victoria Daily Times*, October 1, 1953, page 10.

1333 "Cougars Win, But Lose, Too," *Victoria Daily Times*, October 3, 1953, page 8.

1334 "Cougars Again Edge Bombers," *Victoria Daily Times*, October 5, 1953, page 8.

1335 "Worsley's 'Big Save' Helps Cheat Cougars," *Victoria Daily Times*, October 7, 1953, page 10.

1336 "One Line Found, Two More Sought," *Victoria Daily Times*, October 10, 1954, page 8.

1337 "Cougars Lose Again; Stamps Take WHL Lead," *Victoria Daily Times*, October 13, 1954, page 10.

1338 "Cougars Get Defense Aid," *Victoria Daily Times*, October 14, 1954, page 8.

1339 "Ralph Helps Bob in Cougar Debut," *Victoria Daily Times*, October 17, 1953, page 8.

1340 "Bombers Roar Again; Canucks Pay Here," *Victoria Daily Times*, October 19, 1953, page 8.

1341 "One Goal, No Win, And … No Foolin'," *Victoria Daily Times*, October 20. 1953, page 8.

1342 "Cats Again Fire Blanks," *Victoria Daily Times*, October 24, 1953, page 8.

1343 "Cougars on Spot; Changes Rumoured," *Victoria Daily Times*, October 26, 1953, page 8.

1344 "Cougars Surprise, Trip Stampeders," *Victoria Daily Times*, October 27, 1953, page 8.

1345 "Cougars Edge Flyers, Seek Hat Trick Tonight," *Victoria Daily Times*, October 28, 1953, page 10.

1346 "Cougars Tie Quakers; Royal Stop Canucks," *Victoria Daily Times*, October 29, 1953, page 10.

1347 "Cougars Keep Streak Alive, Tie Quakers," *Victoria Daily Times*, October 31, 1953, page 8.

1348 "But He'll Play Tonight," *Victoria Daily Times*, November 2, 1953, page 8.

1349 "Mathematically, 'Yes,' But in Billy's Book, 'No,'" *Victoria Daily Times*, November 3, 1953, page 8.

1350 "Manson Repays Debt, Almas Earns Dividend," *Victoria Daily Times*, November 7, 1953, page 8.

1351 "Royals Halt Cougar Streak," *Victoria Daily Times*, November 9, 1953, page 8.

1352 "'Names' Named in Cougar Loss," *Victoria Daily Times*, November 12, 1953, page 11.

1353 "Reay's Bad Boys Ask Forgiveness," *Victoria Daily Times*, November 14, 1953, page 8.

1354 "Sam's Prophecy Comes True," *Victoria Daily Times*, November 16, 1953, page 8.

1355 "Rogers' Claim Recalled by Andy's Spree," *Victoria Daily Times*, November 17, 1953, page 8.

1356 "Hebenton Close To Point Lead," *Victoria Daily Times*, November 17, 1953, page 8.

1357 "Billy Worried and for a Reason," *Victoria Daily Times*, November 20, 1953, page 10.

1358 "Maybe Billy Was Right," *Victoria Daily Times*, November 21, 1953, page 8.

1359 "Cougars Sixth as Double-0 Applied," *Victoria Daily Times*, November 23, 1953, page 8.

1360 "70 Seconds Keep Cougars From Win," *Victoria Daily Times*, November 25, 1953, page 10.

1361 "Nightmare for Marcel, Sweet Dream for Cats," *Victoria Daily Times*, November 28, 1953, page 8.

1362 "Cougars Clip Flyers; Climb to Fourth Spot," *Victoria Daily Times*, December 1, 1953, page 8.

1363 "Cougars Blanked - Billy Knows Why," *Victoria Daily Times*, December 5, 1953, page 12.

1364 "Perfectionists Beware, Cougars Like It Rough," *Victoria Daily Times*, December 8, 1953, page 8.

1365 "Reay Likened to Sage, Calls Turn for Cougars," *Victoria Daily Times*, December 12, 1953, page 8.

1366 "Royals Maintain Hex on Cougars," *Victoria Daily Times*, December 14, 1953, page 8.

1367 "Cougars Roll Over For Canucks Again," *Victoria Daily Times*, December 16, 1953, page 10.

1368 "Cougars Yell 'Help' In Drop to Basement," *Victoria Daily Times*, December 19, 1953, page 8.

1369 "Reay's Case Stronger Now," *Victoria Daily Times*, December 21, 1953, page 10.

1370 "Quakers Close to WHL Lead," *Victoria Daily Times*, December 24, 1953, page 8.

1371 "Bombers Put Hole In Cougars' Sock," *Victoria Daily Times*, December 26, 1953, page 8.

1372 "Cougars Meet Canucks Here," *Victoria Daily Times*, December 28, 1953, page 8.

1373 "Cougars Bleed Again In Defeat by Canucks," *Victoria Daily Times*, December 29, 1953, page 6.

1374 "Cougars Awe Critics; Whip Royals Handily," *Victoria Daily Times*, January 2, 1954, page 8.

1375 "Patrick Goes to Rangers; Cougars Break Jinx," *Victoria Daily Times*, January 6, 1954, page 8.

1376 "New Year Happy One For Cougars So Far," *Victoria Daily Times*, January 8, 1954, page 8.

1377 "Flyers Nip Cougars, End Prairie Streak," *Victoria Daily Times*, January 9, 1954, page 8.

1378 "Hockey Standings," *Victoria Daily Times*, January 11, 1954, page 8.

1379 "Canucks Tough, Cougars Tougher," *Victoria Daily Times*, January 12, 1954, page 8.

1380 "Cougar Tale Fails As Plot Goes Awry," *Victoria Daily Times*, January 15, 1954, page 8.

1381 "Cougars Tie Bombers, Give Royals Whipping," *Victoria Daily Times*, January 18, 1954, page 8.

1382 "Sure Eddie Helps As Canucks Routed," *Victoria Daily Times*, January 20, 1954, page 8.

1383 "Cougars Shouldn't Be Any Worse Here Monday,' *Victoria Daily Times*, January 23, 1954, page 8.

1384 "Cougars Ring True, Blank Stampeders," *Victoria Daily Times*, January 24, 1954, page 8.

1385 "Flyers Get Battle And One Big Break,' *Victoria Daily Times*, January 30, 1954, page 8.

1386 "Cougars Hold Quakers Even," *Victoria Daily Times*, February 2, 1954, page 8.

1387 "Bonin and Co. Irk Cougars," *Victoria Daily Times*, February 3, 1954, page 8.

1388 "Cougars Split With Calgary," *Victoria Daily Times*, February 4, 1954, page 10.

1389 "Cougars Beat Old 'Big One' Jinx With Smart Win Over Quakers," *Victoria Daily Times*, February 6, 1954, page 8.

1390 *Victoria Daily Times*, February 9, 1954, page 8.

1391 "Ed Aids Cats On His 'Night'," *Victoria Daily Times*, February 13, 1954, page 8.

1392 "Almas Gone, Evans Due; Kilburn Switched, Anderson, Too," *Victoria Daily Times*, February 19, 1954, page 8.

1393 "Cougar Critics Cringe, Thanks to Claude," *Victoria Daily Times*, February 20, 1954, page 8.

1394 "Stamps Share WHL Lead, Cougars Bid for Fifth," *Victoria Daily Times*, February 22, 1954, page 8.

1395 "Stamps Big, But Still Fall Hard," *Victoria Daily Times*, February 23, 1954, page 8.

The History of Professional Hockey in Victoria, BC: 1911-2011

1396 "Cougars Halt Cougar Move," *Victoria Daily Times*, February 24, 1954, page 8.

1397 "Gods Were Fickle But No One Cared," *Victoria Daily Times*, February 27, 1954, page 8.

1398 "Cougars Bidding For Fourth Place," *Victoria Daily Times*, March 2, 1954, page 6.

1399 "Cougars Get Torrid Like," *Victoria Daily Times*, March 6, 1954, page 9.

1400 "Hall's Outstanding Work Helps Flyers to a 4-2 Win," *The Calgary Herald*, March 8, 1954, page 20.

1401 "Cougars Stalled, Bombers Blanked," *Victoria Daily Times*, March 11, 1954, page 8.

1402 "Cougars Face Loss of 'Hurrying Sam'," *Victoria Daily Times*, March 12, 1954, page 10.

1403 "Sam's Loss Felt More by Quakers," *Victoria Daily Times*, March 13, 1954, page 8.

1404 "With Playoffs Due Soon, Lowe's Left, and Clune," *Victoria Daily Times*, March 26, 1954, page 8

1405 "Clippers Square Series; Stamps Tie for WHL Lead," *Victoria Daily Times*, March 18, 1954, page 8.

1406 "Cougar-Stamp Playoff Looms," *Victoria Daily Times*, March 20, 1954, page 6.

1407 "Final Hockey Standings," *Victoria Daily Times*, March 22, 1954, page 8.

1408 "Cats Throttle Cowboys - And Make 'Em Like It," *Victoria Daily Times*, March 24, 1954, page 8.

1409 "Cats May Play Without Colin," *Victoria Daily Times*, March 25, 1954, page 8.

1410 "Cougars' Toes Pinched As Show On Other Foot," *Victoria Daily Times*, March 26, 1964, page 10.

1411 "Cats on Mend, Home Tonight," *Victoria Daily Times*, March 27, 1954, page 14.

1412 "Cats on Spot Tonight, Abbott Latest Casualty," *Victoria Daily Times*, March 29, 1954, page 8.

1413 "Cougars Do the Most Work, But Stamps Get the Most Results," *Victoria Daily Times*, March 30, 1954, page 8.

1414 "Cats Eliminated; Stamps in Semis," *Victoria Daily Times*, *Victoria Daily Times*, April 2, 1954, page 8.

1415 "Hockey," *Victoria Daily Times*, September 4, 1954, page 12.

1416 "Cougars Shy Three Players," *Victoria Daily Times*, September 21, 1954, page 8.

1417 "Cougars Drill Here, Acquire Defense Help," *Victoria Daily Times*, September 27, 1954, page 8.

1418 "Cougars Trifle Short In Test With Rangers," *Victoria Daily Times*, September 29, 1954, page 12.

1419 Bill Walker, "It's My View," *Victoria Daily Times*, September 29, 1954, page 12.

1420 "Out Cats Do Try But Show Real Sad," *Victoria Daily Times*, October 6, 1954, page 10.

1421 Central Registry was the clearing house for all hockey transactions.

1422 "Cats Surprise Stamps; Hand Jolt to Canucks," *Victoria Daily Times*, October 7, 1954, page 8.

1423 "Dorohoy May Rejoin Cougars," *Victoria Daily Times*, October 9, 1954, page 12.

1424 "Leader Disallows Cougars' Protest," *Victoria Daily Times*, October 12, 1954, page 8.

1425 "Wayne Brown Breaks Leg; Bucyk Out for Five Weeks," *Victoria Daily Times*, October 12, 1954, page 8.

1426 "Pete Durham To Join Cats," *Victoria Daily Times*, October 13, 1954, page 10.

1427 "Marcel Got Some Help But 'Some' Not Enough," *Victoria Daily Times*, October 14, 1954, page 10.

1428 "Cougars Get Aid; Ashbee Acquired," *Victoria Daily Times*, October 16, 1954, page 10.

1429 "Royals Whip Cats," *Victoria Daily Times*, October 18, 1954, page 8.

1430 "Cougars Earn Dues; Canucks Just Bruise," *Victoria Daily Times*, October 21, 1954, page 10.

1431 The club would lose three consecutive games three more times in the season—likely the best record any modern-era Cougar team had accumulated.

1432 "Everything Turns 'Black' for Cats," *Victoria Daily Times*, October 23, 1954, page 14.

1433 "Cats Claw Bower," *Victoria Daily Times*, October 25, 1954, page 8.

1434 "Don Here After Grim Trip," *Victoria Daily Times*, October 26, 1954, page 8.

1435 "Cougars in Three-Ring Victory Over Quakers," *Victoria Daily Times*, October 28, 1954, page 8.

1436 "Cougars Plain Forgot To Go the Other Way," *Victoria Daily Times*, October 30, 1954, page 8.

1437 "Royals Like Cats, Show Why Tonight," *Victoria Daily Times*, November 3, 1954, page 10.

1438 *"Cats Had It Real Good; Ask Luke, He'll Agree," Victoria Daily Times, November 4, 1954, page 8.*

1439 *"One Cougar Must Go After Visit to Royals," Victoria Daily Times, November 6, 1954, page 9.*

1440 *"Cougars Who Win, Stick, So Ashbee on Way Now," Victoria Daily Times, November 8, 1954, page 8.*

1441 *"Cougars Trip Cougars In What Else - A Brawl," Victoria Daily Times, November 13, 1954, page 8.*

1442 *"Cougars Stay Close in Tight WHL Race," Victoria Daily Times, November 15, 1954, page 8.*

1443 *"Cougars Trounce Stampeders," Victoria Daily Times, November 18, 1954, page 12.*

1444 *"Bucyk In, Wall Out, For Cougars," Victoria Daily Times, Victoria Daily Times, November 19, 1954, page 12.*

1445 *"WHL Race Tightens; Pelletier Bids for New Shutout Mark," Victoria Daily Times, November 22, 1954, page 10.*

1446 *"Cats Down Stamps," Victoria Daily Times, November 24, 1954, page 12.*

1447 *"Flyers End Cougar Streak," Victoria Daily Times, November 25, 1954, page 10.*

1448 *"'Dad' Does It Up Proud In Big Cougar Premiere," Victoria Daily Times, November 26, 1954, page 12.*

1449 *"Quakers Blast Cougars," Saskatoon Star-Phoenix, November 29, 1954, page 21.*

1450 *"Cougars Home; Tie Canucks," Victoria Daily Times, December 1, 1954, page 10.*

1451 *"Cougars Throw Real Homecoming," Victoria Daily Times, December 2, 1954, page 10.*

1452 *"Royal Handiest Clutch Men Here," Victoria Daily Times, December 4, 1954, page 8.*

1453 *"Cougars Crowd Leaders; Dorohoy Point Behind Horvath," Victoria Daily Times, December 6, 1954, page 8.*

1454 *"'Even Bill Got One' As Cats Rip Canucks," Victoria Daily Times, December 9, 1954, page 10.*

1455 *"Kuzma Shines for Cougars," Saskatoon Star-Phoenix, December 13, 1954, page 12.*

1456 *"Cougars Drub Canucks; Start Gift-Hunting Now," Victoria Daily Times, December 16, 1954, page 12.*

1457 *"Cougars Roll On, And Over Canucks," Victoria Daily Times, December 18, 1954, page 10.*

1458 *"Stamps Stop Cougar Streak," Victoria Daily Times, December 22, 1954, page 8.*

1459 *"Horvath On Big Scoring spree," Saskatoon Star-Phoenix, December 23, 1954, page 12.*

1460 *"Cougars Bow to Stampeders," Victoria Daily Times, December 27, 1954, page 6.*

1461 *"Cougars Bounce back to Blank Stampeders," Victoria Daily Times, December 28, 1954, page 8.*

1462 *"Royals the Best, But Little More," Victoria Daily Times, December 30, 1954, page 6.*

1463 *"Stamps Finally Score To Halt Cougar Jinx," Victoria Daily Times, January 3, 1955, page 8.*

1464 *"Fresh Deck Could Solve Cougar Ills," Victoria Daily Times, January 5, 1955, page 10.*

1465 *"All's Up to Date With Cougars Now," Victoria Daily Times, January 6, 1955, page 8.*

1466 *"Cougars Don't Win But Canucks Lose," Victoria Daily Times, January 8, 1955, page 8.*

1467 *"Cougars Sight On Third Place," Victoria Daily Times, January 10, 1955, page 6.*

1468 *"Quakers Muss Up Cougars As Doug Talks Up Quakers," Victoria Daily Times, January 13, 1955, page 8.*

1469 *"Things Not Rosy For Cougars Now," Victoria Daily Times, January 14, 1955, page 8.*

1470 *"Cougars Looking Far Ahead As Canucks Sneak Up Behind," Victoria Daily Times, January 15, 1955, page 10.*

1471 *"Canucks Really Crowding Cougars," Victoria Daily Times, January 19, 1955, page 8.*

1472 *"Quakers Blank Victoria," Saskatoon Star-Phoenix, January 20, 1955, page 13.*

1473 *"Cougars Snarling At Tormentors," Victoria Daily Times, January 22, 1955, page 8.*

1474 *"Cougars Get Schedule Break," Victoria Daily Times, January 24, 1955, page 8.*

1475 *"Reay Pleased for Sure, Hints Better to Come," Victoria Daily Times, January 27, 1955, page 10.*

1476 *"Royal Bounce Back," Victoria Daily Times, January 31, 1955, page 8.*

1477 *"Marcel Willing to Wait Until Favor Needed More," Victoria Daily Times, February 3, 1955, page 8.*

1478 *"Cougars Reap Dividends In Win Over Canucks," Victoria Daily Times, February 7, 1955, page 6.*

1479 *The previous scoreless tie was February 24, 1951, with Tacoma and Vancouver the teams involved.*

1480 "Cougars Match Flyers In Playoff Preview," *Victoria Daily Times*, February 10, 1955, page 8.

1481 "Cougars Sever Link With Canucks," *Victoria Daily Times*, February 11, 1955, page 10.

1482 "Cougars Won't Say So, But Bruin Pact Rumored," *Victoria Daily Times*, February 14, 1955, page 8.

1483 "Cougars Get Bradley, Win Player Concession," *Victoria Daily Times* February 16, 1955, page 8.

1484 *These numbers came from an analysis of the season, which I compiled using newspaper articles as the basis for facts.*

1485 "Cougars Escape Flames, Put Royals on Hot Seat," *Victoria Daily Times*, February 17, 1955, page 8.

1486 "Stamps Stop Cougar Surge," *Victoria Daily Times*, February 18, 1955, page 10.

1487 "WHL May Expand To Ten Teams," *Victoria Daily Times*, February 18, 1955, page 10.

1488 "Cougars Bid High Again," *Victoria Daily Times* February 19, 1955, page 10.

1489 "Cougars Share Second as Stamps Beaten; Canucks Tie," *Victoria Daily Times*, February 21, 1955, page 8.

1490 "Royals Slight Hurdle For Bounding Cougars," *Victoria Daily Times*, February 24, 1955, page 8.

1491 "Cougars Pass Stampeders," *Victoria Daily Times*, February 28, 1955, page 10.

1492 "Cougars' Fat Sizzles For Stew With Canucks," *Victoria Daily Times*, March 3, 1955, page 8.

1493 "Cougars Tie With Canucks," *Victoria Daily Times*, March 5, 1955, page 10.

1494 "Flyers May Hold Key To Cougars' Ranking," *Victoria Daily Times*, March 7, 1955, page 8.

1495 "Cougar Club Records Teeter," *Victoria Daily Times*, March 9, 1955, page 10.

1496 *According to the newspaper account of the event, the Hebentons received the following gifts and wishes: a 21-inch television, automatic washer and dryer, dinette and bedroom suites, silver tea set (from the club), two cancelled cheque stubs from Frank Selke of the Montreal Canadiens and owner Lester Patrick of the Cougars, sweater, jacket, fishing tackle (from the Times), table lighter, steak knives, steam, electric fryer, car cushion rug. Also, a water-colour painting, a giant Panda bear and car for 2-year-old Clayton Hebenton (Andy's son), sugar tongs, smoking stand, and a year's passes to two of Victoria's theatres.*

1497 "Cougars Do It Up Brown for Andy," *Victoria Daily Times*, March 10, 1955, page 8.

1498 "Cougars 'In' Now, Hold Playoff Key," *Victoria Daily Times*, March 14, 1955, page 8.

1499 "Our Marcel Now Second; But Stamps Suffer More," *Victoria Daily Times*, arch 16, 1955, page 10.

1500 "Cougars Lose, But Still Win," *Victoria Daily Times*, March 17, 1955, page 8.

1501 "Canucks Nail Third With 1-0 Blanking," *Victoria Daily Times*, March 19, 1955, page 10.

1502 "Royals Miss Out," *Saskatoon Star-Phoenix*, March 21, 1955, page 17.

1503 "Cougars Meet Stamps; 'Up to Players' - Reay," *Victoria Daily Times*, March 21, 1955, page 8.

1504 "Cougars 'Disappoint' Bev; But Flyers Get Lumped Too," *Victoria Daily Times*, March 22, 1955, page 10.

1505 "Cougars Go Two Down, But So Were '51 Champs," *Victoria Daily Times*, March 25, 1955, page 10.

1506 "Andy's Goal (for Marcel) Gives Cougars New Life," *Victoria Daily Times*, March 29, 1955, page 8.

1507 "Just One Chance Left For Battered Cougars," *Victoria Daily Times*, March 30, 1955, page 12.

1508 "Cougars Bow to Stamps In Battle of Pill Bottle," *Victoria Daily Times*, April 1, 1955, page 10.

1509 "Cats' Andy, Peter Named All-Stars," *Victoria Daily Times*, April 2, 1955, page 2.

1510 "Lester Locks Up a Career," *Victoria Daily Times*, September 3, 1955, page 8.

1511 "Lester Patrick Vacates Post With Cougar Outfit," *Saskatoon Star-Phoenix*, September 3, 1955, page 19.

1512 "WHL Gravy Train Ready To be Caught," *Victoria Daily Times*, September 10, 1955, page 11.

1513 Andy Hebenton was sold to the Rangers in the spring of 1955, in return for cash and two players to be named later.

1514 "Cougars Get Player Aid," *Victoria Daily Times*, September 19, 1955, page 5.

1515 "Cougars Report to Camp Today," *Victoria Daily Times*, September 24, 1955, page 10.

1516 Returning players were goaltender Marcel Pelletier, defenceman Bill Davison, and forwards Colin Kilburn, Wayne Brown, Doug Macauley, and Mark Marquess.

1517 "Cougars Tie With Vees, But Finish Never Came," *Victoria Daily Times*, October 1, 1955, page 12.

1518 "Cougars Answer Queries With 5-1 Win Over V's," *Victoria Daily Times*, October 4, 1955, page 8.

1519 "Cats Lose In Fun, But Fun Over Now," *Victoria Daily Times*, October 6, 1955, page 8.

1520 "Cats Meet Royals In Opener Tonight," *Victoria Daily Times*, October 7, 1955, page 10.

1521 "'Nice,' But 'Real Nice' As Cougars Jump Royals," *Victoria Daily Times*, October 8, 1955, page 10.

1522 "Cougars Edge Canucks For Third Straight Win," *Victoria Daily Times*, October 11, 1955, page 10.

1523 "Danny's 'First' Gives Cougars Their 'Fourth'," *Victoria Daily Times*, October 12, 1955, page 10.

1524 "Old Cougars Show New Cougars How," *Victoria Daily Times*, October 15, 1955, page 10.

1525 "Cougars Not Too Neat In Slim Loss to Flyers," *Victoria Daily Times*, October 19, 1955, page 10.

1526 "Cougars Give Quick Reply," *Victoria Daily Times*, October 12, 1955, page 10.

1527 "WHL Trailers Move Up; Royals Shade Cougars," *Victoria Daily Times*, October 24, 1955, page 8.

1528 "Cougars Survive Rugged ice Joust," *Victoria Daily Times*, October 29, 1955, page 10.

1529 "Americans (Hodge) Stop Cats; Wings Remain in NHL cellar," *Victoria Daily Times*, October 31, 1955, page 8.

1530 "Cats Did It Proud Against Quakers," *Victoria Daily Times*, November 5, 1955, page 12.

1531 "Cougars Roll in High Gear; Stamps Lead Eastern Section," *Victoria Daily Times*, November 7, 1955, page 8.

1532 "Olson Quick To Praise Kids; Reay Quick Too - To Leave!" *Victoria Daily Times*, November 9, 1955, page 10.

1533 "Currie Was Too Modest," *Victoria Daily Times*, November 12, 1955, page 8.

1534 "Cougars Can Recoup All Against Canucks Here," *Victoria Daily Times*, November 14, 1955, page 10.

1535 "Eddie Errs, Cat No Worse (Friday)," *Victoria Daily Times*, November 25, 1955, page 8.

1536 "Cougars Warned; Check Those Cheques," *Victoria Daily Times*, November 18, 1955, page 10.

1537 "Hockey (Or Fists) Cougars Still Won," *Victoria Daily Times*, November 19, 1955, page 12.

1538 "Cougar Protest Keeps Seattle Feud Brewing," *Victoria Daily Times*, November 21, 1955, page 8.

1539 "Cougars Jarred, Mostly by Canucks," *Victoria Daily Times*, November 23, 1955, page 13.

1540 "As Fred Would Say—Somebody's Gotta Go," *Victoria Daily Times*, November 26, 1955, page 12.

1541 "Cougars Keep Second Place," *Victoria Daily Times*, November 28, 1955, page 11.

1542 "But Olson Just Says 'Nothing'," *Victoria Daily Times*, November 30, 1955, page 14.

1543 Bill Walker, "It's My View," *Victoria Daily Times*, November 30, 1955, page 14.

1544 "Cougar Pride Triumphs - Last Time for Some?" *Victoria Daily Times*, December 3, 1955, page 12.

1545 "Three-Man Cats Conform to Style," *Victoria Daily Times*, December 6, 1955, page 8.

1546 "Cougars Clicking on More Cylinders," *Victoria Daily Times*, December 7, 1955, page 12.

1547 "Cats Don't Use Chance," *Victoria Daily Times*, December 8, 1955, page 10.

1548 "Cougars Click On, Off, Ice," *Victoria Daily Times*, December 10, 1955, page 12.

1549 "Second Player To Join Cougars," *Victoria Daily Times*, December 1, 1955, page 12.

1550 "Jim Looked On to Set Cougars Right Again," *Victoria Daily Times*, December 13, 1955, page 8.

1551 "Regals On Move?" *Victoria Daily Times*, December 13, 1955, page 8.

1552 "'No Place Like Home' Dulcet Cougar Ditty," *Victoria Daily Times*, December 14, 1955, page 12.

1553 "'Cats' Swallow The Canary Whole," *Victoria Daily Times*, December 17, 1955, page 12.

1554 "Cougars Bounce Ahead, But Canucks Don't Wait," *Victoria Daily Times*, December 19, 1955, page 10.

1555 "No Yule Goodies Yet for Cougars," *Victoria Daily Times*, December 24, 1955, page 13.

1556 "Canucks Blank Cats," *Victoria Daily Times*, December 27, 1955, page 6.

1557 "Cougars Recall Past With Gritty Display," *Victoria Daily Times*, December 28, 1955, page 8.

1558 "Seattle Wins 4-3," *Saskatoon Star Phoenix*, December 31, 1955, page 25.

1559 "Cougars Off and Running," *Victoria Daily Times*, January 3, 1956, page 8.

1560 "Brandon Adopts Regals; Club Seeks Player Aid," *Victoria Daily Times*, January 5, 1956, page 8.

1561 Bill Walker, "It's My View," *Victoria Daily Times*, January 5, 1956, page 8.

1562 "Canucks Beware - Cougars on Prowl," *Victoria Daily Times*, January 7, 1956, page 8.

1563 "Who's Gonna Score In This Crazy Feud," *Victoria Daily Times*, January 11, 1956, page 10.

1564 "Bang! Goes Marcel's Bubble as Vancouver Scores Early," *Victoria Daily Times*, January 14, 1955, page 12.

1565 "Cats Add Strength as Berg Joins Club," *Victoria Daily Times*, January 16, 1956, page 8.

1566 "Macauley Bags Three in 6-2 Win," *Saskatoon Star-Phoenix*, January 16, 1956, page 15.

1567 "Cougar Win Rankles Bud," *Victoria Daily Times*, January 17, 1956, page 6.

1568 "Cats Good, Lucky, To Beat Saskatoon," *Victoria Daily Times*, January 18, 1956, page 10.

1569 "Lynn Not Inspired, Nor Were Cougars," *Victoria Daily Times*, January 19, 1956, page 8.

1570 "Cougar Win 'Much Better' But Pity Those Poor Royals," *Victoria Daily Times*, January 21, 1956, page 10.

1571 "Cougars Successful, But for Those Stamps," *Victoria Daily Times*, January 23, 1956, page 8.

1572 "Cheryl Got Hers And Pete Got His," *Victoria Daily Times*, January 25, 1956, page 10.

1573 "Cougars Click On, Off Ice," *Victoria Daily Times*, January 28, 1956, page 6.

1574 "Cats Stick With Canucks," *Victoria Daily Times*, January 30, 1956, page 8.

1575 "Frank Didn't Hedge' Cougars Got 'Better'," *Victoria Daily Times*, February 1, 1955, page 10.

1576 "WHL Prexy Confirms L.A. Bid," *Victoria Daily Times*, January 31, 1956, page 6.

1577 "No thanks to Charles: Cougar Task Toughens," *Victoria Daily Times*, February 4, 1956, page 6.

1578 "Cats Take Big Step," *Victoria Daily Times*, February 7, 1956, page 10.

1579 "A Hockey Paradox: Cougars Can't Win When Winning," *Victoria Daily Times*, February 8, 1956, page 12.

1580 "Cougars One Point From Canucks," *Victoria Daily Times*, February 11, 1956, page 12.

1581 "Cougars Stopped In Bid for Lead," *Victoria Daily Times*, February 13, 1956, page 6.

1582 "Cougars Plan Showdown With Canucks Tuesday," *Victoria Daily Times*, February 16, 1956, page 10.

1583 "At Stake: First Place; Where? Here on Tuesday," *Victoria Daily Times*, February 18, 1956, page 10.

1584 "Cougars Hit Crest; To Stay, Says Eddie," *Victoria Daily Times*, February 22, 1956.

1585 "Cougars Had It - They Proved It," *Victoria Daily Times*, February 25, 1956, page 6.

1586 "Cougars Take Lumps - - - But So Do Canucks," *Victoria Daily Times*, February 27, 1955, page 8.

1587 "Cougars and Canucks Fail to Reach Division," *Saskatoon Star-Phoenix.*, February 29, 1956, page 28.

1588 "Cats Cheer Fred, But Mourn Doug," *Victoria Daily Times*, March 3, 1956, page 10.

1589 "Judge Said 'Yes' But Ref Said 'No'," *Victoria Daily Times*, March 5, 1956, page 8.

1590 "Canucks Real Top Dogs; Injury Hex Hinders Cat," *Victoria Daily Times*, March 7, 1956, page 12.

1591 "Junior Players Bolster Cougars," *Victoria Daily Times*, March 8, 1956, page 8.

1592 "Speaking of 'Rookies', Colin Lends Larry Hand," *Victoria Daily Times*, March 10, 1956, page 10.

1593 "Let's Face Facts: Canucks Were Hot," *Victoria Daily Times*, March 14, 1956, page 10.

1594 "Trust Marcel How Got What He Wanted Too!" *Victoria Daily Times*, March 17, 1956, page 12.

1595 "WHL Playoffs Open; Cougars to Host Royals Tuesday," *Victoria Daily Times*, March 19, 1956, page 8.

1596 *"Job Wanted—Job Done! Key to Cougar Victory," Victoria Daily Times, March 21, 1956, page 8.*

1597 *"Royals Surprise; Edge Canucks; Stampeders Rally to Nip Flyers," Victoria Daily Times, March 22, 1956, page 10.*

1598 *"Ball-of-Fire Nels Sparks Cats' Win," Victoria Daily Times, March 24, 1956, page 12.*

1599 *"Cougars 'In'; Now Seek To Spoil Canuck Hopes," Victoria Daily Times, March 26, 1956, page 9.*

1600 *"All or Nought Puck Theme," Victoria Daily Times, March 28, 1956, page 10.*

1601 *"It's Canucks And Cats," Victoria Daily Times, March 29, 1956, page 10.*

1602 *"Cougars Weren't Laughing In Playoff Series Opener," Victoria Daily Times, March 31, 1956, page 10.*

1603 *"Cats Bristling At Tough Loss," Victoria Daily Times, April 2, 1956, page 8.*

1604 *"Cougars Study History Books," Victoria Daily Times, April 3, 1956, page 8.*

1605 *"Kilburn Hopeful'; With Reservations," Victoria Daily Times, April 4, 1956, page 10.*

1606 *"Cougars Refuse to Die; Egan Has Nothing to Say," Victoria Daily Times, April 7, 1956, page 12.*

1607 *"Cats Out, Canucks in And Goodbye Hockey," Victoria Daily Times, April 9, 1956, page 8.*

1608 *Victoria Daily Times, April 10, 1956, page 8.*

1609 *"Habs on Hockey Throne; Canucks Lead WHL Final," Victoria Daily Times, April 15, 1956, page 12.*

1610 *"Royals 'Peg In Final," Victoria Daily Times, April 28, 1956, page 8.*

1611 *The Edinburgh Trophy was given to the winner of a series between the WHL champions and the Quebec Hockey League champions. It was presented in only four years: 1954-1957.*

1612 *Victoria Daily Times, September 1, 1956, page 12.*

1613 *"Allan Cup Champions To Meet Cougars Here," Victoria Daily Times, September 1, 1956, page 13.*

1614 *The Allan Cup was awarded annually to the national senior amateur men's champion.*

1615 *"'Hutch' Died as He Lived - Sports Was His Life," Victoria Daily Times, September 4, 1956.*

1616 *Deny Boyd, "What's The Score?" Victoria Daily Times, September 3, 1954, page 13.*

1617 *"Cougars Hit Camp Sunday," Victoria Daily Times, September 23, 1916, page 12.*

1618 *"Colin Scores Trio; Pains Canuck Fans," Victoria Daily Times, November 12, 1956, page 12.*

1619 *"Colin Passes Word: 'Be Ready to Skate'," Victoria Daily Times, September 24, 1956, page 8.*

1620 *"…Here in Body, Not in Spirit," Victoria Daily Times, September 26, 1956, page 4.*

1621 *"Colin Smiles In the Rain," Victoria Daily Times, September 29, 1956, page 6.*

1622 *"First Easy Enough For Colin's Cats," Victoria Daily Times, October 5, 1956, page 10.*

1623 *"Colin 'Satisfied', Opener Monday," Victoria Daily Times, October 6, 1956, page 8.*

1624 *"Cougars Top Canucks—Impress in Opener," Victoria Daily Times, October 9, 1956, page 8.*

1625 *"Colin Request Aid; Bruins Send Beckett," Victoria Daily Times, October 11, 1956, page 12.*

1626 *"Cats Back In School," Victoria Daily Times, October 13, 1956, page 8.*

1627 *"Cats Still Seek Second Victory," Victoria Daily Times, October 15, 1956, page 8.*

1628 *"Cougars Defeat Ice-Machine; Rally to Tie With Warriors," Victoria Daily Times, October 17, 1956, page 12.*

1629 *"Cougars Get Day Off To Ponder Off-Night," Victoria Daily Times, October 18, 1956, page 10.*

1630 *"Cats Popular Losers; Edmonton Loves 'Em," Victoria Daily Times, October 20, 1956, page 12.*

1631 *Saskatoon Star-Phoenix, October 22, 1956, page 18.*

1632 *"A Goal Is a Goal Is a Goal And Cougars Didn't Quibble," Victoria Daily Times, October 23, 1956, page 8.*

1633 *"Souvenirs Get New Look," Victoria Daily Times, October 25, 1956, page 12.*

1634 *"Cougars Drop Overtime Duel On Cummings' Coming of Age," Victoria Daily Times, October 27, 1956, page 12.*

1635 *"10 lbs. or Else … Bulloch Warned," Victoria Daily Times, October 30, 1956, page 8.*

1636 *"Colin Can't Wait For 'Perfect Game'" Victoria Daily Times, October 31, 1956, page 14.*

The History of Professional Hockey in Victoria, BC: 1911-2011

1637 "Cats, One and All Evacuate Hot-Seat," *Victoria Daily Times*, November 3, 1956, page 1.

1638 "Cats, 'Pegs Match Streak," *Victoria Daily Times*, November 5, 1956, page 10.

1639 "Hockey Ignored In Pike's Pique," *Victoria Daily Times*, November 6, 1956, page 8.

1640 "No Action Expected For Warrior Tactics," *Victoria Daily Times*, November 7, 1956, page 8.

1641 "Amerks Leave Little Doubt—They Really Belong Up there," *Victoria Daily Times*, November 10, 1956, page 12.

1642 *Saskatoon Star-Phoenix.*, November 12, 1956, page 15.

1643 "Dorohoy Did the Damage Kilburn Shoulders Blame," *Victoria Daily Times*, November 7, 1956, page 12.

1644 "Colin Issues SOS As Axe Sharpened," *Victoria Daily Times*, November 19, 1956, page 8.

1645 "Hungry Cats End Starvation; Swallow Canucks in One Bite," *Victoria Daily Times*, November 20, 1956, page 6.

1646 "Colin Score Trio, Pains Canuck Fans," *Victoria Daily Times*, November 21, 1956, page 12.

1647 "Nellie's Jaw Worst 'Break'," *Victoria Daily Times*, November 24, 1956, page 14.

1648 "Cats Risk Skein Against Flyers," *Victoria Daily Times*, November 26, 1956, page 6.

1649 "Prairie Clubs Hold Key to Cat Fortunes," *Victoria Daily Times*, November 27, 1956, page 9.

1650 "Stamps Go Thirsty With Marc Pouring," *Victoria Daily Times*, December 1, 1956, page 14.

1651 "Regals Reduce Cougar Bulge," *Victoria Daily Times*, December 5, 1956, page 14.

1652 "Colin Shows Cougars Do-It-Yourself Drill," *Victoria Daily Times*, December 6, 1956, page 10.

1653 "Respect Elders? Not Flyer Rookie," *Victoria Daily Times*, December 8, 1956, page 12.

1654 "Warriors Blow 3-0 Edge As Flyers Win in Overtime 4-3," *Saskatoon Star-Phoenix*, December 10, 1956, page 16.

1655 "PNE Buys Canucks; Coley Sells Interest," *Victoria Daily Times*, December 7, 1956, page 11.

1656 "Woes Pile Still Higher For Beleaguered Cougars," *Victoria Daily Times*, December 11, 1956

1657 "Whitney Joins Cougars; Canucks Climb to Third," *Victoria Daily Times*, December 12, 1956, page 12.

1658 "Cats Edge Royals; Protest Possible," *Victoria Daily Times*, December 15, 1956, page 15.

1659 "Cougars Lick Wounds As Canucks Hit Prairie Road," *Victoria Daily Times*, December 17, 1956, page 10.

1660 *Saskatoon Star-Phoenix.*, December 22, 1956, page 17.

1661 "Cougars Going Up—Top Floor in View," *Victoria Daily Times*, December 24, 1956, page 9.

1662 "Cats Fogbound Everywhere; Winnipeg Equals THAT Record," *Victoria Daily Times*, December 27, 1956, page 8.

1663 "Cat Get New Centre; Wilson Joins Team," *Victoria Daily Times*, December 27, 1956, page 8.

1664 "It Could Have Been Sweet But Pete Turned It Sour," *Victoria Daily Times*, December 30, 1956, page 12.

1665 *Saskatoon Star-Phoenix.*, December 31, 1956, page 24.

1666 "Maybe Lynn Has Overtime Solution," *Victoria Daily Times*, January 2, 1957, page 12.

1667 "Warriors Arrived Angry - But Left Even More So," *Victoria Daily Times*, January 5, 1957, page 12.

1668 "Cats Real Puzzler to Lynn," *Victoria Daily Times*, January 7, 1957, page 8.

1669 "'Rook' George Did It—Couldn't Believe It," *Victoria Daily Times*, January 8, 1957, page 6.

1670 "Cougars Had It—Seattle Stole It," *Victoria Daily Times*, January 12, 1957, page 12.

1671 "Blue-Line Mix May Be Answer," *Victoria Daily Times*, January 14, 1957, page 8.

1672 "Cougars Give Lynn Big Going-Away Gift," *Victoria Daily Times*, January 15, 1957, page 6.

1673 "Whitney Joins Needy Warriors," *Victoria Daily Times*, January 16, 1957 page 10.

1674 "Cats Cut Partridge; to Join Kingston Club," *Victoria Daily Times*, January 19, 1957, page 12.

1675 "Table Manners Ignored As Cougars Eat and Run," *Victoria Daily Times*, January 19, 1957, page 12.

1676 "Ray's Buddy Role Ends; Same Old Villain Again," *Victoria Daily Times*, January 21, 1957, page 8.

1677 "Cats Just Can't Explain All Those Extra Minutes," *Victoria Daily Times*, January 22, 1957, page 6.

1678 "Winning Goal Looked Goofy But It Suited Vern Buffey," *Victoria Daily Times*, January 26, 1957, page 12.

1679 "Cougars Squash Suspension Tale," *Victoria Daily Times*, January 23, 1957, page 10.

1680 *"Cats' Home Brew Chokes Up Flyers," Victoria Daily Times, January 30, 1957, page 14.*

1681 *"Cats Prove Errors Not Always Costly," Victoria Daily Times, January 31, 1957, page 8.*

1682 *"Warriors Out-Battle Cougars For Penalty-Studded 3-1 Win," Victoria Daily Times, February 2, 1957, page 12.*

1683 *"Cats Face Salvage Job On Own Skins tonight," Victoria Daily Times, February 4, 1957, page 8.*

1684 *"Cougar Have New Look on Hockey Life Today," Victoria Daily Times, February 5, 1957, page 6.*

1685 *"Marcel Shows Upstarts He Can Still Be the Best," Victoria Daily Times, February 6, 1957, page 8.*

1686 *"Cats Blanked As Francis Steals Show," Victoria Daily Times, February 9, 1957, page 12.*

1687 *"Cats in Home Stand," Victoria Daily Times, February 10, 1957, page 8.*

1688 *"7,000 See Regals Win in Test Game," Victoria Daily Times, February 10, 1957, page 8.*

1689 *St. Paul Saints (USHL) - Wikipedia, https://en.wikipedia.org/wiki/St._Paul_Saints_(USHL).*

1690 *"Remember Chips? Well, Flyers Will," Victoria Daily Times, February 16, 1957, page 12.*

1691 *"Lapse Costly to Victoria," Saskatoon Star-Phoenix, February 10, 1957, page 12.*

1692 *"Don't Say 'Crucial'—But It Will Be," Victoria Daily Times, February 23, 1957, page 12*

1693 *"Park Avenue Cat Leave Skid Road Vancouverites," Victoria Daily Times, February 26, 1957, page 8.*

1694 *"Dig That Hole Deeper—Vancouver Has Company," Victoria Daily Times, February 27, 1957, page 12.*

1695 *"Don't Sell That Shovel Yet, The Cats Are Alive Again," Victoria Daily Times, March 2m 1957, page 12.*

1696 *"Cats Get 3 Cracks," Victoria Daily Times, March 4, 1957, page 8.*

1697 *"The Fog Was The Same Only Date Was Changed," Victoria Daily Times, March 6, 1957, page 10.*

1698 *Saskatoon Star-Phoenix., March 7, 1957, page 14.*

1699 *"Kilburn Won't Name Names, But …," Victoria Daily Times, March 8, 1957, page 10.*

1700 *"Wire-Climbing Pete Rises to Challenge," Victoria Daily Times,*

1701 *After reviewing the Durham incident, league president Al Leader decided that there would be no additional discipline. He was fined for his misconduct penalties, but the cost would have been more serious had any fans been injured. This information was found in an article in the Victoria Daily Times, March 12, 1957, page 8.*

1702 *"Cougar Pockets Jingle; Sport Three-Point Lead," Victoria Daily Times, March 12, 1967, page 8.*

1703 *"Canucks Snatch Padding Out From Under Cougars," Victoria Daily Times, March 13, 1957, page 12.*

1704 *"Cats, Amerks Mix; Usual Sparks Fly," Victoria Daily Times, March 16, 1957, page 12.*

1705 *"Near Riot At Victoria," Saskatoon Star-Phoenix, March 16, 1957, page 18.*

1706 *"This One Could Be THE One," Victoria Daily Times, March 18, 1957, page 8.*

1707 *"Cats No Longer Wall-flowers As Canucks Heed Home Waltz," Victoria Daily Times, March 19, 1957, page 8.*

1708 *"Cats' Script Too Early? Francis Lost to Amerks," Victoria Daily Times, March 23, 1957, page 12.*

1709 *"Kilburn's Formula for Success … 'If 4 Guys Work …,'" Victoria Daily Times, March 25, 1957, page 8.*

1710 *"140 Pounds of Arnie Crushes Cats' Chance," Victoria Daily Times, March 27, 1957, page 10.*

1711 *"One-Game Series Now," Victoria Daily Times, March 29, 1957, page 10.*

1712 *"Royals Knock Cougars Back to Lunch-Bucket League," Victoria Daily Times, April 1, 1957, page 9.*

1713 *"Three Colin Kilburns Sum Up Hockey Season; the Coach, the Manager, the Player," Victoria Daily Times, April 3, 1957.*

1714 *"Patrick Says Retirement Permanent This Time," Saskatoon Star-Phoenix, March 16, 1957, page 18.*

1715 *Archie Wills, "The Lester Patrick Story," Victoria Daily Times, March 16, 1957 to March 28, 1957.*

1716 *Companies File No. 39,619, British Columbia Museum and Archives, Victoria, BC.*

1717 *"Regals at Edmonton Tonight," Saskatoon Star-Phoenix., October 16, 1957, page 23.*

1718 *"Rearguards Boost Victoria's Stock," Victoria Daily Times, September 27, 1957, page 10.*

1719 *http://www.sihrhockey.org/member_player_sheet.cfm?player_id=4686&mode=2*

1720 *"Royals 'Old Reliables' Forget Times Marches On," Victoria Daily Times*, October 15, 1957, page 12.

1721 *"Arena Officials Promise Ice for Victoria Opener," Victoria Daily Times*, October 12, 1957, page 10.

1722 *"Cracked Ice Purchased To Assist Ice Machine," Victoria Daily Times*, October 15, 1957, page 12.

1723 *"Royals 'Old Reliables' Forget Times Marches On," Victoria Daily Times*, October 15, 1957, page 12.

1724 *"Cougars Buy New Claws' 'The Cat' in Net Friday," Victoria Daily Times*, October 17, 1957, page 10.

1725 *"Even Forum Fans Cheer Our Emile," Victoria Daily Times*, October 19, 1957, page 8.

1726 *"Cougars Overdraw Account; Can't Pay in Third Period," Victoria Daily Times*, October 21, 1957, page 8.

1727 *"Most Victoria Fans Take Optimistic View of Cougars," Victoria Daily Times*, October 22, 1957, page 6.

1728 *"Colin Wide Open But Nobody Fires," Victoria Daily Times*, October 22, 1957, page 6.

1729 *"Young Centre on Way to Bolster Cougars," Victoria Daily Times*, October 22, 1957, page 6.

1730 *"Hal May Still Use Towel; Next Time to Dry Tears," Victoria Daily Times*, October 24, 1957, page 10.

1731 *"Luckless Cougars Hit by Influenza," Saskatoon Star-Phoenix*, October 28, 1957, page 18.

1732 *"Colin Continues Search For Seasoned Rearguard," Victoria Daily Times*, October 29, 1957, page 8.

1733 *"Health? It's Wonderful—Cougars Back at Work," Victoria Daily Times*, October 31, 1957, page 12.

1734 *"Kilburn Quits as Coach; Egan New Cougar Mentor," Victoria Daily Times*, November 4, 1957, page 8.

1735 *"What Pat Did Isn't for Cats," Victoria Daily Times*, November 6, 1957, page 12.

1736 *"Pat Plots Right Course; Colin Keeps Ship Steady," Victoria Daily Times*, November 7, 1957, page 12.

1737 *"Canucks Fan Wondering Why Cougars at Bottom," Victoria Daily Times*, November 12, 1957, page 8.

1738 *"Egan Sets Objective for Cats," Victoria Daily Times*, November 13, 1957, page 14.

1739 *"Fans to Select Teams in WHL All-star Game," Victoria Daily Times*, November 13, 1957, page 14.

1740 *"Extra Man, says Pat, Helps … And He Did!" Victoria Daily Times*, November 14, 1957, page 12.

1741 *"But Two Points Would Be Better!" Victoria Daily Times*, November 16, 1957, page 12.

1742 *"Liked by Fans But Not Refs," Victoria Daily Times*, November 18, 1957, page 8.

1743 *"Cats' Move May Pay 'Dividend'," Victoria Daily Times*, November 19, 1957, page 8.

1744 *"Please, Don't Be Polite When You're Starving!" Victoria Daily Times*, November 21, 1957, page 10.

1745 *"Switch May Upset Art's Plans," Victoria Daily Times*, November 27, 1957, page 10.

1746 *"Maybe Chapman Was Psychic; Cougars Still Most Trouble," Victoria Daily Times*, November 23, 1957, page 12.

1747 *"Right Guess Was Wrong As Far as Cats Concerned," Victoria Daily Times*, November 25, 1957, page 12.

1748 *"Royals' Delayed Punch Pounds Cougars Deeper," Victoria Daily Times*, November 28, 1957, page 14.

1749 *"Cougars Show Profit; Fred Brown Suspended," Victoria Daily Times*, November 29, 1957, page 12.

1750 *"Canucks Kids Light Fuse In Time to Sink Canucks," Victoria Daily Times*, November 30, 1957, page 10.

1751 *"Cougars in Double Win; Dorohoy Provides Spark," Victoria Daily Times*, December 2, 1957, page 8.

1752 *"Pistol Could Start Rewriting Record Book Tonight," Victoria Daily Times*, December 4, 1957, page 10.

1753 *"Doug Won't Find Old Spot Empty," Victoria Daily Times*, December 6, 1957, page 10.

1754 *"Ed Won't Sell At Usual Price," Victoria Daily Times*, December 9, 1957, page 10.

1755 *"Bev's Breakaway Saves Rough on Cougar Cause," Victoria Daily Times*, December 12, 1957, page 6.

1756 *"Cougar Rally Barely Misses; Billy Keeps Warriors Rolling," Victoria Daily Times*, December 14, 1957, page 8.

1757 *"Dorohoy Back on Beam; Kilburn Moved Up Front," Victoria Daily Times*, December 16, 1957, page 10.

1758 *"Cats Should Get Kick Out of This Practice," Victoria Daily Times*, December 16, 1957, page 10.

1759 *"Club Hockey Nights Come Up Next Week," Victoria Daily Times*, December 14, 1957, page 8.

1760 *"Just a Little Security Was All Bev Wanted," Victoria Daily Times*, December 19, 1957, page 12.

1761 "Cougars Make Room for New Defenceman," *Victoria Daily Times*, December 19, 1957, page 12.

1762 "Club Hockey Nights Come Up Next Week," *Victoria Daily Times*, December 14, 1957, page 8.

1763 "Cougars' Setback Not as Sad as Ref," *Victoria Daily Times*, December 23, 1957, page 8.

1764 *Saskatoon Star-Phoenix*, December 23, 1957, page 16.

1765 "Bev, Royals Didn't Have That Traditional Spirit," *Victoria Daily Times*, December 27, 1957, page 10.

1766 "Headquarters Quiet, So Pistol May Play," *Victoria Daily Times*, December 28, 1957, page 10.

1767 "Amerks Spoil '57 Finale; Cats' Plan for New Year," *Victoria Daily Times*, December 30, 1957 page 8.

1768 *Victoria Daily Times*, December 31, 1957, page 8.

1769 "Pat's Newest Medicine May Have Bitter Taste," *Victoria Daily Times*, January 2, 1958, page 10.

1770 "Cats Acquire Yanchuk; Colin Kilburn Injured," *Victoria Daily Times*, January 2, 1958, page 10.

1771 "That Bad Period Still Plaques Cats," *Victoria Daily Times*, January 4, 1958, page 6.

1772 "Cats Continue Search And Nobody Unpacking," *Victoria Daily Times*, January 6, 1958.

1773 "Bev Struts Stuff For Prairie Types," *Victoria Daily Times*, January 9, 1958, page 8.

1774 "WHL Acts to Speed Up Play; Adopts New Playoff System," *Victoria Daily Times*, January 10, 1958, page 8.

1775 "Cougars Compete For New Trophy," *Victoria Daily Times*, January 7, 1958, page 6.

1776 "Cats Make Cut As Layoff Over," *Victoria Daily Times*, January 10, 1958, page 8.

1777 "Emile Could Steer Cats Around Royal Roadblock," *Victoria Daily Times*, January 11, 1957, page 8.

1778 "Royals Eat Well At Cougar Table," *Victoria Daily Times*, January 12, 1958, page 6.

1779 "Cougars Cub Shareholder Seek Meeting," *Victoria Daily Times*, January 13, 1958, page 1.

1780 "Sizzling Debate Takes Place Over Move to Oust Kilburn," *Victoria Daily Times*, January 13, 1958, page 6.

1781 "Colin Flails Club Methods," *Victoria Daily Times*, January 13, 1958, page 6.

1782 "Cougars to Call General Meeting," *Victoria Daily Times*, January 14, 1958, page 6.

1783 "Colin in action Tonight As Cats Tackle Amerks," *Victoria Daily Times*, January 15, 1958, page 10.

1784 "Colin's Pride Picks Up, But Points Go to Amerks," *Victoria Daily Times*, January 16, 1958, page 10.

1785 "Flyers Also Want Kilburn," *Victoria Daily Times*, January 17, 1958, page 10.

1786 "Flyers Give Up Two Forwards To Get Kilburn From Cougars," *Victoria Daily Times*, January 18, 1958, page 14.

1787 The speed at which this trade was negotiated is in direct contrast to the lengthy, drawn-out negotiations in today's hockey world.

1788 "Talent Transfusion Late But Patient Perks Up," *Victoria Daily Times*, January 20, 1958, page 8.

1789 "If Howie Was Shorter Pat Would Be Happier," *Victoria Daily Times* January 27, 1958, page 8.

1790 "Hart May Help Cats Start Climb," *Victoria Daily Times*, January 28, 1958, page 6.

1791 "Blueline Corps Critics Due for Argument Today," *Victoria Daily Times*, January 30, 1948, page 12.

1792 "Pat Weighs Problem of Balanced Squad," *Victoria Daily Times*, February 1, 1958, page 10.

1793 "Stamps Grab Third Place," *Saskatoon Star-Phoenix*, February 3, 1958, page 12.

1794 "Maybe Pat Should Have A Get-Acquainted Party," *Victoria Daily Times*, February 6, 1958, page 10.

1795 "Amerks Can Thank Cats," *Victoria Daily Times*, February 10, 1958, page 8.

1796 "Hugh Won't Be Included in Cats' Worries Tonight," *Victoria Daily Times*, February 12, 1958, page 10.

1797 "Youthful Trio on Spree As Royals Clobber Cats," *Victoria Daily Times*, February 13, 1958, page 8.

1798 "Don, Blinky Won't Be Our Valentines," *Victoria Daily Times*, February 15, 1958, page 6.

1799 "Canucks Make It Unhappy Week," *Victoria Daily Times*, February 17, 1958, page 8.

1800 "Cougars Had Dull Party Until Serving Dessert," *Victoria Daily Times*, February 20, 1958, page 10.

1801 "It Should Appear Quiet After Hassle at Forum," *Victoria Daily Times*, February 22, 1958, page 14.

1802 "Amerks, 10 ('Ouch'), *Victoria Daily Times*, February 24, 1958, page 6

The History of Professional Hockey in Victoria, BC: 1911-2011

1803 "Party-Wrecking Cats Don't Mind the New Role," *Victoria Daily Times*, February 26, 1958, age 12.

1804 "Cougars Feel Royals' Pinch," *Victoria Daily Times*, February 27, 1958, page 10.

1805 "Pat May Have to Revise Plans; Cars Suspend Dorohoy, Bulloch," *Victoria Daily Times*, March 3, 1958, page 10.

1806 "It Was Bright Start But a Dreary Finish," *Victoria Daily Times*, March 5, 1958, page 11.

1807 "Cougars Expect Warm Greeting," *Victoria Daily Times*, March 7, 1958, page 8.

1808 "Colin Also Likes That Prairie Ice," *Victoria Daily Times*, March 8, 1958, page 12.

1809 "Cats No Match For Stampeders," *Victoria Daily Times*, March 10, 1958, page 8.

1810 "Cats Tackle Regals Wednesday," *Victoria Daily Times*, March 11, 1958, page 8.

1811 "Kubica Can Thank Mr. Francis, But It Works Both Ways, Too!" *Victoria Daily Times*, March 13, 1958, page 10.

1812 "Cats Fired More Than Jim's Four," *Victoria Daily Times*, March 17, 1958, page 10.

1813 "Cats Can Take Two Decisions," *Victoria Daily Times*, March 18, 1958, page 8.

1814 "Cougars May Give Amerks New Life," *Victoria Daily Times*, March 19, 1958, page 10.

1815 "Royals Mighty Mites Make Pilfering Pay Off," *Victoria Daily Times*, March 20, 1958, page 10.

1816 "'Honest Works' Earn Their Pay," *Victoria Daily Times*, March 24, 1958, page 8.

1817 "Cougars Aren't Planning Contributions For Marcel," *Victoria Daily Times*, March 27, 1958, page 10.

1818 *Saskatoon Star-Phoenix*, March 29, 1958, page 25.

1819 "WHL Playoffs Open Tuesday," *Saskatoon Star-Phoenix*, March 31, 1958, page 16.

1820 "Cats' Worst Year One of Ed's Best," *Victoria Daily Times*, April 2, 1958, page 12.

1821 "Great to be Popular, But Who'll Get Him?" *Victoria Daily Times*, September 12, 1958, page 10.

1822 "Bionda With Cats?" *Victoria Daily Times*, September 12, 1958, page 10.

1823 "Lacrosse Standout Joins Cougar Cub," *Victoria Daily Times*, September 15, 1958, page 10/

1824 "Egan Satisfied; Marcel Missing," *Victoria Daily Times*, September 29, 1958, page 10.

1825 "Cougars Acquire Repka; Seek More Defence Help," *Victoria Daily Times*, October 2, 1958, page 10.

1826 "Egan Crosses Fingers Waiting for Good Word," *Victoria Daily Times*, October 6, 1958, page 10.

1827 "Marcel, Steady Forwards Carry Pat's Early Hopes," *Victoria Daily Times*, October 9, 1958, page 10.

1828 "Pat's Outlook Grows Brighter," *Victoria Daily Times*, October 10, 1958, page 10.

1829 "They Agree With Marcel; Art May Have Argument," *Victoria Daily Times*, October 11, 1958, page 10.

1830 "Stampeders Show Cats Skating Paves the Way," *Victoria Daily Times*, October 14, 1958, page 10.

1831 "Cats to Try New Tactics," *Victoria Daily Times*, October 17, 1958, page 12.

1832 "No Need to ask if Cougars Approve of Sunday Hockey," *Victoria Daily Times*, October 20, 1958, page 10.

1833 "Pat's Swing Final Proof Cars Ruined Royals' Aim," *Victoria Daily Times*, October 22, 1958, page 12.

1834 "Now Pat Can Think About First Place for Cougars," *Victoria Daily Times*, October 23, 1958, page 14.

1835 "Seattle Speed Stops Cougars," *Victoria Daily Times*, October 27, 1958, page 10.

1836 "Denny's Dream Defence Nightmare for Cougars," *Victoria Daily Times*, October 29, 1958, page 10.

1837 "New Cougars Trend Ends Totem Skein," *Victoria Daily Times*, November 1, 1958, page 12

1838 There was considerable confusion about having two teams in the league with the same name. Spokane used the name of their previous senior hockey league team even though Edmonton had used the name Flyers in the WHL for years. The media often called the new team the Spokes, but this was never their official name. The team was renamed the Comets after the league decided that Edmonton had the sole right to use the name in a ruling on September 21, 1959. Spokane's team name was changed to the Comets for the 1959-60 season.

1839 "Emile Almost Ended Search," *Victoria Daily Times*, November 3, 1958, page 8.

1840 "New Rearguard on Way as Cats Await Quakers," *Victoria Daily Times*, November 4, 1958, page 6.

1841 "Lucien Played His Aces But Marc Grabbed Chips," *Victoria Daily Times*, November 6, 1958, page 12.

1842 "Run of Injuries Breaks of Game," *Victoria Daily Times*, November 10, 1958, page 10.

1843 "Billy Didn't Pass Up Chance to Beat Cats," *Victoria Daily Times*, November 12, 1958.

1844 "Luce Squares Count; Quakers Edge Cats," *Victoria Daily Times*, November 13, 1958, page 12.

1845 "Last Chance for Cats To Grab Prairie Point," *Victoria Daily Times*, November 15, 1958, page 12.

1846 "Baliuk's Play Consoles Pat," *Victoria Daily Times*, November 17, 1958, page 8.

1847 "Marc Couldn't Find a Friend," *Victoria Daily Times*, November 20, 1958, page 14.

1848 "Gordie's Back With Cougars," *Victoria Daily Times*, November 21, 1958, page 12.

1849 "Portland Ready For Franchise," *Victoria Daily Times*, November 21, 1958, page 12.

1850 "Old Pros Splash Paint; Brighten Cougar Scene," *Victoria Daily Times*, November 24, 1958, page 8.

1851 "Baliuk, Pelletier Provide Cougars with a 'Natural'," *Victoria Daily Times*, November 26, 1958, page 12.

1852 "Royal Find Hole in Marc's Armour," *Victoria Daily Times*, November 27, 1958, page 12.

1853 "Ford Scored All Goals as Cougars Beat Seattle 3-1," *Saskatoon Star-Phoenix*, December 1, 1958, page 16.

1854 "Big Luce Was Sizzling; Extends Cougar String," *Victoria Daily Times*, December 3, 1958, page 12.

1855 "Ford's Turn Again With Balancing Act," *Victoria Daily Times*, December 5, 1958, page 12.

1856 "Cats Lose in Overtime; Ford Fires Two More," *Victoria Daily Times*, December 6, 1958, page 12.

1857 "Cougars to Use Wilson Tonight," *Victoria Daily Times*, December 6, 1958, page 12.

1858 "Rest Best Cure For Weary Cats," *Victoria Daily Times*, December 8, 1958, page 10.

1859 "Egan's Grading System Pays Cats Quick Profit," *Victoria Daily Times*, December 11, 1958, page 12.

1860 "They Picked Wrong Night," *Victoria Daily Times*, December 15, 1958, page 12.

1861 "Flyers Level Off Into Fourth Slot," *Victoria Daily Times*, December 18, 1958, page 16.

1862 "Totems Cash In On Cougar Sins," *Victoria Daily Times*, December 20, 1958, page 12.

1863 "Careful rimming Helps Clip Royals," *Victoria Daily Times*, December 27, 1958, page 8.

1864 "Cats Solve Road Puzzle; Tie Canucks for Second," *Victoria Daily Times*, December 29, 1958, page 10.

1865 "Baliuk Snares Share of Lead," *Victoria Daily Times*, December 30, 1958, page 6.

1866 "Red Ink May Down Royals," *Victoria Daily Times*, December 10, 1958, page 14.

1867 "Pros Predicting Longer Grind," *Victoria Daily Times*, December 13, 1958, page 12.

1868 "Edinburgh Cup Series Given Cool Reception," *Victoria Daily Times*, December 18, 1958, page 16.

1869 "Maxwell Applies Pin; Cats' Balloon Bursts," *Victoria Daily Times*, January 2, 1959, page 8.

1870 "Cats Must Solve Riddle To Stay in Third Place," *Victoria Daily Times*, January 5, 1959, page 8.

1871 "Spokane Flyers Take Big Jump," *Saskatoon Star-Phoenix*, January 3, 1959, page 13.

1872 "Emile Had Last 'Words' But Cats Had 'Victory'," *Saskatoon Star-Phoenix*, January 7, 1959, page 10.

1873 Much to the club's relief, the injury to Wilson's eye would not keep him out of the lineup for very long. His eye was bruised with some haemorrhaging of the eye socket, but the club doctors said he would only be out of action for a week. This information was reported in the *Victoria Daily Times*, January 8, 1959, page 10.

1874 "Pat Accustomed To Cougar Antics," *Victoria Daily Times* January 12, 1959, page 6.

1875 All statistics are taken from spreadsheets I compiled from newspaper accounts of individual games from Victoria, Seattle, Spokane, and Vancouver. The analysis of data is mine alone as are any errors.

1876 "That Right Hop Overdue, Says Hal," *Victoria Daily Times*, January 13, 1959, page 6.

1877 "Nick Isn't a Smoothie But He Paved the Way," *Victoria Daily Times*, January 15, 1959, page 10.

1878 "Cats, Stamps Tradin' Again," *Victoria Daily Times*, January 15, 1959, page 10.

1879 "Coast Breezes Revive Totems," *Victoria Daily Times*, January 19, 1959, page 6.

1880 "Manager Pat Singing Blues; Pilot Pat Croons Gay Tune," *Victoria Daily Times*, January 22, 1959, page 8.

1881 "Cougars Miss Sunday Punch," *Victoria Daily Times*, January 26, 1959, page 6.

1882 "Do Cats Play Better Away," *Victoria Daily Times*, January 28, 1959, page 18.

1883 "Tight Reins Keep Cowboys in Check," *Victoria Daily Times*, February 2, 1959, page 8.

1884 "Aspirin May Help Bing, But Cats Must Suffer," *Victoria Daily Times*, February 5, 1959, page 10.

1885 "Cats Frolic at Forum; Keep Hex Over Canucks," *Victoria Daily Times*, February 7, 1959, page 12.

1886 "This Time, Claims Egan, Cougars Will Stay Warm," *Victoria Daily Times*, February 9, 1959, page 8.

1887 "Which Way Will Cats Pick to Jump Tonight?" *Victoria Daily Times*, February 12, 1959, page 14.

1888 *Victoria Daily Times*, February 12, 1959, page 14.

1889 "Good Points Don't Outweigh Bad One," *Victoria Daily Times*, February 13, 1959, page 8.

1890 "Cougars' Roving Ways Could Help Stamps, Too," *Victoria Daily Times*, February 16, 1959, page 6.

1891 "Well, Then, Let's Try That Slow Start Again," *Victoria Daily Times*, February 18, 1959, page 12.

1892 "Cats Doing Their Part To Stop Scenery Switch," *Victoria Daily Times*, February 19, 1959, page 10.

1893 "Baliuk May Be Back With Cats Saturday," *Victoria Daily Times*, February 20, 1959, page 8.

1894 "Marcel Went a-Walking, Kent Came a-Shooting," *Victoria Daily Times*, February 23, 1959, page 8.

1895 "Can Cats Repeat Success at 'Peg?" *Victoria Daily Times*, February 25, 1959, page 10.

1896 "Pat Would Feel Warm Only if Cats Got Hot," *Victoria Daily Times*, February 26, 1959, page 10.

1897 "Will Stamps Follow Script?" *Victoria Daily Times*, February 28, 1959, page 12.

1898 "Fight For Spots," *Victoria Daily Times*, March 2, 1959, page 8.

1899 "Players' Fund Easy Winner?" *Victoria Daily Times* March 3, 1959, page 6.

1900 "Guyle's the Guy To Chill Prairies," *Victoria Daily Times*, March 4, 1959, page 8.

1901 "Plenty of Life In The Old Boys," *Victoria Daily Times*, March 5, 1959, page 12.

1902 "Cats Get Chance To Regain Cash," *Victoria Daily Times*, March 6, 1959, page 8.

1903 "Egan Prefers Hungry Cats," *Victoria Daily Times*, March 9, 1959, page 8.

1904 "Bell Almost Earned Spot On Marcel's Hate Slate," *Victoria Daily Times*, March 12, 1959, page 16.

1905 "Now's a Good Time As Any To Get Warm," *Victoria Daily Times*, March 14, 1959, page 10.

1906 "Would Be Hard to Top Saturday Night's Bargain," *Victoria Daily Times*, March 16, 1959, page 10.

1907 "Earlier in the Season Hal Might Have Smiled," *Victoria Daily Times*, March 18, 1959, page 8.

1908 "Cats Use Hustle Formula To Grab Overtime Win," *Victoria Daily Times*, March 19, 1959, page 10.

1909 Doug Peden, "Sideline Slants," *Victoria Daily Times*, March 19, 1959, page 10.

1910 "Wild Windup For Cougars," *Victoria Daily Times*, March 23, 1959, page 10.

1911 "We'll Be Ready, Says Pat, But Schedule 'For Birds'," *Victoria Daily Times*, March 24, 1959, page 10.

1912 "Rudy Found Weak Spot in Cats' Playoff Plans," *Victoria Daily Times*, March 28, 1959, page 10.

1913 "Cougars Bow Out of Playoff Fight," *Victoria Daily Times*, March 30, 1959, page 8.

1914 "New Ice Arena Would Open Door for WHL Expansion," *Victoria Daily Times*, January 22, 1959, page 1.

1915 Doug Peden, "Sideline Slants," *Victoria Daily Times*, September 9, 1959, page 10.

1916 "After League Offers Approval, Piggott Can Reach for Cheque," *Victoria Daily Times*, September 17, 1959, page 12.

1917 "Finer Details Settled So Hal Back at Work," *Victoria Daily Times*, September 18, 1959, page 10.

1918 "Jim Piggott Takes Aim On WHL Title for Cats," *Victoria Daily Times*, September 19, 1959, page 10.

1919 "Finer Details Settled So Hal Back at Work," *Victoria Daily Times*, September 18, 1959, page 10.

1920 "Jim Piggott Takes Aim On WHL Title for Cats," *Victoria Daily Times*, September 19, 1959, page 10.

1921 "Pete Makes Sure Cougars Will Pay," *Victoria Daily Times*, September 21, 1959, page 8.

1922 "There's Another Reason Why Pete Watched Diet," *Victoria Daily Times*, September 22, 1959, page 8.

1923 "Nick on Way To Join Cats," *Victoria Daily Times*, September 25, 1959 page 11.

1924 "Hockey's 'Nice Guy' Comes Home Saturday," *Victoria Daily Times*, September 24, 1959, page 12.

1925 *"Pint-Sized Cougars Proved Big Trouble," Victoria Daily Times, September 28, 1959, page 8.*

1926 *"Cougars Bolster Blue-Line Corps," Victoria Daily Times, September 29, 1959, page 8.*

1927 *"Tiny Tigers Top Wings' Pest List," Victoria Daily Times, October 1, 1959, page 12.*

1928 *"What Now, Mr. Wilson?" Victoria Daily Times, October 5, 1959, page 10.*

1929 *"Spokes Hope New Look Helps," Victoria Daily Times, October 6, 1959, page 10.*

1930 *This conclusion is easily reached after an examination of the Cougars' schedule I produced using newspaper accounts from several sources. Any errors or omissions are mine alone.*

1931 *"Canucks Not Fooling; Hand Cats 3-2 Beating," Victoria Daily Times, October 10, 1959, page 10.*

1932 *"Cats Got Just Reward When Art Fired 'Winner," Victoria Daily Times, October 13, 1959, page 8.*

1933 *"Cats Ready to Feed Largest Puck Family," Victoria Daily Times, October 8, 1959, page 12.*

1934 *"Cats Got Just Reward When Art Fired Winner," Victoria Daily Times, October 13, 1959, page 8.*

1935 *"Forward Balance Slate With Checking Efforts," Victoria Daily Times, October 15, 1959, page 10.*

1936 *"'Watch Now, Pay Later …'," Victoria Daily Times, October 15, 1959, page 10.*

1937 *"Starting to Grow," Victoria Daily Times, November 7, 1959, page 10.*

1938 *"Rivals Keeping Close Watch on Cats' Cards," Victoria Daily Times, November 13, 1959, page 11.*

1939 *"Totems Short-Changed At Thrifty Marc's Shop," Victoria Daily Times, October 19, 1959, page 10.*

1940 *"Flyers' Finishing Kick Didn't Help Hals' Heart," Victoria Daily Times, October 22, 1959, page 10.*

1941 *"Fash Proves Point—Only Time Tells," Victoria Daily Times, October 26, 1959, page 8.*

1942 *"Even Hal's Optimistic After Seven-Goals Spree," Victoria Daily Times, October 28, 1959, page 14.*

1943 *"Flyers, Cats Win," Saskatoon Star-Phoenix, October 28, 1959, page 31.*

1944 *"Luck Fickle Pal For Agile Emile," Victoria Daily Times, October 19, 1959, page 12.*

1945 *The basis for these records is a detailed examination of the Cougars' schedule, which I produced using newspaper accounts from several sources. Any errors or omissions are mine alone. In the 1950-51 season they were unbeaten in ten games, with nine victories and one tie; in 1952-53, they were unbeaten in nine games, with seven victories and two ties; and in 1953-54, they were unbeaten in seven games, with four victories and three ties.*

1946 *"Stitches Slip on Cats' Trip," Victoria Daily Times, November 2, 1959, page 8.*

1947 *"Alfie Has Praise For Prize Rookie," Victoria Daily Times, November 4, 1959, page 10.*

1948 *The Winnipeg coach was certainly correct about Ted Green. He went on to a successful professional career with the Boston Bruins of the NHL, as well as the New England Whalers and Winnipeg Jets of the WHS. Gary Bergman was also successful. After five seasons in the AHL, he became a star with the Detroit Red Wings and was a member of Team Canada in 1972. He also played with the Minnesota North Stars and the Kansas City Scouts. On the other hand, Wasklowski never made it to the NHL but spent many years with the Fort Wayne Komets of the IHL.*

1949 *Doug, Peden, "Alfie Should Have Scattered Some Praise Among Old Pros," Victoria Daily Times, November 5, 1959, page 12.*

1950 *"Y' Gotta Respect Chaps With Ships," Victoria Daily Times, November 7, 1959, page 10.*

1951 *"Hal Warming Up to Idea of First Prairie Jaunt," Victoria Daily Times, November 9, 1959, page 8.*

1952 *"Agile Cat Enough To Tame Cougars," Victoria Daily Times, November 12, 1959, page 8.*

1953 *"Cats Could Use Big Fire Earlier," Victoria Daily Times, November 14, 1959, page 10.*

1954 *"Totems Make Hay On Prairie Jaunt," Victoria Daily Times, November 16, 1959, page 8.*

1955 *"He Doesn't Look Part, But Artie's an Artist," Victoria Daily Times, November 18, 1959, page 12.*

1956 *"Pep, Punch Missing As Cats Clipped Again," Victoria Daily Times, November 20, 1959, page 12.*

1957 *"Sings of Life By 'Lost Line?'" Victoria Daily Times, November 21, 1959, page 10.*

1958 *"Cougars Must Present Work For Their Present," Victoria Daily Times, November 23, 1959, page 10.*

1959 *"Al the Cats Deserved A Few of Hal's Tears," Victoria Daily Times, November 26, 1959, page 12.*

The History of Professional Hockey in Victoria, BC: 1911-2011

1960 "Cougars Push Hoodoo Hank For All-Star," *Victoria Daily Times*, November 28, 1959, page 8.

1961 "Guyle Has Turn Wearing Horns," *Victoria Daily Times*, November 30, 1959, page 12.

1962 "Cougars Win, 5-2, Coach Confident," *Victoria Daily Times*, December 3, 1959, page 12.

1963 "Cougars Extended By Trail Smokes, But Triumph, 7-5," *Victoria Daily Times*, December 4, 1959 page 10.

1964 "Comets' 3-2 Victoria Labelled 'Ridiculous' By Cougars' Coach," *Victoria Daily Times*, December 6, 1959, page 12.

1965 "More Goals Major Need For Third-Place Cougars," *Victoria Daily Times*, December 8, 1959, page 10.

1966 "Marcel's First Shutout Sets Up Second-Place Battle Saturday," *Victoria Daily Times*, December 10, 1959, page 12.

1967 "Nicholson Shipped To Winnipeg Club," *Victoria Daily Times*, December 10, 1959, page 12.

1968 "Revitalized Cougar Front Line Carries Club to a 4-1 victory," *Victoria Daily Times*, December 13, 1959, page 21.

1969 *Saskatoon Star-Phoenix*, December 19, 1959, page 19.

1970 "No Mask (Yet) For Pelletier," *Victoria Daily Times*, December 11, 1959, page 12.

1971 "Goalie Riggin Takes it on Ear And Cougars Take It on Chin," *Victoria Daily Times*, December 20, 1959, page 12.

1972 "Cougars, Canucks Split Doubleheader; Next Stop Seattle," *Victoria Daily Times*, December 27, 1959, page 10.

1973 "Old Scores to settle With Seattle's Visit," *Victoria Daily Times*, December 29, 1959, page 10.

1974 "Fisticuff-Filled First Period Highlight of 5-3 Cougar Win," *Victoria Daily Times*, December 31, 1959, page 6.

1975 "The Right Foot, Losers, And Move on the Double!" *Victoria Daily Times*, January 3, 1960, page 8.

1976 "Forum Jinx Test For Cougar Punch," *Victoria Daily Times*, January 4, 1960, page 8.

1977 "Marcel Sharp As Cats Prove Hal Has a Point," *Victoria Daily Times*, January 6, 1960, page 10.

1978 "Comets Run Out of Gas; Roy Buys Extra Ticket," *Victoria Daily Times* January 7, 1960, page 10.

1979 "Seattle Perks Up in Third To Gain Tie With Warriors," *Victoria Daily Times*, January 11, 1960, page 8.

1980 "Three-Goal Crop Jinx for Prairies," *Saskatoon Star-Phoenix*, January 13, 1960, page 26.

1981 "Three-Goal Cop Jinx for Prairies," *Victoria Daily Times*, January 23, 1960, page 10.

1982 "Busy Little 'Cat' Real Cool Cookie," *Victoria Daily Times*, January 16, 1960, page 10.

1983 "Flyers Slip at Seattle In Race to Catch Cats," *Victoria Daily Times*, January 18, 1960, page 10.

1984 "Few Complaining About This Rut," *Victoria Daily Times*, January 21, 1960, page 10.

1985 "WHL Summaries," *Saskatoon Star-Phoenix*, January 23, 1960, page 20.

1986 "Arnie Started Wrecking Job," *Victoria Daily Times*, *Victoria Daily Times*, January 25, 1960, page 8.

1987 "Luce Closed the Door and Terry Did the Rest," *Victoria Daily Times*, January 28, 1960, page 10.

1988 "Gordie Agrees 'Duncan Night' Was Fine Idea," *Victoria Daily Times*, February 1, 1960, page 8.

1989 "'Peg Plot Upset By Little Things," *Victoria Daily Times*, February 4, 1960, page 10.

1990 "Noise in Cellar Can Scare Feller," *Victoria Daily Times*, February 6, 1960, page 6.

1991 "Fash's Bat Snaps Cat's Forum Jinx," *Victoria Daily Times*, February 10, 1960, page 10.

1992 "Prize Pony Promises Sellout for Cougars," *Victoria Daily Times*, February 9, 1960, page 8.

1993 "They'll Know Fash Was Slickest Cat," *Victoria Daily Times*, February 11, 1960, page 10.

1994 "George Has Pony; Reg Has Problem," *Victoria Daily Times*, February 11, 1960, page 10.

1995 "Cats Next Target For Colin's Needle," *Victoria Daily Times*, February 13, 1960, page 10.

1996 "Canucks Collar Policy Benefits," *Victoria Daily Times*, February 15, 1960, page 10.

1997 "Arnie Can't Help For Three Weeks," *Victoria Daily Times*, February 17, 1960, page 10.

1998 "Arnie Through For Rest of Year," *Victoria Daily Times*, February 18, 1960, page 10.

1999 "Earlier Call Might Have Suited Cats," *Victoria Daily Times*, February 19, 1960, page 12.

2000 "Gerry Likes Work Diet But Flyers Down Cats," *Victoria Daily Times*, February 20, 1960, page 10.

2001 "Spokes Blanked; Matthews Drive Wins for Cougars, Victoria Daily Times, February 11, 1960, page 8.

2002 "Arnie 'Satisfactory' Following Operation," Victoria Daily Times, February 22, 1960, page 8.

2003 "Cougars Facing Difficult Grind," Victoria Daily Times, February 23, 1960, page 8.

2004 "Cats Just Forgot To Guard Shutout," Victoria Daily Times, February 24, 1960, page 10.

2005 "Four Magic Digit For Stampeders," Victoria Daily Times, February 25, 1960, page 10.

2006 "Masnick to Play For Cats Tonight," Victoria Daily Times, February 27, 1960, page 10.

2007 "Hemlines Slip But Effect Was Pleasing," Victoria Daily Times, February 29, 1960, page 10.

2008 "Four Days With Cats 'Shrine Night' Award," Victoria Daily Times, February 17, 1960, page 10.

2009 "Marcel Had to Work While Cougars Romped," Victoria Daily Times, March 3, 1960, page 120.

2010 "Stamps' Fat Man Just Won't Move," Victoria Daily Times, March 7, 1960, page 10.

2011 "Art's Still a Star In 'Big Goal' Role," Victoria Daily Times, March 10, 1960, page 10.

2012 "Most-Valuable Label Will Be Worth $500," Victoria Daily Times, March 9, 1960, page 10.

2013 "Power Play Cools Cats In Scramble for Second," Victoria Daily Times, March 14, 1960, page 8.

2014 "Cats' Best Road Show Chalks Up Club Record," Victoria Daily Times, March 18, 1960, page 10.

2015 "Hockey 'Night' For the Ladies," Victoria Daily Times, March 15, 1960, page 8.

2016 "Comets Clout Confident cats," Victoria Daily Times, March 17, 1960, page 10.

2017 "Cats Receive Dividend On Don's Summer Toil," Victoria Daily Times, March 21, 1960, page 8.

2018 "Extra Dividend for Cougars Aces," Victoria Daily Times, March 21, 1960, page 8.

2019 "Late Getting to Work; Cats Win in Overtime," Victoria Daily Times, March 26, 1960, page 10.

2020 "Cougars in Driver's Seat After Third Straight Win," Victoria Daily Times, March 28, 1960, page 8.

2021 "Flyers Ousted in Four," Victoria Daily Times, March 31, 1960, page 10.

2022 "Marcel expect to Play as Final Opens Tonight," Victoria Daily Times, April 2, 1960, page 10.

2023 "Terriers Again Provide Cougars' Payoff Punch," Victoria Daily Times, April 4, 1960, page 12.

2024 "The Great Expansion Experiment," Victoria Daily Times, April 6, 1960, page 12.

2025 "Little Cats Fire 'Big' Goal Again," Victoria Daily Times, April 7, 1960, page 10.

2026 "Piggott Ponders California Shift," Victoria Daily Times, April 7, 1960, page 10.

2027 "Canucks Snap Cougar Skein Trim Deficit to One Game," Victoria Daily Times, April 8, 1960, page 10.

2028 "Cougars Forget Teamwork And Canucks Square Series," Victoria Daily Times, April 11, 1960, page 12.

2029 "Dan Gets In Last Word So Canucks Up One Now," Victoria Daily Times, April 13, 1960, page 12.

2030 "Piggott Wants To Move," Victoria Daily Times, April 13, 1960, page 12.

2031 "Scotty's Last Verdict Has Them All Guessing," Victoria Daily Times, April 14, 1960, page 10.

2032 "Canucks Wrap Up Title With Fifth Straight Win," Victoria Daily Times, April 16, 1960, page 12.

2033 "WHL Announced Eight Starters," Saskatoon Star-Phoenix, May 13, 1960, page 23.

2034 I determined these facts from a detailed analysis of the teams in question and team-scoring numbers I acquired from a variety of sources, particularly newspapers.

2035 "Hockey," Victoria Daily Times September 26, 1960, page 10.

2036 "George Has Hopes For New 'Kid' Line," Victoria Daily Times, September 30, 1960, page 6.

2037 "'Like the Pirates, We May Surprise'," Victoria Daily Times, September 28, 1960, page 12.

2038 "No Invitation, But Charlie Joins Cougars' Puck Party," Victoria Daily Times, October 1, 1960, page 10.

2039 "Fizzell, McLeod Sharpest Cats," Victoria Daily Times, October 3, 1960, page 10.

2040 "Cougars Can Show George In Opener Against Totems," Victoria Daily Times, October 13, 1960, page 12.

2041 "New Edition of Cougars Tackles Totems Tonight," Victoria Daily Times, October 14, 1960, page 10.

2042 "Cougar Kids Steal Glamor From Vets," Victoria Daily Times, October 15, 1960, page 10.

2043 "Totems Trip Cats On Boileau's Pair," *Victoria Daily Times*, October 17, 1960. page 10.

2044 "Some Credit to Fizzell Because Comets Fizzle," *Victoria Daily Times*, October 18, 1960, page 10.

2045 "Piggott Agrees Cats Need Help," *Victoria Daily Times*, October 20, 1960, page 8.

2046 "Pelletier Had Best Answers," *Victoria Daily Times*, October 24, 1960, page 10.

2047 "William Is Willing to Supply Nags," *Victoria Daily Times*, October 27, 1960, page 12.

2048 "Just a Bit of Needling Gets Ford in High Gear," *Victoria Daily Times*, October 29, 1960, page 10.

2049 "Perrin Slaps NHL Telecasts," *Victoria Daily Times*, October 31, 1960, page 10.

2050 "Cats Acquire New Forward," *Victoria Daily Times*, November 1, 1960, page 10.

2051 "That Payoff Habit is OK With Cats," *Victoria Daily Times*, November 1, 1960, page 10.

2052 "Hal's Trademark Shows As Bucks Throw Cats," *Victoria Daily Times*, November 5, 1960, page 10.

2053 "Defence Sparkles In first Road Win," *Victoria Daily Times*, November 9, 1960, page 10.

2054 "Moro One Short Of Comet Total," *Victoria Daily Times*, November 10, 1960, page 10.

2055 "New Starting Time For Cougars Games," *Victoria Daily Times*, November 9, 1960, page 10.

2056 "Winning Tally by Ching Was Happy One for Bing," *Victoria Daily Times*, November 12, 1960, page 10.

2057 "Pat Ginnell Goes to Bucks," *Victoria Daily Times* November 19, 1960, page 10.

2058 "Marc's New Pal (Roy's His Name) Real 'Color' Guy," *Victoria Daily Times*, November 17, 1960, page 12.

2059 "Flyers, Cougars Guilty as Charged," November 19, 1960, page 10.

2060 "Pat Adds New Chapter To Old Hockey Story," *Victoria Daily Times*, November 21, 1960, page 10.

2061 "Cats Travel in Ford Fashion; Finally Turn Tables on Bucks," *Victoria Daily Times*, November 23, 1960, page 12.

2062 "Grey Cup Spirit Prevails on Ice," *Victoria Daily Times*, November 26, 1960, page 12.

2063 "All Art Missed Was First Zero," *Victoria Daily Times*, November 28, 1960, page 11.

2064 "Gus Rates Assist For Calgary Spree," *Victoria Daily Times*, December 3, 1960, page 8.

2065 "Power-Play Tally Ruins Cougar Rally," *Victoria Daily Times*, December 5, 1960, page 10.

2066 "Cougars Pick Up Big One for Road," *Victoria Daily Times*, December 10, 1960, page 12.

2067 "Luc Misses Mark But Take Points," *Victoria Daily Times*, December 14, 1960, page 12.

2068 "Manager Flop In Prophet Loop," *Victoria Daily Times*, December 15, 1960, page 10.

2069 "Cats Can't Prove Riggin's Slippin'," *Victoria Daily Times*, December 17, 1960, page 10.

2070 "Cats Trampled By Stampeders," *Victoria Daily Times*, December 19, 1960, page 12.

2071 "Cougars Pulling Out? Leader Denies Report," *Victoria Daily Times*, December 16, 1960, page 12.

2072 "Agar Talks Like Kitten; Cats Check Like Tigers," *Victoria Daily Times*, December 20, 1960, page 8.

2073 "Cat Coach Has Busy Day In Hunt for New Talent," *Victoria Daily Times*, December 21, 1960, page 10.

2074 "Ed's One That Got Away But Cats' Hunt Success," *Victoria Daily Times*, December 22, 1960, page 8.

2075 "Canucks Shut Out Road-Weary Cats," *Victoria Daily Times*, December 21, 1960, page 10.

2076 "Hal's Even Sorrier Now Bucks Didn't Get Gerry," *Victoria Daily Times*, December 27, 1960, page 8.

2077 "It Certainly Was a Rousing Party!" *Victoria Daily Times*, December 31, 1960, page 8.

2078 "All Those Goals Added Dividend," *Victoria Daily Times*, January 3, 1961, page 10.

2079 "Gilles Must Like Idea of Having Steady Job," *Victoria Daily Times*, January 5, 1961, page 8.

2080 "Road-Trip Blues Haunt Cats Again," *Victoria Daily Times*, January 9, 1961, page 6.

2081 "Cats Easy to Nip If They Take Nap," *Victoria Daily Times*, January 11, 1961, page 10.

2082 "Totems Would More of That Luck," *Victoria Daily Times*, January 14, 1961, page 8.

2083 "Bucks Need Rally to Down Cougars," *Victoria Daily Times*, January 16, 1961, page 8.

2084 "Flyers' Fading Fortunes Confusin', Not Amusin'," *Victoria Daily Times*, January 18, 1961, page 10.

Endnotes

2085 "Masnick Dealt For Rearguard," *Victoria Daily Times*, January 18, 1961, page 10.

2086 "Fash'll Tell You Goals Are Goals," *Victoria Daily Times*, January 21, 1961, page 10.

2087 "Cats Get Breaks; Hold On for Win," *Victoria Daily Times*, January 25, 1961, page 12.

2088 "Hal Is Willing to Risk That Kind of Problem," *Victoria Daily Times*, January 28, 1961, page 10.

2089 "Rocket, James to Spice Clash With Warriors," *Victoria Daily Times*, January 30, 1961, page 8.

2090 "Now Agar Has Two New Ones," *Victoria Daily Times*, January 26, 1961, page 10.

2091 "Harry Really Tried To Wreck New Deal," *Victoria Daily Times*, February 1, 1961, page 10.

2092 "Cats' New Punch Still Producing," *Victoria Daily Times*, February 4, 1961, page 10.

2093 "Barrie Is Success In Haunting League," *Victoria Daily Times*, February 7, 1961, page 8.

2094 "'Peg Patrons Finally See Cats Tripped," *Victoria Daily Times*, February 9, 1961, page 10.

2095 "That Cool Prairie Air Like Tonic for Cougars," *Victoria Daily Times*, February 11, 1961, page 10.

2096 "Cat Coach Can Afford To Smile Despite Loss," *Victoria Daily Times*, February 13, 1961, page 10.

2097 "Apprentice Days Over for Leopold," *Victoria Daily Times*, February 15, 1961, page 10.

2098 "Flyers Still Threat For Playoff Berth," *Victoria Daily Times*, February 16, 1961, page 10.

2099 "Route Rougher, But Buckaroos Supply Cushion," *Victoria Daily Times*, February 13, 1961, page 10.

2100 "Cats in Same Spot As Road Trip Ends," *Victoria Daily Times*, February 20, 1961, page 8.

2101 "Larry Made It Tougher For Cats to Open Door," *Victoria Daily Times*, February 22, 1961, page 12.

2102 "Colin Fires Best Shots In Duel With Pelletier," *Victoria Daily Times*, February 23, 1961, page 10.

2103 "Cats Need Fast Finish To Get Tie With Totems," *Victoria Daily Times*, February 25, 1961, page 8.

2104 "Canucks Unfair To Hockey Labor," *Victoria Daily Times*, March 1, 1961, page 8.

2105 "Agar Shuffles Cougar Lineup," *Victoria Daily Times*, March 3, 1961, page 8.

2106 "Frank Could Be Sorry He Touched Off Alarm," *Victoria Daily Times*, March 4, 1961, page 10.

2107 "One Point Better Than None, Cougars Salvage 2-2 Draw," *Victoria Daily Times*, March 6, 1961, page 8.

2108 "Cougars Can Shoulder Blame For Shutting That Back Door," *Victoria Daily Times*, March 8, 1961, page 10.

2109 "Agar Counting on A Happy Reunion," *Victoria Daily Times*, March 10, 1961, page 8.

2110 "Barry Isn't Complaining But How About Comets?" *Victoria Daily Times*, March 11, 1961, page 10.

2111 "Marcel Keeps Cats Smiling," *Victoria Daily Times*, March 13, 1961, page 8.

2112 "Fash Looked Part—Cats Had Heart," *Victoria Daily Times*, March 128, 1961, page 10.

2113 "Two absent, But Cats Clip Bucks at Portland," *Victoria Daily Times*, March 20, 1961, page 8.

2114 "Cats Call Two Juniors To Aid in Closing Drive," *Victoria Daily Times*, March 21, 1961, page 8.

2115 "End of Line for Warriors? Perrin Ready to Sell Team," *Victoria Daily Times*, March 23, 1961, page 10.

2116 "Ed's Fondness for Cats Is One-Sided Friendship," *Victoria Daily Times*, March 25, 1961, page 10.

2117 "A Tie Tuesday Would Clinch Berth for Cats," *Victoria Daily Times*, March 27, 1961, page 10

2118 "Camera Delays Cougars' Start," *Victoria Daily Times*, March 28, 1961, page 10.

2119 "Flyers Eager to Let Cats Have the Exclusive Rights," *Victoria Daily Times*,

2120 "Canucks Open the Back Door, May Tackle Cats in playoffs," *Victoria Daily Times*, March 30, 1961, page 10.

2121 "At Least Arthur Won't Be Around," *Victoria Daily Times*, April 1, 1961, page 10.

2122 "Jones Wins Point Title; Cougars Face Canucks," *Victoria Daily Times*, April 3, 1961, page 10.

2123 "Cats Sharp on Defence But Get Only One Goal," *Victoria Daily Times*, April 5, 1961, page 10.

2124 "Shots Aimed at McLeod Help Cool Off Canucks," *Victoria Daily Times*, April 6, 1961, page 10.

2125 "'Little Train' Carries Cats to Gruelling Overtime Win," *Victoria Daily Times*, April 8, 1916, page 10.

2126 "All Chips on Line Tuesday; Confidence in Cougars Camp," *Victoria Daily Times*, April 10, 1961, page 9.

The History of Professional Hockey in Victoria, BC: 1911-2011

2127 "Claude Soothes Critics; Ends Season for Cats," *Victoria Daily Times*, April 12, 1961, page 12.

2128 "Claude Soothes Critics; Ends Season for Cats," *Victoria Daily Times*, April 12, 1961, page 12.

2129 "Piggott Still Interested, But …," *Victoria Daily Times*, April 6, 1961, page 10.

2130 "Victoria Out as WHL Eyes Big-League Status," *Victoria Daily Times*, April 24, 1961.

2131 "City Fans Saw Cougars Win World Crown," *Victoria Daily Times*, April 24, 1961, page 10.

2132 *In reality, the franchise asked for, and received, permission for a leave of absence from the league, but never returned. Thus, the WHL lost two Canadian markets at the same time.*

2133 "Spokane's Western Hockey Franchise Moves to Denver; Toronto Maple Leafs Purchase Mel Smith's Comet Stock," *Spokane Spokesman-Review*, June 5, 1963, page 12.

2134 "Denver Loses Club," *Spokane Spokesman-Review*, June 26, 1964, page 14.

2135 "New Seats Installed for Hockey Season," *Victoria Daily Colonist*, October 1, 1960, [age 10.

2136 "Leafs Whip Canucks, 7-3," *Victoria Daily Colonist*, October 4, 1964, page 12.

2137 "Maple Leafs Fly For LA 'Double'," *Victoria Daily Colonist*, October 8, 1964, page 9.

2138 "Maple Leafs Bow To Los Angeles," *Victoria Daily Colonist*, October 10, 1964, page 10.

2139 "Maple Leafs Take Second Setback," *Victoria Daily Colonist*, October 11, 1964, page 10.

2140 "Leafs Lose in Overtime, 5-4 Before Sad, Sad-Sized Crowd," *Victoria Daily Colonist*, October 14, 1964, page 8.

2141 "Artificial Ice Pioneer Dies," *Victoria Daily Colonist*, October 15, 1964, page 6.

2142 "Leafs Win First One At Expense of Seals," *Victoria Daily Colonist*, October 18, 1964, page 12.

2143 "WHL Summaries," *Saskatoon Star-Phoenix*, October 19, 1964, page 14.

2144 "Maple Leafs Scintillate In 3-1 Win Over LA," *Victoria Daily Colonist*, October 21, 1964, page 8.

2145 "Outmanned Leafs Prove Just a Promise Away," *Victoria Daily Colonist*, October 25, 1964, page 12.

2146 "Lou Finds Range For Overtime Win," *Victoria Daily Colonist*, October 28, 1964, page 12.

2147 "First Real Test Here for Leafs," *Victoria Daily Colonist*, Daily Colonist, October 30, 1964, page 16.

2148 "High-Scoring Canucks Snow Leafs Under, 6-3," *Victoria Daily Colonist*, October 31, 1964, page 10.

2149 "Leafs Fall to Buckaroos, 4-3 Last Period Their Waterloo," *Victoria Daily Colonist*, November 1, 1964, page 12.

2150 "Leafs Lose in Overtime," *Victoria Daily Colonist*, November 3, 1964, page 14.

2151 "Leaf Penalties Cause Fifth Odd-Goal Loss," *Victoria Daily Colonist*, November 7, 1964, page 10.

2152 "Shoutout Best Method Leafs Find It Works," *Victoria Daily Colonist*, November 8, 1964, page 12.

2153 "Maple Leafs Find Things Even Up," *Victoria Daily Colonist*, November 11, 1964, page 12.

2154 "Leafs Lose in Overtime," *Victoria Daily Colonist*, November 15, 1964, page 13.

2155 "To Join Leafs," *Victoria Daily Colonist*, November 15, 1964, page 15.

2156 "Maple Leafs Collapse Point Easy for Bucks," *Victoria Daily Colonist*, November 18, 1964, page 10.

2157 "Seals Tie Leafs for Fifth Place," *Victoria Daily Colonist*, November 21, 1964, page 10.

2158 "Leafs Win First Road Game To Escape League Basement," *Victoria Daily Colonist*, November 22, 1964, page 12.

2159 "High-scoring Winger Joins Maple Leafs," *Victoria Daily Colonist*, November 24, 1964, page 12.

2160 "Maple Leafs Stun Seattle Totems," *Victoria Daily Colonist*, November 26, 1964, page 39.

2161 "Leaf Bow to Canucks Face Totems Tonight," *Victoria Daily Colonist*, November 28, 1964, page 10.

2162 "Totems Knife Through Shaky Leaf Defence," *Victoria Daily Colonist*, November 29, 1964, page 20.

2163 "Leafs Cooking Up Trade," *Victoria Daily Colonist*, December 4, 1964, page 14.

2164 "Hucul Quits Maple Leafs and Hockey," *Victoria Daily Colonist* December 5, 1944, page 10.

2165 "Maple Leafs Collapse Before Canucks," *Victoria Daily Colonist*, December 6, 1964, page 12.

2166 "Canucks and Bucks Hurting Leafs Most," *Victoria Daily Colonist*, December 8, 1964, page 12.

2167 "Leading Totems Score Little, But Triumph," *Quebec Chronicle-Telegraph*, December 14, 1964, page 8.

2168 "'Pilous' Pills for Pale People Fix Up Maple Leaf's Trouble," Victoria Daily Colonist, December 13, 1966, page 12.

2169 "Leafs' Legs Just Too Tired," Victoria Daily Colonist, December 15, 1964, page 14.

2170 "Leafs Shade Seals 6-5 Keenan Pots Hat-Trick," Victoria Daily Colonist, December 17, 1964, page 41.

2171 "Blades Trample Maple Leafs, 6-4," Victoria Daily Colonist, December 19, 1964, page 12.

2172 "Maple Leafs Fade Away In 6-3 Win for Seals," Victoria Daily Colonist, December 24, 1964, page 14.

2173 "Leafs May Have to Be Their Own Santa Claus," Victoria Daily Colonist, December 22, 1964, page 12.

2174 "Leafs Edge Seals, 4-3 Thrive Under Pressure," Victoria Daily Colonist, December 23, 1964, page 10.

2175 "Leafs Solve Buckaroos After Four Reversals," Victoria Daily Colonist, December 27,

2176 "'Rampaging' May Not Quite Fit—But It Could After Tonight," Victoria Daily Colonist, December 29, 1964, page 10.

2177 "Victoria Centre 'Player of Week'," Victoria Daily Colonist December 29, 1964, page 10.

2178 "Four Straight Victories Spark Bigger Crowds," Victoria Daily Colonist, December 30, 1964, page 10.

2179 "Tie in Portland." Victoria Daily Colonist, January 3, 1965, page 10.

2180 "WHL Summaries," Saskatoon Star-Phoenix, January 2, 1965, page 16.

2181 "Leafs Go to Six As 4,000 Road," Victoria Daily Colonist, January 3, 1965, page 1.

2182 "Streaking Maple Leafs Skate Over Vancouver," Victoria Daily Colonist, January 3, 1965, page 10.

2183 "Leafs' Goaltender Stops Buckaroos," Victoria Daily Colonist, January 6, 1965, page 8.

2184 "Maple Leafs Set Up Grudge Game As Canucks Tear Unbeaten Streak," Victoria Daily Colonist, January 9, 1965, page 12.

2185 "Two Goals by Keenan Start Leafs to Victory," Victoria Daily Colonist, January 10, 1965, page 11.

2186 "Tulsa Bound," Victoria Daily Colonist, January 10, 1965, page 22.

2187 "Leafs Get Another Streak Started Blades Here Tonight to Challenge," Victoria Daily Colonist, January 12, 1965, page 12.

2188 "Leg-Tired Leafs Lose to Blades," Victoria Daily Colonist, January 13, 1965, page 8.

2189 "Don Chiupka Given Trial," Victoria Daily Colonist, January 13, 1965, page 8.

2190 "Fred Hucul Back With Maple Leafs," Victoria Daily Colonist, January 14, 1965, page 10.

2191 "Vancouver Goalie Stops Leaf Cold," Victoria Daily Colonist, January 16, 1965, page 8.

2192 "Millar's One Big Save Give Leafs Inspiration," Victoria Daily Colonist, January 17, 1965, page 12.

2193 "Victoria Leafs Maintain Hold of WHL's 4 Place," Quebec Chronicle-Telegraph, January 18, 1965, page 8.

2194 "Leafs Take Third Spot Nine Point from Lead," Victoria Daily Colonist, January 20, 1965, page 8.

2195 "A Good Move," Victoria Daily Colonist, January 22, 1965, page 12.

2196 "Perreault Produces Big Game As Leafs Edged by Seals, 3-2," Victoria Daily Colonist, January 24, 2965, page 12.

2197 "Leafs Win, 6-3 Over Sad Seals," Victoria Daily Colonist, January 27, 1965, page 10.

2198 "Leafs Chill Bucks, 7-4 Before Biggest Crowd," Victoria Daily Colonist, January 31, 1965, page 12.

2199 "California Clubs' Big Chance Now," Victoria Daily Colonist, February 2, 1965, page 22.

2200 "Shvetz Pulls Ambush That Finishes Blades," Victoria Daily Colonist, February 10, 1965, page 8.

2201 "Leafs Drop Seattle Thriller Face Buckaroos Here Tonight," Victoria Daily Colonist, February 13, 1965, page 10.

2202 "Maple Leafs Back in Running For chance at Higher Spot," Victoria Daily Colonist, February 14, 1965, page 14.

2203 "Two tries Against Totems Could Be Crucial to Leafs," Victoria Daily Colonist, February 16, 1965, page 16.

2204 "Leafs Defeat Seattle On Sheer Doggedness," Victoria Daily Colonist, February 17, 1965, page 6.

2205 "Totems' Tight Checking Stops Maple Leafs, 1-0," Victoria Daily Colonist, February 21, 1965, page 12.

2206 "Winger Joins Leafs For Weekend Series," Victoria Daily Colonist, February 23, 1965, page 10.

2207 "Leafs Can't Win In Vancouver," Victoria Daily Colonist, February 27, 1965, page 12.

The History of Professional Hockey in Victoria, BC: 1911-2011

2208 "Little Leafs Tall Men In Overtime Victory," *Victoria Daily Colonist*, February 28, 1965, page 12.

2209 "Leafs Blow One, 4-3 To Portland Buckaroos," *Victoria Daily Colonist*, March 7, 1965, page 10.

2210 "Leafs on Their Own For Rest of Schedule," *Victoria Daily Colonist*, March 9, 1965, page 12.

2211 "Wild Passes Finish Off Leafs; Rugged Trip Adds to Woes," *Victoria Daily Colonist*, March 10, 1965, page 10.

2212 "Maple Leafs Snap Back To Defeat Los Angeles," *Victoria Daily Colonist*, March 11, 1065, page 14.

2213 "Leafs Back in Fourth Spot Tangle with seals Tonight," *Victoria Daily Colonist*, March 13, 1965, page 12.

2214 "Tired Leafs Fall At San Francisco," *Victoria Daily Colonist*, March 14, 1965, page 12.

2215 "Leafs Meet Challenge With Standout Effort," *Victoria Daily Colonist*, March 16, 1965, page 19.

2216 "Bucks Jolt Leafs Seattle Saves Day," *Victoria Daily Colonist*, March 18, 1965, page 33.

2217 "Win Tonight 'Must' For Leafs' Hopes," *Victoria Daily Colonist*, March 20, 1965, page 12.

2218 "Leafs Roll Past Vancouver In Best Display of Season," *Victoria Daily Colonist*, March 21, 1965, page 12.

2219 "Leafs Pass Big Test Face Another Tonight," *Victoria Daily Colonist*, March 23, 1965, page 12.

2220 "Just One More Victory And Leafs in Series," *Victoria Daily Colonist*, March 24, 1965, page 14.

2221 "Leafs Certain of Playoff Tie Could End all Doubt Tonight," *Victoria Daily Colonist*, March 27, 1965, page 12.

2222 "Leafs Capture Playoff Spot," *Victoria Daily Colonist*, March 28, 1965, page 12.

2223 "Victoria Settles for Seattle; Fielder Champ Eighth Time," *Victoria Daily Colonist*, March 30, 1965, page 13.

2224 "Pilous Picks His Leafs 'If We Stay Sound'," *Victoria Daily Colonist*, March 31, 1965, page 12.

2225 "Leafs Leave Goal Wide Open And Totems Pounce at Chance," *Victoria Daily Colonist*, April 1, 1965, page 14.

2226 "Maple Leafs Down 2-0 Another Chance Tonight," *Victoria Daily Colonist*, April 2, 1965, page 14.

2227 Jim Tang, "Maple Leafs Dazzle Totems, Fans," *Victoria Daily Colonist*, April 4, 1965, page 12.

2228 Jim Tang, "Maple Leafs Dazzle Totems, Fans," *Victoria Daily Colonist*, April 4, 1965, page 12.

2229 Jim Tang, "Leafs on Edge of Oblivion Need Comeback in Seattle," *Victoria Daily Colonist*, page 12.

2230 George Wilson, "Sleaver's Last-Period Goals Bring Totems Here Tonight," *Victoria Daily Colonist*, April 10, 1965, page 14.

2231 Eric Wesselby, "Keenan Sparks Victoria Club Playoff Clincher Set Tonight," *Victoria Daily Colonist*, April 11, 1965, page 12.

2232 "Hot Leafs Invade Portland Wednesday Host Bucks Saturday in Second Game," *Victoria Daily Colonist*, April 12, 1965, page 19.

2233 Jim Tang, "Leafs Bow, 5-1 To Open Series With Portland," *Victoria Daily Colonist*, April 15, 1965, page 16.

2234 Robin Jeffrey, "Portland Two Up In Final Series Leafs Bow, 3-1," *Victoria Daily Colonist*, April 18, 1965, page 12.

2235 "Who Plays In Goal Wednesday?" *Victoria Daily Colonist*, April 20, 1965, page 12.

2236 Jim Tang, "Another Miracle Needed If Leafs to Survive," *Victoria Daily Colonist*, April 22, 1965, page 14.

2237 "Portland Wins Patrick Cup With Shutout," *Victoria Daily Colonist*, April 25, 1965, page 12.

2238 "Hebenton Selected For Trophy," *Victoria Daily Colonist*, April 6, 1965, page 12.

2239 "Western League Approves Plan," *Victoria Daily Colonist*, March 12, 1965, page 14.

2240 "Phoenix Next for Canucks," *Victoria Daily Colonist*, March 31, 1965, page 12.

2241 Jim Tang, "Maple Leafs Back Next Year; But Pilous, Most Players Just Maybe," *Victoria Daily Colonist*, Aril 25, 1965, page 12.

2242 Al Eaton, "Western Hockey League Still Has Big Ideas," *Victoria Daily Colonist*, September 9, 1965, page 14.

2243 "French Kindergarten Here in Victoria?" *Victoria Daily Colonist*, September 16, 1965, page 10.

2244 "Surgery for Keenan End to NHL Trial," *Victoria Daily Colonist*, September 18, 1965, page 14.

2245 "Optimism Pervades Arena as Leafs start Workouts," *Victoria Daily Colonist*, September 28, 1965, page 12.

2246 "Leafs Lose To Canucks." *Victoria Daily Colonist*, October 3, 1965, page 12.

Endnotes

2247 "Houle Cocks Ear As Imlach Plans," *Victoria Daily Colonist*, October 5, 1965, page 11.

2248 "Ghost of Guyle Fielder Haunting Leafs' Barlow," *Victoria Daily Colonist*, October 6, 1965, page 12.

2249 Water Krevenchuk, "Mazur Too Proud to Continue," *Victoria Daily Colonist*, October 7, 1965, page 17.

2250 Jim Taylor "Leafs Look Sharp In Beating Totems," *Victoria Daily Colonist*, October 10, 1965, page 14.

2251 "Add Litzenberger To Leaf Lineup," *Victoria Daily Colonist*, October 13, 1965, page 15.

2252 "Leafs Hustle and Hit To Beat Canucks 4-2," *Victoria Daily Colonist*, October 16, 1965, page 12.

2253 Jim Taylor, "Leafs Impress Even Canucks," *Victoria Daily Colonist*, October 17, 1965, page 16.

2254 "Two New Players To Face Buckaroos," *Victoria Daily Colonist*, October 21, 1965, page 18.

2255 Jim Tang, "Leafs Share Lead Defeat Bucks, 3-2," *Victoria Daily Colonist*, October 24, 1965, page 14.

2256 "Leafs Laugh Off Woes Sit Atop WHL Tables," *Victoria Daily Colonist*, October 26, 1965, page 14.

2257 Jim Tang, "Leafs Storm Back for 3-3 Tie," *Victoria Daily Colonist*, October 28, 1965, page 37.

2258 "Leafs, Seals Tie For Second Time," *Victoria Daily Colonist*, November 4, 1965, page 18.

2259 Jim Tang, "Leafs Cash In On Seattle Errors," *Victoria Daily Colonist*, November 7, 1965, page 18.

2260 "Rookie Joins Leafs," *Victoria Daily Colonist*, November 7, 1965, page 18.

2261 "Penalties No Big Worry To High-Flying Leafs," *Victoria Daily Colonist*, November 9, 1965, page 16.

2262 "Bucks Shut Out Leafs To Share First Place," *Victoria Daily Colonist*, November 11, 1965, page 18.

2263 Jim Tang, "Sick Goaltender Leads Leafs To Brilliant Win Over Bucks," *Victoria Daily Colonist*, November 14, 1965, page 18.

2264 Jim Tang, "These Blades Were Sharp; Leafs Survive Close Shave," *Victoria Daily Colonist*, November 18, 1965, page 18.

2265 "Leafs Win, 5-4 Over Vancouver," *Victoria Daily Colonist*, November 20, 1965, page 12.

2266 Jim Tang, "Leafs Manage Another Rally," *Victoria Daily Colonist*, November 21, 1965, page 14.

2267 Jim Tang, "Maple Leafs Win Shooting Contest," *Victoria Daily Colonist*, November 13, 1965, page 12.

2268 "Leafs Make Hay As Buck's Away," *Victoria Daily Colonist*, November 27, 1965, page 10.

2269 "LA Blades Solve Leaf Magic Showing New-Found Legs," *Victoria Daily Colonist*, November 28, 1965, page 14.

2270 "Interlocking Schedule Proves WHL Contention of Equality," *Victoria Daily Colonist*, November 30, 1965, page 16.

2271 For more information on Eddie Shore including his time as owner of the Springfield Indians, visit https://www.thoughtco.com/all-about-eddie-shore-2778714

2272 "Indians Walloped, 8-3 By Free-Skating Leafs," *Victoria Daily Colonist*, December 2, 1965, page 18.

2273 Jim Tang, "Leafs Answer Totems With Even More Zip," *Victoria Daily Colonist*, December 5, 1965, page 20.

2274 "Leafs Get their Cushion For The Rough Ride Ahead," *Victoria Daily Colonist*, December 7, 1965, page 12.

2275 Ad, *Victoria Daily Colonist*, December 10, 1965, page 14.

2276 Jim Tang, "Leafs Burn Up Bears With Red-Hot Attack," *Victoria Daily Colonist*, December 12, 1965, page 18.

2277 "Will Leafs Lose Two in a Row," *Victoria Daily Colonist*, December 14, 1965, page 16.

2278 Jim Tang, "Woeful Blades No Big Worry Shorthanded Leaf Still Fly," *Victoria Daily Colonist*, December 15, 1965, page 12.

2279 George Gibson, "Seals Even with Leafs Win in Overtime, 4-3," *Victoria Daily Colonist*, December 18, 1965, page 12.

2280 George Gibson, "Seals Have Their Turn at Christmas Getaway," *Victoria Daily Colonist*, December 19, 1965, page 20.

2281 "Maple Leafs, San Francisco Continue Private War Here," *Victoria Daily Colonist*, December 29, 1965, page 12.

2282 Jim Tang, "Mistakes Spell Doom To Maple Leaf Hustle," *Victoria Daily Colonist*, December 30, 1965, page 14.

2283 "Old Nemesis Under Control," *Victoria Daily Colonist*, January 4, 1966, page 8.

2284 Jim Tang, "Leafs Rout Seals With Sharp Show," *Victoria Daily Colonist*, January 6, 1966, page 14.

2285 "Leafs Stretch Margin With Los Angeles Win," *Victoria Daily Colonist*, January 7, 1966, page 12.

2286 "Marcetta Injured," *Victoria Daily Colonist*, January 7, 1966, page 12.

2287 "Seals Finally Recover Their Whitewash Brush," *Victoria Daily Colonist*, January 8, 1966, page 10.

2288 "Leafs On Their Own Tonight Providence Could Help Later," *Victoria Daily Colonist*, January 11, 1966, page 14.

2289 Jim Tang, "Limping Leafs Beat Buckaroos To Preserve First-Place Sport," *Victoria Daily Colonist*, January 12, 1966, page 8.

2290 "Leafs Rip Into Reds For Easy 5-1 Victory," *Victoria Daily Colonist*, January 16, 1966, page 12.

2291 Jim Tang, "Andy Barrels In To Sink Canucks," *Victoria Daily Colonist*, January 20, 1966, page 16,

2292 "Leafs To Try New Line Against Blades Tonight," *Victoria Daily Colonist*, January 22, 1966, page 10.

2293 Jim Tang, "Blades Head Back Home Sure They Were Bilked," *Victoria Daily Colonist*, January 23, 1966, page 12.

2294 "Leafs Could Be Angry Red And Not Embarrassed Pink," *Victoria Daily Colonist*, January 25, 1966, page 10.

2295 "Seattle Skirmish Won Leafs Gird for Bucks," *Victoria Daily Colonist*, January 29, 1965, page 10.

2296 Jim Tang, "Fans Jam Rink To Cheer Leafs," *Victoria Daily Colonist*, January 30, 1966, page 12.

2297 Ad, *Victoria Daily Colonist*, February 2, 1966, page 14.

2298 Doug Peden, "Not End of the World, but Maybe End of Something," *Victoria Daily Colonist*, February 3, 1966, page 10.

2299 "Leader Fired Blast at NHL," *Victoria Daily Colonist*, February 4, 1966, page 12.

2300 Hal Malone, "Gear and Maple Leafs Late But Job Is Done," *Victoria Daily Colonist*, February 4, 1965, page 12.

2301 Hal Malone, "Strange Tunes on Flute While Leafs Tie Bucks," *Victoria Daily Colonist*, February 7, 1966, page 12.

2302 Doug Peden, "Goal That Wasn't Left Portal Open for Bucks," *Victoria Daily Colonist*, February 10, 1966, page 12.

2303 *I remember this as if it were yesterday and recall how I was enraged that an NHL team could hurt a WHL team so badly. The fact that Toronto offered no high-level help for the Victoria Leafs—offering lower-calibre players—spoke volumes about how the parent team really felt about the WHL team.*

2304 "Comeback by Canucks Keeps Leafs in Slump," *Victoria Daily Colonist*, February 12, 1966, page 16.

2305 Doug Peden, "Merry Marcel Steals 'Amateur Night' glory," *Victoria Daily Colonist*, February 14, 1966, page 22.

2306 "HOB Line Plays Cain With Leafs," *Victoria Daily Colonist*, February 17, 1966, page 12.

2307 "Switch in Goalies Doesn't Halt Skid," *Victoria Daily Colonist*, February 19, 1966, page 14.

2308 Doug Peden, "Goalkeeping Switch Certain As Dispute Rocks Leafs' Camp," *Victoria Daily Colonist*, February 23, 1966, page 14.

2309 Doug Peden, "Gary Rates Full Marks; Other Leafs Flunk Test," *Victoria Daily Colonist*, February 24, 1966, page 10.

2310 Doug Peden, "Challenge From Americans Was Like Tonic for Leafs," *Victoria Daily Colonist*, February 28, 1966, page 10.

2311 "Leafs Prepare To Chase Bucks," *Victoria Daily Colonist*, March 1, 1966, page 14.

2312 "Seals in Town Tonight; Al Millar Goes to Tulsa," *Victoria Daily Colonist*, March 2, 1966, page 12.

2313 Doug Peden, "Revolving-Door Tactics Made It Tough on Leafs," *Victoria Daily Colonist*, March 3, 1966, page 10.

2314 "No luck With Canucks, Leafs Will Try Totems," *Victoria Daily Colonist*, March 5, 1966, page 12.

2315 Doug Peden, "Leafs Take A Good One 'For Road'," *Victoria Daily Colonist*, March 7, 1966, page 12.

2316 "Seals Retain Hex on Leafs," *Victoria Daily Colonist*, March 10, 1965, page 15.

2317 "No Excess Baggage As Leafs Fly East," *Victoria Daily Colonist*, March 11, 1966, page 14.

2318 "Leafs Succumb to Providence On Fluke Goal," *Victoria Daily Colonist*, March 14, 1966, page 13.

2319 "Leafs Get Rave Notices But Other Guys Winning," *Victoria Daily Colonist*, March 16, 1966, page 14.

2320 "Hershey Too Rich For Weary Leafs," *Victoria Daily Colonist*, March 17, 1966, page 14.

2321 "Leafs Head Home After Rough Trip," *Victoria Daily Colonist*, March 21, 1966, page 12.

2322 "Long 'At Home' Favors Leafs," *Victoria Daily Colonist*, March 22, 1966, page 12.

2323 Doug Peden, "It Was Like Old Times As Leafs Trip Canucks," *Victoria Daily Colonist*, March 24, 1966, page 10.

2324 "Chevvy's Checks Tonic for Leafs," *Victoria Daily Colonist*, March 25, 1966, page 14.

2325 "Hurting Hucul Shifts the Pain Onto Portland," *Victoria Daily Colonist*, March 28, 1966, page 10.

2326 "Redahl Child Dies," *Victoria Daily Colonist*, March 28, 1966, page 10.

2327 "Conacher's Goal Beats Bears, 5-4," *Vancouver Evening Sun*, March 31, 1966, page 29.

2328 Jim Tang, "Leafs Shatter Totems To Give Seals Chance," *Victoria Daily Colonist*, April 3, 1966, page 12.

2329 Jim Tang, "Leafs Rack Up Blades Redahl Leads Attack," *Victoria Daily Colonist*, April 7, 1966, page 14.

2330 "Totes Took Points," *Victoria Daily Colonist*, April 10, 1066, page 12.

2331 Robin Jeffrey, "Hebenton Ends Schedule Without Missing Game," *Victoria Daily Colonist*, April 10, 1966, page 12.

2332 "Who's Afraid of Big Bad Seals?" *Victoria Daily Colonist*, April 12, 1966, page 10.

2333 Jim Tang, "Leafs Fly Past Seals For Playoff Opener," *Victoria Daily Colonist*, April 14, 1966, page 14.

2334 "Seals Protest Loss Over Goalie Ruling," *Victoria Daily Colonist*, April 14, 1966, page 14.

2335 Jim Tang, "Pelletier Likely in Nets As League Gives Okay," *Victoria Daily Colonist*, April 10, 1066, page 12.

2336 Jim Tang, "Leafs Go Two Up On Seals," *Victoria Daily Colonist*, April 17, 1966, page 12.

2337 Jim Tang, "Seal Comeback Fashioned On Leaf Errors," *Victoria Daily Colonist*, April 19, 1966, page 10.

2338 Jim Tang, "Seals Just Flipping But Fans Reluctant," *Victoria Daily Colonist*, April 21, 1966, page 12.

2339 Jim Tang, "Grimness Grips Leafs After Loss," *Victoria Daily Colonist*, April 22, 1966, page 12.

2340 Jim Tang, "Seals' Amateur Plays Like Pro," *Victoria Daily Colonist*, April 23, 1966, page 14.

2341 Jim Tang, "Leafs Win Heart-Tugger Semi-Final Goes Limit," *Victoria Daily Colonist*, April 24, 1966, page 12.

2342 "Caches Quiet But Burns Eyes Barlow," *Victoria Daily Colonist*, April 26, 1966, page 12.

2343 Jim Tang, "Maple Leafs In WHL Finals After Finally Subduing Seals," *Victoria Daily Colonist*, April 27, 1966, page 14.

2344 "New Leaf Joins Club For Series," *Victoria Daily Colonist*, April 28, 1966, page 12.

2345 "Victoria Handled Buckaroos But Now It's Playoff Time," *Victoria Daily Colonist*, April 29, 1966, page 17.

2346 "Everybody Wants Hockey Tickets," *Victoria Daily Colonist*, April 30, 1966, page 14.

2347 Jim Tang, "Labrosse Scores Big One Late in Second Overtime," *Victoria Daily Colonist*, May 1, 1966, page 14.

2348 George Gibson, "Series Takes Brand-New Look As Leafs Get 6-2 Raking-Over," *Victoria Daily Colonist*, May 3, 1966, page 12.

2349 George Gibson, "Leafs Manage It Again Win the One They Need," *Victoria Daily Colonist*, May 4, 1966, page 12.

2350 "Ticket Sale Starts," *Victoria Daily Colonist*, May 4, 1966, page 12.

2351 Jim Tang, "Leafs Beaten, 3-0 Series All Square," *Victoria Daily Colonist*, May 7, 1966, page 14.

2352 "Leafs Roar Back, 4-2," *Victoria Daily Colonist*, May 8, 1966, page 1.

2353 Jim Tang, "Leafs Just Great When It Counts," *Victoria Daily Colonist*, May 8, 1966, page 10.

2354 George Gibson, "Leafs Falter with Title Near Decider in Portland Tonight," *Victoria Daily Colonist*, May 10, 1966, page 12.

2355 George Gibson, "Leafs End Cliff-Hanging Playdowns By Crushing Buckaroos in Decider," *Victoria Daily Colonist*, May 11, 1966, pages 1 and 12.

2356 George Gibson, "Something of Value Found; Victoria Welcomes Leafs," *Victoria Daily Colonist*, May 12, 1966, page 12.

2357 *Victoria Daily Colonist*, May 12, 1966, page 1.

2358 "City's Luggage Gift for Leafs," *Victoria Daily Colonist*, May 12, 1966, page 12.

2359 *Victoria Daily Colonist*, May 14, 1966, page 16.

2360 Jim Tang, "It Beats Me," *Victoria Daily Colonist*, May 13, 1966, page 14.

2361 "Two Leafs on All-Star Team But a Third Was Overlooked," *Victoria Daily Colonist*, May 5, 1966, page 16.

2362 George Inglis, "Victoria Leafs Look Like This," *Victoria Daily Colonist*, September 24, 1966, page 11.

2363 George Inglis, "Leaf's Premiere Packed," *Victoria Daily Colonist*, September 27, 1966, page 8.

2364 "Victoria Leafs Start With Win," *Victoria Daily Colonist*, October 2, 1966, page 14.

2365 Ron Holland, "Rookies Look Good In Easy Leaf Victory," *Victoria Daily Colonist*, October 6, 1966, page 16.

2366 Ron Holland, "Hucul Leads Leafs As Seattle Falls," *Victoria Daily Colonist*, October 9, 1966, page 14.

2367 "Leafs Stay Undefeated," *Victoria Daily Colonist*, October 12, 1966, page 14.

2368 "Smith Arrives, Keenan Due; Leafs Take Fifth in Trail," *Victoria Daily Colonist*, October 13, 1966, page 18.

2369 Jim Tang, "Portland Victoria Top Teams But There May Be Surprises," *Victoria Daily Colonist*, October 14, 1966, page 12.

2370 Jim Tang, "Star-Short Leafs Start Year Right," *Victoria Daily Colonist*, October 14, 1966, page 14.

2371 "Only Huculs Still Unsigned," *Victoria Daily Colonist*, October 18, 1966, page 12.

2372 Jim Tang, "Huculs Join Leaf Fold Bucks Here Tonight," *Victoria Daily Colonist*, October 19, 1966, page 10.

2373 Jim Tang, "Leafs, Smith Make It Two," *Victoria Daily Colonist*, October 20, 1966, page 14.

2374 "Smith Yields But Leafs Hold; New Club Plays Here Tonight," *Victoria Daily Colonist*, October 22, 1966, page 14.

2375 Jim Tang, "Gull Goalkeeper Proves Tough But Leafs Remain Undefeated," *Victoria Daily Colonist*, October 23, 1966, page 14.

2376 "Leafs Deal Parenteau Preparing for Gulls," *Victoria Daily Colonist*, October 25, 1966, page 12.

2377 Jim Tang, "Gulls Earn First Point Just By Trying Harder," *Victoria Daily Colonist*, October 27, 1966, page 16.

2378 The streak was really over 1,000, but playoff games were not counted as part of the streak.

2379 "A Dollar A Game Committee Aim For Andy's Night," *Victoria Daily Colonist*, October 29, 1966, page 12.

2380 Jim Tang, "Blades Hand Victoria First Loss of Season," *Victoria Daily Colonist*, October 30, 1966, page 14.

2381 "Keenan Sidelined For Eight Weeks," *Victoria Daily Colonist*, November 1, 1966, page 10.

2382 Jim Tang, "Leafs' Winless Streak Reaches Three Games," *Victoria Daily Colonist*, November 3, 1966, page 14.

2383 "Hustling Maple Leafs Battle To Draw with Oakland Seals," *Victoria Daily Colonist*, November 6, 1966, page 14.

2384 "Selby Heads West But to Vancouver," *Victoria Daily Colonist*, November 8, 1966, page 14.

2385 "Leafs Win Over Blades Clark, Marcetta Pace," *Victoria Daily Colonist*, November 10, 1966, page 14.

2386 "Wilcox Lifts Victoria Over Blades, 4-1," *Los Angeles Times*, November 12, 1966, Part II, page 3.

2387 "Hebenton reaches milestone tonight," *Saskatoon Star-Phoenix*, November 12, 1966, page 25.

2388 "Hebenton Makes 1,000 But Seals Are Spoilers," *Victoria Daily Colonist*, November 13, 1966, page 18.

2389 "Leafs Return Healthy After Road-Trip Cure," *Victoria Daily Colonist*, November 15, 1966, page 19.

2390 "Merger on Minds of WHL Owners," *Victoria Daily Colonist*, November 16, 1966, page 12.

2391 Jim Tang, "How Good Are Canucks? Better Wait for Replay," *Victoria Daily Colonist*, November 17, 1966, page 16.

2392 "Canucks Prove Better Than Tired Maple Leafs," *Victoria Daily Colonist*, November 19, 1966, page 12.

2393 "Bucs Clobber Canucks And Threaten Runaway," *Victoria Daily Colonist*, November 20, 1966, page 16.

2394 "Leafs Comeback Fails Totems Escape Cellar," *Victoria Daily Colonist*, November 24, 1966, page 20.

2395 "Canucks Win Third in Row," *Victoria Daily Colonist*, November 26, 1966, page 10.

2396 Jim Tang, "Leafs Look Better But Lose Again," *Victoria Daily Colonist*, November 27, 1966, page 16.

2397 Brian Doherty, "All Hockey to Honor Andy Hebenton Tomorrow," *Victoria Daily Colonist*, November 29, 1955, page 12.

2398 "Fans Play Tribute to Hockey's Iron Andy," *Victoria Daily Colonist*, December 1, 1966, page 14.

2399 Gary Ronberg, "The Thousand and One Night of Andy Hebenton," Sports Illustrated, April 24, 1967, retrieved online from https://www.si.com/vault/1967/04/24/637862/the-thousand-and-one-nights-of-andy-hebenton# on May 7, 2017.

2400 Robin Jeffrey, "Totems Hand Maple Leafs Sixth Loss in a Row," https://www.si.com/vault/1967/04/24/637862/the-thousand-and-one-nights-of-andy-hebenton#, November 1, 1966, page 14.

2401 "Leafs' Country Cousins Come Calling Tonight," Victoria Daily Colonist, December 3, 1966, page 12.

2402 Jim Tang, "Shakeup Coming Says Buck Houle," Victoria Daily Colonist, December 4, 1966, page 14.

2403 "Leafs Ready to End Losing Streak Tonight," Victoria Daily Colonist, December 10, 1928, page 12.

2404 Jim Tang, "A Little More Effort Gives Maple Leafs Win," Victoria Daily Colonist, December 11, 1966, page 14.

2405 Jim Tang, "Leafs Show Old Ability With Hard 3-1 Victory," Victoria Daily Colonist, December 14, 1966, page 14.

2406 "Hockey's Bad Boy Sharp As Leafs Dropped 5-2," Victoria Daily Colonist, December 16, 1966, page 14.

2407 "Laughton Shining Light As Leafs Dump Gulls," Victoria Daily Colonist, December 17, 1966, page 12.

2408 "Leafs Move Up Ladder With Shutout Over Gulls," Victoria Daily Colonist, December 18, 1966, page 12.

2409 "Weary Leafs Shut Out As Injured List Grows," Victoria Daily Colonist, December 21, 1966, page 14.

2410 "Shaky Second Period Gets Leafs 6-4 Loss," Victoria Daily Colonist, December 22, 1966, page 14.

2411 Brian Doherty, "Missed Chances Costly As Leafs Lose Another," Victoria Daily Colonist, December 24, 1966, page 14.

2412 "Something Different in Air Leafs May Be Ready to Rise," Victoria Daily Colonist, December 28, 1966, page 14.

2413 Kevan Hull, "Leafs Nearing Old Form Turn In Smart Victory," Victoria Daily Colonist, December 29, 1966, page 12.

2414 "Weary Victorians Go Through Lost Weekend," Victoria Daily Colonist, January 3, 1967, page 12.

2415 " 'Hesitation Waltz' Has Been Killing Mariomen," Victoria Daily Colonist, January 4, 1967, page 14.

2416 Hal Malone, "Free Parking Privilege Gives Bucks Tight Win," Victoria Daily Colonist, January 5, 1967 page 10.

2417 "For Moment, Leaf Lines Set," Victoria Daily Colonist, January 6, 1967, page 10.

2418 "Canucks May Learn Holiday Has Ended," Victoria Daily Colonist, January 7, 1967, page 14.

2419 Doug Peden, "For Canucks, Leaf Shutout Was Promise of Torture," Victoria Daily Colonist, January 9, 1967, page 10.

2420 Doug Peden, "Lebrun's Hasty Act Opened Victory Gates for Victoria," Victoria Daily Colonist, January 12, 1967, page 12.

2421 Doug Peden, "Mike Enjoyed Every Bruise," Victoria Daily Colonist, January 16, 1967, page 12.

2422 Hal Malone, "Holdings Hands or Hockey Sticks Leaf Rookie Cuts Fancy Figures," Victoria Daily Colonist, January 18, 1967, page 10.

2423 Doug Peden, "Totes Not Seeking The Reason Why…," Victoria Daily Colonist, January 19, 1967, page 12.

2424 Ernie Fedoruk, "Smith Shares In Marcetta's Hour of Glory," Victoria Daily Colonist, January 23, 1967, page 8.

2425 Hockey rules were later changed to prohibit goaltenders skating out to centre ice. However, it was one of the most unusual plays I ever witnessed.

2426 "Whack! … and Keenan's Out—Again," Victoria Daily Colonist, January 24, 1967, page 8.

2427 Doug Peden, "Bob's Finally Convinced Woe Can Last All Year," Victoria Daily Colonist, January 25, 1967, page 12.

2428 "Gulls Stop Leafs," Victoria Daily Colonist, January 26, 1967, page 12.

2429 "Leafs Can't Find Sun in California," Victoria Daily Colonist, January 28, 1967, page 12.

2430 "Blades Enjoy Open Spaces; Clip Leafs 5-3," Victoria Daily Colonist, January 30, 1967, pages 8 and 9.

2431 Doug Peden, "Leafs Walk Softly, Carry a Big Stick," Victoria Daily Colonist, February 3, 1967, page 12.

2432 "Stuttering Leafs Swan Dive Twice," Victoria Daily Colonist, February 6, 1967, page 8.

2433 "Leafs Start Too Late To Spoil Guyle's Party," Victoria Daily Colonist, February 9, 1967, page 14.

2434 "Labadie Is Key Figure In Bid to Crack Slump," Victoria Daily Colonist, February 10, 1967, page 14.

2435 "Let Rivals Shoot Most Might Be Best System," Victoria Daily Colonist, February 13, 1967, page 10.

2436 "Mario's Road-Runners Revive Playoff Chances," *Victoria Daily Colonist*, February 16, 1967, page 12.

2437 "Seals Must Remember Nightmare Days of '65," *Victoria Daily Colonist*, February 18, 1967, page 12.

2438 Doug Peden, "'Blah-Blah' Line Hits Stride, Gaffs Diegans," *Victoria Daily Colonist*, February 23, 1967, page 14.

2439 "Al's Fractured Fractions Buoy Leaf Playoff Hopes," *Victoria Daily Colonist*, February 27, 1967, page 11.

2440 "Maple Leaf Loss only a Half Step," *Victoria Daily Colonist*, March 2, 1967, page 12.

2441 "One Smith Great … Now We Have Two," *Victoria Daily Colonist*, March 4, 1967, page 12.

2442 "Leafs Pull on Line In the Nick of Time," *Victoria Daily Colonist*, March 6, 1967, page 12.

2443 Doug Peden, "Seal Morale Murdered By Barn-Burning Finish," *Victoria Daily Colonist*, March 9, 1967, page 12.

2444 "Seals Bounce Past Leafs As Totes Win," *Victoria Daily Colonist*, March 11, 1967, page 12.

2445 Ernie Fedoruk, "Missing Fifth 'Man' Costly To Maple Leafs," *Victoria Daily Colonist*, March 13, 1967, page 12.

2446 Doug Peden, "Leafs Manage a Draw After Mario's Shuffle," *Victoria Daily Colonist*, March 16, 1967, page 12.

2447 "Seattle's MacFarland Pushes Right Button In Naming Armstrong," *Victoria Daily Colonist*, March 20, 1967, page 12.

2448 "200 Tars Will Cheer Leafs on at Oakland," *Victoria Daily Colonist*, March 17, 1967, page 14.

2449 "Tie With Oakland Keeps Leafs' Hopes Flickering," *Victoria Daily Colonist*, March 23, 1967, page 12.

2450 "A League First? Rotation of Goalies by San Diego," *The Petaluma Argus-Courier*, March 24, 1967, page 11.

2451 "Maple Leafs Run Out of Tomorrows," *Victoria Daily Colonist*, March 27, 1967, page 11.

2452 "Smith Better Thief Without His Mask," *Victoria Daily Colonist*, March 30, 1967, page 12.

2453 "Rollie Sheds Blues With Winning Shot," *Victoria Daily Colonist*, April 1, 1967, page 12.

2454 Doug Peden, "Everybody's An Expert But Owners," *Victoria Daily Colonist*, April 3, 1967, page 10.

2455 "Houle Suffers Heart Attack," *Victoria Daily Colonist*, April 4, 1967, page 10.

2456 "Victoria Team to Phoenix," *The Montreal Gazette*, May 17, 1867, page 25.

2457 Cox, Damien and Stellick, Gord, "'67: The Maple Leafs, Their Sensational Victory, and the End of an Empire," HarperCollins e-books, 2004.

2458 Dave Hicks, "Puck Team Now The Roadrunners," *Arizona Republic*, July 1, 1967, page 56.

2459 "Roadrunners Report To Camp Tomorrow," *Arizona Republic*, September 17, 1967, page 80.

2460 Dave Senick, "Victoria may land IHL team," *Victoria Times Colonist*, December 12, 1996, page B1.

2461 San Francisco Spiders on Wikipedia, https://en.wikipedia.org/wiki/San_Francisco_Spiders.

2462 Darren Kloster, "Victoria has competition for IHL," *Victoria Times Colonist* December 13, 1996, page B3.

2463 Dave Senick, "Victoria may land IHL team," *Victoria Times Colonist*, December 12, 1996, page B1.

2464 Cleeve Dheenshaw, "IHL and Victoria a good fit—Barlow," *Victoria Times Colonist*, November 3, 1996.

2465 Richard Watts, "Victoria is tops on Spiders' list, team owner says," *Victoria Times Colonist*, February 7, 1997, page A1.

2466 Darren Kloster, "Spider Infestation," *Victoria Times Colonist* February 7, 1997, page B1.

2467 Darron Kloster and Richard Watts, "Spider man ready to buy shares of Arena," *Victoria Times Colonist*, April 11, 1997, page A1.

2468 Richard Watts, "IHL team arrives to inspect Victoria," *Victoria Times Colonist*, October 28, 1997, page A3.

2469 Richard Watts, "Caught in the web: IHL committee pledges to back Victoria proposal," *Victoria Times Colonist*, October 30, 1997, page A1.

2470 Bev Wake, "IHL commissioner says Victoria would make a great IHL city, but financing must be in place before any deals are made," *Victoria News*, October 31, 1997, page 29.

2471 Norman Gidney, "Study boosts arena plan: Sports specialist predicts more jobs, more spending," *Victoria Times Colonist*, October 28, 1997, page A3.

2472 "Arena naysayers can't fault legwork: Pasant has done what he can to make this work." *Victoria Times Colonist*, October 31, 1997, page A14.

Endnotes

2473 Denise Helm, "It's do or die time for promoters of new arena deal," *Victoria Times Colonist*, November 3, 1997, page A4.

2474 "Victoria's ready to embrace the IHL," *Victoria Times Colonist*, November 4, 1997, page xx

2475 Richard Watts and Bill Cleverley, "Arena Stalled Again," *Victoria Times Colonist*, November 14, 1997, page A1.

2476 "Dear Harry: Show us the money," *Victoria Times Colonist*, November 14, 1997, page A16.

2477 Richard Watts, "Delays cause problems for Salsa," *Victoria Times Colonist*, November 15, 1997, page A3.

2478 "Arena project team member resigns," *Victoria Times Colonist*, November 15, 1997, page A3.

2479 *Victoria Times Colonist*, November 17, 1997, page 2.

2480 Cleeve Dheenshaw, "Arena principals calling the shots," *Victoria Times Colonist*, November 17, 1997, page 17.

2481 Richard Watts, "Arena closer to money target but another extension granted," *Victoria Times Colonist*, December 16, 1997, page A1.

2482 *Victoria Times Colonist*, December 14, 1997, page A10.

2483 "Council's word is all we've got," *Victoria Times Colonist*, December 16, 1997, page A10.

2484 Richard Watts, "Home stretch," *Victoria Times Colonist*, February 16, 1998, page A1.

2485 Richard Watts, "Missed date frustrates councillors," *Victoria Times Colonist*, February 17, 1998, page A1.

2486 Richard Watts, "Arena deal still on ice," *Victoria Times Colonist*, April 17, 1998, page A1.

2487 *Victoria Times Colonist*, April 16, 1998, page A11.

2488 Judith Lavoie, "B.C. won't guarantee arena loan," *Victoria Times Colonist*, April 19, 1998, page A1.

2489 Carla Wilson, "Pasant mounts big arena push," *Victoria Times Colonist*, September 18, 1998, page C1.

2490 Carlo Wilson, "Business group dispute arena's viability," *Victoria Times Colonist*, October 20, 1998, page D1.

2491 Carla Wilson, "Bungled!" *Victoria Times Colonist*, October 28, 1998, page D1.

2492 *Victoria Times Colonist*, October 30, 1998.

2493 Carla Wilson, "Regret won't stop arena boss," *Victoria Times Colonist*, November 19, 1998, page A1.

2494 Carla Wilson, "Sihota rules out cash for new arena," *Victoria Times Colonist*, November 23, 1998, page C1.

2495 *Victoria Times Colonist*, November 27, 1998, pages A7 and C1.

2496 "Business leaders unite to oppose multiplex," *Victoria Times Colonist*, December 2, 1998, page A15.

2497 Carla Wilson, "Critics take arena battle to premier." *Victoria Times Colonist*, December 2, 1998, pages A1, A2, and A15.

2498 "Time to stop the multiplex game," *Victoria News*, December 4, 1998, page 6.

2499 Carla Wilson, "Ex-finance minister joins arena critics," *Victoria Times Colonist*, December 3, 1998, page B1.

2500 Carla Wilson, "Stage set for arena debate," *Victoria Times Colonist*, December 10, 1998, page A3.

2501 Cindy E. Harnett, "Multiplex hearing draws hot debate," *Victoria Times Colonist*, December 11, 1998, page A1.

2502 Russ Francis, "If the arena deal collapses, will Mayor Cross find himself in the Political Penalty Box?" *Monday Magazine*, December 10-16, 1998, Volume 24, Issue 50, pages 1 and 8.

2503 Cindy E. Harnett, "Developers' dance fires up councillors," *Victoria Times Colonist*, December 12, 1998, page A1.

2504 Carla Wilson, "Cross snubs challenge for arena critique team," *Victoria Times Colonist*, December 12, 1998, page A2.

2505 Minutes, Victoria City Council, Special Meeting of Tuesday, December 18, 1998, at 3:00 pm.

2506 Carla Wilson, "Multiplex developer faces 'hard' date," *Victoria Times Colonist*, December 16, 1998, page A1.

2507 Carla Wilson, "Vancouver firm wooed by multiplex developer," *Victoria Times Colonist*, February 4, 1999, page F6.

2508 Cindy Harnett, "Arena ambitions grow," *Victoria Times Colonist*, February 12, 1999, page A2.

2509 Carla Wilson, "Kingdome managers sign deal on arena," *Victoria Times Colonist*, February 18, 1999, page A5.

2510 Bev Wake/Jeanine Soodeen, "Multiplex naming rights sold to Pacific Coast Net," *Victoria News*, February 24, 1999, page 1.

2511 Susan Danard, "Multiplex gets name but loan still unclear," *Victoria Times Colonist*, February 23, 1999, page A1.

2512 Norman Gidney, "Multiplex naming deal nets interest," *Victoria Times Colonist*, February 24, 1999, page A1.

The History of Professional Hockey in Victoria, BC: 1911-2011

2513 Jeff Rud, "VSEA: It's time to put up or shut up," *Victoria Times Colonist*, February 24, 1999, page C13.

2514 Carla Wilson, "Council rejects extension of arena financing deadline," *Victoria Times Colonist*, February 26, 1999, page A1.

2515 Bev Wake, "Arena's future up to banks," *Peninsula News Review*, February 26, 1999, page 1.

2516 Carla Wilson, "Major recovery awaits if city loses arena deal," *Victoria Times Colonist*, March 3, 1999, pages C1 and C2.

2517 Carla Wilson, "Council grants extension for multiplex financing," *Victoria Times Colonist*, March 12, 1999, page A1.

2518 "Multiplex gets new lease on life," *Peninsula News Review*, March 12, 1999, page 1.

2519 Jeanine Soodeen, "City accepts VSEA financing agreement for now," *Victoria News*, June 2, 1999, page 2.

2520 King Lee and Richard Watts, "No cash, no multiplex, $85 million dream dies," *Victoria Times Colonist*, July 1, 1999, page A1.

2521 Carla Wilson, "VSEA plans to keep its door open," *Victoria Times Colonist*, July 3, 1999, page B1.

2522 Carla Wilson, "VSEA finally closes its city office," *Victoria Times Colonist*, September 5, 1999, page C3.

2523 Jeanine Soodeen, "Memorial Arena is being booked through August 2000," *Victoria News*, August 25, 1999.

2524 Carla Wilson, "New backers emerge for arena," *Victoria Times Colonist*, August 25, 1999, page A1.

2525 Carla Wilson, "WHL brass upbeat on return to Victoria," *Victoria Times Colonist*, August 26, 1999, page B1.

2526 Jeff Bell, "City council to set rules for arena," *Victoria Times Colonist*, August 27, 1999 page D1 and D4.

2527 Matt Ramsey, "Multiplex review approved," *Victoria News*, September 15, 1999, page 4.

2528 https://en.wikipedia.org/wiki/Alan_Lowe

2529 Cindy E. Harnett, "Multiplex deal flawed from start," *Victoria Times Colonist*, December 17, 1999, page A1.

2530 Matt Ramsey, "Review says arena was doomed to fail," *Victoria News*, December 22, 1999, page 3.

2531 *2006 BC Supreme Court 1441 Victoria Sports / Entertainment Associates and Arachnid Hockey Canada, U.L.C. and The Toronto-Dominion Bank and The Bank of Nova Scotia before The Honourable Mr. Justice Bauman*, July 6, 2006, accessed at http://www.courts.gov.bc.ca/jdb-txt/sc/06/14/2006bcsc1441.htm

2532 Cindy E. Harnett, "Arena queries await answers," *Victoria Times Colonist*, January 26, 2000, page C3.

2533 Matt Ramsey, "Review process for new arena starts July 8," *Victoria News*, June 28, 2000, page 9.

2534 Carla Wilson, "Multiplex gets big nod from survey," *Victoria Times Colonist*, November 17, 2000, page B1 and B2.

2535 Cindy E. Harnett, "Arena facility to be subject of independent assessment," *Victoria Times Colonist*, December 8, 32000, page C3.

2536 "Arena ideas wanted," *Victoria Times Colonist*, February 22, 2001, page B3.

2537 Grant Thornton, "Market Feasibility Study - Proposed Multi-Purpose Facility (Victoria)," March 2001.

2538 "City of Victoria - Multipurpose Facility Mayor's Blue Ribbon Panel" accessed from https://web.archive.org/web/20051201114328/http://city.victoria.bc.ca:80/cityhall/currentprojects_multipurpose_archives_terms.shtml on May 16, 2017.

2539 Cindy E. Harnett, "Multiplex attracts four prime suitors," *Victoria Times Colonist*, April 13, 2001, pages A1 and A2.

2540 Cindy E. Harnett, "Arena proposals narrowed to one bid, mayor says," *Victoria Times Colonist*, May 18, 2001, page C1.

2541 "City to Proceed with Negotiations for a New Multipurpose Facility," Press release, City of Victoria, http://www.city.victoria.bc.ca:80/cityhall/press5oom_rel_010614.shtml.

2542 Cindy E. Harnett, "Talks get under way on multiplex deal," *Victoria Times Colonist*, June 15, 2001, page B1.

2543 Interview with Alan Lowe, June 5, 2017.

2544 http://www.city.victoria.bc.ca:80/cityhall/pressroom_ref_011025.shtml

2545 Cindy E. Harnett, "Deadline set for arena deal," *Victoria Times Colonist*, October 26, 2001, page D1.

2546 http://www.city.victoria.bc.ca:80/cityhall/pressroom_rel_011122.shmtl.

2547 Cindy E. Harnett, "Arena deal hinges on WHL franchise," *Victoria Times Colonist*, November 23, 2001, page A1.

2548 Info Sheet, "A New Multipurpose arena for Victoria."

2549 "A New Multipurpose Arena for Victoria," *Victoria Times Colonist*, April 18, 2002, page B2.

2550 "Other Municipalities Contributions Towards A New Regional Multipurpose Arena," http:web.archive.org/web/2005.

2551 "Notice of Other Voting Assent of the Electors 2002 - Multipurpose Arena Facility," http:web.archive.org/web/2005.

2552 Malcolm Curtis, "71% say yes to new arena," *Victoria Times Colonist*, April 21, 2002, page A1.

2553 "Council Agrees to Remove WHL," http:web.archive.org/web/2005.

2554 Malcolm Curtis, "Multiplex developer drops WHL stipulation," *Victoria Times Colonist*, July 12, 2002, page A1.

2555 "City Wins Legal Challenge of Arena Referendum Result," http://www.city.bc.ca:80/cityhall/pressroom_rel_020710a.shtml.

2556 "Celebrate: Thanks for the Memories," *Victoria News Weekend Edition*, September 20, 2002, page 9.

2557 "Thanks for the Memories" program for September 28, 2002 event, in the author's collection.

2558 "Current Projects > Multipurpose Facility> Introduction," https://web.archive.org/web/2005040808.

2559 Don Descoteau, "Arena demo inches closer," *Victoria News*, November 13, 2002, page 3.

2560 Brennan Clarke, "Teams in a bind after arena vote," *Victoria News Weekend Edition*, November 22, 2002, page 17.

2561 Cleve Dheenshaw, "Memorial Sports: The Time of Your Life," *Victoria Times Colonist*, February 2, 2003, page D4.

2562 Adrian Chamberlain, "Memories, Music: The Barn, as live as it gets," *Victoria Times Colonist*, February 2, 2003.

2563 Cleve Dheenshaw, "Wrecking ball turns Memorial to rubble," *Victoria Times Colonist*, February 18, 2003, pages A1 and A2.

2564 Half an Arena to Go," *Victoria Times Colonist*, February 20, 2003, page B1.

2565 "It's Game Over for arena," *Victoria Times Colonist*, March 2, 2003, page A1.

2566 Cleve Dheenshaw, "Arena gone but not forgotten," *Victoria Times Colonist*, March 2, 2003, page B1.

2567 "Deconstructing Memorial," *Victoria News*, May 21, 2003, page 3.

2568 Jeff Bell, "West Shore arena gets head start," *Victoria Times Colonist*, May 8, 2003, page B1.

2569 Cleve Dheenshaw, "It's not a race—so why is West Shore gloating?" *Victoria Times Colonist*, June 4, 2003, page D1.

2570 Gerard Young, "In Victoria, impressions of courage," *Victoria Times Colonist*, June 7, 2003, page A1.

2571 Nicole Fitzgerald, "Veterans make mark on future arena," *Victoria News*, June 11, 2003, page 1.

2572 Cleve Dheenshaw, "Arena developer eyes U.S. team," *Victoria Times Colonist*, June 19, 2003, page A1.

2573 Gerard Young, "Sports pages, cold coffee inspire new arena sculpture," *Victoria Times Colonist*, June 27, 2003, page A1.

2574 Richard Watts, "Arena art outrage sways Lowe," *Victoria Times Colonist*, July 2, 2003, page A1.

2575 Richard Watts, "Give sculpture a chance, U.S. art expert says," *Victoria Times Colonist*, July 3, 2003, page B2.

2576 *Victoria Times Colonist*, July 3, 2003, age A11.

2577 Gerard Young, "Sculpture choice cast in stone," *Victoria Times Colonist*, July 11, 2003, page A1.

2578 Cleve Dheenshaw, "Pouring of arena foundation delayed over site preparation," *Victoria Times Colonist*, July 5, 2003, page D1.

2579 Cleve Dheenshaw, "365 days and counting 'til new arena opens," *Victoria Times Colonist*, August 28, 2003, pages C1 and C2.

2580 Cleve Dheenshaw, "Size of the times," *Victoria Times Colonist*, September 14, 2003, page D1.

2581 Cleve Dheenshaw, "Spectator's Guide to Victoria's New Arena," *Victoria Times Colonist*, September 14, 2003, pages D6 and D7.

2582 "What's In a Name? Gr-r-r-r- Says the 'Cougar'," *Victoria Daily Times*, November 17, 1922, page 10.

2583 Cleve Dheenshaw, "Victoria nets hockey team: Fans asked to name new pro franchise," *Victoria Times Colonist*, September 23, 2003, page A1.

2584 Cleve Dheenshaw, "Thousands tout names for hockey franchise," *Victoria Times Colonist*, October 7, 2003, page A1.

2585 Cleve Dheenshaw, "Hooked on the Salmon Kings," *Victoria Times Colonist*, October 11, 2003, page A1.

2586 "Those feared Salmon Kings," *Victoria Times Colonist* October 11, 2003, page A14.

2587 Cleve Dheenshaw, "Arena GM has impressive resume," *Victoria Times Colonist*, September 23, 2003.

2588 Cleve Dheenshaw, "Maxwell's the man in Victoria," *Victoria Times Colonist*, October 1, 2003, page B4.

2589 Ron Rauch, "New arena scores big win with world curling event," *Victoria Times Colonist*, October 22, 2003, pages A1 and A2.

2590 "The top curlers are coming," *Victoria Times Colonist*, October 22, 2003, page A12.

2591 Cleve Dheenshaw, "Big plans for Victoria Sports Hall," *Victoria Times Colonist*, October 31, 2003, page B9.

2592 Cleve Dheenshaw, "Lee isn't worried about hole on Blanshard," *Victoria Times Colonist*, October 27, 2003, page B1.

2593 Malcolm Curtis, "Veterans closing in on $80,000 target for memorial at new arena," *Victoria Times Colonist*, November 26, 2003, page B1.

2594 Cleve Dheenshaw, "Arena's luxury boxes don't go cheaply," *Victoria Times Colonist*, November 29, 2003, page C11.

2595 Cleve Dheenshaw, "Luxury boxes move quickly," *Victoria Times Colonist*, December 9, 2003, page B6.

2596 Cleve Dheenshaw, "Arena set to rise as foundation work ends," *Victoria Times Colonist*, December 19, 2003, page B2.

2597 Malcolm Curtis, "Building deadline extended for arena," *Victoria Times Colonist*, January 23, 2004, page A1,

2598 Dave Senick, "Companies, not fans, play arena name gamer," *Victoria Times Colonist*, March 6, 2004, pages A1 and A2.

2599 Cleve Dheenshaw, "Victoria joins the sporting name game," *Victoria Times Colonist*, April 1, 2004, page A1 and A4.

2600 Malcolm Curtis, "Arena to carry Save-On colours," *Victoria Times Colonist*, April 1, 2004, page A4.

2601 Jeff Bell, "Veterans granted wish on arena name," *Victoria Times Colonist*, August 19, 2004, page A1.

2602 "Everybody like the latest name change," *Victoria Times Colonist*, August 13, 2004, page A2.

2603 "True Memorial once again," *Victoria Times Colonist*, August 13, 2004, page A10.

2604 "Memorabilia of Memorial wanted for time capsule," *Victoria Times Colonist*, April 3, 2004, page D12.

2605 Malcolm Curtis, "City sets ice rates for new arena," *Victoria Times Colonist*, April 20, 2004, pages B1 and B2.

2606 "Current Projects > Multipurpose Facility > Newsletter >Arena Update – Vol.2 No. 3 – June 14, 2004," City of Victoria, 2004.

2607 Malcolm Curtis, "Traveller's Inn sues RG group over arena name," *Victoria Times Colonist*, July 14, 2005, pages B1 and B3.

2608 Malcolm Curtis and Gerard Young, "Little hope arena will be ready," *Victoria Times Colonist*, August 18, 2004, page A1.

2609 Malcolm Curtis, "Developer Lee hope arena ready in February," *Victoria Times Colonist*, page A1.

2610 Jack Knox, "Small wonder we feel skittish about arena," *Victoria Times Colonist*, September 11, 2004, page C1.

2611 Malcolm Curtis, "Arena target date is now March 31," *Victoria Times Colonist*, October 15, 2004, page B4.

2612 Malcolm Curtis, "Signs to sprout outside arena," *Victoria Times Colonist*, October 22, 2004, page A1.

2613 "Current Projects > Multipurpose Facility > Newsletter > Arena Update > Vol. 2 No. 5 – October 29, 2004," City of Victoria, http://www.city.victoria.bc.ca:80/cityhall/currentprojects_multipurpose_news.shtml.

2614 "McLachlan to christen new arena," *Victoria Times Colonist*, November 17, 2004, page B1.

2615 "Arena takes shape," *Victoria Times Colonist*, December 3, 2004, page A2.

2616 *Victoria Times Colonist*, December 23, 2004, page A1.

2617 Malcolm Curtis, "Crews focus on arena's interior," *Victoria Times Colonist*, December 23, 2004, page B1.

2618 Malcolm Curtis, "Arena delays not costing ratepayers," *Victoria Times Colonist*, February 1, 2005, page A1.

2619 Malcolm Curtis, "Of 501 arena tasks, more than 400 to go," *Victoria Times Colonist*, February 2, 2005, page B1.

2620 Norman Gidney, "Developer promises arena will be ready on time," *Victoria Times Colonist*, February 8, 2005, page A1.

2621 Darron Kloster, "Arena scrambles to fill 300 jobs," *Victoria Times Colonist*, February 125, 2005, page A1.

2622 Malcolm Curtis, "Builder insists Victoria's new arena will be ready for pop star's show," *Victoria Times Colonist*, February 26, 2005, page A1 and A2.

2623 "Ice meets metal," *Victoria Times Colonist*, March 1, 2005, page A1

2624 Malcolm Curtis, "Arena patrons face a long walk," *Victoria Times Colonist*, March 4, 2005, pages B1 and B2.

2625 Jeff Bell, "They'll have a ticket to Rod," *Victoria Times Colonist*, March 16, 2005, page B1.

2626 Jeff Bell, "Security first as arena jobs fill up," *Victoria Times Colonist*, March 17, 2005, page B1.

2627 Lindsay Kines, "Arena down to the wire," *Victoria Times Colonist*, March 26, 2005, page A1.

2628 Gerard Young, "Missed deadlines 'will soon be a distant memory'," *Victoria Times Colonist*, March 26, 2005, page A1.

2629 "A Place to create fresh memories," *Victoria Times Colonist*, March 26, 2005, page A20.

2630 Gerard Young, "Crowd flows in to new arena," *Victoria Times Colonist*, March 27, 2005, page A1.

2631 Max Devlin, "Rod rocks new arena," *Victoria Times Colonist*, March 27, 2005, page B1.

2632 Gerard Young and Lindsay Kines, "Victoria's verdict? Arena rocks," *Victoria Times Colonist*, March 28, 2005, page A1.

2633 "From the court of public opinion," *Victoria Times Colonist*, March 28, 2004, page A3.

2634 Malcolm Curtis, "Arena-goers largely bypass free bus service to concert," *Victoria Times Colonist*, March 29, 2005, page B1.

2635 Malcolm Curtis, "It's safety first with arena inspections," *Victoria Times Colonist*, March 30, 2005, page C1.

2636 "Eyes of the world are on Victoria," *Victoria Times Colonist*, April 2, 2005, page A10.

2637 Gavin Fletcher, "Minor glitches plague arena shakedown," *Victoria Times Colonist*, April 5, 2005, page A1.

2638 Sherrie Epp, "Ferbey sends fan home happy," *Victoria Times Colonist*, April 11, 2005, page A1.

2639 Gavin Fletcher, "Curling worlds a success off ice too," *Victoria Times Colonist*, October 28, 2005, page B5.

2640 "Plaques ensure arena is really memorial," *Victoria Times Colonist*, March 30, 2005, page C1.

2641 Louise Dickson, "Memorial wall to fallen graces lobby of centre," *Victoria Times Colonist*, April 17, 2005.

2642 Malcolm Curtis, "Disputes sideline arena completion," *Victoria Times Colonist*, October 24, 2005.

2643 Malcolm Curtis, "Mayoral candidate slams contract, urges second look," *Victoria Times Colonist*, October 24, 2005, page C2.

2644 https://en.wikipedia.org/wiki/British_Columbia_municipal_elections,_2005#Victoria.

2645 Malcolm Curtis, "Deal will see arena finished in March," *Victoria Times Colonist*, November 11, 2005, page F1.

2646 Malcolm Curtis, "Arena developer avoid penalties as occupancy permits issued," *Victoria Times Colonist*, March 10, 2006, page B2.

2647 http://sofnc.com/past-events-2/

2648 Darron Kloster, "Shaw TV moves to Victoria arena," *Victoria Times Colonist*, March 13, 2008, page B1.

2649 Cleve Dheenshaw "Hooked on the Salmon Kings," *Victoria Times Colonist*, October 11, 2003, page A2.

2650 Cleve Dheenshaw "Salmon Kings spawn ticket rush," *Victoria Times Colonist*, October 15, 2003, pageA1.

2651 Cleve Dheenshaw "Salmon King could land many Island products." *Victoria Times Colonist*, October 17, 2003, page B6.

2652 I produced a spreadsheet of all players to suit up for the Salmon Kings during their time in Victoria and was thus able to determine who from the list had actually played.

2653 Cleve Dheenshaw, "Maxwell the man for ECHL Salmon Kings," *Victoria Times Colonist*, November 4, 2003, page B8.

2654 Cleve Dheenshaw, "Boss not one to pull punches," *Victoria Times Colonist*, November 6, 2003, page B9.

2655 Cleve Dheenshaw, "Canucks' Nonis says no to ECHL. Salmon Kings," *Victoria Times Colonist*, June 11, 2004, page B16.

2656 Cleve Dheenshaw, "Maxwell begins building a hockey team," *Victoria Times Colonist*, April 5, 2004, page B2.

2657 Cleve Dheenshaw "Salmon Kings get next season's marching orders," *Victoria Times Colonist*, June 16, 2004, page C5.

2658 Cleve Dheenshaw, "Hockey fans pony up for next season," *Victoria Times Colonist*, June 18, 2004, page B5.

The History of Professional Hockey in Victoria, BC: 1911-2011

2659 Cleve Dheenshaw "Salmon Kings about to sign first player," Victoria Times Colonist, July 2, 2004, page D9.

2660 Cleve Dheenshaw, "Salmon Kings sign up Islanders," Victoria Times Colonist, July 7, 2004, pages A1 and A2.

2661 Cleve Dheenshaw, "Maxwell building team one contract at a time," Victoria Times Colonist, July 27, 2004, page B7.

2662 Cleve Dheenshaw, "Salmon Kings sign homegrown talent," Victoria Times Colonist, July 30, 2004, page C8.

2663 Cleve Dheenshaw, "Salmon Kings sign veteran pro Williams," Victoria Times Colonist, August 12, 2004, page B10.

2664 Malcolm Curtis and Gerard Young, "Little hope arena will be ready," Victoria Times Colonist, August 18, 2004, page A1.

2665 Cleve Dheenshaw, "Kings of the Mountain," Victoria Times Colonist, September 10, 2004, page B12.

2666 Cleve Dheenshaw, "Quandary for Kings and Salsa," Victoria Times Colonist, September 12, 2004, page C5.

2667 Cleve Dheensha, "New King on the Block," Victoria Times Colonist, September 14, 2004, page B7.

2668 "Chilliwack gets first crack at Salmon Kings," Victoria Times Colonist, September 28, 2004, page B5.

2669 Cleve Dheenshaw, "Salmon Kings net home base for training camp," Victoria Times Colonist, September 24, 2004, page D8.

2670 Cleve Dheenshaw, "Proving his net worth, over and over again," Victoria Times Colonist, October 8, 2004, pages C9 and C11.

2671 Cleve Dheenshaw, "Salmon Kings a homecoming for Colwood player," Victoria Times Colonist, October 9, 2004, page F1.

2672 Cleve Dheenshaw, "Salmon King hopeful has to make more adjustments than most," Victoria Times Colonist, October 10, 2004, page F1.

2673 Cleve Dheenshaw, "Goaltender battles to keep dream alive," Victoria Times Colonist, October 12, 2004, page B8.

2674 Cleve Dheenshaw, "Salmon King looks to make the cut," Victoria Times Colonist, October 14, 2004, page C5.

2675 Cleve Dheenshaw, "Let the ECHL games begin," Victoria Times Colonist, October 16, 2004, pages A1 and A2.

2676 Cleve Dheenshaw, "Kings take to the ice," Victoria Times Colonist, October 16, 2004, page C1.

2677 Cleve Dheenshaw, "Injuries thin Salmon King' ranks," Victoria Times Colonist, October 17, 2004, page A10.

2678 Cleve Dheenshaw, "Kings of the Rink," Victoria Times Colonist, October 18, 2004, pages B1 and B2.

2679 Cleve Dheenshaw, "Salmon Kings sign a roadrunner for road trip," Victoria Times Colonist, October 21, 2004, pages D9 and D10.

2680 Cleve Dheenshaw, "First flight fraught with drama for S-Kings," Victoria Times Colonist, October 22, 2004, pages A1 and A2.

2681 Cleve Dheenshaw, "Kings take a bow, and fall," Victoria Times Colonist, October 23, 2004, pages A1 and A2.

2682 Cleve Dheenshaw, "Condors feast on Salmon Kings," Victoria Times Colonist, October 23, 2004, page D8.

2683 Cleve Dheenshaw, "Olympian helps launch S-Kings era," Victoria Times Colonist, October 23, 2004, page D9.

2684 Cleve Dheenshaw, "Oh, so close!" Victoria Times Colonist, October 24, 2004, page D1.

2685 Cleve Dheenshaw, "Kings get first win," Victoria Times Colonist, October 25, 2003, page D4.

2686 "New Jersey star Gomez signs deal with ECHL Aces," Nanaimo Daily News, October 24, 2004, page 10.

2687 Cleve Dheenshaw, "Gomez Alaska's Ace-in the-hole," Victoria Times Colonist, October 28, 2004, page B1.

2688 Cleve Dheenshaw, "Salmon Kings clear up ticket confusion," Victoria Times Colonist, October 30, 2004, page D9.

2689 Cleve Dheenshaw, "Salmon Kings boast strong Island flavour," Victoria Times Colonist, November 1, 2004, page B4.

2690 Cleve Dheenshaw, "Next stop, Boise," Victoria Times Colonist, November 5, 2004, pages A17 and A19.

2691 Cleve Dheenshaw, "Salmon Kings leave Steelheads floundering," Victoria Times Colonist, November 6, 2004, page F8.

2692 Cleve Dheenshaw, "Steelheads bury Salmon Kings," Victoria Times Colonist, November 7, 2004, page D1.

2693 Cleve Dheenshaw, "Travel woes add extra burden to Salmon Kings' freshman year," Victoria Times Colonist, November 9, 2004, page B4.

2694 Cleve Dheenshaw, "'Kings short in Long Beach," Victoria Times Colonist, November 11, 2004, pages C9 and C10.

2695 Cleve Dheenshaw, "First-period lapse costs Salmon Kings," Victoria Times Colonist, November 13, 2004, page F8.

2696 Cleve Dheenshaw, "Kings post last-minute loss," Victoria Times Colonist, November 14, 2004, page D1.

2697 Cleve Dheenshaw, "Alaska too hot for Kings," Victoria Times Colonist, November 18, 2004, page C7.

2698 Cleve Dheenshaw, "Alaska comes up Aces against Victoria," Victoria Times Colonist, November 20, 2004, pages D1 and D3.

2699 Cleve Dheenshaw, "Salmon Kings net Aces for third win of season," Victoria Times Colonist, pages C1 and C4.

2700 "Cheyne calls it quits," Victoria Times Colonist, November 24, 2004, page C4.

2701 Cleve Dheenshaw, "A tough night in Fresno," Victoria Times Colonist, November 26, 2004, page B9.

2702 "Salmon Kings on the road," Victoria Times Colonist, November 27, 2004, page F1.

2703 Cleve Dheenshaw, "Kings end road trip right where it began," Victoria Times Colonist, November 28, 2004, page D1.

2704 "Goalie Brumby waived," Victoria Times Colonist, December 2, 2004, page C8.

2705 Cleve Dheenshaw, "Beefing up the blueline," Victoria Times Colonist, December 4, 2004, pages E5 and E6.

2706 Ron Rausch, "Bean counter laces up skates for Kings," Victoria Times Colonist, December 5, 2004, page A10.

2707 Gavin Fletcher, "Up here, it's about the hockey," Victoria Times Colonist, December 5, 2004, page A1 and A2.

2708 "Room for 400 to stand at the start of every game," Victoria Times Colonist, December 5, 2004, page A2.

2709 Cleve Dheenshaw, "The Kings are home! Long live the Kings!" Victoria Times Colonist, December 5, 2002, pages D1, D4, and D5.

2710 Judith Lavoie, "It's awesome," Victoria Times Colonist, December 6, 2004, page A1.

2711 Cleve Dheenshaw, "There's no place like home," Victoria Times Colonist, December 6, 2004, page B1.

2712 Cleve Dheenshaw, "Kings bite back," Victoria Times Colonist, December 8, 2004, page B14.

2713 Cleve Dheenshaw, "Kings feast on Condors," Victoria Times Colonist, December 9, 2004, page B9.

2714 "Elbow victim out of hospital after suffering a concussion," Victoria Times Colonist, December 9, 2004, page B9.

2715 "Salmon Kings' defenceman Purinton suspended six games for elbowing," Victoria Times Colonist, December 10, 2004, page C12.

2716 Ron Rauch, "Salmon Kings on a winning roll," Victoria Times Colonist, December 11, 2004, page F9.

2717 Cleve Dheenshaw, "Sea Wolves nip Kings," Victoria Times Colonist, December 12, 2004, page A9.

2718 Cleve Dheenshaw, "Sea Wolves sink Salmon Kings," Victoria Times Colonist, December 14, 2004, page B5.

2719 Cleve Dheenshaw, "Victorians love talking hockey, watching it it's a different story," Victoria Times Colonist, December 15, 2004, pages C1 and C2.

2720 "Salmon Kings' Dexter ECHL player of week," Victoria Times Colonist, December 15, 2004, page C2.

2721 Ron Rauch, "Gulls edge under-manned Kings," Victoria Times Colonist, December 18, 2004, page D6.

2722 Ron Rauch, "High-flying Gulls too much for Kings," Victoria Times Colonist, December 19, 2004, page A9.

2723 Gavin Fletcher, "Salmon Kings edge San Diego Gulls," Victoria Times Colonist, December 21, 2005, page B5.

2724 Sharie Epp, "Dogs ice Salmon Kings," Victoria Times Colonist, January 2, 2005, page A7.

2725 Gavin Fletcher, "Penalty woes slow flow for salmon Kings," Victoria Times Colonist, January 3, 2005, page B1.

2726 Gavin Fletcher, "No such thing as an easy game for Salmon Kings," Victoria Times Colonist, January 4, page C1.

2727 Sharie Epp, "Kings' rally falls short," Victoria Times Colonist, January 5, 2005, page C4.

2728 Sharie Epp, "Salmon Kings flounder," Victoria Times Colonist, January 6, 2005, page B6.

2729 Sharie Epp, "Salmon Kings captain makes ECHL all-stars," Victoria Times Colonist, January 7, 2005, page B4.

2730 Sharie Epp, "It's light out in 'Alaska as Kings bow to Aces," Victoria Times Colonist, January 8, 2005, page D10.

2731 "Aces give lowly Kings a thrashing," Victoria Times Colonist, January 9, 2005, page A7.

The History of Professional Hockey in Victoria, BC: 1911-2011

2732 Cleve Dheenshaw, "Shell-shocked Salmon Kings can't find shelter from storms," *Victoria Times Colonist*, January 12, 2005, page B6.

2733 Cleve Dheenshaw, "Salmon Kings lose eighth straight," *Victoria Times Colonist*, January 18, 2005, page D8.

2734 Cleve Dheenshaw, "Kings get burned in Vegas," *Victoria Times Colonist*, January 15, 2005, page B4.

2735 Cleve Dheenshaw, "Dogs give Kings reason to wail," *Victoria Times Colonist*, January 16, 2005, page A12.

2736 Cleve Dheenshaw, "Kings crowned with another loss," *Victoria Times Colonist*, January 17, 2005, pages B1 and B2.

2737 Cleve Dheenshaw, "Salmon Kings mauled by dogs again," *Victoria Times Colonist*, January 19, 2005, page B3.

2738 Cleve Dheenshaw, "Kings drowned again," *Victoria Times Colonist*, January 20, 2005, page C1.

2739 Gavin Fletcher, "Fans not fickle with Kings in pickle," *Victoria Times Colonist*, January 21, 2005, pages B6 and B9.

2740 Ron Rauch, "Salmon Kings punished for too many penalties," *Victoria Times Colonist*, January 22, 2005, page B5.

2741 Cleve Dheenshaw, "Pain continues, Aces beat Kings," *Victoria Times Colonist*, January 23, 2005, page A10.

2742 Cleve Dheenshaw, "Aces victory gives Kings share of winless record," *Victoria Times Colonist*, January 24, 2005, page B1.

2743 Cleve Dheenshaw, "Salmon King wins with ECHL all-stars," *Victoria Times Colonist*, January 27, 2005, page B9.

2744 Cleve Dheenshaw, "Salmon Kings roll the dice in Vegas," *Victoria Times Colonist*, January 29, 2005, page B5.

2745 "Fish blanked in shootout," *Victoria Times Colonist*, January 30, 2005, page A9.

2746 Cleve Dheenshaw, "Skid continues on Strip for Kings," *Victoria Times Colonist*, February 1, 2005, page B3.

2747 Cleve Dheenshaw, "Falcons swallow Kings," *Victoria Times Colonist*, February 3, 2005, page C8.

2748 Cleve Dheenshaw, "Blackburn flies on wounded wing," *Victoria Times Colonist*, February 4, 2005, page B8.

2749 Cleve Dheenshaw, "Kings fall prey again to buzzer beating birds," *Victoria Times Colonist*, February 5, 2005, page D13.

2750 Cleve Dheenshaw, "Salmon Kings finally put an end to shame," *Victoria Times Colonist*, February 6, 2005, page A8.

2751 Cleve Dheenshaw, "Kings blow first-period lead, returning to their losing ways," *Victoria Times Colonist*, February 8, 2005, page B6.

2752 Cleve Dheenshaw, "Kings victim of fishy play," *Victoria Times Colonist*, February 10, 2005, page B9.

2753 "Salmon Kings land new forward," *Victoria Times Colonist*, February 12, 2005, page B6.

2754 Cleve Dheenshaw, "ECHLError! No bookmark name given. seeks Island rivalry," *Victoria Times Colonist*, February 14, 2005, page B1.

2755 This information is based on an analysis of all the teams that have been part of the ECHLError! No bookmark name given.. As a season-ticket holder, I was well aware of the team with whom the Salmon Kings had the most significant rivalry. They struggled every year to beat the Aces who always fielded a strong, fast skating team that brought out the best in the Kings. They were always entertaining games.

2756 Cleve Dheenshaw, "Kings win shootout," *Victoria Times Colonist*, February 16, 2005, page B5.

2757 http://dropyourgloves.com/fights/TeamSeason.aspx?L=11&S=2005&T=278.

2758 Cleve Dheenshaw, "Kings, Fresno clear benches in brawl," *Victoria Times Colonist*, February 17, 2005, pages B9 and B10.

2759 Cleve Dheenshaw, "Hockey brawlers to be hit hard," *Victoria Times Colonist*, February 18, 2005, page B13.

2760 Cleve Dheenshaw, "From bad to worse," *Victoria Times Colonist*, February 19, 2005, page F6.

2761 Cleve Dheenshaw, "From bad to worse," *Victoria Times Colonist*, February 19, 2005, page F6.

2762 "Depleted Kings lose again to Steelheads," *Victoria Times Colonist*, February 20, 2005, page B11.

2763 "Mullen let go," *Victoria Times Colonist*, February 22, 2005, page B4.

2764 Cleve Dheenshaw, "Salmon Kings flying high," *Victoria Times Colonist*, February 23, 2005, pages B4 and B6.

2765 Cleve Dheenshaw, "Kings run out of steam," *Victoria Times Colonist*, February 24, 2005, page B9.

2766 Cleve Dheenshaw, "A Year for the Record Books," *Victoria Times Colonist*, February 25, 2005, pages B3 and B4.

2767 Cleve Dheenshaw, "Wranglers edge Salmon Kings with dramatic last-minute goal," Victoria Times Colonist, February 26, 2005, pages F1 and F4.

2768 Cleve Dheenshaw, "Kings lose another heartbreaker," Victoria Times Colonist, February 27, 2005, page A9.

2769 Cleve Dheenshaw, "Las Vegas thrashes Salmon Kings," Victoria Times Colonist, March 1, 2005, page B4.

2770 Cleve Dheenshaw, "Purinton dumped off the Fish wagon," Victoria Times Colonist, March 2, 2003, page C3.

2771 Cleve Dheenshaw, "Condors feast on Salmon Kings," Victoria Times Colonist, March 5, 2005, page F8.

2772 Cleve Dheenshaw, "Third-period collapse leaves Kings gasping," Victoria Times Colonist, March 6, 2005, page A9.

2773 Cleve Dheenshaw, "Steelheads fend off Salmon Kings for key victory," Victoria Times Colonist, March 10, 2005, page B8.

2774 Cleve Dheenshaw, "S-Kings pull out O.T. win," Victoria Times Colonist, March 11, 2005, page B9.

2775 Cleeve Dheenshaw, "'Patient' fans give Kings a rousing send-off despite blowout," Victoria Times Colonist, March 13, 2005, page A9.

2776 Cleve Dheenshaw, "On the road again," Victoria Times Colonist, March 14, 2005, page D1.

2777 Cleve Dheenshaw, "Fish fried in Florida," Victoria Times Colonist, March 16, 2005, page B4.

2778 Cleve Dheenshaw, "Kings show they're best of the worst," Victoria Times Colonist, March 18, 2005, page D9.

2779 Sherrie Epp, "Kings skates to second road win," Victoria Times Colonist, March 20, 2005, page B1.

2780 "S-Kings dominate but can't beat Gators," Victoria Times Colonist, March 21, 2005, page B4.

2781 "Ice Pilots sink Kings," Victoria Times Colonist, March 23, 2005, page C1.

2782 "S-Kings lose third in a row Down South," Victoria Times Colonist, March 24, 2005, page C7.

2783 "Kings beat the Blades," Victoria Times Colonist, March 26, 2005, page E7.

2784 "Salmo Kings fall to Florida," Victoria Times Colonist, March 27, 2005, page A13.

2785 Cleve Dheenshaw, "Maxwell's team not exactly as he planned," Victoria Times Colonist, April 1, 2005, page B5.

2786 Cleve Dheenshaw, "Wranglers hog tie Kings," Victoria Times Colonist, April 2, 2005, page E4.

2787 Cleve Dheenshaw, "Kings' plunge continues," Victoria Times Colonist, April 3, 2005, page F4.

2788 Cleve Dheenshaw, "Kings wrap up season to remember," Victoria Times Colonist, April 9, 2005, page E4.

2789 Cleve Dheenshaw, "Kings end season with OT win," Victoria Times Colonist, April 10, 2005, page C4.

2790 Cleve Dheenshaw, "Better luck next year starts with skill," Victoria Times Colonist, April 12, 2005, page B5.

2791 Cleve Dheenshaw, "Salmon Kings haven't lost faith in Maxwell," Victoria Times Colonist, April 1, 2005, page B8.

2792 Cleve Dheenshaw, "Salmon Kings land a couple of frequent flyers," Victoria Times Colonist, September 1, 2005, page B9.

2793 Cleve Dheenshaw, "S-Kings net an old Cougar," Victoria Times Colonist, September 6, 2005, page B1. n

2794 Cleve Dheenshaw, "Salsa break the ice at new arena," Victoria Times Colonist, September 11, 2005, page A1.

2795 Cleve Dheenshaw, "With new ice, let the games begin," Victoria Times Colonist, September 12, 2005, page B1.

2796 Cleve Dheenshaw, "Finnerty's a Texan; Kings get two D-men," Victoria Times Colonist, September 13, 2005, page B6.

2797 Cleve Dheenshaw, "Salmon King dodged disaster down south," Victoria Times Colonist, September 15, 2005, page C16.

2798 Cleve Dheenshaw, "S-Kings net a big one," Victoria Times Colonist, September 16, 2005, page D11.

2799 Cleve Dheenshaw, "Injury forces Salmon Kings firebrand to hang up his skates," Victoria Times Colonist, September 20, 2005, page C1.

2800 Cleve Dheenshaw, "Salmon Kings fail to land radio broadcast deal," Victoria Times Colonist, September 22, 2005, page B1.

2801 Cleve Dheenshaw, "Salmon Kings forward feels right at home," Victoria Times Colonist, September 23, 2005, page D10.

2802 "ECHL adopts NHL-instigated rule changes," Victoria Times Colonist, September 25, 2005, page C13.

2803 Victoria Times Colonist, September 26, 2005, page B5.

2804 Cleve Dheenshaw, "Salmon Kings enter camp with high hopes," *Victoria Times Colonist*, October 2, 2005, page F1.

2805 Cleve Dheenshaw, "Cougar on last team comes back as a Salmon King," *Victoria Times Colonist*, October 6, 2005, page C4.

2806 Cleve Dheenshaw, "Rita ruins season for Wildcatters," *Victoria Times Colonist*, October 7, 2005, page C6.

2807 Cleve Dheenshaw, "Kings at Camp: This is nothing like last year," *Victoria Times Colonist*, October 12, 2005, page B8.

2808 Cleve Dheenshaw, "Campbell shoots for next level," *Victoria Times Colonist*, October 13, 2005, page B9.

2809 Cleve Dheenshaw, "Salmon Kings' reputation on line," *Victoria Times Colonist*, October 15, 2005, page C12.

2810 Cleve Dheenshaw, "S-Kings win pair in preseason," *Victoria Times Colonist*, October 17, 2005, page B1.

2811 Cleve Dheenshaw, "With roster set, S-Kings get down to business," *Victoria Times Colonist*, October 20, 2005, page B1.

2812 Cleve Dheenshaw, "A fresh start for Salmon Kings," *Victoria Times Colonist*, October 21, 2005.

2813 Cleve Dheenshaw, "Salmon Kings open close," *Victoria Times Colonist*, October 22, 2005, page B5.

2814 Sharie Epp, "Condors feast on Salmon Kings miscues," *Victoria Times Colonist*, October 23, 2005, page A8.

2815 Cleve Dheenshaw, "Victoria's hockey future on the line," *Victoria Times Colonist*, October 23, 2005, page D6.

2816 Cleve Dheenshaw, "Barring hurricanes, ECHL will roar in," *Victoria Times Colonist*, October 25, 2005, page D7.

2817 Cleve Dheenshaw, "Salmon Kings seek first W in E Center," *Victoria Times Colonist*, October 28, 2005, page B7.

2818 Cleve Dheenshaw, "Salmon Kings win first," *Victoria Times Colonist*, October 29, 2005, page B7.

2819 Cleve Dheenshaw, "Penalties lead to late collapse," *Victoria Times Colonist*, October 30, 2005, page A8.

2820 Cleve Dheenshaw, "Muntain a mountain in S-Kings win," *Victoria Times Colonist*, November 3, 2005, page C4.

2821 Cleve Dheenshaw, "Salmon Kings fall before faithful," *Victoria Times Colonist*, November 5, 2005, page C9.

2822 Cleve Dheenshaw, "Kings hit third-period Storm," *Victoria Times Colonist*, November 6, 2005, page C12.

2823 Cleve Dheenshaw, "Wheeling nails Salmon Kings," *Victoria Times Colonist*, November 6, 2005, page B1.

2824 Cleve Dheenshaw, "Wheeling coach keeps up a family tradition," *Victoria Times Colonist*, November 7, 2005, page B3.

2825 Cleve Dheenshaw, "Salmon Kings ready for a little hometown love," *Victoria Times Colonist*, November 8, 2005, page B6.

2826 Cleve Dheenshaw, "Thunder underwhelmed," *Victoria Times Colonist*, November 12, 2005, page C13.

2827 *Victoria Times Colonist*, November 11, 2005, page A1.

2828 Cleve Dheenshaw, "House swarming," *Victoria Times Colonist*, November 11, 2005, page C1.

2829 Cleve Dheenshaw, "Salmon Kings offence stifled," *Victoria Times Colonist*, November 12, 2005, page C7.

2830 Cleve Dheenshaw, "Kings steal more Thunder," *Victoria Times Colonist*, November 13, 2005, page A11.

2831 Cleve Dheenshaw, "Steelheads take Game 1 in battle of the fish," *Victoria Times Colonist*, November 17, 2005, page E11.

2832 Cleve Dheenshaw, "Steelheads wield a hammer," *Victoria Times Colonist*, November 29, 2005, page C7.

2833 Cleve Dheenshaw, "Lingren breaks deadlock," *Victoria Times Colonist*, November 20, 2005, page A11.

2834 Cleve Dheenshaw, "S-Kings pull out a loss in Phoenix," *Victoria Times Colonist*, November 22, 2005, page D7.

2835 Cleve Dheenshaw, "Salmon Kings sink Gulls," *Victoria Times Colonist*, November 24, 2005, page D12.

2836 Cleve Dheenshaw, "Wranglers hold Salmon Kings to just one goal," *Victoria Times Colonist*, November 27, 2005, page A9.

2837 Cleve Dheenshaw, "Dogs have S-Kings collared," *Victoria Times Colonist*, November 28, 2005, page C3.

2838 Cleve Dheenshaw, "Phoenix makes roadkill of S-Kings," *Victoria Times Colonist*, November 30, 2005.

2839 Sharie Epp, "Stanley's mug on show at Salmon Kings game," *Victoria Times Colonist*, December 2, 2005, page B8.

2840 Sharie Epp, "S-Kings edge Grizzlies," *Victoria Times Colonist*, December 3, 2005, page D13.

2841 Cleve Dheenshaw, "Salmon Kings let one get away," *Victoria Times Colonist*, December 4, 2005, page A8.

2842 Cleve Dheenshaw, "Grizzlies feast on Salmon by dominating third period," *Victoria Times Colonist*, December 5, 2005, page C1.

2843 Gavin Fletcher, "Canucks ship Rob McVicar to Victoria; they'll take him," *Victoria Times Colonist*, December 7, 2005, page C3.

2844 Sharie Epp, "McVicar steals a win for S-Kings in Idaho," *Victoria Times Colonist*, December 8, 2005, page C12.

2845 Gavin Fletcher, "S-Kings add grit, but lose McVicar," *Victoria Times Colonist*, December 10, 2005, page F1.

2846 "S-Kings at home on the road," *Victoria Times Colonist*, December 10, 2005, page F1.

2847 "Steelheads avoid the sweep," *Victoria Times Colonist*, December 11, 2005, page A8.

2848 Ron Rauch, "Salmon Kings trump Aces," *Victoria Times Colonist*, December 17, 2009, page C9.

2849 Ron Rauch, "Aces all over sluggish Kings," *Victoria Times Colonist*, December 18, 2005, page A7.

2850 Ron Rauch, "Aces take S-Kings to school," *Victoria Times Colonist*, December 20, 1005, page C8.

2851 "Grizzlies' bite lethal," *Victoria Times Colonist*, December 22, 2005, page C9.

2852 "Grizzlies' bite lethal for Salmon Kings," *Victoria Times Colonist*, December 23, 2005, page B1.

2853 "Alaska's Minard feasts on S-Kings," *Victoria Times Colonist*, December 29, 2005, page C9.

2854 "Aces edge S-Kings," *Victoria Times Colonist*, December 31, 2005, page A15.

2855 "S-Kings end '05 on a high," *Victoria Times Colonist*, January 2, 2006, page D1.

2856 Cleve Dheenshaw, "Salmon Kings hope to turn it around at home," *Victoria Times Colonist*, January 5, 2006, page C9.

2857 Gavin Fletcher, "S-Kings shoot down high-flying Falcons," *Victoria Times Colonist*, January 6, 2006, page D1.

2858 Cleve Dheenshaw, "Falcons take flight again," *Victoria Times Colonist*, January 7, 2006, page F9.

2859 Cleve Dheenshaw, "Falcons prey on S-Kings," *Victoria Times Colonist*, January 8, 2006, page A8.

2860 Cleve Dheenshaw, "Hope floats," *Victoria Times Colonist*, January 9, 2006, page D1.

2861 Gavin Fletcher, "Must Maxie go?" *Victoria Times Colonist*, January 12, 2006, page C9.

2862 "Offence to the rescue," *Victoria Times Colonist*, January 13, 2006, page D9.

2863 Cleve Dheenshaw, "Salmon Kings lovin' it in Idaho," *Victoria Times Colonist*, January 14, 2006, page F11.

2864 Cleve Dheenshaw, "Salmon Kings fire Maxwell," *Victoria Times Colonist*, January 17, 2006, page B5.

2865 Cleve Dheenshaw, "Time for accountability," *Victoria Times Colonist*, January 18, 2006, page D8.

2866 Cleve Dheenshaw, "Players welcome 'change in system'," *Victoria Times Colonist*, January 18, 2006, page D8.

2867 Cleve Dheenshaw, "Maxwell leaves with head high," *Victoria Times Colonist*, January 20, 2006, page B3.

2868 "Ward a winner in S-Kings debut," *Victoria Times Colonist*, January 21, 2006, page D8.

2869 "Fun on road comes to an end," *Victoria Times Colonist*, January 22, 2006, page B1.

2870 Cleve Dheenshaw, "Where have the goals gone?" *Victoria Times Colonist*, January 23, 2006, page C3.

2871 Cleve Dheenshaw, "Runners shoot way to Victoria," *Victoria Times Colonist*, January 27, 2006, page D11.

2872 Cleve Dheenshaw, "Overtime heartbreak," *Victoria Times Colonist*, January 29, 2006, page A9.

2873 Cleve Dheenshaw, "Top scorer finished in Victoria," *Victoria Times Colonist*, January 31, 2006, page C1.

2874 Cleve Dheenshaw, "It's crowded in the crease," *Times Colonist*, February 1, 2006, page D7.

2875 Cleve Dheenshaw, "Huxley's first buries Lynx," *Victoria Times Colonist*, February 2, 2006, page C5.

2876 Cleve Dheenshaw, "Lynx bite S-Kings in OT," *Victoria Times Colonist*, February 4, 2006, page E1.

2877 Sharie Epp, "Lynx master S-Kings," *Victoria Times Colonist*, February 8, 2006, page A8.

2878 "S-Kings ink two players from Europe," *Victoria Times Colonist*, February 7, 2006, page C2.

2879 Sharie Epp, "Time to crank it up," *Victoria Times Colonist*, February 2, 2006, page D8.

2880 Cleve Dheenshaw, "Dogs maul S-Kings," *Victoria Times Colonist*, February 9, 2006, page C1.

2881 Sharie Epp, "Dogs feast on Salmons again," *Victoria Times Colonist*, February 11, 2006, page C4 and C5.

2882 Gavin Fletcher, "Dogs put S-Kings on ice," *Victoria Times Colonist*, February 12, 2006, page D4.

2883 Cleve Dheenshaw, "S-Kings go down in desert," *Victoria Times Colonist*, February 18, 2006, page D6.

2884 Cleve Dheenshaw, "Gulls' power play punishes S-Kings," *Victoria Times Colonist*, February 19, 2006, page C4.

2885 Gavin Fletcher, "S-Kings steal the show," *Victoria Times Colonist*, February 22, 2006, page C5.

2886 Cleve Dheenshaw, "S-Kings must contain Aces," *Victoria Times Colonist*, February 24, 2006, page B5.

2887 Cleve Dheenshaw, "Boxma proves his point," *Victoria Times Colonist*, February 25, 2006, page F4.

2888 Cleve Dheenshaw, "Wade shoots down Aces," *Victoria Times Colonist*, February 26, 2006, page C4.

2889 Cleve Dheenshaw, "Black 'n Blue," *Victoria Times Colonist*, February 28, 2006, page C9.

2890 "Stellar play nets Boxma goalie of week honours," *Victoria Times Colonist*, March 1, 2006, page D3.

2891 Cleve Dheenshaw, "Condors come back to bite S-Kings," *Victoria Times Colonist*, March 4, 2005, page F7.

2892 Cleve Dheenshaw, "McVicar back, sharp as a tack," *Victoria Times Colonist*, March 2, 2006, page C9.

2893 Cleve Dheenshaw, "Condors leave K-Kings reeling," *Victoria Times Colonist*, March 6, 2006, page C5.

2894 Cleve Dheenshaw, "Las Vegas just too hot to handle," *Victoria Times Colonist*, March 9, 2006, page B5.

2895 Cleve Dheenshaw, "Las Vegas comes up aces against Salmon Kings," *Victoria Times Colonist*, March 11, 2006, page A18.

2896 Cleve Dheenshaw, "Wranglers wrestle up another," *Victoria Times Colonist*, March 12, 2006, page A9.

2897 Cleve Dheenshaw, "It's 'next season' time for S-Kings," *Victoria Times Colonist*, March 13, 2006, page B3.

2898 "Lingren off to AHL again," *Victoria Times Colonist*, March 1, 2006, page D8.

2899 Ron Rauch, "Newest S-King saves day," *Victoria Times Colonist*, March 16, 2006, page C9.

2900 Ron Rauch, "Here's a switch, Salmon Kings close door in the third," *Victoria Times Colonist*, March 18, 2006, page F7.

2901 Ron Rauch, "S-Kings rally falls just short," *Victoria Times Colonist*, March 19, 2006, page A9.

2902 Cleve Dheenshaw, "S-Kings lose two, gain one," *Victoria Times Colonist*, March 20, 2006, page D4.

2903 Cleve Dheenshaw "Salmon Kings stay hot in desert heat," *Victoria Times Colonist*, March 21, 2006, page B5.

2904 Cleve Dheenshaw, "Salmon Kings tame Ice Dogs," *Victoria Times Colonist*, March 23, 2006, page F7.

2905 Cleve Dheenshaw, "S-Kings cooled by rising Thunder," *Victoria Times Colonist*, March 25, 2006, page E1.

2906 "Salmon Kings steal Stockton's Thunder," *Victoria Times Colonist*, March 26, 2006, page A10.

2907 Cleve Dheenshaw, "Salmon Kings fall to flying Falcons," *Victoria Times Colonist*, March 28, 2006, page B4.

2908 Cleve Dheenshaw, "Salmon Kings earn OT win," *Victoria Times Colonist*, April 1, 2006, page E4.

2909 Cleve Dheenshaw, "Aces' success story blueprint for S-Kings," *Victoria Times Colonist*, April 2, 2006, page A10.

2910 Cleve Dheenshaw, "Late success has S-Kings smilin'," *Victoria Times Colonist*, April 7, 20006, page D10.

2911 Cleve Dheenshaw, "Stingy Grizzlies grind Salmon Kings to a halt," *Victoria Times Colonist*, April 8, 2006, page E1.

2912 Cleve Dheenshaw, "Salmon Kings sizzle in finale," *Victoria Times Colonist*, April 9, 2006, page F1.

2913 Cleve Dheenshaw, "S-Kings wanting on ice, but a success at the gate," *Victoria Times Colonist*, April 10, 2006, page C3.

2914 Cleve Dheenshaw, "Fan-tastic season for S-Kings," *Victoria Times Colonist*, April 12, 2006, page C5.

2915 Cleve Dheenshaw, "Is the AHL heading to Victoria?" *Victoria Times Colonist*, April 18, 2006, page B5.

2916 Cleve Dheenshaw, "No Victoria yet, AHL boss says," *Victoria Times Colonist*, April 19, 2006, page C11.

2917 Cleve Dheenshaw, "Ward says thanks, but no thanks," *Victoria Times Colonist*, April 2, 2006, page C10.

2918 https://www.echl.com/echl-coachs-biographytony-macaulay-victoria-salmon-kings.

2919 Cleve Dheenshaw, "MacAulay handed reins," *Victoria Times Colonist*, June 9, 2006, page C5.

2920 Cleve Dheenshaw, "Back home, on a mission," *Victoria Times Colonist*, September 3, 2006, page A9.

2921 Cleve Dheenshaw, "More offence for S-Kings," *Victoria Times Colonist*, September 7, 2006, page B9.

2922 Cleve Dheenshaw, "S-Kings all eyes," *Victoria Times Colonist*, September 8, 2006, page A17.

2923 Cleve Dheenshaw, "Prospect shoots for big pond," *Victoria Times Colonist*, September 10, 2006, page A9.

2924 Cleve Dheenshaw, "Prospect camp ideal setting to begin new relationships," *Victoria Times Colonist*, September 11, 2006, page B1.

2925 Cleve Dheenshaw, "Taylor first Salmon King to land NHL deal," *Victoria Times Colonist*, September 15, 2006, page D1.

2926 Cleve Dheenshaw, "S-Kings add leadership," *Victoria Times Colonist*, September 16, 2006, page D1.

2927 Cleve Dheenshaw, "Salmon Kings ink AHL veteran Morisset," *Victoria Times Colonist*, September 20, 2006, page D9.

2928 Cleve Dheenshaw, "NHL teams buy ECHLError! Bookmark not defined. clubs," *Victoria Times Colonist*, September 21, 2006, page B4.

2929 Cleve Dheenshaw, "S-Kings add CIS star," *Victoria Times Colonist*, September 22, 2006, page D1.

2930 Cleve Dheenshaw, "S-Kings continue to bolster back-end," *Victoria Times Colonist*, September 26, 2006, page B6.

2931 Cleve Dheenshaw, "S-Kings add veteran goalie to mix," *Victoria Times Colonist*, September 27, 2006, page D6.

2932 Cleve Dheenshaw, "S-Kings' roster takes shape," *Victoria Times Colonist*, September 29, 2006, page D10.

2933 Cleve Dheenshaw, "Salmon Kings land big ones in McLeod, Moose cuts," *Victoria Times Colonist*, October 3, 2006, page B8.

2934 Cleve Dheenshaw, "Another speedster comes West," *Victoria Times Colonist*, October 5, 2006, page C8.

2935 Cleve Dheenshaw, "Rule changes arrive in ECHL," *Victoria Times Colonist*, September 9, 2006, page D11.

2936 Cleve Dheenshaw, "S-Kings land in the West," *Victoria Times Colonist*, September 30, 2006, page C10.

2937 Cleve Dheenshaw, "New attitude, new expectations," *Victoria Times Colonist*, October 6, 2006, page D9.

2938 Cleve Dheenshaw, "Tough blueline to crack," *Victoria Times Colonist*, October 7, 2006, page D12.

2939 Cleve Dheenshaw, "S-Kings' cut painful," *Victoria Times Colonist*, October 13, 2006, page B4.

2940 "Idaho tops S-Kings," *Victoria Times Colonist*, November 14, 2006, page D12.

2941 Cleve Dheenshaw, "Preseason not kind to S-Kings," *Victoria Times Colonist*, October 15, 2006, page A11.

2942 Cleve Dheenshaw, "'High-end catch' let go by S-Kings" *Victoria Times Colonist*, October 17, 2006, page C11.

2943 Cleve Dheenshaw, "Salmon Kings finalize roster," *Victoria Times Colonist*, October 18, 2006, page C9.

2944 *Victoria Times Colonist*, October 22, 2006, page B9.

2945 "S-Kings come up short in Alaska," *Victoria Times Colonist*, October 21, 2006, page D12.

2946 Gavin Fletcher, "Rough start rattles S-Kings," *Victoria Times Colonist*, October 23, 2006, page C1.

2947 *Victoria Times Colonist*, October 23, 2006, page C4.

2948 Gavin Fletcher, "The Franchise," *Victoria Times Colonist*, October 22, 2006, pages D1 and D5.

2949 Cleve Dheenshaw, "The Players," *Victoria Times Colonist*, October 22, 2006, pages D1 and D5.

2950 Cleve Dheenshaw, "Feelin' right at home," *Victoria Times Colonist*, October 25, 2006, page B5.

2951 Gavin Fletcher, "Good hockey, so-so mascot," *Victoria Times Colonist*, October 26, 2006, page B9.

2952 Cleve Dheenshaw, "Idaho steels the show," *Victoria Times Colonist*, October 26, 2006, page B9.

2953 Cleve Dheenshaw, "S-Kings let one slip," *Victoria Times Colonist*, October 28, 2006, page A16.

2954 Cleve Dheenshaw, "S-Kings halt skid," *Victoria Times Colonist*, October 29, 2006, page A9.

2955 Cleve Dheenshaw, "S-Kings hope to show true colours," *Victoria Times Colonist*, October 30, 2006, page D4.

2956 Rob Shaw, "Police raid Salmon Kings' locker room," *Victoria Times Colonist*, October 31, 2006, page A2.

2957 Cleve Dheenshaw, Gavin Fletcher, and Sandra McCulloch, "Allegations swirl around Salmon Kings," *Victoria Times Colonist*, November 1, 2006, page A1.

2958 Rob Shaw, "Crown gets Salmon Kings' evidence," *Victoria Times Colonist*, November 10, 2006, page B1.

2959 Rob Shaw, "Salmon Kings won't face charges," *Victoria Times Colonist*, February 10, 2007, page A1.

2960 Rob Shaw, "Team's image put to test in high-profile case," *Victoria Times Colonist*, February 10, 2007, page A2.

2961 Cleve Dheenshaw, "Salmon Kings deal for Devils' pick," *Victoria Times Colonist*, October 31, 2006, page B7.

2962 Cleve Dheenshaw, "S-Kings release goalie to make room for Canucks prospect," *Victoria Times Colonist*, November 1, 2006, page D7.

The History of Professional Hockey in Victoria, BC: 1911-2011

2963 Cleve Dheenshaw, "Another Moose comes west to Salmon Kings," *Victoria Times Colonist*, November 2, 2006, page B6.

2964 *Victoria Times Colonist*, November 1, 2006, page D7.

2965 Brian Drewry, "S-Kings lose in Sin City," *Victoria Times Colonist*, November 4, 2006, page D2.

2966 Cleve Dheenshaw, "Ellis helps Salmon Kings bounce back in Vegas," *Victoria Times Colonist*, November 5, 2006, page C3.

2967 "Bridges helps wrangle up win," *Victoria Times Colonist*, November 8, 2006, page D8.

2968 Cleve Dheenshaw, "Heshka gets call from Moose," *Victoria Times Colonist*,

2969 Cleve Dheenshaw, "S-Kings keep Falcons from taking off," *Victoria Times Colonist*, November 10, 2006, page D10.

2970 Cleve Dheenshaw, "Falcons fly past S-Kings," *Victoria Times Colonist*, November 12, 2006, page A11.

2971 Cleve Dheenshaw, "S-Kings rebound for win," *Victoria Times Colonist*, November 13, 2006, page B4.

2972 *Victoria Times Colonist*, Novembers 13, 2006, page B2.

2973 Cleve Dheenshaw, "Ellis steals Stockton's thunder," *Victoria Times Colonist*, November 17, 2006, page A17.

2974 Sharie Epp, Thunder strike back," *Victoria Times Colonist*, November 18, 2006, page D10.

2975 Cleve Dheenshaw, "S-Kings up against familiar face," *Victoria Times Colonist*, November 24, 2006, page A20.

2976 "Utah upends Salmon Kings," *Victoria Times Colonist*, November 25, 2006, page C11.

2977 "Stutzel hat trick sparks S-Kings," *Victoria Times Colonist*, November 26, 2006, page A11.

2978 *Victoria Times Colonist*, November 26, 2006, page A12.

2979 Cleve Dheenshaw, "Taylor gets his wish," *Victoria Times Colonist*, November 29, 2006, page B1.

2980 Cleve Dheenshaw, "The New Kings of the road," *Victoria Times Colonist*, December 5, 2006, page D6.

2981 Cleve Dheenshaw, "Aces school S-Kings," *Victoria Times Colonist*, November 30, 2006, page C11.

2982 Cleve Dheenshaw, "Ellis, and nothing else," *Victoria Times Colonist*, December 2, 2006, page C16.

2983 Cleve Dheenshaw, "Aces complete sweep," *Victoria Times Colonist*, December 3, 2006, page A9.

2984 Cleve Dheenshaw, "Oh, Brothers," *Victoria Times Colonist*, December 6, 2006, page D1.

2985 Cleve Dheenshaw, "Dogs nip Salmon Kings," *Victoria Times Colonist*, December 7, 2006, page C1.

2986 Cleve Dheenshaw, "Kelly helps S-Kings keep Dogs at bay," *Victoria Times Colonist*, December 9, 2006, page C14.

2987 Cleve Dheenshaw, "S-Kings grin and bear it," *Victoria Times Colonist*, December 10, 2006, page A11.

2988 "Ellis's heroics not enough," *Victoria Times Colonist*, December 13, 2006, page B6.

2989 "Ice Dogs top S-Kings," *Victoria Times Colonist*, December 16, 2006, page B4.

2990 "S-Kings drop third in a row," *Victoria Times Colonist*, December 17, 2006, page A11.

2991 Cleve Dheenshaw, "'B' word back as losses mount," *Victoria Times Colonist*, December 18, 2006, page C1.

2992 Cleve Dheenshaw, "Help on way for Salmon Kings," *Victoria Times Colonist*, December 21, 2006, page C5.

2993 Cleve Dheenshaw, "S-Kings drop fifth straight," *Victoria Times Colonist*, December 22, 2006, page B10.

2994 Cleve Dheenshaw, "Ellis shows he has all-star stuff," *Victoria Times Colonist*, December 23, 2006, page C13.

2995 Cleve Dheenshaw, "Road woes continue for S-Kings," *Victoria Times Colonist*, December 24, 2006, page B1.

2996 Ron Rauch, "Salmon Kings fire coach," *Victoria Times Colonist*, December 29, 2006, page A1.

2997 Ron Rauch, "S-Kings' new faces ready for Aces," *Victoria Times Colonist*, December 29, 2006, page D9.

2998 Sharie Epp, "Salmon Kings back on track," *Victoria Times Colonist*, December 30, 2006, page D7.

2999 Sharie Epp, "Aces fly high in rematch," *Victoria Times Colonist*, December 31, 2006, page A11.

3000 Sharie Epp, "Last minutes dynamite for S-Kings," *Victoria Times Colonist*, January 2, 2007, page C9.

3001 Sharie Epp, "Goldie helps gun down Dogs," *Victoria Times Colonist*, January 4, 2007, page B7.

3002 Sharie Epp, "S-Kings look to declaw Falcons," *Victoria Times Colonist*, January 5, 2007, page B5.

3003 "Falcons feast on 'S-Kings," *Victoria Times Colonist*, January 6, 2007, page D9.

3004 "S-Kings hit another road block," *Victoria Times Colonist*, January 7, 2007, page A12.

3005 Sharie Epp, "Salmon Kings' coach upbeat despite latest loss," *Victoria Times Colonist*, January 8, 2007, page C1.

3006 Cleve Dheenshaw, "Victoria squad continues its hot streak in Las Vegas," *Victoria Times Colonist*, January 10, 2007, page D1.

3007 Cleve Dheenshaw, "Gajic headed to all-star game," *Victoria Times Colonist*, January 11, 2007, page C12.

3008 "Aces dump S-Kings, *Victoria Times Colonist*, January 13, 2007, page B12.

3009 Cleve Dheenshaw, "S-Kings struggle at Sullivan Arena," *Victoria Times Colonist*, January 14, 2007, page A12.

3010 Cleve Dheenshaw, "Mighty Aces rout Salmon Kings," *Victoria Times Colonist*, January 15, 2007, page C1.

3011 Cleve Dheenshaw, "Abbotsford sets sights on ECHL team for arena," *Victoria Times Colonist*, January 26, 2007, page B4.

3012 "A line change for Salmon Kings," *Victoria Times Colonist*, January 17, 2007, page A10.

3013 Cleve Dheenshaw, "S-Kings add Canucks' draft pick," *Victoria Times Colonist*, January 19, 2007, page D9.

3014 Cleve Dheenshaw, "Condors take bite out of S-Kings," *Victoria Times Colonist*, January 20, 2007, page C12.

3015 Cleve Dheenshaw, "Salmon Kings clip Condors in overtime shootout," *Victoria Times Colonist*, January 21, 2007, page A9.

3016 Cleve Dheenshaw, "From now on, every win crucial for S-Kings," *Victoria Times Colonist*, January 22, 2007, page D1.

3017 Cleve Dheenshaw, "Condor vet swoops on Salmon Kings," *Victoria Times Colonist*, January 23, 2007, page C3.

3018 Cleve Dheenshaw, "Salmon Kings hit road looking for answers," *Victoria Times Colonist*, January 24, 2007, page B11.

3019 Cleve Dheenshaw, "Bridges takes bite out of Ice Dogs," *Victoria Times Colonist*, January 25, 2007, page C9.

3020 Cleve Dheenshaw, "S-Kings solve Condors," *Victoria Times Colonist*, January 27, 2007, page B12.

3021 Cleve Dheenshaw, "Salmon Kings keep it rolling in California," *Victoria Times Colonist*, January 28, 2007, page A9.

3022 Cleve Dheenshaw, "What's this? S-Kings make it four straight," *Victoria Times Colonist*, January 29, 2007, page C1.

3023 Cleve Dheenshaw, "S-Kings acquire blueliner," *Victoria Times Colonist*, February 1, 2007, page B11.

3024 Sharie Epp, "S-Kings push streak to five," *Victoria Times Colonist*, February 3, 2007, page D8.

3025 Cleve Dheenshaw, "Steelheads rout Victoria," *Victoria Times Colonist*, February 4, 2007, page C1.

3026 "Goalie steals one for Idaho," *Victoria Times Colonist*, February 8, 2007, page C1.

3027 "S-Kings triumph in Ellis's return," *Victoria Times Colonist*, February 1, 2007, page C11.

3028 "S-Kings lose, but still in playoff hunt," *Victoria Times Colonist*, February 111, 2007, page A9.

3029 Cleve Dheenshaw, "S-Kings silence Thunder," *Victoria Times Colonist*, February 15, 2007, page B10.

3030 Cleve Dheenshaw, "This time, S-Kings let their offence do the talking," *Victoria Times Colonist*, February 17, 2007, page B3.

3031 Cleve Dheenshaw, "Goldie golden for Salmon Kings," *Victoria Times Colonist*, February 18, 2007, page A9.

3032 Cleve Dheenshaw, "Salmon Kings look to douse Fames farm team," *Victoria Times Colonist*, February 21, 2007, page B9.

3033 Cleve Dheenshaw, "Wranglers wallop S-Kings," *Victoria Times Colonist*, February 22, 2007, page B5.

3034 Cleve Dheenshaw, "S-Kings out-gun Wranglers," *Victoria Times Colonist*, February 24, 2007, page D10.

3035 Cleve Dheenshaw, "Vegas goalie shuts the door again," *Victoria Times Colonist*, February 25, 2007, page A9.

3036 Cleve Dheenshaw, "S-Kings face crucial road trip," *Victoria Times Colonist*, March 2, 2007, page D9.

3037 Sharie Epp, "S-Kings ground Falcons," *Victoria Times Colonist*, March 3, 2007, page D10.

3038 Cleve Dheenshaw, "S-Kings finish off Fresno," *Victoria Times Colonist*, March 4, 2007, page A9.

3039 Cleve Dheenshaw, "S-Kings blue-line given huge boost," *Victoria Times Colonist*, March 7, 2007, page C11.

3040 Cleve Dheenshaw, "Thunder storm back and strike S-Kings in OT," *Victoria Times Colonist*, March 8, 2007, page C9.

3041 Cleve Dheenshaw, "Thunder outgun S-Kings," *Victoria Times Colonist*, March 10, 2007, page D9.

3042 Cleve Dheenshaw, "S-Kingz get the point," *Victoria Times Colonist*, March 11, 2007, page A10.

3043 Cleve Dheenshaw, "S-Kings looking good for games with Utah," *Victoria Times Colonist*, March 12, 2007, page D4.

3044 Cleve Dheenshaw, "Now or never for Grizzlies," Victoria Times Colonist, March 15, 2007, page C6.

3045 Cleve Dheenshaw, "S-Kings spring to life," Victoria Times Colonist, March 16, 2007, page B8.

3046 Cleve Dheenshaw, "Utah steals Victoria's thunder," Victoria Times Colonist, March 18, 2007, page A9.

3047 Cleve Dheenshaw, "Salmon Kings tame Utah," Victoria Times Colonist, March 19, 2007, page B1.

3048 Cleve Dheenshaw, "S-Kings feel pain of Manitoba goalies' injury," Victoria Times Colonist, March 20, 2007, page C1.

3049 Victoria Times Colonist, March 22, 2007, page C11.

3050 Ron Rauch, "Another big step toward playoffs," Victoria Times Colonist, March 24, 2007, page C13.

3051 Cleve Dheenshaw, "S-Kings keep Dogs at bay," Victoria Times Colonist, March 25, 2007, page A9.

3052 Cleve Dheenshaw, "Postseason wait is over," Victoria Times Colonist, March 29, 2007, page B9.

3053 Cleve Dheenshaw, "Good news comes in pairs for S-Kings," Victoria Times Colonist, March 31, 2007, page B10.

3054 Victoria Times Colonist, March 31, 2007, page B11.s

3055 Cleve Dheenshaw, "S-Kings set team record with sixth win in a row," Victoria Times Colonist, April 1, 2007, page A9.

3056 Victoria Times Colonist, April 3, 2007, page C1.

3057 Cleve Dheenshaw, "One for the record book," Victoria Times Colonist, April 5, 2007, page B8.

3058 Cleve Dheenshaw, "S-Kings pluck Roadrunners," Victoria Times Colonist, April 7, 2007, page B7.

3059 Cleve Dheenshaw, "S-Kings finish with flair," Victoria Times Colonist, April 8, 2007, page A9.

3060 Cleve Dheenshaw, "Salmon Kings stun Aces in series opener," Victoria Times Colonist, April 10, 2007, page B5.

3061 Cleve Dheenshaw, "Aces come roaring back," Victoria Times Colonist, April 11, 2007, page C7.

3062 Cleve Dheenshaw, "Aces climb back into driver's seat," Victoria Times Colonist, April 13, 2007, page A18.

3063 Cleve Dheenshaw, "One more chance for S-Kings," Victoria Times Colonist, April 14, 2007, page C10.

3064 Cleve Dheenshaw, "S-Kings stay alive," Victoria Times Colonist, April 15, 2007, page D11.

3065 Cleve Dheenshaw, "Aces finish off Salmon Kings," Victoria Times Colonist, April 17, 2007, page B4.

3066 Names were gleaned from emails to season-ticket holders dated August 15, 2007, August 24, 2007, and August 30, 2007.

3067 "S-Kings bring back Gomez," Victoria Times Colonist, September 5, 2007, page D7.

3068 Email from the Victoria Salmon Kings, dated September 14, 2007.

3069 "More than hockey to Canucks' visit," Victoria Times Colonist, September 15, 2007, page A14.

3070 Cleve Dheenshaw, "Canucks wow the fans," Victoria Times Colonist, September 17, 2007, page D1.

3071 Cleve Dheenshaw, "S-Kings expect battles at camp," Victoria Times Colonist, September 18, 2007, page C5.

3072 "Salmon Kings ink former BCHLer," Victoria Times Colonist, September 9, 2007, page D1.

3073 "Salmon Kings deal Young," Victoria Times Colonist, September 20, 2007, page C6.

3074 "Salmon Kings pick up some grit," Victoria Times Colonist, September 26, 2007, page C15.

3075 Cleve Dheenshaw, "Salmon Kings' camp roster taking shape," Victoria Times Colonist, October 1, 2007, page D2.

3076 Cleve Dheenshaw, "Salmon Kings add former AHLer to goaltending mix," Victoria Times Colonist, October 2, 2007, page D7.

3077 Cleve Dheenshaw, "Let the competition begin," Victoria Times Colonist, October 5, 2007.

3078 Cleve Dheenshaw, "Salmon Kings' prospect LaPointe proud to see dad's plaque at arena," Victoria Times Colonist, October 7, 2007, page A10.

3079 Cleve Dheenshaw, "Battle in crease heats up," Victoria Times Colonist, October 11, 2007, page C8.

3080 Cleve Dheenshaw, "Salmon Kings hopefuls have two games to strut their stuff," Victoria Times Colonist, October 12, 2007, page A21.

3081 Cleve Dheenshaw, "Salmon Kings get exhibition season off to a good start with win in Utah," Victoria Times Colonist, October 13, 2007, page C15.

3082 Cleve Dheenshaw, "S. Kings split series with Utah," Victoria Times Colonist, October 14, 2007, page A11.

3083 Cleve Dheenshaw, "S-Kings get boost form Moose," Victoria Times Colonist, October 16, 2007, page D5.

3084 Cleve Dheenshaw, "Cole odd man out as Salmon Kings finalize roster," Victoria Times Colonist, October 27, 2007, page B1.

3085 Cleve Dheenshaw, "S-Kings aim to spoil the party," Victoria Times Colonist, October 19, 2007, page B8.

3086 Cleve Dheenshaw, "Salmon Kings start with a bang," Victoria Times Colonist, October 20, 2007, page C16.

3087 Cleve Dheenshaw, "Bad Bounces cost S-Kings," Victoria Times Colonist, October 21, 2007, page A15.

3088 Cleve Dheenshaw, "Goldie's big week recognized," Victoria Times Colonist, November 9, 2007, page B5.

3089 Cleve Dheenshaw, "Salmon Kings set to wrangle with Vegas," Victoria Times Colonist, October 24, 2007, page D9.

3090 Cleve Dheenshaw, "Wranglers edge S-Kings in home debut," Victoria Times Colonist, October 27, 2007, page C1.

3091 Cleve Dheenshaw, "Salmon Kings give fans something to cheer about," Victoria Times Colonist, October 28, 2007, page B1.

3092 Cleve Dheenshaw, "Salmon Kings deal for defenceman," Victoria Times Colonist, October 30, 2007, page C6.

3093 Cleve Dheenshaw, "Goldie's trick a real treat," Victoria Times Colonist, November 1, 2007, page C6.

3094 Cleve Dheenshaw, "Super Goldies," Victoria Times Colonist, November 3, 2007, page C15

3095 Brian Drewry, "S-Kings nip Condors in shootout," Victoria Times Colonist, November 4, 2007, page D1.

3096 Cleve Dheenshaw, "Goldie's big week recognized," Victoria Times Colonist, November 9, 2007, page B5.

3097 Information was gained from an examination of the 2007-2008 schedule.

3098 Cleve Dheenshaw, "S-Kings take a drubbing in Utah," Victoria Times Colonist, November 10, 2007, page D10.

3099 Cleve Dheenshaw, "Ellis saves the day for S-Kings," Victoria Times Colonist, November 11, 2007, page C5.

3100 Cleve Dheenshaw, "Ellis slams door on Grizzlies," Victoria Times Colonist, November 13, 2007, page D5.

3101 Cleve Dheenshaw, "Bernier ignites offence," Victoria Times Colonist, November 15, 2007, page C5.

3102 Email dated November 16, 2007, from the Salmon Kings.

3103 Cleve Dheenshaw, "Salmon Kings thunder ahead of Stockton," Victoria Times Colonist, November 17, 2007, page C15.

3104 Cleve Dheenshaw, "Salmon Kings sweep series with Thunder," Victoria Times Colonist, November 18, 2007, page A12.

3105 Cleve Dheenshaw, "Salmon Kings take act on the road," Victoria Times Colonist, November 21, 2007, page D1.

3106 Cleve Dheenshaw, "Ellis helps Salmon Kings win battle of fish," Victoria Times Colonist, November 22, 2007, page C5.

3107 Email dated November 22, 2007, from Salmon Kings.

3108 Cleve Dheenshaw, "S-Kings win streak snapped at six games," Victoria Times Colonist, November 24, 2007, page D11.

3109 Cleve Dheenshaw, "Idaho hands S-Kings a dose of reality," Victoria Times Colonist, November 25, 2007, page B10.

3110 Email dated November 26, 2007, from Salmon Kings.

3111 Cleve Dheenshaw, "Help on the way for S-Kings," Victoria Times Colonist, November 26, 2007, page C2.

3112 Cleve Dheenshaw, "Help on the way for S-Kings," Victoria Times Colonist, November 26, 2007, page C2.

3113 Cleve Dheenshaw, "Help arrives for blue-line," Victoria Times Colonist, November 28, 2007, page C9.

3114 Cleve Dheenshaw, "Goldie plays hero again," Victoria Times Colonist, November 29, 2007, page C5.

3115 Cleve Dheenshaw, "S-Kings love that home cooking," Victoria Times Colonist, November 30, 2007, page C15.

3116 https://www.echl.com/stats/daily-schedule/2007-11-29?league=1&season=45

3117 Cleve Dheenshaw, "Ash Goldie does it again," Victoria Times Colonist, December 1, 2007, page C5.

3118 Cleve Dheenshaw, "S-Kings' offence gets a boost," Victoria Times Colonist, December 4, 2007, page D5.

3119 Cleve Dheenshaw, "Comeback kids at it again," Victoria Times Colonist, December 7, 2007, page C15.

3120 Cleve Dheenshaw, "Phoenix bursts S-Kings' bubble," Victoria Times Colonist, December 8, 2007, page C13.

3121 Cleve Dheenshaw, "Salmon Kings' Ellis, Gajic get Moose call," Victoria Times Colonist, December 12, 2007, page D1.

3122 Cleve Dheenshaw, "High-flying Falcons clip Salmon Kings," Victoria Times Colonist, December 15, 2007, age B1.

3123 Cleve Dheenshaw, "S-Kings clip Condors wings," Victoria Times Colonist, December 16, 2007, page B3.

3124 Cleve Dheenshaw, "S-Kings prey on Falcons," Victoria Times Colonist, December 17, 2007, page D1.

3125 Email dated December 18, 2007, from the Salmon Kings.

3126 Cleve Dheenshaw, "S-Kings up for the test," Victoria Times Colonist, December 19, 2007, page B1.

3127 Cleve Dheenshaw, "S-Kings' rally falls short," Victoria Times Colonist, December 20, 2007, page B5.

3128 Cleve Dheenshaw, "Salmon Kings put Alaska on ice," Victoria Times Colonist, December 22, 2007, page A19.

3129 Cleve Dheenshaw, "Aces trump S-Kings in shootout," Victoria Times Colonist, December 23, 2007, page B3.

3130 Cleve Dheenshaw, "Salmon Kings muffle Thunder," Victoria Times Colonist, December 29, 2007, page C15.

3131 Cleve Dheenshaw, "S-Kings fight for OT win," Victoria Times Colonist, December 30, 2007, page C11.

3132 Sharie Epp, "Outgunned Salmon Kings come up short against Falcons," Victoria Times Colonist, December 31, 2007, page D1.

3133 Ron Rauch, "ECHL hands all-star reins to S-Kings coach," Victoria Times Colonist, January 2, 2008, page B6.

3134 Sharie Epp, "Salmon Kings continue their winning ways," Victoria Times Colonist, January 4, 2008, page B4.

3135 Cleve Dheenshaw, "Salmon Kings fall to Utah," Victoria Times Colonist, January 6, 2008, page B1.

3136 Cleve Dheenshaw, "Overtime haunts S-Kings again," Victoria Times Colonist, January 7, 2008, page B1.

3137 Cleve Dheenshaw, "S-Kings land former junior star," Victoria Times Colonist, January 8, 2008, page C5.

3138 Cleve Dheenshaw, "Wranglers tie S-Kings in knots," Victoria Times Colonist, January 12, 2008, page B11.

3139 Sharie Epp, "Salmon Kings' Ellis keeps Wranglers at bay," Victoria Times Colonist, January 123, 2008, page B1.

3140 Cleve Dheenshaw, "Salmon Kings feeling Canucks' pain," Victoria Times Colonist, January 14, 2008, page B1.

3141 Cleve Dheenshaw, "Lowly Condors take it to S-Kings," Victoria Times Colonist, January 16, 2008, page B1.

3142 Cleve Dheenshaw, "Estrada save days for S-Kings," Victoria Times Colonist, January 17, 2008, page B4.

3143 Cleve Dheenshaw, "Salmon kings clip Falcons' feathers," Victoria Times Colonist, January 19, 2008, page B15.

3144 Victoria Times Colonist, January 19, 2008, page B11.

3145 Cleve Dheenshaw, "Falcons edge salmon Kings in OT," Victoria Times Colonist, January 20, 2008, page B1.

3146 Cleve Dheenshaw, "S-Kings clip Falcons' wings," Victoria Times Colonist, January 21, 2008, page B1.

3147 Email dated January 24, 2008, from Salmon Kings.

3148 Cleve Dheenshaw, "Goldie brightest of stars," Victoria Times Colonist, January 24, 2008, page B6.

3149 Cleve Dheenshaw, "Balance shifting in western rivalry," Victoria Times Colonist, January 26, 2008, page B12.

3150 Cleve Dheenshaw, "S-Kings find a spark," Victoria Times Colonist, January 27, 2008, page C8.

3151 https://www.echl.com/stats/daily-schedule/2007-11-29?league=1&season=45

3152 Cleve Dheenshaw, "Goldie does trick again," Victoria Times Colonist, January 28, 2008, page C3.

3153 Victoria Times Colonist, January 28, 2008, page C2.

3154 "ECHL honours Goldie," Victoria Times Colonist, January 31, 2008, page B4.

3155 Cleve Dheenshaw, "S-Kings rested, ready for stretch run," Victoria Times Colonist, February 5, 2008, page B5.

3156 Cleve Dheenshaw, "S-Kings shoot down 'Condors," Victoria Times Colonist, February 6, 2008, page B3.

3157 Cleve Dheenshaw, "S-Kings stay hot in California," Victoria Times Colonist, February 8, 2008, page B4.

3158 Cleve Dheenshaw, "Condors feast on tired S-Kings," Victoria Times Colonist, February 9, 2008, p page B16.

3159 Cleve Dheenshaw, "Falcons fend off Salmon Kings," Victoria Times Colonist, February 12, 1008, page B5.

3160 Brian Drewry, "Salmon Kings nip Falcons," Victoria Times Colonist, February 13, 2008, page B6.

3161 Cleve Dheenshaw, "S-Kings edge rivals in Vegas," Victoria Times Colonist, February 16, 2008, page B11.

3162 Cleve Dheenshaw, "S-Kings split series with Vegas," Victoria Times Colonist, February 17, 2008, page C1.

3163 Cleve Dheenshaw, "Salmon Kings ride into Phoenix in style," Victoria Times Colonist," February 18, 2008, page B1.

3164 Brian Drewry, "S-Kings' offence heats up," *Victoria Times Colonist*, February 19, 2008, page B5.

3165 Ron Rauch, "Playoff hockey here a bit early," *Victoria Times Colonist*, February 20, 2008, page B5.

3166 Sharie Epp, "Steelheads close the gap," *Victoria Times Colonist*, February 121, 2008, page B4.

3167 Sharie Epp, "Salmon Kings sink Idaho," *Victoria Times Colonist*, February 23, 2008, page B11.

3168 Sharie Epp, "Steelheads take rubber match," *Victoria Times Colonist*, February 24, 2008, page B1.

3169 Cleve Dheenshaw, "Captain leaves on winning note," *Victoria Times Colonist*, February 28, 2008, page B4.

3170 Cleve Dheenshaw, "Salmon Kings aim to step up in captain's absence," *Victoria Times Colonist*, February 29, 2008, page B5.

3171 Cleve Dheenshaw, "Last-second goal gives S-Kings a lift," *Victoria Times Colonist*, March 1, 2008, page B12.

3172 Cleve Dheenshaw, "Las Vegas comes up a winner," *Victoria Times Colonist*, March 2, 2008, page C1.

3173 Cleve Dheenshaw, "ECHL suspends S-Kings' forward, police investigating on-ice punch," *Victoria Times Colonist*, March 5, 2008, page B8.

3174 Cleve Dheenshaw, "S-Kings head north without Gomez," *Victoria Times Colonist*, March 7, 2008, page B9.

3175 Cleve Dheenshaw, "Aces trump Salmon Kings," *Victoria Times Colonist*, March 8, 2008, page B13.

3176 Cleve Dheenshaw, "Aces squeak by Salmon Kings once again," *Victoria Times Colonist*, March 9, 2008, page C3.

3177 Cleve Dheenshaw, "S-Kings save face in Alaska," *Victoria Times Colonist*, March 10, 2008, page B1.

3178 Cleve Dheenshaw, "S-Kings on tricky road to playoffs," *Victoria Times Colonist*, March 14, 2008, page B5.

3179 "Roadrunners leave S-Kings high and dry," *Victoria Times Colonist*, March 15, 2008, page B12.

3180 Brian Drewry, "S-Kings come up dry in desert," *Victoria Times Colonist*, March 17, 2008, page B1.

3181 Ron Rauch, "Turnaround time is now or S-Kings," *Victoria Times Colonist*, March 19, 2008, page B9.

3182 Ron Rauch, "S-Kings get their groove back," *Victoria Times Colonist*, March 20, 2008, page B9.

3183 Sharie Epp, "S-Kings take bite out of Utah," *Victoria Times Colonist*, March 22, 2008, page B6.

3184 Sharie Epp, "Salmon Kings pull off the sweep," *Victoria Times Colonist*, March 23, 2008, page C1.

3185 Email dated March 26, 2008, from Salmon Kings.

3186 Cleve Dheenshaw, "S-Kings road trip off to good start," *Victoria Times Colonist*, March 27, 2008, page B9.

3187 Cleve Dheenshaw, "Condors feast on Salmon Kings," *Victoria Times Colonist*, March 29, 2008, page B12.

3188 Cleve Dheenshaw, "Thunder nip S-Kings in shootout," *Victoria Times Colonist*, March 30, 2008, page C1.

3189 Cleve Dheenshaw, "S-Kings in epic battle for top spot in division," *Victoria Times Colonist*, March 31, 2008, page C1.

3190 Cleve Dheenshaw, "Salmon Kings come up short at wrong time," *Victoria Times Colonist*, April 3, 2008, page B7.

3191 https://lscluster.hockeytech.com/game_reports/official-game report.php?client_code=echl&game_id=5184&lang_id=1

3192 Cleve Dheenshaw, "Late-season slide must be halted," *Victoria Times Colonist*, April 4, 2008, page B9.

3193 Cleve Dheenshaw, "S-Kings deliver in high drama," *Victoria Times Colonist*, April 5, 2008, page B13.

3194 Cleve Dheenshaw, "Salmon Kings take Western Division title," *Victoria Times Colonist*, April 6, 2008, page C1.

3195 "Salmon Kings lose Game 1 in overtime," *Victoria Times Colonist*, April 11, 2008, page A1.

3196 Cleve Dheenshaw, "Condors clip S-Kings in OT," *Victoria Times Colonist*, Times Colonist, April 11, 2008, page B8.

3197 Cleve Dheenshaw, "S-Kings roar back even series," *Victoria Times Colonist*, April 13, 2008, page C3.

3198 "Salmon Kings win Game 3 in OT," *Victoria Times Colonist*, April 16, 2008, page A1.

3199 Cleve Dheenshaw, "Bernier gives Salmon Kings the edge," *Victoria Times Colonist*, April 16, 2008, page B7.

3200 Cleve Dheenshaw, "Salmon Kings in control on the road," *Victoria Times Colonist*, April 17, 2008, page B8.

3201 Cleve Dheenshaw, "Condors edge S-Kings, stave off elimination," *Victoria Times Colonist*, April 20, 2008, page C3.

3202 "Historic win sends Salmon Kings to next playoff round," *Victoria Times Colonist*, April 22, 2008, page A1.

3203 Cleve Dheenshaw, "Goldie's goal KOs Condors *Victoria Times Colonist*, April 22, 2008, page B9.

3204 Email dated April 23, 2008, from Salmon Kings.

3205 "Salmon Kings blanked in Game 1," *Victoria Times Colonist*, April 26, 2008, page A1.

3206 Sharie Epp, "Grizzlies rout Salmon Kings," *Victoria Times Colonist*, April 26, 2008, page B14.

3207 Sharie Epp, "Now, that's more like it," *Victoria Times Colonist*, April 28, 2008, page C1.

3208 *Email dated May 1, 2008, from Salmon Kings.*

3209 Sharie Epp, "Salmon Kings collapse," *Victoria Times Colonist*, May 2, 2008, page B4.

3210 Sharie Epp, "S-Kings play 'real well,' but Grizzlies finish on top," *Victoria Times Colonist*, May 4, 2008, page C1.

3211 Sharie Epp, "Grizzlies finish off S-Kings," *Victoria Times Colonist*, May 5, 2008.

3212 Sharie Epp, "S-Kings headed in right direction," *Victoria Times Colonist*, May 6, 2008, page B5.

3213 Cleve Dheenshaw, "Salmon Kings' brass will likely be busy," *Victoria Times Colonist*, May 6, 2008, page B5.

3214 *Email dated May 30, 2008, from Salmon Kings.*

3215 *Email dated June 23, 2008, from Salmon Kings.*

3216 *Email dated July 7, 2008, from the Salmon Kings.*

3217 *Emails dated July 24, 2008, July 28, 2008, July 31, 2008, and August 6, 2008, from the Salmon Kings.*

3218 "S-Kings beef up roster," *Victoria Times Colonist*, September 5, 2008, page B4.

3219 *Email dated September 9, 2008, from the Salmon Kings.*

3220 Cleve Dheenshaw, "Ellis injury has S-Kings scrambling," *Victoria Times Colonist*, September 18, 2005, page B8.

3221 "S-Kings assistant resigns," *Victoria Times Colonist*, September 8, 2008, page B1.

3222 Cleve Dheenshaw, "Wade trades skates for clipboard," *Victoria Times Colonist*, September 12, 2008, page B4.

3223 *Email dated September 26, 2008, from the Salmon Kings.*

3224 Cleve Dheenshaw, "Salmon Kings' roster taking shape," *Victoria Times Colonist*, September 29, 2008, page B3.

3225 Cleve Dheenshaw, "Benn comes full circle as Moose send him to Salmon Kings," *Victoria Times Colonist*, October 2, 2008, page B6.

3226 Cleve Dheenshaw, "Can Salmon Kings take the next step?" *Victoria Times Colonist*, October 3, 2008, page B7.

3227 Cleeve Dheenshaw, "Moose send familiar foe S-Kings' way," *Victoria Times Colonist*, October 8, 2008, page B9.

3228 Cleve Dheenshaw, "S-Kings win first exhibition contest," *Victoria Times Colonist*, October 11, 2008, page B13.

3229 Cleve Dheenshaw, "S-Kings perfect in preseason," *Victoria Times Colonist*, October 12, 2008, page B1.

3230 Cleve Dheenshaw, "Decision day is here for Salmon Kings," *Victoria Times Colonist*, October 15, 2008, page C15.

3231 Cleve Dheenshaw, "These S-Kings pure Goldie," *Victoria Times Colonist*, October 16, 2008, page B9.

3232 Cleve Dheenshaw, "New Salmon King feels right at home," *Victoria Times Colonist*, October 17, 2008, page B6.

3233 Cleve Dheenshaw, "Phoenix runs over Salmon Kings," *Victoria Times Colonist*, October 18, 2008, page B12.

3234 Cleve Dheenshaw, "Roadrunners sneak by S-Kings," *Victoria Times Colonist*,

3235 Cleve Dheenshaw, "Salmon Kings save best for last," *Victoria Times Colonist*, October 20, 2008, page B1.

3236 Cleve Dheenshaw, "S-Kings get some homegrown talent," *Victoria Times Colonist*, October 21, 2008, page C1.

3237 Cleve Dheenshaw, "Salmon Kings welcome familiar face," *Victoria Times Colonist*, October 22, 2008, page B7.

3238 Cleve Dheenshaw, "Thunder rolls over Salmon Kings," *Victoria Times Colonist*, October 25, 2008, page B13.

3239 Cleve Dheenshaw, "Rookies show they're pros," *Victoria Times Colonist*, October 26, 2008, page B1.

3240 Cleve Dheenshaw, "Thunder rock Salmon Kings again" *Victoria Times Colonist*, October 27, 2008, page B1.

3241 Cleve Dheenshaw, "Labelle burns old 'mates," *Victoria Times Colonist*, October 30, 2008, page B9.

3242 Cleve Dheenshaw, "Salmon Kings still waiting to fulfil potential," *Victoria Times Colonist*, October 31, 2008, page B7.

3243 Cleve Dheenshaw, "Grizzlies take a bite out of Salmon Kings," *Victoria Times Colonist*, November 1, 2008, page B13.

3244 Cleve Dheenshaw, "Salmon Kings drop another one," *Victoria Times Colonist*, November 3, 2008, page C1.

3245 "ECHL investigating after S-King kicked in face," *Victoria Times Colonist*, November 4, 2008, page A1.

3246 Cleve Dheenshaw, "League set to rule on kick to face," *Victoria Times Colonist*, November 4, 2008, page C1.

3247 "Nine-game suspension for kicking incident," *Victoria Times Colonist*, November 6, 2008, age B7.

3248 *Cleve Dheenshaw, "Salmon Kings get early wake-up call," Victoria Times Colonist, November 5, 2008, page B8.*

3249 *Cleve Dheenshaw, "Boutin slams door on Condors Victoria Times Colonist, November 6, 2008, age B7.*

3250 *Cleve Dheenshaw, "Salmon Kings; newcomer happy to help out," Victoria Times Colonist, November 7, 2008, page B7.*

3251 *Cleve Dheenshaw, "Stockton nips S-Kings in shootout," Victoria Times Colonist, November 8, 2008, page B13.*

3252 *Cleve Dheenshaw, "S-Kings hold Thunder at bay," Victoria Times Colonist, November 9, 2008, page B1.*

3253 *Cleve Dheenshaw, "S-Kings find their powerplay," Victoria Times Colonist, November 15, 2008, page B13.*

3254 *Cleve Dheenshaw, "Salmon Kings blank Phoenix Victoria Times Colonist, November 16. 2008, page B1.*

3255 *Email dated November 19, 2008, from Salmon Kings.*

3256 *Cleve Dheenshaw, "Aces cool off Salmon Kings," Victoria Times Colonist, November 20, 2008, page B9.*

3257 *Cleve Dheenshaw, "League-leading Aces fall to Salmon Kings," Victoria Times Colonist, November 22, 2008, page B15.*

3258 *Cleve Dheenshaw, "Penalty calls leave S-Kings in the lurch," Victoria Times Colonist, November 23, 2008, page B1.*

3259 *Cleve Dheenshaw, "Salmon Kings' goalie gets Moose call thanks to Luongo injury," Victoria Times Colonist, November 24, 2008, page B1.*

3260 *Cleve Dheenshaw, "S-Kings get Ellis back in nick of time," Victoria Times Colonist, November 25, 2008, page B5.*

3261 *Cleve Dheenshaw, "Labelle summoned by Moose," Victoria Times Colonist, November 26, 2008, page D1.*

3262 *Email dated November 26, 2008, from the Salmon Kings.*

3263 *Cleve Dheenshaw, "S-Kings start road trip on high note," Victoria Times Colonist, November 27, 2008, page B7.*

3264 *Cleve Dheenshaw, "Salmon Kings nip Utah in OT," Victoria Times Colonist, November 29, 2008, page B1.*

3265 *Cleve Dheenshaw, "Goldie, Ellis lead S-Kings to win in Utah," Victoria Times Colonist, November 30, 2008, page B1.*

3266 *Cleve Dheenshaw, "Salmon Kings' captain in high gear again," Victoria Times Colonist, December 3, 2008, page B7.*

3267 *Cleve Dheenshaw, "S-Kings can't take the Reign," Victoria Times Colonist, December 4, 2008, page B9.*

3268 *Cleve Dheenshaw, "S-Kings feeling at home on the road," Victoria Times Colonist, December 5, 2008, page B5.*

3269 *Ron Rauch, "Salmon Kings fall short in Fresno, Victoria Times Colonist, December 6, 2018, page B13.*

3270 *Ron Rauch, "Salmon Kings snap two-game losing streak," Victoria Times Colonist, December 7, 2008, page B1.*

3271 *Cleve Dheenshaw, "Salmon Kings pour it on against Reign," Victoria Times Colonist, December 8, 2008, page B1.*

3272 *Cleve Dheenshaw, "Ellis slams door on CondorsError! Bookmark not defined.," Victoria Times Colonist, December 10, 1008, page D1.*

3273 *Cleve Dheenshaw, "S-Kings flatten Roadrunners," Victoria Times Colonist, December 13, 2008, page B13.*

3274 *Cleve Dheenshaw, "Goldie tosses hat-trick at Roadrunners," Victoria Times Colonist, December 15, 2008, page B1.*

3275 *Cleve Dheenshaw, "Revolving goalie door swings open again," Victoria Times Colonist, Times Colonist, December 17, 2008, page B7.*

3276 *Cleve Dheenshaw, "Goldie at it again: Strikes down Aces," Victoria Times Colonist, December 18, 1008, page B9.*

3277 *Cleve Dheenshaw, "Salmon Kings trump Aces," Victoria Times Colonist, December 20, 2008, page B12.*

3278 *Cleve Dheenshaw, "Salmon Kings edge Aces," Victoria Times Colonist, December 21, 2008, page B1.*

3279 *Cleve Dheenshaw, "Mother Nature plays Scrooge with players' Christmas plans," Victoria Times Colonist, December 22, 2008, page B1.*

3280 *Cleve Dheenshaw, "Falcons fold as ECHL loses another team," Victoria Times Colonist, December 23, 2008, page B5.*

3281 *"S-Kings goalie takes weekly honours," Victoria Times Colonist, December 24, 2008, page D1.*

3282 *Ron Rauch, "Salmon Kings roll over Thunder," Victoria Times Colonist, December 28, 2008, page B1.*

3283 *Ron Rauch, "Beat goes on for red-hot Salmon Kings," Victoria Times Colonist, December 29, 2008, page B1.*

3284 Email dated December 30, 2008, from the Salmon Kings.

3285 "S-Kings win streak hits 11," *Victoria Times Colonist*, January 3, 2009, page A1.

3286 Ron Rauch, "S-Kings stretch streak," *Victoria Times Colonist*, January 3, 2009, page B10.

3287 Ron Rauch, "Home sweet home for Salmon Kings," *Victoria Times Colonist*, January 4, 2009, page C1.

3288 "Salmon Kings' win streak hits 13," *Victoria Times Colonist*, January 5, 2009, page A1.

3289 Email dated January 6, 2009, from the Salmon Kings.

3290 Cleve Dheenshaw, "Salmon Kings stretch win streak to 13," *Victoria Times Colonist*, January 5, 2009, page B1.

3291 Cleve Dheenshaw, "For S-Kings there's rest for the weary," *Victoria Times Colonist*, January 7, 2009, page B6.

3292 Email dated January 8, 2009, from Salmon Kings.

3293 Ron Rauch, "Salmon Kings winning streak hits 14," *Victoria Times Colonist*, January 10, 2009, page D1.

3294 Ron Rauch, "Salmon Kings Reign supreme," *Victoria Times Colonist*, January 11, 2009, page D1.

3295 Cleve Dheenshaw, "Streaking Salmon Kings take act to Alaska," *Victoria Times Colonist*, January 14, 2009, page B6.

3296 Cleve Dheenshaw, "Salmon Kings' win streak ends in Alaska," *Victoria Times Colonist*, January 15, 2009, page B8.

3297 Cleve Dheenshaw, "Salmon Kings' season 'a great ride so far'," *Victoria Times Colonist*, January 17, 2009, page B9.

3298 Cleve Dheenshaw, "S-Kings guard against complacency," *Victoria Times Colonist*, January 18, 2009, page B1.

3299 Cleve Dheenshaw, "Salmon Kings hit all-star break on top," *Victoria Times Colonist*, January 19, 2009, page B1.

3300 Cleve Dheenshaw, "Salmon Kings' Gendur, Yeo collect victories in skills competition," *Victoria Times Colonist*, January 21, 2009, page C13.

3301 Cleve Dheenshaw, "Run and gun and a lot of fun," *Victoria Times Colonist*, January 22, 2009, page B8.

3302 Cleve Dheenshaw, "S-Kings outlast Wranglers," *Victoria Times Colonist*, January 24, 2009, page B13.

3303 Cleve Dheenshaw, "S-Kings' O'Connor sparks win over Vegas," *Victoria Times Colonist*, January 25, 2009, page B1.

3304 Cleve Dheenshaw, "S-Kings' trip to Vegas ends on sour note," *Victoria Times Colonist*, January 26, 2009, page B1.

3305 Cleve Dheenshaw, "Familiar face returns to Salmon Kings," *Victoria Times Colonist*, January 27, 2009, page C1.

3306 Cleve Dheenshaw, "Salmon Kings' offence kicks it up a notch," *Victoria Times Colonist*, January 28, 2009, page B4.

3307 Cleve Dheenshaw, "Thunder strike proves lethal," *Victoria Times Colonist*, January 29, 2009, page B8.

3308 "Moose call up Yeo, Dietrich headed south," *Victoria Times Colonist*, February 2, 2009, page B2.

3309 Cleve Dheenshaw, "Familiar face back with Salmon Kings," *Victoria Times Colonist*, February 3, 2009, page B5.

3310 Cleve Dheenshaw, "No rest for S-Kings' defence," *Victoria Times Colonist*, February 4, 2009, page C1.

3311 Cleve Dheenshaw, "Comeback not in the cards," *Victoria Times Colonist*, February 5, 2009, page B8.

3312 Cleve Dheenshaw, "Wranglers stump Salmon Kings," *Victoria Times Colonist*, February 7, 2009, page B10.s

3313 Cleve Dheenshaw, "Salmon Kings lose fourth straight," *Victoria Times Colonist*, February 8, 2009, page D1.

3314 Cleve Dheenshaw, "Vegas leaves town with four-game sweep," *Victoria Times Colonist*, February 9, 2009, page B1.

3315 Cleve Dheenshaw, "S-Kings deal Gajic for defenceman," *Victoria Times Colonist*, February 11, 2009, page C1.

3316 Cleve Dheenshaw, "Aces edge Salmon Kings," *Victoria Times Colonist*, February 12, 2009, page C3.

3317 Cleve Dheenshaw, "Help on way for Salmon Kings' blue-line," *Victoria Times Colonist*, February 13, 2009, page B7.

3318 Cleve Dheenshaw, "S-Kings' road tip bound to take toll," *Victoria Times Colonist*, February 14, 2009. Page B11.

3319 Cleve Dheenshaw, "Aces edge S-Kings in shootout," *Victoria Times Colonist*, February 15, 2009, page B1.

3320 Sharie Epp, "Aces blitz Salmon Kings to close gap," *Victoria Times Colonist*, February 16, 2009, page B1.

3321 Ron Rauch, "Reign hold off S-Kings," *Victoria Times Colonist*, February 19, 2009, page B9.

3322 "Salmon Kings lose blue-liner to Moose," *Victoria Times Colonist*, February 21, 2009, page B11.

3323 Brian Drewry, "Salmon Kings edge Condors in shootout," *Victoria Times Colonist*, February 22, 2009. Page D3.

3324 Cleve Dheenshaw, "Derlago paces condors past Salmon Kings," *Victoria Times Colonist*, February 23, 2009, page B2.

3325 Cleve Dheenshaw, "S-Kings' road woes continue in Ontario," *Victoria Times Colonist*, February 24, 2009, page C4.

3326 Cleve Dheenshaw, "Salmon Kings' Gendur gets another shot with the Moose," *Victoria Times Colonist*, February 28, 2009, page B9.

3327 Cleve Dheenshaw, "Salmon Kings in unfamiliar territory," *Victoria Times Colonist*, March 4, 2009, page B7.

3328 Cleve Dheenshaw, "Fluke goal does in Salmon Kings," *Victoria Times Colonist*, March 5, 2009, page B9.

3329 Cleve Dheenshaw, "Salmon Kings lead early, then fall late," *Victoria Times Colonist*, March 7, 2009, page B9.

3330 Cleve Dheenshaw, "S-Kings road woes ongoing," *Victoria Times Colonist*, March 8, 2009, page A10.

3331 Cleve Dheenshaw, "S-Kings aim to turn it around at home," *Victoria Times Colonist*, March 11, 2009, page B8.

3332 Cleve Dheenshaw, "S-Kings return with a bang," *Victoria Times Colonist*, March 12, 2009, page B7.

3333 Cleve Dheenshaw, "Ontario nips Salmon Kings," *Victoria Times Colonist*, March 14, 2009, page B10.

3334 Cleve Dheenshaw, "Salmon Kings rally in shootout," *Victoria Times Colonist*, March 15, 2009, page B1.

3335 Cleve Dheenshaw, "Leavold leads the way for Salmon Kings," *Victoria Times Colonist*, March 16, 2009, page B1.

3336 Cleve Dheenshaw, "Still no solving Steelheads," *Victoria Times Colonist*, March 19, 2009, page B9.

3337 Cleve Dheenshaw, "S-Kings nip feisty Steelheads," *Victoria Times Colonist*, March 21, 2009, page B12.

3338 Cleve Dheenshaw, "Steelheads feast on Salmon Kings," *Victoria Times Colonist*, March 22, 2009, page C1.

3339 "Home stand ends on sour note for S-Kings," *Victoria Times Colonist*, March 23, 2009, page A1.

3340 Cleve Dheenshaw, "S-Kings can't solve Steelheads," *Victoria Times Colonist*, March 23, 2009, page B1.

3341 Cleve Dheenshaw, "Fans come through again for S-Kings," *Victoria Times Colonist*, March 24, 2009, page B5.

3342 Cleve Dheenshaw, "S-Kings stick it to Thunder," *Victoria Times Colonist*, March 25, 2009, page D1.

3343 Cleve Dheenshaw, "Salmon Kings stay red-hot in California," *Victoria Times Colonist*, March 26, 2009, page B9.

3344 Cleve Dheenshaw, "Condors glide over S-Kings," *Victoria Times Colonist*, March 28, 2009, page B10.

3345 Cleve Dheenshaw, "S-Kings head into playoffs on a high," *Victoria Times Colonist*, March 29, 2009, page C1.

3346 Cleve Dheenshaw, "Sit and wait time for the Salmon Kings," *Victoria Times Colonist*, March 30, 2009, page B3.

3347 Cleve Dheenshaw, "ECHL loses more teams, but gains one," *Victoria Times Colonist*, March 31, 2009 page B5.

3348 Cleve Dheenshaw, "Yeo makes S-Kings' history with first-team all-star nod," *Victoria Times Colonist*, April 3, 2009, page B6.

3349 Cleve Dheenshaw, "S-Kings start playoff run against Steelheads," *Victoria Times Colonist*, April 5, 2009, page D1.

3350 Cleve Dheenshaw, "Yeo named league's top defenceman," *Victoria Times Colonist*, April 8, 2009, page B6.

3351 Cleve Dheenshaw, "S-Kings in quest of road win," *Victoria Times Colonist*, April 11, 2009, page B10.

3352 Cleve Dheenshaw, "S-Kings playoff run off to strong start," *Victoria Times Colonist*, April 12, 2009, page C1.

3353 Cleve Dheenshaw, "Ford in high gear for S-Kings," *Victoria Times Colonist*, April 13, 2009, page B1.

3354 Cleve Dheenshaw, "S-Kings blitz Steelheads," *Victoria Times Colonist*, April 16, 2009, page B10.

3355 Cleve Dheenshaw, "S-Kings sweep Steelheads," *Victoria Times Colonist*, April 18, 2009, page B12.

3356 Cleve Dheenshaw, "S-Kings' grit too much for Idaho," *Victoria Times Colonist*, April 19, 2009, page C2.

3357 Cleve Dheenshaw, "S-Kings dig themselves a hole," *Victoria Times Colonist*, April 24, 2009, page B11.

3358 Cleve Dheenshaw, "Alaska taking control," *Victoria Times Colonist*, April 26, 2009, page B2.

3359 Cleve Dheenshaw, "Series far from over, Salmon Kings insist," *Victoria Times Colonist*, April 27, 2009, page C8.

3360 Cleve Dheenshaw, "Late collapse leaves S-Kings in a big hole," *Victoria Times Colonist*, April 30, 2009, page B8.

3361 Cleve Dheenshaw, Season now on line for Salmon Kings," *Victoria Times Colonist*, May 1, 2009, page B7.

3362 Cleve Dheenshaw, "S-Kings season not done yet," *Victoria Times Colonist*, May 2, 2009, page B12.

3363 Cleve Dheenshaw, "Aces deliver knockout blow to S-Kings," *Victoria Times Colonist*, May 3, 2009, page C11.

3364 Cleve Dheenshaw, "Once again Salmon Kings were close, but not close enough," *Victoria Times Colonist*, May 4, 2009, page B3.

3365 Email dated July 9, 2009, from the Salmon Kings.

3366 Email dated July 17, 2009, from the Salmon Kings.

3367 Email dated August 11, 2009, from the Salmon Kings.

3368 Email dated August 19, 2009, from the Salmon Kings.

3369 Email dated August 31, 2009, from the Salmon Kings.

3370 Cleve Dheenshaw, "Salmon Kings opt for no pre-season games," *Victoria Times Colonist*, September 4, 2009, page B5.

3371 Cleve Dheenshaw, "Talented Tifu comes west to Salmon Kings," *Victoria Times Colonist*, September 16, 2009. Page D1.

3372 Cleve Dheenshaw, "Coulombe comes back to Salmon Kings," *Victoria Times Colonist*, September 17, 2009, page B9.

3373 "Salmon Kings bring aboard former Kelly Cup champion Deleurme," *Victoria Times Colonist*, September 19, 2009, page B12.

3374 Cleve Dheenshaw, "S-Kings grab former Condor," *Victoria Times Colonist*, September 23, 2009, page C13.

3375 Cleve Dheenshaw, "S-Kings land all-star goalie," *Victoria Times Colonist*, Sept3ember 25, 2009, page C9.

3376 Cleve Dheenshaw, "Canucks send Ellington to Salmon Kings," *Victoria Times Colonist*, September 29, 2009, page B7.

3377 Cleve Dheenshaw, "Decisions, decisions, decisions," *Victoria Times Colonist*, October 3, 2009, page B11.

3378 Email dated October 6, 2009, from the Salmon Kings.

3379 Ron Rauch, "Goaltenders shine bright as Blue outduels White," *Victoria Times Colonist*, October 10, 2009, page B11.

3380 Cleve Dheenshaw, "Warrior from 'Q' joins S-Kings," *Victoria Times Colonist*, October 14, 2009, page B9.

3381 Cleve Dheenshaw, "Talented S-Kings hit road," *Victoria Times Colonist*, October 16, 2009, page C1.

3382 Cleve Dheenshaw, "S-Kings open season in Alaska," *Victoria Times Colonist*, October 17, 2009, page B11.

3383 Cleve Dheenshaw, "S-Kings fall to Alaska," *Victoria Times Colonist*, October 18, 2009, page B1.

3384 Cleve Dheenshaw, "Aces keep Salmon Kings winless on road," *Victoria Times Colonist*, October 20, 2009, page C1.

3385 Cleve Dheenshaw, "S-Kings back home looking for offence," *Victoria Times Colonist*, October 21, 2009, page B9.

3386 "Salmon Kings sink in home opener," *Victoria Times Colonist*, October 22, 2009, page A1.

3387 Cleve Dheenshaw, "Condorsspoil the party at S-Kings' home opener," *Victoria Times Colonist*, October 22, 2009, page C1.

3388 Cleve Dheenshaw, "Fisher saves day for S-Kings," *Victoria Times Colonist*, October 24, 2009, page B11.

3389 Cleve Dheenshaw, "'Big mistakes' cost S-Kings," *Victoria Times Colonist*, October 25, 2009, page B1.

3390 Cleve Dheenshaw"Salmon Kings' coach promises changes," *Victoria Times Colonist*, October 27, 2009, page B6.

3391 http://www.sihrhockey.org/member_player_sheet.cfm?player_id=47605&mode=0

3392 Cleve Dheenshaw, "Tifu exits as Salmon Kings make changes," *Victoria Times Colonist*, October 28, 2009, page B8.

3393 Cleve Dheenshaw, "Thunder storm Salmon Kings in the third," *Victoria Times Colonist*, October 31, 2009, page B11.

3394 Cleve Dheenshaw, "Moose call on S-Kings' forward," *Victoria Times Colonist*, November 2, 2009, page B5.

3395 Cleve Dheenshaw, "Salmon Kings aim to stop the Reign," *Victoria Times Colonist*, November 6, 2009, page B5.

3396 Cleve Dheenshaw, "S-Kings fail to keep Reign away," *Victoria Times Colonist*, November 7, 2009, page B10.

3397 Cleve Dheenshaw, "S-Kings still believe," *Victoria Times Colonist*, November 8, 2009, page B1.

3398 Cleve Dheenshaw, "Gendur gone as S-Kings shake it up," *Victoria Times Colonist*, November 11, 2009, page D1.

3399 Cleve Dheenshaw, "Keetley saves the day for s-Kings," *Victoria Times Colonist*, November 12, 2009, page B1.

3400 Cleve Dheenshaw, "S-Kings can't overcome Reign," *Victoria Times Colonist*, November 124, 2009, page B9.

3401 Cleve Dheenshaw, "S-Kings shut out Reign," *Victoria Times Colonist*, November 15, 2009, page B1.

3402 Cleve Dheenshaw, "Tough task ahead for Salmon Kings," *Victoria Times Colonist*, November 18, 2009, page B6.

3403 Cleve Dheenshaw, "Salmon Kings stick it to Steelheads again," *Victoria Times Colonist*, November 19, 2009, page B1.

3404 Cleve Dheenshaw, "Struggling S-Kings blanked by Steelheads," *Victoria Times Colonist*, November 21, 2009 page B12.

3405 Cleve Dheenshaw, "S-Kings lose battle in overtime," *Victoria Times Colonist*, November 22, 2009, page C1.

3406 Cleve Dheenshaw, "WHL stars keep Russians winless," *Victoria Times Colonist*, November 26, 2009 page B1.

3407 Ron Rauch, "It's unanimous, Victoria wants WHL back," *Victoria Times Colonist*, November 26, 2009, page B1.

3408 Cleve Dheenshaw, "Moose call on Ellington," *Victoria Times Colonist*, November 27, 2009, page C1.

3409 Cleve Dheenshaw, "Salmon Kings rally back for win," *Victoria Times Colonist*, November 28, 2009, page B12.

3410 Cleve Dheenshaw, "S-Kings blank Reign," *Victoria Times Colonist*, November 29, 2009, page B1.

3411 Cleve Dheenshaw, "S-Kings aim to wrangle up a few wins," *Victoria Times Colonist*, December 1, 2009, page B5.

3412 Cleve Dheenshaw, "S-Kings let one slip away," *Victoria Times Colonist*, December 2, 2009, page B6.

3413 Cleve Dheenshaw, "Salmon Kings given boost with Ellington's return," *Victoria Times Colonist*, December 3, 2009, page B1.

3414 Cleeve Dheenshaw, "Wranglers outgun Salmon Kings," *Victoria Times Colonist*, December 4, 2009, page B6.

3415 Ron Rauch, "Wranglers clip S-Kings yet again," *Victoria Times Colonist*, December 5, 2009, page B11.

3416 Brian Drewry, "Salmon Kings get point: wins needed," *Victoria Times Colonist*, December 8, 2009, page C1.

3417 Cleve Dheenshaw, "Leavold back in the fold," *Victoria Times Colonist*, December 10, 2009, page B1.

3418 Sharie Epp, "Finally, Salmon Kings snap out of it," *Victoria Times Colonist*, December 11, 2009, page B8.

3419 Cleve Dheenshaw, "Captain Goldie leads way," *Victoria Times Colonist*, December 12, 2009, page B12.

3420 Cleve Dheenshaw, "Salmon Kings put on show in front of Canucks' brass," *Victoria Times Colonist*, December 17, 2009, page B1.

3421 Cleve Dheenshaw, "Salmon Kings' top guns find their mark," *Victoria Times Colonist*, December 18, 2009, page B6.

3422 Cleve Dheenshaw, "Rumour of AHL moving west heats up again," *Victoria Times Colonist*, December 18, 2009, page B6.

3423 Cleve Dheenshaw, "Salmon Kings stay red-hot at home," *Victoria Times Colonist*, December 19, 2009, page B11.

3424 Cleve Dheenshaw, "S-Kings edge Thunder," *Victoria Times Colonist*, December 20, 2009, page B1.

3425 Cleve Dheenshaw, "S-Kings goalie wins weekly honour," *Victoria Times Colonist*, December 23, 2009, page D1.

3426 Cleve Dheenshaw, "Attendance woes hit Salmon Kings," *Victoria Times Colonist*, December 24, 2009, page B1.

3427 *Victoria Times Colonist*, December 24, 3009, page B2.

3428 Gamesheet for ECHL game #290, December 27, 2009.

3429 Cleve Dheenshaw, "Beat goes on: Salmon Kings trump Aces," *Victoria Times Colonist*, December 29, 2009, page B4.

3430 Cleve Dheenshaw, "Salmon Kings sizzle even on the road," *Victoria Times Colonist*, December 31, 2009, page B1.

3431 Cleve Dheenshaw, "Streaking Salmon Kings take act north," *Victoria Times Colonist*, January 2, 2010, page B11.

3432 Cleve Dheenshaw, "Streak goes on as S-Kings bake Alaska," *Victoria Times Colonist*, January 3, 2010, page B1.

3433 Cleve Dheenshaw, "Salmon Kings brimming with confidence," *Victoria Times Colonist*, January 5, 2010, page C1.

3434 Cleve Dheenshaw, "Aces strike early, cool off Salmon Kings," *Victoria Times Colonist*, January 5, 2010, page C1.

3435 Cleve Dheenshaw, "S-Kings goalie takes weekly honour," *Victoria Times Colonist*, January 8, 2010, page B1.

3436 Cleve Dheenshaw, "New face in lineup as S-Kings return home," *Victoria Times Colonist*, January 8, 2010, page C1.

3437   Cleve Dheenshaw, "Goldie does the trick again," *Victoria Times Colonist*, January 9, 2010, page B1.

3438   Cleve Dheenshaw, "S-Kings see streak snapped," *Victoria Times Colonist*, January 10, 2010, page B1.

3439   Media Advisory, "Salmon Kings Ink D-man Andy Rogers," January 11, 2010.

3440   Media Advisory, "Salmon Kings edge Wranglers," January 12, 2010.

3441   Media Advisory, "Salmon Kings' Sharrow returns from Moose," January 3, 2010.

3442   Cleve Dheenshaw, "S-Kings save best for last," *Victoria Times Colonist*, January 14, 2010, page B1.

3443   Cleve Dheenshaw, "Everything is just ducky with Condors *Victoria Times Colonist*, January 25, 2010, page B6.

3444   Cleve Dheenshaw, "Early burst lifts S-Kings to victory," *Victoria Times Colonist*, January 16, 2010, page B11.

3445   Sharie Epp, "S-Kings rejuvenated for second-half run," *Victoria Times Colonist*, December 28, 2010, page B1.

3446   Cleve Dheenshaw, "Salmon Kings hoping for more January fireworks," *Victoria Times Colonist*, January 5, 2011, page B5.

3447   Media Advisory, "Salmon Kings to auction off commemorative pink in the rink jerseys," January 13, 2010.

3448   Cleve Dheenshaw, "Snipers secure S-Kings win," *Victoria Times Colonist*, January 17, 2010, page C1.

3449   "Salmon Kings help raise over $28,000 for British Columbia Cancer Foundation," Media Advisory dated February 10, 2010.

3450   "Salmon Kings' Shantz and Ellington help National Conference to skills competition victory," Media Advisory, January 19, 2010.

3451   "Salmon Kings' goal featured throughout the world of sports," Media Advisory dated January 18, 2010.

3452   "Salmon Kings enter second half of season on the upswing," Media Advisory dated January 21, 2010.

3453   "Salmon Kings' Wedderburn and Brandt return from loan," Media Advisory dated January 18, 2010.

3454   Cleve Dheenshaw, "Late rally helps Condors clip S-Kings," *Victoria Times Colonist*, January 23, 2010, page B14.

3455   "Salmon Kings' Painchaud loaned to Moose," Media Advisory January 23, 2010.

3456   Cleve Dheenshaw, "Shantz big factor in S-Kings win," *Victoria Times Colonist*, January 24, 2010, page C9.

3457   Cleve Dheenshaw, "Surging Thunder cool off Salmon Kings," *Victoria Times Colonist*, January 28, 2010, page C1.

3458   "Salmon Kings endure whirlwind Thursday," Media Advisory dated January 28, 2010.

3459   "Salmon Kings' Petruic loaned to Binghamton," Media Advisory dated January 28, 2010.

3460   Cleve Dheenshaw, "Thunder rock depleted Salmon Kings," *Victoria Times Colonist*, January 30, 2010, page B12.

3461   Cleve Dheenshaw, "S-Kings win epic shootout," *Victoria Times Colonist*, January 31, 2010, page C1.

3462   Cleve Dheenshaw, "Help is on the way for S-Kings," *Victoria Times Colonist*, February 3, 2010, page B6.

3463   Cleve Dheenshaw, "Shootout goes S-Kings' way," *Victoria Times Colonist*, February 4, 2010, page B1.

3464   Cleve Dheenshaw, "Salmon Kings can't fend off Grizzlies," *Victoria Times Colonist*, February 6, 2010, page 2010.

3465   Cleve Dheenshaw, "Salmon Kings take extra point from Utah," *Victoria Times Colonist*, February 7, 2010, page B1.

3466   "Moose send Ellington back to Salmon Kings," *Victoria Times Colonist*, February 10, 2010, page B7.

3467   Cleve Dheenshaw, "S-Kings short-staffed but read for surging Aces," *Victoria Times Colonist*, February 11, 2010, page B1.

3468   Cleve Dheenshaw, "Another Goldie night in Victoria," *Victoria Times Colonist*, February 12, 2010, page C3.

3469   Cleve Dheenshaw, "Alaska comes up Aces," *Victoria Times Colonist*, February 14, 2010, page C3.

3470   Cleve Dheenshaw, "S-Kings hit road on right foot," *Victoria Times Colonist*, February 1, 2010, page B3.

3471   Cleve Dheenshaw, "Surging Grizzlies clip S-Kings," *Victoria Times Colonist*, February 18, 2010, page B3.

3472   "Salmon Kings' Sharrow loaned to Rampage," Media Advisory dated February 19, 2010.

3473   "Salmon Kings acquire d-man Davey," Media Advisory dated February 19, 2010.

3474   "Salmon Kings assigned Bryan Leitch," Media Advisory dated February 19, 2010.

3475   Sharie Epp, "Taylor hat trick lifts travellin' Salmon Kings past Utah," *Victoria Times Colonist*, February 20, 2010, page B3.

3476 Cleve Dheenshaw, "Utah rebounds to shade S-Kings," Victoria Times Colonist, February 21, 2010, page C3.

3477 Cleve Dheenshaw, "Late rally not enough for S-Kings," Victoria Times Colonist, February 27, 2010, page B3.

3478 Cleve Dheenshaw, "Condors silence S-Kings in Bakersfield," Victoria Times Colonist, February 28, 2010, page B3.

3479 Cleve Dheenshaw, "Thunder strike down S-Kings," Victoria Times Colonist, March 4, 2010, page B5.

3480 Cleve Dheenshaw, "S-Kings running on fumes," Victoria Times Colonist, March 5, 2010, page B5.

3481 "Salmon Kings' loan Brandy to Moose," Media Advisory dated March 5, 2010.

3482 Cleve Dheenshaw, "Depleted Salmon Kings survive Thunder," Victoria Times Colonist, March 6, 2010, page B1.

3483 Cleve Dheenshaw, "Thunder in charge as S-Kings wrap road trip," Victoria Times Colonist, March 7, 2010, page B1.

3484 Cleve Dheenshaw, "Goalie lineup changes again," Victoria Times Colonist, March 10, 2010, page C1.

3485 Cleve Dheenshaw, "Salmon Kings let one slip away," Victoria Times Colonist, March 11, 2010, page B1.

3486 "Salmon Kings sign forward Jeff Lynch," Media Advisory dated March 12, 2010.

3487 Cleve Dheenshaw, "Steelheads too much for Salmon Kings," Victoria Times Colonist, March 13, 2010, page B9.

3488 Cleve Dheenshaw, "Idaho keeps up heat," Victoria Times Colonist, March 14, 2010, page B1.

3489 Cleve Dheenshaw, "Salmon Kings add speedy U.S college star," Victoria Times Colonist, March 17, 2010, page B6.

3490 Cleve Dheenshaw, "S-Kings' struggles continue on road," Victoria Times Colonist, March 18, 2010, page B1.

3491 Cleve Dheenshaw, "S-Kings halt skid against Condors Victoria Times Colonist, March 20, 2010, page B11.

3492 Cleve Dheenshaw, "Late rally not enough for Salmon Kings," Victoria Times Colonist, March 21, 2010, page C1.

3493 Cleve Dheenshaw, "Salmon Kings are nearing must-win time," Victoria Times Colonist, March 24, 2010, page B7.

3494 Cleve Dheenshaw, "S-Kings fading at wrong time," Victoria Times Colonist, March 25, 2010, page B1.

3495 "Salmon Kings sign d-man Bezzo to ATO," Media Advisory dated March 25, 2010.

3496 "Salmon Kings' Brandt returns from Moose," Media Advisory dated March 25, 2010.

3497 Cleve Dheenshaw, "Fisher slams door on Steelheads," Victoria Times Colonist, March 27, 2010, page B11.

3498 Cleve Dheenshaw, "S-Kings' run for playoff spot hits snag," Victoria Times Colonist, March 28, 2010, page B1.

3499 "Salmon Kings' Ellington re-assigned to Moose," Media Advisory dated March 29, 2010.

3500 "Salmon Kings ink d-man David Cianfrini," Victoria Times Colonist, Media Advisory dated March 30, 2010.

3501 Cleve Dheenshaw, "Salmon Kings have little room for error," Victoria Times Colonist, March 31, 2010, page B9.

3502 "Salmon Kings get Ellington back from Moose," Media Advisory dated March 31, 2010.

3503 Cleve Dheenshaw, "S-Kings playoff hopes take a hit," Victoria Times Colonist, April 1, 2010, page B1.

3504 "Salmon Kings' Ellington rejoins Moose," Media Advisory dated April 1, 2010.

3505 "Salmon Kings sign forward Jason Bast," Media Advisory dated April 3, 2010.

3506 "Salmon Kings' Sharrow named to all-ECHL team," Media Advisory dated April 1, 2010.

3507 Sharie Epp, "S-Kings punch ticket to playoffs," Victoria Times Colonist, April 3, 2010, page B9.

3508 "Salmon Kings host 'Sellout Saturday,' tickets as low as $5!!!" Media Advisory dated March 23, 2010.

3509 Sharie Epp, "S-Kings drop finale; cue the playoffs," Victoria Times Colonist, April 4, 2010, page C1.

3510 Cleve Dheenshaw, "Condors load up for battle with Salmon Kings," Victoria Times Colonist, April 6, 2010, page C1.

3511 Cleve Dheenshaw, "Advantage Salmon Kings," Victoria Times Colonist, April 8, 2010, page B1.

3512 Cleve Dheenshaw, "Calder gives Condors upper hand," Victoria Times Colonist, April 9, 2010, page C1.

3513 Cleve Dheenshaw, "S-Kings fend off Condors Victoria Times Colonist, April 11, 2010, page B1.

3514 "Salmon Kings drop game 4," Media Advisory dated April 11, 2010.

3515 "Salmon Kings bumped from playoffs," *Victoria Times Colonist*, April 13, 2010, page A1.

3516 Cleve Dheenshaw, "Heartbreak down in Bakersfield," *Victoria Times Colonist*, April 13, 2010, page C1.

3517 Cleve Dheenshaw, "Up-and-down season tough to take for Salmon Kings," *Victoria Times Colonist*, April 14, 2010, page B6.

3518 Cleve Dheenshaw, "Canucks ship Island prospect to Salmon Kings," *Victoria Times Colonist*, September 17, 2010, page C3.

3519 "Salmon Kings gear up for training camp and pair of exhibitions against UBC," *Victoria Times Colonist*, September 24, 2010, page C1.

3520 Sharie Epp, "S-Kings bolster blue-line," *Victoria Times Colonist*, October 2, 2010, page B9.

3521 Ron Rauch, "S-Kings coach likes what he sees in training," *Victoria Times Colonist*, October 3, 2010, page B1.

3522 Sharie Epp, "Championship or bust for McLeod, Gajic," *Victoria Times Colonist*, October 5, 2010, page C1.

3523 Sharie Epp, "Cleaver aims to make the final cut," *Victoria Times Colonist*, October 6, 2010, page B6.

3524 Ron Rauch, "Hennigar the centre of attraction," *Victoria Times Colonist*, October 8, 2010, page C1.

3525 Ron Rauch, "Crunch time for S-Kings hopefuls," *Victoria Times Colonist*, October 9, 2010, page B9.

3526 Sharie Epp, "Salmon Kings show some fine form," *Victoria Times Colonist*, October 10, 2010, page C1.

3527 Sharie Epp, "S-Kings' new faces begin to gel," *Victoria Times Colonist*, October 12, 2010, page C1.

3528 Sharie Epp, "Milhouse proves he's ready for next step," *Victoria Times Colonist*, October 13, 2010, page B6.

3529 Sharie Epp, "New captain, new attitude for S-Kings," *Victoria Times Colonist*, October 15, 2010, page C1.

3530 Ron Rauch, "Opening night far from special for Salmon Kings," *Victoria Times Colonist*, October 16, 2010, page B11.

3531 Sharie Epp, "Salmon Kings rebound with shutout," *Victoria Times Colonist*, October 17, 2010, page C12.

3532 Cleve Dheenshaw, "Salmon Kings beef up as they get set to take on Wranglers in 'Vegas," *Victoria Times Colonist*, October 21, 2010, page B1.

3533 Cleeve Dheenshaw, "Gill states his case in S-Kings' net," *Victoria Times Colonist*, October 23, 2010, page B11.

3534 Cleve Dheenshaw, "Wranglers turn back S-Kings," *Victoria Times Colonist*, October 24, 2010, page B1.

3535 Cleve Dheenshaw, "Salmon Kings add Canucks' draft," *Victoria Times Colonist*, October 26, 2010, page C1.

3536 http://www.sihrhockey.org/member_player_sheet.cfm?player_id=44172

3537 Cleve Dheenshaw, "S-Kings stop the Reign," *Victoria Times Colonist*, October 28, 2010, page B1.

3538 Cleve Dheenshaw, "Streaking S-Kings put on a show," *Victoria Times Colonist*, October 30, 2010, page D1.

3539 Cleve Dheenshaw, "S-Kings show who rules," *Victoria Times Colonist*, October 31, 2010, page B1.

3540 Cleve Dheenshaw, "Soft seals deal for S-Kings," *Victoria Times Colonist*, November 4, 2010, page B1.

3541 Cleve Dheenshaw, "Victoria-born Irwin now a 'visitor'," *Victoria Times Colonist*, November 5, 2010, page C1.

3542 Cleve Dheenshaw, "Steelheads cool off S-Kings," *Victoria Times Colonist*, November 6, 2010, page B9.

3543 Cleve Dheenshaw, "Penalties take toll on S-Kings," *Victoria Times Colonist*, November 7. 2010, page B1.

3544 Cleve Dheenshaw, "Hockey fans staying away in droves," *Victoria Times Colonist*, November 9, 2010, page C1.

3545 Cleve Dheenshaw, "Salmon Kings have no luck in Las Vegas *Victoria Times Colonist*, November 12, 2010, page C1.

3546 Cleve Dheenshaw, "S-Kings' skid hits four games," *Victoria Times Colonist*, November 13, 2010, page B9.

3547 Cleve Dheenshaw, "Penalties costly as S-Kings' slide continues," *Victoria Times Colonist*, November 14, 20120, page B12.

3548 Cleve Dheenshaw, "Salmon Kings lose captain to suspension," *Victoria Times Colonist*, November 17, 2010, page C1.

3549 Cleve Dheenshaw, "Condorsgive S-Kings wake-up call," *Victoria Times Colonist*, November 18, 2010, page B1.

3550 Cleve Dheenshaw, "Win gives S-Kings some relief," *Victoria Times Colonist*, November 20, 2010, page B9.

3551 Cleve Dheenshaw, "S-Kings starting to turn season around," *Victoria Times Colonist*, November 21, 2010, page B1.

3552 Cleve Dheenshaw, "S-Kings return on winning note," *Victoria Times Colonist*, November 23, 2010, page C1.

3553 Cleve Dheenshaw, "Veteran help arrives for Salmon Kings," Victoria Times Colonist, November 24, 2010, page B6.

3554 Cleve Dheenshaw, "Steelheads fend off S-Kings," Victoria Times Colonist, November 25, 2010, page B1.

3555 Cleve Dheenshaw, "Canucks' prospect Sauve lands in Victoria," Victoria Times Colonist, November 26, 2010, page C1.

3556 Cleve Dheenshaw, "Steelheads strike early and often," Victoria Times Colonist, November 27, 2010, page B9.

3557 Cleve Dheenshaw, "Steelheads sweep S-Kings," Victoria Times Colonist, November 28, 2010, page C1.

3558 Cleve Dheenshaw, "Depleted Salmon Kings salvage a point," Victoria Times Colonist, December 2, 2010, page B1.

3559 Cleve Dheenshaw, "Thunder strike again," Victoria Times Colonist, December 4, 2010, page B11.

3560 Cleve Dheenshaw, "Salmon Kings fall in overtime," Victoria Times Colonist, December 5, 2010, page B1.

3561 Cleve Dheenshaw, "Clock ticking on WHL move to Victoria," Victoria Times Colonist, December 7, 210, page C11.

3562 "Salmon Kings swing deal with 'South Carolina to pick up defenceman," Victoria Times Colonist, December 7, 2010, page C11.

3563 Cleve Dheenshaw, "Goldie eager to face former team," Victoria Times Colonist, December 8, 2010, page D1.

3564 Cleve Dheenshaw, "Siddall sizzles as S-Kings trump Aces," Victoria Times Colonist, December 9, 2010, page B1.

3565 Cleve Dheenshaw, "Never a dull moment at the 'Sully'," Victoria Times Colonist, December 10, 2010, page C1.

3566 Cleve Dheenshaw, "S-Kings' ranks get a little thinner," Victoria Times Colonist, December 12, 2010, page C1.

3567 Cleve Dheenshaw, "Help on way for depleted S-Kings," Victoria Times Colonist, December 15, 2010, page D1.

3568 Cleve Dheenshaw, "Steelheads bounce Salmon Kings again," Victoria Times Colonist, December 16, 2010, page B1.

3569 Cleve Dheenshaw, "No mercy for ailing S-Kings," Victoria Times Colonist, December 17, 2010, page B9.

3570 Cleve Dheenshaw, "Comeback win give Salmon Kings life," Victoria Times Colonist, December 18, 2010, page B8.

3571 Ron Rauch, "S-Kings start break on a high," Victoria Times Colonist, December 19, 2010, page B1.

3572 Sharie Epp, "S-Kings rejuvenated for second-half run," Victoria Times Colonist, December 28, 2010, page B1.

3573 Sharie Epp, "Reign ruin Salmon Kings' night," Victoria Times Colonist, December 29, 2010, page B7

3574 Sharie Epp, "Top line pours it on against Reign," Victoria Times Colonist, December 30, 2010, page B1.

3575 Sharie Epp, "Salmon Kings come up empty in Utah," Victoria Times Colonist, January 2, 2011, page C1.

3576 Cleve Dheenshaw, "Salmon Kings hoping for more January fireworks," Victoria Times Colonist, January 5, 2011, page B5.

3577 Cleve Dheenshaw, "Thunder hold off Salmon Kings," Victoria Times Colonist, January 6, 2011, page B2.

3578 Cleve Dheenshaw, "S-Kings get back on track," Victoria Times Colonist, January 8, 2011, page B8.

3579 ECHL Gamesheet – January 8, 2011, retrieved from echl.com.

3580 Cleve Dheenshaw, "Familiar face returns to Salmon Kings," Victoria Times Colonist, January 11, 2011, page C1.

3581 Ron Rauch, "Bates' big game adds up to nightmare for S-Kings," Victoria Times Colonist, January 12, 2011, page B6.

3582 Cleve Dheenshaw, "Late surge lifts Wranglers," Victoria Times Colonist, January 13, 2011, page B1.

3583 Cleve Dheenshaw, "Salmon Kings lose their top defenceman," Victoria Times Colonist, January 14, 2011, page C12.

3584 Cleve Dheenshaw, "Salmon Kings leave it to Cleaver," Victoria Times Colonist, January 15, 2011, page B9.

3585 Cleve Dheenshaw, "Idaho's power-play goals sink Salmon Kings," Victoria Times Colonist, January 16, 2011, page B1.

3586 Cleve Dheenshaw, "S-Kings bounce back in Idaho," Victoria Times Colonist, January 18, 2011, page C1.

3587 Gamesheet – January 21, 2011, retrieved from echl.com.

3588 Ron Rauch, "Salmon Kings gain confidence while away but fall to Aces in Alaska," Victoria Times Colonist, January 23, 2011, page B1.

3589 Cleve Dheenshaw, "Wranglers too hot to handle," Victoria Times Colonist, January 28, 2011, page B9.

The History of Professional Hockey in Victoria, BC: 1911-2011

3590 Cleve Dheenshaw, "Wranglers have S-Kings fit to be tied," *Victoria Times Colonist*, January 30, 2011, page B1.

3591 Cleve Dheenshaw, "Something positive to build on," *Victoria Times Colonist*, February 1, 2011, page C4.

3592 Cleve Dheenshaw, "Goldie silenced in return," *Victoria Times Colonist*, February 3, 2011, page B1.

3593 Cleve Dheenshaw, "Hot pink for a hot team," *Victoria Times Colonist*, February 5, 2011, page B10.

3594 Cleve Dheenshaw, "Aces trump Salmon Kings," *Victoria Times Colonist*, February 6, 2011, page B1.

3595 Cleve Dheenshaw, "Salmon Kings bring in well-travelled blue-liner," *Victoria Times Colonist*, February 11, 2011, page C12.

3596 Cleve Dheenshaw "Cleaver slices up Wranglers," *Victoria Times Colonist*, February 12, 2011, page B8.

3597 Cleve Dheenshaw, "Salmon Kings hit California flying high," *Victoria Times Colonist*, February 15, 2011, page C1.

3598 Cleve Dheenshaw, "S-Kings' offence stays in high gear," *Victoria Times Colonist*, February 16, 2011, page B6.

3599 Cleve Dheenshaw, "Moose call on S-Kings blue-liner," *Victoria Times Colonist*, February 18, 2011, page C1.

3600 Cleve Dheenshaw, "Salmon Kings silence Thunder," *Victoria Times Colonist*, February 19, 2011, page B10.

3601 Cleve Dheenshaw, "Thunder pound S-Kings," *Victoria Times Colonist*, February 20, 2011, page B1.

3602 Cleve Dheenshaw, "Salmon Kings limp home from California," *Victoria Times Colonist*, February 22, 2011, page C1.

3603 Cleve Dheenshaw, "Butcher, Cleaver help slice up Utah," *Victoria Times Colonist*, February 26, 2011, page B8.

3604 Cleve Dheenshaw, "S-Kings hold off Utah," *Victoria Times Colonist*, February 27, 2011, page C1.

3605 Cleve Dheenshaw, "Rumours swirling again of Victoria's return to WHL," *Victoria Times Colonist*, March 1, 2011, page D1.

3606 Cleve Dheenshaw, "Plenty of juggling in ECHL *Victoria Times Colonist*, March 2, 2011, page B6.

3607 Travis Paterson, "Salmon Kings returnee to bring energy," *Victoria News*, March 3, 2011, online edition.

3608 Cleve Dheenshaw, "Shantz sizzles in return," *Victoria Times Colonist*, March 3, 2011, page B1.

3609 Cleve Dheenshaw, "Condors fed off Salmon Kings," *Victoria Times Colonist*, March 5, 2011, page B8.

3610 Cleve Dheenshaw, "Salmon Kings fall to Condors *Victoria Times Colonist*, March 6, 2011, page B1.

3611 Cleve Dheenshaw, "Possible playoff preview on tap in Alaska," *Victoria Times Colonist*, March 9, 2011, page B6.

3612 Cleve Dheenshaw, "Pair of familiar faces strike down struggling 'Salmon Kings in Alaska," *Victoria Times Colonist*, March 10, 2011, page B1.

3613 Cleve Dheenshaw, "Goldie has Aces soaring," *Victoria Times Colonist*, March 12, 2011, page B9.

3614 Cleve Dheenshaw, "Salmon Kings swept in Alaska," *Victoria Times Colonist*, March 13, 2011, page B12.

3615 Cleve Dheenshaw, "S-Kings shuffle the deck," *Victoria Times Colonist*, March 16, 2011, page B6.

3616 Cleve Dheenshaw, "S-Kings snap skid in style," *Victoria Times Colonist*, March 17, 2011, page B1.

3617 Sharie Epp, "S-Kings stay in high gear," *Victoria Times Colonist*, March 19, 2011, page B10.

3618 Ron Rauch, "Grizzlies nip S-Kings in OT," *Victoria Times Colonist*, March 20, 2011, page B1.

3619 Ron Rauch, "S-Kings will put home stretch to good use," *Victoria Times Colonist*, March 23, 2011, page B7.

3620 Sharie Epp, "Condors edge Salmon Kings, *Victoria Times Colonist*, March 24, 2011, page B1.

3621 Sharie Epp, "Salmon Kings clinch playoff spot," *Victoria Times Colonist*, March 26, 2011, page B9.

3622 Sharie Epp, "S-Kings nip Thunder in shootout," *Victoria Times Colonist*, March 27, 2011, page B1.

3623 Sharie Epp, "Thunder get back at S-Kings," *Victoria Times Colonist*, March 28, 2011, page D1.

3624 Sharie Epp, "S-Kings fall to Alaska," *Victoria Times Colonist*, March 31, 2011, page B1.

3625 Sharie Epp, "WHL team returning to Victoria; report," *Victoria Times Colonist*, April 1, 2011, page A1.

3626 Sharie Epp, "S-Kings trump Aces," *Victoria Times Colonist*, April 2, 2011, page B7.

3627 Sharie Epp, "Aces clinch top spot," *Victoria Times Colonist*, April 3, 2011, page B1.

3628 Sharie Epp, "Salmon Kings storm out of the gate," *Victoria Times Colonist*, April 5, 2011, page C1.

3629 Sharie Epp, "With WHL looming, tonight could be Salmon Kings' swan song," Victoria Times Colonist, April 5, 2011, page C1.

3630 "Salmon Kings take game one against Condors Victoria News, April 5, 2011, online edition.

3631 Sharie Epp, "Next stop Victoria? WHL gives go-ahead for Bruins' sale," Victoria Times Colonist, April 6, 2011, page B6.

3632 Travis Paterson, Island News, April 6, 2011, online edition.

3633 Sharie Epp, "Condorstake upper hand," Victoria Times Colonist, April 6, 2011, page B6.

3634 Sharie Epp, "Shantz puts S-Kings in control," Victoria Times Colonist, April 9, 2011, page C4.

3635 Tyler Olsen, "Bruins hand out pink slips as relocation looms," Victoria Times Colonist, April 9, 2011, page C4.

3636 Ron Rauch, "S-Kings ground Condors Victoria Times Colonist, April 10, 2011, page B1.

3637 Cleve Dheenshaw, "Momentum suddenly on S-Kings side," Victoria Times Colonist, April 13, 2011, page B7.

3638 "Salmon Kings semifinals begin with a win," Victoria Times Colonist, April 16, 2011, page A1.

3639 Cleve Dheenshaw, "S-Kings walk away with win in opener," Victoria Times Colonist, April 16, 2011, page B9.

3640 Cleve Dheenshaw, "S-Kings sweep Grizzlies in Utah," Victoria Times Colonist, April 17, 2011, page B1.

3641 Cleve Dheenshaw, "Long wait for WHL is over," Victoria Times Colonist, April 21, 2011, page B1.

3642 "Capital scores as WHL returns," Victoria Times Colonist, April 21, 2011, page A14.

3643 Cleve Dheenshaw, "Last hurrah: Salmon Kings make pleas for fan support," Victoria Times Colonist, April 19, 2011, page B6.

3644 "WHL announcement unfair to Salmon Kings," Victoria Times Colonist, April 20, 2011, page A13.

3645 Victoria Salmon Kings Game Notes, April 22, 2011.

3646 "Broom and dustpan time?" Victoria Times Colonist, April 21, 2011, page B1.

3647 "Nothing will unseat Salmon Kings," Victoria News, April 21, 2011, online edition.

3648 Cleve Dheenshaw, "Aspenlind puts S-Kings in command," Victoria Times Colonist, April 21, 2011, page B3.

3649 Cleve Dheenshaw, "Salmon Kings make magic, win series," Victoria Times Colonist, April 25, 2011, page A1.

3650 Cleve Dheenshaw, "S-Kings rally to win series," Victoria Times Colonist, April 23, 2011, page B7.

3651 Cleve Dheenshaw, "S-Kings going out with a bang," Victoria Times Colonist, April 24, 2011, page C1.

3652 Cleve Dheenshaw, "S-Kings add pair of AHLers," Victoria Times Colonist, April 26, 2011, page C1.

3653 "AHLers boost Salmon Kings for Western Final," Victoria Times Colonist, Victoria News, April 27, 2011, online edition.

3654 Cleve Dheenshaw, "Late goal gives Aces the opener," Victoria Times Colonist, April 28, 2011, page B1.

3655 Cleve Dheenshaw, "Overtime win puts Aces in command," Victoria Times Colonist, April 29, 2011, page D1.

3656 Cleve Dheenshaw, "S-Kings in a hole," Victoria Times Colonist, May 1, 2011, page B1.

3657 Cleve Dheenshaw, "End of a season; end of an era," Victoria Times Colonist, May 3, 2011, page C1.

3658 Cleve Dheenshaw, "Only fond memories as Salmon Kings bid farewell," Victoria Times Colonist, May 4, 2011, page C6.

3659 Personal interview with Mark Morrison, conducted on June 4, 2018.

3660 Cleve Dheenshaw, "Only fond memories as Salmon Kings bid farewell," Victoria Times Colonist, May 4, 2011, page C6.

3661 Personal interview with Mark Morrison, conducted on June 4, 2018.

INDEX

Symbols

1919 Stanley Cup playoffs
    influenza 40
1940s drive for municipally built arena 85
2005 Mens World Curling Championship
    April 2-10, 2005 258
2010 Olympic gold medal game 350

A

Abbott
    Reg 97, 98, 99, 100, 102, 103, 106, 107,
        108, 110, 112, 113, 116, 117, 118, 119,
        120, 123, 127, 128, 134, 251
Achtymichuk
    Gene 123, 124, 125, 126, 127, 130, 133, 134, 135
Agar
    George 110, 189, 192, 194, 195, 196, 197
Agreement with Montreal Canadiens 94
Alaska
    Aces 96, 265, 266, 269, 270, 271, 273, 281, 284,
        285, 288, 289, 290, 291, 294, 297, 298, 299,
        300, 305, 307, 314, 317, 319, 321, 327, 329,
        331, 332, 333, 335, 337, 338, 339, 341, 342,
        345, 346, 349, 351, 354, 358, 359, 360,
        361, 362, 363, 364, 366, 367, 527, 541
Alberni Valley Bulldogs 279
Alberta Big Four League 43
Allan
    Derek 279, 281
Allan Cup 147
Almas
    Ralph 123, 124, 125, 126
Amadio
    Leo 194, 196, 197, 198
Anaheim Ducks 342
Anaheim Mighty Ducks 287
Anderson
    Dallas 55, 57, 70, 74, 75, 107, 144, 149, 177,
        181, 182, 241, 283, 284, 286, 287
    Doug 108, 109, 110, 111, 113, 116, 117, 119,
        120, 124, 126, 130, 132, 133, 134, 138, 139,
        140, 141, 142, 143, 144, 147, 148, 149, 150,
        152, 154, 160, 163, 164, 167, 169, 170, 171,
        172, 173, 176, 177, 178, 179, 180, 182, 183,
        185, 186, 189, 192, 194, 196, 197, 198
    Ernie 60
    Jocko 51, 55, 56, 58, 60, 61, 63, 67,
        69, 70, 71, 74, 80, 82
    Joel 285
Andresen
    Joel 288, 289
Andrews
    Dave 291
Andy Hebenton Night 229
Anshelm
    Earl 147, 157
Arbour
    Al 220
Arena Gardens
    Toronto 42
arena plan suspended due to the war 84
Armstrong
    Jim 229, 231
Arnett
    Frank 173, 196
Art Ross All-Stars 12
Ashbee
    Don 109, 130, 131
Ashton
    Mark 290
Asmundson
    Oscar 78, 80
Aspenlind
    Josh 354, 358, 362, 363, 366
Asselin
    Kevin 300
Atanas
    Walt 109, 110, 111, 113
Atherton
    P. J. 354, 355, 356, 357, 359, 360

572

Index

Atlantic City
  Boardwalk Bullies 279
Aubrey
  Peter 269
Augusta
  Lynx 287, 295, 330
Auld
  Alex 293

B

Back
  Warren 157, 160
Baden
  Mowry 252
Bakersfield
  Condors 263, 265, 267, 268, 281, 286, 287, 289, 294, 298, 299, 300, 301, 311, 314, 316, 317, 321, 322, 328, 330, 332, 335, 336, 337, 342, 347, 348, 349, 350, 351, 352, 356, 358, 361, 362, 363, 364, 365
Baliuk
  Stan 161, 163, 167, 168, 169, 170, 172, 173
Ballance
  Bob 108, 109, 113
Ballantyne
  Paul 301, 302, 303, 304, 305, 311, 314, 315, 316, 322, 323, 334
Baltimore Clippers 221
Baptie
  Norval 19, 23
Barbour
  Alf 37, 38, 39
Barlow
  Bob 201, 202, 203, 207, 209, 210, 213, 214, 215, 216, 217, 218, 220, 221, 222, 223, 224, 225, 226, 228, 230, 232, 233, 234, 235, 236, 237, 238, 240, 251, 376
Barrett
  Nathan 315, 316, 317, 318
Barrie
  Mike 264, 265, 267, 268, 270, 271
Barrie Flyers 147
Bartlett
  Mike 310
Bartzen
  Casey 275
Bassen
  Hank 148, 158, 159, 161, 179
Bast
  Jason 352
Bates
  Jamie 359
Baton Rouge Kingfish 252
Battaglia

Anthony 284
Battimo
  Max 273
Baxter
  John 88
Bear Mountain Arena 263, 264, 266, 267, 268, 270, 271, 272, 275, 279, 281, 307
Beauchamp
  Jason 280
Beauchemin
  Rejean 338
Beckett
  Bob 147
Beckford-Tseu
  Chris 284, 359, 362, 363
Belisle
  Dan 279, 285, 286, 289, 291, 293, 298, 307, 323, 324
  Danny 169, 179, 186, 187, 203, 204, 205, 206, 207, 208, 209, 210, 211
Belither
  Sidney 155
Belitski
  Dave 293, 294
Belliveau
  Reg 138, 141
Benedict
  Clint 13, 74
Benn
  Jordie 326, 327, 328, 331, 334, 336
Bennefield
  Blue 264, 265, 266, 267, 268, 270, 271, 272
Bennett and White Construction Co. Ltd. 91
Bentley
  Bev 135, 158, 160, 170, 178, 185, 194, 195
  Doug 112, 133
Berg
  Larry 142, 147, 157
Bergen
  David 240
  Jake 240
Bergman
  Gary 178
Berman
  Geoff 99
Bernier
  Marc-Andre 299, 300, 301, 302, 303, 304, 305, 307, 310, 311, 312, 313, 314, 315, 317, 318, 319, 320, 321, 322, 323
Berridge
  Mike 213
Bettio
  Sam 123, 124, 125, 127, 130
Betts

573

Kaleb 341
Beveridge
  Mike 228
Bezzo
  Paul 351
Billsten
  Curtis 328, 329, 331, 332, 333, 334, 336, 341
Binkley
  Les 228, 229
Bionda
  Jack 167, 176, 177, 178, 180, 181, 182,
    183, 184, 185, 189, 197
Black
  Greg 289
  Steve 131
Blackburn
  Dan 272, 273, 275
  Don 167, 168, 169, 171, 172, 180,
    181, 182, 183, 185, 186
Black Eyed Peas 294
Blanchard
  Trevor 320
Boileau
  Marc 189
Boisvert
  Gilles 184, 193
Bonin
  Marcel 126
Borders
  Scott 275, 276
Borgeson
  Don 228
Borland
  Bill 77, 78
Boston Bruins 58, 75, 97, 121, 134, 138, 140, 141,
  142, 144, 147, 149, 150, 151, 157, 167, 176
Bouchard
  Leon 108, 112, 113, 116, 120
Bougie
  Georges 94, 96, 97
Boundary Hockey League 22, 28
Boutin
  Jonathan 326, 327, 328, 329, 331, 332, 333, 334
Bower
  Johnny 131, 132, 133, 135
Bowness
  Bob 106, 108, 109
Box
  George "Trooper" 33, 35, 39
Boxma
  B. J. 280, 281, 283, 286, 287, 288, 289, 290
Boyce
  Blinky 144, 157, 158, 159, 160, 162, 163

Bozak
  Paul 132
Bradley
  Bart 134, 138, 143
Brain
  George 40
Brandon
  Regals 141, 142, 143, 148, 149, 152, 153, 157
Brandt
  Andy 341, 342, 343, 344, 345, 346,
    347, 348, 350, 351, 352
Bremner
  Ryan 280
Briden
  Archie 75
Bridges
  Bryan 293, 294, 296, 298, 299, 300, 301,
    303, 304, 305, 307, 310
Bridgewood
  Bill 88
Briggs
  Kellen 318
Brisson
  David 273
British Columbia Electric Railway Co. Ltd. 155
British National League 279
Brocklehurst
  Aaron 335, 336, 338, 339
Brown
  Fred 143, 157, 159
  Mike 297, 298
  Wayne 130, 134, 138, 140, 141, 143, 144, 147,
    148, 149, 150, 151, 153, 154, 155
Bruce
  Kyle 341
Brumby
  David 263, 264, 265, 266, 267
Bryant
  Tim 240
Bucyk
  Bill 130, 132, 134, 168
Buffalo Bisons 222
Buffey
  Vern 148, 151, 152, 174
Bulloch
  Nelson 141, 142, 143, 144, 147, 148,
    149, 151, 157, 159, 164
Burgoyne
  Mike 341, 342, 343
Burman
  Geoff 102, 103, 104
Burnett
  Gord 357, 358

Index

Burns
    Charlie 224, 235, 237
Burrows
    Alex 293
Burt
    Scott 315
Burton
    Cummings 148, 149
Busch
    Robert 264, 265, 266
business community concerns with the VSEA proposal 243
Butcher
    Matt 359, 360, 361

C

Cabeldu
    Fred 91
Cahan
    Hank 198
Caister
    Jeff 358, 359, 360, 362, 363, 364, 365, 366, 367
Calgary
    Stampeders 106, 107, 108, 109, 110, 117, 118, 119, 120, 123, 124, 125, 126, 127, 128, 130, 132, 133, 134, 135, 139, 140, 142, 148, 149, 152, 153, 158, 164, 167, 168, 169, 170, 171, 172, 177, 179, 182, 184, 190, 191, 194, 195, 196
    Tigers 51, 53, 54, 55, 57, 59, 60, 61, 62, 69, 71, 72
Calgary Flames 296
Calgary Herald, The 43
California
    Seals 229, 230, 232, 235, 236, 237
Cameron
    Bretton 359
    Bryan 361, 362, 363
Campagnola
    Lieutenant Governor Iona 259
Campbell
    Adam 270, 272, 274, 276
    Clarence 230
    Derek 2, 211, 230, 268, 269, 273, 274, 276, 280, 283, 352
    Duncan 266
Carmichael
    Bruce 142, 143, 145, 147, 148, 149, 150, 151, 152, 153, 154, 155, 181, 186, 195, 198, 207, 228, 229, 230, 231, 232, 233, 234, 235, 236, 237
Central Professional Hockey League 203
Ceresino
    Ray 140, 142
CFB Naden 264
CFL Calgary Stampeders 203
Chadwick
    Florence 126
Chamberlain
    Murph 101, 108
Chapman
    Art 159
Charmer 53
Charron
    Rick 225
Cheyne
    Jeremy 265, 267
Chicago Blackhawks 75, 79, 121, 191, 197, 213
Chilliwack Bruins 364, 365
    sold to RG Properties 365
Chipchase
    Jack 210, 219, 228
Chiupka 153
    Don 138, 139, 140, 141, 142, 143, 144, 147, 148, 149, 152, 153, 154, 155, 159, 162, 163, 206
Chorley
    Elliott 190, 191
Cianfrini
    David 351
Cincinnati
    Cyclones 328, 349
Civic election 1944
    voting for new arena 86
Claire
    Fraser 281
Clancy
    King 224, 226
Clark
    Neil 228, 229, 230
    Premier Glen 241, 243, 244
Cleaver
    Rick 354, 355, 356, 357, 358, 359, 360, 361, 362, 363, 364, 365
Cleghorn
    Odie 4, 12
Cleveland Barons 106, 130, 158, 181, 214
Climie
    Matt 338
Cluman
    Joe 106
Clune
    Walter 123, 124, 125, 127, 130, 132
Cobalt Silver Kings 8
Cole
    Phil 270, 295, 296, 297, 300, 301, 303, 307, 310
Coleman
    Councillor Chris 245
Colorado Avalanche 279
Columbia
    Inferno 294

Columbus Blue Jackets 354
Condors 267, 268, 356, 529, 532
Conn
  Joe 123, 130
  Red 78
Connelly
  Wayne 208, 216, 217, 223
Cook
  Bill 59
  Brad 23, 296, 297
  Leo 39
  Lloyd 40, 41, 52
Cooper
  Kevin 307, 310
Corbeau
  Bert 40
Corrigan
  Mike 224
Corrinet
  Chris 271, 274, 276, 277
Cotnoir 103
  Jerry 98, 99, 100, 101, 102, 103, 104, 106, 108, 110, 111, 112, 113, 116, 119, 121, 123
Coulombe
  Patrick 303, 307, 310, 312, 314, 315, 317, 318, 320, 321, 326, 327, 331, 332, 333, 334, 337, 338, 341, 343, 344, 345, 347, 348, 349, 352
Coultice
  Noel 341, 344
Courchaine
  Adam 361
Courtnall
  Geoff 76, 244
  Russ 76
Coutu
  William 63
Couture
  Derek 354, 355, 356, 357, 358, 361, 362, 363, 366, 367
  Gerry 133
Couvelier
  Mel 244
Cowan
  Bob 157
  Gordie 123
Creighton
  Fred 147
Crosby
  Sidney 350
Cross 245
  Mayor Bob 242, 244, 245, 246
Crowder
  Tim 341
Crowley Construction Ltd. 88

Crozier
  Joe 180, 182
Cubs transferred to Tacoma 82
Currie
  Hugh 189, 193, 195, 196, 198, 283, 286, 287
Cyr
  Ray 143, 181

D

Daigneau
  John 295
Dakers
  Dave 255, 277, 286, 291, 323, 331, 364, 366, 368
Daly
  Dan 79
Dandurand
  Leo 62, 65
Daren Machesney 354
Darling
  Curtis 343
Dave Parenteau, 215
Davey
  Bobby 349, 351
Davidson 154
  Bill 130, 132, 138, 139, 141, 143, 144, 147, 150, 153, 154
Davis
  Drew 310
  Lorne 97, 98
Dayton
  Bombers 282, 287, 338
Dea
  Billy 130
deferred-penalty system 37
Deleurme
  Jason 341
DeMone
  James 295, 296, 297, 300
Denman Street Arena 63, 73
Denver Invaders moved to Victoria 201
Derlago
  Mark 317, 322, 366
Deschamps
  Darren 316, 326
Deschenes
  Lucien 168, 182, 191
Deslaurier
  Jacques 94
Desmarais
  Marty 214, 215
  Tony 214
Desmet
  Taggart 289, 290

Detroit Cougars 75, 82
Detroit Red Wings 130, 176, 177, 279
Dexter
    Brad 264, 266, 268, 269, 270, 271, 274, 276
Dheenshaw
    Cleve 242, 336, 367, 527, 532, 543
Dieldal
    Charles Albert 51
Dietrich
    Jacob 320, 321, 323, 326, 327, 329, 330, 331, 332, 334
Dingle
    Ryan 354, 355, 357, 358, 359, 360, 361, 362, 363
Dionne
    Marcel 251
Dobbyn
    Bill 138, 141, 142, 147, 153
Dobson
    Duncan, BC Mayor Jack 182
Dockery
    Pat 94
Donaldson
    Mike 202
Donnelly
    Mark 362
Dorohoy
    Eddie 95, 96, 97, 98, 99, 100, 101, 102, 103, 106, 107, 108, 109, 110, 111, 112, 113, 116, 117, 118, 123, 125, 126, 127, 130, 131, 132, 134, 138, 157, 158, 160, 161, 163, 164, 165, 167, 171, 173, 251
Downie
    Dave 77, 78
Drew
    Stefan 341
Drummond
    Kurt 282, 283, 285, 288, 289
Druxman
    Nate 80
Dubnyk
    Devan 296, 302, 303
Duffy
    Maurice 97
Dulle
    Kurtis 275, 276, 277
Duncan
    Art 40
Dunderdale
    Tommy 4, 5, 6, 10, 11, 12, 13, 15, 16, 17, 18, 19, 20, 21, 22, 23, 25, 26, 27, 28, 30, 31, 32, 33, 37, 38, 41, 42, 44, 46, 47, 48, 51
Dunleavy
    Chip 288, 289
Durham
    Pete 130, 131, 134, 135, 150, 151, 153, 155, 162, 164

Duschenes
    Jacques 169
    Lucien 108
Dutkowski
    Joe 91, 190

E

ECHL 252, 253, 263, 265, 266, 267, 268, 269, 270, 271, 272, 273, 274, 275, 276, 279, 280, 281, 284, 287, 289, 291, 293, 294, 295, 297, 299, 300, 301, 302, 303, 307, 310, 311, 312, 314, 315, 316, 317, 319, 320, 327, 329, 330, 332, 333, 337, 338, 339, 341, 343, 344, 345, 346, 348, 349, 352, 354, 355, 356, 357, 359, 360, 361, 363, 364, 368, 527
ECHL franchise transfeered to Victoria 253
ECHL in Victoria
    name the team contest 253
ECHL in Victoria new name
    Salmon Kings 253
ECHL salaries, season 1 263
economic-impact study, 1996 241
Edgelow
    Alderman Geoffrey 226
Edmonton
    Eskimos 51, 53, 54, 57, 59, 60, 61, 70, 71, 72, 73
    Flyers 106, 107, 108, 109, 110, 117, 118, 119, 120, 124, 125, 126, 127, 130, 131, 132, 133, 134, 138, 140, 141, 142, 148, 149, 152, 162, 163, 164, 167, 168, 169, 171, 172, 177, 178, 179, 181, 182, 183, 184, 191, 193, 194, 195
Edmonton Oilers 76, 296
Egan
    Pat 158, 159, 160, 161, 162, 163, 164, 167, 168, 169, 170, 171, 172, 173, 174, 176
Ehman
    Jerry 145
Ehrenverth
    Edgar 207, 208, 209, 211, 213, 219, 220
Ellington
    Taylor 326, 338, 341, 342, 344, 345, 346, 348, 349, 351, 352, 354, 357, 363
Elliott
    Brandon 275, 276
Ellis
    Julien 293, 295, 296, 297, 298, 299, 302, 303, 304, 305, 307, 310, 311, 312, 313, 314, 315, 316, 317, 318, 319, 320, 323, 326, 329, 330, 331, 333, 334, 335, 336, 337, 339, 532
Elmer
    Wally 59, 60, 67, 69
Elmira
    Jackals 341, 342, 343, 358
Empress of Asia 38

Engman
  Gustav 294, 296, 302, 303
Erickson
  Autrey 213, 214, 215, 216, 218, 219, 221, 225, 228, 230, 232, 233, 235, 237, 238
Esquimalt Military Hospital 38
Esselmont
  Ryan 271, 274
Estey
  Andrew 279
Estrada
  Kevin 307, 310, 311, 312, 313, 314, 315, 316, 317, 318, 319, 320, 322, 334, 532
Evans
  Claude 126, 127, 198, 199
  Jack 78, 135
  Jim 77, 78, 80
  Joe 94, 95, 97, 98, 99, 103, 104, 106, 108, 111, 113, 116, 117, 118

F

Fairburn
  Jim 117, 119, 120
Falloon
  Kevin 341
Farelli
  Lou 192
Fashoway
  Gord 144, 177, 178, 179, 180, 181, 182, 183, 184, 185, 186, 187, 189, 191, 194, 196, 197
  Gordie 176
Favell
  Doug 224
Fehri
  Eddy 269
Ferraro
  Chris 315, 319, 335
  Peter 28, 130, 243, 269, 281, 315, 317, 354
Field
  Richard 91
Fielder
  Guyle 127, 148, 169, 173, 179, 186, 207, 210, 213, 221, 330, 376
Filion
  Olivier 327, 328, 329, 330, 331, 332, 333, 336, 337, 338, 339, 341, 342, 344, 345, 346, 347, 348, 349, 352
  Rudy 173
Finnerty
  Ryan 263, 264, 265, 266, 268, 269, 270, 273, 276, 279
first goal at Save-On-Foods Memorial Centre 279
first home game broadcast in WCHL history 62
first Sunday professional hockey game played in Vancouver 167

Fisher
  Glenn 334, 342, 345, 346, 348, 349, 350, 351
Fit-Rite Stores 9
Fizzell
  Bert 189, 190, 191, 192, 193, 194, 196
Flaherty
  Wade 304
Fletcher
  Douglas 88
  Gavin 299
Fletcher Bros. 72
Flett
  Bill \ 201, 203
Florida
  Everblades 276, 280, 289, 335, 349, 354, 361
Florida Panthers 293
Fodey
  Jerry 94, 95
Folk
  Bill 171, 193
Foote
  Jordan 326, 327, 328
Forbes
  Elizabeth 184
Ford 179
  George 167, 168, 169, 171, 172, 176, 177, 178, 179, 180, 181, 182, 183, 184, 185, 186, 189, 190, 191, 192, 193, 194, 195, 196, 197, 198, 199
  Todd 80, 172, 181, 184, 194, 198, 280, 326, 327, 329, 330, 331, 332, 333, 334, 336, 337, 338, 339
  Todd. 326
Forhan
  Bill 171
Forster
  Carl 167
  Nathan 266, 268, 270, 271, 273, 274, 275, 277, 280, 283, 284, 285, 287, 288, 289, 290
Fowler
  Norman "Hec" 44, 46, 47, 51, 52, 53, 54, 55, 57, 58
Fox
  Ernie 120
Foyston
  Frank 40, 58, 59, 60, 61, 63, 65, 67, 69, 71, 72, 73, 75
Frame
  David C. 87
Frampton
  Bob 98, 99, 101, 106, 107, 108, 110, 111, 112, 113, 134
  Bobby 98
Francis
  Emile \ 152, 154, 157, 159, 161, 163, 165, 168, 170, 178, 179, 185, 186
Frandvold
  Trent 267

Frank the Pembroke Peach Nighbor 23
Fraser
    Gord 58, 60, 61, 63, 65, 67, 69, 70, 71, 72, 73, 74, 75
Fredheim
    Kris 352, 354
Fred Hume Trophy 192, 210, 231
Fredrickson
    Frank "Freddy" 43, 44, 45, 46, 47, 48, 51, 52,
        53, 54, 55, 56, 57, 58, 59, 60, 61, 62, 63,
        65, 66, 67, 69, 70, 71, 72, 74, 75
Freeman
    Scott 362, 363
Fresno
    Falcons 43, 95, 97, 265, 266, 267, 272, 273,
        274, 279, 281, 285, 290, 294, 296, 298,
        299, 303, 313, 314, 315, 316, 317, 318,
        321, 330, 332, 337, 349, 461, 532
Friedland
    Councillor Bob 244, 245
Ftorek
    Robbie 287
    Sam 287
Fukufuji
    Yutaka 322, 337
Fulton
    Marc 326, 327
funding referendum
    April 2002 250

G

Gagnon
    Charles 95
Gajic
    Milan 293, 294, 295, 296, 297, 298, 299, 300, 301,
        302, 303, 304, 305, 307, 310, 311, 312, 313, 315,
        317, 318, 319, 320, 322, 323, 334, 335, 354, 355,
        356, 358, 359, 360, 361, 362, 363, 364, 365
Galbraith
    Jade 282, 283, 284, 285, 286, 288, 289, 290
Gamble
    Bruce 172
Garbutt
    Josh 290, 294, 295
Gardiner
    Pete 279, 281, 283
Gardner
    George 221
    Harry 59
    Jimmy 5, 6, 13
Gare
    Lanny 281, 282, 283, 284, 285, 286, 288, 289, 290
Garrant
    Gord 167

Gattolliat
    Jim 264, 275
Gauthier
    Gabe 355
Gelech
    Randy 343, 344, 345, 346, 347, 348, 349, 350, 351
Gendur
    Dan 326, 327, 328, 329, 330, 331, 332, 333,
        334, 335, 336, 339, 341, 342, 343, 354
Genge
    Bobby 18, 19, 20, 23, 27, 28, 30, 33, 37, 39, 41, 44
Geoffrion
    Bernie 116
Geogan
    Fiori 94
George
    Mayor Percy 86, 90, 94
George Straith Ltd. 155
Gerrard
    George 183
Gibson
    Jimmy 55, 58
Gilbertson
    Stan 223
Gill
    Riley 354, 355
Gillis
    Mike 323
Gilmour
    Lloyd 161, 218, 219, 222, 224
Ginnell
    Pat 189, 190, 191
Gladue
    Gary 307, 310, 312, 314, 316, 319, 327,
        331, 334, 341, 346, 348, 350
Glass
    Frank 4
Glukhov
    Alexei 270, 272, 274, 275, 276
Godoy
    Elias 290, 291, 293
Goegan
    Fiori 94, 97, 99, 100, 101, 103, 104, 107, 108,
        109, 110, 111, 113, 116, 117, 119, 123
Goldie
    Ash 297, 299, 307, 310, 311, 312, 313, 314, 315, 316,
        317, 318, 319, 320, 321, 322, 323, 334, 338
    Wes 15, 18, 20, 21, 293, 294, 295, 296, 297, 298, 299,
        300, 301, 302, 303, 304, 305, 307, 310, 311,
        312, 313, 314, 315, 316, 317, 318, 319, 320, 321,
        322, 323, 326, 327, 328, 329, 330, 331, 332, 333,
        334, 335, 336, 337, 338, 339, 341, 342, 343, 344,
        345, 346, 347, 348, 349, 350, 351, 352, 354,

358, 360, 361, 362, 363, 364, 366, 454, 532
Gomez
　Robin 300, 304, 305, 307, 310, 312, 315, 317, 318, 319
　Scott 265, 266, 271
Gomick
　Brian 269
Goodacre
　Bob 117
Goodwin
　Arlo 176, 177, 178, 179, 180, 182, 184, 186, 189, 198
　Charlie 176
　John 176
Gorman
　Joe 15, 23
Goyer
　Gerry 181, 183, 185, 186, 187, 189, 191, 192, 193, 194, 195, 196, 197, 198, 202, 218, 225
Grand Forks 22
Grant
　Dr. Gordon 155
Gray
　Ben 303
　Betty 193
　Bob 223
Green
　Teddy 178
Greenwood 22
Grenier
　Blake 326
Gretzky
　Wayne 251
Grevious
　Justin 341
Griffiths
　L. H. 10
Grubb
　D. 91
Guenette
　Francois-Pierre 293, 294, 295, 296, 297, 298, 301, 302, 303, 304, 314, 321
Guerico
　Marco 310
Gulutzan
　Glen 315
Gunter
　Ken 107, 251
Gurba
　Andy 154
Gustafson
　Derek 305
Gwinnett
　Gladiators 341, 348

H

Haileybury Comets 8
Hainsworth
　George 73
Halderson
　Harold "Slim" 46, 47, 48, 51, 52, 54, 55, 60, 61, 62, 63, 65, 67, 69, 70, 71, 73, 74, 75
Hale
　Larry 209
Haley
　Len 216, 229
Hall
　Coley 97, 101, 149, 178
　Glenn 125, 132
　Joe 40
Hamilton
　Don 144, 147, 157, 159
　Jackie 120
　Mike 13, 90, 120, 341, 342, 344, 346, 349, 460
Hanson
　Matt 307, 310
Hardaker
　"Red" 79
Harris
　Fred 40, 44, 48
　Ron 224
　Smokey 79
　Ted 168, 170, 173
Hart
　Art 154, 163, 164, 189
　Harold "Gizzy" 55, 56, 57, 59, 60, 61, 63, 65, 67, 69, 73, 75
　Premier John 94
Haskins
　Tyler 323
Haworth 169
　Gord 147, 148, 149, 150, 151, 152, 153, 154, 157, 159, 162, 163, 164, 167, 169, 170, 171, 172, 174, 176, 177, 178, 179, 180, 181, 182, 183, 184, 185, 187, 189, 190, 191, 197
　Gordy 147
Hay
　George 60
　Jim 171, 176, 177, 178, 184, 185, 187, 189, 190, 192, 193, 196, 197
　Jim "Red Eye" 167
Hayes
　George 96
Hayward
　Mayor Reginald 54
Head
　Don 196, 197, 203, 228, 233
Hebenton

Andy 98, 99, 100, 101, 103, 104, 106, 107, 108, 110, 111, 112, 113, 116, 117, 118, 119, 120, 123, 124, 125, 126, 127, 130, 131, 132, 133, 134, 135, 138, 177, 202, 210, 213, 214, 215, 216, 217, 218, 219, 220, 221, 222, 223, 225, 226, 228, 229, 230, 231, 232, 233, 234, 236, 237, 238, 251
   Gail 230, 231
Hegberg
   Jason 264, 265, 266, 267, 270, 274, 275
Heinrich
   Lionel 147, 150, 153
Heintz
   Dustan 279, 281, 283, 284, 285
Heisinger
   Craig 296, 326, 328
Heiskala
   Earl 231, 236
Henderson
   Jack 225
   Jay 342
   John 214, 221, 222, 223, 224, 225
   Mike 107, 223, 226, 281, 282, 283
Hennigar
   Rob 354, 355, 357, 358, 360, 361, 363, 364, 367
Hershey Bears 216, 222
Heshka
   Shaun 295, 296
Hickey
   Les 110, 112, 113
Highton
   Hec 97, 98, 99
Hildebrand
   Fred 94, 97, 98, 106
Hill
   Bunker 218
Hillman
   Floyd 138, 141
Hirsch
   Carl 245
Hockey Hall of Fame 265
Hodge
   Charlie 123, 139, 143, 144
Hodges
   Tom 178
Holland
   Councillor Bea 245
   Gary 213, 215, 220, 221, 228
Holmes
   Harry "Hap" 27, 40, 47, 52, 55, 56, 58, 59, 60, 63, 65, 67, 71
Hooper
   Thomas 6

Hornby
   Greg 294, 296, 301
   Howie 142
Horse Show Buildings at the Willows Fairgrounds 84
Horvath
   Bronco 132, 133
Houle
   Buck 203, 211, 213, 220, 221, 228, 231, 233, 236, 238
Howe
   Gordie 177
Howes
   Scott 328, 329, 331, 332, 333, 334, 336, 337, 338, 339, 341, 342, 343, 344, 345, 346, 347, 348, 351, 362, 366, 367
Hucul
   Fred 133, 142, 145, 171, 201, 202, 203, 206, 207, 208, 209, 211, 213, 214, 216, 217, 218, 219, 220, 221, 222, 223, 224, 225, 226, 228, 229, 231
   Sandy 184, 201, 202, 207, 208, 210, 211, 213, 215, 219, 220, 222, 224, 226, 228, 229, 236
Huddleston
   Denny 97, 98
Hudson
   Gord 153
Huggett
   Jonathan 246, 248
Hughes
   Councillor Helen 245
   Howie 228, 237
Humboldt-Melfort Indians 142
Humboldt Saskatchewan 144
Hunt
   Gareth 327
Hurricane Hazel 131
Hurricane Katrina 279, 280
Hurricane Rita 280
Husband
   Harold 155
Hutchinson
   Fred 94, 96, 99, 106, 109, 117, 131, 134, 138, 139, 140, 142, 147, 155
   Ron 184
Huxley
   Adam 284, 287, 288, 293
Hyland
   Harry 6, 13
Hynes
   Warren 171

I

Idaho
   Steelheads 265, 266, 273, 274, 275, 283, 284, 286, 294, 295, 301, 302, 310, 312, 318, 326,

328, 333, 336, 337, 338, 342, 343, 346, 350, 351, 354, 355, 357, 358, 360, 527
IHL. *See* International Hockey League; *See* International Hockey League; *See* International Hockey League
Ikeda
　Mike 274
Imperial Tobacco Company 98
Indaba Communications and Training Inc. 248
International Hockey League 240
Ion
　Frederick James \ 78, 79
　Frederick James "Mickey" 23, 26, 29, 31, 40, 42, 52, 53, 57, 59, 61, 62, 63, 65, 69, 70, 77
Irvin
　Dick 116
Irvine
　George 53
Irving
　Leland 348, 349, 350
Irwin
　Alex 39
　Dick 41
　Geoff 293
　Ivan 116, 117, 119, 130, 218
　Joel 294
Island Broadcasting Co. Ltd. 155
Island Decorators Co. Ltd. 155

J

Jackson
　Percy 77
Jaeger
　Brett 273
James
　Donald 94
　Douglas 87
　Gerry 194
　Percy Leonard 87
Jankowski
　Lou 172, 184, 201, 202, 203, 204, 205, 206, 207, 208, 209, 210, 211, 213, 214, 215, 216, 217, 218, 219, 220, 221, 222, 223, 224, 225, 228, 229, 230, 231, 232, 233, 234, 235, 236, 237, 238
Jarvis
　Rob 326
Jasper
　Charlie 79
Jefkins
　Kristjan 265
Jelitto
　D. J. 303
Joe Patrick. *See* Patrick, Joseph
Johansen

Bill 190, 191, 192, 193, 194, 196, 198
Johner
　Dustin 272
Johns
　Joey 150, 173
Johnson
　Al 169
　Ching 169
　Earl 141, 150
　Ernie \ 78, 100
　Ernie "Moose" 4, 6, 10, 11, 13, 19, 37, 38, 39, 40, 41, 42, 44, 45, 46, 47, 48, 77
　Ernie "Moose" Night 45
　Norm 184
　Norman 152
　Tyler 305
Johnston Sport Architecture of Victoria 244
Johnstown
　Chiefs 283, 311
Johnstown Chiefs 279
Joliat
　Auriel 63
Jones
　Art 176, 177, 178, 179, 180, 181, 182, 183, 184, 185, 186, 187, 196, 197, 214, 218, 225
　Con 40
　Norm 123
Jordan
　Little 310
Jorde
　Ryan 293, 294
Josephson
　Mike 264, 265, 267, 270, 273, 274, 276, 280, 282, 283, 284, 286, 287, 288, 289, 290
Jukes
　Bing 171
Junior Chamber Commerce Campaign for Forum Funds 84

K

Kaiser
　Carl 157, 159, 164, 167, 168, 176
Kalamazoo
　Wings 349, 355
Kalamazoo Wings
　United Hockey League 280
Kalemba
　Zane 358, 359, 364
Kamloops Elks 142
Karakas
　Tom 106
Keating
　Mike 130, 131
Keats

Duke 75
Keefe
  Adam 296, 301
Keenan
  Larry 201, 202, 203, 204, 205, 206, 207, 208, 209, 210, 211, 213, 216, 217, 218, 219, 220, 225, 228, 229, 231, 232, 233, 234, 235, 236
Keetley
  Matt 343, 350, 351
Keith
  Greg 274, 275
Kell
  Matt 293
Keller
  Wendy 138
Kelly
  Dave 219, 225
  Jack 77, 78, 79, 80, 321, 334, 336, 338
  Matt 225, 235, 270, 271, 272, 275, 287, 295, 296, 297, 299, 301, 303, 304, 307, 310, 312, 314, 317, 318, 320, 326, 327, 328, 330, 331, 335, 337, 339
Kelly Cup 287
Kendall
  Carl 13
Kenny
  Ernie 33, 79, 80
Ker
  Colonel Russell 88
Kerr
  Albert "Dubbie" 12, 15, 23, 26, 27, 28, 30, 31, 33, 34, 37, 41, 44
Kilburn
  Colin 116, 117, 118, 119, 120, 123, 124, 126, 127, 128, 130, 131, 132, 133, 134, 138, 139, 140, 141, 142, 143, 144, 145, 147, 148, 149, 150, 151, 152, 153, 154, 155, 157, 158, 159, 160, 161, 162, 163, 164, 181, 187, 189, 190, 195, 214
  Doug 157, 158
Kinasewich
  Ray 154
King George VI
  burial 110
Kings lack a play-by-play broadcast 279
Kirk
  Jack 117
Klassen
  Chad 364, 365, 367
Kopak 95
  Jerry 95
  Russ 95, 96
Kosick
  Mark 269
Kostadine

Jason 317
Kotsopoulos
  Evan 328
Kowalchuk
  Mel 249
Krake
  Barney 197
Kraus
  Tim 358, 359, 361, 362
Krestanovich
  Derek 281, 297, 298, 302, 304, 305, 307, 312, 313, 314, 315, 317, 320, 321
  Jordan 297, 300, 301, 302, 304, 305, 307, 310, 312, 313, 314, 315, 316, 317, 318, 319, 321, 327, 334
Kurtenbach
  Orland 158, 159, 183, 187
Kuzma
  Alex 123, 125, 127, 128, 130, 131, 132, 133, 134, 138, 143, 148, 153

L

Labadie
  Mike 213, 214, 215, 216, 217, 218, 219, 221, 223, 224, 225, 228, 233, 234, 235, 236, 237
Labelle
  Olivier 326, 327, 328, 329, 332, 333, 334, 335, 336, 337, 338, 339
Labine
  Leo 202, 233
Labrosse
  Claude 202, 204, 206, 208, 209, 211, 213, 216, 217, 218, 220, 221, 222, 225, 228, 232, 233, 237
Lach
  Elmer 118
Lady Byng Trophy 210, 231
Laing
  Quintin 355
Lalonde
  Newsy 4, 10, 13, 53, 56, 72
Lambert
  Simon 321
Lamoureux
  Dick 192, 193, 201, 203, 204, 205, 206, 207, 209, 211, 213, 214, 215, 216, 217, 218, 220, 221, 222, 224, 225, 228, 229, 235, 236, 366
Landolt
  Shaun 326, 327, 329, 330, 331, 334, 335, 337, 338
Lang
  Devon 332
LaPointe
  Danny 310
  Rick 310
Larrivee

583

Christian 288
Lassiter
    Brandon 341
Las Vegas
    Wranglers 266, 270, 271, 272, 274, 276, 283, 284,
        288, 289, 294, 295, 296, 299, 302, 311, 315,
        316, 317, 318, 319, 332, 334, 335, 344, 345,
        347, 351, 354, 355, 356, 359, 360, 361, 532
Latendresse
    Olivier 341, 342, 343, 344, 345, 346, 347, 348, 349
Laughton
    Mike 213, 228, 229, 230, 231, 232, 233,
        234, 235, 237, 238, 512
Laurent
    Paul 205
Laviolette
    Jack 12, 14
Lavitt 138
    Sam 124, 125, 127, 128, 134
Lawson
    Ed 197, 203
Laycoe
    Hal 158, 169, 176, 177, 178, 179, 180, 183,
        184, 185, 186, 187, 189, 190, 234
Lea
    Bruce 170, 171, 172, 173
Leach
    Lawrence \ 144, 147, 148, 153, 157, 158, 161, 202, 235
Leacock
    Ernie 77, 78, 80
Leader
    Al 88, 94, 100, 107, 112, 130, 134, 143, 148, 158,
        161, 170, 174, 176, 189, 191, 201, 213, 219
Leavold
    Brady 321, 327, 328, 332, 335, 336, 337, 338, 344
Leckie
    Major Robert Gilmour Edwards 38
LeClair
    Corey 313
Lee
    Graham 245, 246, 248, 251, 252, 255
Lefley
    Mike 293
Leger
    Roger 97, 100, 101, 102, 103, 104, 106, 107,
        108, 111, 112, 113, 116, 134
Lehman
    Hugh 6, 12, 39, 40, 41, 44, 52, 56, 72
Leitch
    Bryan 349, 350
Leonard
    Seth 87, 209, 264, 266, 268, 269, 270, 274, 276,
        280, 282, 283, 285, 288, 290, 291, 294

Leopold
    Ron 191
Lepine
    Joe 98, 99, 106
Lester Patrick awarded PCHL Victoria franchise 94
Lester Patrick Trophy 210, 225, 226
Levitt
    Sam 123
Lewis
    Bryon 356
Lindsay
    Bert 4, 5, 6, 10, 13, 15, 16, 17, 18, 20, 24, 25, 26, 27, 31
Lineker
    Craig 362, 363
Lingren
    Steve 280, 281, 282, 283, 284, 285, 286, 287, 288, 289,
        290, 293, 294, 296, 298, 301, 304, 305, 338
Litzenberger
    Eddie 214, 215, 216, 220, 228
Lloyd
    Darryl 41, 80, 161, 218, 219, 222, 294, 295,
        296, 297, 298, 299, 302, 304, 305, 313,
        314, 316, 317, 318, 321, 322, 326, 327,
        329, 330, 331, 332, 333, 335, 336, 337
Long
    Stan 102, 104, 116, 117, 118, 120
Long Beach
    Ice Dogs 266, 268, 269, 270, 271, 276, 283, 286, 287,
        288, 290, 294, 297, 298, 299, 301, 304, 310
Lorentz
    Jim 273
Los Angeles
    Blades 201, 202, 204, 205, 207, 208, 215, 216,
        217, 218, 219, 220, 221, 222, 229, 237
    Monarchs 94, 97
Loughlin
    Clem 37, 39, 41, 44, 46, 47, 51, 52, 53, 54, 55, 56, 58,
        59, 60, 61, 65, 66, 67, 69, 70, 71, 72, 73, 74, 75
    Wilf 39, 41, 44, 47, 48, 51, 52, 55
Louisiana
    Ice Gators 276
Love
    Bob 144
Lowe
    Alan 245, 249
    Mayor Alan 248, 251, 252, 259
    Odie 80
    Ross 123, 125, 126, 127, 128
Lowe elected Mayor
    Alan 246
Ludlow
    Laurie 161
Lumley

Harry 190
Lund
 Larry 236
 Pentti 123
Luney Brothers & Hamilton 91
Lunt
 Councillor Jane 244, 245
Luongo
 Roberto 313, 329
Lynch
 Jeff 350

M

MacArthur
 Dalton 144
MacAulay
 Jeff 294
 Tony 291, 293, 294, 295, 297, 298
 Tony fired 298
Macauley
 Doug 125, 127, 130, 131, 132, 133, 134, 138, 139, 140, 142, 143, 144, 147, 148, 149, 150, 151, 152, 154, 157, 158, 160, 161, 162, 163, 164, 167, 168, 169, 171, 172, 173, 176, 177, 180, 181, 182, 183, 184, 185, 186, 189, 190, 191, 192, 193, 194, 195, 196, 197, 198
MacDonald
 Ran 26
MacFarland
 Bill 174
Machesney
 Daren 358
MacInnis
 Aaron 279, 281
 Al 279
MacKay
 Duncan "Mickey" 54
Mackenzie
 C. F. S. 155
 Fred 162
MacLeod
 Don 197
MacMillan
 John 229
MacMurchy
 Ryan 354, 355, 356, 357, 358, 359, 360, 361, 363, 366, 367
MacNeill
 Morley 97, 98
Madden
 Chris 269, 271
Madigan
 Cornelius \ 138, 207

Madoff
 Councillor Pamela 245
Magliarditi
 Marc 272
Magnowski
 Mark 351, 356
Makaw
 Don 189, 197
Making the Cut 265
Mallen
 Ken 6, 26, 33
Maloney
 Phil 143, 145, 150, 151, 157, 168, 205, 218, 222
Mangos
 Simon 279, 280, 281, 283, 284, 285, 286, 287, 290, 291
Maniago
 Cesare 192
Manitoba Moose 293, 296, 326, 341, 342, 344, 346, 348, 358
Manson
 Bob 123, 124, 125
Manzato
 Daniel 315
Marcetta
 Milan 201, 202, 203, 204, 205, 206, 207, 208, 210, 211, 213, 214, 215, 216, 217, 218, 219, 220, 221, 222, 223, 224, 225, 228, 229, 230, 232, 233, 234, 235, 236, 237, 238
Marineau
 Eddie 94, 95
Mario
 Frank 213, 214, 215, 220, 221, 222, 223, 224, 226, 228, 233, 237
Marples
 Stanley "Stan" 38, 39, 41
Marquess
 Mark 130, 131, 132, 133, 138, 140, 141, 145
Marshall
 Jack 4
Martin
 Derek 354, 364, 365, 366, 367
 Louis-Philippe 294
Martini
 Chris 293
Marty the Marmot mascot 295
Masnick
 Paul 109, 184, 185, 186, 187, 192, 194
Matheson
 Gordie 138, 147, 157, 167
Matthews
 Ron 177, 179, 180, 182, 183, 184, 185, 187, 189, 198
Maxner
 Wayne 215

Maxwell
  Bryan 253, 263, 264, 265, 267, 270, 271,
      273, 274, 275, 276, 277, 279, 280, 282,
      283, 284, 286, 291, 365, 517
    fired as coach of Salmon Kings 286
  Stan 111, 118, 119, 120, 123, 124, 204, 263
  Tommy 363
Mayes
  Lance 271, 281
Mayors Blue-Ribbon Panel 248
Mazur
  Eddie 94, 95, 96, 97, 98, 99, 100, 101, 102, 103,
      104, 116, 117, 119, 120, 121, 134, 201, 202,
      204, 205, 206, 207, 208, 209, 210, 211, 213
McAtee
  Red 107
McBride
  Roy 182
McCaig
  Jaime 275
McCartan
  Jack 206, 221, 223, 234
McCarthy
  Tom 162, 163, 164
McColl
  Fraser 246
McCulloch
  Fred 35
McCusker
  Bob 205, 208
McCutcheon
  Warren 293, 294, 295, 297, 304
McDonald
  Harold 66
  Ran 6, 13, 28, 33, 41
McFarland
  Bill 171
McGavin
  Mayor Andrew 84, 85, 86
McGill University 1
McGregor
  Don 138
  Robert 270
McInenly
  Tommy 80, 81
McIntyre
  Drew 313
  Jack 96, 97, 100, 104, 106, 107, 108, 110, 113, 116, 118
McIver
  Nathan 320
McKay
  Mickey 30, 39, 40
  Roy 94, 95, 96, 97, 99

  Skip 167
McKenna
  Mike 302
McKenzie
  Kenny 88
McLachlan
  Sarah 256
McLean
  Archie 6
  Councillor David 245
  Motto 139
Mcleod
  Don 189
McLeod
  Don 167, 168, 171, 172, 189, 190, 191, 196,
      198, 210, 214, 218, 221, 251
  Jack 189
  Jackie 145, 160
  Jim 207, 237
  Kiel 293, 294, 295, 296, 297, 298, 299, 300, 301,
      302, 303, 304, 305, 310, 311, 312, 313, 314,
      315, 316, 317, 318, 319, 323, 327, 334, 354,
      355, 356, 357, 358, 361, 363, 365, 366, 527
McMurchy
  Ryan 356
McNab
  Max 141, 143, 177, 237
McNabb
  Larry 223, 224
McNeill
  Billy 203
  Douglas 106
McVicar
  Rob 284, 286, 287, 289, 290, 296, 303
McVie
  Tommy 189, 204, 208
Medynski
  Joe 99, 100, 103, 106, 108, 113, 116
Meeking
  Gord 69
  Harry 41, 44, 46, 47, 48, 51, 52, 53, 54, 55,
      56, 57, 60, 63, 67, 69, 70, 72, 75, 77
Meger
  Paul 116
Mehalko
  Brad 267
Melanson
  Mathieu 303
  Rollie 303
Meloche
  Rich 300, 301
merger, PCHA and WCHL 58
Messier

586

Doug 202, 207
Metcalf
  Pete 314
Meyer
  Gil 181
Michaluk
  Art 145
Michaud
  Alfie 285
  Olivier 266
Micka
  Tomas 276
Mikulan
  Ray 141, 145, 151
Miles
  Jeff 284
Milhouse
  Jonathan 354, 356
Millar
  Al 201, 202, 203, 204, 205, 206, 207, 208, 209, 210, 211, 213, 214, 215, 217, 218, 219, 220, 221
Milne
  Frank 158, 159, 161, 163, 167
Milwaukee Admirals 289
Milwaukee Sea Gulls 375
Minard
  Chris 270, 285
Mississippi
  Sea Wolves 268, 276, 279, 280, 338
Mitchell
  Mike 23
MKT Development Group 249
Mole
  Mike 323
Montreal Canadiens 8, 23, 26, 34, 36, 40, 62, 69, 94, 95, 97, 104, 106, 116, 121, 189, 194, 197, 213, 231, 266
Montreal Maroons 69
Montreal Royals 124, 145
Montreal Shamrocks 8
Montreal Victorias 1
Montreal Wanderers 1, 4, 8, 11, 29
Moore
  Jacey 294
  Stanley 91
Moran
  Paddy 12
Morenz
  Howie 63
Morisset
  David 293, 294
Morissette
  Jean-Guy 210

Moro
  Jim 183, 189, 190, 191, 195, 196, 198
Morris
  Bernie 23, 28, 30, 33, 40
Morrison
  Lance 341, 342, 347, 349, 351, 352
  Mark 279, 286, 293, 298, 299, 300, 301, 302, 315, 316, 319, 323, 326, 327, 330, 333, 335, 339, 341, 342, 343, 350, 352, 354, 356, 359, 360, 367
  Mark hired as coach 298
  Scott 187
Mortimers Monumental Works 259
Mosienko
  Bill 168
Muldoon
  Peter \ 79, 80
  Peter "Pete" 28, 31, 32, 40, 52
Mullen
  Dennis 271, 272, 273, 274
multipurpose facilitu
  October 25, 2001, council endorsed recommendations 249
multipurpose facility
  four groups submitted expressions of interest 249
  local support 248
  named for Save-On-Foods grcoery chain 254
  only RG Properties met city's criteria 249
  public art 252
  referendum passed April 20, 2002 250
  request for letters of interest 248
  search for anchor hockey tenant 252
Muntain
  Rob 275, 276, 280, 281, 282, 283
Murray
  Garth 357, 358
  John 34, 45, 95, 96, 167, 170, 341, 342, 358
  Tommy 37
Mutcheson
  Len 96
M.V. Chinook 103

N

Nanaimo Clippers 189
Nash
  Steve 283
Nashville Predators 289
Nathe
  Bryan 311
National Hockey Association 4, 8, 11, 13, 19, 22, 49
National Hockey League 8, 36, 130, 174, 199, 241
Neale
  David 263, 267, 270, 274, 275
Neave

Gord 326
Neilson
    Eric 317
Nelson
    Eric 312
    Grace 1
Nelson, BC 1, 2, 3, 97, 167, 228
Nelson, BC Maple Leafs 164
Nesdill
    Mike 326, 327, 328
new arena complex planned, 1996 240
New Jersey Devils 265
New Westminster
    Royals 1, 3, 4, 5, 6, 7, 10, 11, 12, 13, 14, 15, 16, 18, 19, 23, 24, 25, 26, 28, 85, 88, 94, 95, 96, 97, 98, 99, 100, 101, 102, 103, 104, 107, 108, 109, 110, 111, 112, 113, 117, 118, 119, 120, 123, 124, 125, 126, 127, 130, 131, 132, 133, 134, 135, 138, 139, 140, 141, 142, 143, 144, 145, 148, 149, 150, 151, 153, 154, 155, 157, 158, 159, 160, 161, 162, 163, 164, 165, 167, 168, 169, 170, 171, 172, 173, 176, 177, 189, 192, 193, 202, 373
New York Americans 69
New York Rangers 75, 82, 123, 130, 138, 142, 176, 177, 183, 230, 231, 267
NHL adopts some Western rules 46
NHL lock-out 264
Nichols
    Sibby 33
Nicholson
    Al 167, 169, 170, 171, 172, 173, 176, 177, 178, 179, 180, 182, 208, 221
Nighbor
    Frank "The Pembroke Peach" 23
Nissen
    Jason 319
Nixon
    Danny 100
Noakes
    Ken 253
Nonis
    Dave 289
Norris
    Jack 201, 204
North
    Wayne 40, 45, 189, 190, 192, 193, 194, 195, 196, 197, 198, 252, 254, 257

O

Oakland
    Oaks 94, 96
Oatman
    Eddie 26, 31, 37, 38, 39, 40, 41, 42, 44, 45, 46, 47, 48, 51, 52, 54, 55, 60, 69, 70, 71, 72
    Russell 69, 75
O'Brien
    John Ambrose 8
OConnor
    Sean 269, 313, 327, 328, 330, 331, 332, 333, 334, 336, 337, 338, 339
ODette
    Matt 274
Ogden Entertainment of New York 245
Ohata
    Atsushi 310
Olafson
    Mark 290
OLeary
    Mickey 33
Olson
    Barney 84, 85, 88, 91
    Dennis 162, 163, 164
    Eddie 138, 139, 140, 143, 144, 145
    Glenn 273, 274
Olympic Games
    Antwerp 1920 43
OMeara
    Cliff 77, 78, 79
Ontario
    Reign 330, 333, 335, 336, 337, 343, 344, 355, 356, 358, 359, 360, 363, 535
opening dates for Save-On-Foods Memorial Centre
    March 31, 2005 255
    November 15, 2004 255
ORee
    Willie 202, 218, 230
Orlich
    Dan 249
Ottawa Senators 8, 32, 42, 46, 54, 74
Ouzas
    Michael 330
Owens
    Sean 335

P

Pacific Coast Hockey Association 2, 4, 5, 6, 8, 19, 26, 42, 45, 49, 77, 452
Pacific Coast Hockey League 5, 22, 77, 88, 89, 94, 103, 375, 464
Pacific Coast Net Inc. 245
Pacific Coast Net Place 245
Pacific National Exhibition 149
Paille
    Marcel 218
Painchaud
    Chad 341, 342, 343, 344, 345, 346, 347, 348,

349, 350, 351, 352, 355, 356, 357, 358,
359, 360, 361, 362, 363, 364, 365
Pamidi
  Matt 350
Panagabko
  Pete 144
Panama-Pacific Exhibition 15
Papp
  Willie 207
Pappin
  Jim 220
Paradice
  Al 159
Parenteau
  Dave 215, 216, 217, 221, 222, 228, 251
Partridge
  Roy 147, 151
Pasant
  David 240, 241, 242, 243, 245, 255
Paterson
  Lieutenant-Governor Thomas Wilson 5, 6, 15
Paterson Cup 5, 18, 30
Patrick
  Frank 1, 2, 8, 10, 11, 12, 22, 24, 25, 28, 31,
    32, 35, 36, 42, 43, 47, 51, 52, 53, 55,
    63, 65, 67, 75, 77, 80, 82, 226
  Glenn 282
  Joseph 1, 35, 66
  Lester 1, 2, 3, 4, 5, 6, 7, 8, 10, 11, 12, 13, 14, 15, 16,
    18, 19, 20, 21, 22, 23, 24, 25, 26, 27, 28, 29, 30,
    31, 32, 33, 35, 36, 37, 38, 39, 40, 41, 42, 43, 44,
    46, 47, 48, 51, 52, 53, 55, 56, 57, 58, 59, 60,
    62, 65, 66, 67, 68, 69, 70, 71, 72, 73, 74, 75,
    76, 77, 81, 82, 85, 87, 94, 97, 103, 106, 109,
    116, 117, 118, 124, 138, 151, 155, 226, 282
  Lynn 134, 138, 142, 151, 282
  Murray \ 123, 138
  Murray "Muzz" 45
  Stanley 77, 80, 81
Patrick Arena. *See* Victoria Arena
Patterson
  Colin 341
Pavilion Rock and Shell 252
PCHA. *See* Pacific Coast Hockey Association
Pelletier
  Marcel 130, 131, 132, 133, 134, 135, 138, 139, 140,
    141, 142, 143, 144, 145, 147, 148, 149, 150,
    151, 152, 153, 154, 155, 157, 162, 167, 168, 169,
    170, 171, 172, 173, 174, 176, 177, 178, 179,
    180, 182, 183, 184, 185, 186, 189, 190, 192,
    194, 195, 196, 197, 198, 199, 215, 220, 223
Peluso
  Marco 319

penalty-shot goal
  first 46
penalty shot introduced 46
Pendray
  John Carl 65, 88
Pensacola
  Ice Pilots 276, 283, 297, 301
Penticton Vees 138
Pereira
  Joe 274
Perreault
  Bob 204, 206
Perrin
  Jack 192, 197
  J. D. 148
Pete Durham Night 164
Peters
  Blair 139
Petruic
  Neil 343, 346, 348
Pettinger
  Matt 265
Philadelphia Phantoms 295
Phillips
  Tommy 10, 12, 31
Phoenix 502, 503
  Roadrunners 211, 238, 283, 287, 288, 290,
    294, 297, 298, 301, 305, 312, 313, 318,
    320, 327, 329, 331, 338, 359
Phoenix, BC 22
Phoenix Coyotes 354
Picard
  Jean-Marc 167
Piggott
  Jim 176, 186, 187, 189, 199
Pilla
  Jim 164, 167
Pilot Pacific 240
Pilous
  Rudy 201, 206, 209, 211
Pitre
  Didier 14, 23
Pitton
  Bryan 348, 359, 364
Pittsburgh Hornets 221
Plager
  Bob 205
Plante
  Jacques 180
Plett
  Tim 310
Plimley and Ritchies 62
Plumb

Aaron 270, 275
Pogge
  Justin 342
Poile
  Bud 210, 224
Polanic
  Tom 236, 238
Popein
  Larry 214, 218
Portland 205
  Buckaroos 77, 78, 79, 80, 82, 189, 190, 191, 192, 193,
    194, 196, 197, 198, 199, 202, 203, 204, 205,
    206, 207, 208, 210, 214, 215, 217, 218, 219,
    222, 224, 225, 228, 229, 230, 231, 236, 238
  Eagles 98, 99, 100, 101, 102, 103
  Penguins 94, 95, 96
  Rosebuds 28, 30, 31, 32, 33, 34, 37,
    38, 68, 70, 71, 72, 75
Portland, Oregon 48
possible merger of WHL with AHL 230
Poulin
  George "Skinner" 5, 6, 10, 12, 13, 15, 16, 18,
    19, 20, 23, 25, 26, 27, 28, 31, 32, 37
Powell
  Ray 149, 150, 153, 154, 155
Powers
  Eddie 100, 112
  Jim 218
Poynter
  Dr. Arthur 88
Prendergast
  Kevin 328
Pridham
  Norm 78
Prince of Wales
  1919 visit 40
Princess Marguerite 96
Prodger
  Goldie 15, 18, 20, 21
Providence Reds 164, 218, 221
public art
  opposition to 252
Purinton
  Dale 267, 268, 272, 273, 274, 275
Purvis
  Fred 213

Q

Quebec Aces 222
Quebec Bulldogs 8

R

Raglin
  Clare \ 161, 163, 164
Rahimi
  Daniel 310, 312, 313, 316, 317, 320, 326
Rai
  Prab 355, 357
Ramsey
  Travis 328, 331, 335, 338
Ranieri
  George 147, 151
Rawlings
  Cec 162
Reading
  Royals 270, 333, 343, 349
Reardon
  Kenny 110, 118, 120, 123, 151, 189
Reay
  Billy 123, 124, 125, 126, 127, 130, 139, 159
Redahl
  Gordie 183, 201, 202, 203, 204, 205, 206, 207, 208,
    209, 210, 211, 214, 215, 216, 217, 219, 220, 221,
    222, 223, 224, 228, 229, 230, 231, 235, 237, 238
Redpath
  Oliver 77, 78, 79, 80
Reeves
  Ryan 280
Regina
  Capitals 48, 51, 52, 53, 54, 59, 61, 68
  Regals 140
  Regals moved to Brandon 141
Reid
  Dr. Andy N. 155, 162
  Scott 342
Renfrew Creamery Kings 8
Renfrew Millionaires 2, 72
Renfrew, Ontario 8, 27
Repka
  Lionel 167
RG Properties 248, 249, 250, 251, 253, 255, 256, 257,
    258, 259, 277, 291, 357, 362, 364, 365, 368
Rhodes
  Cec 162
Richard
  Maurice 194
Richardson
  H. L. 69, 71
  Murray 95, 96
Richardson & Stephens 8
Riddell
  Riley 273
Riggin
  Dennis 181, 191
Rimstad

Dave 167, 170
Risser International of Atlanta 243
Ritchie
  Cam 2, 62, 69, 363, 364
Roach
  Brandon 341, 343, 345, 347, 348
Roberts
  Gord 42
  Steve 279, 280, 282, 287, 289, 290, 291
Robertson
  Earl 77, 79, 80, 82
  George 80, 95, 96
  Jim 140, 141, 142, 143, 144
Robinson
  Rob 163
Roche
  Ernie 107, 110, 111, 112, 113, 116, 119, 123, 124
Rochester Americans 216, 218, 219, 220
Rochon
  George 23
Rockey
  Tom 94, 96
Rod Stewart concert
  March 26, 2005 257
Rogers
  Andy 346, 347
Rolfe
  Dale 197
Rollins
  Elwin 179, 183
  Geoff 275
Ronan
  Skene 12
Ross
  Barrie 12, 13, 33, 123, 124, 127, 128, 164, 194, 195, 196, 197, 198
Roughley
  Don 244
Rowe
  Bobby 4, 5, 6, 10, 12, 13, 15, 16, 17, 18, 19, 20, 23, 24, 25, 27, 28, 31, 40, 44, 55, 77, 80
Roy
  Georges 191, 192
Royal Canadian Navy 237
Rudkowsky
  Cody 313
Runge
  Herman 77, 78, 79
  Paul 78, 79

S

Sabourin
  Corey 293
Sagert
  Kalvin 320
Salmon Kings first home game in new arena 282
San Diego
  Gulls 95, 213, 219, 228, 229, 230, 232, 233, 234, 235, 237, 269, 274, 276, 283, 288, 289, 290, 512, 513, 514
  Skyhawks 95, 97
Sandiford
  Fred 81, 202
San Francisco
  Seals 201, 202, 203, 204, 206, 208, 214, 215, 216, 217, 218, 219, 221, 223
  Shamrocks 96, 97, 99
  Spiders 240
San Jose Sharks 281
Saskatoon
  Crescents 46, 51, 53, 54, 55, 59, 60, 61, 62, 69, 70, 71, 72, 73
  Quakers 106, 107, 110, 111, 112, 118, 119, 120, 124, 125, 126, 127, 131, 132, 133, 134, 139, 140, 142, 168, 169, 171, 172, 176, 177
Saskatoon-St. Paul
  Regals 157, 161, 164
Sather
  Glen 275
Saunders
  Bill 79, 190, 191, 192, 193, 194, 195, 196, 197, 198, 205, 220
  Frank 79
Sauve
  Yann 357, 358, 361
Save-On-Foods Memorial Centre 254
  new memorial dedicated, April 17, 2005 259
  new memorial with five plaques 259
Schaddelee
  Maarten 252, 259
Schenderling
  Jeremy 326, 327
Schmautz
  Arnie 155, 176, 177, 178, 179, 180, 181, 182, 183, 184, 185, 189, 190, 197, 202
  Cliff 238
Schneider
  Tony 123, 125, 127, 134
Sclisizzi
  Enio 167, 168, 172, 173, 174
Seals
  San Francisco 202
Seattle 237
  Americans 138, 139, 141, 142, 143, 144, 147, 148, 149, 150, 151, 152, 153, 154, 155, 157, 158, 159, 160, 161, 163, 165

Bombers 117, 118, 119, 120, 123, 124, 125, 126, 127
Eskimos 77, 78, 79, 80
Ironmen 95, 96, 97, 98, 99, 101, 102, 103, 106, 107, 108, 109, 110, 111, 112
Kingdome 245
Metropolitans 32, 33, 36, 38, 39, 40, 41, 42, 44, 45, 46, 47, 48, 52, 53, 54, 58, 79
Totems 167, 168, 169, 170, 171, 172, 173, 177, 178, 179, 180, 181, 183, 184, 185, 189, 191, 193, 194, 195, 196, 197, 198, 202, 203, 204, 205, 207, 208, 209, 210, 213, 214, 215, 216, 217, 218, 220, 221, 222, 228, 229, 230, 231, 232, 236, 237

Seattle Arena 58
Seattle Arena Company 28
Seattle Ironmen 106
Selke
  Frank 125
Senior
  Al 95, 251
Serov
  Vlad 265
Shantz
  David 341, 342, 343, 344, 345, 346, 347, 348, 354, 355, 356, 357, 358, 360, 361, 362, 363, 364, 365, 366, 367
Sharrow
  Jimmy 343, 344, 345, 346, 347, 349, 350, 351, 352
Shaw
  Chris 318
Shaw TV 259
Sheptak
  Curtis 273
Shields
  Kelly 270, 271, 272, 275
Shirley
  Jim 106, 107, 108, 109
Shore
  Eddie 75, 168, 216
  Samuel 12
Shrine Hockey Night 160, 184
Shvetz
  Bill 128, 201, 202, 204, 205, 206, 207, 210, 211, 213, 214, 216, 219, 222, 226, 228, 229, 232, 251, 368
Shybunka
  Tyler 287, 288, 289, 290
Siddall
  Matt 348, 349, 350, 351, 352, 354, 355, 357, 358, 359, 360, 362, 363, 364, 365, 366, 367
Sihota
  Moe 243, 244
Silverthorn
  Steve 295, 302
Sinclair
  Colin 312
Sinnett
  Bill 123, 126, 127
six-man hockey 19, 26, 27, 29, 32, 49, 51, 52
Sjerven
  Grant 267, 270
Skate Canada International 295
Skillings
  Alderman Waldo 90
Sleaver
  John 201, 202, 203, 204, 206, 207, 208, 209, 211, 213, 214, 215, 216, 217, 218, 219, 220, 221, 222, 223, 224, 225
Smaill
  Walter 4, 5, 6, 10, 11, 12, 13, 15, 16, 17, 18, 19, 20, 23, 26, 27, 28, 30
Smith
  Al 228, 229, 230, 232, 235, 236, 237, 238
  Corey 264, 269, 270, 274, 275, 279, 280
  Des 228
  Donald 4, 5, 6, 10, 11, 12, 13, 15
  Gary 237
  Gary \ 203, 204, 205, 228, 236
  Joe 77, 79, 82
  Mark 271, 272, 275, 276
  Mel 201
  Rob 341
  Sid 159
Smyl
  Stan 307, 345
Smythe
  Stafford 201
Snetsinger
  Ed 361, 363
Sochor
  Jan 276, 282
South Carolina
  Stingrays 334, 358
Southern
  Dirk 341, 342, 343, 344, 345, 346, 347, 348, 350, 351, 352, 361
Sparrow
  Emory 61
Speck
  Bill 55
Spencer
  Justin 298
  Mrs. David 23
Spenreth
  Greg 274
Spokane
  Canaries 35
  Comets 177, 178, 179, 180, 181, 182, 183,

185, 189, 190, 192, 193, 195, 198
  Flyers 168, 169, 170, 171, 172, 173
Spokane Arena Company 35
Spokane Comets moved to Denver 201
Spratt
  Jimmy 363, 364
Springfield Indians 168, 216, 222
Stankiewicz
  Ed 197
Stanley Cup 1, 4, 11, 18, 19, 20, 22, 25, 26, 27, 28, 32, 34, 36, 40, 42, 46, 48, 49, 52, 54, 57, 58, 62, 63, 64, 65, 66, 67, 69, 70, 71, 74, 75, 76, 79, 95, 102, 104, 109, 145, 155, 170, 197, 199, 213, 238, 282, 283
Stanton
  Kyle 264, 267
Stapleton
  Pat 202, 207
Stefanishion
  Matt 354, 355, 356, 357, 359, 360, 362, 364
Stevenson
  Duncan 258
Stewart
  Dave 164
  Doug 167
St. Jacques
  Chris 311, 312, 313, 315, 318, 319, 320, 321, 322, 326, 327, 328, 329, 330, 331, 332, 334, 335, 336, 339
  Kevin 300
Stockton
  Thunder 271, 282, 283, 290, 293, 294, 296, 302, 303, 311, 312, 314, 316, 317, 320, 321, 327, 328, 329, 332, 333, 334, 337, 342, 343, 345, 348, 350, 351, 357, 359, 361, 363, 364
Stone
  Art 167
  Jason 263, 264, 266, 267, 268, 269, 272, 275
St. Paul, Minnesota 152
St. Paul Saints 152
Strain
  Craig 276
Strasser
  Paul 138, 142
Strongman 116
  Bernie 94, 97, 99, 100, 104, 106, 111, 113, 117, 119, 251
Stuart
  Herb "Red" 60
Stutzel
  Mike 283, 294, 295, 297, 298, 299, 302, 303, 304, 305
Sudbury Wolves 194
suggested replacements for Willows Arena
  Belleville and Douglas 81
  Douglas Street near the Hudsons Bay store 84
  Pandora Avenue at Blanshard 84

  wool mill near Ogden Point docks 84
Sutherland
  Hugh 106
Sutton
  Pat 283, 289, 294
Swanson
  Jeremy 326, 327
Swarbrick
  Bill 189
Syverson
  Henry \ 151

T

Tacoma
  Rockets 94, 95, 97, 98, 99, 100, 102, 103, 107, 108, 109, 110, 111, 112, 117, 118, 119, 120, 123
  Tigers 82, 102
    disbanded 82
Taillefer
  Pete 99
Tambellini
  Steve 326
Tang
  Jim 209
Tansley
  Gordon 176
Taylor
  Adam 6, 211, 280, 281, 282, 283, 284, 285, 287, 288, 289, 290, 291, 293, 294, 296, 297, 303, 326, 334, 335, 336, 337, 338, 341, 342, 343, 346, 347, 348, 349, 350, 359, 360, 363, 364, 365, 366, 452
  Bobby 203, 204, 210
  Fred "Cyclone" 8, 12, 13, 14, 15, 24, 26, 31, 32, 38, 40, 46
Teal
  Skip 138, 139, 140, 142, 143, 144
Tebbs
  Kris 314
Terminesi
  Jeff 363
Texas
  Wildcatters 276, 279, 280, 291, 330
The RPA Group 249
Thibeault
  Larry 94, 95, 97
Thompson
  Billy 55, 307, 310, 311, 312, 313, 314, 316, 317, 318, 320, 321, 322, 323, 334
Thomson
  Dewar 106
Thrussell
  Ryan 287, 294
Thurlby

Tom 197
Tifu
  Yannick 341, 342, 343
Timmis
  Mark 242
Timmons
  K. C. 280, 281, 282, 283, 284, 285, 286, 288, 289
Tobin
  Charlie 24, 37, 38
  Gerald 38
Todd
  Derek C. 155
Toledo
  Storm 282, 349
  Walleye 338
Tolmie
  Premier Simon Fraser 77
Toone
  Alderman Alf 201
  Mayor Alf 228
Toronto Arenas 36, 40
Toronto Blueshirts 11, 23
Toronto Maple Leafs 145, 159, 201, 213, 228
Toronto Maple Leafs sell Victoria Maple Leafs to Phoenix owner 238
Toronto Marlboros 203, 205, 228
Toronto St. Patricks 48, 52
Trail Smoke Eaters 167, 180, 228
Trapp
  Barry 201, 203
  Bear 341
Trenton
  Titans 265, 281, 291, 357
Trihey
  Clem 55, 58
Truelson
  Keith 322
Tulsa Oilers 203, 205, 218, 219, 220, 221, 224, 232
Turek
  Ryan 354, 355, 357, 358, 359, 360, 361, 362, 363, 364, 366, 367
Turner
  Lloyd 80
  Scott 273, 275, 276, 280, 361
  Sean 274

U

Ufer
  Bob 241
  Robert 241
Uksila
  Charlie 77, 79
Uliyot
  Ken 103
Ulrich
  Jack 10, 11, 16, 19, 20, 23, 26, 27, 28, 29
Underhill
  Matt 285
United Hockey League 280
Utah
  Grizzlies 240, 281, 283, 284, 285, 290, 291, 294, 296, 297, 301, 303, 304, 307, 310, 311, 315, 320, 323, 326, 328, 330, 332, 338, 346, 348, 349, 350, 351, 352, 354, 358, 359, 361, 362, 363, 365, 366, 532

V

Valliere
  Ross 197
VanBallegooie
  Dustin 274
Vancouver 127
  Canucks 94, 95, 96, 97, 98, 99, 100, 101, 102, 106, 107, 108, 109, 110, 111, 117, 119, 120, 123, 124, 125, 126, 127, 130, 131, 132, 133, 134, 135, 138, 139, 140, 141, 143, 144, 145, 147, 148, 149, 150, 151, 153, 154, 158, 159, 160, 161, 162, 163, 164, 165, 167, 168, 169, 171, 172, 177, 178, 179, 181, 182, 183, 184, 185, 186, 187, 190, 191, 192, 193, 195, 198, 202, 203, 204, 205, 206, 207, 208, 209, 214, 215, 217, 218, 220, 221, 222, 229, 230, 236, 237, 263, 276, 279, 284, 289, 293, 295, 303, 326, 336, 341, 361, 362
  Lions 77, 78, 79, 82
  Maroons 50, 52, 53, 54, 60, 61, 69, 71, 72
  Millionaires 24, 25, 26, 30, 31, 32, 33, 34, 36, 37, 38, 39, 41, 42, 44, 45, 47, 48, 50, 70
Vandermeer
  Dan 273
  Pete 354, 355, 356, 357, 358, 359, 360, 361, 363
Van Horlick
  Quentin 307, 326
Vanoosten
  Steve 364
Varga
  Ed 147
Veneruzzo
  Gary 237
Vernon Canadians 147
Vezina
  Georges 63
Victoria
  Aristocrats 7, 33, 34, 37, 38, 39, 40, 41, 42, 43, 44, 45, 46, 47, 48, 50, 367
  Cougars 7, 20, 27, 50, 51, 52, 53, 54, 55, 56, 57, 58, 59, 60, 61, 62, 63, 65, 66, 67, 68, 69, 70, 71, 72, 73, 74, 75, 76, 94, 95, 96, 97, 98, 99, 100, 101, 102,

103, 104, 106, 107, 108, 109, 110, 111, 112, 113, 116, 117, 118, 119, 120, 121, 123, 124, 125, 126, 127, 128, 130, 131, 132, 133, 134, 135, 138, 139, 140, 141, 142, 143, 144, 145, 147, 148, 149, 150, 151, 152, 153, 154, 155, 157, 158, 159, 160, 161, 162, 163, 164, 165, 167, 168, 169, 170, 171, 172, 173, 174, 176, 177, 178, 179, 180, 181, 182, 183, 184, 185, 186, 187, 189, 190, 191, 192, 193, 194, 195, 196, 197, 198, 199, 201, 202, 204, 213, 225, 226, 229, 231, 251, 263, 282, 284, 286, 365, 367
  Cubs 77, 78, 79, 80, 81, 82, 367
  Maple Leafs 201, 202, 203, 204, 205, 206, 207, 209, 210, 211, 213, 214, 215, 216, 217, 218, 219, 220, 221, 222, 223, 224, 225, 226, 228, 229, 230, 231, 232, 236, 237, 238, 263, 279, 367
  Salmon kings
    listen to free audio or watch on pay-per-view 300
  Salmon Kings 8, 253, 254, 255, 259, 263, 264, 265, 266, 267, 268, 269, 270, 271, 272, 273, 274, 275, 276, 277, 279, 280, 281, 282, 283, 284, 285, 286, 287, 288, 289, 290, 291, 293, 294, 295, 296, 297, 298, 299, 300, 301, 302, 303, 304, 305, 307, 310, 311, 312, 313, 314, 315, 316, 317, 318, 319, 320, 321, 322, 323, 324, 326, 327, 328, 329, 330, 331, 332, 333, 334, 335, 336, 337, 338, 339, 341, 342, 343, 344, 345, 346, 347, 348, 349, 350, 351, 352, 354, 355, 356, 357, 358, 359, 360, 361, 362, 363, 364, 365, 366, 367, 368, 452, 517, 527, 532, 535, 538, 544, 545
    first year at Bear Mountain Arena 264
    franchise folded 368
  Salmon Kings become Vancouver Canucks farm team 293
  Salsa 240, 279, 293
  Senators 7, 12, 23, 24, 25, 26, 27, 30, 31, 32, 367
  Spiders 240, 241
  Tyees 40, 116
Victoria Arena
  War closure 34
Victoria Arena Company 2
Victoria Cougars credit cards 177
Victoria Cougars franchise moves to Los Angeles 199
Victoria High School 157
Victoria Hockey Club 155
Victoria Hockey Club (1957) 155
Victoria Memorial Area
  Thanks for the Memories,\ 251
Victoria Memorial Arena 157, 240
  architects named 87
  five-man commission 88
  handled poorly by council 89
  interest in team for PCHL 88
  manager hired 91
  new wooden seats installed 201
  officially opened 92
  opening parade 92
  public subscription 87
  refrigeration pipes installed 91
  second arena by-law passed 90
  second vote to approve the arena funding 90
  site acquired 87
  stage show presented 91
  Standing down Ceremony and Parade 243
  start of the demolition, February 17, 2003 251
  tenders "for Completion of Victoria Memorial Arena" 90
  tenders for the construction of the roof and walls 88
  trouble with the roof 91
Victoria Press Ltd. 155
Victoria Sports Entertainment Associates 240, 241, 243, 244, 245
Villeneuve
  Gilles 204, 206, 208, 218, 221
Vincent
  Alexandre 210, 300, 301
Voltera
  Rob 263, 264, 266, 268, 269, 270, 271, 275
VSEA. *See* Victoria Sports Entertainment Associates; *See* Victoria Sports Entertainment Associates; *See* Victoria Sports Entertainment Associates
VSEA agreement terminated
  June 30, 1999 245
VSEA arena
  naming rights 245
VSEA deadlines missed
  December 15, 1997 242
  December 15, 1998 244
  February 16, 1998 243
  May 31, 1999 245
  November 14, 1997 242

W

Waddell
  Matt 341
Wade
  Ryan 263, 264, 265, 267, 268, 269, 272, 273, 275, 276, 280, 281, 282, 284, 285, 286, 287, 288, 290, 291, 294, 296, 298, 299, 300, 301, 302, 303, 304, 305, 307, 310, 311, 314, 316, 317, 318, 320, 321, 322, 326, 359
Wakshinski
  Clare 164, 165, 167
Walker
  Jack "Hookcheck" 40, 58, 60, 61, 62, 63, 67, 69, 71, 75
  Mike 300
Wall
  Dave 130, 132, 138
  Mike 287

Wallis
  Reggie 101
Wally Smith Memorial Trophy 162, 173, 185
Walsh
  Marty 14
Walsky
  Eric 348, 351, 352
Ward
  Troy 85, 286, 287, 288, 290, 291
  Troy turns down offer to coach the club in 2006-07 291
Wares
  Eddie 94, 95, 96, 97
Warshinski
  Clare 167
Washington Capitals 355
Waslowski
  Norm 178
Watson
  Ryan 265, 266, 268, 270, 272, 273, 274
Watt
  Jordan 310, 312, 313
Waugh
  Gary 189
  Geoff 189, 354, 357, 359, 361, 363
WCHL. See Western Canada Hockey League
Webster
  Don 98, 100, 104, 106, 117
Wedderburn
  Tim 326, 327, 333, 334, 335, 341, 344, 347, 348, 350
Weselowski
  Riley 342
Weslosky
  Jase 354
Western Canada Hockey League 46, 48, 51, 68
Western Canada Senior Hockey League 106
Western Hockey League 68, 116
Western Hockey League juniors 246
Western International Hockey League 180
Westholme Hotel 19
Wheeling
  Nailers 269, 282, 307
When Peace Comes 259
Whitney
  Arnott 140, 141, 142, 150, 151
WHL. See Western Hockey League juniors;
      See Western Hockey League juniors;
      See Western Hockey League juniors
WHL Player Benefit Fund 158
Wieckowski
  Krzysztof 268
Wiest
  Bob 94
Wilcox

Rollie 201, 203, 204, 205, 206, 207, 208, 209, 211, 218, 228, 229, 230, 232, 233, 234, 235, 236, 238
Wilkie
  Murray 167, 170
Williams
  Jeff 264, 265, 267, 268, 269
Williamson
  Jason 293
  Ken 80
Willows Arena 7, 57, 78, 79, 80, 81, 84, 85
  fire 80, 81
Willows Hotel 2
Willows Sports Centre and adjacent ice arena
  destroyed by fire 85
Wills
  Archie 66, 73, 74, 86, 88, 155, 470
Wilson
  Cully 40, 41
  Don 189, 190, 193
  Gord 150, 157, 158, 159, 162, 163, 164, 168, 169, 170, 171, 173, 176, 177, 179, 181, 182
  Michael 354
  Mike 354, 358
Winfeld
  Ralph 201
Winkler
  Harold 71
Winnipeg
  Warriors 139, 140, 141, 142, 145, 147, 149, 151, 152, 154, 163, 164, 168, 169, 171, 172, 178, 179, 182, 183, 184, 189, 190, 191, 192, 194, 197
Winnipeg Falcons 43, 46
Wirll
  Mike 281, 282, 283, 284, 285, 286, 287
Witiuk
  Steve 193, 195, 196, 201, 203, 204, 205, 206, 207, 208, 209, 210, 211, 213, 214, 215, 218, 219, 221, 222, 223, 224, 228, 229, 232, 235, 237
Wong
  Danny 138
Wonoski
  Fred 142, 144
Worsley
  Gump 112, 123, 126
Wride
  Dr. Reginald 138
Wright
  Pete 154, 176, 177, 178, 185, 186
Wrigley
  David 293, 294, 296, 297
Wurtele Arena 264

Y

Yanchuk
  John 161, 162, 163, 164
Yeo
  Dylan 307, 310, 311, 312, 314, 315, 316, 317, 318, 319, 320, 321, 322, 326, 327, 328, 330, 331, 332, 333, 334, 337, 338
Young
  Councillor Geoff 245
  Howie 204
  Moe 130
  Seamus 33, 56, 132, 142, 183, 193, 217, 220, 228, 232, 246, 257, 293, 294, 295, 296, 297, 299, 301, 302, 303, 307, 355

Z

Zacharias
  Mike 358
Zajak
  Barry 167
Zanier
  Reno 173, 176
Zanon
  Brad 319
Zubersky
  Craig 270, 272, 275
Zulyniak
  Andy 294, 295, 296

Printed in Canada